# MEXICO

Where to Stay and Eat
for All Budgets

Must-See Sights
and Local Secrets

Ratings You Can Trust

Fodor's Travel Publications   New York, Toronto, London, Sydney, Auckland
**www.fodors.com**

## FODOR'S MEXICO 2005

**Editors:** Carissa Bluestone, Sarah Gold, Laura Kidder, Pamela Lee, Jennifer Paull

**Editorial Contributors:** Rob Aikins, Patricia Alisau, Trudy Balch, Gary Chandler Prado, John Hecht, Michele Joyce, Barbara Kastelein, Amy Gray Kirkcaldy, Sean Mattson, Maribeth Mellin, Jane Onstott, Mark Sullivan

**Editorial Production:** Tom Holton

**Maps:** David Lindroth, *cartographer;* Rebecca Baer and Robert Blake, *map editors*

**Design:** Fabrizio La Rocca, *creative director;* Guido Caroti, *art director;* Melanie Marin, *senior photo editor*

**Production/Manufacturing:** Robert B. Shields

**Cover Photo** (Mexican women): Sexto Sol/PhotoDisc/Getty Images

## SPECIAL SALES

This book is available for special discounts for bulk purchases for sales promotions or premiums. Special editions, including personalized covers, excerpts of existing books, and corporate imprints, can be created in large quantities for special needs. For more information, write to Special Markets/Premium Sales, 1745 Broadway, MD 6-2, New York, New York 10019, or e-mail specialmarkets@randomhouse.com.

## AN IMPORTANT TIP & AN INVITATION

Although all prices, opening times, and other details in this book are based on information supplied to us at press time, changes occur all the time in the travel world, and Fodor's cannot accept responsibility for facts that become outdated or for inadvertent errors or omissions. So **always confirm information when it matters,** especially if you're making a detour to visit a specific place. Your experiences—positive and negative—matter to us. If we have missed or misstated something, **please write to us.** We follow up on all suggestions. Contact the Mexico editors at editors@fodors.com or c/o Fodor's at 1745 Broadway, New York, New York 10019.

PRINTED IN THE UNITED STATES OF AMERICA

10 9 8 7 6 5 4 3 2 1

# DESTINATION: MEXICO

Climbing a pyramid in the magnificent Maya ruins of Uxmal in the Yucatán. Descending into the formidable clefts of the Copper Canyon. Strolling through the shady plaza of a colonial Heartland town in the heat and torpor of siesta time. Dancing until sunrise in glittering Acapulco. Snorkeling in the Caribbean off Quintana Roo. Hitting a classic cantina in the capital. Gawking at the variety of chilies in an Oaxacan market. Any one of these experiences—not to mention dozens of others you may not have dreamed up yet—are quintessentially Mexican. An amazing diversity of cultures, people, and landscapes forms the core of this country's allure. Buen viaje!

*Tim Jarrell, Publisher*

# CONTENTS

## Maps

## CloseUps

# ON THE ROAD WITH FODOR'S

A trip takes you out of yourself. Concerns of life at home completely disappear, driven away by more immediate thoughts—about, say, what new experience you'll have the next day, or where you'll have dinner. That's where Fodor's comes in. We make sure that you know all your options, so that you don't miss something that's just around the next bend. Because the best memories of your trip might well have nothing to do with what you came to Mexico to see, we guide you to sights large and small all over the region. You might set out to hit the beach or climb a Mayan pyramid, but back at home you find yourself unable to forget the sight of a gray whale or the sound of a marimba band in a village square. With Fodor's at your side, serendipitous discoveries are never far away.

Our success in showing you every corner of Mexico is a credit to our extraordinary writers. Although there's no substitute for travel advice from a good friend who knows your style, our contributors are the next best thing—the kind of people you would poll for travel advice if you knew them.

San Diego–based writer Rob Aikins, who updated the Sonora and Copper Canyon chapters, developed a love for the people and culture of Mexico while traveling the Baja and Pacific coasts looking for surfing spots. He later complemented those experiences by attending the Universidad Nacional Autónoma de México (UNAM) in Mexico City and conducting research in various parts of the country. He recently filmed a documentary in Northern Baja California. He has been an editorial contributor to Fodor's *San Diego* and *Brazil* titles.

So drawn to the surrealism of Mexico that she turned a one-week vacation into a 20-year sojourn, Patricia Alisau has traveled just about every inch of the country on assignment for U.S. and Mexican journals. She has written for Mexico's *Vogue*

magazine and, as a foreign correspondent, worked for the *New York Times,* the *Chicago Tribune,* and the Associated Press. This year, she updated the Acapulco chapter and the Where to Eat, Where to Stay, and Sports & the Outdoors sections of the Mexico City chapter.

A trip to Guadalajara in the early 1990s turned into a newspaper reporting job for Trudy Balch, now an enthusiastic "border crosser" who most recently spent a year as a translator and history teacher at the University of Guadalajara. She has written for *Américas* magazine and the *New York Times,* was a freelance correspondent for the *Los Angeles Times,* and has edited various guidebooks to Mexico. She updated Smart Travel Tips A to Z.

Gary Chandler Prado updated the Guadalajara chapter for the second year in a row. A journalist and travel writer, Gary has traveled in (and written about) North, Central, and South America, as well as Southeast Asia and Europe; his previous assignments with Fodor's include Guatemala, El Salvador, and California. Formerly based in San Francisco, Gary relocated to Guadalajara after his first assignment there.

Calling Mexico City his home away from home, John Hecht has lived in Mexico for nearly nine years. During that time, he has kept himself in tacos and cerveza by writing for numerous publications as a freelance journalist. Currently, he is correspondent for *The Hollywood Reporter.* He updated the Nightlife & the Arts section of the Mexico City chapter.

Since earning her B.A. in the History and Culture of Mexican Society at UC Berkeley, Michele Joyce has lived in Mexico City, where she works as an art teacher and freelance writer. She also lectures on Mexican history and is currently working toward a Masters in Modern Art History at Mexico City's Casa Lamm. She updated the Exploring, Shopping, and A to Z sections of the Mexico City chapter.

Barbara Kastelein, who's about to complete her first decade in Mexico, first made her way through the country 20 years ago, with a chaotic journey from Tijuana to Guadalajara. Crossing vast deserts and sierras through sky-splitting thunderstorms, flies, and political campaigns was more than she could resist. After obtaining a doctorate in literary studies in England, she hurried back to start a writing career and family just a few shady blocks away from Frida Kahlo's Blue House. She has a weekly column with *The Herald,* writes for international publications specializing in tourism and environmental law, and has recently authored a book, *Mexico Chic.* For this edition, Barbara updated the Side Trips from Mexico City chapter.

Although still a Bostonian at heart, Amy Gray Kirkcaldy lives and works in Monterrey, Mexico—spicy food, cowboy hats, and crazy accordion music are almost second nature to her now. She teaches English and is working toward a Masters in Education Technology at the Tecnológico de Monterrey. She translates and writes in her free time and her work appears regularly online and in travel and restaurant guides. Amy updated the Northeast section of the Veracruz and the Northeast chapter.

After traveling to impoverished Mexican communities with youth groups during his high school years, Sean Mattson decided to return to Mexico for a year of Spanish-language studies. That was six years ago. Sean is now a writer and photojournalist for Reuters and the *Guadalajara Colony Reporter* and he also freelances for major north-of-the-border dailies and magazines. He updated The Heartland chapter.

Recipient of the prestigious Pluma de Plata award for writing on Mexico, Maribeth Mellin lives in San Diego near the Tijuana border in a home filled with folk art and photos from Latin America—including a snapshot of the 140-pound marlin she caught in the Sea of Cortes. She has authored travel books on Mexico, Costa Rica, Argentina, and Peru and is currently creating a fictional account of her adventures. Maribeth updated this year's Baja California chapter and half of the Yucatán Peninsula chapter.

Since earning a B.A. in Spanish language and literature, Jane Onstott has lived and traveled extensively in Latin America. She worked as director of communications and information for the Darwin Research Station in the Galapagos Islands, and studied painting in Oaxaca between 1995 and 1998. Since 1986 Jane has contributed to Fodor's guides to Mexico and South America; this year, she updated the Pacific Coast Resorts and Yucatán chapters.

Losing his rent-controlled apartment in New York City convinced former Fodor's editor Mark Sullivan to hit the road. In 2002, over the course of six months, he took more than 150 buses to travel from the Mexican border town of Nuevo Laredo to Panama. This year he returned to Mexico and took more buses to update Oaxaca, the Chiapas, and Veracruz. In his past life as a Fodor's full-timer he oversaw the *South America, Central America,* and *UpClose Central America* guides, to name a few.

# ABOUT THIS BOOK

The best source for travel advice is a like-minded friend who's just been where you're headed. But with or without that friend, you'll be in great shape to find your way around your destination once you learn to find your way around your Fodor's guide.

**SELECTION**

Our goal is to cover the best properties, sights, and activities in their category, as well as the most interesting communities to visit. We make a point of including local food-lovers' hot spots as well as neighborhood options, and we avoid all that's touristy unless it's really worth your time. You can go on the assumption that everything in this book is recommended wholeheartedly by our writers. Flip to **On the Road with Fodor's** to learn more about who they are. It goes without saying that no property pays to be included.

**RATINGS**

Orange stars ★ denote sights and properties that our editors and writers consider the very best in the area covered by the entire book. These, the best of the best, are listed in the **Fodor's Choice** section in the front of the book. Black stars ★ highlight the sights and properties we deem **Highly Recommended**, the don't-miss sights within any region. Use the index to find complete descriptions. In cities, sights pinpointed with numbered map bullets ❶ in the margins tend to be more important than those without bullets.

**SPECIAL SPOTS**

**Pleasures & Pastimes** and chapter title pages focus on experiences that reveal the spirit of the destination. Also, watch for **Off the Beaten Path** sights. Some are out of the way, some are quirky, and all are worthwhile. When the munchies hit, look for **Need a Break?** suggestions.

**TIME IT RIGHT**

Check **On the Calendar** up front and chapters' **Timing** sections for weather and crowd overviews and best days and times to visit.

**SEE IT ALL**

Use Fodor's exclusive **Great Itineraries** as a model for your trip. Either follow those that begin the book, or mix regional itineraries from several chapters. In cities, **Good Walks** guide you to important sights in each neighborhood; ▶ indicates the starting points of walks and itineraries in the text and on the map.

**BUDGET WELL**

Hotel and restaurant price categories from ¢ to $$$$ are defined in the opening pages of each chapter—expect to find a balanced selection for every budget. For attractions, we always give standard adult admission fees; reductions are usually available for children, students, and senior citizens.

**BASIC INFO**

**Smart Travel Tips** lists travel essentials for the entire area covered by the book; city- and region-specific basics end each chapter. To find the best way to get around, see the transportation section; see individual modes of travel ("Car Travel," "Train Travel") for details.

| | |
|---|---|
| **ON THE MAPS** | Maps throughout the book show you what's where and help you find your way around. Black and orange numbered bullets ❶ ❶ in the text correlate to bullets on maps. |
| **BACKGROUND** | We give background information within the chapters in the course of explaining sights as well as in CloseUp boxes and in Understanding France at the end of the book. To get in the mood, review Books & Movies. The Vocabulary can be invaluable. |
| **FIND IT FAST** | The chapters in this book begin with Mexico City, then shift up to Baja California and work south to the Yucatán Peninsula. All regional chapters are divided into small areas, within which towns are covered in logical geographical order; interesting places between towns are flagged as En Route. Heads at the top of each page help you find what you need within a chapter. |
| **DON'T FORGET** | Restaurants are open for lunch and dinner daily unless we state otherwise; we mention dress only when there's a specific requirement and reservations only when they're essential or not accepted—it's always best to book ahead. Unless we note otherwise, hotels have private baths, phones, TVs, and air-conditioning and operate on the European Plan (a.k.a. EP, meaning without meals). We always list facilities but not whether you'll be charged extra to use them, so when pricing accommodations, find out what's included. |
| **SYMBOLS** | |

**Many Listings**

- ★ Fodor's Choice
- ★ Highly recommended
- ⊠ Physical address
- ↔ Directions
- ◐ Mailing address
- ☎ Telephone
- 🖶 Fax
- ⊕ On the Web
- ✑ E-mail
- ▦ Admission fee
- ☉ Open/closed times
- ► Start of walk/itinerary
- Ⓜ Metro stations
- ⊟ Credit cards

**Outdoors**

- 🔺 Ruins
- ◭ Camping

**Hotels & Restaurants**

- ▦ Hotel
- ⇦ Number of rooms
- ⚴ Facilities
- ⦿| Meal plans
- ✕ Restaurant
- ⟁ Reservations
- ⚔ Dress code
- ↘ Smoking
- ⦿⚲ BYOB
- ✕▦ Hotel with restaurant that warrants a visit

**Other**

- ⚙ Family-friendly
- ⎆ Contact information
- ⇨ See also
- ⊠ Branch address
- ☞ Take note

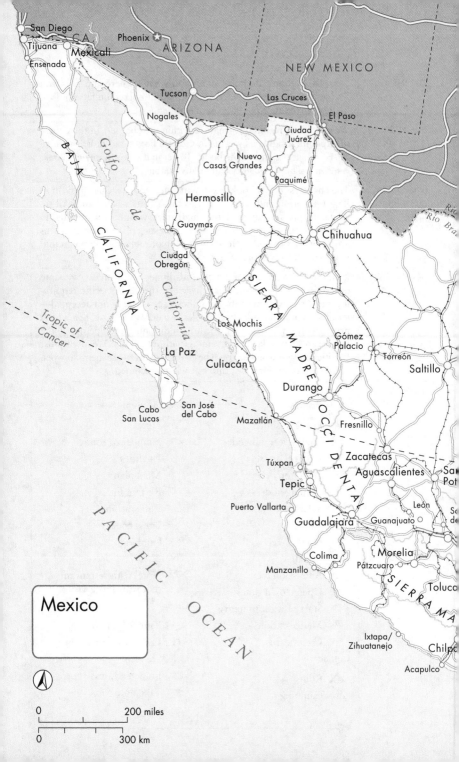

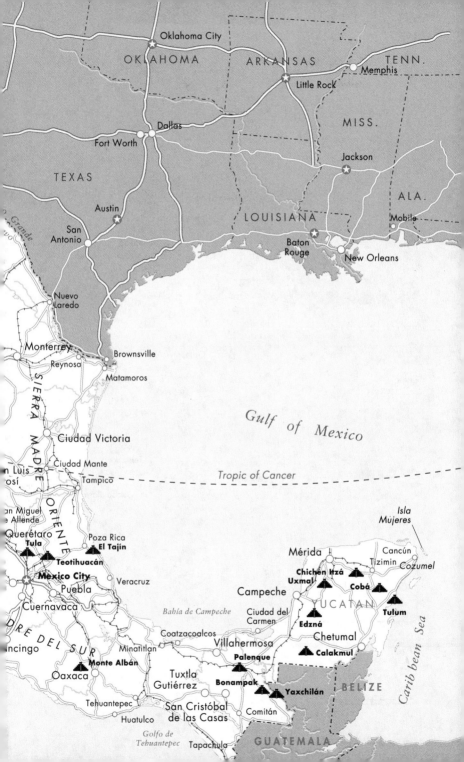

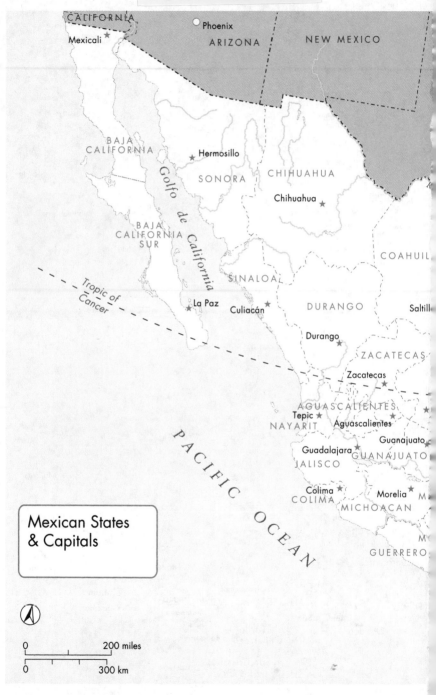

Mexican States & Capitals

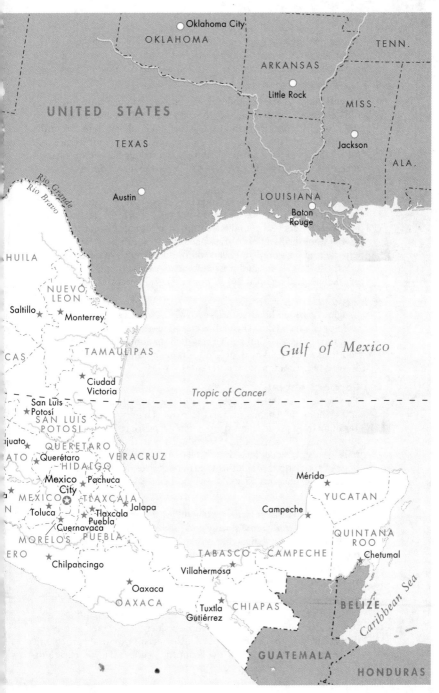

UNITED STATES

OKLAHOMA
Oklahoma City

ARKANSAS
Little Rock

TENN.

MISS.

ALA.

Jackson

TEXAS

Austin

LOUISIANA
Baton
Rouge

*Rio Grande*
*Rio Bravo*

HUILA

NUEVO
LEON

Saltillo
Monterrey

CAS

TAMAULIPAS

*Gulf of Mexico*

Ciudad
Victoria

*Tropic of Cancer*

San Luis
Potosí

SAN LUIS
POTOSI

juato

QUERETARO

ATO   Querétaro    VERACRUZ

HIDALGO

Mexico   Pachuca
City

Mérida

MEXICO   TLAXCALA

N    Toluca         Jalapa
        Tlaxcala
         Puebla
      Cuernavaca

Campeche

YUCATAN

MORELOS   PUEBLA

ERO

Chilpancingo

TABASCO   CAMPECHE

QUINTANA
ROO

Chetumal

Villahermosa

Oaxaca

OAXACA

Tuxtla
Gutiérrez

CHIAPAS

BELIZE

*Caribbean Sea*

GUATEMALA

HONDURAS

The geographical organization of the following paragraphs mirrors the organization of the book. Beginning with Mexico City, coverage then moves up to Baja California and works south to the Yucatán Peninsula.

## 1 Mexico City

Several major volcanoes and a ruined city more than a thousand years old flank Mexico's capital, once the center of Aztec civilization and now the country's cosmopolitan business, art, and culinary hub. From the Alameda, a leafy center of activity since colonial times, to the Zona Rosa, a chic shopping neighborhood, and the marvelous Bosque de Chapultepec, Mexico City offers endless options for exploration.

## 3 Baja California

A lively border culture makes Tijuana an important, if unattractive, city. Just to the south, condo complexes and surf spots lure loafers, retirees, and weekenders year-round, as do the party town of Rosarito and the more established seaport of Ensenada. But you can't say you've really experienced Baja until you head south. Boulder-strewn deserts, mountains, fishing villages, and pristine beaches can be found before reaching the highly developed Los Cabos at the southernmost tip.

## 4 Sonora

Imagine Arizona a hundred years ago, when cowboys drove cattle across wide-open ranch land. Then add a coastline—a fringe of beach washed by a turquoise sea—and you've conjured up Sonora. The sea may lure you for swimming, kayaking, and snorkeling, but the foothills of the Sierra Madre hold their own treasures.

## 5 Copper Canyon

This serpentine system of deep river gorges is easily as diverse, lovely, and exciting as Arizona's Grand Canyon. Here you'll encounter the Tarahumara, a proud cultural group renowned for its long-distance running contests. You won't have to endure a marathon to enjoy the local trails—you can set out for a short stroll or a daylong descent to the canyon floor. A train trip through this largely uncharted region usually begins or ends in Chihuahua City.

## 6 Guadalajara

Mexico's second-largest metropolis fully lives up to its reputation for being *señorial y moderna* (lordly and modern). The city retains a generous measure of colonial charm thanks to its historic center. Some of the country's best arts and crafts can be found at Tlaquepaque, on the city's outskirts, and Tonalá, about 10 minutes farther away. And at Tequila you can drink at the source of Mexico's famous firewater.

## 7 The Heartland

Rich with the history of Mexico's revolution, the Heartland is a treasury of colonial towns and cities whose residents lead quiet, largely traditional lives. Even in San Miguel de Allende, an expatriate art colony, the steep cobblestone streets and beautiful facades take you back hundreds of years.

### 8 Pacific Coast Resorts

People call this jungle-backed coastline the Mexican Riviera and the Gold Coast. Sun worshippers, water-sports lovers, cruise ships, and anglers all converge on the cove-scalloped Pacific coast. Puerto Vallarta is the place for shopping and for diverse, delicious dining; Ixtapa/Zihuatanejo is a two-for-one attraction, a laid-back fishing village adjoining a glitzy resort.

### 9 Acapulco

The beach scene and nightlife of Acapulco have proved their staying power; for decades vacationers have spent their days lying around on beach towels or hammocks and their nights exploring the buzzing restaurants and dance clubs. For those who can rouse themselves to do some sightseeing, the cobblestone streets of nearby Taxco, the silver city, beckon.

### 10 Oaxaca

The prime appeal of Oaxaca state and its eponymous colonial capital is the old and the older. Baroque buildings from the Spanish conquest pass almost for new when compared with the magnificent, millennia-old remnants of the native Zapotec and Mixtec civilizations. The state's coastal developments of Puerto Escondido and Bahías de Huatulco are beloved by surfers and beach bums.

### 11 Chiapas & Tabasco

The state of Chiapas has always been off the beaten path, best known for the mountainous colonial town of San Cristóbal and the jungle-covered ruins of Palenque. Though it may take more careful planning to travel through this region, it certainly has plenty to make you linger, much of it undiscovered by the average adventurer.

### 12 Veracruz & the Northeast

Many Texans get their first taste of Mexico in the northeastern border towns of Nuevo Laredo, Reynosa, and Matamoros. Texan or otherwise, if you venture farther down to Monterrey, you'll find far more sophisticated dining, shopping, and cultural attractions of the country's third-largest city. The superb but little-explored pyramids of El Tajín and the raffish charm of Veracruz, the first European city established on the North American mainland, are among the many reasons to continue south.

### 13 The Yucatán Peninsula

Mexico's most-visited region will reward you with both spectacular beaches and evocative ruins—sometimes simultaneously, as at Tulum. Cancún was purpose-built for pleasure, while Isla Mujeres provides a more peaceful retreat. The world's second-largest barrier reef lies just off the island of Cozumel. Meanwhile, the coastline south of Cancún has been dubbed the Riviera Maya as an increasing number of luxe resorts stake their claim.

## Canyons & Coasts
### 9 to 12 days

Natural wonders never cease in northern and western Mexico. From the heart-stopping views and hikes into the Coppper Canyon to Baja Sur's inland deserts, its annual migrations of whales, and the beaches of Los Cabos, opportunities for adventure and relaxation are everywhere.

**Copper Canyon** *3 to 4 days*. Riding the Chihuahua al Pacífico rail line from west to east affords the most stunning views of the canyons. Start off in Los Mochis or El Fuerte and make the mountain village of Cerocahui your first stop. Continue the next day to Creel, a good base for day hikes or major excursions, such as the 806-foot Basaseachi waterfalls, one of North America's highest. If a dose of urban life

feels like the appropriate tonic after the canyons, spend a night in Chihuahua before catching a plane for La Paz.

**La Paz** *2 days*. Spend the first day in town; as sunset nears, head for the seaside *malecón*, where couples and families stroll beside playgrounds on the sand. Spend the second day kayaking, snorkeling, or diving around Isla Espíritu Santo or Isla Partida in the Mar de Cortés—you're almost guaranteed to spot sea lions and whales. In the winter and early spring, join an all-day tour to Bahía Magdalena, where migrating gray whales give birth.

**Loreto** *1 to 2 days*. Visitors to Loreto are largely intent on fishing in the rich waters off nearby islands, and even nonanglers enjoy a boat ride at dawn. Loreto's laid-back hotels are also the perfect base for exploring the nearby mountains and coast. If you have a sturdy, high-

clearance vehicle, drive about two hours past cattle ranches and boulder-strewn hills to the well-preserved Misión San Javier, or drive a couple of hours north to the incomparably picturesque Bahía Concepción and the town of Mulegé, in an oasis by the sea.

**Los Cabos** *3 to 4 days*. Spend your first day in Los Cabos swimming and sunbathing at Playa Médano and exploring Cabo San Lucas. Sample its theme restaurants and trendy cafés that night. Begin Day 2 with an early fishing trip; late-risers can instead breakfast at one of the Corridor's lavish resorts and later snorkel at Bahía Chileno. Stroll through San José del Cabo's plazas and galleries in the evening, and end the day dining on fresh fish. Spend the rest of your days exploring Baja's incomparable desert and sea scenery: head for the artsy enclave of Todos Santos, or to the East Cape for long drives on sandy desert roads beside the sea.

### BY PUBLIC TRANSPORTATION

Distances here demand a fair amount of air travel: first from Mexico City to Los Mochis, then from Chihuahua to La Paz. The entire rail trip from Los Mochis to Chihuahua is a 15-hour proposition, but it's best to stop at towns along the way and reboard after spending at least one night. There are daily flights from Chihuahua City to La Paz, and flying is by far the best way to travel between these two cities. From La Paz, tour companies will take you to Bahía Magdalena to see whales. To get to Loreto (3 hours north of La Paz), the East Cape (1 hour south), and Los Cabos (2 hours south), rent a car so you can explore the quieter coastal stretches on your own. Buses also run throughout Baja Sur.

## Colonial Mexico
### 6 to 9 days

Remarkably well preserved, these colonial cities are full of atmospheric haciendas and richly decorated cathedrals—along with intriguing juxtapositions of the colonial and the indigenous that are classic Mexico.

**Puebla** *2 to 3 days.* Although Puebla has grown considerably and its downtown can be crowded with traffic, this old city offers unforgettable architecture and regional cuisine, both unique to the destination. You could easily spend a day just admiring the red brick, sculpted stucco, and Talavera tile facades of the city center. To complete the experience, stay at a restored colonial mansion-cum-hotel. After one or two days in Puebla, spend a day at less frenetic Cholula, where you can explore the interior of the great pyramid or visit the lovely baroque churches of Santa María Tonantzintla and San Francisco Acatepec, both just outside town.

**Querétaro** *1 day.* This Heartland city has been called the cradle of independence. Its restored Plaza de la Independencia is filled with grand mansions once belonging to titled friends of the Crown. Amble around the square and nearby streets to see the baroque Museo de Arte de Querétaro, housed in an 18th-century monastery; the Palacio del Gobierno del Estado; and the Jardín de la Corregidora.

**San Miguel de Allende** *1 to 2 days.* A cultural hub of the region, this friendly city is full of bookstores, art galleries, coffee shops, and American expats. Take time to visit some of the churches—the Gothic Revival Parroquia, the churrigueresque Iglesia de San Francisco, and the unique Oratorio de San Felipe Neri. Consider a side trip to the historic village of Dolores Hidalgo, home of the insurgent priest whose cry for Independence started the 1810 war.

**Guanajuato** *2 to 3 days.* Splendid buildings rising above labyrinthine streets give Guanajuato its medieval appearance. Make your way to the main square and the impressive Teatro Juárez. El Museo Casa Diego Rivera, birthplace of the famed muralist, and the hulking Alhóndiga de Granaditas fortress are nearby. On Day 2, visit the Basílica Colegiata de Nuestra Señora de Guanajuato and La Valenciana—the former for its 8th-century statue of the Virgin, the latter for its elaborately carved pink facade and gilded altars.

### BY PUBLIC TRANSPORTATION
The easiest way to get to and between Puebla, Querétaro, San Miguel de Allende, and Guanajuato is by luxury bus. From Mexico City the bus from the Observatorio or Northern bus terminals to Puebla or Querétaro takes about two hours. From Querétaro it's another two hours to San Miguel. San Miguel to Guanajuato is a 2½-hour ride. Nearby León's airport has flights to Mexico City (1 hour).

## La Cocina Mexicana
### 8 to 12 days

Considering the hybridization of Mexican food served in the United States, savoring the true flavors of Mexico can only deepen your appreciation of the country and its culture. By necessity—Mexico is a vast country—this gastronomic tour is limited to a few cities, but keep in mind that every region has its own excellent cuisine.

**Mexico City** *2 to 4 days.* Mexico City chefs turn out everything from cutting-edge to pre-Hispanic dishes for their *chilango* (Mexico City) clientele. Many of the country's most adventurous chefs work in the capital, so you should definitely seek out some *nueva cocina mexicana* (nouvelle Mexican cuisine). There's also plenty of regional cuisine, which means that you'll find delicious Veracruz seafood, Yucatecan *pibíl*, Chihuahua *carne asada*, and more, all without passing the city limits. Wander the city's vast produce markets to gain an appreciation, however slender, of the ingredients that make up your favorite

dishes. Be aware, however, that pickpockets seek out prosperous-looking or foreign shoppers, and guard your valuables well.
**Puebla** *2 days.* From Mexico City, make your way to colonial icons like the Ex-Convento de Santa Rosa, where nuns are credited with the invention of the city's most famous dishes, including *mole negro*, a think, spicy dark sauce, and *chiles en nogadas*, chilies stuffed with a sweet and

highlands to the north; look for "Altura Pluma" (high grown) coffee, the best of Mexico's beans. You should stop in at least one café for *café lechero*, the town's special coffee served ceremoniously with hot milk.
**Oaxaca City** *2 to 3 days.* Several native cultures merge in exotic Oaxaca City, where you can feast on the seven types of *mole* the city is known for, or taste its sweet and savory tamales. Try one of the tra-

chocolate is made, dozens of fresh juices, and much more.

**BY PUBLIC TRANSPORTATION**
The best way to get from Mexico City to Puebla is by luxury bus (2 hrs), from the TAPO terminal. The bus from Puebla over the mountains and into Veracruz City takes four hours. From Veracruz to Oaxaca you can fly back to Mexico City (1½ hrs), then on to Oaxaca (2 hrs), although with airport waits and flying time, this approach may take just as long as driving or taking buses, which at least allow you to enjoy the scenery.

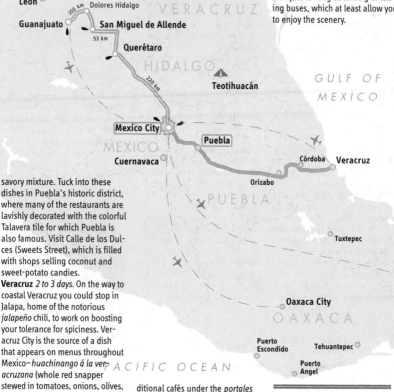

savory mixture. Tuck into these dishes in Puebla's historic district, where many of the restaurants are lavishly decorated with the colorful Talavera tile for which Puebla is also famous. Visit Calle de los Dulces (Sweets Street), which is filled with shops selling coconut and sweet-potato candies.
**Veracruz** *2 to 3 days.* On the way to coastal Veracruz you could stop in Jalapa, home of the notorious *jalapeño* chili, to work on boosting your tolerance for spiciness. Veracruz City is the source of a dish that appears on menus throughout Mexico—*huachinango á la veracruzana* (whole red snapper stewed in tomatoes, onions, olives, and herbs). Seafood is a way of life in Veracruz, and you can expect other mouthwatering dishes like crab *salpicón* (finely chopped with onion, cilantro, and lime), as well as sea bass, prawns, and lobster. The town's lively café society is fueled by the coffee grown in the

ditional cafés under the *portales* (arcades) in the main square: more for the experience than for the food. The local market is an essential stop for its symphony of colors and smells. There you'll find *quesillo*, Oaxaca's rolled string cheese, chocolate and cinnamon cakes from which delicious hot

## Ancient Mexico
**8 to 11 days**

Inhabited by numerous cultures in pre-Hispanic days, Mexico has one of the world's most impressive collections of archaeological sites. The ancient Mayan cities are at their finest on the Yucatán Peninsula and the lowlands of Chiapas, while modern Villahermosa houses ancient altars and sculpture in a mid-city, open-air park. **Villahermosa** *1 to 2 days.* The transportation and commercial hub for modern Mexico's oil industry, Villahermosa was once part a swampy lowland jungle where the Olmec culture held sway a thousand years before the Christian era. See outstanding examples of this little-understood culture at Parque Museo La Venta, where a series of enormous Olmec stone heads are the main attraction. Later in the day, swing north out of town to Comalcalco, a Late Classic Maya site with baked brick temples, so far the only ones known to archaeologists. If you prefer not to rush, visit Comalcalco on the morning of Day 2 before proceding to Palenque, in the lowlands of Chiapas.

and queens who ruled the city, a commercial and transportation hub connecting the region with Tikal, Copán, Calakmul, and other important cities of the lowland Maya. Extensive and graceful, the site is worth an entire day's exploration, with a midday break to escape the heat. If you choose to spend another day in the area, the falls and pools of Agua Azul and Misol-Ha (22 and 62 km [14 and 38 mi] to the south, respectively) give kids and adults some outdoor fun in two beautiful settings.

**Mérida** *6 or 7 days.* A capital city of the Yucatán and the most Maya of all Yucatecan cities, Mérida is a

sions, cathedral, small churches, and shady plazas. On your second day, head to Chichén Itzá, an extensive site built by two different Mayan empires. Spend all of Day 3 at beautiful Uxmal, the sterling example of the graceful Pu'uc architectural style. If time permits, you can spend a day at the smaller Pu'uc ruins of Kabah, Sayil, and Labná. Consider planning your trip around a local Mayan festival to see the intriguing blend of pre-Hispanic beliefs and Catholic rituals.

**BY PUBLIC TRANSPORTATION**
In Villahermosa you can take a cab to the Parque Museo La Venta,

**Palenque** *1 to 2 days.* A visit to these mysterious and beautiful ruins of the Maya kingdom is requisite for lovers of architecture and ancient lore. Intricately carved panels of limestone and stucco, once painted in bright red, black, and ochre, tell stories of the kings

perfect base for seeing the region's ruins. Take in the Museum of Anthropology to preview Mayan art, and walk around the lively main square to view its colonial man-

but unless you have your own wheels, you'll need to book an excursion to Comalcalco as buses to the city are unreliable. To get to Palenque you can catch a luxury bus from the ADO terminal; the trip takes about 2½ hours. There are also full-day excursions to Palenque from Villahermosa. From Tuxtla Gutiérrez there is a one-hour flight to Mérida. You can take day trips to the major Yucatán sites from Mérida.

°C   °F
100 — 212
40 — 105
37 — 98.6
30 — 90
25 — 80
20 — 70
15 — 60
10 — 50
5 — 40
0 — 32
−5 — 20
−10 — 10
−15 — 0
−20

Mexico is sufficiently large and geographically diverse enough that you can find a place to visit any time of year. October through May are generally the driest months; during the peak of the rainy season (June–September), it usually rains for a few hours daily, especially in the late afternoon. But the sun often shines for the rest of the day.

From December through the second week after Easter, the resorts—where most people go—are the most crowded and expensive. This also holds true for July and August, school-vacation months, when Mexican families fill hotels. To avoid the masses, the highest prices, and the worst rains, consider visiting Mexico during November, April, or May.

Mexicans travel during traditional holiday periods—Christmas through January 6 (Three Kings Day), *Semana Santa* (Holy Week, the week before Easter), the week after Easter—and summertime school vacations as well as over extended national holiday weekends, called *puentes* (bridges). Festivals play a big role in Mexican national life. If you plan to travel during a major national event, reserve both lodgings and transportation well in advance.

### Climate

Mexico's coasts and low-lying sections of the interior are often very hot if not actually tropical. The high central plateau on which Mexico City, Guadalajara, and many of the country's colonial cities is springlike year-round—days may be downright hot, however, and evenings chilly or even cold.

🗹 Forecasts **Weather Channel Connection** ☎ 900/932-8437 95¢ per minute from a Touch-Tone phone ⊕ www.weather.com.

## ACAPULCO (PACIFIC COAST)

| Jan. | 88F | 31C | May | 90F | 32C | Sept. | 90F | 32C |
|---|---|---|---|---|---|---|---|---|
| | 72 | 22 | | 75 | 24 | | 75 | 24 |
| Feb. | 88F | 31C | June | 90F | 32C | Oct. | 90F | 32C |
| | 72 | 22 | | 77 | 25 | | 75 | 24 |
| Mar. | 88F | 31C | July | 90F | 32C | Nov. | 90F | 32C |
| | 72 | 22 | | 77 | 25 | | 73 | 23 |
| Apr. | 90F | 32C | Aug. | 91F | 33C | Dec. | 88F | 31C |
| | 73 | 23 | | 77 | 25 | | 71 | 22 |

## COZUMEL (CARIBBEAN COAST)

| Jan. | 84F | 29C | May | 91F | 33C | Sept. | 89F | 32C |
|---|---|---|---|---|---|---|---|---|
| | 66 | 19 | | 73 | 23 | | 75 | 24 |
| Feb. | 84F | 29C | June | 89F | 32C | Oct. | 87F | 31C |
| | 66 | 19 | | 75 | 24 | | 73 | 23 |
| Mar. | 88F | 31C | July | 91F | 33C | Nov. | 86F | 30C |
| | 69 | 21 | | 73 | 23 | | 71 | 22 |
| Apr. | 89F | 32C | Aug. | 91F | 33C | Dec. | 84F | 29C |
| | 71 | 22 | | 73 | 23 | | 68 | 20 |

## ENSENADA (BAJA CALIFORNIA NORTE)

| Jan. | 66F | 19C | May | 70F | 21C | Sept. | 79F | 26C |
|---|---|---|---|---|---|---|---|---|
| | 45 | 7 | | 52 | 11 | | 59 | 15 |
| Feb. | 68F | 20C | June | 73F | 23C | Oct. | 75F | 24C |
| | 45 | 7 | | 54 | 12 | | 54 | 12 |
| Mar. | 68F | 20C | July | 77F | 25C | Nov. | 72F | 22C |
| | 46 | 8 | | 61 | 16 | | 48 | 9 |
| Apr. | 69F | 21C | Aug. | 79F | 26C | Dec. | 68F | 20C |
| | 48 | 9 | | 61 | 16 | | 45 | 7 |

## LA PAZ (BAJA CALIFORNIA SUR)

| Jan. | 73F | 23C | May | 91F | 33C | Sept. | 95F | 35C |
|---|---|---|---|---|---|---|---|---|
| | 54 | 12 | | 59 | 15 | | 73 | 23 |
| Feb. | 77F | 25C | June | 95F | 35C | Oct. | 91F | 33C |
| | 54 | 12 | | 64 | 18 | | 66 | 19 |
| Mar. | 80F | 27C | July | 97F | 36C | Nov. | 84F | 29C |
| | 54 | 12 | | 71 | 22 | | 61 | 16 |
| Apr. | 86F | 30C | Aug. | 97F | 36C | Dec. | 77F | 25C |
| | 55 | 13 | | 73 | 23 | | 54 | 12 |

## MEXICO CITY (CENTRAL MEXICO)

| Jan. | 70F | 21C | May | 79F | 26C | Sept. | 72F | 22C |
|---|---|---|---|---|---|---|---|---|
| | 44 | 6 | | 54 | 12 | | 52 | 11 |
| Feb. | 73F | 23C | June | 77F | 25C | Oct. | 72F | 22C |
| | 45 | 7 | | 54 | 12 | | 50 | 10 |
| Mar. | 79F | 26C | July | 73F | 23C | Nov. | 72F | 22C |
| | 48 | 9 | | 52 | 11 | | 46 | 8 |
| Apr. | 81F | 27C | Aug. | 73F | 23C | Dec. | 70F | 21C |
| | 50 | 10 | | 54 | 12 | | 45 | 7 |

## MONTERREY (NORTHEAST MEXICO)

| Jan. | 68F | 20C | May | 88F | 31C | Sept. | 88F | 31C |
|---|---|---|---|---|---|---|---|---|
| | 48 | 9 | | 68 | 20 | | 70 | 21 |
| Feb. | 73F | 23C | June | 91F | 33C | Oct. | 81F | 27C |
| | 52 | 11 | | 72 | 22 | | 63 | 17 |
| Mar. | 79F | 26C | July | 91F | 34C | Nov. | 73F | 23C |
| | 57 | 14 | | 72 | 22 | | 55 | 13 |
| Apr. | 86F | 30C | Aug. | 93F | 34C | Dec. | 70F | 21C |
| | 64 | 18 | | 72 | 22 | | 50 | 10 |

## SAN MIGUEL DE ALLENDE (HEARTLAND)

| Jan. | 75F | 24C | May | 88F | 31C | Sept. | 79F | 26C |
|---|---|---|---|---|---|---|---|---|
| | 45 | 9 | | 59 | 15 | | 59 | 15 |
| Feb. | 79F | 26C | June | 88F | 30C | Oct. | 79F | 26C |
| | 48 | 9 | | 59 | 15 | | 54 | 12 |
| Mar. | 86F | 30C | July | 82F | 28C | Nov. | 75F | 24C |
| | 54 | 12 | | 59 | 15 | | 50 | 10 |
| Apr. | 88F | 31C | Aug. | 82F | 28C | Dec. | 75F | 24C |
| | 57 | 14 | | 59 | 15 | | 46 | 8 |

# ON THE CALENDAR

Mexico is the land of festivals; if you reserve lodging well in advance, they're a golden opportunity to experience Mexico's culture. January is full of long, regional festivals. Notable are the Fiesta de la Inmaculada Concepción (Feast of the Immaculate Conception), which transforms the city of Morelia into a sea of lights and flowers for much of the month, and a series of folkloric dances in Chiapa de Corzo, Chiapas, that culminates in the Fiesta de San Sebastian, the third week in January.

Several cultural events take place at different times each year. Among these is Cancún's noteworthy Jazz Festival, which happens in the spring or fall and which draws a huge international crowd from the United States, South America, and Europe. The Isla Mujeres International Music Festival, during which the island fills with music and dancers from around the world, is another such event.

## WINTER

| | |
|---|---|
| Dec. | On the 12th, the Fiesta de la Virgen de Guadalupe (Feast of the Virgin of Guadalupe), Mexico's patron saint is honored with processions and native folk dances, particularly at her shrine in Mexico City. In Puerto Vallarta, 12 days of processions and festivities lead up to the night of the 12th. Navidad (Christmas) and the days leading up to it (roughly the 16th through the 24th) see candlelight processions, holiday parties, and the breaking open of piñatas. Mexico City is brightly decorated. |
| Dec. 23 | The Noche de Rábanos (Radish Night), a pre-Christmas tradition in Oaxaca, is one of the most colorful in Mexico: participants carve giant radishes into amusing shapes and display their unusual tableaux in the city's main plaza. |
| Jan. 1 | Día del Año Nuevo (New Year's Day) is traditionally celebrated with large family gatherings. Shops and restaurants may be closed; agricultural and livestock fairs are held in the provinces. |
| Jan. 6 | The Día de los Reyes (Ephiphany) refers to the Day the Three Wise Men brought gifts to the Christ child; on this day Mexican children are traditionally treated to small gifts (although Santa Claus has made inroads in more cosmopolitan cities and border towns). |
| Jan. 17 | The Fiesta de San Antonio Abad (Feast of Saint Anthony the Abbot) honors animals all over Mexico. Pets and livestock are decked out with flowers and ribbons and taken to church for a blessing. |
| Jan. 18 | Taxco's patron saints are celebrated with the Fiesta de Santa Prisca y de San Sebastián (Feast of Saint Prisca and Saint Sebastián) with music and fireworks. |

| | |
|---|---|
| Feb.–Mar. | Día de la Candelaría, or Candlemas Day, means fiestas, parades, bull-fights, and lantern-decorated streets. Festivities include a running of the bulls through the streets of Tlacotalpan, Veracruz. The pre-Lenten Carnaval season is celebrated throughout Mexico—most notably in Mazatlán, Veracruz, and Cozumel—with parades of floats, bands, and all-night parties. |

**SPRING**

| | |
|---|---|
| Mar. 21 | Aniversario de Benito Juárez (birthday of Benito Juárez), a national holiday, is most popular in Oaxaca, birthplace of the beloved 19th-century Mexican president. This is also the day that Cuernavaca's Fiesta de la Primavera (Spring Festival) marks the beginning of the season. |
| Apr. | Semana Santa (Holy Week), the week leading to Easter Sunday, a moveable feast, is observed with parades and passion plays. There are particularly moving and sober ceremonies in Oaxaca and in Taxco. |
| Apr.–May | The Feria Nacional de San Marcos (San Marcos National Fair), held in Aguascalientes, is one of the country's best. It features Indian *matachines* (dances performed by grotesque figures), mariachi bands, and bullfights. The 10-day Festival de las Artes (Arts Festival) brings music, theater, and dance troupes from all over Latin America to San Luis Potosí. |
| May | The first day of May, Día del Trabajo (Labor Day), workers parade through the streets and enjoy family activities. Don't expect to find much of anything open on this day. |
| May 5 | Cinco de Mayo is a bank holiday, although some towns, especially those in the state of Puebla, celebrate the anniversary of the defeat of French invaders in 1862 with speeches and parades. |
| May 15 | The Fiesta de San Isidro Labrador (Feast of Saint Isadore, the Farmer) is noted nationwide by the blessing of new seeds and animals. In Cuernavaca, a parade of oxen wreathed in flowers is followed by street parties and feasting. |

**SUMMER**

| | |
|---|---|
| June 1 | Día de la Marina (Navy Day) is commemorated in all Mexican sea-ports and is especially colorful in Acapulco, Mazatlán, and Veracruz. |
| June 10 | The Fiesta de Corpus Christi (Feast of Corpus Christi) is celebrated in different ways. In Mexico City, children are dressed in native costumes and taken to the cathedral for a blessing. In Papantla, Veracruz, the Dance of the Flying Birdmen—a pre-Hispanic ritual to the sun—is held throughout the day. |
| June 24 | On the Fiesta de San Juan Bautista, (Feast of Saint John the Baptist), a popular national holiday, many Mexicans observe a tradition of tossing a "blessing" of water on most anyone within reach. |

| | |
|---|---|
| July | The Feria Nacional (National Fair) in Durango runs from the Day of Our Lady of Refuge (July 4) to the anniversary of the founding of Durango in 1563 (July 22). The old-time agricultural fair has become known across the country for its carnival rides, livestock shows, and music. Many town celebrate the days preceding the Fiesta de Santiago Apostle (Feast of Saint James the Apostle), on July 25, with *charreadas,* Mexican-style rodeos. |
| July 16 | Fiesta de Nuestra Señora del Carmen (Feast of Our Lady of Mt. Carmel) is celebrated with fairs, bullfights, fireworks, even a major fishing tournament. |
| Aug. | The Fiesta de San Augustine (Feast of Saint Augustine) brings a month of music, dance, and fireworks to Puebla. On the 28th it's customary to prepare the famous *chiles en nogada.* |
| Aug. 15 | Fiesta de la Asunción (Feast of the Assumption of the Virgin) is celebrated nationwide with religious processions. In Huamantla, Tlaxcala, the festivities include a running of the bulls and a carpet of flowers laid out in front of the church. |
| Aug. 25 | The Fiesta de San Luis Potosí honors the town's patron, San Luis Rey, with traditional dance, music, and foods. |
| **FALL** | |
| Sept. 16 | Día de la Independencia, or Independence Day, is celebrated beginning the evening of the 15th. It's marked throughout Mexico with fireworks and parties that outblast those on New Year's Eve. The biggest celebrations are in Mexico City. |
| Sept. 29 | Towns with the name San Miguel naturally celebrate the Fiesta de San Miguel, honoring their patron saint, St. Michael. Colorful parties are held in San Miguel de Allende with bullfights, folk dances, concerts, and fireworks. |
| Oct. | The Fiestas de Octubre (October Festival) means a month of cultural, epicurean, and sporting events in Guadalajara. |
| Oct. 4 | The Fiesta de San Francis de Assisi is a day for processions dedicated to St. Francis in parts of the country. |
| Oct. 12 | The Día de la Raza (Columbus Day) marks the "discovery" of the Americas from an indigenous perspective. Mexicans get a day off of work to contemplate the socio-political ramifications of the Conquest, or merely to party with their *compadres.* |
| Oct.–Nov. | The Festival Internacional Cervantino (International Cervantes Festival) in Guanajuato is a top cultural event that attracts dancers, singers, and actors from various countries. |
| Nov. | On Día de Todos los Santos and Día de Muertos (November 1 and 2), the Day of All Saints and Day of The Dead, families pay respects to departed relatives. Customs vary, but in parts of central and south- |

| | |
|---|---|
| | ern Mexico, families erect elaborate home altars to welcome the dead, refurbish grave sites, and, in some places, hold all-night candlelight cemetery vigils. |
| Nov. 20 | The **Aniversario de la Revolución Mexicana** (Anniversary of the Mexican Revolution) is a major national holiday. |
| Nov.–Dec. | The **Feria de la Plata** (National Silver Fair) is an annual event in Taxco, Guerrero, and an occasion for even more silver selling than usual, the crowning of a Silver Queen, and jewelry exhibitions. |

# PLEASURES & PASTIMES

**Ancient Ruins** Some of the greatest ancient civilizations—among them the Aztecs, the Zapotecs, Mixtecs, and the Maya—left their mark throughout Mexico. Important discoveries in the past few years, such as those at Teotihuacán, have stoked the buzz of inquiry and speculation about these societies. Pick your period and your preference, whether for well-excavated sites or overgrown, out-of-the-way ruins barely touched by a scholar's shovel. The Yucatán Peninsula is, hands down, the greatest source of ancient treasure, with such heavy hitters as Chichén Itzá, Uxmal, Edzná, and Calakmul. However, if you dig deep enough, you're likely to find interesting vestiges of Mexico's pre-Hispanic past in any region in the country. A visit to Mexico City's archaeological museum, one of the best in the world, could ignite the imagination of even those who thought they had no interest in antiquity, and help others focus on the places they'd most like to explore further.

**Arts & Crafts** Mexico is one of the best countries in the world to purchase *artesanías* (handicrafts). Each region has a specialty, be it brightly colored textiles, expressive carved masks, carved wood furniture, or delicately wrought jewelry. There's always souvenir-grade work for sale, but if you shop carefully you can find exceptional, genuine works of folk art. (*See* "Hecho a Mano" in Chapter 7 for more information.) The prizes you'll find—especially in the Yucatan, Chiapas, Oaxaca, Michoacán, and Guanajuato—can give you a deeper appreciation of classic and contemporary folk art made by Mexico's many talented artists.

The contemporary art scene is another hot spot on the cultural map. A wave of young, intrepid artists has drawn much international attention; they've propelled recent Mexican art exhibits in museums from New York to San Diego. To see the latest work at the source, check out the galleries in Mexico City, Oaxaca City, or Puerto Vallarta or visit one of the country's impressive modern-art museums.

**Beaches** A curve of golden sand may well be the first image that pops into your mind when you think of Mexico; the country's beaches are the lure for hundreds of thousands of travelers. Generally speaking, the Pacific is rougher and the waters less translucent than the Caribbean, which is a better choice for snorkeling and scuba diving. Cancún, Cozumel, and Isla Mujeres, as well as what has come to be called the Riviera Maya, are among the best and most popular beach destinations on the Caribbean coast. All beach resorts offer a variety of water sports, including waterskiing, windsurfing, parasailing, and, if the water is clear enough, snorkeling and scuba diving. Surfers favor the beaches south of Rosarito, around Ensenada, and at Puerto Escondido, near Huatulco, as well as myriad secret spots up and down the Pacific coast.

If you want to get in the water, first do a little investigating, as it can be in polluted in some areas. Zihuatanejo, Acapulco, and other popular ports have long fought under-reported pollution problems, which are mostly the result of overtaxed, inadequate infrastructures. Zihuatanejo received some bad press in 2003, and pollution of its once-pristine bay by raw sewage can indeed be a problem. It's best to avoid swimming in closed bays—even those as famous and alluring as Acapulco and Zihuatanejo—for several days after a substantial rainstorm, as post-storm runoff can contaminate otherwise safe seas. Instead hang at the hotel pool or parasail above the waves for a fabulous view.

## Horseback Riding

The dry ranch lands of northern Mexico have countless stables and dude ranches, as do San Miguel de Allende and Querétaro in the heartland. Puerto Vallarta, Mazatlán, and other major resorts have mostly banned horseback riding on the beach, although expeditions can be arranged to cool destinations in the Sierra Madre mountains up and down the Pacific Coast, in the Copper Canyon, and throughout the country.

## Music

From *norteño* to *mariachi* to *banda,* Mexico's varieties of music have at their core expressive power and verve that make their popularity instantly understandable.

**Banda** rose to fame in the 1990s. Brass bands small and large arrange tunes from other styles, including ranchera and cumbia. Among its premier practitioners is Banda del Recodo.

**Cumbia** has its roots in Colombia, where it is also a favorite. Immensely danceable, cumbia was *the* craze before banda came along. Traditional cumbia uses guitars, accordions, brass, and driving African-influenced percussion.

**Danzón** is a dignified dance that originally came to Veracruz from Cuba. The style's popularity there has waned, but not so in Mexico. The music has a special tie to Veracruz City, where couples still dance to it in city parks in the evenings.

**Mariachi** might seem to be Mexico's signature musical style, even though it is just one of many. It originated in the state of Jalisco, by some accounts at a garden party that dictator Porfirio Díaz threw for Americans in 1907. Mariachi bands play in plazas countrywide, their traditional brass sections backed up with guitars, harps, violins, and several unique stringed instruments such as the *requinto.*

**Nortec** is an example of how traditional music forms are being used in a cutting-edge music scene; samples of *norteño* are mixed with electronica dance beats.

**Norteño,** characteristically sung without passion, is known for lyrics that pull no punches when it comes to the tragedies of life. It comes from northern Mexico—border country. Accordions are usually a part of norteño bands.

**Ranchero** is as passionate as Mexican music gets. Ranchero is often compared to American country music; its powerfully direct, relatively simple style was traditionally linked to the working class.

## Regional Cuisine
Mexican gastronomes are dismayed by foreigners' glaring misconceptions of Mexican food as being essentially tacos, enchiladas, and burritos. Mexico's food is as diverse as its geography; distinct specialties typify each region. Using fresh ingredients is the norm rather than the exception, and recipes are passed down through generations.

The staples of beans, chilies, and tortillas on which the poor subsist form the basis for creative variations of sophisticated national dishes but are by no means the only ingredients commonly used. As Mexican cooking continues to develop an international reputation, more people are recognizing its versatility. The increasing interest in *nueva cocina mexicana* (nouvelle Mexican cuisine) prompts chefs to take a fresh look at indigenous ingredients such as crunchy grasshoppers and *huitlacoche* (black corn fungus).

You'll have a wealth of opportunities to try renowned dishes at the source and to sample flavors not readily available elsewhere. Curious about guayaba fruit, roasted kid, or a half dozen kinds of mole sauce? Now's your chance to taste them. Regional chapters describe local specialties; see also "La Cocina Mexicana" in Chapter 1 for more information.

## Soccer
As in Europe, this is Mexico's national sport (known as *futból*). It is played almost year-round at the Estadio Azteca in Mexico City, as well as in other large cities. Soccer fields appear in the most unlikely places, and spirited pick-up games are just as much fun to watch as the professional matches.

# FODOR'S CHOICE

**Fodor'sChoice**
★

The sights, restaurants, hotels, and other travel experiences on these pages are our editors' top picks—our Fodor's Choices. They're the best of their type in the area covered by the book—not to be missed and always worth your time. In the destination chapters that follow, you will find all the details.

## LODGING

| | |
|---|---|
| $$$$ | **Camino Real**, Mexico City. A trifecta of excellence: a design by one of Mexico's best modern architects, renowned artwork, and a branch of Le Cirque. |
| $$$$ | **La Casa Que Canta**, Zihuatanejo. An infinity pool, folk art, and the creative use of flower petals are among the things to sing about. |
| $$$$ | **Danzante Resort**, Loreto. A respect for nature, captivating architecture, and expert area advice from the owners are hallmarks. |
| $$$$ | **Esperanza**, Los Cabos Corridor. It takes tender-loving care seriously with a spa, fab amenities, and personal service. |
| $$$$ | **Fairmont Acapulco Princess**. A tony classic on Playa Revolcadero. Before there was in-room wireless Internet access or aromatherapy treatments, there were guests like Howard Hughes. |
| $$$$ | **Four Seasons Mexico City**. Modeled after an 18th-century palace, but equipped with the most up-to-date amenities, this hotel is the best of both worlds. |
| $$$$ | **Maroma**, Punta Maroma. Peacocks wander the grounds at this lavish hotel, and an exotic "floatarium" awaits you at the spa. |
| $$$$ | **Marquis Reforma**, Mexico City. Ask for a room with a view here and you may never need to venture outside. |
| $$$$ | **One & Only Palmilla**, Los Cabos Corridor. A powerhouse developer gives this place a certain pedigree. But nothing's been left to chance: the setting, grounds, and buildings are gorgeous. |
| $$$$ | **Presidente InterContinental Paraiso de la Bonita Resort and Thalasso**, Puerto Morelos. What's more soothing: the sweeping ocean and jungle views or the thalassotherapy treatments in serene saltwater pools? |
| $$$$ | **Quinta Real**, Guadalajara. Objets d'art and stonework coexist with brick and marble in a hotel that's a great blend of colonial and neocolonial. |
| $$$$ | **Rancho la Puerta**, Tecate. It's a place to corral your cares, and put your stress out to pasture. Eat well, live right, and prosper. |
| $$$$ | **El Tamarindo Golf Resort**, Puerto Vallarta. Enchanting guest villas and an 18-hole golf course are surrounded by jungle on the Costa Alegre. |

| | |
|---|---|
| $$$$ | **Las Ventanas al Paraíso,** Cabo San Lucas. Practically oozes luxury, from the sorbet offered poolside to the decadent spa treatments. |
| $$$$ | **W,** Mexico City. Latin America's first outpost of this chic chain pulls out all the cutting-edge stops. A lounge, a night club, and a late-hours restaurant ensure that the social scene is as sizzling as the design. |
| $$$–$$$$ | **Las Mañanitas,** Cuernavaca. Artisanal work (hand-painted tiles, hand-carved bedsteads) makes these rooms stand out. |
| $$$–$$$$ | **Quinta Real,** Zacatecas. Instead of crowds cheering a toreador, this space, once a bullring, fills with fans of the posh rooms and terrific restaurant and bar. |
| $$–$$$$ | **Casa de la Marquesa,** Querétaro. This 18th-century building may not have won over the woman it was supposedly built for, but it has charmed everyone else since. |
| $$$ | **Casa Natalia,** San José del Cabo. This is a graceful boutique hotel on the town's most charming street. |
| $$$ | **Hacienda de los Santos,** Alamos. The extensive grounds and gracious courtyards around these four linked colonial mansions practically demand a leisurely stroll. |
| $$$ | **Presidente InterContinental Cozumel,** Cozumel. The oceanfront suites at this gorgeous property might succeed in keeping you indoors— if the stone patio and hammock-strung palapas right outside your door weren't so tempting. |
| $$$ | **Westin Regina,** Puerto Vallarta. Public spaces are massy, classy, and colorful; private spaces are intimate, elegant, and subdued. |
| $$–$$$ | **Casa Oaxaca,** Oaxaca City. Stunning details don't always have to be so costly. It seems each room in this colonial house has its own surprise. |
| $$–$$$ | **Hacienda Chichén,** Chichén Itzá, Yucatán. This converted 16th-century hacienda has its own entrance to the ruins. |
| $$–$$$ | **Hotel Santa Fe,** Puerto Escondido. This Oaxaca Coast getaway, with its requisite strip of white sand, provides all the amenities of an all-inclusive resort, without sacrificing its warmth or personality. |

## BUDGET LODGING

| | |
|---|---|
| $$ | **Copper Canyon Sierra Lodge,** near Creel. Kerosene lamps instead of electric lights, the sounds of a waterfall instead of phones ringing— in short: delicious isolation. |
| $$ | **Posada Coatepec,** Coatepec, near Xalapa. Caffeine fiends can live out their dreams in the 19th-century former home of a coffee plantation owner. |

| | |
|---|---|
| $$ | **Las Rosas,** Ensenada. Ocean views, an elegant lobby, and beautiful guest rooms all belie the price. |
| $-$$ | **Casa la Aduana,** Sonora. This B&B takes some scouting to find—down a dirt road in a tiny former mining town—but its comforts are worth the trek. The restaurant, the best in the region, is an experience in itself. |
| $-$$ | **Casa Felipe Flores,** San Cristóbal de las Casas. You'll get all the secrets of the city from the owners of this B&B, which is in an antiques-filled 18th-century mansion. |
| ¢-$$ | **Cabañas Copal,** Tulum. At night, sleep beneath netted palapas, and wander grounds lit by thousands of candles. |
| $ | **Hotel La Escondida,** Huamantla. The middle of nowhere aptly describes this hacienda's location outside of Tlaxcala. The outstanding view of Malinche volcano will ease your separation from civilization. |
| $ | **Hotel Serenidad,** Mulegé. Longevity, simplicity, and lots of bougainvillea are just a few of the draws here. |
| $ | **Museo Parador Santa María,** Chiapas. A stay in this regal former hacienda is the best way to experience the nearby ruins of Chinkultik. |

**RESTAURANTS**

| | |
|---|---|
| $$$$ | **Laja,** Valle de Guadalupe. Polished woods, prix-fixe meals, and premium regional wines. |
| $$$-$$$$ | **Café des Artistes,** Puerto Vallarta. Expect a celebrity chef, sophisticated Euro-Mex dishes, and sleek spaces. |
| $$$-$$$$ | **Kau-Kan,** Zihuatanejo. The Mexican-Mediterranean food melts in your mouth; the amazing bay views simply make you melt. |
| $$$-$$$$ | **Mi Cocina,** San José del Cabo. You'll want to save this spot for after dark, when torchlight casts a compelling glow on this restaurant's intimate dining terrace. |
| $$$-$$$$ | **Laguna Grill,** Cancún. The inventive Asian fusion entrées, top-notch wine list, and decadent desserts here show that Cancún is not just about margaritas on the beach. |
| $$$-$$$$ | **Sancho Panza,** Cabo San Lucas. This jazz-filled Mediterranean bistro has surrealist style. |
| $$$-$$$$ | **Sr. Pepper's,** Mazatlán. Don't let the cute name fool you—this is where locals celebrate life's great events in style. |
| $$$-$$$$ | **La Vela,** Acapulco. Ocean breezes, a sail-like roof, and fabulous red snapper. |
| $$-$$$$ | **Nick San,** Cabo San Lucas. Who would have thought that the flavors of Japan and Mexico could blend so artfully? |

| | |
|---|---|
| $$$ | **Kaiser Maximilian**, Puerto Vallarta. It's all about Austria, with the likes of venison, braised cabbage, and warm apple tarts served in an art nouveau dining room. |
| $$–$$$ | **Aguila y Sol**, Mexico City. Catch the wave of *nueva cocina mexicana*, with its creative new spins on indigenous dishes. |
| $$–$$$ | **El Discreto Encanto de Comer**, Mexico City. Lunch in high Porfiriato style on Mexican-inflected French dishes. |
| $$–$$$ | **Mariscos Villa Rica Mocambo**, Veracruz. An ostensibly casual beachside palapa with seriously good seafood. |
| $$–$$$ | **Ristorante Da Giorgio**, Los Cabos Corridor. Candles flickering on cliffside tables ensure that this spot remains hopelessly romantic long after the amazing sunset is done. |
| $–$$$ | **Cien Años**, Tijuana. Kitchen wizardry adds some more magic to traditional Mexican dishes. |
| $–$$$ | **Gustino Italian Beachside Grill**, Cancún. A sleek, dramatic dining room—often filled with violin music—sets the stage for superb Italian fare. |
| $–$$$ | **Nueva Fonda de San Francisco**, Mexico City. You'll find shark meat lurking between layers of tortillas here—just one of many surprises at this purveyor of creative Mexican cooking. |

## BUDGET RESTAURANTS

| | |
|---|---|
| $–$$ | **Gallos Centenario**, Mexico City. Opulent but young at heart. Kick off a meal of Mexican classics with a chrysanthemum-topped margarita. |
| $–$$ | **Hacienda Del Charro**, Ensenada. Hearty, well-seasoned, aromatic Mexican fare. |
| $–$$ | **Marisquería Mazatlán**, Cabo San Lucas. Locals love the seafood (and the prices) here—you can't get a better recommendation than that. |
| $–$$ | **El Naranjo**, Oaxaca City. Magnificent moles and chiles rellenos are prepared with a contemporary spin. |
| $–$$ | **El Pórtico del Peregrino**, Mérida. Smokers get the street view at this 30-year Mérida institution—but everyone gets incredible local seafood. |
| $–$$ | **La Valentina**, Mexico City. A true champion of traditional indigenous cuisine. |
| $ | **Bistrot Mosaico**, Mexico City. Perennial French favorites mean you'll have to vie with the locals for a table. |
| $ | **Las Monjitas**, Monterrey. A waitstaff in nun costumes serve up whimsical and delicious *comida corrida*. |

¢–$ | **Pachamama,** Loreto. Hard to say what makes it so enticing: the tables right on the plaza or the simple Argentine-Mexican food.

## ARCHAEOLOGY

**Chichén Itzá,** Yucatán. Known worldwide as one of the most magnificent ancient cities built by the Maya.

**Cobá,** Riviera Maya. The Maya stone temples and pyramids here are surrounded by thick, wild jungle.

**Monte Albán,** Oaxaca Valley. Oaxaca State's most fascinating ruin did double duty—first as a major Zapotec city and later as a Mixtec necropolis of lavish tombs.

**Palenque,** Chiapas. Amazing temples and tombs—all bathed in beautiful light and surrounded by jungle.

**El Tajín,** Veracruz state. The extensive site includes the Pyramid of the Niches with its mesmerizing reliefs; unexcavated structures lurk in the surrounding jungle.

**Templo Mayor,** Mexico City. You won't have to trek into the jungle to see these Aztec ruins—they're right in the capital's historic center. The attached museum is more fascinating than the restored pyramid itself.

**Teotihuacán,** north of Mexico City. The history of this ancient site may still be mysterious, but its grandeur is unmistakable. It has one of the world's largest pyramids.

**Tula,** north of Mexico City. Once the capital of the Toltecs, Tula is marked by a statue-topped pyramid.

**Tulum,** Riviera Maya. Even the ancients wanted rooms with a view: this ruined Mayan city is built high on a cliff overlooking the Caribbean.

**Uxmal,** Yucatán. Uncluttered horizontal lines, ornate stone mosaics, soaring vaulted arches—it's all about understated elegance.

**Yaxchilán,** Chiapas. A watery glide along the Río Usumacinta ends at moss-covered temples with finely carved details and grand stairways.

## BEACHES

**Isla Ixtapa,** Pacific Coast. *Pangas* (traditional skiffs) take you from the mainland to this island of beautiful, seafood shanty–lined beaches.

**Pie de la Cuesta,** Acapulco. A wide beach with thatch-roof restaurants and straw palapas for shade. Come for the sunning and boat rides; stay for the sunset.

**Playa de Amor,** Cabo San Lucas. The Pacific and the Sea of Cortés crash together at this secluded spot at the very tip of the Baja peninsula.

**Playa Zicatela,** Puerto Escondido. Surf's up at this beach, where the Mexican Pipeline batters cream-color sand. November sees surfing competitions and bikini contests.

## MUSEUMS

**Acquario de Veracruz,** Veracruz City. One of the best aquariums in Latin America displays all manner of marine life from the Gulf of Mexico.

**Museo de Antropología de Jalapa,** Jalapa. The three main pre-His-panic cultures of Veracruz state are illuminated through an amazing collection of artifacts: everything from delicate murals to whop-ping stone Olmec heads.

**Museo de las Culturas,** Oaxaca City. Themed galleries and salons surround the cloister of a former monastery. Displays cover every-thing from artifacts to language to medicine.

**Museo Na Bolom,** San Cristóbal. What happens when a Danish ar-chaeologist marries a Swiss social activist and they dedicate their lives to the Chiapas and the Lacandón Indians? You get an institute devoted to the study of ecology and of the Maya as well as this museum.

**Museo Nacional de Antropología,** Mexico City. This wonderful in-troduction to pre-Hispanic culture is one of the best archaeological collections in the world, hands down. Between the extraordinary stelae and other monuments detailing royal heritage are the pre-served ephemera of everyday life.

**Museo de la Revolución Mexicana,** Chihuahua City. The former home of Pancho Villa is filled with Revolution-era artifacts, in-cluding the car in which Villa was assassinated.

**Parque Las Maravallas,** Saltillo. The Museo del Desierto at this park gives an interactive look at the desert ecosystems of the Northeast and Chihuahua State.

**Parque Museo La Venta,** Villahermosa. Hefty, Olmec stone heads line pathways at this outdoor park near the aptly named Lake of Illusions.

## PURE MEXICO

**Ballet Folklórico performance,** Mexico City. You won't know where to look first during this swirl of costumes, music, and fast foot-work—a vibrant sampling of Mexico's traditional folk dances.

**Being surrounded by millions of monarch butterflies,** The Heartland. Hike through pine forests that are literally blanketed with migrating butterflies at the Santuario de Mariposas el Rosario, outside of Morelia.

**Cliff divers at La Quebrada,** Acapulco. Daredevil *clavadistas* risk life and limb for your entertainment (and your tips). Arrive early and be generous.

**Dancing—or just watching—the danzón,** Veracruz City. Every Wednesday and Saturday evenings dapper couples practice the city's sensuous claim to fame in Parque Zamora.

**Exploring Cuetzalan, a preserved colonial town.** High in the lush Sierra Norte, you can absorb the sights and smells of the weekly market or wander through a nearby archaeological zone.

**Expanding your idea of "flora and fauna,"** Yucatán. Wildcats, birds, some 350 species of butterflies, and 75 different reptiles make their home in the Reserva de la Biosfera Calakmul, southwest of Xpujil.

**Sunsets in Puerta Vallarta.** Big and fiery, the setting sun seems to spread like orange mercury over Bahía de Banderas.

**Whale-watching in Scammon's Lagoon,** Baja California Sur. Now a national park, this lagoon remains a perfect place to see gray whales up close.

## SHOPPING

**Emilia Castillo,** Taxco (near Acapulco). Innovative silver designs in Mexico's premier "silver city."

**Galería Sergio Bustamante,** Tlaquepaque. The place to shop for Señor Bustamante's magical bronzes and ceramics.

**Mercado Artesanal La Ciudadela,** Mexico City. This daily market packs the double punch of the best selection of crafts and the best bargains in the capital.

**Mujeres Artesanas,** Oaxaca City. Women artists unite at this cooperative and the quality and selection of their crafts are unbeatable.

## WHERE ART COMES FIRST

**Instituto Cultural Cabañas,** Guadalajara. Theater spaces, art galleries, and flower-filled patios complement the large body of work by Mexican muralist José Clemente Orozco.

**Museo de Arte Contemporáneo,** Monterrey. This architectural marvel shows the best in contemporary international art.

**Museo de la Cerámica,** Tlaquepaque. Award-winning pieces large and small hold court in a museum that honors a great modern ceramist.

**Museo de Frida Kahlo,** Mexico City. Kahlo's "Blue House" now guards the trappings of the artist's tumultuous life, from her sketches to her giant papier-mâché skeletons.

**Museo Dolores Olmedo Patino,** Xochimilco. Peacocks strut freely around the grounds of this 17th-century hacienda on the outskirts of Mexico City. The extensive Diego Rivera collection is further enriched by an outstanding sampling of Frida Kahlo's art.

# SMART TRAVEL TIPS

*Finding out about your destination before you leave home means you won't squander time organizing everyday minutiae once you've arrived. You'll be more streetwise when you hit the ground as well, better prepared to explore the aspects of Mexico that drew you here in the first place. The organizations in this section can provide information to supplement this guide; contact them for up-to-the-minute details, and consult the A to Z sections that end each chapter for facts on the various topics as they relate to the country's many regions. Happy landings!*

## ADDRESSES

The Mexican method of naming streets can be exasperatingly arbitrary, so **be patient when searching for addresses.** Streets in the *centro* (downtown or central part of town) of many colonial cities are laid out in a grid surrounding the *zócalo* (main square) and often have different names on opposite sides of the square. Other streets simply acquire a new name after a certain number of blocks or when they cross a certain street. Numbered streets are usually designated *norte/sur* (north/south) or *oriente/poniente* (east/west) on either side of a central avenue.

Blocks are often labeled numerically, according to distance from a chosen starting point, as in "la Calle de Pachuca," "2a Calle de Pachuca," etc. Streets in *colonias* (neighborhoods or districts) outside the *centro* generally have a theme to their names: names of planets, writers, musicians, rivers, or saints, for example. Many Mexican addresses have "s/n" for *sin número* (no number) after the street name. This is common in small towns where there aren't many buildings on a block. Many addresses are cited as "Carretera a . . ., Km 30," which indicates that the property is at the 30th kilometer on the *carretera* (highway) to the named town.

Addresses are written with the street name first, followed by the street number (or "s/n"). A five-digit *código postal* (postal code) precedes, rather than follows, the name of the city: *Hacienda Paraíso, Calle*

*Allende 211, 68000 Oaxaca.* Apdo. (*apartado*) or Apdo. Postal (also abbreviated A.P.) means post-office box.

In Mexico City (and other cities), most addresses include their *colonia,* which is abbreviated as Col. Other abbreviations used in addresses include: Av. (*avenida,* or avenue); Calz. (*calzada,* or road or boulevard); Fracc. (*fraccionamiento,* or subdivision); and Int. (apartment).

Mexican states have postal abbreviations of two or more letters. To send mail to Mexico, you can use the following: Aguascalientes: Ags.; Baja California: B.C.; Baja California Sur: B.C.S.; Campeche: Camp.; Chiapas: Chis.; Chihuahua: Chih.; Coahuila: Coah.; Colima: Col.; Distrito Federal (Federal District, or Mexico City): D.F.; Durango: Dgo.; Guanajuato: Gto.; Guerrero: Gro.; Hidalgo: Hgo.; Jalisco: Jal.; Estado de Mexico: Edo. de Mex.; Michoacán: Mich.; Morelos: Mor.; Nayarit: Nay.; Nuevo Leon: N.L.; Oaxaca: Oax.; Puebla: Pue.; Querétaro: Qro.; Quintana Roo: Q. Roo; San Luis Potosí: S.L.P.; Sinaloa: Sin.; Sonora: Son.; Tabasco: Tab.; Tamaulipas: Tamps.; Tlaxcala: Tlax.; Veracruz: Ver.; Yucatán: Yuc.; Zacatecas: Zac.

## AIR TRAVEL

### BOOKING

When you book, look for nonstop flights and remember that "direct" flights stop at least once. Try to avoid connecting flights, which require a change of plane. Two airlines may operate a connecting flight jointly, so ask whether your airline operates every segment of the trip; you may find that the carrier you prefer flies you only part of the way. To find more booking tips and to check prices and make online flight reservations, log on to www.fodors.com.

### CARRIERS

AeroCalifornia, Aeroméxico, America West, American, Aviacsa, Continental, Delta, Mexicana, Northwest, United, and US Airways all fly from the United States into Mexico City, the nation's main gateway. These airlines also have service to many of the coastal resorts (Acapulco, Cancún, Los Cabos, Mazatlán, Puerto Vallarta, etc.) as well as to such inland communities

as Chihuahua City, Guadalajara, Hermosillo, and Monterrey. Alaska Airlines flies from the United States to Cancún, Guadalajara, Ixtapa/Zihuatanejo, Los Cabos, Manzanillo, Mazatlán, and Puerto Vallarta. American Trans Air (ATA) flies to Cancún, Guadalajara, Ixtapa/Zihuatanejo, and Puerto Vallarta. British Airways goes nonstop from London to Mexico City.

From Canada, you can fly Air Canada to Mexico City and other urban and coastal resort destinations. Aeroméxico, Alaska Airlines, American, Continental, Delta, Mexicana, Northwest, United, and US Airways all fly from major Canadian cities to Mexican destinations via the United States or Mexico City.

Plane travel within Mexico can cost two to four times as much as bus travel, but it will save you considerable time. Aerocalifornia, Aeroméxico, Aviacsa, and Mexicana serve most major cities. Aerocaribe (reserve through Mexicana) serves the Yucatán and the South. Aerolitoral serves the nation's northeastern reaches, and Aeromar covers central Mexico and some northeastern, coastal and southern locations; make reservations on either line through Mexicana or Aeroméxico.

(Note: Some airline toll-free numbers have an 001800 prefix—two zeroes before the "1"—rather than 01800, like most Mexican toll-free numbers. This is entirely correct: what it means is that your call is actually being routed to the United States.) 🎧 From Canada **Air Canada** 🖀 888/247–2262 in the U.S. and Canada ⊕ www.aircanada.com. 🎧 From the U.S. **AeroCalifornia** 🖀 800/237–6225 in the U.S. **Aeroméxico** 🖀 800/237–6639 in the U.S. and Canada ⊕ www.aeromexico.com. **Alaska Airlines** 🖀 800/426–0333 or 800/252–7522 in the U.S. and Canada ⊕ www.alaskaair.com. **America West** 🖀 800/235–9292 in the U.S. ⊕ www.americawest.com. **American** 🖀 800/433–7300 in the U.S. and Canada ⊕ www.aa.com. **ATA** 🖀 800/435–9282 in the U.S. ⊕ www.ata.com. **Aviacsa** 🖀 888/528–4227 in the U.S. ⊕ www.aviacsa.com.mx. **Continental** 🖀 800/231–0856 in the U.S. and Canada ⊕ www.continental.com. **Delta** 🖀 800/241–4141 in the U.S. and Canada ⊕ www.delta.com. **Mexicana** 🖀 800/531–7921 in the U.S., 866/281–3049 in Canada ⊕ www.mexicana.com. **Northwest**

☎ 800/225-2525 in the U.S. and Canada ⊕ www.nwa.com. **United** ☎ 800/241-6522 in the U.S., 800/538-2929 in Canada ⊕ www.united.com. **US Airways** ☎ 800/428-4322 in the U.S., 800/622-1015 in Canada ⊕ www.usairways.com.

↗ From the U.K. **British Airways** ☎ 0845/773-3377 ⊕ www.britishairways.com.

↗ In Mexico **AeroCalifornia** ☎ 55/5207-1392 in Mexico City, 01800/685-5500. **Aeroméxico** ☎ 55/5625-2622 in Mexico City, 01800/021-4010. **Air Canada** ☎ 55/9138-0280 in Mexico City, 01800/719-2827. **Alaska Airlines** ☎ 001800/252-7522. **America West** ☎ 001800/235-9292. **American** ☎ 01800/904-6000. **ATA** ☎ 001800/435-9282. **Aviacsa** ☎ 55/5448-8900 in Mexico City, 01800/006-2200. **British Airways** ☎ 55/5387-0300 in Mexico City. **Continental** ☎ 01800/900-5000. **Delta** ☎ 01800/123-4710. **Mexicana** ☎ 55/5448-0990 in Mexico City, 01800/502-2000. **Northwest** ☎ 55/5279-5390 in Mexico City, 01800/830-7400. **United** ☎ 01800/003-0777. **US Airways** ☎ 55/2623-0100 in Mexico City, 01800/007-8800.

## CHECK-IN & BOARDING
Most airports in Mexico are easy to navigate, with the exception of Aeropuerto Internacional Benito Juárez in Mexico City. This airport's floorplan is confusing; gateways and waiting areas extend from the sides of the main corridors. If you get lost, just be patient and keep asking for directions.

Always **find out your carrier's check-in policy.** Plan to arrive at the airport about two hours before your scheduled departure time for domestic flights and 2½ to 3 hours before international flights. You may need to arrive earlier if you're flying from one of the busier airports or during peak air-traffic times. Also give yourself extra time if flying during the busy winter holiday season, the weeks before and after Easter, and the first two weeks of August. To avoid delays at airport-security checkpoints, try not to wear any metal. Jewelry, belt and other buckles, steel-toe shoes, barrettes, and underwire bras are among the items that can set off detectors.

Assuming that not everyone with a ticket will show up, airlines routinely overbook planes. When everyone does, airlines ask for volunteers to give up their seats. In return, these volunteers usually get a several-hundred-dollar flight voucher, which can be used toward the purchase of another ticket, and are rebooked on the next flight out. If there are not enough volunteers, the airline must choose who will be denied boarding. The first to get bumped are passengers who checked in late and those flying on discounted tickets, so get to the gate and check in as early as possible, especially during peak periods.

Always **bring a government-issued photo ID** to the airport; even when it's not required, a passport is best.

## CUTTING COSTS
The least expensive airfares to Mexico are priced for round-trip travel and must usually be purchased in advance. Airlines generally allow you to change your return date for a fee; most low-fare tickets, however, are nonrefundable. It's smart to call a number of airlines and check the Internet; when you are quoted a good price, book it on the spot—the same fare may not be available the next day, or even the next hour. Always check different routings and look into using alternate airports. Also, price off-peak flights, which may be significantly less expensive than others. Travel agents, especially low-fare specialists (⇨ Discounts & Deals), are helpful.

Consolidators are another good source. They buy tickets for scheduled flights at reduced rates from the airlines, then sell them at prices that beat the best fare available directly from the airlines. (Many also offer reduced car-rental and hotel rates.) Sometimes you can even get your money back if you need to return the ticket. Carefully read the fine print detailing penalties for changes and cancellations, purchase the ticket with a credit card, and confirm your consolidator reservation with the airline.

When you fly as a courier, you trade your checked-luggage space for a ticket deeply subsidized by a courier service. There are restrictions on when you can book and how long you can stay. Some courier companies list with membership organizations, such as the Air Courier Association and the International Association of Air Travel Couriers; these require you to become a member before you can book a flight.

Many airlines, singly or in collaboration, offer discount air passes that allow foreigners to travel economically in a particular country or region. These visitor passes usually must be reserved and purchased before you leave home. Information about passes often can be found on most airlines' international Web pages, which tend to be aimed at travelers from outside the carrier's home country. Also, try typing the name of the pass into a search engine, or search for "pass" within the carrier's Web site.

Mexicana, for instance, offers the "Mexipass" and "Maya-Pass" programs good for 3 to 90 days of travel. The passes, which are only sold outside Mexico, include routes between Mexico City and various other urban and resort destinations; round-trip fares can run as low as $150 between Mexico City and Oaxaca and $240 between Cancún and Oaxaca, not including taxes.

**Consolidators** AirlineConsolidator.com ☎ 888/468-5385 ⊕ www.airlineconsolidator.com; for international tickets. **Best Fares** ☎ 800/880-1234 or 800/576-8255 ⊕ www.bestfares.com; $59.90 annual membership. **Cheap Tickets** ☎ 800/377-1000 or 800/652-4327 ⊕ www.cheaptickets.com. **Exito Travel** ☎ 800/655-4053 ⊕ www.exitotravel.com. **Expedia** ☎ 800/397-3342 or 404/728-8787 ⊕ www.expedia.com. **Hotwire** ☎ 866/468-9473 or 920/330-9418 ⊕ www.hotwire.com. **Now Voyager Travel** ⊠ 45 W. 21st St., Suite 5A, New York, NY 10010 ☎ 212/459-1616 🖷 212/243-2711 ⊕ www.nowvoyagertravel.com. **Onetravel.com** ⊕ www.onetravel.com. **Orbitz** ☎ 888/656-4546 ⊕ www.orbitz.com. **Priceline.com** ⊕ www.priceline.com. **Travelocity** ☎ 888/709-5983, 877/282-2925 in Canada, 0870/876-3876 in the U.K. ⊕ www.travelocity.com.

**Courier Resources** Air Courier Association/Cheaptrips.com ☎ 800/280-5973 or 800/282-1202 ⊕ www.aircourier.org or www.cheaptrips.com; $34 annual membership. **International Association of Air Travel Couriers** ☎ 308/632-3273 ⊕ www.courier.org; $45 annual membership.

### ENJOYING THE FLIGHT
State your seat preference when purchasing your ticket, and then repeat it when you confirm and when you check in. For more legroom, you can request one of the few emergency-aisle seats at check-in, if you're capable of moving obstacles comparable in weight to an airplane exit door (usually between 35 pounds and 60 pounds)—a Federal Aviation Administration requirement of passengers in these seats. Seats behind a bulkhead also offer more legroom, but they don't have underseat storage. Don't sit in the row in front of the emergency aisle or in front of a bulkhead, where seats may not recline.

Ask the airline whether a snack or meal is served on the flight. If you have dietary concerns, request special meals when booking. These can be vegetarian, low-cholesterol, or kosher, for example. It's a good idea to pack some healthful snacks and a small (plastic) bottle of water in your carry-on bag. On long flights, try to maintain a normal routine, to help fight jet lag. At night, get some sleep. By day, eat light meals, drink water (not alcohol), and **move around the cabin** to stretch your legs. For additional jet-lag tips consult *Fodor's FYI: Travel Fit & Healthy* (available at bookstores everywhere).

Smoking policies vary from carrier to carrier. Many airlines prohibit smoking on all of their flights; others allow smoking only on certain routes or certain departures. Ask your carrier about its policy.

### FLYING TIMES
On most direct flights, Mexico City is 5 hours from New York, 4½ hours from Chicago, and 3½ hours from Los Angeles. Cancún is 3½ hours from New York and from Chicago, 4½ hours from Los Angeles. Acapulco is 6 hours from New York, 4 hours from Chicago, and 3½ hours from Los Angeles. From London, Mexico City is a 12½-hour flight. From Sydney, you must fly to Los Angeles (13½ hours) and then change planes (and airlines) for Mexico City.

### HOW TO COMPLAIN
If your baggage goes astray or your flight goes awry, complain right away. Most carriers require that you **file a claim immediately.** The Aviation Consumer Protection Division of the Department of Transportation publishes *Fly-Rights,* which discusses airlines and consumer issues and is available online. You can also find articles

and information on mytravelrights.com, the Web site of the nonprofit Consumer Travel Rights Center.

📋 **Airline Complaints Aviation Consumer Protection Division** ✉ U.S. Department of Transportation, Office of Aviation Enforcement and Proceedings, C-75, Room 4107, 400 7th St. SW, Washington, DC 20590 ☎ 202/366-2220 ⊕ airconsumer.ost.dot.gov. **Federal Aviation Administration Consumer Hotline** ✉ for inquiries: FAA, 800 Independence Ave. SW, Washington, DC 20591 ☎ 800/322-7873 ⊕ www.faa.gov.

## RECONFIRMING

Check the status of your flight before you leave for the airport. You can do this on your carrier's Web site, by linking to a flight-status checker (many Web booking services offer these), or by calling your carrier or travel agent. Always confirm international flights at least 72 hours ahead of the scheduled departure time. Many airlines require that you reconfirm 48 hours ahead of the departure time for flights within Mexico.

## AIRPORTS

The main gateway to the country is Mexico City's Aeropuerto Internacional Benito Juárez (airport code: MEX), a large, modern airport. You can easily exchange money here as well as buy last-minute gifts (although at a higher price) on your way out of the country.

📋 **Airport Information Aeropuerto Internacional Benito Juárez** ☎ 55/5571-3600.

## BUS TRAVEL

Getting to Mexico by bus is no longer for just the adventurous or budget-conscious. In the past, bus travelers were required to change to Mexican vehicles at the border, and vice versa. Now, however, in an effort to bring more American visitors and their dollars to off-the-beaten-track markets and attractions, the Mexican government has removed this obstacle, and more transborder bus tours are available. If you'll be leaving Mexico for points north by bus, you can buy tickets from the Greyhound representative in Mexico City.

Within Mexico, the bus network is extensive. In large cities, bus stations are a good distance from the center of town. Though

there's a trend toward consolidation, some towns have different stations for each bus line.

## CLASSES

Mexican buses can be comfortable air-conditioned coaches with bathrooms, movies, reclining seats with seat belts, and refreshments (first class or deluxe, known as *primera clase* and *de lujo* or *lujo ejecutivo*), or they can be dilapidated "vintage" vehicles (second class, or *segunda clase*). A lower-class bus ride can be interesting if you're not in a hurry and want to experience local culture; these buses make frequent stops. Fares are up to 30% cheaper than those in the premium categories. However, be prepared for cracked windows, litter in the aisles, and pigs and chickens among your busmates. Bring something to eat in case you don't like the restaurant where the bus stops, and **carry toilet paper,** as rest rooms might not have any. For comfort's sake, if you're planning a long-distance haul, **buy tickets for first class or better when traveling by bus within Mexico.** Also ride first class if you're traveling in an area where safety is a concern. Smoking is prohibited on all first-class and deluxe buses.

There are several first-class and deluxe bus lines. ADO and ADO GL (deluxe service) travel from Mexico City to southeastern and Gulf coast destinations, including Cancún, Chiapas, Oaxaca, Tampico, Veracruz, Villahermosa, and Yucatán. Cristóbal Colón goes to Chiapas, Oaxaca, Puebla, and the Guatemala border from Mexico City. Estrella Blanca goes from Mexico City to Manzanillo, Mazatlán, Monterrey, Nuevo Laredo, and other central, Pacific coast, and northern border points. ETN and Primera Plus serve Mexico City, Manzanillo, Morelia, Puerto Vallarta, Toluca, and other central and western cities. Estrella de Oro will take you from Mexico City to Acapulco, Cuernavaca, Ixtapa, and Taxco.

## PAYING

For the most part, plan to pay in pesos, although most of the deluxe bus services have started accepting credit cards such as Visa and MasterCard.

## RESERVATIONS

Tickets for first-class or better—unlike tickets for the other classes—can and should be reserved in advance. You can make reservations for many, though not all, of the first-class bus lines, through the Ticketbus central reservations agency. To travel by bus from the United States, you can buy tickets for destinations served by Estrella Blanca at Greyhound counters in such U.S. gateway cities as San Diego, California, as well as Brownsville, Dallas, Houston, Laredo, and McAllen—all in Texas.

🚌 Bus Information **ADO** and **ADO GL** ☎ 55/5133-2444 or 55/5133-2424, 01800/702-8000 toll free in Mexico ⊕ www.ado.com.mx. **Cristóbal Colón** ☎ 55/5133-2433, 01800/849-6136 toll free in Mexico ⊕ www.cristobalcolon.com.mx. **Estrella Blanca** ☎ 55/5729-0707, 01800/507-5500 toll free in Mexico ⊕ www.estrellablanca.com.mx. **Estrella de Oro** ☎ 55/5549-8520 ⊕ www.autobus.com.mx. **ETN** ☎ 55/5273-8886, 01800/800-3862 toll free in Mexico ⊕ www.etn.com.mx. **Greyhound** ☎ 55/5133-2425, 01800/710-8819 toll free in Mexico, 800/231-2222 in the U.S., 800/661-8747 in Canada ⊕ www.greyhound.com. **Ticketbus** ☎ 55/5133-2424 or 5133-2444, 01800/702-8000 toll free in Mexico ⊕ www.ticketbus.com.mx.

## BUSINESS HOURS

### BANKS & OFFICES

Banks are generally open weekdays 9–3. In larger cities, most are open until 4 or even 7, and some of the larger banks keep a few branches open Saturday from 9 or 10 to 1 or 2:30 and Sunday 10–1:30; however, the extended hours are often for deposits or check cashing only. Government offices are usually open to the public weekdays 9–3; along with banks and most private offices, they're closed on national holidays.

### GAS STATIONS

Gas stations throughout Mexico are normally open 7 AM–10 PM daily. They don't close for lunch. Those near major thoroughfares in big cities stay open 24 hours, including most holidays.

### MUSEUMS & SIGHTS

Along with theaters and most archaeological sights, museums are closed on Monday, with few exceptions. Hours are normally 9 or 10 to 5 or 6.

## PHARMACIES

Pharmacies are usually open daily from 9 AM to 10 PM; on Sundays and in some small towns, they may close several hours earlier. Twenty-four-hour pharmacies are common in larger cities: look for the big-name 24-hour pharmacies such as Farmacia del Ahorro or Fenix.

## SHOPS

Stores are generally open weekdays and Saturday from 9 or 10 AM to 7 or 8 PM; in resort areas, they may also be open on Sunday. In some resort areas and small towns (and even in major cities, though to a lesser degree), stores may close for a two-hour lunch break, roughly 2–4. Airport shops are open seven days a week.

## CAMERAS & PHOTOGRAPHY

Majestic landscapes and varied cityscapes make Mexico a photographer's dream. Although Mexicans generally don't mind having picture-taking visitors in their midst, you should always **ask permission before taking pictures in churches or of individuals.** They may ask you for a *propina*, or tip, in which case a few pesos is customary. (Note that some indigenous peoples don't ever want to be photographed; taking pictures is also forbidden in some churches.) Also, **don't snap pictures of military or high-security installations** anywhere in the country. It's forbidden.

If you're bashful about approaching strangers, photograph people with whom you interact: your waiter, your desk clerk, the vendor selling you crafts. Even better, have a traveling companion or a passerby photograph you *with* them.

To avoid the blurriness caused by shaky hands, get a minitripod—they're available in sizes as small as 6 inches. (Although cameras are permitted at archaeological sites, many of them strictly prohibit the use of tripods.) Buy a small beanbag to support your camera on uneven surfaces. If you plan to take photos on some of the country's many beaches, bring a skylight, 81B, 81C, or polarizing filter to minimize haze and light problems. If you're visiting forested areas, bring high-speed film to compensate for low light under the tree canopy and invest in a telephoto lens to photograph wildlife; standard zoom lenses in the 35–88 range won't capture enough detail.

Casual photographers should **consider using inexpensive disposable cameras** to reduce the risks inherent in traveling with sophisticated equipment. One-use cameras with panoramic or underwater functions are also nice supplements to a standard camera and its gear.

The *Kodak Guide to Shooting Great Travel Pictures* (available at bookstores everywhere) is loaded with tips.
**Ⓕ Photo Help Kodak Information Center** ☏ 800/242–2424 ⊕ www.kodak.com.

### EQUIPMENT PRECAUTIONS
**Don't pack film or equipment in checked luggage,** where it is much more susceptible to damage. X-ray machines used to view checked luggage are extremely powerful and therefore are likely to ruin your film. Try to ask for hand inspection of film, which becomes clouded after repeated exposure to airport X-ray machines, and keep videotapes and computer disks away from metal detectors. Carry an extra supply of batteries, and be prepared to turn on your camera, camcorder, or laptop to prove to airport security personnel that the device is real.

Always **keep your film (and computer disks and videotapes) out of the sun** and on jungle trips keep your equipment in resealable plastic bags to protect it from dampness. As petty crime can be a problem, particularly in the cities, **keep a close eye on your gear.**

### FILM & DEVELOPING
Film—especially Kodak and Fuji brands—is fairly easy to find in many parts of Mexico. If purchased in a major city, a roll of 36-exposure print film costs about the same as in the United States; the price is slightly higher in tourist spots and in more remote places. Advantix is available in Mexico, although developing may take one or two days. It's a good idea to pack more film than you think you'll need on your trip. One-hour and overnight film developing is fairly common.

### VIDEOS
Videotapes are good quality and are easy to find in urban areas. The local standard in Mexico is the same as in the United States: that is, all videos are NTSC (National Television Standards Committee). The best places to buy tapes are Sanborns restaurant-shops (they're all over the place), major pharmacies, and photo shops. A 120-minute tape costs about $3.

### CAR RENTAL
When you think about renting a car, bear in mind that you may be sharing the road with reckless local drivers—sometimes acquiring a driver's license in Mexico is more a question of paying someone off than of having tested skill. Also, be prepared for challenging road conditions, as the highway system is uneven (*see* Road Conditions *in* Car Travel). Check on local road conditions before you rent.

Mexico manufactures Chrysler, Ford, General Motors, Honda, Nissan, and Volkswagen vehicles. With the exception of Volkswagen, you can get the same kind of midsize and luxury cars in Mexico that you can rent in the United States and Canada. Economy usually refers to a Volkswagen Beetle, which may or may not come with air-conditioning.

It can really pay to shop around: in Mexico City rates for a compact car with air-conditioning, manual transmission, and unlimited mileage range from $40 a day and $230 a week to $50 a day and nearly $300 a week, including taxes. In Acapulco and other resort areas, rates generally run $50 a day and more than $300 a week. Insurance averages $18 a day. While shopping for a good deal, avoid local agencies; **stick with the major companies** because they tend to be more reliable.

You can also hire a car with a driver (who generally doubles as a tour guide) through your hotel. The going rate is about $25 an hour within a given town, usually with a three-hour minimum. Limousine service runs about $65 an hour and up, with a three- to five-hour minimum. Rates for out-of-town trips are higher. **Negotiate a price beforehand** if you'll need the service for more than one day. If your hotel can't arrange limousine or car service, ask the concierge to refer you to a reliable *sitio* (cab stand); the rate will be lower.

🚗 **Major Agencies Alamo** ☎ 800/522-9696 ⊕ www.alamo.com. **Avis** ☎ 800/331-1084, 800/879-2847 in Canada, 0870/606-0100 in the U.K., 02/9353-9000 in Australia, 09/526-2847 in New Zealand ⊕ www.avis.com. **Budget** ☎ 800/527-0700, 0870/156-5656 in the U.K. ⊕ www.budget.com. **Dollar** ☎ 800/800-6000, 0800/085-4578 in the U.K. ⊕ www.dollar.com. **Hertz** ☎ 800/654-3001, 800/263-0600 in Canada, 0870/844-8844 in the U.K., 02/9669-2444 in Australia, 09/256-8690 in New Zealand ⊕ www.hertz.com. **National Car Rental** ☎ 800/227-7368, 0870/600-6666 in the U.K. ⊕ www.nationalcar.com.

## CUTTING COSTS

For a good deal, book through a travel agent who will shop around. Do look into wholesalers, companies that do not own fleets but rent in bulk from those that do and often offer better rates than traditional car-rental operations. Prices are best during off-peak periods. Rentals booked through wholesalers often must be paid for before you leave home.

🚗 **Wholesalers Auto Europe** ☎ 207/842-2000 or 800/223-5555 🖨 207/842-2222 ⊕ www.autoeurope.com. **Kemwel** ☎ 877/820-0668 or 800/678-0678 🖨 207/842-2147 ⊕ www.kemwel.com.

## INSURANCE

When driving a rented car you are generally responsible for any damage to or loss of the vehicle. You also may be liable for any property damage or personal injury that you may cause while driving. Before you rent, see what coverage you already have under the terms of your personal auto-insurance policy and credit cards.

Though "innocent until proven guilty" is the law on the books in Mexico, law enforcement officers often work from the opposite premise, which means you could be jailed during investigations after an accident unless you have Mexican insurance.

## REQUIREMENTS & RESTRICTIONS

In Mexico the minimum driving age is 18, but most rental car agencies have a minimum age requirement ranging from 21 to 25. Your own driver's license is acceptable, but an international driver's license is a good idea. It's available from the U.S. and Canadian automobile associations, and, in the United Kingdom, from the Automobile Association or Royal Automobile Club.

## SURCHARGES

Surcharges for additional drivers are around $5 per day plus tax. Children's car seats run about the same, but not all companies have them. Before you pick up a car in one city and leave it in another, ask about drop-off charges or one-way service fees, which can be substantial. Also inquire about early-return policies; some rental agencies charge extra if you return the car before the time specified in your contract while others give you a refund for the days not used. To avoid a hefty refueling fee, **fill the tank just before you turn in the car**, but be aware that gas stations near the rental outlet may overcharge. It's almost never a deal to buy the tank of gas that's in the car when you rent it; the understanding is that you'll return it empty, but some fuel usually remains.

## CAR TRAVEL

There are two absolutely essential points to remember about driving in Mexico. First and foremost is to **carry Mexican auto insurance.** If you injure anyone in an accident, you could well be jailed—whether it was your fault or not—unless you have insurance. Second, **if you enter Mexico with a car, you must leave with it.** In recent years, the high rate of U.S. vehicles being sold illegally in Mexico has caused the Mexican government to enact stringent regulations for bringing a car into the country.

**You must cross the border with the following documents:** title or registration for your vehicle; a birth certificate or passport; a credit card (AE, DC, MC, or V); a valid driver's license with a photo. The title holder, driver, and credit-card owner must be one and the same—that is, if your spouse's name is on the title or registration of the car and yours isn't, you cannot be the one to bring the car into the country. For financed, leased, rental, or company cars, you must **bring a notarized letter of permission** from the bank, lien holder, rental agency, or company. When you submit your paperwork at the border and pay the $25 charge on your credit card, you'll receive a car permit and a sticker to put on your vehicle, all valid for up to six months. Be sure to **turn in the permit and the sticker** at the border prior to their expiration date; otherwise you could incur high fines or even be barred from entering Mexico if you try to visit again.

The fact that you drove in with a car is stamped on your tourist card (visa), which you must give to immigration authorities at departure. If an emergency arises and you must fly home, there are complicated customs procedures to face.

If you bring the car into the country you must be in the vehicle at all times when it is driven. You cannot lend it to another person. Also, although a valid license from home is good in Mexico, an international driver's license isn't a bad idea. These permits are universally recognized, and having one in your wallet may save you a problem with the local authorities.

### EMERGENCY SERVICES

To help motorists on major highways, the Mexican Tourism Ministry operates a fleet of more than 250 pickup trucks, known as the Angeles Verdes, or Green Angels. The bilingual drivers provide mechanical help, first aid, radio-telephone communication, basic supplies and small parts, towing, tourist information, and protection. Services are free, and spare parts, fuel, and lubricants are provided at cost. Tips are always appreciated (figure $5–$10 for big jobs, $2–$3 for minor repairs). The Green Angels patrol fixed sections of the major highways twice daily 8–8 (usually later on holiday weekends). If you break down, **pull off the road as far as possible,** lift the hood of your car, hail a passing vehicle, and ask the driver to **notify the patrol.** Most bus and truck drivers will be quite helpful. If you witness an accident, do not stop to help—inform the nearest official. **Angeles Verdes, Mexico City** ☎ 55/5250-8221.

### GASOLINE

Pemex (the government petroleum monopoly) franchises all of Mexico's gas stations, which you'll find at most junctions and in cities and towns. Gas is measured in liters, and stations usually don't accept U.S.

or Canadian credit cards or dollars. Fuel prices tend to be lower in Mexico City and surroundings and near the U.S. border, increasing the farther you get from these areas. Overall, prices run slightly to moderately higher than in the United States. Premium unleaded gas (called *premium*) and regular unleaded gas (*magna*) are available nationwide, but it's still best to **fill up whenever you can.** Fuel quality is generally lower than that in the United States and Europe, but it has improved enough so that your car will run acceptably. For general opening times, *see* Business Hours, *above*.

Gas-station attendants pump the gas for you and may also wash your windshield and check your oil and tire air pressure. A 5- or 10-peso tip is customary, depending on the number of services rendered. **Keep a close eye on the gas meter** to make sure the attendant is starting it at "0" and that you're charged the correct price.

### INSURANCE

You must **carry Mexican auto insurance,** which you can purchase near border crossings on either the U.S. or Mexican side. Although Mexican law technically considers you innocent until proven guilty, the system often works the other way in reality, so purchase enough Mexican automobile insurance at the border to cover your estimated trip. It's sold by the day, and if your trip is shorter than your original estimate, some companies might issue a prorated refund for the unused time upon application after you exit the country. **Instant Mexico Auto Insurance** ✉ 223 Via de San Ysidro, San Ysidro, CA 92173 ☎ 619/428-3583 or 428-4714, 800/345-4701 in the U.S. and Canada ⎙ 619/690-6533 ⊕ www.instant-mex-auto-insur. com. **Oscar Padilla** ✉ 120 Willow Rd., San Ysidro, CA 92173 ☎ 619/428-4406, 800/258-8600 in the U.S. **Sanborn's Mexican Insurance** ✉ 2009 S. 10th St., McAllen, TX 78503 ☎ 956/686-0711, 800/222-0158 in the U.S. and Canada. ⊕ www. sanbornsinsurance.com.

### PARKING

A circle with a diagonal line superimposed on the letter E (for *estacionamiento*) means "no parking." Illegally parked cars are either towed or have wheel blocks placed on the tires, which can require a trip to the traffic-police headquarters for payment of a fine. When in doubt, **park in a lot instead of on the street**; your car will probably be safer there anyway. Lots are plentiful, and fees are reasonable—as little as $1 for a whole day up to $1 or more an hour, depending on where in the country you are. Sometimes you park your own car; more often, though, you hand the keys over to an attendant. There are a few (very few) parking meters in larger cities; the cost is usually about 10 cents per 15 minutes.

## ROAD CONDITIONS

There are several well-kept toll roads in Mexico—most of them four lanes wide. However, these *carreteras* (major highways) don't go too far out of the capital into the countryside. (*Cuota* means toll road; *libre* means no toll, and such roads are two lanes and usually not as smooth.) Some excellent roads have opened in the past decade or so, making car travel safer and faster. These include highways connecting Acapulco and Mexico City; Cancún and Mérida; Nogales and Mazatlán; León and Aguascalientes; Guadalajara and Tepic; Mexico City, Morelia, and Guadalajara; Mexico City, Puebla, Teotihuacán, and Oaxaca; Mexico City and Veracruz; and Nuevo Laredo and Monterrey. However, tolls as high as $40 one way can make using these thoroughfares prohibitively expensive.

In rural areas, roads are poor: **use caution, especially during the rainy season,** when rock slides and potholes are a problem. **Be alert to animals,** especially untethered cattle and dogs, and to dangerous, unrailed curves. Note that driving in Mexico's central highlands may also necessitate adjustments to your carburetor. *Topes* (speed bumps) are common; slow down when approaching a village.

Generally, driving times are longer than for comparable distances in the United States. Common sense goes a long way, particularly if you have a lot of ground to cover. **Start early and fill up on gas**; don't let your tank get below half full. Allow extra time for unforeseen occurrences as well as for traffic, particularly truck traffic.

Approaches to most large cities are in good condition, but urban traffic can be horren-

dous. As you would in metropolitan areas anywhere, avoid rush hour (7–9 AM and 6–8 PM) and when schools let out (2–3 PM). Signage is not always adequate in Mexico, so **travel with a companion and a good map.** Always lock your car, and never leave valuable items in the body of the car (the trunk will suffice for daytime outings, but don't pack it in front of prying eyes).

## ROAD MAPS

AAA publishes national road maps for Mexico, and Guía Roji publishes current city, regional, and national road maps. The latter are available in bookstores and big supermarket chains for under $10. Gas stations generally don't sell maps.

## RULES OF THE ROAD

When you sign up for Mexican car insurance, you should receive a booklet on Mexican rules of the road. It really is a good idea to read it to avoid breaking laws that differ from those of your country. If an oncoming vehicle flicks its lights at you in daytime, slow down: it could mean trouble ahead. When approaching a narrow bridge, the first vehicle to flash its lights has right of way. One-way streets are common. One-way traffic is indicated by an arrow; two-way, by a double-pointed arrow. Other road signs follow the widespread system of international symbols.

In Mexico City, **watch out for "Hoy no Circula" notices.** Because of pollution, all cars in the city without a Verification "0" rating (usually those built before 1994) are prohibited from driving one day a week (two days a week during high-alert periods). Posted signs show certain letters or numbers paired with each day of the week, indicating that vehicles with those letters or numbers in their license plates aren't allowed to drive on the corresponding day. Foreigners aren't exempt. Cars with license plate numbers ending in 5 or 6 are prohibited on Monday; 7 or 8 on Tuesday; 3 or 4 on Wednesday; 1 or 2 on Thursday; and 9 or 0 on Friday. Cars whose license plates have only letters, not numerals, can't drive on Fridays.

Mileage and speed limits are given in kilometers: 100 kph and 80 kph (62 mph and

50 mph, respectively) are the most common maximums. A few of the toll roads allow 110 kph (68 mph). However, speed limits can change from curve to curve, so watch the signs carefully. In cities and small towns, observe the posted speed limits, which can be as low as 20 kph (12 mph). Seat belts are required by law throughout Mexico.

### SAFETY ON THE ROAD
**Never drive at night** in remote and rural areas. *Bandidos* are one concern, but so are potholes, free-roaming animals, cars with no working lights, road-hogging trucks, and difficulty in getting assistance. It's best to use toll roads whenever possible; although costly, they're much safer.

Driving in Mexico is nerve-racking, with people zigzagging in and out of lanes. Most drivers pay attention to signals and safety rules, but be vigilant. Drunk driving skyrockets on holiday weekends, so be especially cautious if you're on the road at such times.

If you're driving from Manzanillo to Ixtapa/Zihuatanejo—about 8–10 hours with a meal stop—make the trip only during daylight hours, due to reports of carjackings around the area of Playa Azul. Military and police patrols have been increased on Carretera 200 and the number of incidents has dramatically decreased; still, exercise caution. The U.S. State Department's Web site, http://travel.state.gov/mexico/html, gives updates on road safety issues.

Some of the biggest hassles on the road might be from police who pull you over for supposedly breaking the law, or for being a good prospect for a scam. Remember to **be polite**—displays of anger will only make matters worse—and be aware that a police officer might be pulling you over for something you didn't do. Although efforts are being made to fight corruption, it's still a fact of life in Mexico, and the $5 it costs to get your license back is definitely supplementary income for the officer who pulled you over with no intention of taking you down to police headquarters.

If you're stopped for speeding, the officer is supposed to take your license and hold it until you pay the fine at the local police station. But the officer will always prefer a *mordida* (small bribe) to wasting his time at the station. If you decide to dispute a charge that seems preposterous, do so with a smile, and tell the officer that you would like to talk to the police captain when you get to the station. The officer usually will let you go rather than go to the station.

When crossing the streets by foot, **look both ways for oncoming traffic,** even with the light. Although pedestrians have the right of way by law, drivers disregard it. And more often than not, drivers who hit pedestrians drive away as fast as they can without stopping, to avoid jail. Many Mexican drivers don't carry auto insurance, so you'll have to shoulder your own medical expenses.

### CHILDREN IN MEXICO
Mexico has one of the strictest policies about children entering the country. All children, including infants, must have proof of citizenship (a birth certificate) for travel to Mexico. All children up to age 18 traveling with a single parent must also have a notarized letter from the other parent stating that the child has his or her permission to leave their home country. If the other parent is deceased or the child has only one legal parent, a notarized statement saying so must be obtained as proof. In addition, parents must now fill out a tourist card for each child over the age of 10 traveling with them.

If you are renting a car, don't forget to arrange for a car seat when you reserve. For general advice about traveling with children, consult *Fodor's FYI: Travel with Your Baby* (available in bookstores everywhere).

### BABY-SITTING
Most chain and/or luxury hotels can arrange for a hotel staff member to babysit. If you'd like a sitter who speaks English, specify your request and the hotel will try to accommodate you. Rates range from $2 to $5 per hour or more, usually with a three-hour minimum plus taxi fare home. Smaller and budget hotels generally don't have baby-sitters available, and agencies are practically nonexistent.

## FLYING

If your children are two or older, ask about children's airfares. As a general rule, infants under two not occupying a seat fly at greatly reduced fares or even for free. But if you want to guarantee a seat for an infant, you have to pay full fare. Consider flying during off-peak days and times; most airlines will grant an infant a seat without a ticket if there are available seats. When booking, confirm carry-on allowances if you're traveling with infants. In general, for babies charged 10% to 50% of the adult fare you are allowed one carry-on bag and a collapsible stroller; if the flight is full, the stroller may have to be checked or you may be limited to less.

Experts agree that it's a good idea to use safety seats aloft for children weighing less than 40 pounds. Airlines set their own policies: if you use a safety seat, U.S. carriers usually require that the child be ticketed, even if he or she is young enough to ride free, because the seats must be strapped into regular seats. And even if you pay the full adult fare for the seat, it may be worth it, especially on longer trips. Do **check your airline's policy about using safety seats during takeoff and landing.** Safety seats are not allowed everywhere in the plane, so get your seat assignments as early as possible.

When reserving, request children's meals or a freestanding bassinet (not available at all airlines) if you need them. But note that bulkhead seats, where you must sit to use the bassinet, may lack an overhead bin or storage space on the floor.

## FOOD

Most restaurants in Mexico are family-friendly—especially those posting a "Restaurant Familiar" sign. If spicy food is dicey for your children, watch for signs or menus that say *pollo* (chicken) or *carne* (meat, which will feature a variety of steaks and other meat dishes), such as *pollo asado* or *carne asada* (roast chicken or roasted meats). Other familiar choices are *tortas,* sandwiches made on a hard roll, usually with chicken, pork, or cheese, condiments, and a vegetable garnish, and *tacos de bistec,* tacos filled with small

pieces of grilled beef. The Sanborns and VIPs chain restaurants, though not rock-bottom cheap, usually have a good variety of dishes. Many restaurants serve hamburgers and hot dogs, though the latter may be easier to find at smaller lunch counters. As for fast food, most cities and resort areas have all the American chains.

## LODGING

Mexico's major chain and luxury hotels have many child-friendly facilities and options, such as connecting family rooms, play areas and children's pools, and kids' clubs with special activities and outings. Extra beds and cribs are available and often free of charge; you can also arrange for a baby-sitter, though you'll need to specify if you'd like an English-speaking sitter. Ask whether children under a certain age can stay in their parents' room at no extra charge or at a discounted rate. Some hotels only offer children's programs during peak season, so check availability before booking. Also confirm whether children's activities are included in the price or if there's an extra charge.

Smaller and budget hotels generally don't offer such extras, but it never hurts to ask. Children are welcome everywhere except resorts that cater to adults only, such as certain Club Med locations.

## SIGHTS & ATTRACTIONS

Places that are especially appealing to children are indicated by a rubber-duckie icon (🦆) in the margin.

## SUPPLIES & EQUIPMENT

Baby formula, disposable diapers, baby food, and supplies such as bottles and lotions are widely available, especially in big pharmacies and supermarkets. You'll see such familiar powder formula brands as Similac, Nestlé's NAN and Enfamil, with prices ranging from $7 (for 400 grams/14 ounces) to $18–$25 (for 900 grams/31.5 ounces). Premixed formula is not as common, but large stores often have Isomil ($2 for 236 ml, or just under 8 ounces). Fresh milk is readily available in both large and small groceries, as well as convenience stores. American disposable diaper brands such as Pampers and Huggies range from

$4 for a package of 10 to $18 for 64. You'll often find disposable diapers at discounted prices, especially locally made brands.

## COMPUTERS ON THE ROAD

Internet cafés have sprung up all over Mexico, making e-mail by far the easiest way to stay in touch with people back home. If you're bringing a laptop with you, check with the manufacturer's technical support line to see what service and/or repair affiliates they have in the areas you plan to visit. Larger cities have repair shops that service Compac, Dell, Macintosh, SONY, Toshiba, and other major brands, though parts tend to be more expensive than in the U.S.

Carry a spare battery to save yourself the expense and headache of having to hunt down a replacement on the spot. Always check with your hotel about surge protection, especially if the property isn't part of a major chain and/or is in an out-of-the-way place. Extreme electrical fluctuations and surges can damage or destroy your computer. Check with IBM for its pen-size modem tester that plugs into a phone and jack to test if the line is safe.

## CONSUMER PROTECTION

Whether you're shopping for gifts or purchasing travel services, **pay with a major credit card** whenever possible, so you can cancel payment or get reimbursed if there's a problem (and you can provide documentation). If you're doing business with a particular company for the first time, contact your local Better Business Bureau and the attorney general's offices in your state and (for U.S. businesses) the company's home state as well. Have any complaints been filed? Finally, if you're buying a package or tour, always consider travel insurance that includes default coverage (⇨ Insurance).

The Mexican consumer protection agency, the Procuraduría Federal del Consumidor (PROFECO), also helps foreigners, particularly with complaints about goods or services not received in the condition promised (it tries to negotiate settlements or refunds; the process does require written documentation, though). When calling its hotline,

ask for *atención a extranjeros* to get an English-speaking staff member.

**⚑ BBBs** Council of Better Business Bureaus ⊠ 4200 Wilson Blvd., Suite 800, Arlington, VA 22203 ☎ 703/276-0100 🖷 703/525-8277 ⊕ www.bbb.org. **Procuraduría Federal de Consumidor (PROFECO)** ☎ 55/5211-1723 or 55/5625-6700, extension 1317 in Mexico City, 01800/468-8722 toll-free in Mexico.

## CRUISE TRAVEL

Cozumel and Playa del Carmen have become increasingly popular ports for Caribbean cruises. Most lines—including Carnival, Princess, Royal Caribbean International, Norwegian, Cunard, Holland America, and Royal Olympia—leave from Miami and/or other Florida ports such as Fort Lauderdale, Port Manatee, and Tampa. Texas passengers can take Royal Caribbean from Galveston and Royal Olympia or Norwegian from Houston to the Yucatán; Norwegian also has departures from Charleston, South Carolina. Companies offering cruises down the Baja California coast and/or other Pacific coast routes include Carnival, Cunard, Princess, Norwegian, Royal Olympia, Royal Caribbean, and Holland America. Most depart from Los Angeles, Long Beach, or San Diego and head to Los Cabos or Mazatlán, Puerto Vallarta, Acapulco and points south; some trips originate in Vancouver or San Francisco.

To learn how to plan, choose, and book a cruise-ship voyage, consult *Fodor's FYI: Plan & Enjoy Your Cruise* (available in bookstores everywhere).

**⚑ Cruise Lines** Carnival ☎ 888/227-6482 in the U.S. and Canada ⊕ www.carnival.com. **Cunard** ☎ 800/221-4770 in the U.S. and Canada ⊕ www. cunard.com. **Holland America** ☎ 800/426-0327 in the U.S. and Canada ⊕ www.hollandamerica.com. **Norwegian** ☎ 800/327-7030 in the U.S. and Canada ⊕ www.ncl.com. **Princess** ☎ 800/421-0522 in the U.S. and Canada ⊕ www.princess.com. **Royal Caribbean International** ☎ 800/327-6700 in the U.S. and Canada ⊕ www.royalcaribbean.com. **Royal Olympia** ☎ 800/872-6400 in the U.S., 800/368-3888 in Canada ⊕ www.royal-olympic-cruises.com.

## CUSTOMS & DUTIES

When shopping abroad, keep receipts for all purchases. Upon reentering the country, **be ready to show customs officials what**

**you've bought.** Pack purchases together in an easily accessible place. If you think a duty is incorrect, appeal the assessment. If you object to the way your clearance was handled, note the inspector's badge number. In either case, first ask to see a supervisor. If the problem isn't resolved, write to the appropriate authorities, beginning with the port director at your point of entry.

### IN AUSTRALIA

Australian residents who are 18 or older may bring home A$400 worth of souvenirs and gifts (including jewelry), 250 cigarettes or 250 grams of cigars or other tobacco products, and 1,125 ml of alcohol (including wine, beer, and spirits). Residents under 18 may bring back A$200 worth of goods. Members of the same family traveling together may pool their allowances. Prohibited items include meat products. Seeds, plants, and fruits need to be declared upon arrival.

**⟨▸⟩ Australian Customs Service** 🗗 Regional Director, Box 8, Sydney, NSW 2001 🖷 02/9213–2000 or 1300/363263, 02/9364–7222 or 1800/020–504 quarantine-inquiry line 🖷 02/9213–4043 ⊕ www. customs.gov.au.

### IN CANADA

Canadian residents who have been out of Canada for at least seven days may bring in C$750 worth of goods duty-free. If you've been away fewer than seven days but more than 48 hours, the duty-free allowance drops to C$200. If your trip lasts 24 to 48 hours, the allowance is C$50. You may not pool allowances with family members. Goods claimed under the C$750 exemption may follow you by mail; those claimed under the lesser exemptions must accompany you. Alcohol and tobacco products may be included in the seven-day and 48-hour exemptions but not in the 24-hour exemption. If you meet the age requirements of the province or territory through which you reenter Canada, you may bring in, duty-free, 1.5 liters of wine *or* 1.14 liters (40 imperial ounces) of liquor *or* 24 12-ounce cans or bottles of beer or ale. Also, if you meet the local age requirement for tobacco products, you may bring in, duty-free, 200 cigarettes and 50 cigars. Check ahead of time with the

Canada Customs and Revenue Agency or the Department of Agriculture for policies regarding meat products, seeds, plants, and fruits.

You may send an unlimited number of gifts (only one gift per recipient, however) worth up to C$60 each duty-free to Canada. Label the package UNSOLICITED GIFT—VALUE UNDER $60. Alcohol and tobacco are excluded.

**⟨▸⟩ Canada Customs and Revenue Agency** ✉ 2265 St. Laurent Blvd., Ottawa, Ontario K1G 4K3 🖷 800/461–9999 in Canada, 204/983–3500, 506/636–5064 ⊕ www.ccra.gc.ca.

### IN MEXICO

Upon entering Mexico, you'll be given a baggage declaration form and asked to itemize what you're bringing into the country. You are allowed to bring in 3 liters of spirits or wine for personal use; 400 cigarettes, 25 cigars, or 200 grams of tobacco; a reasonable amount of perfume for personal use; one video camera and one regular camera and 12 rolls of film for each; and gift items not to exceed a total of $300. If driving across the U.S. border, gift items must not exceed $50. You aren't allowed to bring firearms, meat, vegetables, plants, fruit, or flowers into the country. You can bring in one of each of the following items without paying taxes: a cell phone, a beeper, a radio or tape recorder, a musical instrument, a laptop computer, a portable copier or printer, and a typewriter. Compact discs and/or audio cassettes are limited to 20 total and DVDs to five.

Mexico also allows you to bring one cat or dog, if you have two things: 1) a pet health certificate signed by a registered veterinarian in the United States and issued not more than 72 hours before the animal enters Mexico; and 2) a pet vaccination certificate showing that the animal has been treated (as applicable) for rabies, hepatitis, distemper, and leptospirosis. For more information or information on bringing other animals or more than one type of animal, contact a Mexican consulate. Aduana Mexico (Mexican Customs) has a striking and informative Web site, though everything is in Spanish. You can also get customs information from the Mexican consulate, which has branches in many major American cities as well as border towns. To find the consulate nearest you, check the Ministry of Foreign Affairs Web site, http://portal.sre.gob.mx/sre; go to the list of embassies, consulates, and delegations and choose the "Consulados de México en el Exterior" option.

**Aduana Mexico** ⊕ www.aduanas.sat.gob.mx. **Mexican Consulate** ⊠ 2401 W. 6th St., Los Angeles, CA 90057 ☎ 231/351-6800 ⊕ www.consulmex-la.com ⊠ 27 E. 39th St., New York, NY 10016 ☎ 212/217-6400 ⊕ www.consulmexny.org.

## IN NEW ZEALAND

All homeward-bound residents may bring back NZ$700 worth of souvenirs and gifts; passengers may not pool their allowances, and children can claim only the concession on goods intended for their own use. For those 17 or older, the duty-free allowance also includes 4.5 liters of wine or beer; one 1,125-ml bottle of spirits; and either 200 cigarettes, 250 grams of tobacco, 50 cigars, *or* a combination of the three up to 250 grams. Meat products, seeds, plants, and fruits must be declared upon arrival to the Agricultural Services Department.

**New Zealand Customs** ⊠ Head office: The Customhouse, 17–21 Whitmore St., Box 2218, Wellington ☎ 09/300-5399 or 0800/428-786 ⊕ www.customs.govt.nz.

## IN THE U.K.

From countries outside the European Union, including Mexico, you may bring home, duty-free, 200 cigarettes, 100 cigarillos, 50 cigars, 100 cigarillos, or 250 grams of tobacco; 1 liter of spirits or 2 liters of fortified or sparkling wine or liqueurs; 2 liters of still table wine; 60 ml of perfume; 250 ml of toilet water; plus £145 worth of other goods, including gifts and souvenirs. Prohibited items include meat products, seeds, plants, fruits, and dairy products.

**HM Customs and Excise** ⊠ Portcullis House, 21 Cowbridge Rd. E, Cardiff CF11 9SS ☎ 0845/010-9000 or 0208/929-0152 advice service, 0208/929-6731 or 0208/910-3602 complaints ⊕ www.hmce.gov.uk.

## IN THE U.S.

U.S. residents who have been out of the country for at least 48 hours may bring home, for personal use, $800 worth of foreign goods duty-free, as long as they haven't used the $800 allowance or any part of it in the past 30 days. This exemption may include 1 liter of alcohol (for travelers 21 and older), 200 cigarettes, and 100 non-Cuban cigars. Family members from the same household who are traveling together may pool their $800 personal exemptions. For fewer than 48 hours, the duty-free allowance drops to $200, which may include 50 cigarettes, 10 non-Cuban cigars, and 150 ml of alcohol (or 150 ml of perfume containing alcohol). The $200 allowance cannot be combined with other individuals' exemptions, and if you exceed it, the full value of all the goods will be taxed. Antiques, which U.S. Customs and Border Protection defines as objects more than 100 years old, enter duty-free, as do original works of art done entirely by hand, including paintings, drawings, and sculptures. This doesn't apply to folk art or handicrafts, which are in general dutiable.

You may also send packages home duty-free, with a limit of one parcel per addressee per day (except alcohol or tobacco products or perfume worth more than $5). You can mail up to $200 worth of goods for personal use; label the package PERSONAL USE and attach a list of its contents and their retail value. If the package contains your used personal belongings, mark it AMERICAN GOODS RETURNED to avoid paying duties. You may send up to $100 worth of goods as a gift; mark the package UNSOLICITED GIFT. Mailed items do not affect your duty-free allowance on your return.

To avoid paying duty on foreign-made high-ticket items you already own and will take on your trip, register them with Customs before you leave the country. Consider filing a Certificate of Registration for laptops, cameras, watches, and other digital devices identified with serial numbers or other permanent markings; you can keep the certificate for other trips. Otherwise, bring a sales receipt or insurance form to show that you owned the item before you left the United States.

For more about duties, restricted items, and other information about international travel, check out U.S. Customs and Border

Protection's online brochure, *Know Before You Go.*

🔰 **U.S. Customs and Border Protection** ✉ For inquiries and equipment registration, 1300 Pennsylvania Ave. NW, Washington, DC 20229 ⊕ www.cbp. gov ☎ 877/287-8667, 202/354-1000 ✉ For complaints, Customer Satisfaction Unit, 1300 Pennsylvania Ave. NW, Room 5.2C, Washington, DC 20229.

## DISABILITIES & ACCESSIBILITY

Mexico is poorly equipped for travelers with disabilities. There are rarely any special discounts or passes, nor is public transportation, including the Mexico City Metro, wheelchair accessible. Some cities, such as Veracruz and Guadalajara, have ramps and curb cuts. But most roads and sidewalks are often crowded—many have cobblestones—and people on the street won't assist you unless expressly asked. Further, you can't rent vehicles outfitted for travelers with disabilities.

Most hotels and restaurants have at least a few steps, and although rooms considered "wheelchair accessible" by hotel owners are usually on the ground floor, the doorways and bathroom may not be maneuverable. It's a good idea to call ahead to find out what a hotel or restaurant can offer. Despite these barriers, Mexicans with disabilities manage to negotiate places that most travelers outside Mexico would not consider accessible.

One Mexican travel agency that addresses the needs of people with disabilities is Varlo y Mar, which arranges trips to Puerto Vallarta. Trips to Cancún and Cabo San Lucas are in the works. You can also rent the company's van (making your own arrangements for a driver) for trips to nearby Costa Careyes.

🔰 **Varlo y Mar** ✉ Oceana Indico 399, Col. Palmar de Aramara, Puerto Vallarta ☎ 322/224-1868 ⊕ www.accesiblemexico.com.

## LODGING

The best choices of accessible lodging are found in major resort towns such as Acapulco, Cancún, and Mazatlán, and big cities such as Mexico City and Guadalajara.

## RESERVATIONS

When discussing accessibility with an operator or reservations agent, ask hard questions. Are there any stairs, inside *or* out? Are there grab bars next to the toilet *and* in the shower/tub? How wide is the doorway to the room? To the bathroom? For the most extensive facilities meeting the latest legal specifications, opt for newer accommodations. If you reserve through a toll-free number, consider also calling the hotel's local number to confirm the information from the central reservations office. Get confirmation in writing when you can.

## TRANSPORTATION

Mexico's public transportation systems are not wheelchair accessible, and its car rental agencies don't have vehicles equipped for travelers with disabilities.

🔰 **Complaints Aviation Consumer Protection Division** (⇨ Air Travel) for airline-related problems. **Departmental Office of Civil Rights** ✉ For general inquiries, U.S. Department of Transportation, S-30, 400 7th St. SW, Room 10215, Washington, DC 20590 ☎ 202/366-4648 🖷 202/366-9371 ⊕ www.dot. gov/ost/docr/index.htm. **Disability Rights Section** ✉ NYAV, U.S. Department of Justice, Civil Rights Division, 950 Pennsylvania Ave. NW, Washington, DC 20530 ☎ ADA information line 202/514-0301, 800/ 514-0301, 202/514-0383 TTY, 800/514-0383 TTY ⊕ www.ada.gov. **U.S. Department of Transportation Hotline** ☎ For disability-related air-travel problems, 800/778-4838 or 800/455-9880 TTY.

## TRAVEL AGENCIES

In the United States, the Americans with Disabilities Act requires that travel firms serve the needs of all travelers. Some agencies specialize in working with people with disabilities.

🔰 **Travelers with Mobility Problems Access Adventures/B. Roberts Travel** ✉ 206 Chestnut Ridge Rd., Scottsville, NY 14624 ☎ 585/889-9096 ⊕ www.brobertstravel.com ✎ dltravel@prodigy. net, run by a former physical-rehabilitation counselor. **CareVacations** ✉ No. 5, 5110-50 Ave., Leduc, Alberta, Canada, T9E 6V4 ☎ 780/986-6404 or 877/ 478-7827 🖷 780/986-8332 ⊕ www.carevacations. com, for group tours and cruise vacations. **Flying Wheels Travel** ✉ 143 W. Bridge St., Box 382, Owatonna, MN 55060 ☎ 507/451-5005 🖷 507/451-1685 ⊕ www.flyingwheelstravel.com.

🔰 **Travelers with Developmental Disabilities New Directions** ✉ 5276 Hollister Ave., Suite 207, Santa Barbara, CA 93111 ☎ 805/967-2841 or 888/967-2841 🖷 805/964-7344 ⊕ www.newdirectionstravel.com.

## DISCOUNTS & DEALS

Be a smart shopper and compare all your options before making decisions. A plane ticket bought with a promotional coupon from travel clubs, coupon books, and direct-mail offers or purchased on the Internet may not be cheaper than the least expensive fare from a discount ticket agency. And always keep in mind that what you get is just as important as what you save.

### DISCOUNT RESERVATIONS

To save money, look into discount reservations services with Web sites and toll-free numbers, which use their buying power to get a better price on hotels, airline tickets (⇨ Air Travel), even car rentals. When booking a room, always **call the hotel's local toll-free number** (if one is available) rather than the central reservations number—you'll often get a better price. Always ask about special packages or corporate rates.

When shopping for the best deal on hotels and car rentals, look for guaranteed exchange rates, which protect you against a falling dollar. With your rate locked in, you won't pay more, even if the price goes up in the local currency.

🖪 Airline Tickets **Air 4 Less** ☎ 800/AIR4LESS; low-fare specialist.

🖪 Hotel Rooms **Accommodations Express** ☎ 800/444-7666 or 800/277-1064 ⊕ www.acex. net. **Hotels.com** ☎ 800/246-8357 ⊕ www.hotels. com. **Steigenberger Reservation Service** ☎ 800/ 223-5652 ⊕ www.srs-worldhotels.com. **Turbotrip. com** ☎ 800/473-7829 ⊕ www.turbotrip.com.

### PACKAGE DEALS

Don't confuse packages and guided tours. When you buy a package, you travel on your own, just as though you had planned the trip yourself. Fly/drive packages, which combine airfare and car rental, are often a good deal. In cities, ask the local visitor's bureau about hotel and local transportation packages that include tickets to major museum exhibits or other special events.

## EATING & DRINKING

Mexican restaurants run the gamut from humble hole-in-the-wall shacks, street stands, *taquerías,* and American-style fast-food joints to elegant, internationally acclaimed restaurants. Prices, naturally, follow suit. To save money, **look for the fixed-menu lunch** known as *comida corrida* or *menú del día,* which is served from about 1–4 almost everywhere in Mexico.

The restaurants we list are the cream of the crop in each price category. Price categories are based on the least expensive entrée to the most expensive. For more information on local foods throughout Mexico, *see* "La Cocina Mexicana" in Mexico City (Chapter 1) and the cuisine sections that appear under Pleasures & Pastimes in each chapter. Throughout this guide, properties indicated by a ✕⛉ are lodging establishments whose restaurant warrants a special trip.

### MEALS & MEALTIMES

You can get *desayuno* (breakfast) in *cafeterías* (coffee shops), of course, as well as snack bars and other establishments. Choices range from hefty egg-and-sausage dishes to *chilaquiles* (a layered casserole with dried tortilla strips, tomato sauce, spices, cheese, and sometimes meat or eggs). *Comida* (lunch) is the big meal of the day, and usually consists of soup and/ or salad, bread or tortillas, a main dish, one or two side dishes, and dessert. *Cena* (dinner) tends to be lighter; in fact, many people just have milk or hot chocolate and a sweet roll; *tamales* are also traditional evening fare, though it's easy enough to find places that will serve a substantial, multicourse dinner.

Restaurants are plentiful and have long hours. (Note, however, that seafood places often close by late afternoon.) Lunch is usually served from 2 PM to 4 PM; dinner is rarely served before 8 PM. Unless otherwise noted, the restaurants listed in this guide are open daily for lunch and dinner.

### PAYING

Credit cards—especially American Express, MasterCard, and Visa—are widely accepted at pricier restaurants. Bargains are usually cash only.

### RESERVATIONS & DRESS

Reservations are always a good idea; we mention them only when they're essential or not accepted. Book as far ahead as you can, and reconfirm as soon as you arrive. (Large parties should always call ahead to check the reservations policy.) We mention dress only when men are required to wear a jacket or a jacket and tie.

## WINE, BEER & SPIRITS

Mexican drinking establishments range from raucous cantinas, reserved for hard-drinking men, to low-key cafés. Be sure to sample some locally made tequila or mezcal (the one with the worm at the bottom). Both potent spirits are made from the agave plant, which is similar to but, in fact, not a cactus. Ask for a *reposado* (aged 2–12 months) or *añejo* (aged 1–3 years) tequila for a smoother—and more expensive—taste. Locally brewed beers are mostly of the Corona category though the Negra Modelo and Indio brands are darker. Mexico's Baja California region has gained a reputation for its wines; ask your waiter to recommend a vintage.

## ECOTOURISM

*Ecoturismo* is fast becoming a buzzword in the Mexican tourism industry, even though not all operators and establishments employ practices that are good for the environment. For example, in the so-called Riviera Maya, an area south of Cancún, hotel developments greatly threaten the ecosystem, including the region's coral reefs. Nevertheless, President Vicente Fox has pledged to support more ecotourism projects, and recent national and international conferences have focused on this theme.

Mexico has more than 18 million acres of preserves, national parks, and biosphere reserves. You can visit monarch butterfly sanctuaries, endangered sea-turtle nesting sites, saltwater lagoons where California gray whales breed, deep desert canyons, and volcanoes. To find out more about ecotourism opportunities and issues, contact the Asociación Mexicana de Turismo de Aventura y Ecoturismo (AMTAVE, or Mexican Association of Adventure Travel and Ecotourism). Planeta.com is another great source for information on environmentally conscious travel—including lists of eco-friendly tour operators—in Mexico

and throughout the world. It also has information on trips that involve mountain climbing, rappelling, hiking, cycling, horseback riding, paragliding, and sea kayaking.
🔃 **AMTAVE** ⊕ www.amtave.org. **Planeta.com** ⊕ www.planeta.com.

## DOLPHIN ENCOUNTERS

One of the most heavily advertised activities in parts of Mexico is swimming with dolphins. The water parks offering such encounters often bill the experiences as "educational" and "enchanting," and every year, thousands of tourists who understandably love dolphins pay top dollar to participate in the activity. Several environmental and anticruelty organizations, however, including Greenpeace, the Humane Society of the United States, and the Whale and Dolphin Conservation Society have spoken out against dolphin encounters. One contention is that many water parks have broken international laws regulating the procurement of dolphins from restricted areas; another is that the confined conditions at some parks have put dolphins' health at risk. Some animals are kept in overcrowded pens and suffer from stress-related diseases; some have died from untreated illness; some have even behaved aggressively toward people swimming with them.

These organizations have been pressuring the water parks to adhere to international regulations and treat their dolphins with better care. Until conditions improve you may wish to visit dolphins at facilities such as Xcaret, an ecological theme park on the Caribbean coast, which has a track record of handling animals humanely. You might also opt to apply the $100-plus fee for this activity toward a snorkeling or whale-watching trip, where you can see marine life in its natural state.
🔃 **Greenpeace** ⊕ www.greenpeace.org. **Humane Society of the United States** ⊕ www.hsus.org. **Whale and Dolphin Conservation Society** ⊕ www.wdcs.org.

## ELECTRICITY

For U.S. and Canadian travelers, electrical converters aren't necessary because Mexico operates on the 60-cycle, 120-volt system; however, many Mexican outlets have not been updated to accommodate three-prong and polarized plugs (those with one larger prong), so to be safe **bring an adapter.**

If your appliances are dual-voltage, you'll need only an adapter. Don't use 110-volt outlets marked FOR SHAVERS ONLY for high-wattage appliances such as blow-dryers. Most laptops operate equally well on 110 and 220 volts and so require only an adapter. Blackouts and brownouts—often lasting an hour or so—are fairly common everywhere, particularly during the rainy season.

## EMBASSIES

🛂 Australia **Australian Embassy** ✉ Calle Rubén Darío 55, Col. Polanco, Mexico City ☎ 55/1101-2200 ⊕ www.mexico.embassy.gov.au/quienes/mx/index. html.

🛂 Canada **Canadian Embassy** ✉ Calle Schiller 529, Col. Polanco, Mexico City ☎ 55/5724-7900 ⊕ www.canada.org.mx.

🛂 Mexico **Mexican Embassy in Australia** ✉ 14 Perth Ave., Yarralumla, ACT ☎ 02/6273-3963 or 6273-3905 ⊕ www.embassyofmexicoinaustralia. org. **Mexican Embassy in New Zealand** ✉ 111 Customhouse Quay (level 8), Wellington ☎ 4/472-0555 ⊕ www.mexico.org.nz. **Mexican Embassy in the U.K.** ✉ 42 Hertford St., London ☎ 20/7499-8586 ⊕ www.embamex.co.uk. **Mexican Embassy in the U.S.** ✉ 1911 Pennsylvania Ave. NW, Washington, DC ☎ 202/728-1600 ⊕ www.sre.gob.mx/eua.

🛂 New Zealand **New Zealand Embassy** ✉ Jaime Balmes 8, 4th fl., Col. Los Morales Polanco, Mexico City ☎ 55/5283-9460.

🛂 United Kingdom **British Embassy** ✉ Río Lerma 71, Col. Cuauhtémoc, Mexico City ☎ 55/5207-2089 or 5242-8500 ⊕ www.embajadabritanica.com.mx.

🛂 United States **U.S. Embassy** ✉ Paseo de la Reforma 305, Col. Cuauhtémoc, Mexico City ☎ 55/5080-2000 ⊕ www.usembassy-mexico.gov/emenu. html.

## EMERGENCIES

The emergency number ☎ 060 works best in Mexico City and environs. In other areas, call ☎ 080 or ☎ 066. For roadside assistance contact the Angeles Verdes. If you get into a scrape with the law, you can call your nearest consulate; U.S. citizens can also call the Overseas Citizens Services Center in the United States. The Mexican Ministry of Tourism also has a 24-hour

toll-free hot line, and local tourist boards may be able to help as well. Two medical emergency evacuation services are Air Ambulance Network and Global Life Flight.

🛂 **Air Ambulance Network** ☎ 01800/010-0027 toll-free in Mexico, 800/327-1966 in the U.S. and Canada ⊕ www.airambulancenetwork.com. **Angeles Verdes, Mexico City** ☎ 55/5250-8221. **U.S. Overseas Citizens Services Center** ☎ 317/472-2328 weekdays 8 AM-8 PM EST, 202/634-3600 after hrs and on weekends. **Global Life Flight** ☎ 01800/ 305-9400 or 01800/361-1600 toll-free in Mexico, 888/554-9729 in the U.S., 877/817-6843 in Canada ⊕ www.globallifeflight.com. **Mexico Ministry of Tourism** ☎ 01800/903-9200 toll free in Mexico.

## ETIQUETTE & BEHAVIOR

In the United States and elsewhere in the world, being direct, efficient, and succinct is highly valued. But Mexican communication tends to be more subtle, and the American style is often perceived as curt and aggressive. Mexicans are extremely polite, so losing your temper over delays or complaining loudly will get you branded as rude and make people less inclined to help you.

Remember that things move at a slow pace here and that there's no stigma attached to being late; be gracious about this and other local customs and attitudes. In restaurants, for example, a waiter would never consider bringing you your check before you ask for it; that would be rude. What's not considered rude, however, is dallying in bringing that check once you do ask for it.

Learning basic phrases in Spanish such as *por favor* (please) and *gracias* (thank you) will make a big difference in how people respond to you. Also, being deferential to those who are older than you will earn you lots of points.

If you're visiting a house of worship, forgo shorts and other revealing clothing. You'll probably notice that friends, relatives, and significant others show a fair amount of physical affection with each other, but—if you're a foreigner—be more retiring with people you don't know well.

### BUSINESS ETIQUETTE

Personal relationships always come first here, so developing rapport and trust is essential. A handshake and personal greeting is appropriate along with a friendly inquiry about family, especially if you have met the family. In established business relationships, do not be surprised if you're greeted with a kiss on the cheek or a hug. Always be respectful toward colleagues in public and keep confrontations private. Meetings may or may not start on time, but you should be patient. When invited to dinner at the home of a client or associate, bring a gift and be sure to send a thank-you note afterward. Your offers to pick up the tab at business lunches or dinners will be greatly appreciated but will probably be declined; as a guest in their country most Mexicans will want to treat you to the meal.

Be prepared to exchange business cards, and feel free to offer yours first. Professional attire tends to be on the traditional side. Your offers to pick up the tab at business lunches or dinners will be greatly appreciated but will probably be declined; as a guest in their country, most Mexicans will want to treat you to the meal.

## GAY & LESBIAN TRAVEL

Mexican same-sex couples keep a low profile, and foreign same-sex couples should do the same. Two people of the same gender can often have a hard time getting a *cama matrimonial* (double bed), especially in smaller hotels. This could be attributed to the influence of the Catholic church—Mexico is a devoutly Catholic country. The same rule that applies all over the world holds in Mexico as well: alternative lifestyles in general are more accepted in cosmopolitan areas, such as Mexico City, Acapulco, Cancún, Cuernavaca, Puerto Vallarta, San Miguel de Allende, and Veracruz City. Guadalajara, though a sizeable town, is quite conservative.

⚑ Gay- & Lesbian-Friendly Travel Agencies **Different Roads Travel** ⊠ 8383 Wilshire Blvd., Suite 520, Beverly Hills, CA 90211 ☎ 323/651-5557 or 800/429-8747 (Ext. 14 for both) ⊟ 323/651-5454 ✉ lgernert@tzell.com. **Kennedy Travel** ⊠ 130 W. 42nd St., Suite 401, New York, NY 10036 ☎ 212/840-8659, 800/237-7433 ⊟ 212/730-2269 ⊕ www.kennedytravel.com. **Now, Voyager** ⊠ 4406 18th St., San Francisco, CA 94114 ☎ 415/626-1169 or 800/255-6951 ⊟ 415/626-8626 ⊕ www.nowvoyager.com. **Skylink Travel and Tour/Flying Dutchmen**

**Travel** ⊠ 1455 N. Dutton Ave., Suite A, Santa Rosa, CA 95401 ☎ 707/546-9888 or 800/225-5759 ⊟ 707/636-0951; serving lesbian travelers.

## HEALTH
### AIR & WATER POLLUTION

Air pollution in Mexico City can pose a health risk. The sheer number of cars and industries in the capital, thermal inversions, and the inability to process sewage have all contributed to the high levels of lead, carbon monoxide, and other pollutants in Mexico City's atmosphere. Children, the elderly, and those with respiratory problems should avoid outdoor activities—including sightseeing—on days of high smog alerts. (Information on smog is often published in the daily papers and mentioned on the radio. If Spanish isn't one of your languages, ask a hotel staffer for an update.) If you have heart problems, keep in mind that Mexico City is, at 7,556 feet, the highest metropolis on the North American continent. This compounded with the smog may pose a serious health risk, so check with your doctor before planning a trip.

In the last few years Mexico has had to make tough choices between much-needed development and protecting the environment. In some places the rate of development has exceeded the government's ability to keep the environment safe. Some clean-up action is underway, after studies released in early 2003 indicated that waters near 16 resort areas contained high levels of pollution from trash, sewage, or industrial waste. Of the resorts—which included Acapulco, Puerto Vallarta, Puerto Escondido, and Huatulco—Zihuatanejo was considered the most polluted. Two factors reportedly contributed to the problem: the waters off its shores are in a bay where pollution is more apt to accumulate than it would in open waters, and this area in particular had difficulties properly treating its wastewater. The clean-up efforts have a long way to go, and the September 2003 replacement of environment minister Víctor Lichtinger, an economist and environmental consultant, with career politician Alberto Cárdenas Jiménez has caused some environmentalists to worry.

Polluted waters can give swimmers gastrointestinal and other problems; **ask locals about where it's best to swim.** Some information about coliform and e. coli bacterial levels in beach waters is also available on the Web site of the Environment Secretariat (SEMARNAT). The site is in Spanish, but the color-coded graphs are easy to follow, and there is an English-language section. The site includes a map of Mexico with major beaches; click on the name of the beach you'd like to check. Watch out for *no recomendable* (not recommended) and *riesgo sanitario* (health risk) areas.

🄵 SEMARNAT ⊕ www.semarnat.gob.mex

## ALTITUDE SICKNESS

The higher you go, the lower the oxygen levels in the air—and the oxygen deficiency in your breathing intake can cause *mal de alturas* (altitude sickness). It usually sets in at 8,000 feet, though some people are affected at 6,000 feet; headache, insomnia, and shortness of breath are the most common symptoms. At 7,556 feet, Mexico City is in the altitude sickness zone for many travelers. Mild pain relievers, such as aspirin or aspirin substitutes, should help with headaches. Altitude sensitivity varies, but in general you can expect symptoms to abate after two or three days. Stronger drugs, such as acetazolamide, should only be taken after consulting a doctor. More severe symptoms include nausea, vomiting, dry cough, confusion, and difficulty walking a straight line; at worst altitude sickness can cause pulmonary and cerebral edema. If your symptoms don't go away, get to a lower altitude and consult a doctor. If you're doing any mountain climbing, be especially careful. Stay hydrated (which includes going easy on diuretics, like coffee, tea, and alcoholic beverages) and plan on scaling back your physical activity until you're acclimated.

## DIVERS' ALERT

**Do not fly within 24 hours of scuba diving.**

## FOOD & DRINK

In Mexico the major health risk, known as *turista,* or traveler's diarrhea, is caused by eating contaminated fruit or vegetables or drinking contaminated water. So **watch what you eat.** Avoid uncooked food, and unpasteurized milk and milk products. *Tacos al pastor*—thin pork slices grilled on a spit and garnished with the usual cilantro, onions, and chili peppers—are delicious but dangerous. The cilantro, for instance, may have been rinsed in unpurified water. It's also a good idea to pass up *ceviche,* raw fish cured in lemon juice—a favorite appetizer, especially at seaside resorts. The Mexican Department of Health warns that marinating in lemon juice does not constitute the "cooking" that would make the shellfish safe to eat. Also, be wary of food sold from street stands: utensils and dishes aren't always properly washed, and there's no knowing what the ingredients have come in contact with.

**Drink only bottled water** or water that has been boiled for at least 10 minutes (if you need to ask for boiled water, say *"por favor, quiero que hiervan el agua por diez minutos"*), even when you're brushing your teeth. Hotels with water-purification systems will post signs to that effect in the rooms. Stay away from ice, unless you're sure it was made from purified water; commercially made purified ice usually has a uniform shape and a hole in the center. When in doubt, especially when ordering cold drinks at untouristed establishments, **skip the ice:** *sin hielo.*

Mild cases of *turista* may respond to Imodium (known generically as loperamide), Lomotil or Pepto-Bismol (not as strong), all of which you can buy over the counter; keep in mind, though, that these drugs can complicate more serious illnesses. You'll need to replace fluids, so drink plenty of purified water or tea; chamomile tea (*te de manzanilla*) is a good folk remedy and it's readily available in restaurants throughout Mexico. In severe cases, rehydrate yourself with Gatorade or a salt-sugar solution (½ teaspoon salt and 4 tablespoons sugar per quart of water).

## MEDICAL PLANS

No one plans to get sick while traveling, but it happens, so consider signing up with a medical-assistance company. Members get doctor referrals, emergency evacuation or repatriation, hot lines for medical consultation, cash for emergencies, and other assistance. You can call International SOS Assistance's U.S.-based phone number collect from Mexico.

🔢 **Medical-Assistance Companies International SOS Assistance** ⊕ www.internationalsos.com ✉ 8 Neshaminy Interplex, Suite 207, Trevose, PA 19053 ☎ 215/245-4707 or 800/523-6586 🖷 215/244-9617 ✉ Landmark House, Hammersmith Bridge Rd., 6th floor, London, W6 9DP ☎ 20/8762-8008 🖷 20/8748-7744 ✉ 12 Chemin Riantbosson, 1217 Meyrin 1, Geneva, Switzerland ☎ 22/785-6464 🖷 22/785-6424 ✉ 331 N. Bridge Rd., 17-00, Odeon Towers, Singapore 188720 ☎ 6338-7800 🖷 6338-7611.

## OVER-THE-COUNTER REMEDIES

*Farmacias* (pharmacies) are the most convenient place for such common medicines as *aspirina* (aspirin) or *jarabe para la tos* (cough syrup). You'll be able to find many U.S. brands (e.g., Tylenol, Pepto-Bismol, etc.). There are pharmacies in all small towns and on practically every corner in larger cities. The Sanborns chain stores also have pharmacies.

## PESTS & OTHER HAZARDS

Caution is advised when venturing out in the Mexican sun. Sunbathers lulled by a slightly overcast sky or the sea breezes can be burned badly in just 20 minutes. To avoid overexposure, **use strong sunscreens and avoid the peak sun hours** of noon to 2 PM. Sunscreen, including many American brands, can be found in pharmacies, supermarkets, and resort gift shops.

## SHOTS & MEDICATIONS

According to the U.S. National Centers for Disease Control and Prevention (CDC), there's a limited risk of malaria, dengue fever, and other insect-carried or parasite-caused illnesses in certain rural areas of Mexico. In most urban or easily accessible areas you need not worry. However, if you plan to visit remote regions or stay for more than six weeks, **check with the CDC's International Travelers Hotline.** Malaria and dengue are both carried by mosquitoes; in areas where these illnesses are prevalent, use mosquito nets, wear clothing that covers the body, apply repellent containing DEET, and use spray for flying insects in living and sleeping areas.

Repellents (*repelentes contra mosquitos*) and sprays (*aerosoles repelentes contra mosquitos*) can be purchased at pharmacies. In some places you see mosquito coils (*espirales contra mosquitos*) used; they can be purchased in hardware stores (*ferretería* or *tlalpalería*) as well as in pharmacies. Also **consider taking antimalarial pills** if you are doing serious adventure activities in subtropical areas. There's no vaccine to combat dengue.

🔢 **Health Warnings National Centers for Disease Control and Prevention** (CDC) ✉ Office of Health Communication, National Center for Infectious Diseases, Division of Quarantine, Travelers' Health, 1600 Clifton Rd. NE, Atlanta, GA 30333 ☎ 877/394-8747 international travelers' health line, 800/311-3435 other inquiries, 404/498-1600 Division of Quarantine 🖷 888/232-3299 ⊕ www.cdc.gov/travel. **World Health Organization** (WHO) ⊕ www.who.int.

## HOLIDAYS

Banks and government offices close on January 1, February 5 (Constitution Day), March 21 (Benito Juárez's birthday), May 1 (Labor Day), September 16 (Independence Day), November 20 (Revolution Day), and December 25. They may also close on unofficial holidays, such as Day of the Dead (November 1–2), Virgin of Guadalupe Day (December 12), and during Holy Week (the days leading to Easter Sunday). Government offices usually have reduced hours and staff from Christmas through New Year's Day.

## INSURANCE

The most useful travel-insurance plan is a comprehensive policy that includes coverage for trip cancellation and interruption, default, trip delay, and medical expenses (with a waiver for preexisting conditions).

Without insurance you'll lose all or most of your money if you cancel your trip, regardless of the reason. Default insurance covers you if your tour operator, airline, or cruise line goes out of business—the chances of which have been increasing. Trip-delay covers expenses that arise because of bad weather or mechanical delays. Study the fine print when comparing policies.

If you're traveling internationally, a key component of travel insurance is coverage for medical bills incurred if you get sick on the road. Such expenses aren't generally covered by Medicare or private policies. U.K. residents can buy a travel-insurance policy valid for most vacations taken during the year in which it's purchased (but check preexisting-condition coverage). British and Australian citizens need extra medical coverage when traveling overseas.

Always **buy travel policies directly from the insurance company**; if you buy them from a cruise line, airline, or tour operator that goes out of business you probably won't be covered for the agency or operator's default, a major risk. Before making any purchase, review your existing health and home-owner's policies to find what they cover away from home.

� **Travel Insurers** In the U.S.: **Access America** ✉ 2805 N. Parham Rd., Richmond, VA 23294 ☎ 800/284-8300 🖷 804/673-1491 or 800/346-9265 ⊕ www.accessamerica.com. **Travel Guard International** ✉ 1145 Clark St., Stevens Point, WI 54481 ☎ 715/345-0505 or 800/826-1300 🖷 800/955-8785 ⊕ www.travelguard.com.
🔡 In the U.K.: **Association of British Insurers** ✉ 51 Gresham St., London EC2V 7HQ ☎ 020/7600-3333 🖷 020/7696-8999 ⊕ www.abi.org.uk. In Canada: **RBC Insurance** ✉ 6880 Financial Dr., Mississauga, Ontario L5N 7Y5 ☎ 800/668-4342 or 905/816-2400 🖷 905/813-4704 ⊕ www.rbcinsurance.com. In Australia: **Insurance Council of Australia** ✉ Insurance Enquiries and Complaints, Level 12, Box 561, Collins St. W, Melbourne, VIC 8007 ☎ 1300/780808 or 03/9629-4109 🖷 03/9621-2060 ⊕ www.iecltd.com.au. In New Zealand: **Insurance Council of New Zealand** ✉ Level 7, 111-115 Customhouse Quay, Box 474, Wellington ☎ 04/472-5230 🖷 04/473-3011 ⊕ www.icnz.org.nz.

## LANGUAGE

Spanish is the official language, although Indian languages are spoken by approximately 8% of the population and some of those people speak no Spanish at all. Basic English is widely understood by most people employed in tourism, less so in the less-developed areas. At the very least, shopkeepers will know the numbers for bargaining purposes.

As in most other foreign countries, knowing the mother tongue has a way of opening doors, so **learn some Spanish words and phrases.** Mexicans welcome even the most halting attempts to use the language.

Castilian Spanish (the dialect spoken in much of Spain) differs from Latin American Spanish in pronunciation, certain aspects of grammar, and vocabulary. Words or phrases that are harmless or everyday in one country can offend in another. (If it's obvious you're a foreigner, however, people may stare and then laugh, but will cut you a lot of slack.) Check out the phrase guide and glossary at the back of this book. For really subtle nuances, consult a native speaker. The *Random House Latin-American Spanish Dictionary* is a good reference.

### LANGUAGES FOR TRAVELERS
A phrase book and language-tape set can help get you started. *Fodor's Spanish for Travelers* (available at bookstores everywhere) is excellent.

### LANGUAGE-STUDY PROGRAMS
Mexico has many language institutes, and attending one is an ideal way not only to learn Mexican Spanish but also to acquaint yourself with the customs and the people. For total immersion, most schools offer boarding with a family, but there's generally flexibility in terms of the type of lodgings and the length of your stay.

We recommend the places listed below for learning Spanish and living with a Mexican family. AmeriSpan Unlimited, based in the United States, can arrange for language study and homestays. Special programs include those at the Centro de Idiomas de la Universidad Autónoma Benito Juárez, which offers classes in Mixtec and Zapotec as well as Spanish. Many programs offer courses in Latin American studies and culture, as well as language.

🔡 **Language Institutes Academia Falcon** ✉ Paseo de la Presa 80, 36000 Guanajuato ☎ 473/731-0745 ⊕ www.academiafalcon.com. **AmeriSpan Unlimited** 🖃 Box 58129, Philadelphia, PA 19102 ☎ 800/879-6640 or 215/751-1100 ⊕ www.amerispan.com. **Cemanáuac** 🖃 A.P. 5-21, CP 62051 Cuernavaca, Morelos ☎ 777/318-6407 ⊕ www.cemanahuac.com. **Centro de Estudios para Extranjeros** ✉ Calle Tomás V. Gómez 125, 44600 Guadalajara, Jalisco ☎ 33/3616-4399 ⊕ www.cepe.udg.mx ✉ Calle Libertad 105, Local 1, 48360 Puerto Vallarta, Jalisco

☎ 322/223-2082. **Centro de Idiomas de la Universidad Autónoma Benito Juárez** ✉ Calle Burgoa s/n, 68000 Oaxaca ☎📠 951/516-5922. **Iberoamerican University Programs for Foreign Students** ✉ Prolongación Paseo de la Reforma 880, C.P. 01210 Lomas de Santa Fe, Mexico, D.F. ☎ 55/5950-4000 and 9177-4400 ⊕ www.uia.mx/ibero/inter. **Instituto Allende** ✉ Ancha de San Antonio 20, 37700 San Miguel de Allende, Guanajuato ☎ 415/152-0190 or 415/152-0929 ⊕ www.instituto-allende.edu.mx. **Instituto de Lenguas Jovel, A.C.** ✉ Calle Ma. Adelina Flores 21 San Cristóbal de las Casas ☎ A.P. 62, 29200 San Cristóbal de las Casas, Chiapas ☎📠 967/678-4069 ⊕ www.institutojovel.com. **National Autonomous University of Mexico School for Foreign Students** ✉ Av. Universidad 3002, Ciudad Universitaria, Deleg. Coyoacón, Mexico City ☎ A.P. 70-391, 04510 México, D.F. ☎ 55/5622-2470 ⊕ www.cepe.unam.mx. **SLI-Spanish Language Institute** ✉ Bajada de la Pradera 208, Col. Pradera 62170 Cuernavaca Morelos ☎ 777/311-0063 ⊕ www.sli-spanish.com.mx ✉ Language Link Inc., Box 3006, Peoria, IL 61612 ☎ 309/692-2961, 800/552-2051 in the U.S. ⊕ www.langlink.com.

## LODGING

The price and quality of accommodations in Mexico vary from superluxurious, international-class hotels, and all-inclusive resorts to modest budget properties, seedy places with shared bathrooms, *casas de huéspedes* (guest houses), youth hostels, and cabanas. You may find appealing bargains while you're on the road, but if your comfort threshold is low, look for an English-speaking staff, guaranteed dollar rates, and toll-free reservation numbers.

The lodgings we list are the cream of the crop in each price category. Properties are assigned price categories based on the range from their least-expensive standard double room at high season (excluding holidays) to the most expensive. We always list the facilities that are available—but we don't specify whether they cost extra; when pricing accommodations, **always ask what's included and what costs extra.** Lodgings are denoted in the text with a house icon, 🏠; establishments with restaurants that warrant a special trip have ✕🏠.

Assume that hotels operate on the European Plan (EP, with no meals) unless we specify that they use the Breakfast Plan (BP, with a full breakfast), the Continental Plan (CP, with a Continental breakfast), the Full American Plan (FAP, all meals), or the Modified American Plan (MAP, with breakfast and dinner) or are all-inclusive (including all meals and most drinks and/or activities).

## APARTMENT & VILLA RENTALS

If you want a home base that's roomy enough for a family and comes with cooking facilities, consider a furnished rental. These can save you money, especially if you're traveling with a group. Home-exchange directories sometimes list rentals as well as exchanges.

🔢 **International Agents At Home Abroad** ☎ 163 Third Ave., No. 319, New York, NY 10003 ☎ 212/421-9165 📠 212/533-0095 ⊕ www.athomeabroadinc.com. **Hideaways International** ✉ 767 Islington St., Portsmouth, NH 03801 ☎ 603/430-4433 or 800/843-4433 📠 603/430-4444 ⊕ www.hideaways.com, annual membership $145. **Vacation Home Rentals Worldwide** ✉ 235 Kensington Ave., Norwood, NJ 07648 ☎ 201/767-9393 or 800/633-3284 📠 201/767-5510 ⊕ www.vhrww.com. **Villanet** ✉ 1251 N.W. 116th St., Seattle, WA 98177 ☎ 206/417-3444 or 800/964-1891 📠 206/417-1832 ⊕ www.rentavilla.com. **Villas and Apartments Abroad** ✉ 183 Madison Ave., Suite 201, New York, NY 10016 ☎ 212/213-6435 or 800/433-3020 📠 212/213-8252 ⊕ www.vaanyc.com. **Villas International** ✉ 4340 Redwood Hwy., Suite D309, San Rafael, CA 94903 ☎ 415/499-9490 or 800/221-2260 📠 415/499-9491 ⊕ www.villasintl.com.

## BOUTIQUE HOTELS & B&BS

Mexico has many intimate and unique properties that put you in close touch with the country's essence *and* cater to your need for pampering. Hoteles Boutique de México (Mexico Boutique Hotels) is a private company that represents 26 such properties. None has more than 80 rooms, and most have fewer than 50. Each place is selected not only for its small size but also for its setting, cuisine, service, and overall allure. Each is also inspected annually to be sure that it continues to meet the high standards set by Hoteles Boutique for inclusion on the roster. You can contact the company to book into one hotel or to help you create a Mexican itinerary—themed or otherwise—with stays in several such properties.

The bed-and-breakfast craze hasn't missed Mexico, and the same delights that you find elsewhere in the world apply here, too—personable service, interesting local furnishings and decorative talent, and tasty morning meals. San Miguel de Allende and other Heartland cities have their share of charming places, as do Mexico City and parts of the Yucatán. If you arrive in Mexico City without a reservation, the Mexico City Hotel and Motel Association operates a booth at the airport that will assist you.

**⏹ Reservation Services** **Hoteles Boutique de México** ☎ 01800/508-7923 toll-free in Mexico, 877/278-8018 in the U.S., 866/818-8342 in Canada ⊕ www.mexicoboutiquehotels.com or www.hotelesboutique.com. **Mexico City Hotel and Motel Association** ☎ 55/5571-3268 or 55/5571-3262

## CAMPING

A host of camping opportunities exist in Mexico, but don't expect the typical U.S.-style campground. Mexico's campgrounds are usually trailer parks with running water, cooking areas, and room to pitch tents; sites can cost $2–$12 (more if you're arriving with a camper or trailer). Usually, you can camp at an *ejido* (farming community) or on someone's land for free or for a modest fee as long as you ask permission first; **ask locals or nearby tourist offices about the safest and best spots.** The beaches at night aren't as safe as they once were; **be alert and don't camp alone.** And don't camp at archaeological sites.

Outside of towns near resort areas or communities with a strong outdoors focus (e.g., Jalapa and Orizaba because of the mountaineering at Pico de Orizaba), camping supplies can be scarce in Mexico. Before you begin packing loads of gear, however, consider how much camping you'll actually do versus how much trouble it will be to haul around your tent, sleeping bag, stove, and accoutrements. Finding a place to store your gear can be difficult—lockers tend to be small.

In many towns along the Pacific and Caribbean coasts, beachside cabanas are an excellent alternative to tent camping. All you'll need for a night in a cabana is a hammock (they don't cost much in Mex-

ico), some mosquito netting, and a padlock for stashing your belongings in a locker. For overall information on camping in Mexico, try Mike and Terri Church's *Traveler's Guide to Mexican Camping* (Rolling Homes Press, 2001).

## HOME EXCHANGES

If you would like to exchange your home for someone else's, join a home-exchange organization, which will send you its updated listings of available exchanges for a year and will include your own listing in at least one of them. It's up to you to make specific arrangements.

**⏹ Exchange Clubs** **HomeLink International** 🏠 Box 47747, Tampa, FL 33647 ☎ 813/975-9825 or 800/638-3841 🖷 813/910-8144 ⊕ www.homelink.org; $110 yearly for a listing, online access, and catalog; $70 without catalog. **Intervac U.S.** ✉ 30 Corte San Fernando, Tiburon, CA 94920 ☎ 800/756-4663 🖷 415/435-7440 ⊕ www.intervacus.com; $125 yearly for a listing, online access, and a catalog; $65 without catalog.

## HOSTELS

No matter what your age, you can save on lodging costs by staying at hostels. In Mexico, however, high-school and college students are more often the norm at hostels than older travelers. In some 4,500 locations in more than 70 countries around the world, Hostelling International (HI), the umbrella group for a number of national youth-hostel associations, offers single-sex, dorm-style beds and, at many hostels, rooms for couples and family accommodations. Membership in any HI national hostel association, open to travelers of all ages, allows you to stay in HI-affiliated hostels at member rates; one-year membership is about $28 for adults (C$35 for a two-year minimum membership in Canada, £14 in the U.K., A$52 in Australia, and NZ$40 in New Zealand); hostels charge about $10–$30 per night. Members have priority if the hostel is full; they're also eligible for discounts around the world, even on rail and bus travel in some countries.

**⏹ Organizations** **Hostelling International–USA** ✉ 8401 Colesville Rd., Suite 600, Silver Spring, MD 20910 ☎ 301/495-1240 🖷 301/495-6697 ⊕ www.hiusa.org. **Hostelling International–Canada**

✉ 205 Catherine St., Suite 400, Ottawa, Ontario K2P 1C3 ☎ 613/237-7884 or 800/663-5777 📠 613/237-7868 ⊕ www.hihostels.ca. **YHA England and Wales** ✉ Trevelyan House, Dimple Rd., Matlock, Derbyshire DE4 3YH, U.K. ☎ 0870/870-8808, 0870/770-8868, 0162/959-2600 📠 0870/770-6127 ⊕ www.yha.org.uk. **YHA Australia** ✉ 422 Kent St., Sydney, NSW 2001 ☎ 02/9261-1111 📠 02/9261-1969 ⊕ www.yha.com.au. **YHA New Zealand** ✉ Level 1, Moorhouse City, 166 Moorhouse Ave., Box 436, Christchurch ☎ 03/379-9970 or 0800/278-299 📠 03/365-4476 ⊕ www.yha.org.nz.

## HOTELS

It's essential to **reserve in advance** if you're traveling during high season or holiday periods. Overbooking is a common practice in some parts of Mexico, such as Cancún and Acapulco. To protect yourself, get a confirmation in writing, via fax or e-mail. Travelers to remote areas will encounter little difficulty in obtaining rooms on a walk-in basis unless it's during a holiday.

Hotel rates are subject to the 15% value-added tax (it's 10% in the states of Quintana Roo, Baja California, and Baja California Sur, and anywhere within 20 km [12⁷⁄₁₀ mi] of the border). In addition, many states charge a 2% hotel tax. Service charges and meals generally aren't included in the hotel rates.

The Mexican government categorizes hotels, based on qualitative evaluations, into *gran turismo* (superdeluxe, or five-star-plus, properties, of which there are only about 30 nationwide); five-star down to one-star; and economy class. Keep in mind that many hotels that might otherwise be rated higher have opted for a lower category to avoid higher interest rates on loans and financing.

High- versus low-season rates can vary significantly. Hotels in this guide have private bathrooms with showers, unless stated otherwise; bathtubs aren't common in inexpensive hotels and properties in smaller towns. Hotels have private baths, phones, TVs, and air-conditioning unless otherwise noted.

### RESERVING A ROOM

If you're particularly sensitive to noise, you should call ahead to learn if your hotel of choice is on a busy street. Many of the most engaging accommodations in Mexico are on downtown intersections that experience heavy automobile and pedestrian traffic. And large hotels are known to have lobby bars with live music in the middle of an open-air atrium leading directly to rooms. When you book, request a room far from the bar.

🎱 **Toll-Free Numbers Best Western** ☎ 800/528-1234 ⊕ www.bestwestern.com. **Choice** ☎ 800/424-6423 ⊕ www.choicehotels.com. **Days Inn** ☎ 800/325-2525 ⊕ www.daysinn.com. **Doubletree Hotels** ☎ 800/222-8733 ⊕ www.doubletree.com. **Four Seasons** ☎ 800/332-3442 ⊕ www.fourseasons.com. **Hilton** ☎ 800/445-8667 ⊕ www.hilton.com. **Holiday Inn** ☎ 800/465-4329 ⊕ www.ichotelsgroup.com. **Howard Johnson** ☎ 800/446-4656 ⊕ www.hojo.com. **Hyatt Hotels & Resorts** ☎ 800/233-1234 ⊕ www.hyatt.com. **Inter-Continental** ☎ 800/327-0200 ⊕ www.ichotelsgroup.com. **Marriott** ☎ 800/228-9290 ⊕ www.marriott.com. **Le Meridien** ☎ 800/543-4300 ⊕ www.lemeridien.com. **Nikko Hotels International** ☎ 800/645-5687 ⊕ www.nikkohotels.com. **Omni** ☎ 800/843-6664 ⊕ www.omnihotels.com. **Radisson** ☎ 800/333-3333 ⊕ www.radisson.com. **Ritz-Carlton** ☎ 800/241-3333 ⊕ www.ritzcarlton.com. **Sheraton** ☎ 800/325-3535 ⊕ www.starwood.com/sheraton. **Westin Hotels & Resorts** ☎ 800/228-3000 ⊕ www.starwood.com/westin. **Wyndham Hotels & Resorts** ☎ 800/822-4200 ⊕ www.wyndham.com.

## MAIL & SHIPPING

The Mexican postal system is notoriously slow and unreliable; **never send packages through the postal service** or expect to receive them, as they may be stolen. (For emergencies, use a courier service). If you're an American Express cardholder, you may be able to receive packages at a branch office, but check beforehand with customer service to find out if this client mail service is available in your destination.

Post offices (*oficinas de correos*) are found in even the smallest villages. International postal service is all airmail, but even so your letter will take anywhere from 10 days to six weeks to arrive. Service within Mexico can be equally slow.

## POSTAL RATES

It costs 8.50 pesos (about 75¢) to send a postcard or letter weighing under 20 grams to the United States or Canada; it's 10.50 (90¢) to Europe and 11.50 ($1) to Australia and New Zealand.

## RECEIVING MAIL

To receive mail in Mexico, you can have it sent to your hotel or use *poste restante* at the post office. In the latter case, the address must include the words "a/c Lista de Correos" (general delivery), followed by the city, state, postal code, and country. To use this service, you must first register with the post office at which you wish to receive your mail. The post office posts and updates daily a list of names for whom mail has been received. Holders of American Express cards or traveler's checks may be able to receive mail in care of the local American Express office; check with customer service beforehand to see whether the office at your destination will do so.

🇫 **American Express** ⊕ www.americanexpress. com/travel.

## SHIPPING PARCELS

Federal Express, DHL, and United Parcel Service are available in major cities and many resort areas. These companies offer office or hotel pickup with 24-hour advance notice (sometimes less, depending on when you call) and are very reliable. From Mexico City to anywhere in the United States, the minimum charge is around $30 for a package weighing about one pound. Starting prices are higher for Australia, Canada, New Zealand, and the United Kingdom, and deliveries take longer. It's best to send all packages using one of these services.

🇫 **Major Services DHL** ⊕ www.dhl.com. **Federal Express** ⊕ www.fedex.com. **United Parcel Service** ⊕ www.ups.com.

## MONEY MATTERS

Prices in this book are quoted most often in U.S. dollars. We would prefer to list costs in pesos, but because the value of the currency fluctuates considerably, what costs 90 pesos today might cost 120 pesos in six months.

If you travel only by air or package tour, stay at international hotel-chain properties, and eat at tourist restaurants, you might not find Mexico such a bargain. If you want a closer look at the country and aren't wedded to standard creature comforts, you can spend as little as $25 a day on room, board, and local transportation. Speaking Spanish is also helpful in bargaining situations and when asking for dining recommendations.

Cancún, Puerto Vallarta, Mexico City, Monterrey, Acapulco, Ixtapa, Los Cabos, Manzanillo, and, to a lesser extent, Mazatlán and Huatulco are the most expensive places to visit. All the beach towns, however, offer budget accommodations; lodgings are even less expensive in less accessible areas such as the Gulf coast and northern Yucatán parts of Quintana Roo some of the less-developed spots north and south of Puerto Vallarta in the states of Jalisco and Nayarit Puerto Escondido and the smaller Oaxacan coastal towns as well as those of Chiapas and Tabasco.

Average costs in major cities vary, although less than in the past because of an increase in business travelers. A stay in one of Mexico City's top hotels can cost more than $200 (as much or more than at the coastal resorts), but you can get away with a tab of $45 for two at what was once an expensive restaurant.

Probably the best value for your travel dollar is in smaller, inland towns, such as Mérida, Morelia, Guanajuato, and Oaxaca. Although Oaxaca lodging can run more than $150 a night, simple colonial-style hotels with adequate accommodations for under $40 can be found, and tasty, filling meals are rarely more than $15.

Prices throughout this guide are given for adults. Substantially reduced fees are almost always available for children, students, and senior citizens. For information on taxes, *see* Taxes.

## ATMS

ATMs (*cajeros automáticos*) are widely available, with Cirrus and Plus the most frequently found networks. Before you leave home, **ask what the transaction fee**

**will be** for withdrawing money in Mexico. (It's usually $3 a pop.)

Many Mexican ATMs cannot accept PINs (personal identification numbers, *número de identificación personal* or NIP in Spanish) with more than four digits. If yours is longer, **ask your bank about changing your PIN before you leave home,** and keep in mind that processing such a change often takes a few weeks. If your PIN is fine yet your transaction still can't be completed—a regular occurrence—chances are that the computer lines are busy or that the machine has run out of money or is being serviced.

For cash advances, plan to use Visa or MasterCard, as many Mexican ATMs don't accept American Express. Large banks with reliable ATMs include Banamex, Bital, BBVA Bancomer, Santander Serfín, and Scotiabank Inverlat. ( ⇨ Safety, on avoiding ATM robberies.)

## CREDIT CARDS

Credit cards are accepted in most tourist areas. Smaller, less expensive restaurants and shops, however, tend to take only cash. In general, credit cards aren't accepted in small towns and villages, except in hotels. The most widely accepted cards are MasterCard and Visa. When shopping, you can usually get better prices if you **pay with cash.**

At the same time, when traveling internationally you'll **receive wholesale exchange rates** when you make purchases with credit cards. These exchange rates are usually better than those that banks give you for changing money. (Before you go, it doesn't hurt to ask your credit card company how it handles purchases in foreign currency.) In Mexico the decision to pay cash or use a credit card might depend on whether the establishment in which you are making a purchase finds bargaining for prices acceptable, as well as whether you want the safety net of your card's purchase protection ( ⇨ Consumer Protection). To avoid fraud, it's wise to **make sure that "pesos" is clearly marked on all credit-card receipts.**

Before you leave for Mexico, be sure to **find out your credit-card companies' toll-free and/or collect-call card-replacement**

**numbers** that work at home as well as in Mexico; they could be impossible to find once you get to Mexico, and the calls you place to cancel your cards can be long ones. **Carry these numbers separately from your wallet** so you'll have them if you need to call to report lost or stolen cards. American Express, MasterCard, and Visa note the international number for card-replacement calls on the back of their cards.

Throughout this guide, the following abbreviations are used: **AE,** American Express; **D,** Discover; **DC,** Diners Club; **MC,** MasterCard; and **V,** Visa.

🔢 Reporting Lost Cards **American Express** ☎ 800/528-2122 in the U.S., 866/549-6426 in Canada ⊕ www.americanexpress.com. **Diners Club** ☎ 800/234-6377 in the U.S., 800/363-3333 in Canada, 303/799-1504 collect for U.S. cardholders abroad, 416/369-6313 collect for Canadian cardholders abroad ⊕ www.dinersclub.com. **MasterCard** ☎ 800/307-7309 in the U.S. ⊕ www.mastercard.com. **Visa** ☎ 800/847-2911 in the U.S. ⊕ www.visa.com.

## CURRENCY

Mexican currency comes in denominations of 20-, 50-, 100-, 200-, and 500-peso bills. Coins come in denominations of 1, 2, 5, 10, and 20 pesos, and 10, 20, and 50 centavos. Many of the coins and bills are very similar, so check carefully.

U.S. dollar bills (but not coins) are widely accepted in border towns and in many parts of the Yucatán, particularly in Cancún and Cozumel, where you'll often find prices in shops quoted in dollars. However, you'll get your change in pesos. Many tourist shops and market vendors as well as virtually all hotel service personnel also accept dollars.

## CURRENCY EXCHANGE

At this writing, the peso was still "floating" after the devaluation enacted by the Zedillo administration in late 1994. Although exchange rates have been as favorable as 11.4 pesos to US$1, 8.7 pesos to C$1, 19.6 pesos to £1, 8.3 pesos to A$1, and 7.3 pesos to NZ$1, the market and prices continue to adjust. Check with your bank or the financial pages of your local newspaper for current exchange rates. For quick estimates of how much something costs in U.S. dollar terms, divide prices given in pesos by 10. For example, 50 pesos would be about $5.

ATM transaction fees may be higher abroad than at home, but ATM currency-exchange rates are the best of all because they're based on wholesale rates offered only by major banks. And if you take out a fair amount of cash per withdrawal, the transaction fee becomes less of a strike against the exchange rate (in percentage terms). However, most ATMs allow only up to $300 a transaction. Banks and *casas de cambio* (money-exchange bureaus) have the second-best exchange rates. The difference from one place to another is usually only a few centavos.

Most banks change money on weekdays only until 1 (though they stay open until 3 or later). Casas de cambio generally stay open until 6 and often operate on weekends also, they usually have better rates and shorter lines. Some hotels exchange money, but for providing you with this convenience they help themselves to a bigger commission than banks.

You can do well at most airport exchange booths (except in Cancún). To avoid lines at airport exchange booths, **get a bit of local currency before you leave home.** You won't necessarily do as well at rail and bus stations, in hotels, in restaurants, or in stores.

When changing money, count your bills before leaving the bank or casa de cambio, and don't accept any partially torn or taped-together notes; they won't be accepted anywhere. Also, many shop and restaurant owners are unable to make change for large bills. Enough of these encounters may compel you to request *billetes chicos* (small bills) when you exchange money.

⁊ **Exchange Services International Currency Express** ⊠ 427 N. Camden Dr., Suite F, Beverly Hills, CA 90210 ☎ 888/278-6628 orders ⎙ 310/278-6410 ⊕ www.foreignmoney.com. **Travel Ex Currency Services** ☎ 800/287-7362 orders and retail locations ⊕ www.travelex.com.

## TRAVELER'S CHECKS

Do you need traveler's checks? It depends on where you're headed. If you're going to rural areas and small towns, go with cash; traveler's checks are best used in cities. Lost or stolen checks can usually be replaced within 24 hours. To ensure a speedy refund, buy your own traveler's checks—don't let someone else pay for them: irregularities like this can cause delays. The person who bought the checks should make the call to request a refund. Traveler's checks aren't available in Mexican pesos; U.S. dollar–denominated checks are your best option.

## PACKING

When traveling internationally, it's good to pack a change of clothes in your carry-on bag in case your other luggage is lost. Take at least a change of underwear, essential toiletries, and a shirt—add to that a bathing suit if you're heading to a beach resort. In your carry-on luggage, pack an extra pair of eyeglasses or contact lenses and enough of any medication you take to last a few days longer than the entire trip. You may also ask your doctor to write a spare prescription using the drug's generic name, as brand names may vary from country to country. In luggage to be checked, **never pack prescription drugs, valuables, or undeveloped film.** And don't forget to carry with you the addresses of offices that handle refunds of lost traveler's checks. Check *Fodor's How to Pack* (available at online retailers and bookstores everywhere) for more tips.

To avoid customs and security delays, carry medications in their original packaging. Don't pack any sharp objects in your carry-on luggage, including knives of any size or material, scissors, nail clippers, and corkscrews, or anything else that might arouse suspicion.

To avoid having your checked luggage chosen for hand inspection, don't cram bags full. The U.S. Transportation Security Administration suggests packing shoes on top and placing personal items you don't want touched in clear plastic bags.

For resorts, bring lightweight sportswear, bathing suits, and cover-ups for the beach. Bathing suits and immodest clothing are inappropriate for shopping and sightseeing, both in cities and beach resorts. Mexico

City is a bit more formal than the resorts and, because of its high elevation, cooler. Men will want to bring lightweight suits or slacks and blazers for fancier restaurants; women should pack tailored dresses or pants suits. Many high-end Mexico City restaurants require jacket and tie; jeans are acceptable for shopping and sightseeing, but shorts are frowned upon for men and women. You'll need a lightweight topcoat for winter and an all-weather coat and umbrella in case of sudden summer rainstorms. Lately the rains have been appearing at other times of the year, so always **pack a small umbrella.**

Cancún and Acapulco are both casual and elegant; you'll see high-style sportswear, cotton slacks and walking shorts, and plenty of colorful sundresses. The sun can be fierce; **bring a sun hat and sunscreen** for the beach and for sightseeing. You'll need a sweater or jacket to cope with hotel and restaurant air-conditioning, which can be glacial, and for occasional cool spells. Few restaurants require a jacket and tie.

Luggage carts are free at the Mexico City airport, practically the only airport where you'll find them; bus and train stations don't have carts. It's a good idea to bring along tissue packs in case you hit a place where the toilet paper has run out. You'll find familiar toiletries and hygiene products, as well as condoms, in shops in cities, resort areas, and most rural areas.

### CHECKING LUGGAGE

You're allowed to carry aboard one bag and one personal article, such as a purse or a laptop computer. Make sure what you carry on fits under your seat or in the overhead bin. Get to the gate early, so you can board as soon as possible, before the overhead bins fill up.

Baggage allowances vary by carrier, destination, and ticket class. On international flights, you're usually allowed to check two bags weighing up to 70 pounds (32 kilograms) each, although a few airlines allow checked bags of up to 88 pounds (40 kilograms) in first class. Some international carriers don't allow more than 66 pounds (30 kilograms) per bag in business class and 44 pounds (20 kilograms) in economy.

On domestic flights, the limit is usually 50 to 70 pounds (23 to 32 kilograms) per bag. In general, carry-on bags shouldn't exceed 40 pounds (18 kilograms). Most airlines won't accept bags that weigh more than 100 pounds (45 kilograms) on domestic or international flights. Expect to pay a fee for baggage that exceeds weight limits. Check baggage restrictions with your carrier before you pack.

Airline liability for baggage is limited to $2,500 per person on flights within the United States. On international flights it amounts to $9.07 per pound or $20 per kilogram for checked baggage (roughly $640 per 70-pound bag), with a maximum of $634.90 per piece, and $400 per passenger for unchecked baggage. You can buy additional coverage at check-in for about $10 per $1,000 of coverage, but it often excludes a rather extensive list of items, shown on your airline ticket.

Before departure, itemize your bags' contents and their worth, and label the bags with your name, address, and phone number. (If you use your home address, cover it so potential thieves can't see it readily.) Include a label inside each bag and **pack a copy of your itinerary.** At check-in, make sure each bag is correctly tagged with the destination airport's three-letter code. Because some checked bags will be opened for hand inspection, the U.S. Transportation Security Administration recommends that you leave luggage unlocked or use the plastic locks offered at check-in. TSA screeners place an inspection notice inside searched bags, which are re-sealed with a special lock.

If your bag has been searched and contents are missing or damaged, file a claim with the TSA Consumer Response Center as soon as possible. If your bags arrive damaged or fail to arrive at all, file a written report with the airline before leaving the airport.

📂 Complaints **U.S. Transportation Security Administration Contact Center** ☎ 866/289-9673 ⊕ www.tsa.gov.

### PASSPORTS & VISAS

When traveling internationally, carry your passport even if you don't need one (it's always the best form of ID) and **make two photocopies of the data page** (one for someone at home and another for you, carried separately from your passport). If you lose your passport, promptly call the nearest embassy or consulate and the local police.

U.S. passport applications for children under age 14 require consent from both parents or legal guardians; both parents must appear together to sign the application. If only one parent appears, he or she must submit a written statement from the other parent authorizing passport issuance for the child. A parent with sole authority must present evidence of it when applying; acceptable documentation includes the child's certified birth certificate listing only the applying parent, a court order specifically permitting this parent's travel with the child, or a death certificate for the nonapplying parent. Application forms and instructions are available on the Web site of the U.S. State Department's Bureau of Consular Affairs (⊕ travel.state.gov).

## ENTERING MEXICO

A tourist visa is required for all visitors to Mexico. If you're arriving by plane, the standard tourist visa forms will be given to you on the plane without your asking for them. They're also available through travel agents and Mexican consulates, and at the border if you're entering by land. A tourist visa costs about $18. The fee is generally tacked onto the price of your airline ticket; if you enter by land or boat, you'll have to pay the fee separately. You're exempt from the fee if you enter by sea and stay less than 72 hours, or by land and do not stray past the 26–30-km (16–18-mi) checkpoint into the country's interior.

In addition to presenting the visa form, you must prove your citizenship. U.S. citizens must prove citizenship by presenting a valid passport, certified copy of a birth certificate, or voter-registration card (the last two must be accompanied by a government-issue photo ID). However, a passport is your best option, because that's what officials are used to dealing with. Minors traveling with one parent need notarized permission from the absent parent (*see* Children in Mexico). You're allowed

to stay 180 days as a tourist; frequently, though, immigration officials will give you less. Be sure to ask for as much time as you think you'll need up to 180 days; going to a Mexican immigration office to extend a visa can easily take a whole day, plus you'll have to pay an extension fee of approximately $18.

Canadians, New Zealanders, Australians, and citizens of the United Kingdom must have a valid passport. Canadians, New Zealanders, and the British may request up to 180 days; Australians are allowed up to 90 days.

## PASSPORT OFFICES

The best time to apply for a passport or to renew is in fall and winter. Before any trip, check your passport's expiration date, and, if necessary, renew it as soon as possible.

🛂 Australian Citizens **Passports Australia** Australian Department of Foreign Affairs and Trade ☎ 131-232 ⊕ www.passports.gov.au.

🛂 Canadian Citizens **Passport Office** ✉ To mail in applications: 200 Promenade du Portage, Hull, Québec J8X 4B7 ☎ 819/994-3500 or 800/567-6868 ⊕ www.ppt.gc.ca.

🛂 New Zealand Citizens **New Zealand Passports Office** ☎ 0800/22-5050 or 04/474-8100 ⊕ www. passports.govt.nz.

🛂 U.K. Citizens **U.K. Passport Service** ☎ 0870/521-0410 ⊕ www.passport.gov.uk.

🛂 U.S. Citizens **National Passport Information Center** ☎ 877/487-2778, 888/874-7793 TDD/TTY ⊕ travel.state.gov.

## REST ROOMS

Expect to find clean flushing toilets, toilet tissue, soap, and running water at public rest rooms in the major tourist destinations and at tourist attractions. Although many markets, bus and train stations, and the like have public facilities, you may have to pay a couple of pesos for the privilege of using a dirty toilet that lacks a seat, toilet paper (keep tissues with you at all times), and possibly even running water. Gas stations have public bathrooms— some tidy and others not so tidy. You're better off popping into a restaurant, buying a little something, and using its rest room, which will probably be simple but clean and adequately equipped. Remember that unless otherwise indicated, you should **put your used toilet paper in the wastebasket** next to the toilet; many plumbing systems in Mexico still can't handle accumulations of toilet paper.

## SAFETY

### CRIME

The U.S. State Department has warned of "high" levels of crime against tourists in Mexico, especially in large cities, noting an increase in the level of violence of the assaults and robberies committed. The largest increase in crime has taken place in Mexico City, where the age-old problem of pickpocketing has been overshadowed by robberies at gunpoint. Other developments have been abductions and robberies in taxicabs hailed from the street (as opposed to hired from a hotel or taxi stand), and even robberies on city buses.

Reports indicate that uniformed police officers have, on occasion, perpetrated nonviolent crimes. The patronage system is a well-entrenched part of Mexican politics and industry, and workers in the public sector—notably police and customs officials—are notoriously underpaid. Everyone has heard some horror story about highway assaults, pickpocketing, bribes, or foreigners languishing in Mexican jails. These reports apply in large part to Mexico City and more remote areas of Oaxaca and Chiapas. So far, crime isn't such a problem in the heartland (cities like San Miguel de Allende), Puerto Vallarta, Cancún, and much of the rest of the country.

Use common sense everywhere, but **exercise particular caution in Mexico City.** In addition, **avoid remote, less-traveled areas of Oaxaca, Chiapas, and Guerrero,** as crime in these areas can be more life-threatening. **Don't wear any jewelry, including watches you care about losing,** and try not to act too much like a tourist. Keep your passport and all valuables in hotel safes, and carry your own baggage whenever possible.

Avoid driving on desolate streets, and don't travel at night, pick up hitchhikers, or hitchhike yourself. Use luxury buses (rather than second- or third-class vehicles), which take the safer toll roads. It's best to take only registered hotel taxis or have a hotel concierge call a radio taxi or *sitio* (cab stand)—**avoid hailing taxis on the street. Avoid urges to get away from it all** on your own (even as a couple) to go hiking in remote national parks; women in particular shouldn't venture alone onto uncrowded beaches.

**Use ATMs during the day and in big, enclosed commercial areas.** Avoid the glass-enclosed street variety of banks where you may be more vulnerable to thieves who force you to withdraw money for them; abduction is also possible. This can't be stressed strongly enough.

Bear in mind that reporting a crime to the police is often a frustrating experience unless you speak excellent Spanish and have a great deal of patience. If you're victimized, contact your local consular agent or the consular section of your country's embassy in Mexico City.

### WOMEN IN MEXICO

If you're on your own, consider using only your first initial and last name when registering at your hotel. **Don't wear a money belt or a waist pack,** both of which peg you as a tourist. If you carry a purse, choose one with a zipper and a thick strap that you can drape across your body; adjust the length so that the purse sits in front of you at or above hip level. Store only enough money in the purse to cover casual spending. Distribute the rest of your cash and any valuables (including credit cards and your passport) between a deep front pocket, an inside jacket or vest pocket, and a hidden money pouch. Do not reach for the money pouch once in public. Better yet, leave your passport and other valuables you don't need immediately in your hotel's safe-deposit box.

Avoid eye contact or smiling at strangers unless you're planning to ask them for directions or something similar. If someone unsavory or otherwise unwanted approaches you, just say "*Con permiso*" ("Excuse me"), and walk away. Or just walk away.

If you're traveling alone or with other women rather than men, you may be subjected to *piropos* (flirtatious compliments).

To avoid this, don't wear provocative clothes or enter street bars or cantinas in some very conservative rural areas, even sleeveless shirts or Bermuda shorts may seem inappropriate to the locals. Your best strategy is to ignore the offender. Piropos are one thing, but more aggressive harassment is another. If the situation seems to be getting out of hand, don't hesitate to ask someone for help. If you express outrage, you should find no shortage of willing defenders.

## ZAPATISTA ACTIVITY
Anti-tourist sentiment continues to bubble in parts of Chiapas where there have traditionally been conflicts, such as the southeastern jungle areas and rural locales east of Ocosingo. It's best to avoid these areas.

## SENIOR-CITIZEN TRAVEL
To qualify for age-related discounts, mention your senior-citizen status up front when booking hotel reservations (not when checking out) and before you're seated in restaurants (not when paying the bill). Be sure to have identification on hand. When renting a car, ask about promotional car-rental discounts, which can be cheaper than senior-citizen rates.

Mexican senior citizens must present a special government-issued credential to obtain discounts at any facility. Some facilities may recognize foreign-issued credentials (such as those from AARP), so make a habit of asking. In any case, it's not enough to simply mention that you are a senior citizen.

**⑦ Educational Programs Elderhostel** ⊠ 11 Ave. de Lafayette, Boston, MA 02111-1746 ☎ 877/426–8056, 978/323–4141 international callers, 877/426–2167 TTY 🖶 877/426-2166 ⊕ www.elderhostel.org. **Interhostel** ⊠ University of New Hampshire, 6 Garrison Ave., Durham, NH 03824 ☎ 603/862-1147 or 800/733-9753 🖶 603/862-1113 ⊕ www.learn.unh.edu.

## SHOPPING
At least four kinds of outlets sell Mexican crafts: indoor and outdoor municipal markets; shops run by Fonart (a government agency to promote Mexican crafts); state-run arts and crafts institutes; and tourist boutiques in towns, malls, and hotels. Be sure to **take your time and inspect merchandise closely.** You'll find bargains, but quality can be inconsistent. Fonart shops and the state-run institutes are a good reference for quality and prices (the latter are fixed); Fonart accepts credit cards. Boutiques also accept credit cards if not dollars. (You may be asked to pay up to 10% more on credit-card purchases; savvy shoppers with cash have greater bargaining clout.) A 10%–15% value added tax, locally called the *impuesto al valor agregado* or IVA (Taxes), is charged on most purchases but is often included in the price; it may be disregarded entirely by eager or desperate market vendors.

Bargaining is widely accepted (even expected) in markets, but you should understand that not all vendors will start out with outrageous prices. If you feel the price quoted is too high, start off by offering half the asking price and then slowly go up, usually to about 70% of the original price. Always **shop around.** In major shopping areas such as San Miguel, shops will wrap and send purchases back to the United States via a package-delivery company.

## KEY DESTINATIONS
Mexico is an arts and crafts paradise, particularly if you're fond of textiles, ceramics, masks, hand-woven baskets, leather goods, wood and metalwork. For copperware, explore the village of Santa Clara del Cobre, south of Pátzcuaro in Michoacán; for silver, head to Taxco, south of Mexico City. Top ceramics towns include Tlaquepaque and Tonalá, outside Guadalajara, and Puebla, the home of brightly colored Talavera pottery. You'll find vivid hand-woven and embroidered textiles in Oaxaca and Chiapas; the latter state is also home to the lacquered and brightly painted gourds known as *jícaras*. The best hammocks are found in Yucatán, Oaxaca, and Chiapas.

## SMART SOUVENIRS
For less-than-obvious souvenirs, go traditional and consider a *molinillo,* a carved wooden beater for frothing hot chocolate; you can find these at street vendors or traditional markets for about $1.50. A set of 10 or so *tiras de papel* (string of colored

tissue-paper cuts) in a gift shop will only set you back about $2. Colorful hand-woven and embroidered napkins from Chiapas start around $3, as do hand-woven baskets.

## WATCH OUT

There are a couple of scams to be wary of if you're shopping with a credit card. Watch that your card goes through the machine only once, so that no duplicates of your slip are made. If there's an error and a new slip needs to be drawn up, make sure the original is destroyed before your eyes. Another favorite scam is to ask you to wait while the clerk runs next door ostensibly to use another business's phone or to verify your number—but really to make extra copies. Don't let your card leave a store without you.

Items made from tortoiseshell (or any sea turtle products) and black coral aren't allowed into the United States. Cowboy boots, hats, and sandals made from the leather of endangered species such as crocodiles will also be taken from you at customs, as will birds or wildlife curios such as stuffed iguanas or parrots. Both the U.S. and Mexican governments also have strict laws and guidelines about the import/export of antiquities. Your best bet? Check with customs beforehand if you plan to buy anything unusual or particularly valuable.

Although Cuban cigars are readily available, American visitors will have to enjoy them while in Mexico. However, Mexico has been producing some fine alternatives to Cuban cigars. If you're bringing any Mexican cigars back to the States, make sure they have the correct Mexican seals on both the individual cigars and on the box. Otherwise they may be confiscated. Finally, if you've bought ceramic plates, bowls, and cups, have them tested for lead if you're not sure about what's in the glaze.

## STUDENTS IN MEXICO

The ISIC student card or GO25 card can get you cut-rate plane tickets to Mexico at youth-oriented travel agencies. Within Mexico, many signs at tourist attractions will state that student discounts are only for Mexican students, but occasionally

you'll get a discount by showing one of these cards. The Mundo Joven travel agency in Mexico City and other areas throughout the country sells ISIC and GO25 cards and offers good deals on plane tickets.

🚪 **IDs & Services Mundo Joven** ✉ Insurgentes Sur 510-D, Col. Crédito Constructor, Mexico City, D.F. 03940 ☎ 55/5615-6300 ⊕ wwwmundojoven.com. **STA Travel** ✉ 10 Downing St., New York, NY 10014 ☎ 212/627-3111, 800/777-0112 24-hr service center 🖷 212/627-3387 ⊕ www.sta.com. **Travel Cuts** ✉ 187 College St., Toronto, Ontario M5T 1P7, Canada ☎ 800/592-2887 in the U.S., 416/979-2406 or 866/246-9762 in Canada 🖷 416/979-8167 ⊕ www. travelcuts.com.

## TAXES

Mexico charges an airport departure tax of US$18 or the peso equivalent for international and domestic flights. This tax is usually included in the price of your ticket, but check to be certain. Traveler's checks and credit cards are not accepted at the airport as payment for this. Many states are charging a 2% tax on accommodations, the funds from which are being used for tourism promotion.

## VALUE-ADDED TAX

Mexico has a value-added tax of 15% (10% in the states of Quintana Roo, Baja California, and Baja California Sur, as well as areas that are up to 20 km, or 12.5 mi, from the border), called IVA (*impuesto al valor agregado*). It's occasionally (and illegally) waived for cash purchases. Other taxes and charges apply for phone calls made from your hotel room.

## TAXIS

Government-certified taxis have a license with a photo of the driver and a taxi number prominently displayed, a meter, and either an orange or green stripe at the bottom of the license plate. Tipping isn't necessary unless the driver helps you with your bags, in which case a few pesos are appropriate.

## AT THE AIRPORT

From most airports you can **take the authorized taxi service.** Purchase the taxi vouchers sold at stands inside or just outside the terminal, which ensure that your fare is established beforehand. Before you purchase your ticket, check the taxi-zone map (it should be posted on or by the ticket stand) and make sure your ticket is properly zoned; if you need a ticket only to Zone 3, don't pay for a ticket to Zone 4 or 5. Don't leave your luggage unattended while making transportation arrangements.

### IN CITIES & BEACH RESORTS
In Mexican cities, **take a taxi rather than public transportation,** which, though inexpensive, is frequently slow and sometimes patrolled by pickpockets. (The exceptions are the air-conditioned buses in Acapulco, Cancún, and Mérida. Also, the Mexico City metro is usually safe and comfortable outside of rush hour, though you should still watch your bags and pockets.)

Always **establish the fare beforehand,** and count your change. In many cities, taxis charge by zones. In this case, be sure to agree on a fare before setting off. (Ask about the price range at your hotel.) In most of the beach resorts, there are inexpensive fixed-route fares, but if you don't ask, or your Spanish isn't great, you may get taken. In cities, especially the capital, be certain that the meter runs before getting in, and remember that there's usually an extra charge after 8 PM. For out-of-town and hourly services, negotiate a rate in advance; many drivers will start by asking how much you want to pay to get a sense of how street-smart you are. In all cases, if you are unsure of what a fare should be, ask your hotel's front-desk personnel or bell captain.

For reasons of security, especially in Mexico City, **hire taxis from hotels and taxi stands (sitios), or use those that you have summoned by phone.** Street taxis might be the cheapest, but an alarming increase in abductions and violent crime involves street cabs, so **do not flag a cab on the street.** And never leave luggage unattended in a taxi.

In addition to private taxis, many cities have bargain-price collective taxi services using minibuses and sedans. The service is called *colectivo* or *pesero.* Such vehicles run along fixed routes, and you hail them on the street and tell the driver where you are

going. The fare—which the driver will then tell you—is based on distance traveled.

## TELEPHONES
Most phones, especially in the better city hotels, have Touch-Tone (digital) circuitry. So do most pay phones. If you think you'll need to access an automated phone system or voice mail in the United States or elsewhere and you don't know what phone service will be available, it's a good idea to take along a Touch-Tone simulator (you can buy one for about $24 at most electronics stores).

### AREA & COUNTRY CODES
The country code for Mexico is 52. When calling a Mexico number from abroad, dial any necessary international access code, then the country code and then all of the numbers listed for the entry.

### DIRECTORY & OPERATOR ASSISTANCE
Directory assistance is 040 nationwide. For assistance in English, dial 090 first for an international operator tell the operator in what city, state, and country you require directory assistance, and he or she will connect you.

### INTERNATIONAL CALLS
To make an international call, dial 00 before the country code, area code, and number. The country code for the United States and Canada is 1, the United Kingdom 44, Australia 61, New Zealand 64, and South Africa 27.

### LOCAL & LONG-DISTANCE CALLS
For local or long-distance calls, you can use either a standard public pay phone or a *caseta de larga distancia,* a telephone service usually operated out of a small business (Public Phones, *below*). To make a direct long-distance or local call from a caseta, tell the person on duty the number you'd like to call, and she or he will give you a rate and dial for you. Rates seem to vary widely, so shop around, but overall they're higher than those of pay phones. If using a pay phone, you'll most often need a prepaid phone card (Phone Cards, *below*). If you're calling long distance within Mexico, dial 01 before the area

code and number. For local calls, just dial the number; no other prefix is necessary.

Sometimes you can make collect calls from casetas, and sometimes you cannot, depending on the individual operator and possibly your degree of visible desperation. Casetas will generally charge 50¢–$1.50 to place a collect call (some charge by the minute); it's usually better to call *por cobrar* (collect) from a pay phone.

### LONG-DISTANCE SERVICES

AT&T, MCI, and Sprint access codes make calling long-distance relatively convenient, but you may find the local access number blocked in many hotel rooms. First ask the hotel operator to connect you. If the hotel operator balks, ask for an international operator, or dial the international operator yourself. One way to improve your odds of getting connected to your long-distance carrier is to travel with more than one company's calling card (a hotel may block Sprint, for example, but not MCI). If all else fails, call from a pay phone.

🎞 **Access Codes AT&T Direct** ☎ 01800/288–2872 or 01800/112–2020 toll free in Mexico. **WorldPhone** ☎ 01800/021–8000 toll free in Mexico. **Sprint International Access** ☎ 01800/234–0000 toll free in Mexico.

### PHONE CARDS

In most parts of the country, pay phones only accept prepaid cards, called Ladatel cards, sold in 30-, 50- or 100-peso denominations at newsstands, pharmacies, or grocery stores. Coin-only pay phones are usually broken or have poor connections. Still other phones have two unmarked slots, one for a Ladatel (a Spanish acronym for "long-distance direct dialing") card and the other for a credit card. These are primarily for Mexican bank cards, but some accept Visa or Master-Card, though *not* U.S. phone credit cards.

To use a Ladatel card, simply insert it in the appropriate slot with the computer chip insignia forward and right-side up, and dial. Credit is deleted from the card as you use it, and your balance is displayed on a small screen on the phone. You'll be charged 1 peso per minute for local calls and more for long-distance and

international calls. Most pay phones display a price list and dialing instructions.

### PUBLIC PHONES

A *caseta de larga distancia* is a telephone service usually operated out of a store such as a *papelería* (stationery store), pharmacy, restaurant, or other small business; look for the phone symbol on the door. Casetas may cost more to use than pay phones, but you tend to be more shielded from street noise. Operators place the call for you (Local & Long-Distance Calls, *above*).

### TOLL-FREE NUMBERS

Toll-free numbers in Mexico start with an 800 prefix. These numbers, however, are billed as local calls if you call one from a private phone. To reach them, you need to dial 01 before the number. In this guide, Mexico-only toll-free numbers appear as follows: 01800/123–4567. The toll-free numbers listed simply 800/123–4567 work north of the border only. Numbers listed as 001800/123–4567 are toll-free numbers that connect you from Mexico to the United States.

### TIME

Mexico has three time zones; most of the country falls in Central Standard Time, which includes Mexico City and is in line with Chicago. Baja California is on Pacific Standard Time—the same as California. Baja California Sur and parts of the northwest coast, including Sonora, are on Mountain Standard Time. Mexico switches to and from Daylight Savings Time on the same schedule as the United States.

### TIPPING

When tipping in Mexico, remember that the minimum wage is the equivalent of $3.50 a day and that most workers in the tourism industry live barely above the poverty line. There are also Mexicans who think in dollars and know, for example, that in the United States porters are tipped about $2 a bag. Many of them expect the peso equivalent from foreigners and may complain if they feel they deserve more— you and your conscience must decide.

What follows are some guidelines. Naturally, larger tips are always welcome: porters and bellhops, 10 pesos per bag at airports and moderate and inexpensive hotels and 20 pesos per person at expensive hotels; maids, 10 pesos per night (all hotels); waiters, 10%–15% of the bill, depending on service (make sure a service charge hasn't already been added, a practice that's particularly common in resorts); bartenders, 10%–15% of the bill, depending on service (and, perhaps, on how many drinks you've had); taxi drivers, 5–10 pesos if the driver helps you with your bags, otherwise the small change from your fare; tour guides and drivers, at least 50 pesos per half day; gas-station attendants, 3–5 pesos unless they check the oil, tires, etc., in which case tip more; parking attendants, 5–10 pesos, even if it's for valet parking at a theater or restaurant that charges for the service.

## TOURS & PACKAGES

Because everything is prearranged on a prepackaged tour or independent vacation, you spend less time planning—and often get it all at a good price.

### BOOKING WITH AN AGENT

Travel agents are excellent resources. But it's a good idea to collect brochures from several agencies, as some agents' suggestions may be influenced by relationships with tour and package firms that reward them for volume sales. If you have a special interest, find an agent with expertise in that area; the American Society of Travel Agents (ASTA; ⇨ Travel Agencies) has a database of specialists worldwide. You can log on to the group's Web site to find an ASTA travel agent in your neighborhood.

Make sure your travel agent knows the accommodations and other services of the place being recommended. Ask about the hotel's location, room size, beds, and whether it has a pool, room service, or programs for children, if you care about these. Has your agent been there in person or sent others whom you can contact?

Do some homework on your own, too: local tourism boards can provide information about lesser-known and small-niche operators, some of which may sell only direct.

### BUYER BEWARE

Each year consumers are stranded or lose their money when tour operators—even large ones with excellent reputations—go out of business. So check out the operator. Ask several travel agents about its reputation, and try to **book with a company that has a consumer-protection program.** (Look for information in the company's brochure.) In the United States, members of the United States Tour Operators Association are required to set aside funds ($1 million) to help eligible customers cover payments and travel arrangements in the event that the company defaults. It's also a good idea to choose a company that participates in the American Society of Travel Agents' Tour Operator Program; ASTA will act as mediator in any disputes between you and your tour operator.

Remember that the more your package or tour includes, the better you can predict the ultimate cost of your vacation. Make sure you know exactly what is covered, and beware of hidden costs. Are taxes, tips, and transfers included? Entertainment and excursions? These can add up.

🛪 Tour-Operator Recommendations **American Society of Travel Agents** (⇨ Travel Agencies). **National Tour Association** (NTA) ✉ 546 E. Main St., Lexington, KY 40508 ☎ 859/226–4444 or 800/682–8886 🖷 859/226–4404 ⊕ www.ntaonline.com. **United States Tour Operators Association** (USTOA) ✉ 275 Madison Ave., Suite 2014, New York, NY 10016 ☎ 212/599–6599 🖷 212/599–6744 ⊕ www.ustoa.com.

### THEME TRIPS

🛪 Adventure Travel **Ceiba Adventures** 📫 Box 2274, Flagstaff, AZ 86003 ☎ 928/527–0171, 800/217–1060 in the U.S. and Canada ⊕ www.ceibaadventures.com.
🛪 Art & Archaeology **Archaeological Conservancy** ✉ 5301 Central Ave. NE, #1218, Albuquerque, NM 87108-9899 ☎ 505/266–1540 ⊕ www.americanarchaeology.com. **Crow Canyon Archaeological Center** ✉ 23390 Rd. K, Cortez, CO 81321 ☎ 970/565–8975, 800/422–8975 in the U.S. and Canada ⊕ www.crowcanyon.org. **Far Horizons Archaeological & Cultural Trips** 📫 Box 91900, Albuquerque, NM 87199-1900 ☎ 505/343–9400, 800/552–4575 in the U.S. and Canada ⊕ www.farhorizons.com.

**Bicycling Backroads** ✉ 801 Cedar St., Berkeley, CA 94710-1800 ☎ 510/527-1555, 800/462-2848 in the U.S. and Canada ⊕ www.backroads.com. **Imagine Tours** ⌂ Box 475, Davis, CA 95617 ☎ 530/758-8782, 800/924-2453 in the U.S. and Canada ⊕ www.imaginetours.com.

**Birding Field Guides** ✉ 9433 Bee Cave Rd., Bldg. 1, Suite 150, Austin, TX 78733 ☎ 512/263-7295, 800/728-4953 in the U.S. and Canada ⊕ www.fieldguides.com. **Victor Emanuel Nature Tours** ✉ 2525 Wallingford Dr., Suite 1003, Austin, TX 78746 ☎ 512/328-5221, 800/328-8368 in the U.S. and Canada ⊕ www.ventbird.com. **Wings** ✉ 1643 N. Alvernon Way, Suite 105, Tucson, AZ 85712 ☎ 520/320-9868, 888/293-6443 in the U.S. and Canada ⊕ www.wingsbirds.com.

**Butterfly Sanctuaries Natural Habitat Adventures** ✉ 2945 Center Green Ct., Boulder, CO 80301 ☎ 303/449-3711, 800/543-8917 in the U.S. and Canada ⊕ www.nathab.com. **Rocamar Tours** ⌂ Box 201, Greely, Ontario, Canada K4P 1N5 ☎ 613/821-2147, 866/762-2627 in the U.S. and Canada ⊕ www.rocamar.com.mx.

**Horseback Riding Equitour FITS Equestrian** ⌂ Box 807, Dubois, WY 82513 ☎ 307/455-3363, 800/545-0019 in the U.S. and Canada ⊕ www.equitours.com.

**Walking Backroads** (⇨ Bicycling). **Butterfield & Robinson** ✉ 70 Bond St., Toronto, Ontario, Canada M5B 1X3 ☎ 416/864-1354, 800/678-1147 in the U.S. and Canada ⊕ www.butterfield.com.

**Whale-Watching American Cetacean Society** ⌂ Box 1391, San Pedro, CA 90733 ☎ 310/548-6279 ⊕ www.acsonline.org. **Baja Discovery** ⌂ Box 152527, San Diego, CA 92195 ☎ 619/262-0700, 800/829-2252 in the U.S. ⊕ www.bajadiscovery.com.

## TRAVEL AGENCIES

A good travel agent puts your needs first. Look for an agency that has been in business at least five years, emphasizes customer service, and has someone on staff who specializes in your destination. In addition, **make sure the agency belongs to a professional trade organization.** The American Society of Travel Agents (ASTA)—the largest and most influential in the field with more than 20,000 members in some 140 countries—maintains and enforces a strict code of ethics and will step in to help mediate any agent-client disputes involving ASTA members if necessary. ASTA (whose motto is "Without a travel

agent, you're on your own") also maintains a Web site that includes a directory of agents. (If a travel agency is also acting as your tour operator, *see* Buyer Beware *in* Tours & Packages.)

**Local Agent Referrals American Society of Travel Agents (ASTA)** ✉ 1101 King St., Suite 200, Alexandria, VA 22314 ☎ 703/739-2782 or 800/965-2782 24-hr hotline 🖷 703/684-8319 ⊕ www.astanet.com. **Association of British Travel Agents** ✉ 68-71 Newman St., London W1T 3AH ☎ 020/7637-2444 🖷 020/7637-0713 ⊕ www.abta.com. **Association of Canadian Travel Agencies** ✉ 130 Albert St., Suite 1705, Ottawa, Ontario K1P 5G4 ☎ 613/237-3657 🖷 613/237-7052 ⊕ www.acta.ca. **Australian Federation of Travel Agents** ✉ Level 3, 309 Pitt St., Sydney, NSW 2000 ☎ 02/9264-3299 or 1300/363-416 🖷 02/9264-1085 ⊕ www.afta.com.au. **Travel Agents' Association of New Zealand** ✉ Level 5, Tourism and Travel House, 79 Boulcott St., Box 1888, Wellington 6001 ☎ 04/499-0104 🖷 04/499-0786 ⊕ www.taanz.org.nz.

## VISITOR INFORMATION

Learn more about foreign destinations by checking government-issued travel advisories and country information. For a broader picture, consider information from more than one country.

**Mexico Tourism Board United States** ☎ 800/446-3942 ⊕ www.visitmexico.com ✉ 375 Park Ave., Suite 1905, New York, NY 10152 ☎ 212/308-2110 ✉ 300 N. Michigan Ave., 4th fl., Chicago, IL 60601 ☎ 312/606-9252 ✉ 2401 W. 6th St., 5th fl., Los Angeles, CA 90057 ☎ 213/351-2075 ✉ 4507 San Jacinto, Suite 308, Houston, TX 77004 ☎ 713/772-2581 ✉ 5975 Sunset Dr., Suite 305, South Miami, FL 33143 ☎ 786/621-2909.

**Canada** ☎ 800/446-3942 ⊕ www.visitmexico.com ✉ 1 Pl. Ville Marie, Suite 1931, Montréal, Québec H3B 2C3 ☎ 514/871-1103 ✉ 2 Bloor St. W, Suite 1502, Toronto, Ontario M4W 3E2 ☎ 416/925-0704 ✉ 999 W. Hastings St., Suite 1110, Vancouver, British Columbia V6C 2W2 ☎ 604/669-2845.

**United Kingdom** ⊕ www.visitmexico.com ✉ Wakefield House, 41 Trinity Sq., London EC3N 4DJ ☎ 207/488-9392.

**Government Advisories U.S. Department of State** ✉ Overseas Citizens Services Office, 2100 Pennsylvania Ave. NW, 4th floor, Washington, DC 20520 ☎ 202/647-5225 interactive hot line or 888/407-4747 ⊕ www.travel.state.gov. **Consular Affairs**

# CONVERSIONS

## DISTANCE

### KILOMETERS/MILES

To change kilometers (km) to miles (mi), multiply km by .621. To change mi to km, multiply mi by 1.61.

| km to mi | mi to km |
|---|---|
| 1 = .62 | 1 = 1.6 |
| 2 = 1.2 | 2 = 3.2 |
| 3 = 1.9 | 3 = 4.8 |
| 4 = 2.5 | 4 = 6.4 |
| 5 = 3.1 | 5 = 8.1 |
| 6 = 3.7 | 6 = 9.7 |
| 7 = 4.3 | 7 = 11.3 |
| 8 = 5.0 | 8 = 12.9 |

### METERS/FEET

To change meters (m) to feet (ft), multiply m by 3.28. To change ft to m, multiply ft by .305.

| m to ft | ft to m |
|---|---|
| 1 = 3.3 | 1 = .30 |
| 2 = 6.6 | 2 = .61 |
| 3 = 9.8 | 3 = .92 |
| 4 = 13.1 | 4 = 1.2 |
| 5 = 16.4 | 5 = 1.5 |
| 6 = 19.7 | 6 = 1.8 |
| 7 = 23.0 | 7 = 2.1 |
| 8 = 26.2 | 8 = 2.4 |

## TEMPERATURE

### METRIC CONVERSIONS

To change centigrade or Celsius (C) to Fahrenheit (F), multiply C by 1.8 and add 32. To change F to C, subtract 32 from F and multiply by .555.

| °F | °C |
|---|---|
| 0 | -17.8 |
| 10 | -12.2 |
| 20 | -6.7 |
| 30 | -1.1 |
| 32 | 0 |
| 40 | +4.4 |
| 50 | 10.0 |
| 60 | 15.5 |
| 70 | 21.1 |
| 80 | 26.6 |
| 90 | 32.2 |
| 98.6 | 37.0 |
| 100 | 37.7 |

## WEIGHT

### KILOGRAMS/POUNDS

To change kilograms (kg) to pounds (lb), multiply kg by 2.20. To change lb to kg, multiply lb by .455.

| kg to lb | lb to kg |
|---|---|
| 1 = 2.2 | 1 = .45 |
| 2 = 4.4 | 2 = .91 |
| 3 = 6.6 | 3 = 1.4 |
| 4 = 8.8 | 4 = 1.8 |
| 5 = 11.0 | 5 = 2.3 |
| 6 = 13.2 | 6 = 2.7 |
| 7 = 15.4 | 7 = 3.2 |
| 8 = 17.6 | 8 = 3.6 |

### GRAMS/OUNCES

To change grams (g) to ounces (oz), multiply g by .035. To change oz to g, multiply oz by 28.4.

| g to oz | oz to g |
|---|---|
| 1 = .04 | 1 = 28 |
| 2 = .07 | 2 = 57 |
| 3 = .11 | 3 = 85 |
| 4 = .14 | 4 = 114 |
| 5 = .18 | 5 = 142 |
| 6 = .21 | 6 = 170 |
| 7 = .25 | 7 = 199 |
| 8 = .28 | 8 = 227 |

## LIQUID VOLUME

### LITERS/U.S. GALLONS

To change liters (L) to U.S. gallons (gal), multiply L by .264. To change U.S. gal to L, multiply gal by 3.79.

| L to gal | gal to L |
|---|---|
| 1 = .26 | 1 = 3.8 |
| 2 = .53 | 2 = 7.6 |
| 3 = .79 | 3 = 11.4 |
| 4 = 1.1 | 4 = 15.2 |
| 5 = 1.3 | 5 = 19.0 |
| 6 = 1.6 | 6 = 22.7 |
| 7 = 1.8 | 7 = 26.5 |
| 8 = 2.1 | 8 = 30.3 |

## CLOTHING SIZE

### WOMEN'S CLOTHING

| US | UK | EUR |
|---|---|---|
| 4 | 6 | 34 |
| 6 | 8 | 36 |
| 8 | 10 | 38 |
| 10 | 12 | 40 |
| 12 | 14 | 42 |

### WOMEN'S SHOES

| US | UK | EUR |
|---|---|---|
| 5 | 3 | 36 |
| 6 | 4 | 37 |
| 7 | 5 | 38 |
| 8 | 6 | 39 |
| 9 | 7 | 40 |

### MEN'S SUITS

| US | UK | EUR |
|---|---|---|
| 34 | 34 | 44 |
| 36 | 36 | 46 |
| 38 | 38 | 48 |
| 40 | 40 | 50 |
| 42 | 42 | 52 |
| 44 | 44 | 54 |
| 46 | 46 | 56 |

### MEN'S SHIRTS

| US | UK | EUR |
|---|---|---|
| 14½ | 14½ | 37 |
| 15 | 15 | 38 |
| 15½ | 15½ | 39 |
| 16 | 16 | 41 |
| 16½ | 16½ | 42 |
| 17 | 17 | 43 |
| 17½ | 17½ | 44 |

### MEN'S SHOES

| US | UK | EUR |
|---|---|---|
| 7 | 6 | 39½ |
| 8 | 7 | 41 |
| 9 | 8 | 42 |
| 10 | 9 | 43 |
| 11 | 10 | 44½ |
| 12 | 11 | 46 |

Bureau of Canada ☎ 800/267-6788 or 613/944-6788 ⊕ www.voyage.gc.ca. **U.K. Foreign and Commonwealth Office** ⊠ Travel Advice Unit, Consular Division, Old Admiralty Building, London SW1A 2PA ☎ 0870/606-0290 or 020/7008-1500 ⊕ www.fco.gov.uk/travel. **Australian Department of Foreign Affairs and Trade** ☎ 300/139-281 travel advice, 02/6261-1299 Consular Travel Advice Faxback Service ⊕ www.dfat.gov.au. **New Zealand Ministry of Foreign Affairs and Trade** ☎ 04/439-8000 ⊕ www.mft.govt.nz.

## WEB SITES

Do check out the World Wide Web when planning your trip. You'll find everything from weather forecasts to virtual tours of famous cities. Be sure to **visit Fodors.com** (⊕ www.fodors.com), a complete travel-planning site. You can research prices and book plane tickets, hotel rooms, rental cars, vacation packages, and more. In addition, you can post your pressing questions in the Travel Talk section. Other planning tools include a currency converter and weather reports, and there are loads of links to travel resources.

Mexico's 31 states and the Federal District (Mexico City) are steadily posting tourism Web sites, though few are in English. Three notable exceptions are: the Mexican Tourism Board's official page (⊕ www.visitmexico.com), with information about popular destinations, activities, and festivals; the Mexico City Tourism Ministry's site (⊕ www.mexicocity.gob.mx/index_EN.html), which lists some of the capital's entertainment and tourist attractions; and the federal Tourism Ministry's Web page (⊕ www.sectorturismo.gob.mx).

The site of the Latin American Network Information Center at the University of Texas at Austin (⊕ http://lanic.utexas.edu/la/mexico) has one of the most complete sets of links to all things Mexican, from archaeology to Zapatista information. Other excellent English-language sites for general history, travel information, facts, and news stories about Mexico are: the United States' Library of Congress well-organized Mexico pages (⊕ http://lcweb2.loc.gov/frd/cs/mxtoc.html and ⊕ www.loc.gov/rr/international/hispanic/mexico/mexico.html); Mexico Online (⊕ www.mexonline.com); Mexico Web (⊕ http://mexico.web.com.mx/english), Mexico Connect (⊕ www.mexconnect.com); the Mexico Channel (⊕ www.trace-sc.com); Mexican Wave ⊕ www.mexicanwave.com; and ⊕ www.eluniversal.com.mx, the online version of the newspaper *El Universal*, which has an English-language edition.

For information on nature and the environment try Ron Mader's Planeta site (⊕ www.planeta.com/mexico.html), which has the latest news on ecotourism and ideas for hiking and adventure travel. If you're interested in visiting and/or climbing Mexico's volcanoes, the U.S. Geological Services and Cascades Volcano Observatory page (⊕ http://vulcan.wr.usgs.gov/Volcanoes/Mexico) is indispensable. For archaeology, two sites stand above others: Mesoweb (⊕ www.mesoweb.com), and the nonprofit site Ancient Mexico (⊕ www.ancientmexico.com).

# MEXICO CITY

Updated by
Patricia Alisau,
Michele Joyce,
and John Hecht

**MEXICO CITY IS A CITY OF SUPERLATIVES.** It is both the oldest (founded in 1325) and the highest (7,350 feet) metropolis on the North American continent. And with nearly 24 million inhabitants, it's the most populous city in the world. At the southern edge of the Mesa Central region of the Plateau of Mexico, the city remains Mexico's industrial, financial, cultural, and political core. Fast, thrilling, and hard to get your head around, it seems permanently in the thrall of turbulent and exciting change—braving the 21st century while clinging to its deeply entrenched Aztec heritage.

As the gargantuan pyramids of Teotihuacán attest, the area around Mexico City was occupied from early times by a great civilization, probably Nahuatl in origin. The founding farther south of the Aztec capital, Tenochtitlán, did not occur until more than 600 years after Teotihuacán was abandoned, around AD 750. Between these periods, from 900 to 1200, the Toltec Empire controlled the valley of Mexico. As the story goes, the nomadic Aztecs were searching for a promised land in which to settle. Their prophecies announced that they would recognize the spot when they encountered an eagle, perched on a prickly pear cactus and holding a snake in its beak. In 1325, the disputed date of Tenochtitlán's founding, they discovered this eagle in the valley of Mexico. They settled on what was then an island in shallow Lake Texcoco and connected it to lakeshore satellite towns by a network of *calzadas* (canals and causeways, now freeways). Even then it was the largest city in the Western Hemisphere and, according to historians, one of the three largest cities on Earth. When he first laid eyes on Tenochtitlán in the early 16th century, Spanish conquistador Hernán Cortés was dazzled by the glistening lacustrine metropolis, which reminded him of Venice.

A combination of factors made the Spanish conquest possible. Aztec emperor Moctezuma II believed the white, bearded Cortés on horseback to be the mighty plumed serpent-god Quetzalcóatl, who, according to prophecy, was supposed to arrive from the east in the year 1519 to rule the land. Thus, Moctezuma welcomed the foreigner with gifts of gold and palatial accommodations. In return, Cortés initiated a massacre. He was backed by a huge army of Indians from other settlements such as Cholula and Tlaxcala, who saw a chance to end their submission to the Aztec empire. With these forces, the European tactical advantages of horses, firearms, and, inadvertently, the introduction of smallpox and the common cold, Cortés succeeded in erasing Tenochtitlán only two centuries after it was founded.

Cortés began building the capital of what he patriotically dubbed New Spain, the Spanish empire's colony that would spread north to cover what is now the southwestern United States, and south to Panama. *Mexico* comes from the word *Mexica* (pronounced *meh*-shee-ka), which was the Aztecs' name for themselves. (Aztec is the Spaniards' name for the Mexica.) At the site of Tenochtitlán's demolished ceremonial center—now the 10-acre Zócalo—Cortés started building a church (the precursor of the impressive Metropolitan Cathedral), mansions, and government buildings. He utilized the slave labor—and the artistry—of the vanquished native Mexicans. On top of the ruins of their city, and using rubble from

Numbers in the text correspond to numbers in the margin and on the Centro Histórico & Alameda Central; Zona Rosa, La Condesa & La Roma; and San Ángel & Coyoacán maps.

**If you have**

**3 days**

Start early with breakfast at the **Casa de los Azulejos** ⑪, which you can follow, if there is a clear sky, with a visit to the top of the **Torre Latinoamericana** ⑫ or with a stroll around the **Alameda Central** ⑯. Visit the **Palacio de Bellas Artes** ⑬ and then wind your way through the historic center on Calle Tacuba to have lunch in the historic Café de Tacuba; here, you are right on the corner of the **Zócalo** ①, with its cathedral, ruins, and museums. Be sure to visit the **Templo Mayor** ④, and then end your day overlooking it all from the bars in either the Hotel Majestic or the Holiday Inn Zócalo. Day 2, head for the **Museo Nacional de Antropología** ㉔ in the morning and enjoy lunch in one of the many swank eateries in the Polanco neighborhood. Then cab it over to the **Mercado Artesanal La Ciudadela** to hit the crafts stalls. Consider an evening in the fashionable **Colonia Condesa** for cocktails and dinner. On Day 3, go to **San Ángel**—start with the Bazar Sábado (if it's Saturday) or the **Museo Estudio Diego Rivera y Frida Kahlo** ㉚. Head east to **Coyoacán,** with its lovely casa-museums, especially the **Museo de Frida Kahlo** ㉞ and **Museo de Leon Trotsky** ㉟. Visit downtown's Plaza Garibaldi for a rousing mariachi send-off, or go for a classy dinner and a few hours of dancing. If the Classic period site of **Teotihuacán** intrigues you, however, you could spend the third day there.

**If you have**

**5 days**

Follow the three-day itinerary, seeing San Ángel and Coyoacán on the third day, then head to **Bosque de Chapultepec** ⑳ on Day 4 to stroll the green pathways and visit the museums and the **Zoológico** ㉓ to see the pandas. On Day 5 take a day trip to climb a pyramid at the ruins of **Teotihuacán.**

**If you have**

**10 days**

Take advantage of having more than a week by visiting more of the fascinating sights beyond the city center. (See also Chapter 2.) Follow the five-day outline and add a visit to the resort town of 🔲 **Cuernavaca,** just over an hour's drive southeast of Mexico City. Spend the day in its museums and browsing its pretty main square, then overnight at one of the town's converted mansions. On Day 7 head back to Mexico City via Highway 95 and stop in **Xochimilco,** where you can ride through the floating gardens on a gondola-like boat. On Day 8 drive north to the ancient Toltec ruins at **Tula;** make an early start if you're traveling in warm weather so that you don't sizzle in the afternoon heat. Continue to the village of **Tepotzotlán,** which has a beautiful Jesuit church, returning to Mexico City for a relaxed dinner. The next day, head to 🔲 **Puebla** for a three-hour tour, then pop over to the nearby town of **Cholula,** once a sacred ceremonial site, before returning to Puebla for the night. Alternatively, book an early trip with Puebla's tourist office to see the beautiful churches between Puebla and Cholula, and try to fit in the convent at Huejotzingo. En route back to Mexico City on the last day, drive to **Cacaxtla** to see some of the best-preserved Mesoamerican murals in Mexico.

**1**

it, they were forced to build what became the most European-style city in North America. But instead of having the random layout of contemporary medieval cities, it followed the grid pattern of the Aztecs. For much of the construction material the Spaniards quarried the local porous, volcanic reddish stone called *tezontle*. The Spaniards also drained the lakes, preferring wheels and horses (which they introduced to Mexico) over canals and canoes for transport. The land-filled lake bed turned out to be a soggy support for the immense buildings that have been slowly sinking into it since they were built.

The city flourished during the colonial period, filling what is now its historic center with architectural treasures. The Franciscans and Dominicans eagerly set about converting the Aztecs to Christianity, but some indigenous customs persisted. Street vending, for instance, is a city signature even today. It is said that the conquering soldiers looked out on them in 1520 and said they had never seen such a market, not even in Rome. In 1571 the Spaniards established the Inquisition in New Spain and burned heretics at its palace headquarters, now a museum in Plaza de Santo Domingo.

It took almost three centuries for Mexicans to rise up successfully against Spain. The historic downtown street 16 de Septiembre commemorates the "declaration" of Independence. On that date in 1810, Miguel Hidalgo, Father of the Catholic Church—and of a couple of illegitimate daughters—rang a church bell and cried out his history-making *grito* (shout): "Death to the *gachupines!* (wealthy Spaniards living in Mexico) Long live the Virgin of Guadalupe!" Excommunicated and executed the following year, Hidalgo is one of many independence heroes who fostered a truly popular movement, culminating in Mexico's independence in 1821. The liberty bell that now hangs above the main entrance to the National Palace is rung on every eve of September 16 by the president of the republic, who then shouts a revised version of the patriot's cry: "¡Viva México!"

Flying in or out of Mexico City, you get an aerial view of the remaining part of Lake Texcoco on the eastern outskirts of the city. In daylight you can notice the sprawling flatness of the 1,480-square-km (570-square-mi) Meseta de Anáhuac (Valley of Mexico), completely surrounded by mountains. On its southeastern side, two usually snowcapped volcanoes, Popocatépetl and Iztaccíhuatl, are both well over 17,000 feet high. After a period of relative tranquility, Popocatépetl awoke and began spewing smoke, ash, and some lava in the mid-1990s; it has remained intermittently active since then.

Unfortunately, the single most widely known fact about Mexico City is that its air is polluted. There's no denying the smog and nightmarish traffic, but strict legislation in recent years has led to cleaner air and, especially after the summer rains, the city has some of the clearest, bluest skies anywhere. At 7,350 feet, the city often has mild daytime weather perfect for sightseeing and cool evenings.

If notoriety for smog brings Los Angeles to mind, so might the fault line that runs through the valley. In 1985 a major earthquake—8.1 on the

1

# Cuisine Old & New
The capital may be able to sate your cravings for blini or sushi, but some of the most intriguing dining experiences stem from Mexican chefs looking forward—or far backward. Some newcomers on the restaurant scene are experimenting with established Mexican favorites; others are bringing ancient dishes out of the archives and onto the table.

Until the 15th century, Europeans had never seen indigenous Mexican edibles such as corn, chilies of all varieties, tomatoes, potatoes, pumpkin, squash, avocado, turkey, cocoa, and vanilla. In turn, the colonization brought European gastronomic influence and ingredients—wheat, onions, garlic, olives, citrus fruit, cattle, sheep, goats, chickens, domesticated pigs (and lard for frying)—and ended up broadening the already complex pre-Hispanic cuisine into one of the most multifaceted and exquisite in the world: traditional Mexican.

The last decade has seen the evolution of *nueva cocina mexicana* (nouvelle Mexican cuisine) from a trend to an established and respected restaurant genre. The style emphasizes presentation and intriguing combinations of traditional ingredients and contemporary techniques. In the more serious or purist restaurants that aim to rescue recipes from the pre-Hispanic past, you can enjoy the delicate tastes of regional dishes gleaned from colonial reports, and indigenous cooking techniques such as steaming and baking. And, irrespective of fashion, market eateries offer pre-Hispanic seasonal delicacies such as crunchy fried grasshoppers and fried *maguey* larva.

# Museums
Mexico City is the cultural as well as political capital of the country, as evidenced by its 80-plus museums—some of the finest in Latin America. In buildings of architectural merit, you can see the stirring murals of such native sons as Diego Rivera, José Clemente Orozco, David Alfaro Siqueiros, and Juan O'-Gorman; the haunting paintings of Frida Kahlo; stunning pre-Hispanic ceremonial pieces; and outstanding collections of religious art.

# Nightlife & the Arts
From high culture to down-and-dirty cantinas, Mexico City has it all. Its folklore ballet is justly renowned; the mariachi duels in Plaza Garibaldi epitomize the tradition of outdoor music. You'll also find trendy discos and steamy dance halls where salsa, merengue, and *danzón* (sensuous Cuban dance music) are headliners. Fine arts are having a moment, too—during the past couple of years, the capital has been touted by the contemporary art world for its modern-art galleries and daring young painters, photographers, video artists, and sculptors.

---

Richter scale—took a tragic toll. The government reported 10,000 deaths, but locally it's said to be closer to 50,000. The last traces of that quake's damage are finally disappearing with the major renovation project in the capital's historic center, an overhaul which includes the application of the latest earthquake-resistant technology.

Glossy magazine ads usually tout Mexico's paradisiacal beach resorts and ancient ruins, but cosmopolitan, historic Mexico City—which goes by just "México" or D.F. (for Distrito Federal) in Mexico—is a fascinating destination in itself. The city's vitality shows in the pace of its changes, such as the restoration of colonial buildings and the crop of new cafés. Other improvements, including new public lighting downtown and a police team specially trained for assisting tourists, make the capital an increasingly better place for an extended visit.

# EXPLORING MEXICO CITY

Most of Mexico City is aligned on two major intersecting thoroughfares: Paseo de la Reforma and Avenida Insurgentes—at 34 km (21 mi), the longest avenue in the city. Administratively, Mexico City is divided into 16 *delegaciones* (districts) and about 400 *colonias* (neighborhoods), many with street names fitting a given theme, such as a river, philosopher, or revolutionary hero. The same street can change names as it goes through different colonias. Hence, most street addresses include their colonia (abbreviated as Col.). Unless you're going to a landmark, it's important to tell your taxi driver the name of the colonia and, whenever possible, the cross street.

The principal sights of Mexico City fall into three areas. Allow a full day to cover each thoroughly, although you could race through them in four or five hours apiece. You can generally cover the first area—the Zócalo and Alameda Central—on foot. Getting around the Zona Rosa, Bosque de Chapultepec and Colonia Condesa will require a taxi ride or two, as will Coyoacán and San Ángel in southern Mexico City.

## Centro Histórico & Alameda Central

The Zócalo, its surrounding Centro Histórico (historic center), and Alameda Central were the heart of both tremendous cities, Aztec and Spanish. There's a palpable European influence in this area, which is undergoing a major refurbishment. Seven hundred years of history lie beneath its jagged thoroughfares. The sidewalks hum with street vendors, hurried office workers, and tourists blinking in wonder. (Some streets have been converted into pedestrian-only zones.) Every block seems energized with perpetual noise and motion.

**a good walk**

*Numbers in the text correspond to numbers in the margin and on the Centro Histórico and Alameda Central map.*

An excellent point of departure for any tour of the city's center is the huge **Zócalo** ❶ ►, the heart and soul of old downtown. From here you can literally see the layers of history in the buildings around you. A pair of buildings, the 1722 **Ayuntamiento,** or city hall, sit on the southern side of the square; on the west side you'll see colonial tiles of the arms of Cortés and other conquistadores. Walk up to the powerful **Catedral Metropolitana** ❷, crammed with religious art and icons. (A bit farther west of the cathedral is the National Pawn Shop in an 18th-century building, the Monte de Piedad, its large glass windows filled with jewelry and electronics.) Angle east across the square to the monumental **Palacio Nacional ❸**, covering two city blocks. Its interior is lined with Diego Rivera's profound mural of Mexican history. Head back north to see the **Templo Mayor ❹**, ruins from the Aztec capital, with its superb museum. Modern-art lovers should walk east on Calle Moneda to Academia to find the **Museo José Luis Cuevas ❺**. From there, backtrack on Calle Moneda one block, turn right to go north on Correo Mayor del Carmen for two blocks, make a left on Calle Justo Sierra, which becomes Donceles, for one block. At Republica de Argentina, turn right to the **Antiguo Colegio de San Ildefonso ❻**, now an art and history museum. Leaving the museum, walk a couple of blocks west on Republica de Cuba until you reach the historic **Plaza de Santo Domingo ❼**, studded with its baroque church, a medical museum, and a gaggle of scribes. Follow Republica de Brasil south to Calle Tacuba; if you haven't had lunch yet, drop in at Café de Tacuba. Then stroll west to the **Museo Nacional de Arte ❽** in the colonial Plaza Manuel Tolsá.

From Calle Tacuba, head two short blocks south to Calle Madero, one of the city's most architecturally varied streets. On the south side of Madero, between Bolivar and Gante, is the 1780 baroque **Palacio de Iturbide ❾**. Go west along on the south side of Madero; less than a block past the palacio you'll come to the **Iglesia de San Francisco ❿**, with its beautifully painted walls. The stunning tilework of the **Casa de los Azulejos ⓫** will draw your eye across Calle Madero.

The ultimate goals of the remainder of this walk are an antiques museum and a Diego Rivera mural museum. From Calle Madero, walk less than a half block west to Eje Central Lázaro Cárdenas, a wide four-lane avenue. At the corner and on your left, you can't miss the 1950s-style skyscraper, the **Torre Latinoamericana ⓬**, which has one of the best aerial views of the city as well as a sky-high aquarium. Cross the avenue and turn right (north) to explore the beautiful **Palacio de Bellas Artes ⓭** opera house, the long side of which skirts Lázaro Cárdenas (its entrance is on Juárez). The 1908 post office building of **Dirección General de Correos ⓮** is up Lázaro Cárdenas another 150 feet, across from Bellas Artes.

Pass the post office to Calle Tacuba and cross Lázaro Cárdenas one last time, where Calle Tacuba turns into Avenida Hidalgo. One block west, you'll come to the antiques-filled **Museo Franz Mayer ⓯**, which often hosts world-class art and photography exhibitions. (It's also a good place for a coffee break.) Across Avenida Hidalgo is the north end of the leafy park **Alameda Central ⓰**. To get to the **Museo Mural Diego Rivera ⓱**, take Juárez west to Calle Balderas. Turn right and walk a short block to Calle Colón to get back to the park. If you're interested in photography, make a detour to **Centro de la Imagen ⓲**; at the end of such a long day, it's best to take a cab.

TIMING    The Zócalo area will be quietest on Sunday, when bureaucrats have their day of rest. But Alameda Park will be jumping with children and their parents enjoying a Sunday outing. The park will be particularly festive during December, when dozens of "Santas" will appear with plastic reindeer to take wish lists. Although Mexicans celebrate on the night of De-

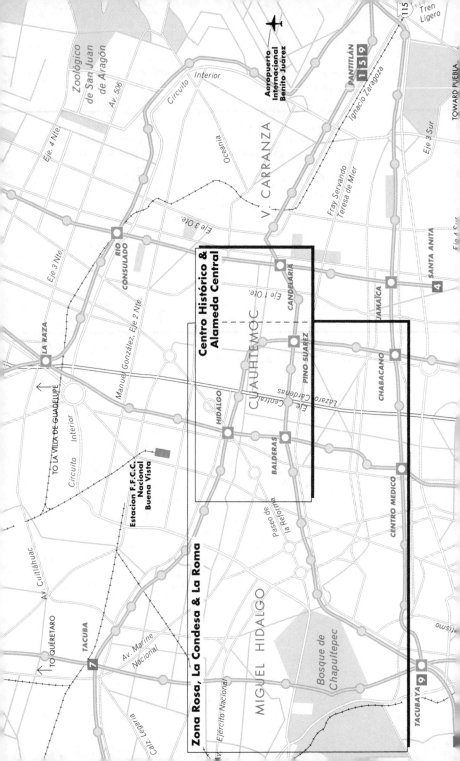

# Mexico City Orientation

TOWARD PUEBLA

IZTACALCO

Rojo Gómez

Av. Lic Javier

Av. Río Churubusco

Circuito Interior

2 miles

3 km

Parque Nacional
Cerro de la Estrella

Av. Cinco

Eje 3 Ote.

Eje 4 Sur

Eje 5 Sur

Eje 6 Sur

Eje 2 Ote.

Calz. de la Viga

Eje 1 Ote.

Av. Santa Ana

Calz. Tasqueña

Av. Plutarco Elías Calles

Calz. de Tlalpan

Country
Club

TASQUEÑA

Tren Ligero

TO XOCHIMILCO

Xola, Eje 4 Sur

BENITO
JUÁREZ

Av. Eugenia

Eje Central Lázaro Cárdenas

Av. División   del Norte

Av. Cuauhtémoc

Av. Río Churubusco

COYOACÁN

Av. Miguel Angel de Quevedo

Eje 10 Sur

TO CUERNAVACO AND
ACAPULCO

Av. de los Insurgentes

Av. A. Urraza

Eje 2 Pte.

Eje 7 Sur

Eje 8 Sur

A. OBREGÓN

BARRANCA DEL
MUERTO

7

San Angel & Coyoacán

Ciudad
Universitaria

UNIVERSIDAD

3

Insurgentes

Av. de la Revolución

Av Patrioti

OBSERVATORIO

1

2

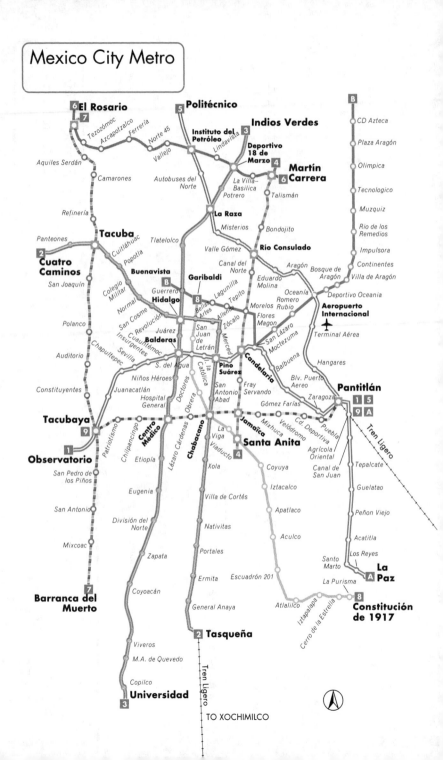

# Mexico City Metro

cember 24, the tradition of giving presents—especially to children—kicks in at dawn on January 6, the Day of the Three Kings, so for about a week beforehand the Three Wise Men of biblical lore replace the Santas in the Alameda. Gorgeous Christmas-light sculptures deck the Zócalo from end to end and stream up Calle Madero past Alameda Park to Paseo de la Reforma beyond the museums in Bosque de Chapultepec. Elaborate decorations also festoon the Zócalo in September for the Independence celebrations known as *Fiestas Patrias* (Patriotic Holidays); on September 16 a military parade marches through.

During the daytime, the downtown area is vibrant with activity. As in any capital, watch out for pickpockets, especially on crowded buses and subways, and avoid deserted streets at night.

The streets in the walking tour are fairly close to one another and can be covered in a day if you don't linger over lunch; otherwise, a couple of days will make for a more leisurely tour. The Palacio Nacional, Templo Mayor and its museum, and the Museo Franz Mayer are each worth an hour of your time; you can cover the Palacio de Bellas Artes in a half hour unless you stumble upon one of its marvelous and epic temporary exhibitions. Remember that most museums close on Monday.

## What to See

CENTRO  **Antiguo Colegio de San Ildefonso.** The college, a colonial building with
HISTÓRICO  lovely patios, started out as a Jesuit school for the sons of wealthy
**6**  Mexicans in the 18th century. It is now a splendid museum that showcases outstanding regional exhibitions. The interior contains murals by Diego Rivera, José Clemente Orozco, and Fernando Leal. ✉ *Calle Justo Sierra 16, almost at the corner of República de Argentina, 2 blocks north of the Zócalo, Col. Centro* ☎ *55/5789–0485* ⊕ *www.sanildefonso. org.mx* ✐ *$3.50, free Tues.* ☉ *Tues.–Sun. 10–6* Ⓜ *Zócalo.*

**2 Catedral Metropolitana.** Construction on this oldest and largest cathedral in Latin America began in the late 16th century and continued intermittently throughout the next three centuries. The result is a medley of baroque and neoclassical touches. Inside are four identical domes, their airiness grounded by rows of supportive columns. There are five altars and 14 chapels, mostly in the ornate churrigueresque style, named for Spanish architect José Churriguera (died 1725). Like most Mexican churches, the cathedral itself is all but overwhelmed by the innumerable paintings, altarpieces, and statues—in graphic color—of Christ and the saints. Over the centuries, this cathedral began to sink into the spongy subsoil, but a major engineering project to stabilize the structure was declared successful in 2000. The older-looking church attached to the cathedral is the 18th-century Sagrario chapel. ✉ *Zócalo, Col. Centro* ☉ *Daily 7–7* Ⓜ *Zócalo.*

**Museo de la Ciudad de México.** The city museum is in a 16th-century building that was once home to Joaquín Clausell, who is widely considered the most important impressionist painter in Mexican history. It displays historical objects from Mexico City, including antique maps, lithographs, and engravings. Clausell's studio is also open to the public and his studio walls are covered with his work. ✉ *Pino Suárez 30, Col. Centro*

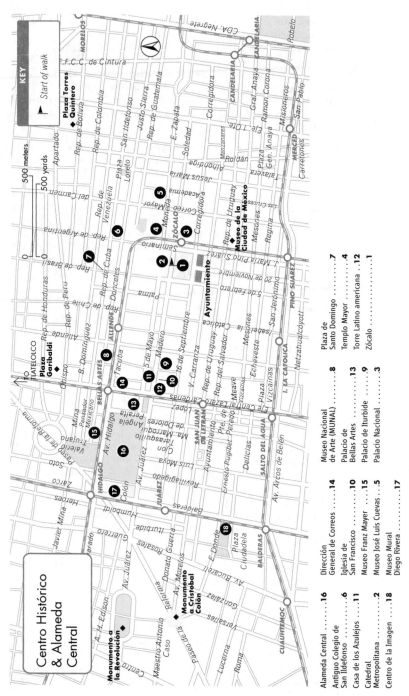

Centro Histórico & Alameda Central

Alameda Central ......**16**
Antiguo Colegio de
San Ildefonso .........**6**
Casa de los Azulejos ....**11**
Catedral
Metropolitana ..........**2**
Centro de la Imagen ....**18**

Dirección
General de Correos .....**14**
Iglesia de
San Francisco .........**10**
Museo Franz Mayer .....**15**
Museo José Luis Cuevas ..**5**
Museo Mural
Diego Rivera ..........**17**

Museo Nacional
de Arte (MUNAL) .......**8**
Palacio de
Bellas Artes ..........**13**
Palacio de Iturbide .......**9**
Palacio Nacional ........**3**

Plaza de
Santo Domingo .........**7**
Templo Mayor ..........**4**
Torre Latino americana ..**12**
Zócalo ................**1**

KEY

▲ *Start of walk*

☎ 55/5542–0083 or 55/5542–0671  🎫 $1.40 ☉ Tues.–Sun. 10–6
Ⓜ Pino Suarez.

**❺ Museo José Luis Cuevas.** Installed in a refurbished former convent, this
attractive museum displays international modern art as well as work by
Mexico's enfant terrible, José Luis Cuevas, one of the country's best-
known contemporary artists. The highlight is the sensational La Giganta
(The Giantess), Cuevas's 8-ton bronze sculpture in the central patio. Up-
and-coming Latin American artists appear in temporary exhibitions
throughout the year. ✉ Academia 13, at Calle Moneda, Col. Centro ☎ 55/
5522–0156 ⊕ www.museojoseluiscuevas.com.mx  🎫 $1 ☉ Tues.–Sun.
10–5:45 Ⓜ Zócalo.

**★ ❻ Palacio Nacional.** The grand national palace was initiated by Cortés on
the site of Moctezuma's home and remodeled by the viceroys. Its current form dates from 1693, although a third floor was added in 1926.
Now the seat of government, it has always served as a public-function
site. In fact, during colonial times, the first bullfight in New Spain took
place in the inner courtyard.

Diego Rivera's sweeping, epic murals on the second floor of the main
courtyard exert a mesmeric pull. For more than 16 years (1929–45), Rivera
and his assistants mounted scaffolds day and night, perfecting techniques
adapted from Renaissance Italian fresco painting. The result, nearly 1,200
square feet of vividly painted wall space, is grandiosely entitled Epica
del Pueblo Mexicano en su Lucha por la Libertad y la Independencia
(Epic of the Mexican People in Their Struggle for Freedom and Independence). The paintings represent two millennia of Mexican history,
filtered through Rivera's imagination. He painted pre-Hispanic times
in innocent, almost sugary scenes of Tenochtitlán. Only a few vignettes—
a man offering a human arm for sale, and the carnage of warriors—acknowledge the darker aspects of ancient life. As you walk around the
floor, you'll pass images of the savagery of the conquest and the hypocrisy
of the Spanish priests, the noble independence movement, and the
bloody revolution. Marx appears amid scenes of class struggle, toiling
workers, industrialization (which Rivera idealized), bourgeois deca-
dence, and nuclear holocaust. These are among Rivera's finest work—
as well as the most accessible and probably most visited. The palace also
houses a minor museum that focuses on 19th-century president Benito
Juárez and the Mexican Congress.

The liberty bell rung by Padre Hidalgo to proclaim independence in 1810
hangs high on the central facade. It chimes every eve of September 16,
while from the balcony the president repeats the historic shout of independence to throngs of chilangos (Mexico City residents) below.
✉ East side of the Zócalo, Col. Centro ☎ No phone 🎫 Free; you'll be
asked to leave an ID at the front desk ☉ Mon.–Sat. 9–6, Sun. 9–2
Ⓜ Zócalo.

**❼ Plaza de Santo Domingo.** The Aztec emperor Cuauhtémoc built a palace
here, where heretics were later burned at the stake in the Spanish Inquisition. The plaza was the intellectual hub of the city during the colonial era. Today, its most charming feature is the **Portal de los Evangelistas,**

whose arcades are filled with scribes at old-fashioned typewriters who are filling in official forms, printing invitations, or composing letters for love-stricken swains.

The gloomy-looking **Palacio de la Escuela de Medicina Mexicana** (⊠ República de Brasil 33, at República de Venezuela, Col. Centro ☎ 55/5529–7543 ⬚ Free ⊘ Daily 9–6), once the headquarters for the Inquisition, is catercorner to the lively portal. Founded by the Catholic Church in 1571 and closed by government decree in 1820, it was a medical school for many years. Now it serves as a fascinating museum portraying the history of medicine in this country.

The 18th-century baroque **Santo Domingo church,** slightly north of the portal, is all that remains of the first Dominican convent in New Spain. The convent building was demolished in 1861 under the Reform laws that forced clerics to turn over all religious buildings not used for worship to the government. ⊠ *Between República de Cuba, República de Brasil, República de Venezuela, and Palma, Col. Centro* ☎ *No phone* Ⓜ *Zócalo.*

❹ **Templo Mayor.** The ruins of the ancient hub of the Aztec empire were
Fodor'sChoice   unearthed accidentally in 1978 by telephone repairmen and have since
★   been turned into a vast archaeological site and museum. At this temple, dedicated to the Aztec cult of death, captives from rival tribes—as many as 10,000 at a time—were sacrificed to the bloodthirsty god of war, Huitzilopochtli. Seven rows of leering stone skulls adorn one side.

The adjacent **Museo del Templo Mayor** contains 3,000 pieces unearthed from the site and from other ruins in central Mexico; they include ceramic warriors, stone carvings and knives, skulls of sacrificial victims, a rare gold ingot, models and scale reproductions, and a room on the Spaniards' destruction of Tenochtitlán. The centerpiece is an 8-ton disk discovered at the Templo Mayor. It depicts the moon goddess Coyolxauhqui, who, according to myth, was decapitated and dismembered by her brother Huitzilopochtli. Call six weeks ahead to schedule free English-language tours by museum staff in the mornings. ⊠ *Seminario 8, at República de Guatemala; entrance on the plaza, near Catedral Metropolitana, Col. Centro* ☎ *55/5542–4784, 55/5542–4785, or 55/ 5542–4786* ⊕ *azteca.conaculta.gob.mx/templomayor* ⬚ *$3.80* ⊘ *Tues.–Sun. 9–5* Ⓜ *Zócalo.*

▶ ❶ **Zócalo.** Mexico City's historic plaza (formally called the Plaza de la Constitución) and the buildings around it were built by the Spaniards, using local slaves. This enormous paved square, the largest in the Western Hemisphere, occupies the site of the ceremonial center of Tenochtitlán, the capital of the Aztec empire, which once comprised 78 buildings. Throughout the 16th, 17th, and 18th centuries, elaborate churches and convents, elegant mansions, and stately public edifices were constructed around the square; many of these buildings have long since been converted to other uses. Clusters of small shops, eateries, cantinas, street stalls, and a few women in native Indian dress contribute to an inimitably Mexican flavor and exuberance.

*Zócalo* literally means "pedestal" or "base": in the mid-19th century, an independence monument was planned for the square, but it was never built. The term stuck, however, and now the word "zócalo" is applied to the main plazas of most Mexican cities. Mexico City's Zócalo (because it's the original, it's always capitalized) is used for government rallies, protests, sit-ins, and festive events. It's the focal point for Independence Day celebrations on the eve of September 16 and is a maze of lights, tinsel, and traders during the Christmas season. Flag-raising and -lowering ceremonies take place here in the early morning and late afternoon. ✉ *Bounded on the south by 16 de Septiembre, north by Av. 5 de Mayo, east by Pino Suárez, and west by Monte de Piedad, Col. Centro* Ⓜ *Zócalo.*

ALAMEDA CENTRAL **⑯** **Alameda Central.** Since Aztec times, when the Indians held their *tianguis* (market) on the site, this park has been one of the capital's oases of greenery and centers of activity. In the early days of the Viceroyalty, the Inquisition burned its victims at the stake here. Later, national leaders, from 18th-century viceroys to Emperor Maximilian and President Porfirio Díaz, envisioned the park as a symbol of civic pride and prosperity: over the centuries, it has been endowed with fountains, railings, a Moorish kiosk imported from Paris, and ash, willow, and poplar trees. The semicircular, white-marble monument, **Hemiciclo a Benito Juárez,** stands on the Avenida Juárez side of the park. There's live music on Sunday and holidays. Ⓜ *Bellas Artes or Hidalgo.*

**⑪** **Casa de los Azulejos.** Built as the palace of the counts of the Valle de Orizaba, an aristocratic family from the early period of Spanish rule, this 17th-century masterpiece acquired its name, the House of Tiles, from its elaborate tilework. The dazzling designs, along with the facade's iron grillwork balconies, make it one of the prettiest baroque structures in the country. The interior is also worth seeing for its Moorish patio, monumental staircase, and a mural by Orozco. The building is currently occupied by Sanborns, a chain store and restaurant, and if you have plenty of time—service is slow—this is a good place to stop for a meal. ✉ *Calle Madero 4, at Callejón de la Condesa, Alameda Central* ☎ *55/5512–9820 Ext. 103* ⊕ *www.sanborns.com.mx/sanborns/azulejos.asp* ⊗ *Daily 7 AM–1 AM* Ⓜ *Bellas Artes.*

**⑱** **Centro de la Imagen.** This pioneering photography center stages the city's most important photography exhibitions, as well as occasional contemporary sculpture and other art or mixed media exhibitions. Photography by international artists is often grouped thematically, drawing parallels between various cultures. ✉ *Plaza de la Ciudadela 2, at Balderas, Col. Centro* ☎ *55/9172–4724* ⊕ *www.conaculta.gob.mx/ cimagen* ▨ *Free* ⊗ *Tues.–Sun. 11–6* Ⓜ *Balderas.*

**⑭** **Dirección General de Correos.** Mexico City's main post office building is a fine example of Renaissance revival architecture. Constructed of cream-color sandstone in 1908, it epitomizes the grand imitations of European architecture common in Mexico during the Porfiriato—the long dictatorship of Porfirio Díaz (1876–1911). Upstairs, the **Museo del Palacio Postal** shows Mexico's postal history. ✉ *Calle Tacuba and Eje*

Central Lázaro Cárdenas, Alameda Central ☎ 55/5510–2999 museum, 55/5521–7394 post office ⊕ www.palaciocorreos.gob.mx ⚞ Free ⊙ Museum weekdays 9–4, weekends 10–2; post office weekdays 8–8, Sat. 9–1 Ⓜ Bellas Artes.

**⑩ Iglesia de San Francisco.** On the site of Mexico's first convent (1524) this church's current 18th-century French Gothic incarnation reflects only one of the site's many incarnations. Its past includes use as a military barracks, hotel, circus, theater, and Methodist temple. On Independence Day in 1856 a conspiracy was uncovered here, leading to a decree to slice through the property with a road named Independencia, and the temporary banishment of the convent's religious folk. ⊠ Calles Madero and 16 de Septiembre, Alameda Central ☎ No phone ⊙ Daily 7 AM–8:30 PM Ⓜ Bellas Artes.

**⑮ Museo Franz Mayer.** Housed in the 16th-century Hospital de San Juan de Dios, this museum exhibits 16th- and 17th-century antiques, such as wooden chests inlaid with ivory, tortoiseshell, and ebony; tapestries, paintings, and lacquerware; rococo clocks, glassware, and architectural ornamentation; and an unusually large assortment of Talavera ceramics. The museum also has more than 700 editions of Cervantes's *Don Quixote*. The old hospital building is faithfully restored, with pieces of the original frescoes peeking through. ⊠ Av. Hidalgo 45, at Plaza Santa Veracruz, Alameda Central ☎ 55/5518–2267 ⊕ www.franzmayer.org.mx ⚞ $3 ⊙ Tues. and Thurs.–Sun. 10–5, Wed. 10–7 ☞ Call 1 wk ahead for an English-speaking guide Ⓜ Bellas Artes or Hidalgo.

**⑰ Museo Mural Diego Rivera.** Diego Rivera's controversial mural, *Sueño de una Tarde Dominical en el Parque Alameda* (*Sunday Afternoon Dream in the Alameda Park*), originally was painted on a lobby wall of the Hotel Del Prado in 1947–48. Its controversy grew out of Rivera's Marxist inscription, "God does not exist," which the artist later replaced with the bland "Conference of San Juan de Letrán" to placate Mexico's dominant Catholic population. The 1985 earthquake destroyed the hotel but not the mural, and this museum was built across the street from the hotel's site to house it. ⊠ Colón 7, at Calle Balderas, Alameda Central ☎ 55/5510–2329 ⊕ www.arts-history.mx/museomural.html ⚞ $1 ⊙ Tues.–Sun. 10–6 Ⓜ Hidalgo.

**⑧ Museo Nacional de Arte (MUNAL).** The collections of the national art museum, which fill a neoclassical building, span nearly every school of Mexican art, with a concentration on work made between 1810 and 1950. On display are Diego Rivera's portrait of Adolfo Best Maugard, José María Velasco's *Vista del Valle de México desde el Cerro de Santa Isabel (View of the Valley of Mexico from the Hill of Santa Isabel)*, and Ramón Cano Manilla's *El Globo (The Balloon)*. ⊠ Calle Tacuba 8, Col. Centro ☎ 55/5130–3400 ⊕ www.cnca.gob.mx/museos.htm ⚞ Free ⊙ Tues.–Sun. 10:30–5:30 Ⓜ Bellas Artes or Allende.

**Museo San Carlos.** The San Carlos collection, in a beautiful, stone building dominated by an open-roof oval courtyard, is one of the most important collections of European art in Latin America. It consists of over 200 pieces, primarily paintings and prints, with a few examples of sculpture and decorative arts. The collection is arranged in small rooms off the main patio according to the wide variety of artistic styles that they represent: Gothic, Renaissance, baroque, rococo, English portraiture, neoclassicism, naturalism, romanticism, impressionism, and realism. The museum offers seminars, workshops, and extraordinary weekend classes for children. ⊠ *Puente de Alvarado 50, Tabacalera* ☎ *55/ 5566–8342 or 55/5592–3721* ⊕ *www.mnsancarlos.inba.gob.mx* ⊠ *$2.50* ⊙ *Wed.–Mon. 10–6* Ⓜ *San Cosme.*

★ ⑬ **Palacio de Bellas Artes.** Construction on this colossal white-marble opera house was begun in 1904 by Porfirio Díaz, who wanted to add yet another ornamental building to his accomplishments. He was ousted seven years later and the building wasn't finished until 1934. The striking structure is the work of Italian Adamo Boari, who also designed the post office; pre-Hispanic motifs trim the art deco facade. Inside the concert hall, a Tiffany stained-glass curtain depicts the two volcanoes outside Mexico City. Today the theater serves as a handsome venue for international and national artists, including the Ballet Folklórico de México. For an entrance fee you can see the interior, with its paintings by several celebrated Mexican artists, including Rufino Tamayo and Mexico's trio of muralists: Rivera, Orozco, and Siqueiros. There are interesting temporary art exhibitions as well, plus an elegant cafeteria. ⊠ *Eje Central Lázaro Cárdenas and Av. Juárez, Alameda Central* ☎ *55/5512–3633* ⊕ *www. conaculta.gob.mx/museos.htm* ⊠ *$3* ⊙ *Tues.–Sun. 10–5:50; cafeteria 11–6* Ⓜ *Bellas Artes.*

⑨ **Palacio de Iturbide.** Built in 1780, this baroque palace—note the imposing door and its carved-stone trimmings—became the residence of Agustín de Iturbide in 1822. One of the heroes of the independence movement, the misguided Iturbide proclaimed himself emperor of a country that had thrown off the imperial yoke of the Hapsburgs only a year before. His own empire, needless to say, was short-lived. Now his home is owned by Banamex (Banco Nacional de México), which sponsors cultural exhibitions in the atrium. ⊠ *Calle Madero 17, Col. Centro* ☎ *55/ 1226–0281* ⊠ *Free* ⊙ *Inner atrium daily 10–7* Ⓜ *Bellas Artes.*

off the beaten path

**TLATELOLCO** – At Paseo de la Reforma's northern end, about 2 km (1 mi) north of the Palacio de Bellas Artes, the area known as Tlatelolco (pronounced tla-tel-*ohl*-coh) was the domain of Cuauhtémoc (pronounced kwa-oo-*teh*-mock)—the last Aztec emperor before the conquest—and the sister city of Tenochtitlán. In modern times its name continues to make residents shudder, as it was here that the Mexican army massacred several hundred protesting students in 1968. In addition, the 1985 earthquake destroyed several high-rise apartments in Tlatelolco, killing hundreds. The center of Tlatelolco is the **Plaza de las Tres Culturas,** so named because Mexico's three cultural eras—pre-Hispanic, colonial, and contemporary—are represented on the plaza in the form of the small ruins of a pre-Hispanic ceremonial center (visible from the roadway); the Iglesia de Santiago Tlatelolco (1609) and Colegio de la Santa Cruz de Tlatelolco (1535–36); and the modern Ministry of Foreign Affairs (1970). The *colegio* (college), founded by the Franciscans after the conquest, was once attended by the sons of the Aztec nobility. ⊠ *Plaza bounded on the north by Manuel González, on the west by Av. San Juan de Letrán Nte., and on the east by Paseo de la Reforma, between Glorieta de Peralvillo and Cuitláhuac, Tlatelolco* Ⓜ *Garibaldi.*

🕉 ⑫ **Torre Latinoamericana.** This 47-story skyscraper, the second-tallest building in the capital, was completed in 1956. On clear days the observation deck and café on the top floors give you terrific views of the city. Small sharks and crocodiles inhabit the 38th floor at the **Fantastic World of the Sea,** a sky-high aquarium. ⊠ *Eje Central Lázaro Cárdenas 2 at Calle Madero, Alameda Central* ☎ *55/5521–0844 observation deck, 55/5521–7455 aquarium* ⊕ *www.arts-history.mx/amex/rutapeatonal/torrelatino1.html* 🗺 *Deck $4; aquarium $2.80* ⊙ *Deck daily 9:30 AM–11 PM; aquarium daily 9:30 AM–10 PM* Ⓜ *Bellas Artes.*

## Zona Rosa, Bosque de Chapultepec & Colonias Condesa & Roma

Bosque de Chapultepec, named for the *chapulines* (grasshoppers) that populated it long ago, is the largest park in the city, a great green refuge from concrete, traffic, and dust. Housing five world-class museums, a castle, a lake, an amusement park, and the Mexican president's official residence, Chapultepec is a saving grace for visitors and locals. If you have time to visit only one of these museums, make it the Museo Nacional de Antropología.

Stores, hotels, travel agencies, and restaurants line the avenues of the Zona Rosa, just east of the park—once a cultural center of Mexico City, it's now a first stop for shopping. Two nearby colonias, known simply as La Condesa and La Roma, are filled with fading 1920s and '30s architecture, shady parks, and inexpensive eateries that cater to the city's young and trendy. The capital's elite concentrated here at the turn of the 20th century before moving on to more-fashionable fields in the 1940s. In the late 1990s a tide of artists, entrepreneurs, and foreigners brought a new wave of energy. La Condesa is the sprucer, hipper area of the two. Grittier La Roma is now home to a group of important art galleries as well as some of the city's best cantinas. A free magazine called *CP06140* (referring to La Condesa's zip code) comes out every two months with up-to-date listings of what to do and where to eat in these neighborhoods. You can pick up a copy in some local cafés and galleries.

*Numbers in the text correspond to numbers in the margin and on the Zona Rosa, La Condesa & La Roma map.*

**a good walk**

Emperor Maximilian built the Paseo de la Reforma in 1865, modeling it after the Champs-Élysées in Paris. Its purpose was to connect the Palacio Nacional with his residence, the Castillo de Chapultepec. At the northeastern end of Reforma are Tlatelolco, the Lagunilla Market, and Plaza Garibaldi, where the mariachis cluster and strut. To the west, Reforma winds its leisurely way west into the wealthy neighborhoods of Lomas de Chapultepec, where posh houses and estates sit behind stone walls.

Start your exploration of the Zona Rosa at the junction of Reforma, Avenida Juárez, and Bucareli, just west of the Alameda Central. Along the stretch of Reforma west of this intersection are a number of statues erected at the request of former Mexican president Porfirio Díaz to honor illustrious men, including Simón Bolívar, Columbus, Pasteur, and the Aztec emperor Cuauhtémoc. The best known, the **Monumento a la Independencia ⑲**, also known as El Angel, marks the western edge of the Zona Rosa. To get the best of the area's sights, walk along Hamburgo, Londres, and Copenhague streets—like others in the Zona, named for Continental cities. There's a crafts market, Mercado Insurgentes, also known as Mercado Zona Rosa, on Londres.

Four blocks southwest of the market, at Avenida Chapultepec, you'll come to the main entrance of **Bosque de Chapultepec ⑳**. Uphill from the park's entrance is the **Castillo de Chapultepec ㉑** with its history museum. North of the Castillo on the near side of Paseo de la Reforma is the **Museo Nacional de Arte Moderno ㉒**. Almost directly across Paseo de la Reforma on its north side and west of Calle Gandhi, you'll see the **Museo Tamayo Arte Contemporáneo ㉓**, in which you'll find Tamayo's paintings as well as those of other outstanding modern artists. West of the Museo Tamayo on the same side of Reforma is the **Museo Nacional de Antropología ㉔**, with its world-renowned collections of Mesoamerican art and artifacts. Cross Reforma again and you'll come to the entrance to the **Zoológico ㉕**.

Southeast of Bosque de Chapultepec are **Colonia Condesa** and **Colonia Roma,** whose attractive, tree-lined streets are peppered with art deco buildings in varying stages of renovation or picturesque decay. Although it's possible to walk to Colonia Condesa from the Bosque de Chapultepec, you'd have to trek along busy, heavily trafficked roads; it's best to take a sitio taxi to the circular Avenida Amsterdam. Loop around Amsterdam until you reach Avenida Michoacán, where you can check out the boutiques and peek down the side streets. On Avenida Michoacán you'll find a sitio taxi stand—hop in for another short cab ride, this time to Colonia Roma's Plaza Río de Janeiro and more atmospheric strolling.

TIMING    You can easily spend an hour at each Bosque de Chapultepec museum, with the exception of the Museo Nacional de Antropología, which is huge compared with its sister institutions. You can have a quick go-through in two hours, but to really appreciate the fine exhibits, anywhere from a half day to a full day is more appropriate. Tuesday to Friday are good days to visit the museums and stroll around the park. On Sunday and Mexican holidays, they're often packed with families. A late-afternoon stroll in La Roma after the museum visits, with dinner in La Condesa, is an excellent way to wind down. Keep in mind that art galleries tend to close on Sunday. The colonias are a must-see in spring, when the jacarandas are in bloom.

## What to See

BOSQUE DE **Bosque de Chapultepec.** This 1,600-acre green space, literally the Woods
CHAPULTEPEC of Chapultepec, draws hordes of families on weekend outings, cyclists,
 joggers, and horseback riders into its three sections. Its museums rank
among the finest in Mexico. This is one of the oldest parts of Mexico

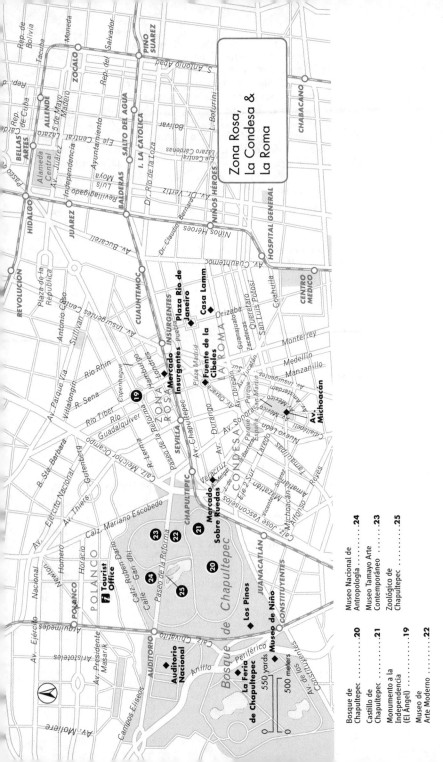

Zona Rosa,
La Condesa &
La Roma

Bosque de
Chapultepec . . . . . . . . . .**20**

Castillo de
Chapultepec . . . . . . . . . .**21**

Monumento a la
Independencia
(El Ángel) . . . . . . . . . . . .**19**

Museo de
Arte Moderno . . . . . . . . .**22**

Museo Nacional de
Antropología . . . . . . . . .**24**

Museo Tamayo Arte
Contemporáneo . . . . . . .**23**

Zoológico de
Chapultepec . . . . . . . . . .**25**

City, having been inhabited by the Mexica (Aztec) tribe as early as the 13th century. The Mexica poet-king Nezahualcóyotl had his palace here and ordered construction of the aqueduct that brought water to Tenochtitlán. Ahuehuete trees (Moctezuma cypress) still stand from that era, when the woods were used as hunting preserves.

At the park's principal entrance, one block west of the Chapultepec metro station, the **Monumento a los Niños Héroes** (Monument to the Boy Heroes) consists of six marble columns adorned with eaglets. Supposedly buried in the monument are the young cadets who, it is said, wrapped themselves in the Mexican flag and jumped to their deaths rather than surrender to the Americans during the U.S. invasion of 1847. To Mexicans, that war is still a troubling symbol of their neighbor's aggressive dominance: it cost Mexico almost half of its territory—the present states of Texas, California, Arizona, New Mexico, and Nevada.

Other sights in the first section of Bosque de Chapultepec include three small boating lakes, a botanical garden, and the Casa del Lago cultural center, which hosts free plays, cultural events, and live music on weekends. **Los Pinos,** the residential palace of the president of Mexico, is on a small highway called Avenida Constituyentes, which cuts through the park; it's heavily guarded and cannot be visited.

The less crowded second and third sections of Bosque de Chapultepec contain a fancy restaurant; the national cemetery; and the Lienzo Charro (Mexican rodeos), held on Sunday afternoon.

**㉑ Castillo de Chapultepec.** The castle on Cerro del Chapulín (Grasshopper Hill) has borne witness to all the turbulence and grandeur of Mexican history. In its earliest permutations, it was an Aztec palace, where the Mexica made one of their last stands against the Spaniards. Later it was a Spanish hermitage, gunpowder plant, and military college. Emperor Maximilian used the castle, parts of which date from 1783, as his residence, and his example was followed by various presidents from 1872 to 1940, when Lázaro Cárdenas decreed that it be turned into the **Museo Nacional de Historia.**

Displays on the museum's ground floor cover Mexican history from the conquest to the revolution. The bathroom, bedroom, tea salon, and gardens were used by Maximilian and his wife, Carlotta, during their reign in the 1860s. The ground floor also contains works by 20th-century muralists O'Gorman, Orozco, and Siqueiros, and the upper floor is devoted to temporary exhibitions, Porfirio Díaz's malachite vases, and religious art. ⊠ *Section 1, Bosque de Chapultepec* ☎ *55/5241–6224* ✆ *$3.70* ⊙ *Tues.–Sun. 9–4:30* ⊕ *www.arts-history.mx/museos/castillo.*

**☾ La Feria de Chapultepec.** This children's amusement park has various games and more than 50 rides, including a truly hair-raising haunted house and a *montaña rusa*—"Russian mountain," or roller coaster. Admission price varies, depending on which rides are covered and whether meals are included. ⊠ *Section 2, Bosque de Chapultepec* ☎ *55/5230–2121 or 55/5230–2112* ✆ *$6–$10* ⊙ *Mon.–Thurs. 10–6, Fri. 10–7, weekends 10–9* Ⓜ *Constituyentes.*

**㉒ Museo de Arte Moderno.** The Modern Art Museum has many important examples of the Mexican School of Painting—including Frida Kahlo, Diego Rivera, José Clemente Orozco, and David Alfaro Siqueiros—as well as a permanent collection of contemporary Mexican art and rotating exhibits. ⊠ *Paseo de la Reforma, Section 1, Bosque de Chapultepec* ☎ *55/5553–6233 or 55/5211–8729* ⬚ *$1.50* ⊙ *Tues.–Sun. 10–6* Ⓜ *Chapultepec.*

**㉔ Museo Nacional de Antropología.** Architect Pedro Ramírez Vázquez's
Fodor'sChoice distinguished design showcases the national archaeological holdings, one
★ of the finest such collections in the world. Each salon on the museum's two floors displays artifacts from a particular geographic region or culture. The collection is so extensive—covering some 100,000 square feet—that you could easily spend a day here, and that might be barely adequate. Explanatory labels have been updated, some with English translations, and free tours are available at set times between 3 and 6. You can also reserve a special tour with an English-speaking guide by calling the museum one week in advance, or opt for an English audio guide ($4) or English-language guidebooks for sale in the bookshop.

A good place to start is in the Orientation Room, where a film is shown in Spanish nearly every hour on the hour weekdays and every two hours on weekends. The film traces the course of Mexican prehistory and the pre-Hispanic cultures of Mesoamerica. The 12 ground-floor rooms treat pre-Hispanic cultures by region—such as Sala Teotihuacána, Sala Tolteca, Sala Oaxaca (Zapotec and Mixtec peoples), Sala Maya (Maya groups from many areas, including Guatemala), and so on. At this writing, the Sala Maya and the Sala Costa del Golfo were closed for renovation. Objects both precious and plebian, including statuary, jewelry, weapons, figurines, and pottery, evoke the intriguing, complex, and frequently bloodthirsty civilizations that peopled Mesoamerica for the 3,000 years that preceded the Spanish invasion. You will find the famous Aztec calendar stone—the original *Piedra del Sol* (Stone of the Sun)—in Room 7, the Sala Mexica, which describes Aztec life. A copy of the Aztec ruler Moctezuma's feathered headdress is displayed nearby in the same salon—strangely, the original headdress is in Vienna. An original stela from Tula, near Mexico City, massive Olmec heads from Veracruz, and vivid reproductions of Mayan murals in a reconstructed temple are some of the other highlights. Be sure to see the magnificent tomb of 8th-century Maya ruler Pacal, which was discovered in the ruins of Palenque. The perfectly preserved skeletal remains lie in state in an immense stone chamber, and the stairwell walls leading to it are beautifully decorated with bas-relief scenes of the underworld. Pacal's jade death mask is also on display nearby.

The nine rooms on the upper floor contain faithful ethnographic displays of current indigenous peoples, using maps, photographs, household items, folk art, clothing, and religious articles. When leaving the museum, take a rest and watch the famous Voladores de Papantla (flyers of Papantla) as they swing by their feet down an incredibly high maypolelike structure. ⊠ *Paseo de la Reforma at Calle Gandhi, Section 1, Bosque de Chapultepec* ☎ *55/5286–2923, 55/5553–6381, 55/5553–6386 for a guide* ⊕ *www.mna.inah.gob.mx* 🎫 *$3.80* ⊙ *Tues.–Sun. 9–7* Ⓜ *Auditorio.*

★ ㉓ **Museo Tamayo Arte Contemporáneo** (Rufino Tamayo Contemporary Art Museum). Within its modernist shell, this sleek museum contains the paintings of the noted Mexican artist and temporary exhibitions on international contemporary artists. The selections from Tamayo's personal collection demonstrate his unerring eye for great art; he owned works by Picasso, Joan Miró, René Magritte, Francis Bacon, and Henry Moore. ⊠ *Paseo de la Reforma at Calle Gandhi, Section 1, Bosque de Chapultepec* ☎ *55/5286–6519* ⊕ *www.museotamayo.org* 🎫 *$1.50* ⊙ *Tues.–Sun. 10–6* Ⓜ *Chapultepec.*

Ⓒ **El Papalote, Museo del Niño.** Five themed sections compose this excellent interactive children's museum: Our World; The Human Body; Con-Sciencia, with exhibits relating to both consciousness and science; Communication, on topics ranging from language to computers; and Expression, which includes art, music, theater, and literature. There are also workshops, an IMAX theater, a store, and a restaurant. ⊠ *Av. Constituyentes 268, Section 2, Bosque de Chapultepec* ☎ *55/5237–1781 or 55/5237–1700* ⊕ *www.papalote.org.mx* 🎫 *$6* ⊙ *Weekdays 9–1 and 2–6, weekends 10–2 and 3–7* Ⓜ *Constituyentes.*

Ⓒ ㉕ **Zoológico de Chapultepec.** During the early 16th century, Mexico City's zoo housed a small private collection of animals belonging to Moctezuma II; it became quasi-public when he allowed favored subjects to visit it. The current zoo opened in the 1920s and has the usual suspects as well as some superstar pandas. A gift from China, the original pair—Pepe and Ying Ying—produced the world's first panda baby born in captivity (much to competitive China's chagrin). In fact, the zoo has one of the world's best mating records for these endangered animals. The zoo includes the Moctezuma Aviary and is surrounded by a miniature train depot, botanical gardens, and lakes where you can go rowing. You'll see the entrance on Paseo de la Reforma, across from the Museo Nacional de Antropología. ⊠ *Section 1, Bosque de Chapultepec* ☎ *55/5553–6263 or 55/5256–4104* ⊕ *www.cnf.org.mx/zoologico/infozoo.html* 🎫 *Free* ⊙ *Tues.–Sun. 9–4* Ⓜ *Auditorio.*

COLONIA  **Around Avenida Michoacán.** Restaurants, cafés, and hip boutiques radi-
CONDESA  ate along and out from La Condesa's main drag, the Avenida Michoacán. It's a great place for a break from a sightseeing slog—just relax at a sidewalk table and watch the hip young world go by. You will be spoiled for choice, if you can find a seat, at the popular **Cafe La Selva** (⊠ Av. Vicente Suárez 38 C and D, off Av. Michoacán, Col. Condesa ☎ 55/5211–5170 Ⓜ Patriotismo). Pick up a quick baguette or sandwich with your coffee at **Mantra** (⊠ Av. Tamaulipas 216, Col. Condesa ☎ 55/5516–0155 Ⓜ Patriotismo).

A snack will fortify you for Avenida Michoacán's other main activity, shopping. The clothing stores often lean toward the trendy; Kulte, for instance, at Atlixco 118, dishes up the latest fads, as does Soho, on Avenida Vicente Suárez between avenidas Michoacán and Tamaulipas. Along the nearby streets you'll find a good mix of temptations—everything from modern furniture to risqué lingerie. As its name (The Open Closet) suggests, the bookstore **El Armario Abierto** (⊠ Agustín Melgar 25, at Pachuca, Col. Condesa ☎ 55/5286–0895 Ⓜ Chapultepec) gives a rare glimpse of progressive Mexico; it specializes in sexuality-related books, videos, and other resources. **El Péndulo** (⊠ Av. Nuevo León 115, at Av. Vicente Suárez, Col. Condesa ☎ 55/5286–9493 ⊕ www.pendulo.com Ⓜ Chilpancingo), meanwhile, acts as a sort of cultural center. The store is stuffed with Spanish-language books and international CDs; classical guitarists and other musicians play on the weekends.

The designer shop Carmen Rion caps Michoacán where it meets the **Parque México,** which has a duck pond, plus one of the city's cheapest and best taxi stands. The park area used to be a racetrack, which explains the circular roads like the looping Avenida México and the occasional references to the Hipódromo (hippodrome) Condesa. From Michoacán you could also turn north on Tamaulipas and walk up a few blocks to visit a smaller park, the **Parque España** for a picnic or a stroll.

If you are in town on Tuesday, stop by Avenida Pachuca, where vendors set up a charming outdoor market, **Mercado Sobre Ruedas,** between Avenida Veracruz and Juan de la Barrera from 9 to 5, just this one day per week. While there are many markets to visit in Mexico, this market is particularly clean and peaceful, since it is set up in a relaxed neighborhood. All tables are set out with pink plastic table cloths and these same cloths are hung above the tables for shade; on a sunny day, the predominance of pink can be strikingly beautiful. Vendors here sell everything from children's clothes, pirated CDs, and ceramic pots to produce, fresh flowers, and take-away food. Sometimes music groups wander through the stalls, singing and strumming their guitars for tips.

COLONIA ROMA Adventurous private art galleries, independent, artist-run spaces, and a rough-around-the-edges atmosphere are the hallmarks of La Roma. Like its western neighbor La Condesa, La Roma was once an aristocratic enclave with stately homes. Now it's known for its lively cantinas, pool halls, dance clubs, and night haunts of questionable repute. Gentrification creeps slowly but steadily onward, though, so enjoy this up-and-comer before it becomes too respectable.

Recently, bookstores and cafés have helped transform this old neighborhood into the capital's full-blown arts district. The **Galería OMR** (⊠ Plaza Río de Janeiro 54, Col. Roma ☎ 55/5511–1080 or 55/5511–1179 ⊕ www.galeriaomr.com Ⓜ Insurgentes) is tucked away in a typical Colonia Roma house, with an early-20th-century stone facade and quirkily lopsided exhibition rooms. This active gallery has a strong presence in international art fairs and art magazines. It's open weekdays 10–3 and 4–7 and Saturday 10–2. A short walk from OMR, **Galería Nina Menocal** (⊠ Zacatecas 93, at Cordoba, Col. Roma ☎ 55/5564–7443 ⊕ www.artnet.com/nmenocal.html Ⓜ Insurgentes) specializes in work by Cuban artists. The gallery is open weekdays 10–7 and Saturday 10–2. The **Casa Lamm Cultural Center** (⊠ Av. Álvaro Obregón 99, at Orizaba, Col. Roma ☎ 55/5525–0019 ⊕ www.casalamm.com.mx Ⓜ Insurgentes), a small mansion and national monument, nurtures artists and browsers with three exhibition spaces, a bookstore, a wide range of courses, and a superb café and restaurant. **Galería Pecanins** (✉ Av. Durango 186 at Plaza Cibeles, Col. Roma ☎ 55/5514–0621 or 55/5207–5661 Ⓜ Insurgentes) may be small but it's a significant local presence for art buyers. It's open weekdays 11–2 and 4–7.

ZONA ROSA   Thanks to a plethora of restaurants, cafés, art and antiques galleries, hotels, discos, and shops, the touristy Zona Rosa has been a favorite part of the city for years. The 29-square-block area is bounded by Paseo de la Reforma on the north, Niza on the east, Avenida Chapultepec on the south, and Varsovia on the west. With the mushrooming of fast-food spots and some tacky bars and stores, however, the area has lost some of its former appeal. Most of the buildings were built in the 1920s, as two- to three-story private homes for the well-to-do. All the streets are named after European cities; some, such as Génova, are garden-lined pedestrian malls accented with contemporary bronze statuary.

To enjoy the Zona Rosa, walk the lengths of Hamburgo and Londres and some of the side streets, especially Copenhague—a veritable restaurant row. The large crafts market on Londres is officially called **Mercado Insurgentes**, although most people refer to it as either Mercado Zona Rosa or Mercado Londres. Opposite the market's Londres entrance is Plaza del Angel, a small upscale shopping mall, the halls of which are crowded by antiques vendors on weekends.

🄌 **Monumento a la Independencia.** Known as El Ángel, this Corinthian column topped by a gold-covered angel is the city's most uplifting monument, built to celebrate the 100th anniversary of Mexico's War of Independence. Beneath the pedestal lie the remains of the principal heroes of the independence movement; an eternal flame burns in their honor. ✉ *Traffic circle between Calle Río Tiber, Paseo de la Reforma, and Calle Florencia, Zona Rosa* Ⓜ *Insurgentes.*

## San Ángel & Coyoacán

Originally separate colonial towns and then suburbs of Mexico City, San Ángel and Coyoacán were both absorbed by the ever-growing capital. But they've managed to retain their original tranquility.

San Ángel is a little colonial enclave of cobblestone streets, stone walls, pastel houses, rich foliage, and gardens drenched in bougainvillea. It became a haven for wealthy Spaniards during the Viceroyalty period, around the time of the construction of the Ex-Convento del Carmen. The elite were drawn to the area because of its rivers, pleasant climate, and rural ambience, and proceeded to build haciendas and mansions that, for many, were country homes. It is now sliced through by the busy Avenida Revolución; visitors usually focus on the area from the cobblestoned Avenida de la Paz, lined with some excellent eateries, to the Ex-Convento on Avenida Revolución, and up to the Plaza San Jacinto and its famous Saturday market.

Coyoacán means "Place of the Coyotes." According to local legend, a coyote used to bring chickens to a friar who had saved the coyote from being strangled by a snake. Coyoacán was founded by Toltecs in the 10th century and later settled by the Aztecs, or Mexica. Bernal Díaz Castillo, a Spanish chronicler, wrote that there were 6,000 houses at the time of the conquest. Cortés set up headquarters in Coyoacán during his siege of Tenochtitlán and kept his famous Indian mistress La Malinche here. At one point he considered making Coyoacán his capital; many of the Spanish buildings left from the two-year period during which Mexico City was built still stand.

Coyoacán has had many illustrious residents from Mexico's rich and intellectual elite, including Miguel de la Madrid, president of Mexico from 1982 to 1988; artists Diego Rivera, Frida Kahlo, and José Clemente Orozco; Gabriel Figueroa, cinematographer for Luis Buñuel and John Huston; film star Dolores del Río; film director El Indio Fernández; and writers Carlos Monsiváis, Jorge Ibargüengoitia, and Nobel laureate Octavio Paz. It's also the neighborhood where the exiled Leon Trotsky met his violent death. Coyoacán's streets buzz with activity, and it has a popular food market, the Mercado Xicotencatl. On weekends families flock to its attractive *zócalo* (central square), second in importance and popularity only to the Zócalo downtown.

*Numbers in the text correspond to numbers in the margin and on the San Ángel and Coyoacán map.*

**a good tour**

Weekends are best for exploring the southern part of the city. Take the metro to M. A. de Quevedo and walk west down Arenal or take a taxi or pesero down Avenida Insurgentes and get off at the **Monumento al General Álvaro Obregón** ▶, the somber gray granite monument marking the spot where the reformer Obregón was gunned down by a religious zealot in 1928. Cross Insurgentes to walk up the cobblestoned, restaurant-lined Avenida de la Paz. Next cross Avenida Revolución, and take the crooked street that leads upwards to the left of the little park until you come to San Ángel's center, **Plaza San Jacinto** ㉖. Stroll to the **Centro Cultural Isidro Favela** ㉗ on the north side of the plaza and, if it's a Saturday, head farther north for arts and crafts at the **Bazar Sábado**.

Retrace your steps on Avenida de la Paz, to Avenida Revolución and Plaza del Carmen, which lies at the corner of Calle Monasterio. Inside is the colonial **Ex-Convento del Carmen** ㉘. Then take Avenida Revolución one long block north past a flower market to see the modern Mexican and European works at the **Museo de Arte Carrillo Gil** ㉙ (known as the Carrillo Gil). Unless you have plenty of energy, get a taxi to take you up Avenida Altavista to the **Museo Casa Estudio Diego Rivera y Frida Kahlo** ㉚ (and to an elegant lunch in the San Ángel Inn or Il Fornaio).

The next part of the tour goes to Coyoacán, which extends east of Avenida Insurgentes about 1 km (½ mi) from San Ángel. You're best off taking a taxi to the **Plaza de Santa Catarina** on Avenida Francisco Sosa, about halfway into the center of Coyoacán.

The pretty 16th-century Iglesia de Santa Catarina dominates this tiny plaza. It contains a bust of Mexican historian Francisco Sosa. Across the street is the **Casa de Jesús Reyes Heroles**; the former home of the

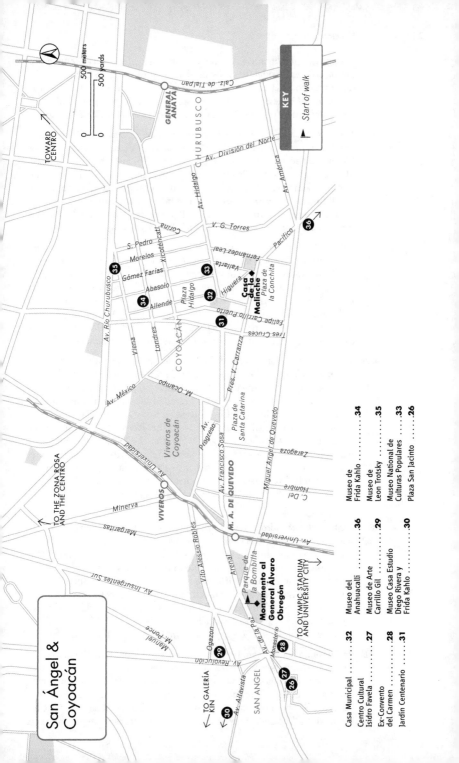

# San Ángel & Coyoacán

500 meters
500 yards

TOWARD CENTRO

Calz. de Tlalpan

GENERAL ANAYA

Av. División del Norte

CHURUBUSCO

Av. Hidalgo

Av. América

Corina

S. Pedro

Xicoténcatl

Morelos

Gómez Farías

Abasolo

Allende

Río Churubusco

Viena

Londres

Av. México

M. Ocampo

COYOACÁN

V. G. Torres

Pacífico

Fernández Leal

Vallarta

Higuera

Plaza Hidalgo

Plaza de la Conchita

Casa de la Malinche

Felipe Carrillo Puerto

Pres. V. Carranza

Tres Cruces

Av. Progreso

Plaza de Santa Catarina

Zaragoza

Miguel Ángel de Quevedo

C. Del Hombre

Av. Francisco Sosa

Viveros de Coyoacán

Av. Universidad

Minerva

Margaritas

VIVEROS

TO THE ZONA ROSA AND THE CENTRO

M. A. DE QUEVEDO

Av. Universidad

TO OLYMPIC STADIUM AND UNIVERSITY CITY

Vto. Alessio Robles

Arenal

Av. de la Paz

Monasterio

Parque de la Bombilla

Monumento al General Álvaro Obregón

Av. Insurgentes Sur

Manuel M. Ponce

Ogazon

Av. Revolución

SAN ÁNGEL

TO GALERÍA KIN

Av. Altavista

Casa Municipal . . . . . . . . **32**
Centro Cultural
Isidro Favela . . . . . . . . . **27**
Ex-Convento
del Carmen . . . . . . . . . **28**
Jardín Centenario . . . . . **31**

Museo del
Anahuacalli . . . . . . . . . **36**
Museo de Arte
Carrillo Gil . . . . . . . . . **29**
Museo Casa Estudio
Diego Rivera y
Frida Kahlo . . . . . . . . . **30**

Museo de
Frida Kahlo . . . . . . . . . **34**
Museo de
Leon Trotsky . . . . . . . . **35**
Museo National de
Culturas Populares . . . **33**
Plaza San Jacinto . . . . . **26**

ex-minister of education is a fine example of 20th-century architecture on the colonial model. It's now used as a cultural center. Continue east on Francisco Sosa and you'll pass **Casa de Diego de Ordaz** at the corner of Tres Cruces. This *mudéjar* (Spanish-Arabic) structure, adorned with inlaid tiles, was the home of a former captain in Cortés's army.

Now you're standing at the entrance of the **Jardín Centenario** ③. The Templo de San Juan Bautista and the **Casa Municipal** ㉜ sit in the larger **Plaza Hidalgo** adjacent to and east of this square. Walk two blocks southeast of Plaza Hidalgo on Calle Higuera, perhaps popping in for a beer at the traditional La Guadalupana cantina, to the corner of Calle Vallarta, where you'll find the **Casa de la Malinche.** The house, darkened with age, faces a picturesque cobbled square called Plaza de la Conchita, which has a tiny, ornate church that Mexican girls long to wed in.

Take Vallarta up from the plaza until you reach Avenida Hidalgo; hang a left and you'll soon find yourself opposite the entrance to the colorful **Museo Nacional de Culturas Populares** ㉝. Retrace your steps to Plaza Hidalgo and walk five blocks north on Calle Allende to the corner of Calle Londres and the **Museo de Frida Kahlo** ㉞. It's linked both historically and romantically with the fortresslike **Museo de Leon Trotsky** ㉟, east of it on Londres, then two long blocks north on Morelos. If you have time, hop in a taxi and head south to the **Museo del Anahuacalli** ㊱.

TIMING You're likely to want to linger in these elegant and beautiful sections of town, especially in Coyoacán. The Frida Kahlo and Leon Trotsky museums give intense, intimate looks at the lives of two famous people who were friends and lovers, and who breathed their personalities into the places where they lived. Allow at least an hour at each. The other museums are much smaller and merit less time. Remember that museums close on Monday. Weekends are liveliest at the Plaza Hidalgo and its neighboring Jardín Centenario (usually referred to as *la plaza* or *el zócalo*), where street life explodes into a fiesta with balloons, clowns, cotton candy, live music, and hypnotic dancing to the sound of drums. On weekends, Plaza Hidalgo hosts a crafts market.

## What to See

SAN ÁNGEL **Centro Cultural Isidro Favela.** Formerly known as La Casa del Risco (the ㉗ Risco House), this 1681 mansion is one of the prettiest houses facing the Plaza San Jacinto. A huge free-form fountain sculpture—exploding with colorful porcelain, tiles, shells, and mosaics—covers the entire eastern wall of its patio. Although it's not ranked among the city's top museums, it has a splendid collection of 17th- and 18th-century European and colonial Mexican paintings. Temporary art exhibitions also rotate through. ⊠ *Plaza San Jacinto 15, San Ángel* ☎ *55/5616–2711* ☒ *Free* ⊙ *Tues.–Sun. 10–5* Ⓜ *M.A. de Quevedo.*

㉘ **Ex-Convento del Carmen.** Erected by Carmelite friars with the help of an Indian chieftain between 1615 and 1628, this convent and church, with its tile-covered domes, fountains, and gardens, is one of the most interesting examples of colonial religious architecture in this part of the city. The church still operates, but the convent is the **Museo Regional del Carmen,** with a fine collection of 16th- to 18th-century religious paintings and icons. Another museum area, the well-designed **Novohispana**, illustrates life in New Spain with work by early colonial artisans and trade guilds. This exhibit has a separate entrance at the back. It's also worth visiting the 12 mummified corpses tucked away in the crypt. ⊠ *Av. Revolución 4, at Monasterio, San Ángel* ☎ *55/5616–2816 or 55/5616–1177* 🖃 *$3.20* ⊘ *Tues.–Sun. 10–5* Ⓜ *M. A. de Quevedo.*

**㉙ Museo de Arte Carrillo Gil.** Considerably superior in terms of design and natural lighting to the city's Museo Nacional de Arte Moderno, this private collection contains early murals by Orozco, Rivera, and Siqueiros; works by modern European artists such as Klee and Picasso; and temporary exhibitions of young Mexican artists. ⊠ *Av. Revolución 1608, at Av. Altavista, San Ángel* ☎ *55/5550–1254* ⊕ *www.mach.inba.gov. mx* 🖃 *$1.50* ⊘ *Tues.–Sun. 10–6* Ⓜ *M.A. de Quevedo.*

**㉚ Museo Casa Estudio Diego Rivera y Frida Kahlo.** Some of Rivera's last paintings are still resting here on ready easels, and his denim jacket and shoes sit on a wicker chair, waiting. The museum that once was home to Diego Rivera and his artist wife, Frida Kahlo, appears as if the two could return at any moment to continue work. Architect Juan O'Gorman, who designed the 1931 building, was a close friend of Rivera. His work reflects his philosophy of progressive socialism and shows the influence of Le Corbusier and other European modernists; the house is now one of the city's architectural landmarks. ⊠ *Calle Diego Rivera, at Av. Altavista, San Ángel* ☎ *55/5616–0996, 55/5550–1518 or 55/5550–1189* 🖃 *$1* ⊘ *Tues.–Sun. 10–6.*

**Museo Soumaya.** This small museum has four rooms, each with a distinct theme. The first has an exhibit of 18th- and 19th-century Mexican portraiture, the second the art of New Spain, including 18th-century ironwork. The Julián Slim Gallery has over 100 sculptures by Auguste Rodin in marble, bronze, terra-cotta, and plaster. The last room has a collection of works from painters like Pierre Renoir, Camille Claudelle, and Paul Gauguin on display. The entrance and exit halls feature 1954 murals by Rufino Tamayo. ⊠ *Avenida Revolución at Rio Magdalena (Eje 10 Sur), San Ángel* ☎ *55/5616–3731 or 55/5616–6620* ⊕ *www. soumaya.com.mx* 🖃 *$1* ⊘ *Wed. 10:30–10:30, Thurs.–Mon. 10:30–6:30.*

**★ ㉖ Plaza San Jacinto.** This welcoming plaza with a grisly history constitutes the heart of San Ángel. In 1847 about 50 Irish soldiers of St. Patrick's Battalion, who had sided with the Mexicans in the Mexican-American War, had their foreheads branded here with the letter *D*—for deserter—and were then hanged by the Americans. These men had been enticed to swim the Río Grande, deserting the ranks of U.S. General Zachary Taylor, by pleas to the historic and religious ties between Spain and Ireland. As settlers in Mexican Texas, they felt their allegiance lay with Catholic Mexico, and they were among the bravest fighters in the war. A memorial plaque (on a building on the plaza's west side) lists their names and expresses Mexico's gratitude for their help in the "unjust North American invasion." Off to one side of the plaza, the excellent arts and crafts market, **Bazar Sábado**, is held all day Saturday. ⊠ *Between Miramon, Cda. Santisima, Dr. Galvez, and Calle Madero, San Ángel* Ⓜ *M.A. de Quevedo.*

COYOACÁN   **Casa de la Malinche.** This somber-looking residence was the home of La Malinche, Cortés's Indian mistress and interpreter, whom the Spaniards called Doña María and the Indians called Malintzín. La Malinche aided the conquest by enabling Cortés to communicate with the Nahuatl-speaking tribes he met en route to Tenochtitlán. Today she is a reviled Mexican symbol of a traitorous xenophile—hence the term *malinchista,* used to describe a Mexican who prefers things foreign. Legend says that Cortés's wife died in this house, poisoned by the conquistador. The house is not open to the public. ⊠ *2 blocks east of Plaza Hidalgo on Calle Higuera at Vallarta, Coyoacán* Ⓜ *M.A. de Quevedo.*

**㉜ Casa Municipal (Casa de Cortés).** The place where the Aztec emperor Cuauhtémoc was held prisoner by Cortés is reputed to have been rebuilt in the 18th century from the stones of his original house by one of Cortés's descendants. Now a sandy color and topped by two coyote figures, it's used for municipal government offices; a small tourist bureau at the entrance offers maps and leaflets publicizing cultural events in the area. Usually you can wander through the wide arches to the pretty tile patio. ⊠ *Plaza Hidalgo 1 between Calles Carillo Puerto and Allende, Coyoacán* ☎ *55/5658–0221* ☉ *Daily 8–8.*

**㉛ Jardín Centenario.** The Centenary Gardens are barely separated from the Plaza Hidalgo by a narrow slow-moving road; both squares are referred to as Coyoacán's zócalo. The Jardín, with its shading trees, a fountain with two snarling coyotes, and a fringe of outdoor cafés, is the place to sit and people-watch. On weekends from 11 AM until about 10 PM it morphs into a lively, hippie-ish handicrafts market, complete with drummers and palm readings. The larger Plaza Hidalgo hosts children's funfairs, amateur musical and dance performances, clowns, bubble blowers, cotton candy, and balloon sellers on weekends and national holidays. It's studded with an ornate old bandstand and the impressive **Templo de San Juan Bautista,** one of the first churches to be built in New Spain. It was completed in 1582, and its door has a baroque arch. During the afternoon of September 15, before the crowds become suffocating at nightfall, this delightful neighborhood zócalo is probably the best place in the capital to enjoy Independence Day celebrations. ⊠ *Between Calle Centenario, Av. Hidalgo, and Caballo Calco, Coyoacán* Ⓜ *Viveros.*

> **need a break?**
>
> Just outside of the Jardín Hidalgo, grab a coffee at **El Jarocho Cafe** (⊠ Cuauhtémoc 134, at Allende, Coyoacán ☎ 55/5658–5029 or 55/5554–5418 ⊠ Av. México 25-C, at Guerrero, Coyoacán ⊠ Centenario 91-B, between Xicotencatl and Malintzin, Coyoacán ⊕ www.cafeeljarocho.com.mx). The Cuauhtémoc branch has been on this corner since 1957, originally selling coffee, mangos, and other items from Veracruz (in Mexico, *jarocho* means "native of Veracruz"). In recent years, demand has grown for this excellent coffee and this corner has become a favorite spot for locals to get their caffeine fix and a front-row seat to people-watching. If you're lucky enough to find a space on the outside benches on the weekends, it's a good place watch the hip Coyoacán crowd walk by and to take a look at the vendors who set up shop here, selling jewelry and art crafts in makeshift stands

on the street and on the top of their cars. With the success of the original locale, there are now a few other branches, but the original is still the most popular—and the best place to get a feel for Coyoacán.

**36** **Museo del Anahuacalli.** Diego Rivera built his own museum for the thousands of pre-Columbian artifacts he collected over the years. The third-floor studio that Rivera did not live long enough to use displays sketches for some of his most controversial murals. The huge dark-gray building, constructed in the 1950s from volcanic rock, resembles an above-ground tomb. If you visit between October and the end of December you'll see one of the city's finest altars to the dead in honor of Rivera himself. ⊠ *Calle del Museo 150, Coyoacán, Col. San Pablo Tepetlapa* ☎ *55/5617–4310 or 55/5617–3797* ⊡ *$3 (includes admission to Museo de Frida Kahlo)* ☉ *Tues.–Sun. 10–6.*

**34** **Museo de Frida Kahlo.** Kahlo has become a sort of cult figure, not only

Fodor'sChoice because of her paintings—55 of 143 are self-portraits—but also because

★ of her bohemian lifestyle and flamboyant individualism. The "Blue House" where she was born in 1907 (not 1910, as she wanted people to believe) and died 47 years later, is both museum and shrine. Kahlo's astounding vitality and originality are reflected in the house, from the giant papier-mâché skeletons outside and the *retablos* (small religious paintings on tin) on the staircase to the gloriously decorated kitchen and the bric-a-brac in her bedroom. You can admire her early sketches, diary entries, tiny outfits, wheelchair at the easel, plus her four-poster bed conveniently fitted with mirror above. Even if you know nothing about Kahlo, a visit to the museum will leave you with a strong, visceral impression of this pivotal feminist artist. ⊠ *Londres 247, at Calle Allende, Coyoacán* ☎ *55/5554–5999* ⊡ *$3 (includes admission to Museo del Anahuacalli)* ☉ *Tues.–Sun. 10–5:45* Ⓜ *Viveros.*

**35** **Museo de Leon Trotsky.** Resembling an anonymous and forbidding fortress, with turrets for armed guards, this house is where Leon Trotsky lived and was murdered. It's difficult to believe that it's the final resting place for the ashes of one of the most important figures of the Russian Revolution, but that only adds to the allure of this austere dwelling, which is owned by Trotsky's grandson. Anyone taller than 5 feet must stoop to pass through doorways to Trotsky's bedroom—with bullet holes still in the walls from the first assassination attempt, in which the muralist Siqueiros was implicated—his wife's study, the dining room, and the study where assassin Ramón Mercader—a man of many aliases—allegedly drove a pickax into Trotsky's head. On his desk, cluttered with writing paraphernalia and an article he was revising in Russian, the calendar is open to that fateful day, August 20, 1940. All informative materials are in Spanish only. ⊠ *Río Churubusco 410, Coyoacán* ☎ *55/5658–8732* ⊡ *$3* ☉ *Tues.–Sun. 10–5* Ⓜ *Viveros.*

**33** **Museo Nacional de Culturas Populares.** A huge *arbol de la vida* (tree of life) sculpture stands in the courtyard of this museum devoted to popular culture and regional arts and crafts. Its exhibitions and events are nicely varied, including children's workshops, traditional musical concerts, and dance performances. On weekends the courtyard becomes a

# CloseUp

# FRIDA KAHLO, A RIBBON AROUND A BOMB

O F COURSE, HE DOES PRETTY WELL for a little boy, but it is I who am the big artist."

Frida Kahlo's tongue-in-cheek comment about her husband to the Detroit News in 1933 seems less and less a joke as the years go by. This petite painter, who has gained international recognition since the 1980s for her colorful but pained self-portraits, has begun to overshadow the massive muralist Diego Rivera. Considered one of the 20th-century's major artistic figures, Rivera created images—especially those rounded peasant women with braided hair, arms brim-full of creamy lilies—that have typified this country for more than a half century. The bizarre Beauty-and-the-Beast dynamics and sordid drama of the couple's relationship ensure the popularity of many of Mexico's museums and murals. But, if Diego dwarfed Frida in stature, he no longer does in fame.

Now, Kahlo's hauntingly beautiful face, broken body, and bright Tehuana costumes, along with a few exotic accessories such as monkeys, parrots, and hairless dogs, have become the trademark of Mexican femininity. Life-size cardboard cutouts with her bat-wing brows, moustache, and clunky ethnic earrings are as familiar here as Marilyn's pout and puffed-up white dress are in the U.S.

In fact, Frida didn't even need to paint to make it into the history books. The controversy and scandal that surrounded her two marriages to Diego include his affair with her younger sister—the same year Frida suffered a third miscarriage and had toes removed from her right foot—and her affair with Communist exile Leon Trotsky. It's hard not to become mired in the tragic twists and turns of her life—from childhood polio to a tram accident that smashed her pelvis, a gangrenous foot that resulted in the amputation of a leg, as well as bouts of anorexia and alcoholism.

But she was also a groundbreaking artist who pioneered a new expressiveness, and her unique iconography of suffering transcended self-pity to create an existential art. Kahlo was the first Latin American woman to have a painting in the Louvre; her work caused a storm in Paris in 1939 (at an exhibition entitled Méxique), and the surrealists claimed it as supremely illustrative of their ideas. It was André Breton who described her art as "a ribbon around a bomb."

Frida, who was always frank about her start in painting—she did it to kill time in one of her many convalescences—had doubts that her paintings were surrealist, saying, "they are the most frank expression of myself." Later she expressed unease with her art for not being suitable to serve the aims of the Communist Party, of which she and Diego were avid supporters. Her husband was more generous, emphasizing how the influence of the religious retablo (ex-voto) that Frida collected was transformed in her art to an exploration of the permanent miracle of life.

And Frida tried hard to be as much the revolutionary as the icon of Mexican femininity. Her last public appearance was 11 days before her death, in a wheelchair at Diego's side, protesting the intervention of the United States in Guatemala.

— Barbara Kastelein

small craft and sweets market. The museum shop stocks art books and high-quality crafts. ✉ *Av. Hidalgo 289, at Calle Allende, Coyoacán* ☎ *55/ 9172–8840* ⊕ *www.cnca.gob.mx/cnca/popul/mncp.htm* 🖃 *Free* ☉ *Tues.–Thurs. 10–6, Fri.–Sun. 10–8* Ⓜ *Viveros.*

# OUTSKIRTS OF MEXICO CITY

As the capital continues to expand, many attractions that used to be side trips are becoming more accessible. To the north of Mexico City stands the Basílica de Guadalupe, a church dedicated to Mexico's patron saint. It can be enjoyed in a half-day tour; if you get an early start, you could combine your visit with a jaunt to the pyramids of Teotihuacán in the afternoon. Xochimilco (pronounced kso-chee-*meel*-co), famous for its floating gardens, lies on the southern outskirts of the city. You can ride in gondola-like boats and get a fleeting sense of a pre-Hispanic Mexico City. The western extremes of the capital offer the popular Parque Nacional Desierto de los Leones—a forested national park with a Carmelite monastery in its center.

## La Villa de Guadalupe

*North of the Zócalo.*

"La Villa"—the local moniker of the site of the two basilicas of the Virgin of Guadalupe—is Mexico's holiest shrine. Its importance derives from the miracle that the devout believe transpired here on December 12, 1531: an Aztec named Juan Diego received from the Virgin a cloak permanently imprinted with her image so he could prove to the priests that he had had a holy vision. The image has become a nationalist symbol of tremendous power and persistence. Although the story of the miracle and the cloak itself have been challenged for centuries, they are hotly defended by clergy and laity alike. As author Gary Wills observed, the story's "authority just grows as its authenticity diminishes." Every December 12, millions of pilgrims arrive, many crawling on their knees for the last few hundred yards, praying for cures and other divine favors. Outside the **Antigua Basílica** stands a statue of Juan Diego, who became the first indigenous saint in the Americas with his canonization in summer 2002. (This canonization was widely seen as a shrewd move on the part of the Catholic church as it tries to retain its position, particularly among Mexico's indigenous population.) The old basilica dates from 1536; various additions have been made since then. The altar was executed by sculptor Manuel Tolsá. The basilica now houses a museum of ex-votos (hand-painted depictions of miracles, dedicated to Mary or a saint in thanks) and popular religious art, paintings, sculpture, and decorative and applied arts from the 15th through 18th centuries.

Because the structure of the Antigua Basílica had weakened over the years and the building was no longer large enough or safe enough to accommodate all the worshipers, Pedro Ramírez Vázquez, the architect responsible for Mexico City's splendid Museo Nacional de Antropología, was commissioned to design a new shrine, consecrated in 1976. In this case, alas, the architect's inspiration failed him: the **Nueva Basílica** is a gigantic, circular mass of wood, steel, and polyethylene that feels like a stadium rather than a church. The famous image of the Virgin is encased high up in its altar at the back and can be viewed from a moving sidewalk that passes below. The holiday itself is a great time to visit if you don't mind crowds; it's celebrated with various kinds of music and dancers. Remember to bring some water with you; you'll need it in the crush. ⊠ *Paseo Zumarraga, Atrio de América, Col. Villa de Guadalupe* ☎ *55/5577–3654* ☉ *Daily 6 AM–9 PM.*

## Xochimilco

*21 km (13 mi) south of Mexico City center.*

When the first nomadic settlers arrived in the Valley of Mexico, they found an enormous lake. As the years went by and their population grew, the land could no longer satisfy their agricultural needs. They solved the problem by devising a system of *chinampas* (floating gardens), rectangular structures akin to barges, which they filled with reeds, branches, and mud. They planted the barges with willows, whose roots anchored the floating gardens to the lake bed, making a labyrinth of small islands and canals on which vendors carried flowers and produce grown on the chinampas to market.

Today Xochimilco is the only place in Mexico where the gardens still exist. Go on a Saturday, when the *tianguis* (market stalls) are most active, or, though it's crowded, on a Sunday. On weekdays the place is practically deserted, so it loses some of its charm. Hire a *trajinera* (flower-painted boat); an arch over each spells out its name in flowers. As you sail through the canals, you'll pass mariachis and women selling tacos from other trajineras.

**Fodor'sChoice** ★ People also flock to Xochimilco for the **Museo Dolores Olmedo Patino,** which holds a superb collection of paintings by Frida Kahlo and the largest private collection of works by Kahlo's husband, the flamboyant muralist Diego Rivera. The museum was established by Olmedo, his lifelong model, patron, and onetime mistress. The lavish display of nearly 140 pieces from his cubist, post-cubist, and mural periods hangs in a magnificent 17th-century hacienda with beautiful gardens. Concerts and entertainment for children are held on weekends, while gaggles of geese and strutting peacocks add to the clamor. This is also the place to see the strange Mexican hairless dog: Ms. Olmedo shares Rivera's passion for these creatures and keeps a few as pets on the grounds. The museum also has works by Rivera's common-law wife, Angelina Beloff. There is a lovely small café in a glassed-in gazebo, good for a cup of coffee or a more substantial meal. The museum is very easy to get to by public transportation; at the Tasqueña metro station, catch the light rail to La Noria (*not* Xochimilco). As you exit the light rail station, cross the street via the the stairway bridge. Walk half a block on 20 de Noviembre until you come to a traffic intersection. Without crossing the street, turn left at this intersection and continue walking down this street (signs will read Antiguo Camino a Xochimilco or Av. Mexico) for two blocks. ⊠ *Av. México 5843* ☎ *55/5555–1016* ⊕ *www.mdop.org.mx* ⊠ *$3, free Tues.* ☉ *Tues.–Sun. 10–6.*

## Parque Nacional Desierto de los Leones

*25 km (16 mi) west of Mexico City center.*

The "Desert of Lions" owes its name to a quarrel in colonial days over land ownership by brothers called "León." Several walking trails criss-cross this 5,000-acre national park's pine forest at 7,511 feet above sea level. Pack a lunch and enjoy it at one of the picnic tables. The park's focal point is the ruined 17th-century **ex-monastery of the Carmelites,** isolated amid an abundance of greenery; it's open Tuesday through Sunday from 9 to 5 and entrance costs 50¢. The park played a signifi-cant role in the War of Independence: in late October 1810, at a spot called **Las Cruces,** Father Hidalgo's troops trounced the Spaniards but resolved not to go on to attack Mexico City, an error that cost the in-surgents 10 more years of fighting.

## Outskirts of Mexico City A to Z

### BUS TRAVEL
Some tour companies offer combination visits to La Villa de Guadalupe and Teotihuacán. Ask at your hotel.

### CAR TRAVEL
To get to **La Villa de Guadalupe,** take Paseo de la Reforma Norte until it forks into Calzada de Guadalupe, which leads directly to the shrine.

Driving to **Xochimilco** doesn't make sense as it's so easily reached via public transportation, but if you must drive, take Periférico Sur to the extension of División del Norte. The trip should take between 45 min-utes and one hour, depending on traffic. (Alternatively, you could take a taxi, but it could cost you up to $25.)

For **Parque Nacional Desierto de los Leones,** follow Paseo de la Reforma all the way west. It eventually merges with the Carretera Libre at Toluca, and after 20 km (12 mi), you'll see signs for the turnoff; it's another 10 km (6 mi) to the park.

### SUBWAY TRAVEL
You can reach **La Villa de Guadalupe** by taking the No. 3 metro line from downtown to Deportivo 18 de Marzo. Here, change to line No. 6 in the direction Martin Carrera, getting off at La Villa–Basílica stop.

For Xochimilco take metro line No. 2 to Tasqueña; here hop on the *tren ligero* ("light" train) that continues south to Xochimilco. Expect a bit of a free-for-all outside the station, as several guides—often on bicycles—will be waiting to direct tourists to the gardens. Official tour guides, em-ployed by the government, wear identifying tags; any other guides offering to take people to the gardens take them to a specific *trajinera* (flower-painted boat) rental business that pays them for bringing in clients. You can cast your lot with a guide (official or not) or catch any bus marked Xochimilco; they usually pick up passengers right outside the train sta-tion. Taking a taxi is not recommended. To walk to the nearest trajin-era *embarcadero* (dock), head down Cuauhtémoc for three blocks, then make a left on Violeta. Continue on Violeta for two blocks (you'll see signs pointing toward "Belen," the embarcadero), and turn right off of Violeta at Nezahualcóyotl.

# WHERE TO EAT

Mexico City has been a culinary capital ever since the time of Moctezuma. Chronicles tell of the extravagant banquets prepared for the Aztec emperor with more than 300 different dishes served for every meal.

Today's Mexico City is a gastronomic melting pot with some 15,000 restaurants. You'll find everything from simple family-style eateries and cantinas to five-star world-class restaurants. The number and range of international restaurants is growing and diversifying—although Spanish, Italian, and Argentine restaurants are dominant.

Mexico City restaurants open 7–11 AM for breakfast (*el desayuno*) and 1–6 for lunch (*la comida*)—although it's rare for Mexicans to eat lunch before 2 and you are likely to feel lonely if you arrive at a popular restaurant before then. Lunch is an institution in this country, often lasting two hours, and until nightfall on Sundays. Consequently, evening meals may often be very light, consisting of sweet bread and coffee or traditional *tamales* and *atole* at home, or a salad and tacos or an appetizer in a restaurant.

When dining, most locals start out at 9 PM for dinner (*la cena*); restaurants stay open until 11:30 during the week and a little later on weekends. Many restaurants are open only for lunch on Sunday. At deluxe restaurants, dress is generally formal (jacket at least), and reservations are almost always advised; see reviews for details. If you're short on time, you can always head to American-style coffee shops (VIPS, Denny's, and Sanborns) or recognizable fast-food chains that offer the tired but reliable fare of burgers, fried chicken, and pizza all over the city; many are open 24 hours.

The popular *Cafe Chino* (Chinese cafés) all over town are a cheap and hearty option for a quick bite. Asian cuisine is still limited here, but you will find some good Japanese and a few real Chinese restaurants. Similarly, there are very few vegetarian restaurants, but you will have no trouble finding nonmeat dishes wherever you grab a bite. Vegans, however, will have a more difficult time as even many meatless dishes are often prepared using lard.

Hygiene practices in food preparation are improving greatly as establishments learn about catering to foreign tourists with more vulnerable stomachs. The Distintivo H, a rigorous standard for disinfection and cleanliness, is an important step in the right direction. It's backed by the Tourism Ministry, and numerous upper-end restaurants are striving to meet its specifications. However, along with the tap water, you should avoid sauces that have fresh tomatoes or cilantro and dishes garnished with lettuce shreds.

# LA COCINA MEXICANA

TO ENTERTAIN THE NOTION that Mexican food is little more than tacos, enchiladas, and burritos would be culinary blasphemy. Regional cooking is the heart and soul of Mexico, multiplied by the republic's 32 states and the provinces within them. Recipes are passed down through generations and labor-intensive preparation requires much patience and loving care. With the staples—rice, beans, chilies, and corn—chefs are turning out ever more sophisticated variations on national dishes.

Maize, which was discovered in Mexico, was sacred to the Indians, who have innumerable ways of preparing it—from faithful tortillas and tamales (cornmeal wrapped in banana leaves or corn husks) to tostadas (lightly fried, open tortillas topped with meat, lettuce, and the like) and tacos (tortillas briefly heated, filled, and wrapped into slim cylinders). Pozole (made with hominy) is a delicious pork-based soup. The sweet, corn-based drink atole is a favorite breakfast or before-bed treat.

You'll find fish not just on the coasts but also in the lake regions around Guadalajara and in the state of Michoacán. Huachinango (red snapper), abalone, crab, and swordfish are all popular. And ceviche—raw fish marinated in lime juice then topped with chopped chilies, onions, and cilantro—is almost a national dish; just make sure it's fresh. Shrimp, lobster, and oysters can be huge and succulent; bear in mind the folk adage and eat oysters only in months with names that contain the letter r. Likewise avoid raw shellfish wherever cholera or water pollution might be a risk.

Mexicans love beef, pork, and barbacoa (barbecued lamb) with a variety of sauces. The complex, spicy mole is one of Mexico's proudest culinary inventions; its

ingredients can number more than 100, including chilies, pumpkin seeds or nuts, and in some cases, cacao. It is usually served over chicken or turkey.

Fresh fruits and vegetables are another Mexican pleasure. Jicama, papaya, mamey, avocado, mango, guayaba, squash, and tomatoes are just some of the produce native to Mexico. (All fresh produce should be washed in water with a commercial disinfectant. For this reason, avoid eating produce at street stalls and beware of uncooked herbs such as cilantro).

Other Mexican specialties are less common abroad: chilaquiles (tortilla strips scrambled with chilies, tomatoes, onions, cream, and cheese), and chiles en nogada (a large poblano chili stuffed with beef or cheese, raisins, onion, olives, and almonds and topped with a creamy walnut sauce and pomegranate seeds). Soups are hearty—particularly pozole, sopa azteca (avocado, chicken chunks, and tortilla in a broth), and don't forget to try the lighter sopa de flor de calabaza (squash–flower soup) or, if you get a chance, sopa de colorin, made from a bright red flower.

The astonishing assortment of breads, sweets, beers, wines (which are fast improving), and agave-based (cactus-related) liquors goes on and on. Sadly, shortage of the blue agave has caused tequila prices to soar, so watch out for cheap varieties that add sugarcane liquor or less digestible substances. Freshly squeezed fruit juices and fruit shakes (licuados) are safe to drink—if ordered in a restaurant with hygienic practices—and taste heavenly.

Colonia Polanco, the upscale neighborhood on the edge of the Bosque de Chapultepec, has some of the best and most expensive dining (and lodging) in the city. Zona Rosa restaurants get filled pretty quickly on Saturday night, especially on Saturdays coinciding with most people's paydays: the 1st and 15th of each month. The same is true of San Ángel, whereas the Condesa neighborhood buzzes with a younger crowd Thursday to Saturday.

| | | WHAT IT COSTS | | | |
|---|---|---|---|---|---|
| | $$$$ | $$$ | $$ | $ | ¢ |
| AT DINNER | over $25 | $15–$25 | $10–$15 | $5–$10 | under $5 |

Prices are per person for a main course, excluding tax and tip.

## Argentine

**$–$$$** ✕ **Cambalache.** If you come with a few people to this ever-busy beef-lover's dream, try the Super Lomo Cambalache, a steak big enough for three or four people. Or try the Don Ignacio, a boneless chicken breast served in a mushroom sauce with pineapple and fresh sweet peppers. And why not sink your fork into the potato soufflé, a house specialty. ⊠ *Arquímedes 85, Col. Polanco* ☎ *55/5280–2080 or 55/5282–2922* ⊟ *AE, MC, V.*

**$–$$$** ✕ **Entrevero.** A Uruguayan may own this friendly eatery on the square of Coyoacán, but all Argentine attractions appear on the menu—the scrumptious *provoleta* (grilled provolone cheese with oregano) among them. Entrevero is also one of the few restaurants in the capital where you will find good pizza, calzones, and gnocchi, and the *crema quemada* (a version of crème brûlée) is sinful. Fair prices and the excellent location guarantee it is always busy, so arrive a little early on weekends to get a table. ⊠ *Jardín Centenario 14-C, Col. Coyoacán* ☎ *55/5659–0066* ⊟ *AE, MC, V* ☺ *No dinner Sun.*

**$–$$$** ✕ **Rincón Argentino.** This established Argentine restaurant is known as much for its decor as for its exquisite cuts of beef. The ceiling is painted to resemble the sky, the bar is covered by a thatch roof, and the dining areas call to mind a stone-and-wood lodge. Most Argentines prefer their beef *bien cocida* (well done), but you can have it any way you like. ⊠ *Av. Presidente Masaryk 177, Col. Polanco* ☎ *55/5531–8617 or 55/5254–8775* ⊟ *AE, MC, V* ☺ *No dinner Sun.*

**$–$$$** ✕ **La Taba.** Smart yet unpretentious, this restaurant in the south of the city is characterized by its generous portions of top-quality beef, done perfectly to your choice of five options—from rare to well done. The flavorful *chistorra* (a semicured chorizo-type sausage) stands out from the wide range of starters; vegetarians can choose from soups, pastas, and salads. The *bife de chorizo* (rump steak) is unforgettable, and big eaters might find room for one of the traditional Argentine desserts. ⊠ *Av. Revolución 1398, Col. Guadalupe Inn* ☎ *55/5662–3165 or 55/5662–2670* ⊟ *AE, MC, V* ☺ *No dinner Sun.*

## Chinese

**$$–$$$** ✕ **Chez Wok.** Above an elegant ladies' boutique on the corner of posh Polanco's Avenida Mazaryk and Tennyson, two Chinese chefs trained in Hong Kong prepare an extensive, excellent menu. Start with exotic frogs' legs Mandarin-style, served with lychees and shiitake mushrooms and steamed in lotus leaves. Three can share a hot pot of leg of venison with bamboo shoots in oyster sauce. A business crowd generates a lively lunchtime bustle. ✉ *Tennyson 117, Col. Polanco* ☎ *55/5281–3410 or 55/5281–2921* ☰ *AE, MC, V.*

**$$–$$$** ✕ **Mandarin House.** Standing proudly at the head of the eateries that line San Ángel's cobbled Avenida de la Paz, this spacious restaurant offers predominantly Mandarin cuisine. The chef's specialties include *pato Pekin* (duck with plum sauce and cucumber in crepes) and *pollo mo su* (chicken with bamboo, cabbage, mushroom, and hoisin sauce). Though there's no strict dress code, you may feel more comfortable in more formal dress. ✉ *Av. de la Paz 57, San Ángel* ☎ *55/5616–4410 or 55/5616–4434* ✉ *Cofre de Perote 205-B, Col. Lomas de Chapultepec* ☎ *55/5520–9870 or 55/5540–1683* ☰ *AE, MC, V* ☾ *No dinner Sun.*

## French

★ **$$–$$$** ✕ **Au Pied de Cochon.** Open round the clock on the ground floor inside the Hotel Presidente, this fashionable bistro continues to seduce well-heeled *chilangos* with everything from oysters to oxtail. The roasted leg of pork with béarnaise sauce is the signature dish; the green-apple sorbet with Calvados is a delicate finish. The daily three-course set menu—which includes a glass of house wine—is only $22. ✉ *Campos Elíseos 218, Col. Polanco* ☎ *55/5327–7756 or 55/5327–7700* ☖ *Reservations essential* ☰ *AE, MC, V.*

★ **$$–$$$** ✕ **Le Bistro Littéraire.** At the far end of a French bookshop, La Bouquinerie, this gem is clearly run for love, not profit. Relish the aromatic escargots, couscous, duck, or moules marinières—but expect slow service. The wine list keeps in tune with the accessible prices of the cuisine. ✉ *Camino al Desierto de los Leones 40, Prolongación Altavista, between Avs. Insurgentes and Revolución, San Ángel* ☎ *55/5616–0632* ☰ *AE, MC, V* ☾ *No dinner weekends.*

**$** ✕ **Bistrot Mosaico.** You may have to wait for a table at this local-favorite restaurant, but the exquisite breads and chipotle mayonnaise that come to your table are just the start of your reward. Try the signature *terrine de berengenas* (eggplant) for a starter. The menu also lists quiche or sausage and lentils depending on whether it's sweltering or raining outside. ✉ *Av. Michoacán 10, between Avs. Amsterdam and Insurgentes, Col. Condesa* ☎ *55/5584–2932* ☰ *AE, MC, V* ☾ *No dinner Sun.*

**Fodor's**Choice ★

## Greek

**$** ✕ **Agapi Mu.** Rambunctious Greek song and dance enliven this small, friendly Greek bistro Thursday through Saturday nights. Tucked away in a snug room of a converted Colonia Condesa home, you'll hum along as you partake of the atmosphere and the *paputsáka* (stuffed eggplant),

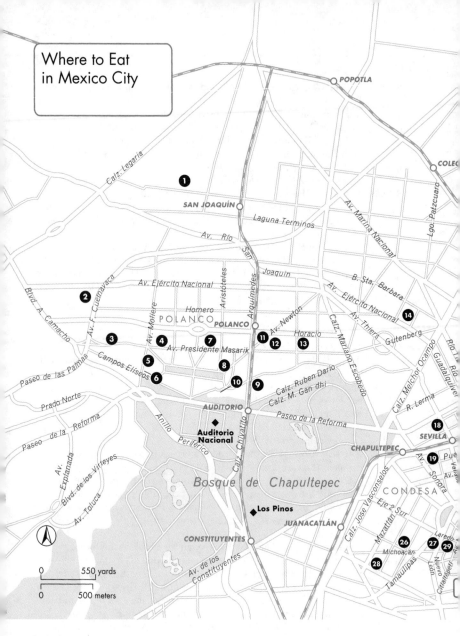

# Where to Eat in Mexico City

POPOTLA

COLEC

Calz. Legaria

SAN JOAQUÍN

Laguna Terminos

Av. Río

San Joaquín

Av. Marina Nacional

Lgo. Patzcuaro

**1**

Blvd. A. Camacho

Av. F. Cuernavaca

Av. Ejército Nacional

Aristóteles

Arquímedes

B. Sta. Barbara

Av. Ejército Nacional

Calz. Mariano Escobedo

**2**

Homero

Av. Molière

POLANCO

POLANCO

Av. Newton

Horacio

Av. Thiers

Gutenberg

**14**

**3**

**4**

**7**

Av. Presidente Masarik

**11**

**12**

**13**

Campos Elíseos

Paseo de las Palmas

**5**

**8**

Calz. Ruben Darío

Calz. M. Gandhi

R. Lerma

Calz. Melchor Ocampo

Río Tíber

Río Guadalquivir

Prado Norte

**6**

**10**

**9**

Paseo

de

la Reforma

AUDITORIO

Paseo de la Reforma

**18**

Av. Explanada

Anillo

Periférico

Auditorio Nacional

Calz. Chivatito

SEVILLA

Blvd. de los Virreyes

Av. Toluca

CHAPULTEPEC

**19** Pue

Av. Sonora

Bosque de Chapultepec

CONDESA

Calz. José Vasconcelos

Eje 2 Sur

Mazatlán

Laredo

**27** **29**

Los Pinos

JUANACATLÁN

Michoacán

**26**

León

Nuevo

Chihuahua

CONSTITUYENTES

**28**

Tamaulipas

Av. de los Constituyentes

0       550 yards

0       500 meters

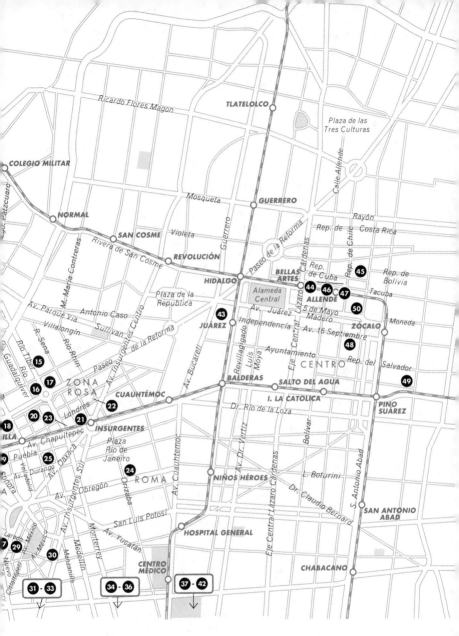

*kalamárea* (fried squid Greek-style), and *dolmádes* (stuffed grape leaves). ⊠ *Alfonso Reyes 96, between Puerto Real and Cuernavaca, Col. Condesa* ☎ *55/5286–1384* ▤ *AE, MC, V* ⊗ *No lunch Sun. and Mon.*

## International

**$$–$$$$**  ✕ **Bellini.** Revolving slowly on the 45th floor of the World Trade Center, Bellini maintains a formal, reserved atmosphere. Any effusiveness will likely be prompted by the spectacular views: romantically twinkling city lights at night and the volcanoes on a clear day. Despite the name, most dishes here aren't Italian but Mexican and international, with lobster as the house special. For a real night out on the town, order the Canadian lobster for $100 a pop. Finish in style with a flambéed dessert, such as strawberries jubilee or crêpes suzette. ⊠ *Av. de las Naciones 1, World Trade Center, 20 mins by car south of Zona Rosa, Col. Napoles* ☎ *55/5628–8305* ▤ *AE, DC, MC, V.*

**$$–$$$$**  ✕ **Hacienda de los Morales.** This Mexican institution, in a former hacienda that dates back to the 16th century, is grandly colonial in style, with dark-wood beams, huge terra-cotta expanses, and dramatic torches. You could start with the delicate walnut soup and follow with one of the chef's highlights, duck in raspberry sauce. Live trio music (three voices and guitars play Mexican ballads) completes the atmosphere. A sporty wood and brass tequila bar with over 200 brands is perfect for a pre-dinner cocktail. ⊠ *Vázquez de Mella 525, Col. Bosque Polanco* ☎ *55/5096–3000 or 55/5096–3054* ▤ *AE, DC, MC, V.*

**$$–$$$**  ✕ **El Discreto Encanto de Comer.** As the name implies, lunch certainly
FodorśChoice   achieves a discreet charm in this elegant upstairs restaurant. The 1910
★     house exemplifies Porfiriato style with its striking stucco and stained glass. The cuisine is largely French with Mexican accents; menus are available in English, but be sure to ask about daily specials. Outstanding dishes include foie gras *con salsa de pera* (with a delicate pear and pistachio sauce), Portobello carpaccio with artichoke, and a unique *camarones a tres pimientos* (shrimp stuffed with Gruyère and topped with a chili sauce touched with cinnamon). For dessert, look for strawberries sprinkled with black pepper or apricots steeped in cognac. ⊠ *Orizaba 76, Col. Roma* ☎ *55/5511–3860 or 55/5533–6074* ▤ *AE, DC, MC, V* ⊗ *No dinner Mon. and Sat. Closed Sun.*

**$–$$**  ✕ **Bellinghausen.** This cherished Zona Rosa lunch spot is one of the capital's classics. The partially covered hacienda-style courtyard at the back, set off by an ivy-laden wall, is a midday magnet for executives and tourists. A veritable army of waiters scurries back and forth serving such tried-and-true favorites as *filete chemita* (broiled steak with mashed potatoes). ⊠ *Londres 95, Zona Rosa* ☎ *55/5207–6149* ▤ *AE, DC, MC, V* ⊗ *No dinner.*

★ **$–$$**  ✕ **Bistro Charlotte.** You may get addicted to dining at this intimate neighborhood bistro, a tiny spot with only 11 tables. At lunch regulars flock here for inspired culinary surprises. Most dishes are prepared with French and Mediterranean accents, yet Thai flourishes appear with increasing regularity. You won't go wrong with the risotto and shrimp bathed in white wine and cream sauce. A small lament: there's only one Charlotte's. ✉ *Lope de Vega 341, Col. Polanco* ☎ *55/5250–4180* ▤ *MC, V* ☉ *Closed Sat. No dinner.*

★ **$–$$** ✕ **La Vinería.** A welcome addition to La Condesa, this dark, cozy restaurant and wine bar is ideal for a light meal and a sip. Try the *rollos de berenjena* (eggplant rolls) with goat cheese, nuts, and red pepper sauce, or the delicious *hojaldre con hongos* (mushroom pastry). Then indulge in a chablis, a tasty strudel, or a cigar. ✉ *Av. Fernando Montes de Oca 52-A, at Amatlán, Col. Condesa* ☎ *55/5211–9020* ▤ *AE, MC, V* ☉ *Closed Sun.*

¢–$ ✕ **Liên.** It's no wonder that in a city short on Asian food, an affordable Vietnamese restaurant in a trendy part of town would become a raging success. Liên's plain interior with cement floors is more than compensated for by the food. The restaurant strikes the right balance between Vietnamese and French cooking without being overly ambitious. Spring rolls are delicately flavored with mint and basil; the double-roasted duck with ginger sauce is so tender it falls off the bone. The place stays full until late, making it a hip spot for a wee-hours snack and drink. ✉ *Av. Tamaulipas 48, at Calle Cadereyta, Col. Condesa* ☎ *55/5553–9901 or 55/5553–9918* ▤ *AE, MC, V.*

## Italian

**$$–$$$** ✕ **Il Fornaio.** A steady stream of well-heeled diners comes here to taste *carpaccio di salmone* dressed with Belgian endive, grapefruit, cress, and a lightly citric vinegar, or enjoy an excellent *linguine ai sapori di mare* (linguine with seafood). The chef refuses to use anything but Italian ingredients; notice the authentic cheeses in dishes like the succulent veal in Gorgonzola sauce. The desserts, such as the sweet crepes (*crespelle al caffè*), are unforgettable. ✉ *Av. Altavista 192, San Ángel* ☎ *55/5616–5985* ▤ *AE, DC, MC, V* ☉ *No dinner Sun.*

**$$–$$$** ✕ **La Lanterna.** The Petterino family has run this two-story restaurant since 1966. The downstairs has the rustic feel of a northern Italian trattoria, with the cramped seating adding to the intimacy. All pastas are made on the premises; the Bolognese sauce is a favorite. Raw artichoke salad, *conejo en Salmi* (rabbit in a wine sauce), and *filete al burro nero* (steak in black butter) are all worthy dishes. ✉ *Paseo de la Reforma 458, at Toledo, Col. Juárez* ☎ *55/5207–9969* ▤ *AE, DC, MC, V* ☉ *Closed Sun. and Dec. 25–Jan. 1.*

## Japanese

**$$$–$$$$** ✕ **Ben Kay.** The silk-clad staff includes a sake sommelier in this prestigious restaurant in the Hotel Nikko. *Kaiseki* is the specialty, a series of small, exquisite dishes. The menu is organized in helpful groupings that limit the anxiety of choice. Prices are high, but you're getting the best. ✉ *Campos Elíseos 204, Col. Polanco* ☎ *55/5280–1111 Ext. 8600* ▤ *AE, DC, MC, V.*

**$$–$$$** ✕ **Suntory.** This main branch of the Suntory restaurants in Mexico welcomes you with a Japanese garden at the entryway. You can choose between the teppanyaki room, the sushi bar, and the shabu-shabu room, with its copper pot of steaming vegetable broth for cooking wafer-thin slices of beef. A daily four-course lunch goes for $36. It closes at 9 PM on Sunday. ☒ *Torres Adalid 14, Col. del Valle* 🕾 *55/5536–9432* ⊟ *AE, DC, MC, V.*

**$–$$$** ✕ **Mikado.** Strategically positioned a few blocks west of the U.S. embassy and close to the Japanese embassy, this notable spot can sate your sushi cravings at very fair prices. Immaculate hygiene, a fine sushi chef, an extensive menu, and a cheerful, bustling atmosphere downstairs make Mikado a real treat. ☒ *Paseo de la Reforma 369, Col. Cuauhtémoc* 🕾 *55/5525–3096* ⊟ *MC, V* ⊘ *No dinner Sun.*

## Mexican

**★ $$–$$$$** ✕ **San Ángel Inn.** During a meal in this magnificent old ex-convent, it may be hard not to fall into gluttony. Dark mahogany furniture, crisp white table linens, and beautiful blue-and-white Talavera place settings strike a note of restrained opulence. For a classic treat, have the *sopa de tortilla* (tortilla soup); note that the *puntas de filete* (sirloin tips) are liberally laced with chilies. Desserts—from light and crunchy meringues to pastries bulging with cream—can be rich to the point of surfeit. ☒ *Calle Diego Rivera 50, at Av. Altavista, San Ángel* 🕾 *55/5616–0537 or 55/5616–2222* ⊟ *AE, DC, MC, V.*

**$$–$$$** ✕ **Aguila y Sol.** Chef/owner Marta Ortiz Chapa brings considerable ex-
**Fodor'sChoice** perience and creativity to this exemplar of nueva cocina mexicana—she's
**★** the author of eight cookbooks on regional Mexican cuisine. Here's your chance to try indigenous produce with a new spin, such as an appetizer of *tortitas de huauzontle* (a green vegetable) with goat cheese, Parmesan, and a *chile pasilla* sauce or a main course of salmon in a maize crust with clams. Portions are not large, so you should have room for a luscious dessert, perhaps the mamey crème brûlée with a carnation-petal jelly. Also look for traditional drinks such as *flor de jamaica* (hibiscus flower drink) or, in cold weather, *ponche de manzana* (apple punch). ☒ *Av. Moliere 42, Col. Polanco* 🕾 *55/5281–8354* ⊟ *AE, MC, V* ⊘ *No dinner Sun. and Mon.*

**$$–$$$** ✕ **Gallos Centenario.** This sublime restaurant near the Zócalo is opulent
**Fodor'sChoice** and popular. For an intimate space reserve the salon *de los anillos de*
**★** *compromiso* (of the engagement rings). For a laugh, ask for the salon *de las tiás* (of the aunts), decorated with black-and-white photos of se-vere-looking ladies. The chrysanthemum-topped margaritas are un-equaled. Outstanding dishes include the beef fillet in *chichilo mole*, the least known of Oaxaca's famed seven moles. A classic dessert is *pastel de zapote* (a cake made with the sweet, black zapote fruit), but perhaps even more seductive is the *espuma de chocolate de metate* (a froth of chocolate) and almond cookies. You should try for a reservation. ☒ *República de Cuba 79, between Chile and Palma, Col. Centro* 🕾 *55/5512–1625 or 55/5512–6868* ⊟ *AE, MC, V* ⊘ *No dinner Sun.*

**$–$$$** ✕ **Los Almendros.** If you can't make it to the Yucatán, try the peninsula's unusual and lively food at one of this restaurant's two locations. The habañero chilies, red onions, and other native Yucatecan ingredients are a delightful surprise for those not yet in the know. Traditional dishes, such as a refreshing lime soup, share the menu with hard-to-pronounce Mayan cuisine. Especially worth trying is the *pescado tikinxic*—white fish in a mild red marinade of achiote seed and bitter orange juice. The branch in

Colonia Guadalupe Inn does not serve dinner on Sunday. ✉ *Campos Elíseos 164, Col. Polanco* ☎ *55/5531–6646* ✉ *Av. Insurgentes Sur 1759, Col. Guadalupe Inn* ☎ *55/5663–5151* ▭ *AE, DC, MC, V.*

★ **$–$$$** ✕ **Izote.** A reservation here is one of the hardest to get, as cookbook author Patricia Quintana has won over the capital with her sophisticated take on pre-Hispanic flavors. Even the likes of Hollywood moguls are seeking out this place. Keep an eye out for the unique fish entrées, such as shark fillet sautéed with chile pasilla, onion, garlic, and epazote, then steamed in chicken stock and *pulque* (a fermented cactus liquor). Tender lamb gets steamed as well, in maguey and banana leaves, after being quickly fried with chilies and a touch of cumin. ✉ *Av. Presidente Masaryk 513, at Socrates, Col. Polanco* ☎ *55/5280–1671* ⚓ *Reservations essential* ▭ *AE, DC, MC, V* ☺ *No dinner Sun.*

**$–$$$** ✕ **Nueva Fonda de San Francisco.** A tried and true favorite that kept its

**Fodor's**Choice following after it relocated from another part of town, the small and very

★ personal Fonda still delights with its creative Mexican cooking. The restaurant's outstanding dish is *pan de cazon* (baby shark layered between tortillas, refried beans, and a tangy salsa). Crepes made with delicate *huitlacoche* (black corn fungus) is the perfect appetizer, as is squash blossom soup served in a squash shell. Light, luscious mamey mousse doesn't disappoint either. Wash it all down with a smooth Santa Emiliana vintage from Chile or an equally good German, French, or Mexican wine. Abstract dishware designed by Lili Margolis graces the tables and piped-in jazz plays softly in the background. ✉ *Amsterdam 105, between Nuevo Leon and Loredo, Col. Condesa* ☎ *55/5211–2361* ▭ *AE, MC, V.*

**$–$$** ✕ **Casa de las Sirenas.** The setting is the calling card here; the 16th-century mansion sits at the foot of the Templo Major ruins, stones from which were incorporated into the building. The atmospheric second-floor terrace is within sight and sound of numerous Indian dances honoring the spirits of the crumbling Aztec temples below. On the menu you'll find such eclectic pairings as Cornish hen with a mango mole sauce—and a plethora of meat and fish dishes. ✉ *Guatemala 32, Col. Centro* ☎ *55/5704–3225 or 55/5704–3465* ▭ *AE, MC, V* ☺ *No dinner Sun.*

**$–$$** ✕ **Fonda Don Chon.** This unpretentious family-style restaurant, deep in a downtown working-class neighborhood, is famed for its pre-Hispanic Mexican dishes. A knowledge of zoology, Spanish, and Nahuatl helps in making sense of a menu that takes in a gamut of ingredients from throughout the republic. *Escamoles de hormiga* (red-ant roe) is known as the "caviar of Mexico" for its costliness, but you may have to acquire a taste for it. Among the exotic dishes are armadillo in mango sauce and fillet of wild boar. ✉ *Regina 160, near La Merced market, Col. Centro* ☎ *55/5542–0873* ▭ *No credit cards* ☺ *Closed Sun. No dinner.*

**$–$$** ✕ **Fonda El Refugio.** This restaurant serves dishes from each major region of the country. Along with a varied regular menu, there are tempting daily specials; you might find a mole made with pumpkin seeds or *huachinango a la veracruzana* (red snapper cooked in onions, tomatoes, and olives). Try the refreshing *aguas* (fresh-fruit and seed juices) with your meal and the *café de olla* (clove-flavor coffee sweetened with brown sugar) afterward. ✉ *Liverpool 166, at Florencia, Zona Rosa* ☎ *55/5207–2732 or 55/5525–8128* ▭ *AE, DC, MC, V.*

★ **$–$$**   ✕ **Fonda del Recuerdo.** The popular *fonda* (modest restaurant) has made a name for itself with fish and seafood platters from the gulf state of Veracruz. Sharing their fame is the *torito*, a potent drink made from sugarcane liquor, and exotic tropical fruit juices. Every day from 1 to 10, five lively *jarocho* (Veracruz-style) and mariachi groups provide festive music and the place is always alive with celebrations and good cheer. ⊠ *Bahía de las Palmas 37, Col. Veronica Anzures* ☎ *55/5260–7339 or 55/5260–1292* ⚔ *Reservations essential* ⊟ *AE, DC, MC, V.*

★ **$–$$**   ✕ **Hostería de Santo Domingo.** This genteel institution near downtown's Plaza Santo Domingo has been serving colonial dishes since the late 19th century in an atmospheric town house. Feast on stuffed cactus paddles, thousand-flower soup, pot roast, and an impressive array of quesadillas. Among some of the best homemade Mexican desserts in town are the flan and *arroz con leche* (rice pudding). The place is open for breakfast and is always full at lunch; it closes at 9 PM on Sunday. Get there early to avoid standing in line. ⊠ *Belisario Dominguez 72, Col. Centro* ☎ *55/5510–1434 or 55/5526–5276* ⊟ *AE, MC, V* ⊗ *No dinner Sun.*

**$–$$**   ✕ **El Tajín.** Named after El Tajín pyramid in Veracruz, this elegant lunch spot sizzles with pre-Hispanic influences. Innovative appetizers include *chilpachole*, a delicate crab and chili soup with epazote, while main dishes could include octopus cooked in its own ink. Prices are quite moderate for this caliber of cooking, and there's an impressive wine list to boot. Ancient Huastecan faces grinning from a splashing fountain add a bit of levity to the dining experience. ⊠ *Centro Cultural Veracruzano, Miguel Angel de Quevedo 687, Coyoacán* ☎ *55/5659–4447 or 55/5659–5759* ⊟ *AE, MC, V* ⊗ *No dinner.*

★ **$–$$**   ✕ **Tecla.** This see-and-be-seen eatery is a popular veteran of Mexico City's nueva cocina mexicana scene and the restaurants' locations and newsprint collage set a hip tone. The appetizers are especially intriguing, including squash flowers stuffed with goat cheese in a chipotle sauce and a spicy crab-stuffed chili. ⊠ *Av. Moliere 56, Col. Polanco* ☎ *55/5282–0010* ⊠ *Av. Durango 186A, Col. Roma* ☎ *55/5525–4920* ⊟ *AE, MC, V* ⊗ *No dinner Sun.*

**$–$$**   ✕ **La Valentina.** The epitome of good taste in all things Mexican, La Valentina devotes itself to rescuing and promoting traditional native cuisine. It avoids gimmicks with balanced dishes that are soft on the palate, yet fragrant with blends of chilies, herbs, nuts, and flowers. Starters reflect specialties from across the country from the Sinaloan Chilorio tacos to the famous *panuchos Yucatecos* (fried tortillas with Yucatan-style spiced chicken or pork). The appetizing tamarind mole intensifies any poultry dish; the seductively titled "Symphony in Mexican Rose" bathes chicken in a walnut and chipotle sauce. ⊠ *Av. Insurgentes Sur 1854B, Col. Florida, San Ángel* ☎ *55/5662–0872 or 55/5662–0177* ⊠ *Av. Presidente Masaryk 393, Col. Polanco* ☎ *55/5282–2297* ⊟ *AE, DC, MC, V* ⊗ *No dinner Sun.*
FodorsChoice
★

**$**   ✕ **Bajío.** Decorated in bright colors, Bajío attracts Mexican families and is run by vivacious Carmen "Titita" Ramírez—a culinary expert who has been featured in various U.S. food magazines. The labor-intensive 30-ingredient mole de Xico is a favorite; also excellent are *em-*

*panadas de plátano rellenos de frijol* (tortilla turnovers filled with bananas and beans) and *carnitas* (roast pork). You may have to go a little off the beaten track to get here, but it's worth it. ⊠ *Cuitláhuac 2709, Col. Azcapotzalco, about a 20-min ride north of Zona Rosa* ☎ *55/5341–9889* ⊟ *AE, MC, V* ☺ *No dinner.*

$ ✕ **Café de Tacuba.** An essential breakfast, lunch, dinner, or snack stop downtown, this Mexican classic has been rewarding the hungry since it opened in 1912 in a section of an old convent. At the entrance to the atmospheric main dining room are huge 18th-century oil paintings depicting the invention of *mole poblano,* a complex sauce with a variety of chilies and chocolate that was created by the nuns in the Santa Rosa Convent of Puebla. A student group dressed in medieval capes and hats serenades Thursday–Sunday 3:30–11:30; mariachis play during dinner on other days. ⊠ *Calle Tacuba 28, at Allende, Col. Centro* ☎ *55/5518–4950* ⊟ *AE, MC, V.*

$ ✕ **Los Girasoles.** Two prominent Mexico City society columnists own this downtown spot. Los Girasoles (which means sunflowers) is on a lovely old square in a restored three-story colonial home and serves light, tasty, and innovative nueva cocina mexicana. There are also pre-Hispanic delicacies such as *escamoles* (ant roe), *gusanos de maguey* (chilied worms), and *mini chapulines* (tiny crispy fried grasshoppers). It closes at 9 PM on Sunday and Monday. ⊠ *Plaza Manuel Tolsá on Xicoténcatl 1, Col. Centro* ☎ *55/5510–0630* ⊟ *AE, MC, V* ☺ *No dinner Sun.–Mon.*

$ ✕ **Sanborns.** The Casa de los Azulejos was among the first of the Sanborns in the country, which now populate every major town in Mexico. The ever-popular restaurant inside the store is perfect for a quick snack or whole meal or just a respite from sightseeing. Burgers, soups, salads, and ice creams for American tastes are just as common on the menu as non-spicy Mexican dishes. Mexicans love to meet friends here for coffee. ⊠ *Reforma 333, across the street from the Angel Monument, Col. Cuauhtémoc* ☎ *55/5752–8061* ⊠ *Reforma 506, near the Diana Monument, Col. Juarez* ☎ *55/5211–6311* ⊠ *Londres 70, inside the Calinda Geneve Hotel, Zona Rosa* ☎ *55/5525–4338* ⊟ *AE, MC, V.*

## Polish

★ $$–$$$ ✕ **Mazurka.** The capital's first and only establishment to offer Polish food enjoys a glowing reputation among older Mexican families. Settle in with complimentary starters of blini with herring paste and cucumber, dill, and cream salad, as Chopin's polonaises trill and leap in the background. The "star of the house" is a crispy, oven-baked duck, stuffed with bitter apple and blueberries. Or try the juicy, sweet duck and pear with cassis. The generous "Pope's Menu" includes two sets of entrées and is only $23 a head. ⊠ *Nueva York 150, between Calles Texas and Oklahoma, Col. Napoles* ☎ *55/5543–4509 or 55/5523–8811* ⊟ *AE, MC, V* ☺ *No dinner Sun.*

## Spanish

$$–$$$ ✕ **Tezka.** This Zona Rosa restaurant specializing in nueva cocina Basque was created by the acclaimed chef Arzac, who transposed many of his

best dishes to Mexico from his restaurant in San Sebastián, Spain. Feast on yellow tuna in a sweet and spicy sauce, or liver prepared with beer, green pepper, and malt. The starters are exquisite; the *caldo de xipiron* (broth of baby squid) is the best in the city. A decent list of Spanish wines includes Cune, Vina Ardanza, and Reserva 904. ⊠ *Royal Hotel, Amberes 78, at Liverpool, Col. Juárez* 🕿 *55/5228–9918 Ext. 5067* ⊟ *AE, DC, MC, V* ☺ *Closed Sun. No dinner Sat.*

**$–$$** ✕ **Círculo Vasco Español.** Dating from the 1890s, this huge, high-ceiling restaurant basks in the faded glamour of the days when dictator Porfirio Díaz dined here regularly. Its founders were Basque and though it has been run by Galicians for over 20 years, the signature dishes are still Basque—look for *rueda de robalo a la donostiarra* (sea bass cooked with parsley and white wine). Galician plates are no slouch either, and a hearty breakfast, like the omelette *de rajas con queso* (with poblano chili and cheese), will set you up for serious sightseeing. ⊠ *Av. 16 de Septiembre 51, Col. Centro* 🕿 *55/5518–2908* ⊟ *MC, V* ☺ *No dinner.*

**$–$$** ✕ **Loyola.** A Basque tour de force, the ample menu with unpronounceable but delicious items includes *kokotxas* (fish cheeks), tapas, black rice simmered in squid ink, oxtail, and many other such regional delicacies. Great salads and wines are another welcome feature. Courteous service, stained glass, Basque coats of arms, and the cozy hum of conversation from contented connoisseurs make this an excellent and authentic dining experience. A weekend buffet is $16. ⊠ *Aristóteles 239, Col. Polanco* 🕿 *55/5250–6756 or 55/5250–9097* ⊟ *AE, MC, V* ☺ *No dinner.*

**$–$$** ✕ **Mesón El Cid.** This charming *mesón* (tavern) exudes an atmosphere of Old Spain highlighted by Spanish stained-glass windows and a roaring fireplace. Weekdays, classic dishes such as paella, spring lamb, suckling baby pig, and Cornish hens with truffles keep customers happy, but on Saturday night this place comes into its own with a four-course medieval banquet, including a procession of costumed waiters carrying huge trays of steaming hot viands for $30 per person. Further entertainment is provided by a student singing group dressed in medieval Spanish capes and hats, a juggler, and magician. For dessert, a real winner is the *turron* (Spanish nougat) ice cream. ⊠ *Humboldt 61, Col. Centro* 🕿 *55/5512–7629* ⊟ *AE, MC, V* ☺ *No dinner Sun.–Mon.*

## Vegetarian

**$** ✕ **Las Fuentes.** This dining landmark is run by Philipe Culbert, a vegetarian who has dedicated his life to providing the tasty, healthy food prescribed under ancient Persian dietary laws. Although you can order à la carte, most diners opt for the various three-course luncheons priced at $7, which might include enchiladas poblanos (poblano pepper stuffed with melted cheese), raw apple salad or mixed vegetables, soup of the day, homemade bread, and coffee or tea. The place is packed at lunch with office workers. ⊠ *Río Panuco 27, at Río Tibur, Col. Cuauhtémoc* 🕿 *55/5207–6414* ⊟ *AE, MC, V* ☺ *No dinner.*

**¢–$** ✕ **El Yug.** This vegetarian spot offers delicious fare to the accompaniment of New Age music. Homemade soups, and main courses such as *chiles rellenos* (poblano chili stuffed with cheese) come with whole-grain bread. A daily *comida corrida* (fixed-price menu) is only $6. The sister restaurant in the Zona Rosa is open daily for breakfast, lunch, and dinner. ⊠ *Puebla 326-6, Col. Roma* ☎ *55/5553–3872* ⊠ *Varsovia 3, at Paseo de la Reforma Zona Rosa* ☎ *55/5525–5330* ⊟ *AE, MC, V* ⊙ *No dinner weekends.*

# WHERE TO STAY

Although the city is huge and spread out, most hotels are clustered in a few neighborhoods. Colonia Polanco has a generous handful of business-oriented hotels; these tend to be familiar major chains. The Zona Rosa has plenty of big, contemporary properties; it's handy to have restaurants and other services right outside the door. La Condesa and La Roma don't have many places to stay, but at this writing, the chic Hotel Condesa was in the works in its namesake neighborhood. The only pleasant tourist areas still poorly served for accommodation are Coyoacán and San Ángel.

Business travelers tend to fill up deluxe hotels during the week; some major hotels discount their weekend rates. Many smaller properties have taken the cue and offer similarly reduced rates as well. If you reserve through the toll-free reservations numbers, you may find rates as much as 50% off during special promotions.

| WHAT IT COSTS | | | | | |
|---|---|---|---|---|---|
| | $$$$ | $$$ | $$ | $ | ¢ |
| FOR 2 PEOPLE | over $250 | $150–$250 | $75–$150 | $50–$75 | under $50 |

Prices are for two people in a standard double room during high season.

## Colonia Polanco

**$$$$** **Camino Real.** About the size of Teotihuacán's Pyramid of the Sun, this
**Fodor's Choice** sleek, minimalist, bright pink and yellow, 8-acre city-within-a-city was
★ designed by Mexico's modern master, Ricardo Legorreta. Impressive artworks embellishing the public spaces include Rufino Tamayo's mural *Man Facing Infinity* and a Calder sculpture. Rooms have gorgeous marble bathrooms and Legoretta's signature bright yellow on one wall. The fifth-floor executive level has 100 extra-large guest rooms with special amenities. El Centro Castellano restaurant offers free child care for long weekend lunchtimes, and Le Cirque opened in 2003. ⊠ *Mariano Escobedo 700, Col. Anzures 11590* ☎ *55/5263–8888* 🖷 *55/5263–8898* ⊕ *www.caminoreal.com.mx* 🛏 *625 rooms, 89 suites* ♿ *3 restaurants, in-room data ports, in-room safes, minibars, cable TV, 4 tennis courts, 2 pools (1 indoor), gym, 3 bars, shops, dry cleaning, laundry service, concierge, concierge floor, business services, meeting rooms, no-smoking floor, travel services, car rental, parking (fee)* ⊟ *AE, DC, MC, V.*

**$$$$** **Casa Vieja.** This sumptuously decorated mansion is simply stunning. Tastefully selected folk art, handsomely hand-carved furniture, and gilded wall trimmings complement patios and splashing fountains. Each one- and two-bedroom suite has a full kitchen, CD player, VCR, high-speed Internet, hot tub, and picture window overlooking an inside garden. The hotel's Mexican restaurant is named after its huge floor-to-ceiling *Árbol de la Vida (Tree of Life)* sculpture. With all the VIPs roosting here, the hotel is also equipped to arrange helicopter and armored car rentals. ⊠ *Eugenio Sue 45, 11560* 🕾 *55/5282–0067* 📠 *55/5281–3780* ⊕ *www.casavieja.com* ➷ *10 suites* ♿ *Restaurant, in-room date ports, in-room fax, in-room safes, kitchens, cable TV, bar, dry cleaning, laundry service, concierge, Internet, meeting room, car rental, travel services, free parking; no a/c* ▭ *AE, MC, V* ⧦ *BP.*

$$$$ 🏨 **J. W. Marriott.** In keeping with its genteel neighborhood, this high-rise hotel has personalized service and small, clubby public areas; nothing overwhelms here. Rooms are done with plenty of wood and warm colors but are otherwise unremarkable in decor. The hotel has a well-equipped 24-hour business center and an ATM machine on the premises. Attractive weekend rates range between $174 and $184. ⊠ *Andrés Bello 29, at Campos Elíseos, 11560* 🕾 *55/5999–0000* 📠 *55/5999–0001* ⊕ *www.marriotthotels.com* ➷ *311 rooms* ♿ *2 restaurants, coffee shop, in-room data ports, in-room safes, minibars, cable TV, pool, gym, bar, dry cleaning, laundry service, concierge, concierge floor, business services, meeting rooms, car rental, travel services, parking* ▭ *AE, DC, MC, V.*

$$$$ 🏨 **Nikko México.** Nikko México occupies a prime Polanco position: adjacent to Bosque de Chapultepec, just a five-minute walk from the anthropology museum. With signage and menus in Japanese, English, and Spanish, it caters especially to business travelers and conferences. It's the second-largest hotel in the city and has marvelous views from the top-floor suites. Each room shines with subdued earth tones and bamboolike walls; a pair of rooms are done in Japanese style, with tatami mats. Among the restaurants is the excellent Ben Kay. Weekend rates are very reasonable. ⊠ *Campos Elíseos 204, 11560* 🕾 *55/5280–1111, 800/908–8800 in the U.S.* 📠 *55/5280–9191* ⊕ *www.nikkohotels.com* ➷ *744 rooms, 24 suites* ♿ *4 restaurants, in-room data ports, in-room fax, in-room safes, minibars, cable TV, driving range, 3 tennis courts, indoor pool, gym, sauna, steam room, health club, 2 bars, shops, baby sitting, concierge, concierge floor, business services, meeting rooms, Internet, car rental, travel services, no-smoking rooms* ▭ *AE, DC, MC, V.*

$$$$ 🏨 **W.** The first W hotel in Latin America grooves with sassy red, black,
Fodor'sChoice and white colors. It manages to be informal and chic at the same time,
★ with the staff clad in casual black rather than the usual stiff uniforms. Guest rooms feature some outside-the-box design: bathrooms are big enough for a dance, strung with hammocks, and feature pressure-point showers; sinks are placed inside the bedroom European-style. Work areas have enormous desks and ergonomic chairs; some rooms are outfitted with faxes and scanners. See and be seen in the red lobby bar or just chill in the Music Lounge. The Away spa has a huge pre-Hispanic temazcal (adobe-domed sweat lodge). ⊠ *Campos Eliseos 252, 11560* 🕾 *55/9138–1800* 📠 *55/9138–1801* ⊕ *www.whotels.com* ➷ *229 rooms, 8 suites* ♿ *Restaurant, in-room data ports, some in-room faxes, in-room safes, cable TV, in-room DVD players, gym, spa, bar, shops, dry cleaning, laundry services, Internet, business services, meeting rooms, travel services, car rental* ▭ *AE, DC, MC, V.*

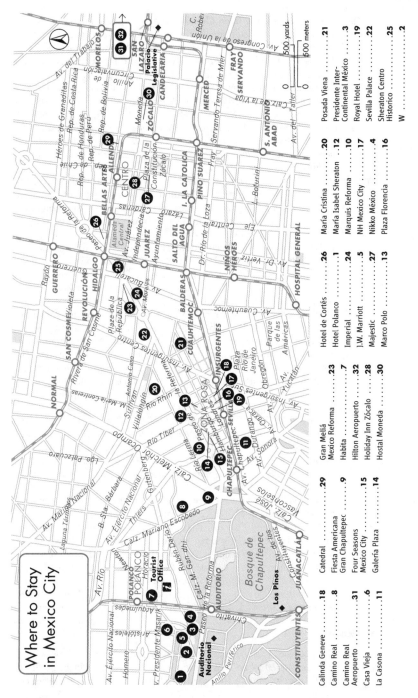

# Where to Stay in Mexico City

**$$$** ▦ **Fiesta Americana Gran Chapultepec.** Sleek and contemporary, this stylish hotel is located opposite the Bosque de Chapultepec, close to the city's main shopping area and five minutes from the Auditorio Nacional. Rooms are angled to maximize views; they're done in muted olives and browns. The spa, beauty salon, and barbershop guarantee you will be presentable for the ultramodern Asian bar, where you can hang out for sushi and cocktails. ⊠ *Mariano Escobedo 756, Col. Anzures 11590* ☎ *55/ 2581–1500* 🖷 *55/2581–1501* ⊕ *www.fiestaamericana.com* ↩ *189 rooms, 14 suites* ⚹ *Restaurant, in-room data ports, minibars, cable TV, gym, spa, hair salon, 2 bars, shop, dry cleaning, laundry services, concierge, business services, meeting rooms, travel services, car rental, free parking* ⊟ *AE, DC, MC, V.*

★ **$$$** ▦ **Habita.** Characterized by pale colors and a spalike atmosphere, Mexico's first design hotel strikes a harmonious balance between style statements and minimalism. New-Age music is piped into the rooms (you can turn it off, of course), and tasteful bowls of limes sit by state-of-the-art TV sets. The swanky tapas bar Área has beautiful open-air views and draws plenty of chic chilangos Thursday to Saturday. ⊠ *Av. Presidente Masaryk 201, 11560* ☎ *55/5282–3100* 🖷 *55/5282–3101* ⊕ *www. hotelhabita.com* ↩ *32 rooms, 4 suites* ⚹ *Restaurant, in-room data ports, in-room safes, minibars, cable TV, gym, spa, bar, concierge, business services, meeting rooms, free parking* ⊟ *AE, MC, V.*

**$$$** ▦ **Presidente Inter-Continental México.** This Inter-Continental has a dramatic five-story atrium lobby—a hollow pyramid of balconies—with music performed daily at the lively lobby bar. Rooms are spacious, decorated in soothing beige, and have two queen beds. On clear days, the top two floors have views of the nearby snow-capped volcanoes. The executive floors have a lounge, concierge, and extra amenities. A number of smart stores and six eateries are on the premises, including Au Pied de Cochon. ⊠ *Campos Elíseos 218, 11560* ☎ *55/5327–7700, 800/447–6147 in the U.S.* 🖷 *55/5327–7730* ⊕ *www.intercontinental. com* ↩ *629 rooms, 30 suites* ⚹ *6 restaurants, coffee shop, in-room data ports, in-room safes, minibars, cable TV, gym, lobby lounge, shops, babysitting, dry cleaning, laundry services, concierge, concierge floor, business services, Internet, meeting rooms, car rental, travel services, parking (fee)* ⊟ *AE, DC, MC, V.*

**$$** ▦ **Hotel Polanco.** This small favorite right off Polanco park has many of the amenities of larger hotels, but a much better price. Marble floors and dark-wood furniture accent the cozy lobby, which leads to five floors of tiny but tidy carpeted rooms with old-fashioned blue flowered bedspreads and cedar furnishings. A pleasant streetside restaurant serves out-of-the-ordinary Italian cuisine. ⊠ *Edgar Allen Poe 8, 11560* ☎ *55/ 5280–8082* ✐ *hotelpolanco@prodigy.net.mx* ↩ *65 rooms, 5 suites* ⚹ *Restaurant, room service, fans, in-room safes, cable TV, gym, bar, laundry services, Internet, meeting rooms, free parking; no a/c* ⊟ *MC, V.*

## Colonia Roma

**$$$** ▦ **La Casona.** This charming hotel is an elegant, understated former mansion, registered as an artistic monument by Mexico's Institute of Fine Arts. From its sunny patios to its sitting rooms, the hotel's interior conveys the spirit of the Porfiriato. The owner loves classical music and has added such whimsical touches as a trumpet turned into a lamp in one room and a portrait of Richard Strauss in another. No two rooms are alike, but all have hardwood floors, elegant furniture, and good-size bathtubs. The two-story hotel building, with its salmon-color facade, looks out onto a tree-lined street. ⊠ *Av. Durango 280, at Cozumel, 06700* ☏ *55/5286–3001* 🖷 *55/5211–0871* ⊕ *www.mexicoboutiquehotels/ lacasona.com* 🛏 *29 rooms* 🔥 *Restaurant, room service, in-room data ports, in-room safes, minibars, cable TV, gym, bar, laundry services, dry cleaning* ⊟ *AE, DC, MC, V* ⧖ *BP.*

## Zona Rosa

**$$$** 🏨 **Galería Plaza.** Location gives this ultramodern hotel an edge; it's on a quiet street, but plenty of shops, restaurants, and nightspots are nearby. Service and facilities are faultless; advantages include a heated rooftop pool with sundeck, a secure underground parking lot, and a 24-hour restaurant. All rooms are fresh and bright, with peach-colored walls, and all have small work areas. ⊠ *Hamburgo 195, at Varsovia, 06600* ☏ *55/5230–1717 or 888/559–4329* 🖷 *55/5207–5867* ⊕ *www.brisas. com.mx* 🛏 *420 rooms, 19 suites* 🔥 *2 restaurants, room service, in-room data ports, in-room safes, minibars, cable TV, pool, gym, lobby lounge, shops, dry cleaning, laundry services, concierge, concierge floor, Internet, business services, meeting rooms, travel services, car rental, parking (fee)* ⊟ *AE, DC, MC, V.*

★ **$$$** 🏨 **Marco Polo.** Modern and intimate, the central Marco Polo has the amenities and personalized service often associated with a small European hotel. North-facing top-floor rooms have excellent views of Paseo de la Reforma and the Angel monument, and the U.S. Embassy is close by. Four penthouse suites have terraces, and are normally rented by the month. ⊠ *Amberes 27, 06600* ☏ *55/5511–1839, 800/448–8355 in the U.S.* 🖷 *55/ 5080–8704* ⊕ *www.marcopolo.com.mx* 🛏 *59 rooms, 16 suites* 🔥 *Restaurant, in-room data ports, in-room safes, minibars, cable TV, gym, bar, dry cleaning, laundry services, Internet, business services, meeting rooms, car rental, parking (fee)* ⊟ *AE, DC, MC, V* ⧖ *CP.*

**$$$** 🏨 **NH Mexico City.** The former Krystal Rosa now belongs to the Spanish NH chain and is still a superbly run high-rise hotel. There's a stylish lobby cocktail lounge and a restaurant, Hacienda del Mortero, which serves excellent classic Spanish and International cuisine. Rooms have business travelers in mind with sober gray and green colors, Scandinavian-style furniture, and hardwood floors. The hotel is in the heart of Zona Rosa and has an excellent view of the neighborhood from the rooftop pool terrace. ⊠ *Liverpool 155, 06600* ☏ *55/5228–9928, 800/ 231–9860 in the U.S.* 🖷 *55/5511–3490* ⊕ *www.nh-hotels.com* 🛏 *267 rooms, 35 suites* 🔥 *Restaurant, in-room data ports, in-room safes, minibars, cable TV with video games, pool, bar, shops, dry cleaning, laundry services, concierge, business services, Internet, travel services, car rental, parking (fee)* ⊟ *AE, DC, MC, V.*

**$$** 🏨 **Calinda Geneve.** This five-story 1906 hotel, referred to locally as El Génova, has a pleasant lobby with traditional Colonial-style carved-wood chairs and tables. Guest rooms are small but comfortable, with modern furnishings. The attractive Salón Jardín, part of the popular Sanborns restaurant chain, has art deco stained-glass flourishes. ⊠ *Londres 130, 06600* ☎ *55/5080–0800* 🖷 *55/5080–0833* ⊕ *www. hotelescalinda.com.mx* 📑 *300 rooms* 🔥 *Restaurant, café, room service, in-room data ports, in-room safes, minibars, cable TV, gym, spa, bar, shop, laundry facilities, business services, meeting rooms parking (fee)* 🖃 *AE, DC, MC, V.*

**$$** 🏨 **Plaza Florencia.** The lobby of this hotel may be weighted with heavy furniture and dark colors, but the rooms upstairs are bright, modern, and, most importantly, soundproofed against the traffic noise of the busy avenue below. Higher floors have views of the Angel monument. Some large family suites are available. ⊠ *Florencia 61, 06600* ☎ *55/5242–4700* 🖷 *55/ 5242–4785* ⊕ *www.plazaflorencia.com.mx* 📑 *134 rooms, 8 suites* 🔥 *2 restaurants, coffee shop, some in-room data ports, in-room safes, minibars, cable TV, bar, pool, dry cleaning, laundry services, business services, meeting rooms, travel services, car rental* 🖃 *AE, DC, MC, V.*

**$$** 🏨 **Royal Hotel.** The immaculate marble lobby of the modern Royal Hotel, beloved by travelers from Spain, is filled with plants and the exuberant conversation of its guests. Spacious rooms have large bathrooms, well-equipped work areas, and interactive TV. Its Spanish restaurant, Tezka, was founded by award-winning chef Arzac and is known for its extraordinary Basque cuisine. ⊠ *Amberes 78, 06600* ☎ *55/5228–9918, 888/740–8314 in the U.S.* 🖷 *55/5514–3330* ⊕ *www.hotelroyalzr.com* 📑 *161 rooms, 1 suite* 🔥 *2 restaurants, in-room data ports, in-room safes, refrigerators, cable TV, gym, hair salon, massage, sauna, bar, shop, baby-sitting, dry cleaning, laundry services, business services, meeting rooms, car rental, travel services, free parking* 🖃 *AE, MC, V.*

**$** 🏨 **Posada Viena.** Hidden away in a quiet neighborhood three blocks from the hustle and bustle of the Zona Rosa, this hotel is convenient to restaurants, bars, and shops, but much more affordable than some of its more central counterparts. Although the elevator and hallways are a little musty, the rooms are fresh and clean, painted with slivers of bright purples, oranges, yellows, and blues. Suites, suitable for up to four people, are ideal for families. The Argentine restaurant offers free tango lessons on Saturday night. The staff couldn't be nicer. ⊠ *Marsella 28, corner of Dinamarca, 06600* ☎ *55/5566–0700, 800/849–8402 in the U.S.* 🖷 *55/5592–7302* ⊕ *www.posadavienahotel.com* 📑 *66 rooms, 20 suites* 🔥 *Restaurant, café, room service, fans, some minibars, cable TV, bar, shop, baby-sitting, dry cleaning, laundry services, meeting room, Internet, car rental, free parking; no a/c* 🖃 *MC, V.*

## Midtown & Along the Reforma

**$$$$** 🏨 **Four Seasons Mexico City.** Among the most luxurious hotels in the capital, this eight-story hotel was modeled after the 18th-century Iturbide Palace—it even has a traditional inner courtyard with a fountain. (Half of the rooms overlook the courtyard.) The rest of the hotel doesn't disappoint: rooms are adorned with palettes of either deep blue and brown or peach and emerald green and the business center is so complete it even has a reference library. The well-stocked tequila bar off the lobby is a perfect pre-dinner option. Excellent cultural tours of the city are of-

**Fodor'sChoice** ★

fered free to guests on weekends. ⊠ *Paseo de la Reforma 500, Col. Juárez 06600* ☎ *55/5230–1818, 01800/906–7500 toll-free in Mexico, 888/304–6755 in the U.S.* 🖷 *55/5230–1808* ⊕ *www.fourseasons.com* 🖬 *200 rooms, 40 suites* ☖ *2 restaurants, in-room data ports, minibars, cable TV, pool, gym, bar, shops, dry cleaning, laundry service, concierge, concierge floor, business services, meeting rooms, Internet, car rental, travel services* ☰ *AE, DC, MC, V.*

**$$$$** 🏨 **María Isabel Sheraton.** Don Antenor Patiño, the Bolivian "Tin King," inaugurated this Mexico City classic in 1969 and named it after his granddaughter, socialite Isabel Goldsmith. The stunning marble lobby has gleaming brass fixtures. All guest and public rooms are impeccably maintained; the former have extra comfy Posturpedic mattresses and goose-down pillows. Penthouse suites in the 22-story tower are extra-spacious and have butler service. The location—across from the Angel monument and the Zona Rosa, with Sanborns next door and the U.S. Embassy a half block away—is prime. ⊠ *Paseo de la Reforma 325, Col. Cuauhtémoc 06500* ☎ *55/5242–5555* 🖷 *55/5207–0684* ⊕ *www.sheraton.com* 🖬 *681 rooms, 74 suites* ☖ *3 restaurants, room service, in-room data ports, in-room safes, minibars, cable TV, pool, gym, massage, sauna, spa, 2 bars, shops, baby-sitting, dry cleaning, laundry services, concierge, concierge floor, business services, Internet, meeting rooms, travel services, car rental, parking (fee), no-smoking rooms* ☰ *AE, DC, MC, V.*

**$$$$** 🏨 **Marquis Reforma.** This plush, privately owned member of the Lead-
**Fodor'sChoice** ing Hotels of the World is within walking distance of the Zona Rosa.
★ Its striking art nouveau facade combines pink stone and curved glass, and the seventh-floor suites afford picture-perfect views of the Castillo de Chapultepec. An art deco theme defines the rooms. You can enjoy Mexican cuisine at La Jolla restaurant and take advantage of hard-to-find holistic massages at the health club. Rates are lower on weekends. ⊠ *Paseo de la Reforma 465, Col. Cuauhtémoc 06500* ☎ *55/5229–1200, 800/235–2387 in the U.S.* 🖷 *55/5229–1212* ⊕ *www.marquisreformahl. com.mx* 🖬 *123 rooms, 85 suites* ☖ *2 restaurants, coffee shop, in-room data ports, in-room safes, minibars, cable TV, pool, gym, spa, bar, shops, business services, meeting rooms, Internet, car rental, travel services, no-smoking rooms* ☰ *AE, DC, MC, V.*

**$$$** 🏨 **Gran Meliá Mexico Reforma.** Convenient to downtown, the Stock Exchange and the Zona Rosa, this gorgeous, 22-floor smoked-glass behemoth answers the call of business travelers looking for location, well-appointed rooms, and high-tech business services. The lobby is certainly a great meeting place, with a brass domed lounge, snug little corners for tête-à-têtes, and a glossy, dove-grey marble floor. Guest rooms are large, with soft blue and auburn colors, oversize TVs, and comfortable sitting areas; the executive floor features butler service. There's also a full-service spa (the largest such spa in a Mexico City hotel). ⊠ *Reforma 1, Col. Tabacalera 06030* ☎ *55/5128–5000, 800/336–3542 in the U.S.* 🖷 *55/5128–5050* ⊕ *www.solmelia.com* 🖬 *424 room, 30 suites* ☖ *2 restaurants, in-room data ports, in-room safes, cable TV, gym, hair salon, spa, theater, shops, concierge, concierge floors, business services, meeting rooms, Internet, car rental, travel services, car rental* ☰ *AE, DC, MC, V.*

$$ 🏨 **Imperial.** Suiting its name, this hotel occupies a stately, cupolaed, late-19th-century building right on the Reforma alongside the Columbus monument. Quiet elegance and personal service are keynotes of this privately owned property; rooms are done in pink and white. The hotel's Restaurant Gaudí serves Continental cuisine with some classic Spanish selections. ⊠ *Paseo de la Reforma 64, Col. Juárez 06600* 🕾 *55/5705–4911* 🖷 *55/5703–3122* ⊕ *www.hotelimperial.com.mx* ⤴ *50 rooms, 10 junior suites, 5 master suites* ⚘ *Restaurant, café, in-room data ports, in-room safes, minibars, cable TV, bar, dry cleaning, laundry services, business services, Internet, meeting rooms, travel services, free parking* ⊟ *AE, DC, MC, V.*

$$ 🏨 **Sevilla Palace.** Five panoramic elevators sweep through the 23 floors of this tower, which is well-priced for its location along Paseo de la Reforma, between Zona Rosa and downtown. The convention halls, meeting rooms, and computer facilities aim to cover the business bases, while a covered rooftop pool with hot tub, a health club, and a terraced rooftop lounge help the suits unwind. The tasteful, sporty rooms have plaid bedspreads and matching coral carpets with a sofa bed for extra guests. ⊠ *Paseo de la Reforma 105, Col. Revolución 06030* 🕾 *55/5705–2800, 800/732–9488 in the U.S.* 🖷 *55/5703–1521* ⊕ *www.sevillapalace.com.mx* ⤴ *413 rooms* ⚘ *2 restaurants, in-room data ports, minibars, pool, gym, 3 bars, shops, baby-sitting, business services, Internet, meeting rooms, travel services, free parking* ⊟ *AE, MC, V.*

★ $ 🏨 **María Cristina.** Brimming with old-world charm, this Spanish colonial-style gem is a Mexico City classic. Impeccably maintained since it was built in 1937, the building surrounds a delightful garden courtyard—the setting for its El Retiro bar. Three apartment-style master suites come complete with hot tubs. In a quiet residential setting near Parque Sullivan, the hotel is close to the Zona Rosa. ⊠ *Río Lerma 31, Col. Cuauhtémoc 06500* 🕾 *55/5703–1212 or 55/5566–9688* 🖷 *55/5566–9194* ⊕ *www.hotelmariacristina.com.mx* ⤴ *140 rooms, 8 suites* ⚘ *Room service, in-room safes, cable TV, hair salon, bar, Internet, travel services, free parking; no a/c in some rooms* ⊟ *AE, MC, V.*

## Downtown

$$$ 🏨 **Sheraton Centro Historico.** The abstract red and blue mural in the lobby and cantilevered grey facade add a dramatic flourish to the city's newest hotel gracing the Historic Center. Geared to conventions, everything is oversize here from the lobby to the seven food and beverage outlets. Plush Italian furniture, grey-green carpeting, and Spanish marble are features of the guest rooms, which come in one of four different color schemes: vanilla, grey, wine, or blue. Suites with a kichenette and dining area are available for long-term stays. Rooms and hallways all have old photos of the Historic Center. The workout facilities and pool will be available by late 2004. ⊠ *Av. Juarez 70, Col. Centro* 🕾 *55/5130–5300* 🖷 *55/5130–5255* ⊕ *www.sheratonmexico.com* ⤴ *375 rooms, 25 suites, 27 extended-stay suites* ⚘ *2 restaurants, café, in-room data ports, in-room safes, cable TV, pool, gym, massage, spa, 4 bars, shops, concierge, concierge floors, business services, convention center, car rental, travel services, parking (fee)* ⊟ *AE, DC, MC, V.*

$$ 📺 **Holiday Inn Zócalo.** This hotel couldn't have a better location—on the Zócalo and close to a gaggle of museums, restaurants, and historic buildings. The building may be historic, but the interior has the feel of a typical Holiday Inn. Although the glass-front lobby lacks personality, there's more flavor to the terrace restaurant, which is set with old-fashioned wrought-iron tables and has an amazing view of the Catedral Metropolitana and Palacio Nacional. ⊠ *Av. 5 de Mayo at Zócalo, Col. Centro 06000* ☎ *55/5521–2121* 🖷 *55/5521–2122* ⊕ *www.holidayinnzocalo.com.mx* ⬥ *100 rooms, 10 suites* ⚫ *2 restaurants, room service, in-room safes, cable TV, gym, bar, meeting rooms, Internet, travel services, parking (fee)* ⊟ *AE, MC, V.*

★ $$ 📺 **Hotel de Cortés.** This darling small hotel, managed by Best Western, is in a 1780 colonial building that's also a national monument. Rooms, in colonial style, are small and simply furnished; they open onto an enclosed central courtyard. Two comfortable soundproof suites overlook Alameda Park. The Museo Franz Mayer is a block away, and it's an easy walk to Palacio de Bellas Artes. Loyal guests reserve many months in advance. ⊠ *Av. Hidalgo 85, Col. Guerrero 06000* ☎ *55/5518–2181, 800/908–1200 in the U.S.* 🖷 *55/5512–1863* ⊕ *www.hoteldecortes.com.mx* ⬥ *19 rooms, 10 suites* ⚫ *Restaurant, bar, baby-sitting, laundry services, concierge, meeting room; no a/c, no room TVs* ⊟ *AE, DC, MC, V.*

$$ 📺 **Majestic.** If you're interested in exploring the historic downtown, the atmospheric, colonial-style Majestic will give you a perfect location. It's also ideal for viewing the Independence Day (September 16) celebrations, for which many people reserve a room a year in advance. Rooms have heavy wooden furniture and bright linens. Although the front units have balconies and a delightful view, they can be noisy with car traffic until about 11 PM. ⊠ *Calle Madero 73, Col. Centro 06000* ☎ *55/5521–8600, 800/528–1234 in the U.S.* 🖷 *55/5512–6262* ⊕ *www.majestic.com.mx* ⬥ *85 rooms* ⚫ *Restaurant, coffee shop, in-room safes, cable TV, bar, dry cleaning, laundry services, business center, meeting room, travel services* ⊟ *AE, MC, V.*

★ ¢ 📺 **Catedral.** In the heart of historic downtown, this refurbished older hotel is a bargain, with many of the amenities of the more upscale hotels at less than half the price. Public areas sparkle with marble and glass. Guest rooms are spacious and clean, if not a little generic. You can get a room with a view of the namesake Catedral, but keep in mind that its bells chime every 15 minutes, late into the night. If your room doesn't have a view, the small terrace is a great place to watch the sun set over the Zócalo. El Retiro bar attracts a largely Mexican clientele to hear live Latin music. ⊠ *Donceles 95, Col. Centro 06000* ☎ *55/5512–8581* 🖷 *55/5512–4344* ⊕ *www.hotelcatedral.com.mx* ⬥ *116 rooms, 8 suites* ⚫ *Restaurant, room service, cable TV, bar, dry cleaning, laundry service, meeting room, Internet, travel services, free parking* ⊟ *AE, MC, V.*

¢ 📺 **Hostal Moneda.** If all you need is a bed, breakfast, and a great location, this no-frills hostel fits the bill, at rock-bottom prices. The careworn marble hallways hold eight separate dormitories, each with 16 beds and a bathroom. Doubles and singles are also available; many are decorated with murals painted by former guests. A rooftop sundeck and restaurant with reasonably priced chicken and vegetarian dishes and beer is the social center of this little community (mainly Europeans). ⊠ *Moneda 8, Col. Centro 06020* ☎ *55/5522–5821* 🖷 *55/5522–5803* ⊕ *www. hostalmoneda.com.mx* ⇨ *153 beds (8 dormitories, 10 doubles, 5 singles)* ⅁ *Restaurant, bar, kitchen, laundry facilities, Internet; no a/c, no room phones, no room TVs* ☴ *No credit cards* ⫟⊙⫟ *BP.*

## Airport

**$$$** 🏨 **Camino Real Aeropuerto.** This sleek hotel can be reached via a short, covered footbridge. Rooms are light and cheery and have sealed double windows to prevent airport noise from entering. A couple of services, including room service and the business center, run 24 hours, useful for travelers on odd-hours schedules. Even if you're only between flights and don't overnight, you can sit in one of the overstuffed chairs in the soothing lobby or catch a meal in the restaurant to get away from the frantic energy of the airport. ⊠ *Benito Juárez International Airport, 15520* ☎ *55/3003–0000, 800/228–9290 in the U.S.* 🖷 *55/3003–0001* ⊕ *www. caminoreal.com* ⇨ *600 rooms, 8 suites* ⅁ *Restaurant, coffee shop, in-room data ports, in-room safes, minibars, cable TV, pool, gym, hair salon, sauna, bar, shops, concierge, business services, Internet, meeting rooms, car rental, parking (fee)* ☴ *AE, DC, MC, V.*

**$$$** 🏨 **Hilton Aeropuerto.** Cool and compact—with a distinctive gray marble lobby and a bar with a wide-angle view of landing planes—the Hilton feels like a private club, enhanced by an attentive but unobtrusive staff. Rooms come with full working gear for a traveling executive: two phone lines, modem connection, ergonomic chairs, oversize desk, and coffeemaker. You can choose from four different views: airstrip, street, atrium, or "garden" (bamboo plants set along a concrete ledge). ⊠ *Benito Juárez International Airport, at international terminal, 15620* ☎ *55/ 5133–0505, 800/774–1500 in the U.S.* 🖷 *55/5133–0500* ⊕ *www. hilton.com* ⇨ *129 rooms* ⅁ *Restaurant, in-room data ports, in-room safes, minibars, cable TV, gym, bar, business services, meeting rooms, no smoking rooms, parking (fee)* ☴ *AE, DC, MC, V.*

# NIGHTLIFE & THE ARTS

A good place to check for current events is *DF por Travesías,* a biweekly entertainment magazine covering bars, clubs, restaurants, and culture. Also available at newsstands is *Tiempo Libre* (www.tiempolibre.com.mx), a weekly magazine listing activities and events (in Spanish).

Citywide festivals with free music, dance, and theater performances by local groups take place year-round, but are especially prevalent in July and August. A three-week cultural and gastronomic festival with international headliners takes place in the Centro Histórico between March and April. Check with the Mexico City Tourist Office for dates and details at ☎ 01800/008–9090 (within Mexico) or visit the festival Web site at www.fchmexico.com. The National Arts Council (CONAC-ULTA) also lists city festivals on its Web site, www.cartelera.conaculta.

gob.mx, along with updates on music, theater, film, and other cultural events of all stripes.

If you'd like to see a film, you can check movie listings by city and neighborhood on the Cinemex Web site, www.cinemex.com. For anti-Hollywood film buffs, duck into Cinemex art-house **Casa de Arte** (⊠ Anatole France 120, at Presidente Masaryk, Col. Polanco ☎ 55/5280–9156). It screens mostly foreign and independent pictures. Films are generally in English with Spanish subtitles.

## Nightlife

Night is the key word to understanding the timing of going out in Mexico City. People generally have cocktails at 7 or 8, take in dinner and a show at 10 or 11, head to discos at midnight, then find a spot for a nightcap or tacos somewhere around 3 AM. (Cantinas are the exception; people start hitting them in the late afternoon and most close by 11 PM.) The easiest way to do this if you don't speak Spanish is on a nightlife tour. **Todo Turismo** (☎ 55/5684–9000 ⊕ www.todoturismo.net) organizes cantina crawls, complete with an English-speaking guide and complimentary brews. You'll need a group of at least four people and must make reservations 24 hours in advance. If you set off on your own you should have no trouble getting around, but for personal safety absolutely avoid hailing taxis on the street—take official hotel taxis or call a sitio (stationed) taxi (☎ 55/5514–7861).

Condesa, Roma, Coyoacán, and Polanco stand out as Mexico City's hippest and trendiest neighborhoods. The Zona Rosa has lost ground to Condesa and Polanco in the past few years but it is still lively on Friday and Saturday nights. Niza, Florencia, and Hamburgo streets are teeming with bars and discos. Outside the Zona Rosa, Paseo de la Reforma and Avenida Insurgentes Sur have a large concentration of nightspots. Remember that the capital's high altitude makes liquor extremely potent, even jolting. Imported booze is expensive, so you may want to stick with what the Mexicans order: tequila, cerveza (beer), and rum, usually as a cuba libre (with Coke). If you order a bottle of hard alcohol (some clubs require this), make sure that the seal hasn't been broken before you're served, as some ill-reputed establishments have been known to sell adulterated booze. Your head will thank you the next day.

### Bars

Nice bars to sit and have a few drinks in used to be hard to come by in Mexico City, but the situation is improving. The rougher cantinas are usually noisy and sometimes seedy, with an early closing time (11 PM), but the better cantinas, full of character and local color, are well worth a visit. The cantinas we list are fairly safe places, but the clientele is predominantly male, so women can expect to get some stares and hellos. Bars are usually open Tuesday–Saturday 8 PM–3 AM and generally don't charge a cover, unless they're offering a good live band.

The most popular neighborhoods for bar-hopping are Polanco, San Ángel, Coyoacán, La Condesa, and, for cantinas, La Roma. Drink prices fluctuate wildly according to area and establishment.

CENTRO HISTÓRICO ★ **El Nivel** (✉ Calle Moneda, near Templo Mayor, Col. Centro ☎ 55/5522–9755), Mexico City's first cantina (opened in 1855), is right off the Zócalo. It's small and traditional; you can get a cheap beer or tequila and be served free appetizers like peanuts and chicharrón (pork rinds) as long as you keep ordering drinks. The bar is named after a water marker outside (called "el nivel") that warned the city about imminent floods during the 20th century.

**La Ópera** (✉ 5 de Mayo 10, at Filomeno Mata, Col. Centro ☎ 55/5512–8959) is one of the city's most elegant watering holes, and it's brought in top personalities since it opened in 1870. Don't forget to have your waiter point out the bullet hole allegedly left in the ceiling by Mexican revolutionary hero Pancho Villa.

A classic downtown cantina, the **Salón Corona** (✉ Calle Bolivar 24, at Madero, Col. Centro ☎ No phone), is one of the friendliest joints in town and is centrally located if you plan to hit other bars in the historic center.

LA CONDESA Get your Guinness on at Irish-style pub **Celtics** (✉ Tamaulipas 36, Col. Condesa ☎ 55/5211–9081)—that is, if you can push your way through the throng to reach the bar.

A good place to start your evening is **El Centenario** (✉ Vicente Suarez 48, at Michoacán, Col. Condesa ☎ 55/5211–0276), a traditional cantina in the heart of the Condesa's restaurant zone. Tables go fast, so prepare to go belly up to the bar, particularly on Friday night. Barhoppers often meet at El Centenario for drinks and song before moving on to late-night haunts nearby.

**El Mitote** (✉ Amsterdam 53, at Sonora, Col. Condesa ☎ 55/5211–9150) is one of those rare Mexico City bars where the music doesn't drown out the conversation. El Mitote's famous vodka sangrias are tasty, but pack a mean punch.

While in the neighborhood, drop by the popular **Pata Negra** (✉ Tamaulipas 30, at Juan Escutia, Col. Condesa). On weekends, it can get pretty crowded, so it's a good idea to get there before 11 if you want a table. On Monday and Wednesday, when the bar thins out, local groups play jazz, bossa nova, and flamenco music.

With glass walls and three split-levels, cocktail lounge **Rexo** (✉ Saltillo 1, at Av. Vicente Suárez, Col. Condesa ☎ 55/5553–1300 or 55/5553–5337) becomes a roaring hive of activity.

Another Condesa favorite is **Rioma** (✉ Insurgentes Sur 377, near Michoacán, Col. Condesa ☎ 55/5584–8288), a basement restaurant-bar formerly owned by renowned Mexican comedian Cantinflas. Local and foreign DJs spin mostly house music.

**St. Patrick's Pub** (✉ Campeche 410, Col. Condesa ☎ 55/5211–3030) is a pleasant bar with a wide selection of Mexican and European suds. The menu also includes pub grub and 20 brands of whiskey.

COYOACÁN **La Guadalupana** (✉ Calle Higuera 14, Coyoacán ☎ 55/5554–6253), a famous cantina dating from 1932, is always packed. The crowd here is overwhelmingly male, so unaccompanied women will definitely draw attention.

Students and hip intellectuals of all ages pack **El Hijo del Cuervo** (✉ Jardín Centenario 17, Coyoacán ☎ 55/5658–5196) for an interesting mix of rock and protest music, known as nueva canción. It also offers the occasional theater show, with cover charges varying (up to $7).

POLANCO   Perched atop the Habita Hotel, **Áera** (✉ Presidente Masaryk 201, at Arquímedes, Col. Polanco ☎ 55/5281–4631) offers a magnificent view of the city from a chic, open-air bar.

The **Camino Real** (✉ Mariano Escobedo 700, Col. Nueva Anzures ☎ 55/5263–8888), southeast of Polanco, has a sophisticated crowd and mellow music.

As the name suggests, **Cosmo** (✉ Presidente Masaryk 410, at Calderón de la Barca, Col. Polanco ☎ 55/5281–4631) specializes in designer cocktails for those who grow tired of the cerveza-and-tequila routine.

LA ROMA   **La Bodeguita del Medio** (✉ Cozumel 37, Col. Roma Norte ☎ 55/5553–0246) is a sit-down joint full of life, with every surface splashed with graffiti. Inspired by the original Havana establishment where Hemingway lapped up mojitos, the place also serves cheap Cuban food—but most people just drink.

The grand cantina **La Covadonga** (✉ Puebla 121, at Córdoba, Col. Roma ☎ 55/5533–2922) has an antique bar and a good restaurant serving up Spanish tapas. Nightly it's filled with the sound of exuberant games of dominoes.

The bar of the restaurant **Ixchel** (✉ Medellín 65, at Colima, Col. Roma ☎ 55/5208–4055) is a great place for a relaxing sip; it's in a beautiful old building.

A fantastic old cantina, **El Portal de Cartagena** (✉ Chiapas 174, at Medellín, Col. Roma ☎ 55/5264–8714 or 55/5584–1113) is ideal for a long lunch and a few beers.

ZONA ROSA   **Bar Milán** (✉ Milán 18, at General Prim, Col. Juárez ☎ 55/5592–0031),
★   northeast of Zona Rosa (a ten-minute walk), is a local favorite with the young and hip. Upon entering you need to change pesos into milagros (miracles), which are notes necessary to buy drinks throughout the night. The trick is to remember to change them back to pesos before last call.

Perhaps the best cantina in the Zona Rosa, **El Trompo** (✉ Hamburgo 87, at Niza, Zona Rosa ☎ 55/5207–8503) has a daily two-for-one drink special from 1 PM to 12 AM.

## Dance Clubs

Dance emporiums in the capital run the gamut from cheek-to-cheek romantic to throbbing strobe lights and ear-splitting music. Most places have a cover charge, but it's rarely more than $10. Friday and Saturday are the busiest club nights, while Thursday's a good option if you'd like a bit of elbow room for dancing. The most popular clubs open

Wednesday, too. Some clubs require that reservations be made one to two days in advance if you want a table.

CENTRO   The so-called cathedral of quebraditas (a fast-paced country dance), **El Pacífico** (⊠ Bucareli 43 at Morelos, Col. Centro ☎ 55/5592–2778), showcases some of the city's most talented dancers as they toss and swing their partners to northern-style *banda* music. El Pacifico could easily win a prize as the noisiest club in Mexico, and its festive atmosphere never disappoints.

**The Pervert Lounge** (⊠ Uruguay 70, between 5 de Febrero and Isabel La Católica, Col. Centro ☎ 55/5518–0976) may not live up (or down?) to its name, but it's funky and fun if you like electronic music.

**Salón Baraimas** (⊠ Filomeno Mata 7, between Av. 5 de Mayo and Calle Tacuba, Col. Centro ☎ 55/5510–4488) is a serious setting for those who know how to salsa. To reserve a table you have to buy a bottle of rum or tequila. Dancing begins around 9, but live bands start at 11.

**Salón Los Ángeles** (⊠ Lerdo 206, Col. Guerrero ☎ 55/5597–5181) takes you back in time to the 1930s. The grand, open dance floor swings to the rhythms of danzón and salsa. When renowned Latin musicians come to town, this is often where they perform.

Local bands play danzón, cha-cha, and mambo upstairs in a converted factory at **Salón México** (⊠ Pensador Mexicano, at San Juan de Dios, Col. Centro ☎ 55/5510–9915), combining nostalgia with fresh energy.

POLANCO   **Box** (⊠ Av. Moliere 425, at Andrómaco, Col. Polanco ☎ 55/5203–3365 or 55/5203–3356) is one of the capital's premier gay discos, playing mostly electronica. For big spenders, there's a special VIP area.

In recent years the huge **Salón 21** (⊠ Moliere, at Andrómaco, Col. Ampliación Granada ☎ 55/5255–1496 or 55/5255–5658), near Col. Polanco, has hosted the best international salsa and Afro-Caribbean bands to visit Mexico City; it's more of an event space than a dance hall, though.

ROMA   In a high-ceilinged colonial mansion, the **Living Room** (⊠ Orizaba 146, Col. Roma ☎ 55/5203–3365 or 55/5203–3356) hosts one of the most popular gay clubs in town. It's open on weekend nights only.

★   So popular you can barely move is the friendly **Mama Rumba** (⊠ Querétaro 230, at Medellín, Col. Roma ☎ 55/5564–6920 ⊠ Plaza San Jacinto 23, San Ángel ☎ 55/5550–8099 or 55/5550–8090), a 10-minute cab ride from the Zona Rosa. A nondescript Cuban restaurant during the day, it turns on the heat Wednesday through Saturday nights. If the Roma location is too crowded, which it usually is, the San Ángel location may give you a little more breathing room.

Many locals consider the tropical sounds at dance hall **La Maraka** (⊠ Mitla 410, at Eje 5, Col. Narvarte ☎ 55/5682–5479), south of Roma, among the city's finest in merengue and salsa music.

**Meneo** (⊠ Nueva York 315, just off Av. Insurgentes Sur, near Eje 5 San Antonio, Col. Napoles ☎ 55/5523–9448) is a modern dance hall for live salsa and merengue, with two dance floors and three orchestras. It's south of Roma.

ZONA ROSA   When it seems as though every place in Zona Rosa has shut down, **El Álamo** (✉ Hamburgo 96, Zona Rosa ☎ 55/5525–8352) is probably just getting started with live tropical music or jukebox picks.

If Latin music isn't your thing, **El Colmillo** (✉ Versalles 52, Col. Juárez ☎ 55/5592–6164), northeast of Zona Rosa (10 minutes on foot), spins techno downstairs and has an acid jazz lounge upstairs. Founded by two Englishmen, El Colmillo draws a variety of foreigners and locals.

**Tandem Pub** (✉ Río Nazas 73, Río Tigris, Col. Cuauhtémoc) was once a quiet British-style pub that has been converted into a hotspot for retro and funk music. Weekend nights alternate between DJs and live music. It's a five-minute walk north of Zona Rosa.

ELSEWHERE   Urban cowboy dance club **El Rodeo** (✉ Santa Fe Av. 5 de Mayo, Col. San Andrés Atenco in Ciudad Satélite ☎ 55/5361–5104) caters to wannabe bronco busters with live norteño music, a huge dance floor, a mechanical bull, and a rodeo show, all bundled up into one knee-slappin' package. It's open Friday through Sunday.

## Dinner Shows

The liveliest shows are in clubs downtown and in the Zona Rosa. At **Focolare** (✉ Hamburgo 87, at Niza, Zona Rosa ☎ 55/5207–8257), you can watch a cockfight, mariachi singers, and traditional folk dancers Thursday through Saturday nights. The show costs $8.50; Mexican dinner and drinks are separate.

**El Arroyo** (✉ Av. Insurgentes Sur 4003, Tlalpan ☎ 55/5573–4344) is a huge complex south of Zona Rosa (40-minute drive), complete with its own bullring. *Novilleros* (novice bullfighters) try out their skills from May to September. An open kitchen serves traditional Mexican specialties and drinks, such as the potent, cactus-derived *pulque,* from 8 to 8. On weekends, mariachi and jarocho musicians add to the buzz.

The mazelike **La Bodega** (✉ Popocatépetl 25, corner of Amsterdam, Col. Condesa ☎ 55/5525–2473) is a lively place for drinks and decent Mexican food. A quirky band of old chaps plays relaxed Latin and Caribbean dance music in the small front room, and the upstairs theater hosts visiting musicians. Try to catch Astrid Haddad, a wild feminist cabaret artiste. You won't get the jokes unless you're fluent in Spanish, but you'll be laughing at her act anyway. Admission starts at $4, not including the theater shows.

## Mariachi Music

The traditional last stop for nocturnal Mexicans is **Plaza Garibaldi** in Colonia Cuauhtémoc east of Eje Central Lázaro Cárdenas, between República de Honduras and República de Perú. Here exuberant, and often inebriated, mariachis gather to unwind after evening performances—by performing even more. There are roving mariachis, as well as norteño (country-style) musicians and white-clad jarocho bands (Veracruz-style) peddling songs in the outdoor plaza, where you can also buy beer and shots of tequila. Well-to-do Mexicans park themselves inside one of the cantinas or clubs surrounding the plaza and belt out their favorite songs.

Note: the square was spruced up in the early 1990s to improve its seedy image, but things still get rough late at night. Furthermore, leaving Plaza Garibaldi can be dangerous—be sure to arrange for transportation ahead of time. You may call a travel agency, drive your car and park on the well-lit ramp below the plaza, or call a safe sitio taxi.

★ **Tenampa** (✉ Plaza Garibaldi 12, Col. Cuauhtémoc ☎ 55/5526–6176) is one of the better cantinas, with some great paintings on the walls of famous Mexican composers. Order a tequila and the musicians will be around shortly, offering to serenade you (a song costs about $5, though Mexicans typically haggle for a dozen), so the bar is rarely without the wailing mariachis for more than 10 minutes. It's open Sunday through Thursday until at least 2 AM, and even later on Friday and Saturday.

A list of upcoming mariachi events and recommended locales can be obtained from the offices of the **Union Mexicana de Mariachis** (✉ Mercados Altos, Plaza Garibaldi, Col. Cuauhtémoc ☎ 55/5526–6256).

If you're up for a few good laughs, don't miss male-bashing balladeer Paquita la del Barrio at **La Casa de Paquita la del Barrio** (✉ Zarco 202, near Estrella, Col. Guerrero ☎ 55/5583–1668). The overweight Paquita sings in the mariachi tradition but her songs, such as "Rata de Dos Patas" (Two-legged Rat), are anything but traditional as they poke fun at macho Mexican society. Paquita usually performs on Friday and Saturday at 7:30 PM and 9:30 PM; however, showtimes are subject to change. You'll probably have to get there about an hour early to avoid long lines.

### Rock & Jazz
**The Bulldog** (✉ Rubens 6, at Av. Revolución, Col. Mixcoac ☎ 55/5611–8818), north of Coyoacán books mostly rock acts. The $27 cover is expensive by Mexican standards, but it includes free drink coupons.

For the fast and furious, **Multiforo Alicia** (✉ Cuauhtémoc 91-A, at Durango, Col. Roma) headlines foreign and local indie bands playing punk, ska, and surf music. In true punk rock fashion, the space is poorly ventilated and the sound system leaves much to be desired, but it's a cheap night out and the scene is entertaining.

**New Orleans** (✉ Av. Revolución 1755, at Altavista, Col. San Ángel ☎ 55/5550–1908) is one of Mexico City's few jazz and blues clubs that has withstood the test of time. It features mostly local acts.

## The Arts

### Dance
FodorsChoice  The world-renowned **Ballet Folklórico de México** (✉ Palacio de Bellas Artes,
★  Av. Juárez at Eje Central Lázaro Cárdenas, Alameda Central ☎ 55/5512–3633 box office, 55/5325–9000 Ticketmaster ⊕ www.balletamalia.com), of Amalia Hernández, is a visual feast of Mexican regional folk dances in whirling colors. Lavish and professional, it's one of the most popular shows in Mexico. Performances are on Wednesday at 8:30 PM and Sunday at 9:30 AM and 8:30 PM at the beautiful Palacio de Bellas Artes—it's a treat to see its Tiffany-glass curtain lowered. Call the box

office or Ticketmaster for information on prices and for reservations. Hotels and travel agencies can also secure tickets.

The **National Dance Theater** (☎ 55/5280–8771) is a good forum for contemporary dance behind the Auditorio Nacional on Paseo de la Reforma.

The **Miguel Covarrubias Hall** (✉ National Autonomous University of Mexico [UNAM], Av. Insurgentes Sur 3000, Ciudad Universitaria ☎ 55/5665–6825), home of the university's dance department, frequently sponsors modern-dance performances.

**Teatro de la Danza** (✉ Centro Cultural del Bosque, off Paseo de la Reforma and Campo Marte, Col. Polanco ☎ 55/5280–8771) stages contemporary and classical dance at a reasonable price.

## Music

Music thrums everywhere in the capital, from itinerant trumpeters and drummers playing in the streets to marimba in the market places. Some of the best street musicians can be found at popular lunchtime eateries, especially in markets. It's customary to offer a tip of small change; at least a few pesos will be appreciated. Free concerts spread through the city's plazas on weekends when, again, donations are in order. Most Mexican music (salsa, son, cumbia, danzón) is for dancing and you will usually find a succession of great live bands in the dance halls and nightclubs.

CLASSICAL  The primary venue for classical music is the **Palacio de Bellas Artes** (✉ Eje Central Lázaro Cárdenas and Av. Juárez, Col. Centro ☎ 55/5512–3633), which has a main auditorium and the smaller Manuel Ponce concert hall. The National Opera performs from February through November at the palace. The National Symphony Orchestra stages classical and modern pieces at the palace in spring and fall.

The top concert hall, often touted as the best in Latin America, is **Ollin Yolitzli** (✉ Periférico Sur 5141, Col. Isidro Favela ☎ 55/5606–0016 or 55/5606–8558); it hosts the **Mexico City Philharmonic** several times a year.

**The National Autonomous University of Mexico's Philharmonic** (✉ Av. Insurgentes Sur 3000, Ciudad Universitaria ☎ 55/5622–7112 or 55/5606–8933) orchestra performs at the university.

Classical concerts (often free) are also held at the **National Music Conservatory** (✉ Auditorio Silvestre Revueltas, Av. Presidente Masaryk 582, Col. Polanco ☎ 55/5280–6347).

Another good venue for classical music is in the south of the city, **Auditorio Blas Galindo** (✉ Av. Río Churubusco, at Calz. de Tlalpan ☎ 55/5521–7960 or 55/5521–0686), in the Centro Nacional de las Artes (CNA, the National Arts Center).

For choral performances, look for one of the free performances of the **Madrigalistas de Bellas Artes** (✉ Calle Moneda 4, Col. Centro ☎ 55/5228–1245) in the Antiguo Palacio del Arzobispado.

POP & ROCK  For pop, rock, and Latin music stars such as Luis Miguel, Peter Gabriel, and Mercedes Sosa, check newspapers for attractions.

The **Auditorio Nacional** (⊠ Paseo de la Reforma 50, across from Nikko México hotel, Col. San Miguel Chapultepec ☎ 55/5280–9250 or 55/5280–9979 ⊕ www.auditorio.com.mx) is smart and modern, with great acoustics.

A choice venue, the **Hard Rock Cafe** (⊠ Campos Elíseos 278, Col. Chapultepec Polanco ☎ 55/5327–7120 or 55/5327–7171) is intimate and has state-of-the-art sound.

**Palacio de los Deportes** (⊠ Av. Río Churubusco and Calle Añil ☎ 55/5237–9999 Ext. 4264) has an open-air venue called the Foro Sol where you can catch the glitzy shows of Madonna or the Rolling Stones.

Though it's in need of an overhaul, the ambience is good at the **Teatro Metropolitano** (⊠ Independencia 90, Col. Centro ☎ 55/5510–1035 or 55/5510–1045). It hosts mostly rock concerts.

### Theater

Good live theater, whether in English or Spanish, is not Mexico City's strong suit. **Centro Cultural Heléico** (⊠ Av. Revolución 1500, Col. Guadalupe Inn ☎ 55/5662–8674) is one of the most reliable bets.

**Centro Cultural Telmex** (⊠ Av. Cuauhtémoc 19, at Av. Chapultepec ☎ 55/5514–1965) stages Spanish-language versions of Broadway plays. Ticket prices range from $18 to $48. Showtimes are Monday, Wednesday, and Friday at 8 PM; Saturday at 5 PM; and Sunday at 1:30 PM and 6 PM.

**El Hábito** (⊠ Madrid 13, Coyoacán ☎ 55/5659–1139), run by the contentious satirist Jesusa Rodríguez, puts on lively music, cabaret, and political theater, but you'll need proficient Spanish to understand the performances.

# SPORTS & THE OUTDOORS

Latin sports such as the *fiesta brava* (bullfighting)—brought to Mexico by the Spanish—have enjoyed popularity for more than four centuries in the capital, which attracts the country's best athletes. And although the roots of *fútbol* (soccer) are probably English, a weekend afternoon game at Mexico City's colossal Estadio Azteca leaves no question that this is the sport Mexicans are craziest about. Baseball and boxing have strong followings, too, as does over-the-top *lucha libre* (wrestling). There are plenty of lovely parks for a safe jog or walk. For more challenging activities, seek out an ecotourism or adventure travel agency for a getaway such as white-water rafting in nearby Veracruz, volcano climbing in Puebla, or mountain biking in the Desierto de los Leones. Some city agencies leave much to be desired, though, so you may need to take extra initiative to find the right group.

### Adventure Sports & Ecotourism

Mexico continues to develop both government offices and private industry groups to promote ecotourism, but these are still nascent. A good starting point for information is the **Asociación Mexicana de Turismo de Aventura y Ecoturismo** (⊠ AMTAVE; Homero 526, Int. 801, at Lamartine, Col. Polanco ☎ 55/5255–4400 or 55/5255–4465 ⊕ www.

amtave.org), a group of ecotourism and adventure travel providers. The association produces an annual catalog and a bilingual (English-Spanish) Web site.

A number of adventure-travel agencies have sprouted up to entice both tourists and locals out of the smog and chaos of Mexico City for a weekend of white-water rafting, rappelling, or biking. One of the best is **México Verde Expeditions** (⊠ Homero 526, Int. 801, at Lamartine, Col. Polanco ☎ 55/5255–4400 or 55/5255–4465 ⊕ www.mexicoverde. com.mx), whose guides speak English and lead tours to the pristine areas of such nearby states as Veracruz and Morelos. Call a week in advance to make reservations and bring a sleeping bag and sunblock.

Marlene Ehrenberg Enriquez, a multilingual certified guide, is a pioneer ecotourism consultant. Her agency, **Marlene Ehrenberg Tours** (⊠ Av. Universidad 1953, edif. 11-203, Universidad ☎ 55/5550–9080 ⊕ www. marlene366.tripod.com), offers specialized tours that focus on Mexico's ecology and culture.

A good bet for rappelling, rafting, rock-climbing, and other extreme sports is **Río y Rapidos** (⊠ Oriente 253, Int. 50, Col. Agricola Oriente ☎ 55/5756–4775 ⊕ http://rioyrapidos.tripod.com.mx), run by affable Carlos Hinojosa. They've been in business since 1980 and offer excursions throughout Mexico.

**Aventura Vertical** (⊠ Juan Bautista 450, Col. La Nopalera ☎55/5863–3363 ⊕ www.aventuravertical.com) offers instruction on weekends in rock-climbing, ice-climbing, and mountain-biking, among others, with certified bilingual guides. Equipment is provided or you can bring your own.

## Boxing

**Arena Mexico** (⊠ Dr. Lavista between Dr. Carmona and Dr. Lucio, Col. Doctores ☎ 55/5588–0508) holds boxing matches most Saturdays starting at around 6:30 PM.

## Bullfighting

The main season for bullfighting is the dry season, around November through March, when celebrated *matadores* appear at **Plaza México** (⊠ Calle Agusto Rodín 241, at Holbein, Col. Ciudad de los Deportes ☎ 55/5563–3959), the world's largest bullring (it seats 40,000). Tickets, which range from $3.50 to $48, can be purchased at hotel travel desks or at the bullring's ticket booths (weekends 9:30–2 and 3:30–7). The show goes on at 4 on Sunday.

## Soccer

Fútbol is the sport that Mexicans are most passionate about, which is evident in the size of their soccer stadium, **Estadio Azteca** (⊠ Calz. de Tlalpan 3465, Tlalpan ☎ 55/5617–8080), the second largest in Latin America. The World Cup Finals were held here in 1970 and 1986. You can buy tickets outside the stadium in the south of the city on the same day of any minor game. For more important games, buy tickets a week in advance. The Pumas, a popular university-sponsored team, play at **Estadio Olímpica** (⊠ Av. Insurgentes Sur at Universidad Nacional Autónoma de México, Ciudad Universitaria).

## Lucha Libre

Wrestling is right up there with soccer as a sport that evokes many emotional outbursts, though it doesn't have as much cachet as the latter. Wrestlers wear masks and dress in costumes depicting good or evil (the devil against the angel, for example), and it's usually good who wins after a couple of acrobatic slams and pitches out of the ring. The debate on whether the fights are fixed rages on. The good guy wrestlers often become folk heroes, appear in comic books and movies, and are role models for young kids. One of the most famous wrestlers was El Santo (The Saint), who has since retired but whose son continues the legacy. Most wrestlers are from the barrios and the sport attracts their compatriots: it's rowdy and loud, and few women attend the matches— if they do, they go in groups or accompanied by a man. Matches take place every Friday night at 8:30 at the **Arena Mexico** (✉ Dr. Lavista between Dr. Carmona and Dr. Lucio, Col. Doctores ☎ 55/5588–0508). Ringside seats fetch $8. Avoid hailing cabs directly outside the arena.

# SHOPPING

The most-concentrated shopping area is the **Zona Rosa,** which is chock-full of boutiques, jewelry stores, leather-goods shops, antiques stores, and art galleries.

**Polanco,** a choice residential neighborhood along the northeast perimeter of Bosque de Chapultepec, has blossomed into a more upscale shopping area. Select shops line the huge, ultramodern **Plaza Polanco** (✉ Jaime Balmes 11, Col. Polanco). You can also head to the **Plaza Masarik** (✉ Av. Presidente Masaryk and Anatole France, Col. Polanco). **Plaza Moliere** (✉ Moliere between Calles Horacio and Homero, Col. Polanco) is another upscale shopping area.

The **Colonia Condesa,** though better known for restaurants and cafés, is sprouting designer clothing boutiques, primarily for a younger crowd. Jewelers, shoe shops, and some hip housewares stores are squeezing in as well. Most cluster along avenidas Michoacán, Vicente Suárez, and Tamaulipas.

Hundreds of shops with more modest trappings and better prices are spread along the length of Avenida Insurgentes and Avenida Juárez.

## Department Stores, Malls & Shopping Arcades

Department stores are generally open Monday, Tuesday, Thursday, and Friday 10–7, and Wednesday and Saturday 10–8.

**Bazar del Centro** (✉ Isabel la Católica 30, just below Calle Madero, Col. Centro), in a restored, late-17th-century mansion built around a garden courtyard, houses several chic boutiques and prestigious jewelers such as **Aplijsa** (☎ 55/5521–1923), known for its fine gold, silver, pearls, and gemstones, and **Ginza** (☎ 55/5518–6453), which has Japanese pearls, including the prized cultured variety. Other shops sell Taxco silver, Tonalá stoneware, and Mexican tequilas and liqueurs.

**Liverpool** (✉ Av. Insurgentes Sur 1310, Col. Guadalupe Inn ✉ Mariano Escobedo 425, Col. Polanco ✉ Plaza Satélite shopping center ✉ Perisur shopping center ⊕ www.liverpool.com.mx) is the largest retailer in Mexico City and often has bargains on clothes.

The upscale department store chain **El Palacio de Hierro** (✉ Av. Durango and Salamanca, Col. Condesa ✉ Plaza Moliere, Col. Polanco ✉ Plaza Coyoacán; Col. Xoco ⊕ www.palaciodehierro.com.mx) is noted for items by well-known designers, as well as its seductive advertising campaigns. **Perisur shopping mall** (✉ Periférico Sur, Perisur ⊕ www.perisur.com. mx), on the southern edge of the city, near where the Periférico Expressway meets Avenida Insurgentes, is posh and pricey.

**Plaza La Rosa** (✉ between Amberes and Génova, Zona Rosa), a modern shopping arcade, has 72 prestigious shops and boutiques, including Aldo Conti and Diesel. It spans the depth of the block between Londres and Hamburgo, with entrances on both streets. **Plaza Loreto** (✉ Avenida Revolución and Río Magdalena, San Ángel ☎ 55/5550–6292) has a strange history. It was built on land that once held a wheat mill owned by Martín Cortés, the son of conqueror Hernán Cortés, and later a paper factory. This small outdoor mall has boutiques, CD stores, a Sanborns, and the Museo Soumaya. **Piccolo Mondo** (☎ 55/5616–4758 ⊕ www. piccolomondo.com.mx) contains a small video arcade for children, with a staff that can supervise kids.

**Portales de los Mercaderes** (Merchants Arcade; ✉ extending the length of the west side of the Zócalo between Calles Madero and 16 de Septiembre, Col. Centro) has attracted merchants since 1524. It's lined with jewelry shops selling gold (often by the gram) and authentic Taxco silver at prices lower than those in Taxco itself, where the overhead is higher. In the middle of the Portales de los Mercaderes is **Tardán** (✉ Plaza de la Constitución 7, Col. Centro ☎ 55/5512–2459), an unusual shop specializing in fashionable men's hats of every shape and style.

**Sanborns** (⊕ www.sanborns.com.mx) is a chain of mini-department stores with some 70 branches in Mexico City. The most convenient are at Calle Madero 4 (its original store in the House of Tiles, downtown); several along Paseo de la Reforma (including one at the Angel monument and another four blocks west of the Diana Fountain); in San Angel (on Avenida de la Revolución and Avenida de la Paz); Coyoacán (at the Jardín Centenario); and in the Zona Rosa (one at the corner of Niza and Hamburgo and another at Londres 130 in the Hotel Calinda Geneve). They carry quality ceramics and crafts (and can ship anywhere), and most have restaurants or coffee shops, a pharmacy, ATMs, and periodical and book departments with English-language publications. They're great spots to meet a friend.

**Santa Fe** (✉ Salida a Toluca, Santa Fe ⊕ www.ccsantafe.com) is the largest mall in Latin America, with 285 stores, a movie theater, an international exhibition center, hotels, and several restaurants. It's in the wealthy Santa Fe district, which in recent years has become the favored office real-estate property in the city. To get here, take the Periférico Expressway south to the exit marked CENTRO SANTA FE.

## Markets

**Fodor's Choice**
★ Open every day from about 10–5, the bustling **Mercado Artesanal La Ciudadela** (⊠ Balderas, one block south of Parque José María Morelos, Col. Juárez) bursts with the widest range of wares and the best bargains in the capital. Browse through the crafts, from Talavera pottery, leather belts, guitars, tile-framed mirrors, hammocks, silverware, and papier-mâché skeletons to rugs, trays from Olinalá, and the ubiquitous sombrero. Prices are good but you can still haggle. A number of casual restaurants serve up hearty set-menu lunches for $3–$5. Covered stalls take up a whole square, a 10–15 minute walk from the Alameda.

★ A "must"—if you are in town on a Saturday—is a visit to the **Bazar Sábado** (Saturday Bazaar; ⊠ Plaza San Jacinto, San Ángel). Hundreds of vendors sell tons of crafts, silver, wood carvings, embroidered clothing, leather goods, wooden masks, beads, *amates* (bark paintings), and trinkets at stalls on the network of cobbled streets outside. Inside the bazaar building, a renovated two-story colonial mansion, are the better-quality—and higher-priced—goods, including *alebrijes* (painted wooden animals from Oaxaca), glassware, pottery, jewelry, and papier-mâché flowers. A patio buffet and an indoor restaurant will help you conquer hunger and thirst. The market is open daily 10–7.

Sunday 10–4, more than 100 artists exhibit and sell their painting and sculpture at the **Jardín del Arte** (Garden of Art; ⊠ Río Nevada, between Sullivan and Manuel Villalongín, Parque Sullivan, northeast of the Reforma-Insurgentes intersection, Col. Cuauhtémoc). Along the west side of the park is a colorful weekend mercado with scores of food stands.

The **Mercado Insurgentes** (also called Mercado Zona Rosa; ⊠ between Florencia and Amberes, Zona Rosa) is an entire block deep, with entrances on both Londres and Liverpool. This typical neighborhood public market distinguishes itself from others in one noticeable way: most of the stalls (222 of them) sell crafts. You can find all kinds of handmade items—including serapes and ponchos, baskets, pottery, silver, pewter, fossils, and onyx. Expect to pay slightly higher prices here than at the Mercado Artesanal de la Ciudadela.

The enormous market **La Lagunilla** (⊠ Libertad, between República de Chile and Calle Allende, Col. Centro) has been a site for local trade and bartering for more than five centuries. The day to go is Sunday, when flea-market and antiques stands are set up outside. Dress down and watch out for pickpockets; it's known affectionately as the Thieves Market—local lore says you can buy back on Sunday what was stolen from your home Saturday.

## Specialty Shops

### Antiques

**Antigüedades Coloniart** (⊠ Estocolmo 37, at Hamburgo, Zona Rosa ☎ 55/5514–4799) has good-quality antique paintings, furniture, and sculpture. **Bazar de Antigüedades** (⊠ Between Londres and Hamburgo, opposite Mercado Insurgentes, Zona Rosa) is a line of antiques stores along a passageway, at its liveliest on a Saturday. **Galería Windsor** (✉ Hamburgo 224, at Praga, Zona Rosa ☎ 55/5525–2881 or 55/5525–2996 ⊕www.galeriawindsor.com.mx) specializes in 18th- and 19th-century antiques. **Rodrigo Rivera Lake** (✉ Campos Elíseos 199-PH, Col. Polanco ☎ 55/5281–5505) collects high-quality antiques and decorative art. It's open by appointment only.

## Art

The best group of modern galleries is in Colonia Roma. Before you go, check out www.arte-mexico.com to find out what events are going on.

The **Galeria de Arte Mexicano** (✉ Gob. Rafael Rebollar 43, San Miguel Chapultepec ☎ 55/5272–5696 or 55/5272–5529 ⊕ www.galeriadeartemexicano.com), founded in 1935, was the first place in Mexico City dedicated full-time to the sale and promotion of art (before its inception, there were no official galleries in the city). The GAM, as it is often referred to, has played an important role in many Mexican art movements and continues to support many of the most important artists in the country. They have also published noteworthy books; these works and catalogs are available at the gallery bookstore. **Praxis Arte International** (✉ Arquimedes 175, Col. Polanco ☎ 55/5254–8813 or 55/5255–5700 ⊕ www.praxis-art.com) also promotes Mexican and Latin American artists. They work with many distinguished artists like Santiago Carbonell and Roberto Cortázar, as well as excellent young artists.

Collectors won't want to miss the best gallery in the south of the city, the **Galería Kin** (✉ Altavista 92, Col. San Ángel ☎ 55/5550–8641 or 55/5550–8910), which exhibits a wide variety of contemporary Mexican painting and sculpture. The **Juan Martín Gallery** (✉ Dickens 33-B, Col. Polanco ☎ 55/5280–0277 ⊕ www.arte-mexico.com/juanmartin) shows avant-garde work. **Misrachi** (✉ Av. Presidente Masaryk 83, at Taine, Col. Polanco ☎ 55/5531–6439 or 55/5531–5052 ✉ Hotel Nikko, Campos Elíseos 204, Col. Polanco ☎ 55/5280–3866 or 55/5280–5728), a long-standing gallery, promotes well-known Mexican and international artists. The **Nina Menocal de Rocha Gallery** (✉ Zacatecas 93, Col. Roma ☎ 55/5564–7209) specializes in up-and-coming Cuban painters. The **Oscar Roman Gallery** (✉ Julio Verne 14, Col. Polanco ☎ 55/5280–0436 ⊕ www.arte-mexico.com/romanosc) is packed with work by good Mexican painters with a contemporary edge. The store and gallery of the renowned **Sergio Bustamante** (✉ Nikko México hotel, Campos Elíseos 204, Col. Polanco ☎ 55/5282–2638 ✉ Camino Real Hotel, Mariano Escobedo 700, Col. Polanco ☎ 55/5254–7372) displays and sells the artist's wild sculpture, jewelry, and interior-design pieces.

## Candy

**Celaya** (✉ 5 de Mayo 39, Col. Centro ☎ 55/5521–1787 ✉ Orizaba 143, Col. Roma ☎ 55/5514–8438 ✉ Colima 143, Col. Roma ☎ 55/5207–5858) is a decades-old haven for those with a sweet tooth. It specializes in candied pineapple, guava, and other exotic fruit; almond paste; candied walnut rolls; and *cajeta,* made with thick caramelized milk.

## Designer Clothing

At first glance, the linen dresses in **Carmen Rion** (⊠ Av. Michoacán 30–A, at Parque México, Col. Condesa ☎ 55/5264–6179) may seem classic, but look closely and you'll find innovative ties and fastenings. The jewelry, often combining wood, silver, and seed pods, is equally unique. The Little Black Dress has a D. F. outpost: **Chanel** (⊠ Presidente Masaryk 450-2, Col. Polanco ☎ 55/5282–3121). **Frattina** (⊠ Presidente Masaryk 420, at Calderón de la Barca and Edgar Allan Poe, Col. Polanco ☎ 55/5281–4036 ⊠ Altavista 52, San Ángel ☎ 55/5550–6830 ⊕ www.frattina.com.mx) carries women-only work by international and top Mexican designers. If the exchange rate goes your way, a trip to **Hermès** (⊠ Presidente Masaryk 422A, between Calderón de la Barca and Edgar Allan Poe, Col. Polanco ☎ 55/5282–2118) may be in order for their legendary silk scarves and leather goods.

## Interior Design & Unique Gifts

Mexico City has several independent furniture stores that offer unique designs and extraordinary gifts. **Dupuis** (⊠ Fuenes 180B, Pedregal ☎ 55/5595–4852 ⊠ Palmas 240, Las Lomas ☎ 55/5540–5349 ⊠ Diego Rivera 50, San Ángel ☎ 55/5550–6178 ⊕ www.dupuis.com. mx) is a pricey furniture store with different styles steeped in different Mexican traditions; indigenous designs, Spanish colonial decorations, and the strong French influence that characterized so much Mexican design at the beginning of the 20th century. They also have unique accessories in subdued colors, including flower pots, lamps, and picture frames, which make excellent gifts—and dupuis is known for elegant gift presentation. **Sant Anooka** (⊠ Vicente Suárez 158, Col. Condesa ☎ 55/5786–7736 ⊕ www.santanooka.com) has kooky furniture designs in wood. This is also a great place to pick up quirky accessories and gifts, like a cutting board for cheese that looks like a mouse trap.

## Jewelry

Taxco silver of exceptional style is sold at **Arte en Plata** (⊠ Londres 162-A, Zona Rosa ☎ 55/5511–1422), with many designs inspired by pre-Columbian art. **Cartier** (⊠ Av. Presidente Masaryk 438, Col. Polanco ☎ 55/5281–5528) sells the sophisticated jewelry and clothes under the auspices of the French Cartier. For unusual jewelry, mostly in silver, glass, and stone, look in at **Entenaya** (⊠ Montes de Oca 47, Col. Condesa ☎ 55/5286–1535). **Pelletier** (⊠ Torcuato Caso 237, Col. Polanco ☎ 55/5250–8600) sells fine jewelry and watches. **Plata Real** (⊠ Goldsmith 56-D, Col. Polanco ☎ 55/5281–0818) aims to preserve silversmith metalwork from the colonial period. In addition to creating replicas of colonial pieces, they offer high-quality contemporary sculptures. **Tane** (⊠ Av. Presidente Masaryk 430, Col. Polanco ☎ 55/5281–4775 ⊠ Santa Catarina 207, San Angel Inn ☎ 55/5616–0165) is a treasure trove of perhaps the best silver work in Mexico—jewelry, flatware, candelabra, museum-quality reproductions of archaeological finds, and bold new designs by young Mexican silversmiths.

## Leather

**Aries** (⊠ Florencia 14, Zona Rosa ☎ 55/5533–2509) is Mexico's finest purveyor of leather goods, with a superb selection of bags and accessories for men and women; prices are high. **Las Bolsas de Coyoacán** (⊠ Carrillo Puerto 9, Coyoacán ☎ 55/5554–2010) specializes in high-quality leather goods. **Gaitán** (⊠ Calle Sarasete 95-B, at Tetracini, Col. Peralvillo ☎ 55/5759–3393) carries an extensive array of leather coats, luggage, golf bags, and saddles. **Via Spiga** (⊠ Hamburgo 136, Zona Rosa ☎ 55/5207–9997 or 55/5208–9224) has a fine selection of shoes, gloves, and handbags.

## Mexican Crafts

**Arte Popular en Miniatura** (⊠ Hamburgo 85, Col. Juárez ☎ 55/5525–8145) is a tiny shop filled with tiny things, from dollhouse furniture and lead soldiers to miniature Nativity scenes. Browse for folk art, sculpture, and furniture in the gallery **Artesanos de México** (⊠ Londres 117, Zona Rosa ☎ 55/5514–7455). Under the auspices of the National Council for Culture and Arts, **Fonart** (National Fund for Promoting Arts and Crafts; ⊠ Juárez 89, Col. Juárez ☎ 55/5521–0171 ⊕ www.fonart.gob.mx ⊠ main store–warehouse ⊠ Av. Patriotismo 691, Col. Mixcoac ☎ 55/5563–4060) operates two stores in Mexico City, and others around the country (see their Web site). Prices are fixed and high, but the diverse, top-quality folk art and handcrafted furnishings from all over Mexico represent the best artisans. The best location is downtown, west of Alameda Park. Major sales at near wholesale prices are held from time to time at the main store–warehouse.

You can find handwoven wool rugs, tapestries, and fabrics with original and unusual designs at **Tamacani** (⊠ Av. Insurgentes Sur 1748B, Col. Florida ☎ 55/5662–7133).

# MEXICO CITY A TO Z

### AIR TRAVEL

AIRPORT  Mexico City's airport, Aeropuerto Internacional Benito Juárez (MEX), is the main gateway to the country.

The airport's newest wing has four banks and seven currency exchanges (*casas de cambio*); Cirrus and Plus ATMs that disburse pesos; places to rent cellular phones; an Internet room; and a food court, pharmacy, bookstore, and pricey shops. A multilevel parking garage charges $4 an hour for short-term parking.

Banks and currency exchanges rotate their schedules to provide 24-hour service. You can also use your ATM card to take pesos directly out of your U.S. account at ATMs (called *cajero automático* locally) here and throughout the city—and you'll get an even better exchange rate. Just remember that your home bank may charge $3 or more per transaction. Free carts are available in the baggage-retrieval areas but they do not fit through the grid once you have cleared customs so you must either hire a porter or carry your luggage yourself. The Mexico City Tourist Office, Mexican Ministry of Tourism (Sectur), and the Hotel Association have stands in the arrival areas that can provide information and find visitors a room for the night.

🛈 **Aeropuerto Internacional Benito Juárez** ☎ 55/5571–3600, 55/5784–0471 for information ⊕ www.asa.gob.mx.

AIRPORT TRANSFERS If you're taking a taxi, be sure to purchase your ticket at an official airport taxi counter marked Transportación Terrestre (ground transportation), located just after the baggage area in national arrivals and in the concourse area (leaving customs to your left) in international arrivals. Under no circumstance take a *pirata* taxi (unofficial drivers offering their services). Government-controlled fares are based on which colonia you are going to and are usually $14–$16 (per car, not per person) to most hotels. A 10% tip is customary for airport drivers if they help with baggage. All major car-rental agencies have booths at both arrival areas.

Taxis are priced by zones; figure out your zone from the big map on the wall (if you're in the central part of the city, you'll probably need Zone 4 or 5, which will cost around $14). To get to the taxi rank, head left from the arrivals area and out of the building. Touts stand at the exit; if you don't have a ticket in your hand, they will attempt to charge you more for the same taxi ride. Do not hand your luggage to anyone offering to help, apart from your driver, unless you are prepared to pay them a tip. The yellow-and-white airport taxis are safe. Avoid the others.

Reaching the city center takes 20 minutes to an hour depending on the traffic. If you're leaving from the city center in the morning, going against traffic, you will reach the airport quickly. In the evening allow at least an hour, count on more time in the rainy season.

Going to the airport, your taxi driver will ask which terminal you want: "Nacional o Internacional?" This question refers to your airline, not your destination. Be careful: some flights have code-sharing between a Mexican and a foreign airline, and check-in could be in either terminal. (Note that you will not lose more than 10 minutes if you arrive at the wrong terminal, since both share the same building.)

Taking the metro between the airport and the city is an impractical option. Although there's a station relatively near the airport, it's in a dodgy neighborhood, and there's no transit service directly to the terminals. Also, heavy luggage is not allowed in the metro during rush hours.

CARRIERS Major North American carriers, including Air Canada, Alaska Airlines, America West, American, Canadian, Continental, Delta, Northwest, Trans World Airlines, United, and USAirways–Air France fly nonstop between Houston and Mexico City.

Mexicana has scheduled service from Chicago, Denver, Las Vegas, Los Angeles, Miami, New York, Orlando, San Antonio, San Francisco, and San Jose, as well as direct or connecting service at 30 locations throughout Mexico. Aeroméxico serves Mexico City daily from Atlanta, Dallas, Houston, Los Angeles, Miami, New Orleans, New York, Orlando, Phoenix, San Antonio, San Diego, and Tucson (as well as Tijuana). Aeroméxico serves some 35 cities within Mexico. Aerolitoral, a subsidiary of Aeroméxico based in Monterrey, serves north-central cities as well as San Antonio, Texas, via Monterrey from Mexico City. Aerocalifornia serves nearly 30 Mexican cities. Líneas Aéreas Azteca, which started up in 2001, connects the capital with a half-dozen other Mexican cities.

**Aerocalifornia** ☎ 55/5208-1457. **Aeroméxico** ☎ 55/5133-4000 ⊕ www.aeromexico. com.mx. **Líneas Aéreas Azteca** ☎ 55/5716-8989. **Mexicana** ☎ 55/5448-0990 ⊕ www. mexicana.com.mx.

## BUS TRAVEL TO & FROM MEXICO CITY

Greyhound buses make connections to major U.S. border cities, from which Mexican bus lines depart throughout the day. Reserved seating is available on first-class coaches, which are comfortable but not nearly as plush as the intercity buses. If you plan stopovers en route, make sure in advance that your ticket is written up accordingly. In Mexico, platform announcements are in Spanish only.

Within Mexico, buses are the most popular way to travel: you can board ultramodern, superdeluxe motor coaches that show U.S. movies and serve soft drinks, coffee, and sandwiches. ETN (Enlaces Terrestres Nacionales) serves cities to the west and northwest, such as Guadalajara, Guanajuato, Morelia, Querétaro, San Miguel de Allende, and Toluca. ADO buses depart southeast to such places as Puebla, Oaxaca, Veracruz, Mérida, and Cancún. Almost every route has reserved seating. Reserved-seat tickets for major bus lines can be purchased at Mexico City travel agencies, at bus stations, on the Internet, or by phone with a service called Ticketbus. Ticketbus sells tickets for the following lines: ADO, ADO-GL, AU, Cristobal Colon, Estrella de Oro, ETN, Greyhound, Linea 1, Plus, and Primera Plus.

Buses depart from four outlying stations (*terminales de autobuses*): Central de Autobuses del Norte, going north; Central de Autobuses del Sur, going south; Central de Autobuses del Oriente, going east; and Terminal de Autobuses del Poniente, going west. Around holidays, you'll need to book your ticket at least a week in advance.

**Bus Depots Central de Autobuses del Norte** ✉ Av. Cien Metros 4907, Col. Magdalena de la Salina ☎ 55/5587-1552. **Central de Autobuses del Sur** ✉ Tasqueña 1320 ☎ 55/5689-9745 or 55/5689-4987. **Terminal de Autobuses del Oriente** ✉ Ignacio Zaragoza 200, Col. 7 de Julio ☎ 55/5762-5977. **Terminal de Autobuses del Poniente** (also known as "Observatorio") ✉ Río Tacubaya and Sur 122, Col. Real del Monte ☎ 55/ 5271-4519.

**Bus Lines ETN** ☎ 55/5577-6529, 55/5271-1262, or 55/5277-6529. **Greyhound** ☎ 55/ 5661-3135, 01800/010-0600 toll-free in Mexico ⊕ www.greyhound.com.mx. **Ticketbus** ☎ 55/5133-2424, 55/5133-2444, 01800/702-8000 toll-free in Mexico ⊕ www.ticketbus. com.mx.

## BUS TRAVEL WITHIN MEXICO CITY

The Mexico City bus system is used by millions of commuters because it's cheap and goes everywhere. Buses are packed during rush hours so, as in all big cities, you should be wary of pickpockets. One of the principal bus routes runs along Paseo de la Reforma, Avenida Juárez, and Calle Madero. This west–east route connects Bosque de Chapultepec with the Zócalo. A southbound bus may be taken along Avenida Insurgentes Sur to San Ángel and University City, or northbound along Avenida Insurgentes Norte to the Guadalupe Basílica. Mexico City tourism offices provide free bus-route maps. The price is usually between 2 and 4 pesos (about 40¢), depending on your destination. Make sure you have some small change, at most a 10-peso coin, loose in your pocket. (Avoid showing a wallet on a bus.) Tell the driver your destination when boarding; he'll tell you the fare, which you pay directly. Some bus stops have shelters with the name of the stop written above, but more often you'll spot a stop by the line or cluster of people waiting. Buses run late but it's best to choose safer forms of transport after dark. There are occasional armed robberies on city buses, but these rarely end in violence. If you are on a bus that is held up, remain calm, and hand over whatever is demanded. If such an incident occurs, your embassy can take a report and suggest ways of following up with local authorities, but don't expect any further investigation or resolution.

### CAR RENTAL

It's usually impractical to rent a car for travel within Mexico City, though it may be a good option for trips outside of the city. Within the city, traffic can be dense and drivers who don't allow other cars room to move (and who are not at all shy about using their horn!) make driving difficult and stressful. Traffic accidents are also difficult to navigate. When accidents happen, both parties involved call their insurance and their insurance companies send representatives to the scene to negotiate responsibility and payment. If someone is injured in a traffic accident, the situation may be even more complicated. In this case, it's advisable to contact your country's embassy so they can recommend the best course of action. Insurance options are available when renting a car through a major agency. All rental companies listed below have offices at Aeropuerto Internacional Benito Juárez.

🚗**Alamo** ⊠ Av. Paseo de la Reforma 157-B, Col. Cuauhtémoc ⊠ Thiers #195, Col. Anzures ☎ 55/5250-0055 ⊕ www.alamo.com. **Avis** ⊠ Atenas 44, Col. Juárez ⊠ Campos Eliseos 218, Col. Polanco ⊠ Insurgentes Sur 730, Col. del Valle ☎ 55/5283-1112 ⊕ www.avis.com.mx. **Budget** ⊠ Campos Eliseos 204, Col. Polanco ⊠ Atenas 40, Col. Juárez ⊠ Hamburgo 71, Col. Juárez ⊠ Mariano Escobedo 700, Col. Anzurez ☎ 55/5566-6800 ⊕ www.budget.com.mx. **Hertz** ⊠ Versalles 6, Col. Juárez ☎ 55/5762-8372 ⊕ www.hertz.com.mx. **Thrifty** ⊠ Av. Paseo de la Reforma 322, Col. Juárez ☎ 55/5207-2833 ⊕ www.thrifty.com.mx.

### CAR TRAVEL

Major arteries into Mexico City include Highway 57 to the north, which starts at Laredo, Texas, and goes through Monterrey and Querétaro. Highway 95 comes in from Cuernavaca to the south, and Highway 190D from Puebla to the east. Highway 15 via Toluca is the main western route.

Millions of intrepid drivers brave Mexico City's streets every day and survive, but for out-of-towners the experience can be frazzling. One-way streets are confusing and rush-hour traffic is nightmarish. Rush hours generally include weekday mornings from 8 to 10 and again from 4:30 to 6:30 PM. Fridays are particularly clogged. You can hire a chauffeur for your car through a hotel concierge or travel service such as American Express.

Also, the strictly enforced law *Hoy No Circula* (Today This Car Can't Circulate) applies to most private vehicles, and may include your rental car. One of several successful efforts to reduce smog and traffic congestion, this law prohibits every privately owned vehicle (including out-of-state, foreign, and rental cars) from being used on one designated weekday. All cars in the city without a Verification "0" rating (usually those built before 1994) are prohibited from driving one day a week (two days a week during alert periods, which are usually in December and January). Cars in violation are inevitably impounded by the police. Expect a hefty fine as well.

The weekday you can't drive is specified by the last number or letter of the license plate: on a nonemergency week, 5–6 are prohibited on Monday; 7–8 on Tuesday; 3–4 on Wednesday; 1–2 on Thursday; and 9–0 on Friday. For further information, contact the Mexican Government Tourism Office nearest you, or log on to ⊕ www.mexicocity.com.mx/nocircula.html or the English-language ⊕ www.t1msn.imeca.com.mx/t1msn_valle_de_mexico/vehicula.asp and plan accordingly.

PARKING  It's easiest to park in a staffed lot; these are especially common in the Centro. You can expect to pay between $1.50 and $3 per hour. Street parking can be hard to find. Police tow trucks haul away illegally parked vehicles, and the owner is heavily fined. Getting your car back is a tedious process. Locatel is an efficient 24-hour service for tracing vehicles that are towed, stolen, or lost (in case you forgot where you parked). There's a chance an operator on duty may speak English, but the service is primarily in Spanish.
🚹 **Locatel** ☎ 55/5658-1111.

### EMBASSIES
The U.S. Embassy is open weekdays 9–5, but is closed for American and Mexican holidays; however, there's always a duty officer to take emergency calls on holidays and after closing hours. The embassy keeps a list of English-speaking local doctors on hand if you need to consult one. The Canadian Embassy is open weekdays 9–1 and 2–5 and is closed for Canadian and Mexican holidays. The British Embassy is open weekdays 8:30–3:30.
🚹 **British Embassy** ⊠ Río Lerma 71, Col. Cuauhtémoc ☎ 55/5242-8500 or 55/5207-2089 ⊕ www.embajadabritanica.com.mx. **Canadian Embassy** ⊠ Schiller 529, Col. Polanco ☎ 55/5724-7900 ⊕ www.canada.org.mx. **U.S. Embassy** ⊠ Paseo de la Reforma 305, Col. Juárez ☎ 55/5080-2000 ⊕ www.usembassy-mexico.gov.

### EMERGENCIES
Most embassies recommend that you register your visit to Mexico with them, so that they're aware of your whereabouts in the event of an emergency. In an emergency, it's also highly recommend that you contact your embassy's consular services before, or in lieu of, calling local authorities. Local emergency numbers are: **060, 065,** or **080** for police, Red Cross, ambulance, fire, or other emergency situations. If you are not able to

reach an English-speaking operator, call the Sectur hot line. For missing persons or cars call Locatel. You'll find English-speaking staff at both the American British Cowdray Hospital and Hospital Español. The Farmacias del Ahorro chain stays open until 10 PM. There are branches throughout the city; you can locate the closest branch by using their Web site www.fahorro.com.mx/d1.html.

🚑 Emergencies **Locatel** ☎ 55/5658-1111. **Sectur** ☎ 55/5212-0260.

🚑 Hospitals **American British Cowdray Hospital** ✉ Calle Sur 136-116, corner of Observatorio, Col. las Américas ☎ 55/5230-8161 for emergencies, 55/5230-8000 switchboard ⊕ www.abchospital.com. **Hospital Español** ✉ Ejército Nacional 613, Col. Granada ☎ 55/5203-3735 ⊕ www.hespanol.com.

### ENGLISH-LANGUAGE MEDIA

The best place for English- and foreign-language newspapers and magazines is Librería e Impresos de Papel Sama, in Zona Rosa. Sanborns carries a few U.S. newspapers and an ample supply of magazines, paperbacks, and guidebooks. The American Book Store has an extensive selection of publications. Remember that most U.S. or foreign-published publications are about double the price you'd pay for them at home.

The Benjamin Franklin Library, actually a part of the U.S. Embassy, was instituted to create greater understanding and cultural exchange between the United States and Mexico. The library, open weekdays 11–7, has a substantial collection of English novels, a good reference section, and many U.S. periodicals. You must be at least 20 years old, fill out an application, and have a Mexican resident sign it in order to check out books, but anyone can browse through the stacks.

Imagen Informativa, 90.5 FM, broadcasts a weekly news program in English called "Living in Mexico," which provides economic, sports, and political information relevant to the English-speaking community in Mexico. It's a good way to learn about current events in the country. Tune in on weekends at 10 AM.

🚑 **American Book Store** ✉ Bolivar 23, Col. del Valle ☎ 55/5512-0306 or 55/5512-6350 ✉ Circuito Médicos 2, Ciudad Satélite ☎ 55/5562-9723 ⊕ www.americanbookstore.com.mx. **Benjamin Franklin Library** ✉ Liverpool 31, Zona Rosa ☎ 55/5080-2733 ⊕ www.usembassy-mexico.gov/bbf/biblioteca.htm. **Librería e Impresos de Papel Sama** ✉ Florencia 57, Zona Rosa ☎ 55/5525-0647 or 55/5208-3125.

### INTERNET

Many hotels have complimentary e-mail service for guests. There's also a proliferation of Internet cafés in areas such as the Colonia Condesa, Coyoacán, and Zona Rosa. Charges can be as little as $3.50 an hour for access. At Bits Café, you can have a cappuccino or a beer and a sandwich, while you catch up on your e-mail. It's open weekdays 10 AM–11 PM, Saturday 11–11, and Sunday 12–11. Open 9 AM–10 PM, Monday through Saturday and noon–9 on Sunday, Coffe Mail is a good place to combine just those two things. After you have spent two hours online, Coffe Mail will offer you free cookies and coffee.

🚑 Internet Cafés **Bits Café** ✉ Hamburgo 165-C, at Florencia, 1 block south of the Angel monument, Col. Juárez ☎ 55/5525-0144. **Coffe Mail** ✉ Amberes 61, Zona Rosa ☎ 55/5207-4537.

**MONEY MATTERS**
There are banks with 24-hour ATMs all over the city. HSBC has the advantage of keeping longer hours than most other banks; for instance, many of its branches are open on Saturday until 3 PM. Avoid banks around lunchtime when they're most crowded. The 15th and 30th or 1st of each month are also unbearably busy, as these are paydays. Banks generally have armed guards, so do not be alarmed by the sight of uniforms and weapons. For safety reasons, it's best to use ATMs in daylight, when other people are nearby. Note that as a safety measure, many ATMs in Mexico City are housed inside the bank, behind more than one locked door. Make sure that you slide your card through as illustrated on the door and that you open the door quickly. These safety measures are for your protection, but they may be awkward to use, making it take longer to access the machine. You may find it easier and safer to use ATMs in Sanborns.

Currency exchanges often have less favorable rates than the banks. They're also harder to find, except in the Zona Rosa and the airport.

**PESERO TRAVEL**
Originally six-passenger sedans, now minibuses, peseros operate on a number of fixed routes and charge a flat rate (a peso once upon a time, hence the name). They're a good alternative to buses and taxis, but be prepared for a jolting ride because many drivers like to turn their buses into bucking broncos. Likely routes for tourists are along the city's major west–east axis (Bosque de Chapultepec–Paseo de la Reforma–Avenida Juárez–Zócalo) and north–south along Avenida Insurgentes, between the Guadalupe Basílica and San Ángel–University City. Peseros pick up passengers at bus stops and outside almost all metro stations. Just stand on the curb, check the route sign on the oncoming pesero's windshield, and hold out your hand. Tell the driver where to stop, or press the button by the back door. If it's really crowded and you can't reach the back door in time, just bang on the ceiling and yell, "*Baja*," which means "getting down." Base fares are 2 pesos (about 20¢) with the price going up to 3.50 pesos (about 35¢) according to how far you travel. Exact change is appreciated by drivers and will save you a lot of fuss. Avoid showing your wallet in a pesero; pickpockets have sharp eyes and there's also the possibility of a hold-up. Peseros are also known as "combis," "micros," and "rutas."

**SAFETY**
Mexico City has a reputation for danger. However, its well-publicized spate of kidnappings have generally targeted successful businesspeople and wealthy local families and the average tourist is not likely to be a victim of this type of crime. Major touristed areas of the city are generally very safe, though it's important for visitors to be on their guard against pickpockets and petty theft. One of the easiest ways to avoid trouble—besides never hailing a taxi on the street—is to avoid standing out as a tourist. This might be difficult for some *gringos,* but recognize that Mexico City is more formal than many other cities, so things like backpacks, shorts, and open-toe shoes will mark you as a

tourist, not just an ex-pat. Of course, it's also important to conceal valuables when walking in the street; keep a close watch on wallets and cameras, especially in crowded metros and buses.

## SIGHTSEEING TOURS

Various travel agencies run tourist-friendly, English-guided tours of Mexico City and surrounding areas. The basic city tour ($39) lasts eight hours and takes in the Zócalo, Palacio Nacional, Catedral Metropolitana, and Bosque de Chapultepec. A four-hour pyramid tour costs around $23 and covers the Basílica de Nuestra Señora de Guadalupe and the major ruins at Teotihuacán. Except for the Tren Turístico, the tours described below can be booked through the agents listed in Travel Agencies; most agencies offer some version of each tour.

BULLRING TOUR    There are trips to the bullring on Sunday with a guide who will explain the finer points of this spectacle. This three-hour afternoon tour can usually be combined with the Ballet Folklórico–Xochimilco trip.

CULTURAL TOUR    A seven-hour cultural tour is run Sunday morning only and usually includes a performance of the folkloric dances at the Palacio de Bellas Artes, a gondola ride in the canals of Xochimilco's floating gardens, and a visit to the modern campus of the National University.

NIGHTLIFE TOUR    Nightlife tours are among the most popular tours of Mexico City. The best are scheduled to last five hours and include transfers by private car rather than bus; dinner at an elegant restaurant (frequently Bellini or at the Del Lago); a drink and a show at the Plaza Garibaldi, where mariachis play; and a nightcap at one of the cantinas around the square, which feature Mexican folk dancers.

TROLLEY TOUR    Mexico City has a new system of red, double-decker, open-top buses called the Turibus, which runs 9–9 daily. An excellent option for tourists is the $11 daily pass (purchased on board), which allows passengers to get on and off as many times as desired. The bus travels up and down Reforma, passes through the Centro, Plaza Río de Janiero in the Colonia Roma, Michoacán in the Colonia Condesa (a great place to stop and eat), and Masaryk in Polanco (a great stop to shop). Most passengers board at the staircase of the Auditorio Nacional, just outside the Auditorio metro stop. Buses leave about every half hour. Two- and three-day passes are also available.

The Paseo por Coyoacán tourist trolleybus goes around the Coyoacán neighborhood, with a guide telling the history of the area in Spanish. It leaves from a stop opposite the Museo Nacional de Culturas Populares whenever there are enough people, so departures are not regular. It costs $3.50 and runs weekdays 10–5, weekends 10–6. Guided tours in English are only available for large groups; reservations must be made in advance.

A good way to see the historic downtown—if you know some Spanish—is on Tren Turístico's charming replicas of 20-passenger trolleys from the 1920s. The 50-minute narrated tour ($3.50) includes the Zócalo, Colegio de San Ildefonso, Plaza de Santo Domingo, Plaza Manuel Tolsá (location of the Palacio de Minería and Museo Nacional

de Arte), Plaza de la Santa Veracruz (Museo Franz Mayer), and the Palacio de Iturbide. Trolleys depart hourly 10–5 daily from the train's offices in front of Alameda Park.

**⚡ Turibus** ☎ 55/5133-2424 ⊕ www.turibus.com.mx. **Paseo por Coyoacán** ✉ Av. Hidalgo, at Calle Allende Coyoacán ☎ 55/5662-8972. **Tren Turístico's** ✉ Av. Juárez 66,
at Revillagigedo, Col. Centro ☎ 55/5512-1013.

### SUBWAY TRAVEL

Transporting 5 million passengers daily, the metro, or STC (Collective
Transportation System), is one of the world's best, busiest, and cheapest transportation systems—a ride costs 2 pesos (about 20¢). The clean
marble-and-onyx stations are brightly lighted, and modern French-de-
signed trains run quietly on rubber tires. Some stations, such as Insurgentes, are shopping centers. Even if you don't take a ride, visit the Zócalo
station, which has large models of central Mexico City during three historic periods. Many stations have temporary cultural displays, from archaeological treasures to contemporary art; the Pino Suárez station has
a small Aztec pyramid inside, a surprise discovery during construction.

There are 10 intersecting metro lines covering more than 160 km (100
mi). Segments of Lines 1 and 2 cover most points of interest to tourists,
including Zona Rosa, Bellas Artes, and Centro Histórico. At the southern edge of the city, the Tasqueña station (Line 2) connects with the electric train (*tren eléctrico*) that continues south to Xochimilco. To the
southeast, the *tren ligero* ("light" train) from the Pantitlán station (Lines
1, 5, and 9) heads east to Chalco in the state of Mexico. The various
lines also serve all four bus stations and the airport; however, only light
baggage is allowed on board during rush hours. User-friendly, color-coded
maps are sometimes available free at metro-station information desks
(if there's an attendant) and at Mexico City tourism offices; color-keyed
signs and maps are posted all around.

Trains run frequently (about two minutes apart) and are least crowded
10–4 and at night. To reduce incidences of harassment during crowded
rush hours, and on crowded lines, regulations may require men to ride
in separate cars from women and children. The cars for women and children are marked "exclusivo para mujeres y niños."

The metro is generally safe, but be careful of pickpockets. Hold on to
your belongings on crowded trains as some thieves will pretend to
bump into you (or even pitch dramatically into you) as a means of dis-
traction. Hours vary somewhat according to the line, but service is essentially weekdays 5 AM–midnight, Saturday 6 AM–2 AM, Sunday and
holidays 6 AM–1 AM. Late at night, it's still best to call a radio taxi or
take a sitio, mostly because many of the neighborhoods surrounding metro
stations are not safe at night.

**⚡ STC (metro)** ⊕ www.metro.df.gob.mx.

### TAXIS

Mexico City taxis come in several colors and sizes. Unmarked, or *turismo,* sedans with hooded meters are usually stationed outside major
hotels and in tourist areas; however, they are uneconomical for short

trips. Their drivers are almost always English-speaking guides and can be hired for sightseeing on a daily or hourly basis (always negotiate the price in advance). Sitio (stationed) taxis operate out of stands, take radio calls, and are authorized to charge a small premium over the meter rate or will offer a set rate. Among these, Servi-Taxis, Radio-Taxi, and Taxi-Mex, which accepts American Express, offer 24-hour service. Most sitio companies offer hourly rates, some for as little as $10 per hour, for a minimum of two hours. Hiring a sitio for a few hours can be an easy way for you to spend a half day or more seeing sights that may be otherwise time-consuming to reach and/or that are of particular interest to you.

Unauthorized cab drivers (sometimes criminals who have stolen the cabs they drive) pose probably the single greatest danger to tourists in the capital. Although the situation has improved slightly, outsiders are especially vulnerable to their assaults, and many have been robbed or forced to withdraw money from ATMs. This danger is easily avoided; simply **do not hail taxis on the street** under any circumstances. If you need a cab but don't speak the Spanish necessary to call one yourself, your best bet is to have a hotel concierge or waiter call you a sitio. Be sure to establish the fare in advance if the sitio does not work with meter and premium. Otherwise, ask for a registered hotel taxi; even though it may be significantly overpriced, it's better than a street-cab rip-off. If you have the time to wait for a radio taxi, this may be a less-expensive option; be sure to ask the price of the ride in advance when you give your destination over the phone.

Taxi drivers are authorized to charge 10% more at night, usually after 10. Tips are not expected unless you have luggage—then 10% is sufficient.

🚩 **Radio-Elite** ☎ 55/5660–1122. **Radio-Taxi** ☎ 55/5566–0077. **Servi-Taxis** ☎ 55/5271–2560. **Taxi-Mex** ☎ 55/5519–7690.

### TELEPHONE CODES
A regional code for Mexico City—55—precedes eight-digit numbers dialed from within the city. To reach Mexico City from elsewhere in Mexico, dial 01 plus the 10-digit number; from abroad, dial 52 plus the 10-digit number. A Mexico City mobile phone normally begins with 044–55. If you call a Mexico City mobile phone (a *celular*) from outside the city, you merely dial 01–55 before the eight-digit number.

### TRAIN TRAVEL
The train system in Mexico is in the process of being privatized and is depressingly moribund given its romantic history. Currently, trains are used almost exclusively for cargo, and there are no longer any passenger services to or from Mexico City to recommend.

### TRAVEL AGENCIES
🚩 **Local Agent Referrals American Express** ✉ Paseo de la Reforma 234, Col. Ciudad de los Deportes ☎ 55/5326–3521 ⊕ www.vacaciones.amex.com. **Grey Line Tours** ✉ Londres 166, at Florencia Zona Rosa ☎55/5208–1163 ⊕www.greyline.com.mx. **Nuevo Mundo** ✉ Marsella 70, at Havre, Col. Juárez ☎ 55/5207–6234 or 55/5207–7988.

**VISITOR INFORMATION**

The Mexico City Tourist Office (Departamento de Turismo del Distrito Federal, or DDF) maintains information booths at the domestic arrival area at the airport. In town, there are plenty of information booths in heavily trafficked areas such as the Zona Rosa, Chapultepec, the Centro and in the south. In addition to the central branches, there are smaller units without phones posted in Plaza San Jacinto, on Paseo de la Reforma outside the Museo Nacional de Antropología, by the cathedral in the Centro, and at La Villa de Guadalupe.

The Secretariat of Tourism (Sectur) operates a 24-hour hotline called Infotur from 9 to 7 daily. Its multilingual operators have access to an extensive data bank with information on both Mexico City and the entire country. If lines are busy, keep trying. From outside Mexico City, call the Sectur Tourist Information Center in Colonia Polanco toll-free weekdays 8–8.

For more info, check out the Web site ⊕ www.mexicocity.com.mx.
🔲Infotur ☎55/5250–0123. **Mexico City Tourist Office** ⊕www.mexicocity.gob.mx ⊠Sala A1, Mexico City Airport, in National Arrivals ☎ 55/5786–9002 ⊠ Amberes 54, at Londres, Zona Rosa ☎ 55/5525–9380 ⊠ Entrada principal, Terminal de Autobuses del Norte, Av. Cien Metros 4907 ☎ 55/5719–1201 ⊠ Casa Municipal, Plaza Hidalgo 1, ground floor, Coyoacán ☎ 55/5659–6009 ⊠ Nuevo Embarcadero, Nativitas Barrio de Xaltocan, Xochimilco ☎ 55/5653–5209. **Secretariat of Tourism (Federal)** ⊠ Av. Presidente Masaryk 172, Col. Polanco ☎ 55/5250–0493, 55/5250–0027, 01800/903–9200 toll-free in Mexico, 800/482–9832 in the U.S. ⊕ www.travelguidemexico.com. **Secretariat of Tourism (DF)** ⊠ Av. Nuevo León 56, at Laredo Col. Condesa ☎ 55/5212–0260.

# SIDE TRIPS FROM MEXICO CITY

2

Updated by
Barbara
Kastelein

**TO ESCAPE THE HUSTLE** of Mexico City, simply strike out in any direction. You'll be pleasantly surprised to find that just outside its borders are villages and towns where the pace is decidedly slower. Many are graced with colonial-era cathedrals whose facades resemble a pastry chef's wildest fantasy. The city of Puebla, for instance, fairly bursts with Baroque flourishes and the colors of its famed Talavera tiles.

You could follow the example of the *chilangos* (Mexico City residents) and visit one of their favorite weekend getaways, such as balmy Cuernavaca or the lakeside community of Valle de Bravo. Or leave behind the modern world altogether and head to one of the ancient ruins found an hour or so outside the capital. Teotihuacán, to the north, is popular for its pair of pyramids dedicated to the sun and moon. Or venture out to the Toltec capital of Tula, where an army of stone warriors stands guard, or east to Cacaxtla, renowned for brilliantly colored murals.

## About the Restaurants

Many of the cities and towns surrounding the capital have delicious local specialties well worth seeking out. *Sopa Tlaxcala,* for example, is a flavorful soup named for the town east of Mexico City. It overflows with black beans, cheese, and tortillas, flavored with *chicharron* (pork scratchings). Puebla is famous for *mole poblano,* a spicy sauce combining the sweetness of chocolate and the heat of chilies.

Restaurants tend not to stay open as late as in Mexico City. In Amecameca and Cuetzalan, restaurants often close for dinner. Even in major hubs, such as Puebla, they may often close early.

## About the Hotels

Most of the interesting spots around Mexico City are less than two hours away, so a hotel won't be absolutely necessary. However, many areas have numerous natural attractions and historic sights and it would be a pity to try to squash them all into one day trip.

Many of these places are popular vacation and *puente* (the Mexican long weekend) destinations for *chilangos* and other Mexicans, and may fill up during major holidays and festivals. Advance reservations are advised for the Christmas period and *Semana Santa.* On the long weekend marking Independence Day (September 16) it's often hard to get a room in Cuernavaca. You should also make advance reservations if you plan to visit Cuetzalan during the town's fair on October 4.

| WHAT IT COSTS | | | | |
|---|---|---|---|---|
| **$$$$** | **$$$** | **$$** | **$** | **¢** |
| RESTAURANTS over $25 | $15–$25 | $10–$15 | $5–$10 | under $5 |
| HOTELS over $250 | $150–$250 | $75–$150 | $50–$75 | under $50 |

Restaurant prices are for a main course excluding tax and tip. Hotel prices are for two people in a standard double room in high season.

# NORTH OF MEXICO CITY

Little more than an hour north of Mexico City in Estado de Mexico (Mexico State) are two of the country's most celebrated ancient cities. The pyramids of Teotihuacán can be enjoyed in a day tour. The ruins of Tula, in the state of Hidalgo, known for its battalion of basalt warriors, can be combined with a visit to the nearby colonial city of Tepotzotlán.

## Teotihuacán

🔺 *50 km (31 mi) northeast of Mexico City center.*

Fodor's Choice ★ There's no doubt about the monumental place Teotihuacán (*teh*-oh-tee-wa-*can*) holds in the region's history. At its peak, somewhere around AD 600, the city controlled much of central Mexico and traded with distant cities such as Tikal in Guatemala and Copán in Honduras. Archaeologists believe that more than 200,000 people called this sprawling metropolis their home.

But by AD 725, the city had been all but abandoned. The reason is unclear, but research indicates that it suffered a massive attack during which all the temples were toppled. Some of the destruction appears to have been at the hands of the city's residents, suggesting that there may have been a revolt caused by overcrowding, a drought-prompted famine, or the iron-fisted leadership.

Just who created this great city isn't known—even its original name has been lost. The Aztecs, who settled here centuries later, remembered how wondrous it had once been. They named it Teotihuacán, meaning "place where men became gods."

Most people enter near the **Cuidadela,** a massive citadel ringed by more than a dozen temples. The **Templo de Quetzalcóatl** (Temple of the Plumed Serpent) is the centerpiece. Here you'll find incredibly detailed carvings of the benevolent deity Quetzalcóatl, a serpent with its head ringed by feathers, jutting out of the facade.

One of the most impressive sights in Teotihuacán is the 4-km-long (2½-mi-long) **Calzada de los Muertos,** the Avenue of the Dead. The Aztecs gave it this name because they mistook the temples lining either side for tombs. It leads all the way to the 126-foot-high **Pirámide de la Luna** (Pyramid of the Moon) which dominates the northern end of the city. Atop this structure, you can scan the entire city. Some of the most exciting recent discoveries, including a royal tomb, have been unearthed here. In late 2002 a discovery of jade objects gave important new evidence of a link between the Teotihuacán rulers and the Maya.

On the west side of the spacious plaza facing the Pyramid of the Moon is the **Palacio del Quetzalpápalotl** (Palace of the Plumed Butterfly); its beautifully reconstructed terrace has columns etched with images of various winged creatures. Nearby is the **Palacio de los Jaguares** (Palace of the Jaguars), a residence for priests. Spectacular bird and jaguar murals wind through its underground chambers.

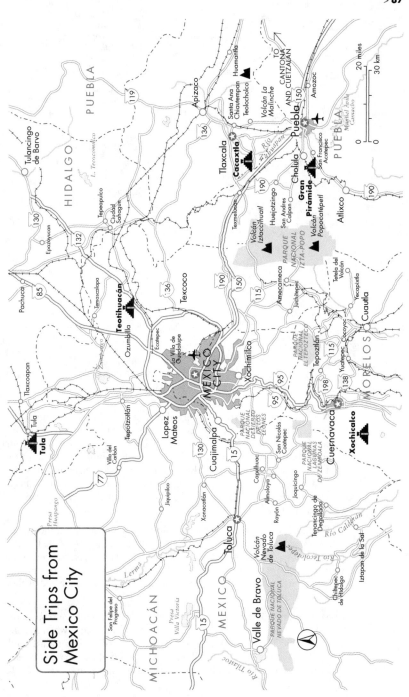

## Side Trips from Mexico City

20 miles

30 km

PUEBLA

HIDALGO

MICHOACÁN

MEXICO

MORELOS

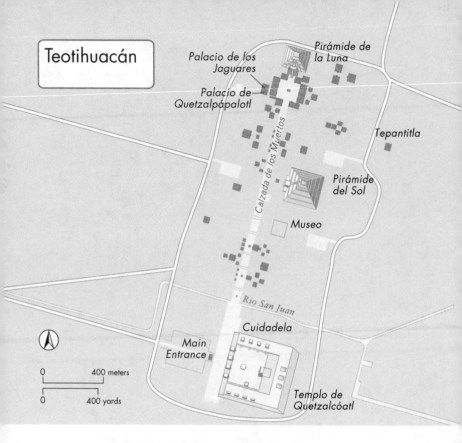

The awe-inspiring **Pirámide del Sol** (Pyramid of the Sun) stands in the center of the city. With a base as broad as that of the pyramid of Cheops in Egypt, it is one of the largest pyramids ever built. Its size takes your breath away, often quite literally, during the climb up 242 steps on its west face. Deep within the pyramid archaeologists have discovered a clover-shape cave that they speculate may have been the basis for the city's religion, and perhaps the reason the city was built in the first place.

The best artifacts uncovered at Teotihuacán are on display at the Museo Nacional de Antropología in Mexico City. Still, the **Museo de la Sitio**, adjacent to the Pirámide del Sol, contains a few good pieces, such as the stone sculpture of the saucer-eyed Tlaloc, some black and green obsidian arrowheads, and the skeletons of human sacrifices arranged as they were when discovered.

More than 4,000 one-story adobe and stone dwellings surround the Calzada de los Muertos; these were occupied by artisans, warriors, and tradesmen. The best example, a short walk east of the Pirámide del Sol, is called **Tepantitla**. Here you'll see murals depicting a watery realm ruled by the rain god Tlaloc. Human figures swim, dance, and even seem to play a game that resembles leapfrog. Restored in 2002, its reds, greens, and yellows are nearly as vivid as when they were painted more than 1,500 years ago.

There are five entrances to Teotihuacán, each near one of the major attractions. If you have a car, it's a good idea to drive from one entrance to another. Seeing the ruins will take several hours, especially if you head to the lesser-known areas. To help you find your way around, a good English-language guidebook is sold at the site. ☎ *594/ 956–0052 or 594/956–0276* ⊕ *archaeology.la.asu.edu/teo* 🎫 *$3.50* ⊙ *Daily 7–6.*

## Tepotzotlán

*35 km (22 mi) north of Mexico City center.*

In pre-Hispanic times, Tepotzotlán was an important stop along the trade route between Toluca and Texcoco. Tepotzotlán (pronounced teh-po-tzot-*lan*), about an hour's car or bus ride from Mexico City, is still a frequent stop for travelers headed to Tula and other nearby sights.

In 1580 a group of Jesuit priests arrived in Tepotzotlán, intent on converting the locals. On the main square they built the **Iglesia de San Francisco Javier,** which ranks among the masterpieces of churrigueresque architecture. The unmitigated Baroque facade will catch your eye immediately; inside, handsome gilded altars stretch from floor to ceiling. Look for the paintings of angels decorating the church—some are dark-skinned, a nod to the indigenous people forced to help in its construction. The Capilla de la Virgen de Loreto glows with gilding and mirrors.

The church is now part of the massive **Museo Nacional del Virreinato.** You're likely to be overwhelmed by the amount of colonial religious art brought here from churches all around the country. Look for the breathtaking 17th-century *Cristo del Arbol* (Christ of the Tree), carved from a single piece of wood. For a break, walk outside to the Claustro de los Naranjos, a lovely patio planted with tiny orange trees. ⊠ *Plaza Hidalgo 99* ☎ *55/5876–0245 or 55/5876–2771* ⊕ *www.inah.gob.mx* ⊙ *Tues.–Sun. 9–6* 🎫 *$2.*

Tepotzotlán is famous for its charming *pastorela,* which has been performed for more than three decades. The drama, which tells of the birth of Jesus Christ. It's staged every year December 16–23 at the church.

### Where to Eat

$ ✕ **Casa Mago.** Across the square from the Museo Nacional del Virreinato next to the town hall, you'll find a row of nearly identical outdoor cafés. This one, with a seemingly endless buffet on the weekends, serves up the best regional fare, such as *filete tampiqueña* (finely sliced tender beef fillet) served with guacamole, beans, tortillas, and rice. ⊠ *Plaza Virreynal 34* ☎ *55/5876–0229* 🖃 *MC, V.*

## Tula

🏛 *75 km (47 mi) north of Mexico City center.*

**Fodor'sChoice** The capital of the Toltecs, Tula is one of the most stunning archaeological
★ sites in central Mexico. Much of the great city—known to its inhabi-
tants as Tollán—was ransacked by the Aztecs. What remains, however,
makes it worth the trip. From afar you can spot the stone sentinels standing guard atop its magnificent pyramid.

Tula rose to power about the same time as the fall of Teotihuacán. It is
bordered on the north and west by carefully reconstructed ball courts.
Between the courts sits the **Templo Quemado**, or Burned Palace. Its dozens
of ruined columns delineate what was once an important governmental building. Directly to the east is the completely restored **Templo de
Tlahuizcalpantecuhtli**, or Temple of the Morning Star. Climb up the uneven steps to reach the cresting row of 15-foot-tall *atlantes*, or warriors.
These awe-inspiring figures gaze southward over the main plaza. 🕿 *773/
732–1183* ⊕ *www.inah.gob.mx* ✉ *$3.50* 🕙 *Tues.–Sun. 9–5.*

## North of Mexico City A to Z

### BUS TRAVEL

To get to Teotihuacán, take one of the Línea Teotihuacán buses that depart every 15 minutes from the Central de Autobuses del Norte in Mexico City. (In the bus station, look for signs marked "piramides"; they
don't say Teotihuacán.) The hour-long trip costs about $2.50. Buses leave
Mexico City from 7 AM–3 PM. The last bus from Teotihuacán leaves
at 8 PM.

Autotransportes Valle Mezquital, which also operates out of Central de
Autobuses del Norte, runs buses to Tula every 15 minutes. The one-and-
a-half hour journey costs about $4.50. The same line serves Tepot-
zotlán every 30 minutes for about $2. The ride to Tepotzotlán takes just
45 minutes—but note that you must get off at the *caseta* (toll gates) where
you can catch a microbus or taxi for the remaining five-minute journey.
🚌 Bus Companies ADO ⊕ www.ticketbus.com.mx. Autotransportes Valle Mezquital
🕿 55/5567–9691. Línea Teotihuacán 🕿 55/5587–0501. Terminal del Norte 🕿 55/
5587–1552 for bus line information.

### CAR TRAVEL

To get to Tepotzotlán from Mexico City, take Highway 57D going
toward Querétaro; the exit for Tepotzotlán is on the left about 40 km
(25 mi) down the highway. Tula is about 8 km (5 mi) north of Tepotzotlán on Highway 57D; its exit is clearly marked. To get to Teotihuacán,
take Highway 85D. Watch out for drunk drivers on the highways surrounding Mexico City, especially around local or national holidays. There's
generally heavy traffic on the way back from Tepotzotlán and Tula after
4 PM on Sunday.

In general, the ruins have free parking but the parking areas are a short
walk from the sites, so be sure not to leave any valuables in your car.

**VISITOR INFORMATION**
For information on the sights north of the capital, it's best to contact the main Mexico City tourism office.

# SOUTH OF MEXICO CITY

Should the multitudes, frenetic activity, and fumes in Mexico City get the best of you, head to sunny Cuernavaca, as locals have for centuries. A thriving city that keeps on growing, the capital of the state of Morelos has a handful of interesting museums, a climate that's glorious year-round, and some excellent hotels. Similarly, Tepoztlán can be visited either as a detour from Mexico City or a destination in its own right—in fact, it seems poised to eclipse Cuernavaca as the retreat of choice, as it's cleaner and more "Mexican" than Cuernavaca. In addition, the village has seen a new spurt of small hotels or *posadas,* restaurants, and Internet cafés. Its attractions include a pretty convent, a lively weekend market, and its own little pyramid perched high in the mountains.

## Cuernavaca

*85 km (53 mi) south of Mexico City center.*

The road to Cuernavaca will likely heighten your anticipation—you'll catch your first glimpse of the city's lush surroundings from a mountain highway, through lacy pine branches. Cuernavaca basks in spring-like temperatures for most of the year, making it perennially irresistible to Mexico City's elite. The area's allure has a long history: Cortés built a summer place—really a massive palace—here, on top of the ruins of the Aztec city he destroyed, and Emperor Maximilian retreated here when the pressures of governing a country where he was despised grew too much to bear.

The best of Cuernavaca's grandeur always lay behind high walls, and its expansion in the last decade has weakened some of its tourist appeal. Public gardens, such as Jardín Borda, only hint at the splendor of centuries past. Today, the best gardens grow in private homes, but the city still has much to recommend it, and the frequency of buses from Mexico City makes it an easy and comfortable day trip.

The city's most traditional square is the **Plaza de Armas,** marked by a hefty, volcanic stone statue of revolutionary hero José María Morelos and a couple of little fountains. On weekdays, the square fills with vendors from neighboring villages. On weekends it is crowded with balloon sellers, amateur painters, and stalls for crafts, jewelry, and knick-knacks. The *tren turístico* (a wooden trolleybus for sightseeing) departs from the southeast opposite the Palacio de Cortés. To the north of the square is leafy **Jardín Juárez** (Juárez Garden), which hosts Sunday concerts at its bandstand.

North of the Plaza de Armas you'll find the **Museo Regional Cuauhnáhuac,** from the Aztec word for the surrounding valley. The fortresslike building was constructed as a stronghold for Cortés in 1522, as the region had not been completely conquered at that time. His palace sits atop the ruins of Aztec buildings, some of which have been partially excavated. There are plenty of stone carvings from the area on display, but the best way to digest all this history is by gazing at the murals Diego Rivera painted on the top floor between 1930 and 1932. ⊠ *Juárez and Hidalgo* ☎ *777/312–8171* ⊕ *www.inah.gob.mx* ✎ *$3.50 (free on Sun.)* ⊙ *Tues.–Sun. 9–6.*

Cortés ordered the construction of the **Catedral de la Asunción,** and like his palace, the cathedral doubled as a fortress. Cannons mounted above the flying buttresses helped bolster the city's defenses. The facade may give you a sense of foreboding, especially when you catch sight of the skull and crossbones over the door. The interior is much less ominous, though, thanks to the murals uncovered during renovations. ⊠ *Hidalgo and Av. Morelos* ⊙ *Daily 8 AM–6 PM.*

⟲ The **Jardín Borda** is one of the most popular sights in Cuernavaca. Designed in the late 18th century for a wealthy family, the Borda Gardens were so famous they attracted royalty. Maximilian and Carlotta visited frequently. Here the emperor dallied with the gardener's wife, called La India Bonita, who was immortalized in a famous portrait. Novelist Malcolm Lowry turned the formal gardens into a sinister symbol in his 1947 novel *Under the Volcano*. A pleasant café sits just inside the gates. ⊠ *Av. Morelos 103, at Hidalgo* ☎ *777/312–9237* ✎ *$3* ⊙ *Tues.–Sun. 10–5:30.*

On a quiet street south of the Plaza de Armas, the **Robert Brady Museum** shows the collection of the artist, antiquarian, and decorator from Fort Dodge, Iowa. Ceramics, antique furniture, sculptures, paintings, and tapestries fill the restored colonial mansion, all beautifully arranged in rooms painted with bright colors. ⊠ *Calle Netzahuacóyotl 4, between Hidalgo and Abasolo* ☎ *777/318–8554* ⊕ *www.geocities.com/bradymuseum* ✎ *$3* ⊙ *Tues.–Sun. 10–6.*

## Where to Stay & Eat

There are plenty of little cafés surrounding the gently sloping Plazuela del Zacate, where Calle Fray Bartolomé de las Casas branches off from Hidalgo.

**$–$$**   ✕ **Casa Hidalgo.** The marvelous view of the Palacio de Cortés helped make this restaurant a big hit among the foreigners in town. The menu mixes Mexican and international foods; you might try the Mexican *sopa fría de mango al agave azul* (cold mango soup with a dash of tequila), followed by the Spanish *filetón hidalgo* (breaded veal stuffed with serrano ham and manchego cheese). A jazz band plays Friday and Saturday nights. Reservations are recommended on weekends. ⊠ *Hidalgo 6, Col. Centro* ☎ *777/312–2749* ▤ *AE, DC, MC, V.*

**$–$$**   ✕ **La Pancha.** This chic restaurant has a startling view over the *barranca* (gulley). For those longing for something fresh and green, the Hesch salad (almonds and Roquefort cheese over mixed greens) will be a treat. A favorite main dish is the *pollo pancha*, a chicken breast filled with mozzarella and spinach in a semi-sweet orange sauce. Reservations are recommended on weekends. ⊠ *Francisco Leyva 94, Col. Centro* ☎ *777/312–7425* ⊙ *No dinner Sun.* ▤ *AE, MC, V.*

**$–$$** ✕ **La Strada.** You can't go wrong with this old-time charmer, on a quiet street beside the Museo Regional Cuauhnáhuac. Choose from a range of pastas after settling in on the candlelit terrace. A guitarist plays Friday and Saturday nights. ⊠ *Salazar 38, around the corner from Palacio de Cortés* ☎ *777/318–6085* ▭ *MC, V.*

**¢** ✕ **La Cueva.** Open from 8:30 AM to midnight (except Sunday when it closes at 10 PM), this dark, cavelike diner is the best place by the zócalo for a cheap *comida corrida* (set lunch) or a quick *torta* and beer to refuel. ⊠ *Galeana 2, at Hidalgo* ☎ *777/312–4002* ▭ *No credit cards.*

**$$$–$$$$** ✕⊡ **Las Mañanitas.** An American expat opened this praised hotel in the 1950s, outfitting the ample rooms with traditional fireplaces, hand-carved bedsteads, hand-painted tiles in the bathrooms, and gilded crafts. The president and European princes stay here, and chilangos drive an hour on weekends just to dine at the restaurant ($–$$$), with its spectacular open-air terraces and garden inhabited by flamingos, peacocks, and African cranes. ⊠ *Ricardo Linares 107, 62000* ☎ *777/314–1466, 01800/221–5299 toll-free in Mexico, 888/413–9199 toll-free in the U.S.* ⊟ *777/318–3672* ⊕ *www.lasmananitas.com.mx* ⟲ *1 room, 21 suites* ⚴ *Restaurant, room service, pool, bar; no room TVs* ▭ *AE, MC, V.*

FodorsChoice
★

**$$$** ✕⊡ **Camino Real Sumiya.** Woolworth heiress Barbara Hutton built this monumental hideaway in the 1950s. The Japanese theme is pleasingly consistent from the imposing entrance to the lobby, bar, bridges, rock garden, wooden paneling, and discreet decor. Restaurante Sumiya ($–$$), which serves international and Japanese food, is an attractive option for nonguests. The rooms are set in the far part of the garden for privacy. Note that the hotel is often taken over by weddings on weekends, so plan ahead. To reach the hotel, which is about 15 minutes south of town at Interior del Fracc. Sumiya, take the Civac-Cuauhtla exit on Acapulco Highway. ⊠ *Col. José Parres, Juitepec, 62550 Morelos* ☎ *777/329–9888* ⊟ *777/329–9866* ⊕ *www.caminoreal.com/sumiya* ⟲ *157 rooms, 6 suites* ⚴ *2 restaurants, cable TV, 7 tennis courts, 2 pools, bar, concierge* ▭ *AE, DC, MC, V.*

★ **$$$** ✕⊡ **Hacienda San Gabriel de las Palmas.** A colorful history pervades the thick walls of this grand hacienda, built in 1529 under Cortés's orders. Now it's a haven of quiet—disturbed only by birdcalls, the splashing of a waterfall, and the ringing of a chapel bell. If you'd like to get even more blissed-out, visit the spa, which includes a temazcal. Antiques fill both the public areas and the guest rooms so be sure to ask for a tour. Outstanding Mexican food is prepared in an attractive open kitchen close to the pool. The hacienda is 25 minutes outside Cuernavaca, making it easy to get to Taxco from here. ⊠ *Carretera Federal Cuernavaca–Chilpancingo, Km 41.8, Amacuzac, 62642* ☎ *751/348–0636, 01800/508–7923 toll-free in Mexico, 1877/278–8018 toll free from U.S.* ⊟ *751/348–0113* ⊕ *www.hacienda-sangabriel.com.mx* ⟲ *15 suites* ⚴ *Restaurant, tennis court, 2 pools, spa, billiards, croquet, horseback riding, bar, meeting rooms; no a/c, no room TVs* ▭ *AE, MC, V.*

★ **$$** ✕⊡ **Hacienda de Cortés.** This 16th-century former sugar mill once belonged to the famed conquistador. Wandering around the gardens and discovering cascades, fountains, abandoned pillars and sculptures is an enchanting experience, especially at dusk. Ask for a room in the old part of the building to immerse yourself in the atmosphere. Rooms have traditional Mexican furnishings and lovely patios or balconies. The restaurant ($–$$) is within old fort walls draped with vines—it's like dining inside a ruined castle. ⊠ *Plaza Kennedy 90, Col. Atlacomulco, 62250* ☎ *777/315–8844* 🖷 *777/315–0035* ⬦ *24 rooms* ♻ *Restaurant, cable TV, pool, bar; no a/c* ⊟ *AE, MC, V.*

**$$–$$$** 🏨 **Hotel Villa Rosa.** This very pink hotel has the advantage of being both very central and yet very tranquil. Although each room is different—you'll find everything from floral patterns to executive-friendly modernity—all have high ceilings with exposed beams and are refreshingly cool, even without air-conditioning. Located at the end of a walled, cobblestoned street, with a grassy garden, shaded pool area, and mini-spa, the Villa Rosa makes a good retreat, particularly midweek when prices dip. ⊠ *2a. Privada de Humboldt 6, Col. Centro, 62000* ☎ *777/312–1632* 🖷 *777/312–9225* ⊕ *www.vrosahotel.com. mx* ⬦ *11 rooms* ♻ *Restaurant, cable TV, pool, spa; no a/c in some rooms* ⊟ *AE, MC, V.*

**$$** 🏨 **Hotel Posada María Cristina.** This delightful hotel, which is popular with foreigners who prefer to stay in town, was constructed in the 16th century as a home for one of Cortez's soldiers. It is full of character, with plenty of alcoves, nooks, and crannies to explore. Lush gardens slope down the steep hill towards the pool. The main restaurant serves Mexican and international cuisine, while the poolside restaurant refreshes loungers with Argentine food. ⊠ *Leyva 20, at the corner of Abasolo, Col. Centro, 62000* ☎ *777/318–5767, 01800/024–5767 toll-free in Mexico* 🖷 *777/318–2981* ⊕ *www.maria-cristina.com* ⬦ *10 rooms, 10 suites* ♻ *2 restaurants, cable TV, pool, bar; no a/c in some rooms* ⊟ *AE, DC, MC, V.*

## Xochicalco

🔺 *23 km (14 mi) south of Cuernavaca.*

★ A trip to the ruins of Xochicalco is one of the best reasons to visit Morelos state. Built by the Olmeca-Xicalanca people, the mighty hilltop city reached its peak between AD 700 and 900. It was abandoned a century later after being destroyed, perhaps by its own inhabitants.

With its several layers of fortifications, the city appears unassailable. The most eye-catching edifice is the **Pyrámide de Quetzalcóatl** (Temple of the Plumed Serpent). Carvings of vicious-looking snakes—all in the style typical of the Mayas to the south—wrap around the lower level, while figures in elaborate headdresses sit above. Be sure to seek out the **Observatorio** in a man-made cave reached through a tunnel on the northern side of the city. Through a narrow shaft in the ceiling the Xochicalco astronomers could observe the heavens. Twice a year—May 14 and 15 and July 28 and 29—the sun passes directly over the opening, filling the room with light.

There are dozens of other structures here, including three impressive ball courts. The site's solar-powered museum has six rooms of artifacts, including beautiful sculptures of Xochicalco deities found nearby. ⊠ *Hwy. 95D, southwest of Cuernavaca* ☎ *777/312–5955* ⊕ *www.inah.gob. mx* ⊠ *$3.50* ☉ *Tues.–Sun. 10–5.*

## Where to Stay & Eat

**$$** ✕⊞ **Casa Marly.** This guest house is rapidly gaining fame for Françoise Ledoux's exquisite cooking—its location just ten minutes from Xochicalco is also quite a plus. All rooms are cheerfully decorated; there is a two-room pavilion suitable for families, as well as a gorgeous penthouse ideal for honeymooners. Guests reserve their meals in advance. ⊠ *Carretera a Xochicalco, Alpuyeca, 62790* ☎ *777/391–5205* ⊕ *www. casamarly.com* ⇋ *5 rooms* ⚲ *Restaurant, pool* ⊟ *No credit cards* ☉ *Closed May and June* ⎸☉⎸ *CP.*

# Tepoztlán

*75 km (47 mi) south of Mexico City center.*

Surrounded by sandstone monoliths that throw off a russet glow at sunset, Tepoztlán is a magical place. No wonder it attracts practitioners of astrology, meditation, yoga, and other New Age pursuits. But Tepoztlán keeps a wary eye on its traditions, so you'll still find women selling homegrown produce in the lively weekend market surrounding the main square and traditional celebrations that predate the conquest. *Danza folklórica* and musical concerts take place many weekends in the **Auditorio Ilhuicalli** (⊠ 5 de Mayo s/n ☎ 739/395–0673). To reach it walk towards the mountains from the right side of the zócalo.

★ The town is famous for its tiny **Pirámide de Tepozteco.** Perched on a mountaintop, this temple is either dedicated to the Aztec deity Tepoztécatl or—depending on whose story you believe—Ome Tochtli, the god of the alcoholic drink, pulque. It attracts hikers and sightseers not afraid of the somewhat arduous climb. The view over the valley is terrific. ⊠ *North end of Av. Tepoztlán* ☉ *Tues.–Sun. 9:30–5:30* ⊠ *$3.50.*

Pulque, a thick, alcoholic beverage made by fermenting juice from the maguey cactus, is a dying drink in modern Mexico, but for those who want to try it, **Alejandro's Pulquería** (⊠ Av. del Tepozteco 23 ☎ No phone) is a true find. On the way back from the Pirámide del Tepozteco (from midday to about 8 PM or whenever the store runs out), you'll have a chance to drink a plastic cup of this strange drink at its freshest. Alejandro Gómez learned the art from his grandfather and offers some unusual flavors, from *nuez* (walnut) to *apio* (celery) and even chocolate. However, the most palatable for those not used to pulque's somewhat slimy texture is *guayaba* (guava). The experience can feel a little sketchy: Alejandro sells his product from a somewhat grimy little room open to the street and there are usually pulque drunkards tottering (harmlessly) about. A cup costs only about 70¢, but it's best to stay with one serving, as this pre-Hispanic drink causes pounding hangovers.

Rising above most of Tepoztlán's buildings is the buttressed **Ex-Convento Dominico de la Natividad.** The former convent, dating from 1559, has a facade adorned with icons dating from before the introduction of Christianity. Every year on September 8 the faithful assemble here to celebrate the town's patron saint. The evening before they climb the mountain for a rowdy celebration. ✉ *Av. Revolución 1910* ⏲ *Tues.–Sun. 10–5.*

Tepoztlán's temperatures fluctuate, from blistering around midday to bitterly cold at night. Visitors who plan an overnight stay in the winter months should bring warmer clothing and a coat.

### Where to Stay & Eat

¢–$ ✕ **Axitla.** This smart establishment in the folds of the mountains is surrounded by ponds and bridges. Among the delicious concoctions are *chile jaral* (ancho chili stuffed with shredded beef and raisins) and lamb in zucchini sauce. You can dine in the pink, high-ceilinged dining room overlooking the trees and river, or alfresco. A lone guitar player adds to the atmosphere weekend lunchtimes. ✉ *Av. del Tepozteco, at the road to the Pyramid* ☎ *739/395–0519 or 739/395–2555* ▭ *MC, V* ⏲ *No dinner. Closed Mon.–Tues.*

★ ¢–$ ✕ **Los Colorines.** Hung with cheery red, white, and green *papel picado* (paper cutouts), this family-friendly restaurant serves great bean soups, stuffed chilies, and grilled meats made in an open kitchen. Special dishes include *huauzontles* (a broccoli-like vegetable you scrape from the stalk with your teeth). Note the restaurant closes at 9 PM. ✉ *Av. del Tepozteco 13* ☎ *739/395–0198* ▭ *No credit cards* ⏲ *No dinner Sun.*

¢–$ ✕ **La Luna Mextli.** You can relax on the patio here with coffee and a newspaper. Fearsome masks and flying mermaids decorate the space, and the sight of local women patting tortillas leaves no doubt that the food is fresh. ✉ *Av. Revolución 16* ☎ *739/395–1114* ▭ *AE, MC, V* ⏲ *No breakfast weekdays.*

¢ ✕ **Café Amor.** This second-story café overlooking the main street is a great place to stop for a cappuccino and a cheese or ham *torta* (sandwich). Nab one of the two tiny tables on the balconies to watch the passing parade—quite literally when there's a festival in town. ✉ *Av. del Tepozteco* ☎ *No phone* ▭ *No credit cards* ⏲ *No dinner.*

$$$ 🏨 **Hostal de la Luz.** A new experiment in "holistic tourism" is making waves at the foot of the Quetzalcóatl mountains in the village of Amatlán. The whole complex, from the traditional adobe structure to the use of feng shui, is designed to blend with the environment and soothe its guests. The guest rooms have wicker meditation chairs set in bay window alcoves from which to absorb the unparalleled views. The resort is roughly a 15-minute drive from Tepoztlán. ✉ *Carretera Federal Tepoztlán-Amatlán, Km 4, Amatlán de Quetzalcóatl, 62520* ☎ *739/395–3374* 📠 *739/395–0323* 🌐 *www.hostaldelaluz.com* 🛏 *13 rooms* 👍 *Restaurant, pool, spa, meeting rooms; no a/c, no room TVs* ▭ *AE, MC, V* 🍽 *BP.*

$$ 🏨 **Posada del Tepozteco.** Enjoy splendid views of both the village and the pyramid as you stroll through this hotel's terraced gardens. A honeymooner favorite, the inn is also a good place for children, with its

# TRADITIONAL MEDICINE MAKES A COMEBACK

**H**ERBAL MEDICINE REMAINS an integral part of Mexican life, and still predominates in remote areas where modern medicines are hard to come by or are too expensive for rural laborers. Even in the capital, most markets will have distinctive stalls piled with curative herbs and plants.

The Aztecs were excellent botanists, and their extensive knowledge impressed the Spanish, who borrowed from Mexico's indigenous herbolarium and cataloged the intriguing new plants. Consequently, medicine remains one of the few examples of cultural practices and indigenous wisdom that has not been lost to history. Visitors to the capital can find a display of medicinal plants used by the Aztecs in the Museum of Medicine, in the former Palace of the Inquisition, at the northwest corner of Plaza Santo Domingo.

A rich variety of herbs is harvested in the 300 rural communities of the fertile state of Morelos, where curanderos (natural healers) flock to the markets on weekends to offer advice and sell their concoctions. Stores in the state capital, Cuernavaca, sell natural antidotes for every ailment imaginable and potions for sexual prowess, lightening the skin, colic in babies, and IQ enhancement.

Chamanes (shamans) and healers abound at the weekend market in the main square of the picturesque mountain village of Tepoztlán. Long known for its brujos (witches), Tepoztlán continues to experience a boom in spiritual retreats and New Age shops. Visitors can benefit from the healing overload without getting hoodwinked by booking a session in one of the many good temazcales (Aztec sweat lodges) in town.

The temazcal is a "bath of cleansing" for body, mind, and spirit; a session consists of a ritual that lasts at least an hour, ideally (for first-timers) with a guide. Temazcales are igloo-shape clay buildings, round so as not to impede the flow of energy. They usually seat 6 to 12 people, who can participate either naked or in a bathing suit. Each guide develops his own style, under the tutelage of a shaman, so practices vary. In general, your aura (or energy field) is cleaned with a bunch of plants before you enter the temazcal, so that you start off as pure as possible. You will have a fistful of the same plants—usually rosemary, sweet basil, or eucalyptus—to slap or rub against your skin. You walk in a clockwise direction and take your place, and water is poured over red-hot stones in the middle to create the steam. Usually silence is maintained, although the guide may chant or pray, often in Nahuatl. The procedure ends with a warm shower followed by a cold one to close the pores.

The experience helps eliminate toxins, cure inflammations, ease pains in the joints, and relieve stress. Consequently, temazcales are growing in popularity, even drawing city executives from the capital on the weekends. You can find some of the most outstanding temazcales in Morelos's top spas, such as the Misión del Sol in Jiutepec and Hostería las Quintas in Cuernavaca. Less pricey are El Centro Mayahuel in Ahuacatitlán, or the temazcales of Teresa Contreras or Dr. Horacio Rojas in Cuernavaca.

— Barbara Kastelein

trampoline, swings, and pair of pet rabbits. Most rooms have balconies and hot tubs. Make reservations for weekend stays two weeks in advance. ☒ *Calle del Paraíso 3, 62520* ☎ *739/395–0010* 🖷 *739/ 395–0323* ☛ *8 rooms, 12 suites* ☖ *Restaurant, room service, tennis court, 2 pools, massage, bar, playground; no a/c, no room TVs* ☰ *AE, MC, V.*

$ ⊡ **Posada Ali.** With unobstructed views of the mountains from the rooms, this family-run inn draws many repeat customers. No two rooms are exactly alike, but all have charming hand-hewn furniture. There's a tiny pool in back. ☒ *Netzahualcóyotl 2, 62520* ☎ *739/395–1971* ☛ *13 rooms* ☖ *Dining room, pool; no a/c* ☰ *No credit cards.*

# Cuautla

*128 km (77 mi) south of Mexico City, 47 km (28 mi) east of Cuernavaca.*

Cuautla's claim to fame is as the birthplace of Emiliano Zapata, one of the heroes of the Mexican Revolution, who rallied his troops with the phrase "Tierra y Libertad" (Land and Liberty). A statue of the moustachioed man stands in shady Plazuela de la Revolución del Sur.

On the south side of the main square you'll find the **Casa de Morelos** (☒ Callejón del Castigo 3 ☎ 735/352–8331), a colonial-era home once occupied by José María Morelos, a priest who fought for the country's independence from Spain. Inside, relics tell the history of the region. It's open Tuesday–Sunday 10–5; admission costs $2.50. Three blocks off the main plaza is the **Museo José María Morelos y Pavón** (☒ Galeana and Bollás sin Cabeza ☎ 735/354–3312), in what was once the town's train station. Here you'll find a hodgepodge of artifacts from the battle for independence, the most interesting of which is a 1904 steam engine once ridden by Zapata. On weekends at 5 PM you can take a ride in a pair of antique wooden carriages. The museum is open Tuesday–Sunday 10–5; admission is 50¢.

One of the region's oldest archaeological sites, **Chalcatzingo** was abandoned in 500 BC, centuries before cities like Teotihuacán and Tula were founded. Built by the Olmecs, the site is best known for its unusual rock carvings, including a depiction of a ruler with an elaborate headdress seated in the mouth of a menacing-looking cave. ☒ *20 km (12 mi) east of Cuautla on Hwy. 160, Km 93* ☎ *No phone* ⊕ *www.inah.gob.mx* ☛ *$2* ☾ *Tues.–Wed. 10–5, Thurs.–Sun. 9–6.*

## Where to Eat

¢–$ ✕ **Las Golondrinas.** On an unpromising street north of the main square, this courtyard restaurant in a colonial-era mansion is a pleasant surprise. Caged songbirds trill while the bow-tied waiters fill you in on the local specialties. Don't pass up the *sopa de flor de calabaza* (squash flower soup) or the *molcajete* (different dishes with grilled meat, cheese, nopal leaves, and sauce, served with tortillas). ☒ *Nicolás Catalán 19* ☎ *735/ 354–1350* ☰ *MC, V.*

## South of Mexico City A to Z

### BUS TRAVEL

Buses run daily every 10 minutes to Cuernavaca, every 40 minutes to Tepoztlán, and every 15 minutes to Cuautla from Mexico City's Central de Autobuses del Sur, at the Taxqueña Metro station. It takes about an hour and a half to reach Cuernavaca, and costs about $5.50. The journeys to Tepoztlán and Cuautla take around two hours, and cost about $5 and $6, respectively. The most reliable company is Grupo Pullman de Morelos, but the Cristobal Colon line has more frequent departures to Tepoztlán. The best option with both lines, if there is no bus departing soon for Tepoztlán, is to ask to be left at the *caseta* (toll booth), a five-minute taxi ride from the town, where you can catch a taxi that will take you down the hill into town for $1.50. Catching the bus at the caseta is also a convenient way to leave Tepoztlán when returning to Mexico City, as officials (identifiable with badges) sell tickets by the snack store on the shoulder, and buses stop every 5 to 10 minutes.

**Grupo Pullman de Morelos** ☎ 55/5549-3505 in Mexico City, 777/318-4638 in Cuernavaca. **Cristobal Colon** ☎ 55/5544-9008.

### CAR TRAVEL

To head toward Cuernavaca from the capital, take Periférico Sur and turn south on Viaducto Tlalpán. The *cuota* (toll road, Route 95D) costs about $10 but only takes about 1½ hours. The *carretera libre* (free road, Route 95) takes much longer.

Tepoztlán is 26 km (16 mi) east of Cuernavaca via Route 95D. Cuautla is about 30 km (18 mi) south of Tepoztlán on the same road.

### EMERGENCIES

**Hospitals Cuernavaca General Hospital** ✉ Av. Domingo Diez s/n, Col. Lomas de la Selva ☎ 777/311-2209. **Cuautla Red Cross** ✉ Angustias de Callejas 53, Col. Centro ☎ 735/352-2195.

**Pharmacies Cuernavaca** ✉ Farmacia Similar, Rayon 2 ☎ 777/312-2725. **Tepoztlán** ✉ Farmacia Villamar, Av. 5 de mayo 45 ☎ 739/395-1006.

### VISITOR INFORMATION

The Cuernavaca Tourist Office is a few blocks north of the Jardín Borda; it's open weekdays 9 to 3 and 5:30 to 7. There are information kiosks in most of Cuernavaca's bus stations, but they open late in the day. The extremely helpful Cuautla Tourism Office is near the entrance of the Museo José Maria Morelos y Pavón. It's open daily 9 to 8.

**Cuautla Tourism Office** ✉ Galeana and Bollás sin Cabeza ☎ 735/352-5221. **Cuernavaca Tourist Office** ✉ Av. Morelos 278, Col. Centro ☎ 777/318-7561.

### TAXIS

**Tepoztlán Radio Taxi Hidalgo** ☎ 739/395-2473 or 739/395-0995. **Radio Taxi Tucan** ☎ 739/395-1454.

# SOUTHEAST OF MEXICO CITY

As you travel east of Mexico City, size up Popocatépetl (poh-poh-kah-*teh*-pettle) and Iztaccíhuatl (ees-tah-*see*-wattle), the twin volcanoes that tower over the valley. The main magnet in this direction is Puebla, a well-preserved colonial town that is capital of the state of the same name. You could be drawn onwards by nearby Cholula, with its dozens of churches, or Tlaxcala, with a pair of shady plazas perfect for spending a lazy afternoon. Farther north in Puebla state you'll find the mountain town of Cuetzalan, with its wonderful Sunday market.

## The Volcanoes & Amecameca

Leaving Mexico City on Route 150D (known as the Carretera to Puebla or the Puebla Highway), you'll see Mexico's second- and third-highest peaks, **Popocatépetl** and **Iztaccíhuatl,** to your right—if the clouds and climate allow. "Popo," 17,887 feet high, is the pointed volcano farther away, sometimes graced with a plume of smoke; "Izta" is the larger, rugged one covered with snow. Popo saw a renewed period of activity since the mid-1990s, which seemed to be coming to an end at the beginning of 2003, and was still quiet at this writing.

As legend has it, the Aztec warrior Popocatépetl was sent by the emperor—father of his beloved Iztaccíhuatl—to bring back the head of a feared enemy in order to win Iztaccíhuatl's hand. He returned triumphantly only to find that Iztaccíhuatl had killed herself, believing him dead. The grief-stricken Popo laid out her body on a small knoll and lit an eternal torch that he watches over, kneeling. Each of Iztaccíhuatl's four peaks is named for a different part of her body, and its silhouette conjures up its nickname, "Sleeping Woman" (although the correct Nahuatl translation is "the white woman").

Popo is strictly off-limits for climbing but several of Izta's rugged peaks can be explored as long as you are accompanied by recommended guides. You'll be rewarded with sublime views of Popo and other volcanoes, with the Pico de Orizaba (or Citlaltepetl) to the east and the Nevada de Toluca to the west. The **Parque Nacional Iztaccíhuatl–Popocatépetl,** or Parque Nacional Izta-Popo for short, has been setting up new paths and picnic areas in its pine forests.

The town of **Amecameca** is the most convenient base for mountaineers and hikers. Its tourism infrastructure is no-frills but adequate, and the offices of the national park and CONANP (the national commission for protected areas) are both here. The best time to visit is the end of October until May; it's bitterly cold at night in the winter months.

### What to See

La Hacienda de Panoaya, also known as Parque de los Venados Acariciables (pettable deer), has plenty of animals for curious kids, with ostriches, emus, and llamas as well as deer. But the menagerie is only part of the game; there are also two museums. The **Museo Internacional de los Volcanes** has some interesting information on volcanoes, but it's primarily a big thrill for kids, who love to scream at the recorded sound of an eruption. Meanwhile, the **Museo Sor Juana Inés de la Cruz** honors its namesake, a nun, scholar, and author who learned to read here and went on to produce some of the most significant poetry and prose of the 17th century. De la Cruz's intellectual accomplishments were truly exceptional in her time, as was her fervent defense of women's right to greater freedom. The hacienda is a 15-minute walk out of town along the boulevard Iztaccíhuatl. ⊠ *Carretera México-Cuautla, Km 58, Amecameca* ☎ *597/978–2670 or 597/978–2813* 🔁 *$2; $2 for animal park* ☉ *Zoo daily 9–5; museums weekends 9–5.*

A cobbled road lined with olive trees and cedars leads to the hilltop **Santuario del Sacromonte,** a church and active seminary known for the *Cristo de Sacromonte.* The black Christ figure, made of sugarcane, is said to date to 1527; it's kept in a cavelike space behind the altar. On clear days, this perch is one of the best spots for breathtaking views over Amecameca towards the volcanoes. Take a bumpy track even higher up to reach the little Guadalupita chapel. ⊠ *Cerro del Sacromonte* ☎ *No phone* ☉ *Daily 9–5.*

## Where to Stay & Eat

¢–$ ✕ **Restaurant Aleman.** This cheerful, surprising throwback to Munich serves up veal knuckle, sauerkraut, and strudel. It's really a lunchtime place, but if you arrive before 7, it will remain open as you finish your dinner. ⊠ *Carretera México-Cuautla, Km 66.5* ☎ *No phone* ☰ *No credit cards.*

¢–$ ✕ **Restaurante El Castillo de los Venados.** The Hacienda Panoaya's restaurant is a large, family-friendly establishment with huge windows for views of the volcanoes and the park's animals. Not surprisingly, venison is the specialty, and the *tostadas de chorizo de venado* (venison sausage) are tasty. The *sopa campesina* (soup with prickly pear leaves, wild mushrooms, and sweet corn) is a hearty starter. There are plenty of vegetarian options. ⊠ *Carretera México-Cuautla, Km 58* ☎ *597/978–2670* ☰ *AE, MC, V* ☉ *No dinner.*

¢–$ ✕ **Ristorante L'Angelo Rosa.** Everything here, from the *bocconcini al salmone* (mozzarella with smoked trout and cream cheese) to the osso buco is delicious, and you can even get an inexpensive Italian table wine, hardly the norm in this neck of the woods. Show up by 7 for dinner. ⊠ *Carretera México-Cuautla, Km 67.5* ☎ *597/976–3037* ☉ *Closed Wed.* ☰ *No credit cards.*

¢ ✕ **Mercado Municipal.** The market next to the left of the church on the zócalo has plenty of acceptable food stalls. You can tuck into local *cecina* (salt pork) or a simple breakfast of *huevos rancheros* served with tortilla and a dollop of mashed beans. The market closes at 3 PM. ⊠ *Plaza de la Constitución s/n* ☎ *No phone* ☰ *No credit cards* ☉ *No dinner.*

¢ 🏨 **Hotel Refugio de la Montaña.** Although it's in need of renovation, this venerable hotel still attracts visitors with its fine patio and splendid views of both volcanoes. Double beds are attractively tucked into cavelike alcoves and all rustic rooms have potbellied stoves. The hotel sees the most action on weekends when a Saturday discotheque brings in young people from town. ⊠ *Blvd. los Volcanes, 56970 Popo Park, Carretera Mexico-Cuautla, Km 66.5* ☎ *597/976–0294* ⇨ *39 rooms* ♨ *Dance club; no a/c, no room TVs* ⊟ *MC, V.*

¢    🏨 **Hotel Rincon del Bosque.** The interior of this brightly painted hotel is plain but pristine. The cheerful rooms, arranged around a car park, cover the basics: TVs, telephones, and gas heaters. Other than a sore lack of morning coffee, the hotel is quite comfortable. ⊠ *Carretera México-Cuautla, Km 37, 56970* ☎🏠 *597/976–2258* ⇨ *5 rooms, 2 suites* ♨ *Free parking* ⊟ *MC, V.*

## Puebla

*120 km (75 mi) east of Mexico City center.*

Puebla, the fourth-largest city in Mexico, overflows with religious structures; it probably has more ex-convents and monasteries, chapels, and churches per square mile than anywhere else in the country. In fact, the valley of Puebla, which includes Cholula, was said to have 224 churches and 10 convents and monasteries in its heyday in the 17th century.

Spain chose the town's location with strategy in mind: it was near major indigenous cities and it was crossed by two major trade routes. The battle of May 5, 1862—resulting in a short-lived victory against French invaders—took place north of town. On Cinco de Mayo, the national holiday, the celebrations include a spectacular procession, and throughout May, bullfights are held in the city's intimate bullring.

Though much of Puebla was destroyed by a French siege in 1863, it was quickly rebuilt and its colonial architecture remains particularly splendid, winning the city's status as a United Nations Patrimony of Humanities site. The idiosyncratic Baroque structures, built with red bricks, gray stone, and white stucco, are decorated with the famously beautiful Talavera tiles produced from local clay. With a population of over 2 million, it remains a prosperous town, with textiles, ceramics, and foreign industrial plants bolstering the local economy.

The city center generally follows a tidy grid pattern. The streets are either avenidas or calles, and most are numbered. Avenidas run east (*oriente*) and west (*poniente*), while calles run north (*norte*) and south (*sur*). Odd-numbered avenidas start south of the zócalo (town square) and even-numbered avenidas start from the square's north side. Odd-numbered calles begin on the west of the zócalo, even-numbered calles to the east.

### A Good Tour

Practically every street in the historic center has something interesting to see—just remember to look up, as that's where you'll see the gargoyles and mortar- and tile-work. Start by having a look at the **Catedral ❶** ►. Turn right on the next block (Avenida 3 Poniente) and at number 201 you will find the historic *Casa del Que Mató al Animal* (The House of He Who Slayed the Beast), now housing the offices of the newspaper *El Sol de Puebla*. It's notable for its stone carved doorway, depicting an old poblana legend of a brave conquistador who killed a giant snake that was plaguing the city. Stroll around the square, then head up Avenida 5 de Mayo to the **Iglesia de Santo Domingo ❷**.

From the Iglesia Santo Domingo, you've got two options. If you've gotten an early enough start, hop in a cab to the intersection of Avenida 4 Poniente and Calle 11 Norte to catch a tour of **Uriarte Talavera ❺**. (From Uriarte, one block west brings you to Calle 11 Norte, which will lead you to the **Museo Nacional de los Ferrocarriles ❻**). If Talavera pottery isn't your cup of tea, walk one block west from Santo Domingo on Avenida 4 Oriente, turn right, and go a few blocks north on Calle 3 Norte to the **Centro Cultural Santa Rosa ❸**. From the cultural center, turn east on Avenida 14 Poniente and make a left on Avenida 5 de Mayo—passing yet another fantastically decorated chapel, on the left side of the street—to reach the mysterious **Ex-Convento Secreto de Santa Mónica ❹**.

After lunch, devote the rest of the afternoon to museums and shopping. The **Museo Amparo ❼** is a must-see, but if modern art is more your thing, head to the **Museo-Taller Erasto Cortés ❽** instead. Callejón de los Sapos is a short walk from either museum; here you can do some shopping or just grab a cold drink in a café. If you want to pick up some folk art, head north along Calle 4 Sur and hang a right at Avenida 4 Oriente to get to the **Mercado de Artesanías El Parián ❾**.

TIMING The length of this walk depends on how much time you spend exploring the streets and shops and peeking into the smaller churches, of which there are far too many to list. Call Uriarte Talavera to confirm what times their tours are given; they're only held three times a day on weekdays. Museo Amparo and Centro Cultural Santa Rosa could each soak up at least an hour and a half. Note that most museums are closed Monday, but the Museo Amparo is closed Tuesday.

Some of the blocks are very long so if you get tired or need to save time, hail a taxi. They're safe and should cost no more than $4 for a ride in the city center—just remember to fix the price before you set off. It can get quite warm around midday, so bring some water and sunblock.

## What to See

**Barrio del Artista.** You can watch painters and sculptors working in the galleries here daily; weekends are the busiest time. You may also purchase pieces, or continue walking down Calle 8 Norte and buy Talavera pottery, cheaper copies of Talavera, and other local crafts and souvenirs from the dozens of small stores and street vendors along the way. ⊠ *Calle 8 Norte and Av. 6 Oriente* ☼ *Daily 10–6.*

**La Calle de las Dulces.** Puebla is famous for *camote,* a candy made from sweet potatoes and fruit. Sweets Street, also known as Calle de Santa Clara, is lined with shops competing to sell a wide variety of freshly made camote and many other sugary treats sometimes in the shape of sacred hearts, guitars, and sombreros. Don't fail to try the cookies—they're even more delicious than they look. ⊠ *Av. 6 Oriente between Av. 5 de Mayo and Calle 4 Norte* ☼ *Daily 9–8.*

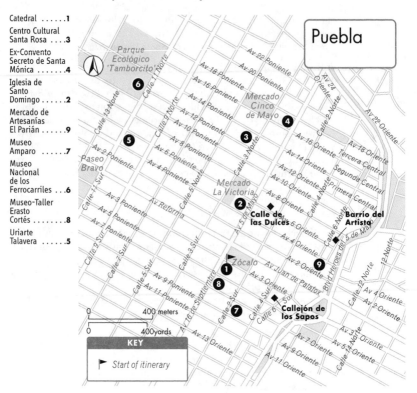

**Callejón de los Sapos.** Toad Alley cuts diagonally behind the cathedral, and the attached square is the up-and-coming antiques market and café area for the trendy. It brims with bright young things on Sunday and is a good place to hang out for a beer and live music on Friday and Saturday nights. ⊠ *Av. 5 Oriente and Calle 6 Sur* ☉ *Daily 10–7.*

▶ ❶ **Catedral.** The cathedral was partially financed by Puebla's most famous son, Bishop Juan de Palafox y Mendoza, who donated his personal fortune to build its famous tower, the second-largest church tower in the country. Palafox was the illegitimate son of a Spanish nobleman who grew up poor but inherited his father's wealth. Onyx, marble, and gold adorn the cathedral's high altar, designed by Mexico's most illustrious colonial architect, Manuel Tolsá. ⊠ *Calle 2 Sur, south of the zócalo* ☉ *Daily 10–6.*

❸ **Centro Cultural Santa Rosa.** The colonial former convent houses a museum of crafts from the state's seven regions; wandering through the well-designed rooms will give you a good introduction to traditional Mexican arts. The museum also contains the intricately tiled kitchen where Puebla's renowned chocolate mole sauce is believed to have been invented by the nuns, as a surprise for their demanding bishop. ⊠ *Av. 14 Poniente* *between Calles 3 and 5 Norte* ☎ *222/232–9242 or 222/232–7792* ⌂ *$1* ⊙ *Tues.–Sun. 10–5.*

🔆 ❹ **Ex-Convento Secreto de Santa Mónica.** Quirky and large, the ex-convent originally opened in 1688 as a spiritual refuge for women whose husbands were away on business. Despite the Reform Laws of the 1850s, it functioned as a convent until 1934, requiring that the nuns withdraw completely from the outside world. You can see the peepholes through which the nuns watched mass in the church next door and tour the crypt where they are buried. Curiosities include the gruesome display of the preserved heart of the convent's founder, and the velvet paintings in the *Sala de los Terciopelos* in which the feet and faces seem to change position as you view them from different angles. ⊠ *Av. 18 Poniente 103, near Av. 5 de Mayo* ☎ *222/232–0178* ⌂ *$2* ⊙ *Tues.–Sun. 9–6.*

❷ **Iglesia de Santo Domingo** (Santo Domingo Church). The beautiful church is especially famous for its overwhelming **Capilla del Rosario,** where almost every inch of the walls, ceilings, and altar is covered with gilded carvings and sculpture. Dominican friars arrived in Puebla as early as 1534, only 13 years after the conquest, and the chapel of La Tercera Orden (The Third Order) was originally called "the chapel of the dark-skinned," so designated for the mixed-race population that shortly ensued. ⊠ *Av. 5 de Mayo at Av. 4 Poniente* ⊙ *Daily 10–6.*

❾ **Mercado de Artesanías El Parián.** This tourist market is the place for kitschy versions of regional craftwork, onyx figures, low-quality Talavera (or Talavera rip-offs), toy guitars, sweets, and, of course, sombreros. Feel free to haggle. For better quality goods, **La Casa del Artesano** alongside the market, is the state-sponsored shop for regional craftwork. ⊠ *Av. 4 Oriente and Calle 6 Norte* ⊙ *Daily 10–7:30.*

★ ❼ **Museo Amparo.** Home to the private collection of pre-Columbian and colonial art of Mexican banker and philanthropist Manuel Espinoza Yglesias, Museo Amparo is one of the most beautiful museums in Mexico. It exhibits unforgettable pieces from diverse regions of the country. Displays are organized clearly and artfully, with evocative videos and ancient poems. Temporary exhibitions often showcase current international work, as well as the museum's own collection of contemporary and modern pieces. ⊠ *Calle 2 Sur at Av. 9 Oriente* ☎ *222/246–4646* ⊕ *www. museoamparo.com* ⌂ *$2.50, free Mon.* ⊙ *Wed.–Mon. 10–6.*

🔆 ❻ **Museo Nacional de los Ferrocarriles.** Occupying the shell of a 19th-century train station, the national railway museum offers a nostalgic treat. Period engines sit on the disused platforms and a couple—from dining cars to kitchen cars and a caboose—can be explored. ⊠ *Calle 11 Norte at Av. 12 Poniente* ☎ *222/232–4988* ⌂ *Free* ⊙ *Tues.–Sun. 10–5.*

❽ **Museo-Taller Erasto Cortés.** Erasto Cortés Juárez was Puebla's most important 20th-century artist. This museum of modern art is a real contribution to the Mexican scene: temporary exhibitions showcase up-and-coming international artists, alongside a permanent display of Cortés' vibrant engravings and bold portraits. ⊠ *Av. 7 Oriente 4,* *between 2 Sur and 16 de Septiembre* ☎ *222/232–1227 or 222/246–6922* 🎫 *Free* ⊗ *Tues.–Sun. 10–5.*

**❺ Uriarte Talavera.** This pottery factory was founded in 1824 and is one of the few authentic Talavera workshops left today. To be authentic, pieces must be hand-painted in intricate designs with natural dyes derived from minerals, which is why only five colors are used: blue, black, yellow, green, and a reddish pink. There's a shop on-site, and free tours in English of the factory are given weekdays at 11, noon, and 1. If you miss the tour, you can only see the shop and the patio. ⊠ *Av. 4 Poniente 911, at Calle 11 Norte* ☎ *222/232–1598* ⊕ *www.uriartetalavera.com* ⊗ *Weekdays 9–6:30, Sat. 10–6:30, Sun. 11–6.*

## Where to Stay & Eat

Puebla is noted for its regional cuisine. Two of Mexico's most popular dishes were supposedly created here to celebrate special occasions, and in both cases, nuns get the credit. One specialty is mole, a sauce made with as many as 100 ingredients, the best-known mole being one with bitter chocolate. The other local specialty is *chiles en nogada,* green poblano chilies filled with ground meats, fruits, and nuts, then covered with a sauce of chopped walnuts and cream, and topped with red pomegranate seeds; the colors represent the red, green, and white of the Mexican flag. Typical snacks are *pelonas,* fried rolls filled with lettuce, shredded beef, cream, and spicy sauce; and the ubiquitous *cemita,* which is like a torta, but usually made with a larger, sweeter bread, and generously filled with avocado, meat, soft cheese, and chilies.

Lunch time is when most *poblanos* eat out, and restaurants tend to be quiet at night unless it's a Friday or Saturday. There is an increasing number of cafés around the zócalo that are good for a quick bite between museum visits. At the restaurants under the *portales* (arches), you can tuck into Mexican and international fare while enjoying some prime people-watching.

**$–$$** ✕ **Villa Rica.** This buzzing eatery evokes its sister restaurant in Veracruz, one of the best seafood restaurants in the country. Specialties such as *chilpachole* (crabmeat soup flavored with epazote) and conch fillet are done with notably fresh ingredients. Note that Villa Rica is busiest at lunchtime and on weekend nights; it's a good idea to make dinner reservations mid-week as the restaurant will sometimes close early if there are no diners present. ⊠ *Calle 14 Sur 3509* ☎ *222/211–2060 or 222/211–2061* ⊟ *AE, DC, MC, V.*

**$** ✕ **Las Bodegas del Molino.** This restaurant's setting—an elegant 16th-century hacienda at the edge of town—is matched by its fine cuisine. If you're not sure about mole, give it a try here: the same woman has been making it since 1982, and her seductive, fruity blend will probably win you over. Make time to request a tour (Matthijs de Kool speaks excellent English) of the fabulous premises. Romantics should book a private dinner in the French Room. ⊠ *Molino de San José del Puente* ☎ *222/249–0483 or 222/249–0399* ⊟ *AE, MC, V.*

**$** ✕ **Fonda de Santa Clara.** Founded in 1965, this popular spot is a classic, with two branches in Puebla (other branches are in Acapulco and

Mexico City). Both of the Puebla locales have great settings and regional dishes. The original, near the zócalo, is cozier, but the larger newcomer at Paseo Bravo still manages a nice colonial feel. The food consists of mole and more mole, but you can also get chalupas, nopal (prickly pear leaf) salad, sopa de medula (marrow bone soup), and other heavy regional fare. ⊠ *Calle 3 Poniente 307* ☎ *222/242–2659* ⊠ *Paseo Bravo, Calle 3 Poniente 920* ☎ *222/246–1919* ☰ *MC, V.*

¢–$ ✕ **La Piccola Italia.** The business lunch crowd jostles with local notable families in this prestigious restaurant, where the specialty is homemade pasta. It's a little quiet in the evening, but tables at the window offer a pleasant view of the winking lights of the city. ⊠ *Teziutlán Norte 1, Col. La Paz* ☎ *222/231–3220* ☰ *AE, V.*

¢–$ ✕ **La Tecla.** Modish, spacious design, and decently priced nouvelle Mexican cuisine has made this branch of the trendy Mexico City restaurant a hit on Puebla's main nightlife drag. Try the duck tacos in green sauce, or fillet of veal bathed in corn fungus and Roquefort. ⊠ *Ave. Juárez 1909, between Calles 19 and 21 Sur* ☎ *222/246–2616* ☰ *AE, MC, V.*

¢ ✕ **Acapulco.** Open from 10 AM to around 11 PM, this takeout eatery close to Catedral is always busy with locals and tourists alike. The specialty is the *pelona,* but the potato-and-cheese tacos are popular, too. When the *señora* asks *cual salsa le pongo?* ("Which sauce do you want?"), the answer is *rojo* (red), *verde* (green), or *ninguna* (none). ⊠ *5 Pte. 114 at Av. 16 de Septiembre* ☎ *No phone* ☰ *No credit cards.*

$$$ ✕▦ **Mesón Sacristía de Capuchinas.** Though this 17th-century building is in the center of Puebla, it's very quiet and cool, thanks to its thick walls. Each room has a slightly different, somewhat monastic, decor. Many have beamed ceilings; some have wrought-iron bedsteads or religious icons. The suites are decorated in a contemporary style. The restaurant (¢–$) is very popular at lunchtime. ⊠ *Av. 9 Oriente 16, 72000* ☎ *222/ 232–8088 or 222/246–6084* ⊕ *www.mesones-sacristia.com* ⇱ *7 suites* ⟁ *Restaurant, cable TV, bar; no a/c* ☰ *AE, MC, V* ⦿ *BP.*

$$$ ✕▦ **Mesón Sacristía de la Compañía.** The antiques that decorate the rooms in this converted colonial mansion are also for sale. Warming touches are both figurative and literal; you'll be welcomed with a plate of cookies, and, if it gets chilly, heaters are brought to your room. The rich colors of folk art pervade the cozy but stylish Confessional bar. The attractive restaurant (¢–$) serves tasty regional dishes such as *carne San Pascual* (steak with corn fungus). ⊠ *Calle 6 Sur 304, at Callejón de los Sapos, 72000* ☎ *222/242–3554* ▤ *222/232–4513* ⊕ *222/232–4513* ⇱ *8 rooms* ⟁ *Restaurant, room service, cable TV, bar, free parking; no a/c* ☰ *AE, MC, V* ⦿ *BP.*

$–$$ ✕▦ **Hotel Royalty.** This well-maintained hotel is always busy because of its popular restaurant (¢–$) under the *portales* (arches) on the main square. The old colonial building is an excellent choice for its central location on the zócalo; the best rooms are the junior suites. The restaurant is a sound choice for breakfast or a pleasant lunch while watching the action in the square. ⊠ *Portal Hidalgo 8, 72000* ☎ *222/242–4740* ▤ *222/242–4743* ⊕ *www.hotelr.com* ⇱ *34 rooms, 11 suites* ⟁ *Restaurant, cable TV, bar; no a/c* ☰ *AE, MC, V* ⦿ *BP.*

**$$$** ⌂ **Camino Real.** Formerly a convent, this 16th-century building radiates historic character, from its luminous restored frescos to its wooden shutters. Large, white rooms have colonial antique furniture and exposed beams. The junior suite was once the convent's chapel, and the presidential suite has original 16th-century gilded furnishings and carpeting. The staff is warm and professional. ☒ *Av. 7 Poniente 105, 72000* ☎ *222/229–0909 or 222/229–0910* 🖷 *222/232–9251* ⊕ *www. caminoreal.com/puebla* ⇱ *75 rooms, 9 suites* ⚬ *2 restaurants, cable TV, in-room data ports, bar, business services* ⊟ *AE, DC, MC, V.*

**$$** ⌂ **Puebla Marriott.** At the city's entrance—a bit far from the attractions— is this quiet and cheery hotel with spacious, colorful gardens. The executive area is designed for business travelers; it consists of a separate building with 70 rooms and its own pool, restaurant, and business area. ☒ *Av. Hermanos Serdan 807, 72100* ☎ *222/223–8300* 🖷 *222/223–8301* ⊕ *www.marriott.com* ⇱ *192 rooms* ⚬ *Restaurant, room service, cable TV, in-room safes, 2 pools, gym, bar, business services, meeting rooms* ⊟ *AE, DC, MC, V* �⊙⫶ *BP.*

**¢** ⌂ **Hotel Santiago.** One of the cheaper central options, this little hotel opposite the Sears department store is modern and clean. The double rooms have two double beds. ☒ *Av. 3 Pte. 106 at 16 de Septiembre, 72000* ☎ *222/242–2860* 🖷 *222/242–2779* ⇱ *37 rooms* ⚬ *Cable TV; no a/c* ⊟ *No credit cards.*

### Nightlife
Puebla's nightlife centers on the bars on Avenida Juárez. Mariachis keep the songs coming at **La Cantina de los Remedios** (☒ Av. Juárez 2504, Col. la Paz ☎ 222/249–0843), a good place for after-dinner drinks.

Additionally, Callejon de los Sapos still offers some spots for drinks and live music, though it's popularity is declining.

## Parque Nacional La Malinche

*80 km northeast of Puebla, 156 km east of Mexico City center.*

Referred to locally as Malintzin (a less Hispanicized version of the same name), La Malinche is Mexico's fourth-tallest mountain at 14,435 feet. The extinct volcano is named for Cortés's notorious mistress, an Indian princess who helped the Spaniards conquer Mexico. Nowadays, only few refer to it by its older and more poetic Nahuatl name of *Metlalcuéyetl* (She of the Long Skirts). From the park's reception area at 10,170 feet, the roundtrip hike to the summit takes five to six hours. Climbers are advised to set off early—if you overnight, you should start around 9 AM (all others should start at 10 AM, as soon as the park opens), as temperatures dive once the sun starts to set. A guide is not required, but be aware that the park does not provide maps, and it is common for inexperienced hikers to get very lost on the way down, ending up in remote Tlaxcalan villages. Guides cost about $100 for a group, and need to be reserved in advance. Have someone who speaks Spanish make the reservation.

If you need to overnight, the park has cabins sleeping six ($52) or nine ($82) people; each has hot water, TV, and fireplace, though you'll need to buy firewood separately. The kitchenettes no longer have gas for cooking, but the on-site restaurant-bar Las Cabañas is very inexpensive and open 9–5 on weekdays and 9–10:30 PM on weekends. The park gets very busy on weekends, but during the week, it's blissfully quiet. To get here from Mexico City, take the Carretera Mexico-Veracruz, making a left on San Martin Texmelucan (heading north towards Apizaco). Head east (right) on Highway 136 after passing Apizaco. You'll see a signpost for the park on your right. From Puebla, take the Carretera 150 Puebla-Amozoc to Highway 129. Follow 129 to Huamantla. ⊠ *Centro Vacacional La Malinche, La Montaña La Malinche, Huamantla–Tlaxcala* 🕿 *246/462–4098* ☉ *Daily 10–5* 🖭 *25¢.*

## Cholula & the Colonial Treasures of Puebla State

Cholula is creeping out from under the shadow of Puebla and gradually being restored to something of its former greatness. Before the Spanish Conquest, this ancient settlement, 8 km (5 mi) west of Puebla, had hundreds of temples and rivaled Teotihuacán as a cultural and ceremonial center. The *mercado santuario* (market sanctuary) system was developed here in AD 1200, whereby satellite cities of Cholula exchanged cultural ideas and began trading with the Gulf region and Oaxaca. On his arrival, Cortés ordered every temple destroyed, and a church built in its place. However, the claim that Cholula has 365 church cupolas, one for every day in the year is to be taken with a grain of salt. Work to preserve the region's heritage is bearing fruit as a number of the 39 churches in Cholula—and the 128 in the surrounding area—have been painstakingly restored. There are also new, clear signposts, and the zócalo is now neat and organized.

Weekends are the liveliest time to visit Cholula, when you can catch the Sunday market and some live music with dinner. The town's even busier during one of its many festivals, especially the *feria de San Pedro,* during the first two weeks of September. This celebration includes *la Bajada de la Virgen,* when the Virgin of Remedies is carried down from her church atop the Gran Pirámide and stays a night in each of the town's neighborhoods. Not to be outdone, the other parish, San Andrés, has a splendid *feria* on the weekend closest to November 30, with a flower-bedecked church, outstanding choir, *ballet folklórico,* fireworks display, fair, and special sweetbreads baked for the occasion.

Thanks in part to the student presence at the respected Universidad de las Americas, some pleasant eateries have popped up under the *portales* (the arches along one side of the zócalo) and on Avenida Hidalgo. The town is divided into three municipalities; most of the major sites of interest are divided between San Pedro Cholula and San Andres Cholula. While Cholula is only a 15-minute taxi ride ($6–$8) from Puebla, it's worth staying a night or two to savor the town's slower, friendlier pace.

�️ The **Gran Pirámide** (Great Pyramid) was the hub of Olmec, Toltec, and Aztec religious centers and is, by volume, the largest pyramid in the world. It consists of seven superimposed structures connected by tunnels and stairways. Ignacio Márquina, the architect in charge of the initial explorations in 1931, decided to excavate two tunnels partly to prove that *el cerrito* (the hill), as many still call it, was an archaeological trove. When seeing the **Zona Arqueológica** you'll walk through these tunnels to a vast 43-acre temple complex, once dedicated to Quetzalcóatl. On top of the pyramid stands the Spanish chapel **Nuestra Señora de los Remedios** (Our Lady of the Remedies). Almost toppled by a quake in 1999, it has been beautifully restored. From the top of the pyramid you'll have a clear view of other nearby churches, color-coded by period: oxidized red was used in the 16th century, yellow in the 17th and 18th, and pastel colors in the 19th. You can obtain an English-language guide for $6. ✉ *Calz. San Andrés at Calle 2 Norte* ☎ *222/247–9081* 🎟 *$3 includes museum* ☉ *Daily 9–6.*

The huge, impressive **Ex-Convento de San Gabriel** includes a trio of churches. The most unusual is the Moorish-style **Capilla Real**, with 49 domes. It was built in 1540 and originally was open on one side to facilitate conversion of huge masses of people. About 20 Franciscan monks still live in one part of the premises, so be respectful of their privacy. ✉ *2 Norte s/n, east of Cholula Zócalo* ☎ *No phone* ☉ *Daily 10–12:30 and 4:30–6.*

★ The exterior of the 16th-century church of **Santa María Tonantzintla** may be relatively simple, but inside waits an explosion of color and swirling shapes. To facilitate the conversion of the native population, Franciscan monks incorporated elements recalling the local cult of Tonantzin in the ornamentation of the chapel. The result is a jewel of the indigenous Baroque. The polychrome wood-and-stucco carvings—inset columns, altarpieces, and the main archway—were completed in the late 17th century and are the essence of churrigueresque. The carvings, set off by ornate gold-leaf figures of plant forms, angels, and saints, were made by local craftspeople. Flash photography is not allowed. ✉ *Av. Reforma, 5 km (3 mi) south of Cholula* ☎ *No phone* ☉ *Daily 9–5.*

The stunning, well-preserved church of **San Francisco Acatepec** has been likened to "a temple of porcelain, worthy of being kept beneath a crystal dome." Construction began in 1590, with the elaborate Spanish Baroque decorations added between 1650 and 1750. Multicolored Talavera tiles cover the exceptionally ornate facade. The interior blazes with polychrome plasterwork and gilding; a sun radiates overhead. Unlike the nearby Santa María Tonantzintla, the ornamentation hews to the standard representations of the Incarnation, the Evangelists, and the Holy Trinity. Look for St. Francis, to whom the church is dedicated, between the altarpiece's spiraling columns. ✉ *6½ km (4 mi) south of Cholula* ☉ *Daily 9–5* ☎ *No phone.*

★ **Huejotzingo** is a must for lovers of religious art and history. The sleepy town, which offers pristine views of Iztaccíhuatl, is known for its cider and monastery, but it explodes in mayhem, pistol shots, and smoke at carnival time (the Saturday before Ash Wednesday and on Shrove Tuesday), when thousands of people, from toddlers to the elderly, celebrate in masks and fancy dress, and re-enact the real and mythic history of the region. It's a wildly cathartic experience, but it's not for the meek, as real gunpowder, very loud explosions, and fires (a wooden hut is built in the square and then burned down) can make it quite frightening. The town also hosts a Festival of Cider from September 22 to October 2, which is much more sedate.

The town's 16th-century Franciscan monastery, the **Ex-Convento de Huejotzingo,** is known for its marvelously decorated corner chapels, each depicting angels. Diffuse light filters through the original onyx windows; the preserved gilded altarpiece is a rarity. ✉ *Plazuela de San Francisco de Asís s/n, 15 km (9 mi) northwest of Cholula on Hwy. 150* ☎ *No phone* 🎫 *$2* ☉ *Monastery daily 8–7.*

## Where to Stay & Eat

¢–$ ✕ **La Lunita.** A stone's throw from the Gran Pirámide, this little eatery has bumped up its prices a bit, but it's still a good place for a cold drink after a sweltering afternoon in the archaeological zone. It's welcoming and cluttered with bric-a-brac; their specialty is *acamayas,* a kind of crayfish. ✉ *Av. Morelos at 6 Norte* ☎ *222/247–0011* 💳 *No credit cards.*

¢ ✕ **Gueros.** This budget eatery to the side of the portales on the zócalo is a local favorite for fresh and hot fast food. The menu includes tacos, *cecina, tacos árabe* (served in pita bread), tortas stuffed with anything from breaded chicken fillet to *riñones* (kidneys), tostadas, *flautas* (stuffed tacos rolled into tubes and deep fried), *pozole* (hominy soup with pork), and fish. It stays open until around midnight. ✉ *Av. Hidalgo 101* ☎ *222/247–2188* 💳 *No credit cards.*

¢ ✕ **Las Mañanitas.** The nicest restaurant under the portales has a handsome bar and a tidy, rustic look. The service is friendly and the portions generous, even for a small *pozole* (hominy soup with pork). Check the board outside for the daily specials, or go for a classic regional dish like mole poblano. ✉ *Portal de Guerrero 17* ☎ *222/261–2537* 💳 *No credit cards* ☉ *Closed Tues.*

★ $$ ✕🏨 **Hotel Quinta Luna.** The elegance of this boutique hotel—only five minutes walk from the zócalo—has been crucial in putting Cholula back on the map. The restored 17th-century mansion was built around a central patio with a fountain. Immaculate rooms have natural colors, polished wood furniture and floors, and high, exposed-beam ceilings. King-size beds are wrapped in luscious, down-filled cotton bedding and supplied with more pillows than you could possibly use. The outstanding restaurant ($–$$) offers Mexican and nouvelle dishes and is worth a visit in its own right. ✉ *3 Sur 702, San Pedro Cholula* ☎ *222/247–8915* 🌐 *www.laquintaluna.com* 🛏 *3 rooms, 3 suites* ⚭ *Restaurant, cable TV, bar, library* 💳 *AE, MC, V* ⎮⍣⎮ *BP.*

¢ 🏨 **Hotel Posada Señorial (Centro Histórico).** This place has the distinction of being the only hotel on the zócalo; look for the small entrance under the arches by a busy coffee shop. The rooms are comfortable, but some are depressingly dark, so ask to see a few before you settle on one. ✉ *Portal de Guerrero 5, San Pedro Cholula* 🏨 *222/247–0341 or 222/247–7719* 🛏 *28 rooms* ♿ *Cable TV; no a/c* ▭ *MC, V.*

## Tlaxcala

*30 km (19 mi) north of Puebla, 120 km (75 mi) east of Mexico City.*

Tlaxcala (pronounced tlas-*ca*-la) is a place where you may well find yourself lingering longer than you had planned, lulled by a few hours spent on the Plaza Xicohténcatl or at a café in one of the colonnades near the zócalo. The distinctive terra-cotta roofs gave the state capital the name *Ciudad Roja*, or the Red City. Climb up to one of the hilltop churches and a sea of ruddy roofs will stretch out around you.

Bordered by Calle Camargo and Avenida Juárez, the **zócalo** has a beautifully tiled bandstand shaded by graceful trees. Adjoining the zócalo at its southeast corner is another square, **Plaza Xicohténcatl.** Souvenir shops line its eastern edge. To the north of the zócalo is the **Palacio de Gobierno** (✉ Between Av. Lira y Ortega and Av. Juárez). Inside the eastern entrance are murals by local painter Desiderio Hernández Xochitiotzin depicting Tlaxcala's pivotal role in the Spanish conquest. The city aligned itself with Cortés against the Aztecs, thus swelling the conqueror's ranks significantly. The palace is open daily 8–8. To the west of the Palacio de Gobierno is the **Parroquia de San José** (✉ Av. Lira y Ortega and Calle Lardizábal), cheerfully decorated in vivid shades of yellow and green. Don't miss the pair of fonts near the entrance that depict Tlaxcalan, a god of war. The church is open daily 9–6.

To the west of Plaza Xicohténcatl is the fascinating **Museo de la Memoria,** with a colonial-era facade but a strikingly modern interior. By focusing on the folklore and festivals of various indigenous cultures, the Museum of Memory recounts the region's past and present. ✉ *Av. Independencia 3* 🏛 *246/466–0791* 🕐 *Tues.–Sun. 10–5* 💲*$1.*

The **Catedral de Nuestra Señora de la Asunción** stands atop a hill one block south of Plaza Xicohténcatl. The cathedral's most unusual feature is its Moorish-style wood ceiling beams, carved and gilded with gold studs. There are only a few churches of this kind in Mexico, as mudéjar flourishes were popular here only during the very early years after the Spanish conquest. Don't miss the view of the city's bullring from the churchyard. The cathedral's austere monastery, now home to the **Museo Regional de Tlaxcala,** displays 16th- to 18th-century religious paintings as well as a small collection of pre-Columbian pieces. A beautiful outdoor chapel near the monastery has notable Moorish and Gothic traces. ✉ *Calz. de San Francisco* 🏛 *No phone* 🕐 *Daily 9–6* 💲 *Museum $3.50.*

On a hill about 1 km (½ mi) northwest of the center of Tlaxcala stands
★ the ornate **Basilica de Ocotlán.** You can see its churrigueresque facade, topped with twin towers adorned with the apostles, from just about everywhere in the city. The church is most notable as a pilgrimage site. In 1541 the Virgin Mary appeared to a poor peasant, telling him to cure an epidemic with water from a stream that had suddenly appeared. Fran-

ciscan monks, eager to find the source of the miracle, ventured into the forest. There they discovered raging flames that didn't harm one particular pine (*ocotlán*). When they split the tree open, they discovered the wooden image of the Virgen de Ocotlán, which they installed in a gilded altar. Many miracles have been attributed to the statue, which wears the braids popular for indigenous women at the time. Behind the altar is the brilliantly painted *Camarín de la Virgen* (Dressing Room of the Virgin) that tells the story. At the base of the hill is the charming **Capilla del Pocito de Agua Santa,** an octagonal chapel decorated with images of the Virgen de Ocotlán. The faithful come to draw holy water from its seven fountains. ⊠ *Calle Guridi y Alcocer* ☎ *246/465–0960* ☉ *Daily 9–6.*

### Where to Stay & Eat

¢–$ ✕ **Fonda del Convento.** In a low stone building on a tree-lined street, this unassuming café is overlooked by most travelers but is always packed with locals. The series of small dining rooms means it won't be hard to find a quiet table. The delicious traditional fare includes such dishes as chicken broth with creamy avocados and strips of cactus flambéed with bits of onion and chilies. ⊠ *Calz. de San Francisco 1* ☎ *246/462–0765* ⊟ *AE, DC, MC, V.*

$ ✕⌂ **Hotel La Escondida.** The Hacienda Soltepec, recently converted into Fodor'sChoice an elegant and welcoming hotel, is a true gem in the middle of nowhere ★ (51 km from Tlaxcala city), with pristine views of the Malinche volcano, mysterious dimly lit corridors, and outstanding service. The stately restaurant (¢–$), watched over by two stuffed bulls' heads, offers delicious regional fare and a cozy fireplace to warm up the chilly winter nights. It is a hive of activity on Sundays when *poblanos* (people from Puebla) come here to lunch. Best of all, the hotel offers tours to other remote haciendas of Tlaxcala state, an eye-opener into the history of the rural region. ⊠ *Carretera Huamantla-Puebla, Km 3, Huamantla 90500* ☎ *247/472–1466 or 247/472–3110* ⊕ *www. haciendasoltepec.com* ⇥ *12 rooms* ⸋ *Restaurant, 3 tennis courts, pool, gym, steam room, billiards, horseback riding, squash, shop, free parking; no a/c* ⊟ *AE.*

# Cacaxtla

⛰ *100 km (63 mi) east of Mexico City center.*

★ At the archaeological site of Cacaxtla you'll see some of Mexico's most vividly colored murals. Accidentally discovered in 1975 by a farmer, the main temple at Cacaxtla contains breathtaking scenes of a surprisingly vicious battle between two bands of warriors. The nearly life-size figures wearing jaguar skins clearly have the upper hand against their foes in lofty feathered headdresses.

The site, dating from AD 650 to AD 900, is thought to be the work of the Olmeca-Xicalanca people. Other stunning paintings adorn smaller structures. The newly restored Templo Rojo, or Red Temple, is decorated with stalks of corn with cartoonlike human faces. Perhaps the most delightful is in the Templo de Venus, or Temple of Venus. Here you see two figures dancing in the moonlight, their bodies a striking blue.

On a hill about 1½ km (1 mi) north of Cacaxtla is the site of **Xochité-catl,** with four Classic period pyramids. You can see both sites with the same admission ticket. Head south from Mexico City toward Puebla on Carretera Federal 119. Veer off to the right toward the town of Na-tivitas. Both sites are near the village of San Miguel del Milagro. ✛ *About 19 km (12 mi) southwest of Tlaxcala on Carretera Federal 119* ☎ *246/416-0477* ▨ *$3.50* ☻ *Tues.–Sun. 10–4:30.*

## Cuetzalan

*320 km (198 mi) north east of Mexico City, 182 km (113 mi) north of Puebla city.*

**Fodor's**Choice ★ The colonial town of Cuetzalan in the Sierra Norte region is one of the most precious and unspoiled attractions in the state of Puebla. The Sierra Norte has been referred to as the *Sierra Mágica* (magical mountain range) for the mystic beliefs held by the pre-Hispanic peoples who inhabited this lush, dramatic swath of land. Cuetzalan's breathtaking landscape is etched with canyons, rushing rivers, and caves, and swaddled in dense, outsize vegetation. Because of its elevation the town is often enveloped in clouds.

The Totonacs first established Cuetzalan as a settlement. The Nahuas then invaded the territory, followed by the Spaniards in 1531. Today the town and its surroundings are still home to a large variety of ethnic groups, who make up over half the local population. These indigenous groups retain many of their traditions, from language and dress to agriculture and social customs and you can enjoy watching this unusual world unfold before you during the Sunday market.

The market is Cuetzalan's main attraction, and weekends are when you will find the most entertainment and tourists. The town is very quiet during the week and some of the restaurants are closed. Tourism is still very ad-lib here, which is part of Cuetzalan's charm. The information office is very basic—and chances are slim that you'll find anyone who speaks English—but has a list of hotels and restaurants, as well as cabins for rent in the surrounding areas. Information on medical services and bus departure times is also available.

The trip up to Cuetzalan is worthwhile, but long—you'll need to be patient, as the winding mountain roads slow things down. Wear sturdy walking shoes and be prepared for cool and damp weather. Note that some people are bothered by the change in altitude. Also, the steep, cobblestoned streets can be dangerously slippery when the weather is misty or rainy. Fortunately, taxis here are very cheap.

At the weekly Sunday market, or **tianguis,** in the town center, local farmers come to sell and trade corn, coffee, beans, spices, and citrus fruits. Most people wear indigenous dress and chatter in Nahuatl, sizing up the cinnamon or bargaining for guavas. The atmosphere, color, and fragrant smells of this lively event are not to be missed.

On the town's **zócalo** you'll find the Renaissance-style church, La Parroquia de San Francisco, as well as the Palacio Municipal. The bandstand and the municipal clock tower were both built in the early 20th century.

The church of **El Santuario de Guadalupe** shows a gothic strain in its needle-slim tower and the pointed arch of the main door. Its common name, La Iglesia de los Jarritos (church of the little pitchers) refers to its landmark spire, prettily adorned by 80 clay vessels. ⊠ *Calz. de Guadalupe* ⊙ *Daily 9–6.*

Originally a coffee processing plant, the **Casa de la Cultura** has been revamped to combine a public library, the town archives, and a somewhat haphazard ethnographic museum, which often displays works by local artists. Opposite the building across Avenida Miguel Alvarado is Cuetzalan's daily crafts market open from 12 to 5. ⊠ *Av. Miguel Alvarado 18* ☎ *No phone* ⊙ *Daily 10–6* ⊡ *Free.*

About 8 km (5 mi) outside Cuetzalan lies the splendid archaeological zone of **Yohualichan,** founded by Totonacs around AD 400. Partly obscured from the road by an austere stone church, Yohualichan (which means the House of Night) consists of a beautiful hilltop grouping of administrative and ceremonial buildings, houses, plazas, and a long ball court. The easiest way to get here is to take a taxi (the ride should cost no more than $6), but *combis* (vans used for public transport) also make regular drop-offs at the top of the road that leads down to the site. To return to Cuetzalan, you can either make arrangements with your taxi driver to wait for you or walk up to the road and hail a combi or taxi. ⊠ *Carretera a Santiago* ☎ *No phone* ⊙ *Tues.–Sun. 9–5* ⊡ *$3.*

off the
beaten
path

**LAS GRUTAS –** Under Cuetzalan's limestone slopes winds an extensive cave system, with over 100 km (62 mi) of passages. Access is limited, but you can arrange for a guide to show you a few caverns bristling with stalactites and stalagmites. Your hotel should be able to arrange for a guide, especially if you mention that you're interested in a tour when you make your reservations or upon your arrival. You can also hire **Agustín López,** an experienced guide (⊠ Farmacia San Francisco, Alvarado 7 ☎ 233/331–0122 or 233/331–0104), though you should try to make reservations with him a week in advance, if possible. The tour takes four to six hours and costs $18 per person (minimum of two people), including water, transport, and a sandwich. López also offers a trip to two of the region's waterfalls, which takes about two hours and costs $8 per person.

## Where to Stay & Eat

¢ ✕ **Café Te Cuento.** This attractive cafeteria and bar serves cappuccinos, pies, and cakes and flans, as well as pizzas, sandwiches, beer, and a range of cocktails and liquors. It's open until 10 PM daily. ⊠ *Calle Hidalgo 38* ☎ *233/331–1259.*

★ ¢ ✕ **Los Jarritos.** This cavelike restaurant is an unforgettable trove of regional cuisine. Even simple items like the salsas and *frijoles* (small black beans) are intensely flavored. There's an exquisite *sopa de setas* (soup of oyster mushrooms) or you could try the signature dish, *enchiladas de picadillo con mole de olla* (ground beef and raisin enchiladas with a savory local mole). ⊠ *Plazuela Lopez Mateo 7* ☎ *233/331–0558* ▭ *MC, V* ◷ *Closed Mon.–Thurs. No dinner Sun.*

¢ ✕ **La Terraza.** Though it's known for its good seafood—like the tasty *pulpos enchipotlados* (octopus in hot chipotle sauce)—this simple, friendly spot caters to various cravings with pasta, hamburgers, and even pancakes for breakfast. ⊠ *Calle Hidalgo 33* ☎ *233/331–0262* ▭ *No credit cards.*

¢ ✕▦ **Hotel Casa de Piedra.** This fine hotel with its sunny, cobblestoned courtyard and appealing restaurant tops the rest. Guest rooms have wooden furniture and small balconies for views over the town or of the flourishing, overgrown yard cackling with turkeys. The staff will help you hire guides to the nearby waterfall or Yohualichan. The hotel is less than two blocks from the zócalo. ⊠ *Calle Lic. Carlos García 11, 73560* ☎ *233/331–0030, 222/249–4089 in Puebla* ⊕ *www.lacasadepiedra. com* ↵ *16 rooms* ⚐ *Restaurant, free parking; no a/c, no room phones, no room TVs* ▭ *MC, V.*

¢ ▦ **Hotel Posada Cuetzalan.** Centrally located and well established, this cheerful hotel has colorful rooms, a pair of pretty patio gardens, and a busy restaurant. The staff can help organize cave tours. ⊠ *Zaragoza 12, 73560* ☎ *233/331–0154 or 233/331–0395* ↵ *37 rooms* ⚐ *Restaurant, cable TV, laundry service, free parking; no a/c* ▭ *MC, V.*

## Nightlife

On Saturday nights, **Los Jarritos restaurant** hosts a spectacular show of Los Voladores, or flyers. Five men brightly dressed as the *hombre pájaro* (bird man) conduct the ritual. They climb a tall pole, then let themselves down twirling on ropes. There's no set fee, but a donation of at least 20 pesos is standard. ⊠ *Plazuela Lopez Mateo 7* ☎ *233/331–0558.*

# Southeast of Mexico City A to Z

### BUS TRAVEL

Buses with the line Los Volcanes, part of the bus company Cristobal Colon, leave for Amecameca from Mexico City's Terminal del Oriente (TAPO) every 20 minutes daily. The trip takes approximately 1¼ hours and costs less than $2. The buses returning to the capital from Amecameca run just as frequently up to 9:30 PM; they leave from a small bus station behind the old flour factory on the northwest side of the zócalo.

Buses from different lines run daily every 20 minutes from TAPO to Puebla's CAPU bus station. It's a two-hour ride and it costs about $8. ADO is the cleanest and most reliable bus line; you can book in advance with the service Ticketbus. Cristobal Colon also runs an hourly first-class service from the Terminal del Sur (Tasqueña) bus station, with departures around half past the hour. The cost is $8.

Autobuses Unidos buses run between TAPO and Cholula several times daily. The ride costs $5 and takes just under two hours. It's "servicio economico," so the buses don't have bathrooms. It's easiest take a bus from Mexico City to Puebla, then take a taxi ride to Cholula.

Autotransportes ATAH buses to Tlaxcala make several daily trips from TAPO. The ride takes just under two hours and costs about $8. To get to Cacaxtla you can take the second class Zacatelo–San Martín bus (Estrella Roja line) from Puebla's bus station; buses leave every 15 minutes from 5:30 AM to 11 PM and cost about $2.

Texcoco/Primera Plus makes the six-hour trip to Cuetzalan from TAPO on weekends only. They generally do two trips each day, but service fluctuates; the ride costs about $10. For those who wish to visit Cuetzalan during the week, the best option is to go to Puebla, and from there take a Via/ADO bus to Cuetzalan; buses leave every two hours. The trip from Puebla to Cuetzalan takes four hours and costs $6. Note that this leg of the journey is on second-class buses only, which means no bathrooms or air-conditioning. Be aware that most buses make two stops in Cuetzalan—the first one is on the outskirts of town, which is quite far from the zócalo and its nearby hotels. The second stop, which is in the town proper, can also be kind of a hike to the central hotels, so you might want to consider hiring a taxi if you're lugging a lot of baggage.

🚌 Bus Depots **Puebla** ✉ CAPU, Blvd. Norte 4222 ☎ 222/249-7211. **Tlaxcala** ✉ Estación de Autobuses Tlaxcala, Camino Tepeinte s/n.

🚌 Bus Lines **ADO** ☎ 55/5133-2424 in Mexico City, 233/331-0411 in Cuetzalan. **Autobuses Unidos** ☎ 55/5133-1100 Ext. 54 in Mexico City. **Autotransportes ATAH** ☎ 55/5571-3422, 55/5542-8907, 55/5542-2007 in Mexico City. **Cristobal Colon** ☎ 55/5544-9008 in Mexico City, 222/225-9007 in Puebla. **Estrella Roja** ☎ 222/249-7099 in Puebla. **Texcoco/Primera Plus** ☎ 233/331-0498 in Cuetzalan. **Ticketbus** ☎ 01800/702-8000 toll-free in Mexico ⊕ www.ticketbus.com.mx. **Los Volcanes** ☎ 55/5133-2433 in Mexico City, 01800/849-6136 toll-free in Mexico ⊕ www.cristobalcolon.mx.

## CAR TRAVEL

From Mexico City, head east on the Viaducto Miguel Aleman toward the airport and exit right onto Calzada Zaragoza, the last wide boulevard before arriving at the airport; this becomes the Puebla Highway at the tollbooth. Route 150D is the toll road straight to Puebla; Route 190 is the scenic—and bumpy—free road. The trip takes about 1½ hours on Route 150D, three hours on Route 190. To go directly to Cholula, take the exit at San Martín Texmelucan and follow the signs; the drive takes roughly an hour and a half.

You'll need to go to Puebla to get to Tlaxcala; from there, take Highway 119 north. To reach Cuetzalan from Puebla, take federal highway 129 to Zaragoza. From there, roads are reasonably well surfaced to Cuetzalan town. Be careful; there are dangerous curves and some of the other vehicles on the road should have been consigned to the scrap yard long ago. To get to Amecameca, take the Puebla Highway and after about 40 minutes, look for an Amecameca signpost on the right.

Puebla has several safe parking lots; it's easy to find spaces in Cholula, too. There's plenty of parking around the ruins of Cholula and Cuetzalan.

## EMERGENCIES

The Brigada del Rescate del Socorro Alpino de México handles emergencies in the Parque Nacional Izta-Popo. You can find pharmacies open until 10 PM in each town, even remote Cuetzalan.

🆘 Hospitals **Cuetzalan** ✉ Miguel Alvarado 85, Centro ☎ 233/331-0127. **Puebla** ☎ 222/219-3300.

🆘 Hot Line **Brigada del Rescate del Socorro Alpino de México** ☎ 55/5392-9299, 55/2698-7557, or 55/3118-1426.

🆘 Pharmacies **Amecameca** ✉ Farmacia Popular, Plaza de la Constitución 7 ☎ 597/978-1026. **Cholula** ✉ Farmacia Nuestra Señora del Sagrado Corazon, Av. Hidalgo 103 B ☎ 222/247-0398. **Cuetzalan** ✉ Farmacia San Francisco, Av. Miguel Alvarado 7, at Privada Miguel Alvarado ☎ 233/331-0122 or 233/331-0104. **Puebla** ☎ 222/220-5254.

## MONEY MATTERS

Puebla has plenty of banks in the city center, including some on Avenida 5 de Mayo. In Cholula, branches of several major banks border the zócalo; all have automatic teller machines. In Cuetzalan, there's a Banamex with an ATM on Avenida Miguel Alvarado at Calle Francisco Madero.

## VISITOR INFORMATION

The CONANP bureau in Amecameca, near the church on the zócalo, is a rich source of information on the volcanoes. It also makes guiding arrangements for climbing Izta.

The Puebla Municipal Tourist Office is open weekdays 9–5 and Sunday 9–3. Be sure to get the state and city map "Puebla Destinos a tu alcance." Ask for Rene Paredes if you'd like to set up a tour in English (perhaps not perfectly fluent but understandable) to churches in the countryside, Cholula, and Huejotzingo.

Cholula has a bureau apiece in the San Pedro and San Andrés areas. Alfredo Torres of the San Pedro office speaks English; that location is open from 9 to 7 daily. The San Andrés office is open only on weekdays from 10 to 5; if you speak fluent Spanish, ask for Refugio Gallegos, whose knowledge and enthusiasm for the area are remarkable.

The Tlaxcala Tourist Office, in the rear of the Palacio de Gobierno, is open weekdays 9–6; on weekends a stand is open downstairs 9–6.

Cuetzalan's tourism information office is pretty bare-bones and chances are slim that anyone will speak English there, but you can pick up a list of hotels and restaurants, leaflets on local attractions, and transit info. It's open daily from 10 to 6.

🆘 **CONANP** ✉ Plaza de la Constitución 10-B, Amecameca ☎ 597/978-3829 or 597/978-3830 ⊕ www.iztapopo.gob.mx. **Cuetzalan** ✉ Dirección Municipal de Turismo, Hidalgo 29 ☎ 233/331-0004 ⊕ www.puebla.gob.mx/cultura/ciudades/cuetzalan.html. **Huejotzingo Consejo Municipal de Turismo** ✉ Ayuntamiento, Zócalo ☎ 227/276-0003. **Puebla Municipal Tourist Office** ✉ Portal Hidalgo 14, Centro Histórico ☎ 222/246-1890 or 222/246-1580 🖷 222/242-4980 ⊕ www.ayuntamiento.pue.gob.mx. **Puebla State Tourism Office** ✉ Av. 5 Oriente 3, Centro Histórico, 72000 Puebla

☎ 222/246-2044 🖷 222/242-3161 ⊕ www.puebla.gob.mx and www.turismopuebla. com.mx. **San Andrés Cholula** ✉ Av. 16 de Septiembre 102 ☎ 222/247-8606 Ext. 205. **San Pedro Cholula Tourist Office** ✉ 12 Oriente at 4 Norte ☎ 222/261-2393 🖷 222/ 247-1969. **Tlaxcala tourist office** ✉ Av. Juárez 18, at Lardizábal ☎ 246/465-0960 ⊕ www.tlaxcala.gob/turismo.com.

# WEST OF MEXICO CITY

Heading west from Mexico City into the state of Mexico, you'll find a string of good day-trip sights, such as the long-extinct volcano, Nevado de Toluca. For a longer excursion, push along through the pine forests to Valle de Bravo, a lovely lakeside colonial town with cobblestone streets. Mexico's wealthy political and business elite keep weekend homes here and barely a weekend goes by without a sailing regatta. It's also popular with fans of ecotourism and extreme sports.

## Parque Nacional Nevado de Toluca

*65 km (40 mi) west of Mexico City center.*

At 15,090 feet, the Nevado de Toluca, an extinct volcano, is Mexico's fifth-tallest mountain. It's one of the few volcanoes with a crater (at 11,800 feet) that can be reached by car, with splendid views all round including Popocatépetl, which looks surprisingly small from here, but is recognizable as a perfect triangle to the east. Two glistening lakes— *La Luna* (the moon) and the larger one, *El Sol* (the sun)—at the top of Nevado are an extra treat. Rainbow trout enjoy swimming here, but the only humans who brave the bitter cold are champion swimmers of the English Channel. It can get crowded on weekends, so for a more contemplative experience you should go during the week.

There are two park entrances. The lower is called *Parque de Los Venados* (Deer Park), although the only fauna you'll see are horses, which can be rented for riding on weekends. If you plan to hike, go to the higher entrance *La Segunda Pluma* (the Second Feather), where two park guards keep a small shop selling soft drinks and snacks. They can familiarize you with the hiking trails. The most popular, called *El Paso del Quetzal* (Quetzal Pass), takes you from the second entrance up to the crater's edge, then down to the lakes inside. If you're hungry for more you can try the tough climb up the far side of the crater to one of the two peaks, *el Pico del Aguila* (Eagle Peak) or the higher *el Pico del Fraile* (Friar's Peak). The trails to the peaks are clear and quite safe, but the sandy inclines and altitude make them harder than they look, and usually only those in excellent physical condition and wearing good climbing shoes have a sporting chance of reaching the summits. ✉ *La Comisión Estatal de Parques Naturales (State Commission of National Parks or CEPANAF) José Vicente Villava 212 Toluca* ☎ *722/213–0375 or 722/214–9919* ⊕ *www.edomexico.gob.mx/portalgem/se/anp/nevado. htm (in Spanish)* ⊙ *Daily 10–5* 💲 *25¢.*

## Valle de Bravo

*75 km (47 mi) west of Mexico City center.*

A few hours here explains why "Valle" is often billed as Mexico's best-kept secret. The pines, clear air, and sparkling Lago Valle de Bravo make it very different from most people's idea—and experience—of Mexico.

This colonial lakeside treasure is peppered with white stucco houses trimmed with wrought-iron balconies and red-tile roofs with long eaves to protect walkers from both the rain and the glaring sun. Connected to Mexico City mostly via a two-lane, winding, mountainous road, the town is visited primarily by wealthy Mexicans—particularly weekenders from the capital—and fans of adventure tourism. The area of La Peña in town and the suburb of Avándaro are enclaves for the country's jet set and politicians.

Valle was founded in 1530 but has no significant historical sights to speak of other than the St. Francis of Assisi cathedral on the town square and the church of Santa Maria, with a huge crucified black Christ on its altar. Rather than sightsee, saunter the streets and check out the bazaars, boutiques, galleries, and markets. Valle is famous for its lacelike fabrics called *deshilados* and earthenware and hand-glazed ceramics.

No visit is complete without a tour of the lake, which is man-made; sailing and windsurfing are the most popular watersports. In November, the monarch butterflies come through the area during their migration to Michoacán and the tourism office can set you up with guided visits to the parts of the forest where they settle.

While Valle de Bravo has a verdant European feel, it is an enclave and for a long time was dead during the week. A couple of new cultural events have spurred a resurgence of tourism, and now the town is full of the sound of hammers and a pleasant buzz of activity. The bus station is being rebuilt, and small posadas have sprung up on the hill into town and along the lake. The town's two major festivals are on May 3 and October 4 and both involve many old Mexican traditional games and dances, as well as elaborate fireworks displays. If you plan to come on these dates, over Christmas, or on a weekend, make sure you make hotel reservations well in advance. To avoid the crowds from the capital and nab lower hotel rates, visit during the week for a quieter experience, more suitable for those who wish to hike and enjoy the pristine views.

### Where to Stay & Eat

¢–$ ✕ **Lagartos Bar.** Right on the edge of the lake, opposite the mall Plaza Valle, this is *the* place for a bite, a beer, and a chat. Most days it's open until 8 PM so you can catch the sunset, but on Saturday you can hang out until midnight, with live trova music rounding out the friendly atmosphere. ⊠ *Prol. Fray Gregorio Jiménez de la Cuenca 6* ☎ *726/262–0986 or 726/262–6691* ▭ *MC, V.*

¢–$ ✕ **La Michoacana.** One of the town's best sources of regional fare is just a short walk from the zócalo, and you can gaze over the town's red-tile rooftops as you dine here. Nibble on a free appetizer of roasted chipotle peppers before tucking into the not-to-be-missed *Cecina Michoacana* (grilled salt beef). Other tasty standbys are the tortilla soup and enchiladas. ⊠ *Calle de la Cruz 100* 🕾 *726/262–1625* 🖃 *AE, MC, V.*

¢–$ ✕ **Los Pericos.** The first of Valle de Bravo's two floating restaurants offers good food and splendid views over the rippling lake, although it may take you a few minutes to get used to the wobbly feeling. It specializes in fish and seafood, with classics being *lobina a la talla* (a sort of freshwater bass) and *trucha a los cuatro quesos* (trout served with cheese sauce). ⊠ *Embarcadero Municipal s/n* 🕾 *726/262–0558 or 262/ 262–5775* 🖃 *AE, MC, V* ⊙ *Closed Mon.*

¢ ✕ **Callejón del Arco.** Everyone knows this sizzling little cobblestone street as *el callejón del hambre* (hunger alley) because of the wonderful beef tacos cooked up here on makeshift stands. With tacos going for a song (90¢ a serving on two tortillas) and long hours (stands are open from 2:30 PM until about midnight) this area couldn't be more convenient for a refueling stop. Remember to avoid the fresh cilantro. ⊠ *Callejon del Arco, off Independencia, one block east of the Iglesia San Francisco* 🕾 *No phone* 🖃 *No credit cards.*

★ ¢ ✕ **Jugos y Barbacoa de Juan.** Everyone is so busy eating and serving steaming tacos that it's hard to tell if there is more than one "Juan" running these two heavenly stalls on the southeast corner of Plaza Independencia. Try the fresh *jugo de naranja con piña* (orange with pineapple juice) or the *barbacoa de puerco* ("barbecued" pork, which here means steamed to succulent perfection). This is stand-up fare, perfect for breakfast or a mid-morning snack. Note that "Juan" closes when the food runs out, which happens well before lunchtime begins (1 PM), so get there before midday to avoid disappointment. ⊠ *Bocanegra s/n, at Pagaza* 🕾 *No phone* 🖃 *No credit cards* ⊙ *No dinner.*

¢ ✕ **Paletería La Michoacana.** This is where everyone comes to buy their fruity ice pops (made with fruit juice and sometimes milk, but no water), some of the best being *zarzamora* (blackberry) and *zapote* (a sweet, inky black fruit). The custom among weekenders is to enjoy these with a bag of *campechanas* (thin sugary pastries) sold on every corner of the zócalo. ⊠ *Plaza Independencia s/n* 🕾 *No phone.*

¢ ✕ **El Torito Willi's.** This hearty weekend restaurant offers tacos and grilled meat in a friendly family atmosphere. Specialties are charcoal-grilled and barbecued beef and the famous *Taco Mar y Tierra* (the equivalent of surf and turf, in a taco). It's open 12 PM to 2 AM Friday through Sunday, as well as on holidays and during festivals and school holidays. ⊠ *Francisco González Bocanegra 200* 🕾 *726/262–2781* 🖃 *AE, MC, V* ⊙ *Closed weekdays Sept.–Easter.*

$ ✕🏠 **Hotel Cueva de Leon.** This cheerful hotel on the corner of Plaza Independencia is an excellent option for its location alone. Rooms are cozy, with brightly colored bedspreads and carved headboards; some have very kitschy Jacuzzis tucked into a corner. The restaurant (¢–$) and bar are by far the most attractive on the square and have wonderful views of the town. ⊠ *Plaza Independencia 2* 🕾 *726/262–4062* 🖨 *726/262– 1361* 🛏 *10 rooms, 3 suites* ♻ *Restaurant, bar* 🖃 *MC, V.*

$$$ 🏠 **Avandaro Golf & Spa Resort.** This former country club morphed into the most upscale resort in Valle. All guest rooms have fireplaces and great

views of the pine forest. If the 18-hole, par-72 golf course doesn't tempt you, perhaps a massage, facial, or yoga class at the high-tech spa will. The property is about 10 minutes from Valle de Bravo, so if you didn't come by car you'll need to take taxis into town. ⊠ *Vega del Río, Fracc. Avándaro, 51200* ☎ *726/266–0366, 55/5280–1532 in Mexico City* 🖷 *726/266–0905* ⊕ *www.grupoavandaro.com.mx* 🛏 *60 rooms* ௴ *Restaurant, room service, cable TV, 18-hole golf course, 7 tennis courts, 2 pools, health club, sauna, spa, bar; no a/c* ⊟ *AE, MC, V.*

**$$** 🏨 **Hotel los Arcos.** Four blocks north of the zócalo, this hotel encircles a patio and, on a lower level, a pool. Guest rooms are cinnamon-colored and some have fireplaces; if you visit in winter, make sure your fireplace works as it's the only heat source. Some rooms have balconies with views of the mountains and village. ⊠ *Francisco González Bocanegra 310, 51200* ☎ *726/262–0042 or 726/262–1363* 🖷 *726/266–0905* 🛏 *24 rooms* ௴ *Cable TV, pool; no a/c* ⊟ *AE, MC, V* ⦁⦁⦁ *BP.*

**¢** 🏨 **Posada Girasoles.** This is a convenient little backpacker's place on the zócalo. Rooms are a little bare and may smell of detergent, but they're clean and the staff is friendly. ⊠ *Plaza Independencia 1* ☎ *726/262– 2967* 🛏 *11 rooms* ௴ *No a/c* ⊟ *No credit cards.*

## Sports & the Outdoors

BOATING  In addition to being a popular restaurant, **Los Pericos** (⊠ Embarcadero Municipal s/n ☎ 726/262–0558 or 262/262–5775) is also the best place to hire a speed boat for a lake tour. Tours in a boat seating up to eight people cost only $15 per hour—you can water-ski for the same price. On weekends, you can take a one-hour tour on their pleasure boat, "Yate Festa Valle," for $3 per person; departures are at 12:30, 2:30, and 3:30. On Saturday a $10 night cruise—9 PM until midnight—includes a disco with bar service.

MOUNTAIN  Valle is ideal for mountain biking, with readily accessible trails. **Cletas**
BIKING  **Valle** (⊠ 16 de Septiembre 200 ☎ 726/262–0291) offers a very good rate for bikes and helmets, and sells other biking gadgets. Owner Carlos Mejía speaks a little English and can recommend places to go.

PARASAILING  Valle is world famous for parasailing, and competitions are held here every year in February. The exhilarating sport is so popular that anyone with a flat, large garden for landing, is prepared for *angelitos* (little angels) to appear out of the sky when winds or misjudgment cause them to miss the standard landing spots. **Vuelos Panorámicos** (⊠ Plaza Valle ☎ 726/262–6382 ⊕ www.alas.com.mx), across the road from the lake (opposite Lagartos Bar) is the approved place for hang gliding and parasailing, with certified instructors. A 30-minute tandem glide down with an instructor costs $130 on weekends and $100 during the week. Bring a jacket or windbreaker, sneakers, and a camera.

# West of Mexico City A to Z

### BUS TRAVEL
Zinacantepec buses depart for Valle de Bravo every 20 minutes daily between 5 AM and 7:30 PM from Mexico City's Terminal Poniente (West Terminal, commonly referred to as Observatorio). The journey takes about

three hours, and a one-way ticket costs about $8. They all stop in Toluca, the journey there taking about 1½ hours and costing $3.50.

🚌 Bus Line **Ticketbus** ☎ 55/5133-2424 in Mexico City, 01800/702-8000 toll-free in Mexico ⊕ www.ticketbus.com.mx. **Zinacantepec** ☎ 55/5271-0344 in Mexico City.

## CAR TRAVEL

By car from Mexico City, follow Paseo de la Reforma all the way west. It eventually merges with the Carretera Libre at Toluca. Alternatively, you can take the toll highway, Highway 15 ($9, but worth it) to Toluca. For the Parque Nacional Nevado de Toluca, make a 44-km (27-mi) detour south on Route 130. The drive takes about an hour. Valle de Bravo is an additional hour and a half away; from Toluca take the Federal 134, otherwise known as the Temascatepc highway. Avoid this drive on Friday and Sunday evenings, when the weekenders are in a frenzied rush. Try to avoid the drive at night, period, as Highway 134 is very windy and has no lighting.

## EMERGENCIES

The guards stationed at the *Segunda Pluma* of the Nevado de Toluca can be reached by radio, through phoning the CEPANAF offices in Toluca.

🚑 Hospitals **Hospital General de Valle de Bravo** ✉ Fray Gregorio Jiménez de la Cuenca s/n ☎ 726/262-1653.

💊 Pharmacies **Valle de Bravo** ✉ Farma Pronto, Pagaza 100, on the corner of Plaza Independencia at Bocanegra ☎ 726/262-1441.

## MONEY MATTERS

Valle de Bravo has plenty of banks with ATMs in the center of the city. Bancomer, on Plaza Independencia is the most central.

## VISITOR INFORMATION

The Mexico State Tourist Office in Toluca is open weekdays 9–6. The municipal tourism office for Valle de Bravo is not very helpful.

ℹ️ **Mexico State Tourist Office** ✉ Urawa 100, Gate 110, Toluca ☎ 722/219-5190 or 722/219-6158 ⊕ www.gem.uaemex.mx/turismo. **Valle de Bravo Turismo Municipal** ✉ Presidencia Municipal, 5 de Febrero 100, entrance opposite the bell tower ☎ 726/262-1678 ⊕ www.valledebravo.com.mx.

# BAJA CALIFORNIA

By Maribeth
Mellin

**SOME OF THE PLANET'S MOST BEAUTIFUL TERRAIN** is on the peninsula that runs south from the California border. Baja (meaning lower) California is only 21 km (13 mi) across at its narrowest point and 193 km (120 mi) at its widest. It's lapped by the Pacific on one side and separated from the Mexican mainland on the other by the Mar de Cortés (Sea of Cortez, also called the Golfo de California or Gulf of California). Great mountain ranges stretch between the two coasts, with one peak soaring more than 10,000 feet. Countless bays and coves, many with pristine beaches, lend shape to the peninsula's 3,364-km (2,086-mi) coastline. There are also stretches of desert as dry as the Sahara as well as cultivated farmlands and vineyards and resorts rife with swaying palm trees.

The peninsula is divided into two states—Baja California (also called Baja Norte, meaning North Baja) and Baja California Sur (South)—at the 28th parallel, about 710 km (440 mi) south of the border. Baja Norte is densely populated. Tijuana has more than 2 million people, making it more populous than all the rest of the peninsula. La Paz, with about 250,000 residents, is the only city of any size south of Ensenada. The two towns at Los Cabos (The Capes) are among the fastest-growing regions in the country. Near the peninsula's tip, a monument marks the spot where the Tropic of Cancer crosses the Carretera Transpeninsular (Transpeninsular Highway, or Mexico Highway 1).

People who traveled to Baja were once considered adventurous, and the peninsula has traditionally been something of a cult destination. Back in the days of Prohibition, the Hollywood crowd began to visit upon realizing the advantages of being so close to another country where liquor wasn't a no-no. John Steinbeck brought attention to La Paz when he made it a setting for his novella *The Pearl.* Bing Crosby is said to have put up some of the money for the first resort hotel in San José del Cabo when the only way to get there was aboard a yacht or private plane.

The rich and famous still often escape to Baja; you might just spot them in secluded hotels along Los Cabos Corridor. But Baja is no longer the exclusive turf of celebs and adventurers. Caravans of motor homes and pickups occasionally clog the Carretera Transpeninsular, and flights into Loreto, La Paz, and Los Cabos are often packed. Plans are also afoot for a series of marinas along the mainland and peninsular coasts of the Mar de Cortés (the project is referred to as the Escalera Nautica, or Nautical Ladder, and is strongly opposed by environmental groups). Although development has made Baja's towns more mainstream, you can still find adventure and solitude on many a hidden bay and sublime beach.

## Exploring Baja California

The border cities of Tijuana, Tecate, and Mexicali have close ties to the southwestern United States. San Felipe, the northernmost Baja town on the Mar de Cortés, is a popular weekend escape and retirement home getaway for Arizonans and southern Californians. Similarly, Rosarito and Ensenada, on Baja's northern Pacific coast, are practically extensions of southern California. South of Ensenada the natural side of Baja appears in desolate mountain ranges and fields of cacti and boulders.

Baja California Sur is more remote, in spite of its strong American influences. The most populated areas are on the gulf coast. The Pacific side is popular with migrating gray whales, who travel by the thousands every winter from the Bering Strait to isolated coves and lagoons here. For those few months, people come from around the world to Guerrero Negro and a few bays and lagoons farther south. Loreto, on the Mar de Cortés, is beloved by sportfishers. La Paz is the capital of Baja California Sur, the region's major port, and a busy center of commerce and government. Los Cabos, made up of the two towns of Cabo San Lucas and San José del Cabo, is one of the country's most expensive resort areas.

If you plan to drive the peninsula, you must have Mexican auto insurance. Always carry water, and make sure your vehicle is in good condition. Keep your gas tank at least half full at all times—remote stations may be out of gas just when you need it. For the most part, the Carretera Transpeninsular is well maintained, although some areas are marred by potholes or gravel and rocks. In addition, the route often has only two lanes, and sharing them with semis and speeding buses can be unnerving.

## About the Restaurants
Restaurants as a rule are low-key and casual, though in Tijuana, Ensenada, and Los Cabos you're as apt to find upscale Continental dining rooms as you are *taquerías* (taco stands). Dress is accordingly informal, and reservations aren't generally required. Moderate prices prevail everywhere but Los Cabos. Some places add a 15% service charge to the bill.

## About the Hotels
Until the 1980s, fishing lodges prevailed along the southern tip of Baja. Now Los Cabos draws golfers, anglers, and sybarites to deluxe hotels that front championship courses and incomparable water views. In the rest of Baja, you can find great deals at small, one-of-a-kind hostelries.

A few out-of-the-way and budget-price hotels don't accept credit cards; some of the more lavish places add a 10%–20% service charge to your bill. Most properties also raise their rates for the December–April high season (and raise them even higher for the days around Christmas). Expect to pay 25% less during the off-season. Many hotels offer midweek discounts of 30%–50% off the weekend rates.

Reservations are a must on holiday weekends for most coastal towns. Some hotels require a minimum two-night stay; resorts might also have minimum-night requirements in high season. Several hotels in Baja have direct toll-free numbers; although the operator may answer in Spanish, there's usually someone who speaks English in the office. Hotels don't always keep their fax machines on, so you may have to call to ask a staffer to connect it. If making a reservation on the Web, ask for a confirmation and print it out before you leave. Note also that several U.S. agencies book reservations at Baja hotels, condos, and time-share resorts, which may cost less than hotels if you're traveling with a group of four or more.

Baja aficionados will tell you that you haven't really explored the peninsula unless you've driven its entire length. That's a major journey, requiring at least a week of travel time—one way. Those who boast of making the drive in two or three days have probably raced down the highway, stopping only to eat and sleep. A leisurely round-trip takes about 14 days, especially as many of Baja's treasures take some extra time and effort to reach. With three days, focus on the area around where you enter the region. If you have five to seven days, you can see the most interesting towns in one state and still linger a bit.

**3**

*Numbers in the text correspond to numbers in the margin and on the Baja California Norte, Tijuana, Ensenada, Baja California Sur La Paz, Los Cabos Coast, San José del Cabo, and Cabo San Lucas maps.*

If you have
## 3 days

In northern Baja, you can explore Tijuana, Rosarito, and Ensenada. Start in **Tijuana** ❶–❿ ☝, then head south before nightfall to a hotel in 🏨 **Playas de Rosarito** ⓫ or **Puerto Nuevo** ⓬ Tour **Ensenada** ⓭–⓴ the next day, and spend the third day in Rosarito before heading back to the border. In Baja Sur, you're best off staying in 🏨 **Los Cabos** ㊳–㊺ ☝ for golf, sportfishing, and snorkeling.

If you have
## 5 days

You can do a thorough tour of northern Baja, starting with a full day and overnight in 🏨 **Tijuana** ❶–❿ ☝. From here head to the small town of **Tecate** ㉑, then on to **Mexicali** ㉒ and 🏨 **San Felipe** ㉔. Overnight in San Felipe, and spend Day 3 checking out the beaches before driving the backcountry to 🏨 **Ensenada** ⓭–⓴. Devote Day 4 to exploring La Bufadora and downtown Ensenada; then head up the coast for a lobster feast at **Puerto Nuevo** ⓬. On Day 5, head back to Tijuana and the border.

If you'd rather tour Baja Sur, begin in 🏨 **Los Cabos** ㊳–㊺ ☝, spending the night there and starting out early the next day for 🏨 **La Paz** ㉚–㊲. Spend Day 2 exploring downtown La Paz and on Day 3, head up the coast to 🏨 **Loreto** ㉙. Spend Days 4 and 5 making your way back to Los Cabos at a leisurely pace.

If you have
## 7 days

Start in **Tijuana** ❶–❿ ☝ on Day 1. Head south before nightfall to a hotel in 🏨 **Playas de Rosarito** ⓫ or **Puerto Nuevo** ⓬. On Day 2, move on to **Ensenada** ⓭–⓴ for a brief tour; then head south to **San Quintín** ㉓ and 🏨 **Guerrero Negro** ㉕. If you're traveling between January and March, arrange for a whale-watching tour for the next day. If not, overnight in Guerrero Negro and then move on for a full-day's trip to 🏨 **Mulegé** ㉘ on the Mar de Cortés. The drive between the two coasts, through stark desert scenery, is one of the most beautiful and desolate in Baja. Spend Night 3 or 4 in Mulegé. Move on to 🏨 **Loreto** ㉙ and spend the next night here. If you didn't stay in Guerrero Negro for whale-watching, spend an extra night in Loreto and arrange a boat tour of the Mar de Cortés. Devote Day 6 of the drive to **La Paz** ㉚–㊲. On Day 7 visit **Los Cabos** ㊳–㊺.

| WHAT IT COSTS | | | | |
|---|---|---|---|---|
| $$$$ | $$$ | $$ | $ | ¢ |
| RESTAURANTS over $25 | $15–$25 | $10–$15 | $5–$10 | under $5 |
| HOTELS over $250 | $150–$250 | $75–$150 | $50–$75 | under $50 |

Restaurant prices are for a main course excluding tax and tip. Hotel prices are for two people in a standard double room in high season, based on the European Plan (EP, with no meals) and excluding service and 17% tax.

### Timing

Baja's climate is extreme, thanks to its desert locale. Temperatures in Tijuana, Ensenada, and Rosarito are similar to those in southern California. Mexicali gets extremely hot in the summer. Northern Baja's resort cities are crowded on holiday weekends, and reservations are a must.

Baja Sur's winters are mild, but not warm; Loreto, La Paz, and Los Cabos can get downright chilly in the evening. Sportfishing aficionados prefer the summer months: although the temperatures are high, the fish are abundant. Loreto and La Paz tend to be crowded only on holiday weekends, but Los Cabos is crowded through much of the year, except at the height of the summer heat.

# BAJA CALIFORNIA NORTE

The peninsula's most populous state is fittingly capped with Tijuana, Baja's largest city, just 29 km (18 mi) south of San Diego. Its promoters like to call it "the most visited city in the world," and the border crossing to Tijuana is the busiest in the United States. By comparison, the state's capital, Mexicali, has a population of only 900,000 residents and attracts few tourists; travelers who pass through it are usually en route to coastal San Felipe.

On Baja's Pacific coast, people stream down the Carretera Transpeninsular (Carretera 1 or Highway 1) to the beach communities of Rosarito and Ensenada. English is spoken as freely as Spanish here, and the dollar is as readily accepted as the peso. Between Baja's towns, the landscape is unlike any other, with cacti growing beside the sea, and stark mountains and plateaus rising against clear blue skies.

Carretera 3 (Highway 3) runs east from Ensenada to San Felipe through the foothills of the Sierra San Pedro Martir. The same highway runs north from Ensenada to Tecate through the Guadalupe Valley and past many of the area's vineyards and wineries. If you're traveling south, Ensenada is the last major city on the northern section of Mexico Carretera 1. San Quintín, 184 km (114 mi) south of Ensenada, is an agricultural community said to be Baja's windiest spot. Sportfishing is particularly good here. Farther south are turnoffs for a dirt road to San Felipe and a paved road to Bahía de los Angeles, a remote bay beloved by fishermen and naturalists. At this writing a marina is in the works on this bay, and the highway to it is being widened to accommodate trailers with large

**3**

## Fishing

Marlin and sailfish leap from the water off Baja's southern tip. Dorado flash their blue and gold heads in the Mar de Cortés. Yellowfin and bluefin tuna weighing 200 pounds or more feed on bait around small Pacific islands. Fishermen flocked to Los Cabos long before developers did. In the 1950s, sportsmen with wealth and a passion for catching big fish flew in private planes to small lodges with airstrips etched in dirt. Word spread, and once the Carretera Transpeninsular was completed in the 1970s, caravans of trucks towing boats headed down the highway to Loreto, La Paz, and Los Cabos. Now Baja is known throughout the world for its excellent fishing and lucrative tournaments.

The fish bite no matter the season. The blazing hot summers are particularly exciting in the Mar de Cortés, when dorado, tuna, and billfish congregate close to shore. Wahoo and blue marlin are abundant off Los Cabos in winter, also the season for the bizarre-looking roosterfish. In northern Baja, off Ensenada and San Quintín, the fishing is best in winter and spring, when the yellowfin and albacore tuna are around.

## Food & Wine

Chefs here prepare a mix of Mexican specialties and rely on the vegetables and fruits grown in Baja's fertile valleys. Beef, pork, and local quail are good as is all the fresh fish. And local chefs can't seem to leave a simple grilled fillet alone: dorado, tuna, and snapper are topped with guajillo and chipotle chilies or tomatillo salsas or mango and papaya relishes. Mexico's best domestic wines are nurtured in the vineyards in the Santo Tomás and Guadalupe valleys outside Ensenada, and a beloved beer, Tecate, comes from the Baja Norte town of the same name.

The peninsula's most popular culinary creation is the *taco de pescado,* or fish taco, made with hunks of battered and fried fish stuffed in a fresh corn tortilla and topped with such fixings as a mayonnaise-based sauce, cilantro, onions, and shredded cabbage. Some say the tacos originated in Ensenada, others insist it was San Felipe. No matter. They now appear on menus throughout Baja and the southwestern United States.

San Felipe is home to Baja's largest shrimping fleet, and cooks in that out-of-the-way town do wonders with the fresh crustaceans. Best are the tacos, with the shrimp sautéed with peppers, onions, and chilies and wrapped in corn tortillas. Shrimp are also used in fajitas, soup, pastas—even omelets.

Lobster, once abundant off both coasts, gets special treatment in Puerto Nuevo, a fishing settlement south of Tijuana. *Langosta Puerto Nuevo* is typically boiled in oil (lard is most common and adds the most flavor) and served with beans, rice, tortillas, and bowls of melted butter. Bowing to tourist tastes, many restaurants in Puerto Nuevo will grill or steam your lobster.

# Golf

Los Cabos has seven public and private golf courses designed by such big names as Jack Nicklaus, Pete Dye, and Robert Trent Jones Jr. With gorgeous topography—holes are often in rocky desert and beside the sea—and another six courses in the planning stages, it's no wonder that *Golf Digest* has ranked Los Cabos as the world's 14th most popular golf destination. Tournaments are now common, and greens fees are reaching Pebble Beach prices.

Los Cabos isn't Baja's only golf destination. The Real del Mar and Bajamar greens south of Tijuana attract weekend visitors from southern California. Loreto's revitalized 18-hole course beside the Mar de Cortés is the centerpiece of a resort development in Nopoló. Golf has become such a draw in Baja that every community wants at least 18 holes. At this writing San Felipe's La Ventana del Mar course is under construction, and rumors about a possible course in La Paz run wild.

# Kayaking

In the northern Pacific, die-hard paddlers can brave cold winds and rough water near Rosarito Beach and Ensenada. The waters off Punta Banda, south of Ensenada, are particularly popular, and in winter you can often see whales.

In the Mar de Cortés you can put into the water around Bahia Concepcion, south of Mulegé, and paddle around the islands that dot the sea from here down to Los Cabos. Week-long kayaking expeditions follow a route from Loreto to La Paz. Manta rays leap and flop onto the sea's surface to shake barnacles from their wings, while dolphin dance in the wake of small boats. On a slow glide around Isla Espíritu Santo, Isla Partida, and other islets off La Paz, you can spot blue-footed boobies, sea turtles, and sea lions. In the afternoon you can beach your craft on sandy island shores, and hike trails past stately cacti and elephant trees. At night you can camp on an isolated beach under the stars.

# Whale-Watching

A small boat glides through clear waters off Baja, its passengers bundled in jackets and scarves. Suddenly, someone spots a dark shape slicing through the water like a submarine. Everyone sits still and silent as the creature moves closer, emitting gusts of air. And then, there she is: a 20-ton mama right by the boat. The interlopers tentatively reach out to touch the gray whale, her skin crusty with mollusks. She opens her enormous eyes, and slowly allows a small form to surface from beneath her fin and nuzzle a human hand. The scene repeats itself as the whale grows comfortable. Cheering and clapping, the enraptured passengers click photos, film videos, and generally perform as if they would around any darling new baby.

Every winter for centuries great gray whales have migrated from the Bering Strait to their birthing grounds in the lagoons off Baja. The boats that follow the whales depart from Ensenada from January to March. The best places for close encounters are Scammon's Lagoon near Guerrero Negro and Magdalena Bay and San Ignacio Lagoon in southern Baja. A few U.S. and Mexican companies offer tours that include overnight stays in small hotels or camps.

boats. Both developments are part of a larger plan to construct a chain of marinas along the Mar de Cortés.

Roughly 595 km (369 mi) south of Ensenada is a steel monument in the form of an eagle, 138 feet high. It marks the border between the states of Baja California and Baja California Sur, and the time changes from Pacific to Mountain as you cross that 28th parallel. Guerrero Negro, Baja Sur's northernmost town, with hotels and gas stations, is 2 km (1 mi) south.

# Tijuana

▶ ❶–❿ *29 km (18 mi) south of San Diego.*

Tijuana is the only part of Mexico many people see—a distorted view of the country's many cultures. Before the city became a gigantic recreation center for southern Californians, it was a ranch populated by a few hundred Mexicans. In 1911 a group of Americans invaded the area and attempted to set up an independent republic; they were quickly driven out by Mexican soldiers. When Prohibition hit the United States in the 1920s and the Agua Caliente Racetrack and Casino opened (1929), Tijuana boomed. Americans seeking alcohol and gambling flocked across the border, spending freely and fueling the region's growth. Tijuana became the entry port for what some termed a "sinful, steamy playground" frequented by Hollywood stars.

Then Prohibition was repealed, Mexico outlawed gambling, and Tijuana's fortunes declined. Although the flow of travelers from the north slowed to a trickle, Tijuana still captivated those in search of the sort of fun not allowed back home. Drivers heading into Baja's wilderness passed through downtown Tijuana, stopping along Avenida Revolución and its side streets for supplies and souvenirs.

When the toll highway to Ensenada was finished in 1967, travelers bypassed the city. But Tijuana began attracting residents from throughout Latin America at the same time, and the population mushroomed from a mere 300,000 in 1970 to more than 2 million today. As the government struggles to keep up with the growth and demand for services, thousands live without electricity, running water, or adequate housing in squatters' villages along the border. Petty crime is a significant problem; moreover, the area has become headquarters for serious drug cartels, and violent crime—reaching the highest levels of law enforcement and business—is booming. You're unlikely to witness a shooting or some other frightening situation, but be mindful of your surroundings, stay in the tourist areas, and guard your belongings.

City leaders, realizing that tourism creates jobs and bolsters Tijuana's fragile economy, are working hard to attract visitors. Avenida Revolución, the main street in the commercial Centro district, is lined with shopping arcades, restaurants, and bars. The Zona Río district—with its impressive Centro Cultural, several shopping complexes, fine restaurants, and fashionable discos—competes with Avenida Revolución for your attention. A massive 10-story-high cathedral dedicated to the Virgin of Guadalupe

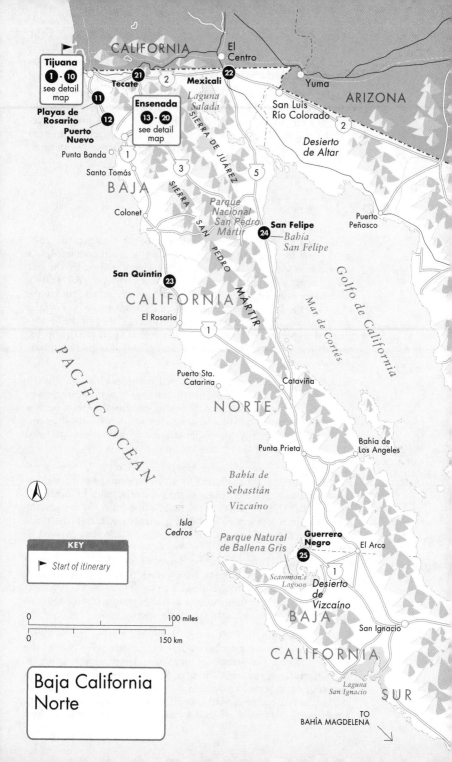

CALIFORNIA
El Centro

Tijuana
1 - 10
see detail map

Tecate
21
2
Mexicali
22
Yuma

ARIZONA

11
Playas de
Rosarito
12
Puerto
Nuevo
Punta Banda
1

Ensenada
13 - 20
see detail map

Laguna
Salada
San Luis
Río Colorado

Desierto
de Altar

2

Santo Tomás

BAJA

3

SIERRA DE JUÁREZ

5

Puerto
Peñasco

Colonet

SIERRA SAN

Parque
Nacional
San Pedro
Mártir

San Felipe
24
Bahía
San Felipe

San Quintín
23

CALIFORNIA

El Rosario

1

PEDRO MÁRTIR

Golfo de California

Mar de Cortés

PACIFIC OCEAN

Puerto Sta.
Catarina

Cataviña

NORTE

Punta Prieta

Bahía de
Los Angeles

Bahía de
Sebastián
Vizcaíno

Isla
Cedros

KEY

► Start of itinerary

Parque Natural
de Ballena Gris

Guerrero
Negro
25

El Arco

Scammon's
Lagoon

Desierto
de
Vizcaíno

1

San Ignacio

0                    100 miles
0                150 km

Baja California
Norte

BAJA

CALIFORNIA

Laguna
San Ignacio

SUR

TO
BAHÍA MAGDELENA

is under construction in this neighborhood. The Avenida Paseo de los Héroes, one of the city's main thoroughfares, cuts through the Zona Río, running parallel to the dry Río Tia Juana (Tia Juana River). The avenue is notable for its large statues of historic figures, including Abraham Lincoln.

The city has an international airport; a fine cultural center that presents international music, dance, and theater groups; and deluxe high-rise hotels. The demand for business-class services has increased with the growth of *maquiladoras* (foreign manufacturing plants). There's even a nascent opera company.

And then there's shopping. From the moment you cross the border, people will approach you or call out and insist that you look at their wares. If you drive, workers will run out from auto-body shops to place bids on new paint or upholstery for your car. All along Avenida Revolución and its side streets, shops sell everything from tequila to Tiffany-style lamps. If you intend to buy food in Mexico, get the U.S. customs list of articles that are illegal to bring back so that your purchases won't be confiscated.

## What to See

**❷ Avenida Revolución.** This infamous strip, lined with shops and restaurants that cater to uninhibited travelers, has long been Tijuana's main tourism zone. Shopkeepers call out from doorways, offering low prices for garish souvenirs and genuine folk art treasures. Many shopping arcades open onto Avenida Revolución; inside the front doors are mazes of stands with low-priced pottery and other crafts.

**★ ☾ ❼ Centro Cultural (CECUT).** The cultural center was designed by architects Manuel Rosen and Pedro Ramírez Vásquez, who also created Mexico City's Museo Nacional de Antropología. The stark, low-slung, tan buildings fronted by the globe-like Omnimax Theater are beloved landmarks. The center's Museo de las Californias provides an excellent overview of Baja's history, geography, and flora and fauna. The Omnimax shows films on a rotating schedule; some are in English. The film *Marine Oasis: The Riches of the Sea of Cortez* has fabulous underwater scenes. Exhibitions on art and culture change frequently, and the center's stage hosts performances by international groups. ☒ *Paseo de los Héroes and Av. Mina, Zona Río* ☎ 664/687–9600 ⊕ *www.cecut.gob.mx* ☒ *Museum $2; museum and Omnimax Theater $4* ☾ *Tues.–Sun. 10–6.*

**❹ L.A. Cetto Winery.** Most of Baja's legendary wineries are in the Ensenada region, but Tijuana does have this branch of one of Mexico's finest wineries. You can tour the bottling plant and sample the wines while watching a video on operations in the Guadalupe Valley. The shop's prices are far lower than those in regular liquor stores. ☒ *Cañon Johnson 2108, at Av. Constitución Sur, Centro* ☎ 664/685–3031 or 664/685–1644 ☒ *$2 for tour and wine tasting* ☾ *Mon.–Sat. 10–5.*

**☾ ❺ Mundo Divertido.** This popular amusement park includes a miniature golf course, batting cages, bumper boats, go-carts, a roller coaster, and a video-game parlor. Admission is free, and the rides cost just a few pesos. ☒ *Calle Velasco 2578, at Paseo de los Heroes, Zona Río* ☎ 664/634–3213 or 664/634–3214 ☾ *Weekdays noon–8:30, weekends 11–9:30.*

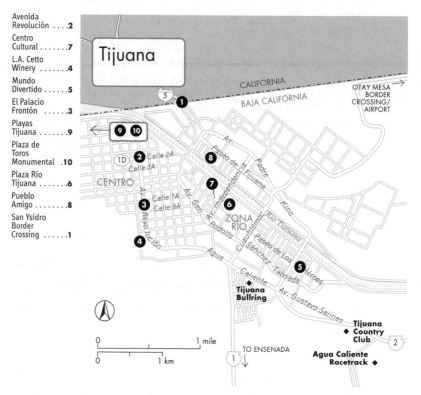

**❸ El Palacio Frontón.** For many years, the magnificent Moorish-style Jai Alai Palace hosted fast-paced jai alai games. The sport has declined in popularity, however, and the palacio is now occasionally used for boxing contests and concerts. ⊠ *Av. Revolución, at Calle 7, Centro* ☎ *664/634–3213* ☺ *Open only for special events.*

**❾ Playas Tijuana.** Along the oceanfront is this mix of modest and expensive residential neighborhoods, with a few restaurants and hotels. The isolated beaches are visited mostly by residents.

**❿ Plaza de Toros Monumental.** The "Bullring by the Sea" is at the northwest corner of the beach area near the U.S. border. It's occasionally used for summer concerts. ☎ *664/688–0125.*

**❻ Plaza Río Tijuana.** The area's largest shopping complex has good restaurants, department stores, hundreds of shops, and the Cineopolis multiplex theater that usually shows English-language films. Shade trees and flowers line the sidewalks that lead from the complex to the Centro Cultural. ⊠ *Paseo de los Héroes, across from Centro Cultural, Zona Río* ☎ *664/684–0402.*

**❽ Pueblo Amigo.** This entertainment center resembles a colonial village, with stucco facades and tree-lined paths leading to a domed gazebo. The complex includes a hotel, several restaurants and clubs, a huge grocery store, and a large branch of the Caliente Race Book, where gambling on televised sporting events is legal. Things get lively at night. ⊠ *Paseo de Tijuana, between Puente Mexico and Av. Independencia, Zona Río.*

**❶ San Ysidro Border Crossing.** Locals and tourists jostle each other along the pedestrian walkway through the Viva Tijuana dining and shopping center and into the center of town. Artisans' stands line the walkway and adjoining streets, offering a quick overview of the wares to be found all over town.

### Where to Stay & Eat

**$$–$$$$** ✕ **Palmazul.** A mural of Baja's cave paintings and a tiled map of the peninsula reflect this restaurant's devotion to all things Baja. Seafood highlights include chocolate clams, red snapper, and shrimp prepared with fruit or chile salsas. Amid the quail, venison, and duck entrées are a few classics such as marinated *arrachera* beef. The wine list has several excellent Baja varieties by the glass; you can sip in the dining room or in the cantina, which is often filled with young professionals. ⊠ *Blvd. Salinas 11154, Colonia Aviación* ☎ *664/622–9773* ▭ *MC, V.*

**$$–$$$** ✕ **El Faro de Mazatlán.** Fresh fish prepared simply is the hallmark of one of Tijuana's best seafood restaurants. This is the place to try ceviche, abalone, squid, and lobster without spending a fortune. Frequented by professionals, the dining room is a peaceful spot for a long, leisurely lunch. Appetizers and soup are included in the price of the meal. ⊠ *Blvd. Sánchez Taboada 9542, Zona Río* ☎ *664/684–8883* ▭ *MC, V.*

**$–$$$** ✕ **Cien Años.** In this Spanish colonial–style restaurant, dishes include crepes
**Fodor'sChoice** filled with *huitlacoche* (fungus that grows on corn), shrimp with nopal
★ cactus, and tender beef with avocado and cheese. An unusual blend of flavors—tamarind, Mexican oregano, mango, poblano chilies—distinguishes the taste of each dish, including the *queso fundido* (melted cheese wrapped in tortillas). ⊠ *Blvd. Sánchez Taboada 10451, Zona Río* ☎ *664/634–7262* ▭ *AE, MC, V.*

**$–$$$** ✕ **La Diferencia.** It's a cozy restaurant that stands out for its bold use of unusual ingredients. If you're feeling adventuresome, go for the rabbit *mixiote,* with the shredded meat marinated in achiote sauce and wrapped in maguey cactus leaves. Also good are the squash-blossom or creamy poblano soups, the chile relleno stuffed with huitlacoche, and the beef fillet with guajillo chile strips. ⊠ *Blvd. Sánchez Taboada 10611 Zona Río* ☎ *664/634–7078* ▭ *AE, MC, V.*

**$–$$$** ✕ **Señor Frog's.** Kitschy license plates, posters, and Mexican crafts cover the walls of this wildly popular restaurant, where waiters encourage patrons to eat, drink, and sing along with the blaring music. Known for its barbecued ribs and chicken, the kitchen also prepares good standards such as tacos and *carne asada* (grilled strips of marinated meat). ⊠ *Pueblo Amigo, Paseo Tijuana 60, Zona Río* ☎ *664/682–4962* ▭ *AE, MC, V.*

**$–$$** ✕ **Chiki Jai.** The Monje family moved to Tijuana from Madrid in 1947, bringing Basque and Spanish cuisine to a tiny restaurant by El Palacio Frontón. They specialize in paella but also have a way with calamari. Meals start with hot homemade bread and Roquefort cheese—the perfect accompaniment to a jug of sangria. ⊠ *Av. Revolución 1388, Centro* ☎ *664/685–4955* ▭ *No credit cards.*

★ ¢–$ ✕ **La Especial.** At the foot of the stairs that run down to an underground shopping arcade you'll find the best place in the tourist zone for home-style Mexican cooking. The gruff, efficient waiters shuttle platters of carne asada, enchiladas, and burritos, all with a distinctive flavor found only at this busy, cavernous basement dining room. ☒ *Av. Revolución 718, Centro* ☎ *664/685–6654* ☰ *MC, V.*

$$–$$$ ✕▦ **Real Del Mar Residence Inn by Marriott.** Golfers and escapists relish this all-suites hotel a short drive south of Tijuana. The suites' living rooms have vaulted brick ceilings, fireplaces, and kitchens. The on-site Rincón San Román restaurant ($–$$$) is excellent and attracts diners from Tijuana and Rosarito. It nods to both France and Mexico; for instance, you could have beef with either an escargot garlic sauce or a chipotle chile sauce. The spa provides ample diversion for nongolfers. ☒ *Ensenada toll road, Km 19.5, 22710* ☎ *661/631–3670, 800/803–6038 in the U.S.* ☏ *661/631–3677* ⊕ *www.realdelmar.com.mx* ⤳ *75 suites* △ *2 restaurants, snack bar, room service, in-room safes, some refrigerators, cable TV, 18-hole golf course, pool, gym, massage, spa, bar, laundry service, meeting rooms, no-smoking rooms* ☰ *AE, MC, V* ¶⃝ *CP.*

$$–$$$ ▦ **Grand Hotel.** The twin, mirrored towers of the hotel and a high-rise office building are Tijuana's most ostentatious landmarks. The rooms could use modernization, but are large; ask for one with good city views. It's an ideal spot for business travelers and anyone looking for a touch of luxury. The hotel mall has an Internet café. A stay here gets you access to the nearby Tijuana Country Club 18-hole golf course. ☒ *Blvd. Agua Caliente 4558, Zona Río 22420* ☎ *664/681–7000, 800/343–7825 in the U.S.* ☏ *664/681–7016* ⊕ *www.grandhoteltij.com.mx* ⤳ *412 rooms, 10 suites* △ *3 restaurants, room service, in-room safes, minibars, cable TV, golf privileges, 2 tennis courts, pool, gym, bar, nightclub, shops, laundry service, business services, meeting rooms, travel services.* ☰ *AE, MC, V.*

$$–$$$ ▦ **Lucerna.** Once one of the most charming hotels in Tijuana, the Lucerna is now showing its age. Still, the lovely gardens, large pool surrounded by palms, touches of tile work, and folk art lend the hotel a distinct Mexican character. ☒ *Paseo de los Héroes 10902, at Av. Rodríguez, Zona Río 22320* ☎ *664/633–3900, 800/582–3762 in the U.S.* ☏ *664/634–2400* ⊕ *www.hotel-lucerna.com.mx* ⤳ *156 rooms, 9 suites* △ *Restaurant, coffee shop, room service, cable TV, pool, gym, nightclub, laundry service, Internet, business services, meeting rooms, travel services* ☰ *AE, MC, V.*

$$ ▦ **Fiesta Inn.** It's a quirky hotel between two boulevards, on a landscaped island and next to the thermal spring for the 1920s-era Agua Caliente Spa. Rooms are modern and comfortable. The Vita Spa has individual and couples' hot tubs fed from the healing spring; it also has spa treatments at reasonable prices. ☒ *Paseo de los Héroes 18818, Zona Río 22320* ☎ *664/634–6360, 800/343–7821 in the U.S.* ☏ *664/634–6912* ⊕ *www.fiestainn.com* ⤳ *122 rooms, 5 suites* △ *Restaurant, coffee shop, room service, in-room data ports, in-room fax, cable TV, pool, gym, hot tubs, massage, spa, laundry service, Internet, meeting rooms, no-smoking rooms* ☰ *AE, MC, V.*

¢–$ ▦ **La Villa de Zaragoza.** This brown stucco motel's strong suit is location; it's near El Palacio Frontón and around the corner from Avenida

Revolución. The neighborhood can be noisy, though, so request a room at the back. The guarded parking lot is a major plus. The motel is used by tour groups, so book ahead for holidays and weekends. ☒ *Av. Madero 1120, Centro 22000* ☎ *664/685–1832* 🖷 *664/685–18327* ⊕ *www.hotellavilla.biz* ➡ *66 rooms* ᝪ *Restaurant, room service, cable TV, some kitchenettes, bar, no-smoking rooms* ☐ *MC, V.*

## Nightlife & the Arts

NIGHTLIFE  Tijuana has toned down its Sin City image, but there are still plenty of boisterous bars on Avenida Revolución. Locals prefer the classier nightclubs in the Zona Río. Tijuana's discos usually have strict dress codes—no T-shirts, jeans, or sandals allowed.

**Baby Rock** (☒ Calle Diego Rivera 1482, Zona Río ☎ 664/634–1313), an offshoot of a popular Acapulco disco, attracts a young, hip crowd. The **Hard Rock Cafe** (☒ Av. Revolución 520, between Calles 1 and 2, Centro ☎ 664/685–0206) has the same menu and decor as other branches of the ubiquitous club.

Businessmen (there's a definite shortage of women here) favor **María Bonita** (☒ Camino Real hotel, Paseo de los Héroes 10305, Zona Río ☎ 664/633–4000). Designed after the L'Opera bar in Mexico City, this small clublike tavern serves several brands of fine tequila along with beer and mixed drinks. You're encouraged to play dominoes, chess, and card games at the tables.

★ Tijuana has its own brand of beer, thanks to the Czech brew master at **Tijuana Brewery Company/La Cervecería** (☒ Blvd. Fundadores 2951, Centro ☎ 664/638–8662). The European-style pub serves Tijuana Claro and Tijuana Oscura, the light and dark beers brewed in the glassed-in brewery beside the bar. *Botanes,* or appetizers, include chiles rellenos and smoked tuna. Bands play some nights.

THE ARTS  Tijuana's cultural scene is thriving, with visiting music and theater groups from around the world performing at the Centro Cultural. **El Lugar del Nopal** (☒ Callejón Cinco de Mayo, at Calle 6, Centro ☎ 664/685–1264) hosts evening performances by jazz groups, classical guitarists, and other performers. The Web site is in Spanish, but you can usually reach an English-speaking person on the phone.

## Shopping

The Avenida Revolución shopping area spreads across Calle 2 to a pedestrian walkway leading from the border. Begin by checking out the stands along this walkway. You may find that the best bargains are closer to the border; you can pick up your piñatas and serapes on your way out of town. Between Calles 1 and 8, Avenida Revolución is lined with establishments that are stuffed with crafts and curios. Bargaining is expected on the streets and arcades, but not in the finer shops.

Over 40 stands display crafts from around Mexico at **Bazaar de Mexico** (☒ Av. Revolución, at Calle 7, Centro). **Importaciones Sara** (☒ Av. Revolución 635, Centro ☎ 664/688–0488) sells imported perfumes and fine clothing at attractive prices. High-quality furnishings and art are tastefully displayed at **Mallorca** (☒ Calle 4, at Av. Revolución, Centro ☎ 664/

688–3502). **El Vaquero** (⊠ Av. Revolución 1006, Centro ☎ 664/685–5236) is a dependable place to buy leather jackets, boots, and saddles. The shops in **Plaza Revolución** (⊠ Calle 1, at Av. Revolución, Centro) sell quality crafts.

You can find great buys on fashionable clothing and shoes at the **Plaza Río Tijuana** (⊠ Paseo de los Héroes 96 and 98, Zona Río ☎ 664/684–0402) center. **Sanborns** (⊠ Av. Revolución at Calle 8, Centro ☎ 664/688–1462) has beautiful crafts from throughout Mexico, an excellent bakery, and chocolates from Mexico City. The **Tijuana Tourist Terminal** (⊠ Av. Revolución, between Calles 6 and 7, Centro ☎ 664/683–5681) is a one-stop center with clean rest rooms. The nicest folk-art store, **Tolán** (⊠ Av. Revolución 1471, between Calles 7 and 8, Centro ☎ 664/688–3637), carries everything from antique wooden doors to ceramic miniature village scenes.

MARKET  The **Mercado Hidalgo** (⊠ Av. Independencia, at Av. Sánchez Taboada, 5
★  blocks east of Av. Revolución, Zona Río) is Tijuana's municipal market, with rows of fresh produce, some souvenirs, and Baja's best selection of piñatas.

## Playas de Rosarito

⓫ *29 km (18 mi) south of Tijuana.*

What was once a suburb of Tijuana, has become a separate self-governed municipality. The region attracted considerable attention when 20th Century Fox built a permanent movie-production studio on the coastline south of town to film the mega-success *Titanic*. Today, the complex doubles as a theme park and a working studio.

Meanwhile, Rosarito's population, now about 100,000, has been growing steadily. The main drag, alternately known as the Old Ensenada Highway and Boulevard Benito Juárez, reflects the unrestrained growth and speculation that have both helped and harmed Rosarito. The street is packed with restaurants, bars, and shops in a jarring juxtaposition of building styles. The building boom has slowed, however, and the town's boosters are attempting to beautify the boulevard.

Southern Californians use Rosarito as a weekend getaway, and the crowd is far from subdued—the town's on the spring break circuit. The police do their best to control the revelers, but spring and summer weekend nights can be outrageously noisy. But hedonism shares the bill with healthier pursuits. Surfers, swimmers, and sunbathers enjoy the beach, which stretches from the power plant at the north end of town to about 8 km (5 mi) south. Horseback riding, jogging, and strolling are popular along this uninterrupted strand, where whales swim within viewing distance on their winter migration. Americans and Canadians continue to swell the ranks in vacation developments and gated retirement communities.

Sightseeing consists of strolling along the beach or down Boulevard Benito Juárez's collection of shopping arcades, restaurants, and motels. Nearly everyone stops at the landmark Rosarito Beach Hotel. It was built during Prohibition and has huge ballrooms, tiled fountains and stairways, murals, and a glassed-in pool deck overlooking the sea. A wooden pier stretches over the ocean; on calm days, there's no better place to watch the sun set than from the café tables along its glassed-in edges.

**Museo Wa-Kuatay.** Rosarito's history is illustrated in exhibits on the Kumiai Indians, the early missions, and ranching in the region at this small museum. ⊠ *Blvd. Juárez, next to the Rosarito Beach Hotel* ☏ *No phone* 🎫 *Free* ⊙ *Open Tues.–Sun. 9–5.*

☺ **Foxploration.** Fox Studios has expanded its operation to include a film-oriented theme park. You learn how films are made by visiting one set that resembles a New York street scene and another filled with props from *Titanic.* Exhibits on filming, sound and light effects, and animation are both educational and entertaining, and Fox's most famous films are shown in the large state-of-the-art theater. The park includes a children's playroom where kids can shoot thousands of foam balls out of air cannons, a food court with U.S. franchises, and a large retail area. ⊠ *Old Ensenada Hwy., Km 32.8* ☏ *661/614–9444, 866/369–2252 in the U.S.* ⊕ *www.foxploration.com* 🎫 *$9–$12* ⊙ *Wed.–Fri. 9–5:30, weekends 10–6:30.*

**Galería Giorgio Santini.** Baja's finest painters and sculptors display their work in this architecturally stunning gallery. Stop by for a glass of wine or an espresso in the coffee shop, and learn something about Baja's vibrant art scene. ⊠ *Old Ensenada Hwy., Km 40* ☏ *661/614–1459* ⊕ *www.giorgiosantini.com* 🎫 *Free* ⊙ *Thurs.–Tues. 11–8.*

## Where to Stay & Eat

★ **$$–$$$** ✕ **La Leña.** The cornerstone restaurant of the Quinta Plaza shopping center, La Leña is spacious and impeccably clean, with tables spread far enough apart for privacy. Try any of the beef dishes, especially the carne asada with tortillas and guacamole or the steak and lobster combo. ⊠ *Quinta Plaza, Blvd. Juárez 2500* ☏ *661/612–0826* ⊟ *MC, V.*

**$–$$$** ✕ **El Nido.** A dark, wood-paneled restaurant with leather booths and a large central fireplace, this is one of Rosarito's oldest eateries. Diners unimpressed with newer, fancier places come here for mesquite-grilled steaks and grilled quail from the owner's farm in the Baja wine country. ⊠ *Blvd. Juárez 67* ☏ *661/612–1430* ⊟ *No credit cards.*

**$–$$$** ✕ **El Patio.** Although it's amid the bustle of the Festival Plaza complex, this tasteful, colonial-style restaurant is the best spot for a relaxed, authentic Mexican meal. The aromas of chilies, mole, and grilled meats spark the appetite. Try the grilled quail, shrimp crepes, or chicken with poblano sauce. The bar is a good place to enjoy a cocktail away from the street-side crowds. ⊠ *Festival Plaza, Blvd. Juárez 1207* ☏ *661/612–2950* ⊟ *MC, V.*

**¢–$** ✕ **La Flor de Michoacán.** Michoacán-style (deep fried) carnitas, served with homemade tortillas, guacamole, and salsa, are the hallmark of this rustic Rosarito landmark, established in 1950. The tacos, *tortas* (sandwiches), and tostadas are great. Takeout is available. ⊠ *Blvd. Juárez 291* ☏ *661/612–1858* ⊟ *No credit cards* ⊙ *Closed Wed.*

**¢–$** ✕ **Tacos El Yaqui.** For true down-home Mexican cooking, nothing beats this taco stand. Carne asada tacos with fresh corn tortillas are superb—the perfect fix for late-night munchies. The stand is clean, and the cooks use purified water. ⊠ *Calle de la Palma, off Blvd. Juárez, across from Rosarito Beach Hotel* ☏ *No phone* ⊟ *No credit cards.*

**$$–$$$** ⊞ **Rosarito Beach Hotel and Spa.** Charm rather than comfort is the main reason for staying here. The rooms in the oldest section have hand-painted wooden beams and heavy dark furnishings. The more modern rooms in the tower have air-conditioning and pastel color schemes. ⊠ *Blvd. Juárez s/n, south end of town* ⌖ *Box 430145, San Diego, CA 22710* ☎ *661/612–0144, 800/343–8582 in the U.S.* ⊕ *www.rosaritobeachhotel. com* ⇦ *180 rooms, 100 suites* ⌂ *2 restaurants, in-room safes, tennis court, 2 pools, gym, spa, beach, racquetball, bar, shops, playground, laundry service; no a/c in some rooms* ▤ *MC, V.*

**$$** ⊞ **Festival Plaza.** The Festival is the perfect place if you have unrestrained fun in mind. The motel-like rooms are in an eight-story building beside the road and bars. A central courtyard serves as a concert stage, playground, and party headquarters. The casitas close to the beach are the quietest accommodations and have small hot tubs as well as living rooms with sofa beds. The villas just south of Rosarito have full kitchens. ⊠ *Blvd. Juárez 1207, 22710* ☎ *661/612–2950, 800/453–8606 in the U.S.* 🖷 *661/612–0124* ⊕ *www.festivalplaza.com* ⇦ *203 rooms, 5 suites, 7 casitas, 13 villas* ⌂ *6 restaurants, cable TV, pool, 2 hot tubs, 7 bars, dance club, shops* ▤ *MC, V.*

**$$** ⊞ **Las Rocas.** This white hotel with blue-tile domes would be the most romantic lodging in town if only it were renovated. The least expensive rooms are small; larger quarters have fireplaces and microwaves. All rooms have ocean views, and the pool and whirlpool seem to spill into the Pacific. An excellent spa offers reasonably priced state-of-the-art treatments. ⊠ *Old Ensenada Hwy., Km 38.5, 22710* ☎ *661/614–0357, 888/527–7622 in the U.S.* 🖷 *661/614–0360* ⊕ *www.lasrocas.com* ⇦ *40 rooms, 34 suites* ⌂ *2 restaurants, some kitchenettes, cable TV, 2 pools, exercise equipment, hot tub, massage, spa, beach, 2 bars* ▤ *MC, V.*

**$** ⊞ **Los Pelicanos Hotel.** Guests return annually to their favorite rooms in this small hotel by the beach. Rooms without ocean views are inexpensive; rates are higher for quarters on the top floors. Some rooms have little outside light. The restaurant is a local favorite for sunset cocktails. ⊠ *Calle Ebano 113, 22710* ☎ *661/612–0445 or 661/612–1757* ⇦ *39 rooms* ⌂ *Restaurant, cable TV, bar* ▤ *AE, MC, V.*

## Nightlife

Rosarito's many restaurants keep customers entertained with live music, piano bars, or *folklórico* (folk music and dance) shows, and the bar scene is hopping as well. Drinking-and-driving laws are stiff. If you drink, take a cab or assign a designated driver. The police also enforce laws that prohibit drinking in the streets; confine your revelry to the bars.

The **Festival Plaza** (⊠ Blvd. Juárez 1207 ☎ 661/612–2950, 661/612–2950 to cantina) presents live concerts on the hotel's courtyard stage most weekends. In the hotel complex are El Museo Cantina Tequila, dedicated to the art of imbibing tequila and stocked with more than 130 brands of the fiery drink. Rock & Roll Taco is an on-site taco stand that's also the town's largest (and most rambunctious) dancing and drinking hangout.

**Papas and Beer** (⊠ On beach off Blvd. Juárez near Rosarito Beach Hotel ☎ 661/612–0444) draws a young, energetic crowd for drinking and dancing on the beach and small stages. **Rene's Sports Bar** (⊠ Carretera Transpeninsular, Km 28 ☎ 661/612–1061) attracts a somewhat quiet, older crowd; the restaurant isn't great, but a few pool tables, TVs broadcasting sporting events, and a convivial gaggle of gringos make the bar a great hangout.

There's a lot going on at night at the **Rosarito Beach Hotel** (⊠ Blvd. Juárez s/n ☎ 661/612–0144): live music at the ocean-view Beach Comber Bar; a Mexican Fiesta on Friday and Saturday nights; and occasional live bands and dances in the cavernous ballroom.

## Sports & the Outdoors

GOLF The **Real del Mar Golf Club** (⊠ 18 km [11 mi] south of border on Ensenada toll road ☎ 661/631–3670) has 18 holes overlooking the ocean. Greens fees are $59 Monday through Thursday and $69 Friday through Sunday. Golf packages are available at some Rosarito Beach hotels.

HORSEBACK You can hire horses at the north and south ends of Boulevard Juárez RIDING and on the beach south of the Rosarito Beach Hotel for $10 per hour. If you're a dedicated equestrian, ask about tours into the countryside.

SURFING Surfers head south of Rosarito on the Old Ensenada Highway to Popotla (Km 33), Calafía (Km 35.5), and Costa Baja (Km 36). The water is chilly most of the year, but it reaches the mid-70s in August and September. The **Inner Reef Surf Shop** (⊠ Old Ensenada Highway, Km 34.5 ☎ 661/613–2065 or 661/615–0841) rents surfboards, boogie boards, and wet suits. Surfboards cost about $20 a day.

## Shopping

Shopping is far better in Rosarito than in most Baja cities, especially for pottery, wooden furniture, and high-end household items favored by condo owners in nearby expat clusters. Curio stands and open-air artisans' markets line Boulevard Juárez both north and south of town. Major hotels have shopping arcades with decent crafts stores.

★ **Apisa** (⊠ Blvd. Juárez 2400 ☎ 661/612–0125) sells contemporary furnishings and iron sculptures from Guadalajara. At **Casa la Carreta** (⊠ Old Ensenada Hwy., Km 29 ☎ 661/612–0502) you can see wood-carvers shaping elaborate desks, dining tables, and armoires. **Casa Torres** (⊠ Rosarito Beach Hotel Shopping Center, Blvd. Juárez s/n ☎ 661/612–1008) sells imported perfumes.

The **Mercado de Artesanías** (⊠ Blvd. Juárez 306 ☎ No phone) is a great place to find manufactured souvenirs—everything from sombreros to serapes. Resembling a colonial church with its facade of hand-painted tiles, **La Misión del Viejo** (⊠ Blvd. Juárez 139 ☎ 661/612–1576) purveys hand-carved chairs, tin lamps shaped like stars, and glazed pottery.

# Puerto Nuevo

⓬ *Old Ensenada Hwy., Km 44, 12 km (7½ mi) south of Rosarito.*

Southern Californians regularly cross the border to indulge in the classic Puerto Nuevo meal: lobster fried in hot oil and served with refried beans, rice, homemade tortillas, salsa, and lime. At least 30 restaurants are packed into this village; nearly all offer the same menu. In most places prices are based on size; a medium lobster will cost you about $15.

Though the fried version is the Puerto Nuevo classic, some restaurants offer steamed or grilled lobsters, which are actually more flavorful. Each October, to mark the start of the season (which ends in March), the town holds a wine and lobster festival.

Artisans' markets and stands throughout the village sell serapes and T-shirts; the shops closest to the cliffs have the best selection. Several long-time favorite inns and restaurants hug the road south to Ensenada.

## Where to Stay & Eat

$$–$$$$ ✕ **La Casa de la Langosta.** Seafood soup and grilled fish are options, but lobster is the star. It's served in omelets and burritos or steamed with a wine sauce. Most tables in the large, noisy dining room are covered with platters of fried or grilled lobster and all the standard accompaniments. There's an actual wine list here, and it has several Baja wines. ⊠ *Tiguron, at Azuelo* ☎ *661/664–4102* ▤ *MC, V.*

☺ $$–$$$$ ✕ **Jatay.** Waiters beckon you from the street to climb the stairs to this second-story dining room, where mariachis play for groups gathered around long dining tables. Jatay may attract diners with its festivities and free margaritas, but it's the lobster that keeps people coming back. Ask for it grilled and served with bowls of melted butter—superb. ⊠ *Calle Azuelo 13* ☎ *661/614–1406* ▤ *MC, V.*

$$–$$$$ ✕ **Ortega's Patio.** Spend a sunny afternoon on the upstairs deck; try for a table with a sea view. Brightly striped serapes hanging about provide some shade and pots of bougainvillea add color. Diners tend to converse between tables as they slowly devour their lobster and well-chilled margaritas. ⊠ *Chinchorro 12* ☎ *661/664–1411* ▤ *MC, V.*

★ $$–$$$$ ✕ **Puerto Nuevo II.** Don't skip the appetizers—including steamed mussels and sautéed octopus with garlic—at this lobster house. The chef doesn't let tradition inhibit his creativity. He chooses whatever is in season and works wonders with chilies and sauces. Order the smallest lobster for your main course so you can thoroughly enjoy the starters. ⊠ *Av. Renteria 2* ☎ *661/644–1454* ▤ *MC, V.*

$–$$$ ✕ **La Fonda.** Landmark La Fonda has faithful guests who love the hotel's simple, ramshackle rooms above the cliffs. But the hotel's maintenance is so poor it's best to stay elsewhere and stop here for a meal. The restaurant is justifiably popular with regulars devouring huge platters of eggs and chorizo sausage in the morning, or Mexican combo plates, grilled fish, or lobster at lunch and dinner. ⊠ *Old Ensenada Hwy., Km 59* ☎ *646/155–0307* ▤ *No credit cards.*

$$–$$$ ▥ **Hacienda Bajamar.** On the grounds of the Bajamar golf resort, south of Puerto Nuevo and about halfway between Rosarito and Ensenada, this hacienda-style hotel surrounds a courtyard. Rooms have hand-carved furnishings and French doors leading to landscaped patios. Junior suites have kitchenettes. Private condos (some for rent) edge the golf course and the cliffs overlooking the ocean. ⊠ *Old Ensenada Hwy., Km 77.5, 22800 Ensenada* ☎ *661/155–0184, 619/222–9104 in the U.S.* ▦ *661/155–0186* ⊕ *www.bajamar.com* ⤳ *71 rooms, 10 junior suites* ⚭ *Restaurant, snack*

*bar, room service, cable TV, driving range, 18-hole golf course, 2 tennis courts, pool, massage, spa, bar, meeting rooms* ⊟ *AE, MC, V.*

**$–$$$** ⊡ **New Port Beach Hotel.** The closest accommodations to the lobster restaurants are in this sand-color complex with ocean views. Rooms have heaters for chilly winter nights, small balconies, and simple blue-gray and white furnishings. The hotel has dance bands in the upstairs lounge, marimba music on the weekend in the lobby bar, and classical music on Sunday. Pets are welcome, and the hotel hosts an obedience competition for dogs in January and July. ⊠ *Old Ensenada Hwy., Km 45, 22712* ☎ *661/614–1166, 800/582–1018 in the U.S.* 🖳 *661/614–1174* ⊕ *www.newportbeachhotel.com* ⟿ *147 rooms* ⌕ *Restaurant, in-room safes, cable TV, 2 tennis courts, pool, gym, bar, laundry service, meeting rooms, some pets allowed (fee), no-smoking rooms* ⊟ *MC, V.*

### Sports & the Outdoors

GOLF **Bajamar** (⊠ Old Ensenada Hwy., Km 77.5 ☎ 661/155–0151, 888/311–6076 toll-free in the U.S. ⊕ www.golfbajamar.com) has 18 holes of championship-level golf on the cliffs above the ocean and another nine holes near the beach. Greens fees are $67 Monday through Thursday and $82 Friday through Sunday.

---

en route  Open views of pounding surf and jagged cliffs are interspersed with one-of-a-kind hotels and restaurants along the coastline between Rosarito and Ensenada. The paved highway (Mexico Carretera 1) between the two cities often cuts a path between low mountains and high oceanside cliffs. Exits lead to rural roads, oceanfront campgrounds, and an ever-increasing number of resort communities. The small fishing villages of **San Miguel** and **El Sauzal** sit off the highway to the north of Ensenada, and you can see the **Coronado Islands** clearly off the coast.

---

## Ensenada

❶❸–❷⓿ *75 km (47 mi) south of Rosarito.*

In 1542 Juan Rodríguez Cabrillo first discovered the seaport that Sebastián Vizcaíno named Ensenada-Bahía de Todos Santos (All Saints' Bay) in 1602. Since then the town has drawn a steady stream of explorers and developers. First ranchers made their homes on large plots along the coast and into the mountains. Gold miners followed in the late 1800s. After mine stocks were depleted, the area settled back into a bucolic state. The harbor gradually grew into a major port for shipping agricultural goods, and today Baja's third-largest city (population 369,000) is one of Mexico's largest seaports. It also has a thriving fishing fleet and fish-processing industry.

There are no beaches in Ensenada proper, but sandy stretches north and south of town are satisfactory for swimming, sunning, surfing, and camping. On summer and holiday weekends the population swells, but the town rarely feels overcrowded. Ensenada tends to draw those who want to explore a more traditional Mexican city.

Many cruise ships stop for at least a few hours in Ensenada to clear Mexican customs; thus, Ensenada is called Baja's largest cruise-ship port. Both the waterfront and downtown's main street are pleasant places to stroll. If you're driving, be sure to take the Centro exit from the highway, since it bypasses the commercial port area.

## What to See

**⑭ Las Bodegas de Santo Tomás.** One of Baja's oldest wineries gives tours and tastings at its downtown winery and bottling plant. The restaurant, La Embotelladora Vieja, is one of Baja's finest. The winery also operates La Esquina de Bodegas, a café, shop, and gallery in a bright-blue building across the avenue. ☒ *Av. Miramar 666, Centro* ☏ *646/174–0836 or 646/174–0829* ☒ *$2* ☉ *Tours, tastings daily at 11, 1, and 3.*

**⑳ Catedral Nuestra Señora de Guadalupe.** The city's largest cathedral is named for the country's patron saint, and is the center of celebrations on December 12, the feast of the Virgin of Guadalupe. Though modest in comparison to mainland cathedrals, the church does have impressive stained-glass windows. ☒ *Av. Floresta at Av. Juárez, Centro.*

★ **⑮ Mercado de Mariscos.** At the northernmost point of Boulevard Costero, the main street along the waterfront, is an indoor-outdoor fish market where row after row of counters display piles of shrimp, tuna, dorado, and other fish caught off Baja's coasts. Outside, stands sell grilled or smoked fish, seafood cocktails, and fish tacos. You can pick up a few souvenirs, eat well for very little money, and take some great photographs. The original fish taco stands line the dirt path to the fish market. If your stomach is delicate, try the fish tacos at the cleaner, quieter Plaza de Mariscos in the shadow of the giant beige Plaza de Marina that blocks the view of the traditional fish market from the street.

**⑯ Muelle de Pescador.** Fishing and whale-watching boats depart from this pier. The area around it has been remodeled, and a broad *malecón* (seaside walkway) with park benches and palms runs along the waterfront. ☒ *Blvd. Costero at Av. Alvarado, Centro.*

**⑬ Parque Revolución.** Revolution Park is Ensenada's most traditional plaza, with a bandstand, playground, and plenty of benches in the shade. The plaza is festive on weekend evenings, when neighbors congregate here to chat and children chase seagulls. ☒ *Av. Obregón between Calles 6 and 7, Centro.*

**⑱ Paseo Calle Primera.** The renamed Avenida López Mateos is the center of Ensenada's traditional tourist zone. High-rise hotels, souvenir shops, restaurants, and bars line the avenue for eight blocks, from its beginning at the foot of the Chapultepec Hills to the dry channel of the Arroyo de Ensenada. The avenue also has cafés and most of the town's souvenir shops. Businesses use one or both street names for their addresses, though most stick with López Mateos. Locals shop for furniture, clothing, and other necessities a few blocks inland on Avenida Juárez, in Ensenada's downtown area.

**⑰ Plaza Cívica.** This block-long concrete park—with sculptures of Mexican heroes Benito Juárez, Miguel Hidalgo, and Venustiano Carranza—

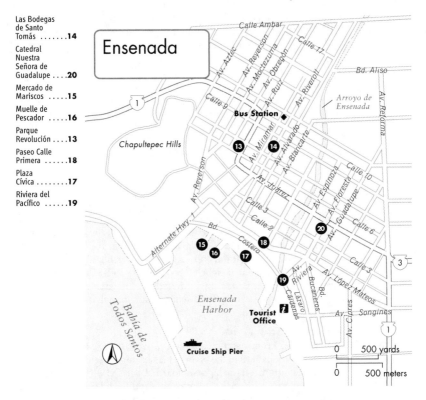

feels more like a monument than a gathering spot. Still, there are benches and horse-drawn carriages at the ready. ✉ *Blvd. Costero at Av. Riveroll, Centro.*

⓲ **Riviera del Pacífico.** Officially called the Centro Social, Cívico y Cultural de Ensenada, the Riviera is a rambling, white, hacienda-style mansion built in the 1920s. An enormous gambling palace, hotel, restaurant, and bar, the glamorous Riviera was frequented by wealthy U.S. citizens and Mexicans, particularly during Prohibition. When gambling was outlawed in Mexico and Prohibition ended in the United States, the palace lost its raison d'être. You can tour some of the elegant ballrooms and halls, which occasionally host art shows and civic events. Many of the rooms are locked; check at the main office to see if someone is available to show you around. The gardens alone are worth visiting, and the building houses the Museo de Historia de Ensenada, a museum on Baja's history. ✉ *Blvd. Costero at Av. Riviera, Centro* ☎ *646/177–0594* ✉ *Building and gardens free; museum donations requested* ⊘ *Daily 9:30–2 and 3–5.*

**off the
beaten
path**

**LA BUFADORA –** Seawater splashes up to 75 feet in the air, spraying sightseers standing near this impressive tidal blowhole (*la bufadora* means the buffalo snort) in the coastal cliffs at Punta Banda. Legend has it that the blowhole was created by a whale or sea serpent trapped in an undersea cave; both these stories, and the less romantic scientific facts, are posted on a roadside plaque here. The road to La Bufadora along Punta Banda—an isolated, mountainous point that juts into the sea—is lined with stands selling olives, tamales, strands of chilies and garlic, and terra-cotta planters. The drive gives you a sampling of Baja's wilderness. There are public rest rooms as well as a few restaurants, including the extremely popular Gordo's, which is open Friday through Sunday. There's a small fee to park near the blowhole. A public bus runs from the downtown Ensenada station to Maneadero, from which you can catch a minibus labeled Punta Banda that goes to La Bufadora. ⊠ *Carretera 23, 31 km (19 mi) south of Ensenada, Punta Banda.*

## Beaches

The waterfront in Ensenada proper is taken up by fishing boats, repair yards, and commercial shipping. The best swimming beaches are south of town. Estero Beach is long and clean, with mild waves; the Estero Beach Hotel takes up much of the oceanfront, but the beach is public. Surfers populate the strands off Carretera 1 north and south of Ensenada, particularly San Miguel, Tres Marías, and Salsipuedes; scuba divers prefer Punta Banda, by La Bufadora. Lifeguards are rare, so be cautious. The tourist office in Ensenada has a map that shows safe diving and surfing beaches.

## Where to Stay & Eat

★ **$$–$$$$**  ✕ **El Rey Sol.** From its chateaubriand *bouquetière* (garnished with a bouquet of vegetables) to the savory chicken chipotle, this family-owned French restaurant sets a high standard. Louis XIV–style furnishings and an attentive staff make it both comfortable and elegant. The sidewalk tables are a perfect place to dine and people-watch. The small café in the front sells pastries, all made on the premises. ⊠ *Av. López Mateos 1000, Centro* ☎ *646/178–1733* ▤ *AE, MC, V.*

**$–$$$**  ✕ **La Embotelladora Vieja.** This elegant restaurant was once the wine-aging room of the Santo Tomás winery. The Baja French menu could include smoked tuna, grilled lobster in cabernet sauvignon sauce, or quail with sauvignon blanc sauce. Some dishes are available without alcohol-enhanced sauces. ⊠ *Av. Miramar 666, Centro* ☎ *646/178–1660* ▤ *AE, MC, V* ☽ *Closed Mon.*

**$–$$$**  ✕ **Mariscos de Bahía de Ensenada.** Red lights flicker around the front door, making this seafood house just off the main drag easy to spot. The place is packed on weekends. Clams, shrimp, lobster, red snapper, squid, and other fresh seafood are fried, baked, broiled, or grilled, and served with a basic iceberg-lettuce salad, white rice, and tortillas made fresh at the window-front tortillería. There are a few canopied sidewalk tables. ⊠ *Av. Riveroll 109, Centro* ☎ *646/178–1015* ▤ *AE, MC, V.*

**$–$$**  ✕ **Hacienda Del Charro.** Hungry patrons hover over platters of chiles rel-
FodorsChoice  lenos, enchiladas, and fresh chips and guacamole at heavy wooden pic-
★  nic tables. Plump chickens slowly turn over a wood-fueled fire by the front window, and the aroma of simmering beans fills the air. ⊠ *Av. López Mateos 454, Centro* ☎ *646/178–2114* ▤ *No credit cards.*

**$–$$** ✕**Oxidos Café.** Baja meets L.A. at this new-wave café, where the metal sculptures and other original art are as interesting as the food. The menu aims to satisfy hunger pangs with hearty burgers, ribs, and pasta. The bar is a gathering spot for local artists—you're sure to get into some interesting conversations if you hang out here. ⊠ *Av. Ruíz 108, Centro* ☎ *646/178–8827* ⊟ *No credit cards.*

**¢–$** ✕**Bronco's Steak House.** A great find near the Riviera del Pacífico, Bronco's serves exceptional steaks and Mexican specialties. Try the *puntas de filete al chipotle*, tender beef tips with smoke-flavored chipotle chilies. Tripe appears frequently on the menu, satisfying the cravings of the locals that fill many of the wood tables. Brick walls, wood-plank floors, and hanging spurs and chaps evoke the Wild West, but the mood is subdued and relaxed. Locals rave about the weekend breakfast buffet. ⊠ *Av. López Mateos 1525, Centro* ☎ *646/172–4892* ⊟ *AE, MC, V.*

**$$** ▤ **Estero Beach Resort.** Families love this long-standing resort on Ensenada's top beach. The best rooms (some with kitchenettes) are by the sand; the worst are by the parking lot. Be sure to check out the outstanding collection of folk art and artifacts in the resort's small museum. Midweek winter rates are a real bargain. There's also an on-site RV park; its 38 sites have hookups for water, sewer, and electricity. ⊠ *Mexico Carretera 1, 10 km (6 mi) south of Ensenada, Estero Beach* ✆ *482 W. San Ysidro Blvd., San Ysidro, CA 92173* ☎ *646/176–6230 or 646/176–6235* 🖷 *646/176–6925* ⊕ *www.hotelesterobeach.com* ↘ *94 rooms, 2 suites* ⚭ *Restaurant, some kitchenettes, cable TV, 4 tennis courts, pool, horseback riding, volleyball, bar, shops, playground* ⊟ *MC, V.*

**$$** ▤ **Hotel Coral & Marina.** This all-suites resort is enormous. It has a spa, tennis courts, a water-sports center, and marina with slips for 350 boats and customs-clearing facilities. All guest quarters have refrigerators and coffeemakers. Suites in the two eight-story towers are done in burgundy and dark green; most have waterfront balconies, seating areas, and international phone service. ⊠ *Mexico Carretera 1, Km 103, Zona Playitas 22860* ☎ *646/175–0000, 800/862–9020 in the U.S.* 🖷 *646/175–0005* ⊕ *www.hotelcoral.com* ↘ *147 suites* ⚭ *Restaurant, room service, refrigerators, cable TV, 2 tennis courts, 3 pools (1 indoor), gym, hot tub, massage, spa, boating, marina, fishing, bar, laundry service, meeting rooms* ⊟ *MC, V.*

**$$** ▤ **Posada El Rey Sol.** A glass elevator rises three floors to rooms that have comfy armchairs, sculpted headboards, and carpeting. The rooms are the loveliest in downtown, and the proximity to restaurants and shops is a big plus. Room service is provided by the El Rey Sol restaurant across the street. ⊠ *Av. Blancarte 130, 22860 Centro* ☎ *646/178–1641, 888/315–2378 in the U.S.* 🖷 *646/174–0005* ⊕ *www.posadaelreysol.com* ↘ *52 rooms* ⚭ *Restaurant, room service, in-room data ports, in-room safes, minibars, pool, hot tub, bar, laundry service, meeting room, no-smoking rooms* ⊟ *MC, V.*

**★ $$** ▤ **Punta Morro.** Just five minutes from Ensenada, this secluded all-suites hotel is a great place to relax. The restaurant overlooks crashing waves and has an excellent combination of Continental cuisine and fresh seafood. All rooms have seaside terraces, fireplaces, coffeemakers, and refrigerators. One-room studios are the least expensive units; the one-bedroom suite costs about $20 more. Two- and three-bedroom suites are also available. ⊠ *Mexico Carretera 1, Km 106, Zona Playitas* ☎ *Box 434263, San Diego, CA 92143* 🖂 *646/178–3507, 800/526–6676 in the U.S.* 🖂 *646/174–4490* ⊕ *www.punta-morro.com* ⤳ *24 suites* ⚘ *Restaurant, in-room data ports, refrigerators, cable TV, pool, hot tub, beach, bar; no a/c* ⊟ *AE, MC, V.*

**$$** 🏨 **Las Rosas.** All rooms in this intimate hotel north of Ensenada face
**Fodor'sChoice** the ocean and pool; some have fireplaces and hot tubs, and even the least
★ expensive are lovely. The atrium lobby has marble floors, mint-green-and-pink couches that look out at the sea, and a glass ceiling that glows at night. Make reservations far in advance. ⊠ *Mexico Carretera 1, north of Ensenada, Zona Playitas* ☎ *374 E. H St., Chula Vista, CA 91910* 🖂 *646/174–4320 or 646/174–4360* 🖂 *646/174–4595* ⊕ *www.lasrosas. com* ⤳ *48 rooms* ⚘ *Restaurant, 2 tennis courts, pool, hot tub, gym, massage, spa, bar, laundry service* ⊟ *AE, MC, V.*

**¢** 🏨 **Hotel del Valle.** Fishermen and budget travelers frequent this small hotel on a quiet side street. Rooms are basic and well maintained. You can use a coffeemaker in the lobby and parking spaces out front. Ask about rate discounts—those posted behind the front desk are about 40% higher than guests in the know normally pay. ⊠ *Av. Riveroll 367, Centro 22800* 🖂 *646/178–2224* 🖂 *646/174–0466* ⤳ *43 rooms* ⚘ *Cable TV; no a/c* ⊟ *MC, V.*

**¢** 🏨 **Joker Hotel.** A bizarre, colorful mishmash of styles makes it hard to miss the Joker. Rooms, which vary in size and level of maintenance, have balconies. The hotel is popular with Mexican families and there may not be an English-speaking staff member on duty. Traffic noise from the highway and from guests leaving at the crack of dawn can be a problem; try to stay away from the road and the busiest parts of the parking lot. ⊠ *Mexico Carretera 1, Km 12.5, Ejido Chapultepec 22800* 🖂 *646/ 176–7201* 🖂 *646/177–4460* ⤳ *40 rooms* ⚘ *Restaurant, some refrigerators, TV, pool, hot tub, bar, nightclub* ⊟ *MC, V.*

## Nightlife

Ensenada is a party town for college students, surfers, and other young tourists, though it's also possible to enjoy a mellow evening out. **La Capilla** (⊠ Hotel El Cid, Paseo Calle Primera 997, Centro ☎ 646/178–2401 Ext. 104) attracts an older crowd that enjoys live Cuban music and romantic
★ ballads in a relaxed setting. **Hussong's Cantina** (⊠ Av. Ruíz 113, Centro ☎ 646/178–3210) has been an Ensenada landmark since 1892 and has changed little since then. A security guard stands by the front door to handle the often rowdy crowd—a mix of locals and visitors of all ages over 18. The noise is usually deafening, pierced by mariachi and ranchera musicians and the whoops and hollers of the pie-eyed. **Papas and Beer** (⊠ Av. Ruíz 102, Centro ☎ 646/174–0145) attracts a collegiate crowd.

## Sports & the Outdoors

FISHING  Boats leave the Ensenada sportfishing pier regularly. The best angling is from April through November, with bottom fishing good in winter. Charter vessels and party boats are available from several outfitters along Avenida López Mateos and Boulevard Costero and off the sportfishing pier. Mexican fishing licenses for the day or year are available at the tourist office or from charter companies.

**Ensenada Clipper Fleet** (✉ Sportfishing Pier, Blvd. Costero at Av. Alvarado, Centro ☎ 646/178–2185) has charter and group boats. The fee for a day's fishing is $50 including a fishing license. **Sergio's Sportfishing** (✉ Sportfishing Pier, Blvd. Costero at Av. Alvarado, Centro ☎ 646/178–2185 ⊕ www.sergios-sportfishing.com), one of the best sportfishing companies in Ensenada, has charter and group boats as well as boat slips for rent. The fee for a day's fishing is $50 per person on a group boat, including the cost of a license.

HIKING  **Expediciones de Turismo Ecológico y Aventura** (✉ Blvd. Costero 1094-14,
★ Centro ☎ 646/178–3704 or 619/279–7503 ⊕ www.mexonline.com/ecotur.htm) runs hiking and camping trips in the San Pedro de Martir National Park. Prices start at $150.

WATER SPORTS  Estero Beach and Punta Banda (en route to La Bufadora south of Ensenada) are both good kayaking areas, although facilities are limited. **Dale's La Bufadora Shop** (✉ Rancho La Bufadora, Punta Banda ☎ 646/154–2092) offers scuba diving trips (with all gear available for rent) to seamounts and walls off Punta Banda. They also have whale-watching trips in winter.

Some of the best surf on the coast is found off Islas de Todos Santos, two islands about 19 km (12 mi) west of Ensenada. Only the best and boldest challenge the waves here, which can reach 30 feet in winter. Surfers must hire a boat to take them to the waves. Calmer, but still exciting, waves crash on the beaches at San Miguel, Tres Marías, and Salsipuedes. **San Miguel Surf Shop** (✉ Av. López Mateos, at Calle Ruíz, Centro ☎ 646/178–1007) is the unofficial local surfing headquarters. They can guide you toward the best areas and to gear rental.

WHALE-  Boats leave the Ensenada sportfishing pier for whale-watching trips
WATCHING  from December through February. The gray whales migrating from the north to bays and lagoons in southern Baja pass through Todos Santos Bay, often close to shore. Binoculars and cameras with telephoto capabilities come in handy. The trips last about three hours. Vessels and tour boats are available from several outfitters at the sportfishing pier. A three-hour tour costs about $30.

## Shopping

Most of the tourist shops are along Avenida López Mateos beside the hotels and restaurants. There are several two-story shopping arcades, many with empty shops. Dozens of curio shops line the street, all selling similar selections of pottery, serapes, and more.

**Artes Don Quijote** (✉ Av. López Mateos 503, Centro ☎ 646/174–4082) has carved wood doors, huge terra-cotta pots, and crafts from Oaxaca. It's closed on Tuesday. **Bazar Casa Ramirez** (✉ Av. López Mateos 510, Centro ☎ 646/178–8209) sells high-quality Talavera pottery and other ceramics, wrought-iron items, and papier-mâché figurines. Be sure to check out the displays upstairs. At **Los Castillo** (✉ Av. López Mateos 1076, Centro ☎ 646/178–2335), the display of silver jewelry from Taxco is
★ limited but of excellent quality. The **Centro Artesenal de Ensenada** has a smattering of galleries and shops. By far, the best shop there is **Galería**

de Pérez Meillón (✉ Blvd. Costero 1094–39, Centro ☎ 646/174–0394), with its museum-quality Casas Grandes pottery and varied folk art by indigenous northern Mexican peoples.

**La Esquina de Bodegas** (✉ Av. Miramar at Calle 6, Centro ☎ 646/178–3557) is an innovative gallery, shop, and café in a century-old winery building. **Los Globos** (✉ Calle 9, 3 blocks east of Reforma, Centro ☎ No phone) is a daily open-air swap meet. Vendors and shoppers are most abundant on weekends. **Mario's Silver** (✉ Calle Primera 1090-6, Centro ☎ 646/178–2451) has several branches along the main street tempting shoppers with both silver and gold jewelry. **La Mina de Salomón** (✉ Av. López Mateos 1000, Centro ☎ 646/178–1733) carries elaborate jewelry in a tiny gallery next to El Rey Sol restaurant. It also has a pastry shop.

## Side Trip to the Valle de Guadalupe

The Valle de Guadalupe, northeast of Ensenada on Carretera 3 to Tecate, is filled with vineyards, wineries, and rambling hacienda-style estates. A few wineries are open to the public; some require appointments. Baja California Tours conducts tours that include visits to several wineries, a historical overview of the valley, transportation from the border, and lunch. The cost is about $80 per person. An area of the valley that was originally settled by the Russians is now called Colonia Rusa (also called Guadalupe and Francisco Zarco); it's about 32 km (20 mi) from Ensenada.

**Chateau Camou** (✉ Carretera 3, Km 70 ☎ 646/177–3303 ⊕ www. chateau-camou.com.mx) is a good example of the new wave of valley wineries. It's open Monday through Saturday 8–3 and Sunday 9–2. Tours start at $5; a tour with a winemaker or owner and lunch costs $40 (reservations required). **Domecq** (✉ Carretera 3, Km 73 ☎ 646/165–2249 ⊕ www.vinos-domecq.com) offers free wine tastings and tours on weekdays 10–4 and Saturday 10–1:30. **L.A. Cetto** (✉ Carretera 3, Km 73.5 ☎ 646/155–2264) has free wine tastings and tours daily 10–4. Serious oenophiles should call ahead to visit **Monte Xanic** (✉ Carretera 3, Km 70 ☎646/174–6155 ⊕www.montexanic.com.mx), one of Mexico's finest wineries. Its wines were served at President Vicente Fox's inaugural dinner. Tastings and tours ($2) are available by appointment.

The **Museo Comunitario del Valle de Guadalupe** (✉ Carretera 3, Km 70 ☎646/155–2030), open Tuesday–Sunday 9–5, is a 1905 house containing a display of Russian household items from the local settlements. If it's not open, ask around for the caretaker. Entry donations are appreciated, though admission is technically free.

WHERE TO STAY & EAT

$$$$

Fodor'sChoice

★

✗ **Laja.** One sign that the Valle de Guadalupe has its sights on Napa is this extraordinary restaurant. The ambitious prix-fixe menu changes frequently, but may include *escabeche* (pickled) mussel salad, ling cod with crab sauce, and braised apples with vanilla and honey ice cream, all served with excellent regional wines. Polished woods and windows overlooking the valley make the dining room as sleek as the menu. A meal here is well worth the drive. ✉ *Carretera 3, Km 83* ☎ *646/155–2556* ⚅ *Reservations essential* ☐ *No credit cards* ☉ *Closed Mon.–Wed. No dinner Thurs. or Sun.*

★ **$$** ⊞ **Adobe Guadalupe.** Brick archways, white-stucco walls, and fountains set a peaceful tone at this inn surrounded by vineyards. Owners Don and Tru Miller have won several awards for their wines and have helped bring outside attention to the valley. Staying here is like being in the California wine country at half the price. ⊠ *Off Carretera 3 (turn at the sign and drive 6 km [4 mi]), Guadalupe* ☎ *646/155–2094, 949/733–2744 in the U.S.* 🖶 *646/155–2093* ⊕ *www.adobeguadalupe.com* 🛏 *6 rooms* ♨ *Dining room, pool, hot tub; no room phones, no TV* ⊟ *MC, V* ⭐ *CP.*

## Tecate

**㉑** *32 km (20 mi) east of Tijuana, 112 km (69 mi) northeast of Ensenada.*

Tecate is a quiet border community with a population of about 100,000. Visitors stop by on day trips from Tijuana, Ensenada, or San Diego to shop and to have lunch at modest cafés facing the pleasant Parque Hidalgo. Tecate's most famous attraction is the Rancho la Puerta spa. Downtown Tecate is centered on the Parque Hidalgo. A few cabdrivers, shoe-shine boys, schoolchildren, and snuggling couples hang out around the small gazebo. On summer evenings, dance and band concerts are held in Parque López Mateos, on Carretera 3 south of town.

One of Mexico's most popular beers comes from the **Tecate Brewery** (⊠ Av. Hidalgo, at Calle Carranza ☎ 665/654–9478). Now part of the huge Cervecería Cuauhtémoc-Moctezuma corporation, the brewery has been updated and produces several brews, including the famed red cans of Tecate beer. Tours are available only for groups and must be arranged in advance, but you can visit the beer gardens and quaff two free beers. It's open weekdays 10–5, weekends 10–2.

Home owners from both sides of the border shop for floor tiles, garden fountains, and flower pots at **Baja-Mex-Tile** (⊠ Blvd. Juárez 9150 ☎ 665/ 654–0204).

### Where to Stay & Eat

¢–$ ✕ **El Jardín.** Nearly everyone who wanders through town on a day trip ends up stopping here. The setting is plain, and the food is Mexican and simple, but the café tables outside have a great view of the plaza. Musicians stop by in the evening, offering to play for a few pesos. ⊠ *Callejón Libertad 274* ☎ *665/654–3453* ⊟ *No credit cards.*

¢ ✕ **Panadería de Tecate.** Open 24 hours every day except Christmas and New Year's, this simple bakery is famed throughout the region. The kitchen whips up more than 100 types of cookies, doughnuts, *pan dulce* (sweet bread), crunchy *bolillos* (rolls), and cakes. ⊠ *Av. Juárez 331* ☎ *665/ 654–0040* ⊟ *No credit cards.*

$$$$ ⊞ **Rancho la Puerta.** Spanish-style buildings and modern glass-and-wood
Fodor'sChoice structures are spread out on the grounds of a sprawling ranch. You stay
★ in luxurious cottages and check in for at least a week to indulge in the perfect blend of exercise, diet, and pampering. Reservations are absolutely essential. Free transportation is available to and from the San Diego airport. ⊠ *Carretera 2, 5 km (3 mi) west of Tecate, 21275* ☎ *665/654– 9155, 760/744–4222 or 800/443–7565 in the U.S.* 🖶 *760/744–5007 in the U.S.* ⊕ *www.rancholapuerta.com* 🛏 *80 rooms* ♨ *Restaurant, fans,*

*in-room safes, refrigerators, some kitchenettes, 4 tennis courts, pool, fitness classes, 2 health clubs, hair salon, massage, spa, hiking, laundry facilities, Internet, airport shuttle; no a/c, no room phones, no TVs, no smoking* ▭ *MC, V* ⫿⃝⫾ *All-inclusive.*

$ 🏨 **Rancho Tecate Resort.** The long, low buildings of this handsome resort are in the hills outside Tecate. The lobby is filled with antiques (the original owner was an avid collector) and the guest rooms are carpeted and comfortable. Diversions include a 3-hole golf course, a man-made lake, and hiking trails. ⊠ *Carretera 3, Km 10, 11 km (7 mi) south of Tecate, 21275* ☎ *665/654–0011* 🖷 *665/654–0241* ⊕ *www.ranchotecateresort.com* 🛏 *45 rooms* ⚒ *Restaurant, 3-hole golf course, tennis court, pool, hot tub, hiking* ▭ *MC, V.*

## Mexicali

**㉒** *136 km (84 mi) east of Tijuana.*

Mexicali, with a population of about 850,000, shares the Imperial Valley farmland and the border crossing with Calexico, a small California city. As the capital of Baja California, Mexicali sees a great deal of government activity. The number of maquiladoras continues to grow, so most visitors are on business; sights are few and far between. A tourist-oriented strip of curio shops, restaurants, and bars is along Avenida Francisco Madero, a block south of the border.

## San Quintín

**㉓** *191 km (118 mi) south of Ensenada.*

Cultivated fields line the highway as you enter San Quintín, the largest producer of tomatoes in Baja. The Oaxacan migrant workers who plant and pick the fertile valley's produce live in squalid camps out of the view of travelers. Bahía de San Quintín, which fronts a few small hotels, is among northern Baja's best fishing grounds, along with Bahía Falsa and Bahía Santa Maria, and the area's few hostelries tend to cater to anglers. Roadside stands sell the local delicacy, Pismo clams, fresh and cooked. Travelers often stop here for essentials en route farther south; this is the last major outpost until Guerrero Negro (a drive of about six hours).

### Where to Stay

¢–$ 🏨 **Old Mill.** Anglers ease their boats into the sheltered bay at this longtime favorite hideaway and set up housekeeping in a variety of rooms, some with kitchens. The lodge-style bar with its huge fireplace is packed on weekend nights. ⊠ *South of San Quintín on a dirt road leading to the bay* ✉ *Box 2631, Spring Valley, CA 91979* ☎ *800/479–7962 in the U.S., 01800/025–5141 toll-free in Mexico* 🖷 *616/165–3376* 🛏 *28 rooms, 2 suites* ⚒ *Restaurant, fans, some kitchens, fishing, bar; no a/c, no room TVs* ▭ *No credit cards.*

¢ 🏨 **Don Eddie's Landing.** Catering mainly to fishermen, Don Eddie's has all the right amenities; its clean, no-frills rooms have TVs, fans, and heaters. Most important, it's got a launching ramp for boats and can arrange charters. Naturally, conversation in the restaurant and bar is rather one-dimensional. ⊠ *Off Carretera 1 on the bay, 22930, follow the signs for* *turnoff and drive 5 km (3 mi)* ☎ *616/162–2722 or 616/162–3143* ⊕ *www.doneddies.com* ⇨ *17 rooms* ⚘ *Restaurant, fans, pool, fishing, bar; no a/c, no room TVs* ▭ *No credit cards.*

## San Felipe

**㉔** *198 km (123 mi) south of Mexicali, 244 km (151 mi) southeast of Ensenada.*

San Felipe (population 25,000) is the quintessential fishing village with one main street (two if you count the highway into town). It's at the edge of the northern Mar de Cortés, which is protected as an ecological reserve in this region. A malecón runs along a broad beach with a swimming area. Taco stands, bars, and restaurants line the sidewalk across the street from the malecón and beach.

In 1948 the first paved road from Mexicali was extended into town, at which point San Felipe became significant. Prior to that time only a few fishermen and their families lived along the coast; now there are impressive shrimping fleets which bring in shrimp served all over the peninsula. Shrimp is so important here that there's an annual festival and cooking competition honoring it in November.

San Felipe has several campgrounds and modest hotels, which fill up quickly in winter and during spring holidays. Snowbirds arrive in recreational vehicles, setting up huge vacation communities in local trailer parks. The character of San Felipe is changing, however, as more and more retirees are building homes at the 35,000-acre El Dorado Ranch development north of town. At this writing, an 18-hole golf course, La Ventana del Mar, is expected to open in summer 2004 at El Dorado, which now has 1,400 homes.

Gringos with temporary Mexican resident status make up one-quarter of San Felipe's population, and the number is increasing. But the town itself retains a fishing village flavor, with a few paved streets and dozens of fishing skiffs on the beach. On holiday weekends San Felipe can be boisterous—dune buggies, motorcycles, and off-road vehicles abound—but most of the time it's quiet and relaxing. The town also appeals to sportfishers, especially in spring. It's easy to find launches, bait, and supplies.

The **Bahía San Felipe** has dramatic changes in its tides. They crest at 20 feet, and because the beach is so broad, the waterline can move in and out up to 1 km (about ½ mi).

San Felipe's main landmark is the **shrine of the Cerro de la Virgen** (Virgin of Guadalupe), at the north end of the malecón on a hill overlooking the sea. A steep stairway leads to it; fishermen traditionally light a candle to the Virgin here before heading out. There's an awesome view of the bay and beach from the hilltop.

### Where to Stay & Eat

**$–$$** ✕ **BajaMar.** The bartender mixes a mean margarita, and the chef has a magic touch with shrimp at this large restaurant on the malecón. The shrimp fajitas with homemade tortillas are fabulous, and most of the shrimp entrées include nearly a dozen fat shrimp. Enchiladas, tacos, and several beef and chicken entrées satisfy carnivores. The corner fireplace is a delight on chilly nights. ☒ *Malecón at Av. Chetumal* ☎ *686/577–2991* ☐ *MC, V.*

★ **$–$$** ✕ **Rosita.** Settle in at an outdoor table across from the malecón and order a plate of some of the finest shrimp tacos in town. Sautéed with onions, peppers, and chilies, the shrimp are a bit spicy and absolutely divine. The green salad topped with shrimp is also good. ☒ *Av. Mar de Cortés 381* ☎ *686/540–6218* ☐ *MC, V.*

¢–$ ✕ **Rice and Beans.** The name nearly says it all—the word "fish" should precede it. This is the place to try *mantaraya* (stingray) tacos and fish soup, along with San Felipe's famous shrimp. It's a casual hangout for the expat-retiree gang. ☒ *Malecón at Av. Chetumal* ☎ *686/577–1770* ☐ *No credit cards.*

$$ 🏨 **El Cortez.** Easily the most popular hotel in San Felipe, El Cortez has several types of setups, including moderately priced bungalows and modern hotel rooms. The beachfront and second-floor bars are both enduringly beloved, and the restaurant has great water views. The hotel is a five-minute walk from the malecón. ☒ *Av. Mar de Cortés s/n, 21850* ✉ *Box 1227, Calexico, CA 92232* ☎ *686/577–1055* 🖨 *686/577–1752* ⤺ *77 rooms, 4 suites, 24 bungalows* ♻ *Restaurant, room service, cable TV, pool, 2 bars, laundry facilities, shop* ☐ *MC, V.*

$–$$ 🏨 **San Felipe Marina Resort.** Most rooms at this low-slung terra-cotta building facing the sea have kitchens, woven rugs on white-tile floors, folk-art decorations, and water views. Many of the rooms are used by timeshare owners for weeklong stays. The pool is above the beach next to a *palapa* (thatched-roof) bar; there's also an indoor pool. The resort is a five-minute drive south of town and has an RV campground next door. ☒ *Carretera San Felipe Aeropuerto, Km 4.5, 21850* ☎ *686/577–1568, 800/291–5397 in the U.S.* 🖨 *686/577–1569* ⤺ *11 standard rooms, 27 studios, 33 suites, 2 villas, 123 RV spaces* ♻ *Restaurant, some kitchenettes, cable TV, 2 tennis courts, 2 pools (1 indoor), hot tub, gym, beach, marina, bar, shops* ☐ *AE, MC, V.*

$ 🏨 **La Hacienda de la Langosta Roja.** This simple hotel is one block from the waterfront and has the town's fanciest restaurant, though its Italian and Mexican dishes are of uneven quality. Rooms are motel basic: the beds are rather hard, but the heaters are powerful, and the showers have plenty of hot water. Groups of fishermen stay here before their long trips. ☒ *Av. Mar de Cortés at Av. Chetumal, 21850* ☎ *686/577–0483, 800/967–0005 in the U.S.* 🖨 *686/577–0484* ⊕ *www.sanfelipelodging. com* ⤺ *41 rooms* ♻ *Restaurant, cable TV, bar* ☐ *MC, V.*

¢–$ 🏨 **El Capitan Motel.** San Felipe's most reasonably priced rooms are in this comfortable motel a block from the water. Rooms are clean and have small desks, green linoleum floors, and portable heaters. ☒ *Av. Mar de Cortés 298, 21850* ☎☎ *686/577–1303* ⤺ *44 rooms* ♻ *Restaurant, cable TV, pool, bar; no room phones* ☐ *MC, V.*

## Sports & the Outdoors

The northern part of the Mar de Cortés has lots of sea bass, snapper, corbina, halibut, and other game fish. Clamming is good here as well. **Alex Sportfishing** (☎ *686/577–1442*) runs day trips on small skiffs for about $150 for three people. **Gone to Baja Adventure Tours** (☎ *619/370–4506 in the U.S.*) runs tours to Puertocitos, a small community with natural hot springs south of San Felipe. A three-day tour, including transportation from San Diego to San Felipe, camping on the beach, and fishing, is $700. **Tony Reyes Sportfishing** (☎ 714/538–9300 in the U.S.), one of the most reputable companies, has six-day trips that cost about $775.

## Baja Norte A to Z

**AIR TRAVEL**

There are few international flights into Baja Norte; most travelers access the area from the border at San Diego. Several airlines fly between mainland Mexico and Tijuana or Mexicali.

AIRPORTS  Tijuana's Aeropuerto Alberado Rodriguez (TIJ) is on the city's eastern edge, near the Otay Mesa border crossing. Mexicali's international airport, Aeropuerto Internacional General Rodolfo Sánchez Taboada (MXL), is about 11 km (7 mi) east of the city. Both airports have all the key facilities, such as currency exchange booths and restaurants, but they can be confusing for first-timers. You must show your ticket before reaching the airline counter. Don't rely on electronic tickets, since airport computers here frequently malfunction.

🛈 **Aeropuerto Alberado Rodriguez** ☎ 664/684-2876. **Aeropuerto Internacional General Rodolfo Sánchez Taboada** ☎ 686/553-5071.

AIRPORT TRANSFERS  Private taxis and *colectivos* (shared vans) serve both airports. Buy your tickets from the taxi counters, where fares are posted. Colectivos to most hotels in both cities cost about $5–$10, taxis about double that.

CARRIERS  Mexicana flies from Tijuana to Mexico City, Guadalajara, and Zacatecas connecting with other national and international flights. Aeroméxico flies to Los Cabos, La Paz, and Mexicali on the Baja Peninsula and to several cities in mainland Mexico. AeroCalifornia flies between Tijuana and La Paz.

🛈 **AeroCalifornia** ☎ 664/682-8754, 664/684-2876 in Tijuana. **Aeroméxico** ☎ 664/685-2230 in Tijuana, 686/557-2551 in Mexicali ⊕ www.aeromexico.com. **Mexicana** ☎ 664/634-6596 in Tijuana, 686/552-9391 in Mexicali ⊕ www.mexicana.com.

**BUS TRAVEL**

Greyhound buses head to Tijuana from downtown San Diego several times daily. Buses to San Diego and Los Angeles depart from the Greyhound terminal in Tijuana 14 times a day. Fares are $5 to San Diego and $18 to Los Angeles. Mexicoach runs buses from the trolley depot in San Ysidro and the large parking lot on the U.S. side of the border to the Tijuana Tourist Terminal at Avenida Revolución between Calle 6 and 7. These shuttles make the circuit every 15 minutes between 8 AM and 9 PM; the fare is $1.50.

Buses connect all the towns in Baja Norte and are easy to use; stations are in Ensenada, Mexicali, San Felipe, Tecate, and Tijuana. There are usually three buses a day. Those traveling to Rosarito stop at a small terminal on Boulevard Juárez across from the Rosarito Beach Hotel. There's no official bus station here; check at the hotels for schedule information.

Buses to destinations in Baja and mainland Mexico depart from Tijuana's Central de Autobuses. Autotransportes de Baja California covers the entire Baja route and connects in Mexicali with buses to Guadalajara and Mexico City. Elite has first-class service to mainland Mexico. Transportes del Pacífico goes to Mexico City and other points on the mainland from Mexicali.

Tijuana's Camionera de la Línea station is just inside the border and has service to Rosarito and Ensenada along with city buses to downtown. The downtown station is at Calle 1a and Avenida Madero. To catch the bus back to the border from downtown, go to Calle Benito Juárez (also called Calle 2a) between Avenidas Revolución and Constitución.

*Colectivos* (small, often striped vans) cover neighborhood routes in most Baja cities and towns. The destination is usually painted on the windshield; look for them on main streets. You can flag the vans down anywhere along their routes; fares are 3 pesos and up, depending on the distance you travel.

🚌 Bus Lines **Autotransportes de Baja California** ☎ 664/686-9010. **Elite** ☎ 664/688-1979 ⊕ www.abc.com.mx. **Greyhound** ☎ 664/686-0697, 664/688-0165 in Tijuana, 800/231-2222 in the U.S. ⊕ www.greyhound.com. **Mexicoach** ☎ 664/685-1440, 619/428-9517 in the U.S. ⊕ www.mexicoach.com. **Transportes del Pacífico** ☎ 664/621-2983.

🚌 Bus Stations **Ensenada bus station** ✉ Av. Riveroll 1075, between Calles 10 and 11, Centro, Ensenada ☎ 646/178-6680. **Mexicali bus station** ✉ Centro Cívico, Av. Independencia, Centro, Mexicali ☎ 686/557-2410. **San Diego** ✉ 120 W. Broadway ☎ 619/239-2366. **San Felipe bus station** ✉ Av. Mar Caribe, at Av. Manzanillo, San Felipe ☎ 686/577-1516. **Tecate bus station** ✉ Av. Benito Juárez, at Calle Abelardo Rodríguez, Tecate ☎ 665/654-1221. **Tijuana city bus station** ✉ Calle 1a, at Av. Madero, Centro, Tijuana ☎ 664/688-0752. **Tijuana Camionera de la Línea** ✉ Centro Comercial Viva Tijuana, Vía de la Juventud Oriente 8800, Zona Río, Tijuana ☎ No phone. **Tijuana Central de Autobuses** ✉ Calz. Lázaro Cárdenas, at Blvd. Arroyo Alamar, La Mesa, Tijuana ☎ 664/621-2982 or 664/621-7640.

## CAR RENTAL

Many U.S. car-rental companies don't allow you to drive their cars into Mexico. Avis permits its cars to go from San Diego into Baja as far as 724 km (450 mi) south of the border. You must declare your intention to take the car into Mexico and buy Mexican auto insurance; the person who rents the car must be the one to return it back in San Diego. Southwest Car Rentals allows its cars as far as Ensenada. California Baja Rent-A-Car rents four-wheel-drive vehicles, convertibles, and sedans for use throughout Mexico (the only company to do this). If you plan to rent your car in Tijuana or San Diego and drop it in Los Cabos, be prepared to pay a hefty sum (up to $900) on top of the rental price.

Fiesta Rent-a-Car and Hertz have offices in Ensenada. The larger U.S. rental agencies have offices at Tijuana's Aeropuerto Alberado Rodriguez, and Avis and Budget have offices in downtown Tijuana. Thrifty has an office in San Felipe.

🚗 **Avis** ✉ Blvd. Cuauhtémoc 1705, Zona Río, Tijuana ☎ 664/683-0605 ⊕ www.avis.com. **Budget** ✉ Paseo de los Héroes 77, Zona Río, Tijuana ☎ 664/634-3303 ⊕ www.budget.com. **California Baja Rent-A-Car** ✉ 9245 Jamacha Blvd., Spring Valley, CA 91977

✉ 619/470–7368, 888/470–7368 in the U.S. ⊕ www.cabaja.com. **Fiesta Rent-a-Car** ✉ Hotel Corona at Blvd. Costero, Centro, Ensenada ☎ 646/176–3344. **Hertz** ✉ Av. Blan-carte, between Calles 1 and 2, Centro, Ensenada ☎ 646/178–2982 ⊕ www.hertz.com. **Southwest Car Rentals** ✉ 2975 Pacific Hwy. ☎ 619/497–4811, 800/476–8849 in the U.S. ⊕ www.southwestcarrental.net. **Thrifty** ✉ Av. Mar de Cortés 75 at the malecón, San Felipe ☎ 686/577–1277 ⊕ www.thrifty.com.mx.

## CAR TRAVEL

The best way to thoroughly tour Baja Norte is by car, although the driving can be complicated. If you're just visiting Tijuana, Tecate, or Mexicali, it's easiest to park on the U.S. side of the border and walk across.

From San Diego, U.S. 5 and I–805 end at the San Ysidro border crossing; Highway 905 leads from I–5 and I–805 to the Tijuana border crossing at Otay Mesa. U.S. 94 from San Diego connects with U.S. 188 to the border at Tecate, 57 km (35 mi) east of San Diego. I–8 from San Diego connects with U.S. 111 at Calexico—203 km (126 mi) east—and the border crossing to Mexicali. San Felipe is on the coast, 200 km (124 mi) south of Mexicali via Carretera 5.

To head south into Baja from Tijuana, follow the signs for Ensenada Cuota, the toll road (also called Carretera 1 and, on newer signs, the Scenic Highway) that runs south along the coast. There are two clearly marked exits for Rosarito, and one each for Puerto Nuevo, Bajamar, and Ensenada. The road is excellent, although it has some hair-raising curves atop the cliffs and is best driven in daylight (the stretch from Rosarito to Ensenada is one of the most scenic drives in Baja). Tollbooths accept U.S. and Mexican currency; tolls are about $3. Rest rooms are available near toll stations. The alternative free road—Carretera 1D or Ensenada Libre—may be difficult for first-timers to navigate. (The entry to the 1D is on a side street in a congested area of downtown Tijuana, and the highway is quite curvy.) Carretera 1 continues south of Ensenada through San Quintín to Guerrero Negro, at the border between Baja California and Baja Sur, and on to Baja's southernmost; there are no tolls past Ensenada.

Mexico Carretera 2 runs east from Tijuana to Tecate and Mexicali. There are toll roads between Tijuana and Tecate and between Tecate and Mexicali. The 134-km (83-mi) journey from Tecate east to Mexicali on La Rumorosa, as the road is known, is as exciting as a roller-coaster ride, with the highway twisting and turning down steep mountain grades and over flat, barren desert.

If you're traveling only as far as Ensenada or San Felipe, you don't need a tourist card, unless you stay longer than 72 hours. If you're heading south of Ensenada, you can get the card at the Mexican Customs Office. You must have Mexican auto insurance, available at agencies near the border.

The combination of overpopulation, lack of infrastructure, and heavy winter rains makes many of Tijuana's streets difficult to navigate by automobile. It's always best to stick to the main thoroughfares. Most of Rosarito proper can be explored on foot, which is a good idea on weekends, when Boulevard Juárez has bumper-to-bumper traffic. To reach Puerto

Nuevo and other points south, continue on Boulevard Juárez (also called Old Ensenada Highway and Ensenada Libre) through town. Most of Ensenada's attractions are within five blocks of the waterfront; it's easy to take a long walking tour of the city. A car is necessary to reach La Bufadora and most of the beaches.

When driving farther south to San Quintín, Guerrero Negro, and Baja Sur, be sure to fill your gas tank when it's half empty. Few towns appear on the highway, and—unless you're following a caravan of RVs—you quickly have the feeling you are headed into the unknown. Don't drive at night, and watch your speed. You never know when a pothole or arroyo will challenge your skills. Also, the cattle on the ranches abutting the highway tend to wander onto the road, an especially dangerous situation at night when they're nearly impossible to spot.

PARKING    Large lots stretch on both sides of I-5 at San Ysidro, close to the border. They charge $8 to $12 per day; though most have an attendant, they aren't actually guarded, so don't leave any valuables in your car. In Tijuana, there are lots along Avenida Revolución and at most major attractions. There's plenty of waterfront parking along Avenida Costera in Ensenada. Parking spaces are harder to find in Rosarito; try the large lot on Avenida Juárez by the Commercial Mexicana grocery store.
🚩 **Mexican Customs Office** ✉ Inside San Ysidro border crossing ☎ 664/682-3439 or 664/684-7790.

### CONSULATES
🚩 **Canadian Consulate** ✉ Calle Germán Gedovius 10411, Zona Río, Tijuana ☎ 664/684-0461 ⊕ www.dfait-maeci.gc.ca. **U.K. Consulate** ✉ Av. Salinas 1500, Fracc. Aviación, Tijuana ☎ 664/686-5320 ⊕ www.fco.gov.uk. **U.S. Consulate** ✉ Tapachula 96, Zona Río, Tijuana ☎ 664/622-7400 ⊕ www.usembassy-mexico.gov/tijuana/Tenglish.htm.

### EMERGENCIES
In an emergency anywhere in Baja Norte, dial 066. The operators speak at least a bit of English. For tourist assistance with legal problems, accidents, or other incidents dial the Tourist Information and Assistance hotline at 078.

The Tijuana government publishes a small guide to crime for tourists, available at information desks. It lists the agencies to contact if you've been involved in a crime, and lists the crimes that tourists most often commit (carrying weapons, purchasing illegal drugs, public drunkenness). Crime victims should contact the State District Attorney's Office or the U.S. Consulate General.
🚩 **State District Attorney** ☎ 664/638-5206.

### LANGUAGE
A great way to get to know Ensenada is to attend weekend or weeklong classes at one of the schools catering to those who wish to improve their Spanish.
🚩 Spanish Classes **Baja California Language College** ☎ 646/174-5688, 877/444-2252 in the U.S. ⊕ www.bajacal.com. **International Spanish Institute of Ensenada** ☎ 646/176-0109.

## LODGING

RESERVING A
ROOM

Several companies specialize in arranging hotel reservations in northern Baja. Baja Information is one of the oldest and best agencies working with Baja hotels and tourism departments. Baja California Tours books hotel rooms in the cities and outlying areas. Mexico Condo Reservations books hotel and condo accommodations and represents La Pinta Hotels, a chain with several hotels on the peninsula.

**Baja California Tours** ⊠ 7734 Herschel Ave., Suite 0, La Jolla, CA 92037 ☎ 858/454-7166 or 800/336-5454 ⊕ www.bajaspecials.com. **Baja Information** ⊠ 6855 Friars Rd., Suite 26, San Diego, CA 92108 ☎ 619/298-4105, 800/522-1516 in CA, NV, AZ, 800/225-2786 elsewhere in the U.S. **Mexico Condo Reservations** ⊠ 4420 Hotel Circle Ct., Suite 230, San Diego, CA 92108 ☎ 619/275-4500 or 800/262-9632 ⊕ www.mexicocondores.com.

## MONEY MATTERS

Dollars are as prevalent as pesos in Baja Norte, and many visitors don't bother changing money. If you wish to deal in pesos, change money at your hotel or a currency exchange point. Be sure to keep some cash on you if you're traveling south, since some places don't accept credit cards and ATMs are nearly nonexistent.

## TOURS & PACKAGES

Baja California Tours has comfortable, informative bus trips throughout northern Baja. Seasonal day and overnight trips focus on whale-watching, fishing, shopping, wineries, sports, dude ranches, and art and cultural events in Tijuana, Rosarito, Ensenada, and San Felipe. Rainbows Over Baja has bust tours to the major towns in Baja, starting and ending in Phoenix, Arizona. Cali-Baja Tours runs bus trips to La Bufadora from Ensenada, and offers transportation between Baja. Five Star Tours runs a daily Tijuana shuttle and tours to Rosarito Beach, Puerto Nuevo, and Ensenada. San Diego Scenic Tours offers half- and full-day bust tours of Tijuana, with time allowed for shopping.

**Baja California Tours** ⊠ 7734 Herschel Ave., Suite 0, La Jolla, CA 92037 ☎ 858/454-7166 or 800/336-5454 ⊕ www.bajaspecials.com. **Rainbows Over Baja** ⊠ 416 W. San Ysidro Blvd., San Ysidro, CA 92173 ☎ 888/311-8034 ⊕ www.rainbowsoverbajatours.com. **Five Star Tours** ⊠ 1050 Kettner Blvd., San Diego, CA 92101 ☎ 619/232-5049 ⊕ www.efivestartours.com. **Cali-Baja Tours** ⊠ Av. Macheros at Blvd. Costero, Centro, Ensenada, BC 92037 ☎ 646/178-1641. **San Diego Scenic Tours** ⊠ 2255 Garnet Ave., San Diego, CA 92109 ☎ 858/273-8687 ⊕ www.sandiegoscenictours.com.

## TROLLEY TRAVEL

The San Diego Trolley travels from the Santa Fe Depot in San Diego, at Kettner Boulevard and Broadway, to within 100 feet of the border every 15 minutes from 5 AM to midnight. The 45-minute trip costs $2.50.

**San Diego Trolley** ☎ 619/233-2004.

## VISITOR INFORMATION

Baja tours, Mexican auto insurance, a monthly newsletter, and workshops are available through Discover Baja, which is a membership club for Baja travelers.

Baja's largest cities have tourism offices operated by different agencies. These offices are usually open weekdays 9–7 (although some may close in early afternoon for lunch) and weekends 9–1. Some of the smaller areas don't have offices. The excellent Baja California State Secretary of Tourism distributes information on the entire state.

Of Ensenada's two tourist bureaus, the one on Boulevard Costero has the most information. Mexicali has both a Convention and Tourism Bureau and a State Secretary of Tourism office, as does Tijuana. Tijuana Convention and Tourism Bureau has two offices, one within the San Ysidro border crossing, and one on Avenida Revolución. The Tijuana Tourist Trust operates an office in the Zona Río. Rosarito, San Felipe, and Tecate also each have a tourist office. The best Web sites for different cities are often private ones that are casually linked to the tourism bureau.

**⑦ Baja California State Secretary of Tourism** ⊠ Paseo de los Héroes 10289, Zona Río, Tijuana ☎ 664/634-6330 ⊕ www.discoverbajacalifornia.com. **Discover Baja** ⊠ 3089 Clairemont Dr., San Diego, CA 92117 ☎ 619/275-4225 or 800/727-2252 ⊕ www.discoverbaja. com. **Ensenada Tourism** ⊠ Blvd. Costero 1477, Centro, Ensenada ☎ 646/172-3022 ⊕ www.ensenada-tourism.com. **Ensenada Tourist Board** ⊠ Blvd. Cárdenas 609, Centro, Ensenada ☎🖶 646/178-8578 ⊕ www.enjoyensenada.com. **Mexicali Convention and Tourism Bureau** ⊠ Calz. López Mateos, at Calle Compresora, Mexicali ☎ 686/554-8912 ☎🖶 686/555-6975 ⊕ www.mexicaliturismo.com. **Mexicali State Secretary of Tourism Office** ⊠ Blvd. Benito Juárez 1, Mexicali ☎ 686/566-1277 ⊕ www.mexicaliturismo. com. **Rosarito Tourist Board** ⊠ Blvd. Juárez 907, Oceana Plaza Shopping Center, Rosarito ☎ 624/612-0396 ⊕ www.rosarito.org. **San Felipe Tourist Information Office** ⊠ Av. Mar de Cortés, San Felipe ☎ 686/577-1155, 686/577-1865, or 686/577-1155 ⊕ www. sanfelipe.com.mx. **Tecate Tourist Information** ⊠ Callejón Libertad, Tecate ☎ 665/654-1095 ⊕ www.tecatemexico.com.mx. **Tijuana Convention and Tourism Bureau** ⊠ Inside the San Ysidro border crossing, Border, Tijuana ☎ 664/683-1405 ⊠ Av. Revolución, between Calles 3 and 4, Centro, Tijuana ☎ 664/684-0481 or 664/688-0555 ⊕ www. tijuanaonline.org. **Tijuana Tourist Trust** ⊠ Paseo de los Héroes 9365-201, Zona Río, Tijuana ☎ 664/684-0537, 888/775-2417 in the U.S. ⊕ www.seetijuana.com.

# BAJA CALIFORNIA SUR

With the completion in 1973 of the Carretera Transpeninsular (Mexico Carretera 1), travelers gradually started finding their way down the 1,708-km (1,059-mi) road, drawn by the wild terrain and the pristine beaches of both coastlines. Baja California Sur became Mexico's 30th state in 1974, and the population and tourism have been growing ever since. Still, Baja Sur remains a rugged and largely undeveloped land. Many people opt to fly to the region rather than brave Carretera 1. The road is in fairly good repair, but there are potholes in some stretches, and services (gas, rest rooms) may not be available. Those venturing on the Carretera Transpeninsular should be well prepared with water and other provisions for a long drive in desolate but beautiful country.

Whale-watching in Scammon's Lagoon, San Ignacio Lagoon, Magdalena Bay, and throughout the Mar de Cortés is a main attraction in winter. History buffs enjoy Loreto, where the first mission in the Californias was established. La Paz, today a busy governmental center and sportfishing city, was the first Spanish settlement in Baja. At the southernmost tip of the peninsula, fishing aficionados, golfers, and sun worshippers gather in Los Cabos, one of Mexico's most popular and most expensive coastal resorts.

## Guerrero Negro

**㉕** *720 km (446 mi) south of Tijuana, 771 km (478 mi) north of La Paz.*

Every December through March, gray whales swim 8,000 km (5,000 mi) south from Alaska's Bering Strait to the tip of the Baja Peninsula. Up to 6,000 whales swim past and stop close to the shore at several spots—including Scammon's Lagoon near Guerrero Negro—to give birth to their calves. These newborns each weigh about half a ton and consume nearly 50 gallons of milk a day. In the past, Guerrero Negro was the headquarters for whale-watching trips, but many operators have moved south to Laguna San Ignacio and Bahía Magdalena. If you're driving, though, it's still easiest to arrange for a boat in Guerrero Negro.

If it weren't for the whales and the Carretera Transpeninsular, which passes near town, few would venture to Guerrero Negro, a town of 10,000. Those traveling south can easily bypass the town. The name, which means Black Warrior, was derived from a whaling ship that ran aground in Scammon's Lagoon in 1858. Near the Desierto de Vizcaíno (Vizcaíno Desert), on the Pacific Ocean, the area is best known for its salt pans, which provide work for many people in town and produce one-third of the world's salt supply. Salt water collects in some 780 square km (300 square mi) of sea-level ponds and evaporates quickly in the desert heat, leaving great blocks of salt. The town is dusty, windy, and generally unpleasant, but it happens to be a favored roosting spot for osprey, which build huge nests on power poles around town.

Fodor'sChoice **Scammon's Lagoon** is about 27 km (17 mi) south of Guerrero Negro, down
★ a rough but passable sand road that crosses the salt flats. The lagoon got its name from U.S. explorer Charles Melville Scammon of Maine, who came here in the mid-1800s. On his first expedition, Scammon and his crew collected more than 700 barrels of valuable whale oil, and the whale rush was on. Within 10 years nearly all the whales in the lagoon had been killed, and it took almost a century for the population to increase to what it had been before Scammon arrived. It wasn't until the 1940s that the U.S. and Mexican governments took measures to protect the whales.

These days, whale-watching boats—most of them *pangas* (small skiffs)—must get permission from the Mexican government to enter Scammon's Lagoon, now a national park called Parque Natural de la Ballena Gris (Gray Whale Natural Park). The other major whale-watching spots (also protected by the government) are farther south, at Laguna San Ignacio and Bahía and Laguna Magdalena, both on the Pacific coast. If traveling on your own, you can reach Laguna San Ignacio from the town of San Ignacio or Loreto. Bahía Magdalena—regulars call it "Mag Bay"—is about a four-hour drive across the peninsula from La Paz and two hours from Loreto. Fishermen will take you out in their boats to

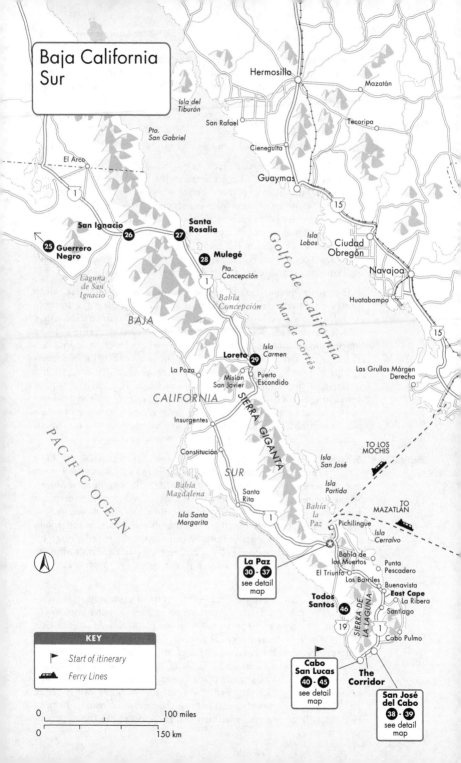

# Baja California Sur

Hermosillo
Mazatán
Isla del
Tiburón
San Rafael
Tecoripa
Pta.
San Gabriel
Cienegulta
El Arco
1
Guaymas
15
San Ignacio
26
Santa
Rosalía
Isla
Lobos
Ciudad
Obregón
25 Guerrero
Negro
27
28 Mulegé
1
Pta.
Concepción
Navajoa
Laguna
de San
Ignacio
Bahía
Concepción
Golfo de California
Huatabampo
BAJA
Mar de Cortés
15
Loreto
29
Isla
Carmen
La Poza
Misión
San Javier
Puerto
Escondido
Las Grullas Márgen
Derecha
CALIFORNIA
SIERRA GIGANTA
Insurgentes
Constitución
SUR
Isla
San José
TO LOS
MOCHIS
Bahía
Magdalena
Santa
Rita
1
Isla
Partida
TO
MAZATLAN
Isla Santa
Margarita
Bahía
la
Paz
Pichilingue
Isla
Cerralvo

**La Paz**
**30 - 37**
see detail
map

Bahía de
los Muertos
Punta
Pescadero
El Triunfo
Los Barriles
Buenavista
**Todos**
**Santos**
46
**East Cape**
La Ribera
19
SIERRA DE LA LAGUNA
Santiago
1
Cabo Pulmo

**Cabo**
**San Lucas**
**40 - 45**
see detail
map

**The**
**Corridor**

**San José**
**del Cabo**
**38 - 39**
see detail
map

PACIFIC OCEAN

## KEY
⚑ *Start of itinerary*
🚢 *Ferry Lines*

| 0 | | 100 miles |
|---|---|---|
| 0 | | 150 km |

get closer to the whales at both places. But for a better view, and an easier stay in this rugged country, travel with an outfitter who will arrange your transportation, accommodations, and time on the water. Whales will come close to your boat, rising majestically from the water, and sometimes swim close enough to be patted on the back.

## Where to Stay & Eat

There are several hotels in Guerrero Negro, none of which is worth visiting for its own sake. Rates tend to increase during the peak whale-watching season from January through March. None of the hotels has heat, and winter nights can be downright frigid. Credit cards aren't normally accepted, but the hotels do take traveler's checks.

¢ ✕🖩 **Malarrimo.** This trailer park–cum–Mexican and seafood restaurant has motel rooms and cabanas. It fills up quickly and is one of the best deals in town. The cabanas are the comfortable accommodations, and they have sleeping lofts along with regular beds. Maps and photos of Baja cover the walls in the dining room ($); give the grilled or steamed fresh fish, lobster, and clams a try. Immensely popular whale-watching excursions from the hotel are run by knowledgeable local guides. ✉ *Blvd. Zapata, 23940* ☎ *615/157–0250* ⊕ *www.malarrimo.com* ➥ *10 rooms, 6 cabanas* ⚐ *Restaurant, fans, cable TV; no a/c, no room phones* ⊟ *No credit cards.*

$ 🖩 **La Pinta.** This inn a few kilometers outside town and looks like an oasis of palms in the desert. The clean, functional rooms are dependable, the setting is more attractive than that of other local lodgings, and the American-Mexican restaurant is decent. Whale-watching excursions can be arranged here. ✉ *La Pinta Carretera 1 at 28th parallel, Domicilio Conocido, 23940* ☎ *619/275–4500 or 800/800–9632 in the U.S.* 🖷 *616/165–9008* ⊕ *www.lapintahotels.com* ➥ *28 rooms* ⚐ *Restaurant, room service, cable TV, pool, beach, Internet, laundry service, no-smoking rooms* ⊟ *MC, V.*

## Sports & the Outdoors

The gray whales that migrate from the Bering Strait are Guerrero Negro's biggest attraction. With a sturdy vehicle, you can drive the 24-km (15-mi) washboard dirt and sand road to Scammon's Lagoon and arrange a trip with the boat captains who await passengers there. Trips usually cost $25–$40 per person depending on the type of boat and length of tour. Start early to take advantage of the calmest water and best viewing conditions. Whale-watching from the shores of the lagoon can be disappointing without binoculars, but it is still an impressive sight to see the huge mammals spouting water high into the air.

**Eco-Tours Malarrimo** (✉ Blvd. Zapata, 23940 ☎ 615/157–0100 ⊕ www.malarrimo.com) is the area's best tour operator. It offers four-hour trips with bus transportation to and from the lagoon and lunch for $45 per person. About 75% of the trip is spent in small skiffs among the whales with English-speaking guides. Reserve several months in advance, especially for February, a peak whale-spotting time.

**Ecological 4 Wheeling Adventures** (🖃 Box 1213, Costa Mesa, CA 92627 ☎ 949/645–7733 ⊕ www.eco4wd.com) runs an annual road trip down Baja to Guerrero Negro for whale-watching. Participants drive their own cars in a caravan and visit towns and cave paintings along the way. The six-day journey costs $835–$1,025 for two people and includes hotels and the whale-watching excursion.

## San Ignacio

**㉖** *227 km (141 mi) southeast of Guerrero Negro.*

Although San Ignacio is amid the Desierto de Vizcaíno, date palms, planted by Jesuit missionaries in the late 1700s, sway gently, in sync with the town's laid-back rhythms. San Ignacio is primarily a place to organize whale-watching and cave-painting tours or to stop and cool off in the shady *zócalo* (town square).

### Where to Stay

$ 🏨 **La Pinta.** This simple, functional hotel is a pleasant place to stay on your transpeninsular journey—although you may wish for a bit more for the money. White arches frame the courtyard and pool, and the rooms are decorated with folk art and wood furnishings. Both the river and town are within walking distance. The staff can set up whale-watching trips with local guides. ⊠ *2 km (1 mi) west of Carretera 1 on an unnamed road into town, 23920* ☎ *624/154–0300, 619/275–4500 or 800/800–9632 in the U.S.* ⊕ *www.lapintahotels.com* ⤳ *28 rooms* ⚖ *Restaurant, room service, cable TV, pool, bar, laundry service, no-smoking rooms* ☐ *MC, V.*

### Sports & the Outdoors

San Ignacio is the base for trips to Laguna San Ignacio, 59 km (35 mi) from San Ignacio on the Pacific coast. The lagoon is one of the best places to watch the gray-whale migration, and local boat captains will usually take you close enough to pet the new baby whales. Tours arranged through

★ **Baja Discovery** (📬 Box 152527, San Diego, CA 92195 ☎ 619/262–0700 or 800/829–2252 ⊕ www.bajadiscovery.com) include round-trip transport from San Diego to San Ignacio Lagoon, by van to Tijuana and private plane to the company's comfortable camp at the lagoon. Accommodations are in private tents facing the water, and there are solar-heated showers. The cost of a five-day package—including transportation, tours, and meals—is $1,975.

★ **Baja Expeditions** (⊠ 2625 Garnet Ave., San Diego, CA 92109 ☎ 858/581–3311 or 800/843–6967 ⊕ www.bajaex.com) operates a camp at the lagoon and offers tours including air transportation from San Diego. The fee is $1,925 including transport, meals, and tours. **Ecoturísticos Kuyima** (⊠ Av. Morelos 23 ☎ 615/154–0070 ⊕ www.kuyima.com) in San Ignacio offers transportation between the town and the lagoon, operates a campground at an isolated area of the lagoon, and has adventure tours to caves with prehistoric paintings that include overnights in San Ignacio and at the lagoon.

## Santa Rosalia

**㉗** *77 km (48 mi) southeast of San Ignacio.*

The architecture in this dusty mining town is a fascinating mix of French, Mexican, and American Old West styles. Santa Rosalia is known

# THE BOOJUM TREES OF BAJA

**MEXICO'S BOOJUM TREES,** *shaped like upside-down carrots, seem like something out of a Dr. Seuss book. These odd trees only grow in a tiny section of the Baja California desert, near Carretera 1, one hour south of Guerrero Negro. You can't miss them, since boojum trees can grow to be 90 feet tall and tower awkwardly over other desert flora such as datillos, elephant trees, and even giant cardón cacti.*

*The boojum's common name, "cirio," was given by Spanish missionaries who* *thought its hanging yellow flowers resembled the slender candles (cirios) used in churches. Naturalist Godfrey Sykes gave the trees their English common name in the 1920s; the story goes that when he first saw one he exclaimed, "it must be a boojum!," referring to an ominous creature in Lewis Carroll's poem "The Hunting of the Snark."*

for its **Iglesia Santa Barbara** (⊠ Av. Obregón at Calle Altamirano), a pre-fabricated iron church designed by Alexandre-Gustave Eiffel, creator of the Eiffel Tower. The iron panels of the little church are brightened by stained-glass windows. Be sure to stop by **El Boleo** (⊠ Av. Obregón at Calle 4), where fresh breads tempt customers weekday mornings at 10.

### Where to Stay

¢ 🏨 **Hotel Frances.** The glory days of this 1886 French hillside mansion shine through despite the modest furnishings. Many rooms open onto a second-story porch with views of town and the sea. There's a small pool and classy restaurant in the courtyard. ⊠ *Av. 11 de Julio at Calle Jean M. Cousteau, 23920* ☎ *615/152–2052* ☞ *17 rooms* ㊂ *Restaurant, pool, laundry service; no cable TV* ☐ *MC, V.*

¢ 🏨 **El Morro.** Santa Rosalia's version of a resort is on the waterfront a bit south of town. Rooms, in a series of one-story buildings connected by rock arches and tile mosaics, are large and comfortable; some have terraces and tile bathrooms. Accommodations are a bit worn, but the reasonable price and the proximity to the sea even the score. The restaurant serves excellent Mexican dishes, and seafood with French sauces. ⊠ *1½ km (1 mi) south of Santa Rosalia on Carretera 1, 23900* ☎ *615/152–0414* ☞ *40 rooms* ㊂ *Restaurant, pool, bar* ☐ *No credit cards.*

## Mulegé

**28** *64 km (40 mi) south of Santa Rosalia.*

Mulegé is a popular base for exploring the nearby Sierra de Guadalupe mountains, the site of several prehistoric rock paintings of human and animal figures. Access to the paintings is good, though you must have a permit and go with a licensed guide. Tours typically involve a bumpy ride followed by an even bumpier climb on *burros* (donkeys). Kayaking in Bahía Concepción, the largest protected bay in Baja, is spectacular. Once a mission settlement, this charming tropical town of some 3,500 residents swells in winter, when Americans and Canadians fleeing the cold arrive in motor homes. There are several campgrounds outside town.

## Where to Stay

$ | **Hotel Serenidad.** A Mulegé mainstay for Baja aficionados since the
**Fodor's**Choice late 1960s, the Serenidad is owned by the Johnson family, longtime res-
★ idents. The hotel is a delightful escape, with simple rooms in brick and stucco buildings scattered under bougainvillea vines and fruit trees. Some suites have fireplaces and separate bedrooms. The Saturday-night pig roast is a tradition. ⊠ *2½ km (1½ mi) north of Mulegé, Carretera 1, 23900* ☎ *615/153–0530* ⧉ *615/153–0311* ⊕ *www.hotelserenidad. com* ⇌ *48 rooms* ♤ *Restaurant, cable TV, pool, bar, airstrip; no a/c in some rooms, no room phones* ☱ *MC, V.*

¢ | **Hacienda.** You can read and lounge in rocking chairs by the pool or along the bar at this modest hotel steps from the town plaza. Kayak trips and tours to cave paintings in the mountains can be arranged. Rooms are spartan but work fine for a night or two. ⊠ *Calle Madero 3, 23900* ☎ *615/153–0021* ⧉ *615/153–0377* ⇌ *24 rooms* ♤ *Restaurant, pool, bar, travel services; no a/c in some rooms, no room phones, no room TVs* ☱ *No credit cards.*

## Sports & the Outdoors

DIVING **Cortez Explorers** (⊠ Calle Moctezuma 75A ☎ 615/153–0500 ⊕ www. cortez-explorer.com) conducts dive trips to the rocky reefs off the Santa Inez Islands in the Mar de Cortés. You can rent dive equipment, mountain bikes, and all-terrain vehicles (ATVs), and take resort courses and snorkeling trips. A two-tank dive trip with rented gear costs $80. Bikes rent for $15 a day, ATVs for $20 an hour.

KAYAKING **EcoMundo/Baja Tropicales** (⊠ Carretera 1, Km 111, Bahía Concepción ☎ 615/153–0320 ⊕ home.earthlink.net/~rcmathews/EcoMundo_.html) rents kayaks, wet suits, and other gear and has several types of kayaking tours, including day and overnight trips in the area of Mulegé. Whale-watching trips on the Pacific coast are also available. The EcoMundo complex on Bahía Concepción includes a learning center, a touring center, and a cafeteria. You can go by the center and get a map and instructions, rent a kayak, and take a four-hour self-guided tour for $20. **Mountain Trips** (⊠ Hotel Las Casitas, Av. Madero 50 ☎ 615/153–0232) is run by Salvador Castro Drew, a Mulegé native who leads tours to the cave paintings and working ranches in the mountains. Trips to the caves start at $35.

# Loreto

㉙ *134 km (83 mi) south of Mulegé.*

Loreto's setting on the Mar de Cortés is spectacular: the gold and green hills of the Sierra de la Giganta seem to tumble into cobalt water. According to local promoters, the skies are clear 360 days of the year, and the desert climate harbors few bothersome insects.

The Kikiwa, Cochimi, Cucapa, and Kumiai tribes first inhabited the barren lands of Baja. Jesuit priest Juan María Salvatierra founded the first

California mission at Loreto in 1697, and not long after, the indigenous populations were nearly obliterated by disease and war. Seventy-two years later, a Franciscan monk from Mallorca, Spain—Father Junípero Serra— set out from here to establish a chain of missions from San Diego to San Francisco, in the land then known as Alta California.

In 1821 Mexico achieved independence from Spain, which ordered all missionaries home. Loreto's mission was abandoned and fell into disrepair. Then in 1829, a hurricane virtually destroyed the settlement, capital of the Californias at the time. The capital was moved to La Paz, and Loreto languished for a century. In the late 1970s, when oil revenue filled government coffers, the area was tapped for development. An international airport was built and a luxury hotel and tennis center opened, followed a few years later by a seaside 18-hole golf course. The infrastructure for a resort area south of town at Nopoló was set up. But the pace of development slowed as the money dried up.

Loreto is once again flush with developments, thanks to an influx of money from FONATUR, the federal government's tourism development fund. The downtown waterfront now has a pristine seawall and sidewalk malecón with park benches. Entrepreneurs are opening small hotels and restaurants, and investors are buying up land. Some say little Loreto will be another Los Cabos someday.

For now, Loreto has a population of around 13,000 full-time residents and an increasing number of part-timers who winter at hotels, homes, and trailer parks. It's still a good place to escape the crowds, relax, and go fishing or whale-watching. The Parque Marítimo Nacional Bahía de Loreto protects much of the Mar de Cortés in this area, but there are a few cruise ships that use Loreto as a port of call, and the marina at Puerto Escondido is central to the government's plans for a series of marinas. With any luck, new developments will be contained in the Nopoló area.

The **malecón** along Calle de la Playa is a pleasant place to walk, jog, or sit watching the sunset. A small marina shelters yachts and the panga fleet; the adjoining beach is popular with locals, especially on Sunday afternoons, when kids hit the playground.

Loreto's main historic sight is **La Misión de Nuestra Señora de Loreto** (✉ Calle Salvatierra at Calle Misioneros ☎ 613/135–0005). The stone church's bell tower is the town's main landmark, rising above the main plaza and reconstructed pedestrian walkway along Salvatierra.

**El Museo de los Misiones,** also called the Museo de Historia y Antropología (Missions Museum or Museum of History and Anthropology), contains religious relics, tooled leather saddles used in the 19th century, and displays on Baja's history. ✉ *Calle Salvatierra s/n, next to La Misión de Nuestra Señora de Loreto* ☎ *613/135–0441* ✍ *$2.70* ☙ *Tues.–Sun. 9–1 and 3–6.*

A major developer is transforming **Nopoló** (⊕ www.loretobay.com), about 8 km (5 mi) south of Loreto, into a resort area called Loreto Bay. Condo complexes and private homes continue to rise on the lots laid out back in the 1970s. The existing nine-court tennis complex and 18-

hole golf course have been spiffed up, and the classy Camino Real hotel attracts many first-time visitors.

**Puerto Escondido,** 16 km (10 mi) down Carretera 1 from Nopoló, has an RV park, **Tripui** (☎ 613/133–0818), with a good restaurant, a few motel rooms, a snack shop, bar, stores, showers, laundry, a pool, and tennis courts. There's a boat ramp at the Puerto Escondido marina close to Tripui; you pay the fee required to launch here to the attendant at the parking lot. The **port captain's office** (☎ 613/135–0656) is just south of the ramp, but it's rarely open.

**Isla Danzante,** 5 km (3 mi) southeast of Puerto Escondido, has good reefs and diving opportunities. You can arrange picnic trips to **Coronado Island,** inhabited only by sea lions, in Loreto, Nopoló, or Puerto Escondido. The snorkeling and scuba diving on the island are excellent. Danzante and other islands off Loreto are now part of the Parque Marítímo Nacional Bahía de Loreto. Commercial fishing boats are not allowed within the 60-square-km (23-square-mi) park.

★ ☾ A trip to **Misión San Javier,** 32 km (20 mi) southwest of Loreto, shows Baja at its best. A high-clearance vehicle is useful for the two-hour drive to the mission—don't try getting here if the dirt and gravel road is muddy. The road climbs past small ranches, palm groves, and the steep cliffs of the Cerro de la Giganta. Marked trails lead off the road to remnants of a small cluster of Indian cave paintings. The mission village is a remote community of some 50 full-time residents, many of whom come outdoors when visitors arrive.

The mission church (circa 1699), which is amid orchards, is built of blocks of gray volcanic rock and topped with domes and bell towers containing three bells from the 18th and 19th centuries. The side stained-glass windows are framed with wood. Inside a gilded central altar contains a statue of St. Javier; side altars have statues of St. Ignacio and the Virgen de los Dolores. Vestments from the 1700s are displayed in a glass cabinet. The church is often locked; ask anyone hanging about to find the person with the keys. Slip a few pesos into the contribution box as a courtesy to the village's inhabitants, who need all the help they can get to keep the church well maintained. Loreto residents make pilgrimages to the mission for the patron saint's festival, celebrated December 1–3. Although you can drive to San Javier on your own, it helps to have a guide along to lead you to the caves and Indian paintings. Many hotels and tour companies can arrange trips. You can spend the night in a small bungalow at **Casa de Ana** (☎ 613/135–1552 in Loreto) and get a rare view into a small Baja community ($34 per night).

## Where to Stay & Eat

$–$$$ ✕ **El Nido.** If you're hungry for steak, chicken, and hearty Mexican combo plates, then this is your place. It's as close as you'll get to a steak house in these parts. The brass and woodwork and courteous waiters make up for prices that seem outrageously high for the neighborhood. ✉ *Calle Salvatierra 154* ☎ *613/135–0027* ▭ *No credit cards.*

¢–$ ✕ **Café Olé.** Locals and gringos hang out here for terrific breakfasts of scrambled eggs with *chorizo* (sausage), and huevos rancheros. It also serves good burgers, ice cream, and french fries. ⊠ *Calle Francisco Madero* ☎ *613/135–0496* ⊟ *No credit cards.*

★ ¢–$ ✕**Canipole.** Sofía Rodríguez reigns over the open kitchen of this down-home Mexican restaurant. The 34 ingredients she uses in her savory mole are displayed in tiny bowls on one table, the ingredients for her home-made Mexican hot chocolate are in bowls on another. Pots of posole (a hominy stew) and tortilla soup simmer over a gas fire on the patio while Sofía pats out fresh tortillas for each order. Specialties include *conejo* (rabbit), quesadillas with *flor de calabaza* (squash blossoms), and un-usual carnitas made with lamb. ⊠ *Pino Suárez s/n, beside the mission* ☎ *613/135–1886* ⊟ *No credit cards* ☉ *No lunch.*

¢–$ ✕**Pachamama.** The owners (she's from Argentina, he's from Mexico City)
Fodor'sChoice have combined their cultures and cuisines to create a place worth repeated
★ visits. Sit at one of the wooden tables in front of the small plaza and nib-ble on regional cheeses or empanadas, then move on to a salad of goat cheese and sliced homegrown tomatoes or a marinated *arrachera* (skirt) steak. Sandwiches on homemade bread make you wish the place were open for lunch. ⊠ *Calle Davis 13, at Calle Salvatierra* ☎ *613/135–1655* ⊟ *No credit cards* ☉ *Closed Sept. Closed Tues. No lunch.*

$$$$ ⊡**Danzante Resort.** This hilltop resort facing Isla Danzante is architecturally
Fodor'sChoice stunning and ecologically sensitive. Owners Michael and Lauren Farley
★ are Baja experts, writers, and underwater photographers. Guest rooms have bent-twig furnishings, wrought-iron bedsteads, patios with hammocks, and such thoughtful items as binoculars and books. Phones and TVs are nonexistent, except for sporadic cellular phone access. There are plenty of activities to pursue, including hikes, kayaking, and bird-watching. An activities center hosts weddings, yoga retreats, and other gatherings. ⊠ *32 km (20 mi) south of Loreto off Carretera 1* ☎ *Box 1166, Los Gatos, CA 95031* ☎ *408/354–0042 in the U.S.* ☏ *408/354–3268 in the U.S.* ⊕ *www. danzante.com* ⇨ *9 junior suites* ☺ *Restaurant, fans, pool, massage, beach, dive shop, hiking, horseback riding, kayaking, no-smoking rooms; no a/c, no room phones, no room TVs, no kids under 8* ⊟ *MC, V* ⦿ *FAP.*

$$–$$$$ ⊡**Hotel Posada de los Flores.** The rose-color walls of this surprisingly chic hotel rise beside downtown's plaza. The public areas are its forte. A glass-bottom pool doubles as a skylight above the atrium lobby, and the rooftop sundeck and restaurant have huge planters of bougainvillea. Ex-posed beams and locally crafted tile adorn the lobby and hallways. Guest rooms, however, are less inviting, and can be very dark and noisy. ⊠ *Calle Salvatierra at Calle Francisco Madero, 23880* ☎ *613/135–1162, 877/ 245–2860 in the U.S.* ⊕ *www.posadadelasflores.com* ⇨ *10 rooms, 5 ju-nior suites* ☺ *2 restaurants, in-room safes, minibars, pool, 2 bars, laun-dry service, car rental; no kids, no smoking* ⊟ *MC, V* ⦿ *BP.*

$$ ⊡**Camino Real.** Loreto's fanciest resort is on the waterfront, at the edge of Nopoló's golf course. A battalion of water toys awaits at the pool area. The bright guest rooms have double sinks in the bathrooms and large closets, but confoundingly small balconies and showers that spray water everywhere. The rooftop suites, however, have terraces complete with hot tubs. The restaurants are good and reasonably priced—a good thing since there are no other dining choices within walking distance. ⊠ *Blvd. Mis-ión de Loreto s/n, 23880* ☎ *613/133–0010, 800/873–7484 in the U.S.*

🖨 *613/133–0020* ⊕ *www.loretobaja.com* 🛏 *149 rooms, 6 suites* ♿ *2 restaurants, room service, in-room safes, minibars, cable TV, pool, beach, 2 bars, shop, laundry service, Internet, business services, meeting rooms, car rental, travel services, no-smoking rooms* ☰ *AE, MC, V.*

**$$** 🏨 **Hotel Oasis.** One of the original in-town hostelries, the Oasis remains an ideal base for those who want to be in town and spend plenty of time on the water. Rooms vary greatly in size and comfort; the best have coffeemakers, water views, and hammocks on the front terraces. Guests gather in the large bar in the evening to exchange fishing tales and wish each other luck over breakfast. The hotel has its own fleet of skiffs. The owners also operate Casa de Ana in San Javier. ⊠ *Calle de la Playa, Apdo. 17, 23880* ☎ *613/135–0112, 800/497–3923 in the U.S.* 🖨 *613/135–0795* ⊕ *www.hoteloasis.com* 🛏 *39 rooms* ♿ *Restaurant, refrigerators, cable TV, pool, boating, fishing, bar* ☰ *MC, V* ❧ *BP, EP, FAP.*

**★ $$** 🏨 **Villas de Loreto.** You'd be hard pressed to miss a TV in this hideaway. There are plenty of activities, from biking to kayaking to lolling in a hammock with a book. Fishing tours can be arranged, and there's a PADI dive shop on premises. Rooms have brightly colored quilts, coffeemakers, and porches; the beach house has a fireplace (as do five other rooms) and a full kitchen. ⊠ *Antonio Mijares at beach, Colonia Zaragoza, 23880* ☎ *613/135–0586* 🖨 *613/135–1355* ⊕ *www.villasdeloreto.com* 🛏 *12 rooms, 1 beach house* ♿ *Restaurant, refrigerators, pool, beach, dive shop, bicycles, laundry service, Internet, some pets allowed; no room phones, no room TVs, no smoking* ☰ *MC, V.*

**$** 🏨 **Motel el Dorado.** The necessary amenities plus ceiling fans and a congenial bar are available at this spanking-clean motel. All that's missing is a pool, but the waterfront is a block away. ⊠ *Paseo Hidalgo at Calle Pipila, 23880* ☎*613/135–1500* 🖨*613/135–1700* ⊕*www.moteleldorado.com* 🛏 *11 rooms* ♿ *Cable TV, fishing, bar; no room phones* ☰ *MC, V.*

## Sports & the Outdoors

FISHING  Fishing put Loreto on the map. You can catch cabrilla and snapper year-round; yellowtail in spring; and dorado, marlin, and sailfish in summer. If you're a serious angler bring tackle. Some sportfishing fleets do update their equipment regularly. All Loreto-area hotels can arrange fishing, and many own skiffs. Local anglers congregate with their small boats on the beach at the north and south ends of town. **Arturo's Fishing Fleet** (⊠ Paseo Hidalgo, between the plaza and marina ☎ 613/135–0766 ⊕ www.arturosport.com) has several types of boats and fishing packages and operates the water-sports concession at the Camino Real hotel. The **Baja Big Fish Company** (⊠ Paseo Hidalgo 19, by the plaza ☎ 613/104–0781 ⊕ www.bajabigfish.com), which specializes in light tackle and fly-fishing, has packages from the United States and fishing trips from Loreto. Day-long excursions cost from $205 to $350, depending on the size of the boat.

GOLF  The 18-hole **Loreto Campo de Golf** (☎ 613/135–0788 or 613/133–0554) is along Nopoló Bay. Several hotels in Loreto have golf packages and reduced or free greens fees. Greens fees are $25 for 9 holes, and $40 for 18 holes. The Loreto Bay Company, which is developing Nopoló, has plans to improve the course.

TENNIS   The **Loreto Tennis Center** (⌧ Blvd. Misión de Loreto s/n ☎ 613/135–0408), 8 km (5 mi) south of town, has nine lighted clay courts open to the public. The cost is $8 an hour.

WATER SPORTS   You can arrange kayaking excursions, whale-watching tours, scuba-certification courses, dive and snorkeling trips, and hikes through the **Baja Outpost** (⌧ Blvd. Mateos, near the Oasis Hotel ☎ 613/135–1134, 888/ 649–5951 in the U.S. ⊕ www.bajaoutpost.com). A two-tank boat dive costs $80; snorkeling trips cost $52. A tour to San Javier is $75. **Paddling South Tours** (✉ Box 827, Calistoga, CA 94515 ☎ 707/942–4550 or 800/398–6200 ⊕ www.tourbaja.com) runs eight- to nine-day kayaking trips for $995 including camping along the coast and meals. The company also offers mountain-biking trips from Loreto. Loreto outdoor specialists **Las Parras Tours** (⌧ Calle Salvatierra at Calle Francisco Madero ☎ 613/135–1010) provides experienced local guides for kayaking, as well as for whale-watching, scuba diving and certification, visiting San Javier, and hiking to cave paintings in the mountains. Day trips in the desert cost $29, and tours to San Javier run $49. The U.S.-based company **Sea Quest** (☎ 360/378–5767 ⊕ sea-quest-kayak.com) has several trips that begin in Loreto. Options include kayaking with gray whales in Magdalena Bay or San Ignacio Lagoon. Weeklong trips start at $1,059.

## Shopping

Loreto's shopping district is along the pedestrian zone on Calle Salvatierra, where there are several souvenir shops and stands, plus the town's only ★ supermarket. **El Alacrán** (⌧ Calle Salvatierra 47 ☎ 613/135–0029) has remarkable folk art, jewelry, and sportswear.

# La Paz

**30**–**37**  *354 km (220 mi) south of Loreto.*

In the slowest part of the off-season, during the oppressive late summer heat, you can easily see how La Paz received its name: "The Peace." It's the peninsula's most traditional city, even as it has grown to a population of 250,000, with a large contingent of retirees from the United States and Canada. Travelers use La Paz as both a destination in itself and a stopping-off point en route to Los Cabos. There's always excellent scuba diving and sportfishing in the Mar de Cortés—La Paz is the stop off for divers and fishermen headed for Cerralvo, La Partida, and the Espíritu Santo islands, where parrot fish, manta rays, neons, and angels blur the clear waters by the shore, and marlin, dorado, and yellowtail leap from the sea.

Hernán Cortés and his soldiers were drawn to La Paz in 1535 by stories of magnificent pearls found in local oysters. In 1720, missionaries arrived to deliver salvation to the indigenous Pericú people. Instead, they introduced smallpox, which decimated the local populace within 30 years. La Paz became the capital of the Californias in 1829. In 1853 a group of U.S. southerners, led by William Walker, tried to make La Paz a slave state, but Mexicans quickly banished them. In 1940 disease wiped out the oyster beds, and with the pearls gone, La Paz no longer attracted prospectors.

La Paz officially became the capital of Baja California Sur in 1974 and is now the state's largest settlement. It is the site of the governor's house and the state's bureaucracy, jail, and power plant, as well as the ferry port to Mazatlán.

## What to See

**㉝** The **Biblioteca de las Californias** specializes in the history of Baja California and has an outstanding collection of historical documents. The library has, however, been relegated to a small section of the building, which has been turned into a children's cultural center. ⊠ *Av. Madero, at Calle 5 de Mayo Centro* ☎ *612/122–0162* ⊙ *Weekdays 9–6.*

**㉞** **La Catedral de Nuestra Señora de la Paz,** the downtown church, is a simple stone building with a modest gilded altar. The church was built in 1860 near the site of La Paz's first mission, which was established that same year by Jesuit Jaime Bravo. ⊠ *Calle Juárez* ☎ *No phone.*

**㉚** At La Paz's west end is the construction zone for the **Fidepaz Marina,** the 500-acre marina, which is part of a long-term development that has yet to reach completion. FONATUR, the government's tourism trust, has taken over the project, which may bring further development to the area. There's a resort hotel by the waterfront.

**㉛** The **Malecón** is La Paz's seawall, tourist zone, and main drag all rolled into one. It runs along Paseo Alvaro Obregón, and has a sidewalk as well as several park areas with benches. Marina La Paz, at the malecón's southwest end, is an ever-growing development that's home to condominiums, vacation homes, and a pleasant walkway lined with cafés.

**㉜** A two-story white gazebo is the focus of **Malecón Plaza,** a small concrete square where musicians sometimes appear on weekend nights. Across the street Calle 16 de Septiembre leads inland to the city center.

**㊱** La Paz's culture and heritage are well represented at the **Museo de Antropología,** which has re-creations of Comondu and Las Palmas Indian villages, photos of cave paintings found in Baja, and copies of Cortés's writings on first sighting La Paz. Many exhibit descriptions are written only in Spanish, but the museum's staff will help you translate. ⊠ *Calle Altamirano, at Calle 5 de Mayo, Centro* ☎ *612/122–0162* ⊠ *Donation requested* ⊙ *Daily 9–6.*

**㊲** Since the time of Spanish invaders, **Pichilingue** was known for its preponderance of oysters bearing black pearls. In 1940 a disease killed them off, leaving the beach deserted. Today Pichilingue is a pleasant place for sunbathing and watching sportfishing boats bring in their hauls. Palapa restaurants on the beach serve oysters *diablo* (raw oysters steeped in a fiery-hot sauce) and inexpensive grilled fish. The road to Pichilingue curves northeast along the bay about 16 km (10 mi) to the terminals where the ferries from Mazatlán and Topolobampo arrive and many of the sportfishing boats depart.

**㉟** **Plaza Constitución,** the true center of La Paz, is a traditional zócalo, which also goes by the name Jardín Velazco. Concerts are held in the park gazebo and locals gather here for art shows and fairs.

## Beaches

Off a dirt road just past Pichilingue, Playa Tecolote and Playa Coyote are adjacent crystal-blue coves with clean beaches. Both have restaurants, water-sports equipment rentals, and palapas for shade. Camping is allowed in the parking lots. Playa Balandra, on a side road between Pichilingue and Tecolote, is a peaceful cove favored by kayak and snorkeling operations from town.

## Where to Stay & Eat

**$–$$$**   ✕ **El Bismark II.** You've got to go a bit out of your way for a local home-style Mexican restaurant. Tuck into seafood cocktails, enormous grilled lobsters, or carne asada served with beans, guacamole, and homemade tortillas. Families settle down for hours at long wood tables, while waitresses divide their attention between patrons and soap operas on the TV above the bar. The desultory service is a drawback. A smaller Bismark is on the malecón. ⊠ *Av. Degollado and Calle Altamirano, Centro* ☎ *612/122–4854* ▣ *MC, V.*

★ **$–$$$**   ✕ **La Mar y Peña.** The freshest, tastiest seafood cocktails, ceviches, and clam tacos imaginable are served in this nautical restaurant crowded with locals. If you can come with friends, go for the *mariscada,* a huge platter of shellfish and fish for four. ⊠ *Calle 16 de Septiembre, between Isabel de la Catolica and Albañez, Centro* ☎ *612/122–9949* ▣ *AE, MC, V.*

**$–$$**  ✕ **El Cangrejo Loco.** A few sidewalk tables sit outside this tiny family-run café; seats are hard to come by at lunchtime. A long list of seafood cocktails offers shrimp, crab, and clams with lime, chilies, or soy sauce. Entrées include a great quesadilla with cheese and crab, manta ray tacos, and stuffed crab. ✉ *Paseo Obregón, between Bravo and Ocampo, Malecón* ☎ *612/122–1359* ⊟ *No credit cards.*

**$–$$**  ✕ **La Pazta.** Locals who crave international fare rave about this trattoria with a sleek black-and-white color scheme and excellent homemade pasta and pizzas. Imported cheeses and wines, and bracing espresso and cappuccino are all welcome changes from the local seafood and taco fare. ✉ *Allende 36, Centro* ☎ *612/125–1195* ⊟ *MC, V* ☻ *No dinner Tues.*

**★ ¢–$**  ✕ **Taco Hermanos Gonzalez.** La Paz has plenty of great taco stands, but the Gonzalez brothers still corner the market with their hunks of fresh fish wrapped in corn tortillas. Bowls of condiments line the small stand, and the top quality draws crowds of sidewalk munchers. ✉ *Mutualismo and Esquerro, Centro* ☎ *No phone* ⊟ *No credit cards.*

**¢–$**  ✕ **El Quinto Sol Restaurante Vegetariano.** El Quinto's brightly painted exterior is covered with snake symbols and smiling suns. The all-vegetarian menu includes fresh juices and herbal elixirs. The four-course prix-fixe *comida corrida* (daily special) is a bargain; it's served from noon to 4. The back half of the space is a bare-bones natural-foods store. ✉ *Belisario Domínguez and Av. Independencia, Centro* ☎ *612/122–1692* ⊟ *No credit cards.*

**☾ $$$–$$$$**  ✕▥ **Crowne Plaza Resort.** La Paz's most modern resort is a hacienda-style inn beside the Fidepaz Marina. Its suites vary in size and style; the largest have two bedrooms and a kitchenette. The pool flows through several levels in the courtyard. The restaurant, with its cordial service and fine cuisine, is a favorite among local executives. ✉ *Lote A, Marina Fidepaz, Apdo. 482, Centro 23000* ☎ *612/124–0830, 800/227–6963 in the U.S.* 🖷 *612/124–0837* ⊕ *www.crowneplaza.com* ↻ *54 suites* ⚒ *Restaurant, room service, in-room data ports, in-room safes, minibars, cable TV, pool, gym, bar, nightclub, playground, business services, travel services* ⊟ *AE, MC, V.*

**★ $$**  ▥ **el angel azul.** Owner Esther Ammann converted La Paz's courthouse into a charming bed-and-breakfast whose rooms frame a central courtyard and are decorated with original artwork. The rooftop suite overlooks the city. ✉ *Av. Independencia 518, at Guillermo Prieto, Centro 23000* ☎ *612/125–5130* ⊕ *www.elangelazul.com* ↻ *10 rooms, 1 suite* ⚒ *Bar, no-smoking rooms; no TVs in some rooms, no kids under 12* ⊟ *MC, V* ❑ *CP.*

**☾ $$**  ▥ **La Concha Beach Resort.** It's on a long beach with calm water, and it has a water-sports center and a notably good restaurant. Rooms can be dark and uninviting, so if you can, splurge on a condo unit with separate bedroom and kitchen; the smallest run around $135 per night. There's a shuttle to town. ✉ *Carretera a Pichilingue, Km 5, between downtown and Pichilingue, 23010* ☎ *612/121–6344 or 612/121–6161, 800/999–2252 in the U.S.* 🖷 *612/121–6218* ⊕ *www.laconcha.com* ↻ *107 rooms* ⚒ *Restaurant, minibars, cable TV, pool, beach, dive shop, snorkeling, 3 bars, laundry service, shops, car rental, travel services* ⊟ *AE, MC, V.*

**$$**  ▥ **Hotel Marina.** Gardens surround the pool and Jacuzzi, and a seaside promenade lines the property. The full-service marina offers fishing, scuba diving, and kayaking. Private charters are available. Most rooms have terraces with water views and are airy, clean, and functional. ⌧ *Carretera a Pichilingue, Km 2.5, 23000* ☎ *612/121–6254, 800/826–1138 in the U.S.* ☒ *612/121–6177* ⊕ *www.hotelmarina.com.mx* ⇥ *86 rooms, 5 suites* ♿ *Restaurant, cable TV, tennis court, pool, hot tub, marina, boating, fishing, bar, car rental* ⊟ *AE, MC, V.*

$–$$ ▦ **Los Arcos.** This colonial-style 1950s hotel is a La Paz landmark. The lobby leads to the courtyard, where the rush of water in the fountain drowns out street noise. Most rooms have balconies, some facing the bay. The Cabañas de los Arcos next door consists of several small brick cottages surrounded by gardens and a small hotel with a pool. ⌧ *Paseo Obregón 498, between Rosales and Allende, Malecón 23000* ☎ *612/122–2744 or 520/529–4529, 800/347–2252 in the U.S.* ☒ *612/125–4313, 520/529–4549 in the U.S.* ⊕ *www.losarcos.com* ⇥ *93 rooms and 18 suites at hotel; 20 bungalows and 23 rooms at Cabañas* ♿ *Restaurant, coffee shop, minibars, cable TV, 2 pools, sauna, bar, meeting rooms, travel services* ⊟ *MC, V.*

$–$$ ▦ **La Perla.** This brown low-rise hotel is a La Paz fixture. Rooms have white walls and light-wood furnishings; some have king-size beds. The pool is on a second-story sundeck away from main street traffic. Noise is a factor in the oceanfront rooms; the trade-off is wonderful sunset views over the malecón. ⌧ *Paseo Obregón 1570, Malecón 23010* ☎ *612/122–0777 or 800/716–8799, 888/242–3757 in the U.S.* ☒ *612/125–5363* ⊕ *www.hotelperlabaja.com* ⇥ *116 rooms* ♿ *Restaurant, cable TV, minibars, pool, bar, playground, shops, meeting rooms* ⊟ *AE, MC, V.*

$ ▦ **Hotel Suites Club El Moro.** A vacation-ownership resort with suite rentals on a nightly and weekly basis, El Moro has a palm-filled garden and a densely landscaped pool area. You can recognize the building by its stark-white turrets and domes. Rooms are Mediterranean style, with arched windows, Mexican tiles, and private balconies. Some rooms have kitchens and can sleep up to five people. A small café serves light fare. ⌧ *Carretera a Pichilingue, Km 2, between downtown and Pichilingue, 23010* ☎ *612/122–4084* ☒ *612/125–2828* ⊕ *www.clubelmoro.com* ⇥ *21 suites* ♿ *Café, cable TV, pool, bar* ⊟ *AE, MC, V* ⫶ *CP.*

¢ ▦ **Pensión California.** You can nab a bed here for less than $20; although the hacienda is run-down, the blue-and-white rooms have baths and are clean. The courtyard has picnic tables and a TV. ⌧ *Av. Degollado 209, Centro 23000* ☎ *612/122–2896* ⇥ *25 rooms* ♿ *Picnic area; no a/c, no room TVs* ⊟ *No credit cards.*

### Nightlife & the Arts

**El Teatro de la Ciudad** (⌧ Av. Navarro 700, Centro ☎ 612/125–0004) is La Paz's cultural center. The theater seats 1,500 and stages shows by visiting performers and local ensembles. **La Terraza** (⌧ La Perla hotel, Paseo Obregón 1570, Malecón ☎ 612/122–0777) is the best spot for both sunset- and people-watching along the malecón. The hotel also has a disco

★ on weekend nights. **Las Varitas** (⌧ Calle Independencia 11, Centro ☎ 612/125–2025), a lively Mexican rock club, heats up after midnight.

### Sports & the Outdoors

BOATING &   The considerable fleet of private boats in La Paz now has room for docking at three marinas: Fidepaz Marina at the north end of town, and the Marina Palmira and Marina La Paz south of town. Most hotels can arrange sportfishing trips. Tournaments are held in August and November. The **Jack Velez Fleet** (✉ Apdo. 402, Centro 23000 ☎ 612/128–7518) has cabin cruisers; charters start around $100 per person. The company also offers whale-watching, snorkeling, and scuba trips.

KAYAKING   The calm waters off La Paz are perfect for kayaking, and you can take multiday trips along the coast to Loreto or out to the nearby islands.

★ **Baja Expeditions** (✉ 2625 Garnet Ave., San Diego, CA 92109 ☎ 858/581–3311 or 800/843–6967 ⊕ www.bajaex.com), one of the oldest outfitters working in Baja, offers several kayaking tours, including multinight trips between Loreto and La Paz. A support boat carries all the gear, including ingredients for great meals. A day trip costs around $75 per person. **Baja Quest** (✉ Sonora 174, Centro ☎ 612/123–5320) has day and overnight trips. Day trips cost about $70 per person. **Fun Baja** (✉ Carretera a Pichilingue, Km 2 ☎ 612/121–5884 ⊕ www.funbaja. com) offers kayak trips around the islands, scuba and snorkel excursions, and land tours. A half-day of kayaking will run about $35. **Nichols Expeditions** (✉ 497 N. Main, Moab, UT 84532 ☎ 435/259–3999 or 800/648–8488 ⊕ www.nicholsexpeditions.com) arranges kayaking tours to Isla Espíritu Santo and between Loreto and La Paz, with camping along the way. A nine-day trip costs $1,200.

SCUBA DIVING &   Popular diving and snorkeling spots include the coral banks off Isla Es-
SNORKELING   píritu Santo, the sea lion colony off Isla Partida, and the seamount 14 km (9 mi) farther north (best for serious divers). **Baja Expeditions** (✉ 2625 Garnet Ave., San Diego, CA 92109 ☎ 858/581–3311 or 800/843–6967 ⊕ www.bajaex.com) runs daylong and multiday dive trips. Day trips cost around $125; seven-day excursions where you live aboard a boat

★ start at $1,495. The **Cortez Club** (✉ La Concha Beach Resort, Carretera a Pichilingue, Km 5, between downtown and Pichilingue ☎ 612/121–6344 or 612/121–6161) is a full-scale water-sports center with equipment rental, and scuba, snorkeling, kayaking, and sportfishing tours. A two-tank dive costs about $125. **Fun Baja** (✉ Carretera a Pichilingue, Km 2 ☎ 612/121–5884 ⊕ www.funbaja.com) offers scuba and snorkel trips with the sea lions. Scuba trips start at $100.

WHALE-   La Paz has become a center for whale-watching expeditions to Bahía Mag-
WATCHING   dalena on the Pacific coast. Note, however, that such trips entail about six hours of travel from La Paz and back for two to three hours on the water. Many people opt to stay overnight in San Carlos, the small town by the bay. Most hotels can make arrangements for excursions or you can head out on your own by taking a public bus from La Paz to San Carlos and then hiring a boat captain to take you into the bay. The whale-watching experience itself entails a trip into the lagoon in a small boat. It's usually chilly, and passengers are bundled up but ready to take off their gloves if a whale comes near. Captains must keep their boats away from the whales, who may approach so closely you can reach out and touch them. Bring along a telephoto lens and lots of film. Binoculars come in handy as well.

An easier expedition is a whale-watching trip in the Mar de Cortés from La Paz, which involves boarding a boat in La Paz and sailing around till whales are spotted. They most likely won't come as close to the boats and you won't see the mothers and newborn calves at play, but it's still fabulous watching the whales breeching and spouting nearby.

**Baja Expeditions** (✉ 2625 Garnet Ave., San Diego, CA 92109 ☎ 858/581–3311 or 800/843–6967 ⊕ www.bajaex.com) runs whale-watching trips to the bay. Seven-day trips to Magdalena Bay including boat trips, camping, and meals start at $1,250 per person. You can also arrange a trip through **Baja Quest** (✉ Sonora 174, Centro ☎ 612/123–5320). The water-sports center **Cortez Club** (✉ La Concha Beach Resort, Carretera a Pichilingue, Km 5, between downtown and Pichilingue ☎ 612/121–6344 or 612/121–6161) runs extremely popular whale-watching trips in winter.

### Shopping
**Artesanías la Antigua California** (✉ Paseo Obregón 220, Malecón ☎ 612/125–5230) has the nicest selection of Mexican folk art in La Paz, including wooden masks and lacquered boxes from Guerrero Negro. It also has good supply of English-language books on Baja. **Artesanía Cuauhtémoc** (✉ Av. Abasolo between Calles Nayarit and Oaxaca, south of downtown, Centro ☎ 612/122–4575) is the workshop of weaver Fortunado Silva, who creates and sells cotton place mats, rugs, and tapestries.
★ Julio Ibarra oversees the potters and painters at **Ibarra's Pottery** (✉ Calle Prieto 625, Centro ☎ 612/122–0404). His geometric designs and glazing technique result in gorgeous mirrors, bowls, platters, and cups. There's unusual pottery at **Mexican Designs** (✉ Calle Arreola 41, at Av. Zaragoza, Centro ☎ 612/123–2231). The boxes with cactus designs are particularly good souvenirs. **La Tiendita** (✉ Malecón, Centro ☎ 612/125–2744) has embroidered guayabera shirts and dresses, tin ornaments and picture frames, and black pottery from Oaxaca.

## The East Cape

*Los Barriles is 105 km (65 mi) south of La Paz.*

Anglers and adventurers have long visited the Mar de Cortés coast north of Los Cabos. The area known as the East Cape consists of a string of settlements and fishing villages between La Paz and San José del Cabo—including Los Barriles, Buena Vista, and La Ribera, all accessible from Carretera 1. From Punta Pescadero in the north to Cabo Pulmo in the south, the cape is renowned for its rich fishing grounds, top-notch diving, and, when the wind kicks up, excellent windsurfing. Hotels and restaurants tend to be modest, and most hotels have meal plans.

There's an outback feel to the East Cape, with a robust group of American "settlers" making their presence known. Many communities are accessible via paved road from Los Cabos. If you're intrepid you can make the three-hour drive on a dirt washboard of a road along the coast to La Ribera, Punta Colorado, and Cabo Pulmo—the latter a superb dive site within a national marine reserve. (This route is *not* recommended for those bothered by dust or long stretches of precipitous driving conditions.)

Cabo Pulmo is home to 100 or so residents, depending on the season. It's a magnet for serious divers, kayakers, and windsurfers, and remains one of southern Baja's natural treasures. Power comes from solar panels, and drinking water is trucked in over dirt roads. Near the beach, solar-powered cottages are for rent at the **Cabo Pulmo Beach Resort** (⊠ Cabo Pulmo ☎ 624/141–0244 ⊕ www.cabopulmo.com), which also has a full-service PADI dive facility.

## Where to Stay & Eat

**$–$$**   ✕**Otra Vez.** It's a great little California-style café with simple grilled seafood, omelets, and lobster New Orleans on the menu. This may be the only time you see sprouts in Baja, so stock up. The clientele is mostly expat retirees and tourists who gossip freely while listening to the Beach Boys. ⊠ *Calle 20 de Noviembre, Los Barriles* ☎ *624/141–0249* ▤ *MC, V* ☽ *Closed Aug.–Sept.*

☸ **$$–$$$**   🏨 **Hotel Buena Vista Beach Resort.** Tile-roof bungalows sit along flower-lined paths next to pools, fountains, and lawns. Some rooms have private terraces. The fishing fleet is excellent, as are other diversions, such as diving, snorkeling, kayaking, horseback riding, and trips to natural springs. A European plan without meals is available from November through March, which cuts the rate in half. ⊠ *Carretera 1, Km 105, 23500 Buena Vista* ☎ *624/141–0033 or 619/429–8079, 800/752–3555 in the U.S.* 🖨 *624/141–0133* ⊕ *www.hotelbuenavista.com* 🛏 *60 rooms* ⟁ *Restaurant, tennis court, 2 pools, hot tub, massage, beach, snorkeling, boating, fishing, horseback riding, meeting rooms, car rental; no room phones, no room TVs* ▤ *MC, V* 🍽 *FAP.*

**$$**   🏨 **Hotel Palmas de Cortés.** The Palmas is the cultural and social center for the East Cape. Often featured on sportfishing shows, the hotel is near the famed Cortez banks and has its own fleet. Its enormous pool has a swim-up bar. Some guest rooms have fireplaces and/or kitchens. Special events, including an annual arts festival in March, are big draws. This company has two other hotels in the area. ⊠ *On the beach; take the road north through Los Barriles and continue to the beach, Los Barriles* ✎ *Box 9016, Calabasas, CA 91372* ☎ *624/141–0214, 800/368–4334 in the U.S.* 🖨 *624/141–0046* ⊕ *www.bajaresorts.com* 🛏 *20 rooms, 15 suites, 10 condos* ⟁ *Restaurant, tennis court, pool, gym, fishing, playground, Internet, airstrip, meeting rooms* ▤ *MC, V* 🍽 *FAP.*

**$$**   🏨 **Hotel Punta Pescadero.** This secluded resort is one of the most peaceful spots in Baja. Rooms have private waterfront terraces, separate living rooms, and fireplaces and are reserved far in advance by regulars who enjoy the sense of complete escape—miles of windswept beach and calm coves with superb snorkeling. The staff can arrange tours to local sights. ⊠ *Camino de Los Barriles a El Cardonal, 23000 Punta Pescadero, 12 km (7 mi) north of Los Barriles* ☎ *624/121–0101, 800/426–2252 in the U.S.* 🖨 *624/126–1771* ⊕ *www.puntapescadero.com* 🛏 *21 rooms* ⟁ *Restaurant, refrigerators, in-room VCRs, pool, beach, dive shop, fishing, airstrip* ▤ *MC, V.*

## Sports & the Outdoors

Water-sports equipment and boat trips are available through area hotels, although regulars tend to bring their own gear and rent cars to reach isolated spots. Windsurfers take over the East Cape in winter, when stiff breezes provide ideal conditions. **VelaWindsurf** (☎ 800/223–5443 in the

U.S. ⊕ www.velawindsurf.com) offers windsurfing and kite-boarding lessons and trips to the East Cape from November to March.

## Shopping

The **Plaza Del Pueblo** (✉ Carretera 1, Los Barriles) is the area's most complete shopping opportunity. The small shopping center includes an Internet café, a tackle store, an ice cream parlor, and a bakery.

# Los Cabos

**38**–**45** *195 km (121 mi) south of La Paz.*

At the southern tip of the Baja California peninsula, the land ends in a rocky point called El Arco (The Arch), a place of stark beauty. The desert ends in sandy coves, with cactus standing at their entrances like sentries under the soaring palm trees, and the warm waters of the Mar de Cortés swirl into the Pacific Ocean's rugged surf.

The conquistadors focused their attention on La Paz during expeditions from mainland Mexico in the mid-1500s. Well aware of the loot to be had, pirates found the peninsula's tip ideal for spotting Spanish galleons traveling from the Philippines to central Mexico. In their turn, missionaries came to convert the few thousand local Indians who lived in mountain villages. The Jesuits established the mission of San José del Cabo in the mid-18th century, but their settlements didn't last long. The missionaries (and other Europeans) brought syphilis and smallpox along with their preachings, and the susceptible indigenous population was nearly wiped out after a few decades.

Anglers discovered this remote region in the 20th century. When pilots flew over Baja during World War II, they spotted the swirling waters and fertile fishing grounds from the air, and word soon spread. Wealthy adventurers with private planes and boats created a demand for fishing lodges, airstrips, and other services, and the region became a cult destination. By the 1960s a half dozen exclusive resorts were thriving on the cliffs and shores amid the barren landscape.

Connected by a 32-km (20-mi) stretch of highway called the Corridor, the two towns of Cabo San Lucas and San José del Cabo were distinct until the late 1970s, when the Mexican government's office of tourism development targeted Baja's southern tip for resort development and dubbed the area Los Cabos. The destination now consists of three major areas: San José del Cabo, Cabo San Lucas, and the Corridor.

Los Cabos has become one of Mexico's most popular and most expensive coastal getaways, with deluxe hotels, championship golf courses, and some of the world's best sportfishing. Hotels in this area have some of the highest room rates in the country. A few elegant spots command $500 or more a night for enormous suites; more mainstream accommodations run $200 or more per night. Budget rooms are extremely difficult to find. Expect to pay $60 for the most basic lodgings.

The population growth rate here is among the fastest in Mexico. The area's infrastructure received much-needed improvements when APEC

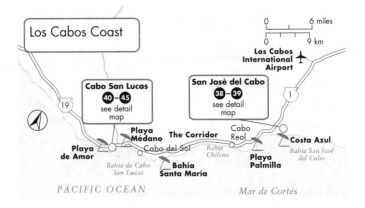

(the Asian Pacific Economic Conference) brought world leaders to town for a conference in 2002. For instance, a toll road was built from the airport to the Corridor, reducing driving time (though local cab drivers don't feel it's worth the $3 toll). But despite all the development that has taken place, and the steep prices that have come along with it, the area remains a natural hideaway.

The best way to see the sights of Los Cabos is on foot. Downtown San José and Cabo San Lucas are compact, with the plaza, church, shops, and restaurants a few blocks from one another. Bus service runs between the towns, with stops along the Corridor. If you plan to dine at the Corridor hotels or travel frequently between the two towns, it's a good idea to rent a car for a few days. As for the beaches, remember that red flags warn of unsafe swimming conditions, yellow flags indicate that you should use caution, and green flags show safe swimming areas. There are no lifeguards on area beaches.

### San José del Cabo

San José del Cabo is the municipal headquarters for Los Cabos. The hotel zone faces a long stretch of waterfront on the Mar de Cortés. The downtown area with its adobe houses and jacaranda trees is the loveliest part of Los Cabos. Entrepreneurs have converted old homes into stylish restaurants and shops, and the government has enlarged and beautified the main plaza. A 9-hole golf course and residential community are south of the town center. Despite the development—and bumper-to-bumper traffic that often clogs streets on weekdays—San José remains the more peaceful of the two towns. If you want exciting nightlife and a rowdy beach scene, consider staying in Cabo San Lucas.

**38** **Boulevard Mijares,** the main street in town, runs roughly perpendicular to the sea. Its north end abuts Avenida Zaragoza, a spot marked by a long fountain; the modest yellow city hall, the Palacio Municipal, is also here. The boulevard's south end has been designated a tourist zone, with Los Cabos Club de Golf as its centerpiece. A few reasonably priced hotels and large all-inclusives are perpendicular to the boulevard (about a 10-minute walk from shops and restaurants) on a long beach that's beautiful but whose rough surf makes swimming dangerous. The estuary at the end of the hotel zone, once a good spot for bird-watching, has dried up. A large marina development is underway north of here.

**39** Locals and travelers mingle at the large, central **Plaza Mijares,** which has a white wrought-iron gazebo and green benches in the shade. Small concerts and art shows are sometimes held here. The town's church, Iglesia San José, looms above the plaza. Be sure to walk up to the front and see the tile mural of a captured priest being dragged toward a fire by Indians.

BEACHES **Playa Hotelera** is the stretch of beach where most of San José's hotels are. It's beautiful, but the current is dangerously rough, and swimming isn't advised. The best swimming beach near San José is **Playa Palmilla,** which is protected by a rocky point south of town. The northern part of the beach is cluttered with boats and shacks, but if you walk south you'll reach the Hotel Palmilla beach, a long stretch of tan sand and calm sea.

WHERE TO STAY ✕ **Mi Cocina.** Torches glow on the dining terrace here, and the tables are
& EAT spaced far enough apart so that you don't have to share your sweet noth-
**$$$–$$$$** ings with a neighbor. You could start with a tequila martini and a
Fodor'sChoice tequila-cured salmon appetizer. Main courses, such as filet mignon with
★ a potato-leek galette (flat cake), look beyond Mexico. ⊠ *Casa Natalia, Blvd. Mijares 4, Centro* ☎ *624/142–5100* ▭ *AE, MC, V.*

**$$–$$$** ✕ **Tequila Restaurante.** An old adobe home serves as the setting for this classy restaurant. The lengthy tequila list gives you a chance to savor the finer brands of Mexico's national drink, and the menu challenges you to decide between excellent Mexican dishes and innovative Pacific Rim spring rolls, salads, and seafood with tequila sauces. ⊠ *Manuel Doblado s/n, Centro* ☎ *624/142–1155* ▭ *No credit cards.*

**$–$$$** ✕ **Damiana.** At this small hacienda beside the plaza, past the center of town, bougainvillea wraps around the tall pines that surround wrought-iron tables, and pink adobe walls glow in the candlelight. Start with fiery oysters diablo, then move on to the tender chateaubriand, charbroiled lobster, or the signature shrimp steak, made with ground shrimp. ⊠ *Blvd. Mijares 8* ☎ *624/142–0499* ▭ *AE, MC, V.*

**$–$$$** ✕ **Tropicana Bar and Grill.** Start the day with coffee and French toast at this enduringly popular restaurant. The back patio quickly fills for every meal with a loyal clientele that enjoys the garden setting. The menu includes U.S. cuts of beef and imported seafood along with fajitas, chiles rellenos, and lobster, always in demand. ⊠ *Blvd. Mijares 30, Centro* ☎ *624/142–1580* ▭ *AE, MC, V.*

**$$** ✕ **Fandango.** This quirky restaurant has an excellent reputation with residents, and its eclectic menu should please almost everyone. Try the sweet-potato fritters, Greek salad, or baby green beans with chilies and toasted almonds. A festive mural, Chinese umbrellas, and a candlelit patio bespeak Fandango's carefree style. ⊠ *Obregón 19, at Av. Morelos, Centro* ☎ *624/142–2226* ▭ *MC, V* ☺ *Closed Sun.*

★ **$–$$** ✕ **Baan Thai.** The aromas alone are enough to lead you through the door, where you're then greeted with visual and culinary delights. The formal dining room has Asian antiques, and a fountain murmurs on a patio. The chef blends Asian spices with aplomb, creating sublime pad thai,

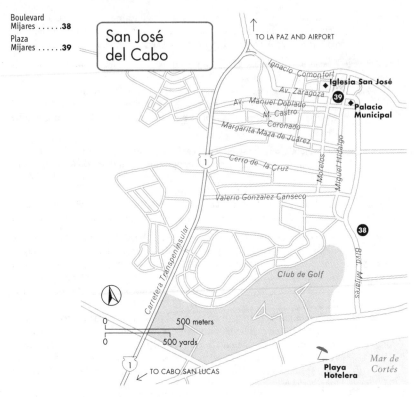

San José
del Cabo

↑
TO LA PAZ AND AIRPORT

Ignacio Comonfort
◆ **Iglesia San José**
Av. Zaragoza
**39**
Av. Manuel Doblado
◆**Palacio
Municipal**
M. Castro
Coronado
Margarita Maza de Juárez

① 

Cerro de la Cruz

Valerio González Canseco

Moretos

Miguel Hidalgo

**38**

Blvd. Mijares

*Club de Golf*

0  500 meters
0  500 yards

①  TO CABO SAN LUCAS

**Playa
Hotelera**

*Mar de
Cortés*

brandy and garlic lamb chops with peanut sauce, and the catch of the
day with lemon black bean sauce. Prices are reasonable for such memorable food. ⊠ *Morelos and Obregón, across from El Encanto Inn, Centro* ☎ *624/142–3344* ☰ *MC, V* ⊘ *Closed Sun.*

⟲ ¢–$  ✕ **Baja Natural.** Tucked down a flight of steps away from the busy
streets, this low-key kid-pleaser is a good place to cool off with fresh-
fruit smoothies, juices, shakes, or power drinks. Hamburgers, hot dogs,
and veggie burgers round out the options. ⊠ *Manuel Doblado, between
Morelos and Hidalgo, Centro* ☎ *624/142–3105* ☰ *No credit cards*
⊘ *Closed Sun. No dinner.*

$$$   ☷ **Casa Natalia.** Standing gracefully on San José's most charming street
**Fodor'sChoice**   is this beautiful boutique hotel. Rooms are done in regional Mexican
★   motifs and have king-size beds, remote-control a/c, private patios, and
cushy robes. Suites have hot tubs and hammocks on large terraces. A
free shuttle takes you to a beach club in the Corridor. The staff mem-
bers—as well as as the owners, who live on the premises—are welcoming,
and the service is personalized. The restaurant, Mi Cocina, noteworthy.
⊠ *Blvd. Mijares 4, Centro 23400* ☎ *624/142–5100, 888/277–3814 in
the U.S.* 🖷 *624/142–5110* ⊕ *www.casanatalia.com* ⇝ *14 rooms, 2 suites*
☖ *Restaurant, room service, in-room safes, cable TV, pool, massage,
bar, concierge, laundry services* ☰ *AE, MC, V* ⧉ *CP.*

✿ **$$–$$$** ⊞ **Presidente Inter-Continental Los Cabos.** Cactus gardens surround this hotel, which seems odd as water is never far away. The hotel is next to the estuary and has three sections centered by pools and lounging areas. Ground-floor rooms, which have terraces, are the best. All rooms have showers instead of tubs. There's no end to the dining options: room service; elegant restaurants; themed buffets; and food carts that sell nachos, hot dogs, and fries. ⊠ *Paseo San José, at end of hotel zone, 23400* ☎ *624/142–0211, 800/327–0200 in the U.S.* 🖷 *624/142–0232* ⊕ *hotels. loscabos.interconti.com* ➥ *395 rooms, 7 suites* ⚖ *3 restaurants, room service, in-room data ports, in-room safes, cable TV, 3 tennis courts, 3 pools, beach, fishing, horseback riding, children's programs (ages 5–12), shops, laundry services, business services, meeting rooms, car rental, travel services, no-smoking rooms* ⊟ *AE, MC, V* ⵔ⍈ *All-inclusive.*

**$** ⊞ **Posada Terranova.** San José's best inexpensive hotel is a friendly place where guests return so frequently they're almost part of the family. The large rooms have two double beds and tile bathrooms. You can congregate at the front patio tables or in the restaurant and it still feels like a private home. ⊠ *Calle Degollado at Av. Zaragoza, Centro 23400* ☎ *624/142–0534* 🖷 *624/142–0902* ⊕ *www.hterranova.com.mx* ➥ *25 rooms* ⚖ *Restaurant, room service, cable TV, bar* ⊟ *AE, MC, V.*

**$** ⊞ **Tropicana Inn.** This small hotel is a great option if you aren't desperate to be on the beach. The stucco buildings, which have tile murals of Diego Rivera paintings, frame a pool and palapa bar in a quiet enclave behind San José's main boulevard. Rooms are maintained to look brand-new. ⊠ *Blvd. Mijares 30, Centro 23400* ☎ *624/142–1580* 🖷 *624/142–1590* ⊕ *www.tropicanacabo.com* ➥ *39 rooms, 2 suites* ⚖ *Restaurant, room service, minibars, cable TV, pool, bar, free parking* ⊟ *AE, MC, V* ⵔ⍈ *CP.*

**¢–$** ⊞ **Posada Señor Mañana.** Accommodations at this eccentric place run the gamut from small, no-frills rooms to larger rooms with air-conditioning, fans, cable TV, coffeemakers, and refrigerators. Hammocks hang on an upstairs deck, and you can store food and prepare meals in the communal kitchen. The owners also have inexpensive cabañas by the beach. ⊠ *Obregón. by the Casa de la Cultura, Centro 23400* ☎ *624/142–0462* 🖷 *624/142–1199* ⊕ *www.srmanana.net* ➥ *11 rooms* ⚖ *Fans; no a/c in some rooms, no TV in some rooms* ⊟ *MC, V.*

NIGHTLIFE San José's nightlife is subdued; there are no bars like the raucous joints in San Lucas. At **Havanas** (⊠ Carretera 1, Km 29 ☎ No phone), the excellent jazz band of owner-singer Sheila Mihevic plays in the hip club Wednesday through Friday. Guides who work with kayaking and adventure-tourism companies hang out at **Rawhide** (⊠ Obregón, at Guerrero ☎ 624/142–3626). Tropicana Inn guests, other visitors, and locals mingle at the **Tropicana Bar and Grill** (⊠ Blvd. Mijares 30 ☎ 624/142–1580), an old standby.

SPORTS & **Ecotours. Baja Wild** (⊠ Obregón, at Guerrero ☎ 624/148–2222 or 624/
THE OUTDOORS 142–5300 ⊕ www.bajawild.com) offers hikes to canyons, hot springs,
★ a fossil-rich area, and caves with rock paintings. It also runs diving, whale-watching, rock-climbing, and rappelling trips. A six-hour hike in the mountains costs $65. An ATV tour in the desert with rappelling runs $85.

**Fishing.** Most hotels in San José can arrange fishing trips. There's no marina in town, so you board your boat at the marina in Cabo San Lucas. The boats at **Gordo Banks Pangas** (✉ La Playa, near San José del Cabo ☎ 624/142–1147, 800/408–1199 in the U.S. ⊕ www.gordobanks.com) are near some of the hottest fishing spots in the Mar de Cortés: the famed Outer and Inner Gordo Banks. The price for three anglers runs from $180 to $220.

**Kayaking. Baja Wild** (✉ Obregón, at Guerrero, San José ☎ 624/148–2222 or 624/142–5300 ⊕ www.bajawild.com) has kayak tours at Cabo Pulmo that cost $95 for a full-day tour. Kayak tours and rentals are available through **Los Lobos del Mar** (✉ Brisas del Mar RV park, on the south side of San José ☎ 624/142–2983). The tours paddle along the Corridor's peaceful bays and are especially fun in winter when gray whales pass by offshore. Prices start at $30.

**Surfing.** For good surfing tips, rentals, and lessons, head to **Costa Azul Surf Shop** (✉ Carretera 1, Km 28, along the Corridor ☎ 624/142–2771 ⊕ www.costa-azul.com.mx). Surfboards rent for $20 a day.

SHOPPING  San José's shops and galleries carry gorgeous, high-quality folk art, jewelry, and housewares. In fact, serious shoppers staying elsewhere should plan on splurging here. **ADD** (✉ Av. Zaragoza at Hidalgo ☎ 624/143–2055), an interior-design shop, sells hand-painted dishes from Guanajuato and carved wood furniture from Michoacán. Across from City Hall is **Almacenes Goncanseco** (✉ Blvd. Mijares 18 ☎ No phone), where you can get film, postcards, groceries, and liquor. **Amigos Smokeshop and Cigar Bar** (✉ Calle Doblado at Av. Morelos ☎ 624/142–1138) is a classy shop and cigar bar that sells fine Cuban and Mexican cigars and Casa Noble tequila. Look for visiting celebs here.

**Los Castillo** (✉ Av. Zaragoza at Hidalgo ☎ 624/142–4717) carries original jewelry pieces from the famed Taxco designers. **Copal** (✉ Plaza Mijares ☎ 624/142–3070) has carved animals from Oaxaca, masks from Guerrero Negro, and heavy wooden furnishings. For fresh produce, flowers, meat, fish, and a sampling of local life in San José, visit the **Mercado**
★ **Municipal,** off Calle Doblado. **Veryka** (✉ Blvd. Mijares 6B ☎ 624/142–0575) is associated with galleries in San Miguel de Allende and Oaxaca, two of Mexico's finest art centers. This shop's *huipiles* (embroidered blouses), masks, tapestries, and pottery are coveted by collectors.

## The Corridor
Many of the legendary fishing lodges and exclusive resorts built before the government stepped in were along the wild cliffs between San José del Cabo and Cabo San Lucas. Since the mid-1980s the area has developed as a destination unto itself. It has several private communities, large-scale resorts, and championship golf courses. Much of the development has taken place in Cabo Real and Cabo del Sol. The venerable 1950s Palmilla hotel is emblematic of recent changes; at this writing it's being renovated and is slated to have a spa, a new restaurant, and villas. The highway along the Corridor has four lanes and well-marked turnoffs for the hotels.

BEACHES  **Bahía Chileno,** 16 km (9 mi) west of San José del Cabo and 16 km (9 mi) east of Cabo San Lucas, is ideal for swimming and snorkeling. Its beach skirts a small, crescent-shape cove with aquamarine water. The Hotel Cabo San Lucas is on a rocky cliff at the beach's western end. Along the eastern edge, some 200 yards away, are boulders you can climb. On the trek down you may see some stray wrappers and cans, but the beach itself is clean and usually not too crowded. In winter this part of the Mar de Cortés gets chilly.

Rugged brown cliffs protect the tan-sand cove of **Bahía Santa María,** which is 19 km (11 mi) west of San José del Cabo and 13 km (8 mi) east of Cabo San Lucas. This bay is a great place to snorkel: hundreds of brightly colored fish swarm through chunks of white coral. There's usually someone on the beach renting gear for $10 per day. From San José del Cabo, take a left off Carretera 1 about 2½ km (1½ mi) after the Hotel Cabo San Lucas; from San Lucas, watch for a sign on the right of Carretera 1 designating the beach turnoff. Take your second left at the sign that reads ACCESSO A ZONA FEDERAL (ACCESS TO FEDERAL ZONE).

**Costa Azul,** east of Cabo Real, is the most popular surfing beach in Los Cabos. A few small campgrounds and casual restaurants line the beach. **Playa Palmilla** is one of the Corridor's best swimming beaches.

WHERE TO STAY
& EAT
$$$–$$$$

✕ **C.** Famed Chicago chef Charlie Trotter is behind this restaurant in the One & Only Palmilla resort. Cylindrical aquariums separate the open kitchen from the dining room. An open-air bar has seating areas overlooking the rocky coastline. Trotter's menu emphasizes vegetables—salsify, wax beans, turnips—and creative fish and meat side dishes. Tuna with crispy polenta, grouper with jasmine rice and napa cabbage, or squab with butternut-squash risotto might appear on the menu, which changes daily. ✉ *Carretera 1, Km 7.5* ☎ *624/146–7000* ⚓ *Reservations essential* ▭ *MC, V* ✆ *No lunch.*

★ $$$–$$$$

✕ **Pitahayas.** This elegant restaurant occupies a lovely niche above the beach at Cabo del Sol. The dishes are an unusual blend of Thai, Polynesian, and Chinese influences. Lobster might have a vanilla bean sauce, octopus turns up in a spicy salad, and the catch of the day comes with a refreshing mango relish. Soft live jazz plays in the background, and the service is impeccable. Dress to impress. ✉ *Sheraton Hacienda del Mar, Carretera 1, Km 10* ☎ *624/145–8010* ▭ *AE, MC, V.*

$$–$$$
Fodor'sChoice
★

✕ **Ristorante Da Giorgio.** Tables along the cliffs have full-on views of El Arco, making this the best possible place to toast the sunset. The food in the handsome candlelit dining room is outstanding as well. Lobster pasta, crab with garlic and olive oil, and pasta with anchovies and capers are all great choices. Dinner reservations are essential at this romantic place. ✉ *Carretera 1, Km 5.5* ☎ *624/145–8160* ▭ *MC, V.*

$–$$

✕ **Zippers.** Home to the surfing crowd and those who don't mind a bit of sand in their burgers, this casual palapa-roof restaurant is on Costa Azul beach just south of San José. It's the place to be to watch sporting events on TV. ✉ *Carretera 1, Km 18.5* ☎ *No phone* ▭ *No credit cards.*

★ $$$$

🏨 **Casa del Mar Beach, Golf & Spa Resort.** It's all about luxurious privacy at this hacienda-style hotel. A hand-carved door leads into the courtyard-lobby, and stairways curve up to the rooms, spa, and library. Guest quarters have bathrooms with whirlpool bathtubs a few steps above the main bedroom. A series of flowing streams, fountains, and gardens leads around the pool to a wide stretch of beach. The restaurant is excellent. ⊠ *Carretera 1, Km 19.5, 23410* ☎ *624/145–7700, 888/227–9621 in the U.S.* 🖷 *624/144–0034* ⊕ *www.casadelmargolfandspa.com* ↘ *25 rooms, 31 suites* ♢ *Restaurant, room service, in-room data ports, in-room safes, cable TV, in-room hot tubs, golf privileges, pool, spa, beach, 4 tennis courts, airport shuttle* ⊟ *AE, MC, V.*

**$$$$** 🏨 **Esperanza.** Created by the prestigious Auberge Resorts, this inn is ut-
**Fodor's Choice** terly polished. Rooms have handcrafted furnishings, Frette linens, and
★ dual-head showers; villas take the luxe even further with private pools and butler service. French and Mexican recipes get a Baja twist in the restaurant. At the spa you can relax with a stone massage or bask in a steam cave; it's open to nonguests by appointment. ⊠ *Carretera 1, Km 3.5, 23410* ☎ *624/145–8641, 866/311–2226 in the U.S.* 🖷 *624/145–8651* ⊕ *www.esperanzaresort.com* ↘ *50 suites, 6 villas* ♢ *Restaurant, in-room data ports, in-room safes, minibars, cable TV, in-room DVD players, pool, gym, spa, beach, shops, concierge, laundry service, meeting rooms* ⊟ *AE, MC, V.*

★ **$$$$** 🏨 **Marquis Los Cabos.** Stunning architecture, attention to detail, and loads of luxurious touches attract a wealthy clientele to the Marquis. Suites have Bulgari toiletries, reversible mattresses (hard or soft), high-speed Internet connections, and original art. Casitas also have private pools and are right on the beach. The serpentine swimming pool curves along the edge of the sand, beneath waterfalls. Food is excellent and reasonably priced. ⊠ *Carretera 1, Km 21.5, 23410* ☎ *624/144–0906, 877/238–9399 in the U.S.* 🖷 *624/144–0905* ⊕ *www.marquisloscabos.com* ↘ *209 suites, 28 casitas* ♢ *3 restaurants, room service, in-room data ports, in-room safes, in-room hot tubs, minibars, cable TV, golf privileges, pool, gym, spa, beach, bar, shop, concierge floor, Internet, business services, meeting rooms, airport shuttle, car rental, travel services, no-smoking rooms* ⊟ *AE, MC, V* ⦿❘ *CP.*

**$$$$** 🏨 **One & Only Palmilla.** Developer Sol Kerzner (Sun City, Atlantis) spent
**Fodor's Choice** $90 million transforming a small hotel into a world-class resort with a
★ spa, a Charlie Trotter restaurant called C, and a Jack Nicklaus golf course. Two pools seem to flow over low cliffs to the sea. Tiled stairways lead to rooms and suites, where beds are overloaded with pillows, bathtubs are deep, and water in the shower truly rains down upon you. Your quarters also have Bose sound systems, flat-screen TVs, and high-speed Internet access (at this writing wi-fi is in the works). Some patios and terraces have daybeds and straight-on sea views. ⊠ *Carretera 1, Km 7.5, 23400* ☎ *624/146–7000, 800/637–2226 in the U.S.* 🖷 *624/146–7001* ⊕ *www.oneandonlypalmilla.com* ↘ *61 rooms, 91 junior suites, 20 1-bedroom suites* ♢ *2 restaurants, room service, fans, in-room data ports, in-room safes, minibars, cable TV, in-room DVDs, 27-hole golf course, putting green, 2 tennis courts, pro shop, 2 pools, outdoor hot tub, fitness center, massage, spa, beach, snorkeling, boating, 3 bars, shop, baby-sitting, laundry service, concierge, business services, meeting rooms, airport shuttle, car rental, travel services, no-smoking rooms* ⊟ *AE, MC, V.*

★ **$$$$** 🏨 **Las Ventanas al Paraíso.** All suites have hot tubs, fireplaces, and telescopes for viewing whales at sea and stars at night. The hotel is filled with handcrafted lamps and doors, sculpture, and paintings. The service is sublime, the restaurants are outstanding, and the spa has the latest treatments. There's even a program for pets. There's a minimum night stay for weekends depending on the season. ⊠ *Carretera 1, Km 19.5, 23400* ☎ *624/144–0300, 888/767–3966 in the U.S.* 📠 *624/144–0301* ⊕ *www.lasventanas.com* 🛏 *61 suites* ⚐ *2 restaurants, in-room data ports, in-room safes, in-room hot tubs, cable TV, in-room VCRs, 2 tennis courts, 2 pools, hot tub, spa, beach, fishing, 2 bars, some pets allowed* ▭ *AE, MC, V* ⧆ *EP, FAP, MAP.*

**$$$–$$$$** 🏨 **Hotel Cabo San Lucas.** Looking like a mountain lodge nearly buried in palms, this long-standing Corridor hotel is a favorite of Baja devotees. Rooms are furnished with cheery yellow and blue fabrics and light-wood pieces; suites and villas are more luxurious with large terraces. The hacienda-style buildings are right above Chileno Beach, one of the best diving spots in Los Cabos. The gift shop is worth a look even if you're not staying here. ⊠ *Carretera 1, Km 14.5, 23410* ☎ *624/144–0014, 323/512–3799 or 866/733–2226 in the U.S.* 📠 *624/144–0015, 323/512–3815 in the U.S.* ⊕ *www.hotelcabo.com* 🛏 *89 rooms, 7 villas* ⚐ *Restaurant, in-room safes, minibars, cable TV, pool, beach, dive shop, fishing, bar, shop, laundry service* ▭ *AE, MC, V.*

**$$** 🏨 **Casa Terra Cotta.** In the hills above Playa Costa Azul, this tiny bed-and-breakfast consists of four small villas, secluded in gardens. All have arched brick roofs, terra-cotta tile floors, and verandas ideal for whale-watching. The enormous breakfasts, made entirely with homegrown or organic ingredients, are legendary. You can use the kitchen facilities for a fee. Reserve at least six weeks in advance. ⊠ *Carretera 1, Km 28.5, ½ km (¼ mi) up hill, 23410* ☎ *624/142–4250* ⊕ *www.terracotta-mex. com* 🛏 *5 rooms, 1 suite* ⚐ *Dining room, no in-room TVs, massage, bar, laundry service* ▭ *MC, V* ⧆ *BP.*

SPORTS &
THE OUTDOORS
**ATV Tours. Desert Park** (⊠ Cabo Real, across from Meliá Cabo Real hotel, Corridor ☎ 624/144–0127) leads ATV tours through the desert arroyos and canyons on the inland side of the Cabo Real development. Fees start at $50 per person.

**Diving and Snorkeling. Bahía Chileno,** a white-sand cove protected by towering brown cliffs, has superb snorkeling. There's a concession stand on the beach with snorkeling-gear rental run by Cabo Acuadeportes; you can also rent gear at the outfitter's Cabo San Lucas shop.

**Fishing.** Most Corridor hotels have excellent fishing fleets, with the boats anchored at the marina in Cabo San Lucas. Hotels can set up the trips and provide box lunches and transportation to the marina. **Jig Stop Tours** (☎ 800/521–2281 in the U.S.) books fishing trips for several Los Cabos fleets. **Victor's Sport Fishing** (☎ 624/142–1092) has a fleet of pangas on the Palmilla resort's beach. Rates start at $180.

**Golf.** Los Cabos has been the sight of many tournaments, including the PGA Senior Grand Slam. The courses that have brought so much attention this way are all centerpieces for mega-resort developments. Expect to pay exorbitant greens fees—nearly $200 in winter, and $140 in summer. **Cabo del Sol** (☎ 624/145–8200, 800/386–2405 in the U.S.) has an 18-hole Jack Nicklaus course and an 18-hole Tom Weiskopf course.

The Robert Trent Jones Jr.–designed **Cabo Real Golf Club** (✉ Meliá Cabo Real hotel ☎ 624/144–0040, 800/393–0400 in the U.S.) has 18 holes.

★ The **El Dorado** (☎ 624/144–5451, 800/393–0400 in the U.S.), an 18-hole Jack Nicklaus course, covers rough seaside terrain in Cabo Real. Among the most spectacular golf courses is the 27-hole Jack Nicklaus–designed

★ course at the **Palmilla Golf Club** (✉ Palmilla resort, Carretera 1, Km 1 ☎ 624/144–5250, 800/637–2226 in the U.S.).

★ **Horseback Riding.** The **Cuadra San Francisco Equestrian Center** (✉ Carretera 1 across from Cabo Real development ☎ 624/144–0160) is a professional center with lessons and trail rides. Treks through back canyons are more interesting than those along the beach, and the horses and guides are both excellent. Trail rides begin at $35; reservations are a must.

## Cabo San Lucas

Cabo San Lucas is decidedly *in*—for its rowdy nightlife, its slew of trendy restaurants, and its shopping. The sportfishing fleet is headquartered here, cruise ships anchor off the marina, and there seems to be a massive hotel on every available plot of waterfront turf—alas, a five-story condo-hotel complex along the bay blocks the view from the town's side streets. Most of the shops, services, and restaurants are between Avenida Cárdenas and the waterfront. The area around the Cárdenas stoplight leading into town by the Puerto Paraíso mall is also busy.

🔞 The main downtown street, Avenida Lázaro Cárdenas, passes the **Plaza Amelia Wilkes,** with its white wrought-iron gazebo. Buildings around the plaza house galleries and restaurants.

🔞 Across from Plaza Amelia Wilkes, a whale skeleton sits outside the small **Museo de Las Californias,** which houses exhibits on southern Baja's fossils and indigenous communities. It's a modest endeavor, but worth your interest and support. ✉ *Av. Hidalgo* ☎ *624/143–0187* 💲 *$1* 🕑 *Tues.–Sat. 8–3.*

🔞 The sportfishing fleet is docked in **Bahía de Cabo San Lucas,** and glass-bottom boats are available at the water's edge.

🔞 Paved walkways run from the busy Boulevard Marina to the hotels and beaches on the east end of town and west to **Mercado de Artesanías** (Artisans Market) at the marina.

★ 🔞 **El Arco,** the most spectacular sight in Cabo San Lucas, is a natural rock arch. It's visible from the marina and from some hotels, but it's more impressive from the water. To fully appreciate Cabo, take at least a short boat ride out to the arch and Playa de Amor, the beach underneath it.

🔞 **El Faro de Cabo Falso** (Lighthouse of the False Cape) was built in 1890 amid sand dunes and on cliffs above the Pacific coast. You need a four-wheel-drive vehicle to reach it by land; most hotels can arrange tours.

BEACHES **Playa de Amor,** at the very end of the peninsula, has a peaceful azure
FodorśChoice cove on its Mar de Cortés side and pounding white surf on its Pacific
★ Ocean side. The contrast is dramatic. **Playa Hacienda,** in the inner harbor by the Hacienda Hotel, has the calmest waters of any beach in
🕗 town, and there's good snorkeling around the rocky point. **Playa Mé-**

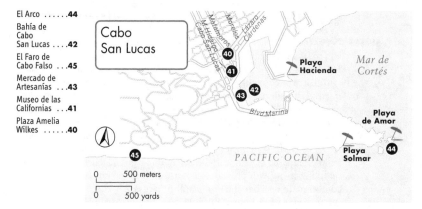

**dano,** just north of Cabo San Lucas, is the most popular stretch in Los Cabos (and possibly in all Baja) for sunbathing and people-watching. The 3-km (2-mi) span of white sand is always crowded, especially on weekends. **Playa Solmar,** on the fringe of the Solmar Hotel, is a beautiful wide beach but it has dangerous surf with a swift undertow. Stick to sunbathing here.

WHERE TO STAY
& EAT
☺ **$$$–$$$$**

✕ **Edith's Café.** The Caesar salad and flambéed crepes are served tableside at this small café, where dinners are accompanied by Mexican trios or soft jazz. Even the simplest items are enhanced: quesadillas have Oaxacan cheese and homemade tortillas, and meat and fish dishes are given unusual chili or tropical fruit sauces. The place sometimes bustles with families in early evening, so dine later if you're looking for romance. ✉ *Paseo del Pescador, near Playa Médano* ☎ *624/143–0801* ▭ *MC, V.*

**$$$–$$$$**
Fodor'sChoice
★

✕ **Sancho Panza.** The sophisticated menu, decor, and live jazz make this small bistro an excellent spot for a lingering dinner. Try the steamed mussels, flank steak stuffed with goat cheese, and sublime wahoo in a savory broth. The menu changes constantly, as does the art in the Dalíesque bar and the extraordinary selection of imported wines in the wine warehouse. Wine and tequila tastings are held frequently. ✉ *Blvd. Marina, behind KFC and Plaza Las Glorias* ☎ *624/143–3212* ▭ *AE, MC, V.*

**$$–$$$$**
Fodor'sChoice
★

✕ **Nick San.** A creative fusion of Japanese and Mexican cuisines truly sets this place apart. How about panfried curry-flavored oysters in cucumber sauce, lobster and vegetable tempura, or a platter of rosy pink sashimi? The lunch menu includes noodle and curry dishes. Watch the chefs at work in the open kitchen or at the handsome mahogany sushi bar, where everything is deftly prepared. ✉ *Blvd. Marina, next to Plaza Las Glorias Centro* ☎ *624/143–4484* ▭ *MC, V.*

☺ **$$–$$$**

✕ **Mi Casa.** One of Cabo's best restaurants is in a cobalt-blue building painted with a mural of a burro, near the main plaza. The fresh tuna and dorado, served with tomatillo salsa or Yucatecan achiote, both shine, as does the sophisticated poblano chiles *en nogada* (stuffed with a meat-and-fruit mixture and covered with white walnut sauce and pomegranate seeds). The large back courtyard is especially nice at night, when it glows with candlelight. ✉ *Av. Cabo San Lucas* ☎ *624/143–1933* 🖃 *MC, V* ☺ *No lunch Sun.*

☺ **$$–$$$** ✗ **Pancho's.** Owner John Bragg has an enormous collection of tequilas, and an encyclopedic knowledge of the stuff. Sample one or two of the 500 labels and you may feel truly festive amid the Oaxacan tablecloths, murals, painted chairs, and streamers than you did when you first arrived. Try regional specialties like tortilla soup or chiles rellenos. The breakfast and lunch specials are a bargain. ✉ *Hidalgo, between Zapata and Serdan* ☎ *624/143–2891* 🖃 *AE, MC, V.*

**$$–$$$** ✗ **Sea Queen.** The service is attentive at this seafood restaurant, despite the fact that the staff must move through an enormous dining room. Fresh sushi is prepared in view, and the chef adds a regional flair to his fish dishes by fixing them with poblano, guajillo, or chipotle chilies. The Mexican combo plate or Thai chicken salad should satisfy those who shun fish. ✉ *Av. Cabo San Lucas at Blvd. Marina* ☎ *624/144–4731* 🖃 *MC, V.*

**$–$$$** ✗ **Mocambo.** Veracruz—a region known for its seafood preparations— meets Los Cabos in an enormous dining room packed with locals. The menu has such hard-to-find regional dishes as octopus ceviche, shrimp empanadas, and a heaping mixed seafood platter that includes sea snails, clams, and octopus, with lobster and shrimp. Musicians stroll among the tables and the chatter is somewhat cacophonous, but you're sure to have a great dining experience here. ✉ *Leona Vicario at Calle 20 de Noviembre* ☎ *624/143–2122* 🖃 *AE, MC, V.*

**$–$$** ✗ **Marisquería Mazatlán.** The crowds of locals lunching at this simple
**Fodor'sChoice** seafood restaurant are a good sign—as are the huge glasses packed
★ with shrimp, ceviche, and other seafood cocktails. You can dine inexpensively on wonderful seafood soup, or spend a bit more for tender *pulpo ajillo* (marinated octopus with garlic, chilies, onion, and celery). ✉ *Mendoza at Calle 16 de Septiembre* ☎ *624/143–8565* 🖃 *MC, V.*

**$–$$** ✗ **The Office.** Playa Médano is lined with cafés on the sand, some with lounge chairs, others with more formal settings. All serve the same basics—cold beer, snacks, fish tacos, french fries—and most accompany the meal with loud American rock. The Office, which has provided perfect vacation photo opportunities for more than a decade, is the best. ✉ *Playa Médano, Centro* ☎ *624/143–3464* 🖃 *MC, V.*

**¢–$** ✗ **Señor Greenberg's Mexicatessen.** Pastrami, chopped liver, knishes, bagels, lox, cheesecake—you can find them all behind the glass counters of this decent Mexican incarnation of a New York deli. It's open 24 hours; the a/c, stacks of newspapers, and soft music might pull you back more than once. ✉ *Plaza Nautica on Blvd. Marina* ☎ *624/143–7808* 🖃 *MC, V.*

**¢** ✗ **Gordo's Tortas.** Listen for the blaring Beatles' tunes to find Gordo's tiny sidewalk stand. His tacos and tortas (sandwiches) are made with loving care, and his fans are loyal enough to chow down on their feet as there are only two small plastic tables by the stand. You can have two or three ham and cheese tortas for the price of one elsewhere. ✉ *Guerrero at Zapata* ☎ *No phone* 🖃 *No credit cards.*

**$$$$** 🏨 **Meliá San Lucas.** The most popular beach in Los Cabos is the site of the Meliá and its huge, ever-packed pool areas, a hot tub under the palms, and all the equipment you could need for playing on and in the water. Rooms have easygoing light-wood furnishings and heavy drapes to block out the midday sun. Early reservations are essential. ⊠ *Playa Médano, 23410* ☎ *624/143–4444, 800/336–3542 in the U.S.* 🖷 *624/143–0418* ⊕ *www.solmelia.com* ⬐ *144 rooms, 6 suites* ⚐ *3 restaurants, in-room safes, minibars, cable TV, 2 pools, hot tub, beach, laundry service* ⊟ *AE, MC, V.*

★ **$$$–$$$$** ▦ **Solmar Suites.** The Solmar is against cliffs, facing the Pacific. Rooms are done in a Mexico–Santa Fe style, with tile baths. The adjacent condo units have kitchenettes and a private pool area. The surf here is far too dangerous for swimming, but don't miss a stroll along the wide strip of beach. The Solmar's sportfishing fleet is first-rate. The good restaurant hosts a Saturday-night Mexican fiesta and buffet dinner. ⊠ *Av. Solmar at Blvd. Marina* ⚐ *Apdo. 8, 23410* ☎ *624/143–3535, 310/459–9861 or 800/344–3349 in the U.S.* 🖷 *624/143–0410, 310/454–1686 in the U.S.* ⊕ *www.solmar.com* ⬐ *82 junior suites, 14 studios, 27 deluxe suites* ⚐ *Restaurant, in-room safes, minibars, cable TV, 3 pools, beach, fishing, bar, laundry service* ⊟ *AE, MC, V.*

☾ **$$$** ▦ **Hotel Hacienda.** The Hacienda resembles a Spanish colonial inn with white arches and bell towers, stone fountains, and statues of Indian gods set amid hibiscus and bougainvillea. The white rooms have red-tile floors, tile baths, and folk art. The water-sports center has any gear you might need. Though tiny, the wellness center offers excellent massages and holistic healing treatments. ⊠ *Playa Médano, 23410* ☎ *624/143–0665 or 624/143–0666, 800/733–2226 in the U.S.* 🖷 *624/143–0666* ⊕ *www.haciendacabo.com* ⬐ *60 rooms, 12 suites, 30 beachfront cabanas* ⚐ *Restaurant, in-room safes, some kitchenettes, cable TV, pool, gym, massage, beach, bar, shops, laundry service* ⊟ *AE, MC, V.*

☾ **$$$** ▦ **Pueblo Bonito Rosé.** Mediterranean-style buildings curve around elegant grounds, statues reminiscent of Roman busts guard reflecting pools, and Flemish tapestries adorn the lobby. Even the smallest suites can accommodate four people, and all have private balconies overlooking the grounds. (Not that many suites are time-share units; the salespeople here are sometimes too aggressive, so make it clear from the start if you don't want to be bothered.) ⊠ *Playa Médano, 23410* ☎ *624/143–5500, 800/990–8250 in the U.S.* 🖷 *624/143–5979* ⊕ *www.pueblobonito. com* ⬐ *260 suites* ⚐ *2 restaurants, in-room safes, kitchenettes, minibars, cable TV, pool, spa, beach, laundry service* ⊟ *MC, V.*

**$$** ▦ **Bungalows Breakfast Inn.** If solitude and a reasonable room rate are more important than being in the center of the action, this is your place, 10 blocks from the beach. Several two-story buildings frame a small, heated pool. Mexican textiles and art ornament the rooms. ⊠ *Calle Constitución, 5 blocks from main plaza, 23410* ☎ *888/424–2252 in the U.S.* 🖷🖷 *624/143–5035* ⊕ *www.cabobungalows.com* ⬐ *16 suites* ⚐ *Cable TV, in-room VCRs, pool; no smoking* ⊟ *No credit cards* ❙◐❙ *BP.*

**$** ▦ **Cabo Inn.** The small, comfortable rooms at this palapa-roof hotel have tangerine and cobalt sponge-painted walls and stained-glass windows above the headboards. The eight rooms on the lower level have refrigerators; a kitchen, barbecue and picnic area, and a television round out the communal amenities. ⊠ *Calle 20 de Noviembre and Vicario, 23410* 🖷🖷 *624/143–0819* ⬐ *21 rooms* ⚐ *Picnic area, refrigerators; no room TVs* ⊟ *No credit cards.*

**$** 🏨 **Los Milagros.** A mosaic sign (made by Ricardo Rode) near the entrance hints at the beauty inside this small inn in the town center. Brilliant purple bougainvillea and orange lipstick vines line the patio, which showcases more of Rode's works by the fountain and small pool. *Boveda*-style (arched brick) roofs top the rooms, which have terra-cotta–tile floors and handmade Guadalajaran furniture. One room is accessible to travelers with disabilities. Book early at this Cabo bargain. ⊠ *Matamoros 116, 23410* ☎ *718/928–6647 in the U.S.* ☎🖶 *624/143–4566* ⊕ *www. losmilagros.com.mx* ⇨ *11 rooms* ⌂ *Some kitchenettes, cable TV, pool, library, laundry service, Internet, business services* ▭ *No credit cards.*

**$** 🏨 **Siesta Suites.** The proprietors keep a close eye on this three-story hotel—a calm refuge two blocks from the marina—and they offer great budget tips. There's no pool, but the suites have full-size refrigerators, and between the two double beds and wide padded couches that make excellent beds even for grown-ups, there's room to sleep quite a crew. A small restaurant and wine bar beside the hotel serves tapas and full dinners. ⊠ *Calle Zapata* ✉ *Apdo. 310, 23410* ☎🖶 *624/143–6494; 866/ 271–0952 in the U.S.* ⊕ *www.cabosiestasuites.com* ⇨ *5 rooms, 15 suites* ⌂ *Kitchenettes, cable TV* ▭ *AE, MC, V.*

NIGHTLIFE    Some travelers choose Cabo San Lucas for its nightlife, which consists mainly of noisy bars with blaring music and plenty of dancing, flirting, and imbibing. The latest U.s. rock plays over an excellent sound system at **Cabo Wabo** (⊠ Calle Guerrero ☎ 624/143–1198), but the impromptu jam sessions with appearances by Sammy Hagar—an owner—and his many music-business friends are the real highlight. **El Galeón** (⊠ Blvd. Marina ☎ 624/143–0443) is a welcome refuge for the quieter crowd, who sip brandy by the piano bar. **Giggling Marlin** (⊠ Blvd. Marina ☎ 624/ 143–1182) seems to have been around forever as the favorite watering hole for anglers. **Sancho Panza Wine Bistro** (⊠ Plaza Las Glorias Hotel, Blvd. Marina ☎ 624/143–3212) is the place to sip imported wines served ★ by the glass while listening to live soft jazz or salsa. **Squid Roe** (⊠ Av. Cárdenas ☎ 624/143–0655) is packed with young foreigners who work in the local tourist industry and know how to party. **La Varitas** (⊠ Calle Gomez, behind Puerto Paraíso ☎ 624/143–9999) is a branch of a La Paz rock club favored by young Mexicans who love to dance.

SPORTS &    **Diving.** El Arco is a prime diving and snorkeling area, as are several rocky
THE OUTDOORS    points off the coast. Divers consider the sandfalls, an underwater cascade of sand that flows from 90 feet to 1,200 feet below sea level, an essential experience; many also undertake the two-hour boat trip to the coral reefs off Cabo Pulmo, off the East Cape. Most hotels can arrange diving trips and equipment rental.

The area's oldest and most complete dive shop is **Amigos del Mar** (⊠ Blvd. Marina, across from sportfishing docks ☎ 624/143–0505, 800/344–3349 in the U.S.). A one-tank dive costs $40; a two-hour snorkeling trip runs $25. **Cabo Acuadeportes** (⊠ Hotel Hacienda, Playa Médano ☎ 624/ 143–0117) offers dive trips (prices start at $40), rents snorkel gear, and can outfit you for just about every other water sport imaginable. **JT Water Sports** (⊠ Playa Médano ☎ 624/144–4566) rents all sorts of water- and land-sports equipment, including diving gear ($40), wave runners ($80 an hour), Windsurfers ($60 an hour), and parasails ($40 for roughly 10 minutes).

★ **Ecotours. Eco Tours de Baja** (✉ Zaragoza, at 5 de Febrero ☎ 624/143–0775) offers ecotours to Caduaño, a small community near the Sierra de la Laguna mountains. The tour includes a ride in a four-wheel-drive vehicle to a region rich in fossils. Other excursions include visits to the woodworking and leather factories in Miraflores and the waterfalls and lakes in the mountains. Trips, which start at $60, include a great barbecue lunch at a small ranch.

**Fishing.** More than 800 species of fish teem in the waters off Los Cabos. Most hotels will arrange fishing charters, which include a captain and mate, tackle, bait, licenses, and drinks. Prices start at about $325 per day for a 25-foot cruiser. Some charters provide lunch, and most can arrange to have your catch mounted, frozen, or smoked. Most of the boats leave from the sportfishing docks in the Cabo San Lucas marina. Usually there are a fair number of pangas for rent at about $30 per hour with a six-hour minimum.

The **Gaviota Fleet** (✉ Bahía Condo Hotel, Playa Médano ☎ 624/143–0430, 800/932–5599 in the U.S. ⊕ www.grupobahia.com) holds the record for the largest marlin caught in Cabo's waters. The company has charter cruisers and pangas. Minerva and John Smith oversee **Minerva's** (✉ Av. Madero, between Blvd. Marina and Guerrero ☎ 624/143–1282 ⊕ www.minervas.com), a renowned tackle store. The Minerva fleet has three charter fishing boats. Some of the Corridor's priciest hotels choose the **Pisces Sportfishing Fleet** (✉ Cabo Maritime Center, Blvd. Marina ☎ 624/143–1288 ⊕ www.piscessportfishing.com) for their guests. The fleet includes the usual 31-foot Bertrams and extraordinary 50- to 70-foot Hatteras cruisers with tuna towers and staterooms. The **Solmar Fleet** (✉ Blvd. Marina, across from sportfishing dock ☎ 624/143–0646 or 624/143–4542, 800/344–3349 in the U.S. ⊕ www.solmar.com) is one of the area's oldest and most reputable companies. The boats and tackle are always in good shape, and many regulars wouldn't fish with anyone else.

**Horseback Riding.** Cantering down an isolated beach or up a desert trail is one of Baja's great pleasures (as long as the sun isn't beating down on your head). Rates are $25–$40. Horses are available for rent in front of the Playa Médano hotels; contact **Rancho Collins Horses** (☎ 624/143–3652). **Red Rose Riding Stables** (✉ Carretera 1, Km 4 ☎ 624/143–4826) has horses for all levels of riders as well as impressive tack.

**Whale-Watching.** The gray-whale migration doesn't end at Baja's Pacific lagoons. Plenty of whales of all sizes make it down to the warmer waters off Los Cabos and into the Mar de Cortés. To watch whales from shore, go to the beach at the Solmar Suites or any Corridor hotel, or the lookout points along the Corridor highway. Several companies run trips (about $40) from Cabo San Lucas. Check with **Cabo Acuadeportes** (✉ Hotel Hacienda, Playa Médano ☎ 624/143–0117) about whale-watching excursions. **Cabo Expeditions** (✉ Plaza Las Glorias hotel, Blvd. Marina ☎ 624/143–2700) offers snorkeling and whale-watching tours in rubber boats.

SHOPPING Boulevard Marina and the side streets between the waterfront and the main plaza are filled with an ever-changing parade of small shops. At the crafts market in the marina, you can pose for a photo with an iguana, plan a ride in a glass-bottom boat, or browse to your heart's content through stalls packed with blankets, sombreros, and pottery.

★ **El Callejón** (✉ Guerrero, between Cárdenas and Av. Madero ☎ 624/143–1139) has multiple showrooms with gorgeous furniture, lamps, dishes, and pottery. **Cartes** (✉ Plaza Bonita, Blvd. Marina ☎ 624/143–1770) sells hand-painted pottery and tableware, pewter frames, handblown glass, and carved furniture. **Dos Lunas** (✉ Plaza Bonita, Blvd. Marina ☎ 624/143–1969) is full of trendy, colorful sportswear and straw hats.

**Galería Gatemelatta** (✉ On dirt road to Hotel Hacienda ☎ 624/143–1166) specializes in colonial furniture and antiques. **Golden Cactus Gallery** (✉ Calle Guerrero, at Madero ☎ 624/143–6399) exhibits paintings and sculptures by local artists. Need a new bathing suit? Check out the selection at **H2O de los Cabos** (✉ Av. Madero at Guerrero ☎ 624/143–1219), where you can choose from skimpy thongs and modest one-pieces.

The walk-in humidor at **J&J Habanos** (✉ Av. Madero, between Blvd. Marina and Guerrero ☎ 624/143–6160) is stocked with pricey cigars. The shop also sells expensive tequilas. **Magic of the Moon** (✉ Hidalgo, near Blvd. Marina ☎ 624/143–3161) has handmade women's sundresses, skirts, and lingerie. **Mama Eli's** (✉ Av. San Lucas ☎ 624/143–1616) is a three-story gallery with fine furnishings, ceramics, appliquéd clothing, and children's toys. **Necri** (✉ Blvd. Marina, between Av. Madero and Ocampo ☎ 624/143–0283) sells folk art and furnishings.

The palatial entrance of **Puerto Paraíso** (✉ Av. Cárdenas ☎ 624/143–0000) leads into a three-story marble-and-glass-enclosed mall. There are a few U.S. chains and an ever-growing number of clothing, jewelry, and home-furnishing shops. Consider visiting Galeria de Kaki Bassi, which has works by one of Baja's leading painters. One of the area's oldest folk-art shops, **Faces of Mexico** (✉ Cárdenas beside the Mar de Cortés hotel ☎ 624/143–2634) has masks from Oaxaca and Guerrero.

## Todos Santos

**㊻** *72 km (45 mi) north of Cabo San Lucas.*

The small agricultural town of Todos Santos is a haven for artists, architects, and speculators, contributing to a rapid rise in real-estate prices. It's a bit inland from the rugged coast and is classically charming with its 19th-century brick-and-stucco buildings and small central plaza. Most of the older adobe buildings are on calles Centenario, Legaspi, and Topete around the main plaza.

In high season, tour buses often clog the streets around the plaza, as this is a pit stop on trips between Cabo San Lucas and La Paz. When the buses leave, the town is a peaceful place to wander. Entrepreneurs have turned some of the plaza-front buildings into galleries and cafés, and there's always a new spot to check out. Business hours are erratic, especially in September and October. Be sure to pick up *El Calendario de Todos San-*

# PEOPLE IN GLASS HOUSES

**A** **BEAUTIFUL GLASS MOSAIC** *over the entrance to La Fábrica de Vidrio Soplado (Blown-Glass Factory) welcomes Los Cabos's most famous artisans every day. Founded in 1988 by engineer Sebastian Romo, the factory uses a glass-making process close to the one first developed in western Asia 4,000 years ago, later refined into glass-blowing during the Roman empire.*

*At the factory, 35 artisans produce more than 450 pieces a day from hundreds of pounds of locally recycled glass. Tourists watch while crushed recycled glass is liquefied in gas-fired ovens and, seconds later, transformed into exquisite figures. Secrets for making the thick glassware's deep blues, greens, and reds—the result of special mixtures of metals and gold— are passed from generation to generation.*

*You're sometimes invited to make your own glassware by blowing through a*

*hollow rod to shape a glob of molten glass at the end. The results are usually not impressive. The factory is in the industrial area of Cabo San Lucas and is usually open to the public Monday through Saturday 8 AM to 2 PM.*

*tos,* a free guide (published eight times a year, in English) with events and developments. It's available at many hotels, shops, and restaurants.

Los Cabos regulars typically take day trips to Todos Santos, stopping to watch surfers at Playa Migriño, Playa Los Cerritos, and Punta Gaspareo. El Pescadero, the largest settlement before Todos Santos, is populated by ranchers and farmers who grow herbs and vegetables for Los Cabos restaurants. They also sell their produce at small roadside stands. Be sure to head back to Cabo from Todos Santos before dark, because Carretera 19 between the two towns is unlighted and prone to high winds and flooding. And don't be tempted to try the dirt roads that intersect the highway unless you're in a four-wheel-drive vehicle. Sands on the beach or in the desert stop conventional vehicles in their tracks.

### Where to Stay & Eat

★ $$$–$$$$  ✕ **Cafe Santa Fe.** The setting, with tables in an overgrown courtyard, is as appealing as the food: salads and soups made from organic vegetables and herbs, homemade pastas, and fresh fish with light herbal sauces. Many Cabo residents lunch here weekly. The marinated seafood salad is a sublime blend of shrimp, octopus, and mussels with olive oil and garlic, with plenty for two to share before dining on lobster ravioli. ⊠ *Calle*

*Centenario* ☎ *612/145–0340* 🖃 *No credit cards* ⊗ *Closed Tues. and parts of Sept. and Oct.*

**$–$$$** ✕ **Los Adobes.** Locals swear by the fried, cilantro-studded local cheese and beef fajitas at this pleasant outdoor restaurant. The menu is a bit ambitious, but it does have several vegetarian options—rare in these parts. At night the place sparkles with star-shape lights. The Internet café within the restaurant has high-speed access. ⊠ *Calle Hidalgo* ☎ *612/ 145–0203* 🖃 *MC, V* ⊗ *No dinner Sun.*

**$–$$$** ✕ **Caffé Todos Santos.** Omelets, bagels, granola, and delicious whole-grain breads delight the breakfast crowd at this small café; deli sandwiches, fresh salads, and an array of tamales, *flautas* (tortillas rolled around savory fillings), and combo plates are lunch and dinner highlights. Check for fresh seafood on the daily specials board, and pick up a loaf of bread for the road. ⊠ *Calle Centenario 33* ☎ *612/145–0300* 🖃 *MC, V.*

**$–$$** ✕ **Mi Costa.** Locals crave the shrimp with garlic and oil served at this concrete-floor, palapa-covered café. On Sunday, families fill the dining area, feasting on peeled shrimp, fish tacos, and grilled fish fillets. It's oh so Mexican casual—feel free to fetch your own napkins and condiments. ⊠ *Militar, at Ocampo* ☎ *No phone* 🖃 *No credit cards.*

**$$** ✕🏨 **Posada La Poza.** The Swiss owners aim to please with their chic posada beside a bird-filled lagoon and the open sea. The handsome suites have rust-tone walls, modern furniture, and Swiss linens; you'll find a CD player and binoculars on hand, but no TVs or phones. Even if you're not staying, stop by the restaurant ($$–$$$; closed Thurs.) for fettuccine with white truffle sauce and organic salads. ⊠ *Follow signs on Carretera 19 and on Av. Juárez to the beach, 23305* ☎ *612/145–0400* 📠 *612/145–0453* ⊕ *www.lapoza.com* 🛌 *7 suites* ⚥ *Restaurant, in-room safes, minibars, pool, massage, bar, Internet; no room phones, no room TVs* 🖃 *MC, V* ⦿ *BP.*

**$$** 🏨 **Hotel California.** Ignore rumors that the Eagles song originated here—this handsome, well-kept place has plenty of true draws. A deep blue and ocher color scheme runs throughout, and the rooms, some of which are blessed with ocean views, have eclectic mixes of antiques and folk art. (At this writing five more rooms are being added.) The bar is a local hot spot. ⊠ *Calle Juárez, at Morelos, 23305* ☎ *612/145–0525* 📠 *612/ 145–0288* 🛌 *6 rooms* ⚥ *Restaurant, pool, bar; no a/c, no room phones, no room TVs* 🖃 *MC, V.*

**$$** 🏨 **Todos Santos Inn.** The six guest rooms in this converted 19th-century house are unparalleled in design and comfort. Gorgeous antiques are set against stone walls under brick ceilings. Ceiling fans and the shade from garden trees keep the rooms cool and breezy. The absence of telephones and TVs makes a perfect foil for the conceits of Los Cabos. The wine bar is open in the evening, and good restaurants are within easy walking distance. ⊠ *Calle Legaspi, 23305* ☎📠 *612/145–0040* 🛌 *6 rooms* ⚥ *Bar; no a/c in some rooms, no room phones, no room TVs* 🖃 *No credit cards.*

**¢–$** 🏨 **Hostería Las Casitas.** If Los Cabos has got you feeling like turning down the volume (and the cash flow), this garden-surrounded B&B is just the thing—and it has great breakfasts, too. Two of the rooms share a shower but have their own toilets and sinks; the other two rooms share all facilities. The buildings' traditional Mexican architecture makes for cool accommodations. Owner Wendy Faith's art-glass studio is also on-site. ☒ *Calle Rangel, at Obregón and Hidalgo* ⊕ *Apdo. 73, 23305* ☎☎ *612/ 145–0255* ☏ *4 rooms, 2 suites with bath* ⚅ *No a/c, no room phones, no TV* ☱ *No credit cards* ⎮⊘⎮ *BP.*

## Baja Sur A to Z

### AIR TRAVEL

Baja Sur has airports in La Paz, Los Cabos, and Loreto, all served by many domestic and international airlines.

AIRPORTS  In La Paz the Márquez de León Aeropuerto Internacional (LAP) is about 16 km (10 mi) north of town. Loreto's airport, Aeropuerto Internacional Loreto (LTO), is 7 km (4½ mi) southwest of town. Aeropuerto Internacional San José del Cabo (Los Cabos International Airport; SJD) is about 11 km (7 mi) north of San José del Cabo and about 48 km (30 mi) from Cabo San Lucas. At Los Cabos, timeshare hustlers assault you with offers of free transportation, which implies a commitment to tour their properties. To avoid the sales pitch, go directly to the transportation desk by the exit to arrange a ride into town.
🛈 **Aeropuerto Internacional Loreto** ☎ 613/135–0565. **Aeropuerto Internacional San José del Cabo** ☎ 624/146–5013. **Márquez de León Aeropuerto Internacional** ☎ 612/ 112–0082.

AIRPORT   Taxis between the La Paz and Loreto airports and their respective towns
TRANSFERS  are inexpensive and convenient. In Los Cabos, cabs to and from the airport are outrageously expensive. Expect to pay at least $25, but a ride can cost over $50 depending on the distance. Some Los Cabos hotels offer airport transfers for a fee, which is usually less than a cab. Ask about the availability of such a service when you make your reservation. Some hotels have sign-up sheets with which you can arrange to share the expense of a cab with other travelers.

CARRIERS  AeroCalifornia serves La Paz airport from Tijuana, Tucson, and Los Angeles; has daily flights from Los Angeles to Loreto's airport; and flies to Los Cabos from Los Angeles and Tijuana. Aeroméxico flies to La Paz from Los Angeles, Tucson, Tijuana, Mexico City, and other cities within Mexico; it flies to Los Cabos and Loreto from San Diego and Mexico City. Mexicana has flights to Los Cabos airport from Guadalajara, Mexico City, and Los Angeles. Alaska Airlines operates its own terminal at Los Cabos airport and has flights from Anchorage, Fairbanks, Portland, Phoenix, San Francisco, San Diego, Los Angeles, and Seattle. America West flies into Los Cabos from Phoenix, Continental from Houston and Newark. Delta and American have seasonal nonstop flights, but— like many U.S. carriers—they don't have offices in Los Cabos. Other international airlines may have service in winter.
🛈 **AeroCalifornia** ☎ 612/125–1023 in La Paz, 624/143–3700 in Los Cabos, 613/135–0500 in Loreto, 800/237–6225 in the U.S. **Aeroméxico** ☎ 612/122–0091 in La Paz, 624/142–

0398 in Los Cabos, 800/237-6639 in the U.S. ⊕ www.aeromexico.com. **Alaska Airlines** ☎ 624/142-2362 in Los Cabos ⊕ www.alaskaair.com. **America West** ☎ 01800/363-2597 toll free in Mexico ⊕ www.americawest.com. **Continental** ☎ 624/142-3840 in Los Cabos, 800/525-0280 in the U.S. ⊕ www.continental.com. **Mexicana** ☎ 624/142-0230 in Los Cabos, 800/531-7921 in the U.S. ⊕ www.mexicana.com.

## BOAT & FERRY TRAVEL

The ferry system connecting Baja to mainland Mexico constantly undergoes rate and schedule changes. Sematur ferries connect La Paz and Mazatlán every day except Saturday; it's an 18-hour trip. Ferries also head from La Paz to Topolobampo, the port at Los Mochis, every day but Sunday; this is a 17-hour trip. You can buy tickets for both ferries at La Paz Terminal at the dock on the road to Pichilingue or at the Sematur Office. The Sematur Web site *should* have the most up-to-date information, but isn't always accurate. Purchase your ticket in advance—it's probably best to use a Mexican travel agent—and expect confusion. Continuous changes in Sematur procedure and pricing make it difficult for even ferry personnel to keep up with the latest policy. At this writing one-way fares range from about $30 to $120, depending on whether you spring for a berth with a bathroom or just a seat on the boat. Baja Ferries operates between Santa Rosalia and Guaymas. A one-way ticket costs about $40; fees for vehicles vary according to size.

If you plan to take a car or a motor home on the ferry to the mainland, you must obtain a vehicle permit before boarding the ferry and must have Mexican auto-insurance papers; everyone crossing to the mainland also needs a tourist card. Tourism officials in La Paz strongly suggest that you obtain the vehicle permit when crossing the U.S. border into Baja; although permits aren't needed in Baja, offices at the border are better equipped to handle the paperwork than those in La Paz. Tourist cards also are available at the border. It's wise to take copies of the following, in triplicate, plus the original: passport, tourist card, birth certificate, and vehicle registration. Also, you'll need to make a reservation for vehicle transportation on a ferry at least a few weeks in advance.
🚢 **Baja Ferries** ✉ La Paz Terminal, La Paz ☎ 612/123-0508 ⊕ www.bajaferries.com. **La Paz Terminal** ☎ 612/122-5005. **Sematur Office** ✉ Calle 5 de Mayo 502 ☎ 612/125-2366 ⊕ www.ferrysematur.com.mx.

## BUS TRAVEL

Autotransportes de Baja California buses runs from Tijuana to La Paz, stopping at towns en route; the peninsula-long trip takes 22 hours. This company also has a route from La Paz to Guerrero Negro (the buses stop at the highway entrance to town). This trip takes anywhere from six to nine hours. Loreto is serviced by both Autotransportes de Baja California and the local Aguila bus company, which also runs from Todos Santos and La Paz to Los Cabos. The Loreto bus terminal sits at the entrance to town. Buses run several times daily and overall they're clean, safe, and comfortable. You don't need to make reservations.

In La Paz it's fairly easy to get around by bus: city buses run along the malecón and into downtown. Buses run between Cabo San Lucas and San José del Cabo, and will stop along the Corridor if you ask the driver.

There are covered bus stops with benches (but no signs) along Carretera 1 in the Corridor. The easiest place to catch a bus in San José is at the stoplight at the intersection of Calle Doblado and Carretera 1. In San Lucas, you can catch one at the stoplight on Carretera 1 in front of the Puerto Paraíso mall. A ride costs $2.

🚌 **Aguila** ☎ 612/122-4270 or 612/122-3063. **Autotransportes de Baja California** ☎ 612/122-6476 or 612/122-7094. **Loreto bus terminal** ✉ Calle Salvatierra at Calle Tamaral ☎ 613/135-0767.

## CAR RENTAL

California Baja Rent-A-Car rents four-wheel-drive vehicles, convertibles, and sedans for use throughout Mexico; you can pick up a car in San Diego and drop it off in Los Cabos, but expect to pay a hefty additional charge. Thrifty has an office south of Loreto in Nopoló. They'll deliver your car to town. Budget in Loreto has a few four-wheel-drive vehicles available. Avis and Hertz have desks at La Paz airport. Hertz has an additional office on Avenida Obregón in town. Avis, Hertz, and Thrifty all have 4-wheel-drive vehicles, but they need to be reserved well in advance.

Several car-rental agencies have desks at Los Cabos airport and in San José or Cabo San Lucas. Reserve a car in advance during high season, especially if you want a van, four-wheel-drive, or air-conditioning. Most agencies rent VW bugs and topless VW bugs, which seem like fun until you're under the blazing sun for several hours.

🚗 **Avis** ☎ 612/124-6312, 612/122-2651 in La Paz, 624/146-0388 at Los Cabos airport ⊕ www.avis.com. **Budget** ✉ Paseo Hidalgo near the malecón, Loreto ☎ 613/135-1090 ✉ Paseo Obregón at Hidalgo, La Paz ☎ 612/122-1919 or 612/122-7655 ⊕ www.budget.com. **California Baja Rent-A-Car** ✉ 9245 Jamacha Blvd., Spring Valley, CA 91977 ☎ 619/470-8368, 888/470-7368 in the U.S. ⊕ www.cabaja.com. **Dollar** ☎ 624/142-0100, 624/143-1250 in Los Cabos ⊕ www.dollar.com. **Hertz** ☎ 612/124-6330 at La Paz airport, 624/142-0375 at Los Cabos airport ✉ Av. Obregón 2130, La Paz ☎ 612/122-5300, 612/122-0919 at La Paz airport ⊕ www.hertz.com. **Thrifty** ✉ Loreto airport ☎ 613/133-0612 ⊕ www.thrifty.com.

## CAR TRAVEL

Mexico Carretera 1, also known as the Carretera Transpeninsular, runs 1,700 km (1,060 mi) from Tijuana to Cabo San Lucas. The highway's condition varies depending on the weather and intervals between road repairs. Don't drive it at high speeds or at night—it's not lighted. There are exits for all the principal towns in Baja Sur. The road between San José del Cabo and Cabo San Lucas is four lanes and reinforced; elevated bridges have eliminated the flooding problems that long plagued the road.

PARKING  It's easy to find street parking in La Paz. In the resort hotspots, though, it's a different story. San José del Cabo's congested streets make finding a spot difficult; park outside the town center rather than trying to navigate narrow one-way streets. It can also be tricky to find parking in Cabo San Lucas, but there's a large, free lot by the marina.

## CRUISE TRAVEL

Several cruise lines use Cabo San Lucas as a port of call. Carnival makes a short stop during its cruise between Los Angeles and Mexico's mainland Pacific coast. Princess has cruises to Los Cabos and the Mexican Riviera from Los Angeles and San Francisco. Lindblad Expeditions, and Clipper Cruise Line run nature cruises in the Mar de Cortés and combine the Mar de Cortés ports of La Paz and Loreto with the Barrancas del Cobre on the mainland. Baja Expeditions has live-aboard ships for diving and whale-watching trips.

🗂 **Baja Expeditions** ✉ 2625 Garnet Ave., San Diego, CA 92109 ☎ 858/581-3311 or 800/843-6967 ⊕ www.bajaex.com. **Carnival** ☎ 800/327-9501 in the U.S. **Clipper Cruise Line** ☎ 800/325-0010 in the U.S. **Cruise West** ☎ 800/888-9378 in the U.S. **Lindblad Expeditions** ☎ 212/765-7740, 800/397-3348 in the U.S. ⊕ www.expeditions.com. **Princess** ☎ 800/421-0522 in the U.S.

### EMERGENCIES

The state of Baja California Sur has instituted an emergency number for police, fire, and medical problems: 060. The number can be used throughout the state and there are English-speaking operators.

### INTERNET

Galería Don Tomás in La Paz has Internet access in artful surroundings. Baja Net in La Paz has ports for laptops along with many computer terminals. Both places charge about $10 an hour. Cabo Mail Internet in Cabo San Lucas has several computers and charges $10 an hour. Cabocafe in San José del Cabo offers access for $9 an hour.

🗂 Internet Cafés **Baja Net** ✉ Av. Madero 430, La Paz ☎ 612/125-9380. **Cabocafe** ✉ Plaza José Green, Suite 3, Blvd. Mijares, San José del Cabo ☎ 624/142-5250. **Cabo Mail Internet** ✉ Blvd. Cárdenas, Cabo San Lucas ☎ 624/143-3797. **Galería Don Tomás** ✉ Av. Obregón 229, La Paz ☎ 612/128-5508.

### MONEY MATTERS

As in Baja Norte, finding ATMs in heavily touristed areas isn't a problem, and some places use dollars as well as pesos. If you're going to a less developed area, though, go equipped with cash.

### TAXIS

In Loreto, taxis are in good supply and fares are inexpensive; it costs $5 or less to get anywhere in town. Taxi fares in Los Cabos, however, are outrageous. It costs at least $40 to take a taxi between the two towns and $20 from a Coridor hotel to either town. Try to share a cab whenever possible. In La Paz, taxis are readily available and inexpensive. A ride within town costs under $5; a trip to Pichilingue costs between $7 and $10. If you'd like to explore the remote beaches, however, *see* Car Rental. Illegitimate taxis are not a problem in this region. The cars are often Volkswagen bugs, except in Los Cabos, where vans are commonly used.

### TOURS

Most tours involve getting into a boat and diving or fishing. It's a must to take a ride to El Arco, the natural rock arches at Land's End, and Playa de Amor, where the Mar de Cortés merges with the Pacific. Nearly all hotels have boat trips to these destinations; the fare depends on how far your hotel is from the point. Tour vessels dock by the arts-and-crafts market in the Cabo San Lucas marina, and the sidewalk along the water is lined with fleet salespeople. Check out the boat before you pay, and make sure there are life jackets aboard.

Contactours has group land and sea tours of Los Cabos and booking agents at several hotels. TourCabos runs boat trips, offers horseback riding, and can provide information on water sports. Nomadas de Baja offers hiking, snorkeling, and kayaking tours of Los Cabos with an ecological bent. Pez Gato, on the marina near Plaza Las Glorias hotel in Los Cabos, has sailing and sunset cruises on a 46-foot catamaran, with live music as well as snorkeling and sailing tours. All trips depart from the marina in Cabo San Lucas; call or stop by the booth at the marina for further information. Discover Baja Travel Club is a great source of info for travel throughout the peninsula.

🚩 **Tour Operators Contactours** ☎ 624/143-3333 or 624/143-2439 in Los Cabos ⊕ www. contactincentives.com. **Discover Baja Travel Club** ✉ 3089 Clairemont Dr., San Diego, CA 92117 ☎ 619/275-4225 or 800/727-2252 ⊕ www.discoverbaja.com. **Nomadas de Baja** ☎ 624/148-1468 in Los Cabos ☎🖨 624/142-4388 ⊕ www.nomadasdebaja.com. **Pez Gato** ☎ 624/143-3797 in Los Cabos. **TourCabos** ☎ 624/142-4040 in Los Cabos ⊕ www. tourcabos.com.mx.

## VISITOR INFORMATION

The Baja California Sur State Tourist Office is in La Paz near the Fidepaz Marina. There's also an information stand on the malecón across from Los Arcos hotel. The booth is a more convenient spot, and it can give you info on Scammon's Lagoon, Santa Rosalia, and other smaller towns. The Loreto Tourist Information Office is in the Palacio Municipal on the main plaza. Both offices and the booth are open weekdays 9–5.

There are no official tourist-information offices in Los Cabos; hotel tour desks are the best sources of information. Avoid tour stands on the streets; they are usually associated with time-share operations. The Web site of the *Gringo Gazette* (www.gringogazette.com) can be helpful.

In Todos Santos, pick up a copy of *El Calendario de Todos Santos* for information on local events. Local residents maintain a Web site, ⊕ www. todossantos-baja.com.

🚩 **Baja California Sur State Tourist Office** ✉ Mariano Abasolo s/n, La Paz ☎ 612/ 124-0100, 612/122-5939, or 612/124-0100 ⊕ www.bajacalifornia.gob.mx. **Loreto Tourist Information Office** ✉ Municipal Building on Plaza Principal, Loreto ☎ 613/135-0411 ⊕ www.gotoloreto.com. **La Paz Hotel Association** ✉ Obregón at Calle 16 de Septiembre, La Paz ☎ 612/125-6844, 866/733-5272 in the U.S. ⊕ www.vivalapaz.com.

# SONORA

4

Updated by
Rob Aikins

**SONORA,** Mexico's second-largest state, is also its second richest. Ranch lands feed Mexico's finest beef cattle, and rivers flowing west from the Sierra Madre are diverted by giant dams to irrigate a low-rainfall area. Among Sonora's many crops are wheat and other grains, cotton, vegetables, nuts, and fruit—especially citrus, peaches, and apples. Hermosillo, Sonora's capital, bustles with agricultural commerce in the midst of the fertile lands that turn dry again toward the coast.

In the more rural areas, this stretch of the Mexican northwest is reminiscent of the American Wild West: *rancheras,* ballads of love and deception, blare from saloons and truck radios, and *ranchitos* (small ranches) dot the cactus-strewn countryside.

The Sonoran desert dominates the landscape through northern Sonora and into southern Arizona. Long stretches of flat scrub are punctuated by brown hills and mountains, towering saguaros, and organ-pipe cacti. This arid landscape, especially at the sea, is a vacation and retirement paradise for neighbors in Arizona, for whom the beaches of Sonora are closer, cheaper, and more interesting than those of southern California. In fact, good highways south of Nogales, Mexico, make the beaches of Puerto Peñasco (Rocky Point) and San Carlos–Guaymas as accessible to Tucson natives as those of Los Angeles or San Diego, California.

Highway 15 begins at the border town of Nogales, Sonora, adjacent to the U.S. town of Nogales, Arizona. It continues south through Hermosillo and reaches the Mar de Cortés (officially called the Golfo de California) at Guaymas, 418 km (259 mi) from the Arizona border. South of Guaymas, the harsh Sonoran desert is left behind, and the landscape begins to take on a more tropical character as it enters the state of Sinaloa just north of the city of Los Mochis. Except in the mountains, the entire region is hot between May and late September, with afternoon temperatures in midsummer sometimes exceeding 120°F (49°C).

In 1540 Francisco Vázquez de Coronado, governor of the provinces to the south, became the first Spanish leader to visit the plains of Sonora. More than a century later, Father Francisco Kino led a missionary expedition to Sonora and what is now southern Arizona—an area referred to as the Pimería Alta for the band of Pima Indians still living there. The Italian-born padre and his fellow friars founded half a dozen missions there. Although Alamos, in the south of Sonora, boomed with silver-mining wealth in the late 17th century, no one paid much attention to the northern part of the region. When the United States annexed a giant chunk of Mexico's territory after the Mexican-American War (1846–48), northern Sonora suddenly became a border area—and a haven for Arizona outlaws. International squabbles bloomed and faded over the next decades as officials argued over issues such as the right to pursue criminals across the border. Porfirio Díaz, dictator of Mexico for most of the years between 1876 and 1911, finally moved to secure the state by settling it.

Settlers from Sonora, however, proved a hardy and independent bunch ill-suited to accepting the dictums of politicos in faraway Mexico City. Sonorans and their neighbors, the Chihuahenses, were major players in the Mexican Revolution, and the republic was ruled by three Sonorans: Plutarco Elías Calles, Adolfo de la Huerta, and Abelardo Rodríguez. Despite the enormous cost and destruction to railroads and other infrastructure, the Mexican Revolution brought prosperity to Sonora. With irrigation from the state's dams, inhabitants have been able to grow enough wheat and vegetables not only for Mexico but also for export. Today, Sonora's economy continues to flourish with growth in agriculture and manufacturing, though tourism is the fastest growing sector, with visitors coming to enjoy not only Sonora's abundance of beaches and sea life, but also the seclusion and tranquility of its mountains and deserts.

## Exploring Sonora

Sonoran landscapes are as varied as the state is vast, with seemingly endless tracts of desert, the mountains of the Sierra Madre, and the fields and valleys that nurture produce and livestock.

Mexico Highway 2 enters Sonora's far northwest from Baja California, paralleling the U.S. border. There are several crossing points, but most people entering Sonora from the United States do so at Nogales, south of Tucson, Arizona.

### About the Restaurants

Restaurants in this neck of the woods are often laid-back; you'll find family-run establishments virtually everywhere. Casual dress (but not beachwear) is always acceptable, and reservations are rarely needed.

### About the Hotels

In Sonora you might find yourself sleeping in a converted mansion or convent in fashionable Alamos, growing a Hemingway beard in a beach bungalow at Bahía Kino, or luxuriating in a posh resort in San Carlos. Lodging in Sonora is no longer the bargain it once was, and winter prices are similar to those of comparable accommodations in other parts of Mexico. Hotels rates sometimes include the 17% tax; so be sure to check this when you're quoted a price.

| WHAT IT COSTS | | | | |
|---|---|---|---|---|
| **$$$$** | **$$$** | **$$** | **$** | **¢** |
| RESTAURANTS over $25 | $15–$25 | $10–$15 | $5–$10 | under $5 |
| HOTELS over $250 | $150–$250 | $75–$150 | $50–$75 | under $50 |

Restaurant prices are for a main course excluding tax and tip. Hotel prices are for two people in a standard double room in high season.

### Timing

Summer temperatures in Sonora are as high as they are in southern Arizona, so unless you're prepared to broil, plan your trip for sometime between October and May. Even in winter, daytime temperatures can rise above 80°F (27°C), though at night the temperature drops considerably. Winter on the coast can also bring strong, steady winds that make temperatures seem much colder than they actually are.

**4**

Because it is so large and spread out, the state of Sonora demands eight days or more to really do it justice. With less time, you'll do best to concentrate on one area. Most visitors to Sonora choose the sea, where desert landscapes collide with the shimmering blue Gulf of California.

*Numbers in the text correspond to numbers in the margin and on the Sonora map.*

**If you have 3 days**

Take Highway 15 south from Nogales to the state capital, ▣ **Hermosillo** ❹ ▶, where you will find a variety of good hotels and restaurants. Overnight here and spend the next morning touring the city or browsing through the Centro Ecológico, which is of special interest to children. After lunch, drive west on Highway 16 to ▣ **Bahía Kino** ❺, a perfect beach for a one- or two-night retreat. The drive back to the Arizona border from Bahía Kino is about six hours.

An alternative three-day itinerary is to cross the U.S. border at Lukeville-Sonoyta and head straight for the beaches of ▣ **Puerto Peñasco** ❸ ▶ for the rest of the first day. The next day you can continue to lounge, lunch overlooking the beach, and tap your feet to live jazz in the evening, or spend the day exploring the lunarlike regions of the **El Pinacate** ❷. On your last day, admire the formidable desert scenery as you loop east to **Nogales** ❶. Spend an afternoon shopping there before you cross the U.S. border.

**If you have 5 days**

Take Highway 15 from **Nogales** ❶ ▶ to **Guaymas** ❼; the drive will take six or seven hours. Exploring the town of Guaymas and the adjacent resort area of ▣ **San Carlos** ❽ will give you plenty to do for two days and nights. Continue south and then east for 3½ hours to charming colonial ▣ **Alamos** ❾, in the foothills of the Sierra Madre. After one or two nights in Alamos, head back north. You might consider spending the night along the tranquil shores of **Bahía Kino** ❺ on your way home. Alternatively, take a day trip through the **Ruta de Rio Sonora** to Aconchi, where you can take a 4-km (2½-mi) hike through ranch country to thermal springs.

**If you have 8 days**

Combine the second of the three-day itineraries with the five-day itinerary, but stop off at ▣ **Hermosillo** ❹ on the way down to **Guaymas** ❼. If you have extra time, you might want to take a short side trip from Alamos to **Aduana** ❿, former site of a thriving silver mine and current location of a thriving restaurant.

## Nogales

▶ ❶ *100 km (62 mi) south of Tucson via Hwy. 19, on the Arizona-Mexico border.*

Bustling Nogales can become fairly rowdy on weekend evenings, when underage Tucsonans head south of the border to drink. It has some good restaurants, however, and visitors can find fine-quality crafts in addition to the usual souvenirs. If you're just coming for the day, it's best to park on the Arizona side of the border—you'll see many guarded lots that cost about $8 for the day—and walk across. Most of the good shopping is within easy strolling distance of the border.

The shopping area centers mainly on Avenida Obregón, which begins a few blocks west of the border entrance and runs north–south; just follow the crowds. Most of the good restaurants are also on Obregón. Take Obregón as far south as you like; you'll know you have entered workaday Mexico when the shops are no longer fronted by English-speaking hustlers trying to lure you in the door.

### Where to Eat

★ $–$$$  ✕ **La Roca.** You'll find this elegant restaurant within walking distance of the border. The old stone house, built against a cliff, has several dining rooms, some with fireplaces; a balcony overlooks a patio with a fountain and magnolia trees. Look for the excellent seafood dishes and the *queso la Roca* (seasoned potato slices covered with melted cheese) appetizer. Reservations are suggested weekend nights. ⊠ *Calle Elias 91, Centro* ☎ *631/312–0891* ⊟ *MC, V.*

$$  ✕ **Elvira.** The dining room of this long-established restaurant bursts with color and bristles with stamped tin stars. Choose from half a dozen different moles, from the rich and dark *mole poblano* to the *manchamanteles,* a sweet stew built around pineapple, banana, and apple. A free shot of tequila comes with each meal. ⊠ *Av. Obregón 1, Centro* ☎ *631/312–4773* ⊟ *MC, V.*

$–$$  ✕ **El Cid.** For more than 20 years, this clean, festive restaurant has earned its reputation for good food and service. Menu staples include burgers, fresh seafood, and traditional Mexican specialties like *camarones ajo* (grilled garlic shrimp) and carne asada. A few more exotic items such as frogs' legs and quail add to the mix. ⊠ *Av. Obregón 124, upper level, Centro* ☎ *631/312–1500* ⊟ *MC, V.*

### Shopping

Nogales's wide selection of crafts, furnishings, and jewelry makes for some of Sonora's best shopping. At more informal shops, bargaining is not only acceptable but expected. The following shops tend to have fixed prices. East of the railroad tracks, **El Changarro** (⊠ Calle Elias 93, below Restaurant La Roca, Centro ☎ 631/312–0545) carries high-quality furniture, including both antiques and rustic-style modern pieces, blown glass, stone carvings, and ceramics. **Mickey** (⊠ Av. Obregón 128–130, Centro ☎ 631/312–2299) has two floors of handcrafted Mexican treasures, *equipale* (pigskin) furniture, Talavera ceramic dishes, pottery, and glassware. **El Sarape** (⊠ Av. Obregón 161, Centro ☎ 631/312–0309) specializes in sterling-silver jewelry from Taxco and pewter housewares and crafts from all over Mexico.

## El Pinacate

❷ *52 km (31 mi) southwest of Sonoyta.*

Midway between the Arizona border and the beach town of Puerto Peñasco, this reserve is best known for its volcanic rock formations and

**4**

## Beaches

Lively hotels and restaurants line the coastal areas around San Carlos, Guaymas, and Puerto Peñasco, but if you are willing to take more time for travel and forgo facilities, you'll find miles and miles of more-secluded beaches along the Mar de Cortés. Most of Sonora's main beaches have paved access roads, but some of the best—like pristine Playa San Nicolás just south of Bahía Kino (Kino Bay)—await the adventurous at the end of rutted, washed-out dirt tracks.

## Local Specialties

Sonoran cuisine has all the makings for stellar surf and turf: it's distinguished by its terrific steaks and, on the coast especially, its fresh fish and seafood. Sonora is also the home of the giant flour tortilla, *machaca* (air-dried beef), and some of the best *carne asada* (thin, grilled, marinated meat) in Mexico. Seafood lovers will find shrimp, scallops, octopus, clams, and fish, both freshwater and ocean species. There's an abundance of enchiladas, tacos, and tamales—the style of Mexican cooking with which most Americans are familiar derives from this region.

---

craters so moonlike that they were used for training the Apollo 14 astronauts. (The area's official name is La Reserva de Biosfera El Pinacate y El Gran Desierto de Altar, but it's generally called El Pinacate.) The diversity of the lava flows makes Pinacate unique, as does the striking combination of Sonoran desert and volcanic field. Highlights of the area include **Santa Clara peak,** a little more than 4,000 feet high and 2.5 million years old, and **El Elegante crater,** 1½ km (1 mi) across and 750 feet deep, created by a giant steam eruption 150,000 years ago. Don't try recreating the moon walk, though—going into the craters damages them.

There are no facilities of any kind at Pinacate. You'll need to bring your own water—take plenty of it—food, and extra gasoline, as well as a good map, which you can get at Si Como No bookstore in Ajo, Arizona, Tucson's Map and Flag Center, or at the Intercultural Center for the Study of Desert and Oceans (CEDO) in Puerto Peñasco, Mexico. A high-clearance vehicle is strongly advised, and four-wheel-drive is recommended. Keep in mind that the desert is no stranger to drug traffickers and illegal border crossings, so use common sense and don't risk getting stranded. Primitive camping is allowed in designated areas with a permit obtainable from the ranger station at the entrance on Highway 8 (☎ no phone). Regardless of whether you intend to camp, you must register at the park entrance, where a ranger's station provides informative displays, a basic map and brochures, as well as a list of rules and tips for visitors. For current park information, contact the International Sonoran Desert Alliance in Ajo, Arizona, at ☎ 520/387–6823.

Summer temperatures can be blistering. The best time to visit is between November and March, when daytime temperatures range between 60°F (16°C) and 90°F (32°C). Tours can be arranged through CEDO or at the tourism office in Puerto Peñasco. Excellent three-day, naturalist-led

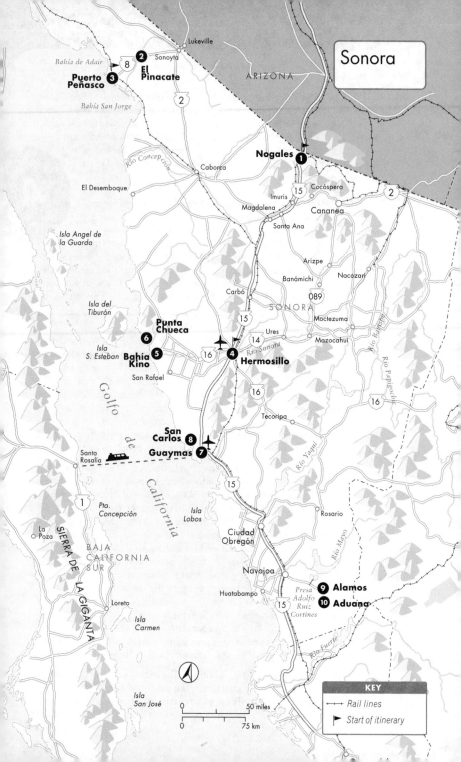

Sonora

ARIZONA

Lukeville

Bahía de Adair

**2** Sonoyta

8

**El Pinacate**

**Puerto Peñasco** **3**

Bahía San Jorge

2

Río Concepción

Caborca

**Nogales** **1**

15 Cocóspera

Imuris

Magdalena

Cananea

El Desemboque

Santa Ana

Isla Angel de la Guarda

Arizpe

Banámichi

Nacozari

Carbó

089

SONORA

Moctezuma

Isla del Tiburón

Punta Chueca **6**

**5**

Bahía Kino

Isla S. Esteban

San Rafael

16

14

**4**

**Hermosillo**

Ures

Río Sonora

Mazocahui

Río Bavispe

Río Papigochic

15

Golfo

de

Tecoripa

16

16

San Carlos **8**

Guaymas **7**

Santa Rosalía

California

Pta. Concepción

1

Isla Lobos

15

Río Yaqui

SIERRA DE LA GIGANTA

La Poza

BAJA CALIFORNIA SUR

Loreto

Isla Carmen

Ciudad Obregón

Rosario

Navojoa

**Alamos** **9**

**Aduana** **10**

Huatabampo

Presa Adolfo Ruiz Cortines

15

Río Mayo

Río Fuerte

Isla San José

0          50 miles

0          75 km

| KEY |
|-----|
| ├──┤ Rail lines |
| ⚑ Start of itinerary |

tours can be arranged through **La Ruta de Sonora** (☎ 520/792–4693) in Tucson. ⊠ *Highway 8 at Km 52, near Ejido Nayarit* ☎ *No phone* 🖃 *Donation requested* ☉ *Daily 8–5.*

## Puerto Peñasco

▶ ❸ *104 km (65 mi) south of the Arizona border at Lukeville on Mexico Hwy. 8.*

Puerto Peñasco was dubbed Rocky Point by British explorers in the 18th century, and that's the name most Americans know it by today. The town itself was established about 1927, after Mexican fishermen found abundant shrimp beds in the area and American John Stone built the first hotel. Al Capone was a frequent visitor during the Prohibition era, when he was hiding from U.S. law.

The real appeal of Puerto Peñasco, at the north end of the Mar de Cortés (Sea of Cortes), is the miles of sandy beaches punctuated by stretches of black, volcanic rock. A remarkably high tide change—as much as 23 feet—makes for great exploring among countless tide pools.

To the beaches add low prices for accommodations, food, and drink, and you've got a popular wintering spot for American RVers and retirees and a favorite weekend getaway for Arizonans. Although Rocky Point is rather faceless, the "old town" has a number of interesting shopping stalls, fish markets, and restaurants.

This coastline is rapidly changing, however. A number of major projects have been developed—including a complex with a shopping center, a luxury hotel, condos and villas, a yacht club, a golf course, and a marina—all designed to attract an upscale clientele. Even more dramatic changes to the landscape may result from the "Escalera Náutica" (Nautical Ladder), a series of high-end marinas up and down the Baja Peninsula and Sonora and Sinaloa coasts, being pushed by President Fox's administration. Only time will tell whether these plans will reach fruition, and what their impact on ecology and the local economy will be.

The northern Gulf area forms an impressive desert-coast ecosystem, and scientists from both the United States and Mexico conduct research programs at the **Intercultural Center for the Study of Desert and Oceans** (known as CEDO, its acronym in Spanish), about 3 km (2 mi) east of town on Fremont Boulevard in the Fraccionamiento Las Conchas neighborhood. You can take an English-language tour of the facility to learn about the ecology of the area and its history, or just pick up a tide calendar (useful if you're planning beach activities) or field guide from the gift shop. Talks and nature outings—including tide-pool walks, Pinacate excursions, and kayaking expeditions of area estuaries—are offered sporadically. ⊕ *Turn east at municipal building and follow signs for Fremont Rd., where there will be signs for Las Conchas Beach and CEDO* ☎ *638/382–0113* ⊕ *www.cedointercultural.org* 🖃 *Free, donation for tours* ☉ *Mon.–Sat. 9–5, Sun. 10–2; tours Tues. at 2, Sat. at 4.*

☾ Not far from CEDO you'll find the **Acuario Cet-Mar,** which focuses on the Mar de Cortés ecosystem and the local intertidal zone. The tanks, filled with many kinds of fish, invertebrates, and turtles, have information in both Spanish and English. You can buy a bag of feed for the sea lions and turtles. Since all of the sea creatures on display are wild, the displays often change as some animals are released. ☒ *Las Conchas* ☎ *638/ 382–0010* ⊕ *www.cedointercultural.org* ☜ *$3* ☉ *Daily 10–5.*

## Where to Stay & Eat

**$–$$$** ✕ **La Casa del Capitán.** Perched atop Puerto Peñasco's tallest point, this restaurant has the best views over the bay and the town below. There's indoor dining, but the long outdoor porch overlooking the sea is the place to be, especially at sunset when it can be packed with locals and visitors alike. A wide-ranging menu includes everything from nachos and quesadillas to flaming brandied jumbo shrimp. ☒ *Av. del Agua 1, Cerro de la Ballena* ☎ *638/383–5698* ⊟ *MC, V.*

**$–$$** ✕ **La Curva.** This friendly family restaurant with great Mexican food is easy to spot if you look for the large green and yellow building or the mermaid on the sign. Traditional Mexican dishes are the best bargain, but seafood lovers will have plenty to choose from: the menu lists 12 different shrimp dishes, such as Hawaiian-style shrimp wrapped in bacon and served in a sweet apple-and-pineapple sauce. ☒ *Blvd. Kino and Comonfort, Centro* ☎ *638/383–3470* ⊟ *MC, V.*

**$–$$** ✕ **Friendly Dolphin.** This bright blue-and-pink palace feels like a home, with its nicely stuccoed ceilings, hand-painted tiles, and upstairs porch with a harbor view. Unique family recipes include foil-wrapped shrimp or fish prepared *estilo delfín*—steamed in orange juice, herbs, and spices. Gaston, the operatic owner, can easily be coaxed into singing traditional rancheras in a baritone as rich and robust as the food. ☒ *Calle José Alcantar 44, Col. Puerto* ☎ *638/383–2608* ⊟ *MC, V.*

**$$–$$$** ✕▦ **Sonoran Spa Resort.** One of the first megacomplexes in Rocky Point, this massive pink resort operates much like a hotel, but it offers one-, two-, and three-bedroom, fully furnished condominiums in place of standard rooms. Best of all, prices—and facilities—are comparable to the hotels in the area. The Sonoran Grill ($–$$) serves steaks and seafood, as well as a great spicy lasagna made with chipotle chilis. The beach fronting the resort is never crowded and you can do plenty here without leaving the resort—a good thing since it is a bit far from the center of town. ☒ *Camino La Choya, Km 3.7, 83550* ☎ *638/383–1044; 877/976–2599 in the U.S.* ⊕ *www.sonoransparesort.com* ⇥ *204 rooms* ⌂ *Restaurant, room service, kitchens, cable TV, in-room VCRs, tennis court, 3 pools, gym, spa, beach* ⊟ *MC, V.*

**$$** ✕▦ **Playa Bonita.** One of the first three hotels in Puerto Peñasco, Playa Bonita is beginning to show its age, though rooms are still clean and comfortable. Ask for a room facing the hotel's broad, sandy beach. An RV park offers 300 hookups at $17–$20 a day. As the name of the Puesta del Sol restaurant ("setting of the sun") implies, this is a perfect place to see the sun set, with plenty of beachfront patio seating. Don't miss the divine margaritas. ☒ *Paseo Balboa 100, Playa Hermosa, 85550* ☎ *638/383–2586; 888/232–8142 in the U.S.* ⊕ *www.playabonitaresort. com* ⇥ *120 rooms, 6 suites* ⌂ *Restaurant, cable TV, pool, hot tub, beach, bar* ⊟ *MC, V.*

**$$** 🏨 **Plaza Las Glorias.** Sitting like a sand-color fortress overlooking the beach, Plaza Las Glorias was the first large chain hotel to hit town. Its open lobby with towering quadrangular ceiling and bamboo-covered skylights draws gasps of admiration from the busloads of tourists who flock here. Rooms are standard; for just a bit more money, junior suites offer refrigerators, microwaves, and ocean views. ⊠ *Paseo Las Glorias 1, Playa Hermosa 83550* ☎ *638/383–0300 or 800/614–9484; 888/ 598–9866 in the U.S.* 🖷 *638/383–6015* ⊕ *www.plazalasglorias.com. mx* ⟲ *210 rooms, 40 suites* ∆ *Restaurant, cable TV, pool, hot tub, beach, snorkeling, bar* ➪ *MC, V.*

**$$** 🏨 **Viña del Mar.** With an old-town location and sweeping ocean views, this tidy hotel gives you an opportunity to sample most of Puerto Peñasco's pleasures without venturing too far from your room. You'll be right by the beach and the shops and restaurants of the malecón. Rooms are bright but sparsely decorated; some face the ocean for excellent sunset views. ⊠ *Av. Primer de Junio, Col. Puerto 83550* ☎ *638/383–0100 or 638/383–3600* 🖷 *638/383–3714* ⟲ *110 rooms* ∆ *Restaurant, cable TV, pool, hot tub, beach, 3 bars, dance club, meeting room* ➪ *MC, V.*

### Nightlife

Puerto Peñasco's nightlife centers around drinking. The sports bar **Latitude 31** (⊠ Blvd. Benito Juárez, en route to Col. Puerto ☎ 638/388–4311) has a great view of the harbor and a host of TVs showing American sports. **The Lighthouse** (⊠ Lote 2, Fracc. el Cerro ☎ 638/383–2389), a pretty restaurant-bar overlooking the harbor, appeals to a more sophisticated crowd. You can dance to live music between 6 and 10 every night except Monday. Popular among the young and those who don't want to put too much distance between the water's edge and their next margarita is **Manny's Beach Club** (⊠ Blvd. Matamoros s/n, Playa Miramar ☎ 638/383–3605). Recorded music blares constantly in this local landmark and it's often packed when other spots are deserted.

### Sports & the Outdoors

WATER SPORTS At **Sun and Fun Dive and Tackle** (⊠ Blvd. Benito Juárez s/n at Calle Lauro Contreras ☎ 638/383–5450) you can rent fishing, diving, or snorkeling equipment or receive PADI and NAUI scuba instruction. Sunset cruises, fishing charters, and snorkeling trips can all be booked here.

## Hermosillo

▶ ❹ *185 km (115 mi) south of Magdalena on Hwy. 15.*

Hermosillo (population 850,000) is the capital of Sonora, a status it has held on and off since 1831. It's the seat of the state university and benefits from that institution's cultural activities. If you know a bit of Spanish, you might think the city's name means "little beauty." In fact, it honors José María González Hermosillo, one of the leaders in Mexico's War of Independence.

Settled in 1742 by Captain Augustín de Vildosola and a contingent of 50 soldiers, Hermosillo was originally called Pitic, the Pima Indian name for "the place where two rivers meet." The city's most prestigious neighborhood—home to the governor and U.S. consul, among other prominent citizens—still bears the name Pitic. Located immediately north of the highway into town and behind the Hotel Bugambilia, the area is worth an hour's stroll to view the creative handling of concrete, tile, and other materials in the homes of Hermosillo's affluent residents.

As the state's business center, Hermosillo is largely modern, but some lovely plazas and parks hark back to a more graceful past.

At the center of town, look for charming **Plaza Zaragoza,** a town square shaded by orange trees and towering figs. Edging the plaza are the town hall and a lovely Moorish-style wrought-iron gazebo. On the plaza's south side stands the **Catedral de Nuestra Señora de la Asunción.** The church was built between 1877 and 1912; during the extended construction time, its neoclassic style was somewhat diluted.

Atop the Cerro la Campana (Hill of Bells), which offers the best viewpoint in the city, stands a former penitentiary, now the **Museo de Sonora.** The cells hold 18 permanent exhibits on astronomy, anthropology, history, geology, geography, and culture, all with a Sonoran slant. The bulk of the exhibits are graphic displays, including charts and maps of trade routes and native populations. Each display has a short summary in English. ⊠ *Jesús García Final s/n, Col. La Matanza* ☎ *662/217–2714* ✍ *$3* ☉ *Tues.–Sat. 10–5, Sun. 9–4.*

☾ On the highway south of town sits the **Centro Ecológico,** an environmental and ecological park with more than 500 species of plants and animals. The outdoor park is best visited November through March because of the heat and lack of shade the rest of the year. The zoo section has a wide variety of animals, but they're sadly cramped in small cages. An observatory holds shows on weekends. ⊠ *Carretera a Guaymas, Km 2.5, 5 km (3 mi) south of Hermosillo* ☎ *662/250–1225* ⊕ *www.centroecologico.com.mx* ✍ *$2* ☉ *Daily 8–5.*

## Where to Stay & Eat

**$$** ✕ **Xochimilco.** If you want to try regional specialties and are willing to go with the set meal, come to this large, institutional-looking place on a narrow side street near the town center. Popular with locals and regulars from across the border, Xochimilco's meals are designed for two or more, and include carne asada, ribs, tripe, vegetable salad, beans, and fresh flour tortillas. ⊠ *Av. Obregón 51, at Gutiérrez, Col. Villa de Seris* ☎ *622/250–4089* ▤ *MC, V.*

**$–$$** ✕ **Sonora Steak.** Come to this sophisticated, understated old house to slice into the finest cuts of the famous Sonoran beef at reasonable prices. The specialty, rib-eye steak, is aged 28 days. Vegetarians can graze on a variety of salads, or opt for cream of green chili soup or fettucine with pasillo chili and garlic. The restaurant is a good spot for a late-night meal—it's open until 2 AM. ⊠ *Blvd. Kino 914, Zona Hotelera* ☎ *662/210–0313* ▤ *MC, V.*

**$$$** ▥ **Fiesta Americana.** Hermosillo's premier hotel, this property is the largest in town and popular among business travelers. The guest rooms stick to a safely tasteful beige-and-forest-green decor. The adjacent disco is one of the most popular in town. ⊠ *Blvd. Kino 369, Col. Lomas Pitic 83010* ☎ *622/259–6000; 800/343–7821 in the U.S.* ▤ *622/259–6062*

⊕ *www.fiestaamericana.com* ⤴ *221 rooms* ♨ *Restaurant, cafeteria, cable TV, tennis court, pool, gym, bar, dance club, shop, business services, meeting rooms, car rental, travel services* ⊟ *AE, MC, V.*

**$$** 🖵 **Holiday Inn Hermosillo.** Two-thirds of the attractive rooms in this contemporary, two-story hotel surround a large green lawn and a good-size pool. With all the amenities and a location in the heart of the hotel zone, it's a bargain. ⊠ *Blvd. Kino and Ramón Corral 1110, Zona Hotelera 83010* ☎ *662/289–1700; 800/623–3300 in Mexico; 800/465–4329 in the U.S.* 🖶 *662/214–6473* ⊕ *www.holidayinnhermosillo.com. mx* ⤴ *123 rooms, 9 suites* ♨ *Restaurant, cable TV, pool, gym, bar, business services, meeting rooms, travel services, airport shuttle, free parking* ⊟ *AE, MC, V.*

**$** 🖵 **Hotel Bugambilia.** This pleasant small property has a trio of top assets: comfortable rooms, a convenient location in the hotel zone, and a good restaurant. The bougainvillea-covered bungalows facing the parking spaces are most popular; other rooms surround the pool. Guests can use the facilities at the Holiday Inn, across the street. ⊠ *Blvd. Kino 712, Zona Hotelera 83010* ☎ *662/289–1600* 🖶 *662/214–5252* ⤴ *104 rooms* ♨ *Restaurant, room service, cable TV, pool, free parking* ⊟ *AE, MC, V.*

### Nightlife & the Arts

**Bar Freedom** (⊠ Blvd. Kino 1012, Zona Hotelera ☎ 662/215–0640) is popular with an upscale, young crowd that comes to dance to various types of Mexican music: Friday and Saturday is disco, Sunday through Tuesday is *banda,* and mariachi music fills in Wednesday and Thursday. **Marco n' Charlie's** (⊠ Blvd. Rodríguez at Calle San Luis Potosí, Zona Hotelera ☎ 662/215–3061) is a watering hole for the town's upper crust. **La Trova Arte–Bar** (⊠ Calle Guerrero and Tamaulipas, Zona Hotelera ☎ 662/214–2861) has romantic music for dancing Wednesday through Saturday.

### Shopping

In the downtown markets of Hermosillo, particularly along Avenidas Serdán and Monterrey, you can buy anything from blankets and candles to wedding attire, as well as a selection of cowboy boots. The variety of goods concentrated in this area equals what you'll find in Nogales, and the prices are better. Local sweets, called *coyotas* (pie crust surrounding brown sugar or a molasses-like sweet), can be purchased in the Villa de Seris neighborhood, near restaurant Xochimilco. At **Ehui!** (⊠ Av. Serdán at Pino Suárez, Centro ☎ 662/212–4010) the friendly Mexican and American owners will tell you the history behind *torote* grass baskets, beautifully carved rain sticks, reproductions of Yaqui testaments, and more typical souvenirs like Talavera dishware.

## Ruta de Río Sonora

*300 km (180 mi) between Hermosillo and Cananea.*

The state highways that follow the state's namesake river are a terrific, adventurous way to see a less-touristy side of Sonora. Between Hermosillo and Cananea, the riverbanks are speckled with small towns, each with its own charm. Some are known for their thermal springs, others for their rich histories. This was the region's first inhabited area; it was settled by the Pima and Opata groups. The *ruta* (route) is also linked to the arrival of the Europeans; the Spanish explorer Alvar Núñez Cabeza de Vaca followed the Río Sonora during his travels between central Mexico and what is now the United States in the mid-16th century. The main towns on this route were all founded around the time of the Coronado expedition in the 1640s. Upon entering each town, signs will give you the exact year. The towns of Ures and Banámichi are two of the largest and oldest towns on the route, both offering a glimpse of traditional Sonoran life. As is typical of the area, each has a colonial church and a heart-of-town square. When people come into town from the surrounding ranches, they end up in the squares for both business and pleasure—you'll see plenty of cowboy boots and hats.

The region is known for its hospitality. It is common for townspeople to wave to you as you pass by. It's easiest to drive up the valley from Hermosillo; driving part of the route makes a great day trip, especially in autumn when the trees along the river turn golden. It's also possible to drive south from Cananea, but you'd have to go over mountain roads, which are particularly difficult in bad weather. *To follow the route from Hermosillo, take Sonora 14 east to Mazocahui, passing through Ures and continue north on Sonora 089.*

## Bahía Kino

➎ *107 km (64 mi) west of Hermosillo on Sonora Hwy. 100.*

On the eastern shore of the Mar de Cortés lies Bahía Kino, home to some of the prettiest beaches in northwest Mexico. For many years, Bahía Kino was undiscovered except by RV owners and other aficionados of the unspoiled. In the past decade or so, great change has come at the hands of North Americans who have been building condos and beach houses here. More change is in the planning as land has been acquired and designs have been submitted for a marina, although no date has been set for construction to begin. The moniker "Bahía Kino" actually refers to twin towns: Kino Viejo (Old Kino, the Mexican village) and Kino Nuevo (New Kino), where facing a long strand of creamy beach you'll find private homes, condos, RV sites, and other tourist facilities.

There's little to do in Bahía Kino, so after hanging around a few days, you might consider taking a run across the narrow channel to **Isla del Tiburón** (Shark Island), designated an ecological preserve in 1963. Permission to visit Tiburón may be obtained from the Seri Indian government; they can also provide a reliable boatman-guide. Only the Seri Indians, for whom Isla del Tiburón is a traditional fishing ground, are permitted to ferry travelers across and guide them around the island. The trip, which is of most interest to anglers and bird-watchers, costs about $250 per boatload of one to four passengers. ⊠ *Seri Indian government: main street, across from the Pemex station, Kino Viejo* ☎ *662/242–0557 or 662/242–0590.*

For a crash ethnography lesson, poke around the interesting if haphazard collection of photographs, musical instruments, artwork, baskets, clothing, and dioramas in the **Museo de los Seris.** Be prepared to practice your Spanish as there are no descriptions in English. ⊠ *Blvd. Mar de Cortés at Calle Progreso* ☎ *No phone* 🎫 *50¢* ⊙ *Wed.–Sun. 8–5.*

If you'll be in town a week or more, it's worthwhile to obtain a temporary membership to the **Club Deportivo.** For $15 a month, you'll be introduced to most of the town's temporary residents and some locals as well. The club offers everything from quilting and Spanish classes to dances and other social activities. There's also a golf course; for a $5 fee you can use the 9-hole sand course with artificial greens. ⊠ *Calle Cadiz s/n at Plaza del Mar RV Park* ☎ *662/242–0321.*

## Where to Stay & Eat

$–$$$  ✕ **El Pargo Rojo.** Fishnets and realistic reproductions of the fish you'll be eating decorate this restaurant, whose name means "red snapper." The catch of the day varies, but you can depend on consistent quality. Classics like a brimming shrimp cocktail could be followed by fish stuffed with shrimp, clams, squid, and octopus. Depending on your luck, you'll be serenaded either by Mexican musicians or by the ceaseless wailing of recorded, polkalike *norteña* music on Mexican MTV. ⊠ *Blvd. Mar de Cortés 1426, Kino Nuevo* ☎ *662/242–0205* ▤ *MC, V.*

★ $–$$$  ✕ **Restaurant Marlyn.** Though this place may be a bit hard to find at first, you may well find yourself returning, drawn by the clean, unpretentious atmosphere and congenial service—not to mention margaritas as big as fishbowls. Superb seafood dishes include *sopa de siete mares* (soup of the seven seas) and *jaiba a la diabla* (a spicy hot crab dish). ⊠ *Calles Tastiota and Guaymas, Kino Viejo* ☎ *662/242–0111* ▤ *MC, V* ⊙ *Closed Mon.*

$–$$  ✕ **Jorge's Restaurant.** This clean, comfortable family restaurant overlooks the bay—a perfect spot for morning coffee, pancakes, and pelican viewing. At other meals portions tend to be small, but the food is quite good, and the owner and his daughters play the guitar and sing in the evening. ⊠ *Near the end of Blvd. Mar de Cortés at Alecantres, Kino Nuevo* ☎ *662/ 242–0049* ▤ *No credit cards.*

$–$$  ✕ **La Palapa.** This thatch-roof spot may be plain, but the food's delicious. The shrimp brochette with green chilies and the breaded oysters are memorable; this is also *the* place for a great, juicy cheeseburger. ⊠ *Blvd. Mar de Cortés and Wellington, on the way into Kino Nuevo* ☎ *662/ 242–0210* ▤ *MC, V.*

$  🛏 **Posada del Mar.** A beachfront location is the bright spot here; you can see the sea from the wide second-story balcony. Rooms, on the other hand, are dark and could use some sprucing up. On the grounds, cacti and stone walkways surround a central fountain. ⊠ *Blvd. Mar de Cortés and Calle Creta, Kino Nuevo 83340* ☎☎ *662/242–0155* ⊕ *www. hotelposadadelmar.com* 🛏 *42 rooms, 2 suites, 2 bungalows* ♻ *Picnic area, pool; no room TVs* ▤ *MC, V.*

$  🛏 **Posada Las Aves.** There's a lot to love about these one- and two-bedroom apartments. They're a great deal: the two largest units—which sleep five or six comfortably in two bedrooms—have a fireplace in the living room, full kitchen and dining room, and cost just over $100 a night. All of the units are spacious, with sturdy wood cabinets, clunky wood and vinyl couches, and sparkling tile bathrooms. ⊠ *Calle Veracruz between Calles Nautla and Tecolutla, Kino Nuevo 83340* ☎ *662/242–0242*

⊕ *www.posadalasaves.com* ⤸ *11 apartments* ⌂ *Picnic area, kitchens, cable TV, pool, playground, free parking* ☰ *No credit cards.*

## Shopping

Kino has little in the way of crafts or even souvenirs, but **Alcatraz** (⊠ Calle Tastiota 12, Kino Nuevo ☎ 662/242–0570), which is Mexican Spanish for calla lily, offers Talavera-style plates, shell ornaments, and plenty of gift items and housewares from all over Mexico.

## Punta Chueca

**❻** *27 km (17 mi) north of Bahía Kino.*

This rustic Seri fishing village perches at the end of a long, bumpy, winding dirt road. (You'll need a sturdy high-clearance vehicle to make this scenic drive.) You'll pass exquisite vistas of the bay, distant empty beaches, and rolling mountains. The inhabitants of this community live a subsistence lifestyle, relying on the sea and desert much as they have for hundreds of years.

With fewer than 700 remaining members, the Seri tribe represents an ancient culture on the verge of dying out. The Seris' love for their natural surroundings is evident in the necklaces that they have traditionally worn and now create to sell. Pretty little shells are wound into the shape of flowers and strung with wild desert seeds and tiny bleached snake vertebrae. Seri women also weave elaborate *canastas* (baskets) of torote grass, which are highly prized and expensive.

As you get out of your car anywhere in town, be prepared to encounter an entourage of Seri women dressed in colorful ankle-length skirts, their heads covered with scarves and their arms laden with necklaces for sale. The Seri are best known, however, for the carved ironwood figurines that represent the animal world around them, including dolphins, turtles, and pelicans. Many Mexican merchants have taken to machine-making large figures out of ironwood for the tourist trade, thereby seriously depleting the supply of the lilac-blossomed tree that grows only in the Sonoran desert. (If the bottom of the statuette is clean cut, it was cut with an electric saw and not made by the Seri.) For this reason, the Seri now carve figures out of several types of stone.

## Guaymas

**❼** *128 km (79 mi) south of Hermosillo.*

The buzz and bustle of Guaymas—Mexico's seventh-largest port—has a pleasant backdrop of rusty red, saguaro-speckled mountains that nudge the deep-blue waters of a sprawling bay on the Mar de Cortés. The Spanish arrived in this "port of ports" by the mid-16th century. In 1701, two Jesuit priests, Father Kino and his colleague Juan María Salvatierra, erected a mission base here intended to convert the native Guaimas, Seri, and Yaqui Indians.

Guaymas was declared a commercial port in 1814 and became an important center of trade with Europe as well as within Mexico. In 1847,

# THE MAQUILA'S MARCH TO MODERNITY

**W**HEN MEXICO BEGAN ITS Border Industrialization Program in 1965, few could have imagined the social and environmental ills that open markets and prosperous free-trade deals would spawn three decades later. Mexico's maquiladoras (also known as maquilas) are foreign-owned assembly plants that produce cars, electronics, and garments for export to the First World; the passage of the North American Free Trade Agreement (NAFTA), which relaxed tariffs on goods moving across North American borders, made the maquila a profitable tool for U.S. companies. Even prior to NAFTA, repeated recessions and peso devaluations in the 1980s, combined with drought and chronic poverty in many of the northern and central agricultural states, brought both multinational companies and desperate migrant workers to Tijuana and Ensenada in Baja California, Nogales in Sonora, Matamoros in Tamaulipas, and above all, Ciudad Juárez in the state of Chihuahua.

Shantytowns sprang up, most of which are still lacking in clean water, sanitation, schools, electricity, and other basic infrastructure; companies and city governments have had no legal obligation, no financial incentive, and in the case of the local governments, no tax revenue, to provide for inhabitants. With time, the living conditions have improved marginally in some areas, but even with meager allowances for housing or health care, workers here are still exploited by American labor standards. And because NAFTA has only an impotent Commission on Environmental Cooperation (CEC) to evaluate, but not enforce, the safe environmental procedures outlined in the agreement, hundreds of maquilas regularly dump hazardous waste along the border. It's estimated that less than half of American maquilas follow Mexican law and return their toxic waste to the United States.

Though the maquila industry created hundreds of thousands of jobs, it effectively threw a grenade in the midst of rural Mexico's family mores and values—for better and worse. Academic studies chart devastating social disintegration, but Mexican women—who for the first time earn a wage and decide what to do with it—are viewed by many to have finally found some liberation.

Ciudad Juárez sits above anonymous swathes of the huge state of Chihuahua, just over the Río Bravo (or Rio Grande) from El Paso, Texas. Over the last three decades more than a million souls have come to toil in the maquilas. Juárez became a magnet for young women, lured from the interior of the country by plentiful jobs. As it turned out, though, not only was their labor cheap, but so were their lives. Since 1993, there have been over 370 officially recognized murders of young women. Hundreds of others have disappeared and are presumed dead. The maquila murders in Juárez have become a scandal of international proportions, and although most cases remain unsolved, local, state, and even international protest is beginning to mount.

The maquila zone poses problems with no easy answers, which still look a long way from resolution. Every day hopeful young men and women are carted in from their rank little huts every day to make gadgets for others, before they can make a life for themselves.

— Barbara Kastelein

during the Mexican-American War, U.S. naval forces attacked and occupied the town for a year. Bumbling filibuster William Walker also managed to take Guaymas for a short time in 1853, and in 1866, during Maximilian's brief reign, the French took control. Today's foreign invaders are mostly travelers passing through on their way somewhere else. Given its proximity to the beaches of San Carlos and Mazatlán, modern Guaymas is more a stepping-stone than a destination. That said, it's a congenial seaside town that some folks prefer to the more tourist-oriented, spread-out San Carlos.

No visit to a Mexican town is complete without a trip to the *mercado,* or municipal market, bursting with colors and smells and a glimpse at daily life. After the throngs, you'll find quiet at the 19th-century church **Parroquia de San Fernando.** Or you might relax across the street at **Plaza 13 de Julio,** a typical Mexican park with a Moorish-style bandstand and matching benches. Follow the signs to Playa Miramar and take advantage of the free tours offered by the pearl farm, **Perlas del Mar de Cortez** (⊠ Bahía de Bacochibampo s/n ☎ 622/221–0136), which has over 200,000 native pearl oysters in cultivation—it's the only pearl farm of its scale in the Americas. Tours are conducted on the hour from 9 AM to 3 PM Monday through Friday and 9 AM to 11 AM on Saturday.

## Where to Stay & Eat

**$–$$** ✕ **Los Barcos.** Los Barcos offers a predictable seafood-and-steak menu. The main room is large and somewhat sterile, with an enormous bar along the back wall. The fan-cooled, thatch-roof adjoining room is more relaxed, with its jukebox and walls painted with smiling dolphins and octopi. The crab tostadas are especially recommended. ⊠ *Calle 22 and Malecón, Centro* ☎ *622/222–7650* ▭ *MC, V.*

**$** ✕▥ **Hotel Armida.** On the edge of town but still close to downtown, this sand-color hotel has a large, well-kept pool, and a good coffee shop where locals gather for power breakfasts. At the excellent steak house, El Oeste ($$–$$$), the stuffed and mounted heads of mountain goats, cougars, and bison gaze down at diners. Large, bright accommodations are plain but serviceable, with comfortable beds; many have balconies overlooking the pool. The economy rooms at the back are a great bargain. ⊠ *Carretera Internacional, Salida Norte 85420* ☎ *622/222–5220* 🖷 *622/224–0448* ⊕ *www.hotelarmida.com* ⤴ *125 rooms* ⚭ *Restaurant, coffee shop, room service, cable TV, pool, bar, meeting rooms, free parking* ▭ *MC, V.*

## Nightlife

**Equus Disco Bar** (⊠ Carretera a Guaymas 1200 ☎ 622/222–3232) has DJs who spin dance and electronica for a young, upscale crowd. It's only open Friday and Saturday.

# San Carlos

❽ *20 km (12 mi) northwest of Guaymas.*

Long considered an extension of Guaymas, and still occasionally referred to as San Carlos, Nuevo Guaymas, this resort town—on the other side of the rocky peninsula that separates Bahía de Bacochibampo from

Bahía de San Carlos—has a personality of its own. Whitewashed houses with red-tile roofs snuggle together along the water where countless yachts and motorboats are docked. The town is a laid-back favorite among professional anglers, North American tourists, and the time-share crowd, as well as wealthy Mexican families from Guaymas. There's a growing assortment of hotels and condominiums, as well as two marinas and a country club with an 18-hole golf course.

The overlapping of desert and semitropical flora and fauna has created a fascinating diversity of species along this coast. Among marine life, more than 650 species of fish exist here. Whales have occasionally been spotted in Bahía de San Carlos, but more common are dolphins and pelicans. The water is calm and warm enough for swimming through October. Scuba, snorkeling, fishing, and boat excursions are popular, too.

The quiet 5-km (3-mi) stretch of sandy beach at **Los Algodones,** where the San Carlos Plaza Hotel and Club Med are now, was in the 1960s a location site for the film *Catch 22.* (In fact, it's still called the Catch 22 beach on many maps.) San Carlos lies in the shadow of the jagged twin-peak **Tetakawi mountain,** a sacred site where native warriors once gathered to gain spiritual strength. The **Mirador Escénico,** or scenic lookout, is the best place in San Carlos to view the Mar de Cortés. Take the steep road up here for a great photo op or just to get an idea of the lay of the land. Just north of the Mirador is Zorro Cove, a great place to snorkel. An interesting day trip (by boat) is the pristine **Isla de San Pedro Nolasco,** an ecological reserve where sea lions claim the rocks.

San Carlos itself has no real city center; instead, it stretches for miles along the four-lane **Corredor Escénico** (Scenic Corridor), which is officially called Boulevard Manlio Fabio Beltrones, or more commonly, Boulevard Beltrones, after a former governor of Sonora.

## Where to Stay & Eat

$–$$ ✕ **Rosa's Cantina.** The walls at this cozy, pink, laid-back restaurant are decorated with historical photos from Mexico's past, including many of Mexican revolutionaries. Ask anyone in town and they'll tell you Rosa's ample breakfasts are the best way to start the day. Try the machaca (dried beef) with eggs and yummy salsa; the tortilla soup is great for lunch or dinner. Gringos who miss being pampered will appreciate the nonsmoking section, decaf coffee, and a safe, sanitary salad bar. ⊠ *Calle Aurora 297, Creston* ☎ *622/226–1000* ▣ *MC, V.*

$$ ✕▦ **Marinaterra.** This hotel complex overlooks the San Carlos marina and has a commanding view of Cerro Tetakawi. Pastels soften the rooms, and most accommodations have a tiny kitchenette. Some corner rooms have hot tubs on outdoor patios available for no extra cost. A shuttle takes guests to the hotel beach club. El Embarcadero restaurant ($–$$) is a good place to try hearty, traditional Mexican soups, like the *caldo Xochitl,* a steaming chicken consommé with white rice, avocado, garnished with chili. ⊠ *Calle Gabriel Estrada s/n, Sector La Herradura 85506* ☎ *622/225–2020; 888/688–5353 in the U.S.* ▣ *622/226–1035* ⊕ *www.marinaterra. com* ⇄ *87 rooms, 18 suites* ₫ *Restaurant, snack bar, refrigerators, cable TV, 2 pools, baby-sitting, car rental, travel services* ▣ *AE, MC, V.*

$$$  🏨 **San Carlos Plaza Hotel and Resort.** Rising from Bahía de San Carlos, this huge, striking pink edifice is the most luxurious hotel in Sonora. The arresting atrium lobby opens onto a large pool and beach. Attractive rooms—all with at least a partial ocean view—have contemporary, if uninspiring, furnishings, and rooms on the first two floors have balconies overlooking the sea. Children love the swimming-pool slide and horseback riding on beautiful Algodones beach. ✉ *Paseo Mar Barmejo Norte 4, Los Algodones 85506* 🖀 *622/227–0077; 800/854–2320 in the U.S.* 🖷 *622/ 227–0098* ⊕ *www.guaymassancarlos.net* 📞 *132 rooms, 41 suites* ◊ *3 restaurants, snack bar, in-room safes, minibars, cable TV, 2 tennis courts, 2 pools, gym, hot tub, beach, 2 bars, meeting rooms* ▭ *AE, MC, V.*

$  🏨 **Fiesta San Carlos.** Every room in this small, beachfront, family-run hotel soaks up views of the gulf. The minimally decorated rooms are clean and comfortable. Some rooms with kitchens are available. ✉ *Blvd. Beltrones, Km 8.5, Carretera Escénico 85506* 🖀 *622/226–0229 or 662/ 226–1318* ⊕ *www.fiestasancarlos.com* 📞 *33 rooms* ◊ *Restaurant, pool, bar, free parking; no room phones, no room TVs* ▭ *MC, V* ¶◎ *BP.*

$  🏨 **Hacienda Tetakawi.** This hotel and trailer park across from the beach on the main street of town is part of the Best Western chain. Rooms are generic but clean, and each has a balcony, a few with a view of the sea. ✉ *Blvd. Beltrones, Km 10, San Carlos 85000* 🖀 *622/226–0248* 📞 *22 rooms* ◊ *Restaurant, pool, bar, cable TV* ▭ *MC, V.*

## Nightlife & the Arts

For two floors of paintings and sculpture by a variety of Mexican and foreign artists, stop by the **Galería Bellas Artes** (✉ Villa Hermosa 111, Sector Villahermosa 🖀 622/226–0073), where their work is for sale. It's open Monday–Saturday 9:30–5. Every Tuesday the **San Carlos Plaza Hotel** (🖀 622/227–0077) hosts an evening of folkloric dancing and singing along with dinner buffet and open bar ($18). Reservations are encouraged; transportation from some hotels is provided.

The **Mai-Tai Bar** (✉ Hotel Marinaterra 🖀 622/225–2030) has live music until 2 AM Friday and Saturday. **Ranas Ranas** (✉ Carretera San Carlos, Km 9.5, Carretera Escénico 🖀 622/226–0610) is a party-down bar with a beach view. **Tequilas Bar** (✉ Gabriel Estrada 1, Marina San Carlos 🖀 622/226–0545) is a popular nightspot with a small dance floor, big crowd, and live music on weekends.

## Sports & the Outdoors

GOLF  Anyone can get a tee time at the par-72, Pete Dye–designed, 18-hole golf course at the **Club de Golf San Carlos** (✉ Av. de los Yaquis, between Loma Bonita and Solimar 🖀🖀 622/226–1102); the $52 greens fee includes a cart. People staying in area hotels usually get lower greens fees.

WATER SPORTS  **Gary's Dive Shop** (✉ Blvd. Beltrones, Km 10 🖀 622/226–0049; 622/226– 0024 after hours ⊕ www.garysdivemexico.com) is lovingly run by American owners Gary and Donna Goldstein, who have been residents and business owners here for over 30 years. They provide free information about the area and run excellent fishing, snorkeling, and PADI-certified diving excursions. You can also book sunset cruises, and whale-watching and customized expeditions.

## Shopping

**Kiamy's Gift Shop** (✉ Blvd. Beltrones, Km 10 ☎ 622/226–0400) is like a bazaar, with something for everyone: silver jewelry, earrings, leather bags, ceramics, Yaqui Indian masks, and T-shirts. **Sagitario's Gift Shop** (✉ Blvd. Beltrones 132 ☎ 622/226–0090) features clothing and a variety of crafts, including wood carvings, baskets, high-quality rugs, and Talavera tile.

## Alamos

★ ❾  *257 km (160 mi) southeast of Guaymas.*

With its cobblestone streets, charming central plaza, 250-year-old Baroque church, and thoughtfully restored haciendas, Alamos is the most authentically restored colonial town in Sonora. In the ecologically rich zone where the Sonoran desert meets a dry tropical forest (also called the semitropical thorn forest) in the foothills of the Sierra Madre, the entire town is designated a national historic monument.

Coronado camped here in 1540, and a Jesuit mission (later destroyed in an Indian rebellion) was established in 1630, but the town really boomed when silver was discovered in the area during the 1680s. Wealth from the mines financed Spanish expeditions to the north—as far as Los Angeles and San Francisco during the 1770s and '80s—and the town became the capital of the state of Occidente, which combined the provinces of Sinaloa and Sonora, from 1827 to 1832. A government mint was established here in 1864. The mines closed by the end of the 19th century, and the town went into decline.

These days, Alamos has reinvented itself as a tourist spot. Leading the movement is a relatively large number of expats who have bought and restored sprawling haciendas near the center of town, turning some into luxurious private homes, others into hotels.

Points of interest include the impressive **Parroquia de Nuestra Señora de la Concepción,** constructed on the site of a 17th-century adobe church destroyed in an Indian uprising. Fronting the parish church is the beautiful central square, the **Plaza las Armas;** its ornate Moorish-style wrought-iron gazebo was brought from Mazatlán in 1904. To the west of the square, on the Cerro de Guadalupe, the old Alamos **jail** is still in use. South of the square is Cerro del Perico, on the top of which is **El Mirador,** which provides a scenic view of the city.

If possible, time your trip to Alamos to include a Saturday **house and garden tour** ($8 suggested donation) of some of the superbly restored mansions and their interior patios and gardens. You can get a tour schedule from the tourist office or any of the local hotels.

Don't miss the **Museo Costumbrista de Sonora** for an excellent overview of the cultural history of the state of Sonora. The numerous well-marked (some in English) displays include artifacts from the nearby silver mines and coins from the mints of Alamos and Hermosillo, as well as typical examples of the clothing and furnishings of prominent local families.

✉ *Calle Guadalupe Victoria 1, on Plaza las Armas* ☎ *647/428–0053* 🎟 *$1* 🕐 *Wed.–Sun. 9–6.*

**Casa de Maria Felix** is a house/museum on the property rumored to be the birthplace of Mexican film star Maria Felix. As such, it has become somewhat of a pilgrimage destination for her legions of fans. On the property is an adobe wall from the original house, numerous paintings honoring the star and some large objects recovered during the building of the current house. Smaller objects (some with relation to the actress, some without), including coins, weapons, and household items are on display in the museum. The owner also rents out comfortable rooms in the house that she shares with her five dogs and two cats. ✉ *Calle Galeana 41* ☎ *647/428–0929* 🎟 *$3* 🕐 *Thurs.–Sun. 2–4 or by appointment.*

## Where to Stay & Eat

★ $ ✕ **Las Palmeras.** This Mexican family restaurant is crammed onto the sidewalk across the street from the Museo Costumbrista de Sonora on the main square. Here you might get homemade *rosca* bread (a sweet, round loaf) with your coffee and an assortment of daily specials. The corn tamales are hard to beat; other specialties include the *chiles relleno* (cheese-stuffed chile peppers) and the *carne milanesa* (similar to chicken-fried steak). ✉ *Lázaro Cárdenas 9* ☎ *647/428–0065* ⚐ *Reservations not accepted* ☰ *No credit cards.*

$ ✕ **Polo's.** Locals, gringos, and expats all converge here; the owner can generally be found roaming the restaurant chatting it up with everyone. The food is simple but very good: sandwiches, shish kebab, and Sonoran steaks. ✉ *Calle Zaragoza 4* ☎ *647/428–0001* ⚐ *Reservations not accepted* ☰ *No credit cards.*

$ ✕ **Los Sabinos.** This small, unpretentious family home–turned–mini café has seating indoors and out, and an extensive menu. House specials include beef tips and ranch-style shrimp, along with fried fillet of sole in garlic butter and lots of kid-favorites like quesadillas and burgers. No alcoholic beverages are sold here. ✉ *Calle 2 de Abril Poniente 15* ☎ *647/428–0598* ⚐ *Reservations not accepted* ☰ *No credit cards.*

$$$ 🏨 **Hacienda de los Santos.** Alamos's most opulent hotel rambles across the grounds of four restored and linked colonial mansions; you'll be well secluded from the outside world by the walls of these former haciendas. In gracious courtyards and lining long porticos are centuries-old pieces of religious art and hand-carved antique furniture, all collected by the American owners. The spacious bedrooms also have antiques, as well as fireplaces. A spa offers massage and beauty treatments. ✉ *Calle Molina 8, 85763* ☎ *647/428–0222; 800/525–4800 in the U.S.* 🖷 *647/428–0367* ⊕ *www.haciendadelossantos.com* 🛏 *8 rooms, 5 suites* ⚐ *Restaurant, cable TV, putting green, 3 pools, gym, spa, bar; no kids under 16, no smoking* ☰ *AE, MC, V* ⏏ *CP.*

FodorsChoice
★

$$ 🏨 **Casa de los Tesoros.** This hotel, the House of Treasures, is a picturesque and romantic converted 18th-century convent. The rooms were once nuns' cells, but they're no longer austere—they've now got fireplaces, tile baths, antique furnishings, and striking local art. The restaurant is excellent. ✉ *Av. Obregón 10, 85763* ☎ *647/428–0010* 🖷 *647/*

428–0400 ⊕ *www.tesoros-hotel.com* ⤴ *13 rooms, 2 suites* △ *Restaurant, pool, bar; no room phones, no room TVs* ☰ *MC, V* ⧠ *BP.*

¢–$ ⊡ **Los Amigos.** The American-expat owner of this cozy B&B a block from Plaza de las Armas treats you like a friend who's come to visit. Three attractive rooms share space with a huge collection of English-language books, glass art, and a fine collection of Mata Ortiz pottery. "Rooftop Camping" on comfy Sonoran cots ($10) is a budget option for the frugal traveler. ✉ *Obregón 3, 85760* ☎ *647/428–1014* ⊕ *www. alamosmexico.com/losamigos* ⤴ *3 rooms* △ *Coffee shop, library, shop; no a/c, no room phones, no room TVs* ☰ *No credit cards* ⧠ *CP.*

## Shopping

It's worth a peek into the three crowded rooms of **El Nicho Curios** (✉ Calle Juárez 15 ☎ 647/428–0213), filled with treasures ranging from Mexican religious paintings to old jewelry and regional pottery. Small stores lining **Plaza Alameda** (northwest of the central plaza) sell Mexican sweets, fabrics, belts, and hats, among other items. *Tianguis* (market stalls) line **Plaza las Armas** every day, but Sunday brings artisans and vendors from the surrounding area.

# Aduana

⑩ *10 km (6 mi) west of Alamos.*

Tucked a couple of miles down a dirt road off the main road to Alamos, Aduana was once the site of one of the richest mines in the district. The village lacks the revitalized charm of Alamos, but it's worth a visit nonetheless—especially for a meal at one of Sonora's best restaurants.

On the main plaza is the **Iglesia de Nuestra Señora de Balvanera.** A cactus that grows out of one of the church's walls is said to mark the spot where the Virgin appeared to the Yaqui Indians in the late 17th century, an event that is celebrated by a procession every November 21 and festivities that bring tens of thousands of the faithful.

## Where to Stay & Eat

$–$$ ✕⊡ **Casa la Aduana.** Though in an unlikely spot 2 mi down a dirt road
Fodor'sChoice off the highway into Alamos, the restaurant here has a reputation as
★ one of the best in Sonora. The restored 17th-century customs house hosts exceptional four-course, prix-fixe menus, with entrées such as chicken in an apple-chipotle cream sauce. Although the walls and floors of the B&B here are the restored originals, modern luxuries haven't been overlooked: soft linens, comfortable beds, and thick bath towels add to the charm. Guest rooms have four-foot-thick walls, which reflect their former duties as vaults for the riches that came from this area's mines. ✉ *Domicilio Conocido* ☎ *647/404–3473* ⊕ *www.casaladuana.com* ⤴ *3 rooms* △ *Restaurant, pool; no a/c, no room phones, no room TVs, no kids under 16* ☰ *MC, V* ⊙ *Closed May–June.*

# SONORA A TO Z

*To research prices, get advice from other travelers, and book travel arrangements, visit www.fodors.com.*

## AIR TRAVEL

AIRPORTS  Both Hermosillo and Guaymas have international airports: General Ignacio L. Pesqueira International Airport (HMO) and General José M. Yanez International Airport (GYM), respectively.

**⚑ General José M. Yanez International Airport** ⊠ Domicilio Conocido, Carretera a San José de Guaymas Guaymas ☎ 622/221-0634. **General Ignacio L. Pesqueira International Airport** ⊠ Carretera Hermosillo a Bahía Kino, Km 9.5, Hermosillo ☎ 662/261-0000.

AIRPORT  To get between the airports and their respective towns, you'll need to
TRANSFERS  take a taxi. Take only the licensed taxis available at the airport taxi stands. A ride from Hermosillo's airport to the town center takes about 15 minutes and should cost about $6. A trip from the Guaymas airport to Guaymas's center should cost $5 and take about 10 minutes. To get to San Carlos from the Guaymas airport should take 20 minutes and cost $10. Local hotels sometimes offer shuttles.

CARRIERS  AeroCalifornia offers daily nonstop jet service from Los Angeles and Monday, Wednesday, and Saturday service from Tucson to Hermosillo. Aeroméxico and its subsidiary Aerolitoral have daily flights to Hermosillo from Tucson, and flights from Los Angeles to Hermosillo. Aeroméxico has direct flights to Hermosillo from many cities in Mexico—including Mexico City, Tijuana, Chihuahua, and Guadalajara, with connections to Guaymas. Mexicana offers domestic service between Hermosillo and other major Mexican cities as well. America West Express has daily flights to Hermosillo and Guaymas from Phoenix.

**⚑ AeroCalifornia** ☎ 662/260-2555, 800/237-6225 in the U.S. **Aeroméxico** ☎ 01800/021-4050 toll free in Mexico, 800/237-6639 in the U.S. ⊕ www.aeromexico.com. **America West Express** ☎ 800/235-9292, 800/235-9292 in the U.S. ⊕ www.americawest.com. **Mexicana** ☎ 662/261-0112, 01800/849-1529 toll free in Mexico ⊕ www.mexicana.com.

## BOAT & FERRY TRAVEL

A privately run ferry makes the trip from Guaymas to Santa Rosalía on the Baja Peninsula every Monday and Thursday. Departing at 8 PM from the ferry terminal on Avenida Serdán, the trip takes approximately 10 hours. The fare is $50 for adults. Cars 10 feet or less in length are $150 and require at least a two-day advance notice. Passenger tickets can be purchased the day of travel.

**⚑ Ferry Terminal** ⊠ Av. Serdán s/n ☎ 622/222-0204.

## BUS TRAVEL

Frequent buses travel to Hermosillo and Guaymas from Nogales, Tijuana, and Mexicali via Grupo Estrella Blanca, which has a network that covers 27 of the 31 states of Mexico. Transportes Baldomero Corral (TBC) offers direct service from Tucson to Nogales, Hermosillo, Guaymas, and Alamos. TUFESA has frequent service between Hermosillo and Guaymas, Nogales, and other destinations within Sonora and northern

Mexico. Transportes del Pacifico (TAP) connects Hermosillo to other Sonoran cities as well as to Mazatlán, Guadalajara, Tepic, and Tijuana. Greyhound Mexico has service to Hermosillo, where you can transfer to one of their corporate partners for a trip anywhere in Mexico.

A bus trip from Nogales to Hermosillo takes approximately five hours. The trip to Guaymas from Nogales is about six hours, and the ride from Nogales to Alamos will take roughly nine hours. Tickets for these long-range trips start around $20. If you're crossing the border and don't already have a tourist visa, ask if the bus driver will make a stop at the Km 21 checkpoint to allow you to acquire one.

⏩ **Greyhound Mexico** ☎ 800/710–8819 in Mexico, 800/229–9424 in the U.S. **Grupo Estrella Blanca** ☎ 662/213–4050. **Transportes Baldomero Corral (TBC)** ☎ 520/903–2801. **Transportes del Pacifico (TAP)** ☎ 662/212–6870. **TUFESA** ☎ 662/213–0442.

## CAR RENTAL

In Guaymas, the agencies to contact are Budget and Hertz, both on the main highway. Budget and Hertz are also in Hermosillo, with branches at the airport.

⏩ **Budget** ✉ Garmendia 46, at Tamaulipas, Col. San Benito, Hermosillo ☎ 662/222–1430 ✉ General Ignacio L. Pesqueira International Airport, Hermosillo ☎ 662/261–0141 ✉ Blvd. Augustín García López s/n, Col. Delicias, Guaymas ☎ 662/222–1450 or 622/222–5500 ⊕ www.budget.com. **Hertz** ✉ General Ignacio L. Pesqueira International Airport, Hermosillo ☎ 662/261–0110 ✉ Calz. Agustin Garcia Lopez 625 Norte, Col. Las Villas, Guaymas ☎ 622/222–1000 ⊕ www.hertz.com.

## CAR TRAVEL

Many visitors to Sonora travel by car from Tucson via I–19 to the border in Nogales, Arizona. Mexico's Highway 15, a divided four-lane toll road, begins in Nogales. This highway is the fastest way to get to Hermosillo and Guaymas–San Carlos, but expect to pay approximately $15 in tolls. The alternative "Libre" (free) routes are generally slower and not as well maintained, though by no means problematic.

There are two points of entry into Nogales. Most drivers take I–19 to the end and then follow the signs. This route, however, will take you through the busiest streets of Nogales, Mexico. It's better to take the Mariposa Road/Arizona Highway 189 exit west from I–19, which leads to the international truck crossing and joins a small peripheral highway that connects with Highway 15 after skirting the worst traffic.

The official checkpoint for entering Mexico is 21 km (13 mi) south of Nogales. It's here that you have to buy insurance and complete paperwork to bring in your car if you haven't already done so in Tucson at either Sanborn's Mexico Insurance or the Arizona Automobile Association.

As a result of the Only Sonora program, tourists driving into Mexico through Nogales and not intending to leave the state need not make a deposit for the vehicle (though insurance is still required). Fill out necessary paperwork at the Only Sonora booth at the Km 21 checkpoint. Bring a valid driver's license and vehicle registration. You will need to get your tourist visa and insurance prior to applying for the Only Sonora program. You will also need copies of your vehicle registration, driver's license, passport, and tourist visa. Copies can be made at the Only Sonora checkpoint, but it's far less expensive to make them before entering Mexico. A six-month tourist visa ($21) is required of anyone planning to stay longer than three days; this is also available at the Km 21 checkpoint. Ask to have it validated for 180 days and keep the receipt if you'll be making more than one foray into Mexico over a period of six months.

Driving in Sonora is best on the toll roads; these are well maintained and have gas stations at regular intervals. Highways between major destinations are in generally good condition, and towns and turn-offs are usually clearly marked. Roads in remote areas range from smooth pavement to dirt track. Avoid driving at night since roads (even toll roads) are not well-lit and often lack shoulders.

🚘 **Arizona Automobile Association** ✉ 8204 E. Broadway, Tucson, AZ ☎ 520/296-7461 ✉ 6950 N. Oracle Rd., Phoenix, AZ ☎ 520/885-0694 or 800/352-5382. **Sanborn's Mexico Insurance** ✉ 105 W. Grant, Tucson, AZ ☎ 520/882-5000.

### CONSULATES
There is a U.S. Consulate in Hermosillo, in back of the Telcel office building near downtown. There is also one in Nogales, one block west of the main bus station.

🚘 **U.S. Consulate** ✉ Calle Monterrey 141, Hermosillo ☎ 662/217-2375 ✉ Calle San José s/n, Nogales ☎ 631/313-4820.

### EMERGENCIES
For emergency fire, police, or medical attention call **060**.

The Green Angels in Hermosillo is a very helpful state-run roadside assistance service for travelers in distress.

🚘 **Green Angels** ☎ 662/212-3253 in Hermosillo, 01800/903-9200 toll free in Mexico. **Red Cross** ☎ 662/214-0010 in Hermosillo, 622/222-5555 in San Carlos, 638/383-2266 in Puerto Peñasco.

🚘 **Hospitals** **Hospital CIMA de Hermosillo** ✉ Paseo Rio San Miguel s/n, Centro ☎ 662/259-0900. **Hospital General de Guaymas** ✉ Calle 12 s/n, Centro ☎ 622/224-0138.

### MONEY MATTERS
In the border towns, including Nogales and Puerto Peñasco, American dollars are readily accepted and usually preferred. Elsewhere, you can change money at local banks and at some larger hotels. ATMs are easy to find in most towns, with the exception of remote villages.

### TOURS
Arizona Coach Tours runs mostly senior-citizen package tours to Alamos, San Carlos, Puerto Peñasco, Baja, and the Copper Canyon. Mexico Tours offers escorted and unescorted bus tours, hotel and condo reservations, and general advice about Pacific coast destinations. Solipaso is run by an American expat couple based in Alamos; they offer set or custom itineraries and specialize in birding, soft adventure, and natural-history tours throughout Mexico.

🚘 **Arizona Coach Tours** ✉ 200 E. 35th St., Tucson, AZ ☎ 520/791-0210 ⊕ www.azcoachtours.com. **Mexico Tours** ✉ 1604 E. Seneca, Tucson, AZ ☎ 520/325-3284,

800/347-4731 in the U.S. ⊕ www.mexi-tours.com. **Solipaso** ⊠ Calle Cardenas #15, Alamos ☎ 647/428-0466 ⊕ www.solipaso.com.

## TRANSPORTATION AROUND SONORA

By far the easiest way to get around is by car—San Carlos and Bahía Kino are particularly spread out, and Bahía Kino has no taxi service of any kind. Most hotels have car-rental agencies. Buses between towns are frequent and inexpensive.

## VISITOR INFORMATION

In addition to the tourism offices listed below, the Sonora Department of Tourism, in Hermosillo, will send you mounds of information and a helpful, full-color magazine. The tourism folks at Hermosillo, Bahía Kino, and San Carlos speak great English and take their jobs seriously. The Hermosillo and San Carlos bureaus are open weekdays 9–5. The Bahía Kino office is open weekdays 9–3. The office in Guaymas is ostensibly open weekdays 8–4 but often closes for no apparent reason. The Alamos tourism office is open weekdays 8–5, and the Puerto Peñasco office stays open weekdays 9–4.

🚺 **Alamos** ⊠ Main Plaza, Calle Juárez 6, Alamos ☎ 647/428-0450. **Bahía Kino** ⊠ Calle Mar de Cortez at Calle Catalina, Kino Nuevo, Bahía Kino ☎ 662/242-0447. **Guaymas** ⊠ Calle 19 and Av. 6, Guaymas ☎ 622/226-0313. **Hermosillo** ⊠ Paseo del Canal at Comonfort, Edificio Sonora, 3rd floor, Hermosillo ☎ 662/217-0076, 800/476-6672 in the U.S. ⊕ www.sonoraturismo.gob.mx. **Puerto Peñasco** ⊠ Blvd. Juárez 320-B at V. Estrella, Puerto Peñasco ☎ 638/383-6122. **San Carlos** ⊠ Blvd. Beltrones, Edificio Hacienda Plaza, San Carlos ☎ 622/226-0202.

# THE COPPER CANYON

## FROM LOS MOCHIS TO CHIHUAHUA CITY

5

Updated by
Rob Aikins

**THE MAGNIFICENT** series of gorges known collectively as Las Barrancas del Cobre (the Copper Canyon) is the real treasure of the Sierra Madre. Inaccessible to the casual visitor until the early 1960s and still largely uncharted, the canyons may now be explored by taking one of the most breathtaking rides in North America. The Chihuahua al Pacífico railroad passes through 87 tunnels and crosses 39 bridges on its journey through country as rich in history and culture as it is in physical beauty.

The canyons of the Sierra Tarahumara, as this portion of the Sierra Madre Occidental is known, form part of the Pacific "Ring of Fire," a belt of seismic and volcanic activity ringing the globe. As a result of its massive geologic movement, a large quantity of the earth's buried mineral wealth was shoved toward the surface. The canyons were then carved over eons by the Urique, Septentrión, Batopilas, and Chínipas rivers and further defined by wind erosion. Totaling more than 1,452 km (900 mi) in length and roughly four times the area of the Arizona Grand Canyon, the gorges are nearly a mile deep and wide in places. The average height of the peaks is 8,000 feet, and some rise to more than 12,000 feet. Four of the major canyons—Cobre, Urique, Sinforosa, and Batopilas—descend deeper than the Grand Canyon. The area's name refers to the color of the lichen on the canyon walls.

The idea of building a rail line to cross this region was first conceived in 1872 by Albert Kinsey Owen, an idealistic American socialist. Owen met with some success initially. More than 1,500 people came from the States to join him in Topolobampo, his utopian colony on the Mexican west coast, and in 1881 he obtained a concession from Mexican president General Manuel Gonzales to build the railroad. Construction on the flat stretches near Los Mochis and Chihuahua presented no difficulties, but eventually the huge mountains of the Sierra Madre got in the way of Owen's dream, along with the twin scourges of typhoid and disillusionment within the community.

Owen abandoned the project in 1893, but it was taken up in 1900 by American railroad magnate and spiritualist Edward Arthur Stilwell. One of Stilwell's contractors in western Chihuahua was Pancho Villa, who ended up tearing up his own work during the Mexican Revolution in order to impede the movement of government troops. By 1910, when the revolution began, the Mexican government had taken charge of building the railroad line. Progress was painfully slow until 1940, when surveying the difficult Sierra Madre stretch finally began in earnest. Some 90 years and more than $100 million after it was started, the Ferrocarril Chihuahua al Pacífico was dedicated on November 23, 1961.

The railroad no longer starts at Topolobampo but at nearby Los Mochis, and Chihuahua City—capital of the eponymous state—is at the other end of the line. Chihuahua was established in 1709, after the Spanish discovered silver in the area around 1649. Chihuahua still derives some wealth from mining—and from ranching, agriculture, and lumber.

Mexico's largest state was once heavily populated by the Tarahumara, close relatives of the Pima Indians of southern Arizona. They are renowned for their running ability and endurance—Tarahumara is a Spanish corruption of their word Rarámuri, which means "running people." Today winners of international marathon races, the Tarahumara in earlier times hunted deer by chasing them to the point of collapse. During festivals they still engage in a game called *rarajípame* in which Tarahumara men run while kicking a handcarved wooden ball for up to 40 hours non-stop. Like other native groups, the Tarahumara's way of life was totally disrupted by the arrival of the Europeans. The Spanish forced them to labor in the mines, and later both Mexicans and Americans put them to work on the railroads. The threat of slavery and the series of wars that began in the 1600s and continued until the 20th century forced them to retreat deeper into the canyons, where they are still at the mercy of outsiders: nowadays, it's loggers and drug lords. Some families are still seminomadic, moving to the high plateaus of the Sierra Madre in summer and down to the warmer canyon floor in winter. Their population, diminished over the years by disease, drought, and poverty, is estimated today at 50,000 to 60,000. Note that the Tarahumara can be uncomfortable having their picture taken; always ask politely first.

## Exploring Copper Canyon

Imagine visiting the Grand Canyon in the days before it was tamed by tourist facilities and you'll have some sense of what a trip through the Copper Canyon will be like—for better or for worse. That is, with the opportunity to encounter a relatively untouched natural site come some of the discomforts of the rustic experience. But if you are careful in your choice of time to visit and are properly prepared, the trip's myriad rewards should far outstrip any inconveniences.

### About the Restaurants

Outside small villages such as Creel and Batopilas, there are few eateries except those connected with lodges; hearty meals are generally included in room rates. There are a few more dining options in Creel, where, in addition to hotel dining rooms, you'll find small cafés along the town's main street, Avenida López Mateos.

You'll have the greatest choice of restaurants in Chihuahua City. The state is a large producer of beef, so steak houses and informal eateries serving *carne asada* (thin, charbroiled or grilled slices of marinated beef) abound, but seafood flown in from the coast is also available. In Los Mochis your best bet is seafood.

### About the Hotels

The hotels in Chihuahua City, including several international chains, cater to both tourists and business travelers. In Cerocahui, Divisadero, Posada Barrancas (*posada* means "inn"), and Creel, most hotels are pine-log types heated by gas furnaces or wood-burning stoves. The lodges send buses or cars to meet the train, and for this reason, reservations are recommended. In summer, October, and around Christmas and Easter, it's important to book in advance.

**5**

Most people make their way into the canyon via Los Mochis, which is the easiest route if you're coming from California or Arizona. The most dramatic canyon scenery is at the western end of the ride, and you're likely to miss it if you approach Los Mochis in the evening. Train delays of three hours or more are not unusual, so you can't count on reaching the scenic end of the route before dark.

Even if you drive down to either Los Mochis or Chihuahua, your itinerary will be largely dependent on the schedule of the Chihuahua al Pacífico train: it runs in each direction only once a day. (Alternatively, you can drive or take a bus as far as Creel from Chihuahua, and arrange hikes or ride the train from there through some of the canyon's best scenery.) The following itineraries assume you will add on a day's train ride to return to your starting point—unless you catch one of the daily Aerolitoral flights between Los Mochis and Chihuahua.

Note: The Sinaloa-Chihuahua state border divides two time zones: Mountain Time to the west and Central Time to the east.

*Numbers in the text correspond to numbers on the Copper Canyon map.*

**If you have 3 days**
Departing from **Los Mochis ①** (or better yet, **El Fuerte ②** ⌐), take the morning Chihuahua al Pacífico train and get off at Bahuichivo, where you can explore the 18th-century church at **Cerocahui ③** and the overlook into the Barranca de Urique. The next day, continue to **Divisadero ④**. Spend your last day exploring **Creel ⑤** and taking a short hike to the falls near Cusárare. If you begin the trip in **Chihuahua City ⑧**, make Cerocahui your final stop.

**If you have 5 days**
Spend a day and night in the old colonial town of **El Fuerte ②** ⌐, catching the train the next morning. Follow the three-day itinerary above, and use the last day and night to extend your time in **Creel ⑤**, with a visit to the mission church of San Ignacio or a drive and hike to the Cascada de Basaseachi.

**If you have 8 or more days**
Spend a day each in **El Fuerte ②** ⌐, **Cerocahui ③**, and **Divisadero ④**, then extend your stay in **Creel ⑤** to include a trip down to **Batopilas ⑥**. It's six to eight hours each way by car (preferably four-wheel-drive) or bus, so you'll want to spend two nights to make the trip worthwhile. (Alternately, extend your stay in Cerocahui to allow an overnight visit to the small town of Urique.) You'll be ready for modern conveniences after that, so plan to enjoy the restaurants and museums of **Chihuahua City ⑧** for an additional day. Another option would be to visit the Mennonite museum near **Cuauhtémoc ⑦** and tour one of the surrounding farms before going on to Chihuahua.

| | WHAT IT COSTS | | | | |
|---|---|---|---|---|---|
| | $$$$ | $$$ | $$ | $ | ¢ |
| RESTAURANTS | over $25 | $15–$25 | $10–$15 | $5–$10 | under $5 |
| HOTELS | over $250 | $150–$250 | $75–$150 | $50–$75 | under $50 |

Restaurant prices are for a main course excluding tax and tip. Hotel prices are for two people in a standard double room in high season.

## Timing

Unless you're planning to head deep into the canyons, winter—December through February—is not the best time to come. Although the scenery can be breathtaking in the snow, some of the hotels in the region are inadequately prepared for the cold. The warmest months are May, June, and July. The rainy season, late June through September, brings precipitation for a short period every day, but this normally won't impede plans to hike or sightsee. It's temperate in the highlands in summer. If you're planning to hike down into the canyons, however, summer temperatures at the bottom can be broiling. Overall, the best months to visit are September and October, when the weather is still warm and rains have brought out all the colors in the Sierra Tarahumara.

Many people come during Easter and Christmas, specifically to see the Tarahumaras' colorful take on church holidays. On these and other religious feast days, many Tarahumara communities dance throughout the night, and villages challenge one another in races that can go for days. The men run in small groups, upward of 161 km (100 mi) or more, all the while kicking a wooden ball. It's not *just* fun and games—each village places a huge communal wager for this winner-take-all event.

## Los Mochis

❶ *763 km (473 mi) south of Nogales on the Arizona-Mexico border.*

At the western end of the rail line, Los Mochis (population 331,000) is an agricultural boomtown. The rail terminus and the city's location about 19 km (12 mi) from the harbor at Topolobampo make it the export center of the state of Sinaloa. As such it is not terribly attractive, and most visitors just use it as an overnight before boarding the train.

The **Museo Regional del Valle del Fuerte,** formerly a doctor's house, is home to permanent exhibits covering the area's history from prehistoric times to present. It also rotates work by local, regional, national, and international artists. Labels are in Spanish only. Occasionally the museum will host music or poetry events on an outdoor patio area. ⊠ *Blvd. Rosales s/n at Av. Obregón, Centro* ☎ *668/812–4692* 🖃 *50¢, free Sun. and holidays* ⊙ *Tues.–Sat. 9–1 and 4–7, Sun. 10–1.*

Cottonwood trees and bougainvillea line the highway from Los Mochis to **Topolobampo.** Fields en route are planted with crops ranging from sugarcane to marigolds and mangoes. Once the site of Albert Owen's utopian colony and the center of the railroad-building activity in the area, it is now a suburb of Los Mochis. **Isla El Farallón,** off the coast, is a

**5**

# Hiking

Hiking in the Copper Canyon is fantastic if you take the proper precautions. *Mexico's Copper Canyon Country,* by M. John Fayhee, is a good source of information. But even the most experienced trekkers should enlist the help of local guides, who can be contacted through area hotels or through travel agents in Los Mochis, El Fuerte, and Chihuahua. Also, the presence of well-guarded marijuana plantations throughout the canyon makes it safer to travel with a local guide who knows which areas to avoid.

La Barranca de Urique is most easily reached—by horse, bus, truck, or on foot—from Cerocahui. Hotels in Creel, Divisadero, and Posada Barrancas offer tours ranging from easy rim walks to a 27-km (17-mi) descent to the bottom. If you're in Cusárare, a gentle and rewarding hike is the 6-km (4-mi) walk from the Copper Canyon Lodge to 100-feet-high Cusárare Falls. More challenging but also more impressive is a full-day trek to the base of the Cascada de Basaseachi. The descent to Batopilas—not for acrophobes—requires an overnight stay.

# Horseback Riding

Hotels throughout the canyons can arrange for local guides and reasonably gentle horses; however, these trips aren't for couch potatoes. The trails into the canyon are narrow and rocky as well as slippery if the weather is icy or wet. At rough spots you might be asked to dismount and walk part of the way. A fairly easy and inexpensive ride is to Wicochic Falls at Cerocahui, about two hours round-trip, including a half-hour hike at the end, where the trail is too narrow for the horses. From Divisadero, horses can be hired to the tiny settlement of Wakajípare, deep within the canyon.

# Local Crafts

A main source of cash income for the Tarahumara is their crafts, including simple handwoven baskets made from sotol (an agave-like plant) or pine needles, carved wooden dolls, rustic pottery, brightly colored woven belts and sashes made on back-strap looms, and wooden fiddles from which the men produce haunting music. The Tarahumara women sell their wares throughout the canyon area, especially at train stops and tourist lodges. Their prices are fair, so bargaining is unnecessary. Chihuahua is known for affordable cowboy boots.

---

breeding ground for the sea lions that gave the town its name: in the language of the Mayo Indians who once dominated the area, *Topolobampo* means "watering place of the sea lions." While the town itself is in need of a facelift, the bay, one of the largest natural bays in the Americas, harbors a nature preserve with many varieties of birds and pods of playful dolphins. Tours can be arranged either through hotels in Los Mochis or from licensed tour operators located adjacent to the ferry landing. The tour operators will almost certainly want to take you to interact with Pechocho, a wild bottlenose dolphin who uncharacteristically chooses to isolate himself from other dolphins in a small inlet near the mouth of the bay.

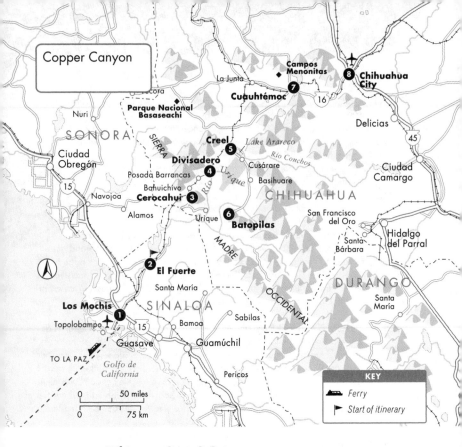

## Where to Stay & Eat

**$-$$** ✕ **El Farallón.** Nautical decor and murals set the tone for the excellent fish served at this simple downtown restaurant. The taquitos of marlin or shrimp are excellent, and you'll also find nigiri sushi and sashimi—rare in Mexico despite the abundance of seafood. For dessert sample some *pitalla* (cactus fruit) ice cream. ⊠ *Av. Obregón 593, at Calle Angel Flores* ☎ *668/812–1428 or 668/812–1273* ▤ *AE, MC, V.*

**$-$$** ✕ **La Fuente.** This unpretentious, colonial-style restaurant specializes in Sinaloan and U.S. beef cuts. Try the local favorite, *cabrería,* a thinly cut, tender fillet. Yummy *queso fundido* (cheese fondue) is made with fresh flour tortillas. Corn tortillas are made on the premises throughout the day. ⊠ *Blvd. López Mateos 1070 Norte, at Jiquilpan* ☎ *668/812–4770* ☺ *Closed Good Friday–Easter* ▤ *AE, MC, V.*

**$-$$** ✕ **Restaurante España.** This slightly upscale restaurant in downtown Los Mochis pulls in the local business crowd. The house specialty is paella with seafood, pork, and chicken; it serves at least two people. The $7 breakfast buffet, served until noon, lines up hearty Mexican favorites such as *chilaquiles* (tortilla strips cooked with cheese, mild chilies, and chicken) along with the usual suspects (omelets). ⊠ *Av. Obregón 525 Poniente* ☎ *668/812–2221 or 668/812–2335* ▤ *AE, MC, V.*

**$$** ⌂ **Hotel Plaza Inn.** Another link in the ubiquitous Balderrama chain, Los Mochis's only five-star hotel caters to businesspeople and tourists alike. Suites have bathtubs and kitchenettes. Standard guest rooms are also spacious, but suffer from a disconcerting color palette combining various hues of pink, coral, and sea-foam green. Duck hunters and fishermen are lured here with sporting packages. ⊠ *Av. Leyva at Cárdenas, 81200* ☎ *668/816–0800, 800/862–9026 in the U.S.* 🖷 *668/818–1590* ⊕ *www.plazainnhotel.net* ⌁ *100 rooms, 27 suites* ⌂ *2 restaurants, in-room safes, pool, gym, bar, nightclub, meeting rooms, travel services, free parking* ⊟ *AE, DC, MC, V.*

**$$** ⌂ **Hotel Santa Anita.** The central reservations link of the Balderrama chain, this downtown hotel will book tours in its sister hotels in El Fuerte, Cerocahui, and Divisadero. The four-story property, built in 1959, has mid-size rooms that are somewhat dim but fitted with comfortable modern furniture; most have air-conditioning. ⊠ *Av. Leyva at Hidalgo, 81200* ☎ *668/818–7046, 800/896–8196 in the U.S.* 🖷 *668/812–0046* ⊕ *www.mexicoscoppercanyon.com/santaanita.htm* ⌁ *125 rooms, 5 suites* ⌂ *Restaurant, cable TV, bar, business services, Internet, meeting rooms, travel services, free parking; no a/c in some rooms* ⊟ *AE, MC, V.*

**$** ⌂ **Corintios Hotel.** Rooms here are plain and looking a bit worn, but this modern-style hotel with a dark-glass facade and a lime-green exterior is centrally located and offers services often not available in this price range. Junior suites differ from regular rooms only in that they have a king-size bed. Note that the three-story hotel has no elevator. ⊠ *Av. Obregón 580 Poniente, 82000* ☎ *668/818–2300* ⌁ *35 rooms, 6 suites* ⌂ *Restaurant, cable TV, gym, hot tub, bar, free parking* ⊟ *AE, MC, V.*

**¢** ⌂ **Taj Majal.** The younger sister to the aging Corintios offers free Internet access on a common computer, comfortable beds, and room service. Despite the graceful effect of the pointed arches of the building's facade and interior hallways, expect the rooms to be small and standard. ⊠ *Av. Obregón 400 Oriente, 81200* ☎ *668/818–7095* 🖷 *668/818–6095* ⌁ *23 rooms, 3 suites* ⌂ *Restaurant, in-room data ports, cable TV, Internet* ⊟ *AE, MC, V.*

## Nightlife

**Friends** (⊠ Hotel Plaza Inn, Av. Leyva at Cárdenas ☎ 668/818–7046), the most popular bar and disco in town, is open to the public on Friday and Saturday nights only. The music, sometimes live, varies from techno to rock en español. **Yesterday** (⊠ Av. Obregón 579 at Guerrero ☎ 668/815–3810) is a convivial nightclub. Live bands, both local and touring, play different types of music (predominantly oldies) Wednesday–Sunday 9 PM–2 AM (often later on Saturday night).

## Shopping

Avenida Obregón between Av. Gabriel Leyva and Av. Guillermo Prieta has a huge number of small shops selling apparel and consumer goods. A walk through this area will allow you to pick up any last-minute items you may need for your journey further into the canyon. If you're headed to Divisadero, Creel, or beyond, snacks and reading material can help pass the long train journey. **VH** (⊠ Av. Obregón at Ignacio Zaragoza ☎ 668/815–7285) is a large supermarket in the center of town.

**La Cava Deli** (✉ Av. Hidalgo 408 ☎ 614/410–9940) sells American and Mexican beers, a good selection of wines and liquors, Cuban cigars, and snack foods. **Librería Los Mochis** (✉ Calle Madero 402 Poniente, at Av. Leyva) has a limited selection of English-language magazines and plenty of Spanish-language books, magazines, and daily newspapers.

## El Fuerte

► ❷ *80 km (50 mi) northeast of Los Mochis.*

If you prefer a peaceful, laid-back small town to the bustle and traffic of commercial Los Mochis, take a bus to El Fuerte, stay the night, and sleep in an hour longer before grabbing the 7:30 train to points east.

Originally named for Saint John the Baptist, this small colonial town is known today as El Fuerte for its 17th-century fort, built by the Spaniards to protect against attacks by the local Mayo, Sinaloa, Zuaque, and Tehueco Indians. Conquistador Don Francisco de Ibarra and a small group of soldiers founded it as San Juan Bautista de Carapoa in 1564. Located along El Camino Real (literally, the "Royal Road"), El Fuerte was one of the frontier outposts from which the Spanish set out to explore and settle New Mexico, Arizona, and California. For three centuries, it was a major trading post for gold and silver miners from the nearby Sierras and the most important commercial and farming center of the area. It was chosen as Sinaloa's capital in 1824 and remained so for several years.

Now a rather sleepy town of some 45,000 residents, El Fuerte has intact colonial mansions, two of the most accessible being the Posada del Hidalgo and El Fuerte Lodge. Most of the historic houses are set off the cobblestone streets leading from the central plaza. A replica of a portion of the original fort has been built on the Cerro de Las Pilas, not far from the main plaza. It houses the **Museo de El Fuerte** (☎ 698/893–1501 ☉ Daily 9–8 in winter; daily 9–9 in summer ☎ 50¢), where several salons display objects representing the history of the area and its flora and fauna, and works from local artists, past and present.

Tour operators use El Fuerte as a base for hiking, birding, fishing, or tubing excursions. Some area hotels get in on the action by organizing float trips on the river outside town. You'll see heron and egrets as well as magpies, kingfishers, and many other birds as you float downstream past willow trees, cacti, and lilac bushes that grow along shore. One popular tour is to a nearby site where hundreds of rock paintings and petroglyphs have been preserved and are being studied.

★ As the train ascends almost 6,000 feet from El Fuerte to Bahuichivo, it passes through or over the majority of the rail line's tunnels and bridges. The scenery shifts from Sinaloan thorn forest, with cactus and scrublike vegetation, to the pools, cascades, and tropical trees of the Río Septentrión canyon. Past Temoris, where a plaque marks the 1961 dedication of the railroad by President López Mateos, the setting shifts to the oak and pine forest that characterizes the higher elevations.

## Where to Stay & Eat

**$–$$**  ✕ **El Mesón del General.** Just a block off the main plaza, this sparely dec-
orated restaurant is the best bet in town for black bass (*lobina*) from
the nearby reservoirs or, in summer, crayfish (*cauque*) from nearby
rivers. If someone in your party craves Chinese instead of Mexican
food, you can order it from the restaurant at the back, run by the same
owners. ⊠ *Benito Juárez 202* ☎ *698/893–0260* ▤ *MC, V.*

★ **$$**  ▥ **El Fuerte Lodge.** Years ago, hunting guide Robert Brand married a local
woman and revived this 380-year-old mansion as an inn. His widow
now tends the lodge, its charm heightened by an antique grandfather
clock and hand-stenciled furniture. *Artesanías* (folk art) decorate the high-
ceiling guest rooms; the beds have beautifully carved and painted head-
boards. Clusters of chairs and tables on wide verandas invite socializing.
⊠ *Montesclaro 37, 81820* ☎ *698/893–0226* ▤ *698/893–1246* ⌑ *32
rooms* ⚭ *Restaurant, bar; no room TVs* ▤ *MC, V.*

**$$**  ▥ **Posada del Hidalgo.** With its gardens and cobblestone paths, this restored 1895 hacienda harks back to a more gracious era. It's difficult
to choose between the larger rooms with balconies and the slightly
more modern rooms that open onto the flower-filled gardens. All are
decorated with rough-hewn handcrafted furniture. ⊠ *Hidalgo 101*
▥▥ *698/893–1194* ⌂ *Reservations: Hotel Santa Anita, Av. Leyva and
Hidalgo, Apdo. 159, 81200 Los Mochis* ☎ *800/896–8196 in the U.S.*
▤ *668/812–0046* ⊕ *www.mexicoscoppercanyon.com* ⌑ *48 rooms, 3
suites* ⚭ *Restaurant, pool, bar, dance club; no room phones, no room
TVs* ▤ *AE, MC, V.*

**¢**  ▥ **Río Vista Lodge.** On the Cerro de las Pilas, the highest spot in El Fuerte,
perches this small, adobe-and-wood posada. Rooms are rustic but cre-
atively decorated with family heirlooms and antiques donated by friends
in town. The wall of one room is actually part of the cerro. So many
hummingbirds frequent the feeders on the patio that you can often see
and hear them as they buzz about your head. Great river views, low prices,
and a relaxed, family-friendly feel make this a favorite. ⊠ *Cerro de las
Pilas, 81820* ☎ *698/893–0413* ⌑ *11 rooms* ⚭ *Restaurant; no room
TVs* ▤ *No credit cards.*

## Cerocahui

❸ *160 km (100 mi) northeast of El Fuerte.*

The quiet mountain village of Cerocahui, just inside the Chihuahua state
border, is a good place to get a sense of how people live in the canyon
area. It's also a favorite stop of birders—over 200 species of birds have
been seen in this part of the Sierras. Across the dirt street from the Hotel
Misión is **Misión San Francisco Javier,** a graceful little temple established
by the Jesuits. Although the order arrived in the area in 1680, Tarahumara Indian uprisings and other difficulties delayed construction of the
church until 1741. It is said that this was the favorite church of the founder,
Father Juan María de Salvatierra, because the Tarahumara were the most
difficult Indians to convert. Nearby is a boarding school for Tarahumara
children, which tour groups sometimes visit. Both of the town's hotels

238 <    **The Copper Canyon**

provide transportation to and from the train station at Bahuichivo, about a 40-minute drive along a bumpy, mostly unpaved road.

The prime reason to come to Cerocahui is its accessibility to **La Barranca de Urique.** It's a lovely ride to the **Cerro del Gallego lookout,** one of the best spots for magnificent views. From there you can make out the slim thread of the Río Urique and the old mining town of Urique, a dot on the distant canyon bottom. A public bus makes the trip from Cerocahui daily after the late arrival of the second-class train, but many people opt for the local hotels' full-day or overnight tours.

off the
beaten
path

★

**URIQUE –** A journey to the small town of Urique offers a fascinating glimpse into canyon life. At the bottom of the system's deepest canyon—1,640 feet above sea level—Urique enjoys an excellent, semitropical climate. Residents plant orchards of citrus and guava trees, and sycamore and fig trees dot the area. The Río Urique, which carved the great canyon, slides lazily along in the dry season but races briskly after the summer rains. Browse in the old general store, El Central, and the town church, and then have lunch at the town's best restaurant, **La Plaza,** on the main square. Rafting expeditions can be arranged through Paraíso del Oso, in Cerocahui.

In the surrounding countryside, the Tarahumara eschew town life, preferring to live in separate family enclaves throughout the valley or in small communities such as Guadalupe, 7 km (4½ mi) from Urique. The most direct path to this town is across a 400-foot-long suspension bridge that rocks and sways above the river. It's not for the faint-of-heart, although the tiny town can also be accessed by car.

You can visit Urique as a day trip from Cerocahui, two to three hours each way by car, or ride horses or hike down into the canyon. Tours are offered through Cerocahui hotels Paraíso del Oso and Misión. The best lodgings in Urique are at **Hotel Estrella del Río** ($35 double), which has large rooms and hot water.

### Where to Stay

$$$$ 🏨 **Hotel Misión.** Part of the Balderrama chain, this is one of just two lodges in Cerocahui. The main house, which looks like a cross between a ski lodge and a hacienda, contains the hotel's office, small shop, and a combined dining room, bar, and lounge surrounding two large fireplaces. The plain, whitewashed rooms have beamed ceilings, Spanish colonial–style furnishings, and wood-burning stoves. Wide verandas draw guests outside to sit in leather rocking chairs, perhaps to sip a glass of wine from the hacienda's own vineyard. ⊠ *Cerocahui* ☎ *Reservations: Hotel Santa Anita, Av. Leyva and Hidalgo, Apdo. 159, 81200 Los Mochis* ☎ *668/818–7046 Ext. 432, 800/896–8196 in the U.S.* 🖷 *668/ 812–0046* ⊕ *www.mexicoscoppercanyon.com* ➳ *38 rooms* ☼ *Restaurant, bar, lounge, shop; no room TVs* ⊟ *AE, MC, V* ⦿ *FAP.*

$$$ 🏨 **Paraíso del Oso Lodge.** Doug "Diego" Rhodes runs this down-to-earth lodge, which is perfectly situated for bird-watching, walks in the woods, or a horseback ride into the canyons. Ranch-style rooms with handmade

wooden furniture and wood-burning stoves face a grassy courtyard. A generator provides electricity for guest rooms; a fireplace in the bar and kerosene lamps in the restaurant-lounge give the common areas a glow. Doug, a loquacious U.S. transplant, gives horseback, hiking, and ATV tours. ⊠ *5 km (3 mi) outside of Cerocahui* ⌖ *Reservations: Box 31089, El Paso, TX 79931* ☎ *800/884–3107 in the U.S.* 🖷 *915/585–7027* ⊕ *www.mexicohorse.com* 🛏 *21 rooms* ⚒ *Dining room, hiking, horseback riding; no a/c, no room phones, no room TVs* ⊟ *MC, V* ⊠| *FAP.*

## Divisadero & Posada Barrancas

**❹** *80 km (50 mi) northeast of Cerocahui, in the state of Chihuahua.*

There's little to do in Divisadero and Posada Barrancas, two whistle-stops five minutes apart on the Continental Divide. Nonetheless, the canyon scenery and refreshing lack of man-made distractions provide a breath of fresh air, and it's impossible to be unmoved by their vistas—especially marvelous at sunset. A popular excursion that takes about seven to eight hours round-trip on foot is to Wakajípare, a Tarahumara village in the canyon.

### Where to Stay

★ $$$$ 🏨 **Hotel Posada Barrancas Mirador.** This beautiful pink hotel perches on the edge of the canyon. The dining room and all the guest rooms have spectacular views; balconies seem to hang right over the abyss. Although on the small side, accommodations are bright and comfortable, with lovely tile floors, old-fashioned chunky chimneys, and a small terrace with table and two chairs. While all the rooms have incredible views, the third floor has the best. ⊠ *Posada Barrancas train station* ⌖ *Reservations: Hotel Santa Anita, Av. Leyva and Hidalgo 81200 Los Mochis* ☎ *668/818–7046, 800/896–8196 in the U.S.* 🖷 *668/812–0046* ⊕ *www.mexicoscoppercanyon.com* 🛏 *49 rooms, 2 suites* ⚒ *Restaurant, hiking, bar, meeting room, travel services; no a/c, no room phones, no room TVs.* ⊟ *AE, MC, V* ⊠| *FAP.*

$$$ 🏨 **Hotel Divisadero Barrancas.** Rooms 1–10 in the old section and 35–52 in the newer section of this canyon-rim hotel have panoramic views. There's a reading room, a café, and a second-story dining room and lounge with magnificent views. Rates include several walking tours; for an extra fee you could tackle a seven-hour guided descent into the canyon (October–March only). ⊠ *Divisadero train station* ⌖ *Reservations: Av. Mirador 4516 31000 Chihuahua City, Chihuahua* ☎ *614/415–1199* 🖷 *614/415–6575* ⊕ *www.hoteldivisadero.com.mx* 🛏 *52 rooms* ⚒ *Restaurant, bar, hiking, meeting room, travel services; no a/c, no room phones, no room TVs* ⊟ *MC, V* ⊠| *FAP.*

★ $$$ 🏨 **Hotel Mansión Tarahumara.** It's a bit disconcerting to come across a red-turreted castle out in canyon country, but somehow this whimsical hotel works. All rooms (15 in separate cabins) have Spanish contemporary–style light-pine furniture and individual heaters, with walls of stone and pine paneling and exposed-beam ceilings. ⊠ *Posada Barrancas train station* ⌖ *Reservations: Av. Juárez 1602-A, Col. Centro, 31000 Chihuahua City, Chihuahua* ☎ *614/415–4721* 🖷 *614/416–5444* 🛏 *57 rooms, 1 suite* ⚒ *Restaurant, some room TVs, indoor pool, sauna,* *steam room, bar, dance club, meeting room, travel services, helipad; no a/c ☲ MC, V ◯ FAP.*

**$$ ☒ Rancho Posada Mirador.** The first hotel in the area, this is a good base from which to explore the canyons. Rooms have ocher stucco walls, ceramic-tile floors, and colonial-style, hand-painted furniture; some have cozy fireplaces. The lobby has a massive stone fireplace, beamed ceiling, and wood furniture. With the exception of large groups, meals are served at Hotel Posada Barrancas Mirador. *☒ Posada Barrancas train station ☎ Reservations: Hotel Santa Anita, Apdo. 159, 81200 Los Mochis ☎ 668/818–7046 Ext. 432, 800/896–8196 in the U.S. ☎ 668/ 812–0046 ⊕ www.mexicoscoppercanyon.com ↩ 37 rooms ☖ Hiking; no a/c, no room TVs. ☲ AE, MC, V ◯ BP, FAP.*

# Creel

❺ *60 km (37 mi) northeast of Divisadero.*

Surrounded by pine-covered mountains, Creel is a mining, ranching, and logging town that grew up around the railroad station. The largest settlement in the area, it's also a gathering place for Tarahumara seeking supplies and markets for their crafts. It's easy to imagine American frontier towns at the turn of the 20th century looking like Creel—without, of course, the international backpacking contingent that makes this town its base. For the number of lodgings and restaurants, the availability of nearby excursions, and the existence of simple yet sound infrastructure for overnight guided trips into the canyon, Creel is the most convenient base for visitors to the Sierra Tarahumara.

On the plaza, **Casa del Artesano Indigena/Museo de Paleontología** (☎ 635/ 456–0080) is actually two museums under one roof. There are exhibits focusing on traditional Tarahumara life, including a beautiful exhibit of black-and-white photographs, as well as dinosaur bones, Spanish-era artifacts and mementos from the area's mining days.

The **Museo de las Tarahumaras** is devoted to the history and philosophy of the Tarahumara peoples. Various exhibitions include original artifacts and replicas of Tarahumara dwellings, traditional clothing, weapons, and musical instruments. Another salon is devoted entirely to photos, both historical and current, of Creel and the Sierra Tarahumara. Descriptions are in English and Spanish. *☒ Domicilio Conocido, across from train station ☎ 635/456–0080 ☒ $1.*

Right in the middle of the town plaza, a cooperative group of tour guides specializes in day trips to areas of interest around Creel. One of the most common day tours is a visit to **Lake Arakeko,** a nearby mission church, a Tarahumara cave dwelling, and rock formations in a variety of weird shapes. The lake visit is little more than a "stop and look," with a chance to buy Tarahumara crafts. The better parts of the two- to three-hour tour are visits to **Valle de los Hongos** (Valley of the Mushrooms), where rocks perch atop each other precariously, and the nearby **Valle de los Monjes** (Valley of the Monks), where monolithic rocks resemble towering figures. (The Tarahumara call this the Valley of the Erect Penises, but tourism pundits have changed the name.) Before you reach this spot you'll stop at **Valle de las Ranas** (Valley of the Frogs), where a few of the formations do look quite froglike. Each stop provides great photo-ops.

Many half-day tours also include a visit to **Cusárare,** whose Tarahumara name means "eagle's nest." Located 26 km (16 mi) from Creel, it's the site of a Jesuit mission, built in 1741, that still serves as a center for religious and community affairs for the Tarahumara who live in the area. Inside the simple whitewashed structure, men and women stand for the Sunday service, women on one side, men on the other. While in the village, a visit to the **Loyola Museum** provides a glimpse at a unique collection of religious-themed oil paintings, painstakingly collected and restored for exhibition here. The main reason most people visit, however, is to take the easy 6-km (4-mi) hike through a lovely piñon forest to see the **Cusárare waterfall,** most impressive during the rainy months.

A popular way to spend the day is to hike to **Recohuata hot springs,** which involves climbing down from the canyon rim into the Barranca de Tararecua. Some tour guides leave their clients at the rim to be guided down to a series of pools by youngsters stationed at the trailhead for this purpose. This tour can be combined with a trip to the magnificent canyon lookout point at **Divisadero,** some 43 km (27 mi) away.

Several other worthwhile day trips along the way to the colonial town of Batopilas are **Basihuare,** where wide horizontal bands of color cross huge vertical outcroppings of rock; the **Barranca de Urique overlook,** a perspective that differs from the one at Divisadero; and **La Bufa,** site of a former Spanish silver mine. Seventy-three kilometers (45 mi) northwest of Creel, along an unpaved, winding road, the 806-foot **Cascada de Basaseachi** are among the highest cascades in North America.

## Where to Stay & Eat

★ ¢–$  ✕ **Tungar.** "The Hangover Hospital," as it is nicknamed, is a home-style, no-smoking, counter-only café with probably the best, most authentic Mexican food in town. The shack-like construction of the restaurant may be unnerving to the uninitiated, but the quality of the food will win over most skeptics. The menu includes such traditional morning pick-me-ups—and hangover cures—as *menudo* (tripe soup), *ari,* a type of ant excrement that, when mixed with chili is said to cure many ills, or the more palatable pozole (hominy soup with chunks of pork, doctored with lime and chili). For lunch consider a few delicious stingray tostadas or a *burro montado,* flour tortillas with melted cheese, beans, and beef stew. ⊠ *Calle Francisco Villa s/n, next to train depot* ☎ *No phone* ▭ *No credit cards* ⊙ *No dinner. No lunch Sun.*

¢–$  ✕ **Veronica's.** This clean, simple eatery on the main street may take its time with service, but remains popular nonetheless. Order up one of the *comidas corridas* (set meals with soup and main course), or à la carte staples like the *discada* (mixed grilled meats and veggies served with hot tortillas) or vegetable soup. This is the best place in town to find vegetarian fare. ⊠ *Av. López Mateos 34* ☎ *635/456–0631* ▭ *No credit cards.*

$$  ▥ **Best Western The Lodge at Creel.** This simple lodge has several wings of log cabin–like rooms with pine floors and walls. Gas-log heaters controlled by wall thermostats are disguised as wood-burning stoves, giving cheer to otherwise plain accommodations. Bathrooms are small

and cramped, but this is still the most luxurious hotel in town. ✉ *Av. López Mateos 61, 33200* ☎ *635/456–0071, 877/844–0409 in the U.S.* 📠 *635/456–0082* 🌐 *www.thelodgeatcreel.com* 🛏 *28 rooms, 1 suite* ♿ *Restaurant, cable TV, gym, hot tub, massage, sauna, spa, bar, travel services, free parking, no-smoking rooms; no a/c* ▭ *AE, MC, V.*

**$$**   🏨 **Copper Canyon Sierra Lodge.** In a peaceful piñon forest near the
**Fodor'sChoice** Cusárare falls, and across the highway from an old mission church and
★ the village of Cusárare, this is a natural beauty with no electricity. The pine-panel and white stucco rooms have red tile floors and area rugs; bathrooms are romantically equipped with kerosene lamps and woodstoves or fireplaces. The excellent meals are served in a beautiful, simple dining room. This spot is best for those with wheels or who want a night or two of isolation; it's 26 km (16 mi) from Creel. ✉ *Cusárare* 📠 *635/456–0036* ✉ *Copper Canyon Lodges, Box 85, Leonard, MI 48367* ☎ *800/776–3942 in the U.S.* 📠 *248/236–0960* 🌐 *www. sierratrail.com* 🛏 *22 rooms* ♿ *Restaurant, bar, travel services, free parking; no a/c, no room phones, no room TVs* ▭ *No credit cards* ⭐ *FAP.*

**$$**   🏨 **Sierra Bonita.** Perched on a hill just outside Creel, this spot is quite self-contained, with a restaurant, bar, and even a disco (open on the weekends). Rooms and suites have less of a rustic look than most in the canyon area, with polyester bedspreads, tile floors, and no real attempt to "go Western." Vans make the five-minute jaunt to Creel on demand. ✉ *Carretera Gran Visión s/n, 33200* ☎ *635/456–0615* 🌐 *www.sierrabonita. com.mx* 🛏 *8 rooms, 10 cabins, 2 suites* ♿ *Restaurant, room service, cable TV, bar, dance club, shop, travel services, free parking; no a/c* ▭ *MC, V* ⭐ *FAP.*

**$**   🏨 **Cabañas Pueblo Viejo.** This funky complex has cabins individually designed to resemble an old Mexican village. Owner-manager don Francisco swears newlyweds love the squeaky, steel-framed bed in the "jail" room. Despite the whimsy, rooms are comfortable and have TVs and heaters; each small breakfast area has a toaster, coffeemaker, and sink. ✉ *Calle Jiménez 5085, behind KOA Hotel, 33200* ☎ *635/456–0295, 614/411–3706 reservations in Chihuahua City* 📠 *614/418–2516* 🛏 *15 rooms, 5 suites* ♿ *Restaurant, cable TV, bar, travel services, free parking; no a/c* ▭ *MC, V* ⭐ *BP, FAP.*

★ ¢   🏨 **Margarita's.** Tiny touts at the train station will guide you to one of the best deals in town. Catercorner from the town plaza, this backpackers' haven has a single, coed dorm room (about $7 gets you a bunk, breakfast, and dinner) as well as private rooms with bath. The rooms—with wrought-iron lamps and light-wood furnishings—are as pleasant as anything at three times the price. ✉ *Av. López Mateos 11, 33200* ☎ *635/456–0045* 🛏 *17 rooms, 1 dorm* ♿ *Restaurant, bicycles, travel services; no a/c, no room TVs* ▭ *No credit cards* ⭐ *MAP.*

¢   🏨 **Margarita's Plaza Mexicana.** This pretty, two-story hotel is one of the town bargains. Each room has a heater and a different wall mural. One disadvantage is that the tequila-and-mariachi parties, often hosted for tour groups in the central courtyard, can get quite noisy. The restaurant always bustles with tour groups, travelers, and a smattering of locals. ✉ *Calle Elfido Bautista s/n, off Av. López Mateos, 33200* ☎ *635/ 456–0245* 🛏 *26 rooms* ♿ *Restaurant, bar, travel services; no a/c, no TV in some rooms* ▭ *No credit cards* ⭐ *MAP.*

## Nightlife

Most people hang out in the hotels where they are staying, as there are only a few other options. When the sun goes down on weekend evenings, **Laylo's Lounge** (✉ Av. López Mateos 25, next to El Caballo Bayo restaurant ☎ 635/456–0136) has music and sometimes other types of performers; it can get rowdy at times. The hotel **Sierra Bonita** (✉ Carretera Gran Visión s/n ☎ 635/456–0615), on a hill west of town, has a disco Friday through Sunday that sometimes hosts live bands playing *norteño* (northern Mexican) tunes or Caribbean *cumbia*. When the music is canned, you might get some pop or rock thrown in.

## Shopping

At the west end of Avenida López Mateos, **Artesanías Victoria** (☎ 635/ 456–0030) sells huge Tarahumara pots and other artifacts, some from elsewhere. Be sure to pay a visit to **Misión Tarahumara** (☎ 635/456–0097), on the east side of the plaza. The shop sells only Tarahumara handiwork, including violins, woven belts, and simple pots of pine needles or unglazed clay. Here you'll also find English-language books on the culture. Proceeds benefit the mission hospital.

# Batopilas

**6** *80 km (50 mi) southeast of Creel.*

Veins of silver—mined on and off from the time of the conquistadors—made this remote village of fewer than 800 people one of the wealthiest towns in colonial Mexico. At one time it was the only place in the country besides Mexico City that had electricity. The hair-raising, 80-km (50-mi) ride down a narrow, unpaved road to the languid town at the bottom of the Barranca de Batopilas takes five or six hours by pickup truck from Creel (closer to seven hours on the local bus, which runs back and forth every day except Sunday). Sights in this relatively lush oasis, in the middle of the semitropical thorn forest, include the ruined **hacienda of Alexander Shepherd,** built in the late 1800s by one of the town's wealthiest mine owners; the original **aqueduct,** which still serves to water some of the townspeople's gardens; and the triple-dome 17th-century **Templo de San Miguel Arcangel,** also known as the Satevó mission church, mysteriously isolated in the Satevó Valley—a scenic 16-km (10-mi) round-trip hike from town. Although the church still serves the surrounding communities, it is generally locked most times. Visitors can obtain the key from the residents of a cluster of houses located directly behind the church. Ask the townspeople to point you in the right direction. Because it takes most of the day to get down to Batopilas, you'll need to spend at least one night at one of the town's modest posadas. Allow more time to explore the canyon's depths, and be sure to take a local guide, as drug traffic makes wandering the area alone unwise.

## Where to Stay & Eat

¢–$ ✕ **Restaurant Carolina.** Hidden at the end of the main road into town, in Plaza Constitución, Restaurant Carolina is a great place to enjoy a quiet conversation or watch the sleepy pace of Batopilas. It's also an excellent place to go for large portions and authentic homestyle Mexican food—and it's one of only two restaurants in town that serves full dinners. Daily specials include such basics as *enchiladas* and *tacos* or more involved dishes such as chicken in a *mole poblano* sauce. ⊠ *Domocilio Conocido* ☎ 649/456–9096 ⊟ *No credit cards.*

$ ▦ **Real de Minas.** Owner Martín Alcaraz earned his stripes during his years as a hotel manager before opening his own small place. It's a charming spot, and more accessible than before—it now has a phone. Each room has decent beds and rustic furnishings but no TV or telephone, which is as it should be—guests come here to experience nature with few distractions. ⊠ *Donato Guerra at Pablo Ochoa* ☎☎ 649/456–9045 ↪ *8 rooms* ♿ *No a/c, no room phones, no room TVs* ⊟ *No credit cards.*

## Cuauhtémoc

**❼** *128 km (79 mi) northeast of Creel, 105 km (65 mi) southwest of Chihuahua.*

A rather anomalous experience in Mexico is a visit to the **Campos Menonitas,** individual family farms of a large Mennonite community surrounding Cuauhtémoc. Some 20,000 Mennonites came to the San Antonio Valley in 1922 at the invitation of President Alvaro Obregón, who gave them the right to live freely and autonomously in return for farming the land. Set up a tour in Chihuahua City through **Divitur Chihuahua** (⊠ Rio de Janeiro 310-1, Col. Panamericana ☎☎ 614/414–6046).

Also worth a visit is the **Mennonite Museum and Cultural Center** (⊠ Carretera a Rubio, Km. 2.5 ☎ 625/582–1382), which shows a typical house from the first pioneers, combining living quarters, kitchen, and stable under one roof.

### Where to Stay & Eat

$–$$ ✕ **Rancho Viejo.** People from Chihuahua City make regular trips to Cuauhtémoc just to dine at this simple country restaurant in the town center. Steaks are the specialty—rib eye, T-bone, or New York cuts—but seafood and Mexican *antojitos* (enchiladas, tacos, and the like) are also served. Roving musicians sing ballads during dinner, and although the kitchen closes at midnight the bar stays open until at least 2 AM. ⊠ *Av. Vicente Guerrero at Calle Tercera 303* ☎ 625/582–4360 ⊟ *MC, V.*

¢ ▦ **Motel Tarahumara Inn.** You'll find most of the creature comforts you need at this two-story motel just a few blocks from the main plaza. Rooms have heat; suites have sofa beds and kitchenettes with refrigerator and stove. The friendly front-desk staff will lend guests dishes and pots and pans as needed. ⊠ *Av. Allende 373* ☎☎ 625/581–1919 ⊕ *www.tarahumarainn.com* ↪ *51 rooms, 4 suites* ♿ *Restaurant, some kitchenettes, cable TV, gym, bar, meeting room, free parking* ⊟ *AE, MC, V.*

## Chihuahua City

**❽** *375 km (233 mi) south of El Paso–Ciudad Juárez border, 1,440 km (893 mi) northwest of Mexico City.*

If you're arriving from the peaceful canyons, the sprawling city of Chihuahua—with more than 670,000 inhabitants—might come as a bit of a jolt. But then, the city is known for its revolutionary nature: two of Mexico's most famous war heroes are closely tied to Chihuahua. The father of Mexican independence, Father Miguel Hidalgo, and his co-conspirators were executed here by the Spanish in 1811. And Chihuahua was home to General Pancho Villa. His revolutionary army, the División del Norte (Northern Army Division), helped overthrow dictator Porfirio Díaz in 1910 and was extremely active in the ensuing civil war. A half century earlier, Benito Juárez, the Abraham Lincoln of Mexico, made Chihuahua his base when the French invaded in 1865.

FodorśChoice ★ Whatever you do, don't miss the **Museo de la Revolución Mexicana,** better known as La Casa de Pancho Villa. Villa lived in this 1909 mansion, also called the "Quinta Luz" (*quinta* means "manor," or "country house"), with his wife, Luz Corral. Although Villa married dozens of women, Corral was considered his only legitimate wife, as the couple was married in both civil and church ceremonies. She lived in this house until her death on June 6, 1986. The 50 small rooms that used to board Villa's bodyguards now house a vast array of artifacts of Chihuahua's cultural and revolutionary history. Parked in the museum's courtyard is the bullet-ridden 1919 Dodge in which Villa was assassinated in 1923 at the age of 45. Don't be shocked by all the uniformed soldiers, the museum is run by the Mexican Army. ⊠ *Calle Décima 3010, near Calle Terrazas, Col. Santa Rosa* ☎ *614/416–2958* 💲 *$1* ⊙ *Tues.–Sat. 9–1 and 3–7, Sun. 10–4.*

Known as the **Parroquia del Sagrado,** the cathedral is also worth a visit. Construction on this stately baroque structure on the Plaza de Armas was begun by the Jesuits in 1726 and—because of local Chichimeca Indian uprisings and the expulsion of the Jesuits—not completed until 1825. The opulent church has Carrara marble altarpieces and a ceiling studded with 24-karat gold ornaments; the huge German-made pipe organ from the late 18th century is still used on special occasions. In the basement, the small **Museo de Arte Sacro** displays 18th-century paintings, primarily those with religious themes. ⊠ *Plaza de Armas, Centro* ☎ *No phone* 💲 *Museum $2* ⊙ *Weekdays 10–2 and 4–6.*

The **Palacio de Gobierno** was built by the Jesuits as a monastery in 1882. Converted into government offices in 1891, it was destroyed by a fire in the early 1940s and rebuilt in 1947. Murals around the state capitol's patio depict famous episodes from the history of the state of Chihuahua, and a plaque commemorates the spot where Father Hidalgo was executed on the morning of July 30, 1811. ⊠ *Calle Aldama at Plaza Hidalgo, Centro* ☎ *614/410–1077* 💲 *Free* ⊙ *Daily 8–8.*

The **Palacio Federal** houses the city's main post office and telegraph office, as well as the *calabozo,* or dungeon, where Hidalgo was imprisoned by the Spanish prior to his execution. His pistols, traveler's trunk, crucifix, and reproductions of his letters are on display. ⊠ *Av. Juárez between Calles Neri Santos and Carranza, Centro* ☎ *614/429–3300 Ext. 1056* 💲 *50¢* ⊙ *Tues.–Sun. 9–7.*

Consecrated in 1721, the **Iglesia de San Francisco** is the oldest church in Chihuahua. Father Hidalgo's decapitated body was interred in the chapel here from 1811 until 1827, when it was sent to Mexico City. (His head was publicly displayed for 10 years by Spanish Royalists in Guanajuato on the Alhóndiga de Granaditas.) Although the church's facade is relatively sober, its baroque altarpieces, decorated with 18th-century paintings, are worth perusal. ☒ *Av. Libertad at Calle 15, Centro* ☎ *No phone* 🎫 *Free* 🕙 *Daily 7–2 and 5–7.*

Slightly outside the center of town but worth a visit is the cultural center of the Universidad de Chihuahua, known as **Quinta Gameros.** This hybrid French Second Empire–art nouveau mansion, with stained-glass windows, ornate wooden staircases, rococo plaster wall panels, and lavish ironwork, was begun in 1907 by architect Julio Corredor Latorre, a Colombian architect, for Manuel Gameros, a wealthy mining engineer. On the ground floor are changing archaeological or fine-arts exhibits; on the second floor are exhibits by Chihuahuan artists, a collection of art nouveau furniture, and the mismatched and rather amateurish contemporary paintings belonging to the state university. ☒ *Calle Bolívar 401, at Calle de la Llave, Centro* ☎ *614/416–6684* 🎫 *$2.80* 🕙 *Tues.–Sun. 11–2 and 4–7.*

A restoration project has made the site of the town's original settlement, **Santa Eulalia,** particularly appealing. The 30-minute drive southeast of town, about $40 one-way by taxi (significantly less by bus), is repaid by the colonial architecture and cobblestone streets of this village, which was founded in 1707 when huge silver deposits were found. The religious artwork in the 18th-century cathedral is noteworthy.

The **Nombre de Dios caverns** are just outside the northeast side of the city, about 20 minutes from the city center. An illuminated, 1.6-km (1-mi) path takes you through 17 separate chambers, past rock formations and stalactites and stalagmites, which have been given names such as Christ, the Waterfall, and the Altar. The tour takes about an hour. Comfortable clothing and walking shoes are recommended. ☒ *H. Colegio Militar s/n, Sector Nombre de Dios* ☎ *614/400–7059* 🎫 *Weekdays $2.50, weekends $3* 🕙 *Tues.–Fri. 9–4, weekends 10–5.*

off the
beaten
path

**CASAS GRANDES –** Some 300 km (186 mi) northwest of Chihuahua, the twin towns of Nuevo Casas Grandes and Casas Grandes are the gateways to the ancient area known as Paquimé, declared a UNESCO World Heritage site in 1998. Nuevo Casas Grandes, a two-horse town with dusty streets and cowboys in regalia, has hotels, shops, and most of the local restaurants. An archaeological site and museum are in Casas Grandes, a one-horse town 8 km (5 mi) away.

Near the aspen-lined Casas Grandes River, sheltered by the burnt-sienna peaks of the Sierra Madre Occidental, Paquimé was inhabited by peoples of the Oasis America culture between AD 700 and 1500. The trading and ceremonial city was poised between the Pueblo cultures of today's Southwestern United States (to whom they were related) to the north and their Mesoamerican neighbors to the south. Architecture and cultural traditions were borrowed from each. Paquimé was a cosmopolitan commercial center whose residents manufactured jewelry and raised fowl and macaws imported from the tropics. Evidence of their engineering and architectural savvy still stands, in the form of heat-shielding walls, T-shape doorways for defense, and intricate indoor plumbing systems. The high-tech museum on-site shows Paquimé artifacts and ceramics and has bilingual (English and Spanish) videos, displays, and interactive computers describing local cultural, religious, and economic practices and Mexican history until the Revolution of 1910. ☎ *636/692–4140* 🎫 *Museum $3.50* ⊙ *Tues.–Sun. 10–5.*

In Nuevo Casas Grandes, **Restaurante Constantino** (⊠ Minerva 112, across from Hotel Paquimé ☎ 636/694–1005) makes great enchiladas and has a full breakfast menu. Family-style **Hotel Piñon** (⊠ Av. Juárez 605, Nuevo Casas Grandes ☎ 636/694–0655) has a swimming pool (closed in winter), a restaurant, bar, and a private collection of ancient *ollas* (clay pots) from Paquimé. **Hotel Hacienda** (⊠ Av. Juárez 2603 Norte, Nuevo Casas Grandes ☎ 636/694–1046), with a restaurant, bar, and swimming pool, is one of the best places to stay in town.

Omnibus de México makes the five-hour trip from Chihuahua to Nuevas Casas Grandes (about $20). To get to the ruins, it's easiest to hail a taxi from the bus station in Nuevas Casas Grandes. Once there, head for the *zócalo* (main square). Paquimé is a 10-minute walk from town—follow the PAQUIMÉ sign on Avenida Constitución.

## Where to Stay & Eat

**$$–$$$** ✕ **La Calesa.** A large, dim, and rather elegant room with wood paneling and red tablecloths and curtains, La Calesa looks every bit the classic steak house. The filet mignon and rib-eye steaks are particularly recommended; try the former cooked with mushrooms. ⊠ *Av. Juárez 3300, Centro* ☎ *614/416–0222* ☷ *AE, MC, V.*

**$–$$** ✕ **Rincón Mexicano.** Chihuahua residents return repeatedly to this traditional eatery for dependable Mexican food and a perennially cheerful atmosphere. Mariachis serenade patrons in both the bright blue-and-yellow restaurant and the adjacent bar. Popular dishes include T-bone and rib-eye steaks, carne asada, and northern Mexico staples such as cactus salad and sizzling platters of fajitas. ⊠ *Av. Cuauhtémoc 2224, Col. Cuauhtémoc* ☎ *614/411–1510* ☷ *AE, MC, V.*

**$** ✕ **Café del Paseo.** Two doors down from Quinta Gameros, this casual, friendly evening hot spot is known for good service. Original art decorates walls painted Santa Fe pinks, peaches, and ochers, and a *trova* group sings popular ballads Wednesday to Sunday after 9 PM. The specialty is *arrachera a la borracha*, tenderized beef marinated in beer and grilled with mushrooms and onions. The restaurant opens daily at 4 PM. ⊠ *Bolivár 411, Centro* ☎ *614/410–3200* ☷ *AE, MC, V* ⊙ *No lunch.*

**¢–$** ✕ **Café Mandala.** If you need your palm read, or just want to sit back and smell the incense, head for this informal New Age eatery at a lookout above Chihuahua. (It's best to call ahead to make an appointment for Spanish card, palm, or coffee-ground readings.) The tables on the outdoor terrace fill quickly on summer evenings, when the city lights provide a romantic backdrop. The food—tacos, tostadas, and other Mexican fare—has a healthful and sometimes vegetarian slant. Try the non-traditional tacos, with a mix of grilled green peppers, tomatoes, mushrooms, and cheese. ✉ *Calle Urquidi 905* ☎ *614/416–0266* ⚱ *Reservations not accepted* ▭ *No credit cards* ✇ *No lunch.*

★ ¢–$ ✕ **La Casa de los Milagros.** According to legend, the owner of this Revolution-era house fell in love with one of Pancho Villa's "girls." His wife prayed to Saint Anthony, and when her husband returned, the house was dubbed "House of Miracles." Today it's *the* place for light snacks, coffee, drinks, and, Thursday through Sunday after 8 or 8:30 PM, live *música de trova* (romantic ballads). Although most come for just a bite, you can also get soup or a steak. The high-ceilinged rooms are often hung with paintings or photos by local talent. ✉ *Victoria 812, near Ocampo, Centro* ☎ *614/437–0693* ▭ *No credit cards* ✇ *No lunch.*

★ $$$ ▦ **Holiday Inn Hotel & Suites.** This appealing property combines comfort and convenience; it's 10 minutes from the downtown sights. Each guest room has a kitchen with stove, refrigerator, dishwasher, and coffeemaker, and a long counter where you can eat or work. A TV with VCR swivels between the living area and the bedroom. The English-speaking staff is friendly and helpful. ✉ *Calle Escudero 702, Fracc. San Felipe 31000* ☎ *614/439–0000, 800/465–4329 in the U.S.* ▤ *614/414–3313* ⊕ *www.sixcontinentshotels.com* ⤴ *74 suites* ⚱ *Restaurant, kitchens, cable TV, in-room VCRs, pool, gym, sauna, basketball, free parking, no-smoking rooms* ▭ *AE, DC, MC, V* ⧲ *CP.*

$$$ ▦ **Westin Soberano Chihuahua.** Atop a rise that has magnificent views of the city and surrounding mountains, Chihuahua's most elegant hotel sparkles. Designed around an atrium with a cascading waterfall, the hotel is a distinct contrast to the rustic accommodations of the canyons. Rooms are plush yet understated, with richly patterned textiles, TVs in tall chests, and baths with both tub and shower. ✉ *Barranca del Cobre 3211, Fracc. Barrancas 31125* ☎ *614/429–2929, 888/625–5144 in the U.S.* ▤ *614/429–2900* ⊕ *www.starwood.com/westin* ⤴ *194 rooms, 10 suites* ⚱ *2 restaurants, cable TV, tennis court, pool, gym, steam room, racquetball, 2 bars, business services, meeting rooms, free parking, no-smoking rooms* ▭ *AE, DC, MC, V.*

★ $$ ▦ **Hotel San Francisco.** A favorite of Mexican business travelers, this modern five-story hotel has a prime location behind the Plaza de Armas. Clean and comfortable rooms have firm mattresses, large TVs, bathtubs, and desks. The lobby is dotted with classic-style statues and urns, and massive floral arrangements. As this is a business-oriented hotel, weekend rates are almost half the weekday rate. ✉ *Victoria 409, Centro 31000* ☎ *614/416–7550, 800/847–2546 in the U.S.* ▤ *614/415–3538* ⊕ *www.hotelsanfrancisco.com.mx* ⤴ *111 rooms, 20 suites* ⚱ *Restaurant, in-room data ports, cable TV, bar, Internet, business services, meeting rooms, free parking, no-smoking rooms* ▭ *AE, MC, V.*

$$ ▦ **Palacio del Sol.** The high-rise downtown hotel looks faded from the outside, but inside, rooms and public spaces are redecorated on a regular basis. From the revolving front door to the stained-glass "sun" mural in the lobby bar, the public spaces seem permanently stuck in an earlier, less sophisticated era. ✉ *Independencia 116, Centro 31000* ☎ *614/416–6000, 800/852–4049 in the U.S.* ▤ *614/416–9947* ⊕ *www.*

*hotelpalaciodelsol.com* ⇆ *174 rooms, 26 suites* ⚷ *2 restaurants, in-room data ports, cable TV, gym, bar, shop, laundry service, meeting rooms, car rental, travel services, free parking* ⊟ *AE, MC, V.*

$  🖫  **Posada Tierra Blanca.** Across the street from the Palacio del Sol but considerably less expensive, this modern motel-style property is convenient to downtown sights. Rooms in wings surrounding the gated swimming pool have firm mattresses, pseudo-antique furnishings, and large TVs. ⊠ *Niños Héroes 102, Centro 31000* ☎ *614/415–0000* 🖷 *614/ 416–0063* ⇆ *90 rooms, 3 suites* ⚷ *Restaurant, cable TV, pool, piano bar, free parking* ⊟ *MC, V.*

### Nightlife & the Arts

This large city is more sedate than one might expect; and its hard-working residents generally wait for the weekends to kick up their heels. At the neon-laced **Bar La Taberna** (⊠ Av. Juárez 3331, Centro ☎614/ 416–8332) you can play pool or, on Friday and Saturday nights, dance to a DJ. **La Casa de los Milagros** (⊠ Victoria 812, Centro ☎ 614/437– 0693) starts to groove after 8:30 PM. At **Hotel Sicomoro** (⊠ Blvd. Ortiz Mena 411, Col. Unidad Presidentes ☎ 614/413–5445) the lobby bar has romantic and folk music Wednesday–Saturday.

### Shopping

In addition to selling gems and geodes from the area, **Artesanías y Gemas de Chihuahua** (⊠ Calle Décima 3015, across from the Museo de la Revolución Mexicana, Col. Santa Rosa ☎ 614/415–2882) carries exceptional silver jewelry and a variety of other crafts. It's closed Monday. Across the street from the *calabozo* (jail) where Father Hidalgo was held, the **Casa de las Artesanías del Estado de Chihuahua** (⊠ Av. Niños Heroes 1101, Centro ☎ 614/437–1292) carries the best selection of Tarahumara and regional crafts in the city, as well as handcrafted wooden furniture and a selection of Mata Ortiz pottery. **Mercado de Artesanías** (⊠ Calle Victoria 506 [another entrance on Calle Aldama 511], between Calles Quinta and Guerrero, Centro ☎ 614/416–2716), a block wide with two entrances, sells everything from inexpensive jewelry, candy, and T-shirts to mass-produced crafts from all over the region.

# COPPER CANYON A TO Z

**AIR TRAVEL**

You can fly into either Chihuahua or Los Mochis from Los Angeles, Tucson, Mexico City, or other major U.S. and Mexican cities.

AIRPORTS   The Chihuahua airport (CUU) is a roughly 10-minute drive from the city center. The Los Mochis–Topolobambo airport (LMM) is about 30 minutes outside Los Mochis on the road to Topolobambo.

🛪 **Aeropuerto de Chihuahua** ⊠ Blvd. Juan Pablo II, Km 14 ☎ 614/420–5104. **Aeropuerto Los Mochis Topolobampo** ⊠ Carretera Los Mochis Topolobampo, Km 12.5 ☎ 668/815–3070.

AIRPORT   The trip from the Chihuahua airport into town costs $10 in a shared
TRANSFERS   van taxi and $16 for a private taxi. The cost of a taxi between Los Mochis airport and the city is about $14.

CARRIERS   Aeroméxico and its feeder airline, Aerolitoral, have daily flights to Chihuahua from Los Angeles, Phoenix, Las Vegas, Atlanta, and El Paso. Within Mexico, Aeroméxico and Aerolitoral have daily flights from Mexico City, Monterrey, Guadalajara, and Tijuana. AeroCalifornia has daily flights to Los Mochis from Los Angeles, Tucson, Tijuana, Mexico City, and Guadalajara.

🛈 **AeroCalifornia**  ⊠ Av. Leyva 99 Norte, Centro, Los Mochis  ☎ 668/818–1616  ⊠ Lateral Periférico Ortíz Mena 1809, Col. Campestre Virreyes, Chihuahua  ☎ 614/437–1022. **Aeroméxico**  ⊠ Paseo Bolívar 405, next to Quinta Gameros, Centro, Chihuahua  ☎ 614/415–6303 in Chihuahua,  ⊠ Av. A. Obregón 1104, Los Mochis  ☎ 668/815–2575  ⊕ www.aeromexico.com.

## BOAT & FERRY TRAVEL

The Topolobampo–La Paz passenger ferry has been replaced with a swift Baja Speed catamaran which makes the journey six times per week, weather permitting. The 5-hour sailing costs $58 for tourist-class seats and $130 for a private cabin. Both fares include one meal, either breakfast or dinner. Boats leave Topolobampo at midnight every day but Saturday, arriving in La Paz around 5 AM. Boats depart the same day from La Paz at 4 PM and arrive in Topolobampo at 9 PM. The schedule is changeable, though, so be sure to contact the terminal ahead of time for information and reservations. Cars now cross on the same ferry. Cost varies by vehicle, but those up to 5 meters (16 feet) in length cost $90 each way and include the driver's fare and dinner.

🛈 **Terminal Topolobampo**  ⊠ Muelle Fiscal s/n, Topolobampo  ☎ 668/862–0141 or 668/812–3922.

## BUS TRAVEL

The Omnibus de México lines run clean, air-conditioned first-class buses from Ciudad Juárez, just across the border from El Paso, Texas, to Chihuahua City. These leave every few hours from 4 AM to about 8 PM. Ask for one that makes at most one or two stops. The cost of the 4½-hour trip is approximately $27. This line also links these and other northern Mexico cities to Guadalajara, Mexico City, San Miguel de Allende, and others in the central region.

Grupo Estrella Blanca (which includes Chihuahuense, Elite, and other lines) buses connect the border cities to Puerto Peñasco, Chihuahua, and Creel, and as far south as Huatulco, in Oaxaca state.

You can take a bus from Los Mochis inland to El Fuerte; the 89-km trip takes about an hour and a half. Local buses depart from the corner of calles G. Prieto and Cuauhtémoc, in downtown Los Mochis.

🛈 Bus Depots **Chihuahua City**  ⊠ Terminal Central de Autobuses de Chihuahua, Carretera al Aeropuerto, Km 2.5  ☎ 614/420–5398. **El Fuerte**  ⊠ Mercado Independencia, Avs. Independencia and Degollado. **Los Mochis**  ⊠ Rosendo G. Castro at Calle I. Zaragoza  ☎ 668/815–0062.

🛈 Bus Information **Grupo Estrella Blanca**  ☎ 614/429–0218 in Chihuahua, 668/812–1757 in Los Mochis. **Omnibus de México**  ☎ 614/420–1580 in Chihuahua.

## CAR RENTAL

Avis, Budget, and Hertz all have offices at the airport in Chihuahua. Car-rental companies at the airport in Los Mochis and in town include Budget and Hertz.

🚗 **Avis** ⊠ Av. Agustín Melgar 1909, Chihuahua ☎ 614/414-1999 ⊕ www.avis.com. **Budget** ⊠ Ortíz Mena 3322, Col. Magesterial, Chihuahua ☎ 614/414-2171 ⊠ Guillermo Prieto 850 Norte, Los Mochis ☎ 668/815-8300 ⊕ www.budget.com. **Hertz** ⊠ Av. Revolución 514, at Josue Neri Santos, Centro, Chihuahua ☎ 614/416-6473 ⊠ Av. Leyva 167 Norte, Los Mochis ☎ 668/812-1122 ⊕ www.hertz.com.

## CAR TRAVEL

Most U.S. visitors drive to Chihuahua via Mexico Highway 45 from El Paso–Ciudad Juárez border, a distance of 375 km (233 mi). The four-lane toll road, Carretera 15, between Nogales on the Arizona border and Los Mochis is 763 km (473 mi).

Paved roads connect Chihuahua City to Creel and Divisadero: take Mexico Highway 16 west to San Pedro, then State Highway 127 south to Creel. The 300-km (186-mi) trip takes 3½–4 hours in good weather. This drive, through the pine forests of the Sierra Madre foothills, is more scenic than the railroad route via the plains area. Driving is a good option if you have a four-wheel-drive vehicle, because there are many worthwhile, if difficult, excursions into the canyons from Creel. From Divisadero to Bahuichivo, the dirt road is full of potholes and is especially dangerous in rain or snow.

## EMERGENCIES

To contact the police, fire department, or an ambulance in Chihuahua or Los Mochis dial **066.**

Chihuahua has an abundance of pharmacies with late-night service in the city center, including Farmacia del Ahorro. In Los Mochis, Farmacia Internacional will deliver for a fee.

🚑 **Red Cross** ☎ 668/815-0808 in Los Mochis, 614/411-1619 in Chihuahua.

🚑 Hospitals **Centro Médico** ⊠ Blvd. Castro 30 Poniente, Los Mochis ☎ 668/812-0198. **Hospital Central del Estado** ⊠ Calle 33 and Rosales, Col. Obrera, Chihuahua ☎ 614/415-9000.

🚑 Pharmacies **Farmacia del Ahorro** ⊠ Calle Aldama at Calle 13, Centro, Chihuahua ☎ 614/410-9017. **Farmacia Cosmos** ⊠ Av. A. Flores at Blvd. Jiquilpan, Los Mochis ☎ 668/812-5161.

## INTERNET

Internet access in this region can be slow, but it is inexpensive, at less than $2 per hour. You can find Internet cafés in the area's larger towns.

💻 Internet Cafes **Café Internet Club** ⊠ Calle Degollado 737 Sur, Los Mochis ☎ 668/821-8960. **Papelería de Todo** ⊠ Calle López Mateos 30, Creel ☎ 635/456-0122. **Quik Acces** ⊠ Calle Aldama 109, Chihuahua City ☎ 614/415-3377.

## MONEY MATTERS

Be sure to change money before you get into the Copper Canyon: there are no banks in Cerocahui, Divisadero, or Posada Barrancas, and no guarantee that the hotels in those places will have enough cash to accommodate you. All of the banks listed below have ATMs. In Creel, the Banco Serfín is open weekdays 9–4. In Los Mochis, business hours for major banks such as Banamex are generally weekdays between 8:30 and 4:30; some banks are open Saturday morning and some change traveler's checks until 1 or 2 PM only. In Chihuahua, most banks are open weekdays 9–1:30 and 3:30–7:30, and Saturday 9–1:30. Banco Bital in downtown Chihuahua is open Monday–Saturday 8–7. In El Fuerte, Bancomer is open weekdays 8:30–4. Hotels have slightly lower exchange rates but normally you won't have to wait in line.

🖪**Banamex** ✉ Av. Guillermo Prieto at Calle Hidalgo, Los Mochis ☎ 668/812–0116. **Banco Bital** ✉ Av. Libertad 1922, Centro, Chihuahua ☎ 614/416–0880. **Bancomer** ✉ Av. Constitución at Av. Juárez, El Fuerte ☎ 698/893–1145. **Banco Serfín** ✉ Av. López Mateos 17, Centro, Creel ☎ 635/456–0060.

### TAXIS
In Chihuahua and Los Mochis, taxis are easy to find and can be engaged at hotels or hailed on the street. Always agree on a price before getting into the cab. In smaller towns and at lodges throughout the Copper Canyon, it's best to make taxi arrangements through your hotel.

### TOURS
Most large hotels in Los Mochis and Chihuahua have in-house travel agencies that arrange tours of the Barrancas del Cobre area, as well as hiking, hunting, and fishing expeditions. In Los Mochis, tours arranged by Hotel Santa Anita will book you almost exclusively into their own line of hotels throughout the canyon region. In El Fuerte, contact Copper Canyon Adventures, which offers individualized and group tours from sedate to adventurous. In Chihuahua, Rojo y Casavantes and Turismo Al Mar offer plane and train tickets as well as city tours, Mennonite Camps, and canyon sojourns. Divitur offers booking services as well as kayaking, mountain biking, and hiking. Doug Rhodes, of Paraíso del Oso Hotel in Cerocahui, leads horseback tours into the Barranca de Urique. He also offers day rentals of mountain bikes and, between July and September, rafting trips. (Communications to Cerocahui are spotty, so contact him with plenty of lead time.)

From the United States, the oldest operator in the area is Pan American Tours. Prices for tours between Los Mochis and Chihuahua range from about $410 to $875 per person (three to seven nights); custom tours can be arranged. Synergy Tours runs individual and group trips about 10 times a year, including off-the-beaten-path treks. The California Native runs independent and small-group escorted trips through the barrancas. Four- to 11-day trips for individuals start around $650; group trips last one to two weeks and begin at $1,870. Adventure Bike Tours does seven-day guided mountain bike descents to Batopilas.

🖪**Adventure Bike Tours** ✉ 220 E. Palmdale St., Tucson, AZ 85714 ☎ 520/807–0706, 800/926–1140 in the U.S. ⊕ www.adventurebiketours.com. **The California Native** ✉ 6701 W. 87th Pl., Los Angeles, CA 90045 ☎ 800/926–1140 in the U.S. ⊕ www.calnative.com. **Copper Canyon Adventures** ☎🖶 698/893–0915, 800/530–8828 in the U.S. ⊕ www. coppercanyonadventures.com. **Divitur** ✉ Rio de Janeiro 310-1, Col. Panamericana, Chihuahua ☎🖶 614/414–6046 ⊕ www.divitur.com.mx. **Pan American Tours** ☏ 5959

Gateway W. 160-B, El Paso, TX 79925 ☎ 800/876-3942 in the U.S. 🌐 www.panamericantours.com. **Paraíso del Oso** 📫 Box 31089, El Paso, TX 79931 ☎ 800/884-3107 in the U.S. 📠 915/585-7027 🌐 www.mexicohorse.com. **Rojo y Casavantes** ✉ Av. Vincente Guerrero 1207, Centro, Chihuahua ☎ 614/439-5858 or 614/415-5787 🌐 www.rycsa.com.mx. **Synergy Tours** ✉ 7335 E. Indian Plaza, Suite 120, Scottsdale, AZ 85251 ☎ 800/569-1797 in the U.S. 📠 480/994-4439 🌐 www.synergytours.com. **The 3 Amigos** ✉Av. Lopez Mateos 46, Creel ☎635/456-0036 🌐www.the3amigoscanyonexpeditions.com. **Turismo Al Mar** ✉ Calle Verna 2202, Col. Mirador, Chihuahua ☎📠 614/416-6589 ☎ 614/416-5950.

TRAIN TOURS Sierra Madre Express of Tucson runs its own deluxe trains (with dome-dining and Pullman cars) to the Copper Canyon from Tucson via Nogales on eight-day, seven-night trips about six times a year. Its trips combine the charm of sleeping on the train with first-class accommodations, starting at $2,795 per person. The trips are geared toward older folks and those who want to view the canyon scenery and experience Tarahumara culture without roughing it.

The American Orient Express II began tours through the canyon in early 2003. The experience evokes the days of more glamorous train travel; travelers dress for dinner. The eight-day trip begins in Tucson, Arizona, and makes stops in Nogales, San Carlos, Alamos (Sonora), and El Fuerte before entering the canyon proper, where it stops at Divisadero and Creel. Rates begin at $2,890.

**American Orient Express II** 📫 5100 Main St., Suite 300, Downers Grove, IL 60515 ☎ 800/320-4206 in the U.S. 🌐 www.americanorientexpress.com. **Sierra Madre Express of Tucson** 📫 Box 26381, Tucson, AZ 85726 ☎ 520/747-0346, 800/666-0346 in the U.S. 🌐 www.sierramadreexpress.com.

### TRAIN TRAVEL

Other than the private train cars of the Sierra Madre Express and the American Orient Express, there is no passenger service from any U.S. border city to either Los Mochis or Chihuahua.

The Ferrocarril Chihuahua al Pacífico line (CHEPE) runs a first-class and a second-class train daily in each direction from Chihuahua and Los Mochis through the canyon. The first-class train departs from Los Mochis at 6 AM (sit on the right side of the train for the best views) and arrives in Chihuahua about 15 hours later. You can bypass Los Mochis and depart 1½ hours later from El Fuerte, a smaller town nestled in the foothills. Delays of several hours are not unusual, as the cargo trains with which CHEPE shares the rails tend to break down often. Westbound, the passenger train departs from Chihuahua at 6 AM and arrives in Los Mochis around 9 PM. The price of a first-class ticket is about $110 each way; you should arrange stopovers when you buy tickets.

State police with automatic weapons travel aboard to discourage would-be thieves. Food and drink in the dining car and bar are predictably expensive, and although it is technically forbidden to bring your own food and drink, conductors generally ignore this bending of rules.

Make reservations a week or more in advance during the busy months of July, August, and October, and around Christmas and Easter. Some find it most convenient to book through a hotel, tour company, or travel agency, although you can also buy tickets at the train station or major hotels in Los Mochis or Chihuahua.

The second-class train leaves an hour later from each terminus but makes many stops and is scheduled to arrive 3½ hours later in both directions than the first-class train. It is rarely crowded and quite comfortable; the train's cars were on the first-class route a few years ago, until the first-class dining and passenger cars were upgraded. Instead of a sit-down restaurant there is a snack car selling burritos, sandwiches, and soft drinks. No reservations are needed; tickets are $55 each way.

If you're driving down to Los Mochis, you're better off leaving your car there and taking the train round-trip. El Fuerte is a more charming starting point than Los Mochis, and if you board there, you'll get another hour's sleep on departure day. If you want to avoid taking the train both directions, you could hop a flight between Chihuahua City and Los Mochis. The most dramatic scenery is found between El Fuerte and Creel, so it's best to take the trip from west to east. If you decide to begin your trip in the east, consider driving to Creel or Divisadero and doing a round-trip from there. The scenery between Chihuahua City and Creel is mainly farmland.

**Ferrocarril Chihuahua al Pacífico** ☎ 614/439-7210, 614/439-7212 in Chihuahua, 668/824-1167 in Los Mochis, 01800/367-3900 toll free in Mexico ⊕ www.ferromex.com.mx.

## VISITOR INFORMATION

The government tourist office in Chihuahua is open weekdays 9–4. A smaller office at the Palacio de Gobierno, on Plaza Hidalgo, is open weekdays 8:30–6, weekends 10–5. At the former, Sonia Estrada, who speaks fluent English, will answer questions and help visitors (in person or over the phone) make travel arrangements all over the state.

The Oficina de Turismo in Los Mochis, on the first floor of the Unidad Administrativa del Gobierno del Estado building, is generally lacking in information.

**Government Tourist Office** ⊠ Av. Libertad and Calle 13, 2nd floor, Centro, Chihuahua ☎ 614/429-3421, 614/429-3300 Ext. 4511, or 4512 ⊠ Palacio de Gobierno, Calle Aldama between Avs. Vicente Guerrero and Carranza, Centro, Chihuahua ☎ 614/429-3596 or 614/429-3300 Ext. 4515 ⊕ www.coppercanyon-mexico.com. **Oficina de Turismo** ⊠ Av. Allende at Calle Ordoñez, Los Mochis ☎ 668/815-1090, 01800/508-0111 in Mexico.

# GUADALAJARA

6

Updated by
Gary Chandler
Prado

**TRADITIONS ARE PRESERVED AND CUSTOMS PERPETUATED** in Guadalajara; it's a place where the fiesta is an art form and the siesta is an institution—as are mariachi bands, tequila, and the Mexican hat dance.
Yet the nation's second-largest city and Jalisco State's capital struggles
to retain its provincial character and colonial charm as its population
surpasses 7 million. Émigrés who left Mexico City after the devastating 1985 earthquake and a steady influx of unemployed rural poor contribute to a population explosion that strains public services and increases
pollution. Amid these problems, however, the city retains its stately churrigueresque architecture and tree-lined boulevards, parks, and plazas.

Once a strategic area of the *cristeros*, a movement of Catholic zealots
in western Mexico in the 1920s, Guadalajara is among Mexico's most
socially traditional and politically conservative cities. Tapatíos, as residents are called (the name may derive from *tlapatiotl*, three purses of
cacao or other commodities used as currency by the area's Indians), take
pride in their rather straight and narrow outlook. Nevertheless, today
Guadalajara has a sizeable gay community, and its numerous gay bars
and clubs testify to a relative open-mindedness.

Though fond of tradition, Tapatíos are historically accustomed to
change. Within 10 years of its founding in 1531, Guadalajara's location shifted three times. In 1542 the city council followed the advice of
Doña Beatriz Hernández to build the community in the center of the
Atemajac Valley, where it could expand. It was thus placed on a mile-
high plain of the Sierra Madre, bounded on three sides by rugged cliffs
and on the fourth by the spectacular Barranca de Oblatos (Oblatos
Canyon). Geographically removed from the rest of the republic during
nearly 300 years of Spanish rule, the city cultivated and maintained a
political and cultural autonomy.

By the end of the 16th century, money was flowing into Guadalajara
from the region's farms and silver mines, creating the first millionaires
of what was then New Galicia. Under orders from Spain, much of the
wealth was lavished on magnificent churches, residences, and monuments.
Remnants of this golden era stand in downtown Guadalajara.

The suburbs of Tlaquepaque (pronounced tla-kay-*pah*-kay) and Tonalá
(pronounced toe-na-*la*) produce Mexico's finest and most popular traditional crafts and folk art. Lago de Chapala (Lake Chapala)—Mexico's largest body of fresh water—and the nearby towns of Chapala and
Ajijic have lured American and Canadian retirees, who enjoy most of
the amenities they were accustomed to north of the border.

# EXPLORING GUADALAJARA

Despite its size Guadalajara maintains a small-town pace and personality. Around 1960 20th-century architecture started to threaten the city's
aesthetic, and Guadalajara acted accordingly in the 1980s by designat-
ing 30 downtown blocks a cultural sanctuary. The result is the restored
Centro Histórico, an area whose 16th-century buildings are connected
by a series of large Spanish-style plazas.

| If you have **3 days** | Spend your first day in the Centro Histórico. The next day, spend the morning and have lunch in Tlaquepaque, and visit Tonalá in the afternoon. These two towns are the best places in Guadalajara to shop. On your third day, see some of the city sights outside the Centro Histórico and take in a show. |

| If you have **5 days** | Tour the Centro Histórico on your first day, and then devote a day to Tlaquepaque and another to Tonalá. Visit Lago de Chapala on Day 4. Spend your final day back in Guadalajara, perhaps visiting the Zoológico Guadalajara, or the Basílica de la Virgen de Zapopan and nearby sights, for which several hours are required. Plan an afternoon of strolling past the mansions that were built by Guadalajara's upper classes in the glorious twilight before the 1910 revolution; the best area is in a six-block radius around Avenida Vallarta west of Avenida Chapultepec. If you'd like to get your feet on the ground in more natural surroundings, hike in the nearby Barranca de Oblatos. |

**6**

| If you have **7 days** | Spend a day in Guadalajara's Centro Histórico and two days exploring and shopping in Tlaquepaque and Tonalá. On Day 4 head to Chapala, a village on the lake of the same name. Head west to Ajijic and make it your base for further lake region explorations. Spend Day 5 in San Juan Cosalá, with its thermal spas, and Day 6 in Tequila. Return to Guadalajara to spend your last day taking in some sights outside the Centro Histórico. |

The Centro is overflowing with elegant buildings and gurgling fountains, from the misting border of the Fuente Minerva (Minerva Fountain; at the intersection of Avenida Vallarta and Avenida López Mateos Sur) to the bubblers flanking the Teatro Degollado. Look for statues and sculptures, too—favorites include La Estampida (The Stampede; at Avenida Niños Hées and Avenida López Mateos Sur) and the whimsically anthropomorphic furniture in front of Instituto Cultural las Cabañas. Many of the trees lining the streets and plazas are often loaded with extremely bitter oranges.

Sights and large hotels are concentrated in three areas: the Zona Centro, which includes the Centro Histórico and extends west to Calle Federalismo and east to Calzada Independencia; the Zona Minerva, which surrounds the Fuente Minerva and Los Arcos monument; and the Zona Plaza del Sol, near the Plaza del Sol shopping mall and ExpoGuadalajara convention center. Guadalajara also has three autonomous municipalities—Zapopan, Tlaquepaque, and Tonalá—within its borders. An hour away are the tranquil villages on Lago de Chapala's receding shores, and Tequila, home of Mexico's notorious liquor.

### Timing
A near-perfect semitropical climate and proximity to the Pacific Ocean—240 km (149 mi) away—ensure warm, sunny days and cool, clear nights. The rainy season is from July to September; afternoon downpours can be fierce, but usually last no more than an hour.

With great weather and frequent events, Guadalajara's high season is officially from September to February. September's Festival Internacional de Mariachi y Tequila attracts traditional troubadours from as far as Japan and runs daily train trips to Tequila. (Tequila has its own festival in late November.) In October the city holds the Fiestas de Octubre, a month-long country fair–like event. Most museums and some other sights are closed on Monday—always check ahead.

## Centro Histórico

Guadalajara's historical buildings and several state and municipal offices lie in this 30-square-block pedestrian area. Bordered by Calle Federalismo to the west, Calzada Independencia to the east, Avenida Independencia to the north, and Avenida Niños Héroes to the south, the Centro Histórico is popular for its wide plazas, shady benches, and entertainment. Here you can glimpse ordinary Tapatío life and indulge in the delights of a quintessentially Mexican city.

### Timing

Allot at least two hours for the Centro. It's best to visit in the morning, but you could spread the walk over several afternoons (when the light is especially beautiful), and reserve your mornings for trips to outlying areas.

### A Good Walk

*Numbers in the text correspond to numbers in the margin and on the Guadalajara Centro Histórico map.*

Start your exploration of downtown at the 17th-century **Catedral ❶** ⌐, on the north side of the Plaza de Armas. After you've marveled at the interior, exit and cross Avenida Alcalde to Plaza de la Ciudad de Guadalajara, with its large fountain, café, and benches scattered beneath laurel trees. To your right (with your back to the cathedral) across Avenida Hidalgo is the **Palacio Municipal ❷**, which often features cultural exhibits on its second floor, the Salón Guadalajara.

From the corner of Avenidas Alcalde and Hidalgo, head one block east to Calle Liceo, until you reach the **Museo Regional de Guadalajara ❸**. The Rotunda de los Hombres Ilustres de Jalisco covers a mausoleum with the remains of 17 of Jalisco's most eminent citizens. After you leave the museum, turn right and walk three blocks on Calle Liceo to the small **Casa-Museo López Portillo ❹** and then the **Museo del Periodismo y de las Artes Gráficas ❺** on Avenida Alcalde.

Backtrack to the Museo Regional, make a left, and head east along Avenida Hidalgo, past the Palacio Legislativo—a former customhouse, tobacco warehouse, and inn that today houses Jalisco's state legislature—and the Palacio de Justicia, which was built in 1588 as part of Guadalajara's first convent and is now the state courthouse. Across Avenida Hidalgo on your right sprawls the Plaza de la Liberación, at the east end of which rises the **Teatro Degollado ❻**. Behind it is the start of the Plaza Tapatía, a five-block-long pedestrian mall. At the end, visit the **Instituto Cultural Cabañas ❼**. Then proceed back west to the modernistic Fuente Quet-

**6**

The Arts  A phenomenal spectrum of art awaits you in Guadalajara. In the soaring main dome of the Insituto Cultural Cabañas is *Hombre de Fuego* (Man of Fire), José Clemente Orozco's most famous mural. A gripping image of a man rising from (or perhaps descending into) a sheet of flames, the painting is a masterpiece of perspective: though the dome's surface is deeply concave, the painting itself appears flat. A hundred meters from the institute, a covered passageway faces Plaza Tapatía, where Huichol families sell wooden masks and figures decorated with thousands of tiny beads.

Guadalajara is filled with stunning churches, most dating from Mexico's colonial era. There's one every few blocks—nearly 15 in the downtown area alone. In the Teatro Degollado you can see performances by dance troupes as diverse as the Ballet Folklórico and the Moscow Ballet. Craftspeople in Tlaquepaque and Tonalá produce fine ceramics, blown glass, and metal work. The Museo del Premio Nacional Panteon Panduro displays winning pieces from Tlaquepaque's annual ceramics competition.

Edibles  Even with a population of 6 million, many outsiders still think of Mexico's second-largest city as a *rancho* (farm town), and view its residents as rough around the edges. Although Guadalajara may be less cosmopolitan than Mexico City, its variety of restaurants testify to a genuine worldliness. Look for excellent Italian, Chinese, and French dishes as well as creative and truly exceptional Mexican food. But there's a true touch of provincialism in the city's hearty, simple street food. *Tortas ahogadas* are a local creation and a lunchtime favorite. Sold mainly from street-corner carts, these "drowned sandwiches" consist of roast pork (a staple here) in a french roll, often with mayo and chili, doused in runny, lukewarm tomato sauce. Tequila comes in hundreds of varieties, many quite refined, and is nowhere more appreciated.

Shopping  Tlaquepaque is full of master craftspeople whose blown-glass, hand-carved wood furniture, fine leather, hand-glazed pottery, and inventive metal creations are sold in pleasant shops. With a church, a quiet plaza, and plenty of eateries, it's the perfect place for a day of browsing and buying. Tonalá has many of the same crafts. Consider hunting for them in the Thursday and Sunday markets (Thursday's is less crowded). Amid knickknacks and outright junk there are some incredible pieces and the prices will probably be better than in Tlaquepaque. Look for mirrors framed in tin and ceramic tiles, handblown and hand-painted pitcher-and-glass sets, animals shaped out of steel, and *bajilla*—exquisitely painted services of plates, bowls, cups, and saucers.

Shoes are big business in Guadalajara. Shops on Calle Pedro Morelos, west of the cathedral, sell stylish, durable, and affordable footwear. Head to Mercado Libertad for *huaraches* (woven leather sandals). The city also has scores of jewelry shops, including several jewelry malls bordering Plaza Tapatía. Traditional malls include the modern, multilevel Centro Magno and the open-air Plaza del Sol. A final word about bargaining—it's customary (and advisable) in markets and Mercado Libertad, but less so in Tlaquepaque and not at all in the malls.

## Sports

Soccer (*futbol* or just *fut*) is without question an obsession. Guadalajara's two main teams, Atlas and Las Chivas (the She-Goats), nurse a healthy rivalry—as do their fans. Atlas appeals more to the middle and upper classes; working-class Tapatís and students (whose parents are surely Atlas fans) prefer Las Chivas. Think carefully before buying a team hat or shirt—it's an important choice here. Bicycle races are occasionally held downtown—you may find streets blocked off, especially early on weekends. Other favored sports include bullfighting and *charreadas*, traditional and highly stylized equestrian events with elegantly clad riders. Both are presented weekly, though the bullfights are only held in October and November.

---

zalcóatl (Quetzalcóatl Fountain) in the plaza's center and outside the institute. Turn left and walk down the stairs to the sprawling Mercado Libertad. Turn left again when you leave the market to reach the **Plaza de los Mariachis** ⓼.

Return to Plaza Tapatía, walk a block to Calle Morelos, and pass numerous bridal shops. Continue west to the **Templo de San Agustín** ⓽. As you leave the church, walk west on Calle Morelos and then turn left onto Avenida Corona. A half block south is the **Palacio de Gobierno** ⓾, with its striking murals. Exit the palacio back onto Avenida Corona and cross to the Plaza de Armas, where you can imagine yourself in the Porfiriato—Mexico's Victorian period—when *dons* and *doñas* strolled by the ornately sculpted kiosk, a gift from France in 1910. With the cathedral to your right, you've come full circle back to the plaza's north side.

### What to See

❹ **Casa-Museo López Portillo.** Guadalajara's López Portillo family included prominent writers and politicians, such as an early-20th-century Jalisco governor and his grandson, José López Portillo, Mexico's president from 1976 to 1982. French Baroque–style rooms in their former home display antique furniture and household items. In the rear is a small art gallery. ⊠ *Calle Liceo 177, at Calle San Felipe, Centro Histórico* ☎ *33/3613–2411 or 33/3613–2435* 🖾 *Free* ☉ *Tues.–Sun. 10–6.*

★ ⌐ ❶ **Catedral.** Begun in 1561 and consecrated in 1618, this downtown focal point is an intriguing mélange of baroque, Gothic, and other styles. Its emblematic twin towers replaced the originals, felled by the earthquake of 1818. Ten of the silver-and-gold altars were gifts from King Fernando VII for Guadalajara's financial support of Spain during the Napoleonic Wars. Some of the world's most beautiful *retablos* (altarpieces) adorn the walls; above the sacristy (often closed to the public) is Bartolomé Esteban Murillo's priceless 17th-century painting, *The Assumption of the Virgin*. In a loft above the main entrance is a magnificent late-19th-century French organ. ⊠ *Av. Alcalde, between Av. Hidalgo and Calle Morelos, Centro Histórico* 🖾 *No phone* 🖾 *Free* ☉ *Daily 8–7.*

🔊 ❼ **Instituto Cultural Cabañas.** This landmark neoclassical-style cultural cen-
FodorśChoice ter was designed by famed Spanish architect-sculptor Manuel Tolsá. Orig-
★ inally a shelter for widows, the elderly, and orphans, the Instituto's 106
rooms and 23 flower-filled patios now house art exhibitions (ask for an
English-speaking guide). The main chapel displays murals painted by
José Clemente Orozco in 1938–39, including *The Man of Fire*, his masterpiece. In all, there are 57 murals by Orozco, plus many of his smaller
paintings, cartoons, and drawings. Kids will wonder at the institute's
enormous murals and can explore its labyrinthine compound. ⊠ *Calle
Cabañas 8, Centro Histórico* ☎ *33/3668–1640* 🖪 *$1; free Sun.*
🕑 *Tues.–Sat. 10:15–5:45, Sun. 10:15–2:30.*

❺ **Museo del Periodismo y de las Artes Gráficas.** Guadalajara's first printing press was set up here in 1792; in 1810 it printed the first 2,000 copies
of "El Despertador Americano," which impelled would-be Mexicans to
join the War of Independence. You can see historic newspapers, printing presses, and recording equipment in this mansion, known as the Casa
de los Perros for the two wrought-iron *perros* (dogs) guarding its roof.
⊠ *Av. Alcalde 225, between Calle Reforma and Calle San Felipe, Centro Histórico* ☎ *33/3613–9285 or 33/3613–9286* 🖪 *$1* 🕑 *Tues.–Sat.
10–6, Sun. 10–3.*

★ ❸ **Museo Regional de Guadalajara.** Constructed as a seminary and public
library in 1701, this has been the Guadalajara Regional Museum's
home since 1918. First-floor galleries contain artifacts and memorabilia
tracing western Mexico's history from prehistoric times through the Spanish conquest. Five 19th-century carriages, including one used by General Porfirio Díaz, are on the second-floor balcony. There's an impressive
collection of European and Mexican paintings, including ones by Bartolomé Esteban Murillo. Unfortunately there are no English-language
materials. ⊠ *Calle Liceo 60, Centro Histórico* ☎ *33/3614–9957* 🖪 *$3;
free Sun.* 🕑 *Tues.–Sun. 9–5:30.*

❿ **Palacio de Gobierno.** The adobe structure of 1643 was replaced with this
churrigueresque and neoclassical stone structure in the 18th century.
Within are Jalisco's state government offices and two of José Clemente
Orozco's most passionate murals. One just past the entrance, depicts a
gigantic Father Miguel Hidalgo looming amid shadowy figures—including
the pope, Hitler, and Mussolini—representing oppression and slavery.
Upstairs is the other mural (look for a door marked CONGRESO), which
portrays Hidalgo, Juárez, and other 1850s Reform era figures. ⊠ *Av.
Corona, between Calle Morelos and Pedro Moreno, Centro Histórico*
☎ *No phone* 🖪 *Free* 🕑 *Daily 9–8:45.*

❷ **Palacio Municipal.** Inside City Hall are murals of the city's founding, painted
by Guadalajara native Gabriel Flores. Free walking tours of the Centro
begin here Saturday at 10 AM (in Spanish only). ⊠ *Av. Hidalgo, at Av.
Alcalde, Centro Histórico* ☎ *No phone* 🖪 *Free* 🕑 *Weekdays 9–8.*

❽ **Plaza de los Mariachis.** This small, triangular plaza just south of the Mercado Libertad was once the ideal place to tip up a beer and experience
the most Mexican of music. The once placid spot is now boxed in by a
busy street, a market, and a run-down neighborhood. It's safest to visit

# Guadalajara
## Centro Histórico

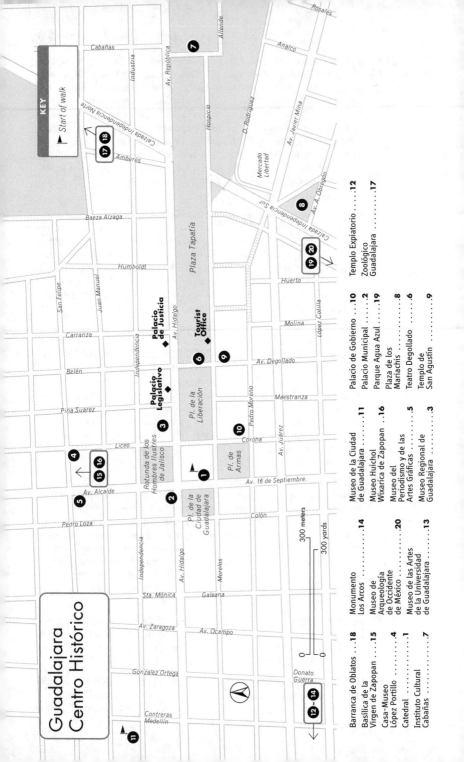

**KEY**

▲ Start of walk

300 meters

300 yards

in the day or early evening; mariachi serenades start at about $8 a song. Use the pedestrian overpass from the south side of Plaza Tapatía to avoid heavy traffic. ⊠ *Calz. Independencia Sur, Centro Histórico.*

★ ⑥ **Teatro Degollado.** Inaugurated in 1866, this magnificent theater was modeled after Milan's La Scala. The refurbished theater preserves its traditional red-and-gold color scheme, and its balconies ascend to a multitier dome adorned with Gerardo Suárez's depiction of Dante's *Divine Comedy*. The theater is home to the Jalisco Philharmonic and the University of Guadalajara's Ballet Folklórico and hosts visiting companies. According to legend, Guadalajara was founded at what is now the Plaza de los Fundadores, on the theater's east side. A sculpted frieze on the theater's rear wall depicts the event. ⊠ *Av. Degollado, between Av. Hidalgo and Calle Morelos, Centro Histórico* ☎ *33/3614–4773 or 33/ 3613–1115* 🖃 *Free; ticket prices for show vary* ⊙ *Weekdays 10–2.*

⑨ **Templo de San Agustín.** One of the city's oldest churches has been remodeled many times since its consecration in 1573, but the sacristy is original. The building to the left of the church, originally an Augustinian cloister, is now the Escuela de Música (School of Music) of the University of Guadalajara. Free recitals and concerts are held on its patio. ⊠ *Calle Morelos 188, at Av. Degollado, Centro Histórico* ☎ *33/3614–5365* 🖃 *Free* ⊙ *Daily 8–1 and 5–8.*

## Elsewhere in Guadalajara

West of the Centro is Zona Minerva, which you can access by walking west on Avenida Juarez (it becomes Avenida Vallarta) or by taking the westbound Trolley 400 or 500 on Calle Independencia. In Zona Minerva are a church, a museum, and two distinctive landmarks—Fuente Minerva (Minerva Fountain) and Monumento Los Arcos. North of the Centro is Zona Huentitán, which contains a zoo and Barranca de Oblatos. You can reach this neighborhood by cab or the northbound Trolley 600 on Calzada Independencia. Finally, there's Zapopan, a municipality of Guadalajara. Northwest of the Centro (take a mint-green Tur bus marked "Zapopan," Bus 275, or taxi), Zapopan makes for a great day trip. You can walk to or between some places on this tour, but you're better off hopping a cab or a bus as there's plenty of walking within some of the sights themselves.

### A Good Tour

Heading west from the Catedral, you'll first arrive at the **Museo de la Ciudad de Guadalajara** ⑪ ➤, with its exhibits on Guadalajara's founding. Continuing west on Avenida López Cotilla, across Avenida Federalismo, you'll reach the Gothic **Templo Expiatorio** ⑫—several eateries around the plaza serve tamales and fruit drinks. Behind Templo Expiatorio is a collection of contemporary art in the **Museo de las Artes de la Universidad de Guadalajara** ⑬. Farther west along Avenida Vallarta, is the **Monumento Los Arcos** ⑭, which you can climb for a spectacular view of the Fuente Minerva. This tour is walkable, but it's not short; all these sites are on or near the route of Trolley 400 or 500, which both head back to the Centro Histórico on Avenida Hidalgo.

You can easily fill a day exploring Zapopan, including visits to the **Basílica de la Virgen de Zapopan** ⑮, 7 km (4½ mi) northwest of downtown, and the neighboring **Museo Huichol Wixarica de Zapopan** ⑯. Near the basilica is Zapopan's municipal palace (with occasional art exhibits), plus a smaller church and an art museum. Restaurants on the pedestrian walkway farther east specialize in seafood. If you prefer to probe the natural world, head northeast to the **Zoológico Guadalajara** ⑰, a huge zoo, and the **Barranca de Oblatos** ⑱, a canyon with waterfalls, hiking trails, and scenic lookouts. South of the Centro Histórico are the **Parque Agua Azul** ⑲, with its paleontology museum, and the nearby **Museo de Arqueología de Occidente de México** ⑳.

## Timing

An hour is ample time for browsing the relatively small Museo de la Ciudad de Guadalajara. A 10-minute walk west is the larger Museo de las Artes de la Universidad de Guadalajara. Art lovers can spend two hours here when all the exhibits are open. Budget an hour for the Templo Expiatorio across the street. The Monumento Los Arcos and the Fuente Minerva make quick single-afternoon tours, but are more distant; from Templo Expiatorio it takes a half hour by foot or five minutes by bus or cab.

Zapopan's central plaza is near many sights and is 15 minutes by cab from the Centro, or 25 minutes by bus. It takes about 20 minutes to soak in the basilica, and the Huichol Museum another 45–60 minutes. Allot a half hour for Zapopan's municipal palace. Take another hour or two to explore the market, additional churches, and art museum (it keeps irregular hours). The zoo is a 20-minute cab-ride away, more by bus because you have to walk about 500 meters to the entrance; the zoo takes about two hours. To avoid crowds and leave before dark, go to the Barranca de Oblatos in the late morning. The Parque Agua Azul's museums are small and require less than an hour.

## What to See

⑱ **Barranca de Oblatos.** The multipronged 2,000-foot-deep Oblatos Canyon has hiking trails and the narrow Cola de Caballo waterfall, named for its horse-tail shape. A portion of the canyon complex called Barranca de Huetitán (Huetitán Canyon) has a steep, winding, 5-km (3-mi) trail to the river below. The trails are less strenuous at Barranca de Oblatos (the name of this entrance as well as the whole canyon). Both areas can be crowded on mornings and weekends. Take a northbound electric bus from in front of the Mercado Libertad and get off at Parque Mirador Indepencia if you're only interested in the view; alternatively, get off at Periférico and catch any eastbound bus for Huetitán and Oblatos. You can see the Cola de Caballo from the Zoológico Guadalajara, but for a closer look catch an Ixcantantus-bound bus from Glorieta La Normal, a traffic circle 10 blocks north of the cathedral, and ask to be let off at the *mirador de la cascada* (waterfall viewpoint).

⑮ **Basílica de la Virgen de Zapopan.** This vast church, with an ornate plateresque facade and *mudéjar* (Moorish) tile dome, was consecrated in 1730. It's the home of La Zapopanita, Our Lady of Zapopan: a 10-

# THE STRUGGLE OF THE HUICHOL

**HE HUICHOL (WEE-CHOL) INDIANS'
TRUE NAME** is the Wirraritari, or
"people who populate places of
thorny plants." It's a fitting name for
this hardy and reclusive group, whose
independence has helped them preserve
their traditions better than many of
Mexico's native communities. (As a
measure of their isolation, some Huicholes
communities only had electricity installed
in 2003.) Most notable among Huichol
traditions is the use of peyote, a
hallucinogenic cactus fruit, in complex
spiritual ceremonies. Huichol artists also
create magical and remarkable
"paintings," by pressing colorful beads or
yarn onto wood molds smeared with sap.

The Huicholes fiercely resisted Spanish—
and later Mexican—intrusion; nowadays,
most live in northern Jalisco, southern
Nayarit, and Zacatecas, in a remote
592,800-acre reservation established in
1953. In recent years, however, the
ownership and boundaries of some
Huichol lands, much of it rented out to
farmers and cattle breeders, have come
under dispute. The conflict has not been
peaceful, with allegations of human rights
violations perpetrated by Nayarit police
as well as by the current "tenants." In the
mid-1990s, after a long investigation,
Mexico's Human Rights Commission
(CEDH) corroborated many of the Huichol
allegations, and a recent constitutional
amendment affirmed the autonomy of the
Huichol and other indigenous communities
within Mexico. But problems continue—
there remains intense pressure to develop
some Huichol lands, and the Mexican
Army, in its highly visible war on drugs,
has arrested Huicholes coming back from
religious pilgrimages in the San Luis Potosí
desert, where they collect peyote.

inch-high statue venerated as the source of many miracles. Every October 12 over a million people crowd the streets up to the basilica, where the Virgin is returned after a five-month tour of the state's parish churches. In 2003 the stunning plaza in front was razed to enlarge an underlying parking structure—it should be restored by early 2005. Catch a taxi, Bus 275, or a northbound Tur. Alternatively, take the light rail to Avila Camacho (Line 1), cross the street, and catch Bus 631. ⊠ *Av. Hidalgo, at Calle Morelos, Zona Zapopan Norte* ☎ *33/3633–0141 or 33/3633–6614* ☜ *Free* ☉ *Daily 10–8.*

🕙 **Monumento Los Arcos.** The double arches of this distinctive monument span Avenida Vallarta, a block east of Fuente Minerva. Reminiscent of the Arc de Triomphe, the neoclassical structure has an intriguing mural inside, and a winding stairway to the roof, where there's a broad view of the fountain and the avenue below. Enter through the south leg, which has a small but helpful tourist office. ⊠ *Av. Vallarta 2641, at Lopez Mateos Sur, Zona Minerva* ☎ *33/3616–9150* ☉ *Daily 8–6* ☜ *Free.*

🕙 **Museo de Arqueología de Occidente de México.** The Archaeological Museum of Western Mexico has pottery and clay figures made by ancient peoples from what are presently the states of Colima, Jalisco, and Nayarit. A collection of urns in the shape of dogs is especially notable, though the overall presentation at this tiny museum is lacking. ⊠ *Av. 16 de Septiembre 889, Zona Centro* ☎ *33/3619–0104* 🖭 *30¢* ⊗ *Tues.–Sat. 10–2 and 5–7:30, Sun. 10–2.*

⑬ **Museo de las Artes de la Universidad de Guadalajara.** The University of Guadalajara's contemporary art museum is in this exquisite early-20th-century building. The permanent collection includes several murals by Orozco. Revolving exhibitions have contemporary works from Latin America, Europe, and the U.S. ⊠ *Av. López Cotilla 930, at Av. Díaz de Leon, west of Zona Centro,* ☎ *33/3134–2222 Ext. 1680* 🖭 *Free* ⊗ *Tues.–Sun. 10–8.*

▶ ⑪ **Museo de la Ciudad de Guadalajara.** Rooms surrounding the tranquil interior patio of this spacious, two-story, colonial mansion contain artwork, artifacts, and reproductions of documents about the city's development from pre-Hispanic times through the 20th century. Ask about English-language materials at the entrance or in the library upstairs. ⊠ *Calle Independencia 684, Zona Centro* ☎ *33/3658–2531 or 33/3658–3706* 🖭 *45¢; free Sun.* ⊗ *Tues.–Sat. 10–5:30, Sun. 10–2:30.*

★ ⑯ **Museo Huichol Wixarica de Zapopan.** The Huichol Indians of northern Jalisco and neighboring states of Zacatecas and Nayarit are famed for their fierce independence and exquisite bead and yarn mosaics. In this small but well-designed museum are many examples of Huichol artwork. Bilingual placards explain tribal history as well as the art. ⊠ *Av. Hidalgo, at Calle Morelos, Zona Zapopan Norte* ☎ *33/3636–4430* 🖭 *50¢* ⊗ *Mon.–Sat. 9:30–1:30 and 3–5:45; Sun. 10–3.*

☉ ⑲ **Parque Agua Azul.** This popular park has playgrounds, caged birds, an orchid house, and acres of trees and grass crisscrossed by walking paths. There aren't many butterflies in the huge, geodesic *mariposario* (butterfly sanctuary), but the semitropical garden inside is still worth a visit. The **Museo de la Paleontología** (⊠ Av. Dr. R. Michel 520, Zona Centro ☎ 33/3619–7043), on the park's east side, has plant and animal fossils as well as exhibits—some hands-on for kids—on the origin of the planet. Admission is 70¢, and the museum is open Tuesday through Sunday from 10 to 6. Free guided Spanish-language tours are at 11, 12:30, and 4:30. (There's no museum entrance inside Agua Azul; you must walk to the park's north side.) ⊠ *Calz. Independencia Sur, between González Gallo and Las Palmas, south of Zona Centro* ☎ *33/3619–0332* 🖭 *40¢* ⊗ *Mon.–Sat. 10–6, Sun. 11–6.*

⑫ **Templo Expiatorio.** The striking, Gothic Church of Atonement is possibly Guadalajara's most beautiful church. Modeled after Italy's Orvieto Cathedral, it has phenomenal stained-glass windows—observe the rose window above the choir and pipe organ. Fronted by a large plaza, the church is backed by the Museo de las Artes de la Universidad de Guadalajara. ⊠ *Calle Díaz de León 930, at Av. López Cotilla, Zona Minerva* ☎ *33/3825–3410* 🖭 *Free* ⊗ *Daily 7 AM–10 PM.*

☉ ⑰ **Zoológico Guadalajara.** On the edge of the jagged Barranca de Huetitán, the city's zoo has over 1,500 animals representing 360 species. There are a kids' zoo, two aviaries, and a herpetarium with 130 species of reptiles, amphibians, and fish. For 50¢ you can take a guided train tour of the grounds. Admission to the adjacent Selva Mágica (Magic Jungle) amusement park is $1.30. ⊠ *Paseo del Zoológico 600, off Calz. Independencia, Zona Huetitán* ☎ *33/3674–4488 or 33/3674–3976* ☞ *$3.50* ☉ *Wed.–Sun. 10–6.*

# WHERE TO EAT

Regional specialties and a growing contemporary food scene, spearheaded by expats and U.S.-trained Mexican chefs, yield a diverse dining experience. Select from Chinese dishes, Continental delicacies, Argentine-style steaks, fresh seafood, or local favorites like *tortas ahogadas,* "drowned sandwiches" in warm tomato sauce; *birria,* spicy stew with goat, lamb, or beef in light tomato broth; *pozole,* thick pork and hominy soup; and *carne en su jugo,* clear spicy broth with steak bits, bacon, beans, and cilantro.

| WHAT IT COSTS | | | | |
|---|---|---|---|---|
| | $$$$ | $$$ | $$ | $ | ¢ |
| AT DINNER | over $25 | $15–$25 | $10–$15 | $5–$10 | under $5 |

Prices are per person for a main course, excluding tax and tip.

★ **$$–$$$** ✕ **Pierrot.** Nose through this quiet French dining room's extensive wine list for a drink to accompany the mouth-watering pâté, the trout almandine, or the pâté-stuffed chicken breast in tarragon sauce. Wall-mounted lamps and fresh flowers on each table are among the restaurant's gracious touches. ⊠ *Calle Justo Sierra 2355, Zona Minerva* ☎ *33/3630–2087 or 33/3615–4758* ☐ *AE, MC, V* ☉ *Closed Sun.*

**$$** ✕ **La Estancia Gaucha.** Tapatíos adore Argentine cuisine and come to this first-rate steak house for its no-nonsense cuts, including the *churrasco estancia* (rib eye) and the *bife de chorizo* (essentially New York strip steak). Don't miss the delicious empanadas or Sunday lunch's homemade ravioli. Piano music accompanies dinner Wednesday through Saturday. ⊠ *Av. Niños Héroes 2860, Zona Minerva* ☎ *33/3122–6565 or 33/3122–9985* ☐ *AE, MC, V* ☉ *No dinner Sun.*

**$$** ✕ **Formosa Gardens.** Guadalajara's Asian residents visit Formosa Gardens, which has sister restaurants in Beijing and Taiwan, for the familiar tastes of home: the menu has Chinese, Japanese, and Thai dishes. The Peking duck is crisp, and the deep-fried orange beef is sweet and tangy. The restaurant is in a mansion and has several dining rooms as well as a pleasant garden area. ⊠ *Av. Union 322, Zona Minerva* ☎ *33/3615–7415* ☐ *AE, DC, MC, V* ☉ *No dinner Sun.*

**$$** ✕ **Santo Coyote.** Faux waterfalls, folk art-crammed walls, and the gift shop may be more reminiscent of Walt Disney World than a popular Guadalajara restaurant. Nevertheless, city jet-setters have given this place the nod for its new Mexican cuisine, first-rate service, and elegant presentation. Try the wood-fired roast or grilled *cabrito* (goat) or the baby back ribs topped with tamarind and pepper sauce. ⊠ *Calle Lerdo de Tejada 2379, Zona Minerva* ☎ *33/3616–6978* ☐ *MC, V.*

**$–$$$** ✕ **El Farallón de Tepic.** Out in the open air and beneath a bright-blue awning, this restaurant specializes in fresh *pescado*—usually red snapper or an equally mild fish—grilled with garlic or butter, in classic tomato sauce, breaded, or stuffed with seafood and cheese. The pescado *sarandeado* (Jalisco-style whole barbecued fish stuffed with vegetables) is worth the 30-minute wait. Go with the homemade flan for dessert. ✉ *Av. Niño Obrero 560, Zona Zapopan* ☎ *33/3121–2616 or 33/3121–9616* ⊟ *AE, MC, V* ☻ *No dinner.*

**$–$$** ✕ **Casa Bariachi.** Expect waiters and diners to sing along with the mariachi bands at this stately restaurant. Expect waiters and diners to sing along. The menu emphasizes steak, and the fiesta continues until 3 AM. A bar by the same name and catercorner to the restaurant stays open late. ✉ *Av. Vallarta 2221, Zona Minerva* ☎ *33/3615–0029* ⊟ *AE, MC, V* ☻ *Closed Sun.*

★ **$–$$** ✕ **La Destilería.** If you can't make it to the village of Tequila, here's the next best thing: a friendly restaurant–cum–tequila museum that serves decent Mexican fare and 220 varieties of the fiery liquor. Antique photos of tequila distilleries and bilingual plaques explaining tequila's history line the brick walls. ✉ *Av. México 2916, Zona Minerva* ☎ *33/3640–3110* ⊟ *AE, MC, V* ☻ *No dinner Sun.*

★ **$–$$** ✕ **La Fonda de San Miguel.** Perhaps the Centro's finest restaurant, La Fonda serves inventive Mexican food in a soaring courtyard, hung with a spectacular array of shining tin stars (the kind made in Tonolá and Tlaquepaque). Try the *molcajete del mar*, a fish stew with beef or chicken, and served in a three-legged stone bowl (the molcajete). ✉ *Donato Guerra 25 Centro Histórico* ☎ *33/3613–0809* ⊟ *AE, D, MC, V.*

★ **$–$$** ✕ **El Sacromonte.** Come here for creative Mexican food, excellent service, and reasonable prices. You're surrounded by *artesanía* in the bright dining area, and there's live music every afternoon and evening. Try a juicy steak or *La Corona de Reina Isabel*—a crown of intertwined shrimp in lobster sauce; there are such classic dishes as chicken mole or *chiles en nogada*, a large mild chili stuffed with a semisweet ground beef mixture, and topped with creamy walnut sauce and pomegranate seeds. Many Mexicans consider it their national dish because the colors match those of the Mexican flag. Reservations are recommended. ✉ *Pedro Moreno 1398, Zona Minerva* ☎ *33/3825–5447* ⊟ *MC, V* ☻ *Closed Sun.*

★ **$–$$** ✕ **Tacos Providencia del Centro.** Tacos here are as delectable as they are unique (try *trompa*, a.k.a. pig snout), but this isn't merely a taco joint. Most people come for the steak, quail, and extensive beer and tequila offerings. Better known as La Riconada for the corner building it occupies, this grand old restaurant has appeared in numerous Mexican movies and TV comedies. Come early because it closes at 6. ✉ *Calle Morelos 86, at Plaza Tapatía, Centro Histórico* ☎ *33/3613–9914 or 33/3613–9925* ⊟ *AE, MC, V.*

★ **$–$$** ✕ **La Trattoria.** Guadalajara's top Italian restaurant is a bustling family place. The menu's highlights include spaghetti *frutti di mare* (with seafood), *scaloppine alla Marsala* (beef medallions with Marsala and mushrooms), and fresh garlic bread. All meals include a trip to the salad bar. Arrive before 8 PM to beat the crowd. ✉ *Av. Niños Héroes 3051, Zona Minerva* ☎ *33/3122–1817* ⊟ *AE, MC, V.*

$  ✕ **Karne Garibaldi.** In the *1996 Guinness Book of World Records,* this Tapatío institution held the record for world's fastest service: 13.5 seconds for a table of six. Lightning service is made possible by the menu's single item: *carne en su jugo,* a combination of finely diced beef and bacon simmered in rich beef broth and served with grilled onions, tortillas, and refried beans mixed with corn. Don't be put off by the somewhat gritty area surrounding the restaurant. ⊠ *Calle Garibaldi 1306, Zona Minerva* ☎ *33/3826–1286* ➾ *AE, MC, V.*

★ $  ✕ **La Pianola.** Signature piano music and appealing dining areas (view the avenue from the front, or unwind in the large, airy courtyard in the back) provide a soothing backdrop for you to sample specialties from this restaurant's varied Mexican menu, which includes pozole and *chiles en nogada* (chiles in walnut sauce). ⊠ *Av. México 3220, Zona Minerva* ☎ *33/3813–1385 or 33/3813–2412* ➾ *AE, MC, V.*

¢–$  ✕ **Antigüedades Café Bazar del Carmen.** It's on Plaza del Carmen—whose serenity seems to have affected the speed of the service—and it's great for coffee, tea, pastries, a light lunch, and, of all things, antiques (there's a small on-site store). Savor the *trensas de champignon* (braided bread stuffed with mushrooms), which comes with a small salad, and follow it with a cappuccino and a slice of chocolate cake. On Saturday night a group of elderly folks smoothly dance *danzón* (a classic Cuban rhythm) nearby. ⊠ *Calle Jacobo Galvez 45-B, off Av. Juárez, Zona Centro* ☎ *33/3658–2266* ➾ *No credit cards.*

# WHERE TO STAY

Choosing a place to stay is a matter of location and price; tourists are often drawn to the Centro, where colonial-style hotels are convenient to the historical center and other sights, or to Tlaquepaque's genial B&Bs, like the Quinta Don José. Business people head for the area around Avenida López Mateos Sur, a 16-km (10-mi) strip extending from the Minerva Fountain to the Plaza del Sol shopping center, where they can take advantage of modern office facilities. Several hotels, like the polished Hilton, are near the ExpoGuadalajara convention center.

Call ahead if you're apprehensive about noise levels; many hotels are on busy intersections, in which case rooms higher up or in the back tend to be less noisy. Some hotels have windows that won't open, so ask for a room with a balcony if fresh air is important to you. Expect hotels in the $$$ and $$$$ categories to have purified-water systems and English-language TV channels among other amenities.

| WHAT IT COSTS | | | | |
| --- | --- | --- | --- | --- |
| | **$$$$** | **$$$** | **$$** | **$** | **¢** |
| FOR 2 PEOPLE | over $250 | $150–$250 | $75–$150 | $50–$75 | under $50 |

Price categories are assigned based on the range between the least and most expensive standard double rooms in high season based on the European Plan (EP, with no meals) unless otherwise noted. Tax (17%) is extra.

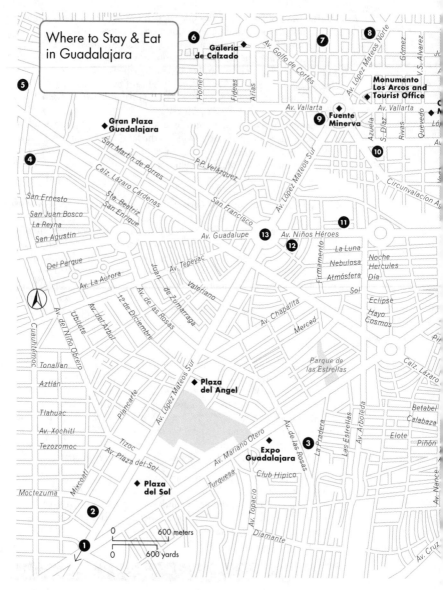

## Where to Stay & Eat in Guadalajara

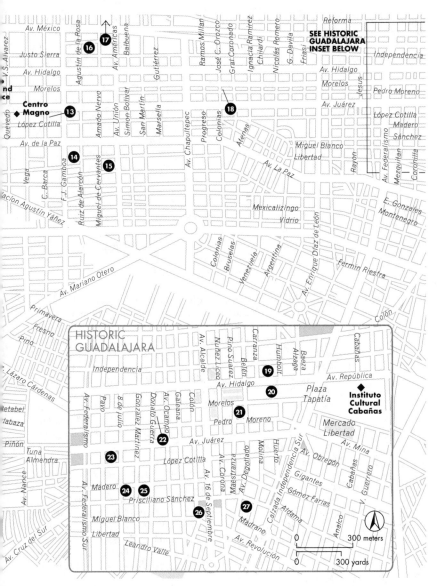

**$$$$** 🏨 **Quinta Real.** Stone and brick walls, colonial arches, and objets d'art
**Fodor'sChoice** fill this luxury hotel's public areas. Suites are plush, though on the
★ small side, with neocolonial-style furnishings, glass-top writing tables,
and faux fireplaces. Junior suites are larger (and slightly more expensive) than master suites. The hotel provides free passes to a nearby
Gold's Gym. ⊠ *Av. México 2727, at Av. López Mateos Norte, Zona
Minerva, 44680* 🕾 *33/3669–0600, 01800/362–1500 in Mexico* 🖷 *33/
3669–0601* ⊕ *www.quintareal.com* 🖙 *76 suites* ⛄ *Restaurant, in-
room data ports, pool, bar, baby-sitting, concierge, business services, meeting rooms, travel services, no-smoking rooms* ▤ *AE, D, DC, MC, V.*

**$$$–$$$$** 🏨 **Camino Real.** A 15-minute cab ride from downtown will bring you
to the first of Guadalajara's luxury hotels. Guest rooms are large and
reasonably well decorated, some have opulent glass and marble bath-
rooms. Many rooms and suites surround the pools and gardens, where
trios serenade the Sunday-morning buffet brunch crowd. Rear rooms
face noisy Avenida Vallarta. ⊠ *Av. Vallarta 5005, Zona Minerva, 45040*
🕾 *33/3134–2424, 01800/901–2300 in Mexico, 800/722–6466 in U.S.*
🖷 *33/3134–2404* ⊕ *www.caminoreal.com/guadalajara* 🖙 *195 rooms,
10 suites* ⛄ *2 restaurants, golf privileges, putting green, tennis court, 4
pools, gym, bar, baby-sitting, playground, concierge, no-smoking rooms*
▤ *AE, D, DC, MC, V.*

**$$$** 🏨 **Crowne Plaza Guadalajara.** Gardens encircling the pool add a bit of
nature to this family-friendly hotel near Plaza del Sol. A mix of antiques
and reproductions fills the public spaces. Rooms have marble baths and
natural lighting; those in the tower have city views. (Rooms near the
playground area can be loud.) Plaza Club room rates include a buffet
breakfast. The top-floor restaurant is the only one in Guadalajara with
a panoramic view. ⊠ *Av. López Mateos Sur 2500, Zona Plaza del Sol,
45050* 🕾 *33/3634–1034, 01800/365–5500 in Mexico* 🖷 *33/3631–9393*
⊕ *www.crownegdl.com.mx* 🖙 *290 rooms, 4 suites* ⛄ *3 restaurants, in-
room data ports, golf privileges, 2 tennis courts, pool, gym, hair salon,
bar, shops, baby-sitting, playground, concierge floor, business services,
car rental, kennel, no-smoking floor* ▤ *AE, DC, MC, V.*

**$$$** 🏨 **Hilton.** Adjacent to the ExpoGuadalajara convention center is this pre-
mier business destination. Among its many business services are a mul-
tilingual staff, a business center, and an executive floor (with free
breakfast in a private dining area). There are excellent spa facilities. ⊠ *Av.
de las Rosas 2933, Zona Plaza del Sol, 44540* 🕾 *33/3678–0505, 01800/
003–1400 in Mexico, 800/445–8667 in U.S.* 🖷 *33/3678–0511* ⊕ *www.
guadalajara.hilton.com* 🖙 *402 rooms, 20 suites* ⛄ *2 restaurants, in-room
data ports, golf privileges, pool, gym, hair salon, massage, spa, bar, con-
cierge floor, business services, meeting rooms, no-smoking rooms* ▤ *AE,
DC, MC, V.*

**$$$** 🏨 **Presidente Inter-Continental.** With its mirrored facade and 12-story atrium
lobby, this bustling hotel attracts a sophisticated business clientele. For
the best city view, request a room on an upper floor facing the Plaza del
Sol shopping center. A Tane silver shop is one of the many on-site stores,
and the health club is one of the city's best. ⊠ *Av. López Mateos Sur
3515, Zona Plaza del Sol, 45050* 🕾 *33/3678–1234, 01800/502–0500
or 01800/363–3000 in Mexico* 🖷 *33/3678–1268* ⊕ *www.interconti.com*

⇗ *379 rooms, 30 suites* ☼ *2 restaurants, coffee shop, in-room data ports, golf privileges, pool, health club, massage, sauna, spa, steam room, bar, shops, baby-sitting, concierge floor, business services, meeting rooms, airport shuttle, car rental* ☰ *AE, D, DC, MC, V.*

★ **$$–$$$** ▦ **Fiesta Americana.** The dramatic glass facade of this high-rise faces the Minerva Fountain and Los Arcos monument. Four glass-enclosed elevators ascend dizzyingly above a 14-story atrium lobby to the enormous guest rooms, which have modern furnishings, marble bathrooms, and arresting views. The lobby bar has live music every night but Sunday. On the *piso ejecutivo* (executive floor) rooms come with breakfast, and there's a business center. ⊠ *Av. Aurelio Aceves 225, Zona Minerva, 44100* ☎ *33/3825–3434 or 33/3630–3671, 01800/504–5000 in Mexico* ⊟ *33/3630–3725* ⊕ *www.fiestamericana.com* ⇗ *387 rooms, 4 suites* ☼ *Restaurant, in-room data ports, 2 tennis courts, pool, gym, hair salon, bar, shops, baby-sitting, concierge, business services, meeting rooms, car rental, no-smoking floor* ☰ *AE, DC, MC, V.*

★ **$$** ▦ **Hotel de Mendoza.** Elegant with its postcolonial architecture, this refined hotel is on a calm side street a block from the Teatro Degollado. Hand-carved furniture and doors and wrought-iron railings adorn the public areas and clean, comfortable rooms. Because standard rooms are small, suites are worth the extra cost. Balconies overlook the courtyard pool (next to the hotel's renowned restaurant) from some rooms. ⊠ *Calle Venustiano Carranza 16, Centro Histórico, 44100* ☎ *33/3613–4646, 01800/361–2600 in Mexico* ⊟ *33/3613–7310* ⊕ *www.demendoza.com.mx* ⇗ *87 rooms, 17 suites* ☼ *Restaurant, gym, pool, meeting rooms* ☰ *AE, MC, V.*

**$$** ▦ **Hotel Plaza Diana.** At this modest hotel two blocks from the Minerva Fountain standard-size rooms have white walls and bright, patterned fabrics, and some suites have saunas. Stay on the upper floors in the rear for the quietest rooms. ⊠ *Circunvalación Agustín Yáñez 2760, Zona Minerva, 44100* ☎ *33/3540–9700, 01800/024–1001 in Mexico* ⊟ *33/3540–9715* ⊕ *www.hoteldiana.com.mx* ⇗ *136 rooms, 15 suites* ☼ *Restaurant, bar, airport shuttle, travel services* ☰ *AE, DC, MC, V.*

**$$** ▦ **Santiago de Compostela.** The more expensive rooms in this 19th-century building face the Parque San Francisco across the street and have tall, narrow windows with iron balconies. For the most part the hotel has simple, modern accommodations, though the suites have Jacuzzis. From a fifth-floor terrace, a pool looks onto Guadalajara's south side. Service can be quite unfriendly. ⊠ *Av. Colón 272, Centro Histórico, 44100* ☎ *33/3613–8880, 01800/365–5300 in Mexico* ⊟ *33/3658–1925* ⇗ *84 rooms, 8 suites* ☼ *Restaurant, pool, bar, shop* ☰ *AE, DC, MC, V.*

**$** ▦ **El Aposento.** Flowers often decorate this small hotel's bright central courtyard, providing a cozy space for relaxing over complimentary Continental breakfast. The old-fashioned rooms are comfortable and have high ceilings, but because some are smaller and shabbier than others, look at a few before deciding. Avoid rooms on the street. TV sets aren't standard. ⊠ *Francisco Madero 545, Zona Centro, 44100* ☎ *33/3614–1612 or 33/3614–0580* ⊕ *www.elaposento.com* ⇗ *15 rooms* ☰ *AE, MC, V* ☯ *CP.*

$ ⊡ **Hotel Cervantes.** This hotel's comfortable, carpeted rooms are adorned with old-time photos and bright Mexican-style linens. All rooms have sofa beds, and the suites have terraces. Off the lobby is the hotel's relaxed restaurant with its excellent breakfast buffet. Nearby are several pastry shops and bookstores, and the Centro Histórico is a short walk away. ⊠ *Calle Priciliano Sánchez 442, Zona Centro, 44100* ☎ *33/ 3613–6686 or 33/3613–6816* ⊕ *www.hotelcervantes.com.mx* ⤙ *95 rooms, 5 suites* ⌂ *Restaurant, pool, bar, laundry service, meeting rooms* ⊟ *AE, DC, MC, V.*

$ ⊡ **Hotel Francés.** Dating from 1610, Guadalajara's oldest hotel is a national monument. Stone columns and colonial arches girdle an attractive three-story atrium lobby and dining area, with a marble fountain and an old-fashioned gated elevator. However, the charm ends outside the guest room, where threadbare linens, dingy bathrooms, and thin walls are serious drawbacks. Rooms facing Calle Maestranza have tiny 17th-century balconies, as well as street noise. ⊠ *Calle Maestranza 35, Centro Histórico, 44100* ☎ *33/3613–1190 or 33/3613–0936, 01800/718–5309 in Mexico* ⊞ *33/3658–2831* ⊕ *www.hotelfrances.com* ⤙ *50 rooms, 10 suites* ⌂ *Restaurant, fans, bar, dance club, car rental* ⊟ *AE, MC, V.*

¢ ⊡ **San Francisco Plaza.** On a quiet side street, this attractive two-story colonial-style hotel faces a small triangular plaza. Potted palms and geraniums surround a gurgling stone fountain in the courtyard sitting area. High ceilings and arches, as well as friendly service, make up for somewhat worn furnishings. ⊠ *Calle Degollado 267, Centro Histórico, 44100* ☎ *33/3613–8954 or 33/3613–8971* ⊞ *33/3613–3257* ⤙ *74 rooms, 2 suites* ⌂ *Restaurant, laundry service* ⊟ *AE, MC, V.*

# NIGHTLIFE & THE ARTS

Guadalajara is active 24/7. All of the Centro seems to hum when the sun sets, and nightclubs attracting an under-30 crowd line Avenida Vallarta. Numerous modern, multiscreen movie theaters play Hollywood's latest films—most in English with Spanish subtitles—plus a sprinkling of Mexican, Latin American, and European movies. Tickets are generally $4–$5 (half price on Wednesday). The major malls—Magno Centro, Gran Plaza, and Plaza del Sol—all have theaters.

The city is also a dynamic cultural and performing-arts hub, attracting local talent *and* internationally known artists and entertainers. There are lots of English-language cultural events around Lago de Chapala, because that's where the American and Canadian expats live. Pick up *Ocio* and *InformArte* for free at any tourist office for listings.

## Nightlife

### Bars

★ Don't miss **La Fuente** (⊠ Calle Pino Suarez, Zona Centro ☎ No phone), a charming, unpretentious cantina. Opened in 1921 and moved to its present site in 1950, the bar attracts business types, intellectuals, and blue-collar workers, all of whom come for the cheap drinks, animated conversation, and live traditional music. Above the bar, look for an old bicycle caked in dust. It's been here since 1957 when, legend has it, one of a long list of famous people (most say it was the father of local newspaper baron Jesus Alvarez del Castillo) arrived without any money, and left the bike to pay for his drinks.

Live tropical tunes Tuesday through Saturday after 10 draw crowds to **Cubilete** (⊠ General Río Seco 9, Centro Histórico ☎ 33/3613–2096). The bustling **Hard Rock Cafe** (⊠ Centro Magno mall, Av. Vallarta 2425, 1st floor, Zona Minerva ☎ 33/3616–4560) has live rock bands from Wednesday through Sunday from 8:30 PM to 12:30 AM, and even later on Saturday. The Fiesta Americana hotel's sleek **Lobby Bar** (⊠ Av. Aurelio Aceves 225, Zona Minerva ☎ 33/3825–3434) has live, low-key entertainment—usually jazz—Monday through Saturday after 8.

For some local color, stop at **La Maestranza** (⊠ Calle Maestranza 179, Zona Centro ☎ 33/3613–5878), a renovated 1940s cantina full of bullfighting memorabilia. After 9 Tuesday through Sunday, patrons cluster around the small stage at **La Peña Cuicacalli** (⊠ Av. Niños Héroes 1988, at Suarez traffic circle, Zona Centro ☎ 33/3825–4690). There's *rock en español* on Tuesday and folk music from Mexico, Latin America, and Spain most other nights.

### Dance Clubs

**Maxim's** (⊠ Hotel Francés, Calle Maestranza 35, Zona Centro ☎ 33/3613–1190 or 33/3613–0936) is open until the wee hours and is one of the better downtown discos. Cover is $3 Thursday through Sunday, but free otherwise. Well-dressed professionals over 25 go to **El Mito** (⊠Centro Magno mall, Av. Vallarta 2425, 2nd floor, Zona Minerva ☎33/3615–7246); there's '70s and '80s music Wednesday, Friday, and Saturday from 10 PM to 4 AM. Wednesday is ladies night, with free entry for women, a $17 entry for men, and an open bar.

**Salón Veracruz** (⊠ Calle Manzano 486, behind the Hotel Misión Carlton, Zona Centro ☎ 33/3613–4422) is a spartan, old-style dance hall where a 15-piece band keeps hoofers moving to Colombian *cumbia;* Dominican merengue; and *danzón,* a waltz-like dance invented in Cuba. It's open Wednesday, Friday, and Sunday from 9:30 PM to 3:30 AM, Thursday and Sunday from 6 PM to 3 AM; cover is $4.50 You can dance to popular Latin and European music at the multilevel **Tropigala** (⊠Av. López Mateos Sur 2188, Zona Minerva ☎ 33/3122–5553 or 33/3122–7903), across from the Plaza del Sol mall.

## The Arts

### Dance

**Ballet Folklórico of the University of Guadalajara.** The university's internationally acclaimed troupe performs traditional Mexican folkloric dances and music in the Teatro Degollado every Thursday at 8:30 PM and Sunday at 10 AM. ☎ 33/3614–4773 ⌨ $2.50–$11.

### Performance Venues

**Ex-Convento del Carmen.** Classical music performances are held in the former convent Tuesday at 8:30 PM; Wednesday is dedicated to book presentations or poetry readings. Friday and Saturday at 8:30 PM and Sunday at 6 PM see theatrical presentations. There's also a spacious art gallery and bookshop. ✉ *Av. Juárez 638, Zona Centro* ☎ *33/3614–7184.*

**Instituto Cultural Cabañas.** Large-scale theater, dance, and musical performances take place on a patio here. The Tolsá Chapel hosts more intimate events. Exhibitions of both Mexican and foreign art are on display, and there are free art classes. ✉ *Calle Cabañas 8, Centro Histórico* ☎ *33/3618–2800 Ext. 31014.*

★ **Plaza de Armas.** The State Band of Jalisco, the Municipal Band, and sometimes the Philharmonic play at the bandstand on Tuesday, Thursday, and Sunday around 6:30 PM. ✉ *Av. Corona between Calle Morelos and Pedro Moreno, across from Palacio de Gobierno, Zona Centro.*

**Teatro Degollado.** Nationally and internationally famous artists perform here year-round. ✉ *Calle Degollado between Av. Hidalgo and Calle Morelos, Zona Centro* ☎ *33/3614–4773 or 33/3613–1115.*

### Symphony
**Orquesta Filarmónica de Jalisco.** Conducted by Maestro Guillermo Salvador, performances are in the Teatro Degollado on Sunday at 12:30 PM and Friday at 8:30 PM. ☎ *33/3658–3812 or 33/3658–3819* 🎟 *$2–$12.*

# SPORTS & THE OUTDOORS

## Bullfighting
*Corridas* (bullfights) are held Sunday at 4:30 from October to December at **Plaza Nuevo Progreso** (✉ Calle M. Pirineos 1930 and Calz. Independencia Nte., across from Estadio Jalisco, Zona Huentitán ☎ 33/3637–9982 or 33/3651–8506), which is 5 km (3 mi) northeast of downtown (Buses 60, 60A, and 600 will get you here). Tickets are sold for the *sol* (sunny) or *sombra* (shady) side of the bullring, and prices are $9–$60. Buy tickets at the bullring or its booth in Plaza México. *Novilleros* (apprentice matadors) often work the cape mornings between 7 AM and 1 PM, and it's free to watch them practice.

## Charreadas
🐎 Charreadas run year-round at the **Lienzo Charros de Jalisco** (✉ Av. Dr. R. Michel 577, Zona Centro ☎ 33/3619–0315 or 33/3619–3232), next to Parque Agua Azul, Sunday at noon. Competitors participate in 10 equestrian and roping events, mariachis or *bandas* (brass bands) perform during breaks, and edibles are available. Admission is about $2.

## Golf
Guadalajara's top golf clubs—El Palomar and Santa Anita—are technically for members only, but hotels such as the Hilton, Camino Real, Crowne Plaza, and Inter-Presidente arrange for their guests to play, or you can call to get approval and reserve a tee-time. Clubs tend to be less crowded on Wednesday and Thursday; all rent equipment for

around $10 to $15. **Atlas Chapalita Golf Club** (⊠ Carretera Guadalajara-Chapala, Km 6.5, El Salto ☎ 33/3689–2620 or 33/3689–2752) is an 18-hole, par-72 course designed by Joe Finger that's on the way to the airport. Greens fees are $80 on weekdays, and $100 on weekends and holidays. **Las Cañadas Country Club** (⊠ Av. Bosques San Isidro 777, Zapopan ☎ 33/3685–0285 or 33/3685–0412) is a rolling, 18-hole course in an exclusive area of Zapopan. Greens fees are $45–$65.

The private **El Palomar Country Club** (⊠ Paseo del la Cima 437 ☎ 33/3684–4434 or 33/3684–4436), on a hill outside town, is an 18-hole, 6,771-yard, par-72 course blissfully removed from the city's din and with several challenging holes and water features. Greens fees are $105 and include a golf cart. Just down the hill from El Palomar is the **Club de Golf Santa Anita** (⊠ Carretera a Morelia, Km 6.5 ☎ 33/3686–0321), a private club with an 18-hole, 6,872-yard course—the region's longest. Greens fees are $60 on weekdays, $82 on weekends and holidays. Guest passes are necessary at both of these clubs: call ahead or ask your concierge.

## Health Clubs

**Gold's Gym** has three convenient locations (⊠ Av. Vallarta 1791, Zona Minerva ☎ 33/3630–2220 ⊠ Av. Xóchitl 4203, Zona Plaza del Sol ☎ 33/3647–0420 ⊠ Av. Niños Héroes 2851, Zona Centro ☎ 33/3647–4960). The Vallarta location is the most convenient to the Centro and has the best hours (weekdays 6 AM–11 PM, Saturday 8–5, and Sunday 8–3). The Xóchitl branch is the best equipped, with a pool, climbing wall, and basketball court. The smaller Niños Héroes location is for women only. Guest passes cost about $7.50 a day. The health club at the **Presidente Inter-Continental** (⊠ Av. López Mateos Sur 3515, Zona Plaza del Sol ☎ 33/3678–1227) hotel allows nonguests to use its facilities for about $13 a day. It's open daily 5:30 AM–11 PM.

## Soccer

Two professional teams and a university team play at **Estadio Jalisco** (⊠ Calle Siete Colinas 1772 at Calz. Independencia Nte., Zona Huentitán ☎ 33/3637–0301 or 33/3637–0299), including one of Mexico's favorite teams, Las Chivas (The She-Goats) de Guadalajara. Games are generally on weekends. The two regular seasons run January through April or May and July through December. Tickets cost $3.50–$32.

## Tennis

Nonguests can use courts at several top hotels for a small fee. Most places have some equipment for rent, but it's best to bring your own. The court at the **Camino Real** (⊠ Av. Vallarta 5005, Zona Minerva ☎ 33/3134–2424) is open daily 7 AM–11 PM, and costs $9/hour until 7 PM and $13/hour until closing. Reservations are essential. You can play on the two courts at the **Crowne Plaza Guadalajara** (⊠ Av. López Mateos Sur 2500, Zona Plaza del Sol ☎ 33/3634–1034) daily from 7 AM until 10 PM or so; fees are $8/hour until the lights come on and $10/hour after that. The **Fiesta Americana** (⊠ Av. Aurelio Aceves 225, Zona Minerva ☎ 33/3825–3434) also has two courts with similar hours and prices.

## Water Parks

Approximately 50 km (31 mi) southwest of Guadalajara are two water parks with thermal pools and lots of entertainment for adults and children. You can reach them by taxi, although buses run from the bus terminals to Villa Corona. **Agua Caliente** (⊠ Carretera a Barra de Navidad, Km 56, Villa Corona ☎ 33/3778–0022 or 33/3778–0784) has a wave pool and water slides, gardens, and restaurants. All facilities are open on weekends, but some are closed midweek. Admission is $2. The entrance fee to the intimate **Chimulco** (⊠ Camino Real, Km ½, Villa Corona ☎ 33/3778–0014) is $4. It has water slides, boat rides, and a large children's play area.

# SHOPPING

Stores tend to open Monday through Saturday 9 or 10 until 8, and Sunday 10–2; some close during lunch, usually 2–4 or 2–5, and others close on Sunday. Guadalajara has over 50 malls; their stores generally stay open during lunch and on weekends. *Tianguis* (street markets) occur daily throughout the city. If you're interested in high-quality arts and crafts, head for the satellite communities of Tlaquepaque and Tonalá.

Serious art-, crafts-, and antiques-lovers may want to consult with Roberto Alvarado of **El Antiquario** (⊠ Calle Argentina 73, ½ block off Av. Vallarta, Zona Minerva ☎ 33/3827–1990 ⊕ www.elantiquario. com). Alvarado has devoted decades to the art and antiques business, and he runs personalized buying tours for around $100 a day. One week's advance notice is requested.

State-government-run **Instituto de Artesanía Jalisciense** (⊠ Calz. González Gallo 20, at Calz. Independencia Sur, Zona Centro ☎ 33/3619–4664) is on the northeast side of Parque Agua Azul, and has a wide selection of the exquisite blown glass and hand-glazed pottery typical of Jalisco artisans. Prices here are fixed.

### Malls

**Centro Magno.** Upscale boutiques and bistros, along with a large cineplex, a dance club, and a Hard Rock Cafe, make this a trendy shopping and dining spot. It's a few blocks east of the Minerva Fountain. ⊠ *Av. Vallarta 2425, Zona Minerva* ☎ *33/3630–1113 or 33/3630–1776.*

**Galería del Calzado.** The 60 stores in this west-side complex all sell high-quality shoes and accessories, often at lower prices than those in the States. ⊠ *Av. México 3225, Zona Minerva* ☎ *33/3647–6422.*

**La Gran Plaza.** This sleek structure contains 334 commercial spaces, a 14-theater cineplex, and a food court. It's east of the Camino Real hotel. ⊠ *Av. Vallarta 3959, Zona Minerva* ☎ *33/3122–3004.*

**Plaza del Sol.** One of the city's largest malls sprawls like a park, with 270 commercial spaces, outdoor patios, trees and garden areas, and parking for 2,100 cars. It's across from the Presidente Inter-Continental hotel. ⊠ *Av. López Mateos Sur 2375, at Mariano Otero, Zona Minerva* ☎ *33/3121–5950.*

## Markets

The best markets are definitely in Tlaquepaque and Tonalá, but there are some options in town as well. West of the cathedral are dozens of shoe shops; several huge jewelry malls border Plaza Tapatía, and you can find anything—anything at all—at Mercado Libertad.

**Mercado Libertad.** What's commonly known as the Mercado San Juan de Dios covers three square blocks and is one of Latin America's largest enclosed markets. Browse more than 1,000 stalls selling everything from clothing and crafts to live animals and gold watches. It's particularly good for leather shoes and silver jewelry. Bargain hard. The hours are daily 10 to 8. ⊠ *Calz. Independencia Sur, use pedestrian bridge from south side of Plaza Tapatía, Zona Centro.*

# SIDE TRIPS FROM GUADALAJARA

Shop Tlaquepaque and Tonalá, probe the Lago de Chapala region, or unlock the secrets of Mexican firewater in Tequila. Guadalajara's proximity to these adjacent regions provides an extraordinary opportunity for such excursions.

## Tlaquepaque & Tonalá

Inveterate shoppers should explore the crafts meccas of Tlaquepaque and Tonalá for their selection of jewelry, pottery, and other artwork. If you like to shop till you drop, there are at least two comfy B&Bs in Tlaquepaque, a town that's reminiscent of Guadalajara, but less congested and more scenic. Stay in Tlaquepaque for a more tranquil base of operations, and take trips into Guadalajara, just a 15–20 minute cab ride away.

### Tlaquepaque
*7 km (4½ mi) southeast of downtown Guadalajara.*

Offering such wares as leather and hand-carved wood furniture, blown-glass miniatures, and handwoven clothing, Tlaquepaque is famed for its arts and crafts. Pedestrian malls and plazas are lined with over 300 shops, most run by families with centuries-old traditions of workmanship. It's also home to one of Guadalajara's finest museums, which displays prize-winning pieces from its annual ceramics competition.

Tonaltecan Indians inaugurated the community's craft legacy in the mid-16th century with their distinctively decorated pottery. After local authorities signed a regional proclamation of independence from Spain in 1821, the village emerged from obscurity and wealthy Tapatíos began constructing palatial summer houses—many now contain shops and restaurants. Weavers, jewelers, and wood-carvers established workshops here as more people came to Tlaquepaque to purchase pottery and complex glass creations. In 1973 the downtown underwent a major renovation, which culminated in the wide Calle Independencia pedestrian mall. More shops can be found on Calle Juárez, a block south, as well as on side streets.

A GOOD WALK   Begin your tour near the west end of pedestrian-only Calle Independencia, at the **Museo Regional de la Cerámica** ㉑ ▶, with its modest but worthwhile collection of regional pottery. Walk east on Calle Independencia for three blocks, through Tlaquepaque's shopping district. Admire the contemporary ceramics at **Galería Sergio Bustamante,** the eclectic collection at nearby **La Casa Canela,** and the Baroque-style statues and wood-and-gilt altarpieces at **Agustín Parra Diseño Novohispano.** A block farther along is the lively main plaza; after visiting the modest **Templo Parroquial de San Pedro Apóstal** ㉒, walk north on Calle Priciliano Sánchez to the **Museo del Premio Nacional de la Cerámica Pantaleon Panduro** ㉓, a high-light for any trip to Tlaquepaque. Stop in at the Folklor Gastronómico on your way to the museum for a delicious comida corrida, or return to the plaza for a more festive meal at El Parián. End your visit by perusing the shops off the main drag, including **Bazar Hecht,** before catching a bus or cab back to Guadalajara proper.

WHAT TO SEE

㉓

Fodor'sChoice

★

**Museo del Premio Nacional de la Cerámica Pantaleon Panduro.** The museum's moniker honors its namesake, Pantaleon Panduro, who was the father of modern ceramics in Jalisco. On display are prize pieces from Tlaquepaque's national ceramics competition, held every June. The art collection includes giant, intricately painted urns and nativity scenes. You can request an English-speaking guide. ⊠ *Calle Priciliano Sánchez at Calle Flórida* ☎ *33/3639–5646, 33/3635–1089, or 33/3659–2858 Ext. 217* ▦ *Free* ☉ *Tues.–Sat. 10–6, Sun. 10–3.*

▶ ㉑ **Museo Regional de la Cerámica.** Exhibits in this colonial mansion track the evolution of ceramic wares in the Atemajac Valley during the 20th century. The presentation isn't always strong, but the bilingual displays discuss six common processes used by local ceramics artisans, including *bruñido*, which involves polishing large urns with smoothed chunks of *pirita* (a mineral). ⊠ *Calle Independencia 237* ☎ *33/3635–5404* ▦ *Free* ☉ *Mon.–Sat. 10–6, Sun. 10–3.*

㉒ **Templo Parroquial de San Pedro Apóstal.** Franciscan friars founded this tiny parish church during the Spanish Conquest and named it after the apostle San Pedro de Analco. Adhering to the Mexican custom of adding the name of its patron saint to the town's name, Tlaquepaque was officially changed to San Pedro Tlaquepaque in 1915. The altars of Our Lady of Guadalupe and the Sacred Heart of Jesus are intricately carved in silver and gold. ⊠ *Calle Guillermo Prieto at Calle Morelos, bordering main plaza* ☎ *33/3635–1001* ☉ *Daily 7 AM–9 PM.*

need a break?

**El Parián.** For a few dollars local mariachis will treat you to a song or two as you sip margaritas at this enormous, partly covered cantina diagonal from the main plaza. Once a marketplace dating from 1883, it has traditional *cazuela* drinks, which are made of fruit and tequila and served in ceramic pots. ⊠ *Jardín Hidalgo* ☎ *33/3659–2362.*

WHERE TO EAT

$–$$

✕ **Casa Fuerte.** Relax with tasty Mexican dishes at the tables along the sidewalk or among the palms and fountain in the patio. Try the chicken stuffed with *huitlacoche* (a corn fungus that's Mexico's answer to the truffle) and shrimp in tamarind sauce. ⊠ *Calle Independencia 224* ☎ *33/3639–6481* ▤ *AE, MC, V.*

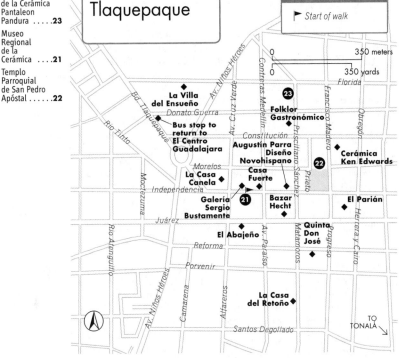

**$ ✕ El Abajeño.** Mexican specialties are served on this converted hacienda's tree-shaded patio. Good bets include *carnitas* (shredded pork) or *filete tapado* (cheese-topped beef fillet) for two. Mariachis play at 3:30 most days; Mexican dance performances begin at 4:30 on weekends. ⊠ *Calle Juárez 231* ☎ *33/3635–9015 or 33/3635–9097* ▭ *MC, V.*

**¢ ✕ Folklor Gastronómico.** Only open on weekday afternoons, this little restaurant serves *comida corridas* (lunch specials) in a peaceful courtyard. The menu changes daily but always includes soup or rice, a main dish, a dessert, and *agua fresca* (sparkling water). Profits support a local ballet folklórico group, whose members help with the service and practice in the back. ⊠ *Calle Priciliano Sánchez 113* ☎ *33/3635–3314* ▭ *No credit cards.*

WHERE TO STAY   **▦ Quinta Don José.** This B&B is just blocks from Tlaquepaque's main
**$–$$**   plaza and shopping area. Natural lighting and room size vary, so look at a few before you choose one. Suites face the pool, and are spacious but a bit dark. There's remarkable tile work in the master suite. Hearty breakfasts are served in an inner courtyard, but will move to the restaurant, which will be Tlaquepaque's only choice for fine Italian dining, once it's complete. ⊠ *Av. Reforma 139, 45500* ☎ *33/3635–7522, 01800/777–2468 in Mexico, 800/537–9567 in the U.S. and Canada* 🖷*33/*

# SIP IT, DON'T SLAM IT

**M**EXICO'S NATIONAL DRINK has long had a reputation as either a mixer or a party drink consumed in quick shots with salt and lime. However, people north of the border are finally discovering what tequila aficionados have known for years: a fine tequila deserves a place among the world's premium spirits.

Tequila's history can be traced back to the Aztec drink pulque, the fermented juice of the agave, a large, spiny plant often mistaken for a cactus, but actually a member of the lily family. When the Spanish conquered Mexico, they applied their knowledge of the distilling process to pulque. With time, it was discovered that the best distillates came from the blue agave grown in the volcanic soils surrounding the town of Tequila, in what is now Jalisco state. Eventually, the drink came to be called by the name of this town.

Tequila was produced by small distilleries for about 200 years until 1821, when Mexico achieved independence from Spain. Without the imports of Spanish liquors to provide competition, tequila became more popular and an industry developed. By the beginning of the 20th century, the industry had adopted standards, but it wasn't until the 1970s that strict laws, known as NORMAS, were adopted to govern tequila production. Today, production is overseen by the Mexican Tequila Regulatory Council.

To earn its name, tequila must meet specific criteria: it must be composed of at least 51% blue agave (agave tequiliana weber, variety azul), and that agave can only be grown in a specific region that is still centered around the town of Tequila. In fact, in 1977, the Mexican government established a Denomination of Origin, which states that all tequila must come from this region of Mexico. In 1997, the

European Union officially recognized tequila's Denomination of Origin status. Only three other alcoholic beverages (Cognac, champagne, and sherry) share this distinction.

Tequila production begins when the agave has matured, a process that can take from eight to twelve years. Once ready for harvest, the 6- to 8-foot spines are cut away from the plant, exposing its core, or piña, so called because of its resemblance to a pineapple. The piñas, weighing from 80 to 300 lbs, are slow-roasted or steamed until soft and then mashed into a pulpy concoction, which is allowed to ferment in vats. At this point, some producers mix in other types of agave sugars. (Tequilas resulting from these batches are called mixtos, or mixed, thus lacking the 100% agave designation that tequila connoisseurs seek.) The resulting concoction is then double distilled in copper pots. All tequila is clear when it emerges from the distilling process. The golden tone of some tequilas is usually due to its aging in wooden casks, although some unscrupulous producers will add caramel coloring to give the appearance of aging.

There are four main classes of tequila. Unaged, clear tequila is called blanco (white); if it's been left in the tanks to age for a few weeks, it's called suave (smooth). Tequila that's been aged in wooden casks for two months to a year is called reposado (rested). Añejo (aged) has been aged from one to four years in wooden casks. Generally, the best and most expensive tequilas are añejos comprised of 100% blue agave.

As connoisseurs continue to rescue tequila from its lamentable Spring Break status, the industry faces a new demand for premium brands. Hampering the fulfillment of this demand is a shortage of blue agave. A fungus, coupled with devastating frosts, hit agave farms in the late 1990s, resulting in the loss of a significant portion of plants. Given that new plants take a minimum of eight years to reach maturity, the industry projects continuing shortages until at least 2009. The result of these shortages can already be seen on the shelves—tequila prices have skyrocketed as much as 3000% since 1998.

To keep prices reasonable and meet the growing demand, some producers have started to downgrade their products. Brands that have traditionally been 100% agave are now being produced as mixtos, and former añejos are now produced as reposados, so it pays to read the labels closely. However, even purists acknowledge that what comprises a good tequila is still largely a matter of taste. Some aficionados prefer the unbridled taste of a blanco or the smoothness of a reposado over an añejo. Either way, a good tequila is meant to be sipped slowly from a tall, slender shot glass known as a caballito. Añejo is often served in a brandy snifter, so the aroma can be savored. Blanco and reposado are sometimes served with a sangrita of tomato and orange juice with salt and lime.

When buying tequila it's best to first try a few types in your favorite bar or restaurant. Take your time and savor each sip and cleanse your palate with some tortillas between drinks. A leisurely tasting will help you decide which class of tequila you prefer, greatly narrowing down the sometimes dizzying selection. When in the stores, don't be fooled by a popular name or fancy bottle: always look for 100% puro de agave on the label. Generally, reposados and añejos are more expensive, but price isn't always the best indicator, as some manufacturers will use eye-catching packaging to sway inexperienced buyers. Some of the best tequilas include Cuervo's

Reserva de la Familia, Sauza's Tres Generaciones, and Patron añejo, though there are many worthy tequilas out there to be discovered. Reserva is notable not only for its quality, but for its role in promoting Mexican artists. Each year a limited number of bottles are produced, and a local artist is commissioned to design the stunning wooden gift boxes, which are hand-painted.

On a side note, the shortage of blue agave, while threatening to the tequila industry, may actually be a boon for distilleries that produce spirits from one of the 135 other types of agave found in Mexico. In 1994, Mexico officially acknowledged several other regional agave distillates including bacanora, produced from the wild agave yaqui of Sonora, and sotol, produced from the agave sotol of Chihuahua. Both of these drinks, while still produced on a small scale, are now available for export and may someday become as well-known as their counterpart from Jalisco. More famous and more widely distributed than these is Oaxaca's mezcal (or mescal), made from the agave espadin. Mezcal is best known for having a worm at the bottom of the bottle (yep, that's not tequila you're drinking), though producers are seeking to refine the drink's image in the hopes of capturing some of tequila's market share as shortages continue to drive tequila prices higher.

— Rob Aikins

*3659–9315, 800/537–9567 in the U.S.* ⊕ *www.quintadonjose.com* ⟐ *6 rooms, 5 suites* ⟐ *Pool, bar, laundry service* ⊟ *AE, MC, V* ⟐ *BP.*

$    ⊡ **La Casa del Retoño.** On a quiet street, several blocks from the shopping district is this newer B&B. Smallish rooms are made of cinder block, but are clean and painted in cheerful hues. Rooms in the back overlook a large garden, while the ones upstairs have terraces. There's a small open-air reading area, and breakfast is served in the small courtyard. ⊠ *Matamoros 182, 45500* ☎ *33/3587–3989* 🖷 *33/3639–6510* ⊕ *www. lacasadelretono.com.mx* ⟐ *8 rooms, 1 suite* ⊟ *MC, V* ⟐ *CP.*

$    ⊡ **La Villa del Ensueño.** Even with the 10-minute walk from Tlaquepaque's center, this intimate B&B is near the town's ample shops. The restored 19th-century hacienda has thick, white adobe walls, exposed-beam ceilings, and plants in huge, unglazed pots. Smokers should request a room with private balcony, as smoking isn't allowed inside. ⊠ *Florida 305, 45500* ☎ *33/3635–8792* 🖷 *33/3659–6152* ⊕ *www.mexonline.com/ ensueno.htm* ⟐ *14 rooms, 4 suites* ⟐ *2 pools, bar, no-smoking rooms* ⊟ *AE, MC, V* ⟐ *BP.*

SHOPPING    Influenced by the unique baroque style of 17th-century New Spain, artist Agustín Parra creates everything from ornate tables and doors to religious icons at **Agustín Parra Diseño Novohispano** (⊠ Calle Independencia 158 ☎ 33/3657–8530 or 33/3657–0316). **Bazar Hecht** (⊠ Calle Juárez 162 ☎ 33/3659–0205) is one of several excellent stores on Juárez, a less-trafficked side street. The Hecht family is known throughout Mexico for its high-quality, ornately sculpted tables, armoires, and chairs.

Colors explode at **La Casa Canela** (⊠ Calle Independencia 258 ☎ 33/ 3635–3717 or 33/3657–1343). Each of its more than 24 rooms is filled with vivid papier-mâché flowers, finely glazed pottery, and elegant furniture. Free tequila and snacks are served on Saturday. Sergio Bustamante's work is found in galleries throughout the world, but you can purchase his magical sculptures or silver- and gold-plated jewelry for less at

Fodor'sChoice    **Galería Sergio Bustamante** (⊠ Calle Independencia 238 ☎ 33/3639–5519,
★    33/3659–7110, or 33/3657–8354, 01800/024–2727 in Mexico).

## Tonalá
*8 km (5 mi) east of Tlaquepaque.*

Among the region's oldest pueblos is the quiet but prosperous Tonalá, a place of dusty cobblestone streets and stucco-covered adobe houses. Formerly, the village was the pre-Hispanic capital of the Atemajac Valley Indians as well as the capital of New Spain when Captain Juan de Oñate moved Guadalajara here in 1532. Within three years, however, Indians and a lack of water forced the Spaniards out.

Although it's been swallowed by ever-expanding Guadalajara, Tonalá remains independent and industrious. Municipal officials estimate that more than 6,000 artisans live and work here. Indeed, most ceramics and pottery sold in Tlaquepaque (and in many other parts of the world) are made in Tonalá. Over 20 distinct moulding and firing techniques—many of them centuries old—are used to create the intricately painted flatware and whimsical figures found here.

On Thursday and Sunday, Tonalá merchandise is sold at bargain prices at a terrific street market, with block after block packed with vendors from 8 AM to 4 PM. Except for a concentration of shops on Avenida de los Tonaltecas, the main drag into town, most of Tonalá's shops and factories are spread out; the town also has unusually long blocks, so wear your most comfortable walking shoes. Many stores are open daily 10–2 and 4–7. Some no longer close for a siesta, but some are closed on Monday. Thursday is less crowded than Sunday.

**A GOOD WALK**  Begin your tour at the assortment of workshops in **La Casa de los Artesanos** ㉔ ▶, on Avenida de los Tonaltecas between Calle 16 de Septiembre and Calle Matamoros. From here proceed past scores of stands, stores, and workshops as you head north along the broad, busy avenue. Turn right onto Avenida Juárez and enter downtown where the town church, the **Santuario** ㉕, and the Palacio Municipal face the Plaza Principal. Walk north on Avenida Morelos to **Artesanías Erandi** ㉖ and **Galería José Bernabe** ㉗, both specializing in local ceramics. Continue north on Morelos several long blocks, turning east (right) on Calle La Paz and left onto Avenida Alvaro Obregón to see handmade wooden masks at **El 7** ㉘. Return the way you came, this time turning west (right) onto Avenida López Cotilla. Not far past Avenida de los Tonaltecas is **La Casa de Salvador Vásquez Carmona** ㉙, where the owner sells fanciful ceramic pottery.

**WHAT TO SEE**  **Artesanías Erandi.** One of Tonalá's biggest hand-painted ceramics exporters
㉖ has its exhibition center in founder Jorge Wilmot's former workshop. To view artisans in action, stop by the factory three blocks away. ⊠ *Calle Morelos 86* ☎ *33/3683–0101* ☉ *Mon.–Sat. 9–6* ⊠ *Factory* ⊠ *Av. López Cotilla 118* ☎ *33/3683–0253* ☉ *Weekdays 9:30–6, Sat. 9:30–2.*

▶ ㉔ **La Casa de los Artesanos.** This virtual department store of Mexican folk art and crafts has an excellent selection of pieces by Tonalá's best artisans. Prices are reasonable, and the staff can direct you to local artisans' studios. ⊠ *Av. de los Tonaltecas Sur 140* ☎ *33/3284–3066 or 33/3284–3068* ☉ *Weekdays 9–8.*

㉙ **La Casa de Salvador Vásquez Carmona.** On a small patio behind his home, Carmona molds enormous ceramic pots and glazes them with intricate designs. ⊠ *López Cotilla 328, west of Av. de los Tonaltecas* ☎ *33/3683–2896* ☉ *Weekdays 8–4, Sat. 8–2, Sun. 10–4.*

㉗ **Galería José Bernabe.** For generations the Bernabe family has produced exquisite petatillo ceramics and simple stoneware. The sprawling workshop behind the gallery is open to visitors. ⊠ *Av. Hidalgo 83, between Zapata and Constitución* ☎ *33/3683–0040 or 33/3683–0877* ☉ *Weekdays 10–3 and 4–7, weekends 10–3. Workshop closed Sun.*

㉕ **Santuario.** Moorish arches form the nave and Stations of the Cross paintings line the walls in the parish church. Next door is the simple Palacio Municipal (City Hall), and the Plaza Principal is across the street. ⊠ *Av. Juárez at Av. Hidalgo.*

㉘ **El 7.** Tonalá native J. Cruz Coldívar Lucano, who signs his work and named his shop El 7 (*el siete*), makes striking hand-painted clay masks and other wall hangings. His work has been exhibited throughout North

and South America as well as Europe. The Spanish Crown owns some of his pieces. His studio is several long blocks from the plaza on Privado Alvaro Obregón, off the main avenue of the same name. ⊠ *Privado Alvaro Obregón 28* ☎ *33/3683–1122* ☾ *Weekdays 9–6, Sat. 9–2.*

WHERE TO EAT ✕ **El Boquinete.** Turn down a narrow passageway, lined with small shops,
**$** to be delivered from the commotion of the market to this tranquil, airy, and pleasant restaurant. Typical Mexican-style chicken and meat dishes are served along with a wide selection of tequila, whiskey, and beer. ⊠ *Passageway between Juárez and Zaragoza* ☎ *33/3683–2525* ☰ *MC, V.*

**$** ✕ **Restaurant Jalapeños.** Steaks are the specialty in this small but clean restaurant whose walls are adorned with brightly painted ceramic vegetables. The daily lunch special, with soup, main dish, drink, and dessert is less than $5. ⊠ *Av. Madero 23, ½ block south of Plaza Principal* ☎ *33/ 3683–0344* ☰ *MC, V.*

**$** ✕ **El Rincón del Sol.** A peaceful covered patio invites you to sip margaritas while listening to live guitar music (afternoons from Thursday to Sunday). Try one of the steak or chicken dishes or the classic chiles *en nogada* (in walnut sauce) in the colors of the Mexican flag. ⊠ *Av. 16 de Septiembre 61* ☎ *33/3683–1989 or 33/3683–1940* ☰ *MC, V.*

## Around Lago de Chapala

Jagged mountains and tranquil towns ring Lago de Chapala, Mexico's largest inland lake. Sunsets are spectacular, and there's just enough humidity to keep the abundant bougainvillea thriving. Spanish settlement in the area dates from 1538, when Franciscan friar Miguel de Bolonio arrived to convert Taltica Indians to Christianity. The Taltica chief was named Chapalac, from which the name Chapala probably originated.

In the 1960s, Mexico's favorable rate of exchange and Lago de Chapala's springlike climate attracted U.S. and Canadian retirees to the area. More than 40,000 expats now call this region home at least part of the year. In the 1990s, however, upstream water was diverted to serve Mexico City, Guadalajara, and other regions, and the lake, which was never very deep, began to shrink. By 2002 it had retreated as much as a half mile in places and once-premier waterfront property was left facing a muddy marshland. An unusually wet summer in 2003 refilled the lakebed in a matter of months. Dry for years, the old pier and boardwalk were suddenly back in use. This might be a good time to visit the once-pristine natural wonder, terribly maltreated but restored, for now, to its former glory.

The town of Chapala is the area's largest settlement; Ajijic, 8 km (5 mi) to the west, is somewhat less developed and has a community of expat artists and writers. Towns and villages along the lake are linked by one highway with multiple names (e.g., Carretera Chapala-Ajijic or Carretera Ajijic-Jocotepec).

### Chapala
*45 km (28 mi) south of Guadalajara.*

This was a placid weekend getaway for aristocrats in the late 19th century, but when then-president Porfirio Díaz got in on the action in 1904, other wealthy Mexicans followed suit. More and more summer homes were built, and in 1910 the Chapala Yacht Club opened. Along Avenida Madero, Chapala's main street, is the still-functioning (but now decrepit) Hotel Nido, built in the early 1900s to accommodate Díaz and his entourage. In the 1940s, Mexican film star María Félix kicked off the first of several honeymoons at this hotel.

On weekends the town still fills with Mexican families, but the once-bustling promenade is a shadow of its former self. Vendors sell refreshments and souvenirs, while dilapidated buses carry visitors across mudflats to the lake's edge—now nearly a half mile away.

Avenida Madero is lined with restaurants, shops, and cafés. On Madero, three blocks north of the promenade, the plaza, at the corner of López Cotilla, is a relaxing spot to read the paper, or to succumb to sweets from surrounding shops. Two blocks south of the plaza, the Iglesia de San Francisco is easy to spot by the blue neon crosses on its twin steeples. The church was built in 1528 and reconstructed in 1580.

On weekends, the rather forlorn Parque la Cristianía, on the south side of the *malecón* (boardwalk), fills with Tapatíos taking respite from the city. Boys compete in games of volleyball, while kids play on jungle gyms and swings. Indoor/outdoor cafés at the end of the promenade serve seafood (but—because of the shrinking lake—no longer the native whitefish, *pescado blanco*).

WHERE TO STAY
& EAT
$–$$

✕ **Mariscos Guicho's.** The best of the waterfront seafood joints, Guicho's serves savory caviar tostadas, frogs' legs, garlic shrimp, and spicy seafood soup. Bright orange walls and checkerboard tablecloths lend the place an authentic Mexican charm. ⊠ *Paseo Ramón Corona 20* ☎ *376/765–3232* ▤ *No credit cards* ✆ *Closed Tues.*

$ ✕ **Cozumel.** Ajijic residents regularly drive to Chapala on Wednesday and Friday for live mariachi music and well-prepared specials, which include a free cocktail and appetizers. Wednesday is chicken cordon bleu night; on other days, choose from seafood and international dishes. (You still get the free drink.) Reservations are essential for Friday and recommended for Wednesday night. ⊠ *Paseo Corona 22-A* ☎ *376/765–4606* ▤ *MC, V* ✆ *Closed Mon.*

$ ✕ **Restaurant Cazadores.** This grandly turreted brick building was once the summer home of the Braniff family, former owners of the defunct airline. The menu includes slightly overpriced seafood and beef dishes. A lovely patio overlooks the boardwalk and is especially pleasant in the evening. ⊠ *Paseo Ramón Corona 8, northeast corner* ☎ *376/765–2162* ▤ *AE, MC, V* ✆ *Closed Mon.*

¢–$ ✕ **El Arbol del Café.** Expatriates cherish this modest café for its roasted-on-the-premises coffee, imported teas, and homemade cakes. Sip a decaffeinated cappuccino (rare in Mexico) and peruse the English-language papers. The bulletin board has rental, for-sale, and other listings. The café closes at 3 on weekdays and at noon on Saturday. ⊠ *Av. Hidalgo 236* ☎ *376/765–3908* ▤ *No credit cards* ✆ *Closed Sun.*

¢ ▦ **Hotel Villa Montecarlo.** The hotel's simple, clean rooms are in three-story contiguous units, all with patios or terraces. The grounds are enormous and well maintained, with several eating and play areas. One of the two swimming pools (the biggest in the area) is filled with natural thermal water. Popular with Mexican families, the hotel offers frequent discounts and packages. ⊠ *Av. Hidalgo 296, about 1 km (½ mi) west of Av. Madero, 45900* ☎ *376/765–2216, 376/765–2120, or 376/765–2025* ➫ *46 rooms, 2 suites* ♢ *Restaurant, 2 tennis courts, 2 pools, bar, laundry service, free parking; no a/c* ▤ *AE, MC, V.*

★ ¢ ▦ **Lake Chapala Inn.** Especially enjoyable now that the lake is back is this European-style inn. Three of the four rooms in this restored mansion face the shore; all have high ceilings and whitewashed oak furniture. Rates include an English-style breakfast (with a Continental breakfast on Sunday). ⊠ *Paseo Ramón Corona 23, 45900* ☎ *376/765–4786* 🖷 *376/765–5174* ⊕ *www.mexonline.com/chapalainn.htm* ➫ *4 rooms* ♢ *Dining room, pool, library, laundry service; no a/c* ▤ *No credit cards* ⊺⊙⊦ *BP.*

## Ajijic
*8 km (5 mi) west of Chapala.*

Ajijic has narrow cobblestone streets, pastel buildings, and gentle pace. Still, the foreign influence is unmistakable: English is spoken almost as widely here as Spanish and license plates run the gamut from British Columbia to Texas. Although Lago de Chapala has also receded here, the change is less dramatic and desultory than in nearby Chapala, and the arts scene gives Ajijic its very own raison d'être.

The Plaza Principal (also called the Plaza de Armas or El Jardín) is a tree- and flower-filled central square at the corner of Avenida Colón and Avenida Hidalgo. The Iglesia de San Andrés (Church of St. Andrew) sits on the plaza's north side. In late November the plaza fills for the saint's nine-day fiesta.

Walk down Calle Morelos (the continuation of Avenida Colón) toward the lake and peruse the boutiques. Turn left onto Avenida 16 de Septiembre or Avenida Constitución, to find several art galleries and studios.

Northeast of the plaza, along the highway, activity centers around the soccer field, which doubles as a venue for bullfights and concerts. Locals and visitors frequent the movie theater, cybercafé, athletic club, and Salvador's restaurant—a local institution.

WHERE TO STAY & EAT

★ $–$$ ✕ **Ajijic Grill.** Order yakitori and tempura from the Japanese side of the menu (though the sushi leaves much to be desired), or a fine cut of meat, prepared on a mesquite-wood grill. The large patio in the center is prettiest at night, when it's softly lighted by tiny white lights. ⊠ *Calle Morelos 5* ☎ *376/766–2458* ▭ *MC, V* ☉ *Closed Tues.*

$–$$ ✕ **La Bodega de Ajijic.** Eat in a covered patio overlooking a grassy lawn and a small pool at this low-key restaurant. The menu has Italian and Mexican dishes, which are a bit small and overpriced. Still, service is friendly, and there's live music—usually guitar or harp—most nights. ⊠ *Av. 16 de Septiembre 124* ☎ *376/766–1002* ▭ *MC, V* ☉ *Closed Mon.*

$–$$ ✕ **Johanna's.** Come to this intimate bit of Bavaria on the lake for authentic German cuisine like sausages and goose or duck pâté. Main dishes come with soup or salad, applesauce, and cooked red cabbage. For dessert indulge in plum strudel or blackberry-topped torte. ⊠ *Carretera Chapala-Jocotepec, Km 6.5* ☎ *33/3766–0437* ▭ *No credit cards* ☉ *Closed Mon.*

¢–$ ✕ **Salvador's.** An old mainstay that's showing its years, this cafeteria-like eatery is a popular expat hangout. There's a well-kept salad bar and specialties from both sides of the border. A pianist performs during the fabulous Sunday brunch as well as at lunch on Wednesday. On Friday people flock here for the fish-and-chips lunch special. ⊠ *Carretera Chapala-Jocotepec Ote. 58* ☎ *33/3766–2301* ▭ *No credit cards.*

$–$$ ▦ **Los Artistas.** Surrounded by an acre of splendid gardens, this spacious yet intimate inn has rooms with brightly painted walls and red tile floors. Each is has colorful handwoven Mexican bedspreads, wrought-iron or carved-wood bed frames, and fresh-cut flowers. Most rooms have patios shaded by bowers of blooming plants. There are no televisions or radios to spoil the tranquility. ⊠ *Calle Constitución 105, 45920* ☎ *33/3766–1027* 🖶 *33/3766–1762* ⊕ *www.losartistas.com* 🛏 *7 rooms* ♧ *Room TVs, pool; no a/c* ▭ *No credit cards* ⦿ *BP.*

★ $ ✕▦ **La Nueva Posada.** The well-kept gardens framed in bougainvillea define this charming inn. Rooms are spacious, with carpet, high ceilings, and local crafts. Villas share a private courtyard and have tile kitchenettes. The bar has jazz or Caribbean music most evenings. Out in the garden restaurant ($), strands of tiny white lights set the mood for an evening meal, where anything from the eclectic menu is recommended. ⊠ *Calle Donato Guerra 9* ⎙ *A.P. 30, 45920* ☎ *376/766–1344* 🖷 *376/766–1444* ⊕ *www. mexconnect.com/MEX/rest/nueva/posada.html* ⤸ *19 rooms, 4 villas* ⌂ *Restaurant, fans, pool, bar, laundry service* ▤ *MC, V* ⍾| *BP.*

$   🖼 **Swan Inn.** Don't be deterred by the sterile foyer and dining room of this small B&B. Back rooms face a Japanese garden and have sloping ceilings, modern furnishings, and paintings by the late founder. Casitas have kitchenettes and open onto the pool. The inn is next to the Lake Chapala Society's tree-filled grounds and close to several art galleries. ⊠ *Av. 16 de Septiembre 18, 45920* ☎ *376/766–0917 or 376/766–2354* ⊕ *www.mexconnect.com/amex/swan* ⤸ *6 rooms, 2 casitas* ⌂ *Some kitchenettes, pool, laundry service; no a/c* ▤ *No credit cards* ⍾| *BP.*

**La Bodega** (⊠ Calle 16 de Septiembre 124 ☎ 376/766–1002 ⧉ $3 cover Fri. and Sun.) has dancing Friday and Sunday, and live guitar or trio music the rest of the week; closed Monday. The rambling, hacienda-style **Posada Ajijic** (⊠ Calle Morelos ☎ 33/3766–0744 or 33/3766–0430) is a restaurant, bar, and popular weekend dance place with an unobstructed view of the lake bed.

Several art galleries offer painting and sculpture lessons. Many are on Avenida 16 de Septiembre and Calle Constitución. Luisa Julian shows her work and offers classes at **Estudio Arte Galaría** (⊠ Calle Ramon Corona 11, at Av. 16 de Septiembre ☎ 376/766–1292).

Ajijic's main shopping strip is on Calle Morelos, but there are many galleries and shops east of Morelos, on Avenida 16 de Septiembre and Calle Constitución. **Artesanía Huichol** (⊠ End of Calle Donato Guerra 🖷 No phone) sells Huichol artwork. There's a crafts shop at the local branch of the state-run **Instituto de Artesanía Jalisciense** (⊠ Carretera Chapala-Jocotepec, Km 6.5 ☎ 33/3766–0548). The **Mi México** (⊠ Calle Morelos 8 ☎ 33/3766–0133) boutique sells women's clothing and jewelry as well as other crafts.

Five kilometers (3 mi) west of Ajijic on the main highway, a **cactus vivero** (nursery) sells some 300 types of cactus. Entrance to the garden and nursery is free. It's open daily 8–2 and 3–5:30.

The **Rojas family** (⊠ Paseo Del Lago and Camino Real, 4 blocks east of Los Artistas B&B ☎ 376/766–4261) has been leading horseback trips for more than 30 years. A ride along the lakeshore or in the surrounding hills costs around $7 an hour.

## San Juan Cosalá
*2 km (1 mi) west of Ajijic.*

San Juan Cosalá is known for its natural thermal-water spas along ⌚ Lago de Chapala. The **Hotel Balneario San Juan Cosalá** (⊠ Calle La Paz Ote. 420, at Carretera Chapala-Jocotepec, Km 13 🖷🖷 376/761–0222 or 376/761–0302) has four large swimming pools and two wading pools; admission is $7. Weekends get crowded and loud.

WHERE TO STAY   ⊞ **Villas Buenaventura Cosalá.** You can relax for free in the hotel's out-
**$$**   door thermal pools or rent time in the private hot tubs or private pools.
The large one- and two-bedroom suites clean, if a bit sterile. The grounds
are dotted with sculpture. On many weekends during high season the
hotel requires a two- or three-night minimum stay. ⊠ *Carretera Cha-
pala-Jocotepec, Km 13.5, 45920* ☎ *376/761–0202* 🖷 *387/761–0364*
🛏 *19 suites* ⌂ *Restaurant (weekends only), some kitchenettes, 4 pools,
hot tub, massage, sauna; no a/c* ☰ *MC, V.*

**$**   ⊞ **Hotel Villa Bordeaux.** This hotel is adjacent to and operated by the
same people as the Hotel Balneario. Rooms are small but attractive, with
brick walls and high ceilings. The pools are reserved for guests and are
quiet. A stay here gets you access to the Hotel Balneario facilities as well.
⊠ *Calle La Paz Ote. 420, at Carretera Chapala-Jocotepec, Km 13, 45900*
☎ *387/761–0494* 🛏 *11 rooms* ⌂ *Restaurant, pool, massage, sauna;
no a/c* ☰ *MC, V.*

## Jocotepec
*15 km (10 mi) west of Ajijic.*

At the western end of Lago de Chapala, small Jocotepec is a world away
from its tourist-impacted neighbors, Ajijic and Chapala. The town has
long been famous for its white serapes, but the delicate shawls are in-
creasingly rare. It remains a refreshingly traditional Mexican town,
though. An example of this is the Sunday *paseo,* where adolescents cir-
cle the main plaza in opposite directions, flirting under the supervision
of older relatives sitting in the middle or along the edges.

WHERE TO STAY   ⊞ **Los Dos Bed & Breakfast.** On a hillside overlooking Jocotepec and the
**$–$$**   lake, Los Dos has a well-kept garden and a pleasant terrace where
breakfast is served. The suites—one is a tri-level cottage—are spacious
and filled with artwork by the owner-operators, Phyliss Rauch and her
husband, Austrian painter Georg Rauch. Georg's studio is on-site; be
sure to ask for a tour. ⊠ *Calle Rico 191, 45800 Nestipac* ☎🖷 *387/763–
0657* ⊕ *www.mexconnect.com/MEX/losdos/losdos.html* 🛏 *3 suites*
⌂ *Kitchenettes, pool, small pets allowed; no a/c* ☰ *No credit cards* ⦿ *BP.*

# Tequila

*56 km (35 mi) northwest of Guadalajara.*

For an in-depth look at how Mexico's most famous liquor is cultivated
from the spiny blue agave plant that grows in fields alongside the highway, stop by this tidy village, about 59 km (37 mi) from Guadalajara.
It's believed that centuries ago, the Tiquilas, a small Nahuatl-speaking
tribe, discovered the fermenting powers of the agave heart's juice. When
distilled (an innovation introduced after the Spanish arrived in the 16th
century), the fermented liquid turns into the heady liquor, which can be
rightfully labeled tequila only in this and a few other regions.

**Museo Nacional del Tequila** (⊠ Calle Ramon Corona 34 ☎ 374/742–2410)
is open Tuesday through Sunday 10 to 5; admission is $1.50. The **Sauza
Museum** (⊠ Calle Albino Rojas 22 ☎ 374/742–0247) has memorabilia
of the Sauza family, a tequila-making dynasty second only to the Cuer-

vos. Admission to the museum, which is open Tuesday through Sunday 10 to 4, is $1.

Opened in 1795, the **José Cuervo Distillery** (⊠ Calle José Cuervo 73 ☎ 374/742–2442) is the world's oldest tequila distillery. Every day, 150 tons of agave hearts are processed into 74,000 liters of tequila here. Hard-hat tours are offered daily every hour from 10 AM to 2 PM; the tours at noon are normally in English, but English-speakers can often be accommodated at other times as well. Admission is $5.75.

# GUADALAJARA A TO Z

### AIR TRAVEL

AIRPORT   The Aeropuerto Internacional Libertador Miguel Hidalgo is 16½ km (10 mi) south of Guadalajara, en route to Chapala.
**🚹 Aeropuerto Internacional Libertador Miguel Hidalgo** ⊠ Carretera Guadalajara-Chapala ☎ 33/3688-5248.

AIRPORT   The Carretera Guadalajara–Chapala (Guadalajara–Chapala Highway)
TRANSFERS stretches north from the airport to the city and south to the Lago de Chapala. It's 30 minutes to Guadalajara and 45 minutes to Chapala, but the trip can be delayed in either direction by slow-moving caravans of trucks and weekend recreational traffic.

Autotransportaciones Aeropuerto operates a 24-taxi stand with service anywhere in the Guadalajara area; buy tickets at the counters at both the national and international exits. A ride to the Centro is $15; it's $20 to $25 to Lago de Chapala. To the airport, the trip should cost $12–$15, using the meter. Up to four people normally fit into a cab; larger vehicles cost $25 to the Centro.
**🚹 Taxi & Shuttles Autotransportaciones Aeropuerto** ☎ 33/3812-4278.

CARRIERS   AeroCalifornia serves Tucson and Los Angeles as well as many Mexican cities. Aeroméxico has nonstop service to Guadalajara from Los Angeles and extensive internal flights. Mexicana has direct flights from Chicago, Los Angeles, San Francisco, and San José. Through Dallas, American Airlines provides service to Guadalajara from all cities in its system. Flights on Continental are routed through the Houston hub. Delta Air Lines flies direct from Los Angeles and Atlanta. Most major airlines, as well as several smaller ones, have offices in the small commercial center across from Centro Magno on Avenida Vallarta.
**🚹 AeroCalifornia** ⊠ Av. Vallarta 2440 ☎ 33/3616-2525. **Aeroméxico** ⊠ Av. Vallarta 2440 ☎ 33/3669-0202. **American Airlines** ⊠ Av. Vallarta 2440 ☎ 33/3688-5394 or 01800/904-6000. **Continental** ⊠ Hotel Presidente Inter-Continental, Av. López Mateos Sur 3515 ☎ 33/3647-4251. **Delta Air Lines** ⊠ Av. López Cotilla 1701 ☎ 33/3630-3530. **Mexicana** ⊠ Av. Vallarta 2440 ☎ 33/3615-3227 or 01800/366-5400.

### BUS TRAVEL TO & FROM GUADALAJARA
First-class, air-conditioned buses with rest rooms run daily to Guadalajara from most major border cities. Greyhound has schedule and fare in-

formation for service into Mexico, although you'll have to change to a Mexican carrier at the border. Guadalajara's Nueva Central Camionera (New Central Bus Station) is 10 km (6 mi) southeast of downtown. Elite has first-class service to Mexico City and other destinations. ETN is the most upscale line, and its prices match its service. Primera Plus has first- and second-class buses serving mainly central and western Mexico. Omnibus de México serves the U.S. border and intermediate destinations.

Buses to and from such nearby destinations as Chapala, Ajijic, and Tequila depart from the Antigua Central Camionera (Old Central Bus Station), northeast of the Parque Agua Azul on Avenida Dr. R. Michel, between Calle Los Angeles and Calle 5 de Febrero. Autotransportes Guadalajara Chapala has service to lakeside towns for $3. It's about 45 minutes to Chapala and another 15 minutes to Ajijic; there are departures every half hour from 6 AM to 9:30 PM. Make sure you ask for the *directo* (direct) as opposed to *clase segunda* (second class), which stops at every little pueblo en route. Most buses continue on to Jocotepec; otherwise, catch a local line from either Chapala or Ajijic.

🚩 **Autotransportes Guadalajara Chapala** ☎ 33/3619-5675. **Estrella Blanca** ☎ 33/3679-0404. **ETN** ☎ 33/3600-0477. **Greyhound** ☎ 01800/712-8819 toll-free in Mexico, 800/231-2222 in the U.S. **Omnibus de México** ☎ 33/3600-0469. **Primera Plus** ☎ 33/3600-0398 or 01800/375-7587.

### BUS TRAVEL WITHIN GUADALAJARA

Buses run every few minutes between 6 AM and 11 PM to all local attractions, including those in Tlaquepaque, Tonalá, and Zapopan; most buses pass through or near the Zona Centro. Unlike many Mexican cities, Guadalajara has actual bus stops, or *paradas,* marked by signs or sheltered benches. Fares are roughly 35¢, making buses the preferred mode of transportation for residents; expect to stand during the day. For Zapopan, Tlaquepaque, and Tonalá, large mint-green Tur buses (Greyhound-like buses) cost around 70¢ and are generally faster, less crowded, and more comfortable than other buses. Window signs indicate the destinations. Tur buses take a limited number of passengers; if one doesn't stop, it's either full or you're not at a proper stop.

Main destinations that you can reach from the Zona Centro include: Zapopan (northbound Tur bus from Avenida Alcalde and Calle Juan Manuel or Avenida 16 de Septiembre and Calle Madero); Tonalá and Tlaquepaque (green southbound Tur bus from Avenida Alcalde and Calle Juan Manuel or Avenida 16 de Septiembre and Calle Madero); Zona Minerva (electric, westbound Par Vial buses numbered 400 or 500 from Calle Independencia); Zona Plaza del Sol (westbound Bus 258 from Alcalde and Calle San Felipe); Zoológico, Barranca de Oblatos, Parque Mirador Independencia, and the soccer and bullfighting stadiums (electric, northbound Par Vial Bus 600 from Calzada Independencia in front of Mercado Libertad or Bus 60, which goes as far as the zoo); Parque Agua Azul (southbound Bus 62-A or C from Calzada Independencia).

### CAR RENTAL

🚩 **Major Agencies Alamo** ☒ Av. Niños Héroes 982, south of Zona Centro, Guadalajara ☎ 33/3613-5531 or 33/3613-5560, 33/3688-6630 at the airport. **Avis** ☒ Hilton, Av.

de las Rosas 2933, Zona Cruz del Sur, Guadalajara ☎ 33/3671-3422, 33/3688-5656 to the airport. **Budget** ☒ Av. Niños Héroes 934, at Av. 16 de Septiembre, Zona Centro, Guadalajara ☎ 33/3613-0027 or 33/3613-0287, 33/3688-5216 at the airport. **Dollar** ☒ Av. Federalismo Sur 480, at Av. de la Paz, Zona Centro, Guadalajara ☎ 33/3825-5080. **Express Rent a Car** ☒ Calle Manzano 444, Zona Centro, Guadalajara ☎ 33/3614-1465 or 33/3614-1865. **Hertz** ☒ At the airport only ☎ 33/3688-5633.

## CAR TRAVEL

Major routes include Ruta 54 (Route 54), which leads south to Colima (220 km [136 mi]) and north to Zacatecas (320 km [198 mi]). Ruta 15 hugs the southern shore of Lago de Chapala before continuing southeast to Morelia (255 km [58 mi]) and Mexico City (209 km [130 mi]). Ruta 15D is the toll road to Mexico City. Heading northwest from Guadalajara, both 15 and 15D pass through some of the most beautiful country in Jalisco and neighboring Nayarit state.

To reach Tlaquepaque, take Avenida Revolución southwest. At the Plaza de la Bandera, turn right onto Calzada del Ejército and cross the plaza to the first light. Turn left onto Boulevard General Marcelino García Barragán (also known as Boulevard Tlaquepaque). Follow the *glorieta* (traffic circle) around to Avenida Niños Héroes. The first intersection is Calle Independencia, the pedestrian mall in Tlaquepaque. From the Plaza del Sol area, take Calzada Lázaro Cárdenas southeast toward the airport and pick up the Carretera Guadalajara–Chapala. (*Note:* bypass the airport/highway exit and take the next one, to the Alamo glorieta). Fork off to the north onto Avenida Niños Héroes. Either trip should take about 25 minutes. To travel from Tlaquepaque to Tonalá, take Avenida Río Nilo southeast directly into town and the intersection of Avenida de los Tonaltecas (5 minutes).

In Guadalajara, beware of heavy traffic and *topes* (speed bumps). Traffic circles are common at many busy intersections. Parking in the city center can be scarce, so take a taxi or bus if you're not staying nearby; otherwise, try the underground lots across from the Palacio Municipal (Avenida Hidalgo and Calle Pedro Loza) and below the Plaza de la Liberación (Avenida Hidalgo and Calle Belén, in front of the Teatro Degollado). Park illegally and the police may tow your vehicle, necessitating a visit to the municipal transit office to pay a fine and then to one of the *correlones* (holding areas) to pay the tow charge (around $15) and retrieve your car.

## CONSULATES

🚩 **British Consulate** ☒ Calle Jesus de Rojas 20, Zona Zapopan, Guadalajara ☎ 33/3343-2296. **Canadian Consulate** ☒ Fiesta Americana, Av. Aurelio Aceves 225, Zona Centro, Guadalajara ☎ 33/3616-5642, 33/3615-6215, 01800/706-2900 toll-free in Mexico for after-hours emergencies. **U.S. Consulate** ☒ Calle Progreso 175, between Av. López Cotilla and Av. Libertad, Zona Centro, Guadalajara ☎ 33/3825-2700, 33/3825-1717, 33/3826-5553 after-hours emergencies.

## EMERGENCIES

🚩 Emergency Services **Cruz Verde** (Green Cross municipal emergency medical service) ☎ 33/3614-5252 central dispatch or 33/3812-5143 or 33/3812-0472. **Federal High-**

**way Patrol** 33/3629-5082 or 33/3629-5085. **General Emergencies** 080 or 065 for ambulance. **Guadalajara City Police** 33/3668-0800 or 33/3617-0770. **Red Cross** 33/3614-5600 or 33/3614-2707. **State Police** 33/3675-3060. **Tourist Police** 3818-3640 or 3818-3600.

**Hospitals Hospital del Carmen** Calle Tarascos 3435, Zona Minerva, Guadalajara 33/3813-1224 or 33/3813-0025. **Hospital México-Americano** Calle Colomos 2110, Zona Centro, Guadalajara 33/3641-3141. **Hospital San Javier** Av. Pablo Casals 640, Col. Providencia, Zona Minerva, Guadalajara 33/3669-0222.

**Late-Night Pharmacies Benavides** Calle Morelos 468, near el Palacio Municipal, Zona Centro, Guadalajara 33/3614-7676 Av. Hidalgo 307-A, Zona Centro, Guadalajara 33/3637-7280. **Farmacias Guadalajara** Av. Javier Mina 221, between Calle Cabañas and Vicente Guerrero, Zona Centro, Guadalajara 3618-9383.

### ENGLISH-LANGUAGE MEDIA

The *Guadalajara Reporter,* a weekly paper sold for 90¢ at newsstands and hotels, is light on news but has community and cultural listings. It's on the Web at www.guadalajarareporter.com. The monthly newspapers *Ojo del Lago* and *Lake Chapala Review* cover the Lago de Chapala area. Many top-end hotels have CNN in English.

**Bookstores Libros de Chapala** Av. Madero 230, Chapala No phone. **Sanborn's** Av. 16 de Septiembre 127, Centro Histórico, Guadalajara 33/3613-6693 Av. López Mateos 2718, Plaza del Sol mall, Zona Cruz del Sur, Guadalajara 33/3647-2510.

### MAIL, INTERNET & SHIPPING

The main *correos* (post office) is open weekdays 8–7. American Express cardholders can receive mail at the AmEx office in Zona Minerva, which is open weekdays 9 to 6 and Saturday 9 to 1. Note that the Mexican postal system is notoriously slow and unreliable; for important letters or packages, use a courier service such as Federal Express or DHL.

There are several decent Internet cafés in the heart of the Zona Centro. The cost is usually $1.20 to $1.50 per hour, and most places charge in 15-minute increments. Alteck has fast Internet connections as well as national and international fax and phone service. It's open weekdays 9 to 8 and Saturday 9 to 7. Compu-Flash, another place with fast Internet connections, is one block east of the Hotel Cervántes. Its hours are weekdays 9:30 AM–10 PM and Saturday 9–8.

**Courier Services Federal Express** Av. Washington 1129, Zona Centro, Guadalajara 01800/900-1100 toll-free in Mexico. **DHL** Plaza del Sol, Local 20, in front of Banamex, Plaza del Sol, Guadalajara 33/3669-0214.

**Cybercafés Alteck** Calle Pedro Mereno 702, Zona Centro, Guadalajara 33/3613-1198 33/3614-4934. **Compu-Flash** Calle Priciliano Sánchez 402, Zona Centro, Guadalajara 33/3614-7165 33/3124-1072.

**Postal Information American Express** Av. Vallarta 2440, Zona Minerva, Guadalajara 33/3818-2323 33/3616-7665. **Correos** Av. Alcalde 500, Zona Centro, Guadalajara 33/3614-4770.

### MONEY MATTERS

ATMs are the most convenient way to get cash, and offer the best exchange rates. (Be sure your PIN has only four digits.) There are several ATMs at the airport. You can also change foreign cash and traveler's checks at a *casa de cambio*; there are dozens on Calle López Cotilla, east of Avenida 16 de Septiembre. They generally open weekdays 9–7 and Saturday 9–1.

### SUBWAY TRAVEL

Guadalajara's underground *tren ligero* (light train) system is clean, safe, and efficient. Line 1 runs north–south along Avenida Federalismo from the Periférico (city beltway) Sur to Periférico Norte, near the Benito Juárez Auditorium. Line 2 runs east–west along Juárez from Tetlán in eastern Guadalajara to Avenida Federalismo, with stops at Avenida 16 de Septiembre (Plaza Universitario) and Mercado Libertad. Lines 1 and 2 form a "T," meeting at the Juárez station at Parque Revolución, at the corner of Avenida Federalismo and Avenida Juárez. Trains run every 15 minutes from 6 AM to 11 PM; a token for one trip costs about 35¢.

### TAXIS

In Guadalajara taxis are safe, readily available, and reasonably priced. All cabs are supposed to use meters (in Spanish, *taximetro*)—you can insist the driver use it or else agree on a fixed price at the outset. *Sitios* (cab stands) are near all hotels and attractions. Fares go up about 25% after 10 PM. Cabs hailed at hotels are more expensive.

A cab to the airport costs $12–$15, and $7 to the new bus station. The fare from downtown Guadalajara to Tlaquepaque is about $5 and about $7 to Tonalá; a cab from one to the other runs about $4.

🚖 Taxi Companies **Taxi Aguirre** ✉ Calle Etopia #660, Zona Centro, Guadalajara ☎ 33/3644–4818. **Taxi Express** ☎ 33/3637–4525. **Taxi Sitio Miverva no. 22** ☎ 33/3124–0920.

### TOURS

The city tourism office conducts a free, two-hour, guided walking tour every Saturday, starting at 10 AM at the Palacio Municipal Palace (Spanish only). The Tourist Board of Zapopan offers free guided trolley tours of Zapopan weekends at 10 AM; call ahead to arrange an English-speaking guide. You can hire a *calandria* (horse-drawn carriage) in front of the Museo Regional, the Mercado Libertad, or Parque San Francisco. The charge is about $15 for an hour-long tour for up to five passengers; it's $10 with a coupon available at the tourist office. Few drivers speak English, though.

Panoramex offers bus tours of Guadalajara and Tlaquepaque, and excursions to Lago de Chapala and Tequila ($13–$20 per person). The bilingual guides of Ajijic's Charter Club Tours lead tours of Guadalajara, shopping and factory trips in Tlaquepaque and Tonalá, and treks to lesser known towns in Jalisco state. Sonrisa Tours is another reliable tour operator. With a day's notice, you can visit many home studios on free tours offered by the Tonalá municipal tourist office.

Each Saturday the *Tequila Express*—the only train to travel to or from the city—leaves Guadalajara on a 10-hour trip (from 10:30 AM to 8:30 PM) that includes a tour of the Hacienda San José del Refugio distillery in Amatitlán (not Tequila), a satisfying lunch, a mariachi and ballet folk-lórico performance, and an unlimited supply of Mexico's most famous liquor. Tickets are $55 and are available through Guadalajara's Cámera de Comercio (Chamber of Commerce) or Ticketmaster.

**⏹ Cámera de Comercio** ✉ Av. Vallarta 4095, Zona Minerva, Guadalajara ☎ 33/3122-7920 or 33/3880-9099. **Charter Club Tours** ✉ Carretera Chapala-Jocotepec, Plaza Montaña mall, Ajijic ☎ 376/766-1777. **Panoramex** ✉ Av. Federalismo Sur 944, Zona Centro, Guadalajara ☎ 33/3810-5057 or 33/3810-5005 ⊕ www.panoramex.com.mx. **Sonrisa Tours** ✉ Paseo del Hospicio 63, Plaza Tapatía, Zona Centro, Guadalajara ☎ 33/3618-9601, 33/3617-2511, or 33/3617-2590. **Ticketmaster** ☎ 33/3818-3800.

## TRAVEL AGENCIES

**⏹ Local Agent Referrals American Express** ✉ Av. Vallarta 2440, Zona Minerva, Guadalajara ☎ 33/3818-2323. **Copenhagen Tours** ✉ Av. J. Manuel Clouthier 156, Col. Prados Vallarta, Zona Minerva, Guadalajara ☎ 33/3629-7957 or 33/3629-4758.

## VISITOR INFORMATION

The Guadalajara branches of the Jalisco state tourist office have information about the city and other parts of Mexico; there's also a branch in Chapala. All branches are open on weekdays and weekends, though hours vary. Guadalajara's municipal tourist office is in front of the Palacio Municipal; it has kiosks downtown in the Plaza Guadalajara, near Los Arcos monument on Avenida Vallarta east of the Minerva Fountain, in Parque San Francisco, in front of the Instituto Cultural Cabañas, in front of Mercado Libertad, at Calle Vicente Guerrero 233 (closed weekends), and at the airport. Hours are generally Monday–Saturday 9–7.

The Tourist Board of Zapopan (weekdays 9 to 7:30) provides information and maps about metropolitan Guadalajara, including Zapopan, Tonalá, and Tlaquepaque. Both the Tlaquepaque (weekdays 9 to 7) and Tonalá (weekdays 9 to 3) tourist offices dispense maps and brochures—look for them in kiosks in the main plazas. One of the attendants usually speaks some English. In Ajijic, the nonprofit Lake Chapala Society, open Monday–Saturday 10–2, provides information about the area.

**⏹ Guadalajara Municipal Tourist Office** ✉ Monumento Los Arcos, Av. Vallarta 2641, 1 block east of Minerva Fountain, Zona Minerva, Guadalajara ☎ 33/3616-9150 or 33/3615-1182 ⊕ www.vive.guadalajara.gob.mx. **Jalisco state tourist offices** ✉ Calle Morelos 102, in Plaza Tapatía, Centro Histórico, Guadalajara ☎ 33/3668-1600, 01800/363-2200 toll-free in Mexico ⊕ http://visita.jalisco.gob.mx ✉ Palacio de Gobierno, Centro Histórico, Guadalajara ☎ No phone ✉ Calle Madero 407-A, 2nd floor, Chapala ☎ 376/765-3141. **Lake Chapala Society** ✉ Av. 16 de Septiembre 16, Ajijic ☎ 376/766-1582 ⊕ www.mexconnect.com/mex_/chreares.html. **Tlaquepaque Municipal Tourist Office** ✉ Calle Morelos 288, Tlaquepaque ☎ 33/3635-5756 or 33/3657-3846. **Tonalá Municipal Tourist Office** ✉ Av. de los Tonaltecas Sur 140, in La Casa de los Artesanos, Tonalá ☎ 33/3284-3092. **Tourist Board of Zapopan** ✉ Av. Vallarta 6503, Ciudad Granja, Zona Zapopan, Guadalajara ☎ 33/3110-0754 or 33/3110-0755 ⊕ www.zapopan.gob.mx.

# THE HEARTLAND

7

Updated by
Sean Mattson

**NAMED FOR ITS CENTRAL** position, the Heartland is known for its well-preserved colonial architecture, its fertile farmland and encircling mountains, and its salient role in Mexican history, particularly during the War of Independence (1810–21). The Bajío (ba-*hee*-o), as it is also called, corresponds roughly to the state of Guanajuato and parts of Querétaro and Michoacán states.

Intense Spanish colonization of the hills surrounding the cities of Guanajuato, Zacatecas, Querétaro, and San Miguel de Allende followed their discovery of silver in the area in the 1500s. Wealthy Creoles (Mexicans of Spanish descent) in Querétaro and San Miguel took the first audacious steps toward independence from Spain three centuries later. When their clandestine efforts were uncovered, two of the early insurgents, Ignacio Allende and Father Miguel Hidalgo, began in earnest the War of Independence.

Another native son, José María Morelos, rallied for independence when Allende and Hidalgo were executed in 1811. This mestizo (mixed race) mule skinner–turned–priest–turned–soldier nearly gained control of the land with his army of 9,000 before he was killed in 1815. Thirteen years later, the city of Valladolid was renamed Morelia in his honor.

Long after the War of Independence ended in 1821, cities in the Bajío continued to figure prominently in Mexico's history. Three major events occurred in Querétaro alone: in 1848 the Mexican-American War ended with the signing of the Treaty of Guadalupe Hidalgo; in 1867 Austrian Maximilian of Hapsburg, whom France's Napoleon III had crowned Emperor of Mexico, was executed in the hills north of town; and in 1917 the Mexican Constitution was signed here.

The Heartland continually honors the events and people that helped shape modern Mexico. In ornate cathedrals or bucolic plazas, down narrow alleyways or atop high hillsides, you'll find monuments—and remnants—of a heroic past. You can savor the region's historic spirit during its numerous fiestas. On a night filled with fireworks, off-key music, and tireless celebrants, it's hard not to be caught up in the vital expression of national pride.

Unlike areas where attractions are specifically designed for tourists, the Bajío relies on its historic ties and the architectural integrity of its cities to appeal to travelers. Families visit parks for Sunday picnics, youngsters tussle in school courtyards, old men chat in shaded plazas, and Purépecha women in traditional garb sell their wares in crowded *mercados* (markets).

## Exploring the Heartland

Travelers often barrel past the Heartland to spots north or west of Mexico City, but there are plenty of reasons to stop here: shops in San Miguel and Guanajuato have bargains on silver and other local crafts, and Michoacán is renowned for its folklore and folk crafts, especially ceramics and lacquerware. Extend your stay and linger over the varied architectural styles that each of the colonial cities has to offer. Although it may be most convenient to tour by car, there is frequent and inexpensive bus service between cities throughout the Bajío.

## About the Restaurants

Restaurants in this neck of the woods don't stay open quite as late as they do in the capital. Locals usually have lunch between 1 and 5 PM and dinner between 7 and 10 PM. Dress is casual, but the line is generally drawn at shorts.

## About the Hotels

In the colonial cities the best lodgings are in the restored haciendas of fabulously rich residents from centuries past. Often near the town's center, many facing directly onto plazas, some of these mansions date from the 16th century. There are also deluxe modern high-rises and functional, low-cost hotels. Except for five-star hotels, most properties in the region aren't heated; bring warm clothes for indoor wear, or inquire in advance if heating is important to you. Likewise, most haciendas-turned-hotels lack air-conditioning because the thick-walled construction keeps interior temperatures low. Room size and furnishings tend to vary dramatically in these restored properties, so if you aren't satisfied with a room you're shown, ask to see another. Most moderate and inexpensive hotels quote prices with 17% value-added tax already included.

| WHAT IT COSTS | | | | |
|---|---|---|---|---|
| **$$$$** | **$$$** | **$$** | **$** | **¢** |
| RESTAURANTS over $25 | $15–$25 | $10–$15 | $5–$10 | under $5 |
| HOTELS over $250 | $150–$250 | $75–$150 | $50–$75 | under $50 |

Restaurant prices are for a main course excluding tax and tip. Hotel prices are for two people in a standard double room in high season, based on the European Plan (EP, with no meals) and excluding service and 17% tax.

# Timing

Among the Heartland's most pleasing attributes is its superb climate—rarely does it get overly hot, even in midsummer, and although winter days can get nippy, especially in northern Zacatecas, they are generally temperate. Average temperatures in the southern city of Morelia range from 20°C (68°F) in May to just under 10°C (49°F) in January. Zacatecas is more extreme, with winter temperatures as low as 0°C (32°F) and snow flurries every several years, and summer highs of 28°C–30°C (81°F–85°F). Expect cool nights year-round in most of the region's cities. The heartland's rainy season hits between June and October and is generally strongest in July and August. Millions of monarch butterflies arrive near Morelia between early November and early March.

For the most part, high season is limited to specific dates near Christmas, Easter, and regional festivals. Consider visiting the Heartland's cultural festivals or religious events: in October Guanajuato's three-week-long International Cervantes Festival attracts actors, musicians, painters, and hundreds of thousands of visitors; in late November is San Miguel's Jazz Festival International; and November 1–2 on the island of Janítzio,

Short on time? With only a few days on your hands, make a point of stopping in one of the Heartland's several colonial cities—each has its own particular flavor. Should you fall under the Heartland's peaceful, friendly spell, you'll need a week to 10 days to drink in the atmosphere of two or three of the region's cities.

*Numbers in the text correspond to numbers in the margin and on the San Miguel de Allende, Guanajuato, Zacatecas, Querétaro, Morelia, and Pátzcuaro maps.*

**7**

**If you have 3 days**

Head to ⊞ **Guanajuato** ⑫–㉔ ▶, the Heartland's most architecturally dramatic city. From here take a day trip to the enchanting town of **San Miguel de Allende** ①–⑪ to shop for crafts.

Alternatively, you could go from Mexico City to the Michoacán capital of ⊞ **Morelia** ㊷–㊿ ▶ and spend a day admiring its stately architecture and café-lined plaza. The next day, drive to **Pátzcuaro** ㊾–㊿, set among volcanoes in the center of Purépecha Indian country. Spend the morning in the bustling market or strolling in the surrounding countryside before returning to Mexico City in the late afternoon.

**If you have 5 days**

Set ⊞ **Guanajuato** ⑫–㉔ ▶ as your base and allow an extra day to see its churches and museums—perhaps even the gruesome Mummy Museum. Stop at the town of Dolores Hidalgo, home of Mexican independence, on your way to a day of shopping in ⊞ **San Miguel de Allende** ①–⑪. Overnight in San Miguel and the next morning head for ⊞ **Querétaro** ㉞–㊶. This quiet colonial city is considered the capital of the Bajío. After a night in a downtown hotel, return to Mexico City or to the airport outside Guanajuato (2½ hours).

If you decide to spend several days in Michoacán, you can easily fill your time exploring the state's colonial towns and its lush, mountainous countryside. After three days in ⊞ **Morelia** ㊷–㊿ ▶ and ⊞ **Pátzcuaro** ㊾–㊿, take a day trip to explore the crater on an extinct volcano in **San Juan Parangaricútiro** or the ruins of an ancient Purépecha Indian capital, **Tzintzuntzan** (both are easy day trips from Pátzcuaro), before returning on the final day to Morelia and Mexico City.

**If you have 7 days**

From your base in ⊞ **Guanajuato** ⑫–㉔ ▶, consider adding to the first of the five-day itineraries a round-trip flight from León's Guanajuato International Airport to ⊞ **Zacatecas** ㉕–㉝. This would give you a day and a half to explore the northern colonial mining city. Because it lies off the main tourist track, Zacatecas has a refreshingly unself-conscious attitude. Another possibility for a week in the heartland would be to make a loop from Mexico City that includes both ⊞ **Morelia** ㊷–㊿ ▶ and ⊞ **Guanajuato.** You'd have time for leisurely side trips to **Pátzcuaro** ㊾–㊿ and ⊞ **San Miguel de Allende** ①–⑪ and a stop in ⊞ **Querétaro** ㉞–㊶. When in Pátzcuaro, take a boat out to the island town of Janítzio on nearby Lake Pátzcuaro, home of Mexico's most famous Day of the Dead festival (lasting up to two days), or to the island of Yunuen, which isn't as yet besieged by tourists.

local Purépecha (also called Tarascan) Indians hold a Day of the Dead to honor their ancestors.

# SAN MIGUEL DE ALLENDE

San Miguel de Allende began luring foreigners in the late 1930s when American Stirling Dickinson and prominent local residents founded an art school in this mountainous settlement. The school, now called the Instituto Allende, has grown in stature over the years—as has the city's reputation as a writers' and artists' colony. Walk along any cobblestone street and you're likely to see residents of a variety of national origins. Some come to study at the Instituto Allende or the Academia Hispano-Americana, some to escape the harsh northern winters, and still others to retire.

Cultural offerings in this town of about 110,000 reflect its large American and Canadian community. There are literary readings, art shows, a yearly jazz festival, psychic fairs, aerobics and past-life regression classes, and a lending library. International influence notwithstanding, San Miguel, declared a national monument in 1926, retains its Mexican characteristics. Wandering past 18th-century mansions, you'll also discover fountains, monuments, and churches—all reminders of the city's illustrious, and sometimes notorious, past. At the corner of Calles Hernández Macías and Pila Seca, for example, is the onetime headquarters of the Spanish Inquisition in New Spain. The former Inquisition jail stands across the way. Independence Day is San Miguel's biggest celebration, with fireworks, dances, and parades on September 15 and 16; bullfights and cultural events, including the running of the bulls, fill out the remainder of the month.

## Exploring San Miguel de Allende

Most of San Miguel's sights are in a cluster downtown, which you can visit in a couple of hours.

**a good walk**

Begin at the main plaza, otherwise known as **El Jardín ❶** ▶. After ambling around for a bit, stop into **La Parroquia ❷**, the sandstone church on the square's south side. Three blocks northeast of La Parroquia (make a right onto Calle San Francisco, on the north side of El Jardín, to Calle Juárez) is the heavily ornamented facade of the **Iglesia de San Francisco ❸**. Take a few steps north on Calle Juárez to Calle Mesones, then east to Calle Colegio, where the colorful **Mercado Ignacio Ramírez** occupies a cavernous structure off the west side of the street. The dome of the **Oratorio de San Felipe Neri ❹** is visible just before the market.

A block west of the church on Calle Insurgentes, **La Biblioteca Pública ❺** is a great place to catch up on town events. Continue west from the library two blocks to Calle Hernández Macías, then head south to the **Bellas Artes ❻** cultural center at No. 75 and the ornate **Iglesia de la Concepción ❼** behind it. Take Hernández Macías south for a block and turn left on Calle Umarán to reach the **Casa de Ignacio Allende ❽**, birthplace of the Mexican national hero. Now you've circled back to the southwest corner of El Jardín.

7

## Architecture

Financed largely by the region's fabulously wealthy silver mines, the cities of the Heartland are rife with architectural masterpieces richly worked with curvaceous lines, human, animal, plant, and geometric motifs, and sculptural depth that accents the play of light and shadow. No two towns are alike: there's the stately, almost European grandeur of Morelia; the steep, labyrinthine allure of Guanajuato; and the pink sandstone splendor of Zacatecas. San Miguel de Allende's Gothic-style parish church puts a Gallic touch on an otherwise very Mexican skyline. And in Pátzcuaro and Querétaro, the ornate 16th-century colonial mansions surrounding the city squares have been converted into hotels and government offices, making their interior patios accessible to the public.

## Cuisine

Culinary tastes vary widely in the Heartland, which spans a large area across central Mexico. Purépecha Indian influences predominate in the state of Michoacán. Tomato-based *sopa tarasca* (a soup with cheese, cream, and tortillas) is one of the best-known regional specialties. Because of the numerous lakes and rivers in the state, several types of freshwater fish are often served in Michoacán restaurants.

At the Heartland's northern end, in Zacatecas, the hearty, meat-eating tastes of the *norteños* (northerners) rule the dinner table. Although beef is the favored dish, other specialties include *asado de boda* (wedding barbecue), pork in a spicy but semisweet sauce. The region is also known for its cheese and wine. And because of San Miguel's expatriate community, the city has a wealth of worthy eateries.

## Hiking & Walking

With its rolling farmland, lofty volcanoes, lakes, and Indian villages, Michoacán is a perfect area for day hikes. Trails near Pátzcuaro wind up to nearby hilltops for great views across town and the surrounding countryside, and in Uruapan—64 km (40 mi) away and 2,000 feet lower in elevation—you can walk along a lush river valley. And no tour of the heartland would be complete without a few days of leisurely strolling on the avenues and backstreets of colonial cities and towns.

---

After making your way around the town's center, consider a leisurely stroll to sights farther afield. From the south side of the plaza (by La Parroquia), head west four blocks on Calle Umarán until you reach Calle Zacateros. Turn south on this narrow cobblestone street for some of the town's most interesting crafts shops—stocked with intriguing items like silver jewelry or Mexican ceremonial masks.

Past the shops, Calle Zacateros becomes Ancha de San Antonio. On your left at No. 20 is the renowned **Instituto Allende** 🟢, where many of San Miguel's foreign visitors come to study. From the institute, continue farther south on Ancha de San Antonio, then turn left onto Callejón del Cardo. Make your way past St. Paul's Episcopal Church, an expat house of worship, until you arrive at the cobblestone Calle Aldama on

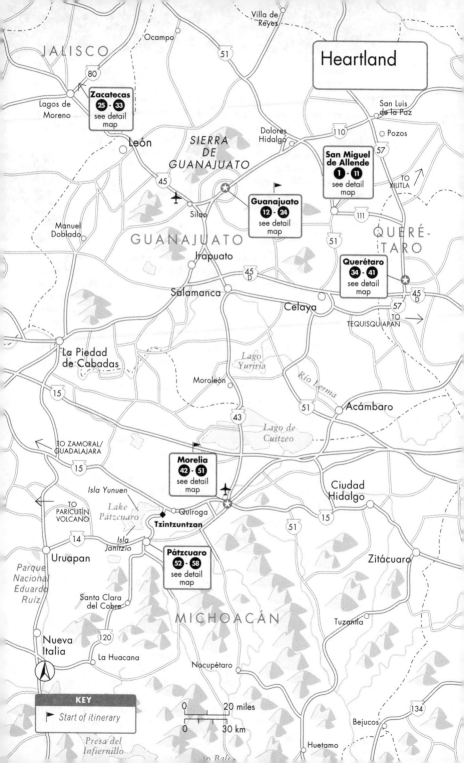

your left. Head downhill and walk briefly through a neighborhood of whitewashed houses before reaching the north entrance to the five-acre Parque Benito Juárez, an oasis of evergreens, palm trees, and gardens.

From the north edge of the park, follow Calle Diezmo Viejo to the terracotta–color mansion known as La Huerta Santa Elena. From here turn left and walk one block uphill on Calle Recreo to the **Lavaderos Públicos** ⑩, San Miguel's outdoor laundry and a favorite gathering spot for local women. Calle Recreo, above the *lavandería,* heads north back toward the plaza, passing the town's bullfighting ring. If you'd like a view of the entire city, turn right off Calle Recreo onto Calle Hospicio, follow Hospicio three blocks to Calle Pedro Vargas, turn right, and go uphill to **El Mirador**'s ⑪ overlook. Otherwise, follow Recreo until reaching Calle Correo, turn left, and walk three blocks to return to El Jardín.

TIMING  A walk through San Miguel takes two to three hours—more if you linger over coffee or a meal. Don't forget that the public library and the Instituto Allende close on Sunday, and the Casa de Ignacio Allende is closed Monday.

## What to See

⑥ **Bellas Artes.** Since 1938 this impressive cloister has been an institute for the study of music, dance, and the visual arts. This building, once the Royal Convent of the Conception, is across the street from the U.S. Consulate and has rotating exhibits and a patio cafeteria. Cultural events are listed on a bulletin board at the entrance. ⊠ *Calle Hernández Macías 75, El Centro* ☎ *415/152–0289* ⊡ *Free* ☉ *Mon.–Sat. 9–8, Sun. 10–2.*

⑤ **La Biblioteca Pública** (Public Library). Within the library's walls are a lovely courtyard café, the offices of the English-language newspaper *Atención San Miguel,* and reading rooms with back issues of popular publications and books in English. On Sunday at noon a two-hour house-and-garden tour (about $15) of San Miguel leaves from the library. Notices, about such things as literary readings and yoga and aerobics classes, are posted on the bulletin board in the library's entranceway. ⊠ *Calle Insurgentes 25, El Centro* ☎ *415/152–0293* ⊡ *Free* ☉ *Weekdays 10–2 and 4–7, Sat. 10–2.*

⑧ **Casa de Ignacio Allende.** A series of statues will leave no doubt as to this building's former resident: this is the birthplace of Ignacio Allende, one of Mexico's great independence heroes. Allende was a Creole aristocrat who, along with Father Miguel Hidalgo, plotted in the early 1800s to overthrow the Spanish regime. Spanish Royalists learned of their plot and began arresting conspirators in Querétaro on September 13, 1810. In turn, Allende and Hidalgo hastened their plans. At dawn on September 16, they rang out the cry for independence, and the fighting began. Allende was captured and executed by the Royalists the following year. As a tribute to his brave efforts, San Miguel El Grande was renamed San Miguel de Allende in the 20th century. ⊠ *Calle Cuna de Allende 1, El Centro* ☎ *415/152–2499* ⊡ *$3* ☉ *Tues.–Sun. 10–4.*

**El Charco del Ingenio.** San Miguel's botanical garden, northeast of the city's center, has five-odd miles of pathways winding past more than 1,500

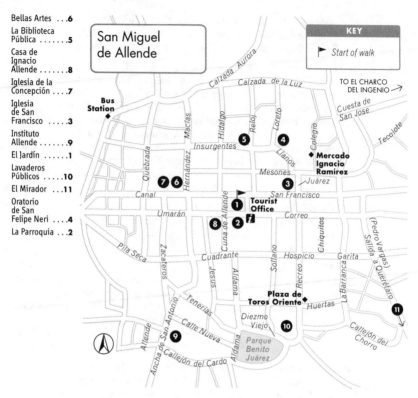

species of cacti and succulents. It's an enjoyable place to walk or cycle, particularly in the early morning or late afternoon. ⊠ *1½ km (1 mi) northeast of El Jardín; signs point the way off Cuesta de San Jose, El Centro* ☎ *No phone* 💲 *$1* ☉ *Sunrise–sunset.*

**❼ Iglesia de la Concepción.** Just behind the Bellas Artes cultural center is this church, which has one of the largest domes in Mexico. The two-story dome (completed in 1891) and the elegant Corinthian columns and pilasters gracing its drum are said to have been inspired by Paris's dome of the Hôtel des Invalides. Ceferino Gutiérrez (of La Parroquia fame) is credited with its design. ⊠ *Calle Canal between Calles Hernández Macías and Zacateros, El Centro* ☎ *No phone.*

**❸ Iglesia de San Francisco.** This church has one of Guanajuato state's finest churrigueresque facades. The term for this style refers to José Churriguera, a 17th-century (baroque) Spanish architect, noted for his extravagant surface decoration. Built in the late 18th century, the church was financed by donations from wealthy patrons and by bullfight revenue. Topping the elaborately carved exterior is the image of Saint Francis of Assisi. Below, along with a crucifix, are sculptures of Saint John and Our Lady of Sorrows. ⊠ *Calle Juárez between Calles San Francisco and Mesones, El Centro* ☎ *No phone.*

**9  Instituto Allende.** Since the school's founding in 1951, thousands of students from around the world have come to learn Spanish and to take classes in the arts. The institute is in the former country estate of the Count of Canal. Abundant with bougainvillea, rosebushes, and ivy vines, the grounds provide a quiet refuge for students and visitors alike. ⌂ *Ancha de San Antonio 20, El Centro* ☎ *415/152–0190* ⊕ *www. instituto-allende.edu.mx* ⊠ *Free* ⊙ *Weekdays 8–6, Sat. 9–1.*

▶ **1  El Jardín.** San Miguel's heart is the plaza commonly known as El Jardín (the garden). Get a feel for the town just by sitting on one of its wrought-iron benches: old men with canes exchange tales, and bells from nearby La Parroquia pierce the thin mountain air at each quarter hour. At dusk thousands of grackles make a fantastic ruckus as they return to roost in the laurel trees. ⌂ *Bounded by Calle Correo on the south, Calle San Francisco on the north, Portal Allende on the west, and Portal Guadalupe on the east, El Centro.*

> **need a break?**
>
> On the southwest corner of the main plaza is **Café del Jardín** (⌂ Portal Allende 2, El Centro ☎ 415/152–5006). This unassuming little café has excellent coffee, cappuccino, hot chocolate, and, in the evening, pizza. Breakfasts are tasty and inexpensive, and the service is friendly.

**10  Lavaderos Públicos.** This collection of red concrete tubs above Parque Benito Juárez is a public laundry where local women gather daily to wash clothes and chat as their predecessors have done for centuries. Some women claim to have more-efficient washing facilities at home, but the lure of the spring-fed troughs, and the chance to catch up on the news, brings them to this shaded courtyard. ⌂ *Calle Diezmo Viejo at Calle Recreo, El Centro.*

**11  El Mirador.** Climb El Mirador (The Lookout) for a panorama of the city, mountains, and reservoir below. The vista is stunning at sunset, and chances are you won't be alone. Locals and tourists like to join Pedro Vargas, whose bronze image commands this spot. ⌂ *Calle Pedro Vargas, El Centro.*

**4  Oratorio de San Felipe Neri.** Built by local Indians in 1712, the original chapel can still be glimpsed in the eastern facade, made of pink stone and adorned with a figure of Our Lady of Solitude. The newer, southern front was built in an ornate baroque style. The wealthy Count of Canal financed an addition to the Oratorio in 1734. Just behind the Oratorio is his **Templo de Santa Casa de Loreto,** dedicated to the Virgin of Loreto. Its main entrance, now blocked by a grille, is on the Oratorio's left rear side. Peer through the grille to see the heavily gilded altars and effigies of the count and his wife, under which they are buried. ⌂ *Calles Insurgentes and Loreto, El Centro* ☎ *No phone.*

**2  La Parroquia.** Designed in the late 19th century by self-trained mason Ceferino Gutiérrez, who sketched his designs in the sand with a stick, this towering Gothic Revival parish church is made of local *cantera* sandstone. Gutiérrez was purportedly inspired by postcards of European Gothic cathedrals. Since the postcards gave no hint of what the back of those cathedrals looked like, the posterior of La Parroquia was done in quintessential Mexican style. La Parroquia still functions as a house of worship, although its interior has changed over the years. Gilded wood altars, for example, were replaced with neoclassical stone altars. The original bell, cast in 1732, still calls parishioners to mass several times daily. ⊠ *South side of El Jardín on Calle Correo, El Centro* ☎ *No phone.*

## Where to Eat

Given its size, San Miguel has a surprisingly large number of international restaurants. The steady influx of American and Canadian visitors supports a variety of Tex-Mex and health-food places. A European influence has contributed to variations on French, Italian, and Spanish themes.

**$$–$$$** ✕ **Bugambilia.** Founded in 1945, Mercedes Arteaga Tovar's restaurant has a well-earned reputation for its fine traditional Mexican cuisine and its romantic setting. Try such classic specialties as *pollo en mole poblano* (chicken coated in a traditional mole sauce) and *sopa azteca* (classic tortilla soup served with a variety of toppings) while listening to the live classical guitarist in the candlelit, tree-filled colonial courtyard. ⊠ *Calle Hidalgo 42, El Centro* ☎ *415/152–0127* ⊟ *MC, V.*

**$$–$$$** ✕ **La Capilla.** Nab a table in the plant-filled courtyard for a nouvelle spin, with choices such as wild mushroom ravioli and carefully crafted desserts. ⊠ *Calle Cuna de Allende 10, El Centro* ☎ *415/152–0698* ⊟ *AE, MC, V* ☉ *Closed Tues.*

**$$–$$$** ✕ **El Market Bistro.** Take your pick of dining spaces here: either a stone-paved garden with a piano or a private dining room with a glowing fireplace. The French menu includes such classics as leek and potato soup, goat cheese salad, and *tournedos rossini,* a marinated sirloin smothered in foie gras, red wine sauce, and mushrooms. ⊠ *Calle Hernández Macías 95, El Centro* ☎ *415/152–3229* ⊟ *AE, MC, V.*

**★ $–$$** ✕ **Harry Bissett's.** This New Orleans–style café and oyster bar reels in the local crowd. The menu is extensive but weekend brunches stand out. Look for the duck gumbo, crab cakes Benedict, and the chocolate truffle cake. ⊠ *Calle Hidalgo 12, El Centro* ☎ *415/152–2645* ⊟ *AE, MC, V.*

**$** ✕ **Bella Italia.** Two pieces of advice for a meal at this family-owned restaurant: ask about the daily specials, and save space for the tiramisu. Lunch is served on the patio, dinner indoors. The staff takes care to recommend a bottle from the rotating list of Italian wines to match the homemade pastas or fish brought from the Sea of Cortez. ⊠ *Calle Hernández Macías 59, El Centro* ☎ *415/152–4989* ⊟ *AE, MC, V.*

**¢–$** ✕ **La Buena Vida.** Don't miss the mouthwatering orange scones, chocolate-chip cookies, lemon bread, baguettes, and breakfast specials at this fabulous bakery and tiny coffee shop. If the few patio tables are full, take your treats to the Jardín. ⊠ *Calle Hernández Macías 72–5, El Centro* ☎ *415/152–2211* ⊟ *No credit cards* ☉ *No dinner.*

## Where to Stay

San Miguel's hotels fill up quickly in summer and winter, when northern tourists migrate here in droves. Make reservations several months in advance if you plan to visit at these times or during the September Independence Day festivities.

**$$$–$$$$** 🏨 **Casa de Sierra Nevada.** Built in 1580 as the archbishop of Guanajuato's residence, this elegant country-style inn still attracts ambassadors, diplomats, film stars, and other luminaries; however, the formerly attentive service has declined. Lace curtains, handwoven rugs, and chandeliers adorn some rooms; fireplaces, cozy terraces, and skylights enhance others. The hotel runs the separate **Casa de Sierra Nevada en el Parque,** an exquisitely restored 18th-century hacienda with five guest rooms. Its restaurant serves refined versions of traditional Mexican dishes and has a sweeping view of Parque Benito Juárez. ⊠ *Calle Hospicio 46, El Centro 37700* ☎ *415/152–7040* 🖷 *415/152–1436* ⤶ *17 rooms, 16 suites* ᗕ *2 restaurants, cable TV, pool, massage, spa, bar, no kids under 10* ⊟ *AE, MC, V* ⊠ *Santa Elena 2, Casa de Sierra Nevada en el Parque, El Centro.*

★ **$$$–$$$$** 🏨 **Casa Quetzal.** Three blocks from the main square, this boutique hotel offers eclectic suites, each with its own characteristic style. A Guatemalan mask or a Chiapan rug might decorate your guest room. ⊠ *Calle Hospicio 34, El Centro 37700* ☎ *415/152–0501* 🖷 *415/152–4961* ⊕ *www. casaquetzalhotel.com* ⤶ *6 suites* ᗕ *Minibars, cable TV, airport shuttle* ⊟ *AE, MC, V* ⦿ *BP.*

**$$$–$$$$** 🏨 **Casa Rosada.** This hotel has the best location in San Miguel, just half a block from the main square. Formerly the Hospital de Naturales de la Purisima Concepción, the colonial building dates from 1792. Guest rooms have a soothingly calm cream-color decor. Two suites have balconies with views of the countryside. ⊠ *Calle Cuna de Allende 12, El Centro 37700* ☎ *415/152–0382* 🖷 *415/152–0382* ⊕ *www. casarosadahotel.com* ⤶ *13 rooms, 4 suites* ᗕ *In-room safes, cable TV, bar* ⦿ *BP* ⊟ *AE, MC, V.*

★ **$$–$$$** 🏨 **Casa Luna Pila Seca.** Each room in this restored 300-year-old Spanish colonial house has antiques or bright folk art, such as painted gourd masks or a carved wooden headboard. Some have vaulted ceilings, others have private patios. The rooftop honor bar is spectacularly lighted by dozens of miniature tin star lights at night. A three-night minimum stay is required; children are allowed only when the entire house is rented to one party. For an open-air, hacienda-style experience, try Casa Luna Quebrada. ⊠ *Calle Pila Seca 11, El Centro 37700* ☎🖷 *415/152–1117* ⊕ *www.casaluna.com* ⤶ *8 rooms, 1 suite* ᗕ *Dining room, massage, shop; no room TVs* ⊟ *MC, V* ⦿ *BP* ⊠ **Casa Luna Quebrada** ⊠ Quebrada 117.

**$$–$$$** 🏨 **Casa Schuck.** American expatriates designed Casa Schuck as a reincarnation of a 19th-century villa. All rooms open onto a gorgeous jacaranda-filled courtyard; from the choicest suite, "The Royal," you'll also have a view of the town's prestigious church. The B&B is just a few blocks off the town's main square. ⊠ *Bajada de Garita 3, El Centro 37700* ☎ *415/152–0657* ⊕ *www.casaschuck.com* ⊟ *MC, V* ⦿ *BP.*

**$** 🏨 **Aristos Hotel.** Positioned on a tranquil, rolling property overlooking downtown San Miguel, Aristos helps you escape the congested town center while still remaining close to the action. Many second-floor rooms have excellent views of La Parroquia and its surrounding area. Rooms are clean and comfortable and the staff is friendly. ⊠ *Calzada del Cardo*

2, *El Centro 37000* ☎ *415/152–0392 or 415/152–3510* ➘ *73 rooms, 4 suites* ᐊ *Restaurant, tennis courts, pool, baby-sitting, laundry service* ▤ *AE, MC, V.*

¢–$ ⊞ **Posada de las Monjas.** Rooms in this 19th-century inn are simply furnished in a colonial style. Several in the old wing are uncomfortably dark and cramped. Head up to the rooftop public terrace for city views; the building is near the hulking dome of the Iglesia de la Concepción. Some rooms have fireplaces, and there's a communal TV in the lobby, which looks like a formal Mexican living room. ✉ *Calle Canal 37, El Centro 37700* ☎ *415/152–0171* 🖷 *415/152–6227* ⊕ *www.posadalasmonjas. com* ➘ *65 rooms* ᐊ *Restaurant, bar, laundry service, free parking; no a/c, no room TVs* ▤ *MC, V.*

# Nightlife & the Arts

## Nightlife

On most evenings in San Miguel you can readily satisfy a whim for a literary reading, an American movie, a theatrical production, or a turn on a dance floor. The most up-to-date listings of events can be found in the English-language paper *Atención San Miguel*, published every Sunday. Biblioteca Pública's bulletin board is also a useful source of current events.

**Agave Azul** (✉ Calle Mesones 99, El Centro ☎ 415/152–1958) draws a crowd for live music, dancing, and, of course, tequila. **Mama Mia** (✉ Calle Umarán 8, El Centro ☎ 415/152–2063) plays everything from Peruvian folk music, classical guitar, and flamenco to salsa and rock. The rotating art exhibitions and comfortable leather chairs at **El Petit Bar** (✉ Calle Hernández Macías 95, El Centro ☎ 415/152–3229) attract a mix of locals and tourists.

## The Arts

Long known as an artists' colony, San Miguel continues to nurture that image today. Galleries, museums, and arty shops line the streets near El Jardín; most close weekdays between 2 and 4 and are open weekends 10 or 11 to 2 or 3. Two government-run salons—at **Bellas Artes** and **Instituto Allende**—feature the work of Mexican artists. The **Galería de Arte Contemporáneo** (✉ Plaza Principal 14, El Centro ☎ 415/152–0454) sells works by contemporary Mexican artists. The two collectors behind the regional and international talent of **Galería Atenea** (✉ Calle Jesús 2, El Centro ☎ 415/152–0785) have a flair for attractive watercolors and Bustamante jewelry. The rambling rooms of **Galería Duo Duo** (✉ Calle Pila Seca 3, El Centro ☎ 415/152–6211) are filled with an eclectic range of items in all price ranges, from handmade scarves to iconographic pillows. **Galería del Pueblo** (✉ Calle Correo 12A, El Centro ☎ 415/152–1448) exhibits an extensive collection of Huichol beadwork and yarn paintings. For a taste of contemporary Mexican art stop by **Galería San Miguel** (✉ Plaza Principal 14, El Centro ☎ 415/152–0454). **Kligerman Gallery** (✉ Calle San Francisco 11, El Centro ☎ 415/152–0951) has contemporary Mexican and American art.

For more than 20 years, San Miguel has played host to August's world-class **Festival de Musica de Camara,** a feast of classical chamber music that has recently included the illustrious Tokyo String Quartet. The **Jazz Festival International** takes place around the last week in November. Tickets for the concerts, workshops, and after-hour jam sessions may be purchased individually or for the series. Call the tourist office for dates and details.

## Sports & the Outdoors

### Ballooning

**Gone with the Wind Balloon Adventures** (⊠ Calle Recreo 68, El Centro ☎ 415/152–6735) offers hot-air balloon rides over town and the surrounding countryside with licensed-certified pilots from Napa Valley, California. The one-hour flights depart at 6 or 7 AM, depending on the season. The $150 cost includes breakfast upon landing.

### Bullfights

Witness the pageantry of a traditional Mexican bullfight at the **Plaza de Toros Oriente** (⊠ Off Calle Recreo, El Centro), which has events several times a year. The most important contest takes place in the last week of September during *la fiesta de San Miguel.* Tickets cost about $3 for a seat in the sun and $10 for a seat in the shade. Call the tourist office for more information.

### Health Clubs

The **Club de Golf Malanquin** (⊠ Celaya Hwy., Km 3 ☎ 415/152–0516 ⊕ www.malanquin.com) has a heated pool, steam baths, tennis courts, and 9 holes of golf, all of which are open to the public for $45 on weekdays or $70 on weekends; it's closed Monday. The exclusive **Hotel Hacienda Taboada** (⊠ Dolores Hidalgo Hwy., Km 8 ☎ 415/152–0888) has several geothermal pools, manicured grounds, and tennis courts. It's open to the public for about $30, which includes lunch; it's closed Wednesday. **Taboada** (⊠ Dolores Hidalgo Hwy., Km 8) has three outdoor geothermally heated pools, one of which is Olympic-size and good for doing laps. They are open to the public for $3.50; it's closed Tuesday.

### Horseback Riding

**Aventuras San Miguel** (⊠ Calle Recreo 10, El Centro ☎ 415/152–6406) rents horses; a two-and-a-half hour tour costs about $35.

## Shopping

For centuries San Miguel's artisans have been creating crafts ranging from straw products to metalwork. Although some boutiques in town may be a bit pricey, you can find good buys on silver, brass, tin, woven-cotton goods, and folk art. Hours tend to be erratic, but most stores open daily at around 9, shut their doors for the traditional afternoon siesta (2 to 4 or 5), then reopen in the afternoon until 7 or 8, and open for just a half day on Sunday. Most San Miguel shops accept MasterCard and Visa.

### Markets

Spilling out for several blocks behind the Mercado Ignacio Ramírez is the **Mercado de Artesanías** (artisans' market), where you'll find vendors of local work—glass, tin, and papier-mâché—as well silver jewelry at

# CloseUp

# HECHO A MANO

**H**ANDMADE IN MEXICO: *some of the world's finest artesanías (crafts) come from this country. Artisanal work is varied, colorful, and inexpensive, and it supports families who carry on ancient and more recent traditions. Although cheap, shoddy items masquerading as "native crafts" are certainly common, careful shoppers can come away with real works of folk art. Keep in mind that many items are exempt from duty.*

*Each region has its specialty. Cities noted for their crafts are Puebla (Chapter 2); Nogales in Sonora (Chapter 4); Guadalajara, Tlaquepaque, and Tonalá in Jalisco (Chapter 6); San Miguel de Allende, Guanajuato, and Pátzcuaro in the Heartland (Chapter 7); Taxco in Morelos (Chapter 9); Oaxaca City in Oaxaca (Chapter 10); San Cristóbal de las Casas in Chiapas (Chapter 11); and Mérida in Yucatán (Chapter 13).*

**Ceramics.** *Talavera-style tiles (blue majolica) and other ceramic ware are best in Puebla. Oaxaca state is known for its unglazed, burnished black pottery. Inventive masks and figurines come from Valle de Bravo, Pátzcuaro in the state of Michoacán, Tonalá outside of Guadalajara, Taxco, and Chiapas.*

**Jewelry.** *For the best quality silver go to Taxco, San Miguel de Allende, and Oaxaca; check for the "925" stamp, which means 92.5% pure silver. Find gold filigree in Guanajuato and Oaxaca. Oaxaca and Chiapas are known for their amber. Beware that much of what's sold as amber is actually glass or plastic: don't buy amber off the street; and if it seems like a great bargain, it's probably fake. For semiprecious stones, go to jewelers' shops in Puebla and Querétaro. Coral jewelry is sold in the Yucatán and other coastal areas, but because of the massive ecological damage caused by coral harvesting, the practice around it is environmentally unsound.*

**Leather.** *Find quality leatherwork in Guadalajara, Oaxaca (for sandals), Chiapas (for belts and purses), or the Yucatán (for bags).*

**Metalwork.** *Look for copper in Santa Clara del Cobre in Michoacán, and tin in San Miguel de Allende and Oaxaca.*

**Weavings and Textiles.** *You'll find rebozos (shawls) and blankets around Oaxaca, Guadalajara, Jalapa, and Pátzcuaro; huipiles (heavily embroidered tunics worn by Indian women) and other embroidered clothing in Michoacán, Oaxaca state, Chiapas, and the Yucatán; masterfully woven rugs, some colored with natural dyes, in Oaxaca; hammocks and baskets in Oaxaca and the Yucatán; lace in the heartland; guayaberas (embroidered or pleated men's dress shirts) along the Gulf coast; and reed mats in Oaxaca and Valle de Bravo. Also rewarding is the Mezquital region east of Querétaro. Shop for Huichol Indian yarn paintings and embroidery near Puerto Vallarta.*

**Woodwork.** *Look for masks in Mexico City; alebrijes (painted wooden animals) in Oaxaca; furniture in Cuernavaca, Guadalajara, San Miguel de Allende, Querétaro, Tequisquiapan, and Pátzcuaro; lacquerware in Uruapan and Pátzcuaro in Michoacán, Chiapa de Corzo in Chiapas, and Puerto Vallarta for pieces from Olinalá in Guerrero state; and guitars in Paracho, Michoacán.*

bargain prices. **Mercado Ignacio Ramírez,** a traditional Mexican covered market off Calle Colegio, one block north of Calle Mesones, is a colorful jumble of fresh fruits and vegetables, flowers, bloody butchers' counters, inexpensive plastic toys, taco stands, and Mexican-made cassettes. Both markets are open daily from around 8 AM until 7.

## Specialty Shops

FOLK ART **Artes de México** (⊠ Calz. Aurora 47, at Dolores Hidalgo exit, Col. Guadalupe ☎ 415/152–0764) has been producing and selling traditional crafts for more than 40 years. **La Calaca** (⊠ Calle Mesones 93, El Centro ☎ 415/152–3954) focuses on antique and contemporary Latin American folk and ceremonial art. Although the inventory at the **Casa Maxwell** (⊠ Calle Canal 14, El Centro ☎ 415/152–0247) has slipped in quality, there's still a reasonable selection of folk art. **La Guadalupana** (⊠ Calle Jesús 25-A, inside Jasmine Day Spa, El Centro ☎ 415/152–7973) only sells items adorned with images of Mexico's beloved Virgin of Guadalupe—from temporary tattoos to coffee mugs. **Talisman Boutique 2** (⊠ Calle San Francisco 7, El Centro ☎ 415/152–0438) sells beautiful embroidered *huipiles* (tunics or blouses) from southern Mexico and Guatemala. **Zócalo** (⊠ Calle Hernández Macías 110, El Centro ☎ 415/152–0663) has vibrant artwork and furniture at fair prices. It's closed on Sunday.

HOUSEWARES **Casa Canal** (⊠ Calle Canal 3, El Centro ☎ 415/152–0479), in a beautiful old hacienda, sells new furniture, most in traditional styles. **Casa María Luisa** (⊠ Calle Canal 40, El Centro ☎ 415/152–0130) has contemporary Mexican furniture, household items, and art. **Casa Vieja** (⊠ Calle Mesones 83, El Centro ☎ 415/152–1284) has tons of glassware and ceramics, housewares, picture frames, furniture, and more. **CLAN destino** (⊠ Calle Zacateros 19, El Centro ☎ 415/152–1623) vends an eclectic international mix of antiques, contemporary art, and jewelry. **México Lindo** (⊠ Calle Mesones 85, El Centro ☎ 415/152–0730) sells a good selection of hand-painted tiles and ceramics from Dolores Hidalgo. **La Zandunga** (⊠ Calle Hernández Macías 129, El Centro ☎ 415/152–4608) sells high-quality, 100% wool rugs from Oaxaca.

JEWELRY Established in 1963, **Joyería David** (⊠Calle Zacateros 53, El Centro ☎415/152–0056) has an extensive selection of gold, silver, copper, and brass jewelry, all made on the premises. Many pieces contain Mexican opals, amethysts, topaz, malachite, and turquoise. **Platería Cerro Blanco** (⊠ Calle Canal 21, El Centro ☎ 415/152–0502) creates and crafts its own silver and gold jewelry and will arrange a visit to its *taller* (workshop) on request. The reputable **7th Heaven** (⊠ Sollano 31, El Centro ☎ 415/154–4677) fashions its own silver, gold, and carved amber pieces.

# Side Trips from San Miguel de Allende

## Dolores Hidalgo
*50 km (31 mi) north of San Miguel via Rte. 51.*

It was here, before dawn on September 16, 1810, that local priest Father Miguel Hidalgo launched Mexico's fight for independence with an impassioned sermon that concluded with the *grito* (cry), "Death to bad government!" Every September 15 at 11 PM, politicians signal the start of Independence Day festivities with a revised version of the grito—"Viva Mexico! Viva Mexico! Viva Mexico!" (Long Live Mexico!). On September 16 (and only on this day), the bell in Hidalgo's parish church is rung.

Dolores Hidalgo is famous for its lovely hand-glazed Talavera-style ceramics, most notably tiles and tableware. The town's numerous stores and factories have reasonable prices. After shopping, head to the plaza for possibly the most exotic ice creams you'll ever taste—flavors such as mole, avocado, beer, and corn. The town is an easy one-hour bus ride from San Miguel de Allende's Central de Autobuses.

Once Father Hidalgo's home, **Casa Hidalgo** is now a museum. It contains copies of important letters Hidalgo sent or received, and other independence memorabilia. ⊠ *Calle Morelos 1* ☎ *418/182–0171* ✉ *About $3* ☉ *Tues.–Sat. 10–5:45, Sun. 10–4:45.*

### Pozos
*35 km (21 mi) northeast of San Miguel de Allende.*

The captivating, high-desert town of Pozos was a silver-mining center in the late 19th century. Now it's almost a ghost town; you can peek at abandoned buildings or the simple, echoing chapel. Rarely will you see another tourist. The Casa Montana hotel is the hub of information and activity; the owner can arrange a tour of the old mines. It has a collection of photos of Pozos and the surrounding area.

Pozos is a 45-minute drive from San Miguel; look for a road marked "Dr. Mora."

WHERE TO STAY  🏨 **Casa Montana.** Steep yourself in the town's colonial atmosphere with
**$$** an overnight stay on its main square. Guest rooms have local artwork, fireplaces, and wonderful deep tubs. Eat on the bouganvillea-filled terraces and if you get the chance, sip a margarita with the owner and listen to her stories about coming to Pozos. Shuttle service is available to both the Guanajuato and Mexico City airports. ⊠ *Jardín Juárez Plaza 37910* ☎ *442/293–0032 or 442/293–0034* ⊕ *www.casamontanahotel. com* ✑ *5 rooms* ⦿ *BP* ♿ *Restaurant, airport shuttle; no a/c, no room TVs* ▤ *MC, V.*

## San Miguel de Allende A to Z

### AIR TRAVEL
AIRPORT  León's Guanajuato International Airport (BJX) is roughly a 1½-hour drive from San Miguel. It's a small airport, so the check-in desks can have long lines.

AIRPORT  Taxis from Guanajuato International Airport to downtown San Miguel
TRANSFERS  cost about $60.

CARRIERS Aeroméxico flies from Los Angeles; American flies from Dallas–Fort Worth; Continental flies from Houston; Mexicana flies from Chicago. Direct flights are available from these cities; you may have connecting flights, usually through Mexico City, if you fly from other areas.
🛪 **Aeroméxico** ☎ 477/714–7156 or 477/716–6226 ⊕ www.aeromexico. com. **American** ☎ 477/714–0483 or 477/716–5551 ⊕ www.aa.com. **Continental** ☎ 477/718–5254 or 477/718–5199 ⊕ www.continental.com. **Mexicana** ☎ 477/716–3697 or 477/714–9500 ⊕ www.mexicana.com.

### BUS TRAVEL
Daily buses run direct from Mexico City's Central del Norte to the Central de Autobuses in San Miguel. Several major lines have frequent service; tickets cost about $24. They include ETN, Flecha Amarilla, Primera Plus, Herradura de Plata, and Pegasso Plus. Travel time is about four hours.
🛪 **ETN** ☎ 415/154–5135 or 415/152–6407. **Flecha Amarilla** ☎ 415/152–7323. **Herradura de Plata** ☎ 415/152–0725. **Pegasso Plus** ☎ 415/152–0725. **Primera Plus** ☎ 415/152–0084.

### CAR RENTAL
Hola Rent a Car has a limited selection of manual-transmission compacts available.
🛪 **Hola Rent a Car** ✉ Plaza Principal 2, Int. 5, El Centro ☎ 415/152–0198.

### CAR TRAVEL
Driving from Mexico City to San Miguel takes roughly 4 hours via Highway 57 (to Querétaro) then Highway 111. Traveling on Highway 45 from Mexico City, a road connecting to Highway 57 and 111, bypasses Querétaro, saving a half hour. Guanajuato is 100 km (62 mi), about 1½ hours, west of San Miguel.

Driving in San Miguel can be frustrating, especially during rush hours; try to avoid the crowded streets in the morning and evening.

### EMBASSIES
The U.S. Consulate is open weekdays 9–1.
🛪 **U.S. Consulate** ✉ Calle Hernández Macías 72, El Centro ☎ 415/152–2357 during office hours, 415/152–0653 or 415/152–0068 for emergencies 🖷 415/152–1588.

### EMERGENCIES
The staff at Hospital de la Fé can refer you to an English-speaking doctor.

San Miguel has many pharmacies. American residents recommend Botica Agundis, where English speakers are often on hand. It's open daily 10:30 AM–11 PM.
🛪 Emergency Contacts **Ambulance–Red Cross** ☎ 415/152–4121 or 415/152–4225. **Fire Department** ☎ 415/152–2888. **Police** ☎ 415/152–0022. **Traffic Police** ☎ 415/152–0538.
🛪 Hospital **Hospital de la Fé** ✉ El Libramiento at Dolores Hidalgo 43, Mesa el Malanquin ☎ 415/152–2233 or 415/152–2320.
🛪 Pharmacy **Botica Agundis** ✉ Calle Canal 26, El Centro ☎ 415/152–1198.

## ENGLISH-LANGUAGE MEDIA

El Colibrí has an extensive selection of paperback novels, magazines, and a few art supplies. Libros el Tecolote has new and used books on Mexican art, history, literature, and cooking.

**El Colibrí** ⊠ Sollano 30, El Centro ☎ 415/152–0751. **Libros el Tecolote** ⊠ Calle Jesús 11, El Centro ☎☎ 415/152–7395.

## MAIL, INTERNET & SHIPPING

Border Crossings offers 24-hour answering and fax service, a Mexico address for receiving mail, packing and shipping, e-mail, a gift shop and art gallery, and other services. Internet service costs about $1.50 an hour. Internet San Miguel charges $3 an hour for the fastest Internet access in town. Coffee, beer, and fresh juices are available.

**Border Crossings** ⊠ Correo 19, Int. 2, El Centro ☎415/152–2497 ☎415/ 152–3672. **Internet San Miguel** ⊠ Calle Mesones 57, side entrance at Relox, El Centro ☎ 415/154–4634 ⊕ www.internetsanmiguel.com.

## MONEY MATTERS

A better bet for money exchange than the slow-moving bank lines is Intercam, open weekdays 9–6, Saturday 9–2.

**Intercam** ⊠ Calles San Francisco 4, Correo 15, or Juárez 27, El Centro ☎ 415/154–6660.

## TAXIS

You can easily hail a taxi on the street or find one at taxi stands—such as Sitio Allende in the main plaza. Flat rates to the bus terminal, train station, and other parts of the city apply. It's safe to hail taxis on the street in San Miguel.

**Sitio Allende** ☎ 415/152–0192.

## TOURS

Colonial México Tours runs historical tours to Guanajuato, Querétaro, and Dolores Hidalgo. Recommended for local and surrounding area tours is PMC (Promotion of Mexican Culture).

**Information Colonial México Tours** ⊠ Plaza Portal Allende 4, 2nd floor, El Centro ☎☎ 415/152–5794. **PMC** ⊠ Calle Cuna de Allende 11, El Centro ☎ 415/152–1630 ☎ 415/152–0121.

## TRANSPORTATION AROUND SAN MIGUEL DE ALLENDE

San Miguel de Allende is best covered on foot, keeping in mind two pieces of advice. First of all, the city is more than a mile above sea level, so you might tire quickly during your first few days if you aren't accustomed to high altitudes. Secondly, streets are paved with rugged cobblestones, and some have no sidewalks. Wear sturdy footwear, such as athletic or other rubber-sole walking shoes.

## TRAVEL AGENCIES

Viajes Vértiz is the American Express representative in San Miguel.

**Local Agent Referral Viajes Vértiz** ⊠ Calle Hidalgo 1A, El Centro ☎ 415/ 152–1856 or 415/152–1695 ☎ 415/152–0499.

**VISITOR INFORMATION**

Delegación de Turismo, on the southeast corner of El Jardín, in a glassed-in office next to la Terraza restaurant, is open weekdays 10–5, Saturday 10–2. Although the tourism board doesn't have a Web site, ⊕ www.portalsanmiguel.com is a helpful Internet resource, with info on local galleries, restaurants, community events and services, real estate, and so on. For information on Pozos, check ⊕ www.mineraldepozos.com.
🚩 **Delegación de Turismo** ☎ 415/152–6565.

# GUANAJUATO

➤ *100 km (62 mi) west of San Miguel de Allende, 365 km (226 mi) northwest of Mexico City.*

Colonial Guanajuato, formerly Mexico's most prominent silver-mining city, is nestled in the mountains at 6,700 feet. This provincial state capital is distinguished by twisting cobblestone alleyways, colorful houses, 15 shaded plazas, and a vast subterranean roadway where a rushing river once coursed. In the town's center is **Alhóndiga de Granaditas,** an 18th-century grain-storage facility that was the site of Mexico's first major victory in its War of Independence from Spain.

The city is swarmed in mid-October with the Festival Internacional Cervantino (International Cervantes Festival), a three-week celebration of the arts. Things keep a steady, lively pace during the rest of the year. Students rush to class with books tucked under their arms, women eye fresh produce at the Mercado Hidalgo, and old men greet each other from whitewashed doorways. On weekend nights, *estudiantinas* (student minstrels dressed as medieval troubadours) serenade the public in the city squares.

## Exploring Guanajuato

Although they're initially confusing, Guanajuato's many plazas and labyrinthine streets are actually easy to navigate. The center is small, and there are surprises around every corner. Remember that the top of the Alhóndiga (which you can see from many spots in town) points north, and the spires of the Basílica Colegiata Nuestra Señora de Guanajuato, at Plaza de la Paz, point south. Thanks to the underground roads, you can meander the city center without the usual traffic.

**a good walk**

The tourist office, at Plaza de la Paz 14 ➤, is a convenient place to begin a walking tour. Turn right and walk up Obregón to reach **Jardín Unión** ⑫, Guanajuato's central square. The ornate **Teatro Juárez** ⑬ is past the Jardín to your right on Calle Sopeña. Lovers of art and Don Quixote shouldn't miss the **Museo Iconográfico del Quijote** ⑭, which is a short walk east on Sopeña from Teatro Juárez. Hardier visitors may opt for the half-hour climb to **El Pípila** ⑮ as a detour. Honoring one of the heroes of the War of Independence of 1810, this monument looms over the city's center. To reach it, bear right on Calle Sopeña past Teatro Juárez. A sign marked EL PÍPILA will direct you onto Callejón de Calvario, which eventually leads to the hillside memorial. Of course you can also reach El Pípila by cable car. The entrance is behind the theater.

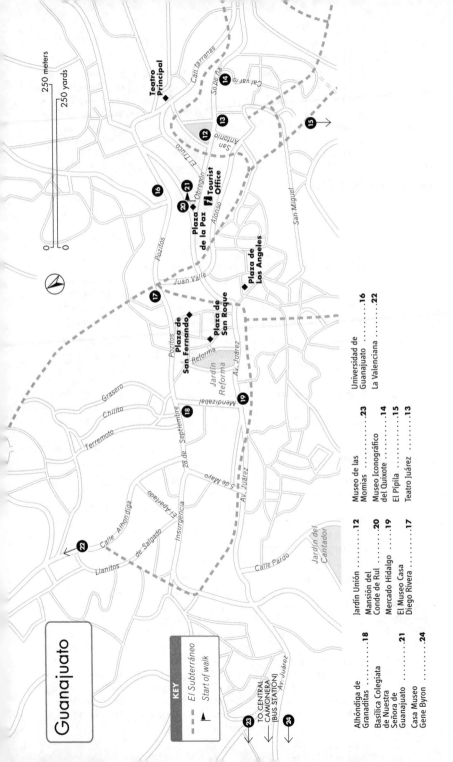

# Guanajuato

**KEY**

- – – El Subterráneo
- ▲ Start of walk

250 meters
250 yards

Teatro Principal ♦

Cantarranas

Soperna

Calvario

**14**

**13**

**12**

El Truco

San Antonio

**15** →

**16**

**21**
**20** ♦
**Plaza de la Paz**
Obregón
**Tourist Office** ℹ
Alonso

Pozitos

Juan Valle

**17**

Pozitos

**Plaza de San Fernando** ♦
**Plaza de San Roque** ♦

San Miguel

**Plaza de Los Angeles** ♦

Jardín Reforma
Reforma
Av. Juárez

Grasero

Chilito

Mendizábal

**19**

Terremoto

28 de Septiembre

**18**

5 de Mayo

Calle Alhóndiga

El Apartado

Insurgencia

de Salgado

**22** ←

Llanitos

Jardín del Cantador

Calle Pardo

**23** ↓
TO CENTRAL
CAMIONERA
(BUS STATION)

**24** ↓
Av. Juárez

Alhóndiga de Granaditas . . . . . . . . . .**18**
Basílica Colegiata de Nuestra Señora de Guanajuato . . . . . . . .**21**
Casa Museo Gene Byron . . . . . . . . . .**24**

Jardín Unión . . . . . . . . .**12**
Mansión del Conde de Rul . . . . . . .**20**
Mercado Hidalgo . . . .**19**
El Museo Casa Diego Rivera . . . . . . . .**17**

Museo de las Momías . . . . . . . . . . . .**23**
Museo Iconográfico del Quixote . . . . . . .**14**
El Pípila . . . . . . . . . .**15**
Teatro Juárez . . . . . . .**13**

Universidad de Guanajuato . . . . . . . .**16**
La Valenciana . . . . . . .**22**

Return to town on Calle Cantarranas, a main street that winds down the hill and around the Jardín Unión. Just before Calle Cantarranas changes its name to Calle Pozitos, you'll see the **Universidad de Guanajuato** ⑯. A short way down from where the name changes is **El Museo Casa Diego Rivera** ⑰, birthplace of Mexico's famous muralist. Calle Pozitos weaves past more residences and eventually becomes Calle 28 de Septiembre. On the left, just past the junction with Mendizabal, is the **Alhóndiga de Granaditas** ⑱, a former fortress converted into a state museum. Go one block south to return to Avenida Juárez and the glassed-in **Mercado Hidalgo** ⑲.

As you leave the market, turn right on Juárez and continue until the road splits near the Jardín Reforma. Bear left and cut down Calle Reforma, a short alley lined with shops. Keep right at the end of the street and you'll arrive at two courtyards: Plaza de San Roque, which hosts outdoor performances during the Cervantes Festival, and Plaza de San Fernando, a shady square where book fairs are held. After the Plaza de San Roque continue southeast and this short detour will return you to Avenida Juárez, where it's a slight climb up to Plaza de la Paz, a 19th-century square surrounded by some of the city's finest colonial buildings, including the 18th-century **Mansión del Conde de Rul** ⑳. The bright-yellow 17th-century baroque **Basílica Colegiata de Nuestra Señora de Guanajuato** ㉑ dominates the plaza. If you continue up Avenida Juárez about a half block past the plaza, you'll pass the tourist office again and arrive back at the Jardín Unión. Catch a bus from the city center to reach the colonial church **La Valenciana** ㉒. If you prefer the macabre to gilding, take a taxi up Avenida Juárez to **Museo de las Momias** ㉓. For a taste of vintage hacienda-style living and modern Mexican art, take a taxi to **Casa Museo Gene Byron** ㉔ on the west side of town.

TIMING    A walk around the center of town will take a couple of hours. Remember that most museums and the theater are closed Monday.

## What to See

⑱ **Alhóndiga de Granaditas.** Previously this 18th-century grain-storage facility served as a jail under Emperor Maximilian and as a fortress during the War of Independence, where El Pípila helped the revolutionaries overcome the royalists. The hooks on which the Spanish Royalists hung the severed heads of Father Hidalgo, Ignacio Allende, and two other independence leaders still dangle on the exterior of this massive stone structure. It's now a state museum with exhibits on local history, archaeology, and crafts. ☒ *Calle 28 de Septiembre 6, El Centro* ☎ *473/732–1112* 🖃 *About $3* ☉ *Tues.–Sat. 10–1:30 and 4–5:30, Sun. 10–2:30.*

㉑ **Basílica Colegiata de Nuestra Señora de Guanajuato.** Painted in a striking yellow, the Basílica is a 17th-century baroque church that dominates Plaza de la Paz. Inside is Mexico's oldest Christian statue: a bejeweled 8th-century Virgin. The venerated figure was a gift from King Philip II of Spain in 1557. On the Friday preceding Good Friday, miners, accompanied by floats and mariachi bands, parade to the Basílica to pay homage to the Lady of Guanajuato. ☒ *Plaza de la Paz, El Centro* ☎ *No phone* ☉ *Daily 9–8.*

**㉔ Casa Museo Gene Byron.** The husband of Canadian artist Gene Byron converted her restored hacienda into this museum following her death in 1987. Byron's home is as she left it, with vintage furniture and accessories and an eclectic art collection, including some of Byron's own sculptures and paintings. Workshops on jewelry-making, theater, stained glass, writing, and art history are held on a regular basis. Rotating exhibits feature up-and-coming Mexican artists. ⊠ *Ex-Hacienda Santa Ana s/n, Marfil* 🕾 *473/733–1029* ☉ *Tues.–Sat. 10–5, Sun. 10–3.*

**⑫ Jardín Unión.** Guanajuato's central square is a tree-lined, wedge-shaped plaza, bordered on three sides by pedestrian walkways. There are musical performances in the plaza's band shell on Tuesday, Thursday, and Sunday evenings; at other times, groups of musicians break into impromptu song along the shaded tile walkways.

> **need a break?** Go to the terrace at the **Hotel Museo Posada Santa Fé** (⊠ Jardín Unión 12, El Centro 🕾 473/732–0084) for alfresco dining at the Jardín. Try the *pozole estilo Guanajuato* (hominy soup to which you can add onions, radishes, lettuce, lime, and chili peppers).

**⑳ Mansión del Conde de Rul.** Once the residence of the count of Rul and Valenciana, who owned Mexico's then-richest silver mine (La Valenciana), this 18th-century mansion is now a courthouse. Famed Mexican architect Eduardo Tresguerras designed this two-story structure in a handsome French Neoclassical design. Though most of the mansion has been taken over by judges and lawyers, the chapel is still in its original state and is open to the public. ⊠ *Plaza de la Paz at Av. Juárez and Callejón del Estudiante, El Centro* 🕾 *No phone* 🎟 *Free* ☉ *Weekdays 8–6.*

**⑲ Mercado Hidalgo.** Don't miss this 1910 cast-iron-and-glass structure, designed by the one-and-only Gustave Eiffel. T-shirts and cheap plastic toys fill the balcony stalls, but the lower level is full of authentic local wares and colorful basketry, as well as fresh produce, peanuts, and honey-drenched nut candies shaped like mummies. ⊠ *Calle Juárez near Mendizabal, El Centro* ☉ *Daily 7 AM–9 PM.*

★ **⑰ El Museo Casa Diego Rivera.** The birthplace of Diego Rivera contains family portraits, furniture, and works by Mexico's foremost muralist; among them are his studies for the controversial mural commissioned for New York City's Rockefeller Center. Completed in 1933 the mural's portrait of Lenin and overall Communist bent prompted Rivera's benefactors to destroy it immediately after it was displayed. The museum's upper galleries show revolving contemporary art exhibitions. ⊠ *Calle Pozitos 47, El Centro* 🕾 *473/732–1197* 🎟 *$1.50* ☉ *Tues.–Sat. 10–6:30, Sun. 10–2:30.*

**㉓ Museo de las Momias.** Mummified human corpses—once buried in the municipal cemetery off Calzada del Panteón—are on display in this unique, though run-down, museum at the town's west end. Until the law was amended in 1858, if a grave site hadn't been paid for after five years, the corpse was removed to make room for new arrivals. Because of the mineral properties of the local soil, these cadavers (the oldest is over 130 years old) were in astonishingly good condition upon exhumation. Some of them are exhibited in glass cases. You'll need to catch a cab to get here; it's atop a steep hill. ⊠ *Panteón Municipal* ☎ *473/732–0639* ⬚ *$5* ☺ *Daily 9–6.*

★ ⓮ **Museo Iconográfico del Quijote.** During his imprisonment in a Spanish concentration camp, Spanish writer and journalist Eulalio Ferrer was so uplifted by Miguel de Cervantes's classic novel that he developed a lifelong passion for *Don Quixote.* This restored 19th-century home is a museum, which displays Ferrer's collection of over 600 pieces, all dedicated to *el hombre de la Mancha* (the man of La Mancha). Gathered after he fled Fascist Spain for Mexico, the star-studded gallery includes works by Salvador Dali, Pablo Picasso, Jose Luis Cuevas, and Alfredo Zalce. ⊠ *Manuel Doblado 1, Centro* ☎ *473/732–6721 or 473/732–3376* ⬚ *www. guanajuato.gob.mx/museo/index.html* ⬚ *$2; free Sun.* ☺ *Tues.–Sat. 10:30–6:30, Sun. 10:30–2:30; closed Mon.*

⓯ **El Pípila.** A half-hour climb or short cable-car ride from downtown is this statue of Juan José de los Reyes Martínez, a young miner and hero of the War of Independence of 1810. Nicknamed El Pípila, de los Reyes crept into the Alhóndiga de Granaditas, where Spanish Royalists were hiding, and set the door ablaze. This enabled Father Hidalgo's army to capture the Spanish troops in this first major military victory for the independence forces. The monument has spectacular city views. Funiculars run daily from 9–10 and cost about $2 for the round-trip. ⊠ *Carretera Panorámica, on bluff above south side of Jardín Unión, El Centro.*

⓭ **Teatro Juárez.** Adorned with bronze lion sculptures and a line of large Greek muses overlooking the Jardín Unión from the roof, the theater was inaugurated by Mexican dictator Porfirio Díaz in 1903 with a performance of *Aïda.* It now serves as the principal venue of the annual International Cervantes Festival. You can take a brief tour of the art deco interior. ⊠ *Calle Sopeña s/n, El Centro* ☎ *473/732–0183* ⬚ *$1.50* ☺ *Tues.–Sun. 9–1:45 and 5–7:45.*

**need a break?**

**El Café** (⊠ Calle Sopeña 10, El Centro ☎ 473/732–2566) has indoor and outdoor tables next to Teatro Juárez and serves soups and sandwiches, as well as an assortment of spiked specialty coffees— among them *cafe diable* (coffee, rum, and lemon juice).

⓰ **Universidad de Guanajuato.** Founded in 1732, the university was formerly a Jesuit seminary. The original churrigueresque church, **La Compañía,** still stands next door. The facade of the university building, built in 1955, was designed to blend in with the town's architecture. If you do wander inside, check the bulletin boards for the town's cultural events. ⊠ *Calle Lascurain de Retana 5, ½ block north of Plaza de la Paz, El Centro* ☎ *473/732–0006* ☺ *Weekdays 8–3:30.*

★ ㉒ **La Valenciana.** Officially called La Iglesia de San Cayetano, this is one of the best-known colonial churches in Mexico. The mid- to late-18th-century pink-stone facade is brilliantly ornate. Inside are three altars, each hand-carved in wood and gilded, in different styles: plateresque, churrigueresque, and baroque. There are also religious paintings from the viceregal period. Near the church is Mina y Bocamina Valenciana, a silver mine discovered in 1529 that yielded ore until the early 1800s. Both the mine and church are included in any of Guanajuato's guided tours, and buses (marked LA VALENCIANA) frequently make the trip from the city center. ⊠ *Carretera Guanajuato–Dolores Hidalgo, Km 2* ☎ *No phone* ☉ *Daily 9–6* 🎫 *Mine tour $3.*

## Where to Eat

The best restaurants in Guanajuato are in hotels near the Jardín Unión and on the highway to Dolores Hidalgo. For simpler fare, private eateries around town offer Mexican and international dishes. Dress tends to be casual.

★ **$$** ✕ **Chez Nicole.** Ask for a garden table at this lovely French restaurant, which has first-rate food and service. One favorite is the sole with white asparagus spears and mashed *camote* (sweet potato). For dessert select the chocolate crepes with kiwis and plums. ⊠ *Calle Arcos de Guadalupe 3, Marfil* ☎ *473/733–1013* 🖃 *AE, MC, V* ☉ *Closed Mon.*

**$-$$** ✕ **Casa del Conde de la Valenciana.** Across the street from La Valenciana is this refurbished 18th-century home, which prepares impeccable, traditional Mexican and international fare. Among the menu's highlights are the fresh gazpacho served in a bowl made of ice, tender *lomo en salsa de ciruela pasa* (pork shoulder in prune sauce), and *pollo a la flor de calabaza* (chicken with poblano chili slices and squash-blossom sauce). Round out the meal with mango ice cream served in the rind. ⊠ *Carretera Guanajuato–Dolores Hidalgo, Km 5, La Valenciana* ☎ *473/ 732–2550* 🖃 *MC, V* ☉ *Closed Sun. No dinner.*

**$-$$** ✕ **El Comedor Real.** Indulge in the chef's namesake special here—the *filete Domenech,* a tender fillet of beef on a potato pancake wrapped in a woven pasta basket. Troubadours perform every Friday and Saturday at 10:30 PM at La Cava, the bar next door. ⊠ *Camino a la Valenciana s/n, Km 1, La Valenciana* ☎ *473/732–0485* 🖃 *AE, MC, V.*

★ **$** ✕ **La Casona Del Cielo.** Crowds come here eager to try the creative menu's bold flavors. For example, there's the *huitlacoche* (a corn fungus delicacy) and crocodile meat. Tamer options exist, too, such as tender beef and homemade ice cream. ⊠ *Calle Pastita 76, Presa* ☎ *473/ 731–2000* 🖃 *AE, MC, V.*

**$** ✕ **El Gallo Pitagórico.** Travail the 100-plus steps up to this restaurant's threshold and you'll be rewarded with an exceptional view of downtown Guanajuato, as well as the mouth-watering house specialty, *filetto Claudio* (fillet marinated in olive oil, capers, parsley, and garlic). Save room for the velvety tiramisu. Weather permitting, have your aperitif in the top-story bar, which has a more dazzling view than that of the restaurant. ⊠ *Constancia 10, behind the Teatro Juárez, El Centro* ☎ *473/732–9489* 🖃 *MC, V.*

**¢** ✕ **El Unicorno Azul.** If you're weary of meat dishes, swing by this food counter behind Jardín Unión: it serves fruit, yogurt, and vegetarian burgers and sandwiches. The owner will cheerfully recommend other health-food places and yoga classes. ⊠ *Plaza del Baratillo 2, El Centro* ☎ *473/732–0700* 🖃 *MC, V* ☉ *Closed Sun.*

## Where to Stay

The least expensive hotels in Guanajuato are along Avenida Juárez and Calle de la Alhóndiga. Moderately priced and upscale properties are near the Jardín Unión and on the outskirts of town. If you plan on attending the Cervantes Festival, which usually runs from mid- to late October, try to secure reservations at least six months in advance.

★ **$$–$$$** 🏨 **La Casa de Espiritus Alegres Bed and Breakfast.** Folk-art lovers are drawn to this "house of good spirits" for its collection of extraordinary crafts from every state in Mexico. Owned by a California artist, the lovingly restored hacienda (circa 1700) has thick stone walls and serene grounds profuse with bougainvillea, banana trees, and calla lilies. Hand-glazed tile baths, fireplaces, and private terraces are standard with each room. Marfil is a 15-minute drive from the center of town—frequent bus service is available. ⊠ *La Ex-Hacienda La Trinidad 1, 36250 Marfil* 🕿 *473/733–1013* ⊕ *www.casaspirit.com* 🛏 *6 rooms, 2 suites* ⚫ *Bar, library, shop, laundry service, free parking; no a/c, no room TVs, no kids under 13* ⊟ *No credit cards* ⦿I *BP.*

**$$–$$$** 🏨 **Hotel Misión Guanajuato.** Built around the former Hacienda San Gabriel's shell, this hotel combines newer rooms with a restored section of the hacienda, which has rooms full of 17th-century furniture and beautiful gardens. Opt for valet parking as the road here is very curvy; self-parking can be precarious and requires a steep cobblestone climb/descent from the hotel's entrance. ⊠ *Camino Antiguo a Marfil, Km 2.5, Marfil 36250* 🕿 *473/732–3980* 🛏 *138 rooms* ⚫ *Restaurant, cable TV, pool, Internet* ⊟ *MC, V* ⦿I *BP.*

**$$** 🏨 **Hostería del Frayle.** Formerly the Casa de Moneda, where ore was taken to be refined after leaving the mines, this quiet four-story lodging was built in 1673 and turned into a hotel in the mid-1960s. It has whitewashed plaster and wood-beam rooms (which nonetheless are somewhat dark) arranged around a small maze of stairways, landings, and courtyards. Some rooms have excellent views of the Pípila, Teatro Juárez, and Jardín Unión, which is a half-block away. The staff is extremely friendly and helpful. ⊠ *Calle Sopeña 3, El Centro 36000* 🕿 *473/732–1179* 🛏 *32 rooms, 5 suites* ⚫ *Restaurant, cable TV, bar, laundry service* ⊟ *MC, V.*

**$$** 🏨 **Hotel Museo Posada Santa Fé.** This colonial-style inn, at the Jardín Unión, has been in operation since 1862. Large historic paintings by local artist Don Manuel Leal hang in the wood-paneled lobby. Rooms facing the plaza can be noisy; quieter rooms face narrow alleyways. ⊠ *Plaza Principal at Jardín Unión 12, El Centro 36000* 🕿 *473/732–0084* 🖶 *473/732–4653* 🛏 *47 rooms, 9 suites* ⚫ *Restaurant, cable TV, bar, laundry service, free parking; no a/c* ⊟ *AE, MC, V* ⦿I *BP.*

**$$** 🏨 **Parador San Javier.** Remnants from the Hacienda San Javier, like a safe and old wood trunks, still decorate the large, plant-filled lobby of this immaculately restored hacienda, which was converted into a hotel in 1971. The rooms are clean and spacious with appealing blue-and-white-tile baths. Several of the 16 colonial-style rooms can be reached via a stone archway and have fireplaces. The adjoining high-rise has newer rooms with satellite TVs. Large convention groups sometimes crowd the facility. ⊠ *Plaza Aldama 92, El Centro 36020* 🕿 *473/732–0626* 🖶 *473/*

*732–3114* 🖀 *99 rooms, 12 suites* ♻ *Restaurant, café, pool, bar, dance club, free parking* 🚬 *AE, MC, V.*

¢ 🖭 **Hotel Socavón.** Don't be put off by the gloomy, tunnel-like entrance of this modest five-story property: open-air walkways, with views of surrounding mountains, lead to guest quarters. Each small room—simply furnished with a bed, desk, and tiny TV—has a wood-beam ceiling and a modern bath. Fourth-floor corner rooms have good views. ⊠ *Calle de la Alhóndiga 41A, El Centro 36000* 🖀 *473/732–6666* 🖭🖭 *473/732–7344* 🖀 *40 rooms* ♻ *Restaurant, bar, free parking* 🚬 *AE, MC, V.*

## Nightlife & the Arts

On most nights a somnolent provincial capital, Guanajuato awakens each fall for the **International Cervantes Festival** (⊠ Plaza de San Francisquito 1, El Centro 🖀 473/731–1150 or 473/731–1161, 532/325–9000 Ticketmaster 🖭 473/732–6775). For three weeks in October world-renowned actors, musicians, and dance troupes perform nightly at the Teatro Juárez and other local venues. Plaza San Roque, a small square near the Jardín Reforma, hosts a series of *Entremeses Cervantinos*—swashbuckling one-act farces by classical Spanish writers. Grandstand seats require advance tickets, but crowds often gather by the plaza's edge to watch for free. If you're going to be among the hundreds of thousands who attend the festivities annually, contact the Festival Internacional Cervantino office at least six months in advance to secure tickets for top-billed events.

When it's not festival season, Guanajuato's nightlife consists of dramatic, dance, and musical performances at **Teatro Juárez** (⊠ Calle Sopeña s/n, El Centro 🖀 473/732–0183). Friday and Saturday at 8 PM, *callejoneadas* (mobile musical parties) begin in front of Teatro Juárez and meander through town (don't forget to tip the musicians). Several nightclubs are in or near the downtown area, including **El Bar** (⊠ Calle Sopeña 10, El Centro 🖀 473/732–2566), where students gather for drinks and salsa dancing. On Friday and Saturday nights there's live music at the **Castillo Santa Cecilia** (⊠ Camino a la Valenciana s/n, Km 1, La Valenciana 🖀 473/732–0485). **La Dama de las Camelias** (⊠ Calle Sopeña 32, El Centro) has lively music and dancing most nights.

## Shopping

**Artesanías Vázques** (⊠ Calle Cantarranas 8 🖭🖭 473/732–5231) has Talavera ceramics from Dolores Hidalgo. Browse the painterly, old-style majolica ceramics at **Capelo** (⊠ Cerro de la Cruz s/n, a dirt road off the Guanajuato–Dolores Hidalgo Hwy., past La Valenciana 🖀 473/732–8964). **Casa del Conde de la Valenciana** (⊠ Carretera Guanajuato–Dolores Hidalgo, Km 5, La Valenciana 🖀 473/732–2550) specializes in brass, tin, ceramic, and wrought-iron home decorations from Mexico and Africa. The **Gorky González Workshop** (⊠ Pastita Ex-huerta de Montenegro s/n, past the baseball stadium 🖀 473/731–0389) offers high-quality ceramics (at a higher price). Some jewelry and regional knickknacks are sold at the **Mercado Hidalgo** (⊠ Calle Juárez near Mendizabal, El Centro). Shops around Plaza de la Paz and Jardín Unión sell ceramics, woolen shawls, and sweaters. Street vendors and shops clustered near La Valenciana and La Valencia sell silver.

## Side Trip to León

*56 km (35 mi) northwest of Guanajuato.*

With over 1 million people, León is the state's most populous urban area. Best known as the shoe-making capital of Mexico, it's also an important center for industry and commerce.

With the time and patience to browse downtown shops, you might find some bargains in León. First try the **Plaza del Zapato,** a mall with 70 stores on Boulevard Adolfo López Mateos, roughly one block from the bus station. From here take a taxi west (about a 10-minute ride) to the **Zona Peatonal,** a pedestrian zone with several shoe stores. On **Calle Praxedis Guerrero,** various artisans' stands sell leather goods.

Flecha Amarilla buses leave Guanajuato's Central Camionera every 15 minutes for León; the ride takes about 45 minutes and costs less than $3. If you opt to drive take Highway 45 directly to León; the drive takes a little more than half an hour.

## Guanajuato A to Z

### AIR TRAVEL

AIRPORT   León's Guanajuato International Airport (BJX) is 40 km (25 mi) west of the city.

AIRPORT TRANSFERS   A taxi ride from the airport to Guanajuato costs about $30 and takes around 30–45 minutes.

CARRIERS   Aeroméxico flies from Los Angeles; American from Dallas–Fort Worth; Continental from Houston; and Mexicana from Chicago.
➤ **Aeroméxico** ☎ 477/714–7156 or 477/716–6226 ⊕ www.aeromexico. com. **American** ☎ 477/714–0483 or 477/716–5551 ⊕ www.aa.com. **Continental** ☎ 477/718–5254 or 477/718–5199 ⊕ www.continental.com. **Mexicana** ☎ 477/716–3697 or 477/714–9500 ⊕ www.mexicana.com.

### BUS TRAVEL

There are several options for direct bus service between Mexico City's Central del Norte and Guanajuato's Central Camionera. Flecha Amarilla offers hourly service daily. For frequent first-class service use Estrella Blanca. The trip takes around five hours and tickets cost $28. Deluxe buses, including those of Primera Plus (Flecha Amarilla's first-class service) and ETN, connect Guanajuato to Mexico City, San Miguel, and Guadalajara. There are several departures daily. The trip between Guanajuato and San Miguel takes a little over an hour; the ride between Guanajuato and Guadalajara lasts four hours. Taxis to downtown Guanajuato from the Camionera cost $2–$3.
➤ **Estrella Blanca** ☎ 473/733–1344. **ETN** ☎ 473/733–1579. **Flecha Amarilla** ☎ 473/733–1332 or 473/733–1333. **Primera Plus** ☎ 473/733–1332 or 473/733–1333.

## CAR TRAVEL

Guanajuato is 365 km (226 mi), or about five hours, northwest of Mexico City via Highway 57 (to Querétaro), then Highway 45. San Miguel de Allende is about an hour and a half away from Guanajuato via Highways 110 and 51.

You won't need a car in central Guanajuato. Many of the attractions are within strolling distance of one another and located between Avenida Juárez and Calle Pozitos, the city's two major north–south arteries. The twisting subterranean roadway—El Subterráneo—also has a primarily north–south orientation.

## EMERGENCIES

Few people in Guanajuato have a good command of English, so in an emergency it's best to contact your hotel manager or the tourist office.

El Fénix (pharmacy) is open Monday–Saturday 8 AM–9:45 PM, Sunday 9–9.

🔒 **Ambulance–Red Cross** ☎ 473/732–0487. **El Fénix** ✉ Av. Juárez 104, El Centro ☎ 473/732–6140. **Hospital General** ☎ 473/733–1577. **Police** ☎ 473/732–0266.

## INTERNET

Redes Internet, open weekdays 9:30–8 and Saturday 10–3, charges $3 an hour for Internet access.

🔒 **Internet Café Redes Internet** ✉ Alonso 70, El Centro ☎ 473/732–0611.

## MONEY MATTERS

There are several currency exchange points and banks with ATMs in Guanajuato's center, mostly along Sopeña and Obregon street.

## TAXIS

You can find taxis at *sitios* (taxi stands) near the Jardín Unión, Plaza de la Paz, and Mercado Hidalgo.

Taxis between León and Guanajuato cost about $17 one way.

## TOURS

The following tour operators give half- and full-day tours with English-speaking guides. These tours typically include the Museo de las Momias, the church and mines of La Valenciana, the monument to Pípila, the Panoramic Highway, subterranean streets, and residential neighborhoods. Night tours often begin at El Pípila for a view of the city lights and end at a dance club. Estudiantinas usually perform during the weekend tours. The state tourism ministry recommends Juvenal Díaz López. Friendly and full of local knowledge, Díaz tailors tours of Guanajuato and its surrounding areas to your specific needs.

🔒 **Tour Operator Recommendations Juvenal Díaz López** ☎ 473/733–3026 or 473/560–1969. **Transporte Exclusivo de Turismo** ✉ Av. Juárez at Calle 5 de Mayo, El Centro ☎ 473/732–5968. **Transporte Turísticos de Guanajuato** ✉ Plaza de la Paz 2, by Basílica de Guanajuato, El Centro ☎ 473/732–2134 or 473/732–2838.

**TRAVEL AGENCIES**

Viajes Georama is the local American Express representative. Viajes Frausto is reliable for hotel and airline reservations.

🔝 Local Agent Referrals **Viajes Frausto** ⊠ Calle González Obregón 10, El Centro ☎ 473/732–3580 🖷 473/732–6620. **Viajes Georama** ⊠ Plaza de la Paz 34, El Centro ☎ 473/732–5909 🖷 473/732–1954.

**VISITOR INFORMATION**

The Guanajuato tourist office is open daily 9–7. You can pick up a map of León there. The local government Web site, ⊕ www.guanajuato. gob.mx, has some basic information in English on the area's historical background, culture, and architecture.

🔝 **Guanajuato tourist office** ⊠ Plaza de la Paz 14, El Centro ☎ 473/732– 1574 or 473/732–1982 Ext. 107 🖷 473/732–4251.

# ZACATECAS

*603 km (375 mi) northwest of Mexico City.*

In colonial days Zacatecas was the largest silver-producing city in the world, shipping the king of Spain great treasures of the precious metal. To this day a silver-mining center, with factories producing jewelry and trade schools training apprentices in the art of handmade silver craft, Zacatecas is relatively undiscovered by foreigners. Designated a UNESCO World Heritage Site in 1993 in recognition of its 18th-century colonial architecture, Zacatecas was also the site of one of Pancho Villa's most spectacular battles.

Although it's a state capital with a population of some 300,000, Zacatecas has a small-town feel with its spotlessly clean streets. Among the town's charms is its *tambora,* a musical parade up and down the streets and alleyways led by a *tamborazo,* a local band that shatters the evening quiet with merriment. Also known as a *callejoneada* (*callejón* means "alley"), the tambora is a popular free-for-all, in which everyone along the way either joins in the procession or cheers from balconies and doorways. During the December *feria* (festival), the tamborazos serenade the Virgin of Zacatecas by playing night and day.

## Exploring Zacatecas

The close proximity of most colonial sights to the city's center, as well as the consistently light traffic, make Zacatecas easy to explore on foot. However, you may need time to acclimate to the high altitude.

**a good walk**

Start your tour at the Plaza de Armas, the city's center, with stops at the impressive **Catedral de Zacatecas** ㉕ ➤ and the **Palacio del Gobierno** ㉖. Across the street from the plaza are two beautiful colonial buildings, one of which is the **Palacio de la Mala Noche** ㉗. Go to the Plaza Santo Domingo, two blocks west of the cathedral, to see the art in the **Museo Pedro Coronel** ㉘ and the baroque **Templo de Santo Domingo** ㉙ next door. To visit the museum of the other Coronel brother—both were equally fanatical art collectors—return to the cathedral, turn left on Avenida Hidalgo, and walk about 1 km (½ mi) north of the plaza to the **Museo Rafael Coronel** ㉚.

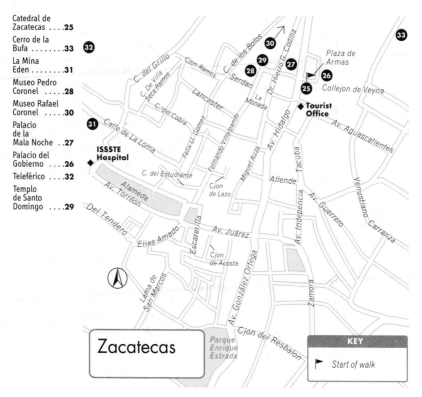

Zacatecas

For a longer walk (or, if you're feeling winded, a quick taxi ride), head
south on Avenida Hidalgo until you come to Juárez, then go right
(roughly west) up the hill, passing the several-block-long Alameda park
and the Social Security Hospital to get to **La Mina Eden** ㉛. After touring the mine, you can take an elevator up to Cerro del Grillo (Cricket
Hill) and catch the **Teleférico** ㉜ cable car across the city to **Cerro de la
Bufa** ㉝, the site of Pancho Villa's famous battle.

TIMING    A walk through the town center clocks in at under two hours, but leave
another couple of hours for the museums. Check the museum schedules because all close at least one day a week; the Museo Pedro Coronel is closed Thursday, for instance, while the Museo Rafael Coronel is
closed Wednesday.

### What to See

▶ ㉕ **Catedral de Zacatecas.** This is one of Mexico's finest interpretations of
baroque style. Each of the facades tells a different legend. According to
one, an anticlerical state governor used the cathedral's silver cross and
baptismal font to mint Zacatecas's first silver coins. ⊠ *South side of
Plaza de Armas on Av. Hidalgo* ☎ *No phone* ☉ *Daily 8–2 and 4–6.*

㉝ **Cerro de la Bufa.** Pancho Villa's definitive battle against dictator Victoriano Huerta occurred on this rugged hill, now a city landmark, in June

1914. The spacious **Plaza de la Revolución** paved with the three shades of pink Zacatecan stone, is crowned with three huge equestrian statues of Villa and two other heroes, Felipe Angeles and Panfilo Natera. Also on-site are the **Sanctuario de la Virgen de Patrocinio** a chapel dedicated to the city's patron, and the **Museo de la Toma de Zacatecas** (☎ 492/922–8066 ☞ $1), which has nine rooms of historic objects such as guns, newspapers, furniture, and clothing from the days of Pancho Villa. It's open daily 10–5. ⊹ *If driving, follow Av. Hidalgo north from town to Av. Juan de Tolosa; turn right and continue until you come to a fountain; take 1st immediate right off retorno (crossover) onto Calle Mexicapan, which leads to Carretera Panorámica. Turn right to signposted Carretera La Bufa, which leads to the top of the hill.*

**❸❶ La Mina Eden.** From 1586 until 1960 this mine supplied Zacatecas with most of its silver. Tours are in Spanish, but you'll have no trouble imagining what life was like for a miner once you're riding in the open mine train down into the underground tunnels. Wear sturdy shoes and bring a sweater. Among the train's stops is, of all places, a discotheque—there's a small gift shop at the entrance. ⊠ *Entrance on Antonio Dovali off Av. Torréon beyond Alameda García de la Cadena* ☎ 492/922–3002 ☞ *$2.50* ☼ *Daily 10–6.*

**★ ❷❽ Museo Pedro Coronel.** Originally a Jesuit monastery, this building was used as a jail in the 18th century, and is now a museum, which exhibits the work of Zacatecan artist and sculptor Pedro Coronel. Also on display is his extensive collection of works by Picasso, Dalí, Miró, Braque, and Chagall, among others, as well as art from Africa, China, Japan, India, Tibet, Greece, and Egypt. ⊠ *Av. Fernando Villalpando at Plaza Santo Domingo* ☎ 492/922–8021 ☞ *$2* ☼ *Fri.–Wed. 10–5.*

**★ ❸⓪ Museo Rafael Coronel.** Concealed by the Ex-Convento de San Francisco's mellow pink 18th-century facade is a rambling structure of open, arched corridors, all leading through garden patios to rooms that exhibit, on a rotating basis, 3,000 of the museum's 10,000 *máscaras* (masks). These representations of saints and devils, wise men and fools, animals and humans were once used in Mexican regional festivals. The museum also has a remarkable display of puppets, pre-Hispanic art, photography, and paintings. It's northeast of the town center, toward Lomas del Calvario. ⊠ *Off Vergel Nuevo between Chaveño and Garcia Salinas* ☎ 492/922–8116 ☞ *About $2* ☼ *Thurs.–Tues. 10–5.*

**❷❼ Palacio de la Mala Noche.** Across from the downtown plaza are a pair of national monuments: two 18th-century colonial buildings with lacy ironwork balconies and built from native pink stone. One is a municipal building known as the Palace of the Bad Night, which, according to legend, was the home of a silver mine–owner who was asked so often to help the needy that he installed a hidden door by which he could enter and leave the palace undisturbed. Up the hill along the side of the palace, you can find the so-called hidden door. The other building is now the Continental Plaza hotel. ⊠ *Av. Hidalgo 639* ☞ *Free* ☼ *Weekdays 8:30–3 and 5–8, weekends 10–2.*

㉖ **Palacio del Gobierno.** The Governor's Palace is an 18th-century mansion with verdant courtyards and, on the main staircase, a poignant mural by António Pintor Rodríguez that depicts the history of Zacatecas. ⊠ *East side of Plaza de Armas* ☑ *Free* ☉ *Daily 9–2 and 5–8.*

---

**need a break?**

**El Teatro Caffé** (⊠ Av. Hidalgo 501, inside Teatro Caldreon ☎ 492/922–8620) is an active coffee shop in a restored 19th-century theater adorned with celestial murals. Students swap ideas here over a cappuccino or a *Neive Opera* (vanilla ice cream topped with chocolate syrup, espresso, and cream).

---

㉜ **Teleférico.** The only cable car in the world to cross an entire city, the Teleféric runs from **Cerro del Grillo** (Cricket Hill) above the Mina Eden to Cerro de la Bufa. Though it crosses at the narrowest point, it showcases the city's magnificent panorama and baroque church domes and spires. It's worth the cost to get the ride up to Cerro de la Bufa, which is quite a climb otherwise. ⊠ *Cerro del Grillo station: Off Paseo Díaz Ordaz, a steep walk from Plaza de Armas* ☎ *492/922–5694* ☑ *$2* ☉ *Daily 10–6, except when there are high winds.*

㉙ **Templo de Santo Domingo.** This 18th-century Jesuit church has an ornamented facade and an opulent interior with gold-leaf religious paintings. In the sacristy is an extensive collection of religious art. ⊠ *Av. Fernando Villalpando at Plaza Santo Domingo* ☎ *No phone* ☉ *Daily 7:30–3 and 5:30–8:30.*

## Where to Stay & Eat

The better restaurants in Zacatecas are actually in its hotels, but some popular eateries are on Avenida Juárez, which intersects Avenida Hidalgo. Your best bet for lodgings are rooms in the attractive, well-preserved 18th- and 19th-century buildings.

★ $$ ✕ **La Cuija.** The Gecko specializes in regional food. Opt for the three-quesadilla appetizer with one each of squash blossoms, cheese, and *huitlacoche* (black corn fungus). Strong entrées include the *crema de labor* (cream soup with corn and squash blossoms) and *asado de boda* (pork in semisweet and spicy sauce). The wine comes from the owner's Cachola Vineyards in Valle de las Arsinas. A traditional Mexican trio performs Thursday–Sunday afternoons. ⊠ *Centro Commercial El Mercado, bottom level* ☎ *492/922–8275* ☐ *AE, V.*

¢–$ ✕ **Café y Nevería Acrópolis.** This diner is trimmed with paintings and sketches given to the owner by famous people who've eaten here, including a small acrylic by Rafael Coronel. Sip a strong Turkish coffee while watching the locals flood in for breakfast. The *chilaquiles verdes* (fried tortilla strips smothered in tangy green sauce and white cheese) comes with a basket of pastries and bread. Traditional café fare, like hamburgers, sandwiches, and fruity shakes, is available for lunch. ⊠ *Av. Hidalgo at Plazuela Candelario Huizar, alongside the cathedral* ☎ *492/922–1284* ☐ *MC, V.*

¢–$ ✕ **El Paraiso.** More than 100 years ago this was a fashionable cantina for Zacatecano elite. Still a town favorite, El Paraiso prepares traditional dishes such as *enchiladas de ayer* (yesterday's enchiladas). The friendly waiters promise that the second day actually enhances the flavor. ⊠ *Av. Hidalgo at Plaza Goitia* ☎ *492/922–6164* ⊟ *AE, MC, V.*

¢–$ ✕ **El Recoveco.** There are 25 steaming plates of traditional Mexican dishes to choose from at this rustic, full-buffet diner. Lunch will likely include Spanish rice, beans, *pollo en mole* (chicken in mole sauce), fresh salads, and fruit water. The staff is friendly and the prices are reasonable: $5 for all-you-can-eat lunch, $4.50 for breakfast. ⊠ *Av. Torréon 513, in front of the Alameda* ☎ *492/924–2013* ⊠ *Jardín Juárez 38, corner of Guadalupe* ☎ *492/923–7174* ⊟ *No credit cards.*

$$$–$$$$ ✕▥ **Quinta Real.** This must be one of the world's more unusual hotels:
FodorsChoice it's built around Mexico's first *plaza de toro* (bullring), which is the sec-
★ ond oldest one in the Western Hemisphere. Pastel fabrics complement dark traditional furniture in the large, bright, and plush rooms. Some of the former bull pens are part of the bar and two levels of the spectator area are now an outdoor café. The elaborate, formal restaurant ($$) has delicious Continental cuisine and an awesome view of the bullring and the aqueduct beyond. ⊠ *Av. Gonzalez Ortega s/n, to the side of the aqueduct, 98000* ☎ *492/922–9104* ▤ *492/922–8440* ⊕ *www. quintareal.com* ↴ *49 suites* ⌂ *Restaurant, minibars, cable TV, bar, shops, laundry service, free parking* ⊟ *AE, MC, V.*

$$–$$$$ ▥ **Mesón de Jobito.** Prior to its conversion into a four-star hotel this was an early-19th-century apartment building, which stood for over a century. There are two levels of guest rooms, all of which are done in tasteful modern decor, with wall-to-wall carpet and striped drapes. The Mesón's placement on a hushed little plaza several blocks from the cathedral enhances its tranquil atmosphere. A city tour, dinner, wine, and an American breakfast for two are included in the higher price. ⊠ *Jardín Juárez 143, 98000* ☎▤ *492/924–1722* ⊕ *www.mesondejobito.com.mx* ↴ *53 rooms, 6 suites* ⌂ *2 restaurants, cable TV, bar, laundry service, parking (fee)* ⊟ *AE, MC, V.*

$$–$$$ ▥ **Emporio Zacatecas.** The 18th-century pink-stone facade of this attractive old colonial building faces the Plaza de Armas and the cathedral. Unfortunately, the hotel's modern interior is rather stark and charmless. During festival season, rooms looking onto the plaza are within earshot of late-night and early-morning tamborazo music. That said, you'll get a great view of the festivities from your small balcony. ⊠ *Av. Hidalgo 703, 98000* ☎ *492/922–6183* ▤ *492/922–6245* ↴ *113 rooms, 1 suite* ⌂ *Restaurant, bar, laundry service, convention center, free parking* ⊟ *AE, MC, V.*

$ ▥ **Hostal del Vasco.** For an authentic Zacatecano hotel, consider this clean, quiet place. The spacious brown-carpeted suites have dark antiques and marble bathrooms; some are equipped with a small kitchen (but no cookware). Sprawling plants and singing birds—Pepe the parrot leads the choir—enliven the two-story interior courtyard. ⊠ *Alameda and Velasco 1, 98000* ☎▤ *492/922–0428* ⊕ *www.hostaldelvasco.com* ↴ *18 suites* ⌂ *Restaurant, some kitchenettes, cable TV, hair salon, laundry service, free parking* ⊟ *AE, MC, V.*

¢ ▥ **Posada de la Moneda.** In the middle of downtown is this tidily polished, albeit somewhat threadbare, Mexican hotel. The rooms are clean and have pint-size balconies. ⌧ *Av. Hidalgo 413, 98000* 🏨 *492/ 922–0881* ⊕ *www.hotelposadadelamoneda.com* 🛏 *34 rooms, 2 suites* ⚒ *Restaurant, cable TV, bar* ☰ *AE, MC, V.*

## Nightlife & the Arts

More than 1,000 feet underground is **El Malacate** (⌧La Mina Eden 🕾492/ 922–3002), the Eden mine's discotheque. Try to make reservations at this must-see hub, which is both crowded and noisy. It's open Thursday–Saturday nights, with a cover charge of around $7. Bands play nightly at the **Quinta Real** (⌧ Av. Gonzales Ortega s/n, 🕾 492/922–9104) in a romantic bar to one side of the old bullring.

## Shopping

Souvenirs in Zacatecas tend toward tacky knickknacks rather than handmade, quality crafts. There's some decent jewelry to be found, although not as much as you would expect for a mining town.

Opposite the east end of Plaza de Armas is **La Cazzorra** (⌧ Av. Hidalgo 713 🕾492/924–0484), a collectibles shop with authentic antiques, books about Zacatecas, Huichol art, *rebozos* (a traditional woven wrap still widely used for warmth), and a fine selection of jewelry from the local silver factory. The owners are a good source of information about the city. The **Centro Comercial El Mercado** (⌧ Calle Hidalgo, next to cathedral) has a few shops with silver goods. **Centro Platero Zacatecas** (🕾 492/923–1007) sells silver jewelry with regional designs produced in its Guadalupe factory. **Güichito** (⌧ Av. Hidalgo 126 🕾492/922– 1907) specializes in handmade traditional candies from the region.

## Side Trips from Zacatecas

### Guadalupe
*7 km (4½ mi) southeast of Zacatecas.*

Guadalupe is a small town rife with colonial art and architecture. Its centerpiece is the **Ex-Convento de Guadalupe,** founded by Franciscan monks in 1707. Currently it houses the **Museo de Arte Virreinal** (*virreinal* means "viceregal," or "colonial") run by the Instituto Nacional de Antropología e Historia. With its baroque **Templo de Guadalupe** and the **Capilla de Nápoles,** the convent itself is a work of art, but even more impressive is its stunning collection of religious art. Exhibits include pieces by Miguel Cabrera, Nicolás Rodríguez Juárez, Cristóbal de Villalpando, and Andrés López. ⌧*Jardín Juárez s/n* 🕾*492/923–2386* 💳*$3* ☉ *Daily 10–4:30.*

In the 18th-century mansion of don Ignacio de Bernárdez is the **Centro Platero Zacatecas,** a school and factory for handmade silver jewelry and other items. Stop in to watch student silversmiths master this tradition. ⌧ *Casco de la Ex-Hacienda Bernárdez* 🕾 *492/923–1007* ☉ *Weekdays 10–6, Sat. 10–2.*

### Zona Arqueológica La Quemada
 *50 km (31 mi) southwest of Zacatecas on Hwy. 54, 3 km (2 mi) off highway.*

By the time the Spaniards arrived in the 16th century this ancient city was a ruin. The site's original name, "Chicomostoc," means "place of the seven tribes." It was previously believed that seven Native American cultures had occupied the area at different times, one community building atop the other. Thin stone slabs wedged into place make up the remaining edifices. The principal draw is a group of rose-colored ruins containing 11 massive, round columns built of the same small slabs of rock. Interesting artifacts can be found in the site's impressive museum. To get here, take a bus toward Villanueva, get off at the entrance to La Quemada, and walk 3 km (2 mi). The bus ride takes about an hour. Alternatively, take a taxi or guided tour. ☎ *No phone* 🎫 *$3* ⊙ *Site and museum daily 10–5.*

## Zacatecas A to Z

### AIR TRAVEL

AIRPORT The Zacatecas La Calera airport (ZCL) is 29 km (18 mi) north of town.

AIRPORT TRANSFERS Aerotransportes shuttles make the trip between Zacatecas and the airport for about $5; private taxis cost about $15.

⛵ **Aerotransportes** ☎ 492/922–5946.

CARRIERS Mexicana has direct service to Zacatecas from Chicago and Los Angeles. It also offers plenty of nonstop flights from other cities in Mexico, including Mexico City, Guadalajara, and Cancún.

⛵ **Mexicana** ⊠ Av. Hidalgo 406 ☎ 492/922–3325 or 492/922–7429 ⊕ www.mexicana.com.

### BUS TRAVEL

Major bus lines run several first- and second-class buses daily from Mexico City's Central de Autobuses del Norte to Zacatecas. The Zacatecas bus depot is a couple of miles southwest of the town center. Estrella Blanca is Futura's first-class service. The trip takes eight to nine hours and costs about $53.

⛵ **Estrella Blanca** ☎ 492/922–0042. **Futura** ☎ 492/922–0042.

### CAR TRAVEL

Zacatecas is about 7½–8 hours by car from Mexico City via Highway 57 (to Querétaro and San Luis Potosí) and Highway 49.

### EMERGENCIES

English is not generally spoken in Zacatecas; contact your hotel manager or the tourist office in case of an emergency. The emergency line for fire, police, or medical attention is **066**.

Pharmacies are abundant; try Farmacia Isstezac, open daily 8 AM–10 PM.

⛵ **Farmacia Isstezac** ⊠ Tacuba 153 ☎ 492/924–0690. **Hospital General** ☎ 492/923–3004. **Police** ☎ 492/922–0180. **Red Cross** ☎ 492/922–3005.

### INTERNET

Cronos charges $1.50 an hour for Internet access and is open Monday–Saturday 9–9 and Sunday 11–8.

🏠 Internet Café **Cronos** ✉ Av. Rayon 212 ☎ 492/922–1548 ✉ Gonzalez Ortega, in front of VIPs restaurant ☎ 492/925–2599.

### MONEY MATTERS

There are several currency exchanges and banks with ATMs in downtown Zacatecas—many are along Avenida Hidalgo.

### TOURS

Viajes Mazzoco, a well-established travel agency and the local American Express representative, gives a four-hour tour of the city center, the Eden mine, the Teleférico, and La Bufa for about $12 a person. There are also tours to La Quemada ruins and environs ($16). Ask in advance for an English-speaking guide.

The tourism office recommends Operadora Zacatecas, which gives tours of the city center and other sites. Juan Dela O of DelaOTours gives lively introductions to sights in Zacatecas and surrounding areas.

🏠 Tour Operator Recommendations **DelaOTours** ✉ Juan de Tolosa 906-A 🏠🏠 492/922–3464. **Operadora Zacatecas** ✉ Av. Hidalgo 630 ☎ 492/924–3676 or 492/924–0050. **Viajes Mazzoco** ✉ Calle Fatima 115 🏠🏠 492/922–0859.

### TRANSPORTATION AROUND ZACATECAS

Most town-center attractions are accessible by foot, although you may want a taxi for visits to farther-flung sights like the Cerro de la Bufa. There's an efficient and inexpensive bus system with clearly marked buses and 30¢ rides.

### VISITOR INFORMATION

The tourist information office is open weekdays 9–8, weekends 9–7.

🏠 Tourist information office ✉ Av. Hidalgo 403, 2nd floor ☎ 492/924–4047 or 492/924–0552.

# QUERÉTARO

*63 km (39 mi) southeast of San Miguel de Allende, 220 km (136 mi) northwest of Mexico City.*

Now a state capital and an industrial center of over 1 million people, Querétaro was once witness to several significant moments in Mexican history, including two of the Mexican-American War's pivotal junctures—its inception and its conclusion. The initial plans for Mexico's independence were hatched in 1810 at the Querétaro home of Josefa Ortiz de Domínguez, a heroine of the independence movement who was also the mayor's wife. Coming full circle, the Mexican-American War concluded here with the signing of the Treaty of Guadalupe Hidalgo in 1848. Additionally, Emperor Maximilian made his last stand north of the town in 1867 when he was executed by firing squad on the Cerro de las Campanas (Hill of the Church Bells). The Austrian government built a small memorial chapel to mark the spot. The Mexican Constitution was signed here in 1917.

Markers, museums, churches, and monuments commemorate Querétaro's heroes and historic moments. The city's impeccably renovated mansions, flower-draped cobblestone walkways, and plazas convey a sense of civic pride. On Sunday evening couples dance to live *danzón* music in the main plaza. Querétaro's citizens are among central Mexico's most congenial people and are quick to share their favorite spots and tales with travelers.

Querétaro is renowned for its opals, which come in red, green, honey, and fire varieties. Because some street vendors sell opals so full of water that they crumble shortly after purchase, you should only make purchases from reputable dealers.

## Exploring Querétaro

Although Querétaro sprawls, the historic district is relatively compact.

Most sights are near the **Plaza de la Independencia** ㉞ ⊩. The **Palacio del Gobierno del Estado** ㉟ is on the plaza's northwest corner. Walk around the square counterclockwise and you'll arrive at the Palacio de Justicia, built as a mansion for the wealthy Domingo Iglesia and, beside it, the **Casa de Ecala** ㊱. Past the Casa de Ecala is Avenida Libertad Oriente, one of the city's bougainvillea-draped pedestrian walkways. Turn west here and walk two blocks to reach Calle Corregidora. Bear right and in the middle of a long block you'll find the entrance to the **Museo Regional de Querétaro** ㊲. Cross the street to Avenida Madero, another "pedway," this one lined with shops. The city's main square, Jardín Obregón, will be on your right.

One block past Avenida Juárez on the corner of Calle Allende Sur and Avenida Madero is the **Casa de la Marquesa** ㊳, an 18th-century mansion converted into a hotel. The neoclassical **Fuente de Neptuno** ㊴ is across from Calle Allende, next to the Templo de Santa Clara. From the fountain, head south on Calle Allende and walk almost a block to an exceptional example of baroque architecture, the **Museo de Arte de Querétaro** ㊵. Retrace your steps to Calle Corregidora, make a left, and walk one block to Avenida 16 de Septiembre. Across the street is the **Jardín de la Corregidora** ㊶.

TIMING   It takes about two hours to walk through Querétaro's compact center. Museums close on Monday.

### What to See

㊱   **Casa de Ecala.** Long ago, as the story goes, the palace's 18th-century owner elaborately adorned his home while engaged in a remodeling war (which he eventually won) with his neighbor. Inside the original facade of this Mexican baroque palace are the offices of DIF, a family-services organization. You're welcome to ramble around the courtyard when the offices are open. ⊠ *Pasteur Sur 6, at Plaza de la Independencia* ☯ *Daily 9–2 and 4–6.*

**Querétaro**

0 ____ 250 meters
0 ____ 250 yards

**KEY**

▶ *Start of walk*

---

**38** **Casa de la Marquesa.** Now a five-star hotel, this beautifully restored 18th-century house was built by the second Marqués de la Villa del Villar del Aguila. Legends about the dwelling suggest that it was constructed to impress a nun with whom the marquis was terribly smitten. He died prior to the casa's completion in 1756, and its first resident was his widow, who had a penchant for things Arabic. The interior is *mudéjar* (Moorish) style, with lovely tile work. Stop in for a drink and the elegant atmosphere of **Don Porfirio's Bar.** ⊠ *Av. Madero 41, El Centro.*

> **need a break?** **Cafeteria El Naranjo** (⊠ Av. Madero 48 ☎ 442/224–0136 Ext. 109) has specialty coffees, including Sexy Coffee (coffee, rum, Kahlúa, and whole cream).

**39** **Fuente de Neptuno.** Renowned Mexican architect and Bajío native Eduardo Tresguerras originally built this fountain in an orchard of the San Antonio monastery in 1797. According to one story, the monks sold some of their land, and the fountain along with it, when they were facing serious economic problems. It now stands next to the Templo de Santa Clara. ⊠ *Calle Allende at Av. Madero.*

**41** **Jardín de la Corregidora.** This plaza is prominently marked by a statue of its namesake and War of Independence heroine—Josefa Ortiz de

Domínguez. Behind the monument stands the **Arbol de la Amistad** (Tree of Friendship). Planted in 1977 in a mixture of soils from around the world, the tree symbolizes Querétaro's hospitality to all travelers. This is the town's calmest square, with plenty of choices for patio dining. ⊠ *Calle Corregidora at Av. 16 de Septiembre.*

**40** **Museo de Arte de Querétaro.** Focusing on European and Mexican artworks, this baroque 18th-century Augustinian monastery-turned-museum exhibits paintings from the 17th through 19th centuries, as well as rotating exhibits of 20th-century art. Ask about the symbolism of the columns and the figures in conch shells atop each arch on the fascinating baroque patio. ⊠ *Calle Allende 14 Sur* ☎ *442/212–2357* ⊕ *www. queretaro-mexico.com.mx/museo-arte* ⊡ *About $1.50, free Tues.* ⊘ *Tues.–Sun. 10–6.*

**37** **Museo Regional de Querétaro.** This bright-yellow, 17th-century Franciscan monastery displays colonial and European artwork in addition to historic memorabilia. For example, there are early copies of the Mexican Constitution and the table on which the Treaty of Guadalupe Hidalgo was signed. ⊠ *Calle Corregidora 3* ☎ *442/212–2031* ⊡ *About $3* ⊘ *Tues.–Sun. 10–7.*

**35** **Palacio del Gobierno del Estado.** Dubbed La Casa de la Corregidora, this building now houses the Palacio municipal government offices, but in 1810 it was home to Querétaro's mayor-magistrate (El Corregidor) and his wife, Josefa Ortiz de Domínguez (La Corregidora). La Corregidora's literary salon was actually a device for conspirators—including Ignacio Allende and Father Miguel Hidalgo—to plot a course for independence. When he discovered the salon's true nature, El Corregidor imprisoned his wife in her room, but not before she alerted Allende and Hidalgo. Soon after, on September 16, Father Hidalgo tolled the bell of his church to signal the onset of the fight for freedom. A replica of the bell caps this building. ⊠ *Northwest corner of Plaza de la Independencia* ⊡ *Free* ⊘ *Weekdays 8 AM–9 PM, Sat. 8–3.*

▶ **34** **Plaza de la Independencia.** Also known as Plaza de Armas, this immaculate square is bordered by carefully restored colonial mansions and is especially lovely at night, when the central fountain is lighted. Built in 1842, the fountain is dedicated to the Marqués de la Villa del Villar, who constructed Querétaro's elegant aqueduct. The old stone aqueduct with its 74 towering arches stands at the town's east end. ✛ *Bounded by Av. 5 de Mayo on the north, Av. Libertad Ote. on the south, Pasteur on the east, and Vergara Sur on the west.*

## Where to Eat

Many of Querétaro's dining spots are near the main plaza (Jardín Obregón), along Calle Corregidora, near the Teatro de la República, and particularly in the Jardín de la Corregidora. The fancier restaurants are in the hotels on the Plaza de la Independencia and off Highway 57, north of the city.

**$$–$$$** ✕ **Restaurante Josecho.** Among the hunting trophies adorning the wood-paneled walls of this highway road stop—next to the bullring at the town's southwest end—are peacocks, elk, bears, and lions. Sports fans stop here for the animated atmosphere as well as the house specialties, which include *filete Josecho* (steak with cheese and mushrooms) and *filete Chemita* (steak sautéed in butter with onions). Save room for the creamy coconut ice cream. A classical guitarist or pianist performs in the evening. Waiters celebrate birthdays by singing and blasting a red siren. ⊠ *Dalia 1, next to Plaza de Toros Santa María* ☎ *442/216–0229 or 442/216–0201* ⊟ *AE, MC, V.*

**$–$$** ✕ **El Mesón de Chucho el Roto.** Named after Querétaro's version of Robin Hood, this restaurant is on the quiet Plaza de Armas. It's strong on regional dishes, like tacos of steamed goat, shrimp with nopal cactus, or squash blossoms. ⊠ *Plaza de Armas* ☎ *442/212–4295* ⊟ *AE, MC, V.*

**¢–$$** ✕ **La Nueva Fonda del Refugio.** Nestled in the Jardín de la Corregidora is this restaurant with intimate indoor and outdoor dining. Fresh flowers top the indoor tables; traditional cowhide *equipale* chairs face the surrounding gardens outside. Order the *filete de huitlacoche* (steak fillet smothered in corn fungus sauce) for a delicious regional twist. You'll be serenaded by guitar-playing trios at night. ⊠ *Jardín de la Corregidora 26* ☎ *442/212–0755* ⊟ *MC, V.*

**¢–$** ✕ **Bisquets Querétaro.** Mexican families come to this friendly spot after church for biscuits, made fresh on the premises. Pick a traditional topping like butter and jelly or go for something more unusual like mole or tuna. There are toothsome enchiladas *Queretanas*, with cheese, potatoes, carrots, and cream, and *huevos al albañil* (eggs with red sauce and beans). ⊠ *Av. Pino Suarez 7* ☎ *442/214–1481* ⊟ *No credit cards.*

**¢–$** ✕ **La Mariposa.** A wrought-iron butterfly (*mariposa*) overlooks the entrance of this cafeteria-like local favorite. Despite its plain appearance, it's the spot for coffee and cake or a light Mexican lunch of tacos, tamales, and *tortas* (sandwiches). ⊠ *Angela Peralta 7* ☎ *442/212–1166 or 442/212–4849* ⊟ *No credit cards.*

## Where to Stay

Querétaro has elegant and unique restored properties. Lower-price hotels are near the main plaza and tend to be noisy; restored colonial mansions are on or near the downtown plazas and deluxe properties are on the town's outskirts.

**$$–$$$$** 🏨 **Casa de la Marquesa.** This used to be an 18th-century private home,
**Fodor'sChoice** but it's now a handsomely restored property in Querétaro's center. Each
★ guest room is large with antiques, tasteful art, parquet floors, and area rugs. The main building's rooms are more elegant and expensive than those in the adjacent La Casa Azul (children under 12 aren't admitted in the main building). The elegant, but austere restaurant, Comedor de la Marquesa, specializes in regional rarities like boar, venison, and *escamole* (ant eggs), as well as more-traditional international cookery. ⊠*Av. Madero 41, 76000* ☎*442/212–0092* 🖷*442/212–0098* 🛏*25 suites* ☖ *2 restaurants, room service, bar, shop* ⊟ *AE, MC, V* ⏏ *BP.*

**$$–$$$** 🏨 **Hacienda Jurica.** Families from Mexico City escape to this sprawling 16th-century ex-hacienda, which has topiary gardens, a horse stable, golf access, and nearly 30 acres of grassy sports fields. Antique horse-drawn carriages dot the grounds and courtyards, and the spacious earth-tone rooms have dark-wood furniture. The hacienda is in Jurica, an upscale residential neighborhood 13 km (8 mi) northwest of the city off Highway 57, and is easiest to reach by car. ⊠ *Carretera Mexico–San Luis Potosí, Km 229, Apdo. 338, 76100* ☎ *442/218–0022* 🖶 *442/218–0136* ⊕ *www.hoteljurica.com.mx* 🛏 *176 rooms, 6 suites* ⚒ *Restaurant, minibars, 2 tennis courts, pool, billiards, horseback riding, bar, laundry service, free parking* ⊟ *AE, MC, V.*

**$$–$$$** 🏨 **Mesón de Santa Rosa.** On the serene Plaza de la Independencia, this elegant property was a stopover for travelers to the north almost 300 years ago. Rooms are clustered around a placid courtyard; lace-hung glass doors and wood-beam ceilings preserve the colonial charm. ⊠ *Pasteur Sur 17, 76000* ☎ *442/224–2623* 🖶 *442/212–5522* 🛏 *5 rooms, 16 suites* ⚒ *Restaurant, minibars, cable TV, pool, bar* ⊟ *AE, MC, V.*

**$$** 🏨 **Holiday Inn Querétaro.** This gracious, well-run establishment has a lot more charm than others in the chain. Located 3 km (about 2 mi) west of the historic district off Highway 57, the contemporary building incorporates many colonial touches such as stone archways and domed *boveda* (vaulted) ceilings. Sunny, ample rooms are comfortably appointed with rustic Mexican furnishings and cheery pastel bedspreads. ⊠ *Av. 5 de Febrero 110, 76000* ☎ *442/216–0202* 🖶 *442/216–8902* ⊕ *www.holidayinn.com.mx* 🛏 *171 rooms, 4 suites* ⚒ *2 restaurants, minibars, cable TV, pool, gym, piano bar, baby-sitting, travel services, free parking, no-smoking rooms* ⊟ *AE, MC, V.*

**$** 🏨 **Hotel Mirabel.** Business travelers and conventioneers favor this reasonably priced modern high-rise. The quiet, carpeted rooms are insulated and have wooden desks. Several double rooms have Alameda Hidalgo park views, and some singles overlook a soccer stadium. ⊠ *Av. Constituyentes Ote. 2, 76000* ☎ *442/214–3099 or 442/214–3444* 🖶 *442/214–3585* ⊕ *www.hotelmirabel.com.mx* 🛏 *170 rooms, 10 suites* ⚒ *Restaurant, cable TV, bar, meeting room, free parking* ⊟ *AE, MC, V.*

## Nightlife & the Arts

Every Sunday evening at 6 there's a band concert in the **Jardín Obregón,** Querétaro's main square. At the tourist office you can pick up a monthly publication called *Tesoro Turístico* (all in Spanish), which provides current information about festivals, concerts, and other cultural events.

## Shopping

Stores around town sell opals (not milky white, like Australian opals, but beautiful nonetheless) and other locally mined gems. If you're looking for loose stones or opal jewelry, do some comparison shopping, since prices beat those in the U.S. **Lapidaria Querétaro** (⊠ Corregidora 149 Nte. ☎ 442/212–0030) is a reputable dealer of loose stones and opals. **Villalone y Artesanos** (⊠ Av. Libertad 24-A ☎ 442/212–8414) has friendly service and authentic stones.

**El Globo** (⊠ Corregidora 41, at Independencia ☎ 442/212–1019 or 442/212–8883) has been around for over a century and offers extravagant cookies, chocolates, freshly baked breads, cakes, and pies.

## Side Trips from Querétaro

### Tequisquiapan

*70 km (43 mi) southeast of Querétaro, off Rte. 120.*

Drenched in sun, bougainvillea, and flowering trees, Tequis (as the locals call it) was once famed for its restorative thermal waters. Recently, the town has experienced a dearth of hot water, reportedly due to a local paper mill's extreme water consumption. As tourism has declined along with the warm water levels, many spas have turned into recreation areas with swimming pools. Though usually deserted midweek, they can liven up on hot weekends. Check with the tourist office for directions to the spas; most are outside of town.

The town's main plaza is punctuated with the neoclassical-style **Templo de Santa María de la Asunción,** which was started in 1874 but not completed until the beginning of the 20th century. Tequis hosts a weeklong wine and cheese festival in late May or early June.

Tequis has a well-deserved reputation for high-quality craftwork like wicker, so you may wish to head to the **Mercado de Artesanías** (⊠ Calz. de los Misterios s/n ☎ No phone) for woven goods, jewelry, and furniture.

### Xilitla

*Approximately 320 km (198 mi) northeast of Querétaro.*

Feel the ordinary world fade away with a trip to the decidedly off-the-beaten path **Las Pozas** (The Pools), the extraordinary sculpture garden of the late, eccentric English millionaire Edward James (1907–84). A friend to artists Dalí and Picasso and rumored to be King Edward VII's illegitimate son, James spent 20 years building 36 surrealist concrete structures deep in the waterfall-filled Xilitla jungle. These astonishing structures are half-finished fantasy castles, gradually falling to ruin as the rain forest slithers in to claim them. It's like the ultimate child's fort. The castles don't have walls—just vine-entwined pillars, secret passageways, and operatic staircases leading nowhere.

It's a 6- to 7-hour thrilling but exhausting mountainous drive to Xilitla, with hairpin turns and spectacular desert, forest, and jungle vistas. Plan on staying at least two nights, as you'll want time to soak up the jungle magic. If you choose not to drive, you can take a bus to Ciudad Valles (1½-hour drive from Xilitla) or fly to Tampico (3½-hour drive from Xilitla), and arrange ahead for the staff of Posada El Castillo to pick you up. ⊹ *From Querétaro, head north on Hwy. 57 (Carretera Mexico–San Luis Potosí). Take the* PEÑA DE BERNAL *turnoff, marked on a bridge overpass and also on a smaller sign at the Cadareyta exit. Continue north through Bernal, after which the road will join Rte. 120. Take 120 through Jalpan and then on to Xilitla, just across the border in the state of San Luis Potosí. The turnoff to Las Pozas is just beyond Xilitla on the left after passing a small bridge* ☜ *$1.50* ☉ *Daily dawn–dusk.*

WHERE TO STAY   🛏 **Posada El Castillo.** When he wasn't living in his jungle hut, Edward
$$   James stayed in town (a 10-minute drive away) in a whimsical house that feels like an extension of the garden structures at Las Pozas—ex-

cept that it has walls. The house, El Castillo (the castle), is now a quirky inn run by Lenore and Avery Danziger, who produced an award-winning documentary film about James that they screen for guests. Rooms are adorned with simple wooden furnishings; the best rooms have huge Gothic windows and panoramic mountain views. You can arrange to have meals here; otherwise, there are few dining options in the area. ⊠ *Ocampo 105, 79900 Xilitla, San Luis Potosí* ☎ *489/365–0038* 🖷 *136/365–0055* ⊕ *www.junglegossip.com* ⇆ *8 rooms* ♨ *Pool* ⊟ *No credit cards.*

## Querétaro A to Z

### BUS TRAVEL

Daily buses run direct between Mexico City's Central del Norte (North Bus Station) and Querétaro's Central de Autobuses, which is a couple of miles southeast of the town center. Major lines have frequent service; travel time is about three hours and tickets cost about $20. Buses also leave several times a day for Guanajuato, San Miguel de Allende, and Morelia.

🚊 **ETN** ☎ 442/229–0078 or 442/229–0019. **Flecha Amarilla** ☎ 442/211–4001. **Grupo Blanco Estrella** ☎ 442/229–0022. **Omnibus de México** ☎ 442/229–0029.

### CAR RENTAL

Budget has an office in downtown Querétaro.

🚊 **Budget** ⊠ Av. Constituyentes Ote. 73 ☎ 442/213–4498 or 441/213–3438 ⊕ www.budget.com.

### CAR TRAVEL

It takes about three hours to get to Querétaro from Mexico City by car via Highway 57. From Querétaro, another hour's drive will get you to Tequisquiapan; take Highway 57 to Route 120. Xilitla is at least six hours away.

### EMERGENCIES

Dial **066** for medical, fire, and theft emergencies. The Green Angels can provide roadside assistance.

🚊 **Ambulance–Red Cross** ☎ 442/229–0545 or 442/229–0665. **Emergency** ☎ 066. **Fire Department** ☎ 442/212–3939 or 442/212–0627. **Green Angels** ☎ 442/213–8424. **Police** ☎ 442/220–8303 or 442/220–9191. **Sanatorio Alcocer Pozo (Hospital)** ⊠ Calle Reforma 23 ☎ 442/212–0149 or 421/212–1787.

### INTERNET

Web Café, open Monday–Saturday 10–10 and Sunday 4–10, charges $3 an hour for Internet access.

🚊 Internet Café **Web Café** ⊠ Ezequiel Montes Sur 67 ☎ 442/216–0250 or 442/216–7272.

**MONEY MATTERS**

Casa de Cambio Acueducto is open weekdays 9–2 and 4–6 and Saturday 9–1.

🛂 **Casa de Cambio Acueducto** ✉ Av. Juárez Sur 58 ☎ 442/212–9304.

**TOURS**

The tourist office runs hour-long trolley tours of the city's historic landmarks at 9, 10, and 11 AM and at 4, 5, and 6 PM Tuesday–Sunday; all commentary is in Spanish. To arrange a city tour in English, call the office—one day in advance if possible. The cost is about $1.50.

**TRANSPORTATION AROUND QUERÉTARO**

Most of Querétaro's historic sites are within walking distance of one another in the downtown district and can be reached by a series of walkways that are closed to car traffic most of the day. If you want to venture farther afield, you'll find that taxis run frequently along the main streets and are inexpensive.

**TRAVEL AGENCIES**

Turismo Beverly offers full travel services; they should have an English-speaking agent.

🛂 **Local Agent Referral Turismo Beverly** ✉ Av. Tecnologia 118 ☎ 442/216–1500 or 442/216–1260 🖶 442/216–8524.

**VISITOR INFORMATION**

Querétaro's Dirección de Turismo del Estado is open weekdays 8–8, weekends 9–8.

Tequisquiapan's Oficina de Turismo is open daily 9–7; its Web site, ⊕ www.tequisquiapan.com.mx, has descriptive information in English. 🛂 **Dirección de Turismo del Estado** ✉ Plaza de Armas ☎ 442/212–1412 or 442/212–0907 🖶 442/212–1094. **Oficina de Turismo de Tequisquiapan** ✉ Andador Independencia 1, Plaza Miguel Hidalgo ☎ 427/273–0295.

# MORELIA

▶ *302 km (187 mi) west of Mexico City.*

With its long, wide boulevards and earth-tone colonial mansions, Morelia is Michoacán state's affable capital—as well as a UNESCO World Heritage Site. Founded in 1541 as Valladolid (after the Spanish city), it changed its name in 1828 to honor José María Morelos, the town's most famous son. The legendary mule skinner–turned–priest led the battle for independence after its early leaders were executed in 1811.

Initially, Morelos had an ill-equipped army of 25 but soon mobilized a contingent of 9,000 that nearly gained control of the country. Although he was defeated and executed in 1815, he left behind a long-standing reformist legacy that called for universal suffrage, racial equality, and the demise of the hacienda system. The city still pays tribute to Morelos—his former home has been turned into a museum, and his birthplace is now a library.

Several annual festivals indulge Morelianos in their love for music. Each May the International Organ Festival is celebrated in the cathedral, giving voice to its outstanding 4,600-pipe organ. Featuring baroque and chamber music, with orchestras from throughout Mexico, the Festival Internacional de Música is held in the last two weeks of July.

Morelia has the delicious distinction of being the candy capital of Mexico. So strong is the sweets-eating tradition that the city has an entire market devoted to confections.

## Exploring Morelia

To thoroughly explore Morelia and its surrounding hillside neighborhoods would require a fair amount of time. However, a stroll through its historic plazas will give you a feel for the city's vitality. Although the vehicle and sidewalk traffic can get heavy at times, Morelia is a pedestrian-friendly place; it also tries to hold back the tide of street vendors that floods most cities.

a good walk

Begin your walk in Morelia's tree-lined downtown **Plaza de Armas** 42 ☞, on the east side of which is the city's famed **Catedral** 43. As you leave the cathedral, cross Avenida Madero Oriente to the **Palacio de Gobierno** 44, a former seminary. From the palace it's four blocks east along Avenida Madero Oriente to Calle de Belisario Domínguez. Make a right and walk one block south to the Templo de San Francisco. To the rear of the church, in the former convent of San Francisco, is the entrance to the **Casa de las Artesanías del Estado de Michoacán** 45, a virtual cornucopia of crafts from around the state.

From the crafts museum, go west to join Calle Vasco de Quiroga, a street lined with vendors, and walk two blocks south until you come to Calle del Soto Saldaña. Head west another two blocks to Avenida Morelos Sur. The corner building on the right is the **Casa Museo de Morelos** 46, which displays memorabilia of the independence leader. It's one block north from the museum to Calle Antonio Alzate and then one block west (where the street name changes to Calle Corregidora) to Calle García Obeso. On this corner stands the **Museo Casa Natal de Morelos** 47, Morelos's birthplace. Continue west on Calle Corregidora until you reach Calle Abasolo. On Calle Allende, one block to the north, is the **Museo Regional Michoacano** 48.

After leaving the museum take Calle Abasolo back to the plaza; 2½ blocks to the north is the **Museo del Estado** 49 on the right side of the street (which changes to Calle Guillermo Prieto at Avenida Madero Oriente). Return to Avenida Madero Oriente and then go 2 blocks to the right to the corner of Avenida Valentín Gómez Farías, to the **Mercado de Dulces** 50.

For a longer stroll, take Avenida Madero Oriente east about a dozen blocks to where it forks. Stay to the right; you'll see the **Fuente de las Tarascas** on a traffic island to your left. Just past the fountain, Morelia's mile-long **aqueduct** begins. This 1875 structure, which consists of 253 arches, once carried the city's main source of drinking water. It's particularly beautiful at night when its arches—some rising to 30 feet— are illuminated. Two blocks farther along (Madero is now called Avenida

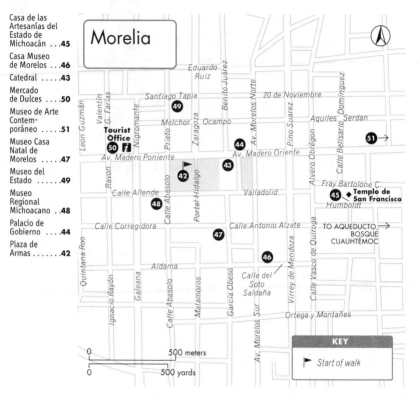

Acueducto) is the entrance to **Bosque Cuauhtémoc,** Morelia's largest park. If you happen by during the week, you may encounter university students studying (or lounging) beneath the palms and evergreens. On weekends, especially Sunday, families on outings take over. Two blocks past the park entrance, you'll see the **Museo de Arte Contemporáneo** ⑤, also on the right side of the street.

TIMING   A tour through Morelia's center will take roughly two hours, not including the time spent in the museums. Remember that most museums, except the Casa de las Artesanías del Estado de Michoacán, close on Monday.

## What to See

㊺ **Casa de las Artesanías del Estado de Michoacán.** In the 16th century, Vasco de Quiroga, the bishop of Michoacán, helped the Purépecha Indians develop artistic specialties so they could be self-supporting. At this two-story museum and store, you can see the work that the Purépechas still produce: copper goods from Santa Clara del Cobre, lacquerware from Uruapan, straw items and pottery from Pátzcuaro, guitars from Paracho, fanciful ceramic devil figures from Ocumicho. In the two main floors around the courtyard of the **Museo Michoacana de las Artesanías,** some of these items are showcased and artists demonstrate how they are made. ✉ *Calle Fray Juan de San Miguel 129* ☎ *443/312–2486 museum, 443/312–1248 store* 🎫 *Free* ⏲ *Mon.–Sat. 10–8 Sun. 10–3:30.*

㊻ **Casa Museo de Morelos.** What is now a two-story museum was acquired in 1801 by José María Morelos and was home to generations of the independence leader's family until 1934. Owned by the Mexican government, it exhibits family portraits, various independence movement artifacts (including a camp bed used by Ignacio Allende), and the blindfold Morelos wore for his execution. The excellent free tour is in Spanish only. ✉ *Av. Morelos Sur 323* ☎ *443/313–2651* 🎫 *$2, free Sun.* ⏲ *Daily 9–7.*

㊸ **Catedral.** Morelia's cathedral is a majestic structure built between 1640 and 1744. Known for its 200-foot baroque towers, which are among Mexico's tallest, it's also home to one of the world's finest organs. With 4,600 pipes, it's the vehicle for the international organ festival held here each May. ✉ *Av. Madero between Plaza de Armas and Av. Morelos* ☎ *No phone.*

㊿ **Mercado de Dulces.** If you have a sweet tooth, don't miss Morelia's candy market. All sorts of local sweets are for sale, such as *ate* (a candied fruit) and *cajeta* (heavenly caramel sauce made from goat's milk). Wooden knickknacks and hand-crafted acoustic guitars are among the nondigestible regional crafts sold from market stalls. ✉ *Av. Madero Pte. at Av. Valentín Gómez Farías* ⏲ *Daily 10–9.*

(51) **Museo de Arte Contemporáneo.** On a beautiful property a stone's throw from both the aqueduct and the Bosque Cuauhtémo, this late-19th-century summer home was restored by the government in 1984 and is now Michoacán's principal contemporary-art museum. The permanent collection has work by famed muralist, lithographer, and illustrator Alfredo Zalce, a Pátzcuaro native. Some of Mexico's leading contemporary artists have temporary exhibitions here. Dance, cinema, theater, and music performances are held regularly in the small auditorium. ✉ *Av. Acueducto 18* ☎ *443/312–5404* 🎫 *Free* ⏲ *Tues.–Sun. 10–2 and 4–8.*

㊼ **Museo Casa Natal de Morelos.** José María Morelos's birthplace is now a national monument and library with mostly literature and history books (as well as two murals by Morelian Alfredo Zalce). Visit the courtyard in back where a marker and an eternal flame honor the fallen hero in a tranquil square. ✉ *Calle Corregidora 113* ☎ *443/312–2793* 🎫 *Free* ⏲ *Tues.–Fri. 10–8, weekends 10–7.*

㊾ **Museo del Estado.** Across from a small plaza with statues of Bishop Vasco de Quiroga and Spanish writer Miguel de Cervantes, this history museum is in a stately mansion that was previously home to the wife of Agustín de Iturbide, Mexico's only native-born emperor. Among the 18th-century home's highlights is a complete Morelia pharmacy from 1868. On permanent exhibition are regional archeological artifacts and displays about mining history and indigenous culture. ✉ *Calle Guillermo Prieto 176* ☎ *443/313–0629* 🎫 *Free* ⏲ *Tues.–Fri. 9–8, weekends 9–7.*

㊽ **Museo Regional Michoacano.** Formerly an 18th-century palace, the museum traces Mexico's history from its pre-Hispanic days through the Cardenista period, which ended in 1940. President Lázaro Cárdenas, a native of Michoacán, was one of Mexico's most popular leaders because he nationalized the oil industry and supported other populist reforms. On the ground floor is an art gallery, plus archaeological exhibits from Michoacán. Upstairs is an assortment of colonial objects, including furniture, weapons, and religious paintings. ⊠ *Calle Allende 305* ☎ *443/ 312–0407* 🖼 *$3, free Sun.* ⊗ *Tues.–Sat. 9–7, Sun. 9–4:30.*

**need a break?** When you've finished your tour of the Museo Regional Michoacano, walk across the street to the colonial stone *portales* (arcades). On one side of the square, the portales are lined with popular sidewalk cafés. For a sandwich, guacamole with chips, or a good selection of juices, coffees, and teas, try **Hotel Casino** (⊠ Portal Hidalgo 229 ☎ 443/ 313–1003).

**㊹ Palacio de Gobierno.** Notable graduates of this former Tridentine seminary, built in 1770, include independence hero José María Morelos, social reformer Melchor Ocampo, and Mexico's first emperor, Agustín de Iturbide. In the 1960s local artist Alfredo Zalce painted the striking murals (on the stairway and second floor), which depict dramatic, often bloody scenes from Mexico's history. Zalce is the last of the great modern muralists still living. ⊠ *Av. Madero 63* ☎ *443/312–8598* 🖼 *Free* ⊗ *Weekdays 8 AM–10 PM, weekends 8 AM–9 PM.*

▶ **㊷ Plaza de Armas.** During the War of Independence, several rebel priests were brutally murdered on this site, and the plaza, known as Plaza de los Mártires, is named after them. Today the square belies its violent past: sweethearts stroll along the tree-lined walks, friends chat under the colossal silver-domed gazebo, and local painters exhibit their work on sunny days. ✛ *Bounded on the north by Av. Madero, on the south by Calle Allende, on the west by Calle Abasolo, and on the east by the cathedral.*

## Where to Eat

Restaurants serve some of Michoacán's tastiest dishes: tomato-based sopa tarasca, corn products such as *huchepos* (sweet tamales) and *corundas* (savory triangular tamales), and game (rabbit and quail). As a rule, more upscale restaurants are in hotels near the plaza and on the outskirts of town.

**$–$$$** ✕ **Fonda Las Mercedes.** Somehow the arty, modern furnishings fit perfectly in this restored colonial mansion's plant-filled stone patio. In chillier weather, you may find the inside dining room to be a cozier option. Offerings from the eclectic menu include lots of soups and six kinds of crepes. If you dare, try the sinfully rich pasta with pistachios and pine nuts in cream sauce. ⊠ *Calle León Guzmán 47* ☎ *443/312–6113* 🍴 *AE, MC, V* ⊗ *No dinner Sun.*

**$–$$** ✕ **Boca del Río.** Fresh seafood for this cheerful yet cafeteria-like restaurant is trucked in daily from Sinaloa and Veracruz. There are light snacks like the popular *coctel de camarones* (shrimp cocktail), along with heartier fare, such as the *jaiba rellena* (mushroom-and-cheese-stuffed crabs liberally seasoned with garlic). For dessert, cross the street to the sprawling Mercado de Dulces. ⊠ *Av. Valentín Gómez Farías 185* ☎ *443/ 313–8691* 🍴 *MC, V.*

**$–$$**  ✕ **Casa de la Calzada.** In a restored weekend home a block and a half from the aqueducts, this elegant restaurant's tables are in a fountain-studded courtyard and in richly painted dining rooms hung with contemporary art. Look for contemporary Mexican dishes like the taste bud fiesta of *pollo del jardín de los naranjos*, chicken stuffed with Mexican sausage and shrimp and coated in a citrus sauce. ⊠ *Calz. Fray Antonio de San Miguel 344* ☎ *443/313–5319* ➟ *AE, MC, V* ◷ *Closed Mon.*

**$–$$**  ✕ **La Casa del Portal.** This venerable restaurant, overlooking the Plaza de Armas, hones in on local dishes. Covered in a succulent red sauce, the corundas are topped with chopped pork, sour cream, and chili poblano strips. Don't miss the *arrachera Valladolid*, a succulent slice of skirt steak with *nopales* (sliced and steamed cactus), guacamole, and beans. ⊠ *Calle Guillermo Prieto 30* ☎ *443/317–4217 or 443/313–4899* ➟ *AE, MC, V.*

**¢–$**  ✕ **Taquería Pioneros.** There's a reason the tables at this positively plain taco shop are packed at lunch: it has delicious grilled meats, prepared Michoacán style, with salsas and mountains of fresh, hot tortillas made on-site. The *pionero* (beef, ham, bacon, onions, and cheese, all grilled) is the only style served in a half portion, which is plenty for most appetites. ⊠ *Calle Aquiles Serdan 7, at Morelos Norte* ☎ *443/313–4938* ⌕ *Reservations not accepted* ➟ *No credit cards.*

## Where to Stay

Several pleasant colonial-style hotels are in downtown Morelia and its outlying areas. Generally, the cheapest properties are near the old and out-of-service bus station; moderately priced selections are clustered around the plaza (or on nearby side streets); deluxe resort hotels are in or near the Santa María hills; and no-nonsense, business-class hotels are on Avenida Camelinas. Downtown hotels are typically the first to fill during the city's organ festival.

**$$–$$$**  🗎 **Hotel Virrey de Mendoza.** Built in 1565 for a Spanish nobleman, this downtown hotel still radiates the atmosphere of a bygone era. A massive stained-glass skylight casts a warm glow over an elegant lobby lounge fitted with an enormous stone fireplace and cushy black leather couches. Guest rooms have dark colonial-style furnishings, lace curtains, soaring ceilings, creaking hardwood floors, and bathrooms with porcelain tubs. ⊠ *Av. Madero Pte. 310, 58000* ☎ *443/312–0633 or 443/312–4940* 🖷 *443/312–6719* ⊕ *www.hotelvirrey.com* ⏎ *40 rooms, 15 suites* ⌂ *Restaurant, coffee shop, cable TV, bar, laundry service, Internet, free parking* ➟ *AE, MC, V.*

**★ $$–$$$**  🗎 **Villa Montaña.** French count Philippe de Reiset fitted this villa with all the trappings of a wealthy Mexican estate. High above Morelia in the Santa María hills, its five impeccably groomed acres are dotted with stone sculptures. Each unit has at least one piece of antique furniture, and most have a fireplace and private patio. The hotel's renowned restaurant serves North American, French, and Mexican cuisine; from its huge windows you'll have a marvelous view of Morelia, especially at night. Children under eight are discouraged from dining in the restaurant. ⊠ *Calle Patzimba 201, 58000* ☎ *443/314–0231 or 443/314–0179* 🖷 *443/315–1423* ⊕ *www.villamontana.com.mx* ⏎ *36 suites* ⌂ *Restaurant, in-*

*room safes, tennis court, pool, gym, piano bar, baby-sitting, laundry service, business services, meeting rooms, free parking* ⊟ *AE, MC, V.*

**$$** 🏨 **Hotel Horizon.** Though it lacks the charm of older, downtown hotels, this four-star, executive-style hotel has great amenities, prices, and service—and usually has vacant rooms even when the downtown hotels are full. In the heart of Morelia's growing modern commercial district, the hotel's a 15-minute, $3 cab ride from downtown. ⊠ *Avenida Camelinas 3325, Oculusen 58270* ☎ *443/324–4646 or 01800/455–5000* ⊕ *www.horizon.com.mx* 📞 *80 rooms* ♻ *Restaurant, minibars, cable TV, pool, gym, hot tub, Internet, business services, meeting rooms, free parking* ⊟ *AE, MC, V.*

**$$** 🏨 **Hotel Posada de la Soledad.** A private mansion built in the 17th century, this is now a charming hotel one block from the Plaza de Armas. In the original section, rooms surround an elegant patio with a large fountain and massive bougainvilleas. Smaller, plainer, and quieter rooms are in the newer section. Rooms on Calle Ocampo get loud traffic noise from the street. Not impressed with the room you're shown? You can always ask to see another. ⊠ *Ignacio Zaragoza 90, 58000* ☎ *443/312–1888 or 443/312–8990* 🖷 *443/312–2111* ⊕ *www.hsoledad.com* 📞 *42 rooms, 9 suites* ♻ *Restaurant, cable TV, bar* ⊟ *AE, MC, V.*

**$–$$** 🏨 **Hotel Mansión Acueducto.** An elaborate wood-and-wrought-iron staircase leads from the elegant lobby to more-modest quarters upstairs. Rooms have dark, colonial-style furniture; older units overlook the aqueduct and nearby park. A motel-like wing has rooms with views of the garden, pool, and surrounding city. At times, student groups book the entire property. ⊠ *Av. Acueducto 25, 58230* ☎ *443/312–3301, 866/589–3411 in the U.S. and Canada* 🖷 *443/312–2020* ⊕ *www.hotelmansionacueducto.com* 📞 *36 rooms, 1 suite* ♻ *Restaurant, cable TV, pool, bar, free parking, no-smoking rooms* ⊟ *MC, V.*

**¢** 🏨 **Hotel Valladolid.** Right on the Plaza de Armas, this property has plain but clean rooms with brick floors and striped bedspreads. Although the accommodations are far from deluxe, this location offers easy downtown access, and the staff is friendly. ⊠ *Portal Hidalgo 245, 58000* ☎ *443/312–0027* 🖷 *443/312–4663* 📞 *25 rooms* ♻ *Restaurant; no room phones* ⊟ *MC, V.*

## Nightlife & the Arts

Morelia has two lively folk-music clubs, both in beautiful downtown locations. **Colibri** (⊠ Galeana 36 ☎ 443/312–2261) has Latin American folk music every night from 9:30 PM to 1 AM. Spirited salsa music is played at **La Porfiriana** (⊠ Calle Corregidora 694 ☎ 443/312–2663) Tuesday–Saturday 9 PM–3 AM.

## Side Trip to Santuario de Mariposas el Rosario

*Approximately 115 km (71 mi) east of Morelia.*

One hundred million monarch butterflies migrate annually from the United States and Canada to winter in the easternmost part of Michoacán, near México state's border. A visit to the **Santuario de Mariposas el Rosario** between early November and early March is an awesome sensory ex-

Fodor's Choice
★

perience. Caked with orange-and-black butterflies, the sanctuary's pine forest looks like it's on fire. Listen closely and you'll hear the rustle of millions of wings beating. The hike to the groves is a steep climb, and the high altitude (10,400 feet) will require that you take it slowly.

This day trip takes about 10 hours, but it's absolutely worth the effort. If you choose not to drive the rough roads, catch a guided tour in Morelia. ✥ *Hwy. 15 east to Zitácuaro, then take marked but unnumbered road north to Angangueo, and on to sanctuary entrance* ☎ *No phone* 💰 *$2 (plus tip for guide)* ⊘ *Daily 10–5.*

## Morelia A to Z

### AIR TRAVEL

AIRPORT  Aeropuerto Internacional Francisco Mujica (MLM) is 24 km (15 mi) north of Morelia.

AIRPORT  A taxi ride between the town center and the airport will probably cost
TRANSFERS  you about $12.

CARRIERS  Aeroméxico flies daily to Morelia from Mexico City's international airport.
🛪 **Aeroméxico** ☎ 800/021–4000 in the U.S. ⊕ www.aeromexico.com.

### BUS TRAVEL

Direct bus service is available daily between the Terminal Poniente (commonly referred to as the Observatorio) in Mexico City and Morelia's Central de Autobuses. Several bus lines have frequent service; the most direct trip ($24) takes four hours on ETN. Herradura de Plata is another bus line. Buses leave every hour or two around the clock.
🛪 **Central de Autobuses** ✉ Periférico de la República 5555, across the street from Estadio Morelos soccer stadium ☎ 443/334–1075. **ETN** ☎ 443/334–1063. **Herradura de Plata** ☎ 443/334–1096.

### CAR RENTAL

Budget has an office at the Francisco Mujica airport. National's office is beside the airport.
🛪 **Budget** ✉ Aeropuerto Internacional Francisco Mujica ☎ 443/313–3399 ⊕ www.budget.com.

### CAR TRAVEL

The drive from Mexico City to Morelia on the toll road, Highway 15, through Toluca, Atlacamulco, Contepec, and Maravatio takes about four hours.

### EMERGENCIES

Dial 070 for medical, fire, and theft emergencies.
🛪 **Ambulance–Red Cross** ☎ 443/314–5151. **Consumer Protection Office** ☎ 443/315–6202. **Fire Department** ☎ 443/320–1780. **Hospital de la Cruz Roja** ☎ 443/314–5073. **Hospital Memorial** ☎ 443/315–1047 or 443/315–1099. **Police** ☎ 443/326–8522.

**INTERNET**
Chat Room Cyber Café, open Monday–Saturday 9 AM–10 PM and Sunday noon–9, charges $2 an hour for Internet access.
🛈 Internet Café **Chat Room Cyber Café** ✉ Calle Nigromante 132-A ☎ 443/313–9984.

**MONEY MATTERS**
Consultoría Internacional Casa de Cambio is open Monday–Saturday 9:30–5:30.
🛈 **Consultoría Internacional Casa de Cambio** ✉ Calle Guillermo Prieto 48 ☎ 443/313–8308 or 01800/230–1111.

**TOURS**
The local tourism department offers 50-minute bus tours of the city's main sights for $3.20—buses leave every half hour from 10 to 7 Tuesday through Sunday on a variety of tour options. Guided by local historians, the impossible-to-miss bus marked "Kuanari" boards on Abasolo off the Plaza de Armas. For tours in English book at least a day ahead.

Several worthy operators conduct tours of Morelia and the butterfly sanctuary. Contact Ayangupani through David Saucedo Ortega at the Villa Montaña front desk.
🛈 Tour Operator Recommendations **Ayangupani** ✉ Calle Patzimba 201 ☎🖷 443/315–4045. **Explora Viajes** ✉ Av. Madero Ote. 493B ☎ 443/312–7766 🖷 443/312–7660. **Kuanari Bus Tours** ☎ 443/400–2993. **Morelia Operadores de Viajes** ✉ Isidro Huarte 481 ☎ 443/312–8723 or 443/312–8747 🖷 443/312–9591.

**TRANSPORTATION AROUND MORELIA**
As in many heartland cities, Morelia's major sights are near the town's center and are easy to reach on foot. Street names in Morelia change frequently, especially on either side of Avenida Madero, the city's main east–west artery. Taxis can be hailed on the street or near the main plaza. Buses run the length of Avenida Madero.

**TRAVEL AGENCIES**
Gran Turismo is the American Express representative.
🛈 **Gran Turismo** ✉ Edificio Ejecutivo Camelinas, Av. Camelinas 3233, Int. 102–103 ☎ 443/324–0484 🖷 443/324–0495.

**VISITOR INFORMATION**
Secretaría Estatal de Turismo is open weekdays 9–8, Saturday 9–7, and Sunday 9–3.
🛈 Tourist Information **Secretaría Estatal de Turismo** ✉ Palacio Clavijero, Calle Nigromante 79 ☎ 443/317–2371 🖷 443/312–9816.

# PÁTZCUARO

*58 km (36 mi) southwest of Morelia.*

The 16th-century capital of Michoacán exists in a time warp. This beautiful lakeside community at 7,250 feet in the Sierra Madre is home to the Purépecha Indians, who fish, farm, and ply their crafts as they have for centuries. Women wrapped tightly in striped wool *rebozos* (shawls) hurry to market in the chilly morning air. Men in traditional straw hats wheel overburdened carts down crooked, dusty backstreets.

The architecture, too, has remained largely unchanged since kindly Bishop Vasco de Quiroga oversaw Pátzcuaro's 16th-century building boom. After he died in 1565, the state capital was moved to Morelia, and the town became a cultural (and architectural) backwater for hundreds of years. These days 16th-century mansions surround the downtown plazas; one-story whitewashed houses with sloping red-tile roofs line the side streets and hills.

Despite the altitude, the weather in Pátzcuaro is temperate year-round. (Autumn and winter nights, however, are cold; sweaters and jackets are a must.) On November 1 the town is inundated with tourists en route to Janítzio, an island in Lake Pátzcuaro, where one of Mexico's most elaborate Day of the Dead graveyard ceremonies takes place. At numerous small towns around the lake you can buy craft items from their makers, in the process absorbing a bit of small-town rural Mexico.

## Exploring Pátzcuaro

You can zip through Pátzcuaro's historic center, but the town and outlying areas merit a more leisurely exploration. There can be some traffic in the Plaza Bocanegra and on the main road coming into town, but elsewhere it is blissfully quiet.

a good walk

Start your walk at the tourist office on the **Plaza Vasco de Quiroga** ㉜ ⌐. Cross to the east side of the square and turn right on Calle Dr. José María Coss; in less than a block you'll see a long cobblestone walkway leading to **La Casa de los 11 Patios** ㉝, a former convent now containing several crafts shops. As you leave the complex, continue up a stone walkway to Calle Lerín. To the north (past Calle Portugal) is the **Templo de la Compañía** ㉞, the state's first cathedral. After visiting the church, continue another half block north to the **Museo de Artes Populares** ㉟ on your right.

Directly down Enseñanza Arciga and across a cobblestone courtyard is **La Basílica de Nuestra Señora de la Salud** ㊱. Walk downhill from the Basílica (take Buena Vista to Calle Libertad and turn left) to reach the **Biblioteca Pública Gertrudis Bocanegra** ㊲. For a nice detour from the library, continue for a half block to the large outdoor mercado sprawled along Calle Libertad and its side streets. At times the road is so crowded with people and their wares—fruit, vegetables, beans, rice, herbs, and other necessities of daily life—that it's difficult to walk. If you press on for about a block, you'll see an indoor market to your left, filled with more produce, large hanging slabs of meat, hot food, cheap trinkets, and locally made wool garments. When you're finished with your market tour, retrace your steps down Calle Libertad. Across the street from the library, you can rest at **Plaza Bocanegra** ㊳, one block north of your starting point, Plaza Vasco de Quiroga.

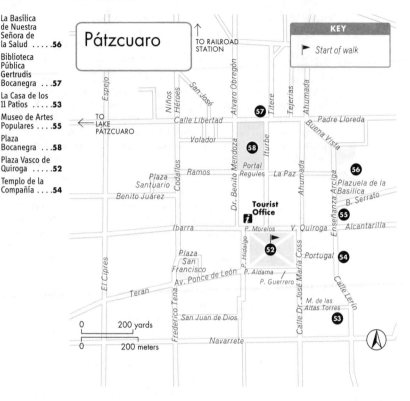

TIMING   A brisk walk through town will take just a couple of hours; allow more
time for Pátzcuaro's dozens of crafts stores, the craft museum (closed
Monday), and for a break in a café.

## What to See

▶ **56 La Basílica de Nuestra Señora de la Salud.** Vasco de Quiroga began this
church in 1554, and throughout the centuries others—undaunted by earthquakes and fires—took up the cause and eventually completed it in honor
of the Virgin of Health. Near the main altar is a statue of the Virgin made
of derivatives of cornstalks and orchids. Several masses are held daily;
the earliest begins shortly after dawn. Out front, Purépecha women sell
hot tortillas, herbal mixtures for teas, and religious objects. Lake
Pátzcuaro is visible in the distance. ⊠ *Enseñanza Arciga, near Calle Be-
nigno Serrato* 🕾 *No phone.*

**57 Biblioteca Pública Gertrudis Bocanegra.** Juan O'Gorman painted a vast
mural, depicting in great detail the history of the region and of the
Purépecha people, in the back of this library in 1942. At the bottom right,
you can see Gertrudis Bocanegra, a local heroine who was shot in 1814
for refusing to divulge the revolutionaries' secrets to the Spaniards.
⊠ *North side of Plaza Bocanegra* ☉ *Weekdays 9–7.*

**53** **La Casa de los 11 Patios.** High-quality shops featuring Purépecha handiwork are housed in this 18th-century convent. As you meander through the shops and courtyards, you'll encounter weavers producing large bolts of cloth, artists trimming black lacquerware with gold, and seamstresses embroidering blouses. If you plan to shop in Pátzcuaro, this is a good place to start. ⊠ *Calle Madrigal de las Altas Torres s/n* ⊘ *Daily 10–2 and 4–8; some shops close Monday.*

**55** **Museo de Artes Populares.** The 16th-century home of the Colegio de San Nicolás Obispo now displays colonial and contemporary crafts, such as ceramics, masks, lacquerware, paintings, and ex-votos in its many rooms. Behind this building is a *troje* (traditional Purépecha wooden house) braced atop a stone platform. ⊠ *Enseñanza Arciga* ☎ *434/ 342–1029* 🎟 *About $3* ⊘ *Tues.–Sat. 9–7, Sun. 9–2:30.*

**58** **Plaza Bocanegra.** The smaller of the city's two squares (it's also called Plaza Chica), this is Pátzcuaro's commercial center. Bootblacks, push-cart vendors, and bus and taxi stands are all in the plaza, which is embellished by a statue of the local heroine, Gertrudis Bocanegra. ⊕ *Bounded by Av. Libertad on the north, Portal Regules on the south, Benito Mendoza on the west, and Iturbe on the east.*

▶ **52** **Plaza Vasco de Quiroga.** A tranquil courtyard girded by towering, century-old ash and pine trees and 16th-century mansions (since converted into hotels and shops), the larger of the two downtown plazas commemorates the bishop who restored dignity to the Purépecha people. During the Spanish conquest, Nuño de Guzmán, a lieutenant in Hernán Cortés's army, committed atrocities against the local population in his efforts to conquer western Mexico. He was eventually arrested by the Spanish authorities, and in 1537 Vasco de Quiroga was appointed bishop of Michoacán. To regain the trust of the indigenous people, he established model villages in the area and promoted the development of *artesanía* (crafts) commerce among the Purépechas. Quiroga died in 1565, and his remains were consecrated in the **Basílica de Nuestra Señora de la Salud.** ⊕ *Bounded by Calle Quiroga on the north, Av. Ponce de León on the south, Portal Hidalgo on the west, and Calle Dr. José María Coss on the east.*

**need a break?** Before heading to Lake Pátzcuaro, sit in **Plaza Vasco de Quiroga** for a moment and savor the rich Michoacán ice cream available under the portals on the west side of the plaza. Or sip a warming Doña Paca cappuccino spiked with *rompope* (egg liqueur) at the sidewalk café in front of Mansión Iturbe.

**54** **Templo de la Compañía.** Michoacán's first cathedral was begun in 1540 by order of Vasco de Quiroga and completed in 1546. When the state capital was moved to Morelia some 20 years later, the church was taken over by the Jesuits. It remains much as it was in the 16th century. Moss has grown over the crumbling stone steps outside; the dank interior is planked with thick wood floors and lined with bare wood benches. ⊠ *Calle Lerín s/n, east end of Portugal* ☎ *No phone.*

**LAKE PÁTZCUARO** – The tranquil shores of Lake Pátzcuaro are just a 10-minute cab ride from downtown. A few lakeside restaurants here serve fresh whitefish and other local catches. Amble along the dock or peek into the waterfront crafts shops. Try to make time for a boat trip to **Janítzio** (the largest of Lake Pátzcuaro's five islands) or to tiny **Yunuen,** which offers a clear-eyed view of island life. Wooden launches, with room for 25 people, depart for Janítzio and the other islands daily 9–6. Purchase round-trip tickets for $3.50 at a dockside office (prices are controlled by the tourist department). The ride to Janítzio takes about 30 minutes and is particularly beautiful in late afternoon, when the sun is low in the sky. Once you're out on the lake, fishermen with butterfly nets may approach your boat. The nets are no longer used for fishing, but for a small donation these locals will let you take their picture.

On most days (November 1 being the exception), Janítzio is a quiet albeit touristy island inhabited by Purépecha Indians. It's crowned by a huge statue of independence hero José María Morelos, which is accessible by a cobblestone stairway. Although the road twists past many souvenir stands as it ascends, don't be discouraged. The view from the summit—of the lake, the town, and the surrounding hills—is well worth the climb. Inside the statue are some remarkable murals that spiral up from the base to the tip of the monument.

Although Janítzio has succumbed to tourism, the small island of Yunuen is just beginning to attract visitors. This tranquil town has a few families, and provides a more accurate picture of island life than does Janítzio. You can take a boat here from the ferry landing, or arrange an overnight stay in simple yet clean visitor cabins. The office of tourism can provide information.

## Where to Eat

Restaurants in Pátzcuaro specialize in seafood, such as whitefish, *trucha* (trout), and *charales* and *boquerones* (two small, locally caught fish served as appetizers). Finding a satisfying meal in Pátzcuaro can be a challenge; focusing on local Purépecha dishes, such as sopa tarasca, may prove most rewarding. As a rule, restaurants are around the two plazas and in hotels. Since the large meal is served at midday, many dining establishments are shuttered by 9.

**$–$$** ✕ **El Primer Piso.** On warm nights you can watch activities in the Plaza Vasco de Quiroga from a balcony table at this second-floor restaurant. Inside, the restaurant doubles as an art gallery. The eclectic menu provides a break from rather monotonous Pátzcuaro fare: try the pear salad with goat cheese, walnuts, and watercress, or the white-chocolate mousse with blackberries and melon cream. ⊠ *Plaza Vasco de Quiroga 29* 🕾 *434/342–0122* ▭ *AE, MC, V* ☾ *Closed Tues.*

**¢–$$** ✕ **Doña Paca.** At this terrific family-run restaurant you'll find some of the best examples of local cuisine. Look for the fish specials and the tamale-like corundas with cream sauce. ☒ *Hotel Mansión Iturbe, Portal Morelos 59* ☎ *434/342–0268* 🖃 *AE, MC, V* ⌦ *No breakfast.*

¢–$ ✕ **El Patio.** It's possible to duck into this low-key restaurant at midday for simply a strong cappuccino or glass of Mexican wine, but you should definitely try the mouthwatering whitefish platters when they're available (these days whitefish is a hard catch). For a late-afternoon snack, go for a plate of quesadillas with a side order of guacamole or the sopa tarasca. ☒ *Plaza Vasco de Quiroga 19* ☎ *434/342–0484* 🖃 *MC, V.*

¢–$ ✕ **El Viejo Gaucho.** Join the crowd for a festive night of live music from North, Central, and South America performed in front of a mural, repainted each season. Try the *churrasco Argentino* (seasoned steak) and don't forget to top it with *chimichurri* (an Argentine sauce made with fresh herbs and olive oil). Most entrées are pseudo-Argentinian, but there are also pizza, hamburgers, and french fries. ☒ *Iturbe 10* ☎ *434/342– 3627* 🖃 *AE, MC, V* ☉ *No lunch.*

## Where to Stay

Although Pátzcuaro has no deluxe hotels, there are several clean, moderately priced properties. Most are on or within a few blocks of the Plaza Vasco de Quiroga. Several more-expensive hotels are on Avenida Lázaro Cárdenas, the road to Lake Pátzcuaro. If you're planning to be in town on or near November 1–2, the Day of the Dead, make hotel reservations at least six months in advance.

★ $$$ ▦ **Hacienda Mariposas.** A friendly bilingual staff and terrific restaurant are just some of the exceptional amenities at this getaway. Low-tech distractions include live music during dinner, horseback riding trips, and birdsong from the surrounding pine forest. Guest rooms have fireplaces (as well as central heating) and beds topped with down comforters, plus CD players with a selection of music. The property is a few minutes' drive from town; transportation to and from Pátzcuaro is included. ☒ *Santa Clara del Cobre Hwy., Km 3, 61600* ☎ *443/333–0762, 800/ 573–2386 in the U.S.* 🖷 *707/575–1166* ⊕ *www.haciendamariposas.com* ⤶ *12 rooms* ♿ *Restaurant, spa, horseback riding; no room TVs* 🖃 *AE, MC, V* ⏺ *BP.*

★ $–$$$ ▦ **La Casa Encantada.** Fans of open-air and colonial-style living should stay in this restored 17th-century home in the heart of Pátzcuaro. Complementing its four distinct, colorful suites, this B&B has a beautifully groomed garden, a large hacienda-style living room with a fireplace, and gourmet breakfast. A half-block from the Plaza de Quiroga, it's got one of the best locations in town. Don't worry, La Casa Encantada isn't haunted—no matter what your Spanish-English dictionary says the name means. ☒ *Dr. Coss 15, Centro 61600* ☎ *434/342–3492* ⊕ *www.lacasaencantada.com* ⤶ *4 suites* ♿ *Cable TV, in-room VCRs, massage* 🖃 *No credit cards.*

$$ ▦ **Hotel Posada La Basílica.** On some mornings, strains from mass at the neighboring Basílica de Nuestra Señora de la Salud filter softly into this inn. The 17th-century building has comfortable, individually decorated rooms, some with fireplaces. Thick wood shutters cover floor-to-ceiling windows, and walls are trimmed in hand-painted colonial designs.

✉ *Enseñanza Arciga 6, 61600* ☎ *434/342–1108* 📠 *434/342–0659* 🖥 *12 rooms* ⚬ *Restaurant, free parking; no a/c* ⊟ *AE, MC, V.*

★ **$$** 🏨 **Mansión Iturbe.** Stone archways ring plant-filled courtyards in this 17th-century mansion, which retains much of its colonial sensibility. Rooms, with large wood-and-glass doors, are partially carpeted. Bicycles are lent to guests for a few hours per stay, and every fourth night is free. The owners are an excellent source of information regarding Pátzcuaro and the surrounding areas. ✉ *Portal Morelos 59, 61600* ☎ *434/342–0368 or 434/342–3628* 📠 *443/313–4593 in Morelia* ⊕ *www.mexonline. com/iturbe.htm* 🖥 *12 rooms* ⚬ *3 restaurants, bicycles, travel services, no-smoking rooms* ⊟ *AE, MC, V* ⊙ *BP.*

**$** 🏨 **Los Escudos.** Originally a 16th-century home, this cozy hotel has courtyards blooming with potted plants and guest rooms adorned with small murals. Ten rooms in the back are shielded from street noise and open onto an outdoor patio; five rooms have fireplaces. ✉ *Portal Hidalgo 73, 61600* ☎ *434/342–0138 or 434/342–1290* 📠 *434/342–0649* 🖥 *42 rooms* ⚬ *Restaurant, free parking* ⊟ *MC, V.*

**¢** 🏨 **Cabañas Yunuen.** This complex was built on the island of Yunuen in collaboration with the Department of Tourism to promote visits to some of the area's more authentic communities. There are six cabins in all: two each for 2, 4, and 16 people; each cabin has a kitchenette with small refrigerator. Breakfast or dinner and round-trip transportation by boat is included in the price. Be sure to call ahead for reservations. ✉ *Domicilio Conocido, Isla de Yunuen* ☎ *434/342–4473* 🖥 *6 cabins* ⚬ *Dining room, kitchenettes, billiards, Ping-Pong* ⊟ *No credit cards.*

## Nightlife & the Arts

The **Danza de los Viejitos** (Dance of the Old Men) is a widely known regional dance performed during Saturday dinner at **Hotel Posada de Don Vasco** (✉ Av. Las Americas 450) for about $15 (includes dinner). It's also performed Saturday night at 8:30 PM at Los Escudos, on Plaza Vasco de Quiroga. On weekends dancers perform for tips in the plaza and outside the boarding area to Janítzio.

## Shopping

With dozens of crafts shops around town, Pátzcuaro has some of Mexico's finest folk-art shopping. There are good deals at the stalls outside the Basílica and the marketplace off Plaza Bocanegra. **Artesanías El Naranjo** (✉ Plaza Vasco de Quiroga 29-2), an intimate group of stores, offers a variety of ceramics, clothing, and folk art. **Bordados Santa Cruz** (✉ Calle Dr. José María Coss 3 ☎ 433/338–1425) is a women's embroidery collective. For fresh-ground local coffee packaged in burlap bags, visit **El Café Uruapan** (✉ Benito Mendoza 3 ☎ 434/342–5061). Since 1898, the family-run **Chocolate Casero Joaquinita** (✉ Enseñanza Arciga 38 ☎ 434/342–4514) has been concocting delectable homemade cinnamon-spiced hot-chocolate tablets. Don't miss the stands in front of the Basílica and at the daily mercado west of Plaza Chica for inexpensive local crafts. **Mantas Tipicas** (✉ Calle Dr. José María Coss 5 ☎ 434/342–1324) sells hand-loomed tablecloths, place mats, and curtain and cushion fabric. Visit the doorway of Jesús García Zavala at **Plateria García** (✉ Enseñanza Arciga 28 ☎ 434/342–2036) for hand-worked silver Purépecha jewelry in the pre-Columbian tradition. **Santa Teresa Velas y Cirios** (✉ Portugal 1 ☎ 434/342–4997) sells handmade candles.

## Side Trips from Pátzcuaro

### Tzintzuntzan

*17 km (10½ mi) northeast of Pátzcuaro.*

When the Spanish arrived to colonize the region in the 16th century, some 40,000 Purépechas lived and worshiped in this lakeshore village, which they called "place of the hummingbirds." The ruins of the pyramid-shape temples, or *yacatas,* found in the ancient capital of the Purépecha kingdom, still stand and are open to the public for $2. There are also vestiges of a 16th-century Franciscan monastery where Spanish friars attempted to convert the Indians to Christianity. Although Tzintzuntzan lost some prominence when Bishop Vasco de Quiroga moved the seat of his diocese to Pátzcuaro in 1540, the village is still well known for the straw and ceramic crafts made by the Purépecha Indians and sold in numerous shops along the main street of town. The bus marked QUIROGA takes a half hour to get from Pátzcuaro's Central Camionera to Tzintzuntzan.

### Santa Clara del Cobre

*20 km (12½ mi) south of Pátzcuaro.*

Even before the conquest, Santa Clara del Cobre was a center for copper arts. Now the local copper mines are empty, but artisans still make gorgeous vessels, plates, napkin rings, and jewelry using the traditional method of hand-pounding each piece of metal. For an introduction to available styles, visit the **Museo del Cobre** (✉ Calles Morelos and Pino Suárez, near the plaza), open Tuesday–Sunday 10–3 and 5–7. Admission is 50¢. Then explore the 50-some little shops and factories in town. The friendly owners speak English at **Arte y Cobre** (✉ Calle Pino Suárez 53 ☎ No phone). Although the selection isn't as extensive as other shops along the square, the prices are often less expensive. The bus to Santa Clara del Cobre from Pátzcuaro's Central Camionera takes 40 minutes.

### Uruapan

*64 km (40 mi) west of Pátzcuaro.*

The subtropical town of Uruapan is distinctly different from its lakeside neighbor: some 2,000 feet lower than Pátzcuaro, although still at an elevation of 5,300 feet, it's a populous commercial center with a warm climate and lush vegetation. The town's name is derived from the Purépecha word *urupan,* meaning "where the flowers bloom." Uruapan celebrates Palm Sunday with a lively procession through the streets, brass bands, and a spectacular, bargain-filled crafts market in the central plaza—one of the best in all of Mexico.

You can get to Uruapan from Pátzcuaro by car or bus. Highway 14 and the toll road are the most direct routes between the two cities. There's frequent bus service on the Flecha Amarilla and other major lines; travel time is about 70 minutes.

You can see several points of interest within a few hours. The **Mercado de Antojitos,** an immense, sprawling market, begins in back of the Museo Regional de Arte Popular and extends farther north on Calle Constitución. Along the road, Purépecha Indians sell large mounds of produce, fresh fish, beans, homemade cheese, and cheap manufactured goods. If you travel south along Calle Constitución, you'll come to a courtyard where vendors sell hot food.

The **Museo Regional de Arte Popular,** opposite the north side of Uruapan's Plaza Principal, was a 16th-century hospital before its conversion. It exhibits crafts from the state of Michoacán, including an excellent display of lacquerware made in Uruapan. 🕾 *452/524–3434* 🕾 *Free* ☉ *Tues.–Sun. 9:30–1:30 and 3:30–6.*

**Parque Nacional Eduardo Ruiz** (about six long blocks from the Plaza Principal off Calle Independencia) is an urban park with paved paths that meander through verdant tropical acreage past abundant waterfalls, fountains, and springs to the source of the Río Cupatitzio. There's also a trout farm and a popular playground.

Eleven kilometers (7 mi) south along the Río Cupatitzio is the magnificent waterfall at **Tzaráracua.** At this point the river plunges 150 feet off a sheer rock cliff into a riverbed below; a rainbow seems to hang perpetually over the site. Buses marked TZARÁRACUA leave sporadically from the Plaza Principal in Uruapan. You can also take a taxi for about $3, or drive there via Avenida Lázaro Cárdenas.

Farther afield, about 32 km (20 mi) north of Uruapan, lies the dormant **Paricutín volcano.** Its initial burst of lava and ashes wiped out the nearby village of San Juan Parangaricútiro in 1943. Today travelers can visit this buried site by hiring gentle mountain ponies and a Purépecha guide in the town of Angahuan. You can also hike over surreal grey sands and volcanic rock to the still-steaming crater. The trail isn't clearly marked, so it's highly advisable to get a guide (there are plenty of local children ready to volunteer at the park entrance for a reasonable price). Get an early start and carry lots of water because the round trip takes all day. Also wear sturdy shoes or hiking boots and be careful with the sometimes treacherous volcanic rock. To reach Angahuan, take Los Reyes bus from Uruapan's Central Camionera or go by car via the Uruapan-Carapan highway.

## Pátzcuaro A to Z

### BUS TRAVEL
Buses run daily between the Terminal Poniente (commonly referred to as the Observatorio) in Mexico City and Pátzcuaro's Central Camionera on the southwestern outskirts of town. Several lines offer frequent service; the most direct trip takes five hours and is on either Herradura de Plata, Pegasso Plus, or ETN. Transportation coming from most

heartland cities goes to Morelia; buses leave about every 15 minutes from there on the 45-minute trip to Pátzcuaro.

**f** Bus Depot **Central Camionera** ⊠ El Libramiento ☎ 434/342–0960.

**f** Bus Information **ETN** ☎ 434/342–1060, 443/313–7440 in Morelia. **Herradura de Plata and Pegasso Plus** ☎ 434/342–1045.

### CAR TRAVEL
The Mexico City–Guadalajara tollway cuts driving time to Pátzcuaro to 4½ or 5 hours, and the trip on to Guadalajara to 4 hours. From Morelia, the excellent free road to Pátzcuaro takes just over an hour. You'll have to rent a car in Mexico City or Morelia, as there are no rental outlets in Pátzcuaro.

### EMERGENCIES
Pharmacies are plentiful; Farmacia Gems is popular with residents. Pátzcuaro offers medical services through Hospital Civil.

**f Farmacia Gems** ⊠ Benito Mendoza 21 ☎ 434/342–0332. **Hospital Civil** ⊠ Romero 10 ☎ 434/342–0285. **Police** ☎ 434/342–0004. **Traffic Police** ☎ 434/342–0565.

### INTERNET
Meganet is a funky café with Internet service daily 9–10 for about $1.20 an hour. Punto Com is open Monday–Saturday 10–9 and charges about $1 an hour for Internet access.

**f** Internet Café **Meganet Internet y Cafetería** ⊠ Benito Mendoza 8. **Punto Com** ⊠ Arciga 20 ☎ 434/342–3596.

### MONEY MATTERS
Bancomer–BBVA has a 24-hour ATM. Banamex has an ATM for use during business hours.

**f Banamex** ⊠ Portal Juárez 32 ☎ 434/342–1550 or 434/342–1031. **Bancomer–BBVA** ⊠ Benito Mendoza 23 ☎ 434/342–0901.

### TOURS
Guide Francisco Castilleja knows a lot about pre-Hispanic philosophy, history, archaeology, and medicinal herbs. He speaks fluent English, German, French, and Spanish. Guide and anthropologist Miguel Angel Nuñez specializes in off-the-beaten-path visits to nearby indigenous communities as well as local sights. He speaks Spanish, English, and German.

**f** Tour Operator Recommendations **Francisco Castilleja** ⊠ Centro Eronga, Profr. Urueta 105 ☎ 434/344–0167. **Miguel Angel Nuñez** ☎ 434/344–0108.

### TRANSPORTATION AROUND PÁTZCUARO
Many of Pátzcuaro's principal sights are near the Plaza Vasco de Quiroga and Plaza Bocanegra in the center of town. Taxis and buses to the lake can also be found at the latter square. If you want to visit surrounding villages, taxi drivers will drive you for a reasonable rate. Be sure to agree on a fee before setting out.

### VISITOR INFORMATION
Delegación de Turismo is the official tourism office, and although you may not find anyone here who speaks English, they do their best to pro-

vide information regarding excursions outside Pátzcuaro. It's open Monday–Saturday 9–3 and 4–8, Sunday 9–3.

Dirección de Orientación y Fomento al Turismo offers maps and can answer basic questions about tourist facilities in Pátzcuaro. It's open daily 9–3 and 5–7.

🇮 **Delegación de Turismo** ✉ Plaza Vasco de Quiroga 50A ☎☎ 434/342–0215 or 434/342–0216. **Dirección de Orientación y Fomento al Turismo** ✉ Portal Hidalgo 1, on Plaza de Quiroga ☎ 434/342–0215 or 434/342–0216 🖷 434/342–0967.

# PACIFIC COAST RESORTS

**BEST PLACE TO SPY ON CELEBS**
Costa Alegre's low-key
Las Alamandas resort ⇨*p.399*

**BEST MARATHON BRUNCH SERVICE**
The 9-to-5 affair at Daiquiri Dick's ⇨*p.391*

**BEST WAY TO DITCH THE CROWDS**
Escape to rustic Zihuatanejo ⇨*p.420*

**SAILFISH CAPITAL OF THE WORLD**
Manzanillo ⇨*p.414*

**MOST CREATIVE CHEF**
Thierry Blouet at Puerto Vallarta's
Café des Artistes ⇨*p.391*

**BEST DEEP-SEA FISHING**
Mazatlán ⇨*p.379*

Updated by
Jane Onstott

**AQUAMARINE SWELLS UNDULATE, BREAKING UPON SANDY BEACHES.**
Lanky coconut trees shade huts thatched in leaves of palm. Waves are
sliced by boogie boarders, jet-skiers, and surfers. Coves shelter schools
of fish followed by curious snorkelers, and mangroves are a haven for
birds of all stripes. Fishermen stand thigh deep in the surf, tossing their
weighted nets into the sea, and each stretch of sand holds the promise
of a glorious sunset. Whatever your pleasure, the Pacific Coast (a.k.a.
the Mexican Riviera or the Gold Coast) is the place to relax, restore,
recharge, or even reinvent yourself.

At the coast's northern end, Mazatlán is a commercial and shipping center. Produce from fertile area farmlands—including melons, cantaloupes,
wheat, and cotton—are shipped from here, as are thousands of tons of
shrimp, tuna, and sardines. The city gained prominence in the mid-19th
century, and its historic downtown has several charming plazas and some
beautifully restored late-19th- and early-20th-century buildings. Proximity to the United States, excellent sportfishing, and nice beaches account for Mazatlán's popularity.

It was at the lovely beach called Mismaloya that late film director John
Huston put Puerto Vallarta on the map, filming Tennessee Williams's
*The Night of the Iguana* in 1963. Although not cast in the picture, Elizabeth Taylor accompanied Richard Burton during filming, and the gossip about their romance (both were married at the time, but not to each
other) brought this tiny fishing village to the public's attention. Since
then the number of residents and visitors has doubled many times.
Creature comforts have arrived, along with reliable Internet access,
Sam's Club, Walmart, and a large foreign population that abandons town
during the dog days of summer. Despite its growth, Puerto Vallarta retains many charms: beautiful beaches, awesome shopping, great restaurants. For a sense of the Eden that once was, visit one of the small towns
north toward Punta de Mita and beyond, or south toward Manzanillo.

The government has worked steadily to develop tourism along the coast
between Puerto Vallarta and Manzanillo, dubbing it La Costa Alegre
(The Happy Coast). A four-lane toll road has cut the driving time between Manzanillo and Guadalajara, Jalisco State's capital and Mexico's
second-largest city, to three hours. About an hour north of Manzanillo,
the Grand Bay Hotel epitomizes the contrast between the area's traditional fishing villages and the modern resorts. The Grand Bay's impeccably groomed grounds, elegant buildings, and white-glove order stand
in stark contrast to the nearby town of Barra de Navidad, with its
sandy streets and humble homes whose thatched roofs disappear during storms.

The least glamorous of the Pacific Coast resorts, Manzanillo was founded
soon after the Spanish conquest. Hernán Cortés envisioned Manzanillo
as a gateway to the Orient: from these shores, Spanish galleons brought
in the riches of Cathay to be trekked across the continent to Veracruz,
where they filled vessels headed for Spain. Bolivian tin magnate Antenor
Patiño chose it for the site of a lavish Moorish-style Las Hadas resort
in 1974. For a while it and its exclusive clientele were better known than

# Beaches

The Pacific coast has inviting beaches, with deliciously warm waters and spectacular sunsets. There are fishing villages where a tiny number of ex-pats have made the switch to unpaved streets and hammocks—the simple life. There are also surf meccas whose praises have long been sung from one surfer to the next as well as on the pages of glossy magazines. There are places to parasail above the waves, jump aboard a brain-bouncing banana boat, or just sip a cold drink brought to you by a uniformed waiter.

**8**

In Mazatlán, long stretches of soft beige sand hug the hotel and condo zones north of downtown; runners love the long boardwalk fronting downtown's less showy beaches, which are frequented by fishermen setting out to sea and surfers catching waves nearer the shore. Puerto Vallarta's expansive Bahía de Banderas has it all. The boardwalk downtown provides views, benches, and lots of whimsical art to admire. Both north and south of downtown are golden-sand stretches where you can dine, party, and parasail; there are also gloriously unpopulated shores and more intimate, craggy coves well suited for snorkeling.

In Manzanillo, container ships hog the commercial end of the crescent-shaped bay, but you can still find plenty of clean, uncrowded beaches on which to relax. The volcanic sands may be black, brown, or beige; the southernmost beaches are the darkest and sometimes flecked with gold. Farther south, Ixtapa has a long, uninterrupted beach fronting the hotel zone. The deep bay of neighboring Zihuatanejo has several lovely beaches lined with informal seafood shanties and in high season, water-sports concessions. A couple of hotels dot the shore here, but many more partake of the breeze and the view from the cliffs above.

# Shopping

You can spend as much time shopping in Puerto Vallarta as you can lazing in the sun. Boutiques and emporiums selling crafts from throughout Mexico vie with clothing and jewelry boutiques for your attention, especially downtown. And there are more than a dozen fine-art galleries. Many of those in the Marina Vallarta area and downtown participate in the Artwalk event, between November and April, when serious buyers wander from shop to shop, often with a cocktail in hand. Shops filled with home furnishings of carved wood, iron, tin, stone, blown glass, and brass may make you want to buy a house in Mexico or open an import–export enterprise of your own.

You should also look for traditional bowls and masks and less traditional statuettes made by the Huichol Indians. Tiny glass (or less desirably, plastic) beads are embedded precisely in hollowed-out gourds or carved wooden pieces with beeswax. Designs such as suns, deer, and peyote buttons each have a symbolic meaning. Jalisco State also has a great tradition of utilitarian pottery, and though you'll find the best variety in Puerto Vallarta (outside the towns where they're made, of course, and in Guadalajara), you can buy beautiful place settings and individual pieces from Mazatlán to Ixtapa.

Other Pacific coast resorts have less sophisticated shops than those of Puerto Vallarta, but you can still find masks, pottery, lacquerware, carved-wood animals, hand-dyed woven rugs, and embroidered clothing. In Mazatlán look for shell art and carved wood items. In Ixtapa/Zihuatanejo shop for masks from Jalisco and Guerrero states and beaded bowls and statuettes made by the Huichol Indians. Each resort has at least one handicrafts market as well as a traditional market that sells everything from produce to cooked food, jeans, mops and buckets, and hundreds of other sundries.

# Water Sports

Sportfishing is good off Puerto Vallarta most of the year, particularly for billfish, rooster fish, mahimahi, yellowtail, and bonito. Manzanillo claims to be the world's sailfish capital; the season runs from mid-October through March. Blue marlin and dorado are also abundant. Ixtapa/Zihuatanejo is one of Mexico's most popular sportfishing destinations. Anglers revel in the profusion of sailfish (November through March), black and blue marlin (May through January), yellowfin tuna (November through June), and mahimahi (November through January). Light-tackle fishing in the lagoons and just off the beach in *pangas* (skiffs) for *huachinango* (red snapper) is also popular. In November, Mazatlán, Puerto Vallarta, and Manzanillo host international tournaments.

Parasailing, swimming, windsurfing, sailing, kayaking, and waterskiing are popular all along the Pacific Coast. Manzanillo, Mazatlán, and San Blas have some of Mexico's finest surfing, and the best diving spots in this area are found around the islands off Puerto Vallarta and Ixtapa. Puerto Vallarta hosts Mexico's annual boat show each November, as well as various sailing regattas in winter.

---

Manzanillo itself. The community is now the country's second-busiest port, and you can see the lights of freighters at anchor along the southern beaches.

Ixtapa and Zihuatanejo represent another juxtaposition of the modern and the traditional. Some 500 km (300 mi) south of Manzanillo, Ixtapa is the newest of the region's tourist destinations. Like Cancún, it was the brainchild of the Mexican government in the early 1970s. Although far smaller and less sophisticated than Cancún or Los Cabos, Ixtapa is nonetheless a modern resort with a string of high-rise hotels along its brief, manicured main boulevard. Its development drew attention to nearby Zihuatanejo, a once-humble fishing village on a gorgeous bay. Zihua, as it's lazily called, is home to the area's fish market and its most inexpensive hotels as well as to such voluptuous properties as La Casa Que Canta, Villas del Sol, and Casa Cuitlateca.

The Pacific Coast is perfect for folks who love nature, Mexican-Mediterranean architecture, and tropical drinks. Lie in the sun with your toes in the pool. Eat seafood by day; by night, quaff aged tequila from the land where tequila-making began. Loll in a hammock with a good book in hand. Or take a more energetic attitude, parasailing, skin diving, kayaking, hiking, or exploring some of the coast's smaller, less touristy destinations.

## Exploring the Pacific Coast Resorts

Although Pacific Coast cultures were in some ways as fascinating as that of the better known Aztecs, they left behind no major monuments, and so have been largely ignored by archaeological research teams. This isn't the place to explore ruins, museums, and cathedrals. Rather it's a place to pick a spot to settle, immersing yourself in the simultaneously bustling and restful resort lifestyle of great dining, shopping, sunbathing, and almost any sort of water sport.

Many of those who head to Mazatlán are content to party in the hotel zone (Zona Dorada); others choose a hotel in the Olas Altas district closer to downtown to enjoy a more authentically Mexican experience. Day tours to El Quelite, Concordia, and Copala afford a glimpse of small-town life and the countryside. A daylong or overnight trip south takes you to the mangroves and estuaries around Teacapán, near the Nayarit border. This is a beachy, mango-and-coconut-filled land of cattle ranches.

On a trip to Puerto Vallarta you can opt for an in-town hotel, hole up in an ultraluxury beach resort just outside town, or rent a shack in a fishing village or a house in a nearby seaside community such as Bucerías. PV is also a great hub for exploring the coast, either on day or overnight trips. Although some vacationers choose Manzanillo, it's most popular with Mexican families and snowbirders settling down for a long winter's nap in the sun.

Although of course there's tons of coast to explore around Ixtapa/Zihuatanejo, travelers there tend to stay put, relaxing at or near their hotel in Ixtapa or Zihua and for adventure, traveling the few short miles to the other town. Snorkel trips head for pretty Manzanillo beach, just behind Zihua's bay, and there's Ixtapa island to be explored—both by boat only. Another great day trip is to Barra de Potosí, about 15 minutes past the Zihuatanejo airport. Those who chose Troncones, a laid back beach about 20 minutes north of Zihua, tend to stay put for a few days at least.

### About the Restaurants

The Pacific Ocean yields a dazzling variety of fresh seafood that coastal dwellers know how to slice, dice, and spice into tasty regional dishes. Shrimp, octopus, oysters, and fresh fish are the highlights; be sure to have a seafood cocktail along the beach. You can savor traditional *pescado sarandeado* (whole fish rubbed with salt and spices and grilled over hot coals) as well as elaborate dishes devised by imported European chefs.

Mazatlán has many casual, lively restaurants that serve surf-and-turf and Mexican favorites. Puerto Vallarta is as known for its multitalented chefs as for its array of restaurants—some with spectacular views, others hidden in the small, romantic patios of former homes. Manzanillo's restaurants lack the sophistication of those in Puerto Vallarta, but most serve fresh, reasonably priced seafood. In Ixtapa/Zihuatanejo, restaurants range from open-air *palapas* (thatch-roof structures) on the beach to deluxe establishments with international chefs.

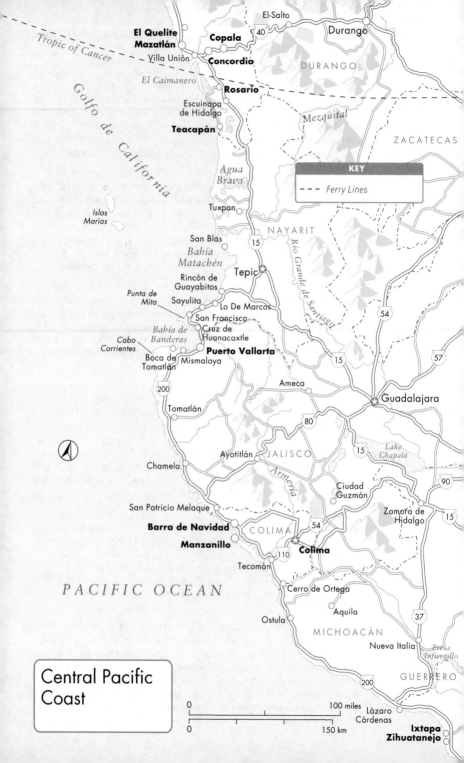

Tropic of Cancer

Golfo de California

Islas Marías

PACIFIC OCEAN

El-Salto

**El Quelite**
**Mazatlán**          **Copala**          Durango

Villa Unión          DURANGO

**Concordia**

El Caimanero          **Rosario**

Escuinapa
de Hidalgo                    Mezquital                    ZACATECAS

**Teacapán**

Agua
Brava

Tuxpan

San Blas          NAYARIT
Bahía
Matachén          15

Rincón de          Tepic
Guayabitos

Punta de          Sayulita          Río Grande de Santiago
Mita
          Lo De Marcos
          San Francisco          54
Bahía de          Cruz de
Banderas          Huanacaxtle          15

Cabo          **Puerto Vallarta**          57
Corrientes
          Boca de          Mismaloya
          Tomatlán

          200          Ameca          Guadalajara

          Tomatlán          80

                    Ayotitlán          JALISCO          15          Lake
                                                          Chapalá
Chamela          Armería                                        90

                    Ciudad
                    Guzmán

San Patricio Melaque                              Zamora de          15
                                                  Hidalgo
**Barra de Navidad**          COLIMA          54

**Manzanillo**                    **Colima**

          110
          Tecomán                              37

                    Cerro de Ortega

          Ostula          Aquila

                    MICHOACÁN
                    Nueva Italia          Presa
                                        Infiernillo

# Central Pacific
# Coast          GUERRERO

                    200

KEY
--- Ferry Lines

0                    100 miles
0          150 km          Lázaro
          Cárdenas
                    **Ixtapa**
                    **Zihuatanejo**

Some hotel restaurants add 15% IVA (value-added tax) as well as a service charge to your tab. Many more humble establishments charge neither, so check your bill and tip accordingly.

## About the Hotels

Mazatlán has its share of comfortable beachfront hotels as well as large concentrations of trailer parks. In Puerto Vallarta, accommodations range from tiny inns to luxury waterfront hotels and spectacular resorts on secluded coves. Like the destination itself, Manzanillo's properties are laid back; more functional than elegant. Many are all-inclusives. Big beachfront properties are the norm in Ixtapa; Zihuatanejo has budget hotels and several of Mexico's most exclusive small hotels.

Hotels raise their rates for the high season (December 15 through Easter week); rates are also on the high side during July and August, when Mexican families swarm the beaches for their summer vacations. In Manzanillo high season corresponds only to specific holidays, especially Christmas, Easter, and summer vacation (July–August). For the best prices, visit in May, June, September, or October. Note, however, that hurricanes may crop up between late September and early November. Price categories are based on high-season rack rates; expect to pay less by asking for "package rates," which include breakfast, or other specials. Prices should be at least 25% less during the off-season.

| WHAT IT COSTS IN DOLLARS | | | | | |
| --- | --- | --- | --- | --- | --- |
| | $$$$ | $$$ | $$ | $ | ¢ |
| RESTAURANTS | over $25 | $15–$25 | $10–$15 | $5–$10 | under $5 |
| HOTELS | over $250 | $150–$250 | $75–$150 | $50–$75 | under $50 |

Restaurant prices are for a main course excluding tax and tip. Hotel prices are for two people in a standard double room in high season, based on the European Plan (EP, with no meals) and excluding service and 17% tax.

## When to Go

Resorts on this coastal stretch are at their best in winter, with temperatures of 20°C–30°C (70°F–80°F) and a bit higher in Ixtapa and Zihuatanejo. The off-season brings humidity, mosquitoes, and higher temperatures (northernmost Mazatlán remains coolest), but also emptier beaches, warmer water (about 20°C/70°F), and less-crowded streets—plus 25%–35% lower room rates and cheaper rental-car costs. During and right after the rainy season (June–October), the countryside, the Sierra Madre Occidental, and the Sierra Madre del Sur turn a brilliant green.

# MAZATLÁN

Mazatlán is the Nahuatl (Aztec) word for "place of the deer," and long ago it did, indeed, shelter many of these creatures. Duck, quail, pheasant, and other wildfowl fed in the lagoons, and mountain lions, rabbits, and coyotes roamed the surrounding hills. Today there's a dearth of deer, and although hunting is still practiced, deep-sea fishing is the main lure: Mazatlán has one of Mexico's largest sportfishing fleets, and anglers haul in some of the coast's biggest catches, both in size and number. Approximately 12,000 billfish are caught and released each year, including some of gargantuan proportions.

More numerous than the visitors who come to fish are those who come to sun, surf, and sail. And although the Zona Dorada—lined with hotels, shops, and tourist-oriented restaurants—certainly has the feel of a tourist town, Mazatlán's post-colonial downtown reminds you that this city of nearly 700,000 souls is also a dignified port with an interest in arts and culture.

The Spanish first visited the Mazatlán region in 1531, and later the colonial government built a small fort and watchtowers to protect Spanish galleons from English and French pirates. The settlement was just a smudge on the map until the mid-19th century, when it became northwestern Mexico's most important city and port. As such, it drew the attention of outsiders seeking to challenge the Mexican government in this sparsely settled part of the country. In 1847, during the Mexican–American War, U.S. forces marched down from the border, occupying the city and closing the port. In 1864, French ships bombarded the city and then controlled it for several years. The British occupied the port for a short period in 1871. Mexico's own internal warring factions took over from time to time. And after the Civil War in the United States, a group of Southerners tried to turn Mazatlán into a slave city.

## Exploring Mazatlán

Though many visitors never leave the Zona Dorada (Golden Zone)—a broad avenue lined with hotels, shops, and party-down restaurants—downtown Mazatlán is a fun place to explore. Mazatlán's historic center consists of distinctive late-19th- and early-20th-century edifices and Italianate mansions built by shipping magnates. Its mainly two-story buildings have fanciful wrought ironwork window grills and balconies, wooden shutters, and thick walls painted in pastel colors. The city's newest resort area, aptly dubbed Nuevo Mazatlán, is north of the Zona Dorada, around Punta Cerritos on a long—and so far lonely—stretch of beachfront property called Emerald Bay.

*Numbers in the text correspond to numbers in the margin and on the Mazatlán map.*

a good tour

Start in the **Zona Dorada ❶** ▶ at Punta Camarón. North along Avenida Camarón Sábalo and the four-block loop closer to the water, Avenida Playa las Gaviotas, is the stuff resorts are made of: bars and restaurants, shell and souvenir shops, beachfront hotels. This route affords a good view of Mazatlán's three islands—Isla de los Pájaros, Isla del Venado, and Isla de los Lobos (also referred to erroneously as Isla de Chivos). At Faro Mazatlán resort, Avenida Camarón Sábalo becomes Avenida Sábalo Cerritos and crosses over the Estero del Sábalo lagoon. The area north of here is slowly being developed as Nuevo Mazatlán (New Mazatlán), an exclusive region slated to be filled with high-end resorts.

Below the Zona Dorada, the coast road changes names frequently. South of Punta Camarón it's called Avenida del Mar. About halfway between Punta Camarón and downtown and a few blocks inland is the city's aquarium, **Acuario Mazatlán** ❷, on Avenida de los Deportes. Avenida del Mar continues past beaches popular with residents and travelers staying at the budget hotels across the street. You're sure to notice the avenue's main landmark, the Monumento al Pescador: an enormous statue of a voluptuous, nude woman reclining on an anchor, her hand extended toward a fisherman dragging his nets.

Soon after the monument, Avenida del Mar becomes Paseo Claussen (named for one of the German originators of Pacífico beer). Calles Juárez and Cinco de Mayo lead from the coast road to Mazatlán's busy downtown. The heart of the city is **Plaza Revolución** ❸, also called *el zócalo* (main square) or Plazuela República. On the square's north side is the twin-spired **Catedral de Mazatlán** ❹; on facing streets are the City Hall, banks, and a post office. About three blocks south of the zócalo is the Teatro Angela Peralta, built between 1860 and 1874. Beautifully restored, the theater is now an official historic monument. Stop for a drink or a bite at any one of the establishments around the nearby Plazuela Machado, known for its lively fiestas, and the restaurants, cafés, and music venues that ring it. The streets around the plaza are closed to vehicular traffic Friday through Sunday after 6 PM. Three blocks west, the unassuming Casa de la Cultura houses the **Museo de Arte de Mazatlán** ❺. Just a few doors away, the **Museo Arqueológico de Mazatlán** ❻ has archaeological pieces from early Pacific coast tribes.

Back along the waterfront, Paseo Claussen and the parallel, very walkable *malecón* (seawalk), continue past several statues, including the *Monumento a la Continuidad de la Vida* (*Monument to the Continuity of Life*), a large fountain with a handsome couple atop a large conch shell and a school of leaping porpoises. Next you'll come to Playa Olas Altas, where, at High-Divers Park, young men plunge into the sea from a small white platform. It's spectacular at night, when the divers leap carrying flaming torches. Continuing south you'll see La Mazatleca, a bronze representation of the beauty of local women, and a small bronze deer, the symbol of Mazatlán. Above the Olas Altas area is **Cerro del Vigía** ❼, a hill with terrific vistas.

## What to See

❷ **Acuario Mazatlán.** A perfect child-pleaser, Mazatlán's aquarium has tanks of sharks, sea horses, and multicolor salt- and freshwater fish. Be sure to take in the skating macaw and penny-pinching parrot at bird shows held several times daily. There's also a sea-lion show as well as botanical gardens, a large playground, an aviary, a gift shop, and snack bars. ✉ *Av. de los Deportes 111, Olas Altas* ☎ *669/981–7815* 💲 *$5* ⊙ *Daily 9:30–6.*

❹ **Catedral de Mazatlán.** The bright yellow spires of the downtown cathedral are a city landmark. Begun in 1855, the church wasn't completed until the end of that century, and embraces a variety of architectural styles. Made a basilica in 1935, it has a gilded and ornate triple altarpiece, with murals of angels overhead and many small altars along the sides. ✉ *Calles Juárez and 21 de Marzo, Centro* ☎ *No phone.*

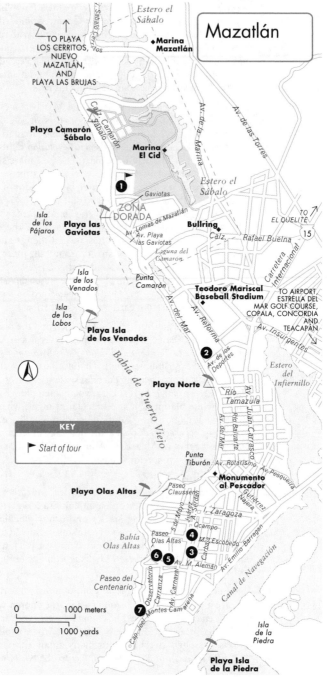

Mazatlán

**7** **Cerro del Vigía** (Lookout Hill). The view from this windy hill above Olas Altas is fantastic: you can see both sides of Mazatlán, the harbor, and the Pacific. The steep road up is better suited for a private car or taxi than for walking. At the top of the hill is a rusty cannon and the Centenario Pérgola, built in 1848 to celebrate the end of the U.S. invasion. The restaurant here may be unexceptional, but it's a great pit stop for a beer or soft drink.

**6** **Museo Arqueológico de Mazatlán.** The archaeological museum has a small but interesting collection of regional artifacts. In addition to the black-and-red pottery of the Totorames, an indigenous tribe that inhabited the area until 200 years before the Spanish arrived, there are displays with the clothing and utensils of regional tribes. Temporary exhibits fill the small main hall. Only some of the information is in English. ⊠ *Calle Sixto Osuna 76, at Av. Venustiano Carranza, Centro* ☎ *669/981–1455* ⬚ *$2.50* ☉ *Mon.–Sat. 10–6, Sun. 10–3.*

**need a break?** The sidewalk tables at **Copa de Leche** (⊠ Paseo Olas Altas, near Calle Sixto Osuna, Centro ☎ No phone), across from the malecón, are perfect for watching sunsets. Like Copa de Leche, **Fonda Santa Clara** (⊠ Olas Altas 1220-A Sur ☎ 669/982–5753) draws tourists wandering along the malecón to its outside tables, though its really the domain of young mothers with kids in tow and old-timers rehashing stories for hours over coffee or a cool beer. Inland near the Angela Peralta Theatre, **El Café Gourmet Memorial** (⊠ Calle Carnaval 1209, Centro ☎ No phone) serves big cups of strong coffee along with cakes, pastries, and paninis. Conversation can be loud, and there's live jazz some weekends.

**5** **Museo de Arte de Mazatlán.** This small museum shows the work of local, regional, and national artists, including Gerardo Santamarino, José Luis Cuevas, and Armando Nava. Varied cultural events in the upstairs gallery draw locals and a smattering of savvy foreigners Thursday evenings; look for posters or flyers here or around town. ⊠ *Calle Sixto Osuna and Av. Venustiano Carranza, Centro* ☎ *669/985–3502* ⬚ *$1* ☉ *Tues.–Sat. 10–2 and 4–6.*

**3** **Plaza Revolución.** At the center of downtown, this square hosts one of the most incongruous gazebos in Mexico—below the traditional, wrought-iron bandstand is what looks like a '50s diner. The multicolor tiles on floors and walls, ancient jukebox, and soda fountain couldn't make a more surprising sight. People surround the bandstand Sunday afternoon to hear local musicians play. ⊠ *Bounded by Calle 21 de Marzo to the north, Calle Flores to the south, Av. Benito Juárez to the east, and Av. Nelson to the west Centro.*

▶ **1** **Zona Dorada.** Marking the beginning of Mazatlán's touristy Golden Zone is Punta Camarón, the rocky outcropping on which the disco Valentino sits, resembling a Moorish palace. To the north, Avenida Playa las Gaviotas (until recently called Avenida Rodolfo T. Loaiza) splits off from Avenida Camarón Sábalo, running closer to the beach before rejoining Camarón Sábalo. In this four-block pocket are many hotels, shops, restaurants, and nightclubs.

## Around Mazatlán

A pleasant though unexceptional town 48 km (30 mi) east of Mazatlán, **Concordia** is known for its furniture makers, 18th-century church, and unglazed clay pottery. The drive into town is lined with organ cactus and mango trees and is especially pretty after the summer rains cover nearby hills and distant mountains in green. **Copala,** a former mining town, is at the foot of the Sierra Madre Occidental, 25 km (15 mi) east of Concordia. A single cobblestone street winds through town to a tiny plaza and 18th-century church. Old homes have colorful facades enlivened with flowering vines and trees and embellished with ironwork. If you really want to get away from it all, several of the small restaurants near the square rent rooms.

The 2,000 inhabitants in the quiet village of **El Quelite,** 29 km (18 mi) northeast of Mazatlán off Carretera 15, are mostly farmers and cattle ranchers. Tours to the area take in a rooster farm, a tortilla factory, and a bakery and include a typical country lunch; some trips also include a demonstration of the preconquest ball game known as *ulama,* or a traditional riding and roping exhibition called *charrería.* If you visit on your own and want to stay overnight, accommodations are available at the home of the town's best known citizen, **Dr. Marcos Osuna** (✉ Callejón Fco. Bernal 1). The cost is roughly $50, including breakfast.

A serene drive south of Mazatlán takes you to cattle and coconut country. Tour companies such as Marlin Tours stop at the 17th-century mining town of **El Rosario,** 72 km (45 mi) south of Mazatlán, to see the magnificent church for which the town is named; trips often include stops at a Spanish cemetery and lovely old church and a visit to nearby thermal springs. RVers find the long, lonely, sandy beaches of **Teacapán,** 59 km (37 mi) south of El Rosario, much to their liking. And off-the-beaten-trackers can easily spend a few days beachcombing, eating fresh fish at informal seaside restaurants, and exploring the nontouristy muncipal seat, Escuinapa. Many people come to bird-watch in the estuary that separates the state of Sinaloa from Nayarit, to the south.

## Beaches

**Playa Camarón Sábalo.** Like the Zona Dorado's Playa las Gaviotas to the south, this beach is backed by hotels with concessions renting Windsurfers and offering parasail rides and other diversions. Most properties have lounge chairs and umbrellas for their guests; nonguests can usually use them if they order drinks or snacks. The beach is protected from heavy surf by islands just offshore.

**Playa los Cerritos.** It's a long stretch of sand running several miles between Marina Mazatlán and Punta Cerritos and just north of the Zona Dorada. Still relatively unpopulated (although the construction of condos may change that), it's great for long, uninterrupted walks; a steep drop-off and undertow make it less than ideal for swimming. Around Punta Cerritos are thatch-roof eateries frequented by surfers.

**Playa las Gaviotas.** Mazatlán's most popular beach parallels the Zona Dorada hotel loop on the street of the same name. Authorized vendors sell pottery, lace tablecloths, and silver jewelry, or rent boats, Windsurfers, and other toys. When you tire of sand and sun, repair to one of the many beachfront hotel restaurants willing to accommodate sandy, skimpily clad customers.

**Playa Isla de la Piedra.** Sixteen kilometers (10 mi) of unspoiled beach allows enough room for everyone to spread out. This is also the place to rent a horse for a good long ride. On holidays and weekends, the beach is packed with picnicking families listening to boom boxes. Small palapas along the beach's north end serve tasty smoked marlin and other seafood treats. You can access the beach in one of the water taxis that cross the navigation canal dividing downtown from Isla de la Piedra; they depart from a pier just behind the Pacifica Brewery. The cost is about $1.50 round-trip; save your ticket for the return voyage.

★ **Playa Isla de los Venados.** An amphibious sort of tank, a relic from WWII, makes regularly scheduled departures from El Cid hotel, in the Zona Dorada, to Deer Island—a 20-minute ride. (You can also get here on snorkeling and day cruises arranged through area tour operators.) The beach is pretty, uncluttered, and clean. For even better snorkeling, you can hike to small, secluded coves covered with shells.

**Playa Norte.** This strip of dark-brown sand runs parallel to the stretch of waterfront road known as Avenida del Mar. It's popular with those staying at hotels across the beachfront boulevard. Palapas selling cold drinks (including whole chilled coconuts), tacos, and seafood line the beach. Fishermen land their skiffs at the sheltered cove at the south end, a section sometimes referred to as Los Pinos (The Pines).

**Playa Olas Altas.** High Waves Beach borders Paseo Claussen south of Playa Norte. Surfers congregate here in summer months, when the waves are at their highest. Men dive into the shallow sea when a paying crowd gathers (often coinciding with tour groups at 11 AM, 3 PM, and sunset) at High Divers Park; nearby is the *Monumento a la Continuidad de la Vida,* a bronze statue of a pair of happy humans joined by a team of playful dolphins.

## Where to Eat

$$$-$$$$ × **Sr. Peppers.** The place that locals go for a fancy night out has forest-green walls, crystal chandeliers, rattan furnishings, and lots of highly polished brass. Candlelight and live piano music lend romance. The short menu focuses on shrimp, lobster, and mesquite-grilled steak. Most dishes come with soup or salad, pasta or potatoes, steamed veggie, and Texas-style toast. ⊠ *Av. Camarón Sábalo across from Faro Mazatlán hotel, Zona Dorada* ☎ 669/914–0101 ⊟ *MC, V* ☉ *No lunch.*

**Fodor'sChoice** ★

★ $$-$$$ × **Angelo's.** With its fresh flowers, cream-and-beige color scheme, and candlelight this Italian restaurant is truly elegant. A piano-accompanied singer stirs up the romance Thursday through Sunday after 7. Try the veal scallopini with mushrooms or the capellini with pesto and grilled scallops. The service is impeccable. ⊠ *Pueblo Bonito hotel, Av. Camarón Sábalo 2121, Zona Dorada* ☎ 669/914–3700 ⊟ *AE, MC, V* ☉ *No lunch.*

$$-$$$ × **La Concha.** A large enclosed palapa has three levels of seating and tables by the sand. Adventurous types might attempt the stingray with black butter or calamari in its ink; the more conservative can opt for a thick filet mignon. In winter there's live music in the evenings, and the spa-

cious dance floor is adorned with twinkling lights. La Concha is open for breakfast as well as lunch and dinner. ⊠ *El Cid Moro, Av. Camarón Sábalo s/n, Zona Dorada* ☎ *669/913–3333* ▭ *AE, MC, V.*

**$–$$$**  ✕ **La Casa Country.** This boisterous, faux-rustic-Western restaurant across from the Holiday Inn serves Mexican dishes as well as steaks grilled over charcoal or firewood. The *arrachera* (skirt steak) and other regional cuts come with kettle beans, quesadilla, and guacamole; the rib eye and American cuts have sides of corn on the cob and baked potato. Early in the evening, waiters abandon their posts for an informal line dance. You can carouse here until 2 AM; it's not hard to do thanks to fresh-fruit margaritas or piña coladas served by the pitcher. ⊠ *Av. Camarón Sábalo s/n, Zona Dorada* ☎ *669/916–5300* ▭ *AE, MC, V.*

**$–$$$**  ✕ **La Costa Marinera.** Fathers, sons, godfathers . . . this seaside spot is a family business, and the commitment and attention to detail are plain to see. It's popular with locals, and its multiple dining rooms often accommodate large groups of cruise ship passengers as well. The seafood menu seems endless, and the presentation is tops. ⊠ *Privada del Camarón, at Privada de la Florida, Zona Dorada* ☎ *669/916–1599 or 669/914–1928* ▭ *MC, V.*

**$–$$$**  ✕ **El Shrimp Bucket.** Social mavens breakfast at this festive old town patio restaurant; at lunch and dinner the clientele switches to businesspeople. The dining room's shrimp motifs aptly represent the menu; try the cheese-stuffed jumbo shrimp wrapped in bacon, sautéed, and served with rice and steamed veggies, or the fried shrimp served in a clay buckets. Barbecue ribs are also a good bet. Traditional trios serenade Thursday through Saturday nights. ⊠ *Hotel Siesta, Paseo Olas Altas 11–126 Sur, Olas Altas* ☎ *669/981–6350* ▭ *AE, MC, V.*

★ **¢–$$$**  ✕ **Pancho's.** You can dine upstairs or down, inside or out at this hopping seaside restaurant, where seafood is the specialty. Choose from enormous platters to share, soups, and ceviche. There's also filet mignon smothered in mushrooms and served with rice, steamed veggies, baked potato, and thick Texas-style toast. Portions are generous, and the food is so good that you'll most likely clean your plate. More great news: it's open from 7 AM to 11 PM. ⊠ *Av. Playa las Gaviotas 408, Centro Comercial las Cabanas, Local 11-B, Zona Dorada* ☎ *669/914–0911* ▭ *MC, V.*

★ **$–$$**  ✕ **Panamá Restaurant y Pastelería.** Low prices, large portions, and lots of choices—for breakfast, lunch, and dinner—make this coffee shop a standout. For not-so-adventurous eaters there are burgers and fries, sandwiches, and pancakes (any time of day). The soups are yummy, the salads are healthful, and the cakes and pastries are baked fresh throughout the day. The lunch specials are such bargains that some office workers eat here every day. ⊠ *Camarón Sábalo 400, Zona Dorada* ☎ *669/913–6977* ▭ *AE, MC, V* ⊠ *Juárez at Canizales, Centro* ☎ *669/985–1853* ▭ *AE, MC, V.*

**$–$$**  ✕ **Pedro & Lola.** Authentic Mexican seafood is served in this 19th-century building that's filled with contemporary art. Try the *papillot,* the day's catch cooked in foil with white wine, shrimp, and mushrooms. As it's named after Mexican *ranchera* singers Pedro Infante and Lola Beltrán, the restaurant has excellent live music (often oldies rock) on weekend evenings. Reservations are recommended Thursday through

Saturday. ⊠ *Calle Carnaval 1303, at Plazuela Machado, Centro* ☎ 669/ 982–2589 ⊟ *AE, MC, V* ⊘ *No lunch.*

¢ ✕ **El Túnel.** The Tunnel, named for its original long, narrow, floor plan, has been in business since 1945 and is open noon to midnight. It's especially beloved by patrons of the nearby Teatro Angela Peralta, who come for such regional snacks as *gorditas* (fried rounds of cornmeal topped with a garnish), tostadas, and meat or potato tacos. All are served at tables covered in bright green and orange oilcloths. Movie posters and stills of María Félix and Pedro Infante adorn the glossy walls. ⊠ *Calle Carnaval 1207 Centro* ☎ *No phone* ⊟ *No credit cards.*

## Where to Stay

$$$–$$$$    ▣ **Pueblo Bonito Emerald Bay.** The first (and, so far, only) major resort in Nuevo Mazatlán offers seclusion to those who eschew the busy Zona Dorada. Forty gardeners tend lakes and gardens. The huge bilevel pool is surrounded by shady pavilions. In late summer sea turtles lay their eggs on the property's long beach. Suites are in freestanding villas, whose neoclassical design elements bring to mind European palaces. Beds with goose-down mattress pads are among the thoughtful touches. ⊠ *Av. Ernesto Coppel Campaña 201, Nuevo Mazatlán 82110* ☎ *669/989–0525, 800/ 990–8250 in the U.S.* ☒ *669/988–0718 or 669/989–0525* ⊕ *www. pueblobonito.com* ⇝ *124 suites* ♧ *Restaurant, café, grocery store, room service, in-room safes, kitchens, cable TV, 2 pools, bar, pub, gym, hair salon, 2 hot tubs, spa, steam room, beach, bar, children's programs (ages 6–12), laundry service, concierge, internet, airport shuttle, car rental, travel services, free parking, no-smoking rooms* ⊟ *AE, MC, V.*

$$–$$$$    ▣ **El Cid Megaresort.** Mazatlán's largest resort has four properties, three of which are together in the Zona Dorada. A free shuttle connects these to the upscale Marina El Cid Hotel and Yacht Club, at the north end of town overlooking the 100-slip marina. A stay at any El Cid property allows you to use the full-service spa and fitness center, the golf school and course, and the aquatics center. The Marina and the El Moro Beach are the most upscale, while the Granada costs less as it's on the opposite side of the street from the beach. ⊠ *Av. Camarón Sábalo s/n, Zona Dorada 82110* ☎ *669/913–3333, 800/525–1925 in the U.S.* ☒ *669/914– 1311* ⊕ *www.elcid.com* ⇝ *1,320 rooms, suites, and studios* ♧ *8 restaurants, cable TV, 27-hole golf course, 11 tennis courts, 8 pools, gym, spa, beach, marina, 3 bars, dance club, shops, children's programs (ages 4–12), laundry service, business services, meeting rooms, car rental, travel services, free parking, no-smoking rooms* ⊟ *AE, DCMC, V.*

★ $$$    ▣ **Pueblo Bonito.** Chandeliers and beveled-glass doors sparkle in this all-suites hotel's enormous lobby. Guest quarters have built-in sofas with earthtone upholstery, beds with egg-crate-foam and pillow-top mattress pads, and pillow menus that give you the chance to choose the cushioning that's best for you. Kitchens are well equipped. Pink flamingos stroll manicured lawns, golden koi swim in small ponds, and bronzed sunbathers repose on padded lounge chairs by the crystal-blue pool. ⊠ *Av. Camarón Sábalo 2121, Zona Dorada 82110* ☎ *669/914–3700, 800/ 990–8250 in the U.S.* ☒ *669/914–1723* ⊕ *www.pueblobonito.com* ⇝ *247 suites* ♧ *3 restaurants, grocery, room service, in-room data* *ports, kitchens, cable TV, 2 pools, gym, hair salon, hot tub, massage, sauna, beach, bar, shops, children's programs (ages 6–12), laundry service, concierge, Internet, car rental, travel services, free parking, no-smoking rooms ⊟ AE, MC, V.*

**$$$** 🏨 **Royal Villas Resort.** Panoramic elevators transport you to the upper floors from the marble-rich atrium lobby of this pyramid-shape, 12-story structure. More ample and functional than elegant, one- and two-bedroom suites are done in bold blues and oranges. All have balconies; those from the third floor up have good ocean views. Access to the inviting pool is by a bridge that crosses over a fish pond. ⊠ *Av. Camarón Sábalo 500, Zona Dorada 82110* ☎ *669/916–6161, 800/898–3564 in the U.S.* 📠 *669/914–0777* ⊕ *www.royalvillas.com.mx* 🛏 *125 suites* ⚒ *2 restaurants, room service, kitchenettes, cable TV, pool, gym, hair salon, hot tub, massage, sauna, beach, bar, recreation room, shops, children's programs, laundry service, internet, business services, meeting rooms, travel services, free parking, no-smoking rooms* ⎁ *BP* ⊟ *AE, MC, V.*

**$$–$$$** 🏨 **Holiday Inn Sunspree Resort.** The Holiday Inn fills its rooms with tour and convention groups that create a party mood by the pool and on the beach. The Kid's Spree program provides activities for children; adults can attend tennis clinics and borrow snorkel equipment or boogie boards. Rooms, which are done in beiges and browns, have quiet, digitally controlled air-conditioners, ironing boards and irons, hair dryers, and coffeemakers. Bathrooms have showers but not tubs. ⊠ *Av. Camarón Sábalo 696, Zona Dorada 82110* ☎ *669/913–2222, 800/465–4329 in the U.S.* 📠 *669/913–7044* ⊕ *www.holiday-inn.com* 🛏 *160 rooms, 23 suites* ⚒ *Restaurant, room service, café, in-room data ports, refrigerators, cable TV, pool, exercise equipment, beach, volleyball, bar, shop, baby-sitting, children's programs (ages 5–12), business services, meeting rooms, no-smoking rooms* ⊟ *AE, MC, V.*

**$$** 🏨 **Best Western Posada Freeman.** One of the nicest things about this restored high-rise landmark is its location across from Playa Olas Altas and a stone's throw from old town. Rooms are bright but small and cramped. You can stretch out beside the rooftop pool, which no one seems to know about (there's also a wonderful bar up here). A sunny breakfast room serves an ample buffet that's popular with guests and nonguests. The staff is helpful and outgoing. ⊠ *Av. Olas Altas 79, Sur Centro 82110* ☎ *669/985–6969* ☎ *866/638–8806 in the U.S.* ⊕ *www.posadadelrio.com* 🛏 *64 rooms, 8 junior suites* ⚒ *Restaurant, fans, in-room data ports, in-room safes, some kitchenettes, cable TV, pool, bar, laundry service, internet, meeting room, free parking, no-smoking rooms* ⊟ *AE, MC, V* ⎁ *BP.*

**$$** 🏨 **Casa Contenta.** One building has seven one-bedroom apartments, and a separate house can accommodate up to eight people with its three bedrooms, three baths, and living–dining room. Throughout the Mexican furniture and fittings are slightly worn, some of the mattresses are thin, and some of the couches are stiffly formal. Still, well-stocked kitchens, an authentic Mexican atmosphere, proximity to the beach, and bargain room rates bring many repeat clients; book well in advance. Monthly rates are available. ⊠ *Av. Playa las Gaviotas 224, Zona Dorada 82110* ☎ *669/913–4976* 📠 *669/913–9986* ⊕ *www.casacontenta.*

*com.mx* 🗗 *8 units* 🛏 *Kitchens, cable TV, pool, beach, free parking; no room phones* ▭ *MC, V.*

★ **$$** 🏨 **Playa Mazatlán.** Families and laid-back singles favor this Playa Gaviotas hotel for its reliable guest quarters and consistently good service. Each sunny, no-frills room has comfy beds with tile headboards, a tile table and chairs by a sliding-glass window, and a terrace or balcony. Palapas line the beach just beyond the first-floor rooms. The pool is large, and the shops—selling folk art, bikinis, and souvenirs—are varied. At night candles flicker in the open-air restaurant, where a trio sets the mood for dining and a larger band shows up later to play dance music. The Mexican Fiesta dinner show is popular. ⊠ *Av. Playa las Gaviotas 202, Zona Dorada 82110* ☎ *669/989–0555, 800/762–5816 in the U.S.* 🖷 *669/914–0366* ⊕ *www.playamazatlan.com.mx* 🗗 *413 rooms* 🛏 *Restaurant, room service, cable TV, 3 pools, gym, hair salon, 2 hot tubs, beach, Ping-Pong, volleyball, 2 bars, shops, dry cleaning, laundry service, concierge, convention center, meeting rooms, car rental, travel services, free parking, no-smoking rooms* ▭ *AE, MC, V.*

**$$** 🏨 **Plaza Marina.** This hotel has standard rooms that overlook the small pool with a swim-up bar that's open only in high season. Rooms have shared balconies with tables and chairs. Both suites and junior suites have kitchens with wraparound breakfast bars and views of Playa Norte across the street; junior suites have an ocean view from the bedroom as well as the living area. The clientele is mainly Mexican businesspeople and, in summer, families from the interior. The staff is professional and friendly. ⊠ *Av. del Mar 73, Playa Norte 82110* ☎ *669/982–3622, 01800/711–9465 toll-free in Mexico* 🖷 *669/982–3499* 🗗 *56 rooms, 43 suites* 🛏 *Restaurant, some in-room data ports, some kitchens, refrigerators, cable TV, pool, exercise equipment, bar, laundry service, meeting rooms, free parking* ▭ *AE, MC, V.*

**$$** 🏨 **El Quijote Inn.** Room sizes and configurations vary at this five-story, beachside inn. Most are one- and two-bedroom suites with full kitchens. All units have shared or private balconies or patios, tile floors, and coffeemakers. Floors are a bit decrepit, as is the elevator, but an outdoor bar and restaurant overlook both the beach and nicely landscaped grounds surrounding a large pool and large hot tub. ⊠ *Avs. Camarón Sábalo and Tiburón, Zona Dorada 82110* ☎ *669/914–1134* 🖷 *669/914–3344* 🗗 *18 rooms, 52 suites* 🛏 *Restaurant, fans, refrigerators, some kitchens, pool, hot tub, beach, bar, meeting room* ▭ *AE, MC, V.*

**$$** 🏨 **Los Sábalos.** This high-rise is on a long, clean beach smack in the center of the Zona Dorada. In the rooms white walls set off bright blue and green fabrics and other details. Perks include coffeemakers and hair dryers. You'll be in the thick of the action here, and it's home to Joe's Oyster Bar, an informal dance club that really revs up on weekends. ⊠ *Av. Playa las Gaviotas 100, Zona Dorada 82110* ☎ *669/983–5333, 800/ 528–8760 in the U.S., 877/756–7532 in Canada* 🖷 *669/983–8156* ⊕ *www.lossabalos.com* 🗗 *85 rooms, 100 suites* 🛏 *3 restaurants, room service, in-room safes, some refrigerators, cable TV, pool, spa, beach, 2 bars, dance club, shops, baby-sitting, concierge, meeting rooms, free parking* ▭ *AE, MC, V.*

**$** 🏨 **Azteca Inn.** Rooms in this three-story low-rise have disconcerting bright-red curtains and plaid bedspreads; beyond that, they're spartan.

The courtyard pool has a hot tub, and the watering hole feels like a cross between a terrarium and an American honkey-tonk. ⊠ *Av. Playa las Gaviotas 307, Zona Dorada 82110* ☎ *669/913–4655* 🏠 *669/913– 7476* ⊕ *www.aztecainn.com.mx* 🔁 *74 rooms* ⚲ *Cafeteria, fans, cable TV, pool, hot tub, bar, free parking* 🚭 *AE, MC, V.*

$ 🏨 **Rancho Los Angeles.** Coconut baron Dr. Ernesto Rivera opens his two-story Teacapán home to lodgers. Rates seem high given the basic rooms and so-so mattresses, but the tradeoff is a sense that you're staying at a lonesome beach house owned by distant relatives. Dr. Rivera's son, Jorge, cooks seafood, including the regional specialty pescado sarandeado. Many visitors opt to stay at the adjacent, 60-spot RV park, right on the beach, with full-hookups ($15 a day). ⊠ *Carretera Escuinapa–Teacapán, Km. 25, Teacapán* ☎ *695/953–1609* 🔁 *20 rooms* ⚲ *Restaurant, grill, fan, refrigerator, pool, wading pool, beach, parking; no room phones, no room TVs* 🚭 No credit cards.

$ 🏨 **Villas María Fernanda.** The homey bungalows and larger apartment are right on the estuary in Teacapán. You can rent kayaks or mountain bikes and arrange for tours through the mangroves. There's no restaurant, but the one next door will prepare takeout meals of fish and Mexican dishes. ⊠ *Calle Reforma s/n at the estuary, Teacapán 82400* ☎ *695/ 953–1343* ⊕ *www.villasmariafernanda.com* 🔁 *6 suites, 1 apartment* ⚲ *Fans, cable TV, some kitchenettes, some kitchens, pool, wading pool, hot tub, laundry service* 🚭 *MC, V.*

¢ 🏨 **Hotel Siesta.** Rooms in this Olas Altas hotel are plain but comfortable, with firm beds and brown-print spreads. The exterior hallway may be lined with damp, artificial-turf carpeting, but it surrounds the sweet-smelling courtyard, where dieffenbachias grow to primeval proportions and doves roost in almond trees. The first-floor patio is ringed by such nonaffiliated businesses as a car rental office and a travel agency. The Shrimp Bucket restaurant, which provides the hotel room service, is also here. ⊠ *Paseo Olas Altas 11 Sur, Playa Olas Altas 82110* ☎ *669/981– 2640* 🏠 *669/982–2633* 🔁 *58 rooms* ⚲ *Room service, dry cleaning, laundry service, car rental, travel services* 🚭 *AE, MC, V.*

## Nightlife

In downtown Mazatlán, **Altazor** (⊠ Constitución 521 at Heriberto Frias, Plazuela Machado, Centro ☎ 669/981–5554) has live or canned Cuban music, blues, and rock. At 7 on Wednesday nights, the place shows art films. **Canucks** (⊠ Paseo Claussen 259, Centro ☎ 669/981–2978) hosts live bands most weekends. Monday is open-mike night. **El Caracol Disco Club** (⊠ Av. Camarón Sábalo s/n, Zona Dorada ☎ 669/913– 3333), at El Cid Castilla, has a high-tech disco, billiards, board and arcade games, and theme nights. A $20 cover includes all drinks and games. **Dionisios** (⊠ Calle Belisario Domínguez 1406, Centro ☎ 669/985– 0333) attracts gays and straights to its softly lighted, minimalist lounge adorned with work by local artists. Weekends see a DJ who spins disks at a volume permitting conversation in a normal tone of voice.

The complex known as **Fiesta Land** (⊠ Av. Camarón Sábalo, at Calz. Rafael Buelna, Zona Dorada ☎ 669/984–1666), on the Zona Dorada's southern edge, has a several bars and restaurants. Valentino has two dance clubs—one geared toward a younger crowd, the other with more tranquil, romantic music—and a karaoke salon. The Bora Borapalapa bar-restaurant is known for its raucous disco music and table-dancing; like Valentino, it opens after 9 PM. Pepe's & Joe is a microbrewery with American-style burgers and dogs. The extravagant Sheik restaurant delights diners with waterfalls, ocean views, stained-glass windows, and marble floors.

★ The **Fiesta Mexicana** (✉ Playa Mazatlán hotel, Av. Playa las Gaviotas 202, Zona Dorada ☎ 669/989–0555) holds dinner shows Tuesday, Thursday (in high season), and Saturday from 7 to 10:30. The $28 entrance fee covers an all-you-can-eat Mexican buffet, an open bar, entertainment, and dancing. **Jazz Bar** (✉ Calle Sixto Osuna 510B, Plazuela Machado, Centro ☎ 669/981–6146) lures excellent entertainers with its commitment to a jazz-only format. Owners Phil and Tracey suggest you bring your horn and horn in on a jam session. **Joe's Oyster Bar** (✉ Los Sábalos hotel, Av. Playa las Gaviotas 100, Zona Dorada ☎ 669/983–5333) is a popular beachfront spot where all sorts of people dance to techno and other popular music.

For a "locals" experience, hit the **palapa bar** at Playa Las Brujas, Punto los Cerritos, to dance to *musica de banda* Friday and Saturday nights, and Sunday after 4 or 5 PM. A favorite with young revelers bent on downing tequila shooters and whooping it up is **Señor Frog's** (✉ Av. del Mar 882, Zona Costera ☎ 669/982–1925). It's also a restaurant that serves good barbecued ribs and chicken with corn on the cob. Bandidos carry tequila bottles and shot glasses in their *bandoliers,* Revolution-era ammunition belts.

## Sports & the Outdoors

### Baseball
The people of Mazatlán loyally support **Los Venados** (☎ 669/981–1710 ✉ Blvd. Justo Sierra, Zona Estadio), a Pacific League Triple A team. Regular season games are played at the Teodoro Mariscal Baseball Stadium October through December, longer if the team makes the playoffs. Purchase tickets at the stadium box office after 1 PM on game day; prices are $1–$8.

### Bullfights & Charreadas
Bullfights are held most Sunday afternoons at 3:30 from December through April in the bullring—Plaza de Toros Monumental—on Calzada Rafael Buelna near Calle de la Marina. *Charreadas* (rodeos) take place during roughly the same time period, also on Sunday. Tickets (about $10–$20 for charreadas; $30–$35 for bullfights) are available at the bullring, through most hotels and travel agencies, and at the nightclub **Valentino** (✉ Fiesta Land complex, Av. Camarón Sábalo, at Calz. Rafael Buelna, Zona Dorada ☎ 669/984–1666).

### Fishing
Sportfishing fleets operate from the docks south of the lighthouse, in Marina Vallarta, and in Marina Mazatlán, near the Faro Mazatlán

hotel. You can arrange deep-sea charters through your hotel, or you can contact the companies directly. Charters include a full day of fishing, bait, and tackle and usually an ice chest with ice. Prices range from $70 to $100 per person on a party boat, or from $270 to $450 to charter a boat for 1 to 6 passengers.

For bass fishing in El Salto Reservoir, a lake northeast of Mazatlán off Carretera 40, contact **Amazing Outdoors Tours** (⊠ El Patio Restaurant, Camarón Sábalo 2601, Zona Dorada ☎ 669/984–3151 ⊕ www. basselsalto.com). Choose a half or full day trip, or stay overnight at their fishing lodge. The reputable **Aries Fleet** (☎ 669/916–3468) is connected with El Cid Hotel and operates from Marina El Cid. The company has shared or charter boats for big-game fishing. **Bill Heimpel's Star Fleet** (☎ 669/982–2665 ⊕ www.starfleet.com.mx), which has fast twin-engine boats, is well regarded.

## Golf

It may be older and dowdier than other area greens, but the 9-hole course at **Club Campestre de Mazatlán** (⊠ Carretera Internacional Sur ☎ 669/ 980–1570) is substantially cheaper. Fees are $18 for 9 holes; caddies ($5 but tip generously) and a limited number of carts ($10) are available. The last 9 holes of the spectacular 27-hole course at **El Cid Golf and Country Club** (☎ 669/913–3333 Ext. 3261) were designed by Lee Trevino. There's a putting green and driving range. Greens fees are $42, plus $40 for a cart and $17 for a caddy. The **Estrella del Mar Golf Club** (⊠ Camino Isla de la Piedra, Km 10 ☎ 669/982–3300), just south of Mazatlán proper on Isla de la Piedra (Stone Island) has an 18-hole Robert Trent Jones Jr. course. Transportation from some of Mazatlán's major hotels is free. There are a pro shop, driving range, and a putting green. Carts and transportation to and from the course are included in the $110 greens fee. Clinics are offered, too.

## Tennis

Many of the hotels have courts, some of which are open to the public, and there are a few public courts not connected to the hotels. Call for reservations at **El Cid Megaresort** (⊠ Av. Camarón Sábalo s/n, Zona Dorada ☎ 669/913–3333), which has nine courts, some clay and others cement. Only a few are illuminated; the cost is $10 per hour per court. The **Racquet Club las Gaviotas** (⊠ Av. Ibis s/n, at Av. Río Bravo, Fracc. Las Gaviotas ☎ 669/913–5939) has three cement and three clay courts for rent by the hour. **Club de Tenis San Juan** (⊠ Av. Camarón Sábalo s/ n, across from Hotel Costa de Oro, Zona Dorada ☎ 669/913–5344), has three unlit courts for rent by the hour ($3 per person).

## Water Sports

You can rent Jet Skis, Hobie Cats (two-person catamarans), kayaks, and Windsurfers at most beachfront hotels. Parasailing is popular along the Zona Dorada, and scuba diving and snorkeling are catching on. There aren't, however, any extraordinary dive spots; the best snorkeling is around Isla de los Venados.

**Aqua Adventures** (⊠ Hotel Royal Villas, Av. Camarón Sábalo 500, Zona Dorada ☎ 669/916–6161) rents motorized and nonmotorized water sports equipment. **Aqua Sport Center** (✉ Av. Camarón Sábalo s/n, next to Hotel La Puesta del Sol, Zona Dorada ☎ 669/913–3333 Ext. 3341) offers parasailing trips and rents Wave Runners, kayaks, boogie boards, sailboats, and banana boats. Its staffers can also arrange half-day tri-maran trips to Isla de los Venados aboard the *Kolonahe,* docked at El Cid Marina.

The 4-acre **Parque Acuático Mazagua** (✉ Av. Sábalo Cerritos and Entronque Habal Cerritos, Nuevo Mazatlán ☎ 669/988–0152) has 20 water ac-tivities—including slides, wading pools, and a pool with man-made waves—as well as picnic facilities that have barbecue grills. Entrance is about $8 per person; the park is open 10 AM–6 PM Wednesday through Sunday for most of the year and daily in July, August, and during school holidays.

## Shopping

Some of the best shops are in the Zona Dorada, particularly along Avenidas Camarón Sábalo and Playa las Gaviotas. Bargaining isn't the norm in shops, but it's expected in markets. The gigantic **Mercado Central,** downtown between Calles Juárez, Ocampo, Serdán, and Leandro Valle, is open daily and filled with produce, meat, and fish. In the first few rows parallel to Juárez Street you'll find shell necklaces, huaraches (Mexican sandals), cowhide children's shoes, T-shirts, and gauzy dresses. Although more along the lines of souvenirs than folk art, the market's inventory has improved in the last few years.

### Crafts

Mexican artist **Elina Chaubert** (✉ Calle Sixto Osuna 24 Centro ☎ No phone) has unique beaded necklaces and bracelets, casual beachwear, Guerrero masks, and embroidered cotton clothing. She's also a renowned painter, who sells acrylic and oil paintings (her own and those of others). **Gallery Michael** (✉ Av. Camarón Sábalo 19, Zona Dorada ☎ 669/916–7816 ✉ Av. Las Garzas 18, Zona Dorada ☎ 669/916–5511) has sil-ver jewelry, handicrafts, and mementos.

**Mazatlán Arts and Crafts Center** (✉ Av. Playa las Gaviotas 417, Zona Do-rada ☎ 669/913–2120) is full of souvenir standards: onyx chess sets, straw sombreros, leather jackets, sandals, coconut masks, and piñatas. Part of Hotel Playa, **México México** (✉ Av. Playa las Gaviotas 202, Zona Dorada ☎ 669/989–0555) is a good place to buy resort wear, costume and shell jewelry, and unique ceramic and metal items. The stylish work at the **Nidart** (✉ Calle Libertad 45 and Calle Carnaval, Centro ☎ 669/981–0002) includes leather masks, ceramic sculptures, contemporary black-and-white photos, and other Mexican arts and craft. Sometimes you can see artisans producing these wares in open workshops.

### Jewelry

Fodor'sChoice **Casa Maya** (✉ Av. Playa las Gaviotas 411, across from Hotel Las Flo-res Zona Dorada ☎ 669/914–0491) has silver and gold jewelry; silver tea sets, platters and urns; and Talavera place settings. **Centro Comercial Las Cabanas** (✉ Av. Playa las Gaviotas 408, Zona Dorada ☎ No phone) consists of two rows of shops—many selling gold, silver, abalone, and enamel jewelry—facing a narrow central patio where worn-out spouses can take a break. **Pardo** (⊠ Av. Playa las Gaviotas, across from Hotel Las Flores, Zona Dorada ☎ 669/914–2389) has a lovely and expansive collection of gold and silver jewelry, and loose stones. **Rubio Jewelers** (⊠ Costa de Oro hotel, Av. Camarón Sábalo L-1, Zona Dorada ☎ 669/ 914–3167) carries fine gold, silver, and platinum jewelry. It's also Mazatlán's exclusive distributor of Sergio Bustamante's whimsical ceramic and bronze sculptures.

## Mazatlán A to Z

### AIR TRAVEL

AIRPORT  Aeropuerto Internacional Rafael Buelna is about 25 km (18 mi) south of town—a good 30-minute drive.

🚩 **Aeropuerto Internacional Rafael Buelna** ☎ 669/982-2177.

AIRPORT  To get to the airport you must take a private taxi, which will cost be-
TRANSFERS  tween $15 and $20. Transportaciones Aeropuerto vans run from the airport to downtown Mazatlán, the hotel zones, and elsewhere for $5–$6 per person. The company also has private cabs (for one to four passengers) that cost $20.

🚩 Shuttles **Transportaciones Aeropuerto** ☎ 669/990-3555.

CARRIERS  Aeroméxico has daily flights from multiple U.S. and Mexican cities, though nothing direct. Alaska Airlines flies nonstop from Los Angeles. Continental flies daily nonstop from Houston, and from other major U.S. airports to Mexico City. AeroCalifornia has direct flights from Los Angeles five to seven days a week; there are also daily direct flights from La Paz in Baja California and from Mexico City. Mexicana flies nonstop daily from Mexico City, and daily direct from Los Angeles. America West links Mazatlán to Phoenix with nonstop flights, daily in high season.

🚩 **AeroCalifornia** ☎ 669/913-2042, 800/237-6225 in the U.S. **Aeroméxico** ☎ 669/ 982-3444, 01800/021-4000 toll-free in Mexico, 800/237-6639 in the U.S. **Alaska Airlines** ☎ 669/985-2730, 800/252-7522 in the U.S. **America West** ☎ 669/981-1184, 800/235-9292 in the U.S. **Continental** ☎ 669/985-1881, 800/523-3273 in the U.S. **Mexicana** ☎ 669/913-0772 or 669/982-2888, 800/531-7921 in the U.S.

### BOAT & FERRY TRAVEL

The car-and-passenger ferry between La Paz in Baja California Sur and Mazatlán takes about 18 hours and is fairly reliable. One-way fares are about $60 for tourist-class passage, $76 for a tiny cabin (bath down the hall), and $91 for berth with bath. Cost for transporting vehicles varies by size, beginning at about $210. Check the schedule and purchase tickets in advance, as prices and times change frequently. Royal Caribbean, Holland America, and Princess, among other cruise lines, include Mazatlán on their seven-day Mexican Riviera cruises.

🚩 **Ferry service** ⊠ Prolongación de Calle Carnaval s/n, Fracc. Playa Sur ☎ 669/981-7020 or 669/981-7023 ⊕ www.bajaferries.com.

## BUS TRAVEL

The Mazatlán bus terminal is at Carretera Internacional 1203 at Calle Chachalacas, three blocks behind the Sands Hotel. Elite, one of the area's best bus lines, has service to the U.S. border and south to Guadalajara, Mexico City, and the southern coast. Transportes del Pacífico (TAP) has service throughout Mexico, including the capital.

Buses and minibuses run frequently along all main avenues. Fares start at about 40¢ and increase slightly, depending on the destination. Look for the bright green buses, which cost just a little more and are new and air-conditioned.

🚌 **Elite** ☎ 669/981-3800 or 669/985-1868. **TAP** ☎ 669/981-4659.

## CAR RENTAL

🚌 **Major Agencies Budget** ✉ Av. Camarón Sábalo 402, Zona Dorada ☎ 669/913-2000. **Hertz** ✉ Av. Camarón Sábalo 314, Zona Dorada ☎ 669/913-4955, 669/985-0845 to the airport. **National** ✉ Av. Camarón Sábalo 7000, Zona Dorada ☎ 669/913-6000 ✉ airport ☎ 669/982-4000.

## CAR TRAVEL

Mazatlán is 1,212 km (751 mi) from the border city of Nogales, Arizona, on the good but expensive (about $30) toll road 15-D, or on the federal highway 15. One overnight stop is recommended. Within the city, it's fairly easy to navigate the coast-hugging roads (one or two lanes in each direction). Parking can be difficult downtown, but most hotels and restaurants in the Zona Dorada have lots.

## CONSULATES

🚌 **Canadian Consulate** ✉ Av. Playa las Gaviotas 202, Zona Dorada ☎ 669/913-7320. **U.S. Consul** ✉ Av. Playa las Gaviotas 202, across from Hotel Playa Mazatlán, Zona Dorada ☎ 669/916-5889.

## EMERGENCIES

🚌 **Balboa Hospital & Walk-In Clinic** ✉ Av. Camarón Sábalo 4480, at Plaza Balboa, Zona Dorada ☎ 669/916-7933. **Farmacias Moderna** ✉ Privada Bugambilias 200 at Av. Camarón Sábalo, Zona Dorada ☎ 669/916-5233. **General Emergency Number** ☎ 060. **Red Cross** ✉ Calle Zaragoza 1801, Zona Dorada ☎ 669/916-5233.

## ENGLISH-LANGUAGE MEDIA

You can find English-language books and maps at Mazatlán Book and Coffee Company, across from the Costa de Oro Hotel, in Plaza Galería. Posted hours are Monday through Saturday 9–6, although it's not terribly loyal to the schedule in low season. Mazatlán's English-language monthly magazine, *Pacific Pearl*, has ads and articles of interest to locals and visitors. El Estanquio newsstand sells magazines and newspapers in English.

🚌 **Bookstore El Estanquio** ✉ Av. Camarón Sábalo at Av. Playa las Gaviotas, Zona Dorada ☎ No phone. **Mazatlán Book and Coffee Company** ☎ 669/916-7899.

## MAIL, INTERNET & SHIPPING

The main post office is downtown, across from the main plaza, and offers MexPost shipping, with rates slightly cheaper than the international shipping companies. DHL is in the heart of the Golden Zone. There are cyber-cafés scattered through the old district and the Zona Dorada; most charge from $1.50 to $3 per hour and are open from 8 or 9 AM until 11 or midnight.

**Ⓜ Mail Services** **DHL** ✉ Av. Camarón Sábalo at Calle Lomas de Mazatlán, Centro ☎ 669/990-0010. **Post office** ✉ Av. Juárez at 21 de Marzo, Centro ☎ 669/981-2121.

**Ⓜ Cybercafés** **Cafe Internet** ✉ Av. Camarón Sábalo 5108 next to Ocean Palace Cafe, Zona Dorada ☎ No phone. **Netscape** ✉ Av. Camarón Sábalo 222, Zona Dorada ☎ 669/990-1289.

### MONEY MATTERS

Credit cards are widely accepted at hotels and restaurants; small, family-run establishments prefer cash. Although many hotels will change your dollars to pesos without charging a commission, they don't offer as good a rate as do banks, most of which have ATM machines and are open weekdays 8:30–4:30. In the Zona Dorada, Servicios Turísticos will exchange currency for you daily 7–6.

**Ⓜ Banks** **Banamex** ✉ Calle Flores at Av. Juárez, Centro ☎ 669/982-7733.

**Ⓜ Exchange House** **Servicios Turísticos** ✉ Av. Camarón Sábalo 980-B, Centro ☎ No phone.

### TAXIS

Taxis cruise the Zona Dorada strip, which is about 3 km (2 mi) north of downtown, regularly. You can hail them on the street. Fares start at $2.50; discuss the fare and conduct any negotiations before setting out. A fun way to get around is in an open-sided *pulmonía*; the fare, for up to three passengers, starts at about $3 for a short trip. There are also several 24-hour radio taxi companies.

**Ⓜ Taxis** **Ecotaxis Rojos** ☎ 669/985-2828. **Ecotaxis Verdes** ☎ 669/986-1111.

### TOURS

Aqua Sport Center has transportation only to Isla de los Venados ($8 round trip), as well as trimaran packages including lunch, snorkeling, and kayaking ($35). King David Tours is one of several operators offering a bay tour that takes in Isla de la Piedra and includes lunch and open bar ($20). The price is $25 with two activities; choose from snorkeling, horseback riding, and banana-boat rides.

Marlin, Olé, Vista Tours, and Pronatours each offer a city tour ($18) and a colonial tour (Copala and Concordia; $32 without lunch, $40 with lunch). Marlin Tours runs a tequila factory tour ($28) as well as an all-day excursion (about $40) ending in Teacapán, near the Nayarit border. The van tour makes stops in towns, ranches, and sometimes a thermal spring, and includes Continental breakfast and drinks. Lunch at a seaside restaurant and an optional boat ride aren't included. Olé Tours can arrange custom trips to the villages of El Quelite and El Rosario as well as to Concordia and Copala.

Die-hard archaeology buffs or those who like an off-road adventure should consider a trip to El Calón, ruins ensconced in a mangrove estuary and accessible only at high tide. An archaeologist from the University of Buffalo spent years investigating the 30-meter-tall pyramid, which is believed to have been built by the Totorame Indians over the course of 100 years. It's made of oyster, clam, and conch shells interspersed with layers of earth, and there may be hundreds of similar undiscovered mounds in the area. You can make plans for a visit through the Rancho Los Angeles hotel.

**Aqua Sport Center** ☎ 669/913-3333 Ext. 3341 in Mazatlán. **King David Tours** ✉ Av. Camarón Sábalo 333, Zona Dorada ☎669/914-1444 or 669/914-0451. **Marlin Tours** ✉Calle de la Laguna 300, Local 2-D, Zona Dorada ☎ 669/913-5301. **Mazatleco Sport Center** ✉ Av. Playa las Gaviotas 408, Zona Dorada ☎ 669/916-5933. **Olé Tours** ✉ Av. Camarón Sábalo 7000, Zona Dorada ☎ 669/916-6288 ⊕ www.oletours.com. **Pronatours** ✉ Av. Camarón Sábalo s/n, Centro Comercial El Cid, Zona Dorada ☎ 669/913-3333 or 660/914-0022. **Rancho Los Angeles** ✉ Carretera Escuinapa-Teacapán, Km. 25, Teacapán ☎695/953-1609 **Vista Tours** ✉ Av. Playa las Gaviotas 413, Local 54, Zona Dorada ☎669/914-0187.

### TRAVEL AGENCY
**Local Agent Referrals American Express** ✉ Av. Camarón Sábalo 1500, Locales 15 and 16, Plaza Balboa, Zona Dorada ☎ 669/913-0600.

### VISITOR INFORMATION
The Sinaloa State Tourism Office is open weekdays 9–5.
**Sinaloa State Tourism Office** ✉ Av. Camarón Sábalo s/n, Banrural Bldg., 4th floor, Zona Dorada ☎ 669/916-5160 through 669/916-5165.

# PUERTO VALLARTA

Puerto Vallarta, which is on the edge of the Sierra Madre range, has been attracting outsiders since the 16th century. Its Bahía de Banderas drew pirates and explorers as early as the 1500s; it was used as a stopover on long trips as a place for the crew to relax (or maybe plunder and pillage). Sir Francis Drake apparently stopped here. In the mid-1850s, don Guadalupe Sánchez Carrillo developed the bay as a port for the silver mines by the Río Cuale. Then it was known as Puerto de Peñas (Rocky Port) and had about 1,500 inhabitants. In 1918 it was made a municipality and renamed for Ignacio L. Vallarta, a governor of Jalisco.

In the 1950s Puerto Vallarta was essentially a pretty hideaway for those in the know—the wealthy, and a few hardy escapists. When it first entered the general public's consciousness, with John Huston's 1964 movie *The Night of the Iguana,* it was a quiet fishing and farming community. After the movie was released, tourism boomed, and today PV (as it's now called) is a city with some 250,000 residents. Airports, hotels, and highways have supplanted palm groves and fishing shacks. About 2 million people visit each year, and from November through April cobblestone streets are clogged with pedestrians and cars.

PV has spread north and south over the years, but every attempt has been made to keep intact the character and image of downtown. City ordinances require houses there to be painted white with red-tile roofs, limit the number of floors, and dictate other architectural details. Pack mules still occasionally clop down the streets and, in the background, velvety green hills look so close they seem to spring from the sea. Above downtown, steep mountain roads curve and twist through jungles of pines and palms, and rivers rush down to meet fine sand beaches and rocky coves.

## Exploring Puerto Vallarta

In downtown PV, a.k.a. Centro or Viejo Vallarta, many two- and three-story houses have been converted to shops, galleries, and restaurants. The malecón is a great place to get your bearings and take the town's pulse. Dividing Centro is the Río Cuale. This river—which can be ebullient or anemic, depending on the rains—embraces a sliver of an island with a cultural center, museum, restaurants, and shops. Just south of the Río Cuale, the sands of Playa Olas Altas and Playa los Muertos are backed by lively restaurants and modest hotels.

The Zona Hotelera, which is divided into southern and northern segments, is the stretch of beach-lined, hotel-laden coast that runs from just north of Centro up to the Marina Vallarata area. The beach along here changes a bit with the character of each resort it fronts; it's particularly nice by the Fiesta Americana and the Krystal hotels. Marina Vallarta is home to the cruise-ship terminal; the Royal Pacific Yacht Club and its 355-slip marina; an 18-hole golf course; condo developments; and such exclusive resorts as the Velas Vallarta, the Marriott, and the Westin. There are a few mini-malls here, with restaurants as well as shops. Farther north is Nuevo Vallarta, just over the state line in Nayarit and at the mouth of the Río Ameca. It has several all-inclusive resorts perfect for those content to simply stay put.

Just south of Centro is a string of resorts, including the Camino Real, and more intimate hotels as well as condos. Many are on their own rocky coves. If you head still farther south, en route to Manzanillo, the coast is sprinkled with some of the region's most exclusive resorts. You won't see them from Carretera 200 (Highway 200); most are on the beach, down manicured gravel roads. Roughly 121 kilometers (75 miles) south of PV is the village of Playa Quemaro, which marks the start of the 92-kilometer-long (57-mile-long) Costa Alegre—Happy or Joyous Coast. This region, which ends at Barra de Navidad just north of Manzanillo, is slowly becoming an internationally known vacation destination and now has a handful of exclusive hotels along its shores. Small, sometimes well-marked roads off Carretera 200, which runs farther inland here than it does to the north, lead to seaside villages and resorts.

A rental car is helpful to fully explore the many beaches and small towns north and south of Centro. That said, at a minimum of about $50 per day for car rental, you'll probably save money using taxis and city buses if you only plan to head just outside town, and thus avoid hassles with parking (not to mention drinking and driving). Taxis cruise up and down the main drags, and buses fly along, most at a terrifying speed. A car is a serious hindrance in Centro and the Río Cuale area. You can see most of the sights on foot—just be sure you wear comfortable shoes for the uneven cobblestone streets.

*Numbers in the text correspond to numbers in the margin and on the Puerto Vallarta map.*

**a good walk**

When you start seeing cobblestone streets, you've reached Centro. Start your walk at the northern end of the **malecón** ❽ ☛, which runs parallel to Paseo Díaz Ordáz beginning at Avenida 31 de Octubre. About nine blocks south, Díaz Ordáz merges with Calle Morelos at the old light-house tower. Two blocks farther south is the town's main square, Plaza de Armas. On the northern side of this busy, tree-shaded plaza you'll see the **Palacio Municipal** ❾ (City Hall), and one block east, **La Iglesia de Nuestra Señora de Guadalupe** ❿, which is topped by a distinctive crown. Across the street from the plaza on the malecón are Los Arcos, the lime-stone arches framing the town's much-loved outdoor amphitheater.

Head south a few blocks and turn left on Calle A. Rodríguez. After a few blocks you'll come to the busy Mercado Municipal at the foot of the old bridge over the Río Cuale. The steep hillside above, dotted with vine-drenched villas, is called Gringo Gulch, named after the hundreds of U.S. expats who settled here in the 1950s and '60s. To reach the area's most famous sight—Elizabeth Taylor's former home, **Casa Kimberley** ⓫—you can climb the steps on Calle Zaragoza. In the middle of the Río Cuale lies the **Isla Río Cuale** ⓬, which is accessible by bridges for both pedes-trians and autos and is a great place to stroll, shop, and eat.

## What to See

⓫ **Casa Kimberley.** Elizabeth Taylor's former home is connected to Richard Burton's former home across the street by the pink-and-white "love bridge" he had constructed. Part of the house has been converted into a bed-and-breakfast, but you can tour other areas of it daily 9–6. Bur-ton bought the 24,000-square-foot home for Taylor's 32nd birthday after their much-publicized romance during his filming of *The Night of the Iguana* with Ava Gardner, Deborah Kerr, and Sue Lyon. Taylor owned the house for 26 years, and left most of her possessions behind (all on display) when she sold it. ⊠ *Calle Zaragoza 445, Centro* ☏ *322/222–1336* ⌸ *$8.*

⓾ **La Iglesia de Nuestra Señora de Guadalupe.** The Church of Our Lady of Guadalupe is topped by an ornate crown that replicates the one worn by Carlota, the empress of Mexico in the late 1860s. The crown top-pled during an earthquake that shook this area of the Pacific Coast in October 1995, but was quickly replaced with a fiberglass version in time for the celebration of the Feast of the Virgin of Guadalupe (December 12). ⊠ *Calle Hidalgo, 1 block east of zócalo, Centro* ⊙ *7:30 AM–8 PM.*

⓬ **Isla Río Cuale.** Surrounded by the Río Cuale, this island effectively slices downtown in two. It has a large market with both shops, outdoor stalls, trendy restaurants, and inexpensive cafés. A bronze statue of film di-rector John Huston dominates the central plaza. Just beyond the statue, at the island's east end, the **Casa de la Cultura** (☎ No phone) sells the work of local artists, offers art and dance classes, and hosts cultural events.

The **Museo Arqueológico** (⊠ Western tip of island, Centro ☎ No phone) has pre-Columbian figures and Indian artifacts. The museum's posted hours are daily 10–6, but it's often closed for one reason or an-other. Admission is free, but a donation is requested. To reach Isla Río Cuale from the town's north side, cross the bridge at Encino and Juárez

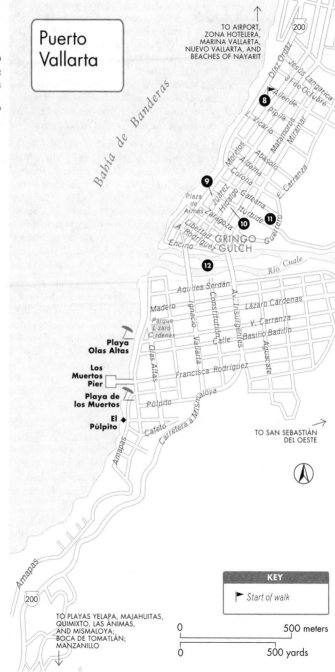

## Puerto Vallarta

TO AIRPORT,
ZONA HOTELERA,
MARINA VALLARTA,
NUEVO VALLARTA, AND
BEACHES OF NAYARIT

200

Bahía de Banderas

Díaz Ordaz

Jesús Langarica

31 de Octubre

Allende

Pipila

L. Vicario

Matamoros

Miramar

Morelos

Abasolo

Aldama

Corona

E. Carranza

Juárez

Hidalgo

Galeana

Plaza
de
Armas

Zaragoza

Iturbide

Guerrero

Libertad

A. Rodríguez

GRINGO
GULCH

Encino

Río Cuale

Aquiles Serdán

Madero

Av. Insurgentes

Lázaro Cárdenas

Ignacio

Constitución

V. Carranza

Parque
Lázaro
Cárdenas

Vallarta

Calle

Basilio Badillo

Aguacate

**Playa
Olas Altas**

Olas Altas

**Los
Muertos
Pier**

Francisca Rodríguez

**Playa de
los Muertos**

Púlpito

Carretera a Mismaloya

**El
Púlpito** ◆

Cafeto

TO SAN SEBASTIÁN
DEL OESTE

Amapas

Amapas

200

TO PLAYAS YELAPA, MAJAHUITAS,
QUIMIXTO, LAS ÁNIMAS,
AND MISMALOYA;
BOCA DE TOMATLÁN;
MANZANILLO

**KEY**

▶ *Start of walk*

0            500 meters

0            500 yards

or at Libertad and Miramar. From the south, cross at Ignacio L. Vallarta and Aquiles Serdán, or at Insurgentes and Aquiles Serdán.

★ ▶ ❽ **Malecón.** The malecón is downtown's main drag, a nice place to rest on a wrought-iron bench and watch the water and the rest of the world. The seaside walkway is faced by restaurants, cafés, and shops. It's also dotted with interesting sculptures, including the bronze sea horse that has become PV's trademark, and *La Nostalgia,* a bronze statue of a seated couple, inspired by the love life of author Ramiz Barquet. The latest addition is *Rotunda del Mar,* a collection of whimsical statues by artist Alejandro Colunga. ⬚ *Parallel to Paseo Díaz Ordáz, extending about 16 blocks from Río Cuale northeast to 31 de Octubre, Centro.*

❾ **Palacio Municipal.** The late Manuel Lepe's 1981 mural depicting PV as a fanciful seaside fishing and farming village hangs above the stairs on City Hall's second floor. Lepe is known for his blissful, primitive-style scenes of the city, filled with smiling angels. The tourism office is on the first floor. ⬚ *Av. Juárez, on Plaza de Armas, the main plaza, Centro* ☎ *No phone* ⊙ *Weekdays 9–5.*

## Beaches

### North of Centro

☾ **Bucerías.** When PV swells with tourists, local families head to the less populated beaches at the north end of Bahía de Banderas in Nayarit State. Twelve kilometers (7 mi) north of Nuevo Vallarta are the sands of the simple town of Bucerías, where a loyal flock of snowbirds has encouraged the growth of small hotels and restaurants. Beyond Bucerías are long stretches of deserted beach around La Cruz de Huanacaxtle and La Manzanilla, where kids play in the shallow waters while their parents sip cold drinks. Destiladeras is a long, semirocky beach with good surf.

**Punta de Mita.** West of the town of Bucerías and its beach, Punta de Mita is home to the posh Four Seasons and the boutique resort Casa Las Brisas. The former fishing enclave has a blue bay that's nice for swimming; around the bend are waves for surfing. This is a prime spot for viewing a sunset; in winter, whales come here to mate and give birth. Scuba divers like the fairly clear waters and abundance of fish and coral on the bay side of the Isla Marietas, about a half hour offshore. Heading north, the coast road leads to the popular beach at El Anclote, with simple restaurants.

★ **Sayulita.** Steadily gaining popularity is Sayulita, which is above the Punta de Mita and El Anclote beaches and about 45 minutes north of PV on Carretera 200. Some say it's like PV was 40 years ago. In addition to hotels and restaurants, Sayulita has excellent surfing and heavenly beaches. Fifteen minutes farther north is San Francisco, unofficially known as San Pancho, with modest rental bungalows and eateries, a 1½-km-long (1-mi-long) barely developed stretch of sand, and more great surfing spots. A half hour beyond San Francisco, the pretty beach at Lo de Marco is also popular with surfers.

### Centro

**Playa los Muertos.** Long ago, Playa los Muertos was the site of a battle between pirates and Indians, hence the name, which means "Beach of the Dead." It begins just south of the Río Cuale ends at a rocky point called El Púlpito (another beach, Olas Altas, is north of the Río Cuale). The area around it is now promoted as the Zona Romántica, but most people still call it Los Muertos. Strolling vendors selling lace table-cloths, kites, and jewelry are almost as abundant as sunbathers. Beach toys for rent include everything from rubber inner tubes to Windsurfers. Walking up the steps (more than 100) at the east end of Calle Púlpito leads to a lookout with a great view of the beach and the bay.

## South of Centro

**Las Ánimas.** This large beach south Boca de Tomatlán appeals to fami-lies and is full on weekends and holidays. Simple seafood eateries line the sand, and you can also rent Jet Skis, ride a banana boat, or soar up into the sky on a colorful parachute.

**Boca de Tomatlán.** At the mouth of the Río Tomatlán and about 17 km (10½ mi) south of PV are this small village and its rocky cove. Water taxis leave from Boca to Los Arcos, an offshore rock formation popu-lar with skin and scuba divers, and the more secluded beaches of Playa las Ánimas and Yelapa, still farther south. About halfway between Boca and Playa de Mismaloya to the north, Chee Chee's, a massive, terraced restaurant and swimming-pool complex, spreads down a steep hillside like a small village. Next door, similarly terraced Le Kliff restaurant is a great spot for a sunset cocktail. Just south of Boca is Chico's Paradise, and a bit farther on, Las Orquidias. Both are riverfront restaurants where you can swim in clear river pools.

**Majahuitas.** With no bathrooms or services for the average Joe, lovely Ma-jahuitas—between the beaches of Quimixto and Yelapa—is the playground of those on day tours and guests of the exclusive Majahuitas Resort. Palm trees shade the white sand beach, and the water is crystal clear.

**Mismaloya.** Playa Mismaloya is the once-pristine cove where *the* movie was made. Offshore is Los Arcos, a protected rock formation great for snorkeling and diving. Major hotels such as Camino Real and La Jolla de Mismaloya have plopped down on some of the primo spots, mean-ing that you can avail yourself of the hotel services while enjoying the public beaches. From Mismaloya you can drive or catch a cab (about a 25-minute ride) on the dirt road to El Edén: a jungle restaurant-bar serving Don Crispin, a regional tequila, where you can swim as well in the river or pool.

**Quimixto.** Between the sandy stretches of Las Ánimas and Majahuitas is rocky Quimixto, whose calm, clear waters attract boatloads of snorkel-ers. These daytrippers also love the 25-minute horse ride or slightly longer walk to a large, clear pool under a waterfall—perfect for a dip.

**Yelapa.** The secluded fishing village and beach of Yelapa is about an hour southeast of downtown. Seafood shanties edge the sand, and para-sailors float high above it all. From here, you can hike 20 minutes into the jungle to see a small waterfall (often dry in winter). Take a day ex-cursion from Marina Vallarta's cruise-ship terminal; you can also hire a motor launch from Boca de Tomatlán. Less expensive water taxis depart from the pier at Los Muertos at 10:30 and 11 AM for Yelapa and return to pick you up at 3 or 4 PM.

## Where to Eat

**$$$–$$$$** ✕ **Bianco.** With its curveaceous glass bar, undulating white-on-white banquettes, and house-special martinis, Martin Good's restaurant seems straight from the hippest part of Miami. Chef Laurent Delorme "plays with his food," using local ingredients and French recipes to create grilled mahimahi in a mussel cream sauce, veal chops with shiitake mushrooms, and roasted lobster tail and grilled beef served with orange polenta and a three-pepper sauce. The bar has an excellent sound system and there's often live salsa or jazz. ⊠ *Calle Insurgentes 109, Centro* ☎ *322/222–2177* ▭ *AE, MC, V* ⊗ *No lunch. Closed Mon. and Aug.–Sept.*

**$$$–$$$$** ✕ **Café des Artistes.** You might say that Thierry Blouet is passionate about
**Fodor'sChoice** food: not only is he a master chef and the owner of this restaurant, he's
★ also a promoter of PV's beloved Festival Gourmet, held each November. In his kitchen Mexican ingredients and European techniques are used to produce such stellar dishes as cream of prawn and pumpkin soup, mussels in a scallop mousse, and roast duck with soy and honey. Special menus combine some of his signature dishes with appropriate wines and, of course, dessert. There are several sleek, intimate dining spaces, including a courtyard garden, as well as a cigar lounge, and a bar. ⊠ *Av. Guadalupe Sánchez 740, Centro* ☎ *322/222–3229* ⌕ *Reservations essential* ▭ *AE, MC, V* ⊗ *No lunch.*

**$$$–$$$$** ✕ **La Palapa.** It's a large, welcoming, thatch-roof place that's open to the breezes of Playa los Muertos. The menu jumps from panfried goat cheese appetizers to tortilla soup, from straightforward Angus beef to seafood prepared in interesting ways. For an expensive but very romantic evening, reserve a table for two right on the sand, and enjoy one of several set menus ($50–$250 for two; reservations are required for this package two days in advance). Regardless of where you sit or what your order, expect to be serenaded by musicians at dinner. ⊠ *Calle Púlpito 103, Los Muertos* ☎ *322/222–5225* ▭ *AE, MC, V.*

**$$–$$$$** ✕ **Blue Shrimp.** The lighting, table and window dressings, and other details are on the blue side, making you feel as if you're underwater. Cushioned booths encourage cozy conversation. Choose your shrimp by size and weight, and the chef will prepare it to order, most likely with rice and steamed veggies. Lobster and a variety of fish plates are also available, or dive into the salad bar (more impressive at night), which costs less than $2. ⊠ *Calle Morelos 779, Centro* ☎ *322/222–4246* ▭ *MC, V.*

★ **$$$** ✕ **Daiquiri Dick's.** The beachside patio dining room of this longtime favorite frames a view of the bay at Playa los Muertos. "Brunch" lasts from 9 to 5 and consists of a long menu of soups, salads, pizza, crab cakes, and ceviche—don't expect traditional American breakfast favorites. The Caesar salad explodes with flavor, and the medallions of beef tenderloin demi-glacé and the lobster tacos are superb. Finish off with a hazelnut daiquiri. ⊠ *Av. Olas Altas 314, Centro* ☎ *322/222–0566* ▭ *MC, V* ⊗ *Closed Sept.*

**$$$** ✕ **Kaiser Maximilian.** The efficient, genuinely friendly staff help to make
FodorśChoice this a top spot. Viennese and other European entrées dominate the
★ menu, which is modified each year when the restaurant participates in
PV's culinary festival. One such menu item is herb-crusted rack of lamb
served with horseradish and pureed vegetables au gratin; another is veni-
son medallions with chestnut sauce served with braised white cabbage
and steamed vegetables. The adjacent café (open all day) has sand-
wiches as well as yummy desserts and great coffee. Try the warm apple
tart with cinnamon ice cream and caramel sauce. ✉ *Av. Olas Altas 380,
Olas Altas* ☎ *322/223–0760* 🖃 *AE, MC, V* ☺ *No lunch; closed Sun.*

★ **$$$** ✕ **Trio.** Founding German chef Bernhard Guth and Uls Henrickson are
known for their avant-garde Mediterranean creations. Try the orange-
crusted sea bass with a sweet puree of garbanzo, dates, olives, and cider
or the rack of lamb and ravioli with lamb ragout. The artsy crowd and
professional staff make each experience here enjoyable. The kitchen often
stays open until just shy of midnight, and there's a rooftop terrace on
which to dine or have drinks. ✉ *Calle Guerrero 264, Centro* ☎ *322/
222–2196* 🖃 *AE, MC, V.*

**$$–$$$** ✕ **Le Kliff.** From a table on one of four tiers, you can watch for whales
in season or boats heading to the docks as the sun sets. (Such fabulous,
180-degree ocean views offset the slightly inflated prices.) The flooring
consists of tree-trunk slices laid down like tiles, and the entire open-sided
restaurant is covered by an enormous palapa. You can come for sunset
hors d'ouevres and cocktails only, a few kilos of lobster, or the specialty
"three friends": lobster, shrimp, and fish fillet served with soup or salad.
✉ *Carretera a Barra de Navidad, Km. 17.5, just south of Playa Mismaloya* ☎ *322/224-0975* 🖃 *AE, MC, V.*

**$$–$$$** ✕ **River Cafe.** At night, candles flicker at white-skirted tables with com-
fortable, cushioned chairs, and tiny white lights sparkle in palm trees
surrounding the multilevel terrace. This riverside restaurant is less impressive during the day, but even then, each plate is a visual as well as
a culinary treat. Attentive waiters serve such international dishes as chicken
stuffed with wild mushrooms and spinach or rack of lamb with polenta.
If you're not into a romantic dinner, stop in for breakfast, or belly up
to the intimate bar for a drink and—Friday through Sunday evenings—
a listen to the live jazz. ✉ *Isla Río Cuale, Local 4, Centro* ☎ *322/223–
0788* 🖃 *AE, MC, V.*

★ **$–$$$** ✕ **Cafe de Olla.** A large tree extends from the dining-room floor through
the roof, local artwork adorns the walls, and salsa music often plays in
the background. This is the place for reasonably priced, down-to-earth
Mexican food—enchiladas, *carne asada* (grilled strips of marinated
meat), and *chiles rellenos* (stuffed, batter-fried chili peppers). The restau-
rant is hugely popular; you may need to wait a short while for a table,
especially for breakfast, which begins at 9 AM. Service is excellent.
✉ *Calle Basilio Badillo 168-A, Los Muertos* ☎ *322/223–1626* ⌂ *Reser-
vations not accepted* 🖃 *No credit cards* ☺ *Closed Tues.*

**$–$$$** ✕ **Chico's Paradise.** It's easy to while away hours—or even the day—
under the huge, multilevel palapa, taking a dip in the river or watching
tortillas being made by hand. Seafood, including fresh jumbo shrimp
and stuffed crab, is a specialty, but chiles rellenos and chicken burritos
are also popular. Or just come for the huge tropical drinks. In the off-

season, Chico's closes just after sunset. ⊠ *Carretera a Manzanillo, Km 20, just south of Boca de Tomatlán* ☎ *322/222–0747* ▭ *No credit cards.*

★ $–$$$  ✕ **Don Pedro's.** Everything is a treat at this giant beachfront palapa in Sayulita, a half hour north of the airport and an hour from Centro, where European-trained chef and co-owner Nicholas Parrillo serves an array of fish, seafood, and poultry sprinkled with herbs and grilled over mesquite. From the crusty herbed breads and pizzas baked in wood-fire ovens to the rich mango ice cream, everything is as fresh as can be. ⊠ *Calle Marlin 2, midway along Sayulita town beach, 35 km (22 mi) north of Puerto Vallarta airport, Sayulita* ☎ *327/275–0229* ▭ *AE, MC, V* ☺ *Closed Aug.–Oct.*

$–$$  ✕ **Andale.** Although many long-timers have been drinking, rather than eating, at this local hangout for years, the restaurant serves great burgers, herb-garlic bread, black-bean soup, and jumbo shrimp as well as nightly drink specials at the chummy bar. The interior is cool, dark, and informal; two rows of tables line the narrow outdoor patio. ⊠ *Av. Olas Altas 425, Olas Altas* ☎ *322/222–1054* ▭ *MC, V.*

$–$$  ✕ **La Bodeguita del Medio.** Near the malecón's north end, this attractive restaurant-bar has a sea view from its second-floor dining room. The specials vary by season; if possible, try the roast pork, the Cuban-style paella, or the pork loin in tamarind sauce; order rice, salad, or fried plantains separately. Like its Havana namesake, it sells Cuban rum and cigars, and the music—like the cuisine—is pure Caribbean. A Cuban sextet performs most nights until past midnight. Try the Havana specialty drink *mojito*: a blend of lime juice, sugar, mint, mineral water, and white rum. ⊠ *Paseo Díaz Ordáz 858, Centro* ☎ *322/223–1585* ▭ *AE, MC, V.*

¢–$  ✕ **Tutifruti.** If you find yourself near the main square at lunchtime, consider having a taco at this little stand a couple blocks up Calle Morelos. It's run by a group of ladies who seem to feed the whole neighborhood at midday. The quesadillas and *machaca* (shredded beef) burritos are delicious; you can get a sandwich or burger, too. Wash it all down with a *licuado* (smoothie) made from fresh fruit and milk. Consider sharing because the portions are large. If you're lucky you might get one of the few stools at the tiled counter. ⊠ *Calle Morelos 552, Centro* ☎ *322/222–1068* ▭ *No credit cards* ☺ *Closed Sun. No dinner.*

## Where to Stay

### Puerto Vallarta

$$$$  ▦ **Four Seasons Resort.** At the northern end of Bahía de Banderas, a 40-minute drive northwest of the PV airport, this hotel was designed for exclusivity. Spacious rooms are in red-tile-roof Mexican-style casitas of one, two, and three stories and fitted with traditional Four Seasons amenities. Each has elegant yet earthy furnishings and a private terrace or balcony—many with a sweeping sea view. The Jack Nicklaus–designed championship golf course has a challenging, optional 19th-island hole. A good variety of sporting and beach equipment is on hand for you to use, and golf and spa packages are available. ⊠ *Bahía de Banderas, Punta de Mita 63734, Nayarit* ☎ *329/291–6000, 800/819–5053 in the U.S.* ◱ *329/291–6015* ⊕ *www.fourseasons.com* ◗ *123 rooms, 27 suites* ⌂ *3 restaurants, room service, in-room data ports, in-room safes, minibars,*

*cable TV, 19-hole golf course, 4 tennis courts, pool, wading pool, hot tub, gym, spa, beach, snorkeling, boating, horseback riding, 2 bars, baby-sitting, children's programs (ages 5–12), laundry service, concierge, internet, business services, meeting rooms, car rental, free parking ⊟ AE, DC, MC, V.*

**$$$$** ▦ **Presidente InterContinental Puerto Vallarta Resort.** In the open-air, palapa-sheltered entryway, you're met by the sounds of waves crashing and thatch rustling. You pass above gardens to seating areas with contemporary furnishings and classic coastal views. There's no front desk; check-in is handled individually, right in your room, with its white-tile floors and citrus-color fabrics. You're asked to choose from among four experiences that involve changing the scents, music, and certain amenities in your room. Pillow menus, bottled-water menus, complimentary red wine or premium tequila, Casablanca lilies or red roses, and L'Occitane toiletries are other stress-reducing touches. Even the activities here are relaxing: yoga, pilates, sunbathing. ⊠ *Carretera a Barra de Navidad, Km 8.6, Mismaloya 48300* ☎ *322/228–0191 or 322/228–0507* 🖷 *322/228–0493* ⊕ *www.intercontinental.com/puertovallarta* 🛏 *97 rooms, 23 suites ᐸ 2 restaurants, snack bar, room service, in-room safes, cable TV, tennis court, pool, fitness classes, health club, massage, spa, beach, bar, dry cleaning, laundry service, concierge, Internet, business services, meeting rooms, free parking, no smoking rooms* ⊟ *AE, MC, V.*

**$$$$** ▦ **Velas Vallarta.** Silky sheets and cozy down comforters, multiple ceiling fans, and large, flat-screen TVs are a few of the creature comforts that set the Velas apart from the rest. Each large living area has two comfortably wide built-in couches in colorful prints and a round dining table. Huichol cross-stitch and modern Mexican art decorate the walls. Studios and 1-, 2-, and 3-bedroom suites offer the same amenities except that the former don't have balconies with a view of the pool and the beach. Tall palms, pink bouganvillea, and wild ginger with brilliant red plumes surround the two enormous pools. The spa, gym, and hair salon are small and unassuming. ⊠ *Av. Costera s/n, 48354* ☎ *322/221–0091, 800/835–2778* 🖷 *322/221–0755* ⊕ *www.velasvallarta.com* 🛏 *339 suites ᐸ 2 restaurants, grocery, 24-hour room service, fans, in-room data ports, in-room safe, some in-room hot tubs, some minibars, some kitchens, some kitchenettes, cable TV, 3 tennis courts, 2 pools, hot tub, beach, bicycles, 2 bars, gym, hair salon, spa, shops, baby-sitting, children's programs (ages 5–12), laundry service, concierge, meeting rooms, car rental, travel services, free parking, no-smoking rooms* ⊟ *AE, MC, V* ⵄ *AI, EP.*

**$$$–$$$$** ▦ **NH Krystal Vallarta.** This full-service resort and separate time-share property resembles a small village, with brick pathways and gardens leading to the pool area, shops, and dozens of 3-story accommodations. All guest quarters exude Mexican character, with tile floors and Spanish colonial-style furnishings combined pleasantly with modern touches. Rooms and suites are pretty and bright, but not all have a balcony. Master villas have separate dining and living rooms as well as private pools. Water sports concessions are available on the commodious, secluded beach. ⊠ *Av. de las Garzas s/n, Zona Hotelera 48300* ☎ *322/224–0202, 800/231–9860 in the U.S.* 🖷 *322/224–0222* ⊕ *www.nh-hotels.com* 🛏 *102 rooms, 54 suites, 99 villas ᐸ 6 restaurants, in-room safes, minibars, cable*

TV *with movies, 2 tennis courts, 3 pools, 3 wading pools, gym, hair salon, spa, massage, beach, racquetball, 2 bars, dance club, baby-sitting, playground, laundry service, concierge, convention center, car rental, travel services, no-smoking rooms* ⊟ *AE, MC, V.*

$$$ 🏨 **Camino Real.** One of PV's first hotels is on a small bay south of town. Fragrant white jasmine and other tropical plants grace the grounds. Rooms have marble floors with white furniture and bright pink, yellow, and purple highlights against stark white walls; plush robes are classy touches. La Brisa restaurant serves superb seafood lunches; other onsite restaurants give you the choice of Italian and various types of Mexican fare. If you stay in the 11-story tower that houses the Camino Real Club, such services as breakfast on a terrace overlooking the sea are included in the rate. ⊠ *Carretera a Barra de Navidad, Km 3.5, Playa las Estacas 48300* ☎ *322/221–5000, 800/722–6466 in the U.S.* 🖷 *322/221–6000* ⊕ *www.caminoreal.com* ⊅ *326 rooms, 11 suites* ⚒ *3 restaurants, 24-hour room service, in-room safes, minibars, cable TV, 2 tennis courts, pool, gym, beach, 2 bars, shops, baby-sitting, children's programs (ages 5–10), laundry service, concierge, meeting rooms, travel services, free parking* ⊟ *AE, DC, MC, V* ❡ *CP, EP.*

$$$ 🏨 **Fiesta Americana.** The dramatically designed terra-cotta building rises above a deep-blue pool that flows under bridges and beside palm oases; a seven-story palapa covers the elegant lobby—paved in patterned tile and stone—and a large round bar. The ocean-view rooms have a modern pink and terra-cotta color scheme, and each has beige marble floors, a balcony, and a tile bath with a powerful shower. The beach bustles with activity and equipment rentals. It's about halfway between the Marina Vallarta complex and Centro. ⊠ *Blvd. Francisco Medina Ascencio, Km 2.5, Zona Hotelera 48300* ☎ *322/224–2010, 800/343–7821 in the U.S.* 🖷 *322/224–2108* ⊕ *www.fiestaamericana.com.mx* ⊅ *255 rooms, 36 suites* ⚒ *3 restaurants, 24-hour room service, in-room safes, cable TV with movies, pool, hot tub, beach, 5 bars, shops, baby-sitting, concierge, meeting rooms, car rental, travel services, free parking* ⊟ *AE, MC, V.*

★ $$$ 🏨 **La Jolla de Mismaloya.** Its guests consistently give this hotel high marks. And why not, considering its location right on beautiful Mismaloya Bay? All the huge, brightly decorated, one-bedroom suites have a separate living area and ample terraces with a table and four chairs; some also have well-equipped kitchens. Two-bedroom suites have two baths, but no kitchen. The pools are surrounded by spacious patios, so there's plenty of room to find the perfect spot in the sun, whether you're on your honeymoon or with the kids. ⊠ *Zona Hotelera Sur, Km 11.5, Mismaloya 48300* ☎ *322/226–0660, 877/868–6124 in the U.S.* 🖷 *322/228–0853* ⊕ *www.lajollademismaloya.com* ⊅ *303 suites* ⚒ *5 restaurants, room service, in-room data ports, in-room safes, some kitchens, minibars, cable TV, tennis court, 4 pools, gym, hair salon, hot tub, spa, beach, dive shop, snorkeling, jet skiing, bicycles, volleyball, 2 bars, sports bar, shops, video game room, baby-sitting, children's programs (ages 5–11), laundry service, dry cleaning, concierge, internet, convention center, meeting rooms, car rental, travel services, free parking, no-smoking rooms* ⊟ *AE, MC, V* ❡ *AI, EP.*

$$$ 🏨 **Paradise Village.** Built like an Aztec pyramid, this Nuevo Vallarta hotel and time-share property has its own marina and hosts an international

sailing regatta each March. All suites have balconies with either marina or ocean views; the smallest, a junior suite, is 700 square feet. Furnishings are functional: there are sofa beds and well-equipped kitchens. Locals like to visit the spa, which is noted for its massages and facials. ✉ *Paseo de los Cocoteros 18, 63732 Nuevo Vallarta* ☎ *322/226–6770, 800/995–5714 Ext. 111 in the U.S.* 📠 *322/226–6752* ⊕ *www. paradisevillage.com* 🛏 *490 suites* ⚐ *6 restaurants, grill, 2 snack bars, room service, kitchens, cable TV, 18-hole golf course, 4 tennis courts, 3 pools, gym, spa, beach, windsurfing, jet skiing, basketball, volleyball, 4 bars, dance club, shops, convention center, car rental, travel services* 🖶 *AE, MC, V.*

**$$$** 🏨 **Sol Meliá Puerto Vallarta.** The sprawling Meliá, on the beach and close to the golf course, is popular with families and just about hums with activity. An enormous birdcage with several parrots dominates the breezy lobby, which also houses an eclectic collection of Mexican art and memorabilia. The plazas beyond have still more artworks as well as garden areas, fountains, ponds, and such bits of whimsy as a supersize chess board with plastic pieces as big as a toddler. There's a huge pool, an outdoor theater with nightly shows, and elaborate children's programs. Rooms are havens in subdued blues, creams, and sands. ✉ *Paseo de la Marina Sur 7, Marina Vallarta 48354* ☎ *322/226–3000, 800/336–3542 in the U.S.* 📠 *322/226–3030* ⊕ *www.solmelia.com* 🛏 *356 rooms, 4 suites* ⚐ *3 restaurants, cable TV, in-room safes, refrigerator, cable TV, 2 tennis courts, pool, gym, hair salon, massage, 2 hot tubs, beach, archery, billiards, 3 bars, video game room, shops, baby-sitting, children's programs (ages 4–12), laundry service, concierge, internet, meeting rooms, travel services* 🖶 *AE, DC, MC, V* ⦿ *AI.*

**$$$** 🏨 **Westin Regina.** Its buildings evoke ancient temples and are about as mammoth. That said, the open-air lobby feels surprisingly low slung, and
**Fodor'sChoice** there's not a bad sightline anywhere—whether you gaze out to the leafy
★ courtyard or down an orange-tiled, brightly painted corridor lined with Mexican art. The jarring echoes here are tempered by the rush of an enormous water feature. In the spacious, balconied rooms concrete-and-stone floors massage bare feet, and top-of-the-line mattresses with whisper-soft duvets make for heavenly siestas. Guest quarters above the sixth floor have ocean views; those below face the 600 palm trees surrounding the four beautiful pools. ✉ *Paseo de la Marina Sur 205, Marina Vallarta 48321* ☎ *322/226–1100, 800/228–3000 in the U.S. and Canada* 📠 *322/226– 1131* ⊕ *www.westinpv.com* 🛏 *266 rooms, 14 suites* ⚐ *2 restaurants, 2 snack bars, room service, in-room data ports, in-room safes, minibars, cable TV with movies, 3 tennis courts, 3 pools, wading pool, gym, 2 hot tubs, sauna, spa, steam room, beach, Ping-Pong, 2 bars, baby-sitting, children's programs (ages infant–12), laundry service, concierge, concierge floor, car rental, travel services, free parking, no-smoking rooms* 🖶 *AE, DC, MC, V.*

**$$–$$$** 🏨 **Marriott Casa Magna.** It's hushed and stately in some places, lively and casual in others. No wonder this unassuming resort has so many fans. Creamy marble, polished and rough, is *everywhere*. In rooms, fabrics with rich accent colors complement yellow walls and furnishings painted pumpkin orange. There's an infinity pool right by the beach, and walkways crisscross grounds planted with herbs, chilies, and fruit trees. The cactus garden has 100 varieties, including enough blue agave to make a small batch of tequila. Guests of all ages can help biologists with the sea turtle rescue project in June and July. ☒ *Paseo de la Marina 5, Marina Vallarta 48354* ☎ *322/226–0000, 800/228–9290 in the U.S.* 🖷 *322/226–0061* ⊕ *www.marriott.com* 🖛 *404 rooms, 29 suites* ♧ *4 restaurants, 24-hour room service, in-room data ports, in-room safes, minibars, cable TV with movies, 3 tennis courts, pool, wading pool, fitness classes, gym, hair salon, hot tub, spa, sauna, beach, boating, boccie, volleyball, 3 bars, shop, baby-sitting, children's programs (ages 5–12), laundry service, concierge, business services, meeting rooms, car rental, free parking, no-smoking rooms* ☰ *AE, DC, MC, V.*

**$$–$$$** ☒ **Quinta María Cortez.** This atmospheric B&B has soul. Its seven levels ramble up a steep hill at Playa Conchas Chinas, about a 15-minute walk south of Playa los Muertos. Most rooms have balconies and kitchenettes; all are furnished with antiques and local art. Other draws are the efficient and welcoming staff, the fortifying breakfast served on a palapa-covered patio, and the views from the rooftop sundeck. ☒ *Calle Sagitario 132, Playa Conchas Chinas 48310* ☎ *322/221–5317, 888/640–8100 for reservations* 🖷 *322/221–5327* ⊕ *www.quinta-maria.com* 🖛 *7 rooms* ♧ *Fans, in-room safes, some kitchenettes, refrigerators, pool, beach, Internet, some free parking; no a/c in some rooms, no room TVs, no kids* ☰ *AE, MC, V* ⏺⧠ *BP* ☞ *5-night minimum winter, 3-night minimum summer.*

**$–$$$** ☒ **Villa Amor.** What began as a home on top of a hill was transformed into luxury palapa suites among the trees, with more outdoor than indoor living and beautiful views of Sayulita's coast. Accommodations range from a basic room for two (with a hot plate and a small fridge) to a honeymoon suite with a terrace and a plunge pool. The restaurant is good and has live music on weekends. The staff is friendly, and a beautiful beach is just a short walk away. You can borrow bikes, surfboards, and fishing and snorkeling equipment. ☒ *Playa Sayulita 63842, Sayulita, Nayarit* ☎ *329/291–3010* 🖷 *329/275–0263* ⊕ *www.villaamor.com* 🖛 *21 villas* ♧ *Restaurant, fans, refrigerators, some kitchenettes, tennis court, massage, snorkeling, fishing, bicycles, horseback riding, bar, laundry service, concierge, free parking, no-smoking rooms; no a/c in some rooms, no room phones, no room TVs* ☰ *No credit cards.*

**★ $$** ☒ **Buenaventura.** The location is ideal: on Centro's northern edge, just a few blocks from the malecón as well as from the airport highway's shops, hotels, and restaurants. Rooms are cheerful and have pale-wood furnishings, bright striped textiles, framed tropical prints, and small baths with sparkling blue and white tile. The beach is small, but there's an area there for adults only. There's also a lively pool scene. ☒ *Av. México 1301, Centro 48350* ☎ *322/226–7000 or 888/859–9439* 🖷 *322/222–3546* 🖛 *232 rooms, 4 suites* ♧ *2 restaurants, room service, cable TV, 2 pools, hot tub, massage, beach, volleyball, 3 bars, baby-sitting, laundry service, concierge, travel services* ☰ *AE, MC, V* ⏺⧠ *AI, EP.*

**$$** ☒ **Casa Iguana Hotel.** Palms and plants edge walkways, which in turn line the swimming pool and goldfish ponds. Balconies look down on this garden scene and on the palapa bar-restaurant. Standard suites have full kitchens; shower-only baths; chunky, bare-wood furniture with cast-iron hardware; and tiles with folkloric patterns. Electric orange and yellow plaids brighten spaces that can be dark at certain times of the day. The hotel is on a dusty, cobblestone street off Carretera 200 (local buses stop here) and 15-minutes south of downtown. The beach is a five-minute walk away; the village of Mismaloya is even closer. ⊠ *Av. 5 de Mayo 455, Mismaloya 48394* ☎ *322/228–0186, 01800/216–2222 in Mexico, 877/893–7654 in the U.S., 877/224–5057 in Canada* 🖷 *322/ 228–0087* ⊕ *www.casaiguanahotel.com* ⤴ *49 2-bedroom suites, 3 3-bedroom suites, 1 dormitory* ⌂ *Restaurant, grocery, kitchens, fans, cable TV, pool, outdoor hot tub, bar, laundry facilities, Internet, meeting room* ⊟ *AE, MC, V* ⦿ *EP, FAP.*

★ **$–$$** 🏨 **Los Arcos.** This hotel, which is right on the beach in town, buzzes. Accommodations range from standard rooms to large suites with kitchens; all have bright color schemes, rustic Mexican furnishings, and white-tile floors. The swimming pool stretches on and on, and bleach-white buildings are fronted by lacy palms and draped in yellow trumpet vines. There's live music nightly until 11:30 and a Mexican fiesta on Saturday evening in the open-air palapa restaurant-bar facing the beach. Kaiser Maximilian, one PV's best restaurants, is steps away. ⊠ *Av. Olas Altas 380, Olas Altas 48380* ☎ *322/222–1583, 800/648–2403 in the U.S., 888/729–9590 in Canada* 🖷 *322/222–2418* ⊕ *www. playalosarcos.com* ⤴ *181 rooms, 100 suites* ⌂ *Restaurant, cable TV, some kitchens, pool, beach, bar, baby sitting, free parking* ⊟ *MC, V.*

**$–$$** 🏨 **Casa Dulce Vida.** Hidden four blocks off the busy malecón, this '60s-era villa has seven suites of various sizes filled with modern Mexican art and comfortable furniture. All have well-equipped kitchens and a few have ocean-view terraces; the largest has three bedrooms, two baths, and a separate dining room. There's a red-tile pool and tropical gardens. In high season, the property only accepts weeklong bookings. ⊠ *Calle Aldama 295, Centro 48300* ☎ *322/222–1008, 800/600–6026 in the U.S.* 🖷 *322/222–5815* ⊕ *www.dulcevida.com* ⤴ *6 suites* ⌂ *Fans, some in-room safes, kitchens, pool; no a/c in some rooms, no phone in some rooms, no room TVs* ⊟ *V.*

**$** 🏨 **Casa Andrea.** One- and two-bedroom apartments in this spiffy property are truly homey. Each is different, but all have ceiling fans and dark-wood beams that contrast with white ceilings and walls. Use the hotel's computer to check your e-mail, or curl up with a book or watch a video in the library. Coffee and pastries are served each morning on the garden patio. The location, just a few blocks from Los Arcos and the boardwalk, is a real plus. The management prefers that you book this property by the week, although exceptions are sometimes made. ⊠ *Calle Francisca Rodriguez 174, Centro 48380* ☎ *322/222–1213* ⊕ *www. casa-andrea.com* ⤴ *11 apartments* ⌂ *Fans, kitchens, pool, hot tub, gym, bar, library, laundry facilities, Internet; no room phones, no room TVs* ⊟ *No credit cards* ⦿ *CP.*

**$** 🏨 **Hotel Rosita.** In 1948, a visionary named Don Salvador Gonzalez Gutiérrez decided that it was time for PV to have a hotel. What started as a sleepy 12-room hostelry is now a busy 115-room downtown hotel, and it's still in the founder's family. A series of brick-framed arches creates breezy passageways in the open-air, terra-cotta-tiled reception area. The tiny pool and the ocean are just beyond. Rooms are very basic; expect shower-only baths, white-tile floors, and fabrics with faint floral prints. Request a room facing the water, as much for the view as for the natural light; rooms facing the street are dark, making them feel cramped. ✉ *Paseo Díaz Ordaz 901, Centro 48300* 🕾 *322/223–2000, 01800/326– 1000 in Mexico* 🖷 *322/223–4393* ⊕ *www.hotelrosita.com* ➪ *115* ⬧ *Restaurant, pool, bar, laundry service* 🖃 *AE, MC, V* ⦿ *BP, EP.*

¢ ⊞ **Posada de Roger.** If you hang around the pool or the small shared balcony overlooking the bay, it's not hard to get to know the other guests—most of them savvy budget travelers from Europe and Canada. A shared, open-air kitchen on the fourth floor has a great view, too. Rooms are spare and vault-like, the showers are hot, and the beds comfortable—if you like a very firm mattress. Freddy's Tucan, the indoor-outdoor bar-restaurant (no dinner) is very popular with locals. The hotel is also in an area that's known for its restaurants and shops. Playa los Muertos is a few blocks away. ✉ *Calle Basilio Badillo 237, Col. E. Zapata 48380* 🕾 *322/222– 0836 or 322/222–0639* 🖷 *322/223–0482* ⊕ *www.posadaroger.com* ➪ *48 rooms* ⬧ *Restaurant, fans, cable TV, pool, bar* 🖃 *AE, MC, V.*

## Costa Alegre

★ $$$$ ⊞ **Las Alamandas.** Personal service and exclusivity lure movie stars and royalty to this low-key resort amid a nature preserve about 1½ hours from both PV and Manzanillo. Although the villas are painted hot pink, they remain hidden by all the vegetation. Suites are filled with folk art, and their indoor-outdoor living rooms have modern furnishings with deliciously nubby fabrics in bright, bold colors and Guatemalan-cloth throw pillows. Although there are no in-suite TVs, you can request one and a VCR for a night, and the property has a movie library. Among the outdoor activities are boat rides along the Río San Nicolás. There's a two-night minimum. ✉ *Carretera 200, Km 85* ⬧ *AP 201, San Patricio Melaque 48980* 🕾 *322/285–5500 or 888/882–9616* 🖷 *322/285–5027* ⊕ *www. alamandas.com* ➪ *14 suites* ⬧ *2 restaurants, room service, fans, minibars, tennis court, pool, gym, beach, snorkeling, fishing, mountain bikes, croquet, horseback riding, Ping-Pong, volleyball, 2 bars, shops, laundry service, concierge, internet, meeting room, airport shuttle, airstrip, car rental, free parking; no room TVs* 🖃 *D, DC, MC, V* ⦿ *EP, FAP.*

$$$$ ⊞ **El Careyes Beach Resort.** It's a boldly painted village of a resort on a gorgeous bay, 98 km (60 mi) north of Manzanillo airport and 172 km (107 mi) south of Puerto Vallarta. Freshly painted rooms and suites are done in yellow ochers, corals, and sapphire blues. The full-service spa has European beauty and body treatments; a deli sells fine wines, prosciutto, and other necessities of the good life. A full range of water-sports equipment awaits you at the beach, and there are dune buggies and kayaks, too. ✉ *Carretera a Barra de Navidad (Carretera 200), Km 53.5, 48983 Costa Careyes, Jalisco* 🕾 *315/351–0000, 800/325–3589 in the U.S.* 🖷 *315/351–0100* ⊕ *www.starwood.com/luxury* ➪ *44 rooms, 4 suites* ⬧ *Restaurant, grocery, room service, some fans, in-room data ports, in-room safes, minibars, cable TV, some in-room VCRs, golf privileges, 2 tennis courts, pool, gym, hot tub, spa, beach, snorkeling, windsurfing, boating, fishing, bar, cinema, shops, laundry service, internet, business services, meeting rooms, free parking* 🖃 *AE, MC, V.*

$$$$ ⊞ **Hotelito Desconocido.** This isolated hotel on a long stretch of beach is an idyllic escape for those willing to pay well for simple pleasures. Rooms and suites are in casitas that incorporate local building styles

and materials, including plank floors, reed mats, bamboo walls, and palm-frond roofs; rustic bathrooms have tile floors. Solar power runs essential equipment, and rooms are cooled by battery-powered fans and lit by lanterns and candles. In the morning, signal for coffee and croissants by running a flag up a pole. Meals plans are available, though they don't include drinks; it also costs extra to use the kayaks and bikes or to go horseback riding. ⊠ *Playón de Mismaloya s/n, Cruz de Loreto Tomatlán* ⌂ *Carretera a Mismaloya 479-102, Edificio Scala, 48380* ☎ *322/222–2526* ⊟ *322/223–0293* ⊕ *www.hotelito.com* ⇆ *16 rooms, 13 suites* ⌂ *2 restaurants, fans, pool, spa, beach, boating, bicycles, billiards, free parking; no a/c, no room phones, no room TVs* ⊟ *AE, MC, V* ⦿I *FAP.*

**$$$$** ⊞ **El Tamarindo Golf Resort.** More than 2,000 acres of ecological reserve
**Fodor'sChoice** and jungle surround this magical resort on 16 km (10 mi) of private coast.
★ The architecture embodies a regional style that first appeared in the 1960s, rendering simple design elements (with a Mediterranean flavor) in local building materials. Many villas have private plunge pools and outdoor living rooms; all have nubby fabrics, oiled wood, and other classy elements. At night, the gracious staff lights more than 1,500 candles around the villas to create a truly enchanting setting. Spa treatments are available in your room or on the beach. ⊠ *Carretera Melaque–Puerto Vallarta (Carretera 200), Km 7.5, 48970 Cihuatlán, Jalisco* ☎ *315/351–5032, 800/325–3589 in the U.S.* ⊟ *315/351–5070* ⊕ *www.starwood. com/luxury* ⇆ *29 villas* ⌂ *Restaurant, room service, fans, in-room data ports, in-room safe, some in-room hot tubs, 18-hole golf course, 2 tennis courts, pool, massage, beach, dive shop, snorkeling, bar, free parking; no room TVs* ⊟ *AE, MC, V.*

# Nightlife

Puerto Vallarta is a party town, where the discos open at 10 PM and stay open until 3 or 4 AM. A $12 cover charge is the norm (at least for men) in the popular discos, many of which are at hotels. Mexican fiestas are popular and can be lavish affairs with buffet dinners, folk dances, and even fireworks. Make reservations with the hotels that host them or with a travel agency.

## Bars

★ **La Bodeguita del Medio** (⊠ Paseo Díaz Ordáz 858, Centro ☎ 322/223–1585) is a wonderful Cuban bar whose friendly vibe makes meeting new friends easy. As its name implies, **Collage** (☎ 322/221–0505), on the highway at the Marina Vallarta complex, has a mishmash of establishments: several restaurants, a bowling alley, billiards, two bars, shuffleboard, a video arcade, and a disco. At romantic **El Faro** (⊠ Royal Pacific Yacht Club, Marina Vallarta ☎ 322/221–0541) you can admire the bay and marina from atop a 110-foot lighthouse. There's often live guitar or other types of music in the evening. The cozy **Kit Kat Club** (⊠ Calle Púlpito 120, Centro ☎ 322/223–0093) has great martinis and a retro-lounge feel.

## Dance Clubs

**Christine** (⊠ Krystal Vallarta, Av. de las Garzas s/n, Zona Hotelera ☎ 322/224–0202) has stunning light shows set to music—from disco to techno. In addition to pretty good Mediterranean dinners in the ground-floor restau-

rant, **de Santos** (✉ Calle Morelos 771, Centro ☎ 322/223–3052) is a club where disco-beat music pounds nightly between 10 PM and 2 AM. If the smoke and noise get to you, head upstairs to the rooftop bar, where you and your friends can fling yourself on the giant futons for some stargaz-
★ ing. **J.B.** (✉ Blvd. Francisco Medina Ascencio 2043, Zona Hotelera ☎ 322/224–4616), pronounced "Jota Bay," is the best club in town for dancing to live salsa. The DJ-spun techno, dance, disco, Latin, and hip hop music at **The Zoo** (✉ Paseo Díaz Ordáz 630, Centro ☎ 322/222–4945), a party-hearty place with a cage for show-off dancers, attracts a mixed crowd of locals and tourists and stays open to nearly dawn.

## Sports & the Outdoors

### Biking

**Bike Mex** (✉ Calle Guerrero 361, Centro ☎ 322/223–1834) provides the gear (24-speed mountain bikes, gloves, and helmets) and snacks for several bike tours, which can be tailored to your experience and fitness level. The most popular excursion is a four-hour trip inland to bathe in an impressive waterfall (4 hours, $46). More ambitious options and mul-tiday excursions can be tailor-made for advanced riders.

### Fishing

The billfish tournament in November draws dedicated fishermen from all over the world. **CharterDreams** (☎ 322/221–0690) offers a variety of trips, from $280 for super pangas for one or two people to $750 for a luxury cruising yacht for as many as eight people.

### Golf

Puerto Vallarta has several impressive courses with first-class services in-cluding driving range and putting greens, lessons, pro shop, and clubhouse. The Four Seasons has an 18-hole course at its Punta de Mita property, as does El Tamarindo, on Carretera 200 south of PV. Both are wonderful courses, but if you're not a guest, tee times can be hard to come by.

Puerta Vallarta's original course is the 18-hole **Los Flamingos Country Club** (✉ 12 km [8 mi] north of airport, Nuevo Vallarta ☎ 329/296–5006), designed by Percy Clifford. The greens fee is $115, including a shared cart and a bucket of balls. Joe Finger designed the 18-hole course at **Ma-rina Vallarta** (☎ 322/221–0545 or 322/221–0073); the $105 greens fee includes a shared cart and tax.

★ About two hours south of Vallarta on the Costa Alegre, **El Tamarindo** (✉ Carretera Melaque–Puerto Vallarta [Careterra 200], Km. 7.5, Ci-huatlán ☎ 315/351–5032 Ext. 500), designed by David Fleming, is breathtaking. The cost to play at the exclusive resort of the same name is $210 and includes the cart and tax. Guests get priority for tee times, so call up to a week ahead of time to check availability.

At the Paradise Village hotel and condo complex, **El Tigre** (✉ Paseo de los Cocoteros 18, Nuevo Vallarta ☎ 322/226–6739), is an 18-hole course with 12 water features. The greens fee of $149 includes a shared cart and practice balls. The 18-hole course at **Mayan Palace** (✉ Paseo de las Moras 1, Nuevo Vallarta ☎ 322/226–1543) includes a golf cart
★ for each player in its $130 greens fees. The **Vista Vallarta** (✉ Circuito

Universidad 653, Col. San Nicolás ☎ 322/290–0030 or 322/290–0040)
course has 18 holes designed by Jack Nicklaus and another 18 by Tom
Weiskopf. It costs $140 to play each of the courses, which are a few miles
northwest of the Marina Vallarta area.

## Horseback Riding

**El Ojo de Agua** (✉ Cerrada de Cardenal 227, Fracc. Aralias ☎ 322/224–
0607) conducts sunset and half-day horseback rides (3 to 5 hours,
$47–$50), some including lunch and time for a swim in a mountain stream.
Also available are five-night excursions in the Sierra Madre ($825). **Ran-
cho Charro** (☎ 322/224–0114) provides transportation to and from
your hotel for rides to area rivers and waterfalls. Choices include three-
hour rides ($47), all-day ($100) rides, and overnight expeditions ($315).

## Scuba Diving & Snorkeling

An underwater preserve surrounding Los Arcos, a rock formation off Playa
Mismaloya, is a popular spot for diving and snorkeling. The rocky bay
at Quimixto, about 32 km (20 mi) south of PV and accessible only by
boat, is a good snorkeling spot. Punta de Mita, about 80 km (50 mi) north,
has Las Marietas Islands, with lava tubes and caves. In winter you might
spot humpback whales; the rest of the year, divers look for manta ray,
sea turtles, and colorful fish. Experienced divers will find big fish lurk-
ing in the underwater pinnacles and caves around El Morro Islands.

Many of the larger resort hotels rent snorkeling and diving equipment
and offer introductory dive courses at their pools. For PADI-certifica-
tion, daylong dive trips, and equipment rentals, contact **Chico's Dive Shop**
(✉ Paseo Díaz Ordáz 772, Centro ☎ 322/222–1895). Trips to Los
Arcos accommodate kids and snorkelers as well as those who want a
two-tank dive ($80). The PADI dive masters at **Pacific Scuba** (✉ Fran-
cisco Medina Ascencio 2486, Centro ☎ 322/209–0364 ⊕ www.
pacificscuba.com.mx) teach courses, rent equipment, and arrange trips.
A two-tank package (at six different sites) costs around $225 and in-
cludes lunch and all gear.

## Tennis

At **Los Tules Tennis Club** (✉ Condominios Los Tules, Carretera al Aeropuerto, Km. 2.5, across from Gigante supermarket, Zona Hotelera
☎ 322/226–1030 Ext. 743) you can take lessons or join organized
tournaments in addition to renting court time ($1 per hour per court,
$3.50 at night). The five asphalt courts are lighted.

## Water Park

☾ Children love **Splash** (✉ Carretera a Tepic, Km 155, Nuevo Vallarta
☎ 322/297–0724), where they can plummet down enormous water slides,
swim, and play on playground equipment and carnival rides. There are
restaurants and bars as well as sea lion and dolphin shows. The park is
open daily 10–6; admission is $12.

# Shopping

Puerto Vallarta has been described as a shopper's paradise punctuated
with hotels and beaches. There are plenty of malls, small specialty shops,

and fine-art galleries. Masks, pottery, lacquerware, carved-wood animals, hand-dyed woven rugs, Huichol bead art, and embroidered clothing are just some of the handicrafts for sale. There's also a good selection of Mexican silver in PV, but watch out for *chapa,* a combination of alloys. Real silver carries the 0.925 stamp required by the government.

In the Mercado Municipal, at Avenida Miramar and Libertad, flowers, piñatas, produce, and plastics share space in indoor and outdoor stands with souvenirs and lesser-quality crafts. Isla Río Cuale is a fun place to shop, with both small indoor shops and outdoor market stalls surrounded by cafés and restaurants. The highway on the north side of town is lined with small commercial plazas. There's a variety of shops at the huge Paradise Plaza, next to Paradise Village Resort in Nuevo Vallarta, as well as a bank, a hair salon, a video arcade, and cafés. Other worthwhile centers include Gigante Plaza, by the Fiesta Americana hotel; Plaza Marina, on the highway at Marina Vallarta; and Villa Vallarta, by the Plaza las Glorias hotel.

Prices in the shops are fixed, and U.S. dollars and credit cards are for the most part accepted. Bargaining is expected in the markets and by beach vendors, who also freely accept American money. If possible comparison shop; quality varies. Most stores are open daily 10–8. A few close for siesta at 1 or 2, then reopen at 4; some close or have reduced hours on Sunday.

## Art

**Galería Arte Latinoamericano** (⊠ Calle Josefa Ortíz Domínguez 155, Centro ☎ 322/222–4406) has contemporary art, sculptures, and lithographs. **Galería Dante** (⊠ Calle Basilio Badillo 269, Col. E. Zapata ☎ 322/222–2477) is a 6,000-square-foot gallery and sculpture garden with classical, contemporary, and abstract works from more than 50 Latin American artists. Oaxacan Guillermo Pacheco and other modernists are represented by **Galería Gradiva** (⊠ Av. Ignacio L. Vallarta 179, Centro ☎ 322/222–7143). **Galería Pacífico** (⊠ Calle Aldama 174, Centro ☎ 322/222–1982) is a pioneer gallery nearly 20 years old.

★ You'll find wonderful, varied art in many media at **Galería Uno** (⊠ Calle Morelos 561, Centro ☎ 322/222–0908). Owners Jan Lavender and Martina Goldberg love to showcase local talent, especially emerging artists. Internationally known Sergio Bustamante—the creator of life-size brass, copper, and ceramic animals and lately, mermaids—has several galleries: **Sergio Bustamante** (⊠ Av. Juárez 275, Centro ☎ 322/222–1129 ⊠ Paseo Díaz Ordáz 716, Centro ☎ 322/223–1407 ⊠ Paseo Díaz Ordáz 542, Centro ☎ 322/222–5480).

## Clothing

**La Bohemia** (⊠ Calle Constitución, at Calle Basilio Badillo, Col. E. Zapata ☎ 322/222–3164 ⊠ Plaza Neptuno Interior, Marina Vallarta ☎ 322/221–2160) sells contemporary resort wear, designer art wear, unique jewelry, and accessories. **Express–Guess** (⊠ Paseo Díaz Ordáz 660, Centro ☎ 322/222–6470) carries its own line of quality sportswear for men and women. There's a well-edited collection of cotton and linen dresses, shawls, purses, hats, and jewelry at **Etnica Boutique** (⊠ Av. Olas Altas 398,

Olas Altas ☎ 322/222–6763). A few items from Indonesia are mixed in with things from different regions of Mexico and Central America.

**Güeros** (✉ Calle Zaragoza 160, Centro ☎ 322/222–0633) sells expensive contemporary clothing with Huichol designs for men, women, and children, as well as shoes, handbags, straw, leather, and home furnishings. **María de Guadalajara** (✉ Puesta del Sol condominiums, Marina Vallarta ☎ 322/221–2566 🖳 Calle Morelos 550, Centro ☎ 322/222–2387) carries comfortable women's clothing in gauzy fabrics and luscious colors. **Oahu** (✉ Calle Juárez 314, Centro ☎ 322/223–1058) has men's surf and casual wear, including well-made flip flops, high-quality T-shirts, and pint-size Hawaiian shirts for children. For over-the-top ethnic clothing, stamped leather purses from Guadalajara, and belt buckles from San Miguel as well as clunky necklaces and bracelets of ★ quartz, amber, and turquoise, don't miss **Serafina** (✉ Calle Basilio Badillo 260, Olas Altas ☎ 322/223–4594).

### Folk Art

**Galería de Ollas** (✉ Calle Morelos 101, Local 3-D, Centro ☎ 322/223–1045 🖳 Paradise Plaza, Nuevo Vallarta ☎ 329/297–1200) is the place to buy wondrous pottery from the village of Mata Ortiz. Good prices and fair dealings with indigenous artisans recommend **Hikuri** (✉ Calle Olas Altas 391, Olas Altas ☎ 322/222–7397 🖳 Paradise Plaza Loc. L-2, Nuevo Vallarta ☎ 322/297–0342), which sells Huichol art. Beaded masks and statuettes, yarn art, and other folk crafts fill the **Huichol Collection Gallery** (✉ Calle Morelos 490, Centro ☎ 322/223–2141)

**El Instituto de la Arte Jalisciense** (✉ Calle Juárez 284, Centro ☎ 322/222–1301) promotes the state's handcrafts, selling signed burnished clay bowls, blown glass, plates and bowls from Tonalá, and other wonderful items at fair prices. Shop for inexpensive, one-of-a-kind folk art from Guerrero, Michoacán, and Oaxaca at **Lucy's CuCú Cabaña** (✉ Calle Basilio Badillo 259, Col. E. Zapata ☎ 322/222–1866). Note that Lucy closes during lunch, on Sunday, and in low season (mid-May through mid-October).

**Mundo de Azulejos** (✉ Av. Venustiano Carranza 374, Col. E. Zapata ☎ 322/222–2675) sells decorative tiles. Their artists can custom-make tile panels in 24 to 48 hours, and the staff is adept at packing pieces to be shipped internationally. Glassblowers at the **Mundo de Cristal** (✉ Av. Insurgentes 333, at Calle Basilio Badillo, Col. E. Zapata ☎ 322/222–4157) create both avant-garde and classic designs. **Olinalá** (✉ Av. Lázaro Cárdenas 274, Centro ☎ 322/222–4995) sells painted ceremonial masks from throughout Mexico and contemporary paintings by the owner. **Querubines** (✉ Av. Juárez 501–A, Centro ☎ 322/222–2988) has utilitarian and decorative items, including painted gourds from Michoacán, Talavera pottery, Oaxacan rugs, vintage posters, and more.

### Jewelry

**Joyas Finas Suneson** (✉ Calle Morelos 593, Centro ☎ 322/222–5715) specializes in silver jewelry and objets d'art by some of Mexico's finest—and most expensive—designers. The worldly **Viva** (✉ Calle Basilio Badillo 274, Col. E. Zapata ☎ 322/222–4078) represents hundreds of jewelry designers from across the globe. The store also sells unique espadrilles, flats, and sandals as well as beach clothing and accessories.

## Puerto Vallarta A to Z

**AIR TRAVEL**

AIRPORT Puerto Vallarta's Aeropuerto Internacional Gustavo Díaz Ordáz is 7½ km (4½ mi) north of town, not far from the resorts at Marina Vallarta.
🛈 **Aeropuerto Internacional Gustavo Díaz Ordáz** ⊠ Carretera a Tepic, Km 7.5, Zona Aeropuerto ☎ 322/221-1298 or 322/221-1325.

AIRPORT TRANSFERS Volkswagen vans provide economical transportation from the airport to PV hotels. Taxis or vans to the exclusive Costa Alegre resorts between PV and Manzanillo can run well over $100.

CARRIERS Mexicana has direct service from Chicago and Mexico City. Aeroméxico has flights from multiple U.S. and Mexican cities. Alaska Airlines serves the western United States, with direct flights from Los Angeles, San Francisco, and Seattle. American has daily nonstop flights from Dallas/Fort Worth and on Saturday and Sunday from Chicago O'Hare. Continental flies nonstop from Houston. America West has nonstop flights from Phoenix.
🛈 **Aeroméxico** ☎ 322/221-1204, 01800/021-4000 toll-free in Mexico, 800/237-6639 in the U.S. **Alaska Airlines** ☎ 322/221-1350, 01800/252-7522 toll-free in Mexico, 800/252-7522 in the U.S. **America West** ☎ 322/221-1333, 800/235-9292 in the U.S. **American** ☎ 322/221-1799, 01800/904-6000 toll-free in Mexico, 800/433-7300 in the U.S. **Continental** ☎ 322/221-1025, 800/523-3273 in the U.S. **Mexicana** ☎ 322/224-8900, 800/531-7921 in the U.S.

**BUS TRAVEL**

One kilometer (½ mi) north of the airport is PV's Central Camionero, or central bus station. ETN has the most luxurious service to Guadalajara, Mexico City, and many other destinations, with roomy, reclining seats. Transportes del Pacífico serves the Pacific Coast region. Elite/Futura has first-class service to Acapulco, Mexico City, the U.S. border, and other destinations. Primera Plus serves destinations throughout Mexico. Southern Jalisco towns such as Barra de Navidad are best reached on Transportes Cihuatlán.

City buses serve downtown, the Zona Hotelera Norte, and the southern beaches. Bus stops—marked by blue-and-white signs—are every two or three blocks along the highway (Carretera Aeropuerto) and in town. Buses to Playa Mismaloya and Boca de Tomatlán run about every 15 minutes from the corner of Avenida Insurgentes and Basilio Badillo downtown.
🛈 **Central Camionero** ⊠ Puerto Vallarta-Tepic Hwy., Km 9, Las Mojoneras ☎ 322/290-1008. **Elite/Futura** ☎ 322/290-1001 or 322/221-0850. **ETN** ☎ 322/290-0996 or 322/290-0119. **Primera Plus** ☎ 322/290-0715. **Transportes Cihuatlán** ☎ 322/290-0994 or 322/221-0021. **Transportes del Pacífico** ☎ 322/290-0119 or 322/290-0993.

## CAR RENTAL
**⚑ Major Agencies Advantage** ✉ Blvd. Francisco Medina Ascencio 1768, Centro ☎ 322/222-7220 ✉ Hotel Velas Vallarta, Marina Vallarta ☎ 322/221-0091 Ext. 5630. **Budget** ✉ Blvd. Francisco Medina Ascencio 1680, Centro ☎ 322/222-3355. **Dollar** ✉ Av. Paseo de las Palmas 1728, Zona Hotelera ☎ 322/223-1354, 322/221-1001 to the airport. **National** ✉ Av. Francisco M. Ascencio 4172, Col. Villa de las Flores ☎ 322/209-0390.

## CAR TRAVEL
Puerto Vallarta is about 1,900 km (1,200 mi) south of Nogales, Arizona, at the U.S.–Mexico border, 354 km (220 mi) from Guadalajara, and 167 km (104 mi) from Tepic. Driving in PV can be unnerving. From December through April—peak tourist season—traffic clogs Centro's narrow, cobblestone streets. During the rainy season, from July through October, the streets may become flooded and the steep hills muddy and slippery. Parking is also a challenge. Unless you're planning extensive exploring outside Centro, consider using taxis and buses to get around.

## CONSULATES
**⚑ Canadian Consulate** ✉ Obelisco Condominio, Av. Francisco M. Ascencio 1951, Int. 100, Zona Hotelera ☎ 322/293-0098. **U.S. Consulate** ✉ Edificio Vallarta Plaza, Calle Zaragoza 160, 2nd floor, Centro ☎ 322/222-0069.

## EMERGENCIES
**⚑ Ambulance/Red Cross** ☎ 322/222-1533. **Farmacia CMQ** ✉ 24-hour pharmacy; Calle Basilio Badillo 365 ☎ 322/222-2941. **General Emergency Number** ☎ 060. **San Javier Marina Hospital** ✉ Blvd. Francisco Medina Ascencio 2760, at María Montessori, Zona Hotelera Norte ☎ 322/226-1010.

## ENGLISH-LANGUAGE MEDIA
There's no shortage of printed English-language information in PV. In addition to lots of slick (and truly helpful) map guides, check out the ad-driven but informative *PV Tribune*. The *Vallarta Voice* is a monthly English-language paper and *Vallarta Today* is a daily.

## MAIL, INTERNET & SHIPPING
For sending and receiving mail and packages, go to Mail Boxes Etc., which also offers fax and e-mail services. The Net House ($3 per hour) is open from dawn to the wee hours seven days a week, and has computers with English-language keyboards. It's air-conditioned and serves coffee, pizza, and dessert.

**⚑ Internet Café The Net House** ✉ Av. Ignacio L. Vallarta 232, Col. E. Zapata ☎ 322/222-6953.

**⚑ Mail Service Mail Boxes Etc.** ✉ Blvd. Francisco Medina Ascencio, Edificio Andrea Mar Local 7, Marina Vallarta ☎ 322/224-9434.

## MONEY MATTERS
Credit cards are widely accepted at hotels and restaurants; expect to pay in cash at small, family-run places. For the best exchange rate go to the bank (most have ATM machines). Most hotels offer a lower exchange rate although they don't charge commissions or ATM fees.

**⚑ Banks Bancomer** ✉ Plaza Marina ☎ 322/221-0662. **Banamex** ✉ Calle Juárez, at Calle Zaragoza, Centro ☎ 322/222-0911. **Eurovallarta** ✉ Centro Comercial Plaza Marina Centro, next to McDonald's ☎ 322/209-0093.

## TAXIS

The ride from the Nuevo Vallarta hotels to Centro costs about $13; from Marina Vallarta to the north of Centro or Mismaloya to the south it's about $5. The minimum fare, for example from one Centro destination to another, is $2.50. Cabs are plentiful, and you can easily hail one on the street. They aren't metered, though, so be sure to agree on a fare before embarking.Water taxis ($9) depart from Boca de Tomatlán for Ánimas, Quimixto, Mahajuita, and Yelapa at around 9 and 10 AM. More convenient for people on the north end of downtown are water taxis leaving from the beach south of Hotel Rosita ($15), although these depart later, at 11:30 AM. Other water taxis ($19) leave the pier at Playa los Muertos pier, at the foot of Calle 31 de Octubre, at 10:15 and 11 AM. All prices are round trip (save your ticket), daily, and return to the same pier from which they decamped at approximately 4 PM. Double check the return time with the boat driver as there's no land route back to PV from most of these beaches.

## TOURS

Daytime bay cruises go to Los Arcos, Yelapa, Quimixto, or Playa las Ánimas, and to Isla Marietas for whale-watching (in winter), snorkeling, swimming, and lunch. Most depart from the Terminal Marítima at around 9 AM (returning midafternoon) and cost around $70.

Local fishermen at Punta de Mita have formed the Sociedad Cooperativa de Servicios Turísticos (Tourist Services Cooperative), which offers various seafaring trips at reasonable rates. The guides may not speak English as well as the more polished PV operators, but they know the local waters, and the fees go directly to them and their families. Sport fishing costs about $43 per hour, with a four-hour minimum for up to five people. Two hours of whale-watching (for up to eight people, $90) and snorkeling around the Marieta Islands ($38 per hour, two-hour minimum, for up to eight people) are available.

The well-respected Vallarta Adventures arranges many types of tours. You can travel by small prop plane to the old mining town of San Sebastian del Oeste, high in the Sierra Madre, for $130 per person. Or you can go on shopping or tequila-tasting expeditions outside Guadalajara or on a cruise to Caleta Bay for dinner on the beach and a show ($70). Harris Tours offers six-hour city tours ($25) as well as a "Hidden Mexico" tour, which takes you to such fishing villages as Bucerías. Another trip heads to Las Juntas, where you can learn about the Mexican *charrería* (rodeo). Both cost about $25 per person.

Natura Tours offers nature-oriented excursions, including bass and deep-sea fishing, scuba diving, hiking, horseback riding, and biking. Villa tours arranged by the International Friendship Club will get you inside the garden walls of some of PV's prettiest homes. Tours depart promptly at 11 AM (arrive by 10:30) from the Posada Río Cuale (Calle Aquiles Serdán 242) on Wednesday and Thursday mid-November through the end of April. The $30 fee benefits local charities. Several companies offer canopy rides: harnessing visitors and sending them slinging from one observation post in the treetops to another. The most impressive of these is

Canopy Tours de Los Veranos, a 200-meter ride through the treetops and across a river. Transportation is provided from the OXXO store in Conchas Chinas or La Jolla de Mismaloya hotel, and the cost is around $60. 🗗 **Canopy Tours de los Veranos** ☎ 322/223-6060. **Harris Tours** ☎ 322/223-2972. **International Friendship Club** ☎ 322/222-5466. **Natura Tours** ✉ Carretera Aeropuerto, Km 5.5, Zona Hotelera 📠 322/224-0410. **Sociedad Cooperativa de Servicios Turísticos** ✉ Av. El Anclote, Manzana 17, No. 1, Corral de Risco, Punta de Mita ☎ 329/291-6298. **Vallarta Adventures** ✉ Av. de las Palmas 39, Nuevo Vallarta ☎ 329/297-1212 ✉ Edificio Marina Golf, Local 13-C, Calle Mástil, Marina Vallarta ☎ 322/221-0836 ⊕ www.vallarta-adventures.com.

### TRAVEL AGENCY
🗗 Local Agent Referrals **American Express** ✉ Calle Morelos 660, Centro ☎ 322/223-2955.

### VISITOR INFORMATION
The municipal tourist office, open weekdays 8–4, is on the Plaza Principal. The Jalisco State Tourism Office is open weekdays 9–5. For information about Nuevo Vallarta and southern Nayarit, contact the Nayarit State Tourism Office.
🗗 **Jalisco State Tourism Office** ✉ Plaza Marina shopping center, Local 144 & 146, Marina Vallarta ☎ 322/221-2676. **Municipal Tourist Office** ✉ Av. Independencia 123, Centro ☎ 322/223-2500 Ext. 131. **Nayarit State Tourism Office** ✉ Paseo de los Cocoteros at Blvd. Nuevo Vallarta, between Gran Velas and Maribal hotels ☎ 322/297-0180. **Puerto Vallata Tourism Board & Convention and Visitors Bureau** ✉ Local 18 Planta Baja, Zona Comercial Continental Plaza ☎ 322/224-1175 ⊕ www.visitpuertovallarta.com.

# MANZANILLO

Clear blue waters lap the black-and-gold volcanic sand on Manzanillo's twin *bahías* (bays), Manzanillo and Santiago. Each is home to a town of the same name, both of which lack polish and have a dearth of shops, museums, and other attractions. It's the very lack of sophistication combined with inviting beaches and some great resorts that attract a certain type of tourist—or rather, traveler.

Manzanillo's fanciest resorts are on and above La Península de Santiago, a spit of land separating Bahía de Santiago and Bahía de Manzanillo. Although less imposing now that it's surrounded by competing hotels, Las Hadas resort is a fanciful collection of white domes and peaks that radiate pink in the midday heat. When Bolivian tin magnate Antenor Patiño conceived of this dazzling palace in the early 1960s, Manzanillo was easier to reach by air or sea than by land; it was a rugged, primitive port that attracted hardy sailors and beachcombers. When Patiño's retreat was completed in 1974, the international social set began to visit Manzanillo, and yet it remained essentially a port city with few attractions.

A government project to beautify downtown has promised a huge garden and pedestrian walkway and an upgrade of the surrounding area. Currently, though, the downtown waterfront area is ho-hum, despite the huge statue of a leaping turquoise sailfish by Chihuahua sculptor Sebastián. What services and restaurants there are, are strung along the boulevard with little sense of connection or community. Many shops and hotel desks close for afternoon siesta; on Sunday most businesses (including restaurants) shut down, and everyone heads for the beach.

North of Manzanillo proper, La Costa Alegre continues to be developed. Travelers on a tight budget or who want a super low-key experience usually head to the small towns of Barra de Navidad and Melaque, about an hour up the coast from Manzanillo. Out of a wild peninsula just across from Barra de Navidad, big-time investors created Isla Navidad, a 1,230-acre resort complex. About 20 minutes north of Manzanillo's airport, the exclusive property looms like a mirage to the surfer transplants and simple shopkeepers across the channel in Barra. Public areas are all plush and classy; outside, multiple swimming pools flow from one to another via falls and slides, all surrounded by inspired landscaping.

## Exploring Manzanillo

The Santiago area, on Bahía de Santiago between the Santiago and Juluapán peninsulas, offers little indication that it's a tourist destination save the string of hotels and restaurants on several pretty beaches. Playa la Audiencia, home to the Gran Bahía Real Resort & Spa, is a nice little cove with dark sand, a restaurant on the beach, and water-sports outfitters. On the far side of the bay, Playa La Boquita is a sheltered cove popular with families.

Directly east of Bahía de Santiago is Bahía Manzanillo, where Las Hadas and Karmina Palace hotels nestle in a sheltered cove and less expensive hotels line such quiet beaches as Playa las Brisas. The so-called Zona Hotelera is less popular than it once was, but it's still great for long walks on the beach. Las Brisas is backed by the Laguna de San Pedrito (San Pedrito Lagoon). On the far side, the highway continues away from the water toward *el centro* (downtown), a busy, jam-packed seaport with little of interest.

At the beginning of the harbor, Carretera 200 jogs around downtown and intersects with Carretera 110 to Colima. Avenida Morelos leads past the shipyards and into town. The zócalo, known as **Jardín de Alvaro Obregón,** is right on the main road by the waterfront. It's sunstruck and shadeless during the day, but can be quite lively in the cool of the evening. Streets leading away from the plaza have ice cream and lingerie stores and shops selling postcards, T-shirts, etched shot glasses, and shell art.

## Beaches

**Playa la Audiencia.** On the east side of the Península de Santiago, below the Gran Bahía Real Resort & Spa and between two rock outcroppings, Playa la Audiencia is small but inviting, with calm water, shade umbrellas, and water sports equipment for rent. The local Indians supposedly granted Cortés an audience here—thus the name. It's a good spot for snorkeling.

**Playa la Boquita.** At the east end of Bahía de Santiago, the popular La Boquita has palm-leaf palapas for shade, informal restaurants, and out-

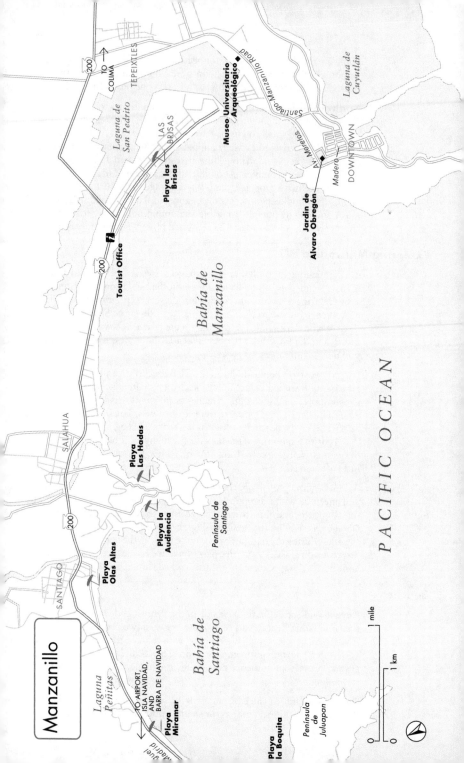

# Manzanillo

TO COLUMA

200

TEPEIXTLES

Laguna de San Pedrito

LAS BRISAS

Playa las Brisas

Museo Universitario Arqueológico ◆

Santiago-Manzanillo Road

Laguna de Cuyutlán

Av. Morelos

Madero ◆

DOWNTOWN

Jardín de Álvaro Obregón

Tourist Office

200

Bahía de Manzanillo

SALAHUA

Playa Las Hadas

Playa la Audiencia

Peninsula de Santiago

PACIFIC OCEAN

SANTIAGO

Playa Olas Altas

200

Bahía de Santiago

TO AIRPORT, ISLA NAVIDAD, AND BARRA DE NAVIDAD

Laguna Peñitas

Playa Miramar

Playa la Boquita

Peninsula de Juluapan

1 mile

1 km

0

fitters that rent water toys. The calm, waveless water is perfect for swimming and snorkeling. The beach in front of Club Santiago, once the favored hangout for locals, is now accessible only by walking north along the beach from the highway or through the club gates. There's no fee to enter; just stop and let the guard write down your car's license number if you're driving.

**Playa las Brisas.** Although not in vogue, long, sandy Playa las Brisas is a good place to stroll or swim. When you tire of walking or playing in the surf, you can take a breather in one of several restaurants, including some in hotels, that are along the beach.

**Playa las Hadas.** Across the Península de Santiago from the Playa la Audiencia, this small, secluded, rocky beach is a good snorkeling spot. It's favored by guests from Las Hadas resort and the adjoining Karmina Palace. Expensive restaurants at both hotels serve drinks, snacks, and full meals. A water-sports concession rents jet skis, small sailboats, and kayaks; it also arranges dive and snorkel trips.

**Playa Miramar.** Miramar means "look at the sea." There are restaurants, water sports outfitters, and horses for hire. Vendors sell jewelry and beachwear from stalls across from the Hotel Maeva. On weekends, families camp out for the day, renting shade umbrellas and lounge chairs from the hotel. Although the waves are a little stronger than at Playa la Boquita, this is still a good spot for swimming.

**Playa Olas Altas.** This beach's name means "high waves." (It's also known as Playa de Oro.) The surfers who come here don't mind the lack of services found at more popular stretches.

## Where to Eat

★ **$$$–$$$$**  ✕ **Legazpi.** Maroon-and-white striped cushions adorn dark-wood chairs and banquets, brass lamps hold thick white candles, and wide windows afford dramatic bay views. The menu is Italian with an emphasis on Mediterranean dishes. Be sure to check out the cozy bar, where there's a mural depicting the history of Manzanillo. ⊠ *Las Hadas Hotel, Av. De los Riscos and Av. Vista Hermosa, Fracc. Península de Santiago* ☎314/ 331–0101 Ext. 3512 ▤ *AE, MC, V* ☾ *Closed Sun. No lunch.*

**$–$$$**  ✕ **El Bigotes.** Waitresses in funky, meter maid–style uniforms serve good seafood to the tune of canned music and the rhythm of waves at this unpretentious restaurant. The specialty is the Jalisco favorite pescado sarandeado. Also recommended are the gigantic portions of ceviche (shrimp or fish) and the *camerón mustache* (butterflied shrimp breaded in shredded coconut and sautéed). ⊠ *Blvd. Miguel de la Madrid 3157, Zona Hotelera* ☎ *314/334–0831* ▤ *MC, V.*

★ **$–$$$**  ✕ **L'Recif.** Waves crash on the rocks below this huge palapa, a 15-minute drive from Manzanillo's Zona Hotelera toward Playa la Boquita. There's a little of everything on the menu—seafood, pasta, chicken, beef—but the signature dish is the camerón L'Recif (shrimp stuffed with cheese, wrapped in bacon, and broiled); it's served with mango sauce and sides of mashed potatoes and sautéed corn, zucchini, and carrots. If you're visiting in March, try to be here at 5 PM, when you might catch a glimpse of a whale. ✉ *Cerro del Cenicero s/n, El Naranjo, Condominio Vida del Mar, Península de Juluapán* ☎ *314/335–0900* ☐ *MC, V* ☺ *Closed May–Oct. No lunch.*

**$–$$$** ✕ **Toscana.** Specialties include seafood shish kebab served with rice and steamed vegetables, a "three lettuce" salad with goat cheese, and a Caesar salad. For dessert, try the tiramisu. Most of the tables sit on the simple outdoor terrace overlooking the beach. There's also a dance floor where electric-guitar music is played nightly after 8:30 PM. ✉ *Blvd. Costero Miguel de la Madrid 3177, Zona Hotelera* ☎ *314/333–2515* ☐ *MC, V* ☺ *No lunch.*

**¢–$** ✕ **Juanito's.** Owned by an American who settled in Manzanillo in 1976, Juanito's is the spot to watch U.S. football and other sporting events in good company. It's the most popular place in town for breakfast, and it also has burgers, milk shakes, fries, barbecued ribs, and fried chicken. Decoration is minimal, but the service is quick and the coffee strong and hot. Check your e-mail or surf the Web on one of two on-site computers. ✉ *Blvd. Costero Km 14, Olas Altas* ☎ *314/333–1388* ⌑ *Reservations not accepted* ☐ *AE, MC, V.*

## Where to Stay

**$$$$** ▦ **Gran Bahía Real Resort & Spa.** This white-stucco giant Playa la Audiencia fills up with families and conventioneers. Rooms have light woods, tile floors, and turquoise fabrics; junior suites are carpeted. All guest quarters have private balconies, but poor design blocks the view from many—ask for a room in the low-rise section, or upgrade to a suite on one of the main building's top two floors. There are a large free-form pool, a spa, and several bars and restaurants, as well as plenty of equipment and activities to keep you occupied. ✉ *Av. Audiencia 1, Playa la Audiencia 28200* ☎ *314/333–2000, 800/448–5028 in the U.S.* ☐ *314/333–2272* ⮑ *328 rooms, 11 suites* ⌂ *3 restaurants, room service, minibars, cable TV, 4 tennis courts, pool, fitness classes, gym, hair salon, hot tub, massage, sauna, steam room, beach, boating, basketball, Ping-Pong, 4 bars, shops, baby-sitting, children's programs (ages 4–12), laundry service, concierge, business services, convention center, travel services, car rental, free parking, no-smoking rooms* ☐ *AE, MC, V* ◉| *AI.*

**$$$$** ▦ **Karmina Palace.** Manzanillo's all-inclusive, all-suites hotel is a short walk from neighboring Las Hadas resort. Cascades, fountains, multitier lagoons punctuate the meandering grounds, and there's a beautiful palapa restaurant at the ocean's edge. Each junior suite has marble floors, a balcony or terrace, a sofa bed, and a large tub with separate shower facilities. Corner suites have two bedrooms, each with a bath, a kitchen, and a dining room as well as a balcony with a plunge pool. ✉ *Av. Vista Hermosa 13, Fracc. Península de Santiago, 28200* ☎ *314/334–1313 or 877/527–6462* ☐ *314/334–1108* ⊕ *www.karminapalace.com* ⮑ *325 suites* ⌂ *3 restaurants, room service, in-room safes, some kitchens, some minibars, cable TV, 8 pools, fitness classes, gym, spa, beach, snorkeling, jet skiing, waterskiing, fishing, bicycles, billiards, Ping-Pong, volleyball, 5 bars, dance club, nightclub, video game room, shops, children's programs (ages 4–12), laundry service, concierge, Internet, business center, meeting rooms, travel services, free parking* ☐ *AE, MC, V* ◉| *AI.*

★ **$$$–$$$$** 🏨 **Las Hadas Golf & Marina.** Las Hadas delights with its exotic, Moorish-style buildings on 15 acres of flower-and-vine-covered grounds. Cream-on-white room decoration is elegant and understated; polished marble, fine sheets, and plush towels are the norm. Amenities include a golf course, a full-service marina with internet connection and satellite TV for boaters, and the Legazpi restaurant (open in high season only)—one of the city's best. ⊠ *Av. de los Riscos and Av. Vista Hermosa, Fracc. Península de Santiago 28867* ☎ *314/331–0101 or 888/559–4329* 🖷 *314/331–0125* ⊕ *www.brisas.com.mx* 🛏 *204 rooms, 29 suites* ⟁ *3 restaurants, 24-hour room service, some fans, in-room safes, minibars, cable TV, 18-hole golf course, 10 tennis courts, 2 pools, wading pool, gym, hair salon, massage, beach, dive shop, snorkeling, waterskiing, boating, fishing, marina, 3 bars, shops, baby-sitting, concierge, travel services, car rental, no-smoking rooms* ⊟ *AE, DC, MC, V.*

**$$–$$$** 🏨 **Dolphin Cove Inn.** The good news is that the rooms and one-bedroom suites are bright, clean, and private, with pretty views from their balconies or terraces. There are also great beaches nearby, as well as some of Manzanillo's best hotels, where you can dine or bar hop for a change of pace. The bad news? The property has endless stairs: leading to the pool, the restaurant, office, small grocery store, and neighboring properties. Guests are asked to smoke only on their balconies, not in rooms. ⊠ *Av. Vista Hermosa s/n, Fracc. Península de Santiago 28860* ☎ *314/334–1692 or 888/497–4138* 🖷 *314/334–1689* ⊕ *www.dolphincoveinn.com* 🛏 *27 rooms, 11 suites* ⟁ *Restaurant, grocery, fans, in-room VCRs, kitchenettes, pool, beach, concierge, free parking* ⊟ *AE, MC, V.*

**$$** 🏨 **Marina Puerto Dorado.** There are excellent views of the bay and harbor from this low-rise, which looks a lot like a condo complex. Each ample two-bedroom suite can presumably accommodate up to six adults and has a kitchen, dining bar, and living room; furnishings in some suites, however, are showing their age. Mix with other guests at the pool, in the whirlpool, or on the shaded or exposed lounge chairs overlooking the beach. Penthouse suites have a second-floor bedroom with a Jacuzzi on the terrace. ⊠ *Av. Lázaro Cárdenas 101, Playa Las Brisas 28200* ☎🖷 *314/334–1480* 🛏 *27 suites, 3 penthouse suites* ⟁ *Restaurant, room service, cable TV, pool, beach, bar, shop, laundry service, free parking* ⊟ *MC, V.*

★ **$$** 🏨 **La Posada.** This bright pink hotel has been a favorite with North Americans since 1957. With only 23 rooms, most guests get to know each other well, mingling in the *sala*, a large, cheery, open-air living-dining area with a communal coffeepot. Rooms are comfortable enough though not fancy (there's only one on the beach), and old iron keys work their antique locks. There's honor-system beer- and soft-drink service. ⊠ *Av. Lázaro Cardenas 201, Fracc. Las Brisas 28200* ☎ *314/333–1899* 🖷 *314/333–6690* 🛏 *23 rooms* ⟁ *Snack bar, fans, pool, beach, bar, Internet; no room phones, no a/c in some rooms, no room TVs* ⊟ *MC, V* ⯑ *BP.*

¢ 🏨 **Marbella.** In one of the few budget accommodations on the beach—which faces the open ocean, not the bay—rooms have tile floors and tiny, palm-shaded balconies. Ask for one of the newer rooms as one section of the hotel has been upgraded, and the cost is the same as for an older room. There's a good Spanish/seafood restaurant, El Marinero, and a buffet restaurant. ⊠ *Coast road between Manzanillo and Santiago, Zona Hotelera 28869* ☎ *314/333–1103* 🖷 *314/333–1222* ✑ *hotmarbella@prodigy.net.mx* ✒*92 rooms* ◊ *2 restaurants, some fans, cable TV, pool, beach, bar, laundry service, internet, free parking* ☰ *AE, MC, V.*

¢ 🖽 **María Cristina.** A clean but drab two-story motel in the Santiago area, the María Cristina is just four blocks from the beach in a mostly commercial area. All rooms have cable TV, but only three—they call them "bungalows"—are air-conditioned; cheaper rooms have ceiling fans. ⊠ *Calle 28 de Agosto 36, Santiago 28860* ☎☎ *314/333–0966 or 314/333–0767* ✒*21 rooms* ◊ *Fan, cable TV, pool, free parking; no a/c in some rooms* ☰ *MC, V.*

## Nightlife

**Bar de Félix** (⊠ Blvd. Miguel de la Madrid 805, Zona Hotelera ☎ 314/333–9277), adjacent to the club VOG, is a large bar with crimson fauxvelvet settees, a dance floor, and a giant-screen TV. For a lively drinking and dancing scene, head for **Colima Bay Café** (⊠ Blvd. Costero 921, Zona Hotelera ☎ 314/333–0168). **VOG** (⊠ Blvd. Miguel de la Madrid 805, Zona Hotelera ☎ 314/333–1875) plays disco music Thursday through Saturday.

## Outdoor Activities & Sports

### Fishing

Billed the "Sailfish Capital of the World," Manzanillo has fleets that regularly hook marlin, dorado, roosters, and tuna. Sportfishing boats are available at major hotels and through tour agencies. **Ocean Pacific Adventures** (☎☎ 314/335–0605) to charter a 26-foot boat (1 to 5 people) for $200, or a 40-foot cruiser (1 to 10 people) for $250. Both tours last five hours and include a fishing license and a case each of beer and soda as well as the usual ice, bait, and tackle.

### Golf

The 9-hole course at **Club Santiago** (⊠ Av. Camarón 1-A, Club Santiago, Santiago ☎ 314/335–0410), designed by Larry Hughes, has the usual amenities, including carts, caddies, pro shop, and snack shop. The greens fee is $42, or $85 with a cart. Robert Von Hagge mapped out
★ the impressive 27-hole **Isla Navidad** (⊠ Paseo Country Club s/n ☎ 315/355–6439) course in the Grand Bay resort complex, about an hour north of Manzanillo. The expansive clubhouse has a pro shop where you can take lessons, and a restaurant-bar as well as men's and women's locker rooms with steam, sauna, and whirlpools. Greens fees are $160 (9 holes) to $210 (27 holes), including cart. Caddies charge $20 per cart. **La Mantarraya** (⊠ Av. De los Riscos and Av. Vista Hermosa, Fracc. Península de Santiago ☎ 314/331–0101), the 18-hole golf course at Las Hadas hotel, designed by Roy Dye, offers club rentals and caddies. The greens fee, including cart, is about $45.

### Water Sports

The rocky points off Manzanillo's peninsulas and coves make for good snorkeling and scuba diving. You can rent snorkel and scuba gear as well as kayaks, paddleboats, Windsurfers at many beachside hotels and outfitters. **Pacific Watersports** (✉ Las Hadas resort, Av. De los Riscos and Av. Vista Hermosa, Fracc. Península de Santiago ☎ 314/333–1848) organizes guided diving tours ($75 for one tank; $100 for two) and snorkeling excursions (about $35 per person for the two–hour tour).

## Shopping

Shopping in Manzanillo is poor. Most hotels offer a small selection of folk art and beachwear, and there are souvenir shops around the main square and in Plaza Manzanillo, a shopping center on the coast road between Santiago and Manzanillo. The newest center is Plaza Salagua, with a Soriana department store and other shops. It's across from the VOG disco on Boulevard Miguel de la Madrid. Most of the shops are closed 2–4; many are open Sunday 10–2. The **Centro Artesenal las Primaveras** (✉ Av. Juárez 40, Santiago ☎ 314/333–1699) has a large assortment of handicrafts of so-so quality.

## Side Trips

### Barra de Navidad
*55 km (34 mi) northwest of Manzanillo.*

Barra, as it's usually called, is a laid-back little surfers' town that's beginning to attract outside attention. Since the luxurious Grand Bay hotel was built in the late 1990s, a well-heeled crowd of yachties has taken to shopping along the two main streets. In fact, shopping here is much better than in Manzanillo, and although the family-owned stores sell largely the same things—carved wooden bowls and ceramic plates from Guerrero, sarongs from Indonesia, and snow globes with mermaid and sealife themes—it's fun to compare bric-a-brac and prices. Interspersed with the shops are informal restaurants that specialize in fresh fish. The brown-sand beaches are also lined with open-air restaurants, perfect retreats from the strong coastal sun. At low tide you can walk along the beach from Barra to San Patricio Melaque, a distance of about 6 km (4 mi).

WHERE TO STAY & EAT
$–$$

✕ **Nacho.** People come to this beachfront family restaurant for delicious seafood and strong, wonderful *cafe de olla* (Mexican coffee). The specialty is charcoal-grilled fish, but also try the *campechana,* an appetizer of clams, shrimp, and fish, or one of several seafood salads or soups. Service is on the slow side, but then there's really no reason to rush when you're staying in Barra. ✉ *Calle Legazpi 100* ☎ *315/355–5138* ▭ *No credit cards.*

★ $$$$

▦ **Grand Bay.** On a 1,200-acre peninsula between the Pacific and the Navidad Lagoon, 30 minutes north of Manzanillo airport, this no-holds-barred resort cascades down to a private, though not terribly scenic, beach. More enticing are the complex's Spanish arches, shady patios, cool fountains, and lush gardens—not to mention the tiered swimming pools connected by slides and waterfalls. Rooms have marble baths, original art, deluxe amenities, and balconies with mountain or sea views. You can play the fabulous Robert Von Hagge–designed golf course, and there's boat service to the fishing village of Barra de Navidad, just across the bay. ✉ *Isla Navidad 48987* ☎ *314/331–0500, 800/996–3426 in the U.S.* ▤ *315/355–6071* ⊕ *www.islaresort.com.mx* ➷ *158* *rooms, 41 suites ♿ 3 restaurants, room service, in-room safes, minibars, cable TV, 27-hole golf course, 3 tennis courts, 3 pools, gym, beach, dive shop, snorkeling, jet skiing, marina, waterskiing, fishing, volleyball, 3 bars, shops, baby-sitting, children's programs (ages 4–12), laundry service, concierge, business services, convention center, meeting rooms, airport shuttle, car rental, free parking ☰ AE, MC, V.*

¢ 🖼 **El Marquez.** Although it's far from fancy, the friendly staff (it's a family operation) and clean rooms make El Marquez a good alternative to some of the pricier—but just as bare bones—accommodations on the beach. It's a few blocks from the center of town and from the shore, and it has a small pool. Choose a room with a ceiling fan or air-conditioning. For only two weeks a year, around Christmas and Easter, does the price creep up into the low side of the $ category. ✉ *Calle Filipinas 75 48987* 📠 *315/355–6300 or 315/355–5304* 🛏 *30 rooms ♿ Some fans, cable TV, pool, free parking; no a/c in some rooms* ☰ *MC, V.*

## Colima

*98 km (61 mi) northeast of Manzanillo.*

Colima, the capital of the eponymous state, is about an hour from Manzanillo via an excellent toll road that continues on to Guadalajara. An easygoing provincial city, Colima is most famous for the pre-Hispanic "Colima dog" figurines, which originated in this region and are on display—along with other archaeological pieces—at the **Museo de las Culturas del Occidente** (Museum of Western Cultures; ✉ Casa de la Cultura, Calz. Galván and Av. del Ejército 📞 312/313–0608). It's open Tuesday–Sunday 9–7, and admission is $1.50.

The **Museo Universitario de Culturas Populares** (University Museum of Popular Culture; ✉ Calles Gabino Barreda and Manuel Gallardo 📞 312/312–6869) has pre-Hispanic and contemporary Indian costumes, masks, instruments, and other artifacts. Entry to the museum, which is open Tuesday–Sunday 10–2 and 5–8, is free. The town of **Comala,** a 15-minute ride north of Colima, is noted for hand-carved furniture and ironwork, and for the charming cafés to which Colima residents flock on holidays and weekends.

WHERE TO STAY 🖼 **Mahakua Hacienda de San Antonio.** Ahhh, the Mahakua. This stun-
$$$$ ning hacienda was built as the home of 19th-century German immigrant Arnold Vogel on his 5,000-acre coffee plantation. It was completely refurbished in the 1970s and is now leased to Aman Resorts, famous for its ultra-luxurious (and *ultra-expensive*) properties around the world. Rooms have 15-foot beamed ceilings and blend European and American appointments with Mexican handicrafts. Have lunch by the enormous pool, drinks around the fire in the convivial library, and dinner in the courtyard or the dining room. The staff is warm and attentive. If you're lucky you'll witness an impressive nighttime display from nearby Volcán de Fuego. ✉ *San Antonio 28450* 📞 *312/313–4411 or 888/802–9127* 📠 *312/314–3727* 🌐 *www.amanresorts.com* 🛏 *22 rooms, 3 suites ♿ Restaurant, room service, in-room data ports, cable TV, pool, exercise equipment, massage, horseback riding, bar, library, laundry service, concierge, Internet, airport shuttle, travel services, free parking; no a/c* ☰ *AE, MC, V.*

## Manzanillo A to Z

### AIR TRAVEL

AIRPORT  Manzanillo's Aeropuerto Internacional Playa de Oro is 32 km (20 mi) north of town, on the way to Barra de Navidad.

🚹 **Aeropuerto Internacional Playa de Oro** ☎ 314/333-2525.

AIRPORT  Volkswagen vans transport passengers from the airport to major resorts;
TRANSFERS  these shuttles are less expensive than taxis.

CARRIERS  Aeroméxico has daily flights from Houston, Los Angeles, and Atlanta, with a plane change in Mexico City. Mexicana serves the region via Mexico City. Alaska Airlines flies from Seattle and direct from Los Angeles, daily in high season and less frequently the rest of the year. America West has weekly direct flights from Phoenix during high season; you must connect in Mexico City between May and December. AeroCalifornia has direct flights from Los Angeles several times a week, continuing on to Mexico City.

🚹 **AeroCalifornia** ☎ 314/334-1414, 800/237-6225 in the U.S. **Aeroméxico** ☎ 314/ 333-015, 01800/021-4000 toll-free in Mexico, 800/237-6639 in the U.S. **Alaska Airlines** ☎ 01800/252-7522 toll-free in Mexico, 800/252-7522 in the U.S. **America West** ☎ 314/ 334-1140, 800/235-9292 in the U.S. **Mexicana** ☎ 314/333-2323, 800/531-7921 in the U.S.

### BUS TRAVEL

The resorts in the Manzanillo area are several miles from the main bus station on Boulevard Costero Miguel de la Madrid, which is no more than a parking lot full of buses. Elite and Estrella Blanca connect Manzanillo with other Pacific coast cities and Mexico City; the former has a longer list of destinations. Primera Plus serves Puerto Vallarta, Guadalajara, Tijuana, Mexico City, Acapulco, and smaller coastal towns. ETN has comfortable buses—with wide, almost totally reclining seats—to Guadalajara, Colima, Morelia, and Mexico City.

🚹 **Elite/Estrella Blanca** ☎ 314/332-0432. **ETN** ☎ 314/334-1050. **Primera Plus** ☎ 314/ 332-0515.

### CAR RENTAL

🚹 Major Agencies **Dollar** ✉ Hotel Karmina Palace, Av. Vista Hermosa 13, Fracc. Península de Santiago ☎ 314/334-1313. **Hertz** ✉ Blvd. Costero Miguel de la Madrid 1246-B, Zona Hotelera ☎ 314/333-3141. **National** ✉ Blvd. Costero Miguel de la Madrid 1070, Zona Hotelera ☎ 314/333-0611.

### CAR TRAVEL

The trip south from the Arizona border to Manzanillo is about 2,419 km (1,500 mi); from Guadalajara, it is 332 km (206 mi) over mostly well-kept highways; from Puerto Vallarta, 242 km (150 mi) on Carretera 200, which winds through the mountains beginning in Tepic, in the state of Nayarit. Streets in downtown Manzanillo are congested, but parking is rarely a problem and having a car is a plus to reach the farther flung beaches and restaurants.

### EMERGENCIES
🔌 **Fire Department** ☎ 314/312-5858. **Hospital de Manzanillo** ☎ 314/336-7272. **Police** ☎ 314/334-0557 or 314/336-7300. **Red Cross** ☎ 314/336-5770.

### MAIL, INTERNET & SHIPPING
The correos is about five blocks south of the main plaza in downtown. It's open weekdays 8–7 and Saturday 9–1. Juanito's restaurant in Santiago has several computers at which you can access the Internet.
🔌 Internet **Juanito's** ✉ Blvd. Costero, Km 14, Olas Altas ☎ 314/333-1388.
🔌 Mail **Correos** ✉ Calle Galindo 30, Centro.

### MONEY MATTERS
There are plenty of banks in downtown Manzanillo and Santiago, most with ATMs. Many visitors prefer to change money at the front desk of their hotel, where the poorer exchange rate is offset by the convenience and the absence of a bank fee for an international ATM transaction.
🔌 Bank **Banamex** ✉ Calle México 136, Centro ☎ 314/332-0115.

### TAXIS
Cabs are unmetered and are easy to hail on the streets. Agree on a price beforehand. The minimum fare will be $1.50, though cabs departing from hotels often charge nearly twice as much.

### TOURS
Manzanillo is spread out; consider a guided orientation tour. More appealing, though, than the city tours are the sportfishing trips, sunset cruises, horseback outings, and excursions to the state capital, Colima, as well as to Comala and the dormant and active volcanoes near the capital.

Agencia de Viajes Bahías Gemelas offers city with shopping ($22), sportfishing ($70), and horseback-riding tours. Viajes Héctours offers the same tours as Bahías Gemelas, plus shopping, bay cruises, tours on four-wheelers ($70), and day excursions to Colima ($60) or area banana plantations ($50).
🔌 **Agencia de Viajes Bahías Gemelas** ✉ Blvd. Costero Miguel de la Madrid 1556, Zona Hotelera ☎ 314/333-1000. **Viajes Héctours** ✉ Blvd. Costero Miguel de la Madrid 3147, Zona Hotelera ☎ 314/333-1707.

### VISITOR INFORMATION
The Colima State Tourism Office is open weekdays 9–3 and 5–7, Saturday 10–2. The municipal tourism office is open weekdays only, 9–3 and 6–8.
🔌 **Colima State Tourism Office** ✉ Blvd. Costero Miguel de la Madrid 1033, Zona Hotelera, Manzanillo ☎ 314/333-2277 or 314/333-2264. **Municipal Tourism Office** ✉ Av. Juárez 100, Centro Manzanillo ☎ 314/332-6238.

# IXTAPA & ZIHUATANEJO

Ixtapa and Zihuatanejo offer a taste of Mexico present and past. Ixtapa (eesh-*tah*-pa), created in the 1970s, is exclusively a vacation resort. Although it's small and tame in comparison to Cancún—also dreamed up in the '70s by Mexico's National Fund for Tourism Development—it's definitely been made-to-order for the tourist trade, with a line of high-rises, and the occasional low-rise, fronted by the Pacific and backed by a row of minimalls harboring restaurants, shops, grocery stores, and pharmacies.

At the time Ixtapa was built, Zihuatanejo (see-wa-ta-*nay*-ho), only 7 km (4 mi) southeast along the coast, was a fishing village, the exclusive domain of locals and adventurers willing to forgo running water, electricity, and paved streets for the chance to live in—or just visit—a rustic paradise. It's still charming even though it has gained more admirers, its streets have been paved, its infrastructure has been brought up to date, and some of its fishermen have become entrepreneurs.

Long before Cortés and Columbus sailed to the Americas, Zihuatanejo was a retreat for indigenous nobility. Figurines, ceramics, stone carvings, and stelae found in the area verify the presence of civilizations dating as far back as the Olmecs (3000 BC). Weaving was likely the dominant industry, as evidenced by pre-Hispanic figurines, bobbins, and other related artifacts. The original Nahuatl name, Cihuatlán, means "place of women." Ixtapa, originally spelled Iztapa, means "white sands," and was ceded to (but not used by) one of the Spanish conquistadors.

In 1527, Spanish conquistadors launched a trade route from today's Bahía de Zihuatanejo (Zihuatanejo Bay) to the Orient. Galleons returned with silks, spices, and, according to some historians, the Americas' first coconut palms, brought from the Philippines. But the Spaniards did little colonizing here. A scout sent by Cortés reported back to the conquistador that the place was nothing great, tagging the name Cihuatlán with the less-than-flattering suffix "ejo"—hence "Zihuatanejo."

Between Ixtapa and Zihua, it's impossible to pigeonhole what type of person chooses which destination. Young and old, party animals and those who crave scuba diving or pure relaxation, are drawn to Ixta or Zihua based on a variety of needs and desires. Budget travelers rarely find rooms in Ixtapa, however, except as part of special packages during the low season. Neither place has much in the way of attractions, but they're both pleasant places to stroll. The beach, of course, is the destination's *raison d'être,* and the best of these are found in Zihuatanejo.

## Exploring Ixtapa & Zihuatanejo

### Ixtapa

The Zona Hotelera extends along a 3-km (2-mi) strip of sandy beach called Playa del Palmar, on the Pacific. It's fun to walk along the shore to check out the various hotel scenes and water-sports activities, though the way the small waves break discourages swimming. You can also walk the length of the zone on Paseo Ixtapa, a landscaped thoroughfare lined with strip malls. At the Zona Hotelera's southeast end is the 18-hole Palma Real Golf Club; at the the resort's northwest end is the Marina Ixtapa development, with a 600-slip yacht marina, the 18-hole Marina Golf Course, and a small enclave of restaurants and shops. Take a taxi 15 minutes up the coast from Ixtapa's Zona Hotelera to Playa Linda.

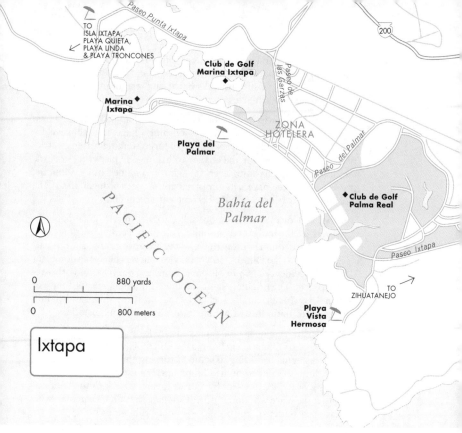

From here it's a 10-minute boat ride to **Isla Ixtapa** (Ixtapa Island), where you can spend the day eating, sunning, and swimming.

### Zihuatanejo

Zihuatanejo hugs a deep, enclosed bay with calm beaches. To tour the town, start at the municipal *muelle* (pier), from which skiffs regularly depart for the 10-minute ride to Playa las Gatas, most easily accessible by water. The sportfishing boats depart from this pier, too, and it's the beginning of the Paseo del Pescador (Fisherman's Walk), or malecón, which runs along the main beach, the most picturesque part of the town itself. Follow the seaside path, which is only ½ km (⅓ mi) long and is fronted by small restaurants and shops. Along the way you'll pass a basketball court that doubles as the town square. Most of the budget accommodations are in downtown Zihuatanejo; the glamorous hotels are on or overlooking Playa la Ropa. For true seclusion, venture to the growing beach town of Troncones, a 20-minute drive northwest of Zihuatanejo.

The malecón ends at the **Museo Arqueológico de la Costa Grande** (⊠ Paseo del Pescador 7 at Plaza Olof Palme ☎ 755/554–7552), where pre-Hispanic murals, maps, and archaeological pieces are on permanent display. It's open Monday–Saturday 10–6; admission is 60¢. Beyond the museum, a footpath cut into the rocks leads to Playa la Madera.

## Beaches

### Ixtapa

**Isla Ixtapa.** The most popular spot on Isla Ixtapa (and the one closest
to the boat dock) is Playa Cuachalalate. An excellent swimming beach,
it was named for a local tree whose bark has been used as a remedy for
kidney ailments since ancient times. A short walk across the island, Playa
Varadero hugs a rocky cove. Guides recommend snorkeling here, but
watch for coral-covered rocks on both sides of the cove. Just behind is
Playa Coral, whose calmer, crystal-clear water is more conducive to swimming. Each of the above beaches is lined with seafood eateries eager to
rent snorkel equipment. Playa Carey, toward the island's south end, is
small and has no services. Pangas ($3.50 round-trip) run between the
boat landings at both Cuachalalate and Varadero beaches and Playa Linda
on the mainland, where you'll find a few all-inclusive, high-rise hotels.

**Playa del Palmar.** Ixtapa's main beach, this broad, 3-km-long (2-mi-long)
sandy stretch runs along the Zona Hotelera. Here many hotel concessions rent water-sports equipment to guests and nonguests. Since this is
essentially open sea, the surf can be strong.

**Playa Quieta.** Thatch-roof restaurants dispense beer, sodas, and the
catch of the day at Playa Quieta, about 10 minutes north of Ixtapa's
Zona Hotelera. It's edged at one end by an estuary with birds and
gators. You can rent horses, and a warren of vendors sells souvenirs and
handcrafts.

**Playa Vista Hermosa.** Intimate Vista Hermosa, south of the Zona Hotelera and framed by rocks, is accessible by boat or via Las Brisas hotel.
In high season, water-sports outfitters open for business here.

### Zihuatanejo

★ **Playa las Gatas.** Named for the *gatas* (nurse sharks) that once lingered
here, this beach is bordered by a long row of hewn rocks that create a
breakwater. Legend has it that a Tarascan king built the breakwater so
that this stretch of sand would be sheltered for his daughter's use.
Snorkelers scope out the rocky coves, and surfers spring to life with the
arrival of small but fun summer swells. The beach is lined with simple
seafood eateries that provide lounge chairs for sunning. You can scram-
ble over rocks separating this beach from Playa la Ropa in about 20 minutes. It's much more common and convenient, however, to take one of
the skiffs that run from the municipal pier every 10 or 15 minutes between 8 and a half-hour before sunset. Buy your round-trip ticket (about
$4) on the pier, and keep the stub for your return trip.

**Playa la Madera.** You can reach small Playa la Madera, which is across
the Bahía Zihuatanejo, via a seaside footpath cut into the rocks or by
car. This pancake-flat, dark-sand beach has a sprinkling of small, inexpensive hotels and restaurants. It was named *madera,* or "wood," beach
because it was a Spanish port for shipping oak, pine, cedar, and mahogany
cut from the nearby Sierra Madre del Sur.

**Playa Principal.** At the edge of town, the picturesque main beach (a.k.a.
Playa Municipal) is rimmed by the Paseo del Pescador. Here local fishermen keep their skiffs and gear, used for nightly fishing journeys. They
return here in the early morning to sell their catches.

FodorśChoice
★

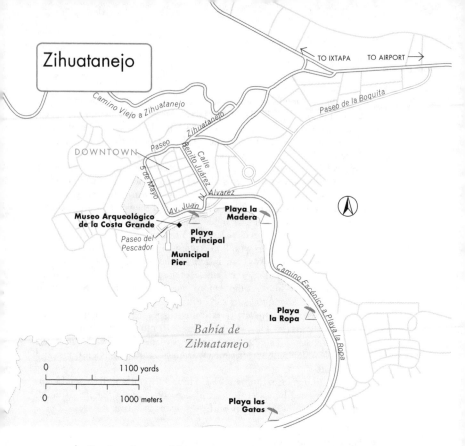

**★ ☾ Playa la Ropa.** The area's most beautiful beach is beyond a rocky point across the bay and a 20-minute walk from Playa la Madera and a 5-minute taxi ride from town. Along this 1-km (½-mi) stretch of soft sand are open-air restaurants—with hammocks for post-meal siestas—a few hotels, and water-sports outfitters. It got its name ("clothing beach") when a cargo of Oriental silks and garments washed on to it from a Spanish galleon shipwrecked offshore. The calm water here is optimum for kids to splash in, and the long, long beach is perfect for tossing a ball or Frisbee.

## Where to Eat

### Ixtapa

**★ $$$–$$$$** ✕ **Beccofino.** This marina-side restaurant is always crowded. You can eat inside, where dark, polished woods contrast with bright white linens, or outside on the canopy-sheltered deck. Among the best dishes on the northern Italian menu are minestrone soup, *caprese* salad (with tomatoes, basil, and mozzarella), fish fillet (usually red snapper or mahimahi) with a champagne sauce, and chicken cacciatore. Many of the pastas are made in-house, and breakfast is available after 9:30 AM. ⊠ *Plaza Marina Ixtapa* ☎ *755/553–1770* ✍ *Reservations essential* 🖃 *AE, MC, V.*

**$-$$$** ✕ **Casa Morelos.** The wooden bar, ocher walls, and handcrafted furnishings make this tiny restaurant seem like a true cantina. Patio tables are more elegant at night than during the day, with potted trees dressed in little white lights and lively tropical music at a level that doesn't drown out conversation. The *chiles rellenos de camarón* (egg-battered peppers stuffed with shrimp), fajitas, and tuna steak topped with three kinds of chilies are all filling and delicious. After dinner, head next door to Señor Frogs for some dancing. Or come really early for a generous breakfast; the restaurant opens at 7:30 AM. ⊠ *La Puerta shopping center, Blvd. Ixtapa s/n* ☎ *755/553–0578* ▭ *MC, V.*

**$-$$$** ✕ **El Galeón.** People-watchers like to settle in at the rope-and-rigging-adorned bar of this Marina Ixtapa restaurant. You can eat on the terrace or in a reproduction galleon right on the water. The tuna steak is outstanding, as are the pastas; upscale Mexican and international fare are also available. The signature dish is *pollo galleón,* medallions of chicken breast stuffed with lobster and bathed in a three-cheese sauce, served with mashed potatoes and steamed vegetables. ⊠ *Plaza Marina Ixtapa* ☎ *755/553–2150* ▭ *AE, MC, V.*

**¢-$** ✕ **Nueva Zelanda.** Although it's open all day, this sparkling little coffee shop is best known for its breakfasts, which, some say, are the best in town. This branch opened after the success of the original eatery in downtown Zihuatanejo. Both kitchens have fresh fruit juices and coconut milkshakes as well as omelets, enchiladas, salads, and *tortas* (sandwiches on large, crusty rolls). ⊠ *Centro Comercial El Kiosko, behind bandstand, Blvd. Ixtapa s/n* ☎ *755/553–0838* ⌚ *Reservations not accepted* ▭ *No credit cards.*

**¢-$** ✕ **Ruben's.** The delicious scent of grilling meats will entrance you from blocks away; as you approach your ears will detect the soft yet persisent sounds of Latin rhythms to which unhurried waiters tap their feet. The music is loud inside, and after sundown most clients dine at the white plastic tables on the grassy front yard. The charcoal-grilled burgers, which are made of top sirloin, and the french fries, deep-fried zucchini, and baked potatoes are delightful American treats. For dessert try the grilled bananas glazed with cinnamon and sugar and served with a dollop of fresh cream. ⊠ *Centro Comercial Flamboyant, next to Bancomer bank, Blvd. Ixtapa s/n* ☎ *755/553–0027 or 755/553–0358* ▭ *No credit cards.*

## Zihuatanejo

**$$$-$$$$** ✕ **Kau-Kan.** Owner-chef Ricardo Rodriguez, who studied in Paris before returning to Mexico and the upscale kitchen of La Casa Que Canta hotel, gives exquisite seafood dishes Mexican and Mediterranean treatments. On the menu you'll find whatever's freshest: perhaps melt-in-your-mouth abalone or grilled mahimahi under a sweet, spicy pineapple sauce. The shrimp-stuffed potatoes and the lobster with fresh basil and a garlic sauce are legendary. A few large oil paintings adorn the walls, but the main visual attraction is the gorgeous view of Bahía Zihuatanejo. ⊠ *Carretera Escénica, Lote 7 en route to Playa La Ropa* ☎ *755/554–8446* ▭ *AE, MC, V* ☾ *Closed Sept. No lunch.*

**Fodor's**Choice
★

★ **$-$$$** ✕ **Coconuts.** Its name is a nod to the region's previous status as a coconut plantation, and under the direction of chef-owner Patricia Cummings, it has become one of Zihuatanejo's top restaurants. You can eat at the horseshoe-shape bar, in one of several areas of the old property (restored by Ms. Cummings' architect husband), or outside on the patio surrounded by tiny white lights. Try the roast pork loin, the sweet and zesty coconut shrimp, or one of the vegetarian items. Five different dessert coffees are prepared flaming at your table. ⊠ *Pasaje Agustín Ramírez 1* ☎ *755/554–2518* ⊟ *AE, DC, MC, V* ✆ *Closed Aug.–early Oct.*

$–$$$    ✕ **Las Gaviotas.** You can join the town's politicos and other bigwigs at this Playa la Ropa eatery. Sit under one of two palm-thatch roofs or on a balcony that's even closer to the sand. Ceiling fans stir up a breeze but can't budge the glass and plastic hanging buoys that serve as the restaurant's principal decoration. On the menu are the usual selection of ceviches, shrimp, and fresh fish fillets served with french fries. For dessert indulge in the crispy fried bananas served with a scoop of conout ice cream or bathed in cinnamon-laced cream. ⊠ *South end of Playa la Ropa* ☎ *755/554–2700* ⊟ *No credit cards.*

¢–$$$    ✕ **La Sirena Gorda.** Oil paintings and a bronze statue depict the namesake "fat mermaid" at this small, friendly restaurant near the pier and the fish market. Specialties include seafood tacos and octopus kebab. The setting is casual, with a lively bar and a wraparound patio opening onto the town's lazy street scene. The place is open for breakfast as well. ⊠ *Paseo del Pescador 90* ☎ *755/554–2687* ⚍ *Reservations not accepted* ⊟ *No credit cards* ✆ *Closed Wed.*

¢–$$    ✕ **Casa Elvira.** This institution is right on the malecón, just a few steps from the fish market. It's not fancy, but the walls radiate bright orange and a courtyard fountain splashes in a minor key. The staff is helpful yet unobtrusive, and the food habitually good. The fare consists of Mexican dishes and such simple seafood plates as fish steamed in foil and served with rice and french fries. Lobster is a specialty, though it and the well-loved seafood platter will push your tab into the $$$ category. The restaurant is open for breakfast December through Easter. ⊠ *Paseo del Pescador 32* ☎ *755/554–2061* ⊟ *MC, V.*

¢–$    ✕ **Atoles y Tamales Any.** Any's is a great place for hot, cinnamony coffee and traditional drinks such as *horchata* (rice water) and *agua de jamaica* (hibiscus water). Six to eight different tamales are offered each day, most savory, some sweet, all huge. Everything about the place is typically Mexican—crockery and coffee mugs, colorful striped table coverings, and local radio music in the background. The roof is thatched, and the walls are painted in vivid rural scenes. ⊠ *Calle Ejido 38, at Calle Vicente Guerrero* ☎ *755/554–7373* ⊟ *No credit cards* ✆ *Closed Sun.*

¢–$    ✕ **Nueva Zelanda.** This restaurant was so successful that it led to the opening of a branch in Ixtapa. Like its counterpart, breakfast is a specialty here, though meals are served all day. Milkshakes, juices, omelets, salads, and sandwiches are all on the menu. ⊠ *Calle Cuauhtémoc 23* ☎ *755/554–2340* ⚍ *Reservations not accepted* ⊟ *No credit cards.*

## Where to Stay

### Ixtapa

★ $$$$    ▦ **Las Brisas Ixtapa.** This immense, pyramid-shape wonder slopes down a hill to its own cove and beach. Although rooms are small and have low ceilings, they're comfortable and modern, with red tile floors, blue tile headboards, and firm but plump mattresses. Each room also has a large balcony with a hammock, a chaise longue, and a table; junior suite balconies have hot tubs. Guests and nonguests enjoy the hotel's excellent Portofino and El Mexicano restaurants, which are open for dinner only. Las Brisas II restaurant's cliffside tables are the perfect spot for a sunset cocktail. The staff is friendly and professional. ⊠ *Playa Vista Hermosa, 40880* ☎ *755/553–2121 or 888/559–4329* 🖷 *755/553–0751* ⊕ *www. brisas.com.mx* ⮝ *423 rooms, 37 suites* ♦ *5 restaurants, 24-hour room service, fans, in-room safes, minibars, cable TV with movies, 4 tennis courts, 3 pools, wading pool, gym, hair salon, beach, fishing, boating, 4 bars, shops, baby-sitting, children's programs (ages 4–12), laundry service, business services, concierge, concierge floor, convention center, car rental, travel services, free parking, no-smoking rooms* ▭ *AE, MC, V.*

**$$$** 🏨 **Riviera Beach Resort.** Furnishings are an adroit mix of rustic and modern in this 11-story resort. Rooms are done in cheerful blues and yellows with framed acrylic paintings. Junior suites have views from both the living room and the bedroom. Neither rooms nor suites have balconies, but windows do open to the sea breezes. A children's pool with a slide lures kids away from the huge, palm-shaded main pool, which has a swim-up bar. El Ancla restaurant serves a dynamite breakfast buffet; El Arrecife, open for dinner only, specializes in steak and fresh seafood. The day spa, open to nonguests, offers facials, massage, and other body and salon treatments; it also has a sauna. ⊠ *Blvd. Ixtapa s/n, 40880* ☎ *755/553–1066 or 888/809–6133* 🖷 *755/553–1991* ⊕ *www.riviera.com.mx* ⮝ *150 rooms, 23 suites* ♦ *2 restaurants, in-room data ports, in-room safes, minibars, cable TV, 2 tennis courts, 2 pools, wading pool, gym, hot tub, massage, sauna, spa, steam room, 2 bars, meeting rooms, travel services, free parking, no-smoking rooms* ▭ *AE, MC, V.*

★ **$$** 🏨 **Barceló.** Attractively landscaped grounds and a veranda restaurant surround the large, geometric pool at this modern high-rise. Rooms are done in rust and navy blue and have tiny, triangular terraces. Thoughtful touches include coffeemakers, hairdryers, and makeup mirrors. The entertainment staff holds some sort of show six nights a week. ⊠ *Blvd. Ixtapa s/n, 40880* ☎ *755/555–2000* 🖷 *755/553–0808* ⊕ *www.barcelo. com* ⮝ *325 rooms, 11 suites* ♦ *4 restaurants, grocery, 24-hour room service, in-room safes, minibars, cable TV with movies, 3 tennis courts, pool, fitness classes, gym, spa, beach, 3 bars, baby-sitting, children's programs (ages 6–12), laundry service, concierge, internet, business services, meeting rooms, travel services, free parking, no-smoking floors* ▭ *MC, V* 🍽 *AI, EP.*

**$$** 🏨 **Best Western Posada Real.** One of the less expensive of Ixtapa's chain hotels, the four-story Posada Real is also one of the more intimate. Shell-shape lamps above the headboards invite you to read in the firm bed; air-conditioning units are quiet and efficient. The infinity pool—heated when necessary—has a view of the beach, a fountain in the middle, and a swim-up bar. Although the rooms have small windows and no balconies this place is a real deal. ⊠ *Blvd. Ixtapa s/n, 40880* ☎ *755/553–1745, 800/528–1234 in the U.S.* 🖷 *755/553–1805* ⊕ *www.bestwestern.com*

🖘*110 rooms* ⚘*Restaurant, room service, in-room safes, cable TV, putting green, pool, hot tub, beach, 2 bars, shop, laundry service, car rental, travel services, free parking, no-smoking rooms* ⊟ *AE, MC, V.*

**$$** 🏨 **NH Krystal Ixtapa.** Each room in this prow-shape, beachfront hotel has a view of the beach from a balcony. What it lacks in charm it makes up for in amenities, although more than one longtime customer has complained of a decline in maintenance over the past few years. Contemporary rooms have comfortable beds with fine sheets. Club Krystalito has children's activities, and the excellent meeting facilities attract many conventions. Bogart's restaurant has good Continental fare as well as soft lighting, palm trees, and a Moorish fountain. The Christine disco is Ixtapa's most popular. ⊠ *Blvd. Ixtapa s/n, 40880* ☎ *755/553–0333, 800/231–9860 in the U.S.* 🖷 *755/553–0336* ⊕ *www.nh-hotels.com* 🖘 *254 rooms, 20 suites* ⚘ *3 restaurants, coffee shop, room service, in-room data ports, in-room safes, minibars, cable TV with movies, 2 tennis courts, pool, wading pool, gym, massage, beach, hair salon, 3 bars, dance club, children's programs (ages 3–10), concierge, meeting rooms, free parking, no-smoking floor* ⊟ *AE, DC, MC, V* ⦿ *BP.*

## Troncones

**$** 🏨 **El Burro Borracho.** Six comfortable stone cottages sit right on the 5-km-long (3-mi-long) beach. Relax in a hammock on your private patio, or go beachcombing, boogie-boarding, hiking, or caving. Afterward, retreat to the congenial bar-restaurant, with menu options ranging from cheeseburgers to fresh lobster. ⊠ *Playa Troncones* 🖂 *A.P. 277 Zihuatanejo, 40880* ☎ *755/553–2800* 🖷 *755/553–2807* 🖘 *6 bungalows* ⚘ *Restaurant, fans, beach, hiking, free parking; no a/c, no room phones, no room TVs* ⊟ *No credit cards.*

**$** 🏨 **Casa Ki.** Each bungalow at this homey haven in the wilds of Troncones has a tiny refrigerator and a patio with hammocks, table, and chairs. There's also a house (for $185 a night), with a full kitchen, a small living room, two bedrooms, two en suite bathrooms, and a long porch looking right onto the sand and waves. All guests have access to a communal kitchen and dining room, as well as barbecue facilities, at the center of the property; there's also a meditation room. ⊠ *Playa Troncones* 🖂 *A. P. 405 Zihuatanejo, 40880* ☎🖷 *755/553–2815* ⊕ *www.casa-ki.com* 🖘 *3 bungalows, 1 house* ⚘ *Dining room, fans, refrigerators, beach, baby sitting, free parking; no room phones, no a/c, no room TVs* ⊟ *No credit cards* ⦿ *CP* ⊙ *Closed mid-Sept.–mid-Oct.*

## Zihuatanejo

**$$$$** 🏨 **Casa Cuitlateca.** Zihuatanejo's smallest boutique hotel affords spectacular bay views. In the guest rooms, inlaid stone floors and whitewashed stucco walls show handmade furnishings, folk art, and such details as tree-trunk lintels to their best advantage. There's an infinity pool and a rooftop, cool-water whirlpool. The staff will arrange nearly any excursion you can think of (including to the beach below, if you don't want to walk), and the patio restaurant, open to the public for dinner only, serves a multicourse, prix-fixe meal ($55–$65, including drinks, appetizers, and wine with dinner; reserve before noon). Children under 16 are not encouraged. ⊠ *Calle Playa la Ropa, 40880* ☎ *755/554–2448 or 877/541–1234* 🖷 *755/554–7394* ⊕ *www.casacuitlateca.com* 🖘 *3* *rooms, 1 suite ⚹ Restaurant, fans, pool, hot tub, concierge, airport transfer, free parking; no room TVs* ⊟ *AE, MC, V* ⦿ *BP.*

**$$$$**  ▦ **La Casa Que Canta.** The "House That Sings" clings to a cliff above
FodorsChoice Playa la Ropa. All guest quarters have lovely furnishings and folk art;
★ suites have bay views from outdoor living areas. Bathrooms are luxurious, as are such touches as flower petals arranged in intricate mosaics on your bed each day. The infinity pool seems to be airborne; below it, a saltwater pool has a waterfall and Jacuzzi. The restaurant serves guests breakfast and lunch; dinners here are more formal and are open to the public (reservations required). ⊠ *Camino Escénico a Playa la Ropa, 40880* ☎ *755/555–7000 or 888/523–5050* 🖷 *755/554–7900* ⊕ *www. lacasaquecanta.com* ⟿ *24 suites, 4 apartments* ⚹ *Restaurant, room service, fans, in-room safes, minibars, pool, saltwater pool, gym, hot tub, spa, 2 bars, library, shop, laundry service, concierge, internet, free parking; no room TVs, no kids under 16* ⊟ *AE, DC, MC, V.*

★ **$$$$**  ▦ **Villa del Sol.** Paths meander through gardens, passing coconut palms and fountains en route to Playa la Ropa. Rooms are artistically and individually designed, with bright but not overpowering textiles and folk art; all have terraces or balconies. Meals at the Villa del Sol restaurant are elegant; the Cantina Bar and Grill is more casual. MAP is required in high season, and only a few suites accommodate children under 14. ⊠ *Playa la Ropa, 40880* ☎ *755/555–5500 or 888/389–3239* 🖷 *755/554–2758* ⊕ *www.hotelvilladelsol.com* ⟿ *35 rooms, 35 suites* ⚹ *2 restaurants, room service, fans, in-room safes, minibars, cable TV, 2 tennis courts, 4 pools, gym, spa, beach, 3 bars, shops, travel services, car rental, no-smoking rooms, some pets allowed* ⊟ *AE, MC, V* ⦿ *EP, MAP.*

**$$$**  ▦ **La Quinta Troppo.** Red tile, inlaid stone, robin's-egg-blue cement flooring, and other wonderful details lend this boutique hotel charm. Each room has a floor-to-ceiling screened window overlooking a semiprivate balcony or porch. From a hammock on the communal terrace you can see everything from downtown Zihua to Playa las Gatas. The location and the views offset the minimalist creature comforts. ⊠ *Camino Escénico s/n, 40880* ☎ *755/554–3423* 🖷 *755/554–7340* ⊕ *www.laquintatroppo. com* ⟿ *8 rooms* ⚹ *Dining room, fan, pool, massage, shop, laundry service, Internet, business center; no a/c in some rooms, no room phones, no room TVs, no children under 15* ⊟ *AE, MC, V* ⦿ *CP.*

**$$**  ▦ **Brisas del Mar.** A once desultory property has been revamped to create this stylish, Mediterranean-chic hotel above Playa la Madera. Follow the stairs up and down the cliff-side grounds to the beach, restaurant, pool, or just to your room. Rooms have Talavera-ceramic sinks in wooden surrounds, carved doors and furnishings from Michoacán, molded plastic bathtubs, and large balconies; most have fabulous beach views. For the money this is now one of Zihua's best beach hotels. Just remember those stairs; if you don't like to hike, don't stay here. ⊠ *Calle Eva Sámano de López Mateos s/n, Playa la Madera, 40880* ☎ *755/554–2142* 🖷 *755/554–6710* ⊕ *www.hotelbrisasdelmar.com* ⟿ *30 rooms* ⚹ *Restaurant, some in-room hot tubs, cable TV, pool, exercise equipment, massage, sauna, billiards, Ping-Pong, 2 bars, library* ⊟ *AE, MC, V.*

**$–$$**  ▦ **Sotavento Beach Resort.** This multilevel oldie-but-goodie is on a cliff overlooking the bay. Below, accessible by more than 200 stairs, are Playa la Ropa and the hotel's beach bar, pool, and lounge chairs. Guest quarters are old and often plain but well maintained, with white cement closet and shelving units. The cheapest rooms are on the first floor and have no view, but most are large and airy and have terraces with hammocks and chaise longues. Mattresses are a bit thin; the sound of the waves may help soothe you to sleep. ⊠ *Playa la Ropa, 40880* ☎ *755/554–2032, 877/699–6685 in the U.S., 877/667–3702 in Canada* 🖷 *755/554–2975* ⊕ *www.beachresortsotavento.com* ↴ *70 rooms, 20 suites* ♿ *2 restaurants, fans, room service, fans, pool, massage, beach, 2 bars, laundry service, free parking; no a/c, no room TVs* ▭ *AE, D, MC, V.*

**$** 📺 **Ávila.** Although institutional in character, this hotel is well situated in the center of town facing the beach at Paseo del Pescador. Rooms are large and clean but are showing signs of age and have hard beds and noisy air-conditioning. Rooms 11 through 13 are the best; they share a wide, furnished patio overlooking the beach. In March this place fills up with fishing-tournament participants. ⊠ *Calle Juan N. Alvarez 8, 40880* ☎ *755/554–2010* 🖷 *755/554–8592* ↴ *27 rooms* ♿ *Fans, some refrigerators, beach* ▭ *MC, V.*

**$** 📺 **Irma.** One of Zihuatanejo's originals, this simple colonial-style hotel is on a bluff overlooking Playa la Madera, which is accessible via a stairway. Rooms have tile floors and plastered-cement wall units for storing clothing. Request an ocean-view room; most of these are better furnished, fresher, and more up to date than those without views. There's a patio overlooking the sea and twin, dark-blue pools surrounded by tables and lounge chairs. In low season the restaurant serves breakfast only. ⊠ *Playa la Madera, 40880* ☎ *755/554–2105* 🖷 *755/554–3738* ↴ *73 rooms* ♿ *Restaurant, room service, in-room safes, 2 pools, bar, laundry service, free parking; no a/c in some rooms, no room phones, no room TVs* ▭ *AE, MC, V.*

## Nightlife

A good way to start an evening is a happy hour at one of the hotel bars. Most bars are informal, but discos have a dress code; you may be turned away if you're wearing shorts, tank tops, or tennis shoes. A number of hotels have Mexican fiesta nights with buffets and folkloric dance performances.

There's live piano music nightly at **Bandidos** (⊠ Calle Pedro Ascencio 2, at Calle Cinco de Mayo, Zihuatanejo ☎ 755/553–8072), which serves drinks, snacks, and full meals at the interior bar and outdoor patio, and usually offers more animated strains of live music after 9. Next to the Best Western Posada Real, **Carlos 'n' Charlie's** (⊠ Blvd. Ixtapa s/n, Ixtapa ☎ 755/553–0085) has late-night dancing on a raised platform

★ by the beach. **Christine** (⊠ Krystal Ixtapa hotel, Blvd. Ixtapa s/n, Ixtapa ☎ 755/553–0333), the town's most popular (and most expensive) disco, has varied music and high-tech light shows.

Tops for sunset viewing (with live music in high season) is the beachfront **Lobby Bar** (⊠ Las Brisas Ixtapa hotel, Playa Vista Hermosa, Ixtapa ☎ 755/553–2121). Like others in the chain, **Señor Frog's** (⊠ Centro Comercial Ixtapa, across from Riviera Beach Hotel, Ixtapa ☎ 755/

553–0272) has innovative decorations, a wild crowd, and several means for getting patrons as drunk as possible.

## Sports & the Outdoors

### Fishing

The area is best known for its feisty sailfish, hooked year-round. Seasonally you'll find yellowfin tuna, dorado, blue and black marlin, mackerel, barracuda, bonito, and others. Before you leave home, you can get information and make bookings through **Ixtapa Sportfishing Charters** (⊠ 19 Depue La., Stroudsburg, PA 18360 ☎ 570/688–9466 ⊕ www. ixtapasportfishing.com). Cost ranges from $210 for one to two people aboard a 25-foot super panga to around $300–$445 for a 28- to 38-foot boat accommodating 4 to 6 fisherpersons.

**Cooperativo de Pescadores Azuete** (⊠ Paseo del Pescador 81, Zihuatanejo ☎ 755/554–2056) charges $150 for up to four passengers in small, fast skiffs or $250 for larger, more comfortable, albeit somewhat slower craft. **Cooperativo Triángulo del Sol** (⊠ Paseo del Pescador 38, Zihuatanejo ☎ 755/554–3758) offers day trips in boats from 26 to 36 feet. Prices are in the $150 to $250 range.

### Golf

Part of the Marina Ixtapa complex, the challenging 18-hole, par-72 course at the **Club de Golf Marina Ixtapa** (⊠ Ixtapa ☎ 755/553–1410) was designed by Robert Von Hagge. Greens fees are $94 (including cart). Caddies charge $20, and you can rent clubs. The **Palma Real Golf Club** (⊠ Blvd. Ixtapa s/n, Ixtapa ☎ 755/553–1163 or 755/553–1703) has an 18-hole, par-72 championship course designed by Robert Trent Jones Jr. It abuts a wildlife preserve that runs from a coconut plantation to the beach; you may glimpse a gator while you play. A round costs $75 mid-December through mid-April and $50 the rest of the year. Carts cost an additional $35. Caddies and club rental available.

### Horseback Riding

Many area tour operators can arrange guided horseback excursions. Costs are high (around $40 for a ride of less than 1½ hours), but they include transportation and usually a soft drink or beer after the ride. You can rent horses with guides for $20 an hour at **Rancho Playa Linda** (☎ 755/554–3085) just up the coast from Ixtapa. Excursions generally leave in the morning and again in the afternoon after the heat has abated, about 4 or 5 PM.

### Tennis

**Club de Golf Marina Ixtapa** (⊠ Ixtapa ☎ 755/553–1410) has one lighted court. Fees are $8 during the day and $10 at night, and you can rent equipment. It costs $4.50 per hour ($16 at night) to play on one of the four cement courts at the **Palma Real Golf Club** (⊠ Blvd. Ixtapa s/n, Ixtapa ☎ 755/553–1163).

### Water Sports

Outfitters line Ixtapa's Playa del Palmar. Parasailing costs about $20 for a 10-minute ride; banana-boat rides are about $5 per person (minimum 4 passengers) for a 15-minute trip. On Playa la Ropa, next to La

Perla restaurant in Zihuatanejo, Hobie Cats rent for about $27 an hour depending on boat size, and classes are $25 per half hour.

SCUBA DIVING   More than 30 dive sites in the area range from deep canyons to shallow reefs. The waters here are teeming with sea life, and visibility is generally excellent. Experienced PADI dive masters run trips ($65 for one tank, $85 for two) and teach courses at **Ixtapa Aqua Paradise** (✉ Centro Comercial Los Patios, Local 137, Ixtapa ☎ 755/553–1510). Owned and operated by NAUI master diver and marine biologist Juan Barnard, the **Zihuatanejo Scuba Center** (✉ Hotel Paraíso Real, Playa La Ropa, Zihuatanejo ☎ 755/554–8156) runs one- and two-tank dives as well as five-day certification courses.

WATER PARK   **Magic World** (✉ Blvd. de las Garzas s/n, Ixtapa ☎ 755/553–1359), next to the Ixtapa Palace Hotel, has such amusements as wave pools and water slides as well as several restaurants. It's open Tuesday–Sunday 10:30–5:30, and admission is $6.50.

# Shopping

## Ixtapa

As you enter Ixtapa from the airport or from Zihuatanejo, you'll see a large handicrafts market, **Mercado de Artesanía Turístico,** on the right side of Boulevard Ixtapa and across from the Hotel Barceló. The result of an ordinance banning vendors from the beach, this market is open weekdays 10–9 and has some 150 stands, selling handicrafts, T-shirts, and souvenirs.

Lining the Zona Hotelera's main street, Paseo del Palmar, are a series of strip malls with boutiques, restaurants, pharmacies, and grocery stores. Everything seems to blend together along here, and even some store proprietors don't know the name of the mall they're in. The most common landmarks for finding the locales within these malls are the hotels directly across the street. One of the few stores that stands out from the rest is ★ **La Fuente** (✉ Centro Comercial Los Patios ☎ 755/553–0812 ✉ Centro Comercial a Puerta ☎ 755/553–1733), with its huge assortment of women's resortwear as well as housewares and gifts. For silver jewelry check out **Santa Prisca** (✉ Centro Comercial Los Patios ☎755/553–0709).

## Zihuatanejo

Downtown Zihuatanejo has a fascinating **mercado municipal** with a labyrinth of small stands on the east side of the town center, on Avenida Benito Juárez between Avenida Nava and Avenida González. On Zihuatanejo's western edge is the **Mercado de Artesanía Turístico** (✉ Calle Cinco ★ de Mayo between Paseo del Pescador and Av. Morelos), with some 250 stands selling jewelry of shell, beads, and quality silver as well as hand-painted bowls and plates, hammocks, gauzy blouses, T-shirts, and souvenirs. Near the main plaza, **Casa Marina** (✉ Paseo del Pescador 9 ☎ 755/554–2373) sells Yucatecan hammocks, Oaxacan rugs, and a smattering of folk art. It's generally closed Sunday except when the cruise ships call.

Ziha's tiny nucleus has several worthwhile shops; most are closed Sunday. Shop for silver and gold jewelry at **Alberto's** (✉ Calle Cuauhtémoc 15, across from Cine Paraíso ☎ 755/554–2161). **Arte Mexicano Nopal**

(⊠ Av. Cinco de Mayo 56 ☎ 755/554–7530) sells Mexican handicrafts, reproductions of ancient art, and natural pine furniture that can be finished according to your tastes. **Coco Cabaña** (⊠ Calle Vicente Guerrero 5, at Av. Agustín Ramírez ☎ 755/554–2518) has a small and somewhat expensive but well-chosen selection of Mexican folk art. The tablecloths, pillowcases, baby clothes, and other lace, crocheted, and embroidered items at **Deshilados** (⊠ Calle Nicolás Bravo 49 ☎ 755/554–2518) make distinctive souvenirs and gifts.

In the Villa del Sol hotel, **Gala Art** (⊠ Playa la Ropa ☎ 755/554–7774) exhibits and sells paintings, jewelry, and bronze, wood, and marble sculptures crafted by artists from throughout Mexico. **Galería Maya** (⊠ Calle Cuauhtémoc 42 ☎ 755/554–4606) is very browseable for its folk art and glad rags from Oaxaca and Chiapas as well as from Guatemala. **Lupita's** (⊠ Calle Juan N. Alvarez 5 ☎ 755/554–2238) has been selling colorful women's apparel—including handmade items from Oaxaca, Yucatán, Chiapas, and Guatemala—for more than 20 years.

## Ixtapa & Zihuatanejo A to Z

### AIR TRAVEL

AIRPORT You can fly to Aeropuerto de Zihuatanejo, 12 km (8 mi) southeast of Zihuatanejo, from Houston, Los Angeles, and other major U.S. cities.
🛈 **Aeropuerto de Zihuatanejo** ☎ 755/553-8864 or 755/554-3298.

AIRPORT From the airport, Autotransporte de Zihuatanejo shuttles deliver passengers
TRANSFERS to Zihua ($6.50) and Ixtapa ($7.50); the trip takes about 25 minutes.
🛈 **Company Autotransporte de Zihuatanejo** ☎ 755/553-8864.

CARRIERS Mexicana has daily flights from U.S. and Mexican cities. Aeroméxico flies from multiple U.S. and Mexican cities. Alaska Airlines has direct flights several times a week from Los Angeles. America West flies direct from Phoenix at least once a week. Houston is the hub for Continental, which offers daily direct flights.
🛈 **Aeroméxico** ☎ 755/553-0555, 01800/021-4000 toll-free in Mexico, 800/237-6639 in the U.S. **Alaska Airlines** ☎ 755/554-8457, 01800/252-7522 toll-free in Mexico, 800/426-0333 in the U.S. **America West** ☎ 755/554-8634, 800/235-9292 in the U.S. **Continental** ☎ 755/554-4219, 800/525-0280 in the U.S. **Mexicana** ☎ 755/554-2208, 01800/502-2000 toll-free in Mexico, 800/531-7921 in the U.S.

### BOAT TRAVEL

Several cruise lines, including Holland America, Princess, and Royal Cruise Lines, sail to Ixtapa and Zihuatanejo as part of their seven-day Riviera Mexicana trips.

### BUS TRAVEL

The Estrella de Oro bus company has deluxe service to Acapulco, Morelia, and Mexico City. Estrella Blanca offers first-class service to the same destinations as well as to a few intermediate destinations. The two bus companies have terminals near each other at the southern edge of

Zihuatanejo on Carretera 200. Estrella de Oro also has a ticket office in Ixtapa's Plaza Ixpamar; Estrella Blanca's Ixtapa office is in Centro Comercial Los Patios.

**🛱 Estrella Blanca** ☎ 755/554-3474. **Estrella de Oro** ☎ 755/554-2175.

### CAR RENTAL

**🛱 Major Agencies Budget** ✉ Centro Comercial Ambiente, Blvd. Ixtapa s/n, Ixtapa ☎ 755/553-0397, 755/553-0517, 755/554-4837 at the airport. **Hertz** ✉ Calle Nicolás Bravo 13, Local 10, Zihuatanejo ☎ 755/554-2255, 755/554-2590 at the airport.

### CAR TRAVEL

The drive south from Manzanillo on Carretera 200 takes about seven hours. The preferred route between Mexico's capital and the coast at Zihuatanejo is the brand new Carretera de Cuota (toll road) connecting Zihuatanejo. Both the Mexico City–Morelia leg and the Morelia–Zihua leg take about 2½ hours, and the divided highways have snack shops and restrooms at toll booths. The free, older route is the Autopista del Sol; it connects Zihuatanejo to Mexico City via Acapulco and takes about eight hours. The 4-hour Zihua–Acapulco leg on Carretera 200 passes through small towns and coconut groves and has spectacular ocean views.

Driving in Ixtapa and Zihuatanejo is a breeze: neither city is congested and no one is any particular hurry. On-street parking is plentiful, and although security isn't really a problem, there are also inexpensive guarded lots.

### CONSULATE

**🛱 United States Consulate** ✉ Paseo Ixtapa, Plaza Ambiente, Local 9, Ixtapa ☎ 755/553-2100.

### EMERGENCIES

**🛱 Hospital General de Zihuatanejo** ✉ Av. Morelos s/n at Mar Egeo, Zihuatanejo ☎ 755/554-3965. **Police** ☎ 755/554-2040. **Red Cross** ☎ 755/554-2009. **Tourist Protection** ☎ 755/554-5641.

### INTERNET

Many hotels in Ixtapa have business centers with Internet access, but cybercafés or Internet connection stores are few and expensive. Ixtapa Conexión, in Plaza Ixtapa, is one of the few. In Zihua try Café Internet, near the center of town. Despite its name there's no coffee; the cost is $2 per hour.

**🛱 Internet Cafés Café Internet** ✉ Calle Benito Juárez Local 2, near Calle Juan N. Alvarez, Zihuatanejo ☎ 755/554-0661. **Ixtapa Conexión** ✉ Plaza Ixtapa, Paseo del Palmar s/n, Ixtapa ☎ 755/553-2253.

### MONEY MATTERS

Although many businesses accept credit cards or U.S. traveler's checks in small denomination, many prefer cash. Change cash or traveler's checks at banks, money exchange booths, or—at a slightly lower rate—hotels. Most area banks have ATMs.

**🛱 Banks Banco Bital** ✉ Blvd. Ixtapa s/n, across from Hotel Riviera Pacífico, Ixtapa ☎ 755/553-0642. **Bancomer** ✉ Av. Benito Juárez, at Calle Nicolás Bravo, Zihuatanejo ☎ 755/554-7490.

**TAXIS & MINIBUSES**

Unless you plan to travel great distances or visit remote beaches, taxis and buses are the best way to get around. Taxis are plentiful, and you can call for one or hail one on the street; fares are reasonable and fixed. The fare from Ixtapa's Zona Hotelera to Zihuatanejo is $4. You can call APAAZ or UTAAZ for a cab; both companies offer 24-hour service. Minibuses run every 10–15 minutes between the Ixtapa hotels and downtown Zihuatanejo until 10 PM; the fare is about 50¢.

🚖 Taxi Companies **APAAZ** ☎ 755/554-3680. **UTAAZ** ☎ 755/554-3311.

**TOURS**

VIPSA and TIP act as both tour operators and travel agencies, offering several popular cruises, snorkeling and horseback-riding expeditions, bus trips, city tours as well as arranging incentive tours and ground transportation. Some of the most popular excursions include the 1½-hour sunset cruises ($45) and four-hour swim and snorkel trip to Isla Ixtapa. Intermar Ixtapa organizes all types of tours in both the town and the country.

To see pink flamingos and other wading birds, head for Barra de Potosí (15 minutes past the airport), where a beautiful *laguna* (lake) is an unofficial bird sanctuary. You can go on a tour, hire a local fisherman, or take a bus or taxi—you'll pay less for the latter, and you'll be able to linger at one of the casual restaurants lining the beach. (There are very informal accommodations here if you want to rough it for a night.) You can hire a fisherman's boat from Zihuatanejo's municipal pier for a trip to the scenic, remote Playa Manzanillo, which is great for snorkeling.

🚖 **Intermar Ixtapa** ✉ Paseo Ixtapa s/n, Centro Commercial Los Patios, Local 105, Ixtapa ☎ 755/553-2666. **TIP** ✉ Calle Juan N. Alvarez, at Calle Benito Juárez, Local 2, Zihuatanejo ☎ 775/554-7511.

**TRAVEL AGENCY**

🚖 Local Agent Referrals **VIPSA** ✉ Hotel Barceló, Blvd. Ixtapa s/n, Ixtapa ☎ 755/553-2480.

**VISITOR INFORMATION**

The Guerrero State Tourism Office is open weekdays 8–9 and Saturday 8–3. Ixtapa's Oficina de Convenciones y Visitantes (Convention and Visitors' Bureau) is helpful with hotel and tour operator recommendations. It's open weekdays 9–2 and 4–7.

🚖 **Guerrero State Tourism Office** ✉ La Puerta shopping center, Blvd. Ixtapa s/n, Ixtapa ☎ 755/553-1967. **Oficina de Convenciones y Visitantes** ✉ Paseo de las Gaviotas 12, Ixtapa ☎ 755/553-1270 or 553-1570 ⊕ www.ixtapa-zihuatanejo.org.

# ACAPULCO

9

Updated by
Patricia Alisau

**DIEGO RIVERA IS SAID TO HAVE BEEN SO ENCHANTED** by Acapulco's sunsets that he re-created them on canvas. In the 1950s, this vibrant port city, which has a beautiful bay, attracted a stream of Hollywood stars. This is also where John and Jackie Kennedy spent their honeymoon, as did Henry and Nancy Kissinger, Liz Taylor and Michael Todd, and Bill and Hillary Clinton. Three of Sylvestor Stallone's *Rambo* flicks were filmed in Acapulco, as was *Blow* with Johnny Depp and Penélope Cruz. Singer Julio Iglesias and other celebrities maintain homes here, carrying on the Hollywood tradition.

The natural harbor of Bahía de Acapulco (Acapulco Bay) is the city's centerpiece. By day this stretch of the Pacific, 433 km (268 mi) south of Mexico City, is a deep tempting blue; at night the water flashes and reflects the city's lights. Warm water, nearly constant sunshine, and balmy year-round temperatures let people plan their day around the beach—whether they're lounging in a hammock or snorkeling, parasailing, fishing, or water-skiing. Still, the city offers plenty of attractions to lure people away from the sands: championship golf courses, tennis courts, food and crafts markets, and fabulous restaurants.

In the 16th century, when Acapulco was a hub of trade under the Spanish Crown, its famous galleons regularly returned from the Orient with the finest silks, spices, and porcelains. As the city grew, it inspired merchant princes to build lavish mansions. Acapulco's wealth also attracted pirates who regularly attacked the city in the 17th and 18th centuries. In the early 19th century, the fort was assailed by both rebels and royalists during the War of Independence. Decades later the city was again assaulted, this time by troops led by Mexican President Antonio Lopez de Santa Ana (of the Alamo fame). It was also overrun by Napoléon III's forces in the 1860s, during what's known as the French Invasion. Peace reigned only after the Mexican Revolution of 1910–20. In the 1930s, a road opened between Acapulco and the capital at Mexico City. The journey, which now takes about 4½ hours, then took several days. But the road's completion still marked the modest beginnings of tourism in the region. In the 1940s, after spying a prime piece of real estate along the stunning Bay of Acapulco, former Mexican President Miguel Alemán Valdés bought up miles of coastline just before the road and airport were built here. By the 1960s, tourism was booming as glittering high-rise hotels were appearing along what is today known as the Costera.

In the evening Acapulco prepares itself for the pleasures of the night and things get more formal. Dining out is one of the city's great pleasures. In addition to the showy places, there are plenty of good no-frills, down-home joints representative of the real Mexico. Acapulco's nightlife is also legendary, with ever more spectacular dance clubs constantly opening. Perpetually crowded, the discos are in groups of twos and threes, and most people hit several places in a single night.

Acapulco has managed to age gracefully over the years even as it's grown into a community of a million inhabitants. Care is lavished on its upkeep. The city fathers initiated a multimillion-dollar beautification program some time ago; the effort helps keep the bay, beaches, and streets landscaped and pristine.

# EXPLORING ACAPULCO

Old Acapulco is on the bay's western edge. Its streets run inland, forming a grid that's easy to explore on foot. Avenida Costera Miguel Alemán, a wide, coastal boulevard, has many major hotels, restaurants, and malls. You need a car to explore this area, which is home to the posh Costera strip, and to visit Acapulco Diamante, still farther east. Running from Las Brisas to Barra Vieja beach, this 3,000-acre expanse encompasses exclusive Punta Diamante and Playa Diamante, with upscale hotels and residential developments, private clubs, and pounding surf.

To the west, Pie de la Cuesta is famous for its fabulous sunsets—reason enough to venture here late in the afternoon. Grab a beach chair, sip a drink, and watch the stream of colors moving across the sky. Although Pie de la Cuesta's main road has been paved and it now has an all-inclusive resort (popular with Canadians and Germans), the tiny area has seen little other development.

Even during a short stay, you can get a feel for Acapulco if you take in some downtown sights along with your beach activities. With more time, you can enjoy excursions to more isolated beaches as well as to Taxco, a colonial town a delightful three-hour drive north of Acapulco, where silversmith shops line cobblestone streets.

### Timing

Temperatures hover at the 30°C (80°F) mark just about year-round, and sunshine is virtually guaranteed anytime. Snowbirds from the United States and Canada show up all winter, but the busiest times are Christmas week, Easter week, and during July and August. Most hotels are booked solid during these times, so make reservations well in advance. Prices during Christmas week rise 30%–60% above those in low season.

## Costera

Avenida Costera Miguel Alemán hugs the Bahía de Acapulco from the Carretera Escénica (Scenic Highway) in the east to Playa Caleta (Caleta Beach) in the southwest—a distance of about 8 km (5 mi). Most of the major beaches, shopping malls, and hotels are along or off this avenue, and locals refer to its most exclusive stretch—from El Presidente hotel to Las Brisas—simply as "Costera." Because many an address is listed only as "Costera Miguel Alemán" and streets off this avenue have no logical pattern, addresses are rarely used; directions are usually given from a major landmark.

*Numbers in the text correspond to numbers in the margin and on the Acapulco map.*

**a good tour**

Take a drive or taxi ride along the Costera Miguel Alemán, starting on its eastern edge at La Base, the Mexican naval base south of Playa Icacos. When you come to Playa Icacos, you'll see the **Casa de la Cultura ❶** ▶ cultural complex on the beach side (just past the Hyatt Regency hotel); a little farther down is **CiCi ❷**, a children's amusement park. About 1 km (½ mi) past it, on the right side of the Costera, lies the Acapulco

**If you have**
**3 days**

Spend the first day parasailing, waterskiing, or simply sunning. That evening take a sunset cruise that includes a bird's-eye view of the hilltop mansions of the rich and famous. The following day pay an early visit to the Mercado Municipal, the waterfront, and the *zócalo* (town square). Head to the beach for some rays and take in some late-afternoon shopping in the boutiques and handicrafts markets along Avenida Costera Miguel Alemán. Come nightfall, "shake off the dust" (as they say in Mexico) at one of the city's glitzy discos. The next day return to the beach or head out fishing. Later, toast Acapulco during a late candlelit dinner.

**9**

**If you have**
**5 days**

Follow the three-day itinerary. On the fourth day visit El Fuerte de San Diego, built in the 18th century to protect Acapulco from pirates, and today is the home of the history museum. Then swing down the street to the Casa de Mascaras, with its collection of Guerrero masks. For a taste of the 1950s Acapulco of John Wayne and Johnny Weissmuller, hire a taxi to take you into the hills above Caleta and Caletilla; make it a point to drop into Los Flamingos hotel, which Weissmuller once owned with others from the Hollywood gang. Head out to Pie de la Cuesta, a beach west of town, for a late lunch and boat ride or waterskiing on Laguna Coyuca (Coyuca Lagoon), and then cross the road and park your body under an umbrella to watch the sun set. Set the next morning aside for the thrilling Shotover Jet boat ride on the Puerto Marques lagoon. Devote a few hours to Mágico Mundo Marino or the ruins at Palma Sola.

**If you have**
**7 days**

Follow the five-day itinerary and, on the sixth day, rent a car or arrange for a tour to Taxco, a colonial treasure of twisting cobblestone streets and some 2,000 silver shops, a three-hour drive north of Acapulco; plan to spend the night. In addition to shopping for silver, visit the Iglesia de San Sebastián y Santa Prisca, the town's most important landmark, on Plaza Borda, and the Casa Humboldt, which houses a museum. Try to get a front-row seat at one of the bars or restaurants on the square and spend an hour watching the activity: weddings, funerals, baptisms, and vendors selling baskets and animal figurines. The following day, tour the Grutas de Cacahuamilpa, an expanse of subterranean chambers.

---

International Center (often called simply the convention center). Continue along through the commercial heart of the Costera until you reach **Parque Papagayo ❸**, one of the country's top municipal parks.

### Timing

This tour should take no more than an hour and it can either be done in the early morning or afternoon. Although you drive only a few miles each way, expect Acapulco traffic to be heavy from around 8 in the morning to 8 at night and worse on the weekends.

### What to See

▶ **❶ Casa de la Cultura.** This cultural complex includes a small archaeological museum, first-class regional and Mexican handicrafts for sale, and the Ixcateopan art gallery. ⊠ *Av. Costera Miguel Alemán 4834, Costera* ☎ *744/484–4004* ✉ *Free* ⊙ *Weekdays 9–2 and 5–8, Sat. 9–2.*

🕐 ❷ **CiCi.** A water-oriented theme park for children, the Centro Internacional para Convivencia Infantil, fondly known as CiCi, has dolphin and seal shows, a freshwater pool with wave-making apparatus, a water slide, mini-aquarium, and other attractions. Transportation from hotels in Acapulco proper is provided for couples who book hour-long swims with the dolphins (it's easy to catch a cab for the return trip). ⊠ *Av. Costera Miguel Alemán, across from Hard Rock Cafe, Costera* ☎ *744/ 484–8210* ✉ *$6* ⊙ *Daily 10–6.*

🕐 ❸ **Parque Papagayo.** Named for the hotel that formerly occupied the grounds, this park is on 52 acres of prime Costera real estate, just after the underpass that begins at Playa Hornos. It has an aviary as well as a jogging path, exercise classes, a library, a roller-skating rink, a race-track with mite-size race cars, a space-shuttle replica, bumper boats in a lagoon, and other rides. ⊠ *Av. Costera Miguel Alemán, Costera* ☎ *744/485–9623* ✉ *No entrance fee; rides $1 each; $5 ride packages available* ⊙ *Park: daily 5–8. Rides section: nightly 4–11.*

## Old Acapulco

Old Acapulco, one of the areas that you can easily tour on foot, is where the locals go to dine, enjoy a town festival, run errands, and worship. Also known as El Centro, it's where you'll find the zócalo, the church, and El Fuerte de San Diego. Just up the hill from Old Acapulco is La Quebrada and its legendary cliff divers. The southern peninsula retains remnants of Acapulco's earliest incarnation. This primarily residential area has been revitalized through efforts such as the reopening of the Caleta Hotel and the opening of the aquarium at Playa Caleta. Although the area is past its prime, it's still popular with budget travelers and those who pine for Acapulco's 1950s glory days. The Plaza de Toros, where bullfights are held on Sunday from the first week of January to Easter, is in the center of the peninsula.

**a good tour**

A few blocks inland from the intersection of Avenida Costera Miguel Alemán and Calle Diego Hurtado de Mendoza is the sprawling **Mercado Municipal** ❹ ▶. To reach it, take the bus marked MERCADO or have a taxi drop you off; it's best to navigate El Centro on foot. A few blocks west, **El Fuerte de San Diego** ❻ is on the hill overlooking the harbor next to the army barracks. At the fort, you can hire a guide for a trip to the **Palma Sola** archaeological site, just northwest of Old Acapulco. Or continue your walking tour by leaving the fort and wandering along the **malecón** ❼, with its series of docks. Adjoining it is the **zócalo** ❽, Old Acapulco's center. A 15-minute walk up the hill from the zócalo brings you to **La Quebrada** ❾, where the famous cliff divers perform their daredevil stunts daily. From here or from the zócalo you can grab a cab to the **Mágico Mundo Marino** ❿ to visit the aquarium.

### Timing

In the morning, start at the municipal market; plan to spend at least an hour there. Follow this with a visit to the El Fuerte de San Diego, al-

**9**

## The Best Rest

You can stay in baronial splendor or chill out in bucolic hostelries. In the days before a/c, Hollywood celebrities often vacationed in Old Acapulco's hotels, built on breezy hillsides. Although many of these places are past their prime, they're fairly well maintained and certainly less expensive than lodgings in Costera. Many also have lots of charm, spectacular sea views, and—nowadays—air-conditioning.

The names associated with Costera's high-rises—Radisson, Hilton, Hyatt, Fairmont—are as familiar and comforting as the facilities they offer. Beach bars, water-sports outfitters, and high-end restaurants are standard, as are such things as in-room safes and Internet access. East of Costera, in Acapulco Diamante, several smashing properties hug Puerto Marques Bay. You'll find exclusivity and higher rates in this area, but the amenities are fit for a king.

Pie de la Cuesta's rustic inns suit the location far from the frenetic activity of downtown and Costera. There's no nightlife—and you may not even get hot water at your hotel—but you'll rarely be more than a few yards from the beach.

## Out on the Town

Acapulco's clubs are open nearly 365 days a year from about 10:30 PM until they empty out. The minute the sun slips over the horizon, the Costera comes alive. People mill around, window-shopping, choosing restaurants, and generally biding their time until the disco hour.

Many resorts have splashy entertainment nightly, sometimes with big-name Mexican or international artists. At the very least such hotels have live music during happy hour, restaurant theme parties, dancing at a beach bar—or all three.

Casual beach restaurants line a section of the Costera known as "the strip." Many have live jazz or tropical music and attract people who are at ease settling in for the night to enjoy the scene. For an even more informal evening, head for the zócolo, where there's usually a band on weekend evenings.

## Shopping

Guerrero State is known for hand-painted ceramics, items made from *palo de rosa* wood, primitive bark paintings depicting scenes of village life and local flora and fauna, and embroidered textiles. Stands in downtown's sprawling municipal market are piled high with handicrafts as well as fruit, flowers, spices, herbs, cheeses, poultry, and other meats. Practice your bargaining skills here or at one of the streetside handicrafts sellers. Prices are almost always inflated for tourists, so don't be shy about asking for reductions.

Boutiques selling high-fashion Mexican designs for men and women are plentiful and draw an international clientele. This is a great place to shop for bathing suits, evening wear, and gems from all over the world. Many shops also sell high-quality crafts from throughout the country. Although many of Acapulco's stores carry jewelry and other items made of silver, aficionados tend to make the three-hour drive to the colonial town of Taxco—one of the world's silver capitals.

# Sun, Sand & Surf

You can tee off at the 9-hole municipal course or at one of four 18-hole championship courses along the Costera. Most hotels have pools, and many have tennis clubs as well. The lure of Acapulco's sands is irresistible, though. You can eat in a beach restaurant, dance, and sleep in a *hamaca* (hammock)—all without leaving the water's edge. There are also plenty of quiet, isolated beaches within reach.

The water teems with sailfish, marlin, shark, and mahimahi, so fishing is as popular here as waterskiing, windsurfing, kayaking, and bronco riding (one-person Jet Skis). But the most traditional Acapulco sporting experience is parasailing, developed here in the 1960s. Although visibility isn't as good as in the Caribbean, scuba diving is an option. It's best in December through February, when the water is the most transparent. A Canadian warship was scuttled to make a trip down more appealing. In Pie de La Cuesta's lagoon, which runs parallel to the ocean, fresh-water fishing, kayaking, and water skiing are options.

# A Taste of Acapulco

Dining in Acapulco is more than eating out—it's the most popular activity in town. You can sample cuisines from around the world or feast on succulent classics from all over Mexico. Fresh seafood is the star on many menus; many of the downtown seafood joints even serve dishes made with catches brought in by fishermen that very day. Top-quality beef from the Mexican states of Sonora and Chihuahua is also popular.

The tone and settings of Acapulco's restaurants is almost as varied as the cuisine. You can have an utterly romantic meal high above the hills, with a gorgeous view of the bay and superb international dishes. Or you can dine in a beachside restaurant, overlooking a sensual, calm sea. Some places attract a casual, fun-loving crowd; at other places the experience is low-key and soothing.

Dining in Old Acapulco will put you in contact with the gracious locals, who are savvy about where to find the best food. You can plan a half-day outing to rustic Barra Vieja east of Acapulco for lunch and take a boat through the mangroves to one of many dining huts, where fish is grilled over hot coals. You can also head to Pie de la Cuesta, a laid-back somewhat isolated area west of downtown. Here you can have lunch at a seaside eatery, go horseback riding, and then linger on the beach for a spectacular sunset.

---

lowing one to two hours to tour the fort's exhibits. Later, stroll the malecón and zócalo. In the afternoon, head for La Calenta and the aquarium, stopping first for lunch at La Cabaña restaurant on the beach. Visit the aquarium and then return to your hotel to rest or hit the beach. At night, head out to La Quebrada to see a cliff-diving performance. The next day, allow a half-day to tour the Palma Sola ruins.

## What to See

**❺ Casa de Mascaras.** A private home has been turned into a gallery for a stunning collection of 550 handmade ceremonial masks, most from the state of Guerrero. Some are representative of those still used in such traditional ritualistic dances as "Moors and the Christians" and "Battle of the Tigers." ⊠ *Calle Morelos s/n, ex-zona militar B, a half block from Fuerte de San Diego, Old Acapulco* ☎ *744/486–5577* ☜ *Free (donation suggested)* ⊙ *Mon.–Sat. 10–6.*

★ ⑥ **El Fuerte de San Diego.** Under the Spaniards, Acapulco became a lucrative port for trade with the Philippines. The original fortress, built in 1616 to protect the wealthy city from pirates, was destroyed by an earthquake in 1776; the current, pentagonal one went up in the 18th century. Today the fort houses the **Museo Historico de Acapulco** (Acapulco History Museum). Bilingual videos and text explain exhibits tracing the city's history from the first pre-Hispanic settlements 3,000 years ago, to the exploits of such pirates as Sir Francis Drake, through the era of the missionaries, and up to Mexico's independence from Spain in 1821. There are also displays of precious silks, Talavera tiles, exquisitely handtooled wooden furniture, and delicate china. A good multimedia show in Spanish (an English version requires a minimum of 15 people) on the history of Acapulco is staged outside the museum grounds on Thursday, Friday, and Saturday at 8 PM for $10 per person. ⊠ *Calle Hornitos and Calle Morelos, Old Acapulco* ☎ *744/482–3828* ☜ *$3.25* ⊙ *Tues.–Fri. 10–5, Sat. 10–5 and 7–9:30, Sun. 10–5.*

🄲 ⑩ **Mágico Mundo Marino.** In addition to an aquarium, Magic Marine World has a free sea-lion show and swimming pools—not to mention clean rest rooms. You can also rent Jet Skis, inner tubes, kayaks, and other equipment here for use on Playa Caleta, a beach connected to this park via a pedestrian bridge. From Playa Caleta you can take the glass-bottom boat to Isla la Roqueta—about 10 minutes each way—for snorkeling. ⊠ *Playa Caleta, Old Acapulco* ☎ *744/483–1215* ☜ *$3. Round-trip boat ride to Isla la Roqueta: $5* ⊙ *Daily 9–6.*

⑦ **Malecón.** A stroll by the docks will confirm that Acapulco remains a lively port. At night Mexicans bring their children to play on the tree-lined promenade. Farther west, by the zócalo, are docks for sightseeing yachts and smaller fishing boats. ⊠ *Av. Costera Miguel Alemán, between Calle Escudero on the west and El Fuerte de San Diego on the east, Old Acapulco.*

▶ ④ **Mercado Municipal.** Locals come to this municipal market to buy everything, from candles and fresh vegetables to plastic buckets and love potions. In addition, you can buy baskets, pottery, hammocks—there's even a stand offering charms, amulets, and talismans. The stalls within the mercado are densely packed together and there's no air-conditioning, but things stay relatively cool. Come early to avoid the crowds. ⊠ *Calle Diego Hurtado de Mendoza and Av. Constituyentes, a few blocks west of Costera, Old Acapulco* ⊙ *Daily 5 AM–7 PM.*

off the
beaten
path

**PALMA SOLA** – Taking the name of the neighborhood closest to it, this archaeological site juts up a mountainside northeast of Old Acapulco. The area is blanketed in 2,000-year-old petroglyphs, executed by the Yopes, Acapulco's earliest known inhabitants. Stone steps with intermittent plazas for viewing the ancient art are set along

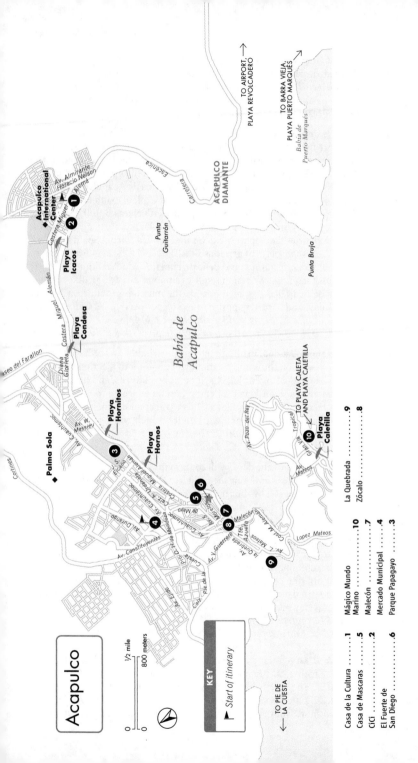

# Acapulco

0 ——— ½ mile
0 ——— 800 meters

TO PIE DE
LA CUESTA ←

→ TO AIRPORT;
PLAYA REVOLCADERO

TO BARRA VIEJA,
PLAYA PUERTO MARQUÉS

Acapulco International Center

Playa Icacos

Playa Condesa

Playa Hornitos

Playa Hornos

Palma Sola

Bahía de
Acapulco

ACAPULCO
DIAMANTE

Punta Guitarrón

Punta Bruja

Bahía de
Puerto Marqués

Playa Caletilla

TO PLAYA CALETA
AND PLAYA CALETILLA

a path through virgin vegetation. A cave used as a ceremonial center is atop the mountain, more than 1,000 feet above sea level and definitely worth the visit. The site is still being studied by the National Institute of Archaeology and History, which built the small information center at the entrance. You need a guide and driver to get here; make arrangements at El Fuerte de San Diego. ☎ 744/482–3828 for tours ⊠ Free ⊙ Daily 9–5.

**❾ La Quebrada.** Way above downtown Acapulco, La Quebrada (literally "gorge"; in this case referring to a canyon surrounded by cliffs) is home to the El Mirador hotel, *the* place for tourists in the 1940s. These days most visitors come to see the *clavadistas* jump from a height of 130 feet daily at 1 PM and evenings at 7:30, 8:30, 9:30, and 10:30. Be sure to arrive early to get a spot with a good view. Before they take the plunge, the divers pray at a small shrine on the cliffs. Sometimes they dive in pairs; often they carry torches. The hotel's La Perla supper club is the most comfortable viewing spot, but you'll be charged a cover of $12 with à la carte dining, or $31, which includes cover and two drinks. (Be forewarned: the tequila, rum, and brandy here are watered down, but the fees include tips for the wait staff and the divers.) You can also see the divers from the general observation deck next to the hotel (about $3). When you exit, divers may be waiting to greet you. Many people tip them; they get paid very little for risking their lives.

*Fodor'sChoice* ★

**❽ Zócalo.** Old Acapulco's hub is this shaded plaza, overgrown with dense trees. All day it's filled with vendors, shoe-shine men, and people lining up to use the pay phones. After siesta, they drift here to meet and greet. On Sunday evening there's often music in the bandstand. The zócalo fronts Nuestra Señora de la Soledad (Our Lady of Solitude), the town's modern but unusual church, with its stark-white exterior and bulb-shaped blue-and-yellow spires. The church hosts the festive Virgin of Guadalupe celebration on December 12. ⊠ *Bounded by Calle Felipe Valle on the north, Av. Costera Miguel Alemán on the south, Calle J. Azueta on the west, and Calle J. Carranza on the east, Old Acapulco.*

## Beaches

In the past few years, city officials made a great effort to clean up the Bahía de Acapulco, and maintaining it is a priority. Although vending on the beach has been outlawed, you'll probably still be approached by souvenir hawkers. Some beaches, such as Revolcadero and Pie de la Cuesta, have very strong undertows and surf, so swimming isn't advised.

**Barra Vieja.** A pleasant drive 27 km (17 mi) east of Acapulco, between Laguna de Tres Palos and the Pacific, brings you to this long stretch of uncrowded beach. Most people make the trip for the solitude and to feast on *pescado à la talla* (red snapper marinated in spices and grilled over hot coals).

**Playa Caleta.** On the southern peninsula in Old Acapulco, this beach and smaller Playa Caletilla (Little Caleta) to the south, once rivaled La Quebrada as the main tourist area. Today, their snug little bays and calm waters make them a favorite with Mexican families. Caleta has the Magico

# CloseUp

## THREE DAYS ON THE CHEAP

A VACATION IN ACAPULCO needn't drain your wallet dry. Some of the best things to do are inexpensive, if not entirely free. And choosing your lodging with care will save still more money. The cliff-side Los Flamingos in Old Acapulco is a good bet; not only do the affordable rates include transportation to the beach and downtown, but a stay here means that you're following in the footsteps of such Hollywood celebrities as Fred MacMurray and Johnny Weissmuller. One of Acapulco's best deals, however, is the charming Boca Chica: it's next to Playa Caleta, and its rates include a full (and substantial) breakfast.

**Day One:** Spend the morning sunning on Playa Caleta. Have lunch at La Cabaña, a beachside seafood place with a bit of history. Early in the afternoon, take the bus into Old Acapulco and tour the Fuerte de San Diego; exhibits in its museum recount Acapulco's history. The neighboring Casa de Mascaras has displays of hand-carved indigenous ceremonial masks. Have dinner at La Casa de Tere, a real local joint.

**Day Two:** Hit Old Acapulco's Mercado Municipal late in the morning. Remember to bargain as you browse through its stalls of crafts, cotton blouses, and leather belts. Drop into one of the zócalo's cafés for a late-afternoon bite. Afterward have a seat on a bench and watch the world go by, before wandering to the waterfront. Splurge on a $20 ticket for a sunset cruise—with drinks and dancing—on the Bonanza or economize and head to the viewing platform at the El Mirador hotel to watch the divers at La Quebrada. Afterward take a cab to Zorrito's for dinner.

**Day Three:** Late in the morning or early in the afternoon, take a bus or cab to Pie de la Cuesta, a strip of beach west of downtown. Spend the day here sunbathing and snacking. Hang around for what is arguably Acapulco's most brilliant sunset or take a cab or bus to Playa Condesa and the Fiesta Americana Condesa hotel—its bar is always fun, particularly during happy hours when drinks are really cheap. Affordable restaurants nearby include Beto's and Carlos 'n' Charlie's.

Mundo Marino entertainment center for children and a large seafood restaurant. Caletilla has lots of food shacks. On both beaches vendors sell everything from seashells to peeled mangos; boats depart from both to Isla de Roqueta.

**Playa Condesa.** Referred to as "the strip," this stretch of sand facing the middle of Bahía de Acapulco has more than its share of visitors, especially singles. It's lined with lively restaurants.

**Playa Hornitos.** Running from the Avalon Excalibur west to Las Hamacas, Hornitos (Little Hornos) and adjacent Playa Hornos are shoulder-to-shoulder with locals and visitors on weekends. Graceful palms shade the sand, and there are scads of casual eateries on the beach, especially on Playa Hornos. A slice of Playa Hornos and Playa Hornitos mark the beginning of the hotel zone to the east.

**Playa Icacos.** Stretching from the naval base to El Presidente hotel, away from the famous strip, this beach is less populated than others on the Costera. The morning waves are especially calm.

FodorsChoice
★

**Pie de la Cuesta.** You need a car or cab to reach this relatively unpopulated spot, about a 25-minute drive west of downtown. A string of simple, thatched-roof restaurants and new, rustic inns border the wide beach, and straw palapas provide shade. What attracts people to Pie de la Cuesta, besides the long expanse of beach and spectacular sunsets, is beautiful Laguna Coyuca, a favorite spot for waterskiing, freshwater fishing, and boat rides (swimming isn't recommended). Boats will ferry you to La Laguna restaurant, where, some people claim, the pescado à la talla is even better than at Barra Vieja.

**Playa Puerto Marqués.** Tucked below the airport highway, this strand is popular with Mexican tourists, so it tends to get crowded on weekends. Beach shacks here sell fresh fish and vendors sell silver, blankets, beach coverups, and other items.

**Playa Revolcadero.** This wide, sprawling beach fronts the Fairmont Pierre Marqués and Fairmont Acapulco Princess hotels. People come here to surf and ride horses. The water is shallow, but the waves are fairly rough and the undertow can be strong, so be careful while swimming.

# WHERE TO EAT

Every night, Acapulco's restaurants fill up, and every night you can sample a different cuisine, whether you opt for a greasy spoon serving regional favorites or an establishment with the finest international dishes. On the Costera Miguel Alemán there are dozens of beachside eateries with *palapa* (palm frond) roofs, as well as wildly decorated rib and hamburger joints popular with visitors under 30—not necessarily in age, but definitely in spirit.

Loud music blares from many restaurants along the Costera, especially those facing Playa Condesa, and proprietors will aggressively try to hustle you inside with offers of drink specials. If you're looking for a hassle-free evening, avoid this area or decide in advance where to dine. Most places that cater to visitors purify their drinking and cooking water.

At the best spots in town, a main dish of meat or fish can run up to $60, and the views are fantastic. Ties and jackets are out of place, but so are shorts and jeans. Unless stated otherwise, all restaurants are open daily for lunch and dinner; dinner-only places open around 6:30 or 7.

| | **WHAT IT COSTS** | | | | |
|---|---|---|---|---|---|
| | $$$$ | $$$ | $$ | $ | ¢ |
| AT DINNER | over $25 | $15–$25 | $10–$15 | $5–$10 | under $5 |

Prices are per person for a main course at dinner, excluding tax and tip.

## Acapulco Diamante

### Italian

$$$–$$$$ ✕ **Casa Nova.** Live piano music lends romance to Casa Nova, which is carved out of a cliff that rises from Bahía de Acapulco. The views, both from the terrace and the air-conditioned dining room, are spectacular, the service is impeccable, and the Italian cuisine is divine. The Mexican chef was trained in Europe and is earning accolades for the cuisine. You can choose the fixed-price *menu turístico* for $35 or order à la carte. Favorites include lobster tail, linguine *alle vongole* (with clams, tomato, and garlic), and *costoletta di vitello* (veal chops with mushrooms). ⊠ *Carretera Escénica 5256, Las Brisas* ☎ *744/446–6237* ⌛ *Reservations essential* ▤ *AE, MC, V* ⊙ *No lunch.*

### Mexican

★ $$–$$$$ ✕ **Hacienda.** Personable, efficient waiters dress as classy *charros* (Mexican cowboys with silver-studded outfits) and mariachis entertain at this restaurant in a colonial hacienda, once a millionaire's estate. The menu has such dishes as sautéed oysters from Loreto (Baja California) served with chile-poblano mousseline. Seafood and chateaubriand made with Black Angus tenderloin are specialities. On Sundays, there's a champagne brunch for $28. ⊠ *Fairmont Acapulco Princess hotel, Playa Revolcadero Revolcadero* ☎ *744/469–1000* ▤ *AE, DC, MC, V* ⊙ *No lunch.*

### Seafood

$$$–$$$$ ✕ **La Vela.** On a wharf that juts out into Bahía de Puerto Marqués, this
FodorśChoice casual, open-air dining spot has wooden floors and a dramatic roof that
★ simulates a huge white sail. It's particularly atmospheric after dark, when the lights of Puerto Marqués flicker in the distance. There are several fish and shellfish dishes on the menu, but the specialty is the red snapper *à la talla* (basted with chili and other spices and broiled over hot coals). ⊠ *Camino Real Acapulco Diamante, Carretera Escénica, Km 14, Acapulco Diamante* ☎ *744/466–1010* ▤ *AE, DC, MC, V.*

## Costera

### American

$$–$$$ ✕ **Carlos 'n' Charlie's.** Although it's part of a large chain, this is an Acapulco landmark. It cultivates controlled craziness: prankster waiters, a joke-filled menu, and eclectic decorations. The crowd is mostly young and relaxed, and the menu straddles the border, with ribs, stuffed shrimp, and oysters among the best offerings. A luncheon buffet on

Wednesday costs $10. ⊠ *Av. Costera Miguel Alemán 112, Costera* ☎ *744/484–1285 or 744/484–0039* ⊟ *AE, MC, V.*

**$–$$$** ✕ **Hard Rock Cafe.** This link in the international Hard Rock chain is one of Acapulco's most popular spots with good reason. The famous New York–cut steaks, hamburgers, and brownies, as well as the Southern-style fried chicken and ribs, are well prepared, and portions are ample. Taped rock music begins at noon, and a live group starts playing at 11 PM (except Tuesday). ⊠ *Av. Costera Miguel Alemán 37, Costera* ☎ *744/ 484–6680* ⊟ *AE, MC, V.*

### Contemporary

★ **$$–$$$$** ✕ **Baikal.** Modern, ultrachic Baikal is *the* place to see and be seen. The dining room has a white-on-white color scheme and 12-foot-high windows that frame the sparkling bay; sea-theme short films are shown from time to time on drop-down movie screens. The menu is small but select, with dishes that fuse French, Asian, and Mexican preparations and ingredients. Try the cold cream of cucumber soup spiced with mint and mild jalapeño; the sliced abalone with a *chipotle* (dried, smoked chilies) vinaigrette is also a good bet. Soft bossa nova and jazz play in the background. ⊠ *Carretera Escénica 22, Costera* ☎ *744/446–6867* ⚘ *Reservations essential* ⊟ *AE, DC, MC, V* ☉ *Closed Mon. May–Nov. No lunch.*

### Continental

**$$$$** ✕ **Madeiras.** At this local favorite, the bar-reception area has dramatic coffee tables whose glass tops rest on carved wooden animals; the dishes and flatware were created by Taxco silversmiths; and all tables have views of Bahía de Acapulco. Dinner is a four-course, prix-fixe meal and there are 15 menus from which to choose. Specialties include tasty chilled soups and a delicious red snapper baked in sea salt (a Spanish dish); there are also steak choices, lobster tail, chicken, and pork. Seatings are every 30 minutes from 7 PM to 11 PM. Reserve well in advance on weekends and for Christmas and Easter week. ⊠ *Carretera Escénica 33-B, just past La Vista shopping center, Costera* ☎ *744/446–5636* ⚘ *Reservations essential* ⊟ *AE, MC, V* ☉ *No lunch.*

### French

**$$$–$$$$** ✕ **Le Jardín des Artistes.** Tables at this thoroughly French garden hideaway have fresh flowers and Tiffany lamps, and discreet waiters deliver dishes made rich by classic cream and butter sauces. The Mexican chef has gained a local following thanks to his delicious escargots in garlic butter, red-snapper fillet with savory mustard sauce, and smoked trout soufflé. After dinner, stroll through the snazzy art gallery. ⊠ *Calle Vicente Yañez Pinzón 11, Costera* ☎ *744/484–8344* ⚘ *Reservations essential* ⊟ *AE, MC, V* ☉ *Closed May 1–Dec. 14. No lunch.*

### Health Food

**¢–$** ✕ **100% Natural.** Along the Costera Miguel Alemán are several of these 24-hour restaurants that specialize in quick service and light, healthful food: sandwiches made with whole-wheat bread, soy burgers, chicken dishes, yogurt shakes, fruit salads. You'll recognize these eateries by their green signs with white lettering. The original—and best—is across from the Costa Club hotel. ⊠ *Av. Costera Miguel Alemán 200, near Acapulco*

# Where to Stay & Eat in Acapulco

**KEY**
**6** *Restaurants*
**1** *Hotels*

**Restaurants** ▼

Baikal . . . . . . . . . . . . . . .**36**
Beto's . . . . . . . . . .**22, 45**
La Cabaña . . . . . . . . . . . .**9**
El Amigo Miguel . . . . . . .**14**
El Cabrito . . . . . . . . . . .**29**
Carlos 'n' Charlie's . . . . .**21**
La Casa de Tere . . . . . . .**13**
Casa Nova . . . . . . . . . . .**38**
Coyuca 22 . . . . . . . . . . . .**6**
El Faro . . . . . . . . . . . . .**25**
Hacienda . . . . . . . . . . .**42**
Hard Rock Cafe . . . . . . .**27**

Le Jardín des Artistes . . .**20**
Madeiras . . . . . . . . . . . .**37**
Mezzanotte . . . . . . . . . .**34**
100% Natural . . . . . .**18, 30**
Pipo's . . . . . . . . . .**12, 28**
Suntory . . . . . . . . . . . .**31**
La Vela . . . . . . . . . . . .**39**
Zapata, Villa y Cia . . . . .**33**
Zorrito's . . . . . . . . . . . .**17**

**Hotels** ▼

Avalon . . . . . . . . . . . . .**16**
Boca Chica . . . . . . . . . . .**8**
Las Brisas . . . . . . . . . . .**35**
Camino Real Acapulco
Diamante . . . . . . . . . . .**40**
Elcano . . . . . . . . . . . . .**26**
Fairmont Acapulco
Princess . . . . . . . . . . . .**43**
Fairmont Pierre
Marqués . . . . . . . . . . . .**41**
Fiesta Americana
Condesa Acapulco . . . . .**23**
Los Flamingos . . . . . . . . .**7**
Hacienda Vayma . . . . . . .**3**

Las Hamacas . . . . . . . . . .**15**
Hyatt Regency
Acapulco . . . . . . . . . . . .**32**
El Mirador . . . . . . . . . . . .**4**
Misión . . . . . . . . . . . . .**11**
Parador del Sol . . . . . . . .**1**
Park Hotel &
Tennis Center . . . . . . . . .**19**
Quinta Real . . . . . . . . . .**44**
Suites Alba . . . . . . . . . .**10**
Suites Etel . . . . . . . . . . . .**5**
Villas Ukae Kim . . . . . . . .**2**
Villa Vera . . . . . . . . . . .**23**

*Plaza, Costera* ☎ *744/485–3982* ✉ *Av. Costera Miguel Alemán 3111, next to Oceanic 2000, Costera* ☎ *744/484–8440* ☐ *MC, V.*

## Italian

**$$–$$$** ✕ **Mezzanotte.** You may end up dancing with your waiter—perhaps atop a table—on a Friday or Saturday evening; you'll definitely end up mixing with the who's who of Acapulco just about any night of the week. The stylish interior has a large sunken dining area, original sculptures, and huge bay windows looking out to sea. Clients rave about the fettuccine with smoked salmon in avocado sauce and the charcoal-grilled sea bass with shrimp and artichokes in a citrus sauce. For a light ending to your meal, try the gelato. Music videos are projected on large screens on weekends. ✉ *Carretera Escénica 28–1, in La Vista shopping center, Costera* ☎ *744/446–5727* ☐ *AE, MC, V* ⊘ *No lunch.*

## Japanese

**$$$–$$$$** ✕ **Suntory.** You can dine either in a blessedly air-conditioned room or in the delightful Asian-style garden. It's one of Acapulco's few Japanese restaurants and one of the few deluxe places that's open for lunch. Many diners opt for the *teppanyaki* (thin slices of beef and vegetables seared on a hot grill), prepared at your table by skilled chefs. Rib eye and seafood have been added to the menu. ✉ *Av. Costera Miguel Alemán 36, across from La Palapa hotel, Costera* ☎ *744/484–8088* ☐ *AE, MC, V.*

## Mexican

**$–$$$$** ✕ **Zapata, Villa y Cia.** The music and the food are strictly local, and the memorabilia recalls the Mexican Revolution—guns, hats, and photographs of Pancho Villa. Often the evening's highlight is a visit from a sombrero-wearing baby burro, so be sure to bring your camera. The menu includes the ever-popular fajitas, tacos, and grilled meats. ✉ *Hyatt Regency Acapulco, Av. Costera Miguel Alemán 1, Costera* ☎ *744/469–1234* ☐ *AE, DC, MC, V* ⊘ *No lunch.*

★ **$–$$$** ✕ **Zorrito's.** When Julio Iglesias is in town, he heads to this open-air, streetside eatery after the discos close. It's open almost all the time, serving Acapulco's famous green-and-white *pozole* (pork and hominy soup) as well as such steak dishes as *filete tampiqueña* (a strip of tender grilled beef), which comes with tacos, enchiladas, guacamole, and beans. ✉ *Av. Costera Miguel Alemán and Calle Anton de Alaminos, next to Banamex, Costera* ☎ *744/485–3735* ☐ *MC, V* ⊘ *Closed 7 AM–9 AM Mon. and Wed.–Sun and 7 AM–2 PM Tues.*

**$–$$** ✕ **El Cabrito.** As the name implies, goat is a specialty of this restaurant—here it's served charcoal-grilled. You can also choose from among such truly Mexican dishes as chicken in *mole* (spicy chocolate-chili sauce); shrimp in tequila; and jerky with egg, fish, and seafood. Top it off with a cold beer or glass of wine. ✉ *Av. Costera Miguel Alemán, between CiCi and Centro Internacional, Costera* ☎ *744/484–7711* ☐ *MC, V.*

## Seafood

**$$–$$$$** ✕ **El Faro.** Classy El Faro resembles a lighthouse, right down to its nautical interior, with portholes and gleaming sculptures that evoke anchors and waves. Spanish chef Jorge Pereira adds Basque and Mediterranean touches to his original creations. For starters, there's a lettuce salad with goat cheese, dried wild fruits, and herb-infused olive oil. Favorite main dishes are haddock with clams and seared tuna medallions with baby onions. ⊠ *Elcano hotel, Av. Costera Miguel Alemán 75, Costera* ☎ *744/ 484–3100* ⊟ *AE, MC, V.*

$–$$$$ ✕ **Beto's.** By day you can eat right on the beach and enjoy live music; by night this palapa-roof restaurant is transformed into a romantic dining area lighted by candles and paper lanterns. Whole red snapper, lobster, and ceviche are recommended. California clams with lime and Tabasco sauce have been added. Live jazz music makes the place more appealing during the high season. At the Barra Vieja beach branch, the specialty is pescado à la talla. ⊠ *Av. Costera Miguel Alemán at Playa Condesa, Costera* ☎ *744/484–0473* ⊠ *Barra Vieja* ☎ *744/444–6071* ⊟ *AE, MC, V.*

★ $–$$$$ ✕ **Pipo's.** On a rather quiet stretch of the Costera, this old, family-run restaurant doesn't have an especially interesting view, but locals come here for the fresh fish, good service, and reasonable prices for most dishes. Try the *huachinango veracruzano* (red snapper baked with tomatoes, peppers, onion, and olives) or the fillet of fish in *mojo de ajo* (garlic butter). The original location downtown is also popular with locals. ⊠ *Av. Costera Miguel Alemán and Nao Victoria, across from Acapulco International Center, Costera* ☎ *744/484–0165* ⊠ *Calle Almirante Bretón 3, Old Acapulco* ☎ *744/482–2237* ⊟ *AE, MC, V.*

## Old Acapulco

### Continental

$$$–$$$$ ✕ **Coyuca 22.** This may well be Acapulco's most beautiful restaurant. You sit gazing down on Doric pillars, statuary, an enormous illuminated obelisk, a small pool, and the bay beyond; it's like eating in a partially restored Greek ruin. Choose from two fixed menus or order à la carte; all dishes are artful. Seafood and prime rib are specialties. ⊠ *Av. Coyuca 22 (10-min taxi ride from the zócalo), Old Acapulco* ☎ *744/482–3468 or 744/483–5030* ⚓ *Reservations essential* ⊟ *AE, MC, V* ☺ *No lunch. Closed Apr. 30–Nov. 1.*

### Mexican

$–$$$ ✕ **La Casa de Tere.** Hidden in a commercial district downtown (signs point the way), this spotless, open-air eatery with the pink walls is in a league of its own—expect beer-hall tables and chairs, colorful Mexican decorations, and photos of Acapulco of yore. The varied menu includes outstanding *sopa de tortilla* (tortilla soup), chicken mole, and flan. ⊠ *Calle Alonso Martín 1721, 2 blocks from Av. Costera Miguel Alemán, Old Acapulco* ☎ *744/485–7735* ⊟ *No credit cards* ☺ *Closed Mon.*

### Seafood

$–$$$ ✕ **La Cabaña.** In the 1950s, this local favorite was a bohemian hangout that attracted renowned bullfighters along with Mexican songwriter Agustín Lara and his lady love, María Félix. You can see their photo over the bar and sample the same dishes that made the place famous back then: baby-shark tamales, seafood casserole, or shrimp prepared with sea salt, curry, or garlic. The restaurant is smack in the middle of Playa Caleta, and there are free lockers for diners who want to take a swim, as well as banana and wave-runner rentals. ⊠ *Playa Caleta Lado*

*Ote. s/n, Fracc. las Playas (a 5-min taxi ride east of town square), Old Acapulco* ☎ *744/482–5007* ⊟ *AE, MC, V.*

**$–$$**  ✕ **El Amigo Miguel.** Locals rave about this place and keep it abuzz at all hours. The seafood is fresh, the portions are ample and well-priced, and it's in a convenient downtown location right off the zócalo. A second-floor balcony provides a view of the bay. Feast on fish soup, whole grilled sea bass, fish fillet in a buttery garlic sauce or lobster. All come with sides of rice and warm bread. ⊠ *Calle Benito Juarez 31, at Calle Anzueta, Old Acapulco* ☎ *744/483–6981* ⊟ *MC, V.*

# WHERE TO STAY

Acapulco Diamante is home to hotels so lush and well equipped that most guests don't budge from the minute they arrive. Farther along towards the airport, there are the divinely luxurious hotels along the Playa Revolcadero beach; the water there is too rough for swimming but the heart of Acapulco is only a 25-minute, $14 taxi ride away.

There's much more activity on Avenida Costera Miguel Alemán, with its many discos, shops, and restaurants. All the Costera properties have freshwater pools and sundecks, and most have restaurants and/or bars overlooking, or on, the beach. Hotels across the street are almost always less expensive than those directly on the beach; because there are no private beaches in Acapulco—or anywhere in Mexico, for that matter—all you have to do is cross the road to enjoy the sand.

Downtown Acapulco's beaches and restaurants are popular with Mexican vacationers. The hotels attract Canadian and European bargain-hunters. To the west, Pie de la Cuesta is peppered with nondescript inns and cute rustic lodges, where a beachside location might just be more a common characteristic than hot running water. For nightlife or shopping, you'll have to go into Acapulco proper.

Wherever you stay, prices will be reasonable compared with those in the United States. Service is generally good as well: Acapulqueños have been catering to visitors for more than half a century.

| WHAT IT COSTS | | | | |
| --- | --- | --- | --- | --- |
| **$$$$** | **$$$** | **$$** | **$** | **¢** |
| LODGING    over $250 | $150–$250 | $75–$150 | $50–$75 | under $50 |

*Price categories are assigned based on the range between the least and most expensive standard double rooms in high season based on the European Plan (EP, with no meals) unless otherwise noted. Tax (17%) is extra.*

## Acapulco Diamante

★ **$$$$**  ▣ **Camino Real Acapulco Diamante.** This stunning hotel is at the foot of a lush hill on exclusive Playa Pichilingue, far from the madding crowd. All rooms are done in pastels and have tile floors, luxurious baths, and such up-to-date amenities as laptop-size safes outfitted with chargers; all rooms also have balconies or terraces with a view of peaceful Puerto

Marqués bay. Eleven extra-spacious club rooms have their own concierge and extra amenities. ⊠ *Calle Baja Catita (off Carretera Escénica at Km 14), Acapulco Diamante 39867* ☎ *744/466–1010, 800/722–6466 in the U.S.* ☐ *744/466–1111* ⊕ *www.caminoreal.com/acapulco* ➪ *145 rooms, 11 suites* ⌂ *3 restaurants, room service, in-room safes, minibars, cable TV, golf privileges, tennis court, 3 pools, gym, spa, beach, snorkeling, boating, waterskiing, fishing, 2 bars, baby-sitting, children's programs (ages 5–15), laundry service, concierge, Internet, meeting room, car rental, travel services, no-smoking rooms* ☐ *AE, DC, MC, V.*

$$$$
Fodor'sChoice
★

**Fairmont Acapulco Princess.** The Princess is one of those places that seems to lure the rich and famous (Howard Hughes once hid away in a suite here). Near the reception desk, fantastic ponds with waterfalls and a slatted bridge hint at the luxury throughout. Large, airy rooms have cane furniture, marble floors, and such high-tech features as wireless Internet access. You can dine in seven excellent restaurants, and get in a match at the tennis center, which hosts international tournaments. The superb spa, open to guests and nonguests, has aromatherapy, thalassotherapy, body wraps, and other treatments as well as a fitness center, hair salon, Jacuzzi, sauna, and Swiss showers. ⊠ *Playa Revolcadero, Revolcadero* ☎ *A.P. 1351, 39300* ☎ *744/469–1000, 800/441–1414 in the U.S.* ☐ *744/469–1016* ⊕ *www.fairmont.com* ➪ *927 rooms, 92 suites* ⌂ *6 restaurants, café, room service, in-room safes, cable TV, 36-hole golf course, 11 tennis courts, 5 pools, health club, hair salon, spa, beach, snorkeling, boating, waterskiing, fishing, basketball, 3 bars, dance club, shops, baby-sitting, children's programs (ages 3–12), laundry service, concierge, Internet, business services, meeting room, car rental, travel services* ☐ *AE, DC, MC, V* ⍾⊙⍾ *BP, EP.*

★ $$$$

**Fairmont Pierre Marqués.** You're doubly blessed if you stay at this hotel, which was built as a beach hideaway for J. Paul Getty in 1958: you have access to all the Fairmont Acapulco Princess's facilities *and* peace and quiet. There's a hint of hacienda here, with the red-tile roofs, natural wood furniture, and ceiling fans. Choose from standard rooms, executive premier (with small refrigerators) rooms, suites, villas, and duplex bungalows (with private patios). ⊠ *Playa Revolcadero, Revolcadero* ☎ *A. P. 1351, 39907* ☎ *744/466–1000, 800/441–1414 in the U.S.* ☐ *744/ 466–1046* ⊕ *www.fairmont.com* ➪ *220 rooms, 74 executive premier rooms, 25 suites, 10 villas* ⌂ *2 restaurants, room service, in-room safes, minibars, some refrigerators, cable TV, 36-hole golf course, 5 tennis courts, 3 pools, beach, bar, shops, baby-sitting, children's programs (ages 3–12), playground, laundry service, concierge, meeting room, car rental, travel services* ☐ *AE, DC, MC, V* ⍾⊙⍾ *BP, EP.*

$$$$

**Quinta Real.** A member of Mexico's most prestigious hotel chain, this low-slung hillside resort overlooks the sea, about a 15-minute drive from downtown. The 74 suites have balconies, marble floors, Mexican-made hardwood furniture, earth-tone rugs and fabrics, and closet door handles shaped like iguanas—a signature motif. The lovely beach is seemingly endless. ⊠ *Paseo de la Quinta Lote 6, Desarrollo Turmstico Real Diamante, Acapulco Diamante 39907* ☎ *744/469–1500, 800/457–4000 in the U.S.* ☐ *744/469–1515* ⊕ *www.quintareal.com* ➪ *74 suites* ⌂ *Restaurant, room service, cable TV, 4 pools, gym, spa, beach, snorkel-*

*ing, boating, fishing, bar, baby-sitting, laundry service, concierge, Internet, car rental* ⊟ *AE, MC, V.*

**$$$–$$$$** 🏨 **Las Brisas.** This hilltop haven is particularly popular with honeymooners. The complex has a variety of quarters—from one-bedroom units to deluxe private casitas complete with small private pools—that all have beautiful bay views. As the facilities are very spread out, transportation is by pink-and-white golf cart, though the wait can be up to 20 minutes. For tooling around town, you can rent the hotel's signature pink-and-white Jeep for $75 a day. A stylish Continental breakfast is delivered to your room each morning. ⊠ *Carretera Escénica 5255, Las Brisas, 39868* ☎ *744/469–6900, 888/559–4329 in the U.S. and Canada* 🖷 *744/484–2269* ⊕ *www.brisas.com.mx* ⤣ *300 units* ♦ *2 restaurants, in-room data ports, 5 tennis courts, 3 pools, exercise equipment, hair salon, hot tub, sauna, snorkeling, boating, fishing, 2 bars, dry cleaning, laundry service, concierge, Internet, meeting room, car rental, travel services* ⊟ *AE, MC, V* ⓞ| *CP.*

## The Costera

**$$$$** 🏨 **Hyatt Regency Acapulco.** The Hyatt is popular with business travelers, conventioneers, and—thanks to its bold Caribbean color schemes and striking design—television producers, who have opted to use it as the setting for many a Mexican soap opera. It has everything you need and more, including four outstanding eateries (one of them a kosher restaurant), a spa, and a deluxe shopping area. It's also the only hotel in Latin America with an on-site synagogue. The west side of the property insulates you from the noise of the maneuvers of the nearby naval base. ⊠ *Av. Costera Miguel Alemán 1, Costera 39869* ☎ *744/469–1234, 800/633–7313 in the U.S. and Canada* 🖷 *744/484–3087* ⊕ *www.hyatt.com* ⤣ *607 rooms, 17 suites* ♦ *4 restaurants, snack bar, room service, in-room safes, minibars, cable TV, 5 tennis courts, 2 pools, gym, spa, beach, 3 bars, shops, baby-sitting, children's programs (ages 8–12) in high season only, laundry service, business services, Internet, meeting room, car rental, travel services, free parking* ⊟ *AE, MC, V.*

**★ $$$** 🏨 **Elcano.** Restored so that it has its original 1950s glamour, this perennial favorite is sparkling and fresh. Rooms are snappy in white and navy blue, with white-tile floors and modern bathrooms. There's a beachside restaurant with an outstanding breakfast buffet, a more elegant indoor restaurant, and a gorgeous pool that not only seems to float above the bay, but also has whirlpools built into its corners. ⊠ *Av. Costera Miguel Alemán 75, Costera 39690* ☎ *744/484–1950, 800/972–2162 in the U.S.* 🖷 *744/484–2230* ⊕ *www.hotel-elcano.com* ⤣ *163 rooms, 17 suites* ♦ *2 restaurants, room service, minibars, cable TV, golf privileges, pool, gym, beach, snorkeling, boating, waterskiing, fishing, 2 bars, baby-sitting, laundry service, concierge, travel services* ⊟ *AE, MC, V.*

**$$–$$$** 🏨 **Villa Vera.** A five-minute drive north of the Costera leads to the place where Elizabeth Taylor married Mike Todd and where Lana Turner settled for three years. That said, the glamour of what was once a very exclusive hotel is all in its history. Although some villas were once private homes and have their own pools, most accommodations are unremarkable. There's no beach, so the main pool with its swim-up bar is the hub. The Villa Vera Spa and Fitness Center, open to guests and nonguests, has exercise machines, free weights, milk baths, algae treatments, and massages. ✉ *Calle Lomas del Mar 35, Costera* ✆ *A.P. 560, 39690* ☎ *744/484–0333 or 888/554–2361* 🖶 *744/484–7479* ⊕ *www. clubregina.com* ⤹ *24 rooms, 25 suites, 6 villas* △ *Restaurant, minibars, cable TV, in-room VCRs, 4 tennis courts, 15 pools, fitness classes, gym, spa, bar, shop, laundry service, Internet, concierge, meeting room, car rental, travel services* ▤ *AE, MC, V.*

**$$** 🏨 **Avalon Excalibur Acapulco.** Suits of armor in the lobby evoke medieval Europe, but the beach, bouncy bars, and flirty, open-air restaurant epitomize Acapulco. Everything—from the floors to the furnishings—is fresh. Rooms have two queen-size beds, dark-wood furniture, pale rose and white walls, and private terraces. Late in the afternoon, many guests head to the bar for a two-for-one happy hour followed by a karaoke session. ✉ *Av. Costera Miguel Alemán 163, Costera 39670* ☎ *744/485– 5050, 800/261–5014 in the U.S. and Canada* 🖶 *998/883–2173* ⊕ *www. avalonvacations.com* ⤹ *400 rooms, 20 suites* △ *2 restaurants, room service, in-room safes, cable TV, tennis court, 2 pools, gym, bicycle rental, beach, snorkeling, boating, jet skiing, parasailing, water skiing, 2 bars, shops, baby-sitting, children's program (4–10), laundry service, concierge, meeting room, car rental, travel services, parking (fee)* ▤ *AE, MC, V.*

**$$** 🏨 **Fiesta Americana Condesa Acapulco.** As it's in the thick of the main shopping and restaurant district, the Condesa is popular with tour groups and singles. It also has a very lively lobby bar and is on Playa Condesa, one of the best and most popular beaches in town. Rooms are done in pastel tones and have light-wood furniture and tile floors. ✉ *Av. Costera Miguel Alemán 97, Costera 39690* ☎ *744/484–2828, 800/343–7821 in the U.S.* 🖶 *744/484–1828* ⊕ *www.fiestaamericana.com* ⤹ *492 rooms, 8 suites* △ *2 restaurants, room service, minibars, cable TV, 2 pools, beach, parasailing, waterskiing, bar, shop, baby-sitting, children's programs (ages 4–12), dry cleaning, laundry service, concierge, business services, meeting room, car rental, travel services* ▤ *AE, MC, V.*

**$$** 🏨 **Las Hamacas.** Rooms at this friendly 1950s Acapulco hotel surround a large inner courtyard. It's across the street from the beach, a three-minute drive from downtown, and it has a lovely garden of coconut palms from its former days as a plantation. The spacious, light-filled rooms have contemporary wood furniture; those facing the leafy courtyard are tranquil. Junior suites sleep two adults and two children. A stay here gets you access to a beach club. ✉ *Av. Costera Miguel Alemán, Costera 39670* ☎ *744/483–7006* 🖶 *744/483–0575* ⊕ *www.hamacas.com.mx* ⤹ *107 rooms, 20 suites* △ *Restaurant, room service, cable TV, golf privileges, 2 pools, hair salon, paddle tennis, Ping-Pong, bar, shop, baby sitting, laundry services, Internet, meeting room, travel services, free parking* ▤ *AE, MC, V.*

**$$** 🏨 **Park Hotel & Tennis Center.** A helpful staff, a savvy Bulgarian manager, and a prime location make this an appealing place to stay. Rooms, which have colonial-style furnishings are around a garden with a good-size pool. Some have kitchenettes and balconies; all are spotlessly clean and well priced. The Park has an excellent tennis center, and it's only a block to the beach. ✉ *Av. Costera Miguel Alemán 127, Costera* ✆ *A. P. 269, 39690* ☎ *744/485–5992* 🖶 *744/485–5489* ⊕ *www.parkhotel-*

*acapulco.com* 🗝 *88 rooms* 👌 *Cable TV, 3 tennis courts, pool, bar, shops, car rental, free parking* 🖃 *MC, V.*

## Old Acapulco

**$$** 🏨 **Boca Chica.** German visitors love this Old Acapulco mainstay, right down to its antique switchboard. It's a few steps from a swimming cove, and the open-air lobby has lovely views of Bahía de Caletilla. Rooms are small—with old-fashioned slats on the door, little balconies, and nondescript furnishings—but they're very clean and fresh. The palapa restaurant serves 20 varieties of sushi; there's also a landscaped jungle garden and a pool. The Mexican breakfasts are ample. ✉ *Playa Caletilla, across the bay from Isla la Roqueta and Mágico Mundo Marino, Old Acapulco 39390* ☎ *744/483–6601 or 744/483–6388, 800/346–3942 in the U.S.* 🖷 *744/483–9513* ⊕ *www.acapulco-bocachica.com* 🗝 *42 rooms, 3 suites* 👌 *Restaurant, pool, beach, dive shop, snorkeling, fishing, bar, shops, laundry service, car rental, free parking* 🖃 *MC, V* ⍾ *BP.*

★ **$$** 🏨 **Los Flamingos.** Almost a historical monument, this hot-pink, cliff-side hotel was the favored hangout of John Wayne, Johnny ("Tarzan") Weissmuller, and the rest of the gang from Hollywood back in the 1950s. Today it draws Europeans for its fine views and its *coco locos*, (tequila drinks served in a green coconut, Acapulco's signature concoctions), which barman Esteban Castañeda will tell you were invented here in the 1960s. Rooms have bright pink walls and spartan, shower-only baths. Weissmuller liked to stay in the circular two-bedroom master suite. The hotel provides free transportation to the beach and downtown. ✉ *Av. López Mateos, Fracc. las Playas, Old Acapulco 39390* ☎ *744/482–0690* 🖷 *744/483–9806* ⊕ *www.acapulco-hotels-online.com* 🗝 *46 rooms, 2 suites* 👌 *Restaurant, pool, bar, laundry service, free parking; no a/c in some rooms* 🖃 *MC, V.*

**$$** 🏨 **El Mirador.** With its white walls, red-tile roofs, and hand-carved Mexican furnishings, El Mirador exudes nostalgia. It's on a hill with a knockout view of Bahía de Acapulco and La Quebrada, where the cliff divers perform. Many suites have refrigerators, hot tubs, and stunning ocean vistas. ✉ *Av. Quebrada 74, Old Acapulco 39300* ☎ *744/483–1155, 800/342–2644 in the U.S.* 🖷 *744/482–4564* ⊕ *www.acapulco-mexico.com* 🗝 *133 rooms, 9 suites* 👌 *2 restaurants, minibars, some refrigerators, cable TV, 3 pools (1 saltwater), hair salon, sauna, bar, shops, children's programs (ages 3–12), laundry service, meeting room, travel services, free parking* 🖃 *AE, MC, V.*

**$$** 🏨 **Suites Alba.** On a quiet hillside, the Alba is an all-white, all-suites hotel that's popular with families. All guest quarters sleep four, six, or eight and have terraces; some have kitchenettes. A cable car to the hotel's beach club, which is on the bay and next to the Club de Yates and its 330-foot-long toboggan run, is available for guests with disabilities. ✉ *Grand Via Tropical 35, Old Acapulco 39390* ☎ *744/483–0073, 877/428–1327 in Canada* 🖷 *744/483–8378* ⊕ *www.acapulcohotelmexico.com* 🗝 *247 suites* 👌 *Restaurant, some kitchenettes, 4 pools, hot tub, beach, bar, shops, laundry service* 🖃 *MC, V.*

**$** 🏨 **Misión.** Two minutes from the zócalo, this charming, colonial-style hotel surrounds a greenery-rich courtyard with an outdoor dining area that's only open for breakfast. Rooms are small and by no means fancy, with wrought-iron beds, tile floors, painted brick walls, and ceiling fans. Every room has a shower, and there's plenty of hot water. The best rooms are on the second and third floors as you can open the windows and fully appreciate the view; the top-floor room is large but hot in the daytime. ⊠ *Calle Felipe Valle 12, Downtown 39300* ☎ *744/482–3643* 🖶 *744/482–2076* ➫ *20 rooms* ⚿ *Fans; no a/c, no room TVs, no room phones* ⊟ No credit cards.

$ 🏨 **Suites Etel.** On Cerro Pinzona (Pinzona Hill), a five-minute walk from La Quebrada, the Etel has outstanding views of Bahía de Acapulco and spacious rooms with sturdy cedar furniture. All accommodations sleep three, and you can rent a full kitchen and dining room to turn your room into a suite. One studio has a kitchenette. There's a garden on the roof and children's play area by the pool. The owner, gracious Senora Etel Alvarez, is the great-grand-niece of John August Suter, whose gold mine launched the Gold Rush of 1849. ⊠ *Av. Pinzona 92, Old Acapulco 39390* ☎ *744/482–2240* 🖶 *744/482–2241* ➫ *12 rooms* ⚿ *Fans, some kitchenettes, cable TV, pool, fishing, car rental* ⊟ No credit cards.

## Pie de la Cuesta

$$$$ 🏨 **Parador del Sol.** Germans and Canadians favor this all-inclusive resort's pink villas scattered throughout gardens along both the lagoon and the Pacific Ocean sides of Carretera Pie de la Cuesta. The ocean is particularly dramatic here with towering waves. The spacious rooms have tile floors and fan-cooled terraces with hammocks. In addition to all meals and domestic drinks, rates include shows, dance and aerobics classes, tennis, and nonmotorized water sports. Motorized water sports cost extra. ⊠ *Carretera Pie de la Cuesta–Barra de Coyuca, Km 5, Pie de la Cuesta* 🕿 *A.P. 1070, 39300* ☎ *744/444–4050* 🖶 *744/444–4214* ⊕ *www. paradordelsol.com.mx* ➫ *150 rooms* ⚿ *Restaurant, fans, cable TV, 4 tennis courts, 2 pools, fitness classes, gym, fishing, soccer, volleyball, 3 bars, dance club, shops, laundry service, meeting rooms, free parking* ⊟ *AE, DC, MC, V* ⫱⊙⫲ All-inclusive.

★ $ 🏨 **Hacienda Vayma.** Congenial host Parwin runs the Vayma with European flair. White stucco bungalows named for musicians and painters line the beach. The plain rooms accommodate two, three, or five people and have huge beds protected by mosquito nets; bathrooms are tiny, and there's no hot water. Suites overlook the ocean and have hot water, hot tubs, a/c, and terraces. The spa has the largest pool in Pie de la Cuesta. Rates spike on weekends when the hotel fills with embassy personnel from Mexico City. ⊠ *Av. Fuerza Aereo Mexicana 356, Pie de la Cuesta 39300* ☎ *744/460–2882* 🖶 *744/460–0697* ✑ *www.vayma@vayma.com. mx* ➫ *20 rooms, 4 suites* ⚿ *Restaurant, fans, pool, hot tub, massage, spa, beach, waterskiing, bocce, horseback riding, volleyball, bar, shop, laundry service, free parking, some pets allowed; no a/c in some rooms, no room phones* ⊟ No credit cards.

¢ 🏨 **Villas Ukae Kim.** You can't miss this colorful, rustic, seaside lodge. The large rooms are painted in bright Mexican hues, and all have terraces and mosquito nets slung over double beds; the honeymoon suite has a private hot tub. ⊠ *Av. Fuerza Aereo Mexicana 356, Pie de la Cuesta*

*39300* 🏨 *744/460–2187* 🛏 *21 rooms, 1 suite* ☖ *Restaurant, fans, pool, beach, waterskiing, fishing, bar, laundry service, free parking; no a/c in some rooms, no room phones, no room TVs* ☰ No credit cards.

# NIGHTLIFE

**Alebrije** (✉ Av. Costera Miguel Alemán 3308, across from Hyatt Regency, Costera ☎ 744/484–5902) can accommodate 5,000 people in its love seats and booths. From 10:30 (opening time) to 11:30, the music is slow and romantic; afterward there's dance music and light shows until dawn. The music ranges from pop to tropical. **O Bleu** (✉ Av. Costera Miguel Alemán 15, at Fragata Yucatán, Costera ☎ 744/484–8815) is entered via a torch-lit moat that leads to the Queen of the Sea's castle; inside, you feel as if you're in a submarine surrounded by mermaids. The place is packed with 18- to 25-year-olds dancing to the latest pop and pop Latino sounds. It's open Wednesday–Sunday from December to April and on weekends only May to November.

**Baby O** (✉ Av. Costera Miguel Alemán 22, Costera ☎ 744/484–7474) is a private club that's known to open its doors to select nonmembers. (You can make a reservation through the hotel concierge). Eschewing the glitz and mirrors of Acapulco's older discos, it resembles a jungle cave. The crowd is 25 to 35 and mostly well-dressed, wealthy Mexi-
★ cans. It's closed Monday to Wednesday in low season. **Cielo Congela** (✉ Carretera Escénica, Costera ☎ 744/484–7164) has lavish mirrors and white walls that make it seem like an ice palace; things heat up quickly, though, thanks to the fantastic sound and light systems. The club accommodates 700 at a central bar and in comfortable booths; a glass wall provides an unbelievable view of Bahía de Acapulco. The music is enough of a mix to make everybody happy; it all starts at 10:30.

As its name suggests **Discobeach** (✉ Playa Condesa, Costera ☎ 744/484–8230) is right on the sands. It's so informal that the under-30 crowd even turns up in shorts. The waiters are young and friendly—some people find them overly so, and in fact, this is a legendary pickup spot. Every Wednesday, ladies' night, all the women receive flowers. During the day,
★ you can try the bungee jump on the beach. At **Palladium** (✉ Carretera Escénica, Costera ☎ 744/446–5490) a waterfall cascades down from the dance-floor level. The dance floor itself is surrounded by 50-foot-high windows, giving dancers a wraparound view of Acapulco.

**Salon Q** (✉ Av. Costera Miguel Alemán 23, Costera ☎ 744/481–0114), the so-called Cathedral of Salsa, is a combination dance hall and disco, where the bands play salsas, merengues, and other Latin rhythms for young and old. Weekends see shows—mostly impersonations of Mex-
★ ican entertainers. **Zucca** (✉ Carretera Escénica, Costera ☎ 744/484–6727), a snug place, attracts a 25-and-older crowd, mainly couples. People really dress up here, with the men in well-cut pants and shirts and the women in racy outfits and cocktail dresses. Patrons dance to music from the '70s, '80s, and '90s. It's open at 11 PM Wednesday through Saturday during high season and Thursday to Saturday in low season.

# SPORTS & THE OUTDOORS

## Bullfights

The season runs from about the first week of January to Easter, and *corridas* (bullfights) are held on Sunday at 5:30. Tickets are available through your hotel or at the window in the **Plaza de Toros** (⊠ Av. Circunvalación, Playa Caleta ☎ 744/482–1181) Monday–Saturday 10–2 and Sunday 10:30–5. Tickets in the shade (*sombra*)—the only way to go—cost about $22. Preceding the fight are performances of Spanish dances and music by the Chili Frito band.

## Fishing

You can arrange trips through your hotel or at the Pesca Deportiva near the *muelle* (dock) across from the zócalo (be sure to ask someone at your hotel about which companies are reliable). For freshwater trips try the companies along Laguna Coyuca. Boats accommodating 4–10 people cost $250–$500 a day, $45–$60 by chair. Excursions leave about 7 AM and return at 1 PM or 2 PM. At the docks, you can hire a boat for $40 a day (two lines). You must get a license ($8–$10, depending on the season) from the Secretaría de Pesca; there's a representative at the dock, but note that the office is closed during siesta, between 2 and 4.

## Golf

There's a public golf course at the **Club de Golf** (☎ 744/484–0781) on the Costera across from the Acapulco Malibú hotel. Greens fees are $40 for nine holes, $60 for 18. A 36-hole championship golf course is shared by the **Fairmont Acapulco Princess and Pierre Marqués hotels** (⊠ Playa Revolcadero, Revolcadero ☎ 744/469–1000). Make reservations well in advance. Greens fees are $93 for guests and $110 for nonguests. A round on the 18-hole course at the **Mayan Palace** (⊠ Playa Revolcadero, domicilio conocido, Revolcadero ☎ 744/469–6000) time-share condo complex is $66 for guests, $103 for nonguests. At **Tres Vidas** (⊠ Carretera al Aeropuerto, domicilio conocido, Tres Vidas ☎ 744/444–5135), greens fees are $180 for 18 holes before 2 PM, $150 afterward but only guests from the Fairmont Princess, Fairmont Pierre Marques, and Las Brisas hotels can play as non-members.

## Tennis

Court fees range from $9 to $26 an hour during the day and double in the evening. At hotel courts, nonguests pay about $6 more per hour. Lessons start at about $15 an hour; ball boys get a $2 tip. **Costa Club** (⊠ Costera ☎ 744/485–9050) has three hard-surface courts, two lighted. In addition to five outdoor courts, the **Fairmont Acapulco Princess** (⊠ Playa Revolcadero, Revolcadero ☎ 744/469–1000) has two air-conditioned synthetic-grass, lighted indoor courts and a stadium that hosts international tournaments. The **Fairmont Pierre Marqués** (⊠ Playa Revolcadero, Revolcadero ☎ 744/466–1000) has five synthetic-grass lighted courts.

Guests at the **Hyatt Regency Acapulco** (⊠ Av. Costera Miguel Alemán 1, Costera ☎ 744/484–1225) have access to three hard-surface lighted courts at the Municipal Golf Club. The **Mayan Palace** (⊠ Playa Revolcadero, domicilio conocido, Revolcadero ☎ 744/469–1879) condo complex has 12 lighted clay courts. There are three lighted asphalt courts at the **Park Hotel & Tennis Center** (⊠ Av. Costera Miguel Alemán 127, Costera ☎ 744/485–5992). You'll find five courts at **Tiffany's Racquet Club** (⊠ Av. Villa Vera 120, Costera ☎ 744/484–7949). Some are asphalt and have lights, others are clay and don't. **Villa Vera** (⊠ Lomas del Mar 35, Costera ☎ 744/484–0333) has two lighted clay courts and two lighted hard-surface courts.

## Water Sports

You can arrange to water-ski, rent broncos (one-person Jet Skis), parasail, and windsurf at outfitters on the beaches. Parasailing is an Acapulco highlight; a five-minute trip costs $60. Waterskiing is about $40 an hour; broncos cost $40–$95 for a half hour, depending on the size. You can arrange to windsurf at Playa Caleta and most beaches along the Costera, but the best place to actually do it is at Bahía Puerto Marqués. The main surfing beach is Revolcadero.

**Hermanos Arnold (Arnold Brothers)** (⊠ Av. Costera Miguel Alemán 205, near El Fuerte de San Diego, Old Acapulco ☎ 744/482–0788) is affiliated with the Asociación Mexican Subacuatico (Mexican Subaquatic Association) and has been running scuba-diving excursions and snorkeling trips for almost 50 years. Scuba trips cost $35; snorkeling costs $20. Lessons are included.

The **Shotover Jet** (⊠ Continental Plaza, Av. Costera Miguel Alemán, Locale 3, Costera ☎ 744/484–1154) is a wild boat ride that's an import from the rivers around Queenstown, New Zealand. An air-conditioned bus takes you to the Pierre Marques Lagoon, about 20 minutes from downtown Acapulco. Twelve-passenger boats provide thrilling 30-minute boat rides on the lagoon, complete with 360-degree turns—one of the Shotover Jet's trademarks—and vistas of local flora and fauna. The cost for the ride and transportation to and from the site is $35. For more thrills, you can shoot the rapids for $50 for an hour-and-a-half to two hours with a guide; there's a four-person minimum.

# SHOPPING

Most shops are open Monday–Saturday 10–7. The main strip is along Avenida Costera Miguel Alemán from the Costa Club to El Presidente Hotel. Here you can find Guess, Peer, Aca Joe, Amarras, Polo Ralph Lauren, and other fashionable sportswear boutiques. The Costera is also home to branches of Aurrerá, Gigante, Price Club, Sam's, Wal-Mart, and Comercial Mexicana, as well as the upscale Liverpool department store (called Fabricas de Francia). These sell everything from liquor and fresh and frozen food to light bulbs, clothing, medicines, garden furniture, and sports equipment. Old Acapulco has inexpensive tailors, patronized by the Mexicans, and lots of souvenir shops.

Sanborns (⊠ Av. Costera Miguel Alemán 1226, Costera ☎ 744/484–4413 ⊠ Av. Costera Miguel Alemán 3111, Costera ☎ 744/484–2025 ⊠ Av. Costera Miguel Alemán 209, Costera ☎ 744/482–6167 ⊠ Av. Costera Miguel Alemán, off zócalo Old Acapulco ☎ 744/482–6168) is a very un-Mexican store that is, nevertheless, an institution throughout Mexico. Among its wares are English-language newspapers, magazines, and books, as well as high-quality souvenirs. All branches are open 7 AM to midnight in high season and 7:30 AM–11 PM the rest of the year.

## Malls

**Aca Mall,** which is next door to Marbella Mall, is all white and marble and filled with the likes of Tommy Hilfiger, Peer, and Aca Joe. The multilevel **Marbella Mall,** at the Diana *glorieta* (traffic circle), is home to Martí, a sporting-goods store; a health center (drugstore, clinic, and lab); the Canadian Embassy; Bing's Ice Cream; and several restaurants. **Plaza Bahía,** next to the Costa Club hotel, is an air-conditioned mall with boutiques such as Dockers, Nautica, and Aspasia.

## Markets

To get the itinerant vendors off the beaches and streets, the local government set up flea markets along the Costera, mostly uninviting dark tunnels of stalls that sell inexpensive souvenirs. The artifact replicas, bamboo wind chimes, painted wooden birds, shell earrings, and embroidered clothes begin to look identical. Although prices are low, it's good to comparison shop; bargaining is essential.

One large flea market with a convenient location is **La Diana Mercado de Artesanías,** a block from the Emporio hotel, close to the Diana monument in Costera. **El Mercado de Artesanías El Parazal** is a 15-minute walk from Sanborns downtown. Look for fake ceremonial masks, the ever-present onyx chessboards, $20 hand-embroidered dresses, imitation silver, hammocks, and skin cream made from turtles (don't buy it, because turtles are endangered and you won't get it through U.S. Customs). From Sanborns downtown, head away from Avenida Costera to Vásquez de León and turn right one block later. The market is open daily 9–9. Don't miss the **Mercado Municipal,** where restaurateurs load up on produce early in the morning, and, later in the day, locals shop for piñatas, serapes, leather goods, baskets, hammocks, amulets to attract lovers or ward off enemies, and velvet paintings of the Virgin of Guadalupe.

## Specialty Shops

### Art

**Edith Matison's Art Gallery** (⊠ Av. Costera Miguel Alemán 2010, across from Club de Golf, Costera ☎ 744/484–3084) shows the works of renowned international and Mexican artists—including Calder, Dalí, Siqueiros, and Tamayo—and crafts. **Galería Rudic** (⊠ Calle Vicente Yañez Pinzón 9, across from Continental Plaza and adjoining Jardín des Artistes restaurant, Costera ☎ 744/484–1004) has works by top contemporary Mexican artists, including Armando Amaya, Leonardo Nierman, Gastón Cabrera, Trinidad Osorio, and Casiano García.

**Pal Kepenyes** (✉ Guitarrón 140, Lomas Guitarrón ☎ 744/484–3738) gets good press for his jewelry and sculpture (some of it rather racy), on display in his workshop. **Sergio Bustamente** (✉ Av. Costera Miguel Alemán 120–9, across from Fiesta American Condesa hotel, Costera ☎ 744/484–4992 ✉ Hyatt Regency Acapulco, Av. Costera Miguel Alemán 1, Costera ☎ 744/469–1234) is known for his whimsical, painted papier-mâché and giant ceramic sculptures.

## Clothing

**Armando's** (✉ Hyatt Regency Acapulco, Av. Costera Miguel Alemán 1, Costera ☎ 744/484–5111 ✉ Av. Costera Miguel Alemán 1252–7, in La Torre de Acapulco, Costera ☎ 744/469–1234) sells its own line of women's dresses, jackets, and vests with a Mexican flavor. It also has some interesting Luisa Conti accessories. **Esteban's** (✉ Av. Costera Miguel Alemán 2010, across from Club de Golf, Costera ☎ 744/484–3084) has a clientele of international celebrities and many important local families. Its opulent evening dresses range from $200 to $3,000; daytime dresses average $120. There's a men's clothing section on the second floor. If you scour the sale racks, you can find some items marked down as much as 80%.

**Nautica** (✉ Plaza Bahía, Costera ☎ 744/484–1650 ✉ Las Brisas hotel, Carretera Escénica 5255, Las Brisas ☎ 744/485–7511) is stocked with stylish casual clothing for men. **Men's and Ladies** (✉ Fairmont Acapulco Princess hotel arcade, Playa Revolcadero, Revolcadero ☎ 744/469–1000) has beach cover-ups and hand-painted straw hats, as well as Israeli bathing suits, Colombian sweaters, Walford body wear, and light dresses. **St. Germaine** (✉ Av. Costera Miguel Alemán, at entrance to Fiesta Americana Condesa hotel, Costera ☎ 744/485–2515 ✉ Costa Club, Av. Costera Miguel Alemán 123, Costera ☎ 744/487–3712) sells a sensational line of swimsuits for equally sensational bodies.

## Handicrafts

**Alebrijes & Caracoles** (✉ Plaza Bahía, Costera ☎ 744/485–0490) consists of two shops designed to look like flea-market stalls. Top-quality merchandise includes papier-mâché fruits and vegetables, Christmas ornaments, wind chimes, and brightly painted wooden animals from Oaxaca. **Arte Para Siempre** (✉ Av. Costera Miguel Alemán 4834, near Hyatt Regency Acapulco, Costera ☎ 744/484–3624), in the Acapulco Cultural Center, sparkles with handicrafts from the seven regions of Guerrero. Look for hand-loomed shawls, painted gourds, hammocks, baskets, Olinalá boxes, and silver jewelry.

## Silver & Jewelry

Buy articles described as being made from semiprecious stones or silver only in reputable establishments, lest you end up with cleverly painted paste or a silver facsimile called *alpaca*. Make sure that 0.925 is stamped on the silver piece; this verifies its authenticity.

**Minette** (✉ Fairmont Acapulco Princess hotel arcade, Playa Revolcadero, Revolcadero ☎ 744/469–1000) has diamond jewelry of impeccable design by Charles Garnier and Nouvelle Bague. There's also jewelry set with Caledonia stones from Africa as well as Emilia Castillo's exquisite line of brightly colored porcelain ware, inlaid with silver fish, stars, and birds. **Suzett's** (⊠ Hyatt Regency Acapulco, Av. Costera Miguel Alemán 1, Costera ☎ 744/469–1234), a tony shop that's been around for years, has a laudable selection of gold and silver jewelry. **Tane** (⊠ Las Brisas hotel, Carretera Escénica 5255, Las Brisas ☎ 744/469–6900) carries small selections of the exquisite flatware, jewelry, and objets d'art created by one of Mexico's most prestigious (and expensive) silversmiths.

# SIDE TRIP

## Taxco

*275 km (170 mi) north of Acapulco.*

In Mexico's premier "silver city," marvelously preserved, white-stucco, red-tile-roof colonial buildings nuzzle cobblestone streets that wind up and down the foothills of the Sierra Madre. Taxco (pronounced *tahss-*ko) is a living work of art. For centuries its silver mines drew foreign mining companies. In 1928 the government made it a national monument. And today its charm, abundant sunshine, flowers, and silversmiths make it a popular getaway.

Hernán Cortés discovered Taxco's mines in 1522 while looking for lead for his armory. The silver rush lasted until the next century. In the 1700s, a Frenchman who Mexicanized his name to José de la Borda, discovered a rich lode that revitalized the silver industry and made him exceedingly wealthy. After Borda, however, Taxco's importance again faded, until the 1930s and the arrival of William G. Spratling, a writer-architect from New Orleans. Enchanted by the city and convinced of its potential as a center for silver jewelry, Spratling set up an apprentice shop. His artistic talent and fascination with pre-Columbian design combined to produce silver jewelry and other artifacts that soon earned Taxco its worldwide reputation as the Silver City once more. Spratling's inspiration lives on in his students and their descendants, many of whom are today's famous silversmiths.

Taxco's biggest cultural event is the Jornadas Alarconianos, which honors one of Mexico's greatest dramatists with plays, dance performances, and concerts in the third week of May. Other fiestas provide chances to honor almost every saint in heaven with music, dancing, and fireworks. A refreshing change is the festival of the grasshopper each November 3 where the townsfolk head to the sierra to catch the jumping critters in droves. They take them home and deep fry them for a tasty protein-laden treat. Oh, yes. The town is also Mexico's fireworks capital, and its citizens demonstrate their pyrotechnic skills with set pieces—wondrous blazing "castles" made of bamboo.

Because of the byways, alleys, and tiny streets, maneuvering anything bigger than your two feet through Taxco is difficult, so it's good that almost everything of interest is within walking distance of the zócalo. Wear sensible shoes for negotiating the hilly streets. Just be advised that city's altitude is 5,800 feet, so if you've come from sea level, take it easy, particularly on your first day.

★ ⓫ The **Iglesia de San Sebastián y Santa Prisca** has dominated the busy, colorful Plaza Borda since the 18th century. Usually just called Santa Prisca, it was built by French silver magnate José de la Borda in thanks to the Almighty for Borda's having literally stumbled upon a rich silver vein. According to legend, St. Prisca appeared to workers during a storm and prevented a wall of the church from tumbling. Soon after, the church was named in her honor. The style of the church—a sort of Spanish baroque known as churrigueresque—and its pale pink exterior have made it Taxco's most important landmark. Its facade, naves, and *bovedas* (vaulted ceilings), as well as important paintings by Mexican Juan Cabrera, are slowly being restored. ⌧ *Southwest side of Plaza Borda* ☎ *No phone* ☉ *Daily 6 AM–9 PM.*

need a break? | Around Plaza Borda are several *neverías* (ice-cream stands) where you can treat yourself to ice cream in exotic flavors such as tequila, corn, avocado, or coconut. **Bar Paco,** directly across the street from Santa Prisca, is a Taxco institution; its terrace is the perfect vantage point for watching the comings and goings on the zócalo while sipping a margarita or a beer.

⓬ The former home of William G. Spratling houses the **Museo Spratling.** This small gallery explains the working of colonial mines and displays Spratling's collection of pre-Columbian artifacts. At the Plazuela de Juan Ruiz de Alarcon plaza on ⌧ *Calle Porfirio Delgado 1* ☎ *762/622–1660* ⌧ *$3* ☉ *Tues.–Sat. 9–6, Sun. 9–3.*

⓭ **Casa Humboldt** or Museo de Arte Virreinal as it is also known, was named for German adventurer Alexander von Humboldt, who stayed here in 1803. The Moorish-style, 18th-century house has a finely detailed facade. It now contains a wonderful little museum of colonial art. ⌧ *Calle Juan Ruíz de Alarcón 6* ☎ *762/622–5501* ⌧ *$2.25* ☉ *Tues.–Sat. 10–6:15, Sun. 10–3:45.*

⓮ Saturday and Sunday mornings locals from surrounding towns come to sell and buy produce, crafts, and everything from peanuts to electrical appliances at the **Mercado Municipal.** It's directly down the hill from Santa Prisca. Look for the market's chapel to the Virgin of Guadalupe.

⓯ Mexico's largest caverns, the **Grutas de Cacahuamilpa** (Caves of Cacahuamilpa) are about 15 minutes northeast of Taxco. These 15 large chambers encompass 12 km (7½ mi) of geological formations. All the caves are illuminated, and a tour takes around two hours. ⌧ *$3 (includes tour).*

## Where to Stay & Eat

You can find everything from tagliatelle to iguana in Taxco restaurants, and meals are much less expensive than in Acapulco. Dress is casual, but less so than at Acapulco resorts. No shorts here, please. This is not a beach resort. There are several categories of hotel to choose from within Taxco's two types: the small inns nestled on the hills skirting the zócalo and the larger, more modern hotels on the outskirts of town.

★ $–$$$ ✕ **El Mural.** You can eat indoors or out on a poolside terrace, where there's a view not only of a Juan O'Gorman mural but of the stunning Santa

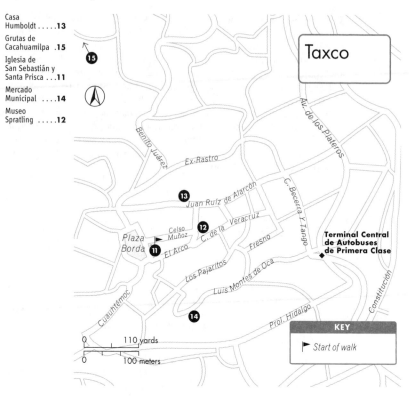

Prisca church. The chef prepares classic international surf-and-turf favorites as well as such Mexican specialties as cilantro soup and crepes with *huitlacoche* (corn fungus, a pre-Hispanic delicacy that really is delicious). The daily three-course fixed-price meal is $16. For breakfast, try the home-baked sweet rolls and marmalade from the fruit of nearby trees. ⊠ *Posada de la Misión, Cerro de la Misión 32* ☎ *762/622–2198* ▤ *AE, MC, V.*

**$–$$$** ✕ **Señor Costilla.** The name of this whimsical restaurant translates as "Mr. Ribs." The Taxco outpost of the zany Anderson chain does, indeed, serve barbecued ribs and chops. There's great balcony seating overlooking the main square. ⊠ *Plaza Borda 1* ☎ *762/622–3215* ▤ *MC, V.*

**$–$$** ✕ **Cielito Lindo.** This charming restaurant has a Mexican-international menu, a cozy patio, and an ideal location on the main square. Give the Mexican specialties a try—for example, *pollo en pipian verde* (chicken simmered in a mild, pumpkin seed–based sauce). ⊠ *Plaza Borda 14* ☎ *762/622–0603* ▤ *MC, V.*

**★ ¢–$$** ✕ **Hostería el Adobe.** It's an intimate place, with excellent food and such exotic details as hanging lamps made of clusters of masks. There are meat and fish dishes but hands-down favorites are garlic-and-egg soup and the *queso adobe,* fried cheese on a bed of potato skins, covered with a green tomatillo sauce. ⊠ *Plazuela de San Juan 13* ☎ 762/622–1416 ☐ *MC, V.*

¢–$ ✕ **Santa Fe.** Mexican family-type cooking at its best is served in this simple place a few blocks from the main square. Puebla-style mole, Cornish hen in garlic butter, and enchiladas in green or red chili sauce are among the tasty offerings. There's a daily *comida corrida* (fixed-price) meal for $6. ⊠ *Calle Hidalgo 2* ☎ 762/622–1170 ☐ *No credit cards.*

$$ ⌂ **Hotel de la Borda.** It may be a bit worn, but de la Borda is still a favorite with bus tours, and the staff couldn't be more hospitable. Ask for a room overlooking town. There's a restaurant and a large marble lobby. ⊠ *Cerro del Pedregal 2* ⌖ *A.P. 6, 40200* ☎ 762/622–0025 ☐ *762/622–0617* ⊕ *www.hotelborda.com* ⊲ *98 rooms, 3 suites* ⌂ *Restaurant, room service, pool, bar, laundry service, free parking* ☐ *AE, MC, V.*

$$ ⌂ **Monte Taxco.** A colonial style predominates at this full-service hotel, which has a knockout view, a funicular, three restaurants, a disco, and nightly entertainment. It's the fanciest hotel in Taxco and a few miles up a mountain from town, so plan to take taxis to get back and forth. There are rooms equipped for guests with disabilities. ⊠ *Lomas de Taxco* ⌖ *A.P. 84, 40210* ☎ 762/622–1300 ☐ *762/622–1428* ⊘ *monte-taxco@silver.net.mx* ⊲ *153 rooms, 6 suites, 32 villas* ⌂ *3 restaurants, cable TV, 9-hole golf course, miniature golf, 3 tennis courts, 3 pools, gym, hot tub, sauna, massages, horseback riding, dance club, laundry service, free parking* ☐ *AE, MC, V.*

★ $$ ⌂ **Posada de la Misión.** Laid out like a colonial-style village, this hotel has well-kept doubles with beamed ceilings and two-bedroom suites that have fireplaces and terraces as well. The pool area is adorned with a mural by noted Mexican artist Juan O'Gorman, and there's a silver workshop and boutique that sells Spratling silver jewelry. ⊠ *Cerro de la Misión 32* ⌖ *A.P. 88, 40230* ☎ 762/622–0063 ☐ *762/622–2198* ⊕ *www.posadamision.com* ⊲ *120 rooms, 30 suites* ⌂ *Restaurant, some kitchenettes, cable TV, pool, bar, dance club, shops, meeting rooms, free parking; no a/c* ☐ *AE, MC, V* ⎢⍥⎥ *MAP.*

$–$$ ⌂ **Rancho Taxco-Victoria.** The Taxco-Victoria exudes a certain charm even though the hotel is past its prime. Its simple rooms are attractive and freshly painted. There's also the requisite splendid view. Furniture in the common areas was designed by William Spratling. ⊠ *Calle Carlos J. Nibbi 5* ⌖ *A.P. 83, 40200* ☎ 762/622–0210 ☐ *762/622–0010* ⊕ *www.victoriataxco.com* ⊲ *63 rooms, 5 suites* ⌂ *Restaurant, some cable TV, pool, bar, free parking* ☐ *AE, MC, V.*

$ ⌂ **Agua Escondida.** Popular with some regular visitors to Taxco, this hotel has cute rooms with pink hues and Mexican-style furnishings. ⊠ *Calle Guillermo Spratling 4, 40200* ☎ 762/622–1166 ☐ *762/622–1306* ⊕ *www.aguaescondida.com* ⊲ *50 rooms* ⌂ *Restaurant, café, cable TV, pool, bar, free parking; no a/c* ☐ *MC, V.*

¢ ⌂ **Hotel Emilia Castillo.** This in-town inn is straightforward, clean, and good for the price. The Emilia Castillo silver shop is off the lobby. There's a restaurant just outside the front door. ⊠ *Juan Ruíz de Alarcón 7, 40200* ☎ 762/622–1396 ⊘ *hotelemilia@hotmail.com* ⊲ *14 rooms* ⌂ *No a/c, no room phones, no TV in some rooms* ☐ *No credit cards.*

# ONE MAN'S METAL

**N LESS THAN A DECADE** *after William Spratling arrived in Taxco, he transformed it into a flourishing silver center, the likes of which had not been seen since colonial times. In 1929 the writer-architect from New Orleans settled in the then sleepy, dusty village because it was inexpensive and close to the pre-Hispanic Mexcala culture that he was studying in Guerrero Valley.*

*For hundreds of years Taxco's silver was made into bars and exported overseas. No one even considered developing a local jewelry industry. Journeying to a nearby town, Spratling hired a couple of goldsmiths and commissioned them to create jewelry, flatware, trays, and goblets from his own designs. Ever the artist with a keen mind for drawing, design and esthetics, Spratling decided to experiment with silver using his designs. Shortly afterward, he set up his own workshop and began producing highly innovative pieces. By the 1940s, Spratling's designs were gracing the necks of celebrities and being sold in high-end stores abroad.*

*Spratling also started a program to train local silversmiths; they were soon joined by foreigners interested in learning the craft. It wasn't long before there were thousands of silversmiths in the town, and Spratling was its wealthiest resident. He moved freely in Mexico's lively art scene, befriending muralists Diego Rivera (Rivera's wife, Frida Kahlo, wore Spratling necklaces) and David Alfaro Siqueiros as well as architect Miguel Covarrubios. The U.S. ambassador to Mexico, Dwight Morrow, father of Anne Morrow who married Charles Lindbergh, hired Spratling to help with the architectural details of his house in Cuernavaca. American movie stars were frequent guests at Spratling's home; once, he even designed furniture for Marilyn Monroe.*

*When his business failed in 1946 relief came in the form of an offer from the United States Department of the Interior: Spratling was asked to create a program of native crafts for Alaska. This work influenced his later designs. Although he never regained the wealth he once had, he operated the workshop at his ranch and trained apprentices until he died in a car accident in 1969. A friend, Italian engineer Alberto Ulrich, took over the business and replicated Spratling's designs using his original molds. Ulrich died in 2002, and his children now operate the business.*

*Spratling bequeathed his huge collection of pre-Hispanic art and artifacts to the people of Taxco, and they're now displayed in a museum carrying his name. The grateful citizens also named a street after their much-beloved benefactor and put a bust of him in a small plaza off the main square.*

¢ ⌂ **Posada de San Javier.** The secluded San Javier sprawls haphazardly around a jungle-like garden with a pool and a wishing well. In addition to guest rooms, there are seven one-bedroom apartments with living rooms and kitchenettes; however, these are often filled by visiting wholesale silver buyers. ⊠ *Calle Estacas 32, 40200* ☎ *762/622–3177* 🖷 *762/622–2351* 📧 *posadasanjavier@hotmail.com* ⇱ *18 rooms, 7 apartments* 🍴 *Restaurant, some kitchenettes, room service, some cable TV, pool, bar, free parking* ▤ *No credit cards.*

## Nightlife

The **Bar Paco** (⊠ Plaza Borda 12 ☎ 762/622–0064) is a traditional favorite. At **Bertha's** (⊠ Plaza Borda 9 ☎ 762/622–0172), Taxco's oldest bar, a tequila, lime, and club soda concoction called a Bertha is the specialty. It's supposedly the forerunner of today's margarita.

**La Pachanga** (⊠ Cerro de la Misión 32 ☎ 762/622–5519), a discotheque at Posada de la Misión, is open Thursday–Sunday and is popular with townsfolk and visitors. **Passagge** (⊠ Av. de los Plateros s/n ☎ 762/627–1177) is a popular disco. Much of Taxco's weekend nighttime activity is at Monte Taxco hotel's discotheque, **Windows** (⊠ Lomas de Taxco ☎ 762/622–1300). On Saturday night, the hotel has a buffet and a fireworks display.

## Shopping

Sidewalk vendors sell lacquered gourds and boxes from the town of Olinalá as well as masks, straw baskets, bark paintings, and many other handcrafted items native to the state of Guerrero. Sunday is market day, which means that artisans from surrounding villages descend on the town, as do visitors from Mexico City. If you find a seat on a bench in Plaza Borda, you're set to watch the show and peruse the merchandise that will inevitably be brought to you by strolling vendors.

Most people come to Taxco with silver in mind. Three types are available: sterling, which is always stamped 0.925 (925 parts in 1,000) and is the most expensive; plated silver; and the inexpensive *alpaca*, which is also known as German or nickel silver. Sterling pieces are usually priced by weight according to world silver prices. Fine workmanship will add to the cost. Bangles start at $4, and bracelets and necklaces cost $10 to $200 and higher.

Many of the more than 2,000 silver shops carry identical merchandise; a few are noted for their creativity. William Spratling, Andrés Mejía, and Emilia Castillo, daughter of renowned silversmith Antonio Castillo, are among the famous names. Designs range from traditional bulky necklaces (often inlaid with turquoise and other semiprecious stones) to streamlined bangles and chunky earrings.

CRAFTS **Arnoldo** (⊠ Calle Palma 2 ☎ 762/622–1272) has ceremonial masks; originals come with a certificate of authenticity as well as a written description of origin and use. For $100 per person, Arnoldo will take you on a tour of the villages where the dances using the masks are performed on February 2, May 15, and December 12. **D'Elsa** (⊠ Plazuela de San Juan 13 ☎ 762/622–1683), owned by Elsa Ruíz de Figueroa, carries a selection of native-inspired clothing for women and a well-chosen selection of crafts.

SILVER
Fodor'sChoice
★

**Emilia Castillo** (✉ Juan Ruíz de Alarcón 7, in the Hotel Emilia Castillo ☎ 762/622–3471) is one of the most exciting silver shops; it's renowned for innovative designs and for combining silver with porcelain (Neiman Marcus sells the wares in its U.S. stores). The stunning pieces at **Galería de Arte en Plata Andrés** (✉ Av. de los Plateros 113A, near Posada de la Misión ☎ 762/622–3778) are created by the talented Andrés Mejía. He showcases his own designs and those of such promising young designers as Priscilla Canales, Susana Sanborn, Francisco Diaz, and Daniel Espinosa, who is the current rage among Hollywood celebrities and just opened a shop in Beverly Hills.

★ **Spratling Ranch** (✉ South of town on Carretera Taxco–Iguala, Km 177 ☎ 762/622–6108) is where the heirs of William Spratling turn out designs using his original molds. You can shop only by appointment. **Talleres de los Ballesteros** (✉ Calle Florida 14 ☎ 762/622–1076 ✉ Joyería San Agustín ✉ Calle Cuauhtémoc 4 ☎ 762/622–3416) and their branch, Joyería San Agustín, carry a large collection of well-crafted silver jewelry and serving pieces.

# ACAPULCO A TO Z

### AIR TRAVEL

AIRPORT
The Aeropuerto Internacional Juan N. Alvarez is 20 minutes east of the city.
🛈 Aeropuerto Internacional Juan N. Alvarez ☎ 744/466–9434.

AIRPORT
TRANSFERS
Private taxis aren't permitted to carry passengers from the airport to town, so most people rely on Transportes Aeropuerto, a special airport taxi service. The system looks confusing, but there are dozens of helpful English-speaking staff members to help you.

Look for the desk with sign that says TAXIS on the walkway in front of the terminal. Tell the attendant what hotel you want, buy your ticket, and follow the directions to reach the dispatcher who will guide you to your transportation. The ride from the airport to the hotel zone on the strip costs about $8 per person for the *colectivo* (shared minivan) and starts at $31 for a nonshared cab. The drivers are usually helpful and will often take you to hotels that aren't on their list. Tips are optional.
🛈 Taxis & Shuttles **Transportes Aeropuerto** ☎ 744/462–1095.

CARRIERS
From the United States, American has nonstop flights from Dallas, with connecting service from Chicago and New York. Continental has nonstop service from Houston and winter and spring service nonstop from Newark. Delta's direct flights are from Los Angeles and Atlanta. Mexicana's flights from Chicago, San Antonio, and Los Angeles stop in Mexico City before continuing on to Acapulco. Aeroméxico has nonstop service from Los Angeles; flights from New York stop in Mexico City.

Aeroméxico also has one-stop or connecting service from Atlanta, Chicago, Houston, Miami, and Orlando. America West has a flight from Phoenix.

🛪 **Aeroméxico** ☎ 744/466-9109. **America West** ☎ 744/466-9257. **American** ☎ 744/466-9227. **Continental** ☎ 744/466-9063. **Delta** ☎ 01800/902-2100 toll-free in Mexico. **Mexicana** ☎ 744/486-7586.

## BOAT TRAVEL

Many cruises include Acapulco as part of their itinerary. Most originate from Los Angeles. Celebrity Cruises is popular with tourists. Crystal P&O is a reliable operator. Cunard Line also offers cruises that include Acapulco. Krystal Cruises plies the Riviera Mexicana, which includes Acapulco. Princess Cruises offers trips several times a year. Bookings are generally handled through a travel agent.

## BUS TRAVEL

Bus service from Mexico City to Acapulco is excellent. Sistema Estrella Blanca has first-class buses, which leave every hour on the hour from the Taxqueña station; they're comfortable and in good condition. The trip takes 4½ hours, and a one-way ticket costs about $26. Estrella de Oro also has deluxe service, called Servicio Diamante, with airplane-like reclining seats, refreshments, rest rooms, air-conditioning, movies, and hostess service. The deluxe buses leave four times a day, also from the Taxqueña station, and cost about $40. Plus service (regular reclining seats, air-conditioning, and a rest room) on the same bus line costs $26.

First-class Estrella de Oro buses leave Acapulco for Taxco five times a day from 7 AM to 6:40 PM from the Terminal Central de Autobuses de Primera Clase (First-Class Bus Terminal). The cost for the approximately 4½-hour ride is about $15 one-way. Sistema Estrella Blanca buses depart Acapulco several times a day from the Terminal de Autobuses. Purchase your tickets at least one day in advance at the terminal if it's a Mexican holiday or Christmas week. A first-class, one-way ticket is $13. Buses depart from Taxco just about every hour starting at 6 AM.

Within Acapulco one of the most useful buses runs from Puerto Marqués to Caleta, making stops along the way. Yellow air-conditioned tourist buses, marked ACAPULCO, run about every 15 minutes along this route. If you want to go from the zócalo to the Costera, catch the bus that says LA BASE (the naval base near the Hyatt Regency). It detours through Old Acapulco and returns to the Costera just east of the Ritz Hotel. If you want to follow the Costera for the entire route, take the bus marked HORNOS. Buses to Pie de la Cuesta or Puerto Marqués say so on the front. The Puerto Marqués bus runs about every 10 minutes and is always crowded. The fare is under $1. Scarlet-with-white-stripe buses are the most common but lack a/c and are often packed. They follow the same routes listed above and are a few cents cheaper.

🛪 **Estrella de Oro** ✉ Av. Cuauhtémoc 158, Old Acapulco, Acapulco ☎ 744/485-8705 or 744/622-0648 ✉ Av. de los Plateros 126, Taxco ☎ 762/485-8705 or 762/622-0648 ✉ Av. Taxqueña 1320, Tlalpan, Mexico City ☎ 55/5689-9745. **Sistema Estrella Blanca** ✉ Calle Ejido 47, Old Acapulco, Acapulco ☎ 744/469-2028 ✉ Av. de los Plateros 104, Taxco ☎ 762/622-0131 ✉ Av. Taxqueña 1320, Tlalpan, Mexico City ☎ 55/5689-9740.

## CAR RENTAL

🏃 Major Agencies **Avis** ☎ 744/466-9190. **Budget** ☎ 744/481-2433. **Dollar** ☎ 744/466-9493. **Hertz** ☎ 744/485-8947. **Quick** ☎ 744/486-3420.

## CAR TRAVEL

The trip to Acapulco from Mexico City on the old route (Carretera Libre a Acapulco) takes about six hours. A privately built and run four-lane toll road is expensive (about $48 one-way) but well maintained, and it cuts driving time between the two cities to 4½ hours. Many people go via Taxco, which can be reached from either road. It takes about three hours to drive to Taxco from Acapulco using the toll road.

If you plan to visit (or stay) in Pie de la Cuesta or Barra Vieja, you might want to rent a car. That said, be prepared for maddening traffic along the Costera from about 8 in the morning until 8 at night. Further it's hard to find a parking spot along the street in town, and there are few lots.

## CONSULATES

🏃 **Canadian Consulate** ✉ Marbella Mall, Suite 23, Costera ☎ 744/484-1305. **U.K. Consulate** ✉ Acapulco International Center, Av. Costera Miguel Alemán 4455 ☎ 744/484-173. **U.S. Consulate** ✉ Continental Plaza Hotel, Av. Costera Miguel Alemán 121-14, Costera ☎ 744/469-0556.

## EMERGENCIES

🏃 **Hospital del Pacífico** ✉ Calle Fraile and Calle Nao 4, Costera ☎ 744/487-7180. **Hospital Privado Magallanes** ✉ Calle Wilfrido Massieu 2, Costera ☎ 744/485-6194. **Police** ☎ 744/485-0034. **Red Cross** ☎ 744/485-4100.

## ENGLISH-LANGUAGE MEDIA

You can find English-language books and periodicals at Sanborns, a reputable chain store, and at the newsstands in some of the larger hotels.
🏃 Bookstores **Sanborns** ✉ Av. Costera Miguel Alemán 1226, Costera ☎ 744/484-4413 ✉ Av. Costera Miguel Alemán 3111, Costera ☎ 744/484-2025 ✉ Av. Costera Miguel Alemán 209, Costera ☎ 744/482-6167 ✉ Av. Costera Miguel Alemán, off zócalo, Old Acapulco ☎ 744/482-6168.

## HORSE-DRAWN CARRIAGES

Buggy rides up and down the Costera are available in the evenings. There are two routes: from Parque Papagayo to the zócalo and from Playa Condesa to the naval base. Each costs about $10 (be sure to agree on the price beforehand).

## MAIL, INTERNET & SHIPPING

More and more Internet facilities are cropping up in Acapulco to keep you connected while traveling. Smart PCs is in a shopping arcade next to Carlos 'n' Charlie's restaurant. The iNternet Cyber Café is near the Marbella Hotel on the Avenida Costera Miguel Alemán.
🏃 Cybercafés **iNternet Cyber Café** ✉ Calle Horacio Nelson 40-7A, Costera ☎ 744/484-8254. **Smart PCs** ✉ Av. Costera Miguel Alemán 112-4, Costera ☎ 744/484-2877.
🏃 Mail & Shipping **Airborne Express** ✉ Av. Costera Miguel Alemán 178, Costera ☎ 744/484-1076. **Correos** (Post Office) ✉ Av. Costera Miguel Alemán 215, Old Acapulco ☎ 744/483-1674 ✉ Acapulco International Center, Av. Costera Miguel Alemán, Costera

☎ 744/484-8029. **DHL** ✉ Av. Costera Miguel Alemán 810, Fracc. Hornos, Old Acapulco ☎ 744/485-9567. **Mail Boxes, Etc.** ✉ Av. Costera Miguel Alemán 40-3, Costera ☎ 744/481-0565.

## MONEY MATTERS

There are many *casas de cambio* (currency exchange offices) around the zócalo and along the Costera. Their hours are generally Monday–Saturday 9–5. Most banks have ATMs and are open weekdays 9–3 and Saturday 9–1.

🏧 Banks **Banamex** ✉ Av. Costera Miguel Alemán 38-A, Costera ☎ 744/484-3381. **Bancomer** ✉ Av. Costera Miguel Alemán, at Calle Laurel, Fracc. Club Deportivo, Costera ☎ 744/484-8055. **Bital** ✉ Calle Jesus Carranza 7, Old Acapulco ☎ 744/483-6113.

🏧 Exchange Offices **Casa de Cambio Austral** ✉ Av. Costera Vieja 3, Old Acapulco ☎ 744/484-6528. **Casa de Cambio Servicio Auxiliares Monetarios** ✉ Av. Costera Miguel Alemán 88, Old Acapulco ☎ 744/481-0218. **Dollar Money Exchange** ✉ Av. Costera Miguel Alemán 151, Costera ☎ 744/486-9688. **Divisa World Center** ✉ Av. Costera Miguel Alemán 999, Costera ☎ 744/484-5516.

## TAXIS & MINIBUSES

Before you go anywhere by cab, find out what the price should be and agree with the driver on a fare. Never let a taxi driver decide where you should eat or shop, since many get kickbacks from small stores and restaurants. Although tipping isn't expected, Mexicans usually leave small change.

Hotel taxis are the most expensive, the roomiest, and in the best condition. A price list that all drivers adhere to is posted in hotel lobbies. Fares in town are $3 to $7; from downtown to the Princess Hotel is about $18; from the hotel zone to Playa Caleta is about $9. Cabs that cruise the streets usually charge by zone, with a minimum charge of $2. A normal fare is about $3 to go from the zócalo to the International Center. Rates are about 30% higher at night. You can also hire a taxi by the hour or the day. Prices vary from about $10 an hour for a hotel taxi to $8 an hour for a street taxi; always negotiate.

Minibuses travel along preset routes through Taxco and charge about 40¢. Volkswagen "bugs" provide inexpensive (average $1.50) taxi transportation.

## TOURS

Operators have offices around town and desks in many of the large hotels. Contact Mexico Travel Advisors at La Torre de Acapulco for tours of Acapulco. Viajes Acuario is another reliable tour company. Both companies offer city tours ($20), day tours of Taxco ($65, including lunch), and nightclub tours ($25–$30, including transportation cover charges).

The *Bonanza*'s sunset cruise, with open-bar domestic alcohol, and live and disco music, costs $19. Boats leave from downtown near the zócalo at 10:30, 4:30, and 10:30. The evening cruise includes a musical Latin show and dancing. Many hotels and shops sell tickets, as do waterfront ticket sellers.

A new open-air trolley added in 2003 is convenient for touring the major attractions along the Costera and in Old Acapulco. Operating daily 10–6, the trolley starts at the Parque Papagayo and stops at the Fuerte de San Diego, La Quebrada, Caleta beach, the zócalo, convention center, and at most hotels along the Costera up until the Hyatt. The cost is $6.50 and passengers can get off and on as many times in a day as they wish. ▐ *Bonanza* ☎ 744/482-4947. **Mexico Travel Advisors** ✉ Av. Costera Miguel Alemán 1252, Costera ☎ 744/484-7400. **Tranvías Turísticas** ✉ Av. Cond. Aries no. 52, Costera 744/481-3685, 744/484-0700. **Viajes Acuario** ✉Av. Costera Miguel Alemán 186-3, Costera ☎ 744/485-6100.

### TRAVEL AGENCIES
▐ Local Agent Referrals **American Express** ✉La Gran Plaza shopping center, Av. Costera Miguel Alemán 1628, Suites 7–9, Costera ☎ 744/469-1166. **Viajes Wagon-Lits** ✉ Carretera Escénica 5255, Las Brisas ☎ 744/484-1650 Ext. 392.

### VISITOR INFORMATION
Procuraduría del Turista, the State Attorney General's Tourist Office, is open 9 AM–11 PM daily. Taxco's tourism office is open weekdays 9–2 and 5–8; Saturday 9–3. ▐ **Procuraduría del Turista** ✉ Acapulco International Center, Av. Costera Miguel Alemán, Costera ☎ 744/484-4416 ⊕ www.visitacapulco.com.mx. **Taxco Tourism Office** ✉ Av. de los Plateros 1 ☎ 762/622-6616.

# OAXACA

Updated by
Mark Sullivan

**A FEAST FOR THE EYES AND EARS,** Oaxaca never fails to fascinate first-time visitors. There's very little in Mexico that can compare to strolling past the colonnades lining the main square of Oaxaca City, listening to the melancholic voices of the mariachis. There's something about the light, and the way it reflects off the pale green stone used in the cathedral and most other buildings, that makes this place seem not quite real.

But what keeps people coming back to Oaxaca year after year is the food, which is without compare even in a country with a rich and varied culinary tradition. Oaxaca is known as "the land of seven moles" because of its seven distinct kinds of this rich, thick sauce. Each type of mole (pronounced *mow*-lay) has dozens of ingredients, and these may include everything from nuts and sesame seeds to pineapples and bananas.

The state of Oaxaca has one the country's largest Indian populations. Two out of three Oaxaqueños descend from Zapotec or Mixtec Indians, whose villages are sprinkled across the valleys, mountains, and coastal lowlands. Within a 40-km (25-mi) radius of the capital, Oaxaca City, the archaeological ruins of Monte Albán, Mitla, Yagul, Lambityeco, and Dainzú bear witness to the highly advanced cultures of their ancestors. Within the large state's borders there are 17 distinct ethnic groups, and 52 dialects are spoken. In the capital many people are fluent in English as well as Spanish, but in the small hamlets, even Spanish is a second language.

In the 15th century much of the region was conquered by the Aztecs, who gave Oaxaca its name: *Huaxyaca*. In the Nahuatl language it means "by the acacia grove." The next century witnessed the Spanish conquest of Mexico, for which the monarch Charles V rewarded Hernán Cortés with the title of Marqués del Valle de Oaxaca in 1528. Cortés preferred to live elsewhere, but his descendants kept the property until Mexico's bloody Revolution, which began in 1910.

Two of Oaxaca's sons figured greatly in Mexican politics: Benito Juárez, the first full-blooded Indian to become president, and Porfirio Díaz, a military dictator who declared himself president-for-life. Juárez was a sheepherder from San Pablo Guelatao, a settlement about 64 km (40 mi) north of Oaxaca. As a child he spoke only his native Zapotec tongue. He was later trained for the clergy but ended up studying law and entering politics. Elected governor of the state in 1847, the stocky statesman became chief justice of the Supreme Court of Mexico in 1857, and then president of the republic in 1858.

In 1864 Napoleon III crowned Austria's Archduke Maximilian emperor of Mexico; Juárez and his supporters resisted the French from a provisional capital city in northern Mexico. When the nascent French empire collapsed in 1867, Juárez returned to Mexico City. He was re-elected shortly thereafter and again in 1871; he died of a heart attack the following year, however. His rival, Porfirio Díaz, rose to power in 1876, maintaining the presidency until 1911. Dissatisfaction among the country's poor had mounted steadily under Díaz's autocratic, elitist government. The revolutionary movement that finally chased Díaz from power was spearheaded by a wealthy but nonconformist intellectual, Francisco I. Madero, who was elected president that same year.

Numbers in the text correspond to numbers in the margin and on the Oaxaca City, Oaxaca Valley, and Oaxaca Coast maps.

**If you have**
**3 days**

If you have only three days to spend in the state, you should stick to **Oaxaca City ①–⑪** ➤ and environs. On the first day take in the Catedral Metropolitana de Oaxaca, the Museo de Arte Contemporáneo de Oaxaca, and the Museo de las Culturas. On Day 2, beat the crowds by catching an early bus to **Monte Albán,** the ruins of an ancient capital of the Zapotec people that sits high in the mountains. After returning to the city for a late lunch, visit the Museo de Arte Prehispánico Rufino Tamayo and the Centro Fotográfico Álvarez Bravo. If you're in the mood for more history, spend Day 3 exploring the nearby ruins of **Yagul** and **Mitla.** If not head to the Central de Abastos—the city's largest market—to shop for some handicrafts. Watch the sun set over Oaxaca from the terrace bar of the Hotel Victoria, on a hill just above the city proper.

**10**

**If you have**
**5 days**

If you have a few more days, you have time for some rest and relaxation at the beach. Follow the three-day itinerary above, exploring the colonial city of 🏙 **Oaxaca City ①–⑪** ➤. On Day 4 head to the beautiful stretch of coastline called the 🏙 **Bahías de Huatulco ⑭–⑰** ➤. Take a boat tour of the breathtaking bays, followed by a sunset cocktail and evening meal at the Camino Real's Chez Binni restaurant. On Day 5, tour the small beaches and hidden bays between Huatulco and 🏙 **Puerto Ángel ⑬**.

**If you have**
**7 days**

You can immerse yourself in the cultural treasures of 🏙 **Oaxaca City ①–⑪** ➤ for a few days before kicking back with some sea and sun. On Day 4, head to 🏙 **Bahías de Huatulco ⑭–⑰**. When you arrive, sign up for a boat tour of the bays. On Day 5, drive west to the pretty port of 🏙 **Puerto Ángel ⑬**, where you can take your pick of several nearly deserted beaches like Playa Zipolite and Playa Mazunte. On Day 6 drive west to 🏙 **Puerto Escondido ⑫**, where you might spend the afternoon touring Laguna Chacahua. On Day 7 you can ride horses on the beach in the morning, then relax with in a soothing *temazcal* (pre-Hispanic sauna) and massage in the afternoon.

Oaxaca (pronounced wah-*hah*-kah) is in one of three adjacent valleys encircled by the majestic Sierra Madre del Sur. Mexico's fifth-largest state, it's bordered by Chiapas to the east, Veracruz and Puebla to the north, and Guerrero to the west. Southern Oaxaca State is blessed with 509 km (316 mi) of Pacific coast, along which are many magnificent beaches. The government is busy transforming Bahías de Huatulco (Bays of Huatulco), 125 km (77 mi) east of Puerto Escondido, into a resort along the lines of Cancún.

## Exploring Oaxaca

Park the car when you pull into Oaxaca City; you won't be needing it in the Centro Histórico, as everything is within walking distance. Besides, the abundance of one-way or pedestrian-only streets make driving a headache. Taxis are easy to hail, if you tire of walking. The only time you should consider driving is if you intend to visit more than one of the villages in Oaxaca Valley.

Several rather narrow and potholed highways follow the tortuous curves of the Sierra de Oaxaca south to Pacific surf spots and palm-lined beaches. Puerto Escondido and the even smaller beach towns nearby are the places to go for a casual, friendly, laid-back vacation. Although relatively unsophisticated by international standards, Huatulco has some incredible scenery and a handful of luxury resorts.

Note: although it's infrequent, highway robbery still occurs in this part of Mexico. Among the most obvious targets are first-class buses, especially on the highways running to and along the coast. Night buses are most vulnerable, so travel by day whenever possible.

## About the Restaurants

Traditional Oaxacan dishes are among the finest and most elaborate in all of Mexico. The home- and factory-made *mezcal*, an alcoholic drink derived from the maguey cactus, differs in flavor with each maker and can be as high as 80 proof. The cream variety, thick and sweet, is flavored with nuts, herbs, or citrus fruits.

The open-air cafés surrounding Oaxaca City's *zócalo* (main square) are good for drinks, snacks, and people-watching, with the scene changing from serene early mornings to crowded parades with brass bands, floats, and *monos* (giant papier-mâché dolls) on holiday evenings. Most serve the economical *comida corrida* (midday set menu) after 1:30 PM.

The dishes that make dining in the capital memorable are less favored along the coast, where seafood reigns. Puerto Escondido has quite a few interesting restaurants. Cuisine is varied, and competition keeps prices low. In Puerto Ángel and surrounding beach towns, expect the simplest of grilled fish dishes served with white rice and few frills.

## About the Hotels

Oaxaca City has magnificently restored properties, including a 16th-century convent and dozens of smaller, moderately priced accommodations. Hotels and rates vary considerably on the coast. Most Puerto Escondido and Puerto Ángel lodgings, even the most luxurious, are quite reasonable. High-end in Huatulco means high-priced, but there are also a respectable number of moderately priced accommodations. Try La Crucecita, a short taxi ride from the more posh properties lining the bays.

| WHAT IT COSTS | | | | |
| --- | --- | --- | --- | --- |
| | $$$$ | $$$ | $$ | $ | ¢ |
| RESTAURANTS | over $25 | $15–$25 | $10–$15 | $5–$10 | under $5 |
| HOTELS | over $250 | $150–$250 | $75–$150 | $50–$75 | under $50 |

Restaurant prices are for a main course excluding tax and tip. Hotel prices are for two people in a standard double room in high season.

**10**

Archaeology Dramatic Zapotec and Mixtec ruins at Monte Albán, Mitla, and Yagul provide insight into ancient civilizations. Their golden era had already passed when they were conquered by the Aztecs in the 15th century; shortly thereafter, the Spaniards arrived. Despite these conquests, indigenous languages are still extensively spoken in dozens of towns surrounding Oaxaca, where traditional lifestyles are slowly infused with modern trends and mores.

Fiestas Oaxaca celebrates holidays and festivals with verve. El Día de los Muertos (Day of the Dead) officially begins on October 31, the eve of All Saints' Day, when both city dwellers and country folk decorate altars for deceased family members. Tradition dictates that they also visit the cemetery with candles and flowers, balloons, and the deceased's favorite food and drink. The most frequently visited graveyard is that of Xoxo; Atzompa and Xochimilco also have colorful celebrations.

December is full of fiestas, including those for Mexico's patron saint, the Virgen de Guadalupe (December 12) and Oaxaca state's patron, la Virgen de la Soledad (December 18). December 23 sees the Noche de Rábanos (Night of the Radishes), when the Oaxaca City's *zócalo* (main square) is packed with growers and artists displaying their hybrid carved radishes, *flores inmortales* (small, dried "eternal flowers"), and *totomoxtl* (corn husks, pronounced to-to-*mosh*-tl)—all arranged in interesting tableaux. December 24 is the Noche de Calendas, in which locals demonstrate their devotion to the Virgin Mary by bearing heavy baskets of flowers from church to church.

Shopping Many of the villages surrounding Oaxaca City are known for the skill of artisans who create pottery, woven rugs, and other utilitarian items that often embody generations of craftsmanship and unique family designs. Look also for wood carvings of skeletons and animals as well as the *alebrijes* (fanciful creatures painted in bright colors and geometric designs). Oaxaca City's galleries exhibit folk and fine art; the city has many painters of international renown. In addition, Oaxaca's marketplaces make for fabulous outings. On market day both *mestizos* (people of mixed European and Indian descent) and indigenous people head to town to buy and sell, barter, and gossip. As large and lively now as it has been for centuries, Oaxaca City's Abastos Market attracted the attention of D. H. Lawrence, who wrote about it in *Mornings in Mexico* (1927).

Surfing Puerto Escondido has been a household name for serious surfers the world over since the 1960s. The town's famous surfing spot, Playa Zicatela, ranks up there with Hawaii's North Shore and Australia's Barrier Reef; waves here roll in with impressive force. Many surfers migrate here annually to ride the waves or participate in an international competition.

### Timing

Whether you stay in Oaxaca City or along the coast, book rooms six months to a year in advance for dates around Day of the Dead celebrations (October 31–November 2), Easter week, and Christmas–New Year's vacations. Although July and August fall in the rainy season, they're popular travel months with Mexican and foreign families, as they coincide with school vacations. Expect discounts of 20%–50% in low season.

# OAXACA CITY

▶ Oaxaca City, officially called Oaxaca de Juárez, is more than an open-air museum. It's a vibrant city of 260,000 that reveres its past and looks forward to its future. It's a study in contrasts, a commingling of sights, smells, and sounds both ancient and new. You'll hear the singsong strains of Zapotec, Mixtec, and other native languages in the markets, Spanish rock in the bars and restaurants, and hip-hop in English blaring from passing cars. Scions of affluent families sip tea or tequila in classy restaurants; out on the streets, men, women, and children of significantly more modest means sell pencils, sweets, and ears of delicious grilled *elote* (corn). Oaxaca is no longer off the beaten path, so you'll also see plenty of tourists in the city center.

## Exploring Oaxaca City

The Centro Histórico is a pastel collage of colonial- and republican-era mansions, civic edifices, and churches that delight the eye. The colonial heart is laid out in a simple grid, with all the attractions within a few blocks of one another. Most streets change names when they pass the zócalo; for example, Calle Trujano becomes Calle Guerrero as it travels from west to east.

a good walk

Begin at the shady **zócalo ❶** ▶. On the south side of this pedestrians-only square step into the **Palacio de Gobierno ❷** and check out the mural by Arturo García Bustos. Afterward walk to the zócalo's northwest corner and the **Alameda de León ❸**, a second square that abuts the central plaza. You can't miss the **Catedral Metropolitana de Oaxaca ❹**. After visiting the cathedral, turn right on Avenida Independencia and left at the next corner. This puts you on Calle Macedonio Alcalá, a pedestrian mall with restored colonial mansions in a palate of pastels, as well as galleries, shops, museums, and restaurants. It's also lively at night, as many of the shops stay open late. On your right, 1½ blocks up, is the **Museo de Arte Contemporáneo de Oaxaca ❺**. Turn right on Calle Murguía and walk 2½ blocks to the **Centro Fotográfico Álvarez Bravo ❻**.

Retrace your steps on Calle Murguía, turning right on the pedestrian-only Calle 5 de Mayo. Taking up the entire block on the street's east side is the exquisite Ex-Convento de Santa Catalina, now the Camino Real Oaxaca. Continue north until Calle 5 de Mayo ends at Calle Gurrión and the beautiful **Iglesia de Santo Domingo ❼**. If you're interested in the plants of the region, head right on Calle Gurrión. At the corner of Calle Reforma is the **Jardín Etnobotánico ❽**. Adjacent to the Iglesia de

Santo Domingo, the **Museo de las Culturas** ❾ contains, among other things, treasure from the tombs of nearby Monte Albán.

Walk south along Calle Macedonio Alcalá, then take a right on Avenida Morelos. Just a few blocks down in a tranquil colonial home is the **Museo de Arte Prehispánico Rufino Tamayo** ❿. After seeing the museum's pre-Hispanic art, continue west on Morelos 2½ blocks. Descend the steps and cross the large plaza to the massive **Basílica de Nuestra Señora de la Soledad** ⓫. On the left side of the church is a small museum with items related to Oaxaca's patron saint. Go east on Avenida Independencia past the post office and you'll be back at the Alameda and the Zócalo.

## What to See

❸ **Alameda de León.** This shady square, a bit smaller than the zócalo, is bordered by the massive cathedral on one side and the beautifully restored post office on the other. Locals gossip on wrought-iron benches or read the newspaper while their children chase pigeons.

⓫ **Basílica de Nuestra Señora de la Soledad.** The baroque basilica houses the statue of the Virgin of Solitude, Oaxaca's patron saint. According to legend, a mule that had mysteriously joined a mule train bound for Guatemala perished at the site of the church; the statue was discovered in its pack, and the event was construed as a miracle—one commemorated by this church, which was built in 1682. Many Oaxaqueños are devoted to the Virgin, who is believed to have more than the usual facility for healing and miracle-working. In the 1980s robbers removed her jewel-studded crown; she now has a replica of the original and a glass-covered shrine. ⊠ *Av. Independencia 107, at Calle Victoria, Centro Histórico* 📷 *No phone* ☉ *Daily 7–7.*

> **need a break?**
>
> In front of the Basílica de Nuestra Señora de la Soledad is a tiny park called Jardín Socrates. Here you'll find half a dozen stands selling some of the best ice cream in Mexico. The hands-down favorite is **Neveria La Niagara** (⊠ Av. Independencia and Calle Victoria, Centro Histórico 📷 No phone). Flavors include *rosas* (roses), *elote* (corn), and the acquired taste of *leche quemada* (burned milk).

❹ **Catedral Metropolitana de Oaxaca.** Begun in 1544, the cathedral was destroyed by earthquakes and fire and not finished until 1733. It honors the Virgin of the Assumption, whose statue can be seen on the facade above the door. The chapel at the back of the church and left of the altar houses the revered crucifix of El Señor del Rayo (Our Lord of the Lightning Bolt), the only piece to survive a fire that started when lightning struck the thatch roof of the original structure. There's no clapper in the bell, supposedly because it started to ring on its own accord back in the 18th century. ⊠ *Av. Independencia 700, Centro Histórico* 📷 *951/516–4401* ☉ *Daily 10 AM–9 PM.*

❻ **Centro Fotográfico Álvarez Bravo.** The center is named for the self-taught Mexico City photographer, Manuel Álvarez Bravo, who won his first photographic competition here in Oaxaca. Exhibitions here change every month or two. The site also houses a darkroom for students who

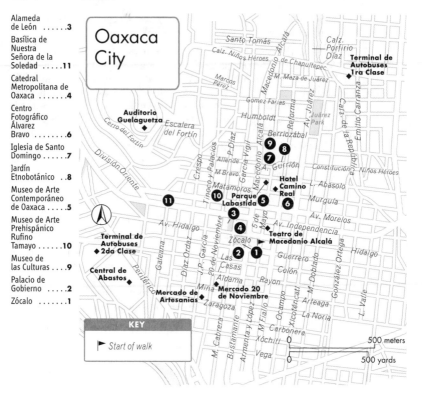

study at the center, a library of music and photography, and, incongruously, a Braille library. ✉ *Calle Murguía 302, at Calle Reforma, Centro Histórico* ☎ *951/516–4523* ✉ *Free* ☉ *Wed.–Mon. 9:30–8.*

★ ⑤ **Museo de Arte Contemporáneo de Oaxaca.** Although it's in an attractive colonial residence, MACO houses changing exhibitions of contemporary art. Inaugurated by graphic artist Francisco Toledo, the museum has in its collection quite a few of his etchings. You'll also find work by fellow Oaxacans Rudolfo Morales and Rufino Tamayo. Be sure to check out the fragments of frescoes that once decorated the walls of this old mansion in the front gallery on the second floor. ✉ *Calle Macedonio Alcalá 202, at Avenida Morelos, Centro Histórico* ☎ *951/514–2228* ✉ *$1* ☉ *Wed.–Mon. 10:30–8.*

★ ⑩ **Museo de Arte Prehispánico Rufino Tamayo.** You'll find a beautifully displayed collection of pre-Hispanic pottery and sculpture at this carefully restored colonial mansion. The courtyard, dominated by a fountain guarded by a quartet of stone lions, is shaded with pink and white oleander. Originally this was the private collection of the painter Rufino Tamayo. Especially interesting are the tiny figurines of women with children from Guerrero, some perhaps dating from more than 3,000 years ago, and the smiling ceramic figures from Veracruz. ✉ *Av. Morelos 503,* *at Calle Porfirio Díaz, Centro Histórico* ☎ *951/516–4750* ✉ *$3* ☉ *Mon. and Wed.–Sat. 10–2 and 4–7, Sun. 10–3.*

**❼ Iglesia de Santo Domingo.** With a 17th-century facade framed by two domed bell towers and an interior that's an energetic profusion of white and real gold leaf (typical of the Mexican baroque style), Santo Domingo is Oaxaca City's most brilliantly decorated church. The interior dome is adorned with more than 100 medallions depicting martyrs of the church. ✉ *Plaza Santo Domingo, Centro Histórico* ☎ *951/516–3720* ✉ *Free* ☉ *Daily 7–1 and 5–8.*

**❽ Jardín Etnobotánico.** This sprawling botanical garden, inside the massive walls of the Ex-Convento de Santo Domingo, was the first of its kind in the Americas. Many plants that are now known throughout the region were first cultivated here. Species found only in Oaxaca are on display, including some particularly beautiful orchids. Hour-long English-language tours are conducted on Tuesday and Thursday at 11 AM and Saturday at 4 PM. Spanish-language tours are on Tuesday at 10 AM and Saturday at 5 PM. You must take a tour to gain admission, after which you can roam the grounds. ✉ *Calle Gurrión and Calle Reforma, Centro Histórico* ☎ *951/516–7615* ✉ *Free.*

**❾ Museo de las Culturas.** This museum is laid out in a series of galleries around **Fodor's**Choice the cloister of the labyrinthine Ex-Convento de Santo Domingo. On the ★ ground floor are temporary exhibits and the Biblioteca Francisco de Burgoa's collection of antique books. On the second floor you'll find rooms dedicated to Oaxacan music, medicine, indigenous languages, and pottery. More than a dozen other salons have been organized chronologically; here you'll find such Monte Albán treasures as the stunning gold jewelry from Tomb 7—among the greatest archaeological finds of all time. ✉ *Plaza Santo Domingo, Centro Histórico* ☎ *951/516–2991* ✉ *$3.50* ☉ *Tues.–Sun. 10–8.*

**need a break?** **Café La Antigua** (✉ Calle Reforma 401, Centro Histórico ☎ 951/ 516–5761), just around the corner from the Iglesia de Santo Domingo, brews a great cup of java. The place is also a little lesson in coffee, as the placemats explain the various types offered.

**❷ Palacio de Gobierno.** The 19th-century neoclassical state capitol is on the zócalo's south side. A fresco mural that was completed in 1988 wraps around the stairwell. In it, altars to the dead, painters of codices, fruit sellers, gods, and musicians crowd together to catalog the customs and legends of Oaxaca's indigenous people. At the top, on the left side of the mural, note the *apoala* tree, which according to Mixtec legend bore the flowers from which life sprang. ✉ *Portal del Palacio, Centro Histórico* ☎ *951/516–0677* ☉ *Daily 9–8.*

▶ **❶ Zócalo.** During the day, it seems as if everyone passes through Oaxaca's shady main plaza, with its green wrought-iron benches and matching bandstand. At night, mariachi and marimba bands play under colonial archways or in the bandstand. It's a historic and truly beloved spot: when McDonald's tried to open a branch on its east side in late 2002, grass-

# CloseUp

# IN SEARCH OF THE DEAD

F YOU ARRIVE IN MEXICO in time for El Día de los Muertos (the Day of the Dead) you might be handed a brochure as you get off the airplane. What at first glance appears to be a guide to holiday observances is really a flyer touting the Día de los Muertos liquor sales at the duty-free shop. Such American-style commercialization has led to this holiday being billed as "Mexican Halloween," but it's much more than that. The festival, which takes place October 31 through November 2, is a hybrid of pre-Hispanic and Christian beliefs that honors the cyclical nature of life and death. Local celebrations are as varied as they are dynamic, often laced with warm tributes and dark humor.

To honor departed loved ones at this time of year, families and friends create ofrendas, altars adorned with photos, flowers, candles, liquor, and other items whose colors, smells, and potent nostalgia are meant to lure their spirits back for a family reunion. The favorite foods of the deceased are also included, prepared extra spicy so that the souls can absorb the essence of these offerings.

Although the ofrendas and the colorful calaveritas (skeletons made from sugar that are a treat for Mexican children) are common everywhere, the holiday is observed in so many ways that a definition of it depends entirely on what part of Mexico you visit.

In Mexico City and the smaller towns surrounding it, people cram the streets Mardi Gras–style and party till dawn. A suburban shopping mall hosts an ofrenda competition in which contestants honor notables from Frida Kahlo to Cervantes. A restaurant owner in rural Yucatán proudly displays his ofrenda, but the folks in its faded black-and-white photo aren't his parents. "I don't know who they are," he admits freely. "I just like the picture."

Chiapas marks Día de los Muertos with trips to the cemetery. In the village of San Juan Chamula, where ancient customs are still closely followed, families spread marigolds on the graves of their loved ones on November 1. The color, one woman explains, symbolizes the sun. But except for a few goats eating the flowers, the same cemetery is eerily quiet on November 2. People are at home, waiting for a visit from the spirits.

In Campeche, families make pilgrimages to their loved ones' graves, remove the bones, dust them off, and carefully place them back for another year. In a sandy Isla Mujeres cemetery, Marta, a middle-aged woman wearing stylish sunglasses, rests on a fanciful tomb. "She is my sister," Marta says, motioning toward the teal-and-blue tomb. "I painted this today." She exudes no melancholy; rather she's smiling, happy to be spending the day with her sibling.

Nearby, Juan puts the final touches—vases made from shells he's collected—on his father's colorful tomb. A glass box holds a red candle and a statue of the Virgin Mary. "This is all for him," Juan says, motioning at his masterpiece, "because he is a good man." The intense late-afternoon sun causes even the fake flowers to wilt, perfuming the cemetery with the smell of heated plastic; the shadows creeping across the tomb fail to diminish the intensity of its newest coat of paint. "This is a good day," says Juan, taking in the merrily festooned city of the dead around him. "This is a very good day."

— David Downing

roots opposition led by painter Francisco Toledo brought the project to a halt. ✉ *Bounded by Portal de Clavería on the north, Portal del Palacio on the south, Portal de Flores on the west, and Portal de Mercaderes on the east, Centro Histórico.*

## Where to Eat

### Centro Histórico

★ **$$–$$$** ✕ **Casa Oaxaca.** There's no more romantic spot in Oaxaca than this candlelit courtyard. You can dine under the pomegranate tree in the center of the main dining area, or if you prefer more privacy, in any of the secluded spots on the terrace upstairs. Many of the entrées, such as the plump jumbo shrimp, come prepared several different ways. Can't decide? Opt for the five-course tasting menu. ✉ *Calle García Vigil 407* ☎ *951/514–4173* ☰ *AE, MC, V.*

**$–$$$** ✕ **La Catedral.** Though this restaurant takes up the entire first floor of a colonial house, the best seats in the house are out on the patio. You can dine beneath the colonnades or in the sun next to the fountain on the wall. Popular dishes include mushroom soup flavored with *epazote* (a pungent local herb), chicken with *salsa de flor de calabaza* (pumpkin-blossom sauce), and *lechón* (suckling pig). There's dancing to live tropical music in the bar Friday and Saturday from 9 PM until 2 or 3 AM. Sunday sees a lavish buffet from 1 to 6. ✉ *Calle García Vigil 105, at Av. Morelos* ☎ *951/516–3285* ☰ *AE, MC, V.*

**$–$$** ✕ **El Asador Vasco.** Nightly serenades by *tunas* (traditionally dressed minstrels) help to evoke medieval Spain, and this restaurant successfully blends the flavors of Mexico and Spain (particularly the Basque region). Try the sumptuous *ostiones en salsa de chipotle* (oysters in a smoked chili sauce). If you want a seat on the second-story balcony, reservations are recommended. ✉ *Portal de Flores 10-A, west side of zócalo* ☎ *951/ 514–4755* ☰ *AE, MC, V.*

**$–$$** ✕ **Las Danzantes.** Named for the dancing figures carved in stone at the nearby ruins of Monte Albán, this restaurant is a modern take on those ancient structures. The three-story-tall walls, consisting of triangular columns of rough stone, are reflected in a pool that takes up about half of the room. There's no ceiling, just sky above. One of the best dishes is *salmón envuelto en hoja de platanos* (salmon wrapped in banana leaves); slices of baked bananas provide a nice contrast to the fish. ✉ *Calle Macedonio Alcalá 403* ☎ *951/501–1184* ☰ *AE, MC, V.*

**$–$$** ✕ **El Naranjo.** A contemporary spin on traditional recipes distinguishes Fodor'sChoice Iliana de la Vega's charming little restaurant. Each day of the week she
★ cooks up one of Oaxaca's seven moles, including *manchamanteles* (tablecloth stainer), so named for its ability to do just that. Specials change daily, but, if you're lucky, one will be medallion of beef with a sauce of oranges, chipotle peppers, and blue cheese. Wines come from as far away as Chile and Spain. ✉ *Calle Trujano 203* ☎ *951/514–1878* ⊕ *www. elnaranjo.com.mx* ☰ *AE, MC, V* ✆ *Closed Sun.*

**$** ✕ **El Mesón.** It's right off the zócalo, so it's no surprise that this storefront restaurant draws in lots of tourists. But it's also popular with locals who come for the sizzling steaks. Your waitress hands you a paper menu, and you simply check off which cut of meat you prefer and how

# CloseUp

# ON THE MENU IN OAXACA

**F**OOD ISN'T TAKEN LIGHTLY in Oaxaca. Traditional recipes, many of which predate the arrival of the Spanish, are passed from generation to generation. Sisters argue over who makes the most authentic version of grandmother's mole.

Oaxacans don't like change, which may be why restaurants like El Naranjo that feature updated versions of classic dishes are inundated by foreigners and ignored by locals. You can imagine the outcry when McDonald's announced it was going to open a restaurant on the zócalo. It didn't take long for the company to rethink its plans.

When it comes to sampling Oaxaca's cuisine, do as the locals do. Oaxaca's markets—and inexpensive eateries near them—are among the most interesting places to sample any of the following regional specialties.

Although the name sounds like an elegant dish, **chapulines** are nothing more than fried grasshoppers seasoned with salt, tangy chili, and a pinch of lime. You find them everywhere from the fanciest restaurant to the humblest vendor's cart. All sizes of grasshoppers are available, depending on the season; the large ones go down a bit easier if you remove the legs first. According to local lore, one taste will charm you into returning to Oaxaca.

**Jicuatote** is a sweet, white gelatinous dessert made with milk, cloves, cinnamon, and cornmeal. It's served in tubs or cut into cubes and is usually colored red on top.

Although you'll find versions of this sauce everywhere in Mexico, **mole** is to Oaxaca as baked beans are to Boston. There are seven major kinds of moles, so many restaurants ladle out a different one every day of the week. If you've had mole back home, it was probably mole oaxaqueña.

Also known as mole negro, or black mole; it is the standard bearer for all moles. It gets it sweetness from cocoa and its fire from peppers. It's found in every kind of dish, both on top of chicken and folded inside enchiladas. Another favorite is manchamanteles, which translates roughly as "tablecloth stainer" (it's not as thick as other moles, so it spills easily). Moles are not always a deep, rich brown. Verde is green, amarillo is yellow, and colorado and coloradito are slightly different shades of red.

Say cheese, or rather, **quesillo.** The stringy cheese made in and around Oaxaca is soft and nutty. It makes its way into many dishes, even those that have nothing to do with Mexico. Hint: that's not mozzarella on your pizza.

Made from the flowers and seeds of the cacao tree, **tejate** is sweetened with corn, coconut milk, sugar, and spices. The result—white clumps suspended in brown liquid—is served in a painted gourd bowl. The concoction may look deadly, but it's actually tasty and nutritious.

**Tlayudas** are huge, flat tortillas spread with refried beans and topped with cheese, salsa, and, if you like, strips of chicken or pork. They're halfway between soft tortillas and crispy tostadas, and they're hard to eat delicately. Put away the knife and fork and break off a piece.

you'd like it cooked. For a sugar fix, have a cup of rich Oaxacan hot chocolate and a slice of nut or cheese pie. ⊠ *Av. Hidalgo 805, at Calle Valdivieso* ☎ *951/516–2729* ▭ *MC, V.*

$ ✕ **La Olla.** The service is a bit slow at this combination gallery-café, so you'll have plenty of time to admire the works by local artists that adorn the walls. The food makes up for any shortcomings, however. Start with the *tlayuda azteca*, a Mexican-style pizza topped with chicken, avocados, and stringy Oaxacan cheese. The sampler plate includes everything from strips of beef to seasoned pork to *chapulines* (grasshoppers). ⊠ *Calle Reforma 402* ☎ *951/516–6668* ▭ *AE, MC, V* ☉ *Closed Sun.*

¢–$ ✕ **El Sagrario.** The Sanctuary is more cavernous than cloistered; the dining area covers three floors of a huge old house, so you'll never have a problem getting seated. It's a popular spot for pizza, pasta, and Caesar salads. After dinner you can show off your moves on the tiny dance floor until 2 AM. ⊠ *Calle Valdivieso 120* ☎ *951/514–0303* ▭ *AE, MC, V.*

### Elsewhere in Oaxaca

$–$$ ✕ **El Colibrí.** A neon sign bearing the namesake hummingbird draws you to this little cafeteria. Mothers who have packed their kids off to school and beeper-toting business executives favor this place, perhaps for its free refills of super-hot coffee and the extensive menu of Mexican favorites. If you're homesick, you can always order a burger with fries. The restaurant is across from the bus station, making it a great escape from the crowded waiting area. ⊠ *Calz. Niños Héroes de Chapultepec 903, Colonia Reforma* ☎ *951/515–8087* ▭ *AE, MC, V.*

★ $ ✕ **La Escondida.** The outdoor lunch buffet, served 1:30–6:30, is a great reason to venture outside the city. Waiters bring you a welcome cocktail and a typical appetizer, such as *taquitos de pollo* (small tacos filled with chicken) or *memelas* (fried discs of corn meal topped with goodies). You then select from more than 70 Mexican dishes, including several kinds of meat fresh from the grill. You can linger here, listening to wandering mariachi and marimba musicians—and let the kids loose on the small playground. ⊠ *Carretera a San Agustín Yatareni, Km 7, San Agustín Yatareni* ☎ *951/517–6655* ▭ *AE, MC, V.*

¢ ✕ **El Biche Pobre.** This little restaurant near Parque Paseo Juárez is packed with locals—sometimes there's not a tourist in sight—who appreciate the traditional fare like *enquiladas suizas* (with sour cream, not swiss cheese) and the rock-bottom prices. It's a ten-minute walk from the zócalo. ⊠ *Calzado de la República 600, Jalatlaco* ☎ *951/513–4636* ▭ *MC, V.*

## Where to Stay

### Centro Histórico

★ $$$–$$$$ ▭ **Camino Real Oaxaca.** Before its restoration in 1975, this 16th-century building—the former Convento de Santa Catalina de Siena—served as the town hall, a jail, and even a movie theater. Many original details, such as the frescoes above many of the arches, remain. A rear patio holds the *pileta*, a font where you'll find the stone basins where the nuns did laundry. Rooms are comfortable, but, as befits a former convent, are rather small. The restaurant is charming, but even nicer is the grassy courtyard where mariachis play. ⊠ *Calle 5 de Mayo 300, 68000* 🕾 *951/ 516–0611* 🖷 *951/516–0732* ⊕ *www.caminoreal.com/oaxaca* 🛏 *84 rooms, 7 suites* ♿ *Restaurant, room service, in-room safes, minibars, cable TV, pool, 2 bars, baby-sitting, laundry service, travel services, no-smoking rooms* ➅ *AE, DC, MC, V.*

**$$–$$$**
**Fodor'sChoice**
★

🏨 **Casa Oaxaca.** A trio of imaginative Europeans poured their hearts and souls into this unusual bed-and-breakfast. Their house combines traditional materials like adobe and cantera stone with minimalist sensibilities. The result is a masterpiece where gleaming white colonnades lead you to your room. Each is different; some have little sun rooms overlooking the indigo-tile pool, while others have sitting areas where you can enjoy a cocktail. All lead out to the private terraces that ring the upper story. Treat yourself to the shaman-sanctioned *temazcal* (pre-Hispanic-style sweat lodge). ⊠ *Calle García Vigil 407, 68000* 🕾 *951/514– 4173* 🖷 *951/516–4412* ⊕ *www.casa-oaxaca.com* 🛏 *6 rooms, 1 suite* ♿ *Restaurant, room service, cable TV, pool, massage, bar, laundry service, Internet, airport shuttle* ➅ *AE, MC, V* 🍽 *CP.*

**$$**
🏨 **Casa de Sierra Azul.** The central courtyard in this colonial-era mansion is certainly memorable, with lush vines tumbling down over the arches. Other touches like a massive wrought-iron gate and leaded-glass windows make this one of the Centro Histórico's prettiest lodgings. Each room is different, so take a look at a few before you decide. Room 1, up an old stone staircase, has a courtyard all to itself. ⊠ *Av. Hidalgo 1002, at Calle Fiallo, 68000* 🕾 *951/514–8412* 🖷 *951/514–7171* ⊕ *www. mexonline.com/sierrazul.htm* 🛏 *12 rooms, 2 suites* ♿ *Cable TV, laundry service, travel services; no a/c, no room phones* ➅ *AE, MC, V.*

**$$**
🏨 **Hostal de la Noria.** The rooms in this restored colonial mansion two blocks west of the zócalo have unique touches; in some rooms, it's carved wooden headboards, in others wrought-iron or hammered-tin ones. They all wrap around a charming central courtyard with a flower-filled fountain; surrounding it are tables topped with lacy umbrellas. Chicken mole and foil-wrapped fish fillets steamed in a mezcal sauce top the list of favorites at the elegant Restaurante Asunción ($–$$). ⊠ *Av. Hidalgo 918, 68000* 🕾 *951/514–7844* 🖷 *951/516–3992* ⊕ *www. lanoria.com* 🛏 *17 rooms, 33 suites* ♿ *Restaurant, room service, cable TV, pool, bar, baby-sitting, laundry service, meeting rooms, free parking* ➅ *AE, MC, V.*

**$$**
🏨 **Hotel Marqués del Valle.** Taking up almost the entire northern edge of the zócalo, this hotel puts Oaxaca at your doorstep. Many of the rooms have views of the Palacio de Gobierno or the Catedral Metropolitana. If you splurge a bit, you can reserve a room with French doors leading out to a small balcony. Rooms are cozy, although not as atmospheric as at most other hotels in town. ⊠ *Portal de Clavería s/n, 68000* 🕾 *951/514– 0688 or 951/516–3474* 🖷 *951/516–9961* ⊕ *www.hotelmarquesdelvalle. com.mx* 🛏 *100 rooms* ♿ *Restaurant, room service, in-room safes, cable TV, laundry service* ➅ *AE, MC, V.*

**$$**
🏨 **Hotel Victoria.** This salmon-color complex, on a hill surrounded by terraced grounds and fragrant gardens, has everything from simple rooms to sprawling suites. Be sure to request one with a view, so you can draw back your curtains at dawn and catch your breath at the mist

over the Sierra Madre. At night, have a drink at the bar overlooking the city lights. A trio often performs at El Tule restaurant. A shuttle bus runs on the half hour to the city center, 10 minutes away. ⊠ *Calle Lomas del Fortín 1, Lomas del Fortín 68000* ☎ *951/515–2633* 🖷 *951/515–2411* ⊕ *www.hotelvictoriaoax.com.mx* ➥ *59 rooms, 57 suites, 34 villas* ⟳ *Restaurant, room service, in-room safes, minibars, cable TV, tennis court, pool, 2 bars, baby-sitting, laundry service, travel services, free parking* ➲ *AE, MC, V.*

¢ 🖼 **Las Azucenas.** This intimate hotel occupies a charmingly restored old home near the Basilica de la Soledad. You can spot that church, and at least half a dozen others, from the plant-filled terrace. The most private room is secluded on the second floor. The others are just as cozy, but one has a skylight rather than a window. Ask for a tiny *tele* (TV) at the reception desk if you can't bear to miss the evening news. ⊠ *Calle Martiniano Aranda 203, at Matamoros, 68000* ☎ *951/514–7918, 877/780–1156 in the U.S., 877/343–8570 in Canada* 🖷 *951/514–9380* ⊕ *www.hotelazucenas.com* ➥ *10 rooms* ⟳ *No room phones, no room TVs* ➲ *MC, V.*

¢ 🖼 **Las Mariposas.** María Teresa Villarreal, the owner and operator of this pleasant little place, proudly shows off her restored colonial-style home. It's not fancy, but the lived-in feeling suits most people just fine. You can mingle with other guests on the open patio gladdened with laurel and lemon trees. Those staying in standard rooms share a brightly colored outdoor kitchen, while those who have booked studios have kitchenettes with coffeemakers and other essentials. ⊠ *Calle Pino Suárez 517, 68000* ☎🖷 *951/515–5854* ⊕ *www.mexonline.com/mariposas.htm* ➥ *7 rooms, 6 studios* ⟳ *Some kitchenettes; no a/c, no room phones* ➲ *No credit cards* ⦿ *CP.*

¢ 🖼 **Posada del Centro.** The best of the budget lodgings, this little colonial house also happens to be smack-dab in the center of the old city. Simple but clean, the rooms surrounding the pair of courtyards have rustic wardrobes and night tables, colorful tile floors, and soaring ceilings. Only the nicer rooms have cable TV, although each room has a color set. The family that runs the place is happy to help you plan your outings in Oaxaca. ⊠ *Av. Independencia 403, 68000* ☎🖷 *951/516–1874* ⊕ *www.mexonline.com/posada.htm* ➥ *23 rooms, some with bath* ⟳ *Café, some cable TV; no a/c* ➲ *No credit cards.*

### Elsewhere in Oaxaca

$$–$$$ 🖼 **Hacienda Los Laureles.** About a 20-minute drive from Oaxaca's historical center, this hotel is a cool, quiet oasis. The spa, which has a hot tub, massage, and traditional temazcal steam baths, helps you regain your inner balance. Staff members will help you arrange horseback excursions, bicycle rides, or ecological tours to the nearby mountains. ⊠ *Av. Hidalgo 21, San Felipe del Agua 68000* ☎ *951/501–5300* 🖷 *951/520–0890* ⊕ *www.hotelhaciendaloslaureles.com* ➥ *16 rooms, 9 suites* ⟳ *Restaurant, room service, cable TV, pool, gym, massage, steam room, bar, library, baby-sitting, Internet, laundry service, free parking* ➲ *AE, MC, V.*

¢ 🖼 **Hotel Cazomalli.** Even the baked-earth floor tiles shine at this sleepy little hostelry, in a cobblestone district close to Parque Paseo Juárez. Clean, quiet rooms have blond-pine furnishings and handwoven fabrics. The only TV is in a small, second-floor salon. Friendly owner Marina Flores and her family serve breakfast 8–10 AM. ⊠ *Calle El Salto 104, at Calle Aldama, Jalatlaco 68080* 🕾🕾 *951/513–3513* ⊕ *www. hotelcazomalli.com* ↜ *15 rooms* ⚮ *No room TVs, no a/c* ⊟ *MC, V.*

# Nightlife & the Arts

On Sunday at 12:30 PM the Oaxaca State Band sets up under the Indian laurel trees in the zócalo, whose open-air cafés often have live marimba, salsa, or flamenco music at night. See the free monthly magazines *Oaxaca Times* and *Oaxaca* for event information.

## Nightlife

BARS **El Sol y La Luna** (⊠ Calle Reforma 502, at Calle Constitución, Centro Histórico 🕾 951/514–8069) is the place to listen to live music, most often jazz, but also flamenco, salsa, and tango. There's a cover charge of $2 to $4 after 9 PM. There's not much to **Freebar** (⊠ Calle Matamoros 100, at Calle García Vigil, Centro Histórico 🕾 951/514–3834)—just a couple of dimly lit rooms—but the alternative music is popular with young people, who pack the place even during the week.

Things can get lively at **La Cucaracha** (⊠ Calle Porfirio Díaz 301, at Matamoros, Centro Histórico 🕾 951/514–2042) mostly because of the dozens of tequilas for sale. A yellow placard outside announces the evening's entertainment. Posters of Subcommandante Marcos, hero of the Zapatistas, make the decor at **La Resistencia** (⊠ Calle Porfirio Díaz 503, at Calle Allende, Centro Histórico 🕾 No phone). The music runs from grunge to techno on weekends, but there's more mellow *trova cubana* (Cuban ballads) during the week.

One of the city's most venerable watering holes, **La Tentación** (⊠ Calle Matamoros 101, at Calle García Vigil, Centro Histórico 🕾 951/514–9521) continues to be popular. There's dancing on the terrace on weekend evenings.

CANTINAS Bastions of macho men and strong spirits, cantinas traditionally aren't places for women. The cantinas in the Centro Histórico tend to be a bit less rough, but single women should still think twice about going in alone. A real hole in the wall, **¡Pues No Que No!** (⊠ Calle Bravo at Calle García Vigil, Centro Histórico 🕾 No phone) doubles its size from two tables to four with a tiny balcony. Push aside the swinging doors of **La Casa del Mezcal** (⊠ Calle Miguel Cabrera 209, between Calle Mina and Calle Aldama, Centro Histórico 🕾 No phone), near the Juárez market, for a classic cantina experience that's diminished only slightly by the presence of a large TV (or two). The cantina prides itself on its stock of *toblada,* a cousin of tequila made from wild agave.

DANCE CLUBS The only gay club in town, **Bar 502** (⊠ Calle Porfirio Díaz 502, at Calle Allende, Centro Histórico 🕾 951/516–6020) also has some of the best DJs. The clientele is pretty evenly mixed between men and women. People arrive late—well after midnight—and stay until the wee hours of the morning. It's open only Thursday to Saturday. Dance to live salsa music every night at one of the city's most popular dance clubs, **Candela** (⊠ Calle Murguía 413, at Calle Pino Suárez, Centro Histórico 🕾 951/514–2010).

The place to be on weekends, **NRG** (✉ Calzado Porfirio Díaz 102, Colonial Reforma ☎ No phone), has a pulsating sound system that packs the dance floor. The music starts at 10 PM, but the bar area is open at 8 PM.

GUELAGUETZA One of Oaxaca's major celebrations is the Guelaguetza, a Zapotec word for "offering" or "gift." It's generally held on the last two Mondays in July. Delegations of traditional dancers from throughout the state perform in authentic costumes at the Auditorio Guelaguetza.

If you're not in Oaxaca in July, you can still get a taste of Guelaguetza. Some of the best dancers perform all year in several places around town. Every Friday night—and more often in busier seasons—the **Camino Real Oaxaca** (✉ Calle 5 de Mayo 300, Centro Histórico ☎ 951/516–0611) hosts a regional dance show that's considered the best in town. The $26 admission includes a buffet dinner (7 PM) and the show (8:30 PM) in the former convent's 16th-century chapel. Reservations are strongly recommended.

Every evening, the rather drab **Casa de Cantera** (✉ Murguiá 102, Centro Histórico ☎ 951/514–7585) transforms itself into the colorful "Casa de Guelaguetza." It's a mesmerizing show, with lots of music and dancing. It starts at 8:30 PM, and the cover charge is $10. The **Hotel Monte Albán** (✉ Alameda de León 1, Centro Histórico ☎ 951/516–2330) has nightly dance shows beginning at 8:30 PM. Admission is about $7.

## The Arts

FILM On the northern edge of the Centro Histórico, **Cinema Pochote** (✉ Calle García Vigil 817, Centro Histórico ☎ 951/513–2087) offers art films in various languages, often English with Spanish subtitles. The metal folding chairs are a bit hard, but, hey—admission is free and there are two shows (usually at 6 and 8 PM) every night but Monday.

THEATER **Centro Cultural Ricardo Flores Magón** (✉ Calle Macedonio Alcalá 302, Centro Histórico ☎ 951/514–0395) hosts performances of music and dance. One of the city's most beautiful buildings, the 19th-century **Teatro de Macedonio Alcalá** (✉ Av. Independencia at Calle 5 de Mayo) is currently undergoing a massive restoration project. When completed in 2005, the theater will present concerts.

# Sports & the Outdoors

## Biking

**Bicicletas Bravo** (✉ Calle Garcí Vigil 409, at Calle Allende, Centro Histórico ☎ 951/516–0953) leads trips as short as a few hours and as long as a few days into the countryside. You can also rent a bike and set out on your own. **Bicicletas Pedro Martínez** (✉ Av. Hidalgo 100, Jalatlaco ☎ 951/518–4452) has trips of varying lengths, including one all the way to Puerto Escondido.

## Hiking

**Tierra Dentro** (✉ Calle Reforma 528, at Calle Constitución, Centro Histórico ☎ 951/501–1363 ⊕ www.tierraventura.com) has hikes through the Sierra Norte as well as opportunities for rock climbing and bird watching. **TierrAventura** (✉ Calle Abasolo 217, Centro Histórico

☎ 951/501–1363  ⊕ www.tierraventura.com) has treks of up to six days to remote parts of the region. Expect to see some villages far off the beaten path.

## Shopping

If you think you'll be buying more folk art than you can carry home, get receipts showing that you've paid the 15% sales tax on all purchases. This will allow you to send your purchases home through shipping services or shops without having to pay extra for them to provide the paperwork. Ask for referrals to shipping agents when you ask for receipts. Also, check out the high-end shops on Calle Macedonio Alcalá first; then compare prices and quality with the items you find in the *mercados* (markets), smaller shops, or in the pueblos where artisans live and work. Note that some stores are closed Sunday and others close at midday.

### Markets

★ Oaxaca's largest and oldest market is held at the **Central de Abastos** (literally the "Center of Supplies") on the southern edge of downtown. Saturday is the traditional market day, but the enormous covered market swarms daily with thousands of buyers and sellers from Oaxaca and the surrounding villages. Along with mounds of multicolored chilies and herbs, piles of tropical fruit, electronics, and bootleg tapes, you'll find intricately woven straw baskets, fragile green and black pottery, and colorful *rebozos* (shawls) of cotton and silk. Don't burden yourself with lots of camera equipment or bags; and keep an eye out for pickpockets and purse-slashers. Polite bargaining is expected.

Close to the zócalo, the daily **Mercado Benito Juárez** (⊠ Between Calles 20 de Noviembre and Miguel Cabrera at Las Calas, Centro Histórico) has stalls selling moles, chocolates, fruits and vegetables, and much more. It's more for locals, but inside the bulky brick building you can find some interesting arts and crafts. It's mostly locals that you'll find chowing down at the lively stalls of the daily **Mercado 20 de Noviembre** (⊠ Between Calles 20 de Noviembre and Miguel Cabrera at Calle Aldama, Centro Histórico), across the street from the Mercado Benito Juárez. No prices are listed, but rest assured that this will be your cheapest meal in Oaxaca.

★ For textiles, don't miss **Mercado de Artesanías** (⊠ Calle J. P. García, near Calle Ignacio Zaragoza, Centro Histórico), a great place to shop for handwoven and embroidered clothing from Oaxaca's seven regions. This is also the place to find the handmade *huipiles* (short, boxy blouses, often made of velveteen) worn in the Isthmus of Tehuantepec.

### Specialty Shops

ART GALLERIES **Galería Arte Mexicano** (⊠ Plaza Santo Domingo, Calle Macedonio Alcalá 407–16, Centro Histórico ☎ 951/516–3255) has local artists' work, and
★ in adjoining rooms, folk art, antiques, and silver jewelry. **Galería Indigo** (⊠ Calle Allende 104, Centro Histórico ☎ 951/514–3889) is a lovely gallery in an enormous restored mansion. Ceramics, graphics, paintings, and other fine art from talented artists from Oaxaca and beyond are for sale.

Across from Iglesia de Santo Domingo, **Galería Quetzalli** (⊠ Calle Constitución 104, Centro Histórico ☎ 951/514–2606) hosts large-scale

# EVERYDAY MARKETS

Almost every neighborhood has its own market day. Check out **Mercado de Conzatti** (⊠ Calle Reforma and Calle Humboldt, Centro) Friday until 4 PM. Sunday is market day for the **Mercado de Merced** (⊠ Calz. de la República and Calle Morelos, Centro).

Some of the best markets are in villages surrounding Oaxaca. Wednesday is market day in San Pablo Etla, which is famous for its fresh white cheese. In addition to cooked food, breads,

groceries, and clothing, Thursday's market at Zaachila has farmers bartering for spotted piglets, braying goats, and still larger animals—all before noon. Friday's tianguis (open-air market) is held in Ocotlán, where you can also admire the restored Dominican church and monastery of Santo Domingo. Sunday is market day in the Zapotec town of Tlacolula.

works, mostly by Mexican artists. **Galería Soruco** (⊠ Plaza Labastida 104, Centro Histórico ☎ 951/514–3938) displays work by up-and-coming artists as well as more established talents such as Sergio Hernández and Shinzaburo Takeda.

**Manuel García Arte Contemporáneo** (⊠ Portal Benito Juárez 110, Centro Histórico ☎ 951/514–1093), on the zócalo, often has interesting photography exhibits.

HANDICRAFTS **ARIPO** (⊠ Calle García Vigil 809, Centro Histórico ☎ 951/514–4030) is a government-run artists cooperative with competitive prices and ex-★ clusively Oaxacan work. **Artesanías Chimalli** (⊠ Calle García Vigil 513-A, Centro Histórico ☎ 951/514–2101) has an excellent selection of crafts, including painted copal-wood animals with comical expressions.

**Fonart** (⊠ Calle Crespo 114, Centro Histórico ☎ 951/516–5764) has a representative selection of quality arts and crafts from elsewhere in Mexico. Doing business since 1961, **Jarciería El Arte Oaxaqueño** (⊠ Calle Mina 317, at J. P. García, Centro Histórico ☎ 951/516–1581) has a small but good assortment of stamped-tin products as well as animals and skele-★ tons carved of feather-light wood; prices are great. **La Mano Mágica** (⊠ Calle Macedonio Alcalá 203, Centro Histórico ☎ 951/516–4275) is a relatively expensive crafts and fine-arts gallery with a large inventory of interesting pieces.

**Milagros Para Ti** (⊠ Calle 5 de Mayo 412, Centro Histórico ☎ 951/501–2009), a shop owned by American transplant Debbie Mounts, sells copper, brass, Talavera pottery, pewter, textiles, and shoes—mainly from Michoacan and Guanajuato—as well as Oaxacan rugs, miniature ceramic figures, woven baskets, art, alebrijes, stained glass, and antique jewelry. You'll support the women artists' co-op (open daily) by shop-Fodor'sChoice ping at the huge warren of shops that makes up **Mujeres Artesanas de**
★ **las Regiones de Oaxaca** (⊠ Calle 5 de Mayo 204, Centro Histórico

☎ 951/516–0670), often referred to as MARO. The selection and quality are excellent, and prices are reasonable.

JEWELRY   The streets west of Mercado 20 de Noviembre between Trujano and Mina are crowded with jewelry shops. Most offer 10- and 12-karat gold.

A family business since 1963, **El Diamante** (✉ Calle García Vigil 106-H, Centro Histórico ☎ 951/516–3983) offers reliable workmanship and courteous service within a few blocks of the Alameda. It carries traditional styles that don't seem dated. **Oro de Monte Albán** (✉ Calle Macedonio Alcalá 403, Centro Histórico ☎ 951/514–3813) sells gold and silver reproductions of pre-Columbian jewelry found in the tombs of royalty at Monte Albán. There's also a shop at the archaeological site.

Facing a pretty promenade, the two rooms of **Go-Go** (✉ Calle Adolfo C. Gurrion 110, Centro Histórico ☎ 951/514–9826) are filled with strikingly original designs. Almost everything here is silver.

## Side Trips to Oaxaca Valley

You can easily fill a week with visits to the colonial towns surrounding Oaxaca City. There are outdoor markets every day, and each is different. And don't forget the striking ruins of Monte Albán, Mitla, and other ancient cities. Renting a car is an easy and delightful way to cover the distances. Buses, *colectivos* (minibuses), and taxis round out the options. Many of the towns and sites are along or just off Carretera 190 (to Mitla) and Carretera 175 (to Ocotlán).

### North & West of Oaxaca City

Fodor'sChoice   The onetime holy city of more than 30,000 Zapotecs, **Monte Albán,** on a small road 9 km (5½ mi) west of Oaxaca, is the state's most interesting and extensively excavated ruin. Despite its size, experts estimate that only about 10% of the site has been uncovered. Digs take place whenever the budget permits.

Monte Albán overlooks the Oaxaca Valley from a flattened mountaintop 5,085 feet high. Either Zapotecs or their predecessors leveled the site around 600 BC. The varying heights of the site follow the contours of distant mountains. The oldest of the four temples is the **Galería de las Danzantes,** or the Dancers' Gallery, so named for the elaborately carved stone figures that once covered the building. Most of the originals are now in the site museum, but some can still be seen in the temple. Experts are unsure whether the nude male figures represent captives, warriors, or some other group; the theory that they were dancers has been discarded because some appear to be bound.

The Zapotecs constructed most of the buildings along a north–south axis, with the exception of one structure called the **Observatorio** (Observatory). The arrow-shaped structure is set at a 45 degree angle, pointing toward the southwest. It is thought to have been an observatory as it's more closely aligned with the stars than with the Earth's poles.

In the **Juego de Pelota,** or Ball Court, one or more games were played. Hips, shoulders, knees, and elbows were probably used to hit a wooden

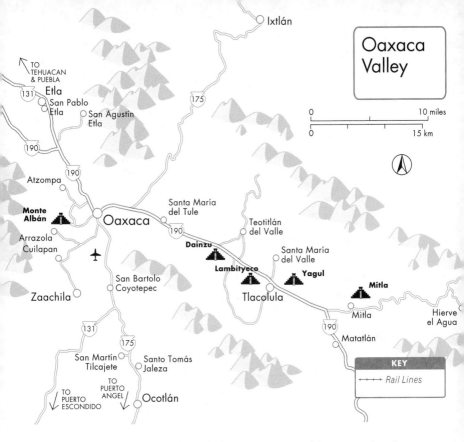

or rubber ball. Although the exact outcome of these games is unknown, there's some speculation that they were a means of solving disputes among factions or villages or of celebrating the defeat of a rival. Experts generally agree that the losing team was sacrificed to the gods.

No one knows for sure whether the Zapotecs abandoned the site gradually or suddenly, but by AD 1000 it stood empty. Years afterward the Mixtecs used Monte Albán as a lofty necropolis of lavish tombs. More than 200 tombs and 300 burial sites have been explored. The most fantastic of these, **Tumba 7,** yielded a treasure unequaled in North America. Inside were more than 500 priceless Mixtec objects, including gold breastplates; jade, pearl, ivory, and gold jewelry; and fans, masks, and belt buckles of precious stones and metals. The tomb is north of the parking lot, but is seldom open.

At Monte Albán you'll find a small site museum with a gift shop. The cafeteria isn't half bad and has a great view of Oaxaca Valley. Direct buses serve Monte Albán from the Hotel Rivera del Ángel (Calle Mina 518) on the half hour from 8:30 to 3:30; the last bus back is at 6 PM. The round-trip fare is about $3; to stay longer than two hours you must pay a small surcharge (you can decide once you're on-site). ☎ 951/516–1215 for museum gift shop ☒ $3.50 ☉ Daily 8:30–6.

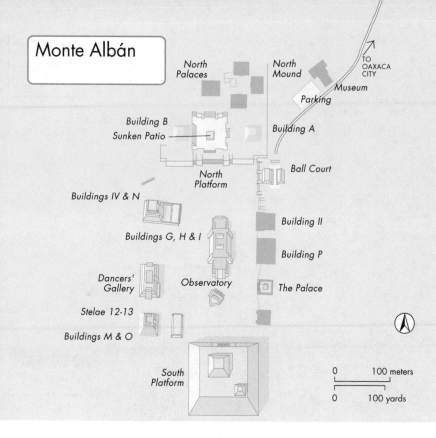

# Monte Albán

North Palaces

North Mound

TO OAXACA CITY

Museum

Parking

Building B
Sunken Patio

Building A

North Platform

Ball Court

Buildings IV & N

Building II

Buildings G, H & I

Building P

Dancers' Gallery

Observatory

The Palace

Stelae 12-13

Buildings M & O

South Platform

| 0 | 100 meters |
|---|---|
| 0 | 100 yards |

Take some time to wander the few main streets of unimposing **Atzompa**, 8 km (5 mi) northwest of Oaxaca en route to Monte Albán. Its inhabitants produce fanciful clay pots and sculptures as well as the more traditional green-glazed plates, bowls, and cups. You can often visit the potters' simple home workshops. More convenient (although the quality of work can be disappointing) is the *mercado artesanal* (artisans market) open daily from 8 to 7.

Carretera 190 leads northwest to several unmarked villages well worth visiting. About 15 km (9 mi) north of Oaxaca, a narrow road leads to the town of **San Pablo Etla**, known for its high-quality white cheese. You can purchase it, along with fresh buns, at the Wednesday market. Just behind the market, La Fonda (open for breakfast and lunch) has excellent stuffed chilies and other regional fare.

About a mile past San Pablo Etla is the turnoff for **San Agustín Etla**, known for its abundance of water. One neighborhood, Vistahermosa, has several sprawling outdoor bathing facilities where you can swim, lie in the sun, lunch in the shade, and sip a cool drink. Balneario Vistahermosa on Calle Hidalgo is one of the nicest facilities; admission is $2.50.

## South & West of Oaxaca City

In prosperous **Arrazola,** 12 km (8 mi) southwest of Oaxaca, off Carretera 131, artists carve angels, devils, and all sorts of fanciful animals out of light, porous copal wood. These brightly colored figures, from tiny to tremendous, are decorated with dots, squiggles, and other artful touches. This craft was developed by Arrazola's best-known artist, Don Manuel Jiménez, and almost everyone in town has jumped on the bandwagon. Some people may invite you into their homes to see their work.

About 4 km (2½ mi) beyond the turnoff for Arrazola you'll come to the dusty little town of **Culiapan.** Its claim to fame are the roofless ruins of a Dominican monastery called the **Ex-Convento de Santiago Apóstol.** The long, narrow structure was begun in 1560 but never finished. Vincente Guerrero, a hero of the country's battle for independence, was executed here in 1831. Admission is $2.50.

**Zaachila** was an important center of Zapotec civic and religious authority at the time of the Spanish invasion. On Thursday, oxcarts loaded with alfalfa or hay head for the area's liveliest livestock market. Get here before noon, or there won't be a pig left in the poke. The town, which is 17 km (11 mi) southwest of Oaxaca on Carretera 131, is known for its colorful church on the main square. Just behind the church is a small archaeological site with a pair of underground tombs that are fun to explore. An eerie carved owl guards one of the graves. Admission is $2.

The Nahuatl name of **San Bartolo Coyotepec** literally translates as "Place of the Coyotes." The town is 12 km (8 mi) south of Oaxaca on Carretera 175. Across from the stately church is a colonnaded square where you can buy the fragile, unglazed black ceramics for which the town is deservedly famous. Keep an eye out for the **Alfarerís Doña Rosa,** a workshop named for the woman who invented the technique for making the pottery. She died in 1980, but remains a revered figure in this town. In **Santo Tomás Jalieza,** 20 km (12 mi) south of Oaxaca and along a small road off Carretera 175, women make belts, sashes, and other woven goods on small back-strap looms. Prices are reasonable.

About 29 km (18 mi) south of Oaxaca on Carretera 175 is **San Martín Tilcajete,** a town full of painted wooden animals as well as cute carved devils, stern saints, and other religious items. **Ocotlán** is known for its handcrafted machetes and knives. The large town, 30 km (18 mi) south of Oaxaca on Carretera 175, has a beautifully restored church and monastery on an attractive main plaza. Friday's market draws buyers and sellers from the surrounding countryside. Near the entrance to town, the four Aguilar sisters—Josefina, Guillermina, Irene, and Concepción—makes distinctive figurines of red clay. The sisters, now elderly, might be there to show you around their adjoining workshops. If not, one of their children or grandchildren will. Buses from the second-class station depart for Ocotlán every 15 minutes or so.

## South & East of Oaxaca City

About 14 km (9 mi) east of Oaxaca on Carretera 190, the hamlet of **Santa María del Tule** is known for the huge *ahuehuete* cypress that towers over the pretty colonial-era church behind it. Thought to be more than 2,000 years old, it's one of the world's largest trees, with roots buried

# CloseUp

## TOURIST YU'US

YOU CAN EXPERIENCE LIFE in the villages around Oaxaca Valley by taking advantage of the **Tourist Yu'u project** (✉ Calle Murguía 204, at Calle 5 de Mayo, Centro Histórico ☎ 951/516–4828), developed by the state tourism board. You stay in basic, comfortable cabins that have semistocked kitchens or access to simple eateries nearby. The Yu'us are the ultimate budget lodging, costing as little as $4 per person per night.

There are Yu'us in nine villages, many quite close to Oaxaca City. Santa Ana del Valle is a Zapotec town with a tradition of making serapes, thick blankets now used as rugs; the Yu'u there at the entrance of the town is lovingly maintained. Two other popular Yu'us are at Hierve el Agua and Benito Juárez. You can visit cold-water springs and fossilized waterfalls at Hierve el Agua. You can rent bikes or horses for

juants into surrounding pine forest at Benito Juárez.

The volunteers in the Oaxaca office, located inside the state tourism office, don't speak much English, but they do have a book with photos of each of the lodgings and lists of the activities in the area. Take a good look before you book, as the accommodations vary greatly. Some are solidly built, while others are wooden cabins that are pretty but let in quite a few bugs. Note that the cabins are attended by volunteers, villagers who usually have other jobs. Don't expect five-star services, though your welcome will be warm. And it's a good idea to bring reading material, drinking water, and a few provisions.

---

more than 60 feet in the ground and a canopy arcing some 140 feet high. It has an estimated weight of nearly 640,000 tons; it would take 35 adults to embrace the trunk. The fee to see it is 20¢. At informal outdoor eateries in the Tule tree's shadow, local ladies tend large griddles, serving *atole* (a nutritious drink of ground cornmeal or rice), soups, and snacks.

Giant rug looms sit in the front rooms of many houses in **Teotitlán del Valle,** 30 km (18 mi) southeast of Oaxaca, just off Carretera 190. The small Museo Comunitario (closed Monday) on the main square focuses on the crafts and culture of the area. For an expensive (by local standards) but memorable lunch of authentic regional food, head for Tlamanalli at Avenida Juárez 39; the restaurant is so good it has been featured in several food magazines. The rug- and *serape*-making town of **Santa Ana del Valle** is less well known than Teotitlán but also worth visiting; prices here may be a bit cheaper. The turnoff for the town is 31 km (19 mi) from Oaxaca on Carretera 190.

Although most often visited during its bustling Sunday market, **Tlacolula,** 31 km (19 mi) east of Oaxaca on Carretera 190, makes an interesting stop midweek. While you're here, visit the baroque-style Capilla del Santo Cristo, a chapel dating from the 16th century.

⚓ There are several smaller archaeological sites along Carretera 190 before you reach Mitla, all worthy of a visit. The first is **Dainzú**, about 20 km (12 mi) outside of Oaxaca. Here you'll find some carvings that may remind you of the Dancers' Gallery at Monte Albán, though these clearly depict a ball game. The most spectacular sight is the *Tumba del Jaguar* (Tomb of the Jaguar), which is open daily 8–5. Admission is $2.

⚓ **Lambityeco,** about 29 km (19 mi) from Oaxaca, was built in the waning years of nearby Mitla. Its outstanding feature is a series of carvings that seem to depict the faces of nobles. There's also a carving of the rain god wearing an impressive headdress. The city flourished until AD 750, when it was abandoned. Many archaeologists believe the inhabitants moved to the better protected city of Yagul. ⊠ *Off of Carretera 190* ☎ *No phone* 🎟 *$2* ☉ *Daily 8–5.*

⚓ The ruins at **Yagul** aren't as elaborate as those at Monte Albán or Mitla, but their position atop a hill makes them more than worth a visit. This city, which is 36 km (22 mi) southeast of Oaxaca off Carretera 190, was predominantly a fortress protecting a group of temples. The *Palacio de los Seis Patios* (Palace of the Six Patios), a maze of hallways leading to hidden courtyards, is fun to explore. If you find the eerie *Tumba Triple* (Triple Tomb) locked, give the guard $1 or so to open it for you. He may even let you borrow a flashlight to get a good look at the carved skulls. ☎ *951/516–0123* 🎟 *$3* ☉ *Daily 8–5.*

★ ⚓ **Mitla,** 46 km (27 mi) southeast of Oaxaca, expanded and grew in influence as Monte Albán declined. Like its precursor, Mitla is a complex of structures started by the Zapotecs and later taken over by the Mixtecs. The striking architecture is almost without equal within Mexico thanks to the exquisite workmanship on the fine local quarry stone, which ranges in hue from pink to yellow. Unlike Monte Albán, Mitla's attraction lies not in its massive scale, but in its unusual ornamentation; the stonework depicts only mesmerizing abstract designs.

The name comes from the Aztec word *mictlan,* meaning "place of the dead." Don't expect to see anything resembling a graveyard, however; the Zapotecs and Mixtecs typically buried their dead under the entrance to the structure where the deceased resided. There are a few underground tombs in the *Grupo de las Columnas* (Group of the Columns), the main section of the ruins, that are fun to climb down into.

The journey on Carretera 190 takes about 50 minutes. If you haven't rented a car, you can catch a *colectivo* (collective taxi) at the side of Oaxaca City's second-class bus station or along the road to Mitla. ☎ *951/ 568–0316* 🎟 *$3* ☉ *Daily 8–5.*

## Oaxaca City A to Z

### AIR TRAVEL

AIRPORT  Oaxaca City's Aeropuerto Internacional Benito Juárez is 8 km (5 mi) south of town.

🛈 **Aeropuerto Internacional Benito Juárez** ☎ 951/511-5422.

AIRPORT
TRANSFERS
At the airport, Transportes Aeropuerto will trundle you into the soonest available van and drop you off at your hotel for $2.50 (more if there are no other passengers). From town, buy a ticket ahead of time (ask to be picked up at your hotel). The company is closed on Sunday; for Monday departures, purchase tickets by the preceding Saturday. Regular cabs cost about $10.

🚐 Shuttles **Transportes Aeropuerto** ⊠ West side of Alameda de León, Centro Histórico ☎ 951/514-4350.

CARRIERS
Mexicana flies from various U.S. cities (including Chicago, Los Angeles, Miami, New York, and San Francisco) to Oaxaca City with a stop in Mexico City, as does Aeroméxico (from Chicago, Dallas–Fort Worth, Houston, Los Angeles, Miami, New York, and Phoenix). Direct service from Oaxaca to Acapulco and Cancún is available on Aviacsa, which flies to other national destinations via Mexico City.

Aero Vega has daily service to Puerto Escondido (sometimes less in low season) and charter service to Huatulco. Aerocaribe has two triangular routes (Oaxaca–Puerto Escondido–Huatulco and in the opposite direction) each day. Aerotucán also has daily flights between Oaxaca City and both Puerto Escondido and Huatulco.

🛩 **Aero Vega** ☎ 951/516-4982 in Oaxaca, 958/582-0151 in Puerto Escondido. **Aerocaribe** ☎ 951/511-5247. **Aeroméxico** ☎ 951/516-1066, 800/237-6639 in the U.S. **Aerotucán** ☎ 951/501-0532. **Aviacsa** ☎ 951/511-5039. **Mexicana** ☎ 951/516-8414, 800/531-7921 in the U.S.

## BUS TRAVEL

Deluxe buses make the six-hour nonstop run from Mexico City to Oaxaca for between $28 and $41. Oaxaca City's first-class terminal is frequently referred to as the ADO, because ADO is the most prominent bus company. UNO and Cristóbal Colón also have frequent service to regional destinations such as Puebla, Veracruz, and Villahermosa. The second-class bus station, Central de Autobuses, serves smaller towns within the state. It's southwest of the zócalo near the Central de Abastos.

🚌 Bus Terminals **Oaxaca City (first-class)** ⊠ Calz. Niños Héroes de Chapultepec 1036, at Calle Emilio Carranza ☎ 951/513-0529. **Oaxaca City (second-class)** ⊠ Prolongación de Trujano at the Periférico ☎ 951/516-1218.

## CAR RENTAL

You won't need a car in Oaxaca City, which is fairly compact. Though outlying sights are easily accessible through many travel agencies, a car is a great way for adventurous souls to see more remote villages and archaeological sites at their own pace.

🚗 Major Agencies **Alamo** ⊠ Calle 5 de Mayo 203, Centro Histórico ☎ 951/514-8534. **Budget** ⊠ Calle 5 de Mayo 315, across from the Camino Real Oaxaca, Centro Histórico ☎ 951/515-0330, 951/511-5252 at the airport. **Hertz** ⊠ Plaza Labastida 115-49, Centro Histórico ☎ 951/516-2434, 951/511-5478 at the airport.

## CAR TRAVEL

If you have plenty of time, you can take Carretera 190 (the Pan-American Highway) south and east through Puebla to Oaxaca City—a distance of 546 km (338 mi) along a rather curvy road. This route takes between 7 to 8 hours if you drive straight through. If you want to get there quicker, the *cuota* (toll road) that connects Mexico City to Oaxaca City cuts the driving time down to about 5 or 6 hours. It costs about $30 one way.

The roads leading out to the Oaxaca Valley are fairly well paved, though be forewarned that the section of Carretera 190 by Tlacolula is riddled with potholes of amazing size and depth. On the roads branching out from Carretera 190, be on the lookout for speed bumps, which often aren't painted (if you see a sign that says "Tope," slow down) and inexplicably placed in areas where there's nothing for miles but cattle. Lastly, make sure to fill up whenever you see a gas station.

### CONSULATES
🖪 **Canadian Consulate** ⊠ Calle Pino Suarez 700, Local 11-B, Centro Histórico ☎ 951/513-3777. **U.S. Consulate** ⊠ Calle Macedonio Alcalá 407, Int. 20, Centro Histórico ☎ 951/514-3054.

### EMERGENCIES
🖪 **General Emergencies** ☎ 066. **Hospital-Red Cross** ⊠ Av. Armenta and López 700, Centro Histórico ☎ 951/516-4455. **Police** ☎ 951/516-0400.

### MAIL, INTERNET & SHIPPING
There are several Internet cafés downtown. Axis, open weekdays 10–8 and Saturday 10–6, charges about $2 an hour. The centrally located *correos* (post office) is open weekdays 8–7 and Saturday 9–1. A good place to ship packages home is Artesanías Chimalli.
🖪 Cyberafé **Axis** ⊠ Calle 5 de Mayo 412, Centro Histórico ☎ 951/514-8024.
🖪 Mail **Correos** ⊠ Av. Independencia at the Alameda, Centro Histórico ☎ 951/516-2661.
🖪 Shipping **Artesanías Chimalli** ⊠ Calle García Vigil 513-A, Centro Histórico ☎ 951/514-2101.

### MONEY MATTERS
There are loads of banks in the Centro Histórico, and most have ATMs. *Casas de cambio* (currency exchange offices) have rates comparable to those at banks; in addition, their lines are shorter and they tend to stay open longer. Most hotels and tourist-oriented restaurants and shops accept credit cards and traveler's checks; markets and smaller establishments in the city and the villages prefer cash.

A block from the zócalo, Banamex is open weekdays 9–4. Banorte has similar hours. Both have reliable ATMs. You can exchange currency at the Casa de Cambio Puebla weekdays 9–6 and Saturday 9–2.
🖪 Bank **Banamex** ⊠ Av. Hidalgo 821, 1 block east of the Zócalo, Centro Histórico ☎ 951/516-5900. **Banorte** ⊠ García Vigil 103, Centro Histórico ☎ 951/516-4940.
🖪 Exchange **Casa de Cambio Puebla** ⊠ Calle García Vigil 106, Centro Histórico ☎ 951/514-5103.

### TAXIS
Taxis are plentiful, clearly marked, and reasonably priced. You can usually find them at any hour of the day cruising on downtown streets. There are also stands on Avenida Independencia at Calle García Vigil,

on the north side of the Alameda, and on Calles Abasolo and 5 de Mayo, near the Camino Real Oaxaca. Cabs aren't metered. Determine the fare ahead of time (in town, usually $2–$3), or pay about $15 an hour for destinations within the city. For outlying destinations, ask the driver to show you the tariff card, or agree on a price before setting out.

### TOURS

There are dozens of travel agencies scattered around Oaxaca City, and all offer guided trips to outlying archaeological sites and villages. Always available are half- and full-day tours of the city, half-day excursions to Monte Albán, and full-day journeys to Mitla that usually stop at the tree in Santa María del Tule on the way back. You can also book trips to villages that coincide with market days. Do some research into the various markets and tell the companies which ones you'd like to see. Otherwise, you'll be pressed to go wherever the company happens to be headed the next day. Viajes Turísticos Mitla and Agencia Marqués del Valle are among the most established agencies.

🖪 **Agencia Marqués del Valle** ⊠ Portal de Clavería s/n, Centro Histórico ☎ 951/514–6970 or 951/514–6962. **Viajes Turísticos Mitla** ⊠ Hotel Rivera del Ángel, Calle Mina 518, Centro Histórico ☎ 951/516–6175.

### VISITOR INFORMATION

The Municipal Tourism Office is open daily 8–8. Although the staff is eager to help you out, few speak English. It's a good idea to know exactly what you need before you go inside. Asking for general information on markets may get you a blank stare; asking for directions to Ocotlán will get you a decent map and information on buses.

🖪 **Municipal Tourism Office** ⊠ Av. Independencia 607, at Calle García Vigil, Centro Histórico ☎ 951/516–0123.

# THE OAXACA COAST

Oaxaca's 520-km (322-mi) coastline is one of mainland Mexico's last Pacific frontiers. The town of Puerto Escondido has long been prime territory for international surfers and its four-block pedestrian walkway, crowded with open-air seafood restaurants, shops, and cafés, is indeed, lively. Across the highway, however, the "real" town above provides a look at local life and a dazzling view of the coast.

Midway between Puerto Escondido and Bahías de Huatulco, tiny Puerto Ángel has a limited selection of hotels and bungalows tucked into the hills. The growing number of accommodations in nearby beach villages such as Zipolite and Mazunte has seduced some of Puerto Ángel's previously faithful sun-lovers.

Bahías de Huatulco (generally called simply Huatulco) covers 51,900 acres, 40,000 of which are dedicated as a nature reserve. The focal point of the development, which was masterminded in the 1980s by Fonatur (the government's tourism developer), is a string of nine sheltered bays that stretches across 35 km (22 mi) of stunning coast. The first in this necklace is Conejos, which has Huatulco's most luxurious private villas and two boutique hotels. The town of La Crucecita, originally built to house the construction crews working on area developments, has the requisite plaza with a Catholic church as well as a thriving market, small shops, budget and moderately priced hotels, and plenty of restaurants.

Bahía Tangolunda is home to Huatulco's most exclusive hotels, whereas Santa Cruz has mid-range hotels as well as a marina and a cruise ship terminal. Development of Bahía Chahué has begun with an 88-slip marina, a luxury spa, and a few small hotels. A parking lot makes the beach accessible, and a public beach club has changing rooms, a restaurant, and a swimming pool. A Best Western and a few other small hotels, bars, and restaurants are near this bay, but most are across the highway on Boulevard Benito Juárez.

## Puerto Escondido

**12** *310 km (192 mi) south of Oaxaca City.*

A coffee-shipping port in the 1920s, Puerto Escondido is now dedicated more to coffee sipping. It was the first beach resort on the *carretera costera* (coastal highway), and it remains the most popular. Playa Zicatela is famous for its waves, drawing surfers from around the world. It doesn't hurt that this beach is also one of the prettiest on the coast.

Although it bills itself as a bustling beach resort, Puerto Escondido is still a fishing village. Little boys still walk from restaurant to restaurant with plastic pails full of fish they have caught, and men sit around repairing their nets and trading tips on the best spots to find barracuda or pompano.

Puerto Escondido is divided into three sections, each attracting a different clientele. El Adoquín, the part of Avenida Pérez Gasga that is reserved for pedestrians, runs right through the center of the town. This area is most popular with Mexican families. You'll find plenty of inexpensive shops, restaurants, and hotels along the four blocks.

Calle de Morro is the domain of foreign teens and twentysomethings, as this road parallels Playa Zicatela. Surfside shacks all claim that they sell the "world's coldest beer." Don't expect much local color; it's indistinguishable from similar stretches of sand worldwide.

Carrizalillo is the least developed of the tourist areas of Puerto Escondido, and the people who stay here like it that way. The hotels, most of them upscale, cater to families. Along Boulevard Benito Juárez are some of the town's best restaurants. Oh, and if you were wondering why this street is as wide as a runway, it used to be the airport. The new one is across the carretera costera.

One of the easiest day trips from Puerto Escondido is the wildlife preserve of **Laguna de Manialtepac.** This lovely lake about 14 km (9 mi) from the center of town is a birder's paradise, with parrots, pelicans, and spoonbills in the surrounding mangrove forests. Several restaurants on the shores of the lake have launches to bring you close to the wildlife.

About 74 km (46 mi) west of Puerto Escondido is the **Parque Nacional Laguna Chacahua** (Chacahua Lake National Park). You can tour the la-

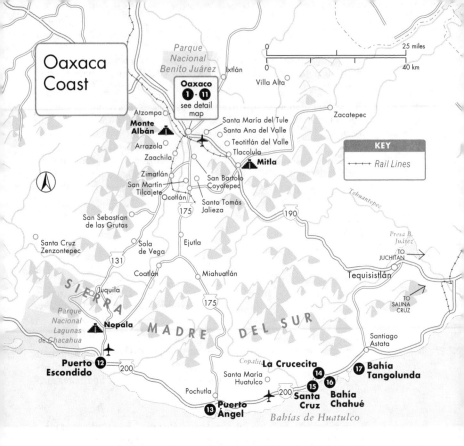

goon in a small motor launch, watching the birds that hunt among the mangroves. The bird population is most numerous during the winter months, when migratory species arrive from the frozen north. Most tours from Puerto Escondido include a visit to a crocodile farm and an hour or two on the beach at Cerro Hermoso.

If you want a bit of pampering, cleanse your body and soul at **Temazcalli,** a spa that claims its treatments combine the energy of wood, fire, rock, and medicinal herbs. Choose an individual (for one or two) steam or a ritualistic group cleansing; the latter involves chants and prayers. Or opt for a good old-fashioned massage with scented oils. ⊠ *Av. Infraganti 28, at Calle Temazcalli* ☎ 📠 *958/582–1023.*

### Beaches

**Playa Bacocho.** This beach west of town is backed by high red cliffs. It's ringed by upscale housing and hotel developments as well as some inviting bars, discos, and restaurants. The rip currents are strong along this stretch of beach, so swimming isn't advised.

**Playa Carrizalillo.** In a region full of beautiful beaches, Playa Carrizalillo can still make you breathless. The high cliffs that surround it ensure that it is never too crowded. The water here is clean and clear.

**Playa Manzanillo.** Of Puerto Escondido's seven beaches, Playa Manzanillo, which rings Puerto Angelito, is one of the safest for swimming and snorkeling. You can reach it on foot from paths west of town, by taxi ($2 per ride), or by boat ($3 per person) from Playa Marinero. It has calm, clean water and informal snack shops selling juices, sodas, and beer.

**Playa Marinero.** The sand is clean but somewhat hard and brown at this strip of sand that runs parallel to Avenida Pérez Gasga. There are restaurants where you can retreat from the sun and treat yourself to a cool drink. Fishing and tour boats leave from Playa Marinero, beyond which, around a jumble of giant rocks creeping out into the surf is the most famous—and dangerous—beach of all, Playa Zicatela.

FodorśChoice
★ **Playa Zicatela.** One of the world's top 10 surfing beaches, Zicatela's cream-color sands are battered by the mighty Mexican Pipeline. In November international surfing championships are held here (followed by the even more popular bikini contest), though the town is just about always filled with sun-bleached aficionados of both sexes intent on serious surfing and hard partying. There are often lifeguards on duty, but only the most confident should swim here; even when the waters appear calm, the undertows and rip currents can be deadly. If you have any doubts about your prowess, settle for watching the surfers.

## Where to Stay & Eat

$–$$ ✕ **La Galería.** Every inch of wall space at this open-air restaurant is filled with works by local artists. And every inch of your table will be covered by platters of homemade pasta, topped with cheese, shrimp, or even smoked salmon. Pizzas are also popular; try the one with eggplant, garlic, mushrooms, and herbs. ⊠ *Av. Pérez Gasga s/n, across from tourist office* ☎ *954/582–2039* ▭ *No credit cards.*

$–$$ ✕ **Junto al Mar.** The name means "Beside the Sea," and that's certainly the case: tables in the open-air dining room overlook kids playing at Playa Marinero. Some of the boats bobbing in the bay probably brought in the fresh seafood on the menu. You get to tell the chef how to prepare it—panfried with some garlic, for example, or sautéed with tomatoes and onions. ⊠ *Av. Pérez Gasga 600* ☎ *954/582–1272* ▭ *AE, MC, V.*

$–$$ ✕ **La Perla.** Because it's a bit of a hike from the beach, this seafood restaurant has some of the best prices in town. The cavernous dining room is prepared to serve multitudes; don't feel put off if you're the only one there. The octopus is tender, and the *ceviche* (marinated raw fish) melts in your mouth. Breakfast is served daily. ⊠ *Calle 3a Poniente s/n, Sector Juárez* ☎ *954/582–0461* ▭ *No credit cards.*

$–$$ ✕ **Perla Flameante.** At the Flaming Pearl, slices of dorado, shark, barracuda, and seven other types of fish come prepared with a multitude of seasonings and accompanied by terrific deep-fried onion rings and zucchini strips. The second-story restaurant is high enough to catch a breeze while those down below are still sweltering. ⊠ *Av. Pérez Gasga, near Mar y Sol* ☎ *954/582–0167* ▭ *MC, V.*

★ $ ✕ **La Torre.** Perhaps the only restaurant in Puerto Escondido with tablecloths, this casually elegant place is popular with travelers in the know and locals who would rather keep it a secret. Its out-of-the-way location at the far end of Boulevard Benito Juárez doesn't seem to deter anyone. Steaks are available anytime, but the *costillas de cerdo* (pork ribs) are only on the menu on Friday. On pleasant evenings there's no better place to sit than beside the fountain in the garden. ⊠ *Blvd. Benito Juárez 427* ☎ *954/582–1119* ⊟ *No credit cards* ☉ *Closed Mon.*

★ ¢ ✗ **El Cafecito.** Not much more than a pair of thatched palapas, El Cafecito, doesn't look like much. In reality, it's the center of the universe and everything you need to know about Puerto Escondido is either tacked to a post or being passed around by word of mouth. Oh, and then there's the food: burgers topped with bacon or avocado for lunch, and more substantial fare, such as grilled fish, for dinner. The restaurant is known for its whole-grain breads and fruit-filled pastries. ⊠ *Calle del Morro s/n, across from Playa Zicatela* ☎ *954/582–0516* ⊟ *No credit cards.*

**$$–$$$** ✗⊡ **Hotel Santa Fe.** An impressive archway leads you to Santa Fe, a hotel
**Fodor'sChoice** that feels more like a small village. A cluster of colonial-style buildings
★ in pastel shades is surrounded by well-tended gardens filled with brilliant red hibiscus. You can catch a glimpse of the surf from the balcony of your room or bungalow. There's no need ever to leave, as you can dine at the excellent restaurant ($–$$) or prepare a meal in your own kitchenette. ⊠ *Calle del Morro s/n, across from Playa Zicatela 71980* ☎ *954/582–0170 or 888/649–6407* ⊟ *954/582–0260* ⊕ *www.hotelsantafe.com.mx* ↪ *59 rooms, 2 suites, 8 bungalows* ⚭ *Restaurant, some kitchenettes, cable TV, 3 pools, wading pool, bar, shops, laundry service, Internet, free parking* ⊟ *AE, MC, V.*

¢ ✗⊡ **Flor de María.** Half a block from Playa Marinero, this colonial-style building couldn't have a better location. The choicest rooms have little balconies. All rooms are reached via a plant-filled courtyard painted vivid shades of gold and red. In La Galera ($), daily dinner specials get Italian and Peruvian touches. There's always at least one vegetarian option on the menu. ⊠ *Entrance to Playa Marinero, 71980* ☎ *954/582–0536* ⊟ *954/582–2617* ⊕ *www.mexonline.com/flordemaria.htm* ↪ *24 rooms* ⚭ *Restaurant, fans, in-room safes, pool, bar, laundry service; no room phones, no room TVs* ⊟ *MC, V* ☉ *Restaurant closed May–Nov. and on Tues. June–Aug. and Oct.–Nov.*

**$$** ⊡ **La Hacienda.** The predominately French country–style suites at this boutique hotel have fresh flowers, a sprinkling of carefully chosen antiques, and blue-and-white Mexican tiles. The kitchenettes are sizable and the patio restaurant serves one or two items for dinner daily during high season (December–March) and with advance notice at other times. ⊠ *Calle Atunes 15, 71980* ☎ *954/582–0096* ↪ *7 suites* ⚭ *Restaurant, kitchenettes, pool, beach, laundry service* ⊟ *MC, V.*

**$$** ⊡ **Hotel Aldea del Bazar.** Like a mirage, this sparkling white Middle Eastern–influenced hotel sits high on a bluff overlooking the calm waters of Playa Bacocho. The rooms either overlook the surf or the manicured lawns. All have tasteful little sitting areas with low couches covered in brightly colored pillows. The pre-Colombian eucalyptus sauna will help you relax before heading to dinner at the Moorish-style restaurant. The food is good and there's a variety of international dishes and seafood specialties. ⊠ *Blvd. Benito Juárez 7, 71980* ☎ *954/582–0508* ↪ *47 rooms* ⚭ *Restaurant, cable TV, pool, massage, sauna, spa, beach, bar, travel services, free parking* ⊟ *AE, MC, V.*

**$$** ▦ **Villas Carrizalillo.** A cluster of bungalows in a little-known part of Puerto Escondido, Villas Carrizalillo is perfect for those in search of a little solitude. The tile-roofed villas are arranged in such a way that you're never looking into someone else's window. They range in size from a small studio to a three-bedroom abode with a private yard. A favorite, called the Puebla, has two balconies overlooking Playa Carrizalillo. ⊠ *Av. Carrizalillo 125, 71980* ☎ *954/582–1735* ⊕ *www.villascarrizalillo.com* ⇗ *10 rooms* ⚭ *Kitchens, beach, snorkeling, boating, bicycles; no room phones* ⊟ No credit cards.

**$$** ▦ **Villa Roca Suites.** Looking a little like a sand castle, Villa Roca certainly has a sense of whimsy. But it's serious about your comfort, so the rooms have more than enough space for two people to spread out. Most have two balconies—one overlooking the street, the other the shore— so you can even have some alone time. Since the hotel is right on the beach, you can have your toes in the water in no time. ⊠ *Av. Pérez Gasga, 71980* ☎ *954/582–3525* ▤ *954/582–3443* ⇗ *6 suites* ⚭ *Cable TV, beach; no room phones* ⊟ *No credit cards.*

**$** ▦ **Paraíso Escondido.** Hidden halfway up the steps of Calle Unión, this colonial-style hotel has the charm of a wealthy—and somewhat dotty— relative's house. Each room has its own mix of folksy wooden furniture, fanciful tin mirrors, and what can only be described as "art." You might, for example, have a hand-carved alligator staring at you while you shave. Five third-floor suites have kitchenettes and private, oceanview terraces, one with a hot tub overlooking the sea. ⊠ *Calle Unión 10, 71980* ☎ *954/582–0444* ⇗ *20 rooms, 5 suites* ⚭ *Restaurant, pool, bar, library; no room TVs* ⊟ *No credit cards.*

**¢–$** ▦ **Arco Iris.** This three-story hotel has something no other lodging on Playa Zicatela has: private verandas hung with hammocks within sight of the surf. On a breezy day almost every hammock is occupied. That makes up for other shortcomings, such as the slightly worn furnishings and dated exterior. There's also a large swimming pool, a video viewing room, and a second-floor vegetarian restaurant. ⊠ *Calle del Morro s/n, across from Playa Zicatela, 71980* ☎☎ *954/582–0432 or 954/582–1494* ⊕ *www.oaxaca-mio.com/arcoiris.htm* ⇗ *32 rooms, 4 suites* ⚭ *Restaurant, pool, beach, bar, laundry service, free parking* ⊟ *MC, V.*

**¢–$** ▦ **Villa Belmar.** Maintenance on the Villa Belmar's array of arches, domes, and cupolas—done in Mediterranean white and blue—is zealous, if not always careful. The one-bedroom apartments, comfortable double rooms, and spartan surfer huts attract a mix of people. Many accommodations have balconies from which to admire Playa Zicatela, a stone's throw away. You can rent by the day in high season and by the week or the month at other times. ⊠ *Calle del Morro s/n, Playa Zicatela 71980* ☎ *954/582– 0244* ▤ *954/582–2520* ⊕ *www.villabelmar.com* ⇗ *18 rooms, 15 suites, 5 apartments* ⚭ *Restaurant, pool, free parking* ⊟ *MC, V.*

**¢** ▦ **Casa Vieja.** The most charming lodging in the older section of Puerto Escondido, this colonial-style building has little balconies overlooking Avenida Pérez Gasga. The rooms have nice touches like decorative borders on the walls. Instead of a fountain, the courtyard has a wishing well. ⊠ *Av. Pérez Gasga s/n, 71980* ☎ *954/582–1454* ⇗ *22 rooms* ⚭ *Shop, no room phones* ⊟ *No credit cards.*

¢ ⊡ **Tabachín.** Well-stocked kitchenettes, shelves filled with books, and an assortment of clocks, vases, and other items make the studios here feel homey. Given the location a block from Playa Zicatela, the room rates are astonishingly low. Owner Don Pablo also manages a small country inn, the Posada Nopala, about two hours inland in the pine forests of the Oaxaca mountains. ⊠ *Calle de Morro s/n, across from Playa Zicatela, 71980* 🕾 *954/582–1179* ⊕ *www.tabachin.com.mx* ⤳ *6 apartments* ⚲ *Restaurant, kitchenettes* 🖃 *MC, V* ⎮◉⎮ *BP.*

## Nightlife & the Arts

NIGHTLIFE You won't have trouble getting yourself into trouble in Puerto Escondido. Simply head down to Playa Zicatela, where dozens of little shacks serve up cold beer. Set under a dramatic dome, **Casa Babylon** (⊠ Calle de Morro s/n, across from Playa Zicatela 🕾 No phone) is certainly the most beautiful bar near Playa Zicatela. While you nurse your beer, you can challenge friends to a game of Scrabble or Monopoly.

For spirited live entertainment, stop by **Son y La Rumba** (⊠ Av. Pérez Gasga s/n 🕾 No phone), behind the tourist information booth. Owner Myka sings every night, but you never know who will drop in to jam with her— a classical violinist or a flamenco guitarist. The bar is open from 10:30 PM until around 2 AM, sometimes later.

THE ARTS On Plazoleta San Raphael, **Cinema Paradiso** (⊠ Calle 3a Poniente 911 🕾 No phone) screens new and old movies every day at 3, 5, and 7 PM, with an added matinee on weekends at noon. If nobody else shows up, you can have the projectionist play any movie they have on hand!

## Sports & the Outdoors

Puerto Escondido's pretty coves aren't as deserted as they seem. For about $80, you and your friends can hire a boat for a three-hour bay tour to look for dolphins and sea turtles. Contact **Adventura Submarina** (⊠ Av. Pérez Gasga 601 🕾 954/588–1682).

FISHING If you're in search of the really big fish—barracudas, marlins, and sailfish— then you've come to the right place. **Omar's Sportfishing** (⊠ Playa Puerto Angelito 🕾954/559–4406 ⊕www.oaxaca-mio.com/omarsportfishing.htm) will take you out on a four-hour tour of the best fishing spots for about $135 for up to four people.

SURFING Playa Zicatela is the best place to hang ten in Puerto Escondido, so it's no surprise the oceanfront walk is crowded with surf shops. You can rent surfboards or buy beachwear at **Mexpipe** (⊠ Calle del Morro s/n, across from Playa Zicatela 🕾954/582–0759). The staff here is also happy to give individual lessons ($20 per hour).

# Shopping

The town's sprawling market, **Mercado Benito Juárez,** is a long walk (but a short cab ride) from the beaches. It's worth checking out on the busiest days, which are Wednesday and Saturday. If you don't feel like going to the market, the market will come to you. Vendors wander down along the beaches selling everything from bracelets to blankets.

If you'd like more than a few beads to take home, **Oro de Monte Albán** (✉ Av. Pérez Gasga, at Marina Nacional ☎ 954/582–0530) sells gold and silver fashioned into ancient designs.

**en route** Off Carretera 131, the road between Puerto Escondido and Oaxaca City, **Juquila** is home to the miracle-working, diminutive Virgen de Juquila. The saint's day, December 8, is preceded by nine days of prayers and festivities, including fireworks, carnival rides, dances, and general gaiety. Any time of year, however, is pleasant to visit the small town in the heart of coffee country. Inexpensive hotels that cater to the constant stream of pilgrims line the hilly streets.

## Puerto Ángel

**⑬** *81 km (50 mi) southeast of Puerto Escondido.*

The state's leading seaport 100 years ago, Puerto Ángel today is simply a tiny town on a stunning bay. Its charms come from what it is not, namely overcommercialized like Huatulco and overgrown like Puerto Escondido.

The **Centro Mexicano de la Tortuga** is at Playa Mazunte. The local economy was based on exploitation of the *golfina* (olive ridley) turtle until the government put a ban on turtle hunting in 1990. Since then the slaughterhouse has been closed, and, poachers aside, Mazunte is now devoted to protecting the species. The beach's name derives from the Nahuatl word *Maxonteita,* which means "please come and spawn" and, indeed, four of the world's eight species of marine turtles come to lay their eggs on Oaxaca's shores. A dozen aquariums are filled with turtle specimens that once again flourish in the nearby ocean. ✉ *Playa Mazunte* ☎ *No phone* 🎟 *$2* ☉ *Tues.–Sun. 9–4.*

### Beaches
**Playa Mazunte.** About 13 km (8 mi) west of Puerto Ángel on Carretera 200, Mazunte is a stunning stretch of sand, which has its share of simple seafood restaurants and low-key accommodations.

**Playa Panteón.** The navy has its installations on this central town beach on Carretera 200. The most popular swimming-and-sunning territory is past the oceanfront cemetery (*panteón* means "cemetery"). Other good and less-populated swimming and snorkeling beaches are nearby.

★ **Playa San Agustanillo.** This long stretch west of town (past Zipolite) is pretty and somewhat safe for swimming, although the current is very strong. Vendors roam the sand selling cool drinks and grilled fish.

**Playa Zipolite.** Though a favorite with surfers, nude sunbathers, and wild young things, Zipolite also appeals to travelers content with a hammock on the beach and little else in the way of creature comforts. The long stretch of creamy sand is 4 km (2 mi) west of town. Note that the undertow is extremely strong and riptides are unpredictable.

### Where to Stay & Eat
**$** ✕ **Rincón del Mar.** A few steps from the soft sands of Playa del Panteón, this restaurant is the envy of all the others. From a table in the open-air dining room you can watch as the fishermen return with the catch

of the day. Choose your fish (the tuna and pompano are good) and how you want it prepared. Or try the *pescado a la cazuela,* a rich seafood stew. ⊠ *Playa del Panteón* ☎ *No phone* ☰ *No credit cards.*

¢ ✕▦ **Posada Cañon Devata.** The simple bungalows at this ecologically minded hideaway are scattered around a wooded canyon. There are even simpler rooms on several floors of the rambling main house. There's no hot water, but there are nice touches like lamps carved to resemble jaguars and other beasts. The thatched-roof restaurant is a find for vegetarians, who sometimes hike over from other hotels. ⊠ *Pedro Sainz de Baranza s/n, off Blvd. Virgilio Uribe, 70902* ☎ *958/584-3137* ✍ *janedarshan@yahoo.com* ⮑ *16 rooms, 6 bungalows* ⚲ *Restaurant, bar; no a/c, no room phones, no room TVs* ☰ *No credit cards.*

¢–$ ▦ **Ángel del Mar.** On a bluff overlooking Playa del Panteón, this hotel doesn't exaggerate when it claims to have the best views. It also has Puerto Ángel's most comfortable accommodations. They aren't fancy, but they're modern and have amenities other local lodgings don't offer, such as hot water. ⊠ *Pedro Sainz de Baranza s/n, off Blvd. Virgilio Uribe, 70900* ☎ *958/584-3008* ☎ *958/584-3014* ⮑ *44 rooms* ⚲ *Restaurant, pool, bar* ☰ *MC, V.*

¢ ▦ **La Buena Vista.** The rooms on the top level of this hillside hotel have a great view of the bay, as well as the best breezes. Some have balconies, others have terraces with hammocks. None have hot water or much of anything that could be called an amenity. The third-floor restaurant (which serves breakfast and dinner) has one of the most dependable kitchens in town, although the service suffers when there's a crowd. ⊠ *Calle la Buena Compañía, 70902* ⊕ *www.labuenavista.com* ☎☎ *958/584-3104* ⮑ *20 rooms* ⚲ *Restaurant, shop; no a/c, no room phones, no room TVs* ☰ *No credit cards.*

### Sports & the Outdoors

**Excursions Cary** (⊠ Muelle Puerto Ángel, Blvd. Virgilio Uribe at Calle José Vasconcelos ☎ 958/584-3053) can take you out to look for sea turtles and dolphins daily at 10:30, 2, and 6:30. Look for them on the main dock.

## Bahías de Huatulco

*277 km (172 mi) south of Oaxaca City, 111 km (69 mi) east of Puerto Escondido, 48 km (30 mi) east of Puerto Ángel.*

☞ Development in the beautiful Bahías de Huatulco (Bays of Huatulco) continues to march slowly forward. Because of the fits and starts of its construction, the area has an unfinished look. Four of the nine bays have been developed, but only Bahía Tangolunda, with its golf course and luxury hotels, has the look of a resort.

If you have a car, you can drive to one of several undeveloped bays and play Robinson Crusoe to your heart's content. Boat tours are also an option. Standard four- to eight-hour trips—depending on how many bays you visit—might include a lunch of freshly caught fish. Fishing, diving, and snorkeling tours visit the beaches and reefs.

⓮ **La Crucecita,** off Carretera 200, is the only place in Huatulco that resembles—in a rather artificial way—a real Mexican town. Its central plaza has a church whose inside walls are covered with naive frescoes. This is also a place where you can dine, hang out at sidewalk cafés, and browse in boutiques. You'll also find a bank, bus station, and Internet cafés here.

⓯ **Santa Cruz,** on the bay of the same name, was the center of a 30-family fishing community until development forced everyone to move elsewhere. Today the bay is the perfect spot for swimming, snorkeling, and boating, and you can arrange boat tours and fishing trips at the marina. Mingle with the locals in the central zócalo—perhaps on the wrought-iron gazebo—or sip a cool drink or cappuccino in the Café Huatulco.

⓰ For a relaxing day on the beach, head to **Bahía Chahué.** The beach parking lot has a lookout point, and the marina has 88 slips, though other services aren't yet in place. You'll find a swimming pool, changing rooms, a restaurant, and shaded lounge chairs at the public beach club; there are also hotels on the main road, Boulevard Benito Juárez.

⓱ The Huatulco of the future is most evident at **Bahía Tangolunda,** where the poshest hotels are in full swing and the sea is abob with sightseeing *lanchas* (small motorboats), kayaks, and sailboats. The site was chosen by developers because of its five beautiful beaches. Although there's a small complex with shops and restaurants across from the entrance to the Barceló hotel on Boulevard Benito Juárez, most of the shopping and dining take place in the towns of Santa Cruz and La Crucecita, each about 10 minutes from the hotels by taxi or bus.

## Where to Stay & Eat

LA CRUCECITA & SANTA CRUZ
$–$$$

✗ **Ve El Mar.** Once a seafood shack, this is now a romantic restaurant where you can wiggle your toes in soft sand by the water's edge. It's a good spot for a casual lunch, candlelight dinner, or a "morning after" ceviche. The specialty is *piña rellena,* a hollowed-out pineapple stuffed with baked shrimp au gratin. ⊠ *Bahía Santa Cruz* ☎ *958/587–0364* ▤ *No credit cards.*

$–$$
✗ **Oasis.** Thought you had to say adios to sushi during your trip to Mexico? Not so: California rolls and other freshly prepared morsels are on this restaurant's Japanese menu. You can also order from the regular menu, which includes favorites such as hamburgers and chicken salad. ⊠ *Calle Flamboyan 211, at Calle Bugambilia, La Crucecita* ☎ *958/587–0045* ▤ *AE, MC, V.*

★ $
✗ **Sabor de Oaxaca.** Almost as popular with locals as it is with visitors, this open-air restaurant is one of the best in La Crucecita. Massive sampler plates introduce neophytes to refried beans, guacamole, tortillas, salsas, stuffed chilies, marinated meats, and more. You can go as far as cactus soup or crunchy grasshoppers (in season) or play it safe with a juicy steak or a burger with fries. It's open until midnight, so this is a good place for a late-night snack. ⊠ *Calle Guamuchil 206, La Crucecita 70989* ☎ *958/587–0060* ▤ *AE, MC, V.*

$–$$
▥ **Posada Arrecife.** This two-story hotel is one of the best deals in La Crucecita, possibly the reason it's so popular with Mexican families. Most of the clean, comfortable rooms have ceiling fans, but for a bit more you can get air-conditioning. The staff is courteous and helpfu. ⊠ *Calle*

*Colorín 510, La Crucecita 70989* ☎ *958/587–1707* 🖷 *958/587–1737*
✆ *hotelarrecife@hotmail.com* 🖵 *28 rooms* ⚲ *Restaurant, fans, cable
TV, pool, laundry service, free parking; no a/c in some rooms, no room
phones* ▤ *MC, V.*

★ ¢–$   🏨 **Misión de los Arcos.** Everything about this hotel is luxurious—except
for the rates. Each room is different, but all have adobe-style rounded
walls and alcoves filled with local handicrafts; most also have small balconies. The honeymoon suite has a huge garden patio filled with plants,
a wrought-iron table and chairs, and a fountain. ✉ *Calle Gardenia 902,
La Crucecita 70989* ☎ *958/587–0165* 🖷 *958/587–1904* ⊕ *www.
misiondelosarcos.com* 🖵 *15 rooms* ⚲ *Café, fans, gym, Internet; no a/c
in some rooms* ▤ *AE, MC, V.*

BAHÍA   ✕ **Don Porfirio.** At this casual eatery, you can grab a table in the dining
TANGOLUNDA   room or out on the covered patio. There's a good variety of Mexican
$–$$$   dishes, such as the grasshoppers fried with garlic. There are also international options, such as shish kebab flavored with tequila. Locals
swear that the lobster is the best in town. ✉ *Zona Hotelera Tangolunda,
across from Hotel Gala* ☎ *958/581–0001* ▤ *AE, MC, V.*

★ $$$–$$$$   ✕🏨 **Camino Real Zaashila.** The free-form pool with built-in lounge
chairs around its rim is an irresistible draw to this gleaming white resort. If you'd like a bit more privacy, ask for one of the 40 rooms with
a private pool. From there you can have a view of the secluded lagoon.
Waterfalls punctuate the property's 27 acres, and a dreamy nature walk
runs from one end of it to the other. The elegant yet casual Chez Binni
($$–$$$) looks out past the pool to the ocean. Try the bouillabaisse for
two. ✉ *Blvd. Benito Juárez 5, 70989* ☎ *958/581–0460, 800/722–6466
in the U.S.* 🖷 *958/581–0461* ⊕ *www.camino-zaashila.com* 🖵 *120
rooms, 10 suites* ⚲ *3 restaurants, in-room safes, minibars, cable TV, tennis court, 2 pools, wading pool, gym, beach, 2 bars, baby-sitting, travel
services* ▤ *AE, DC, MC, V.*

★ $$$   ✕🏨 **Barceló.** You'll have bay views from the balcony of any room in
this resort, which spans the shore of beautiful Bahía Tangolunda. Red-
tile roofs on the low-slung buildings add a touch of Mediterranean elegance. Hardwood accents lend warmth to highly polished marble.
This is an all-inclusive resort, so you'll have free use of most water sports
equipment; dive masters are on hand with all the necessary equipment,
for an extra charge. At night candles flicker in the glamorous Casa Real
restaurant ($$–$$$). The food is northern Italian; reservations are essential. ✉ *Blvd. Benito Juárez, 70989* ☎ *958/581–0055* 🖷 *958/581–
0113* ⊕ *www.barcelo.com* 🖵 *347 rooms, 9 suites* ⚲ *3 restaurants, minibars, cable TV, 4 tennis courts, 2 pools, wading pool, gym, massage,
sauna, beach, dive shop, boating, 4 bars, shops, children's programs (ages
5–12), laundry service, business services, convention center, meeting rooms,
travel services, free parking* ▤ *AE, DC, MC, V.*

$$$$   🏨 **Las Brisas.** Only the spacious, minimalist suites have balconies, but
almost all of the rooms have wonderful views of the ocean. Divided into
four different areas that are romantically named for the mountains, stars,
clouds, and sea, the rooms are far from the hustle and bustle of the main
building. ✉ *Blvd. Benito Juárez s/n, 70989* ☎ *958/581–0355 or 888/
559–4329* 🖷 *958/581–0355* ⊕ *www.las-brisas-hualulco.com* 🖵 *280*

*rooms, 58 suites ⌂ 5 restaurants, minibars, cable TV, 12 tennis courts, 3 pools, 2 wading pools, gym, spa, beach, dive shop, soccer, squash, volleyball, 3 bars, theater, shops, meeting rooms, travel services, free parking, no-smoking rooms ☰ AE, MC, V.*

**$$$–$$$$**    ▦ **Gala.** The emphasis at this resort is on fun; there's a kids' club to entertain the youngsters while the grown-ups play tennis or relax by the pool. The rate includes most outdoor activities—a good deal if you want to do more than just work on your tan. The light-filled guest rooms have plenty of space to spread out. ⊠ *Blvd. Benito Juárez 4, 70989 ☎ 958/583–0400 or 877/888–4252 🖷 958/581–0220 ⊕ www.galaresorts.com ⌂ 300 rooms, 12 suites ⌂ 4 restaurants, room service, in-room safes, cable TV, 3 tennis courts, 3 pools, 2 wading pools, gym, beach, 4 bars, dance club, shops, baby-sitting, children's programs (ages 2–15), meeting rooms, car rental ☰ MC, V* ⦿| *AI.*

★ **$$$–$$$$**    ▦ **Quinta Real.** This hilltop resort takes luxury to almost excessive heights. Each suite has creamy white leather furniture, exquisite handwoven tapestries, a hot tub, and a terrace with a spectacular ocean view. Eight corner suites have plunge pools, and a few are equipped with telescopes for dolphin- and star-gazing. Vans take you to and from the beach, which is a long walk down from the hotel. ⊠ *Blvd. Benito Juárez 2, 70989 ☎ 958/581–0428, 800/457–4000 in the U.S. 🖷 958/581–0429 ⊕ www.quintareal.com ⌂ 54 suites ⌂ 2 restaurants, in-room safes, minibars, cable TV, tennis court, 2 pools, wading pool, bar, shops, baby-sitting, shop, laundry service, business services, meeting rooms, free parking, no-smoking rooms ☰ AE, MC, V.*

### Sports & the Outdoors

BICYCLING    You can rent bikes or take a guided tour of the mountains, beach, or river through **Aqua Terra** (⊠ Plaza las Conchas 6, Bahía Tangolunda ☎ 958/581–0012). An English-speaking guide and all the equipment you need are included. The cost is $18–$40, depending on length of trip. **Aventuras Huatulco** (⊠ Blvd. Guelaguetza 12, Bahía Tangolunda ☎ 958/587–1695) runs bicycle trips, as well as other types of outdoor treks.

FISHING    You can arrange sportfishing trips with the **Sociedad Cooperativa Tangolunda** (⊠ Santa Cruz Marina ☎ 958/587–0081), the boat-owners' cooperative at the marina on Santa Cruz Bay. They also run full-day bay tours.

GOLF    Bahía Tangolunda's challenging 18-hole golf course, the **Campo de Golf Tangolunda** (⊠ Blvd. Benito Juárez and Blvd. Tangolunda, Bahía Tangolunda ☎☎ 958/581–0059), was designed by Mario Schetjnan. The greens fee is $63 for 18 holes; carts rent for $33.

HORSEBACK RIDING    Arturo Casillas of **Rancho Caballo de Mar** (☎ 958/587–0530) will collect you from your hotel. Rates are about $30 for a morning or afternoon ride through the countryside.

RIVER RAFTING    The U.S.-based **Agua Azul** (⊠ 1770 W. State St., #330, Boise, ID 83702 ☎ 208/863–1100 ⊕ www.aguaazul.com) runs whitewater-kayaking trips year-round. The exciting adventure tours of up to eight days encounter plenty of Class III and IV waters. Runs on either the Ríos Copalita or Zimatán begin in the mountains and end just shy of the Pacific ★ Ocean. **Piraguas Aventuras** (☎☎ 958/587–1333 ⊕ www.piraguas.com)

conducts rafting and kayaking trips of different levels of difficulty. Most trips run two to seven days and include meals, activities, and hotel or camping at reasonable rates. The company also offers canyoneering trips (hiking, swimming, and cliff-jumping).

SCUBA DIVING  Most major hotels can arrange dive classes and excursions. The PADI-certified dive masters at **Hurricane Divers** (⊠ Bahía Santa Cruz ☎ 958/587–1107 ⊕ www.hurricanedivers.com) are well-regarded. Eagle rays, green moray eels, and, in winter, gray whales, are frequently spotted.

### Shopping

La Crucecita's **Mercado Municipal** (Municipal Market; ⊠ Calle Guanacaste at Bugambilia, La Crucecita ☎ No phone) is a fun place to shop for postcards, leather sandals, and souvenirs amid mountains of fresh produce. The **Museo de Artesanías Oaxaqueñas** (⊠ Calle Flamboyan 216, La Crucecita ☎ 958/587–1513) is really a store, not a museum, and the artisans who create the wooden alebrijes, woven tablecloths, typical pottery, painted tinware, and rugs from throughout the state are sometimes on hand for demonstrations.

**El Arte Mexicano** (⊠ Calle Guamuchil 210, La Crucecita ☎ 958/587–1223) has a wide array of crafts from around the country. **Paradise** (⊠ Calle Gardenia and Calle Guarumbo, La Crucecita ☎ 958/587–0268) has an excellent selection of casual, stylish beach and resort wear.

In Santa Cruz, **María Bonita** (⊠ Marina Santa Cruz, Santa Cruz ☎ 958/587–1400) is a gallery-like shop that sells silver, platinum, titanium, and gold jewelry as well as diamonds and other precious stones. The store also has fine handicrafts from around the state. For cigars, head to Bahía Tangolunda. There are plenty of *puros* at **Huatulkopka** (⊠ Blvd. Benito Juárez s/n, Bahía Tangolunda ☎ 958/581–0040).

## Oaxaca Coast A to Z

### AIR TRAVEL

AIRPORTS  Aeropuerto Puerto Escondido is a 10-minute taxi ride from town on Carretera 200. Aeropuerto Bahías de Huatulco is about 16 km (10 mi) from Tangolunda on Carretera 200.

🛪 **Aeropuerto Bahías de Huatulco** ☎ 958/581–9004. **Aeropuerto Puerto Escondido** ☎ 954/582–0492 or 958/582–0491.

AIRPORT  Inexpensive taxi service to and from Aeropuerto Puerto Escondido is
TRANSFERS  available through Transportes Turísticos. From Aeropuerto Bahías de Huatulco, try Transportes Terrestre and Autotransportes Turísticos. The cost to reach Bahía Tangolunda hotels from the airport is about $12 per person.

🛪 Taxis & Shuttles **Autotransportes Turísticos** ☎ 954/582–0459. **Transportes Terrestre** ☎ 958/581–9024. **Transportes Turísticos** ☎ 954/582–7343 or 954/582–0914.

CARRIERS  Mexicana flies to Huatulco from Mexico City. Aerocaribe (a subsidiary of Mexicana) and Aerotucán have daily flights that connect Huatulco and Puerto Escondido to Oaxaca City. Aero Vega has daily service between Puerto Escondido and Oaxaca in high season.

🖪 **Aerocaribe** ☎ 954/582-2023 in Puerto Escondido, 958/587-1220 in Huatulco. **Aero-tucán** ☎ 958/582-1725 in Puerto Escondido. **Aero Vega** ☎ 958/582-0151 in Puerto Escondido. **Mexicana** ☎ 958/587-1615 in Huatulco.

## BUS TRAVEL

Direct service between Oaxaca City and Puerto Escondido is available on several first-class lines, including Estrella del Valle. Buses leave from Oaxaca City and Puerto Escondido about four or five times daily. Cristóbal Colón has several first-class buses per day leaving from Oaxaca's first-class bus terminal, frequently referred to as the ADO. Most buses travel to both Huatulco and Puerto Escondido via Salina Cruz. There's one daily direct bus between Oaxaca City and Huatulco (eight hours, $18).

A good alternative are the vans that run between Oaxaca City and either Puerto Escondido or Pochutla, off the highway near Puerto Ángel. They are safe and speedy, often shaving hours off the driving time. Viaje a Oaxaca services the Puerto Escondido route, while Autoexprés Atlántida heads down to Pachutla. Both have about five departures a day and cost about $12 each way.

Frequent, inexpensive second-class buses connect Puerto Escondido, Puerto Ángel, and Huatulco, making a pit stop at Pochutla. Buses come by every 15 minutes or so, and each leg costs about $2.

Note: Although infrequent, attacks by highway bandits still occur in Mexico, with the most obvious targets being first-class buses. Night buses are most vulnerable, so travel by day whenever possible.

🖪 Companies **Autoexprés Atlántida** ✉ Calle La Noria 101, Centro Histórico, Oaxaca City ☎ 951/574-7077. **Cristóbal Colón** ✉ Calz. Niños de Chapultepec 1036, Jalatlaco, Oaxaca City ☎ 951/515-1248, 800/702-8000 toll-free in Mexico. **Estrella del Valle** ✉ Calle Armenta and López 721, Centro Histórico, Oaxaca City ☎ 958/581-0588 ✉ Av. Hidalgo 400 at 3a. Oriente, Puerto Escondido ☎ 954/582-0050. **Viaje a Oaxaca** ✉ Calle Galeana 420, Centro Histórico, Oaxaca City ☎ 951/439-1319.

🖪 Bus Terminals **La Crucecita** ✉ Calle Gardenias and Ocotillo, La Crucecita, Huatulco ☎ 958/587-0261. **Puerto Escondido** ✉ Calle Primera Nte. 201, Puerto Escondido ☎ 954/582-0050.

## CAR RENTAL

Rental cars are easy to come by in Puerto Escondido and Bahías de Huatulco. Fast is a Mexican company.

🖪 Major Agencies **Alamo** ✉ Av. Pérez Gasga 113, Puerto Escondido ☎ 954/582-3003. **Budget** ✉ Blvd. Benito Juárez, next to Hotel Aldea del Bazar, Puerto Escondido ☎ 954/582-0312 ✉ Calle Ocotillo and Calle Jasmín, La Crucecita, Huatulco ☎ 958/587-0010, 958/581-9000 for Aeropuerto Bahías de Huatulco. **Dollar** ✉ Barceló hotel, Blvd. Benito Juárez, Bahía Tangolunda, Huatulco ☎ 958/581-0055 Ext. 787, 958/581-0480, 958/581-9004 for Aeropuerto Bahías de Huatulco. **Fast** ✉ Plaza las Conchas 6, Bahía Tangolunda, Huatulco ☎ 958/581-0002.

## CAR TRAVEL

Several highways make their way to the coast, but the best choice is Carretera 175. The five-hour journey to Pochutla, a small town about 10 minutes from Puerto Ángel, can be nerve-wracking, as there are plenty of sheer cliffs and hairpin turns. From Pochutla, you can drive east to Puerto Ángel and Huatulco or west to Puerto Escondido. Carretera 131, from Oaxaca City to Puerto Escondido may look like a shorter route, but work on the road may add hours to your travel time. Carretera 190 via Salina Cruz is the relatively fast (six–seven hours) route to Huatulco. Leave early; do *not* attempt any of these roads at night.

Although having a car will better enable you to explore secluded beaches, it may be less expensive to hire a taxi for day trips.

### EMERGENCIES
🚺 **Red Cross** ☎ 958/587-1188 in Bahías de Huatulco, 954/582-0550 in Puerto Escondido. **Police** ☎ 958/587-0020 in Bahías de Huatulco, 954/582-0498 in Puerto Escondido. **Tourist Police** ☎ 954/582-3439 in Puerto Escondido.

### INTERNET, MAIL & SHIPPING
In Huatulco, Choco Latté is the most attractive place for a coffee and some time on the Internet. Send letters and packages through MexPost, at the entrance to La Crucecita across from the Pemex station. Puerto Escondido's correos, north of the coast highway, is open weekdays 9–7 and Saturday 9–noon.

🚺 **Cybercafé Choco Latté** ✉ Calle Gardenia 902, at Calle Tamarindo, La Crucecita, Huatulco ☎ 958/587-0165.

🚺 **Mail Correos** ✉ Calle 7 Norte, at Calle Oaxaca, Puerto Escondido ☎ 954/582-0232 ✉ Blvd. Chahué 100 La Crucecita, Huatulco ☎ 958/587-0551.

### MONEY MATTERS
Puerto Escondido has a Banamex on its tourist strip and several more banks up in town near the market. Huatulco's most convenient bank is in La Crucecita. Hours are generally weekdays 9–4.

🚺 **Banks Banamex** ✉ Av. Pérez Gasga 314, Puerto Escondido ☎ 954/582-0626. **Bital** ✉ Calle Bugambilia 1504, La Crucecita, Huatulco ☎ 958/587-0884 ✉ Av. Pérez Gasga, Puerto Escondido ☎ 954/582-1824.

### TOURS
BIRD-WATCHING Tour operators often combine a trip to Puerto Ángel's Playa Mazunte, and its sea turtle center, with a visit to Laguna de Ventanilla to see resident and migratory species of waterbirds, as well as crocodiles. You can also take the 1½-hour, nonmotorized skiff tour. Arrive any day between 8 AM and 4 PM; the lagoon entrance is about five minutes west of the Centro Mexicano de la Tortuga. In Puerto Escondido Canadian ornithologist Michael Malone offers day-long excursions (December–April) into the Laguna Manialtepec. Arrange tours (about $35 per person) through Viajes Ditmar, the most reliable agency in town.

COFFEE PLANTATIONS Visiting the coffee plantations in the mountains is especially alluring when coastal heat and humidity soar. Prices average $40–$50 per day. Contact Azteca Tours for trips to the family coffee plantation of Max Scherenberg. The all-day jaunt includes a typical lunch at the plantation and a visit to the Llano Grande waterfalls with local guides.

SIGHTSEEING Bahías Plus, which has offices in many major hotels in Huatulco, conducts tours to Puerto Ángel and Puerto Escondido and the surrounding sights; prices range from $20 to $50. Paraíso Huatulco has all-day bay cruises for $25 a person.

**⚑ Azteca Tours** ⊠ Calle Gardenia 1302, La Crucecita, Huatulco ☎ 958/583-4041. **Bahías Plus** ⊠ Calle Carrizal 704, La Crucecita, Huatulco ☎ 958/587-0216 or 958/587-0932. **Paraíso Huatulco** ⊠ Barceló hotel, Blvd. Benito Juárez, Bahía Tangolunda, Huatulco ☎ 958/581-0218. **Viajes Ditmar** ⊠ Av. Pérez Gasga 905, Puerto Escondido ☎ 954/582-0734.

## VISITOR INFORMATION

The Puerto Escondido Tourism Office is inconveniently located, unless you happen to be staying west of town in the Aldea del Bazar Hotel. But Gina Machorro, who staffs the small information booth downtown on Avenida Pérez Gasga, is more helpful anyway. The main office is open weekdays 9–3 and 4–7, Saturday 10–3. The information booth is open weekdays 10–2 and 4–6, Saturday 10–1.

The Puerto Ángel Tourism Office is on the second floor of a tiny building at the entrance to the pier. The first floor is a clean public rest room. The office, which stocks maps and brochures, is open daily 9–3 and 4–8.

The Huatulco branch of the state tourism office is open weekdays 8–5 and Saturday 9–1. Sedetur is open Friday 9–5 and Saturday 9–1.

**⚑ Puerto Ángel Tourism Office** ⊠ Blvd. Virgilio Uribe, at Calle José Vasconcelos, Puerto Ángel ☎ No phone. **Puerto Escondido Tourism Office** ⊠ Blvd. Benito Juárez s/n, Playa Bacocho, Puerto Escondido ☎ 954/582-0175 ⊠ Av. Pérez Gasga s/n, at Marina Nacional ☎ No phone. **Huatulco Tourism Office** ⊠ Blvd. Benito Juárez s/n, Bahía Tangolunda, Huatulco ☎ 958/581-0176 or 958/581-0177.

# CHIAPAS & TABASCO

**11**

Updated by
Mark Sullivan **THE SINEWY MOUNTAIN ROADS** that lead through the Chiapas are full of hairpin turns hugging the edges of mist-filled ravines. Along the way you'll still find remote clusters of grass-roofed huts and cornfields planted on near-vertical hillsides. Things haven't changed much in centuries. Women still wrap themselves in traditional deep-blue shawls and coarsely woven wool skirts, and sunburned children sell fruit and flowers by the road. The region has nine distinct linguistic groups, most notably the highland-dwelling Tzotzils and the Tzeltals, who live in both highland and lowland areas. In more isolated regions, many villagers speak only their native language.

World attention was drawn to off-the-beaten-path Chiapas in the mid-1990s, when guerrillas staged a brief but potent rebellion, launching what has turned out to be a long-term equal rights struggle for Mexico's indigenous groups. A bloody past of exploitation by and fierce confrontation with outsiders remains vividly present, as already impoverished communities are forced to compete for their lands with developers and new settlers. In fact, Chiapas has been at the margin of the nation's development and is one of the poorest states. Land distribution is skewed as well: about 1% of landowners hold 15% of the territory—about 50% of the arable land—keeping the colonial system nearly intact.

It was the indifference of the Mexican government to their plight that helped bring the anger of the indigenous people to a boil in 1994, leading the Zapatista National Liberation Army (EZLN) to an armed uprising. The government of President Vicente Fox held meaningful talks with EZLN, and the national and international interest sparked by the movement bodes well for further development in the region. The pipe-smoking Zapatista spokesperson, Subcomandante Marcos, has become a cult figure in Mexico: his ski-masked image appears on everything from magazine covers to children's toys.

But while the Zapatistas are still making headlines, so are the archaeologists working in the region. Although many people have read about Palenque, the regal city in the middle of a thick jungle, relatively few have heard of equally grand ruins such as Toniná and Yaxchilán. A bit harder to reach, they have nothing like the crowds that sometimes choke the narrow paths at Palenque, though more and more people visit each year.

Nominally enriched a half century ago with the discovery of oil in the Gulf of Mexico on its northern border, Tabasco also has a bloody past. During the 1920s and 1930s, Tomás Garrido Canabal, a vehemently anticlerical governor, outlawed priests and had all the churches either torn down or converted to other uses. Riots, deportations, and property confiscations were common. That said, you won't find much evidence of Tabasco's turbulent past today; the spirit that prevails here—at least in modern Villahermosa, Tabasco's capital—is one of commerce.

Most of those who visit Villahermosa are traveling for business, but the city has an excellent pre-Colombian anthropology museum and an unparalleled collection of massive Olmec heads and altars. Both provide a good introduction to the indigenous heritage of Tabasco. Comalcalco, with its interesting Mayan ruins, is culturally and geographically linked to Palenque. Geographically stunning, Tabasco also has lakes, lagoons, caves, and wild rivers that surge through the jungle.

# Exploring Chiapas & Tabasco

The abode of the ancient Olmecs, Tabasco is lush, green, and pastoral; Chiapas, once the domain of the Maya, is for the most part mountainous. The colonial city of San Cristóbal de las Casas dominated both regions when the Spanish conquistadores held sway over the country. Thanks to its petroleum industry, Villahermosa is by far stronger today.

For most, the highlight of a trip to the region is still the Maya city of Palenque. But there are plenty of other ruins worth exploring, from Toniná near Ocosingo and Comalcalco outside of Villahermosa. The once-isolated ruins of Yaxchilán and Bonampak are now more accessible.

*Note:* Although travel in the area is reasonably safe, at this writing the U.S. State Department was advising visitors to "exercise caution" in Chiapas because of the presence of armed rebels and armed civilian groups in some areas. Although none of the sporadic confrontations has been near a main tourist destination—and no tourist has ever been harmed—contact the U.S. State Department or any of the Mexican Government Tourist Offices for an update on the situation before you go. Always carry your tourist card and passport even on day trips throughout the region, as there are military checkpoints along both main and secondary roads. If you're a first-time visitor, you may be more comfortable taking tours of the region—especially if you don't speak Spanish.

## About the Restaurants

Because the weather is warm, meals in Chiapas and Tabasco are often served outdoors. Restaurants are found in flower-filled gardens or tree-shaded courtyards; those that actually have roofs usually have the doors flung open to catch the breeze. Outside a few upscale places in Villahermosa and San Cristóbal de las Casas, people don't dress up for dinner. Change into long pants, though, to protect yourself from the mosquitoes and other insects that come out at sunset.

Prices are reasonable in this part of the country. A filling dinner usually won't cost more than $15, even at fairly fancy places. It's a common practice to eat lunch (the main meal of the day) around 1 or 2 and a light dinner around 7 or 8.

## About the Hotels

In a region this beautiful, it's no surprise that the hotels are oriented toward the outdoors. Open-air lobbies are common, usually leading straight to a swimming pool and often to a lake or stream where you can take a dip.

In Chiapas, San Cristóbal has hotels that are within walking distance of the main plaza. Most are from the colonial era—or if not, at least a century old—in keeping with the rest of the town. Palenque, no longer a jungle outpost, has plenty of inns that let you enjoy views of the misty mountains from your comfortable suite. There are also quite a few *posadas* (guest houses) and other low-cost lodgings in town.

*Numbers in the text correspond to numbers in the margin and on the Chiapas and Tabasco and San Cristóbal de las Casas maps.*

**11**

**If you have 3 days**

Three days is enough time to visit the region's prettiest colonial towns. Spend the first day and night in 🏛 **San Cristóbal de las Casas ❶–❽** ⌐. Spend at least two hours on a walking tour of this enchanting highland town. On Day 2, visit the Maya villages of **San Juan Chamula ⓮**, known for its church where pre-Hispanic rituals are performed, and **Zinacantán ⓯**, famous for its colorful handwoven tunics and shawls. Return to San Cristóbal to visit the market, shop for folk art, and spend the night. From San Cristóbal, you can spend Day 3 in pretty **Comitán ⓫**, stopping along the way at the village of **Amatenango del Valle ❿** to purchase some pottery. You'll want to spend your last night in the breathtaking Museo Parador Santa María.

**If you have 5 days**

Five days will give you just enough time to see the region's best Mayan and Olmec sites. Spend the first day and night in 🏛 **Villahermosa ㉕** ⌐, seeing the giant Olmec heads and the fascinating anthropology museum. About a hour away are the interesting ruins of **Comalcalco ㉗**. On Day 2, drive or take a bus to the Maya city of 🏛 **Palenque ㉑**, visit the ruins, and stay overnight. On Day 3, scale the nearly vertical heights of **Toniná ⓳**, near the frontier town of 🏛 **Ocosingo ⓲**. Spend the night there or return to Palenque. On Day 4 and 5 see the ruins at **Bonampak ㉓** and **Yaxchilán ㉔**. You can arrange to spend the night at the ecotourism lodge called Escudo Jaguar. It's on the Río Usumacinta, near the boat launch for Yaxchilán.

**If you have 7 days**

Like the great outdoors? Then you've come to the right place. Spend the first day and night at the Mayan ruins at 🏛 **Palenque ㉑** ⌐. On Day 2 you can visit the stunning jungle waterfalls at nearby **Agua Azul ⓴**. Tours from Palenque let you see this and other waterfalls in one fun-filled day. If horseback riding is your thing, on Day 3 you can arrange a ride to the ruins of **Toniná ⓳** from your hotel in 🏛 **Ocosingo ⓲**. Head south to 🏛 **San Cristóbal de las Casas ❶–❽** on Day 4, where you can arrange a bicycle ride to the nearby villages of **San Juan Chamula ⓮** and **Zinacantán ⓯**. Using San Cristóbal as your base, head out for a swim at the **Lagos de Montebello ⓭** on Day 5. Head west on your sixth day, touring colonial **Chiapa de Corzo ⓰** en route to the impressive Cañón del Sumidero. On your last day drive to **Tuxtla Gutiérrez ⓱**, which has one of the best zoos in the country.

---

Hotels in Tuxtla Gutiérrez and Villahermosa—two cities with their minds on business—have far less character. But there are many moderately priced places in both cities where you can get a touch of the local culture.

Many, though not all, hotels quote prices that already include the 17% tax. This is especially true of budget and moderately priced lodgings. Be sure to ask about this when you're given a price.

| | WHAT IT COSTS | | | | |
|---|---|---|---|---|---|
| | $$$$ | $$$ | $$ | $ | ¢ |
| RESTAURANTS | over $25 | $15–$25 | $10–$15 | $5–$10 | under $5 |
| HOTELS | over $250 | $150–$250 | $75–$150 | $50–$75 | under $50 |

Restaurant prices are for a main course excluding tax and tip. Hotel prices are for two people in a standard double room in high season.

### Timing

In the highlands, September is the peak of the rainy season, which officially starts in late August and can run until early October. It gets cold at night, and can be chilly during the day as well. It's very hot and humid in the lowlands most of the year, but especially after February, with temperatures peaking in May and June.

# SAN CRISTÓBAL DE LAS CASAS

A pretty highland town in a valley where pine forests are interspersed with fields of corn and other vegetables, San Cristóbal straddles two worlds. Here indigenous women with babies tied tightly in colorful shawls share the main square with teenagers talking on cell phones. Graceful colonial-era buildings house shops selling DVD players.

San Cristóbal makes the perfect hub for exploring the region's villages and towns, lakes and rivers, and archaeological sites. Small enough to see in a day, the town is also captivating enough for a stay of a week or longer. In addition to admiring the town's colorful facades, budget some time to visit to the market, peek into a few churches, and enjoy a cup of locally grown coffee in a shady courtyard.

The town's cool climate is a refreshing change from the sweltering heat of the lowlands. On chilly evenings, wood smoke scents the air, curling lazily over the red-tile roofs of small, brightly painted stucco houses. The sense of the mystical here is intensified by the fog and low clouds that hover over the surrounding mountains.

San Cristóbal and the surrounding communities are the ancestral home of the highland Maya, who at the time of the Spanish conquest were centuries past their golden era. In 1526, the Spaniards, under Diego de Mazariegos, defeated the Chiapan Indians at a battle outside town. Mazariegos founded the city, which was called Villareal de Chiapa de los Españoles, two years later. For most of the colonial era, Chiapas, with its capital at San Cristóbal, was a province of Guatemala. Lacking the gold and silver of the north, it was of greater strategic than economic importance.

Under Spanish rule, the region's resources became entrenched in the *encomienda* system, in which wealthy Spanish landowners forced the locals to work as slaves. "In this life all men suffer," lamented a Spanish friar in 1691, "but the Indians suffer most of all." The situation improved only slightly through the efforts of Bartolomé de las Casas, the bishop of San Cristóbal, who in the mid-1500s protested the torture and mas-

## Archaeological Sites

Ruins of Mayan cities in the middle of mysterious, overgrown jungles are a big draw in Chiapas. Unparalleled Palenque has the most appeal, and the lesser-known sites of Toniná, Bonampak, and Yaxchilán are attracting more attention than ever. In Tabasco you'll find Comalcalco, which resembles Palenque—made of bricks instead of stone.

## Food

The food of Chiapas is influenced by the region's heritage, so many of the dishes have been around since the days of the Maya. Distinctive flavors come from such herbs as *chipilín* and *yerba santa* (or *mumu*, as locals call it). Don't pass up the *cochinito horneado* (smoked pork) or the many local variations of tamales. Wash it all down with *atole* (a slightly sweetened cornmeal drink).

**11**

Tabasco serves lots of fresh fish from the coast as well as from its lakes and rivers. Local specialties include *pejelagarto,* an ugly fish with a head like that of an alligator and a strong, sweet flavor. It's often served whole, so be prepared to face the fearsome beast. Also try *puchero* (beef stew with vegetables and plantains) and *chaya,* a type of green similar to spinach. Make sure to try the region's fresh, white cheese.

## Shopping

The weavers of Chiapas produce striking embroidered blouses, *huipiles* (tunics), bedspreads, and tablecloths. Other artisans create leather goods, homemade paper products, and painted wooden crosses. Lacandon bows and arrows and reproductions of the beribboned ceremonial hats worn by Tzotzil indigenous leaders also make interesting souvenirs.

Chiapas is one of the few places in the world that has amber mines, so finely crafted jewelry made from this prehistoric resin is easy to find in San Cristóbal—as are plastic imitations sold by street vendors (stores usually sell amber and street vendors commonly have the fakes, although there's some crossover). San Cristóbal is also known for the wrought-iron crosses that bless its rooftops. Although many of the iron-working shops have closed, you can still find the crosses in a few old-fashioned stores. Tuxtla Gutiérrez and Palenque, although not known for crafts, have a few shops selling quality folk art from throughout the state.

---

sacre of the local people; these downtrodden protested in another way, murdering priests and other *ladinos* (Spaniards) in infamous uprisings.

Mexico, Guatemala, and the rest of New Spain declared independence in 1821. Chiapas remained part of Guatemala until electing by plebescite to join Mexico on September 14, 1824—the date is still celebrated throughout Chiapas as the Día de la Mexicanidad (Day of Mexicanization). In 1892, because of San Cristóbal's allegiance to the Royalists during the War of Independence, the capital was moved to Tuxtla Gutiérrez. With that shift went all hope that the town would keep pace with the rest of Mexico. It wasn't until the 1950s that the roads into town were paved and the first automobiles arrived.

Bahía de
Campeche

Laguna de
Términos

Ciudad del
Carmen

Frontera

CAMPECHE

186

**Paraíso** 28

**Comalcalco** 27

26

**Comalcalco
Town**

180

**Villahermosa** 25

TABASCO

187

186

Calazajá

199

**Palenque
Town**

**Palenque** 21 22

195

Misol-Há

Tenosique

**Agua Azul**
20

199

Río Usumacinta

198

◆ **Cañon del
Sumidero**

**San Juan
Chamula**

**Ocosingo** 18 19 **Toniná**

Oxchuc

**Yaxchilán** 24

**Tuxtla
Gutiérrez** 17

**Zinacantán** 14

15

Huixtán

Lacanjá

**Bonampak** 23

16

**Las Grutas
de Rancho Nuevo**

Río Colorado

**Chiapa de
Corzo**

9

*SELVA
LACANDONA*

**San Cristóbal
de las Casas**

1 - 8
see detail
map

190

10 **Amatenango
del Valle**

SIERRA

**Comitán**
11

La Trinitaria

**Lagos de
Montebello**

MADRE

12

13

CHIAPAS

**Chinkultik**

*Presa la
Angostura*

190

DE CHIAPAS

GUATEMALA

200

Motozintla

0          20 miles

0          30 km

**Chiapas &
Tabasco**

Tapachula

Puerto
Madera

**KEY**

┼┼┼ *Rail Lines*

▶ *Start of itinerary*

## Exploring San Cristóbal de las Casas

San Cristóbal is laid out in a grid pattern centered on the zócalo. When walking around, remember that street names change on either side of this square: Calle Francisco Madero to the east of the square, for example, becomes Calle Diego de Mazariegos to the west. The town was originally divided into *barrios* (neighborhoods), but they now blend together into a city center that's easy to negotiate.

In colonial times, Indian allies of the triumphant Spaniards were moved onto lands on the outskirts of the nascent city. Each barrio was dedicated to a different occupation. There were Tlaxcala fireworks manufacturers in one part of the town and pig butchers from Cuxtitali in another. Although specific divisions no longer exist, some of the local customs have been kept alive. For example, each Saturday certain houses downtown will put out red lamps to indicate that homemade tamales are for sale.

Surrounding San Cristóbal are many small villages celebrated for the exquisite colors and embroidery work of their inhabitants' costumes. Huixtán (hweesh-*tan*) and Oxchuc (osh-*chuc*) are about 28 km and 43 km (17 mi and 27 mi), respectively, on the road to Ocosingo. The Thursday market in Tenejapa, 27 km (17 mi) northeast of San Cristóbal, is worth seeing.

**a good walk**

Begin in Plaza 31 de Marzo, better known as the **zócalo** ❶ ▶. Note the 16th-century Casa de Diego de Mazariegos on the southeast corner (it's now the Hotel Santa Clara) and, to the northwest, the neoclassical Palacio Municipal, with its numerous arcades. **Catedral de San Cristóbal** ❷, on the north side, has a fascinating facade. Head one block north and one block west to the **Museo del Jade** ❸. Walk east two blocks to Avenida General Utrilla and then north (left) 3½ blocks to the 16th-century **Templo de Santo Domingo** ❹ with its baroque facade. Walk around the complex to its museum and famous textiles cooperative.

Return to Avenida General Utrilla and walk north three blocks to the **Mercado Municipal** ❺. You can catch a cab, or walk nine blocks east on Calle Comitán to the **Museo Na Bolom** ❻, a repository of Indian artifacts. As the museum is shown by tour only, you'll probably want to time your arrival for the 11:30 or 4:30 English- and Spanish-language tours. If you've made prior arrangements, you can end the day at the **Museo Sergio Castro** ❼, where the owner gives nightly slide shows and talks about regional costumes and textiles. Either catch a taxi or walk five blocks south on Avenida Vicente Guerrero and eight blocks west on Calle Real de Guadalupe. If the English-language slide show isn't happening, proceed instead to the **Museo del Ambar** ❽.

### What to See

❷ **Catedral de San Cristóbal.** Dedicated to San Cristóbal Mártir (St. Christopher the Martyr), this cathedral was built in 1528, then demolished, and rebuilt in 1693, with additions during the 18th and 19th centuries. Note the classic colonial traits on the ornate facade: turreted columns, arched windows and doorways, and beneficent-looking statues of saints in niches. The floral embellishments in rust, black, and white accents on the ocher background are unforgettable. Inside, don't miss the painting *Nuestra Señora de Dolores* (*Our Lady of Sorrows*) to the left of the altar, beside the gold-plated *Retablo de los Tres Reyes* (*Altarpiece of the Three Kings*); the Chapel of Guadalupe in the rear; and the gold-washed pulpit. ⊠ *Calle Guadalupe Victoria at the Zócalo* ⊘ *Daily 9–2 and 4–8.*

★ ➎ **Mercado Municipal.** This municipal market occupies an eight-block area. Best visited early in the morning—especially on the busiest day, Saturday—the market is the social and commercial center for the indigenous groups from surrounding villages. Stalls overflow with medicinal herbs, fresh flowers, and bundles of wool, as well as the best coffee in the region for less than $3 a pound. Be careful here, as robberies are common. If you must bring your camera, be discreet, and, as always, ask permission before photographing people. ⊠ *At Avs. General Utrilla, Nicaragua, Honduras, and Belisario Domínguez* ⊘ *Daily 7 AM–dusk.*

➑ **Museo del Ambar de Chiapas.** Next to the pretty Ex-Convento de la Merced, this museum has exhibits showing how and where amber is mined, as well as its function in Maya and Aztec societies. You'll see samples of everything from fossils to recently quarried pieces to sculptures and jewelry. Labels are in Spanish only; ask for an English-language summary. The volunteer staff can explain how to distinguish between real amber and fake. ⊠ *Plazuela de la Merced, Calle Diego de Mazariegos s/n* ☎ *967/678–9716* ⊠ *$1* ⊘ *Tues.–Sun. 10–2 and 4–7.*

➌ **Museo del Jade.** Jade was prized as a symbol of wealth and power by Olmec, Teotihuacán, Mixtec, Zapotec, Maya, Toltec, and Aztec nobility, and this museum shows jade pieces from different Mesoamerican cultures. The most impressive piece is a reproduction of the sarcophagus lid from Pakal's tomb, at Palenque. It's said to be one of the most faithful and brilliant Maya reproductions in the world. ⊠ *Av. 16 de Septiembre 16* ☎ *967/678–2550* ⊠ *$3* ⊘ *Daily noon–9.*

➏ **Museo Na Bolom.** It's doubtful that any foreigners have made as much
**Fodor'sChoice** of an impact on San Cristóbal as did the European owners of this home-
★ turned-library-museum-restaurant-hotel. Built as a seminary in 1891, the handsome 22-room house was purchased by Frans and Gertrude (Trudi) Blom in 1950. He was a Danish archaeologist, and she was a Swiss social activist; together they created the Institute for Ethnological and Ecological Advocacy, which carries on today. It got its name, Na Bolom (House of the Jaguar), from the Lacandon Maya with whom Trudi worked: Blom sounds like the Maya word for jaguar. Both Frans and Trudi were great friends of the small Lacandon tribe, whose traditions and way of life they documented. Their institute is also dedicated to reforestation of the area; it plants thousands of trees each year.

Both Bloms are deceased, but Na Bolom showcases their small collection of religious treasures, which was hidden in attics during the anticlerical 1920s and 1930s. Also on display are findings from the Classic Maya site of Moxviquil (pronounced mosh-vee-*keel*), on the outskirts of San Cristóbal, and objects from the daily life of the Lacandon. Trudi's bedroom contains her jewelry, collection of indigenous crafts, and

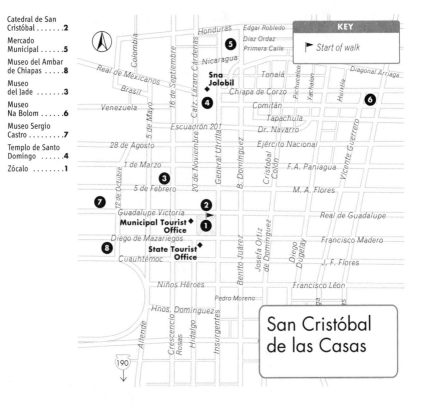

wardrobe of embroidered dresses. A research library holds more than 10,000 volumes on Chiapas and the Maya. Tours are conducted Monday–Saturday in English and Spanish at 11:30 and 4:30.

Across from the museum, the Jardín del Jaguar (Jaguar Garden) store sells crafts and souvenirs. Look for the thatch hut, a replica of local Chiapan architecture. It consists of a mass of woven palm fronds tied to branches, with walls and windows of wooden slats, and high ceilings that allow the heat to rise. The shop here sells Lacandon crafts, as well as black-and-white photos taken by Trudi.

Revenue from Na Bolom supports the work of the institute. You can arrange for a meal at Na Bolom even if you don't stay at the hotel. In addition, the staff is well connected within San Cristóbal and can arrange tours to artisans' co-ops, villages, and nature reserves that are off the beaten path. ⊠ *Av. Vicente Guerrero 33, at Calle Comitán* ☎ *967/ 678–1418* 🖃 *Museum $3.50, tour $4.50* ⊙ *Tours: Daily 11:30 and 4:30. Library: weekdays 10–4. Store: Mon.–Sat. 9:30–2 and 4–7, Sun. 4–7.*

**❼ Museo Sergio Castro.** Sergio Castro, an agronomist from northern Mexico who has dedicated himself to building schools in the highlands of Chiapas, has spent a lifetime working with indigenous peoples; many of the ceremonial costumes were given to him as payment for his work in the communities. There are around 1,000 pieces in the collection, including textiles, weavings, wooden saints, musical instruments, and toys. Sergio gives tours and slide shows in English, Spanish, and French, but you must make reservations in advance. ⊠ *Calle Guadalupe Victoria 61* ☎ *967/678–4289* 🖃 *$2.50* ☺ *Daily 5 PM–7 PM.*

**❹ Templo de Santo Domingo.** This three-block-long complex houses a church, a former monastery, a regional history museum, and the Templo de la Caridad (Temple of the Sisters of Charity). A two-headed eagle—emblem of the Hapsburg dynasty that once ruled Spain and its American dominions—broods over the pediment of the church, which was built between 1547 and 1569. The pink stone facade (which needs a good cleaning) is carved in an intensely ornamental style known as Baroque Solomonic: saints' figures, angels, and grooved columns overlaid with vegetation motifs abound. The interior has lavish altarpieces, an exquisitely fashioned pulpit, a sculpture of the Holy Trinity, and wall panels of gilded, carved cedar—one of the precious woods of Chiapas that centuries later lured Tabasco's woodsmen to the highlands surrounding San Cristóbal. At the complex's southeast corner you'll find the tiny, humble Templo de la Caridad, built in 1715 to honor the Immaculate Conception. Its highlight is the finely carved altarpiece. Indigenous groups from San Juan Chamula often light candles and make offerings here. (Do *not* take photos of the Chamulas.)

The Ex-Convento de Santo Domingo, adjacent to the Santo Domingo church, now houses Sna Jolobil, an Indian cooperative that sells local weavings, embroidered clothing, and colorful postcards. The shop is open Tuesday–Saturday 9–2 and 4–7. The small **Museo de los Altos** (Highlands Museum; ☎ 967/678–1609), also part of the complex, displays a permanent exhibition of historical documents and memorabilia and has two rooms dedicated to changing cultural shows. Hours are Tuesday–Sunday 10–5. Admission is $3. ⊠ *Av. 20 de Noviembre s/n, near Calle Guatemala.*

**need a break?** With more than a dozen organic javas on the menu, it's not surprising that **La Selva Café** (⊠ Av. Crescencio Rosas 9, at Calle Cuauhtémoc ☎ 967/678–7244) is filled with people craving caffeine. You can also munch on baguette sandwiches and other light fare.

▶ **❶ Zócalo.** The square around which this colonial city was built has in its center a gazebo used by marimba musicians most weekend evenings at 8 PM. You can have a coffee on the ground floor of the gazebo; expect to be approached by children and women selling bracelets and other wares. Surrounding the square are a number of 16th-century buildings, some with plant-filled central patios. On the facade of the Casa de Diego de Mazariegos, now the Hotel Santa Clara, are a stone mermaid and lions that are typical of the plateresque style—as ornate and busy as the work of a silversmith. The yellow-and-white, neoclassical Palacio Municipal (Municipal Palace) on the square's west side was the seat of the state government until 1892, when Tuxtla Gutiérrez became the capital. Today it houses a few government offices, including the municipal tourism office. ⊠ *Between Avs. General Utrilla and 20 de Noviembre and Calles Diego de Mazariegos and Guadalupe Victoria.*

## Where to Eat

★ **$$**  ✕ **Na Bolom.** You wouldn't be surprised to see Frans and Trudi Blom, the original owners of this house, join you for a meal in their former dining room. Just off the old-fashioned kitchen, the room looks much as it did when the pair did their research here in San Cristóbal. Today, the communal oak dining table is shared by volunteers, artists, scholars, and travelers. A hearty breakfast is served beginning at 7 AM, and a five-course dinner at 7 PM sharp. Expect such rib-sticking dishes as beef stew or roasted chicken. If you're not staying at the hotel, call several hours ahead for a reservation. ⊠ *Av. Vicente Guerrero 33, at Calle Comitán* ☎ *967/678–1418* ▤ *MC, V* ⊘ *No lunch.*

★ **$–$$**  ✕ **Restaurant L'Eden.** People rave about the delicious dishes—especially the sizzling steaks—at this chalet-style restaurant in the Hotel El Paraíso. The tangerine and cerulean interior has eight cozy candlelit tables surrounding a massive fireplace. Swiss delights include classic *raclette* (melted cheese and potatoes) and fondue bourguignonne (beef with eight different sauces). The service—doting but not distracting—is among the best in the city. ⊠ *Calle 5 de Febrero 19* ☎ *967/678–0085* ▤ *AE, MC, V.*

★ **¢–$**  ✕ **Mayambé.** Brightly colored fabrics hang on the walls and from the rafters at this Asian-influenced restaurant. Grab a seat in the covered courtyard (sit closer to the fireplace if the night is a bit nippy) or a cushion in the traditional Thai dining room off to one side. There are plenty of Indian and Thai dishes on the expansive menu, but one of the best choices is the Vietnamese-style *platillo vietnamita* (tofu, shrimp, or chicken sautéed with peanuts, cashews, and bits of chili and coconut and served with sweet coconut rice). ⊠ *Calle Real de Guadalupe 66* ☎ *967/674–6278* ▤ *MC, V.*

**¢–$**  ✕ **Restaurante el Teatro.** Sunshine streams in the windows here during the day, warming yellow walls hung with theatrical posters and masks from around the world. At night, candlelight presides. The menu features primarily French and Italian dishes—including crepes and chateaubriand. The wood-fired pizzas (some with odd ingredients like Roquefort cheese) are delicious. Wind up the evening with the chocolate mousse. ⊠ *Av. 1 de Marzo 8, at Av. 16 de Septiembre* ☎ *967/678–3149* ▤ *MC, V* ⊘ *Closed Mon.*

**¢**  ✕ **La Casa del Pan.** When you walk in the door, the scent of freshly baked bread is the first thing you notice. You may be tempted to skip the restaurant altogether and just grab a few of the warm rolls and a jar of the locally made preserves. But the House of Bread serves a fabulous, if leisurely, breakfast. For lunch, try the tasty *tamales chiapanecos* (with a spicy cheese filling) or the mild chilies stuffed with corn and herbs. Round out your meal with bean soup and one of the best salads in town. If you like the organic coffee, you can buy a bag to take home. ⊠ *Calle Dr. Navarro 10, at Av. Belisario Domínguez* ☎ *967/678–5895* ▤ *MC, V* ⊘ *Closed Mon.*

**¢**  ✕ **Emiliano's Moustache.** The tortillas here are made fresh by hand throughout the day and go well with the wide variety of traditional Mexican meals. This is a good place to stop late in the evening—the dining room is open until 1 AM. An upstairs bar overlooks the restaurant, which is named for Mexican revolutionary hero Emiliano Zapata; photos and paintings of him abound. ⊠ *Av. Crescencio Rosas 7, at Calle Diego de Mazariegos* ☎ *967/678–7246* ☐ *No credit cards.*

¢ ✕ **La Paloma.** Cozy and relaxing, this café is inside a former home of city founder Diego de Mazariegos. But that doesn't mean it's a musty museum. It's quite modern, with funky chairs and tables scattered about. The curved bar is in what can only be described as a jungle. Start with *sopa de flor de calabaza* (squash flower soup) or *ensalada de nopalitos* (cactus salad), then move on to the tongue-twisting *albondigas enchipotladas* (meatballs in chili sauce). ⊠ *Calle Hidalgo 3, ½ block south of the zócalo* ☎ *967/678–1547* ☐ *MC, V.*

## Where to Stay

**$–$$** 🏨 **Casa Felipe Flores.** Breakfast in this lovingly restored 18th-century man-
Fodor'sChoice sion is served on a sunny courtyard or in the dining room decorated with
★ carefully chosen antiques. It's such a nice way to start the day that you might find yourself lingering until it's time for lunch. David and Nancy Orr, the friendly owners, are happy to share their knowledge of San Cristóbal. Each bedroom has a handsome wardrobe, writing desk, and—adjacent to the corner fireplace—an old-fashioned bed with carved head- and footboards. ⊠ *Calle Dr. Felipe Flores 36, 29230* ☎☎ *967/678–3996* ↪ *5 rooms* ♻ *Dining room, bar, library, laundry service, airport shuttle, travel services* ☐ *No credit cards* �🍽 *BP.*

**$** 🏨 **Casavieja.** Dating from 1740, this colonial-era house has three interior courtyards separated by graceful colonnades. Most of the simple guest rooms have large windows overlooking the courtyards, but a few on the second floor have views of the mountains. The Espinosas, who run the hotel, treat you like members of the family. The hotel is three blocks east of the zócalo, so the location is perfect. ⊠ *Calle Maria Adelina Flores 27, 29230* ☎ *967/678–0385* ☎☎ *967/678–6868* ⊕ *www.casavieja.com.mx* ↪ *38 rooms, 2 suites* ♻ *Restaurant, cable TV, bar, free parking* ☐ *AE, MC, V.*

**$** 🏨 **Casa Mexicana.** A waterfall tumbling into a pond filled with flowers makes this hostelry in a restored colonial mansion stand out. A lovely newer wing across the street, also in a colonial home, has a colonnaded courtyard and large, quiet rooms painted light colors and filled with tasteful photographs of San Cristóbal. The restaurant, which surrounds a courtyard with towering banana trees, serves international dishes. ⊠ *Calle 28 de Agosto 1, at Av. General Utrilla, 29200* ☎ *967/678–0698 or 967/678–0683* ☎ *967/678–2627* ⊕ *www.hotelcasamexicana.com* ↪ *52 rooms, 3 suites* ♻ *Restaurant, room service, cable TV, massage, sauna, bar, laundry service, free parking* ☐ *AE, MC, V.*

★ **$** 🏨 **Na Bolom.** The rooms here aren't just named for local indigenous communities, they are filled with pictures and books detailing their lives, as well as examples of their weavings and pottery. The rooms in the colonial house have quaint touches like corner fireplaces. Na Bolom may be a 15-minute walk from the center of town, but it's so pleasant here you might not want to leave. Book well in advance, and ask for a room with a garden view. ✉ *Av. Vicente Guerrero 33, at Calle Comitán, 29200* ☎ *967/678–1418* ⊕ *www.nabolom.org* ⤳ *15 rooms* ⚐ *Restaurant, library, shop, free parking; no a/c, no rooms TVs* ▤ *MC, V.*

**$** 🏨 **Posada Diego de Mazariegos.** This quaint hotel—really two perfectly preserved 18th-century colonial homes—has covered courtyards, beautiful gardens, and sunlit nooks throughout. Rooms have high ceilings and wide windows; some have fireplaces. Ask for one of the rooms that number in the 300s, which are in an older wing and have high wood-beam ceilings as well as working charcoal stoves. The bar, Tequilazo, stocks more than 115 brands of tequila. ✉ *Calle 5 de Febrero 1, corner of Av. General Utrilla, 29200* ☎ *967/678–0833* 🖷 *967/678–0827* ⊕ *www.diegodemazariegos.com.mx* ⤳ *70 rooms, 4 suites* ⚐ *Restaurant, cafeteria, room service, in-room data ports, cable TV, bar, shop, laundry service, travel services, free parking* ▤ *AE, MC, V.*

**$** 🏨 **Rincón del Arco.** This massive structure takes up most of a city block, but you'd never know it from the intimate little courtyards inside. The unique details in the rooms include freestanding fireplaces, many of them fashioned by local artisans out of clay. With a touch of whimsy, a few have smiling faces. Since each room is different, ask to see several until you find the one you like best. Accommodations in the newer section have a pleasing garden view. Rooms on the top floor share a wide balcony on which you can sit and enjoy a view of red-tile-roof houses clustered around the venerable Iglesia de Guadalupe. ✉ *Calle Ejército Nacional 66, 29200* ☎ *967/678–1313* 🖷 *967/678–1568* ⊕ *www.rincondelarco.com* ⤳ *48 rooms, 2 junior suites* ⚐ *Restaurant, cable TV, bar, laundry service, free parking* ▤ *MC, V.*

**¢** 🏨 **Hotel Santa Clara.** Once the home of city founder Diego de Mazariegos, this rambling 16th-century mansion is now a hotel overlooking the main plaza. It has a tangible air of past grandeur: beamed ceilings, antique oil paintings, saints in niches, and timeworn hardwood floors. Six of the nine roomy units with balconies overlook the zócalo. Despite the somewhat worn furnishings, the hotel's location and history make it popular. ✉ *Av. Insurgentes 1, 29200* ☎ *967/678–0871 or 967/678–1140* 🖷 *967/678–0871* ⊕ *www.estanciascoloniales.com* ⤳ *37 rooms, 2 suites* ⚐ *Restaurant, coffee shop, cable TV, pool, 2 bars, travel services, free parking* ▤ *AE, MC, V.*

**¢** 🏨 **Posada San Cristóbal.** The spacious rooms in this grand old building a block from the main plaza have high ceilings, antique furniture, and heavy French doors; those on the second story have dark wood floors. Enjoy the patio, with its cheery walls, blue and white tiles, and white wrought-iron furniture. Don't miss the charming facade, which has the patron saint in a little nook. ✉ *Av. Insurgentes 3, 29200* ☎ *967/678–6881* ⤳ *20 rooms* ⚐ *Restaurant, room service, cable TV, bar, laundry service, parking (fee); no a/c, no room phones* ▤ *MC, V.*

## Nightlife & the Arts

### Nightlife

In Hotel Santa Clara, **Cocodrilo** (✉ Av. Insurgentes 1 ☎ 967/678–0871 or 967/678–1140) is a laid-back tavern that hosts rock and salsa bands most nights from 9:30 to midnight. You say you want a **Revolución**

# CloseUp

# A VOICE OF MANY VOICES

N THE EARLY HOURS OF JANUARY 1, 1994, while most of Mexico was sleeping off the New Year's festivities, the Zapatista National Liberation Army (EZLN) surprised the world when it captured San Cristóbal de las Casas and several surrounding towns, demanding land redistribution and equal rights for Chiapas's indigenous peoples.

The Zapatista triumph was short-lived. The mostly Tzotzil and Tzeltal troops soon departed San Cristóbal, and on January 12, President Carlos Salinas de Gortari called for a unilateral cease-fire. According to government figures, 145 lives were lost during the 12-day struggle. But hundreds have been killed in years of clashes between rebel supporters and paramilitary groups; thousands have been displaced.

The factors that led to the Zapatista uprising are many. Centuries of land appropriation repeatedly uprooted Chiapas's Maya-descended groups. Also, despite its natural resources (Chiapas provides nearly half of Mexico's electricity and has extensive oil and gas reserves), the state's indigenous residents still suffer appallingly high rates of illiteracy, malnutrition, and infant mortality.

In 1995 President Ernesto Zedillo sent troops into the Lacandon jungle to capture the Zapatista leadership, including charismatic leader Subcomandante Marcos. The ambush failed. The following year negotiations with the rebels resulted in the San Andrés Accords, which called for a constitutional amendment recognizing indigenous cultural rights and limited autonomy. President Zedillo instead pursued a policy of low-intensity warfare—often in the name of "development" or "reforestation"—for the rest of his administration. The policy led to disastrous results, including the massacre

of 45 unarmed Zapatista supporters at the hands of paramilitary forces in the village of Acteal, Chenalho, in December 1997.

During his presidential campaign, Vicente Fox insisted that he could resolve the Zapatista conflict in 15 minutes; during his inaugural address he announced that he was ordering partial troop withdrawals and would submit legislation based on the San Andrés Accords. In turn, Marcos announced three conditions for the restoration of negotiations—further military withdrawals, the release of Zapatista prisoners, and implementation of the accords. The first two have been achieved. Fox, however, continues to be engaged in a media war with Marcos. In early 2001, a Zapatista caravan traveled to the capital to demand negotiations.

Fox, who welcomed the Zapatistas to the capital, has come under attack from members of the Institutional Revolutionary Party (PRI) as well as members of his own National Action Party (PAN). Not everyone is convinced of the Zapatistas' noble motives. In February 2003, a group of Zapatistas chased out the American owners of a guest ranch bordering the archaeological ruins of Toniná. Even though the resulting publicity continues to put a dent in tourism, the state government continues to decline to intervene, saying a heavy-handed approach would backfire. Around the same time, a group of Zapatistas reportedly detained for a few hours tourists on a kayaking trip along the Río Jatate. Whether these are isolated incidents or a series of ongoing events remains to be seen.

(⊠ Av. 20 de Noviembre at Calle Primero de Marzo ☎ No phone)? This bar tries to please everyone, and just about succeeds. It serves great breakfasts and lunches, then opens the bar for happy hour from 5:30 to 7:30. Most nights see live jazz, rock, or ska performances. If that's not enough, there are computers and a video room that screens popular films.

**Latinos** (⊠ Calle Francisco Madero 23, corner of Av. Benito Juárez ☎ 967/678–9927) serves up live Latin jazz, salsa, or tropical music after 9:30 every night but Sunday, when it's closed. **Las Velas** (⊠ Calle Francisco Madero 14 ☎ 967/678–0417) is a disco that pulses with live rock and reggae music. It's open nightly 8 PM until 4 AM.

### The Arts
**Museo Na Bolom** (⊠ Av. Vicente Guerrero 33, at Calle Comitán ☎ 967/678–1418) occasionally sponsors talks and films. The elegant **Teatro Hermanos Domínguez** (⊠ Diagonal Hermanos Paniagua s/n, just outside the city limits ☎ 967/678–3637) features programs such as folkloric dances from throughout Latin America.

## Sports & the Outdoors
### Biking
For a tour of the countryside surrounding San Cristóbal, try the folks at **Los Pingüinos** (⊠ Calle Ecuador 4 ☎ 967/678–0202). You can also rent a bike and strike out on your own.

### Horseback Riding
A horseback ride into the neighboring indigenous villages is good exercise for mind and body. Most hotels can arrange trips, or you can contact **Viajes Chinkultik** (⊠ Calle Real de Guadalupe 34 ☎ 967/678–0957 ⊠ Av. Insurgentes 14 ☎ 967/678–7266). Bilingual guides lead five-hour horseback rides to San Juan Chamula and Zinacantán; the cost is about $12 per person.

## Shopping

Look for the elaborately crafted textiles from communities surrounding San Cristóbal; they incorporate designs that have been around for millennia. San Cristóbal's market, although picturesque, generally sells more produce than arts and crafts. The shops on Avenida General Utrilla, south of the market, have a large selection of Guatemalan goods, the price and quality of which may be lower than Mexican wares. Make sure to check merchandise carefully for imperfections.

Shops are generally open Monday–Saturday 9–2 and 4–8. Indian women and children will often approach you on the streets with their wares— mostly fake amber jewelry, woven bracelets, and small dolls. Their selections might not be as varied as those in the shops, but prices will be a little lower. And you can be assured that these hard-working vendors earn every cent they make.

### Handicrafts
**Artesanías Chiapanecas** (⊠ Calle Real de Guadalupe 46C, at Av. Diego Dugelay ☎ No phone) has an excellent selection of embroidered blouses,

huipiles, tablecloths, and bags. The government-run **Casa de las Arte-sanías** (⊠ Calle Niños Héroes and Av. Hidalgo ☎ 967/678–1180) sells wooden toys, ceramics, embroidered blouses, bags, and handwoven textiles from throughout the state. You'll also find honey, marmalade, and locally made liqueurs.

Among its excellent selection of wares, **Sna Jolobil** (Weaver's House in the Tzotzil language; ⊠ Ex-Convento de Santo Domingo, Calz. Lázaro Cárdenas 42 ☎ 967/678–7178), the regional crafts cooperative, has hand-dyed woolen sweaters and tunics, embroidered pillow covers, and pre-Hispanic-design wall hangings. **Taller Leñateros** (⊠ Calle Flavio A. Paniagua 54 ☎ 967/678–5174), a unique indigenous co-op in an old colonial San Cristóbal home, sells top-quality crafts and lets you observe artisans at work. Look for handmade books, boxes, postcards, and writing paper fashioned out of plants.

### Jewelry
**El Arbol de la Vida** (⊠ Calle Real de Guadalupe 27 ☎ 967/678–5050) is a smart shop that specializes in designer amber jewelry mixed with silver and gold. It also has a small museum displaying the different types of amber found around the world. One of San Cristóbal's best boutiques, **La Galería** (⊠ Calle Hidalgo 3 ☎ 967/678–1547) sells plenty of hand-made jewelry and original artwork.

# SOUTH & EAST OF SAN CRISTÓBAL

Due east of San Cristóbal is one of the least explored and most exotic regions of Chiapas: the Selva Lacandona, said to be the western hemisphere's second-largest remaining rain forest. Incursions of developers, settlers, and refugees from neighboring Guatemala are transforming Mexico's last frontier, which for centuries has been the homeland of the Lacandon, a small tribe descended from the Maya of Yucatán. Some of the indigenous groups maintain their ancient customs, living in huts and wearing long, plain tunics. Their tradition of not marrying outside the tribe is causing serious problems, however, and their numbers, never large to begin with, have been reduced to about 350.

## Las Grutas de Rancho Nuevo
**❾** *13 km (8 mi) south of San Cristóbal off Carretera 190.*

Spectacular limestone stalactites and stalagmites are illuminated along a 2,475-foot concrete walkway inside the labyrinthine caves known as Las Grutas de Rancho Nuevo (or Las Grutas de San Cristóbal), which were discovered in 1960. Kids from the area are usually available to guide you for a small fee. You can rent horses ($5 per half hour) for a ride around the surrounding pine forest, and there's a small restaurant and picnic area on the site. To get here, catch a Teopisca-bound microbus at Boulevard Juan Sabines Gutiérrez, across from the San Diego church, in San Cristóbal. Make sure to tell the driver to let you off at the "grutas." Get off at the signed entrance, and walk about 1 km (½ mi) along the dirt road. Or, you can catch a taxi from town for about $6. For about twice that price, the driver will wait while you explore the caves. ☎ *No phone* 🚗 *$1 per car plus 50¢ per person* ☉ *Daily 9–4:30.*

## Amatenango del Valle

**❿** *37 km (23 mi) southeast of San Cristóbal.*

Amatenango del Valle is a Tzeltal village known for the handsome, primitive pottery made by the town's women, whose distinctive red and yellow huipiles are also much remarked upon. Almost every household has wares to sell. Look for ocher, black, and gray animal figurines—the best known are the doves. Lining the road to Comitán, at the entrance to town, are some simple shelters where other artisans sell their wares. If you go when rain isn't a threat, you might get to see some of the pots being fired over open flames on the ground outside. Spanish is definitely a second language here, and women negotiate without a lot of chitchat or use younger children as interpreters.

## Comitán

**⓫** *55 km (34 mi) southeast of Amatenango del Valle.*

After a string of dusty little towns, Comitán comes as a surprise. The road into the city is lined with laurels and bougainvillea. Founded by the Spanish in 1527, the city flourished early on as a major center linking the lowland villages to the highland towns. Even today it serves as a trading hub for the Tzeltal people. Many of the colonial buildings lining Comitán's pretty plaza and nearby side streets have been preserved. The city also has two notable churches. On the main square, the yellow **Templo de Santo Domingo** (⊠ 1 Av. Oriente at Calle Central Oriente) has Moorish-style architecture. Some of the original stonework is still visible on the facade. The salmon and gold **Templo de San Caralampio** (⊠ 3 Av. Oriente at 1 Calle Norte Oriente) has a highly detailed Spanish baroque facade that reveals the influence of Guatemalan artisans.

In the lovely former home of a hero of the fight for independence, the **Casa-Museo Dr. Belisario Domínguez** is now a museum with a fascinating collection of medical instruments. It also contains photographs, documents, and letters from the Mexican Revolution, during which the doctor was assassinated for his outspoken criticism of President Victoriano Huerta. The town's official name is Comitán de Domínguez in his honor. ⊠ *Av. Central Sur at Blvd. Belisario Domínguez 35* ☎ *963/632–1300* 🚗 *50¢* ☉ *Tues.–Sat. 10–6:45, Sun. 9–12:45.*

The **Museo de Arte Hermila Domínguez de Castellanos** shows work by modern artists, many of them from this part of the country. Look for pieces by master painters Rufino Tamayo and Francisco Toledo, both from Oaxaca. ⊠ *Av. Central Sur at Blvd. Belisario Domínguez 51* ☎ *963/632–2082* 🚗 *20¢* ☉ *Tues.–Sat. 10–6.*

The small but worthwhile **Museo de Arqueología** is dedicated to archaeological finds in the region. Most of the exhibits in its four rooms are of ancient Maya carved stone tablets and ceramic vessels. One of the most interesting is a covered box decorated with a stylized jaguar head that was found in the ruins of Chinkultic. Explanatory texts are only in Spanish. ⊠ *Primera Calle Sur Oriente s/n at Primera Avenida Sur Oriente* ☎ *963/632–5760* ⊞ *Free* ⊙ *Tues.–Sun. 10–5.*

About 7 km (4 mi) south of Comitán, ⛰ **Tenam Puente** is on a hill with a spectacular view of the valley below. This name of this ceremonial center comes from the Nahua word *tenamitl*, which means "fort" or "fortified place." The city, which does resemble a fortress, was built around the same time as nearby Chinkultik and was occupied during the Classic and Postclassic periods. Archaeologists Frans Blom and Oliver LeFarge discovered the ruins in 1926, but it wasn't until restoration in the 1990s that a royal tomb was unearthed. There are three ball courts, apparently one each for the lower, middle, and upper classes. Most of the 2-square-mi site has yet to be explored. ⊞ *Free* ⊙ *Daily 9–4.*

## Where to Stay & Eat

¢ ✕ **Café Quiptik.** Next to the Templo de Santo Domingo, this little café overlooks the main square. Run by a group of organic farmers, it has more than 10 types of coffee to choose from. There are also light dishes like *pollo a la mantequilla* (chicken sauteed in butter and sprinkled with manchego cheese). ⊠ *1 Av. Oriente Sur at 1 Calle Sur Oriente* ☎ *963/ 632–0400* ⊟ *No credit cards.*

¢ ⊡ **Posada del Virrey.** You can tell this is a family-run establishment, because the fountain in the courtyard is filled with pet turtles. There's also a playground in the back where your little ones are welcome to hang out. Rooms at this plum-colored posada aren't fancy, but they are clean and comfy. ⊠ *Dr. Belisario Domínguez 13, at Av. Central Norte* ☎ *963/ 632–1811* ⊳ *15 rooms* ⌂ *Cable TV* ⊟ *No credit cards.*

# Chinkultik

⛰ ⑫ *46 km (29 mi) southeast of Comitán.*

It's a steep hike of about 15 or 20 minutes to the hilltop pyramid that crowns this Maya city. From here you're rewarded with a fabulous view of sheer cliffs that drop into a sparkling lake. In the distance you can see the Lagos de Montebello. The ruins, which are only partially restored, also include a ball court and ceremonial center.

To get here from Comitán, head south on Carretera 190, and turn left at the sign reading LAGOS DE MONTEBELLO outside of La Trinitaria. There's a road on the left leading to the ruins, which are 2 km (1 mi) off the highway. Driving is the best way to get here. A bus runs from Comitán, but you have a long walk to get to the site. ⊠ *Carretera a Lagos de Montebello, Km 30* ⊞ *$3* ⊙ *Daily 10–4.*

## Where to Stay & Eat

$ ✕⊡ **Museo Parador Santa María.** Part of a hacienda from the 1830s, this hotel couldn't be more charming. Enter through the massive stone gate and you'll see the estate's chapel, now a museum filled with 17th-century religious art. Each of the six rooms is regally appointed; one even has a gilt bed whose canopy is held aloft by a crown. The restaurant ($–$$), on a terrace overlooking the mountains, serves excellent dishes

FodorśChoice ★

like *crema de chipilín* (cream soup made with a local herb). Top off your visit to Chinkultik with the fixed-price, three-course lunch. ⊠ *Carretera a Lagos de Montebello, Km 22* 🏠 *963/632–5116* ⤳ *6 rooms, 2 suites* ⚭ *Restaurant, bar, laundry service, free parking* 🖃 *MC, V.*

## Lagos de Montebello

**⓭** *64 km (40 mi) southeast of Comitán.*

The 56 lakes and surrounding pine forest of the Lagos de Montebello (Lakes of the Beautiful Mountain) constitute a 2,437-acre park that's shared with Guatemala. Each lake has a slightly different tint—emerald, turquoise, amethyst, azure, steel gray—thanks to various oxides.

At the park entrance, the paved road forks. The left fork leads to the Lagunas de Colores (Colored Lakes). At Laguna Bosque Azul, the last lake along that road, there's a café; it may be humble, but it's a nice change from all the food stalls set up near every lake with a parking lot. Small boys will approach you to offer a 45-minute horse-riding expedition to a cave within the forest. You can also tour the lake in a rowboat (about $5 for up to four people).

The right fork in the road at the park entrance leads past various lakes to Lago Tziscao and, just outside the park boundaries, a village of the same name. A restaurant near the shore has a spectacular view of the lake, where a 30-minute boat ride costs $2.50 per person.

Although various buses travel to and between the lakes, the tourist office recommends that you take a tour to be on the safe side. Although it isn't common, tourists have been robbed while walking from one lake to another. There are several police checkpoints in the area, so remember to bring along your passport.

# NORTH & WEST OF SAN CRISTÓBAL

On the outskirts of San Cristóbal, San Juan Chamula and Zinacantán are traditional villages well worth exploring. The small colonial town of Chiapa de Corzo is the first major community you come to when you drive west from San Cristóbal along Carretera 190. Here you can catch a motorboat to the stunning Cañón del Sumidero.

## San Juan Chamula

**⓮** *12 km (7½ mi) northwest of San Cristóbal de las Casas.*

Justly celebrated for its religious and cultural traditions, San Juan Chamula is one of the most fascinating of the highland villages. The Chamulas, a subgroup of the Tzotzils, are descendents of the Mayas. More than 80,000 Chamulas live in hamlets throughout the highlands north and west of San Cristóbal; several thousand of them live in San Juan Chamula. Most adults still wear traditional dress—men often don black wool tunics, while women wear colorfully embroidered blouses over wool skirts.

A fiercely independent people, the Chamulas fought against the Spanish beginning in 1524. They are also fiercely devout—practicing a religion that's a blend of Catholic and Maya practices—a trait that has sometimes pitted some members of the community against others. In the past 30 years, thousands who have converted to other religions have been forced to abandon their ancestral lands.

Life in San Juan Chamula revolves around the **Iglesia de San Juan Bautista,** a white stucco building whose doorway has a simple yet lovely flower motif. The church is named for Saint John the Baptist, who here is revered even above Jesus Christ. There are no pews inside, because there are no traditional masses. Instead the floor is strewn with fragrant pine needles, on which the Chamulas sit praying silently or chanting while facing colorfully attired statues of saints. Worshippers burn dozens of candles of various colors, chant softly, and may have bones or eggs with them to aid in healing the sick.

Before you enter, buy a $1 ticket at the tourist office on the main square. Taking photographs and videos inside the church is absolutely prohibited. Some tourists trying to circumvent this rule have had their film confiscated or their cameras smashed. Outside the church cameras are permitted, but most adults resent having their picture taken.

Near the Iglesia de San Juan Bautista is the small museum called **Ora Ton.** Inside are examples of traditional dress, exhibits of musical instruments, and photos of important festivals. Admission is with the same ticket you bought for the church.

On the hill above the Iglesia de San Juan Bautista are the ruins of the **Iglesia de San Sabastian.** This church was built with stones from the Maya temple that once stood on the site. Surrounding it is the old cemetery, an especially colorful place on the Day of the Dead.

To get to San Juan Chamula from San Cristóbal, head west on Calle Guadalupe Victoria, which veers to the right onto Ramón Larrainzar. Continue 4 km (2½ mi) until you reach the entrance to the village.

## Zinacantán

**⑮** *4 km (2½ mi) west of San Juan Chamula.*

The village of Zinacantán is even smaller than San Juan Chamula. The men wear bright pink tunics embroidered with flowers; the women cover themselves with bright pink shawls. If you visit the homes of backstrap loom weavers along the main street you are welcome to take photos. Otherwise, cameras are frowned upon.

The **Iglesia de San Lorenzo,** on the main square, at first looks much more traditional that the church in San Juan Chamula. But you soon notice odd little touches, like ceramic representations of animals sacred to the Maya scattered about. Admission is about 50¢.

The **Museo Ik'al Ojov,** on the street behind the church, is in a typical home and displays Zinacantán costumes through the ages. ☎ *No phone* ✉ *Donation suggested* ☉ *Tues.–Sun. 9–5.*

Zinacantán is reached via a paved road just outside San Juan Chamula. From San Cristóbal, take the Tuxtla road about 8 km (5 mi) and look for the signed turnoff on your right.

## Chiapa de Corzo

**⑯** *70 km (43 mi) west of San Cristóbal, 15 km (9 mi) southeast of Tuxtla Gutiérrez.*

The town of Chiapa de Corzo (then known as Chiapa de los Indios) was founded in 1528 by Diego de Mazariegos, who one month later fled the heat and mosquitoes and settled instead in San Cristóbal de las Casas (then called Chiapa de los Españoles to avoid confusion).

Life in this small town on the banks of the Río Grijalva revolves around the Plaza Ángel Albino Corzo, named for a former governor of the state. In the center is the bizarre **Fuente Mudéjar**, or Moorish Fountain. The structure, built in 1562, once supplied the town with water. Said to be in the shape of the crown of the Spanish monarchs Fernando and Isabella, it is a mishmash of Moorish, Gothic, and Renaissance styles.

About a block south of Plaza Ángel Albino Corzo is a massive church called the Ex-Convento de Santo Domingo de Guzmán. It houses the **Museo de la Laca** (Lacquerware Museum), which has a modest collection of delicately carved and painted *jícaras* (gourds). The foreign examples are from as close as Guatemala and as far away as Asia.  ⊠ *Calle Mexicanidad de Chiapas 10* ☎ *961/616–0055* ⧄ *Free* ⊘ *Tues.–Sun. 10–5.*

★ The **Cañón del Sumidero**, a canyon 38 km (24 mi) north of Chiapa de Corzo, came into being about 36 million years ago, with the help of the Río Grijalva, which flows north along the canyon's floor. The fissure, which meanders for some 23 km (14 mi), is perhaps the most interesting landscape in the region.

You can admire the Cañón del Sumidero from above, as there are five lookout points along the highway. But the best way to see it is from one of the dozens of boats that travel to the canyon from the Embarcadero in Chiapa de Corzo between 8 AM and 4 PM daily. Two-hour rides cost about $9 per person. From the boat you can admire the nearly vertical walls that rise 3,500 feet at their highest point. As you coast along, consider the fate of the Chiapa people who reputedly jumped into the canyon rather than face slavery at the hands of the Spaniards during the 16th century.

### Where to Eat

$  ✕ **Jardines de Chiapa.** An excellent and inexpensive variety of regional dishes is served daily at this patio restaurant. Try the *tasajo* (sun-dried beef served with pumpkin-seed sauce) and the *chipilín con bolita*, a soup made with balls of ground corn paste cooked in a creamy herb sauce and topped with cheese. Don't arrive fashionably late—the restaurant closes at 7:30.  ⊠ *Av. Francisco I. Madero 395* ☎ *961/616–0198* ⊟ *AE, MC, V.*

## Tuxtla Gutiérrez

**⑰** *15 km (9 mi) northwest of Chiapa de Corzo, 85 km (53 mi) northwest of San Cristóbal, 289 km (179 mi) southwest of Villahermosa.*

In 1939, writer Graham Greene characterized Tuxtla Gutiérrez as "not a place for foreigners—the new ugly capital of Chiapas, without attractions." The accuracy of that bleak description is slowly fading, but most people still only pass through Tuxtla on their way to Oaxaca to the west or San Cristóbal de las Casas to the east. But the capital has what is probably Mexico's most innovative zoo. It's also close to the Cañón del Sumidero, making this a good base for exploring the area.

Tuxtla's first name derives from the Nahuatl word *tochtlan,* meaning "abundance of rabbits." Its second name honors Joaquín Miguel Gutiérrez, who fought for the state's independence from Spain and incorporation into the newly independent country of Mexico. The town became the state capital in 1892, taking the honor away from San Cristóbal de las Casas.

To get your bearings, stay on Avenida Central, which becomes Boulevard Belisario Domínguez as it heads west. Where Avenida Central crosses Calle Central is the sprawling **Parque Central,** where the large trees serve as umbrellas for an army of vendors. Across from Parque Central is the gleaming white **Catedral de San Marcos** (⊠ Av. Central at Calle Central ☎ 961/612–0939). Founded in the second half of the 16th century, the modern structure shows some colonial touches. The tower has 98 bells that ring every hour as mechanical figurines resembling the apostles appear above. It's open daily 8–2 and 3–7.

**★ ☺** All the animals at the **Zoológico Regional Miguel Álvarez del Toro,** known to locals as ZooMAT, are native to Chiapas. You'll find more than 100 species on display, include jaguars, tapirs, iguanas, and boa constrictors. Birders will be excited to see the rare resplendent quetzal at close quarters. At this writing, the zoo was closed for renovations through 2004. If work is still in progress when you visit, you can still inquire about taking a guided tour of the grounds. ⊠ *Calz. Cerro Hueco s/n, southeast of town off Libramiento Sur* ☎ 961/614–4701 or 961/614–4765 🖾 *Free* ☉ *Tues.–Sun. 9–5.*

Northeast of Parque Central, the leafy Parque Madero is home to **Museo Regional de Antropología e Historia,** which has an excellent display of pre-Columbian pottery and a salon with revolving cultural exhibits. ⊠ *Calzado Hombres Illustres 350, at Calle Oriente 11a* ☎ 961/612–8360 🖾 *$3* ☉ *Tues.–Sun. 9–4.*

Marimba music is popular in Tuxtla. As its name suggests, the **Jardín de la Marimba** (⊠ Av. Central Poniente at 8a Calle Poniente Sur) hosts marimba bands every evening at 7 and 9.

### Where to Stay & Eat

**$$–$$$** ✕ **Montebello.** Prime rib and Mexican specialties headline the menu at this elegant restaurant, and every roll, cake, dessert, and tortilla is made on the premises. Montebello's earth-tone elegance is set off by an unusual white mural of the Sumidero cliffs sculpted into a wall. It's particularly romantic here at night, when the city lights shimmer. ✉ *Camino Real, Blvd. Belisario Domínguez 1195* ☎ *961/617–7777* ☐ *AE, DC, MC, V* ☉ *Closed Sun.*

★ **$–$$$** ✕ **El Asador Castellano.** Mouthwatering Spanish dishes are the specialty at this pretty little restaurant. The most popular dish is *lechón a la segoviana,* succulent baby pig that you can order as a straightforward dish for one person or have cut and served with a flourish at your table. The extensive wine list favors Spanish wines hard to find in Mexico City, let alone Chiapas. The restaurant is a bit hard to find, as it's tucked behind a bank. ✉ *Blvd. Belisario Domínguez 2320-A* ☎ *961/602–9000* ☐ *AE, MC, V* ☉ *No dinner Sun.*

**$** ✕ **La Carreta.** The scent of sizzling steak wafts from the door of this open-air restaurant. Portions are huge, and the mixed grill for two, four, or six people comes with beans, tortillas, and salsa—a super deal. A beautiful wooden staircase leads to the second-floor terrace that overlooks the marimba players that play most afternoons. To see the floor show late on Friday and Saturday nights, you must book in advance. ✉ *Blvd. Belisario Domínguez 703* ☎ *961/602–5518 or 961/602–5403* ☐ *MC, V.*

**$** ✕ **Las Pichanchas.** An outstanding variety of regional dishes, including the regional favorite cochinito horneado, is served at this little restaurant. The big draw, though is the live marimba music in the afternoon (2:30–5:30) and evening (8:30–11:30). From 9 PM–10 PM folk dancers take to the floor. The restaurant is popular with Mexican families. ✉ *Av. Central Oriente 837* ☎ *961/612–5351* ☐ *AE, MC, V.*

★ **$$$** ⌂ **Camino Real.** You might think you're in the Caribbean when you see this sprawling hotel set around a huge lagoon-style pool and a bar shaded with exotic vegetation. The list of amenities at this hilltop oasis—unmistakable for its purple and orange color scheme—is longer than that at many of its more-expensive counterparts. The Los Azulejos restaurant, open 24 hours, is enclosed in a sky-blue glass dome; its heavenly buffets are well worth the price. All the well-appointed rooms have views of the distant mountains. ✉ *Blvd. Belisario Domínguez 1195, 29060* ☎ *961/617–7777, 800/722–6466 in the U.S.* 🖷 *961/617–7799* ⊕ *www.caminoreal.com* ⤺ *174 rooms, 36 suites* ᐃ *3 restaurants, room service, in-room data ports, in-room safes, minibars, cable TV, 2 tennis courts, pool, spa, health club, hair salon, sauna, 2 bars, shop, concierge floor, business services, meeting rooms, car rental, travel services, no-smoking rooms* ☐ *AE, DC, MC, V.*

**$$** ⌂ **Hotel Arecas.** On the outskirts of town, Hotel Arecas is a haven of quiet gardens with fruit trees, flowering plants, and a secluded swimming pool. Both the rooms and the bungalow-style junior suites have tasteful colonial-style fittings and furnishings. The informal Calabaza Grill serves a buffet breakfast daily and has an à la carte menu of Mexican specialties for lunch and dinner. ✉ *Blvd. Belisario Domínguez, Km 1080, 29020* ☎ *961/615–1122, 961/615–1128, 800/780–7234 in the U.S.* 🖷 *961/615–1121* ⊕ *www.hotelarecas.com.mx* ⤺ *44 rooms, 16 suites* ᐃ *Restaurant, room service, cable TV, pool, bar, shop, business services, Internet, meeting rooms, free parking* ☐ *AE, DC, MC, V.*

**$** ⌂ **Hotel María Eugenia.** Just a few blocks from the main square, this high-rise tries its best to be modern. That it's a bit past its prime doesn't take away from its understated appeal. Rooms have balconies overlooking downtown. The cafeteria serves a scrumptious breakfast buffet of Mexican favorites. ⊠ *Av. Central Oriente 507, 29000* ☎ *961/613–3767 or 961/613–3770* 🖷 *961/613–2860* ⊕ *www.mariaeugenia.com.mx* ⇥ *83 rooms* ⌂ *Restaurant, cafeteria, room service, pool, bar, meeting rooms, travel services, free parking* ⊟ *AE, MC, V.*

# THE ROAD TO PALENQUE & BEYOND

The road from San Cristóbal to Palenque veers slightly east on Carretera 190 upon leaving town, then links up to Carretera 199, which heads north to Palenque. You'll pass Ocosingo and the turnoff to Toniná along the first half of the journey, then Agua Azul and Misol-Há before reaching the ruins. It's sierra country most of the way until the mild valleys around Ocosingo; the climate will get progressively hotter and more humid as you descend from the highland and approach Palenque. The vegetation will also change, from mountain pine to thick, green tropical foliage. To get to Villahermosa from Palenque, head north for 56 km (35 mi) on Carretera 199, and then turn left (west) onto Carretera 186 at Catazajá for a fairly straight, leisurely drive. Frequent buses are available for all routes.

## Ocosingo

**⑱** *98 km (61 mi) northeast of San Cristóbal, 118 km (73 mi) south and east of Palenque.*

Although Ocosingo is literally on the tourist trail, most people pass right by on their way to San Cristobal or Palenque. That's a shame, because Ocosingo sits in one of the prettiest valleys in Chiapas. It's a perfect place for horseback riding through the countryside or bathing in the waterfalls at several rivers. It's also the best base for exploring the Maya ruins of Toniná.

Like many other towns, Ocosingo is centered around a manicured square with a town hall on one end and a cathedral on the other. It hasn't quite caught up with the rest of the world, which is its charm. There's not a single travel agency in the entire town—yet.

Ocosingo is primarily a market town, which is evident when you head to the market area called the **Tianguis Campesino** (⊠ 2 Av. Sur Oriente and 4 Calle Oriente Sur). Brightly dressed Tzeltal and Lacandon women from the surrounding villages kneel on the ground or sit on tiny stools to sell vegetables and fruits from their gardens.

### Where to Stay & Eat

¢–$ ✕ **El Desván.** Through a pair of graceful arches you can gaze down on the main square from this second-story restaurant. There's a certain rustic charm imparted by the wrought-iron wall sconces and the rough-hewn tables and chairs. The menu begins with simple dishes like quesadillas and enchiladas and moves on to more substantial fare like *pollo a la mexicana* (chicken simmered with tomatoes and onions). ⊠ *1 Av. Sur Oriente 10* ☎ *919/673–0117* ⊟ *No credit cards.*

¢ ✕🖼 **Hospedaje y Restaurant Esmeralda.** A half-block away from the main square you'll find this historic house. Accommodations are basic, but owners Glen Wersch and Ellen Jones work hard to make you feel at home, happily doling out lots of travel tips. In the dining room, you can enjoy delicious roasted meats and homemade bread. Work up an appetite with a two-hour horseback ride. ✉ *Calle Central Norte 14, 29950* 📠📞 *919/673–0014* ⊕ *www.ranchoesmeralda.net* ⇆ *5 rooms* ⚐ *Restaurant, fans, horseback riding, bar, laundry service; no room phones, no room TVs* ⊟ *No credit cards.*

## Shopping

Ocosingo is known throughout the region for its cheeses, so it's no surprise that truck drivers passing through call this town "Los Quesos." If you want to sample some of the traditional *queso de bola* (literally, "ball of cheese"), head to **Fabrica de Quesos Santa Rosa** (✉ 1 Oriente Norte 11 📞 919/673–0009). If this waxy sphere catches your fancy, you can even arrange a tour of the adjacent factory. Delicious *queso botanero* (a creamy cheese with chilis, olives, and other items mixed in) is available at **Quesos Laltic** (✉ 2 Poniente Norte 1 📞 919/673–0231).

# Toniná

🏔 ★ ⑲   *14 km (8 mi) east of Ocosingo.*

Between San Cristóbal and Palenque, on a paved road running along the Río Jataté and through the mild Ocosingo Valley, is the ancient Maya city of Toniná. The name means "house of stone" in Tzeltal, and you'll understand why it seemed appropriate once you glimpse this series of temples looming some 20 stories over the valley. Built on a steep hillside, Toniná is even taller than Palenque or Tikal.

Toniná is thought to be the last major Maya ceremonial center to flourish in this area. It thrived for at least a century after the fall of Palenque and Yaxchilán. In fact, it may have contributed to their downfall. Excavations indicate that the vanquished rulers of those cities were brought here as prisoners. Wonderfully preserved sculptures, including the *Mural de las Cuatro Eras* (Mural of the Four Ages) depict bloody executions.

Taxis from Ocosingo's main square cost about $8; for about twice that the driver will wait for you. Colectivos headed to the ruins leave from the market as soon as they are full, which is usually every 20 minutes or so. They cost $1 per person each way. 🎫 *$3* ☉ *Daily 9–4.*

# Agua Azul

★ ⑳   *68 km (42 mi) northwest of Toniná.*

The series of waterfalls and crystalline blue pools at Agua Azul is breathtaking, especially during the dry season (from about November through March), as wet-season waters are often churned up and brown with mud. You can swim in a series of interconnected pools.

If the single cascade at nearby Misol-Há is less grandiose than the series of falls and pools at Agua Azul, it's no less amazing. You can swim

# MAYA ARCHITECTURE

THE MAYA WERE OUTSTANDING ARCHITECTS, without compare in the Americas. They erected palaces and pyramids in less-than-hospitable climates without the aid of metal tools, the wheel, or beasts of burden. The Maya ruled much of southeastern Mexico, Belize, Guatemala, and western Honduras and El Salvador. It's not surprising that the architectural styles in different regions diverged.

**Río Usumacinta.** Builders of pyramids of this style typically gave them additional height by placing them on hillsides. The principal structures in this style were covered with exquisite bas-reliefs carved in stone. The small one-story pyramid-top temples characteristically had vestibules and rooms with vault ceilings. The wide, spacious chambers inside the pyramids had smaller, attached rooms filled with bas-reliefs of important events. Río Usumacinta friezes slope inward, rather than standing perpendicular. Perhaps the most striking architectural element in this style is the large roof comb found on the sacred structures. Finest examples: Palenque, Yaxchilán, Toniná.

**Río Bec.** Influenced by Petén style seen in Guatemalan sites like Tikal, the pitch of these pyramids is rather steep, and the foundations are elaborately decorated. The stairways on the outside of some pyramids were built for aesthetic rather than practical purposes, and were "false" (unclimbable). The principal structures were long, one-story affairs containing two or sometimes three tall towers. Each was capped by a large roof comb emboldened with a dramatic stucco facade. Finest examples: Calakmul, Xpuhil, Río Bec.

**Chenes.** Found mainly in Campeche, this style likewise had long, single-story structures. In this case they were divided into three distinct sections, each with its own doorway charmingly surrounded by a face of the rain god, Chaac, whose mouth forms the entrance. Finest examples: Hochob, Chicanná.

**Puuc.** In the beautifully proportioned Puuc style, the buildings were designed in a low-slung, quadrangle shape and had many rooms. Exterior walls were probably kept plain to show off the friezes above, which were lavishly embellished with stone-mosaic deities surrounded by geometric and serpentine motifs. The corners of buildings were characteristically lined with the curl-nosed Chaac. Pyramids in this region didn't have roof combs. Finest examples: Uxmal, Labná, Kabah, Sayil.

**Northeast Yucatán.** The fusion of two Maya groups—the early Chichén Maya and later Itzá Maya—produced this Late Classic (AD 800–1000) style famously exemplified by Chichén Itzá. Here new forms such as columns and grand colonnades were introduced. Palaces with row upon row of columns carved in the form of serpents looked over private patios, platforms were dedicated to the planet Venus, and pyramids were offered to Kukulcán (the plumed serpent god borrowed from the Toltecs, who called him Quetzalcóatl). Finest examples: Chichén Itzá, Mayapán.

**Quintana Roo Coast.** Although somewhat influenced by the Itzá Maya, a different style eventually evolved here. The large, squat-looking, one-story buildings have interior columns, wood-beam-supported ceilings, and numerous figures of the descending or Upside Down god. Friezes were distinctively decorated with small niches. Finest example: Tulum.

— Patricia Alisa

in the pool formed by the 100-foot cascade, or explore behind the falls, where a cave leads to a subterranean pool. (If there's a guide with flashlight in hand to help you, tip him $1 or so).

Six-hour trips from Palenque, which include visits to Agua Azul and Misol-Há, cost about $10 per person.

## Palenque

*191 km (118 mi) northeast of San Cristóbal de las Casas, 150 km (93 mi) southeast of Villahermosa.*

FodorsChoice

★

Of all the Maya ruins, none is more sublime than Palenque, and only Tikal in Guatemala and Copán in Honduras are its equal. Arrive here on a morning when the fog still shrouds the surrounding hills and you'll know why it's a sacred place for the Maya rulers.

Since the Spanish first heard tales of a colossal city lost in the jungle, there has been no shortage of explorers—some hardy, others foolhardy—determined to uncover the secrets of Palenque. In 1831, an eccentric count named Jean-Frédéric Maximilien de Waldeck set up house with his mistress for a year in what has become known as the Templo del Conde (Temple of the Count). Amateur archeologist John Lloyd Stephens and Frederick Catherwood lived briefly in the sprawling Palacio (Palace) during their 1840 expedition. Serious excavations began in 1923 under the direction of Frans Blom, cofounder of the Na Bolom foundation in San Cristóbal. Work continued intermittently until 1952, when Alberto Ruz Lhuillier, a Mexican archaeologist, uncovered the tomb of the 7th-century ruler Pakal beneath the Templo de las Inscripciones (Temple of the Inscriptions).

Unraveling the story of Palenque has been difficult. Only around 1000 of the thousands of glyphs found here have been deciphered, but they have already revealed the complex history of the Palenque dynasties. Exciting finds by archaeologists from the University of Texas in 1998 introduced a new character, Uc-Pakal-Kinich, into the lineage of Palenque rulers. Other clues unearthed at Templo 19 point to a probable liaison between rulers of Palenque and of Copán.

Although it was inhabited as early as 1500 BC, Palenque's most important buildings date from the Mid- to Late Classic period (AD 300–1000). At its zenith, between AD 600 and AD 700, the city dominated the greater part of what is today Tabasco and Chiapas. This period coincided with the reign of K'inich Hanab Pakal, the king who was buried beneath the Templo de las Inscripciones. But the city that thrived under Pakal's rule was abandoned around AD 900. The reasons for the Mayas' departure are still being debated. Archaeologists think it has something to do with the fierce rivalry between Palenque and Toniná.

Palenque's elegance makes clear why archaeologist Sylvanus Morley called the Maya the "Greeks of the New World"—not only for their remarkable buildings, but also for the supple naturalism of their art. The masters here shaped stone, stucco, and ceramics into ornate, lyrical designs. Instead of the freestanding stelae found at other Maya cities, at Palenque

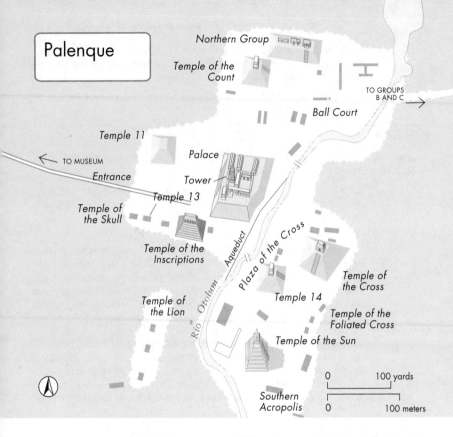

Palenque

Northern Group

Temple of the
Count

TO GROUPS
B AND C →

Ball Court

Temple 11

TO MUSEUM

Palace

Entrance

Tower

Temple 13

Temple of
the Skull

Aqueduct

Plaza of the Cross

Temple of the
Inscriptions

Río Otolum

Temple of
the Cross

Temple 14

Temple of
the Lion

Temple of the
Foliated Cross

Temple of the Sun

0        100 yards

Southern
Acropolis

0        100 meters

you find highly expressive relief sculpture and elaborate glyphs. In its heyday, Palenque encompassed an astonishing 128-plus km (49 square mi). Hills were flattened to support the temples, which were surrounded by wide plazas, a ball court, and burial grounds. The temples themselves contained a complex array of twisting corridors, narrow subterranean stairways, and wide galleries. The design was more than aesthetic, because the buildings also served as fortresses in time of war.

As you enter the site, the first temple on your right is the reconstructed **Templo de la Calavera** (Temple of the Skull). A stucco relief, presumed to be in the shape of a rabbit or deer skull, was found at the entrance to the temple. It now sits at the top of the stairs. Like the rest of the buildings, the Templo de la Calavera is unadorned stone. When it was built, however, it was painted vivid shades of red and blue.

At the eastern end of this cluster of temples is the massive **Templo de las Inscripciones,** dedicated to Pakal. The temple's nine tiers correspond to the nine lords of the underworld. Atop this temple and the smaller ones surrounding it are vestiges of roof combs—delicate vertical extensions that are among the features of southern Maya cities. You can descend the steep, damp flight of stairs to view the king's tomb. One of the first crypts found inside a Mexican pyramid, it contains a stone tube in the shape of a snake through which Pakal's soul was thought to have passed to the netherworld. The intricately carved sarcophagus lid weighs some 5 tons and measures 10 feet by 7 feet. It can be difficult to make out the carvings on the thick slab, but they depict the ruler, prostrate beneath a sacred ceiba tree. There's a reproduction in the site museum.

To enter the Templo de las Inscripciones, you must obtain a permit first thing in the morning at the site museum. If you can't secure a permit, you can always enter the unassuming **Templo XIII**. Attached to the Temple of the Inscriptions, this structure also has a royal tomb hidden in its depths, the Tumba de la Reina Roja, or Tomb of the Red Queen. The sarcophagus, colored with cinnabar, probably belonged to Pakal's wife or mother.

The smaller buildings inside the breathtaking **Palacio** are supported by a 30-foot-high plinth. Stuccowork adorns the pillars of the galleries as well as the inner courtyards. Most of the numerous friezes inside depict Pakal and his dynasty. The palace's iconic tower was built on three levels, thought to represent the three levels of the universe as well as the movement of the stars.

To the east of the palace is the tiny Río Otulum, which in ancient times was covered over to form a 9-foot-high vaulted aqueduct. Cross the river and climb up 80 easy steps to arrive at the reconstructed Plaza de la Cruz (Plaza of the Cross). It contains the **Templo de la Cruz Foliada** (Temple of the Foliated Cross), **Templo del Sol** (Temple of the Sun), and the **Templo de la Cruz** (Temple of the Cross), the largest of the group. Inside the nearby Templo 14, there's an underworld scene in stucco relief, finished 260 days after Pakal's death. The most exquisite roof combs are found on these buildings.

South of the Plaza de la Cruz is another group of buildings called the Acrópolis Sur, or Southern Acropolis. **Templo 19** has yielded some exciting finds, including a large sculpted stucco panel, a carved stone platform with hundreds of hieroglyphics, and a limestone table (in pieces but now restored) depicting the ruler K'inich Ahkal Mo' Nahb' III. The latter is on display in the site museum. In **Templo 20**, ground-penetrating radar helped locate a frescoed tomb covered in murals. Both temples are still being excavated and are sometimes closed to the public.

To reach the cluster called the Grupo Norte (Northern Group) walk north along the river, passing on your left the Palacio and the unexcavated **ball court**. There are five buildings here in various states of disrepair; the best preserved is the **Templo del Conde** (Temple of the Count).

A short hike northeast of the Grupo Norte lies **Grupo C** (Group C), an area containing remains of the homes of nobles and a few small temples shrouded in jungle. To maintain the natural setting in which the ruins were found, minimal restoration is being done. Human burials, funeral offerings, and kitchen utensils have been found here as well as in **Grupo B** (Group B), which lies farther along the path through the jungle. On the way, you'll pass a small waterfall and pool called El Baño de la Reina (The Queen's Bath). By far the most interesting of these seldom-visited ruins is the **Grupo de los Murciélagos** (Group of the Bats). Dark, twisting corridors beneath the ruins are ready to be explored. Just be aware that you might run into a few of the creatures that gave the spooky buildings their name.

A path from the Grupo de los Murciélagos leads over a short extension bridge to the **museum.** (You can also reach it by car, as it's along the same road you took to the entrance.) The museum has a remarkable stucco rendering of Mayan deities in elaborate zoomorphic headdresses, which was discovered in front of the Temple of the Foliated Cross. Also noteworthy are the handsome, naturalistic faces of Mayan men that once graced the facades. Displays here and in the rest of the site are labeled in English, Spanish, and the Maya dialect called Chol. There's also a snack bar and a crafts store.

To get more in-depth information about the ruins, hire a multilingual guide at the ticket booth. Guides charge about $35 for a group of up to 7 people. Tours generally last about two hours. ⌨ *$3.50* ⊙ *Ruins daily 8–5, museum Tues.–Sun. 9–4.*

### Where to Stay

★ **$$** ⌨ **Chan Kah.** If you want to stay near the ruins, this is the place. Amid colorful wild ginger and aromatic jasmine, this cluster of bungalows feels miles from anywhere. Your bungalow has a dressing room and a spacious bedroom with floor-to-ceiling windows overlooking the gardens. If you aren't already close enough to nature, there is a pair of mahogany rocking chairs on your back porch. From many rooms you can see the nearby stream that fills the immense lagoon-style pool. Don't confuse this Chan Kah with the hotel of the same name in town. ⊠ *Carretera Ruinas, Km 3.5, 29960* ☎ *916/345–1100 or 916/345–1134* ☏ *916/345–0820* ⊕ *www.chan-kah.com.mx* ☏ *73 rooms, 6 suites* ☒ *Restaurant, in-room safes, 2 pools, billiards, bar, recreation room, meeting room; no TV in some rooms* ☰ *MC, V.*

## Palenque Town

㉒ *8 km (5 mi) north of the ruins.*

The community of Palenque wraps you in a warm tropical embrace. Its days as a sleepy little town are far behind; the cinder-block structures have been gussied up with coats of vivid yellow, orange, and blue paint. It's not a pretty place, but Palenque tries hard to keep you from noticing.

The dominant landmark is the chalk-white **Cabeza Maya,** a giant sculpture of the head of a Mayan chieftain that graces the traffic circle just west of downtown. It's in the quiet neighborhood of La Cañada.

### Where to Stay & Eat

★ **$–$$** ✕ **Maya Cañada.** This thatch-roof restaurant in La Cañada is one of the prettiest in Palenque. Grab a table on the main level amid the fragrant gardens, or head up to the tiled terrace lit by cast-iron lanterns. Either way, you're in for a treat. Musicians play softly as you choose among the regional dishes like *pollo en mole chiapaneco,* the same dish you might find in Oaxaca but with a bit more spice. There's a full bar where you might sample one of the Mexican wines. ✉ *Calle Merle Green s/n, La Cañada* ☎ *916/345–0216* 🖿 *AE, MC, V.*

**$** ✕ **Maya.** Billed as Palenque's first restaurant, Maya opened for business back in 1958. It sits so close to the main square that you can hear the birds that come home to roost each sunset. The tables in the dining room, swathed in magenta fabric, always seem to be crowded. The three-course set menus at lunch are a good deal. Dishes served à la carte include medallions of *robalo*, a local fish that is equally tasty fried or breaded. The coffees are the best in town. ✉ *Av. Independencia at Av. Hidalgo* ☎ *916/345–0042* 🖿 *AE, MC, V.*

**¢–$** ✕ **Café de Yara.** There's something refreshing about this corner café; maybe it's the doors flung open to catch the breeze, or the walls painted the color of lemons and limes. A good choice is the *pollo a la pasilla con nopales* (boneless chicken breast cooked in a chili sauce and covered with bits of cactus). Make sure to end your meal with a cup of organic coffee. ✉ *Av. Hidalgo 66, at Calle Abasolo* ☎ *916/345–0269* 🖿 *AE, MC, V.*

**¢–$** ✕ **Las Tinajas.** Simple and homey, Las Tinajas serves the type of food that Palenqueños find at their own dining room tables. Locals rave about the panfried shrimp and the strips of beef covered with sizzling onions. You'll usually strike up a conversation with a stranger if you sit at one of two large tables just outside the front door. If you want a bit more privacy, try a table inside. ✉ *Av. 20 de Noviembre 414* ☎ *No phone* 🖿 *No credit cards.*

**¢** ✕ **El Arbolito.** On the main road to Villahermosa, this funky restaurant is full of hacienda memorabilia. There's a wall full of floppy hats, each inscribed with a different Mexican proverb. Other walls have mounted animal heads and pelts. The specialties all come from Puebla, a city well known for its fine cuisine. Favorites include the spicy *consomé de borrego especial,* a broth with barbecued mutton, onions, and fresh cilantro. Beef tips in smoky chipotle sauce are served with beans, rice, and a bowl of piping hot tortillas. There's live marimba music in the afternoon. ✉ *Carretera Palenque–Villahermosa, Km 1.5* ☎ *916/345–0900* 🖿 *MC, V.*

**$$** 🏨 **Calinda Nututún Palenque.** A large natural pool forms in a bend in the Río Nututún, which runs through the grounds of this hotel. The rooms in the low-slung main building are plain but ample. Book a suite and you'll have more space and a terrace overlooking the gardens. The main drawback is the location, which is far from town but not closer to the ruins. ✉ *Carretera Palenque–Ocosingo, Km 3.5* 🖃 *Apdo. 74, 29960* ☎ *916/345–0100, 916/345–0161, 800/221–2222 in the U.S.* 🖷 *916/ 345–0620* 🛏 *55 suites, 12 rooms* ♨ *Restaurant, pool, bar, playground, free parking; no TV in some rooms* 🖿 *AE, MC, V.*

**$$** 🏨 **Maya Tulipanes.** On a quiet street in La Cañada, this hotel is one of the most pleasant in Palenque. The spacious terrace, surrounded by greenery, is marked by a huge thatch-roofed sitting area where people meet before heading off to the ruins. Rooms are standard issue, marred only by the fluorescent lights. ✉ *Cañada 6, 29960* ☎ *916/345–0201* 🖷 *916/ 345–1004* ⊕ *www.mayatulipanes.com* 🛏 *70 rooms* ♨ *Restaurant, room service, cable TV, pool, bar, shop, travel services, meeting rooms* 🖿 *AE, MC, V.*

**$–$$** 🏨 **Ciudad Real Palenque.** This colonial-style hotel, all done up in bright yellows and creams, is surrounded by thriving gardens. A small waterfall and creek run through the grounds. All the rooms, with cheerful fabrics made by local artisans, have balconies facing the gardens. The palm-lined pool has several hammocks where you can spend a lazy afternoon. ⊠ *Carretera Pakal-Na, Km 1.5, 29960* ☎☎ *916/345–1315 or 916/345–1343* ⊕ *www.ciudadreal.com.mx* ⌷ *69 rooms, 3 suites* ⌂ *Restaurant, room service, cable TV, pool, bar, shop, travel services, meeting rooms* ⊟ *AE, MC, V.*

¢ ▣ **Hostal San Miguel.** You can't beat the location of this cheerful little hotel, which is in the heart of Palenque. You can't beat the price either—about $15 for a room with a wrought-iron balcony looking over the tops of the trees. There are no amenities to speak of, but the rooms are spotless and a lot larger than you'll find at any other downtown lodging. ⊠ *Av. Juárez, at Calle Abasolo, 29960* ☎ *No phone* ⌷ *48 rooms* ⌂ *Fans; no room phones, no room TVs* ⊟ *AE, MC, V.*

## Bonampak

🏛 ㉓ *183 km (113 mi) southeast of Palenque.*

Bonampak, which means "painted walls" in Mayan, is renowned for its courtly murals of Mayan life. The settlement was built on the banks of the Río Lacanjá in the 7th and 8th centuries and was uncovered in 1946. Explorer Jacques Soustelle called it "a pictorial encyclopedia of a Maya city." In remarkable tones of blue, red, green, and yellow, the scenes in the three rooms of the fascinating **Templo de las Pinturas** recount subjects such as life at court and the aftermath of battle.

Segments of the murals are deteriorating because of the humidity. In 1984 Mexican experts devised cleaning and restoration processes, and with the help of the National Geographic Society—and computerized, digital amplification techniques—remarkable details and color have come to light. Still, the reproductions at the archaeological museums in Mexico City and Villahermosa are more legible than these on-site specimens. But nothing comes close to seeing them in person.

Until the 1990s, only the most devoted fans of the Maya attempted the trip here. Now, however, you can drive or take a three-hour bus ride from Palenque on the paved Carretera 198. Buses or tour vans will take you all the way to the ruins or drop you at Lacanjá so you can hike the last 3 km (2 mi).

Be sure to wear sturdy shoes, and bring insect repellent, good sunglasses, and a hat to protect yourself from mosquitoes, ticks, sand flies, undergrowth, and the jungle sun. The ruins are open daily 8–5; admission is $7, including transportation from the park entrance to the main structures. Note that only four visitors are allowed in each room of the Templo de las Pinturas at a time, and you can't use a flash.

## Yaxchilán

🏛 ㉔ *50 km (31 mi) northeast of Bonampak, 190 km (118 mi) southeast of* **Fodor'sChoice** *Palenque.*
★

Excavations at Yaxchilán (ya-shee-*lan*), on the banks of the Río Usumacinta, have uncovered stunning temples and delicate carvings. Spider monkeys and toucans are, at this point, more prolific than humans, and howler monkeys growl like lions from the towering gum trees and magnificent 100-year-old ceibas.

Yaxchilán, which means "place of green stones," reached its cultural peak during the Late Classic period, from about AD 800 to 1000. It's dominated by two acropolises containing a palace, temples with finely carved lintels, and great staircases. Several generations ago, the Lacandon who live in the vicinity made pilgrimages to this jungle-clad site to leave "god pots" (incense-filled ceramic bowls) in honor of ancient deities. They were awed by the headless sculpture of Yaxachtun (ya-sha-*tun*) at the entrance to the temple (called Structure 33) and believed that the world would end when its head was replaced on its torso.

Yaxchilán was on the trade route between Palenque and Tikal, and the remains of a 600-foot bridge over the Río Usumacinta to connect Yaxchilán to Guatemalan territory has been discovered.

Getting to Yaxchilán requires a one-hour riverboat ride; you must first drive or take a bus to the small town of Frontera Corozal, off Carretera 198, where boats depart for the ruins and for the Guatemalan border. It's best to arrange trips through travel agencies, tour operators, or tourist offices in Mexico City, Palenque, or San Cristóbal de las Casas; their staffers can also arrange for you to stay at the wonderful Tzeltal Indian cooperative, Escudo Jaguar. Admission to the ruins is $3; they're open daily 8–5.

### Where to Stay

¢ ▦ **Escudo Jaguar.** If you don't mind rustic accommodations, this ecotourism project is the ideal base for exploring Bonampak and Yaxchilán. Each of the wooden, thatch-roof cabins has screened windows, mosquito nets, fans, and a wide concrete veranda with two large, colorful hammocks. The restaurant serves full breakfasts, lunches, and dinners. It's best to book trips to Bonampak and Yaxchilán with travel agents or tour operators ahead of time, mentioning that you want to stay at Escudo Jaguar. ⊠ *Frontera Corozal* ☎ *555/151–1869* ✆ *13 cabins* ⚘ *Restaurant; no a/c, no room phones, no TVs* 🖃 *No credit cards.*

# VILLAHERMOSA & TABASCO

Graham Greene's succinct summation of Tabasco in *The Power and the Glory* as a "tropical state of river and swamp and banana grove" captures its essence. Although the state played an important role in Mexico's early history, its past is rarely on view. Instead, it's Tabasco's modern-day status as a supplier of oil that defines it. On a humid coastal plain and crisscrossed by 1,930 km (1,197 mi) of rivers, low hills, and unexplored jungles, the land is still rich in banana and cacao plantations. Refineries and related structures are, for the most part invisible; what you're more apt to see are small ranches.

The capital city of Villahermosa epitomizes the mercurial development of Tabasco, where the airplane arrived before the automobile. Thanks to oil and the money it brought in, the cramped and ugly neighborhoods in the mosquito-ridden town of the 1970s have largely been replaced by spacious boulevards, shady parks, and cultural centers. Running alongside the fast-flowing Río Grijalva, the Zona Luz has been redone as a brick-paved pedestrian zone, with plenty of cafés, coffee shops, and ice cream parlors that stay packed until late in the evening.

Tabasco contains the route of the Spanish explorations of 1518–19. At that time, the Maya lived along the rivers that served as trade routes between the peoples of the north and those of the south. When the Spaniards came, they had to bridge 50 rivers and contend with swarms of mosquitoes, beetles, and ants—as well as the almost unbearable heat. At the same time, the region was so lush that one early chronicler termed it a Garden of Eden.

The Spanish conquest was made easier by the tribal warfare between the Tabascans and their Aztec overlords. Among the 20 slaves turned over to the Spaniards upon their arrival in the Aztec capital was a Chiapan woman named Malinche (or Malintzín), who was singled out for her ability to speak both the Maya and the Nahuatl languages. Called Doña Marina by the Spaniards, she learned Spanish and became not only Cortés's mistress and the mother of his illegitimate son, but also an interpreter. Malinche's cooperation helped the conquistador vanquish both Moctezuma and Cuauhtémoc, the last two Aztec rulers. Even today, "La Malinche" is synonymous with "traitor" throughout much of Mexico.

After the American Civil War, traders from the southern United States began operating in the region, hauling precious mahogany trees upstream from Chiapas and shipping them north from the small port of Frontera. After this prosperous era, Tabasco slumbered until the oil boom of the 1970s and 1980s. Although it has little infrastructure in place to help attract tourism, Tabasco has beaches, lagoons, caves, and nature reserves worthy of exploration. The fired-brick Mayan ruins of Comalcalco attest to the influence of Palenque, and the region southeast of Villahermosa has rivers and canyons that are home to deer, alligators, and the occasional jaguar.

## Villahermosa

► **㉕** *821 km (509 mi) southeast of Mexico City, 632 km (392 mi) southwest of Mérida.*

Where you wander in Villahermosa depends on your mood. Soak in the local culture in the Zona Luz, the pedestrian-only streets between Parque Juárez and the Plaza de Armas. Travel back 2,000 years or so at the Parque Museo La Venta. Or just shop at the upscale Galería Tabasco.

Most people make a beeline for the **Museo Regional de Antropología Carlos Pellicer Cámara.** On the right bank of the Río Grijalva, the museum is named after the man who donated many of its artifacts. Pellicer, who has been called the "poet laureate of Latin America," was deeply influenced by a love of his native Tabasco; his poems record the region's insistent rhythms and visual intensity.

Much of the collection is devoted to Tabasco and the Olmec people, the "inhabitants of the land of rubber" who flourished as early as 1750 BC and disappeared around 100 BC. The Olmecs have long been honored as inventors of the region's numerical and calendrical systems. The pyramid, later copied by the Maya and Aztec cultures, is also attributed to them. Some of the most interesting artifacts on display here are the remnants of their jaguar cult. The jaguar symbolized procreation, and many Olmec sculptures portray half-human, half-jaguar figures or human heads emerging from the mouths of jaguars.

Many of Mexico's ancient cultures are represented on the upper two floors, from the red-clay dogs of Colima and the nose rings of the Huichol Indians of Nayarit to the huge burial urns of the Chontal Maya, who built Comalcalco, a Maya city near Villahermosa. All the explanations are in Spanish, but the museum is organized in chronological order and is very easy to follow.

The museum is part of the huge Centro de Investigación de las Culturas Olmec y Maya, dedicated to research into Olmec and Maya history. The CICOM complex, about 1 km (½ mi) south of the Zona Luz, also houses a theater, library, and craft shop. ⊠ *Periférico Carlos Pellicer 511, an extension of Malecón Madrazo* ☎ *993/312–6344* ✉ *$1* ☼ *Tues.–Sat. 9–7, Sun. 9–5.*

Covered with dazzling cobalt tiles, the building housing the **Museo de Historia de Tabasco** was originally called the Casa de los Azulejos (House of the Tiles). The mansion would be over the top even without the cherubs reclining along the roof. The museum's collection is a bit sparse, but the individual pieces—an anchor from the days pirates patrolled the Gulf of Mexico, a carriage from the reign of dictator Porfirio Díaz—help bring the past to life. ⊠ *Av. Juárez 402 at Calle 27 de Febrero* ☎ *No phone* ✉ *50¢* ☼ *Tues.–Sat. 10–8, Sun. 10–5.*

Giant stone heads and other carvings were salvaged from the oil fields at La Venta, on Tabasco's western edge near the state of Veracruz. They're on display in the 20-acre **Parque Museo La Venta,** a lush park founded by Carlos Pellicer Cámara in 1958. The views of the misty Lago de las Ilusiones (Lake of Illusions) are stirring, which is probably why young lovers come here to smooch in quiet corners.

The 6-foot-tall stone heads, which have bold features and wear what look like helmets, weigh up to 20 tons. Scholarly debates about them are endless. The least outlandish theory is that the faces—very similar to today's Tabasco Maya—are portraits of athletes, warriors, or, most likely, rulers. The most unnerving carving is an altar depicting a man carrying the lifeless body of a child. Other men seem to be subduing squirming children on the sides of the altar, making you wonder about their fate.

The park also contains a zoo displaying animals from Tabasco and neighboring states. The jaguars—including one that is jet black—always elicit screams from children. Sadly, many of the animals here are in danger of extinction. ⊠ *Blvd. Ruíz Cortines s/n* ☎ *993/314–1652* ✉ *$3* ☼ *Daily 8–4* ☼ *Zoo closed Mon.*

FodorśChoice
★

The compact **Museo de la Historia Natural** (Natural History Museum) is just outside the entrance to the Parque Museo La Venta. Of most interest are the displays of Tabasco's native plants and animals, many of which are now under government protection. Kids love the skull of a triceratops and various bones from other dinosaurs. ⊠ *Blvd. Ruíz Cortines s/n* ☎ *No phone* 🎫 *$1* ⊙ *Tues.–Sun. 9–5.*

**Parque Yumká,** which means "the spirit that looks after the forest" in Chontal Maya, is a popular nature reserve with more than 250 acres of jungle, savannah, and wetlands. Half-hour guided walking tours take you over a hanging bridge and past free-roaming endangered species such as spider monkeys, crocodiles, and native *tepezcuintles* (giant rodents). After the walk there's a narrated tram ride past elephants, zebras, and other Asian and African creatures. Boat tours glide past birds taking flight. ⊠ *16 km (10 mi) east of Villahermosa* ☎ *993/356–0115* 🎫 *$4* ⊙ *Daily 9–5 (ticket window closes at 4).*

## Where to Stay & Eat

**$$$** ✕ **Bougainvillea.** Polished wood, crimson carpets, and lanterns with a vaguely art deco design make the dining room of the Hyatt Regency look like a Chinese restaurant. Some entrées, like the duck in a tamarind sauce, have an Asian flair. But the food here is better termed international, especially on Wednesday and Thursday, when the star attractions are several different kinds of fondue. On ordinary nights start with the paper-thin carpaccio, then move on to the plump shrimp in a garlic sauce. ⊠ *Av. Juárez 106, at Av. Ruíz Cortines* ☎ *993/310–1234* 🖃 *AE, DC, MC, V* ⊙ *Closed Sun.*

**$–$$$** ✕ **El Mesón del Ángel.** You might think you've stumbled into a country inn when you make your way up the blue-tile steps of this local favorite. Inside are cheery brass chandeliers, lacy curtains, and stained-glass windows bearing the image of the namesake cherub. The owner is from Madrid, so the menu is full of dishes like *paella a la valenciana* (rice with seafood and sausage) and *arroz negro* (rice with squid ink). ⊠ *Av. Méndez 1604* ☎ *933/315–8616 or 933/352–1138* 🖃 *AE, MC, V.*

**★ $–$$** ✕ **Los Tulipanes.** Soothing views of the Río Grijalva set this restaurant apart. Choose a table on the shaded patio or in the softly lit salon. The staff tries hard to please, steering you toward regional favorites like *pejelagarto,* a succulent fish, and *carne salada con chaya,* delicious chunks of beef mixed with plantains. Locals turn out in droves for the Sunday afternoon seafood buffet. ⊠ *Periférico Carlos Pellicer 511, in the CICOM complex* ☎ *993/312–9209* 🖃 *AE, MC, V.*

**$** ✕ **La Fontana.** If you've had your fill of beans and rice, head to this trattoria near Parque Museo La Venta. For once the red, white, and green flags hanging in the casual dining room aren't from Mexico, so there's not a tortilla in sight. The specialty here is pasta, which is made daily. The wide range of salads is also good. ⊠ *Av. Ruíz Cortines 1410* ☎🖹 *993/314–3283* 🖃 *AE, MC, V.*

**$$$–$$$$** 🏨 **Camino Real.** You can literally shop till you drop here—a stairway leads directly to the upscale Galería Tabasco. But other than that, this hotel is all work and no play. It's set up for conferences, so the sleek lines of the lobby are often obscured by people fiddling with their name tags. The restaurant, with floor-to-ceiling windows shaded with bamboo, is filled with executives closing a deal. There's a gorgeous pool, but it sits empty much of the time. ✉ *Paseo Tabasco 1407, 86030* ☎ *993/316–4400, 800/722–6466 in the U.S.* 🖷 *993/316–4439* ⊕ *www. caminoreal.com/villahermosa* ⇆ *180 rooms, 16 suites* ⚭ *Restaurant, coffee shop, room service, in-room data ports, in-room safes, minibars, cable TV, pool, laundry service, concierge floor, Internet, business services, convention center, meeting rooms, car rental, travel services, free parking* ⊟ *AE, DC, MC, V.*

**$$$** 🏨 **Hyatt Regency Villahermosa.** Although it's stodgy on the outside, this luxury hotel lightens up once you pass through the front doors. The pleasingly modern Ceiba Café, which serves a superb breakfast buffet, has curlicues of wrought iron that lend it a Victorian feeling. The more formal restaurant, Bougainvillea, is as red as Marilyn Monroe's lipstick. The lobby bar, called Plataforma, is decked out like the inside of an offshore oil platform. Rooms all have marble floors and polished wood furnishings. ✉ *Av. Juárez 106, 86050* ☎ *993/315–1234, 800/228–9000 in the U.S.* 🖷 *993/315–1235* ⇆ *198 rooms, 9 suites* ⚭ *2 restaurants, room service, in-room data ports, in-room safes, minibars, cable TV, 2 tennis courts, pool, 3 bars, shop, laundry service, concierge floors, Internet, business services, convention center, meeting rooms, car rental, travel services, free parking, no-smoking rooms* ⊟ *AE, MC, V.*

**$$** 🏨 **Calinda Viva & Spa Villahermosa.** Across from Parque Museo La Venta, this hotel has an enviable location. After a day exploring the park, you can have someone work out the kinks at the in-house spa. The low-slung building's gleaming white facade is softened a bit by a Spanish tile roof. Although rooms are simply furnished, each is quite comfortable and has a small balcony. ✉ *Av. Ruíz Cortines at Paseo Tabasco, 86050* ☎ *993/315–0000* 🖷 *993/315–3073 or 993/315–1858* ⊕ *www. hotelescalinda.com.mx* ⇆ *239 rooms, 1 suite* ⚭ *Restaurant, in-room safes, minibars, cable TV, pool, gym, hot tub, massage, sauna, steam room, 2 bars, dance club, laundry service, Internet, business services, meeting rooms, travel services, free parking* ⊟ *AE, MC, V.*

**$$** 🏨 **Cencali.** Overlooking the sparkling Laguna de las Ilusiones, this hotel is surrounded by coconut-palm, mango, and cacao trees. What you don't see are the neighboring hotels, which are hidden behind the foliage. The big, cheerful rooms have small balconies. Don't miss the fabulous lobby mural of pre-Columbian indigenous life by Tabascan artist Daniel Montuy. ✉ *Av. Juárez at Paseo Tabasco, 86040* ☎ *993/315–1999* 🖷 *993/315–6600* ⊕ *www.cencali.com.mx* ⇆ *114 rooms, 8 suites* ⚭ *Restaurant, cable TV, pool, bar, Internet, business services, meeting rooms, airport shuttle, car rental* ⊟ *AE, DC, MC, V* ⦿ *BP.*

**$** 🏨 **Casa Inn.** This graceful high-rise sits in the middle of the Zona Luz, not far from all the downtown sights. A waterfall sets the mood as soon as you enter the spacious lobby. Seemingly dozens of employees are ready at a moment's notice to bring a fresh towel or hail a taxi. The best of the tastefully decorated rooms are in the back, with a view of a sliver of the river. ✉ *Av. Madero 480, at Calle Lerdo de Tejada, 86000* ☎ *993/358–0102 or 800/201–0909* 🖷 *993/358–0194* ⊕ *www.casainn.ws* ⇆ *100 rooms* ⚭ *Restaurant, room service, in-room data ports, in-room safes, cable TV, bar, Internet, shop, meeting rooms, free parking* ⊟ *AE, MC, V.*

$ ▥ **Plaza Independencia.** The great location—on a quiet street near the main plaza—puts you close to everything in the Zona Luz. The lobby and common areas are painted in eye-popping shades of bright pink, sky blue, and butter yellow. These hues sneak into guest rooms, which sometimes makes for a clashing color scheme. Ask for a room on one of the upper floors, as they overlook the river. ⊠ *Av. Independencia 123, 86000* ☎ *993/312–1299* 🖷 *993/314–4724* 🖵 *89 rooms, 1 suite* ⚘ *Restaurant, room service, in-room safe, cable TV, pool, lobby lounge, sports bar, laundry service, meeting rooms, free parking* ⊟ *AE, MC, V.*

★ ¢ ▥ **Hotel Madan.** Don't let the exuberant purple facade fool you—this is by far the best budget lodging in Villahermosa. A gently curving staircase covered with hand-painted blue tiles leads to the second floor, where sunny patios filled with greenery are around every corner. The staff is always on its toes, which is why you won't find a speck of dust in the simple but comfortable rooms. ⊠ *Av. Madero 408, at Calle Reforma, 86000* ☎ *993/314–0518* 🖷 *993/314–373* ✎ *madan2002@prodigy.oct.com* 🖵 *40 rooms* ⚘ *Coffee shop, cable TV, bar* ⊟ *AE, MC, V.*

## Nightlife & the Arts

Named for the "empress of operetta," the **Teatro Estado Esperanza Iris** (⊠ Periférico Carlos Pellicer 511, an extension of Malecón Madrazo ☎ 993/314–4210) is a modern theater complex hosting everything from traditional dance to avant-garde films. It is part of the huge CICOM complex.

## Shopping

The pedestrian-only streets of the Zona Luz are great for window shopping. But when locals take out their credit cards, they are heading to the upscale boutiques of **Galería Tabasco** (⊠ Paseo Tabasco ☎ 993/316–4400). So should you.

# Comalcalco Town

② *56 km (35 mi) northwest of Villahermosa.*

There's not much to see in this dusty little town, but it's the center of what's called the "Ruta del Cacao," or the Cocoa Route. Call ahead to arrange a free tour of **Hacienda de la Luz** (⊠ Blvd. Zovirosa Wade ☎ 933/334–1126), which is quite close to downtown Comalcalco. It's also known as Hacienda Hayer, because a German doctor named Otto Wolter Hayer bought it in the 1930s and turned it into the most profitable hacienda in the region. On the tour you'll learn everything about the production of cacao, from the plant to the chocolate stage. There's a small shop that sells products made from cocoa beans, which were used as currency here in pre-Hispanic times.

A visit to Comalcalco is pretty much unavoidable if you are visiting the nearby ruins. From here you can take a taxi to the front gate. For about $10 the driver will wait for you while you explore.

**en route** On your way to Comalcalco you'll pass through the town of Cupilco, home of the **Templo de la Virgin de la Asunción.** The facade, painted in wild colors, is one of the most unusual in Mexico.

## Comalcalco

🏛 ㉗ *3 km (2 mi) northwest of Comalcalco Town.*

The region's abundant cacao trees provided food and a livelihood for a booming Maya population during the Classic period (100 BC to AD 1000). Comalcalco, which was founded in about the 1st century BC, marks the westernmost reach of the Maya; descendants of its builders, the Chontal, still live in the vicinity. Its name, means "place of the clay griddles" (bricks) in Nahuatl, and it's Tabasco's most important Maya site, unique for its use of fired brick (made of sand, seashells, and clay), as the area's swamplands lacked the stone for building. The bricks were often inscribed and painted with figures of reptiles and birds, geometric figures, and drawings before being covered with stucco.

The major pyramid on the Gran Acrópolis del Este (Great Eastern Acropolis) is adorned with carvings as well as large stucco masks of the sun god, Kinich Ahau. The burial sites here also depart radically from Maya custom: the dead were placed in cone-shape clay urns, in a fetal position. Some have been left in situ, others are on display in the site museum along with many of the artifacts that were uncovered here. Admission to the site, which is open daily 10–4:30, is $3.

## Paraíso

㉘ *19 km (12 mi) north of Comalcalco.*

As you head toward the Gulf of Mexico coast and Paraíso, stop at one of the cacao plantations and chocolate factories. On the coast you'll get a glimpse of small-town life. Climb the Cerro Teodomiro (Teodomiro Hill) for a spectacular view of Laguna de las Flores (Las Flores Lagoon) and coconut plantations. Small seafood restaurants and several small hotels dot the shore here; others are a few kilometers inland, in town.

The region's small, dark-sand beaches are not among Mexico's prettiest; the best place to spend your time is 5 km (3 mi) southeast of Paraíso, in **Puerto Ceiba,** a fishing community whose inhabitants breed and harvest oysters. You can take a two-hour boat tour aboard the *Puerto Ceiba I* around the mangrove-lined Laguna Mecoacán (Mecoacán Lagoon) and the coastal rivers. Tours, which cost about $5 for adults, leave from the small Puerto Ceiba Restaurant.

# CHIAPAS & TABASCO A TO Z

### AIR TRAVEL

AIRPORTS   The region has airports in every major city, although they mostly handle domestic flights. Aeropuerto San Cristóbal, 15 km (9 mi) northwest of downtown, is on the road to Palenque. Aeropuerto de Comitán is about 15 km (9 mi) south of the city. El Aeropuerto Terán is 8 km (5 mi) southwest of Tuxtla Gutiérrez. Villahermosa's tidy little Aeropuerto Capitán Carlos A. Rovirosa is 15 km (9 mi) south of the city in Ranchería dos Montes. At this writing, the tiny international airport in Palenque was closed.

◪ Aeropuerto Capitán Carlos A. Rovirosa ☎ 993/356-0157 or 993/356-0156. **Aeropuerto de Comitán** ☎ 963/636-2143. **Aeropuerto San Cristóbal** ☎ 967/674-3016. **Aeropuerto Terán** ☎ 961/615-0498 or 961/615-1437.

AIRPORT
TRANSFERS
You can catch a *colectivo* (shared minivan) from Aeropuerto San Cristóbal to downtown for about $4 per person. Private taxis cost about $8 for up to three passengers. Taxis from Tuxtla Gutiérrez's airport cost $5 into town. The only transportation from Villahermosa's airport is via taxi. A trip downtown costs $15. Taxis from the airport can also drive you straight to Palenque for $75.

CARRIERS
If you want to fly directly to the region from the U.S., your best bet is the daily flight between Houston and Villahermosa on Continental. Otherwise you're going to connect in another Mexican city.

If you want to get to Villahermosa, AeroCalifornia, Aeroméxico, Aviacsa, and Mexicana have daily flights from Mexico City. Aerocaribe, Mexicana's regional line, connects Villahermosa with Tuxtla Gutiérrez, Cancún, Mérida, and Oaxaca.

Aviacsa has direct flights to Tuxtla Gutiérrez from Mexico City, Oaxaca, and Tapachula. Aerocaribe flies between Tuxtla and Oaxaca, Villahermosa, and Mexico City. Aeromar has daily flights between Mexico City and both San Cristóbal and Comitán.

◪ **Aero California** ☎ 993/316-8000 in Villahermosa, 800/237-6225 in the U.S. **Aerocaribe** ☎ 993/316-5046 in Villahermosa, 961/602-5649 in Tuxtla Gutiérrez. **Aeromar** ☎ 967/674-3014 in San Cristóbal, 963/636-2143 in Comitán. **Aeroméxico** ☎ 01800/021-4010 toll free in Mexico, 800/237-6639 in the U.S. **Aviacsa** ☎ 01800/711-6733 toll free in Mexico, 888/528-4227 in the U.S. **Continental** ☎ 800/231-0856 in the U.S. **Mexicana** ☎ 993/356-3132 in Villahermosa, 961/602-5765 in Tuxtla Gutiérrez, 800/531-7921 in the U.S.

## BUS TRAVEL

From Villahermosa, first-class service to Campeche, Chetumal, Mérida, Mexico City, Palenque, San Cristóbal, Tapachula, Tuxtla Gutiérrez, Veracruz, and elsewhere is available at the Terminal Central de 1a Clase. There's frequent second-class service to nearby towns from the Central Camionera de 2a Clase.

From San Cristóbal, Estación Cristóbal Colón has first-class buses to major destinations in Chiapas and beyond. Second-class service on Transportes Tuxtla Express Plus to Tuxtla, Ocosingo, Palenque, and Comitán departs from the terminal at Avenida Ignacio Allende. To avoid bus stations altogether, take one of the Chevy Suburban vans directly across from Estación Cristóbal Colón. They leave for Tuxtla, Ocosingo, and Comitán as soon as they fill up, which is about every 20 minutes. A trip should cost less than $4 per person.

From Palenque, first-class service is available to Ocosingo, Villahermosa, San Cristóbal, Tuxtla Gutiérrez, Mérida, Cancún, and Mexico City. They leave from the main bus terminal on Avenida Juárez. If you can't get a first-class bus, many of the same destinations can be reached on the second-class buses operated by Transportes Rodolfo Figueroa, a few doors away from the main bus terminal.

In Tuxtla, Estación Cristóbal Colón has first-class service to Oaxaca, Palenque, Villahermosa, Tapachula, Mérida, San Cristóbal, Cancún, Puerto Escondido, and Playa del Carmen, among others. First- and second-class transportation within the state is available on Autobuses TRF.

Buses between San Cristóbal and Tuxtla do not stop in downtown Chiapa de Corzo, but will let you off on the highway outside of town, where taxis are plentiful. Buses from Chiapa de Corzo to Tuxtla run along the north side of Plaza Ángel Albino Corzo.

**🚍 Bus Terminals Palenque** ✉ Av. Juárez near Av. de la Vega, Palenque ☎ 916/345-1344. **San Cristóbal** ✉ Av. Insurgentes and Blvd. Juan Sabines Gutiérrez, San Cristóbal ☎ 967/678-0291. **Tuxtla Gutiérrez** ✉ Av. 2a Poniente Norte 268, Tuxtla Gutiérrez ☎ 961/612-2624. **Villahermosa (first class)** ✉ Calle F. J. Mina 297, corner of Calle Lino Merino, Villahermosa ☎ 993/312-7692 or 993/312-1446. **Villahermosa (second class)** ✉ Av. Ruíz Cortines s/n at Prolongación de Mina, Villahermosa ☎ 993/312-0863.

**🚍 Bus Companies Autobuses TRF** ✉ 4a Poniente Sur 1060, Tuxtla Gutiérrez ☎ 916/312-7692. **Transportes Tuxtla Express Plus** ☎ 967/678-4869 in San Cristóbal.

## CAR RENTAL

Budget, Dollar, Hertz, and National have offices in the major cities of Chiapas and Tabasco. The national chains Excellent and Optima often have better prices and will deliver the car to your hotel.

**🚗 Agencies Budget** ✉ Aeropuerto Terán, Tuxtla Gutiérrez ☎ 961/615-6380 ✉ Blvd. Belisario Domínguez 2510 ☎ 961/615-0672 ✉ Aeropuerto Capitán Carlos A. Rovirosa, Villahermosa ☎ 993/356-0118 ✉ Av. 27 de Febrero 712, Villahermosa ☎ 993/314-3790. **Dollar** ✉ Hotel Maya Tabasco, Av. Ruiz Cortines 907, Villahermosa ☎ 993/314-4466. **Excellent** ✉ Calle Real de Guadalupe 5, San Cristóbal ☎ 967/678-7656 ✉ Blvd. Belisario Domínguez 302, Tuxtla Gutiérrez ☎ 961/602-5721. **Hertz** ✉ Aeropuerto Capitán Carlos A. Rovirosa, Villahermosa ☎ 993/356-0200 ✉ Hotel Camino Real, Paseo Tabasco 1407, Villahermosa ☎ 993/316-0163 ✉ Aeropuerto Terán, Tuxtla Gutiérrez ☎ 961/615-7070 ✉ Hotel Camino Real, Av. Belisario Domínguez 1195 ☎ 961/615-5348. **National** ✉ Aeropuerto Terán, Tuxtla Gutiérrez ☎ 961/614-6683 ✉ 11a Poniente Sur 1172, Tuxtla Gutiérrez ☎ 961/614-6681. **Optima** ✉ Calle Hermilo Lopez Sanchez 55, San Cristóbal ☎ 967/674-5409.

## CAR TRAVEL

From Tuxtla Gutiérrez, Carretera 190 goes east through Chiapa de Corzo to San Cristóbal before continuing southeast to Comitán and the Guatemala border. Carretera 199 to Carretera 186 (the turnoff is at Catazajá) is the preferred route from San Cristóbal to Villahermosa; it takes you via Ocosingo and Palenque. The winding drive from San Cristóbal to Palenque takes about five hours; it's another two hours from Palenque to Villahermosa along a fairly straight stretch. On the map, Carretera 195 may look like the most direct way to travel between San Cristóbal and Villahermosa, but it entails hours of hairpin curves.

If you're traveling to the Yucatán, take Carretera 186 from Palenque. To get to Villahermosa from Coatzacoalcos and Veracruz, take Carretera 180. In all cases, exercise caution during the rainy season (June through October), when roads are slick.

You'll want to explore colonial towns like San Cristóbal and Comitán on foot. You won't want the hassle of a car in Villahermosa or Tuxtla, as they are sprawling cities with speeding traffic and few signs. The main road through Villahermosa, Avenida Ruíz Cortines, is almost a highway; exit ramps are about 1 km (½ mi) apart, and destinations aren't clearly marked. Drive with caution.

Should you need help on the highways, contact the Polcía Federal de Caminos (Federal Highway Police).

**Policía Federal de Caminos** ⊠ Blvd. Juan Sabines Gutiérrez s/n, San Cristóbal ☎ 967/678-6466 ⊠ Av. Academia de Policías 295, Tuxtla Gutiérrez ☎ 961/614-3235.

### EMERGENCIES

**Cruz Roja** (Red Cross) ⊠ Prolongación Ignacio Allende 55, San Cristóbal ☎ 967/678-0772.

**Hospitals & Clinics Centro Medico Metropolitano de Tuxtla Gutiérrez** ⊠ 1a Oriente 847, Tuxtla Gutiérrez ☎ 961/612-3041. **Hospital General de Palenque** ⊠ Prolongación Juárez s/n, Palenque ☎ 916/345-0733. **Hospital Regional de San Cristóbal** ⊠ Av. Insurgentes 24, San Cristóbal ☎ 967/678-0770. **Hospital Cruz Roja de Villahermosa** ⊠ Av. Sandino 716, Villahermosa ☎ 993/315-5555 or 993/315-6263.

**Late-Night Pharmacies Farmacia del Ahorro** ⊠ Av. Central Poniente 874, Tuxtla Gutiérrez ☎ 961/602-6677 ⊠ Av. 27 de Febrero 1401, Villahermosa ☎ 933/315-6606. **Farmacia Bios** ⊠ Av. Hidalgo at Av. Cuauhtémoc, San Cristóbal ☎ 967/678-1818. **Farmacia Lastra** ⊠ Av. Juárez, at Calle Abasolo, Palenque ☎ 916/345-1119.

### INTERNET, MAIL & SHIPPING

The region's *correos* (post offices) have MexPost service, a shipping service that's comparable to DHL or FedEx and slightly cheaper. San Cristóbal has at least one Internet café per block near the center of town. You can check e-mail while you eat and listen to music at the Cafetería del Centro ($1 per hour), half a block from the zócalo. It's open daily 7 AM–9:30 PM. The CyberCafe is about 10 blocks from the main bus station in Tuxtla Gutiérrez, but the price is right: $1 an hour for Internet access. It's open daily 9–2 and 4–8. Prodinet, close to the Tuxtla's main square, is open daily 8:30–11. Palenque's Red Maya, open daily 9 AM–10 PM, has a dozen or so fast computers. An hour costs $1. There's a tiny Internet café called Millenium in Villahermosa's Zona Luz. It's open Monday–Saturday 8 AM–10 PM, Sunday 10–6. It charges about $1 an hour.

**Cybercafés Cafetería del Centro** ⊠ Calle Real de Guadalupe 7, San Cristóbal ☎ 967/678-3922. **CyberCafe** ⊠ 3a Norte Poniente 1340, Local 8, Tuxtla Gutiérrez ☎ 961/612-3900. **Millenium** ⊠ Av. Marisco Saenz at Lerdo de Tejada, Villahermosa ☎ 993/314-5684. **Prodinet** ⊠ 2a Norte Poniente 325, Tuxtla Gutiérrez ☎ 961/613-5860. **Red Maya** ⊠ Av. Juárez 133, Palenque ☎ 916/345-0934.

**Post Offices Palenque** ⊠ Calle Independencia at Calle Bravo ☎ 916/345-0143. **San Cristóbal** ⊠ Calle Ignacio Allende 3, at Calle Diego de Mazariegos ☎ 967/678-0765. **Tuxtla Gutiérrez** ⊠ Primera Av. Norte Poniente, at 2a Calle Oriente Norte ☎ 954/582-0232. **Villahermosa** ⊠ Calle 7 Norte, at Calle Oaxaca ☎ 954/582-0232.

### MONEY MATTERS

In Villahermosa and Tuxtla Gutiérrez, most hotels, restaurants, and shops accept credit cards and traveler's checks, while many of those in Palenque, Comitán, and San Cristóbal often prefer cash. In Chiapa de Corzo and other small towns, cash is the name of the game.

Bank hours are generally weekdays 9–4:30, although some open for a short time on Saturday. Many in the downtown areas have ATMs where you can withdraw pesos. They aren't as easy to find in small towns, so it's best not to get down to your last pesos before replenishing your funds.

🖪 Banks **Banamex** ✉ Calle Real de Guadalupe and Av. Insurgentes, San Cristóbal ☎ 967/678-1043 ✉ Av. Juárez 62, Palenque ☎ 916/345-0490 ✉ Av. 1a Sur Poniente 141, Tuxtla Gutiérrez ☎ 961/611-4231. **Bancomer** ✉ Av. Juárez 40, Palenque ☎ 916/ 345-0198. **Banco Inverlat** ✉ Calle Juárez 415, Villahermosa ☎ 993/312-5803.

🖪 Currency Exchange **Agencia de Cambio Lacantún** ✉ Calle Real de Guadalupe 12-A, San Cristóbal ☎ 967/678-2587.

## TAXIS

San Cristóbal has private and colectivo taxi service to outlying villages from the *sitio* (taxi stand) at Boulevard Jaime Sabines and Avenida Ignacio Allende, a short distance from the main bus station. Taxis to downtown destinations cost about $1.50. Within downtown Tuxtla Gutiérrez, taxis cost a minimum of $2. You can take a taxi 20 minutes away to Chiapa de Corzo for about $7; to San Cristóbal, about 1½ hours away, the cost is about $30. Jaguar, one of several radio taxi companies in Tuxtla, will pick you up at your hotel.

In Palenque, the taxis of Sitio Maya Pakal line up along the main square. A ride to the ruins is $5; it's a bit more if you call for a cab from your hotel. Within the city of Villahermosa itself, trips are fixed at $1.50 in yellow colectivo taxis; the minimum fare is $2 in the white *especial* (special or private) taxis.

🖪 **Jaguar** ☎ 961/612-4137. **San Cristóbal Taxis Jovel** ☎ 967/678-6899. **Sitio Maya Pakal** ☎ 916/345-0379. **Villahermosa Radio Taxi** ☎ 993/315-8333.

## TOURS

SAN CRISTÓBAL  Pepe Santiago, a Lacandon native associated with Museo Na Bolom since childhood, leads tours daily to San Juan Chamula, Zinacantán, and San Nicolás Buenavista. (Pepe's name is a veritable ticket of acceptance in the more remote regions of Chiapas.) The group leaves Museo Na Bolom promptly at 10 AM and returns around 3:30; it's well worth the $11 price. If Pepe isn't available, his knowledgeable sister, Teresa Santiago Hernández, also leads tours. Gabriela Gudiño is a reliable private tour guide who specializes in history and indigenous peoples.

Viajes Pakal, Viajes Chinkultik, Posetur, and Viajes Navarra offer local tours around San Cristóbal and beyond, as well as tours of archaeological sites such as Bonampak, Yaxchilán, Palenque, and Chinkultik, and other points of interest like Agua Azul, Lagos de Montebello, and Sumidero Canyon. Chinkultik is especially recommended for its professionalism and its three-day trip to Laguna Miramar: all food, transportation, tents, and even porters (it's a three-hour walk in to the lake) are included in the price of $200 per person.

🖪 **Gabriela Gudiño** ✉ Calz. México 81, San Cristóbal ☎📠 967/678-4223. **Museo Na Bolom** ✉ Av. Vicente Guerrero 33, at Calle Comitán, San Cristóbal ☎ 967/678-1418. **Posetur** ✉ Posada Diego de Mazariegos, 5 de Febrero 1, San Cristóbal ☎ 967/678-0833. **Viajes Chinkultik** ✉ Calle Real de Guadalupe 34, San Cristóbal ☎ 967/678-0957 ✉ Av. Insurgentes 14, San Cristóbal ☎ 967/678-7266. **Viajes Navarra** ✉ Calle Real de Guadalupe 15-D, San Cristóbal ☎ 967/678-1143. **Viajes Pakal** ✉ Calle Cuauhtémoc 6A, San Cristóbal ☎ 967/678-2818.

TUXTLA
GUTIÉRREZ

Viajes Miramar offers city tours of Tuxtla Gutiérrez for about $10. It also has a five-hour tour that allows you to see the Sumidero Canyon from the ridge above and from a boat on the river below. The cost is $70 for up to four people.

🚩 **Viajes Miramar** ✉ Hotel Camino Real, Blvd. Belisario Domínguez 1195, Tuxtla Gutiérrez ☎ 961/617-7777 Ext. 7230.

PALENQUE

Most tour operators run half-day guided tours of Palenque ruins for about $6, which includes a guide and transportation. Full-day tours costing $14 per person begin in Palenque, then move on to the waterfalls at Misol-Há and Agua Azul. Longer trips to San Cristóbal, Toniná, and Cañón de Sumidero can also be arranged.

Transportes Chambalum has six-hour trips to Agua Azul, Agua Clar, and Misol-Há; the cost is about $11 per person. Kichan Bajlum and Kukulcán, both reliable tour operators, have one- and two-day trips to Bonampak and Yaxchilán. A one-day trip costs $50, including transportation by minivan and boat, a guide, and a modest lunch.

🚩 **Kichan Bajlum** ✉ Av. Juárez at Calle Abasolo, Palenque ☎ 916/345-2452. **Kukulcán** ✉ Av. Juárez s/n at Calle 20 de Noviembre, Palenque ☎ 916/345-1506. **Transportes Chambalum** ✉ Calle Allende at Av. Juárez s/n, Palenque ☎ 916/345-2849.

VILLAHERMOSA

Viajes Tabasco, in the Zona Hotelera, is a big travel agency and a good place to buy air tickets. Viajes Villahermosa, in the Zona Luz, is another full-service agency. Creatur Transportadora Turística specializes in multiday excursions that take in Misol-Ha, Cañón de Sumidero, and other sights off the beaten path. Rutas del Usumacinta has tours to Chiapas and Guatemala, including Bonampak and Yaxchilán. Turismo Nieves has tours to Comalcalco and other destinations in Tabasco.

🚩 **Creatur Transportadora Turística** ✉ Av. Paseo Tabasco 715, Villahermosa ☎ 993/315-3999 ⊕ www.creaturviajes.com. **Rutas del Usumacinta** ✉ Calle Remo 215, Residencial Cuidad Deportiva, Villahermosa ☎ 993/351-0405. **Turismo Nieves** ✉ Sarlat 202, Villahermosa ☎ 993/314-1888 ⊕ www.turismonieves.com.mx. **Viajes Tabasco** ✉ Galería Tabasco, Local 173, Zona Hotelera, Villahermosa ☎ 993/316-4154 or 993/316-4090 ⊕ www.viajestabasco.com. **Viajes Villahermosa** ✉ Méndez 724, Villahermosa ☎ 993/312-5456 ⊕ www.turismonieves.com.mx.

## VISITOR INFORMATION

In Villahermosa, the Instituto de Turismo de Tabasco is a bit of a hike—it's on Avenida de los Ríos on the way to Galería Tabasco. The office is open weekdays 9–4. Far more convenient is an auxiliary office at the Parque Museo La Venta, open daily 9–4.

San Cristóbal's municipal tourist office is open Monday–Saturday 8–8 and has some information about the city. For information about attractions throughout the city and state, try the state tourist office, which is open weekdays 8–8, Saturday 9–8, and Sunday 9–2. The folks at the Tuxtla Gutiérrez state tourist office (open weekdays 8–4) are extremely helpful and dole out maps and brochures. The Tuxtla Gutiérrez Municipal

Tourist Office, more conveniently located under the Plaza Central, is open weekdays 8–8 and Saturdays 8–1.

In Palenque, the tourism information office on the main drag is open Monday–Saturday 9–9 and Sunday 9–1. The people in the Comitán tourist office are very knowledgeable. The office is open weekdays 9–7, Saturday 9–2 and 4–7, and Sunday 9–1.

**🔢 Comitán Tourist Office** ✉ Calle Central Benito Juárez Oriente 6, Comitán ☎ 963/632-4047. **Palenque Tourist Information Office** ✉ Av. Juárez at Calle Abasolo, Palenque ☎ 916/345-0356. **San Cristóbal Municipal Tourist Office** ✉ Palacio Municipal, ground floor, on the Zócalo, San Cristóbal ☎ 967/678-0665. **San Cristóbal State Tourist Office** ✉ Av. Miguel Hidalgo 1-B, ½ block from zócalo, San Cristóbal ☎ 967/678-6570 or 967/678-1467. **Tuxtla Gutiérrez Municipal Tourist Office** ✉ Calle Central Norte and 2a Av. Norte Oriente, Tuxtla Gutiérrez ☎ 961/612-5511. **Tuxtla Gutiérrez State Tourist Office** ✉ Edificio Plaza de las Instituciones, ground floor, Blvd. Belisario Domínguez 950, Tuxtla Gutiérrez ☎ 961/602-5127 or 961/602-5269. **Villahermosa State Tourism Office** ✉ Av. de los Ríos at Calle 13, Villahermosa ☎ 993/316-2889 ⊕ www.etabasco.gob.mx/turismo.

# VERACRUZ &
# THE NORTHEAST

**FANCIEST FOOTWORK**
Sunday danzón at Parque Zamora ⇨*p.574*

**GREATEST CATCH**
Mariscas Villa Rica Mocambo,
Veracruz's best seafood spot ⇨*p.571*

**MOST ELEGANT ANCIENT CITY**
The ruins of El Tajín ⇨*p.589*

**COOLEST COOLING-OFF**
A dip in the pools of Texolo,
a majestic waterfall ⇨*p.587*

**BEST OF THE BORDER TOWNS**
Matamoros ⇨*p.599*

**BEST NEWS FOR NIGHT OWLS**
Monterrey's burgeoning nightlife ⇨*p.606*

**BEST COLONIAL QUICK FIX**
The charming town of Saltillo ⇨*p.608*

Updated by
Mark Sullivan

**UNDISCOVERED BY MOST TRAVELERS,** Veracruz is Mexico in miniature. No matter what you're looking for, you're likely to find it in this state straddling the Gulf of Mexico. Interested in ancient civilizations? You can explore El Tajín—its Pyramid of the Niches is one of the country's most enchanting pre-Columbian buildings. Love colonial-era architecture? You can wander around the venerable village of La Antigua, where the Spanish settled in the 16th century. In search of a little culture? Check out the fascinating aerial display of the *voladores* (fliers) of Papantla.

But Veracruz has much more to offer. You can also stroll the plazas of quaint mountain villages, laze on sandy beaches, and dine on some of the best seafood in Mexico. There are festivals year-round, so you're almost guaranteed to enter a town where people are literally dancing in the streets.

In the Northeast, the three border cities of Nuevo Laredo, Reynosa, and Matamoros are industrial areas that lure American day-trippers with moderate-price crafts and authentic Mexican dishes. Improved roads have led more people to take advantage of the opportunity to visit Monterrey, Mexico's third-largest city. With its cultural attractions, five-star hotels and restaurants, modern outlook, and, of course, shops, it's a highlight of the region. In the nearby Sierra Madre, you can explore stunning canyons, cliffs, and caves.

## Exploring Veracruz & the Northeast

The lively port city of Veracruz might not be the city that never sleeps, but it *is* a city that gets very little rest. People listen to music in the squares until late at night, then are found sipping coffee in the sidewalk cafés early the next morning. The exuberance of *jarochos,* as the city's residents are known, does not falter even in the broiling midday heat.

The lush coastal state of Veracruz also harbors pockets of colonial history, as well as fine native ruins and some of Mexico's most outstanding adventure tourism routes. Xalapa, the state capital, is a pretty university town and cultural hub.

Northeastern Mexico consists of a string of border towns across from the United States, the city of Monterrey, and some surrounding natural wonders. The border towns' charm is limited—you might prefer to linger in Monterrey, making side trips into the nearby mountains or to the colonial town of Saltillo.

### About the Restaurants

There's no need to break out your most dashing suit here, as very little in the region is truly formal. A jacket and tie would look out of place almost anywhere, apart from the business hub of Monterrey. Reservations may be needed for the most popular restaurants.

### About the Hotels

The only place you'll find modern high-rises is Boca del Río, a beach resort just south of Veracruz. Veracruz itself offers a number of charming hotels right on the main square, and they are a good value. Downtown

Xalapa has few lodgings that could be called luxurious, but what they lack in amenities they more than make up for with atmosphere. Even more out-of-the-way places usually have an atmospheric hotel or two.

Catering mostly to business travelers and short-term tourists, accommodations in the border towns increasingly tend to fall into two camps: the chains of more standardized small hotels or the wilting individual establishments whose heyday has passed. Monterrey affords more choices in all price ranges.

| WHAT IT COSTS | | | | |
|---|---|---|---|---|
| | $$$$ | $$$ | $$ | $ | ¢ |
| RESTAURANTS | over $25 | $15–$25 | $10–$15 | $5–$10 | under $5 |
| HOTELS | over $250 | $150–$250 | $75–$150 | $50–$75 | under $50 |

Restaurant prices are for a main course excluding tax and tip. Hotel prices are for two people in a standard double room in high season.

### Timing

In Veracruz, the weather is balmy between November and April. The notorious *nortes*—gusty winds that blow in off the Gulf of Mexico— usually appear between October and February, and especially in December. Pack a light jacket for evenings, and a hat. In summer, both the temperature and humidity soar, but the frequent rains afford a respite.

A great time to visit Veracruz is the week before Ash Wednesday for its *Carnaval,* Mexico's major pre-Lenten bash. It's glitzy, merry, and wild, but retains a small-town sanity that keeps it safer than the better-known celebrations in Rio or New Orleans. The biggest problem at such times is finding a room, so make sure to reserve several months in advance. The same is true during Christmas and Easter.

The hottest months in the northeast are June through August. The cooling rains arrive in July and last through November. There are never any crowds at the border towns or in Monterrey except during major U.S. holidays, when Americans head south for a day or weekend.

# THE STATE OF VERACRUZ

A long, slim crescent of land bordering the Gulf of Mexico, Veracruz ranks among the favorite vacation destinations for Mexican families. Although the beaches aren't quite the white-sand wonders of the Yucatán, they're cheerful and vibrant, full of young couples slurping coconut milk and kids laughing at the tiny sand crabs that pop up whenever there's a moment's calm. Moreover, the state holds a romantic allure for those drawn to the sensuous joie de vivre of Xalapa, the blue waters of Lago Catemaco, or the villages at the base of the Cofre de Perote.

As you head inland—the state is only 140 km (87 mi) across at its widest point—you meet the Sierra Madre Oriental, with its stunning 18,400-foot Pico de Orizaba (also called Citlaltépetl), Mexico's highest peak. In the foothills of this range, you'll find the state capital Xalapa, where

**12**

The state of Veracruz and northeast Mexico are separate regions, which is how most travelers approach them when planning a trip. Veracruz is closer to the large cities of Mexico City, Puebla, and Oaxaca, and is a popular getaway for Mexican families. Northeast Mexico is closer to Texas and is more often frequented by Texans hopping across the border than by people using Mexico City as a gateway. Our approach to the northeast is therefore from Texas. The drive up the coast from Veracruz is possible, but the distances—502 km (311 mi) between Veracruz and Tampico and 1,005 km (623 mi) from Veracruz to Monterrey—may be daunting from behind the wheel.

*Numbers in the text correspond to numbers in the margin and on the Veracruz and East Central Mexico, Veracruz, Northeastern Mexico, and Monterrey maps.*

**If you have 3 days**

Head straight for the port of ▦ **Veracruz** ①– ❼ ▶, with the most Caribbean flavor of all the cities lining the Gulf of Mexico. On Day 3, visit the archaeological site of **Cempoala** ⑬, a major Totonac city.

If you're driving down from Texas, you could explore the area around ▦ **Monterrey** ㉓– ㉝ ▶, the cultural and industrial giant of the northeast. Spend the first day walking around the Macroplaza area, with its outstanding modern-art and history museums. Devote the next two days to some of the region's natural attractions, including the Cañon de la Huasteca, the Grutas de García, and the waterfall in the Parque Nacional Cumbres de Monterrey.

**If you have 7 days**

Start in ▦ **Veracruz** ①– ❼ ▶, spending two days exploring the city. On Day 3, drive down the coast to the lakefront village of ▦ **Catemaco** ⑪. If you're visiting at the time of a festival, make sure to stop along the way in the lively town of **Tlacotalpan** ❽. Make your way inland on Day 4 to ▦ **Xalapa** ⑭. Get your feet wet with a trip to the magnificent falls near the village of **Xico** ⑯ or relax with a cup of coffee in the town of **Coatepec** ⑮ on Day 5. On your sixth day you could travel farther north to see the ruins of **El Tajín** ⑱, staying in ▦ **Papantla de Olarte** ⑰. Head back toward Veracruz on your last day, stopping along the way at the riverfront village of **La Antigua** ⑫.

For the northeast, add excursions to **Saltillo** ㉞ and to ▦ **Tampico** ㉟.

university students carrying laptops share the sidewalks with local farmers selling a few ears of corn. Xalapa is a favorite place for foreigners to study Spanish, and the nearby town of Jalcomulco is a base for river-rafting explorations on the Río Pescados.

The state does have some good beaches, but the real reasons to come are the atmosphere, the people, the cuisine, and the history. All these are at their best in the musical, multicultural city of Veracruz. Travelers arrived by ship, then boarded a train to Mexico City, often looking back wistfully. Today the fun-loving town lures domestic vacationers with its excellent seafood and lively nightlife. The city remains a working port and navy base with so many marimba bands in the *zócalo* (main square) on weekend evenings that they have to compete to be heard.

Olmec civilization thrived in Veracruz long before the rise of the Maya. The state's best-preserved ruins, at El Tajín near Papantla, are thought to have been the work of another as yet unidentified civilization, which had its heyday between AD 550 and 1100. By the time Hernán Cortés landed in Veracruz in 1519, the Aztecs held sway, but within a very short time the Indian population was devastated by war and disease.

The state of Veracruz played a pivotal role in Cortés's march to Tenochtitlán. A government-sponsored circuit called the Ruta de los Dioses (Route of the Gods) traces the Spanish conquistador's footsteps, from his Veracruz landing to his arrival in Mexico City, where he defeated the Aztec rulers. It's a mélange of soft adventure excursions, combined with visits to colonial cities and archaeological zones.

## Veracruz

*502 km (311 mi) south of Tampico, 345 km (214 mi) west of Mexico City.*

In 1519 Cortés landed in La Antigua, a slip of a place on the Río Huitzilapan, but it was Veracruz that became the major gateway for the Spanish settlement of Mexico. Its name, also given to many other communities throughout Latin America, means "true cross." Pirates frequently attacked the steamy coastal city, and their battles to intercept Spanish goods add a swashbuckling edge to the history of the oldest port in the Americas. The Spanish brought thousands of African slaves to Veracruz; later, Cuban immigrants flooded the town.

Today Veracruz is still one of the most important ports in Mexico, and you'll immediately sense its extroverted character. Huge cargo ships, ocean liners, and fishing vessels crowd its harbor, and the waterfront *Paseo del Malecón* is always buzzing with strolling couples and sailors with a few hours to kill. In the evening at the zócalo, the sound of marimbas floats through the air.

**a good tour**

Start at the **zócalo** ❶ ➤, the palm-shaded square that's the heart and soul of Veracruz. No matter what time of the day or night you visit, there's sure to be live music. Walk past the tower of the Palacio Municipal and northeast for a block on Calle Lerdo. You'll reach another public park, this one called the Plaza de la República. At the western edge you'll see the Estación de Ferrocarriles, whose halls no longer echo with the sounds of people rushing to catch a train. Another lovely building from the early 20th century, the Edificio Gemelo de Telégrafos y Correos, is still the place to mail a letter. You'll notice its neoclassical entrance on the north side of the plaza.

Head southeast on Plaza de la República, following the crowds that head northeast along the **Paseo del Malecón** ❷. On your right you'll see the Faro Venustiano Carranza, which holds the navy's offices. You can't miss

**12**

## Local Specialties

The state of Veracruz is home to some of Mexico's most accessible and delicious regional dishes. Its signature sauce is the *mole de Xico,* a rich, sweet concoction similar to that which you'd find in Oaxaca, but with seasoned fruits and nuts. Many of the traditional specialties show the influence of the Spanish and African communities of nearby Cuba, including the state's signature dish, *huachinango a la veracruzana* (red snapper in the Veracruz style, which means it's simmered in tomatoes, onions, garlic, green olives, and capers). Leaving without sampling this would be both a shame and a bit of a feat, as every eatery has its own version. Another dish with a similar influence is *salpicón de jaiba,* a spicy crabmeat salad usually prepared with tomatoes, capers, and peppers. Other dishes reflect African ties in their use of beans, plantains, yucca, taro, white sweet potatoes, and especially peanuts, which appear in the classic *puerco encacahuatado* (pork in peanut sauce) and the bracing *salsa macha,* made by grinding peanuts with garlic, chilies, and olive oil.

You'll find peanut ice cream all over the state, as well as other *nieves* made with mangos, papayas, and other local fruits. Another sweet-tooth tempter is *buñuelos veracruzanos,* golden doughnuts that are dipped in a sugar and cinnamon mix. Look out for the charge of *toritos* (little bulls), a heady alcoholic punch made with cane liquor, milk, and tropical fruit pulp or peanuts.

In Veracruz, as befits a hot, breezy port town, the emphasis is on simple, fresh food, mostly *pescado* (fish) and *mariscos* (shellfish). Some of the best places to eat in the region are the family-run seafood shacks you often find lining the beaches. Just ask for the *platillo del día* (daily dish). It's always served with a flourish. Xalapa has the best restaurants in the state, with menus featuring locally caught fish.

The Northeast isn't renowned for the subtlety of its cuisine, but its cattle country ensures an abundance of good beef cuts, the most typical being *arrachera.* A prime regional treat is kid (*cabrito*), which, when well prepared, has a delicate lamblike flavor. If you'd like to try it, Monterrey is the place to give it a go; you cannot be in this city for long without seeing goat sizzling on the grill.

## Volcanoes & Nature Preserves

Veracruz state claims a few national parks—not to mention Mexico's highest peak, the Pico de Orizaba. At over 18,000 feet, this extinct volcano is the third-highest mountain in North America. Climbing season is between November and March.

Another extinct volcano, the Cofre de Perote, lures climbers to its national park area near the state capital Xalapa. In addition to its *alpinismo* (mountaineering) attractions, the park has plenty of facilities, including several campgrounds.

Veracruz's nature preserves give the state enormous potential for ecotourism— from rafting to hiking to bird-watching—and options are growing every year. State and municipal tourism offices have a list of recommended operators. For most activities, particularly mountaineering, you should be sure to go with a guide. Seasonal weather changes can lead to hazardous conditions.

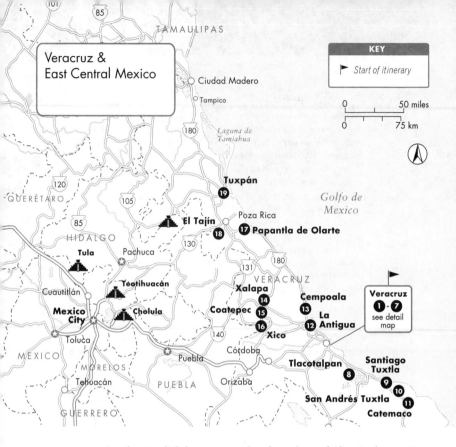

it—there's a lighthouse protruding from the roof. If you're here at 8 AM, you can watch the changing of the guard.

Head southeast on Avenida 16 de Septiembre. In two blocks you'll come to the modern Altar de la Patria, which honors the country's war dead. Turn right onto Calle Arista, and after a block you'll spot the miniature rampart in front of the **Museo Histórico Naval** ③. Continue down Calle Arista, maybe taking a few minutes to sit in the pretty little Parque de Marina, and take a left onto Avenida Zaragoza. After a block you'll reach the **Museo de la Ciudad** ④. Take a left on Calle Canal, and after two blocks you'll be standing in front of the fortress known as the **Baluarte de Santiago** ⑤. Where you go next depends of whether you're more interested in what's above or below sea level. If you liked *The Little Mermaid*, you'll probably head to the **Acuario de Veracruz** ⑥. The aquarium is more than a mile from downtown, so you'll want to hop in a taxi. Wheels are also required to see the **Fuerte de San Juan de Ulúa** ⑦. The old fort is across the harbor from downtown.

TIMING   This tour will take the best part of a day. Veracruz is extremely hot and humid, so you might consider breaking it into parts, seeing the historic downtown one day and the more distant sights the next.

## What to See

🐢 ❻ **Acuario de Veracruz.** Veracruz is home to one of the biggest and best aquar-
**Fodor's**Choice  iums in Latin America. The main exhibits include a tank with 2,000 species
⭐  of marine life native to the Gulf of Mexico, including manta rays, barracudas, and several kinds of sea turtles. Other tanks display tiger
sharks and a quintet of gentle manatees who seem to enjoy interacting
with the crowds. Especially chilling is the 18-foot-long outline of a
great white shark caught off the coast of Tuxpán. ⊠ *Plaza Acuario, Blvd.
Manuel Avila Camacho s/n* ☎ *229/932–7984 or 229/932–8006* ⊕ *www.
acuariodeveracruz.com* ⊠ *$5* ☉ *Mon.–Thurs. 10–7, Fri.–Sun. 10–7:30.*

❺ **Baluarte de Santiago.** This small fortress is all that's left of the old city
walls. Like the Fuerte de San Juan de Ulúa, the colonial-era bulwark
was built as a defense against pirates. The 1635 structure is impressively
solid from the outside, with cannons pointed toward long-gone marauders.
Inside is a tiny museum that has an exquisite exhibition of pre-Hispanic
jewelry—Spanish plunder, no doubt—discovered by a fisherman in the
1970s. ⊠ *Calle Francisco Canal between Av. Gómez Farías and Av. 16
de Septiembre* ☎ *229/931–1059* ⊠ *$2.50* ☉ *Tues.–Sun. 10–4:30.*

⭐ ❼ **Fuerte de San Juan de Ulúa.** This unique coral-stone fort has been witness to some of the most momentous events in Mexican history. During the viceregal era, Veracruz was the only east coast port permitted
to operate in New Spain and, therefore, was attacked by pirates. The
great island fort, the last territory in Mexico to be held by the Spanish
Royalists, is a monument to that buccaneering era. A miniature city in
itself, it is a maze of moats, ramparts, drawbridges, prison cells, and torture chambers. Fortification began in 1535 under the direction of Antonio de Mendoza, the first viceroy of New Spain. A few centuries later,
it was used as a prison, housing such prominent figures as Benito Juárez,
who was held here by conservative dictator Santa Anna before being
exiled to Louisiana in 1853. After independence, it was used in unsuccessful attempts to fight off first the invading French, then the Americans, then the French again, and, in 1914, the Americans yet again.

The fort is under extensive renovation through at least 2005, but remains open to the public. There are no explanatory signs, but you can
explore the former dungeons and store rooms, climb up on the ramparts,
and wander across beautiful grassy patios. It's connected to the city center by a causeway; a taxi here should cost about $5. You could also catch
a bus from the zócalo marked SAN JUAN DE ULÚA. Guides wander around
in the site until about 3 PM—an English-speaking guide will charge
around $2 per person. ⊠ *Via causeway from downtown Veracruz*
☎ *229/938–5151* ⊠ *$2.50* ☉ *Tues.–Sun. 10–4:30.*

❹ **Museo de la Ciudad.** A good place to get oriented, this museum in a lovely
colonial-era building tells the city's history through artifacts, displays,
and scale models. Also exhibited are copies of pre-Columbian statues
and contemporary art. There are no explanatory materials in English,
however. ⊠ *Av. Zaragoza 397, at Calle Esteban Morales* ☎ *229/989–
8873* ⊠ *$2.50* ☉ *Wed.–Mon. 10–6.*

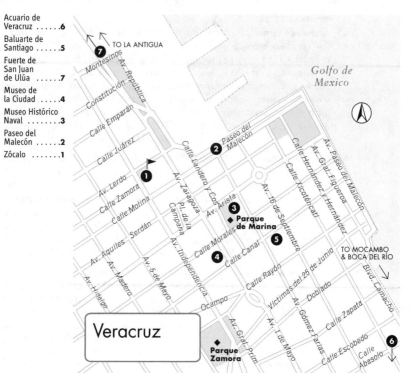

**Museo Histórico Naval.** In an impressive set of buildings that once housed navy officers, the Naval History Museum tells how the country's history was made on the high seas. Veracruz has been dubbed the city that was *cuatro veces heróica*, or "four times heroic," for its part in defending the country against two attacks by the French and two by the Americans. The museum tells of those wars, as well as the life of revolutionary war hero Venustiano Carranza. Explanatory materials are only in Spanish. ⊠ *Av. Arista, between Av. 16 de Septiembre and Av. Landero y Coss* ☎ *No phone* 🎫 *Free* 🕐 *Tues.–Sun., 9–5.*

**2** **Paseo del Malecón.** Everyone seems to come here at night, from cuddling young couples in search of a secluded bench to parents with children seeking the best place for ice cream. Drop by during the day and you'll find boats that will take you out into the harbor for about $5 per person. ⊠ *Northern extension of Av. Molina.*

---

**need a break?**

There are always lines out the door at **Nevería Güero Güero Güera Güera** (⊠ Calle Zamora 15, at Av. Landero y Coss ☎ 229/932–0582), where you can get a huge cup of *cacahuate* (peanut), *fresa* (strawberry), or more than a dozen other flavors of ice cream for only a buck. Locals say the name came about when the owner used to shout *güero* and *güera*, meaning blond-haired man or woman, to catch the attention of passing foreigners.

**❶ Zócalo.** This park, also known as the Plaza de Armas, is known for its distinctive *portales* (colonnades). Two towers have bells that compete for your attention. The hands-down winner is the deafening Catedral de Nuestra Senora de la Asunción, which sits on the southwest corner of the square. It dates from 1721. The runner-up is the 1635 Palacio Municipal, which has a fainter but no less insistent tune. The tower originally did double duty as a lighthouse for the port. ⊠ *Av. Independencia between Calle Lerdo and Calle Zamora.*

## Beaches

Veracruz City's beaches are not particularly inviting, being on the brownish side of gold, with polluted water. Decent beaches with paler, finer sand begin to the south in **Mocambo,** about 7 km (4½ mi) from downtown, and get better even farther down. The beach in front of the Fiesta Americana hotel is particularly well maintained. (Although it may appear to be claimed by the hotel, it's public.) About 4 km (2½ mi) south of Playa Mocambo is **Boca del Río,** a small fishing village at the mouth of the Río Jamapa, which is quickly getting sucked into Veracruz's orbit. A taxi from the city center costs about $4. **Mandinga** is a farther 8 km (5 mi) south of Boca del Río and is less frequented by tourists.

## Where to Eat

In addition to the restaurants around the zócalo, you'll want to head to Boca del Río. Many restaurants here are modest but serve some of the finest seafood in this part of the country. If you'd like to eat with the locals, try the Mercado Hidalgo for breakfast or lunch; it's a 10-block walk south from the zócalo.

**$$$–$$$$** ✕ **Che Tango.** With the huge grill positioned in the front window, even passersby know the specialty of this casual yet elegant Argentine restaurant. Select your cut of rib eye, tenderloin, top sirloin, or strip steak from the chilled display case brought to your table and tell your bow-tied waiter how you'd like it cooked. While it sizzles, nibble one of the flaky empanadas topped with *chimichuri* (sauce made with olive oil and parsley). If the sun and surf have gone to your head, try the refreshing house cocktail—*Rosita* (made with anise). ⊠ *Av. 16 de Septiembre 1938, at Calle Enríquez, Col. Flores Magón* ☎ *229/932–1745 or 229/932–1756* ▭ *AE, MC, V.*

**$–$$$** ✕ **Mariscos Villa Rica Mocambo.** Tucked away in Boca del Río—on a small
**Fodor'sChoice** street that runs parallel to Playa Mocambo—this open-air eatery is one
★ of the best seafood restaurants in the country. Specialties include mussels, grouper, crab claws, and octopus prepared as you wish. For those who relish spicy food, the *ostiones enchilpayados* (oysters in cream and chipotle chili) are sublime. Popular bands play Thursday–Sunday 3–7, so you may need a reservation on these days. ⊠ *Calz. Mocambo 527, Boca del Río* ☎ *229/922–2113 or 229/922–3743* ▭ *AE, DC, MC, V.*

**$–$$$** ✕ **Pardiño's.** Although it looks like a modest eatery, Pardiño's is a local landmark. The place has become so popular that branches have spread throughout the republic. Plain tables in a nondescript storefront belie the elegant preparation of such dishes as crabs *salpicón* (finely chopped with cilantro, onion, and lime), grilled sea bass, and a truly memorable huachinango a la veracruzana. ☒ *Calle Zamora 40, Boca del Río* ☏ *229/986–0135* ▭ *AE, DC, MC, V.*

★ **$–$$** ✕ **Gran Café de la Parroquia.** A leisurely stint in the sun here, watching ships unloading their cargo, is what Veracruz is all about. Try for a sidewalk table under the arches, if you can withstand the competing marimbas and the appeals of women selling crafts. Get here before 11 AM to try the classic *picadas y gordas* (puffy, deep-fried tortillas with beans, onion, mole, and cheese). Service may not always be very speedy or coordinated, though when you want more coffee you don't need to say a word, just tap your spoon against the side of your cup. Best of all is the tradicional lechero, served flamboyantly with the milk poured from silver jugs at a great height. ☒ *Paseo de Malecón, between Hotel Hawaii and Hotel Emporio* ☏ *229/932–2626* ▭ *No credit cards.*

★ **$–$$** ✕ **Gran Café del Portal.** Opened by a Spanish immigrant in 1835, this now-famous sidewalk café in a former monastery eventually grew to cover an entire city block. The menu has a wide selection of dishes, including a delicious huachinango a la veracruzana. The weekday lunch set menu is a great deal at about $8. The Portal has an ongoing rivalry with the Gran Café de la Parroquia as to which place serves the real *tradicional lechero* (coffee with hot milk)—white-jacketed waiters bring you one kettle of strong coffee and another of hot milk, and let you do the mixing. ☒ *Av. Independencia 1185, across from cathedral* ☏ *229/932–9339* ▭ *No credit cards.*

**$** ✕ **Palapa Iguana.** Playa de Hornos, a popular stretch of sand south of the Acuario de Veracruz, is lined with a seemingly endless series of thatch-roofed seafood shacks. They all serve basically the same thing: fish cooked any way you like it. This place, with a giant version of its namesake positioned on the roof, is one of the best. Grab a table in the open-air dining room or one under an umbrella by the surf. ☒ *Playa de Hornos* ☏ *No phone* ▭ *No credit cards* ☼ *No dinner Mon.–Thurs.*

## Where to Stay

The lodgings in the Centro Histórico can be counted on to have a bit of character, especially those surrounding the zócalo. They have relatively few amenities, however—if you're looking for luxury, head to the high-rises in Boca del Río.

CENTRO HISTÓRICO

★ **$$** ⌂ **Hotel Emporio.** It's not hard to imagine that the architect had cruise ships in mind when designing the elegantly curved balconies of this waterfront hotel. Many of the immaculate, light-filled rooms have superb harbor views, as do the gardens on the roof. Dine in the popular restaurant, which is decorated in neoclassical French style, or under the shade of an umbrella at any of the hotel's three pools (one is equipped with a waterfall, slides, and a miniature "ship" for kids). ☒ *Paseo del Malecón 244, 91700* ☏ *229/932–2222 or 800/295–2000* ☒ *229/932–5752* ⊕ *www.hotelesemporio.com.mx* ⇥ *182 rooms, 21 suites* ⌂ *Restaurant, coffee shop, cable TV, 3 pools, gym, sauna, bar, shops, business services, meeting rooms, free parking* ▭ *AE, MC, V.*

**$$** ⌂ **Villa del Mar.** Across from one of the nicer sections of the downtown beach, this hotel lets you enjoy the sun of Veracruz without the scene of Boca del Río. As you might guess when you see the small playground, it caters mostly to families. The spacious rooms surround a garden with a tennis court, swimming pool, and a hot tub. A few bungalows accommodating up to five people are available, but they aren't air-conditioned and are a bit gloomy. ✉ *Blvd. Manuel Avila Camacho at Calle Bartolomé de las Casas, 91910* ☎ *229/989–6500 or 800/322–1212* 🖷 *229/932–7135* ⊕ *www.hotel-villadelmar.com* ➔ *91 rooms, 14 bungalows* ♿ *Restaurant, cable TV, tennis court, pool, hot tub, bar, playground, laundry service, free parking; no a/c in some rooms* ☰ *MC, V* ⧫ *BP.*

**$**  🏨 **Calinda Veracruz.** From the pool on the rooftop patio you have a fantastic view of the mariachis strolling around the zócalo. There's a similar vista from the balconies of many of the immaculate guest rooms. Since this high-rise is a bit removed from the square, the strolling musicians won't keep you awake all night. Sanborn's is one of the most popular downtown restaurants. ✉ *Av. Independencia s/n, at the corner of Av. Miguel Lerdo, 91700* ☎ *229/931–2233 or 800/290–0000* 🖷 *229/931–5134* ⊕ *www.hotelescalinda.com.mx* ➔ *102 rooms, 14 suites* ♿ *Restaurant, cafeteria, room service, in-room data ports, in-room safes, minibars, cable TV, pool, shop, laundry service, business services, meeting rooms, free parking* ☰ *AE, MC, V.*

★ **$**  🏨 **Hotel Hawaii.** You can't miss this hotel, because its profile resembles an arrow pointing straight up. An unusual design, but it means that most rooms have views of the Paseo del Malecón. Hotel Hawaii is one of the best deals in town, offering exceptional comfort and service at a reasonable rate. Rooms have sophisticated designs and are impeccably maintained. The eager-to-please staff makes sure you have a map of the city and a bag of locally grown coffee to take home. ✉ *Paseo del Malecón 458, 91700* ☎ *229/938–0088* 🖷 *229/932–5524* ➔ *30 rooms* ♿ *Coffee shop, room service, cable TV, pool, laundry service, free parking* ☰ *AE, MC, V.*

**$**  🏨 **Hotel Imperial.** Built a century ago, this hotel facing the zócalo has lost little of its charm. The wrought-iron elevator, dating from 1904, was one of the first in Latin America. It runs right up the center of the indoor courtyard toward the eye-popping stained-glass dome. Though a bit dated, the rooms have a certain elegance and many have balconies on the square. ✉ *Av. Miguel Lerdo 153, near Av. Independencia, 91700* ☎ *229/932–1207* 🖷 *229/931–4518* ➔ *54 room* ♿ *Restaurant, room service, cable TV, bar* ☰ *AE, MC, V.*

**BOCA DEL RÍO**  🏨 **Crowne Plaza Torremar.** The lobby in this high-rise on Playa Mo-
**$$$** cambo is adorned with glass sculptures that glitter in the abundant sunlight. Most of the rooms have windows facing the ocean, but the suites also have small balconies. The cascading poolside fountain and the organized activities in the play area make this a good bet for families traveling with young children. ✉ *Blvd. Adolfo Ruíz Cortines 4300, Playa Mocambo, 94260* ☎ *229/989–2100 or 800/712–9900* 🖷 *229/989–2121* ⊕ *www.crowneplaza.com* ➔ *212 rooms, 18 suites* ♿ *Restaurant, room service, in-room safes, cable TV, 2 pools, gym, bar, baby-sitting, children's programs (ages 3–11), laundry service, concierge floor, business services, convention center, meeting room, car rental, free parking* ☰ *AE, DC, MC, V.*

# CloseUp

# A LITTLE NIGHT MUSIC

THE AIR IS HOT AND HUMID, *even though the sun has already set on the pretty port city of Veracruz. Elderly couples seated on the* wrought-iron benches around Parque Zamora barely move, hoping that inactivity will bring some relief. A conductor lifts a languid baton that rouses a group of musicians to life. The sound they make isn't quite in tune, but it is as rich as honey and as radiant as the summer evening. The couples listen for a few moments, then stroll to the bandstand. Men in crisply ironed shirts and dapper straw hats hold out their hands to women in straight skirts and blouses embroidered with birds and flowers. When they begin to dance, there's barely any movement above the waist, just subtle hip movements and the occasional fancy footwork. It's a dance designed for a tropical night.

This is the danzón, a languorous dance brought to Mexico in 1879 by Cubans fleeing their country's Ten Years' War. These refugees ended up living outside the city walls (only aristocrats were allowed to live inside), but the sons of the Mexican elite, looking for thrills, sneaked into the poor neighborhoods at night, and eventually introduced the danzón to high society. Sensuous compared to the stiff dances that were the norm then, the danzón was at first considered scandalous. But soon it won over its detractors and became the most popular dance in Veracruz. It still fills dance halls throughout the city. You can see people of all generations dancing in Parque Zamora every Sunday evening. While their parents and grandparents glide around the bandstand, children practice their steps off to the side.

The city's unique heritage can also be found in its music, swayed by African and Caribbean rhythms. The son jarocho (which literally means "Veracruz sound") is

one of seven different regional variations of Mexican sones. These songs, livelier than danzones, can be in 4/4 or 6/4 time. Doubtless the best known one is "La Bamba," which originated here and dates back to the 17th century. Traditionally, the cantadores (singers) were both singers and wordsmiths, creating endless new coplas (verses) for well-known songs. Between numbers they continue to entertain the audiences, telling jokes and gently ribbing the other musicians.

Son jarocho centers on strings and percussion, employing some combination of violin, arpa (harp), jarana (a 6- or 10-string guitar), requinto (a small rhythm guitar), bocona (a four-string bass), and pandero (tambourine). Musicians will flock into restaurants to energize diners with their vigorous strumming. A young woman often accompanies them, performing flamenco-like steps in a frilly frock; the tarima (wooden dance platform) where dancers pound out the rhythms becomes another essential instrument.

To get a sampling of all the types of music in Veracruz, head to the zócalo. Inevitably there will be strolling mariachis and teams playing marimbas (wooden xylophones that sound like a children's toy). But none of it compares to the bands playing late into the night in Parque Zamora. By the time the musicians are packing up their instruments, the temperature has barely budged. Women wave fans they had hidden in their bosoms, willing to suffer the heat for the spirit of the danzón.

— Mark Sullivan

**$$–$$$** ⌖ **Fiesta Americana.** This splashy high-rise on Playa Costa de Oro has the best business facilities in the state of Veracruz, making it popular for conventions and large groups. The hotel's miles of marble corridors all seem to lead to the giant serpentine pool and lush gardens facing the ocean. Guests have access to a 9-hole golf course 20 minutes away. ⌖ *Blvd. Manuel Avila Camacho s/n, at Fracc. Costa de Oro, 94299* ☎ *229/989–8989 or 800/343–7821* 🖷 *229/989–8904* ⊕ *www.fiestaamericana. com.mx* ⤴ *211 rooms, 22 suites* ⚬ *3 restaurants, room service, in-room data ports, in-room safes, cable TV, tennis court, indoor-outdoor pool, 3 hot tubs, massage, dive shop, 2 bars, shops, baby-sitting, children's programs (ages 4 and up), business services, meeting rooms, free parking, no-smoking rooms* ⊟ *AE, DC, MC, V.*

**$$–$$$** ⌖ **Hotel Lois.** For those with a sense of humor, this Boca del Río landmark is an over-the-top mishmash of '50s kitsch and art deco excess, all done up in garish shades of purple. The coffee shop alone has lavender booths, several random romanesque columns, and lots of gleaming chrome. Guest rooms are more conventional, with subdued pastels; spend a bit more for one with a hot tub. The bar is the place to go for salsa dancing. ⌖ *Blvd. Adolfo Ruíz Cortines 10, 94249* ☎ *229/937–7598 or 229/937–8290* 🖷 *229/937–8089* ⊕ *www.hotellois.com* ⤴ *112 rooms, 17 suites* ⚬ *Restaurants, coffee shop, room service, in-room safes, minibars, cable TV, pool, gym, hair salon, sauna, billiards, squash, 2 bars, baby-sitting, children's programs (ages 3–9), meeting rooms, car rental, free parking* ⊟ *AE, MC, V.*

## Nightlife & the Arts

It's no surprise that people gravitate toward the **zócalo,** which is full of marimba players, mariachi bands, and guitar players. Grabbing a table at one of the sidewalk cafés along the park's northern edge gives you a front-row seat, but it also means that every musician will offer to play you a song for a few dollars. Friday and Sunday nights at 8 PM, local groups perform traditional dances on a makeshift stage.

**Fodor'sChoice** From 6 to 9 on Wednesday and Sunday nights, men in dapper hats and
★ women with fans dance the danzón at **Parque Zamora.** It's a magical evening, as the couples swirl around a Victorian bandstand. If you'd like to learn a few steps, the **Instituto Veracruzano de la Cultura** (Veracruz Cultural Institute; ⌖ Calle Canal at Av. Zaragoza ☎ 229/931–6967) offers danzón classes for a minimal fee. The teachers don't mind visitors watching a class.

For authentic Cuban music, head downtown to the unpretentious **El Rincón de la Trova** (⌖ Plazuela de la Lagunilla 59 ☎ No phone), where people of all ages gather Thursday through Saturday to dance to famous bands until the wee hours. El Rincón de la Trova's six-day Cuban music festival in November draws performers and fans from all over Mexico and the Caribbean.

**La Casona de la Condesa** (⌖ Plazuela de la Lagunilla Lagunilla 61 ☎ No phone), next door to El Rincón de la Trova, caters to a more upscale crowd. Dozens of little round tables surround a stage where musicians play everything from rock to jazz. It's open Thursday through Sunday.

Dance clubs are plentiful along the waterfront. Most are packed Friday and Saturday nights with a young, largely local crowd. **Antra** (✉ Blvd. Adolfo Ruíz Cortines 15 ☎ 229/922–5142) is popular with the young and groovy. For salsa, try **Carioca** (✉ Blvd. Adolfo Ruíz Cortines 10 ☎ 229/937–8290) in the lobby of Hotel Lois. The popular club has live music Thursday through Sunday. **Kachimba** (✉ Blvd. Manuel Avila Camacho, at Médico Militar, Boca del Río ☎ 229/927–1980) is a great spot for live Cuban music. It's open Thursday to Sunday. Another dance club is **Ocean** (✉ Blvd. Adolfo Ruíz Cortines 8 ☎ 229/935–2390), which has indoor pools, though—unless you really tie one on—they're strictly for decoration. It's open Friday and Saturday.

## Sports & the Outdoors

BOATING You can easily charter a *lancha* (boat) to take you to nearby islands like Isla Verde and Isla de los Sacrificios. The best place to find one for a spur-of-the-moment outing is along the Paseo del Malecón. Expect to pay about $5 per person. Longer trips to nearby Isla Verde (Green Island) and Isla de Enmedio (Middle Island) leave daily from the shack marked PASEO EN LANCHITA near Plaza Acuario. If you want to call ahead, contact the friendly folks at **Amphibian** (✉ Blvd. Manuel Avila Camacho 1707, at Calle 1 de Mayo ☎ 229/931–0997).

DIVING The waters near Veracruz are home to nearly two dozen reefs waiting to be explored. **Mundo Submarino** (✉ Blvd. Manuel Avila Camacho 3549 ☎ 229/980–6374) has diving lessons for everyone ranging from newcomers to experts. The company also conducts dives to nearby reefs. **Tridente** (✉ Blvd. Manuel Avila Camacho 165 ☎ 229/931–7924) offers diving trips for around $50 per person; the price includes gear and instruction. If you want to snorkel, the cost is only $23.

WHITE-WATER RAFTING On trips led by **Rio Aventura** (✉ Room 20-E, Las Americas Shopping Mall, Boca del Río ☎ 229/922–8640 ⊕ www.rioaventura.com.mx), you can combine rafting with other sports.

## Shopping

Stands lining the **Paseo del Malecón** sell ocean-related items: seashells and the beauty creams and powders derived from them, black-coral jewelry, and ships-in-a-bottle. You'll also find Coatepec coffee, T-shirts, crucifixes, and tacky stuffed frogs, iguanas, and armadillos. The **Plaza de las Artesanías** market on the Paseo de Malecón purveys high-quality goods, including leather and jewelry, with high prices to match. It's open daily 11–8. For a slice of Mexican life, head to the wildly vibrant **Mercado Hidalgo** (✉ Bounded by Calles Cortés, Soto, Madero, and Hidalgo), where you'll find artful displays of strawberries and chilies beside platters of cow eyeballs and chicken feet.

If you're headed to the Acuario de Veracruz, you enter through a shopping mall called the **Plaza Acuario** (✉ Blvd. Manuel Avila Camacho s/n ☎ 229/932–9950). It's a good place to pick up gifts for the folks back home. One of the more unusual shops in Plaza Acuario is **Fiora** (✉ Blvd. Manuel Avila Camacho s/n ☎ 229/932–9950), a little store that sells beautiful jewelry designed from miniature flowers grown in Veracruz.

Veracruzanos have adopted the fashion of neighboring Yucatán, and its famous embroidered *guayabera* shirts are as popular here as mariscos. **Guayaberas Fina Cab** (⊠ Av. Zaragoza 233, between Calles Arista and Serdán ☎ 229/931–8427) has the best quality goods. This family-run shop has a great selection of hand-stitched shirts and dresses, with embroidery ranging from basic interlocking cables to elaborate floral designs. **El Mayab** (⊠ Calle Zamora 78, at Av. Zaragoza ☎ No phone) has a selection of machine-produced guayaberas, which go for less than the hand-embroidered variety.

With its sizable Cuban population, Veracruz does a brisk business in cigars. Around Plaza de Armas, there are plenty of street-side stands that specialize in both Mexican and Caribbean tobacco. For the largest variety of cigars, try the small kiosk on Avenida Independencia, in front of Gran Café del Portal; it sells Cuban Cohibas for less than a buck. Although Cuban smokes are the big draw, keep in mind that Veracruz upholds its own proud tradition in the tobacco trade. **Cubahi** (⊠ Av. Sarmiento 59 ☎ No phone) has the finest local products.

## Tlacotalpan

**⑧** *90 km (56 mi) south of Veracruz.*

The name Tlacotalpan is of Nahuatl origin and means "in the middle of the earth," referring to the settlement's location on what was then an island. Once a prosperous port city, Tlacotalpan is still very pretty, with century-old houses lining its narrow streets and colorful churches surrounding its tree-shaded square. There are few sights here besides the **Museo Salvador Ferrando** (⊠ Calle Alegre 6 ☎ 288/884–2385), a tiny museum that displays furniture and other items from the 19th century.

The real attractions are the town's festivals, the most thrilling being that of Tlacotalpan's patron saint, the *Virgen de la Candelaria.* Before the conquest, native inhabitants worshipped the water goddess Chalchiutlicua, better known as *Encamisada de Verde* (gowned in green). With the arrival of the Spanish and the subsequent push to convert to Catholicism, she was substituted by the Virgin of the Candelaria. This patron saint of fishermen is honored each year on February 2. Tlacotalpan's fiesta begins January 31 with a display of hundreds of horses, followed by regattas and the famous running of the bulls through the streets. An image of the Virgin floats down the river with a candle, followed by a flotilla of little boats.

Other lively times are *Semana Santa,* the week before Easter; *Carnaval,* in May; and the *Fiesta de San Miguelito,* September 27 to 29.

## Santiago Tuxtla

**⑨** *140 km (87 mi) south of Veracruz.*

Lush and mysterious, Los Tuxtlas is a hilly region where a small volcanic mountain range, the Sierra de Los Tuxtlas, meets the sea. Crystal-clear lakes, tumbling waterfalls, and relaxing mineral springs make this region a popular stopover for travelers heading west to Mexico City or east to the Yucatán. The region's three principal towns—Santiago Tuxtla, San Andrés Tuxtla, and Catemaco—are carved into the mountainside more than 600 feet above sea level, lending them a coolness that's the envy of the perspiring masses on the coastal plain.

Santiago Tuxtla is most charming of the towns in Los Tuxtlas. The Olmec civilization, the oldest in Mexico, flourished here between 900 and 600 BC. Evidence of the Olmec culture is all around you. A huge stone head dominates the attractive central square, known as **Parque Juárez.** Called the Cabeza Cobata, or the Cobata Head, for the field west of town where it was discovered, it is by far the largest of these unusual carvings ever discovered. Facing Parque Juárez is the **Museo Regional Tuxteco,** where you'll find another colossal stone head. The museum is worth a visit to learn about the region's indigenous peoples and its contemporary cultures. ⊠ *Circuito Lic. Angel Carvajal s/n* ☎ *294/947–0196* ⊠ *$2* ⊗ *Mon.–Sat. 9–6, Sun. 9–3.*

About 21 km (13 mi) east of Santiago Tuxtla are the ruins of **Tres Zapotes,** once an important ceremonial center for the Olmec people. Discovered near here was a stone carving bearing a date that revealed that the Olmec culture is at least as old as that of the Mayas. Today there is little to see besides several groups of unreconstructed temples. The site museum, however, holds the first of the massive Olmec heads to be discovered. To reach Tres Zapotes, head southwest on Carretera 179 and turn north after about 8 km (5 mi). Taxis from Santiago Tuxtla travel this route regularly. Admission to the museum is $2.

## San Andrés Tuxtla

⑩ *143 km (95 mi) south of Veracruz.*

With tobacco fields extending in every direction, Los Tuxtlas is known for its cigars. The town of San Andrés Tuxtla is famous for its hand-rolled variety. If you'd like to see them being made, head to the **Puros Santa Clara** (⊠ Blvd. 5 de Febrero 10 ☎ 294/947–9900), just outside town on the highway to Catemaco and Santa Clara. This is where the famous Te-Amo cigars are made.

There's little else to keep you in this regional hub, but there's plenty of interest in the surrounding countryside. About 12 km (7 mi) east of San Andrés Tuxtla is one of the most splendid waterfalls in the region, the 50-meter-tall **Salto de Eyipantla.** To get here, head east on Carretera 180 to the town of Sihuapan. If you head 3 km (1½ mi) northeast of town, you'll reach the **Laguna Encantada** or Enchanted Lagoon. This unusual lake was thought to be magical because its level drops during the rainy season and rises again when the weather is dry.

## Catemaco

⑪ *166 km (103 mi) south of Veracruz.*

Overlooking an immense blue lake, the town of Catemaco is one of the most popular vacation destinations in Los Tuxtlas. Not everyone comes for the breathtaking views, however. The cool, gray fog that slips over the mountains and across the lake provides the perfect setting for the region's most famous attraction: the *brujos* (witches) who claim to be able to cure whatever ails you. Conventional medicine failed to penetrate this jungle area until the 1940s, so the folk traditions have survived, making use of herbal remedies (typically using basil, rosemary, and other ingredients of doubtful origin) to cure diseases and get rid of evil spirits. Catemaco is the place to go for a consultation with a brujo for a ritualistic cleansing. This costs anywhere between $2 and $20, depending on your ailment, which may range from misfortune in love to financial hardships to health problems. The cost also increases according to the brujo's assessment of how much you are able to pay. A convention of brujos takes place here every March.

Tours of **Lago Catemaco,** a lake that was formed from the crater of a volcano, can be arranged through most local hotels. Several small islands are sprinkled across the surface of the deep-blue lake. The most popular is Isla Tanaxpilla, also known as the Island of the Monkeys because it harbors a colorful colony of fish-eating baboons. The creatures were brought here from Thailand by biologists hoping to study them.

Beyond Catemaco, a paved road continues over the hills and down to a lovely stretch of undeveloped coastline. About 20 km (12 mi) east from Catemaco is the village of **Sontecomapan,** where you can take a launch across the lagoon to a desolate beach. A bumpy dirt road follows the coast 19 km (12 mi) north of Sontecomapan to the sleepy fishing village of **Montepío,** which has a wide beach and a couple of inexpensive restaurants.

## Where to Stay

Catemaco is by far the prettiest place to stay in Los Tuxtlas. Upscale lodgings are strung on the lake shore, while more affordable digs are grouped around the small square.

**$$** ▢ **La Finca.** This contemporary hotel is on the shores of Lago Catemaco. The builders knew why people were coming here: they designed the low-slung buildings so that all the rooms face the water, and indeed, each room has a balcony with a lovely view. The hotel is popular with Mexican families; book ahead for summer vacation and other busy times. ✉ *Carretera 180, Km 147, 95870* ☎ *294/943–0322* 📠 *294/943–0888* ⊕ *www.lafinca.com.mx* ↘ *53 rooms, 3 suites* ♺ *Restaurant, cafeteria, cable TV, pool, beach, boating, bar, dance club, business services, meeting rooms, helipad* ▭ *AE, MC, V.*

**$$** ▢ **Hotel Nanciyaga.** These rustic, four-person cabins surrounded by jungle are among the most secluded and attractive accommodations on the shores of Lake Catemaco. While there is no hot water or electricity, you can enjoy the warm, curative *temazcal* steam baths on Saturday. Kayak expeditions, jungle tours, and consultations with brujos can be arranged.  ✉ *Carretera Catemaco, Km 7, 70410* 📠 *294/943–0199* ⊕ *www.nanciyaga.com* ↘ *10 cabins* ♺ *Restaurant; no a/c, no room phones, no room TVs* ▭ *MC, V.*

## La Antigua

⑫ *25 km (16 mi) northwest of Veracruz.*

This sleepy little village, given its name by the Spaniards after they abandoned it, was the conquistadors' capital for 75 years. They left it behind in 1599 after the founding of Veracruz, whose port was a much more convenient place from which to ship their plundered gold to Spain.

A small community still lives here, however, and they are justifiably proud of the treasures their village holds. Although locals call it **Casa de Cortés** (✉ Av. Independencia at Calle Ruiz Cortés), the 16th-century customshouse actually had nothing do to with the conquistador. It once had 22 rooms surrounding a huge courtyard, but now little is left. It's worth seeing if only for its crumbling masonry, taken over by clinging vines and massive tree roots.

★ La Antigua also has the first church of New Spain, the diminutive **Ermita del Rosario** (✉ Av. Independencia at Calle Elodia Rosales). The little white stucco structure has been restored (and enlarged) many times over the years. The oddly placed arch in the middle of the church was actually once the facade. On the outside you can see that two windows near the altar were originally doors.

Heading south on Avenida Independencia you'll soon find a tree with tentacle-like branches blocking the road. This is the **Ceiba de la Noche Feliz** (Tree of the Happy Night). It's said the tree was here when Cortés chose this spot for the village.

La Antigua is roughly half an hour north of Veracruz, off Highway 180. You can take an Xalapa-bound AU bus from the second-class bus station for about $1.

### Where to Stay & Eat

**$–$$** ✕ **Las Delicias Marinas.** All roads in La Antigua seem to lead to this riverfront restaurant, a favorite for years. The huge arches facing the water are hung with nets full of cardboard fish. Try the *cazuela de mariscos,* a seafood stew filled with shrimp, crab, octopus, and mussels in a spicy green sauce. Afternoons at 1:30 and 6:30 there's live marimba music, and on weekends the musicians are joined by colorful dancers. ✉ *On the Río Huitzilapan* ☎ *296/971–6038* ▤ *No credit cards.*

¢ ▦ **La Ceiba.** It's only 45 minutes from Veracruz, so there's no real reason to stay in La Antigua. But if the village casts a spell on you, the best place to lay your head is this simple little hotel near the water. Rooms are as basic as they come, but clean and cozy. ✉ *Av. Independencia s/n* ☎ *No phone* ⟿ *54 rooms* ⟡ *Restaurant, boating; no a/c, no room phones, no room TVs* ▤ *No credit cards.*

### Sports & the Outdoors

Daytrippers from Veracruz and even farther away come to La Antigua to take a leisurely boat ride up the **Río Huitzilapan** (Hummingbird River). There are a dozen or so covered boats at the end of Avenida Independencia under an extension bridge called the Puente Colgate. Captains charge $5 per person for a cruise up the river.

## Cempoala

🏛 ⓭ *42 km (26 mi) northwest of Veracruz.*

Cempoala (often spelled Zempoala) was the capital of the Totonac people, whose influence once spread throughout all of Veracruz. The name means "place of 20 waters," after the sophisticated irrigation system employed by the Totonacs. When Cortés arrived here under the cover of night, the plaster covering of the massive **Templo Mayor** (Main Temple) and other buildings led him to believe the city was constructed of silver. Cortés placed a cross atop this temple—the first gesture of this sort in New Spain—and had mass said by a Spanish priest.

The city's fate was sealed in 1519, when Cortés formed an alliance with the Totonac leader. Chicomacatl—dubbed "Fat Chief" by his own people because of his enormous girth—was an avowed enemy of the more powerful Aztecs, so he decided to fight them alongside the Spanish. The alliance greatly enlarged Cortés's paltry army of 200 men and encouraged the Spaniard to march on Mexico City and defeat the Aztecs. The strategic move backfired, however. The Totonacs could protect themselves again the Spanish swords, but were powerless against the smallpox the invaders brought with them. The population was devastated.

Cempoala was rediscovered by Francisco del Paso y Troncoso in 1891. Ten of the 60 to 90 structures at Cempoala have been excavated and can be visited. All are built of river stones, shells, sand, and "glue" made from the whites of turtle and bird eggs.

Upon entering the ruins, you'll see **Circulo de los Gladiadores,** a small circle of waist-high walls to the right of center. This was the site of contests between captured prisoners of war and Totonac warriors: each prisoner was required to fight two armed warriors. One such prisoner, the son of a king from Tlaxcala, won the unfair match and became a national hero. His statue stands in a place of honor in Tlaxcala. Another small structure to the left of the circle marks the spot where an eternal flame was kept lit during the sacred 52-year cycle of the Totonacs.

At the **Templo de la Luna** (Temple of the Moon), to the far left of Templo Mayor, outstanding warriors were honored with the title "Eagle Knight" or "Tiger Knight" and awarded an obsidian nose ring to wear as a mark of their status. Just to the left of the Moon Temple is the **Templo del Sol** (Temple of the Sun), where the hearts and blood of sacrificial victims were placed.

Back toward the dirt road and across from it is the **Templo de la Diosa de la Muerte** (Temple of the Goddess of Death), where a statue of the pre-Hispanic deity was found along with 1,700 small idols.

There's a small on-site museum housed in a palapa. Voladores from Papantla usually give a performance here on weekends. Well-trained guides offer their services, but tours are mainly in Spanish. ☎ *No phone* ⊕ *www.inah.gob.mx* 🎟 *$2* ☼ *Tues.–Sun. 10–5.*

## Xalapa

🄬 *90 km (56 mi) northwest of Veracruz.*

A ceremonial center for the Aztecs when Cortés swept through the region, Xalapa is still a city of great importance. Take one look at the impressive Palacio de Gobierno and you know this is a political powerhouse. The presence of the Universidad Veracruzana ensures that Xalapa is a cultural capital as well. Its state theater, for instance, attracts performers from around the world. In addition, Xalapa is also an agricultural center. This great mix of interests means that in any sidewalk café you might find farm workers with their machetes, government workers shouting into cell phones, and students tapping on laptap computers.

As with most places in Mexico, Xalapa has had many names over the years. The current name is a slight variation on Xallapan, the name chosen when four neighboring villages decided to pool their otherwise meager resources. You'll sometimes see the name of the city spelled "Jalapa," which is the Hispanic version of the original Nahuatl word. Residents of Xalapa call themselves *xalapeños*. Xalapa is perched on the side of a mountain between the coastal lowlands and the high central plateau. More than 4,000 feet above sea level, the city enjoys cool weather the entire year. But the city also has unpredictable weather changes—sun, rain, and fog are all likely to show themselves over the course of a day. It's a good idea to bring an umbrella and a jacket with you, even if there's not a cloud in the sky.

Much of the city seems to have been built without a plan, and that's the source of its charm. The hills here pose intriguing engineering problems, and major avenues tend to make sharp turns, following the landscape rather than adhering to the strict grid system so beloved by the Spanish. In some places, the twisting cobblestone streets are bordered by 6-foot-high sidewalks to compensate for sudden sharp inclines. Locals refer to the city as a *plato roto* (broken dish) because of its layout.

The gorgeous central square, called **Parque Juárez,** is right in the middle of town, with the neoclassical Palacio de Gobierno on one side and the neocolonial Palacio Municipal on another. Between the governmental palaces is the **Catedral de Xalapa,** a charming church dating from 1772. If it looks a little crooked from the outside, just step inside. A chapel juts out at an odd angle, making the whole place seem askew.

FodorśChoice  The town's prime cultural attraction is the **Museo de Antropología de**
★  **Xalapa.** With 3,000 of 29,000 pieces on display, it is second only to Mexico City's archaeological museum. Its treasure trove of artifacts covers the three main pre-Hispanic cultures of Veracruz: Huasteca, Totonac, and most important, Olmec. Its three sections are filled with magnificent Olmec stone heads, carved stelae and offering bowls, terra-cotta jaguars and cross-eyed gods, and cremation urns in the form of bats and monkeys. Especially touching are the life-size sculptures of women who died in childbirth (the ancients elevated them to the status of goddesses). Tours by English-speaking students are available daily 11–4, but it's best

to call in advance and make an appointment. ⊠ *Av. Xalapa s/n* ☎ *228/815–0920 or 228/815–0708* 💳 *$4* ⊙ *Daily 9–5.*

## Where to Stay & Eat

★ **$–$$** ✕ **La Casa de Mamá.** The antique furnishings and lazily turning ceiling fans almost succeed in giving this popular restaurant the feel of an old-fashioned hacienda, but the insistent street noise reminds you that you're in a busy capital city. Never mind: you'll be focusing on the generous portions of charcoal-broiled steaks and the succulent shrimp and fish dishes, served with *frijoles charros* (black beans cooked in a spicy sauce). The place is known for its desserts, which include flan with caramel and bananas flambéed in brandy. ⊠ *Av. Avila Camacho 113* ☎ *228/817–3144* ▤ *AE, MC, V* ⊙ *No dinner Sun.*

★ **$–$$** ✕ **La Estancia de los Tecajetes.** For fine regional dishes prepared with a dash of creativity, try this rustic restaurant overlooking the tropical Parque Los Tecajetes. Inside, it's cozy and relaxing, always buzzing with diners feasting on *cecina* (paper-thin beef fillet) with refried beans and slices of avocado and *crepas poblanas* (crepes filled with chicken or spinach and topped with poblano chilies). For something more daring, try the *camarones al whisky* (shrimp with bourbon). The restaurant is tucked into a small strip mall, so it's tricky to find. ⊠ *Plaza Tecajetes, Av. Avila Camacho 90* ☎ *228/818–0732* ▤ *MC, V* ⊙ *No dinner Sun.*

**$** ✕ **La Casona del Beaterio.** In contrast to the cafeterias that line Avenida Zaragoza, La Casona del Beaterio dishes up fine local fare in comfort. The restaurant's two spacious rooms, surrounding a courtyard garden with a fountain, have stained-glass windows and plenty of hanging plants. Breakfast specials are a steal, but the house specialty—*cazuela de mariscos* (stew of shrimp, octopus, and clams cooked with chipotle chilies)—draws the crowds. This is java country, so the menu has a dozen different coffee and espresso concoctions. ⊠ *Av. Zaragoza 20* ☎ *228/818–2119* ▤ *AE, MC, V.*

**¢** ✕ **La Fonda.** The entrance to this second-floor restaurant is hidden on a small pedestrian walkway off busy Calle Enríquez, a block from Parque Juárez. Brightly colored streamers, baskets of paper flowers, and paintings of festivals enliven the little cluster of dining rooms. The food is hearty northern Veracruz fare. Delicious *nopales* (cactus strips) and chipotle chilies are essential elements of almost every dish. ⊠ *Callejón del Diamante 1, at Calle Enríquez* ☎ *228/818–7282* ▤ *No credit cards* ⊙ *Closed Sun. No dinner.*

**$$** 🏨 **Fiesta Inn Xalapa.** This brick-red hotel is a bit out of the way—a 10-minute drive from the center of town—but it has hard-to-find (for Xalapa) amenities like a pool. The modern guest rooms in the two-story, colonial-style structure get plenty of morning sunlight. Airport transfers from Veracruz are available for a fee. ⊠ *Carretera Xalapa–Veracruz, Km 2.5, 91000 Fracc. Las Animas* ☎ *228/812–7920, 800/504–5000 in the U.S.* 🖷 *228/812–7946* 🌐 *www.fiestainn.com* ➪ *119 rooms, 3 suites* ⚐ *Restaurant, coffee shop, room service, in-room data ports, in-room safes, cable TV, pool, gym, bar, laundry service, meeting room, free parking* ▤ *AE, DC, MC, V.*

★ **$** 🏨 **Mesón del Alférez.** A royal lieutenant of the Spanish Viceroy lived in this colonial house some 200 years ago. Now it's a gem of a small hotel, restored with earthenware tiles, rustic wood beams, and lime-pigment washes on the walls in such luminous hues as lilac, sky blue, and magenta. Rooms surround three small bougainvillea-covered courtyards and have lovely hand-carved wood headboards, Talavera lamps, and hand-loomed bedspreads. ⊠ *Sebastián Camacho 2, at Av. Zaragoza, 91000* ☎ *228/818–6351 or 228/818–0113* 🖷 *228/812–4703* ⊕ *www.geocities. com/mesondelalferez* ↝ *15 rooms, 6 suites* ⅄ *Restaurant, room service, laundry service, free parking* ▤ *AE, MC, V* ❏◯❏ *CP.*

¢ 🖳 **Hotel Posada El Virrey.** On the plus side, this colonial-style hotel is a short walk from Parque Juárez . . . unfortunately, that walk is mostly uphill, perhaps a reason why the rates are so reasonable. The rooms are quiet, especially those that face away from the street. Some are on the small side, so take a look at a few before you decide. ⊠ *Dr. Lucio 142, Col. Centro 4, north of Parque Juárez, 91000* ☎ *228/818–6100* ⊕ *www. posadadelvirrey.com.mx* ↝ *40 rooms* ⅄ *Restaurant, cable TV, bar, laundry service, Internet, free parking* ▤ *AE, MC, V.*

## Nightlife & the Arts

NIGHTLIFE   If you're in the mood for live music, **Barlovento** (⊠ Av. 20 de Noviembre Oriente 641 ☎ 228/817–8334) heats up with a salsa beat for dancing Wednesday through Saturday nights. **La Corte de los Milagros** (⊠ Av. 20 de Noviembre Oriente 522 ☎ 228/812–3511) is a relaxing haunt where you can listen to Cuban-style ballads. It's open Wednesday through Saturday. **Vertice** (⊠ Av. Murillo Vidal at Calle Zempoala ☎ No phone) is one of the few bars where you can actually hold a conversation. There's live music Tuesday to Thursday.

**La Quimera** (⊠ Blvd. Adolfo Ruíz Cortines 1 ☎ 228/812–3277) throbs with dance music Wednesday through Saturday nights.

THE ARTS   The **Agora** (⊠ Parque Juárez ☎ 228/818–5730) cultural center has art exhibitions and the occasional folk-music performance and shows classic and avant-garde films. Stop by during the day to see what's planned; it's closed Monday. The **Teatro del Estado** (⊠ Ignacio de la Llave s/n ☎ 228/817–3110) is the big, modern state theater of Veracruz. The Orquesta Sinfónica de Xalapa performs here, often giving free concerts during the off-season (early June–mid-August). Check *Diario Xalapa* (the city's Spanish-language newspaper) for dates and times.

## Sports & the Outdoors

CLIMBING   The 18,400-foot **Pico de Orizaba,** Mexico's highest mountain, will virtually become your traveling companion in Veracruz state—you'll feel as though you see it at every turn. The Aztecs called the volcano Citlaltépetl, or Star Mountain, because under the full moon the snowy peak looks like a star. Woodlands spread along its flanks, with a glacier shining above. Tour operators in Xalapa organize climbs to the summit in the dry season, from November to March. Orizaba is 53 km (33 mi) south of Xalapa.

Another option for climbing is the beautiful **Parque Nacional Cofre de Perote**, where the centerpiece is the 14,022-foot-tall extinct volcano. A road leads almost to the summit, so you can either plan a day trip or stay for several days. The park is about 50 km (31 mi) west of Xalapa.

Based in the small village of Coscomatepec, **La Cabaña de Manolo** (☎ 273/737–0215) is a well-regarded tour operator. Ask for Manuel Gutiérrez. In Xalapa, **Veraventuras** (✉ Santos Degollado 81-8, Xalapa ☎ 228/818–9779) runs hiking trips in nearby national parks. Ask for Adolfo Contreras.

WHITE-WATER RAFTING

With access to six rivers for white-water rafting, Veracruz is now an established mecca for the sport in Mexico. The rivers drain the steep slopes rising up to the flanks of Pico de Orizaba and are the usual tropical-storm drains: wide valley floors with shoal-like rapids at every twist and turn. The rafting season runs from August to November.

The **Río Antigua** has five runs, all classed at level IV or under. Not far from the Río Antigua, the **Río Actopan** is a beautiful Class III stream. For pure white-water fun, the **Río Pescados** is the best run in the area. In the rainy season, it has some rapids on the high side of Class IV, but mostly the rapids are Class III. Tight turns against the towering cliffs make for some great splatting.

Base camps with tents, rafting equipment, and dining facilities are near the river at Jalcomulco, 42 km (26 mi) southeast of Xalapa. On trips led by **Amigos del Río** (✉ Calle Chipancingo 205, Xalapa ☎ 228/815–8817 🖷 229/922–8641 ⊕ www.amigosdelrio.com.mx), you can choose trips based on skill level, from newcomer to expert. **Expediciones Mexico Verde** (✉ Av. Murillo Vidal 133, Xalapa ☎ 228/812–0146 or 228/812–0134 ⊕ www.raftingmexicoverde.com) organizes various rafting excursions, from day trips to multiday programs, to Río Pescados, Río Actopan, and other rivers. Most guides speak English.

## Shopping

Mexico's finest export coffee is grown in this region, specifically in the highlands around the picturesque colonial towns of Coatepec and Xico, less than 10 km (6 mi) from Xalapa. Shops selling the prized *café de altura* (coffee of the highlands) abound in the main squares of both places. **Cafécali** (✉ Callejón del Diamante 2 ☎ 228/818–1339) offers a wide selection of excellent coffee at good prices. **Café Colón** (✉ Calle Primo Verdad 15, between Avs. Zaragoza and Enríquez ☎ 228/817–6097) sells 20 varieties of coffee for about $2.50 a pound.

**Callejón del Diamante,** also known as Calle Antonio M. Rivera, is a charming pedestrian street with vendors hawking a variety of wares: inexpensive jewelry, hand-woven baskets, and fleece-lined slippers among them.

The **Mercado Jauregui** (✉ Av. Revolución and Calle Altamirano), open daily, is a wild indoor bazaar with everything from jewelry, blankets, and fresh vegetables to some rather dubious-looking natural "healing" potions and supposedly aphrodisiacal body pastes.

## Coatepec

⓯ *8 km (5 mi) south of Xalapa on Carretera 7.*

The air is cool and refreshing in Coatepec. Residents call their town the "capital mundo del café" (the coffee capital of the world), and this isn't much of an exaggeration. The climate is perfect for growing the sought-after *altura pluma* (mountain grown) coffee, and you'll see bushes with bright red berries on every available scrap of land. The heady scent of roasting beans wafts across the main square. Locals are so immersed in coffee culture that many swear they can distinguish a cup made with beans from Coatepac from one made with beans grown in nearby Xico.

Coatepec, from the Nahuatl phrase Coatl-Tepetl ("snake hill"), grew during the coffee boom years of the early 20th century. The mansions along its elegant streets are pinned with ornate balconies; take a peek inside and you'll see gorgeous courtyards overflowing with greenery.

The wealth of Coatepec town is apparent in its gilt-covered churches. Across from the main square, the 18th-century **Parroquia San Jerónimo** (⊠ Calle 5 de Mayo at Calle Jiménez de Capillo) has low arches trimmed with gold leaf. Don't miss the steeple, which is topped by a tiny onion dome. The **Santuario de Nuestra Señora de Guadalupe** (⊠ Calle Aldama at Calle Hidalgo) hardly has a surface that isn't covered with some precious metal. Make sure to take a look at the dome, which is cleverly painted to look much taller than it actually is.

Getting to Coatepec is easy. Take any of the shuttle buses marked XICO that leave from a traffic circle on Calle Allende, a few blocks west of Parque Juárez in Xalapa. The 10-minute ride costs less than $1.

### Where to Stay & Eat

¢–$   ✕ **La Finca de Andrande.** This pleasant little café is the place where locals come when they have a craving for caffeine. Enjoy a steaming cup of coffee in the sunny courtyard or in one of the understated dining rooms looking out over the main square. Breakfasts are delicious—make sure to share a basket of the freshly baked *panes dulces* (sweet breads). The dinner menu includes such specialties as *pulpo encebollado* (octopus sautéed with onions) and *trucha ahumada* (smoked trout). ⊠ *Calle Lerdo 5* ☎ *228/816–4887* ▭ *MC, V.*

$$    ▣ **Posada Coatepec.** Once the home of a coffee baron, this 19th-century
Fodor'sChoice  mansion—a 15-minute drive from Xalapa—now caters to a privileged
★    few. The lobby, decorated with a fine collection of period antiques, feels like the entrance to a private home. The guest rooms have original tile floors, beamed ceilings, and heaters for Coatepec's often chilly weather. Stained-glass windows bathe the restaurant in warm reds and yellows. True to its roots, the posada can arrange coffee plantation tours. ⊠ *Calle Hidalgo 9, 91500 Coatepec* ☎ *228/816–0544* 🖷 *228/816–0040* ⊕ *www. posadacoatepec.com.mx* ⇱ *7 rooms, 16 suites* ⌂ *Restaurant, room service, cable TV, pool, sauna, bar, laundry service, parking (fee); no a/c* ▭ *AE, MC, V.*

### Shopping

The friendly folks at the **Café de Avelino** (⊠ Calle Aldama, between Calle Cuatemoc and Calle Morelos ☎ 228/816–3401) will turn you into a coffee connoisseur by showing you how the experts rate the beans.

# Xico

★ **⑯** *19 km (12 mi) south of Xalapa, 11 km (7 mi) south of Coatepec.*

If you close your eyes and try to imagine the ideal Mexican small town, you'd probably come up with something very close to Xico. Aside from the occasional passing automobile, this village seems untouched by time: donkeys hauling burlap sacks of fresh beans clip-clop along the cobblestone streets followed by local coffee harvesters, machetes tied to their waists with red sashes. Adding to this back-in-time beauty is the fact that the town is often surrounded by mist.

The village is also known for its raucous summer festival that goes on for just over a week at the end of July, celebrating the town's patron saint, Mary Magdalene. At the end of Avenida Hidalgo, the pretty **Parroquia de Santa María Magdalena** (✉ Calle Benito Juárez at Calle Lerdo) was built on the highest spot in town. Behind the altar is a traditional depiction of the crucifixion with Mary Magdalene, showing a bit more shoulder than usual, laying prostrate beneath. A more demure statue of her is dressed in a different outfit for every day of the festival in her honor. The small museum behind the church has a display of her ensembles.

But Xico is perhaps even better known for its natural wonders, notably the **Cascada de Texolo,** a majestic waterfall set in a deep gorge of tropical greenery. The setting for the 1984 film *Romancing the Stone,* as well as the 2002 *El Crimen del Padre Amaro,* the lush area surrounding the falls is great for exploring; numerous paths lead through forests of banana trees to smaller cascades and crystal-blue pools, perfect for a refreshing swim. There's also a steep staircase that will take you from the observation deck to the base of the falls.

The falls are about 3 km (2 mi) from the center of town. To reach them, start from the red-and-white church where Calle Zaragoza and Calle Matamoros meet and follow the cobblestone street downhill, bearing right when you reach the small roadside shrine to the Virgin Mary. Continue through the coffee plantations, following the signs for LA CASCADA until you reach the main observation deck. Entry is free.

To get to Xico, take one of the shuttle buses marked XICO that leave from a traffic circle on Calle Allende, a few blocks west of Parque Juárez. The 20-minute ride costs less than $1.

## Where to Stay & Eat

Xico is famous for its native cuisine; the tasty *mole xiqueña* is similar to that of Oaxaca, but gets a kick from ground poblano chilies.

¢–$  ✕ **El Mesón Xiqueño.** A macaw named Paco greets you with a squawk when you enter this charming courtyard restaurant. Huge wagon wheels placed here and there remind you that horse-drawn carts once brought all the coffee grown here to market. The kitchen's emphasis is local cuisine, so start with *brujitas xiqueñas,* the "little witches" that are actually pockets of fried corn filled with beans and avocado. Main dishes include *cecina xiqueña,* which is seasoned beef pounded flat and grilled. ✉ *Av. Hidalgo 148* ☎ *228/813–0781* ▭ *MC, V.*

¢ ✕🖃 **Hotel Coyopolan.** Overlooking the Río Coyopolan, this two-story hotel couldn't have a better location. From the colonial-style building you can hear the river as it spills over into a few small waterfalls. Rooms are small, but cheerfully decorated with hand-painted borders and local handicrafts. The open-air restaurant, La Molienda ($), serves up fresh river fish. There's also a satisfying selection of beef and chicken dishes. ⊠ *Calle Venustiano Carranza Sur s/n, 91240* ☎ *228/813–1266* ⊕ *www. hotelcoyopolan.com* ↩ *14 rooms* ⌂ *Restaurant, fans; no a/c, no room phones* ▤ *No credit cards.*

## Shopping

You can find just about anything along Calle Hidalgo, but the one thing not to leave without is mole. **Derivados Acamalín** (⊠ Av. Hidalgo 150 ☎ 288/813–0713) is famous for its moles, as you can tell by the photos on the walls of celebrities who have dropped by for a taste. If you want to buy your mole the old-fashioned way, drop by **Mole Charito** (⊠ Av. Hidalgo 178 ☎ 288/813–0389). There are big tureens filled with different sauces. Try some and take home the one you like best.

# Papantla de Olarte

⑰ *250 km (155 mi) northwest of Veracruz.*

Papantla de Olarte, set on a rather steep hillside, is in the center of a vanilla-producing region. Products made from that particular bean, from candies to liqueurs, are sold everywhere. There's even a vanilla festival that draws people to the town every March. The rest of the year, Papantla de Olarte goes about its business. Totonac men in flowing white shirts and pants lead their donkeys through the crowded streets, and young couples smooch underneath palm trees that ring the zócalo.

★ Papantla is the home of the **voladores,** who twirl off an 82-foot pole in front of the town's ornate cathedral. This ritual was originally performed as a tribute to the god of sun and rain; nowadays you'll have opportunities to see it in various towns in this region. The voladores begin the dance on a platform at the top of the ceremonial pole, each facing one of the cardinal directions. They start their descent from the side of the platform facing east—where the sun rises and the world awakes—twisting left for 13 full rotations each. Between them, the flyers circle the pole 52 times, representing the sacred 52-year cycle of the Totonacs (the Maya calendar had the same 52-year cycle). One man, the prayer giver, sits atop the pole, playing a small flute while keeping rhythm on a drum as the flyers descend. Originally the ceremony was held on the vernal equinox, but now the voladores fly for the crowds every Saturday and Sunday at 12:45 PM.

If you have some time to kill, stop by the **Casa de la Cultura** to peruse a few galleries of regional painting, sculpture, and ceramics. If you're there at 4 PM, you're welcome to take a peek at a traditional dance class. There is information in English. ⊠ *Pino Suárez 216* ☎ *784/842–2427* 🎟 *Free* ⊙ *Weekdays 8–2 and 4–8.*

### Where to Stay & Eat

$ ✕ **Plaza Pardo.** From the balcony of this cheerful second-story restaurant you'll have a great view of the goings-on in the zócalo. Brightly colored cloths adorn the tables, where house specialties—including *cecina con enchiladas* (salted beef with spicy enchiladas), *bocoles* (chicken- or cheese-stuffed tortillas), and *rellenos al gusto* (green chilies stuffed with your choice of chicken, cheese, or beef)—are served. ⊠ *Enríquez 105, Col. Centro* ☏ *784/842–0059* ⊟ *No credit cards.*

$ ✕ **Sorrento.** With more than 200 items on the menu, this is the most popular restaurant in Papantla. It's always crowded with locals who come to enjoy the cheap regional seafood and to catch a few minutes of a *telenovela* (soap opera) on the corner television set. The *platillo mexicano,* a selection of regional appetizers, is big enough for two. ⊠ *Enríquez 107, Col. Centro* ☏ *784/842–0067* ⊟ *No credit cards.*

¢ ▦ **Hotel Provincia Express.** This hotel is in the heart of things, just steps from the main square. Many of the modern rooms have little balconies with views of the mountains. They tend to be a bit noisy, so if you're a light sleeper, ask for a room in the back. ⊠ *Enríquez 103, Col. Centro, 93400* ☏ *784/842–1645 or 784/842–4213* 🖷 *784/842–4214* ➽ *16 rooms, 4 suites* ♦ *Cable TV, bar, laundry service* ⊟ *MC, V.*

¢ ▦ **Hotel Tajín.** The trick at this pretty pink hotel is getting the right room; the baker's dozen of rooms with views of the town are the best. Otherwise, make sure you'll have air-conditioning rather than just a fan, and check the mattress for firmness before you settle in. All rooms are spic-and-span. Although the staff does not speak English, they go out of their way to figure out what you need and deliver it promptly. ⊠ *Nuñez and Domínguez 104, Col. Centro, 93400* ☏ *784/842–0121 or 784/842–1623* ➽ *59 rooms* ♦ *Cable TV, hair salon, laundry service, travel services, free parking; no a/c in some rooms* ⊟ *MC, V.*

### Shopping

A half-block downhill from the main square, is the teeming **Mercado Miguel Hidalgo** (⊠ Av. 20 de Noviembre), which sells Totonac costumes, carvings, baskets, and shoulder bags. It's a daily market, but is much busier on weekends. The real draw is vanilla, the chief product of this region, which is sold in every conceivable form.

## El Tajín

▲ ⑱  *13 km (8 mi) west of Papantla.*

**Fodor'sChoice**
★
The extensive ruins of El Tajín—from the Totonac word for "thunder"—express the highest degree of artistry of any ancient city in the coastal area. The city remained hidden until 1785, when a Spanish engineer happened upon it. Early theories attributed the complex—believed to be a religious center—to a settlement of Maya-related Huasteca, one of the most important cultures of Veracruz. Because of its immense size and unique architecture, scholars now believe it may have been built by a distinct El Tajín tribe with ties to the Maya. Although much of the site has been restored, many structures are still hidden under jungle.

El Tajín is thought to have reached its peak between AD 600 and 1200. During this time, hundreds of structures of native sandstone were built here, including temples, double-storied palaces, ball courts, and hundreds of houses. But El Tajín was already an important religious and administrative center during the first three centuries AD. Its influence is in part attributed to the fact that it had large reserves of cacao beans, used as currency in pre-Hispanic times.

Evidence suggests that the southern half of the uncovered ruins—the area around the lower plaza—was reserved for ceremonial purposes. Its centerpiece is the 60-foot-high **Pirámide de los Nichoes** (Pyramid of the Niches), one of the finest pre-Columbian buildings in Mexico. The finely wrought seven-level structure has 365 coffers—one for each day of the solar year—built around its seven friezes. The reliefs on the pyramid depict the ruler, 13-Rabbit—all the rulers' names were associated with sacred animals—and allude also to the Tajín tribe's main god, the benign Quetzalcóatl. One panel on the pyramid tells the tale of heroic human sacrifice and of the soul's imminent descent to the underworld, where it is rewarded with the gift from the gods of sacred *pulque,* a milky alcoholic beverage made from cactus.

Just south of the pyramid is the I-shaped **Juego de Pelotas Sur** (Southern Ball Court). This is one of more than 15 ball courts—more than at any other site in Mesoamerica—where the sacred pre-Columbian ball game was played. The game, played throughout Mesoamerica, is similar in some ways to soccer—players used a hard rubber ball that could not be touched with the hands, and suited up in knee pads and body protectors—but far more deadly. Intricate carvings at this and other ball courts indicate that the games ended with human sacrifice. It's still a subject of debate whether the winner or loser of the match was the sacrificial victim. It is surmised that the players may have been high-standing members of the priest or warrior classes.

To the north, **El Tajín Chico** (Little El Tajín) is thought to have been the secular part of the city, with mostly administrative and residential buildings. It was likely the location of the elite's living quarters. Floors and roofing were made with a pre-Columbian concrete of volcanic rock and limestone. The most important structure here is the **Complejo de los Columnos** (Complex of the Columns). The columns once held up the concrete ceilings, but early settlers in Papantla removed the stones to construct houses. If you're prepared to work your way through the thick jungle, you can see some more recent finds along the dirt paths that lead over the nearby ridges.

You can leave bags at the visitor center at the entrance, which includes a restaurant and a small museum that displays some pottery and sculpture and tells what little is known of the site. A performance by some voladores normally takes place at midday. Start early to avoid the midday sun, and take water, a hat, and sunblock. To get here, take an EL TAJÍN shuttle bus that departs from Avenida 16 de Septiembre in Veracruz, behind the cathedral. The trip takes about 20 minutes. ☎ *No phone* ✉ *$3* ⊕ *www.inah.gob.mx* ☉ *Daily 9–5.*

## Tuxpán

**⑲** *193 km (120 mi) south of Tampico, 309 km (192 mi) northwest of Ve-racruz, 89 km (55 mi) north of Papantla.*

Tuxpán is a peaceful riverside town with graceful winding streets—and the Río Tuxpán is even clean enough to swim in. Juárez, the main street, running parallel to the river, is lined with diners, hotels, and shops. **Parque Reforma** is the center of social activity in town, with more than 100 tables set amid the cafés and fruit stands. It has a memorial to Fausto Vega Santander, a member of the 201st Squadron of the Mexican Air Force and the first Mexican to be killed in combat during World War II. On the western edge of Parque Reforma is the small **Museo Archae-olóia**. The museum is open weekdays 9–1 and 4–8.

Launches shuttle passengers across the river to the **Casa de Fidel Castro**, where Castro lived for a time while planning the overthrow of Fulgencio Batista. A replica of the *Granma*, the ship that carried Fidel's men from Tuxpán to Cuba, molders outside. Inside, the casa is bare save for some black-and-white photos of Fidel.

### Beaches

Tuxpán's main attraction is the miles of beaches that begin 7 km (4½ mi) east of town. The first, and most accessible beach from Tuxpán, is **Playa Tuxpán.** The surf here isn't huge, but there's enough action to warrant breaking out your surf or boogie board. Of the open-air restaurants along Playa Tuxpán, the most established is Miramar, which has an extensive menu of freshly caught seafood. About 20 km (12 mi) from town is another popular beach called **Playa Norte.**

### Where to Stay & Eat

¢–$  ✕ **Antonio's.** This quiet spot turns out excellent seafood dishes, including the *cazuela de mariscos* (seafood stew) and the *pez espada bella molineras* (swordfish served with a mushroom and shrimp sauce). If you're not in the mood for fish, the place also grills up steaks. On Friday and Saturday nights a trio of musicians swings into action. ⊠ *Av. Juárez 25, at Calle Garizurieta* ☎ *783/834–1602* ▭ *AE, MC, V.*

¢–$  ✕ **Berra de Mariscos.** Don't be fooled by the white plastic tables and chairs—the seafood here easily rivals that at fancier places in town. Hunker down with a cold beer and a plate of *pulpo encebollado* (octopus cooked with onions, butter, and garlic) or the house specialty, *camarones a la diabla* (a spicy concoction of grilled shrimp and chilies). The place is opposite Parque Reforma. ⊠ *Av. Juárez 44, at Calle Mina* ☎ *No phone* ▭ *No credit cards.*

★ $  ▥ **Hotel Florida.** Get past the harsh fluorescent lights in the lobby and you'll find one of the best deals in downtown Tuxpán. The art deco–style structure dating from 1940 has rooms that are, for the most part, spacious and sunny. Some have views of the town's elegant church, so ask to see a few before you decide. ⊠ *Av. Juárez 23, at Calle Garizurieta, 92800* ☎ *783/834–0222 or 783/834–0602* 🖷 *783/834–0650* ⊕ *www.hotelflorida.com.mx* ☞ *75 rooms* ⚐ *Restaurant, room service, cable TV, bar, meeting room, free parking* ▭ *DC, MC, V.*

$  ⊞ **Hotel May Palace.** The most luxurious lodgings in Tuxpán are at this hotel overlooking Parque Reforma. The five-story building—which qualifies as a high-rise here—is geared toward the business executives who meet for drinks in the small video bar or for dinner in the pleasant restaurant. The rooms, all painted in neutral shades, have views of the river. The rooftop pool is a great place to hang out. ⊠ *Av. Juárez 44, at Calle Mina, 92800* ☎☎ *783/834–8882 or 783/834–4461* ⤤ *70 rooms ⅋ Restaurant, room service, cable TV, pool, gym, bar, laundry service, meeting room, free parking* ⊟ *AE, MC, V.*

$  ⊞ **Hotel Plaza Palmas.** In a sleepy neighborhood five minutes from the center of town, this hostelry is a welcome respite from the hustle and bustle of Tuxpán. And although the mounted stag heads guarding the spare lobby give the Palmas a rather incongruous hunting lodge quality, the quirkiness ends there. Two U-shape buildings surround a large palm-lined pool and a small seafood bar. ⊠ *Carretera Tuxpán-Tampico s/n, 92820* ☎ *783/834–3529 or 783/834–3574* ☎ *783/834–3535* ⤤ *97 rooms, 4 suites ⅋ Restaurant, room service, cable TV, 2 tennis courts, pool, bar, shop, playground, laundry service, 3 meeting rooms, free parking* ⊟ *AE, MC, V.*

### Sports & the Outdoors

WATER SPORTS   For scuba diving, head to **Isla Lobos** (Island of the Wolves), a protected ecoreserve that shares its space with a military outpost and a lighthouse. In the shallow water offshore are a few shipwrecks and colorful reefs with puffer fish, parrot fish, damselfish, and barracuda. Generally, the best time to dive is between May and August. **Aqua Sport** (⊠ Carretera la Playa, Km 8.5 ☎ 783/837–0259 or 783/837–0191), west of Playa Tuxpán, arranges diving trips to Isla Lobos.

# VERACRUZ A TO Z

### AIR TRAVEL

AIRPORTS   Aeropuerto Internacional Heriberto Jara Corona is a clean, bright facility about 8 km (5 mi) south of downtown Veracruz. It's a small airport, so you won't have any trouble finding your way around. There's an ATM, as well as a bank where you can exchange currency.

🔀 Aeropuerto Internacional Heriberto Jara Corona ☎ 229/934–5372 or 229/934–9008.

AIRPORT   A cab ride between the airport and the city center costs $12 and takes
TRANSFERS   roughly half an hour. Taxis are readily available at the airport. No city bus serves the airport. An air-conditioned private car ($15) runs between the airport and the downtown office of Transavion.

🔀 Transavion ⊠ Av. Díaz Mirón 3008 ☎ 229/937–8978.

CARRIERS   The only direct international flight into Veracruz is on Continental, which has one flight daily from Houston. All other flights connect through Mexico City. There are several daily nonstop flights on Mexicana and Aeroméxico from Mexico City to Veracruz. Aerocaribe has three flights a day between Veracruz and Monterrey, plus daily flights to Mérida and Cuernavaca. Aerolitoral flies between Veracruz and Tampico and Villahermosa.

🔀 Aerocaribe ☎ 229/934–5888 ⊕ www.aerocaribe.com. **Aerolitoral** ☎ 229/934–3478. **Aeroméxico** ☎ 229/935–0833 or 229/935–0283 ⊕ www.aeromexico.com. **Continen-**

tal ☎ 229/938–6022, 800/900–5000 toll-free in Mexico ⊕ www.continental.com. **Mexicana** ☎ 229/932–2242 or 229/932–8699 ⊕ www.mexicana.com.mx.

## BUS TRAVEL TO & FROM VERACRUZ

Of Mexico City's four bus terminals, the one offering the most departures to Veracruz is the Terminal del Oriente, better known as TAPO. ADO has the most buses heading to Veracruz. The trip costs about $24 and takes about five hours, passing by the magnificent Pico de Orizaba. UNO, the deluxe bus line, also serves this route.

Veracruz's main terminal is on Avenida Díaz Mirón about 4 km (2½ mi) south of the zócalo. ADO, UNO, and other first-class companies operate from the half of the terminal facing Avenida Díaz Mirón, while AU and second-class companies are found in the half facing Avenida La Fragua.

Xalapa's bus station, called TAXA, is 2 km (1 mi) east of downtown. Like Veracruz, it houses first-class and second-class companies under the same roof. Papantla's station is served only by ADO.

To reserve tickets, either go to a local bus terminal or contact Ticketbus, the telephone and online reservation service. There is a small fee for issuing tickets.

🚍 Bus Terminals **Papantla** ✉ Calle Benito Juárez at Calle 20 de Noviembre ☎ No phone. **Veracruz** ✉ Av. Díaz Mirón 1698, at Calle Xalapa ☎ No phone. **Xalapa** ✉ Av. 20 de Noviembre s/n ☎ No phone.
🚍 Bus Line **Ticketbus** ☎ 800/702–8000 ⊕ www.ticketbus.com.mx.

## BUS TRAVEL WITHIN VERACRUZ

ADO, the region's best bus line, travels just about everywhere. Its buses are clean, comfortable, and frequently arrive at your destination a bit early. ADO's GL service is a notch above its regular service, and costs a bit more. UNO, the deluxe bus line, is the most expensive.

ADO runs frequent buses from Veracruz to Xalapa. The trip takes two hours and costs about $10. ADO buses also shuttle between Veracruz and Tuxpán several times a day; it's a four-hour trip and costs about $14. There's service half a dozen times a day from Veracruz up to Papantla; the ride lasts three hours and costs $11. Several daily buses make the journey to Santiago Tuxtla (two hours, $6), San Andrés Tuxtla (2½ hours, $7), and Catemaco (three hours, $7). A handful of buses travel to Tlacotalpan (1½ hours, $5).

As for Xalapa, ADO runs at least six buses a day from CAXA to Tuxpán (five hours, $16) and to Papantla (four hours, $12).

## CAR RENTAL

Several international chains—Avis, Alamo, Budget, and Hertz—have kiosks in the main terminal of Aeropuerto Internacional Heriberto Jara Corona. Avis and Dollar have offices close to the center of Veracruz. Hertz can be found on the main drag in Boca del Río.

🚗 **Alamo** ✉ Aeropuerto Internacional Heriberto Jara Corona, Veracruz ☎ 229/938–3700. **Avis** ✉ Aeropuerto Internacional Heriberto Jara Corona, Veracruz ☎ 229/934–9623 ✉ Calle Collado 241, at 20 de Noviembre, Veracruz ☎ 229/932–6032. **Budget**

✉ Aeropuerto Internacional Heriberto Jara Corona, Veracruz ☎ 229/937-5721. **Dollar** ✉ Aeropuerto Internacional Heriberto Jara Corona, Veracruz ☎ 229/938-7878 ✉ Simon Bolívar 501, at García Auly, Veracruz ☎ 229/935-8807. **Hertz** ✉ Aeropuerto Internacional Heriberto Jara Corona, Veracruz ☎ 229/937-4776 ✉ Hotel Costa Verde, Blvd. Manuel Avila Camacho 3797, Boca del Río ☎ 229/937-4776.

## CAR TRAVEL

From Mexico City, you can reach Veracruz in about five hours on Carretera 150-D. Carretera 140, which branches off Carretera 150-D, leads to Xalapa. Carretera 130 leads past Poza Rica to Papantla.

From Veracruz, Carretera 180 leads north to Papantla and south to Santiago Tuxtla, San Andrés Tuxtla, and Catemaco. Carretera 140 leads from Veracruz to Xalapa.

The highways throughout the state are generally in very good condition. Pay extra attention when driving in Xalapa, since the streets do not follow a traditional grid pattern and getting lost is a real possibility. Finding street parking in the cities is generally not a problem.

## EMERGENCIES

Dial **060** in Veracruz for medical, fire, and theft emergencies. If you have a medical emergency, call the Red Cross (Cruz Roja) for ambulance service. Local police officers can handle most incidents, but if you're on an isolated stretch of road, contact the Angeles Verdes (Green Angels), a highway patrol service.

In Xalapa, Calle Enríquez is lined with pharmacies. For 24-hour service, the Farmacia Plus is your best option. Farmacia Médico, the largest pharmacy in Papantla, is open daily 8 AM–10 PM. In downtown Tuxpán, Farmacia El Fenix is open daily 8 AM–10 PM. In Veracruz, Farmacia del Ahorro is a big, bright drugstore with branches all over town. It offers good prices and does home deliveries; it closes at 10:30 PM daily. For 24-hour home delivery in Veracruz, call Farmacia Las Torres.

🏥 Hospitals **Centro Médico** ✉ Av. Cuauhtémoc 82, Col. del Valle, Tuxpán ☎ 783/834-7400. **Clínica Santa Cruz** ✉ Calle Rodolfo Curti 122, Zona Centro Papantla ☎ 784/842-0557. **Hospital General de Veracruz** ✉ 20 de Noviembre s/n, Veracruz ☎ 229/931-7857.

🏥 Emergency Services **Angeles Verdes** ☎ 229/932-8498. **Papantla Cruz Roja** ☎ 784/842-0126. **Papantla Police** ☎ 784/842-0075. **Tuxpán Cruz Roja** ☎ 783/834-0158. **Tuxpán Police** ☎ 783/834-0252. **Veracruz Cruz Roja** ☎ 229/937-5500. **Veracruz Police** ☎ 229/938-0664 or 229/938-0693. **Xalapa Cruz Roja** ☎ 228/817-8158. **Xalapa Police** ☎ 228/818-7490 or 228/818-7199.

🏥 24-Hour & Late-Night Pharmacies **Farmacia del Ahorro** ✉ Paseo del Malecón 342, at Calle Fariaz, Veracruz ☎ 229/937-3525. **Farmacia El Fenix** ✉ Enrique 103, Zona Centro, Papantla ☎ 784/842-0636 ✉ Calle Morelos 1, at Av. Juárez, Tuxpán ☎ 783/834-0983 or 783/834-3023. **Farmacia Las Torres** ✉ Av. Díaz Mirón 165, Veracruz ☎ 229/932-6363. **Farmacia Médico** ✉ Gutiérrez Zamora 103, Papantla ☎ 784/842-0640. **Farmacia Plus** ✉ Av. Revolución 173, Sayago, Xalapa ☎ 228/817-2797.

## INTERNET

You can find Internet cafés in most of the state, even in small towns such as Papantla. All charge between $1 and $2 an hour. Several blocks from Papantla's main square, PC's Palafox has a speedy connection; it's open weekdays 8 AM–9 PM, Saturday 8–7, and Sunday 8–5. Tuxpán's Sesico, near Parque Reforma, is open Monday–Saturday 9–8:30 and Sunday 10–3.

For Internet access in Veracruz, head to Web Café for the fastest machines; it gives slightly cheaper rates for students. It's open daily 10–10. Café Internet Xalapa, in the center of town, is open daily 9–9. Another conveniently located Internet café is Terra Xalapa.

🖪 Internet Cafés **Café Internet Xalapa** ⊠ Pasaje Enríquez 1, Xalapa ☎ 228/817–5141. **PC's Palafox** ⊠ Aquiles Serdán 500, at Calle Galeana, Papantla ☎ 784/842–1357. **Sesico** ⊠ Av. Juárez 52, off Parque Reforma, Tuxpán ☎ 783/834–4505. **Terra Xalapa** ⊠ Calle 20 de Noviembre 211, Xalapa ☎ 228/818–4043. **Web Café** ⊠ Calle Rayon 579, between Avs. Independencia and Zaragoza, Veracruz ☎ No phone.

## MONEY MATTERS

There are plenty of banks surrounding Papantla's main square, most of which change money weekday mornings. Banamex changes both cash and traveler's checks weekdays 9–noon and has a 24-hour ATM.

The Tuxpán Banamex changes cash and traveler's checks weekdays 9–5; it has a 24-hour ATM. Bancomer has a 24-hour ATM and changes cash and traveler's checks weekdays 8:30–2:30.

The best rates in Veracruz are at Bancomer, but money-changing hours are limited to weekdays 9–noon, so you'll have to arrive early to make it through the lines. The Casa de Cambio Puebla is open weekdays 9–6. Or use the ATMs that are readily available downtown.

🖪 Banks **Banamex** ⊠ Calle Enríquez 102, Papantla ☎ 784/842–0001 or 784/842–1766 ⊠ Av. Juárez at Calle Corregidora, Tuxpán ☎ 783/834–7907. **Bancomer** ⊠ Av. Juárez at Escuela Médico Militar, Tuxpán ☎ 783/834–0009 ⊠ Enríquez 109, Papantla ☎ 784/842–0174 or 784/842–0223 ⊠ Av. Juárez at Av. Independencia, Veracruz ☎ 229/931–0095 or 229/989–8000.

🖪 Currency Exchange **Casa de Cambio Monedas Internacional** ⊠ Elustres 48, Xalapa ☎ 228/817–2060. **Casa de Cambio Puebla** ⊠ Av. Juárez 112, Veracruz ☎ 229/931–2450.

## TOURS

Based in Mexico City, Expediciones Mexico Verde runs 7- to 10-day trips along the Cortés Route, which includes visits to Veracruz City, La Antigua, Cempoala, Xalapa, and Coatepec and other sites in the states of Tlaxcala, Puebla, and Mexico. Guides speak English.

Centro de Reservaciones Veracruz in Boca del Río runs trips to Cempoala, Xalapa, Catemaco, El Tajín, and Papantla. BTT Tours, at Hotel Lois in Boca del Río, offers trips to La Antigua and Los Tuxtlas, Xalapa, Tajín, and Cempoala. Guides for these companies usually speak some English.

In Xalapa, Arqueotours specializes in tours of the ruins around the city. A popular two-day tour includes visits to Cempoala, El Tajín, and several other archeological sites.

🖪 Tour Operator Recommendations **Arqueotours** ⊠ Callejón de la Animas 13, Xalapa ☎ 228/812–5514. **BTT Tours** ⊠ Blvd. Adolfo Ruíz Cortines 10, Boca del Río ☎ 229/935–4192. **Centro de Reservaciones Veracruz** ⊠ Mar Báltico 132, Boca del Río ☎ 229/

935–6422 or 229/935–6423. **Expediciones Mexico Verde** ✉ Homero 526, Int. 801, Col. Polanco, Mexico D.F. 11560 ☎ 55/5255–4400, 01800/362–8800 toll free in Mexico 🖷 55/5255–4465 ⊕ www.raftingmexicoverde.com.

### VISITOR INFORMATION

The Veracruz Tourist Office occupies a room in the Palacio Municipal; it's open daily 10–6. The main Xalapa Tourist Office is in the large office building on the way out of town toward Veracruz and is open weekdays 9–9. There's a more convenient tourist information booth in front of the Palacio Municipal that is open daily 9–9. Both stock slick maps and brochures, but they charge for them.

The Papantla Tourism Office, in the basement of the Palacio Municipal, is open weekdays 8–6 and Saturday 9–noon. The Tuxpán Tourist Office, off Parque Cano, is open Monday–Saturday 8–3 and 4–6. Catemaco's tourism office is open weekdays 9–3 and 7–9 and Saturday 10–noon. Inside the Palacio Municipal, Xico's tourist bureau is open weekdays 9–3 and 6–9.

🔢 **Catemaco Tourism Office** ✉ Av. Venustiano Carraza s/n, Catemaco ☎ 294/943–0258 or 294/943–0016. **Xalapa Tourist Information Booth** ✉ Calle Enríquez 14, Xalapa ☎ No phone. **Xalapa Tourist Office** ✉ Blvd. Cristóbal Colón 5, Jardines de las Animas, Xalapa ☎ 228/812–8500 Ext. 130 🖷 228/812–5936. **Papantla Tourist Office** ✉ Calle Reforma 100, Papantla ☎ 784/842–0176 or 784/842–0026. **Tuxpán Tourist Office** ✉ Av. Juárez 26, Tuxpán ☎ 783/834–0177. **Veracruz Tourist Office** ✉ Palacio Municipal, Veracruz ☎ 229/932–7593. **Xico Tourist Office** ✉ Hidalgo s/n, Xico ☎ 228/813–0327 or 228/813–0334 Ext. 216.

# THE NORTHEAST

Texans and businessmen are among the lucky few that have discovered the charm of Northeastern Mexico; day-trippers cross the border to soak up the local color at border towns like Nuevo Laredo, Matamoros, and Reynosa, and businessmen are delighted by the luxury offered in fast-paced Monterrey. The average tourist to Mexico often overlooks this region of contrasts, natural beauty, wealth, and technology.

That's a shame, as there is much here to enjoy. Nature lovers can explore the waterfalls of Parque Nacional Cumbres de Monterrey and the stalactites and stalagmites of Grutas de García. Culture seekers can immerse themselves in the much-lauded museums in and around Monterrey.

## Nuevo Laredo

**⑳** *1½ km (1 mi) south of Laredo, Texas.*

Nuevo Laredo was founded in 1848, at the end of the Mexican-American War. When the Río Grande was declared the international borderline, the residents of Laredo suddenly found themselves living in the United States. Many simply moved their homes across the river.

Of all the towns along the Texas border, Nuevo Laredo bears the biggest onslaught of Americans. As soon as you cross the International Bridge you'll be approached by hawkers eager to guide you to kitschy keepsakes or cheap prescription drugs.

There are a few charming spots in this rough-and-tumble town. The main square, **Plaza Hidalgo,** is a great place to relax after an afternoon of shopping. The lovely ivory-color clock tower, dating from 1915, never seems to tell the correct time. A few blocks north, **Plaza Juárez** is filled with amorous teens after dark.

## Where to Stay & Eat

★ $$–$$$ ✗ **Victoria 3020.** With its walled garden and candlelit courtyard, this is the place for a romantic dinner. It's also probably the best value in town, since it offers elegant food and a peaceful refuge from vendors in the center. The rich entrées include the *Calendario Azteca,* a colorful palette of beef, quesadillas, flautas (rolled-up, fried tortillas with beef or chicken inside), tostadas (a fried tortilla with a variety of toppings), guacamole, beans, and rice. ✉ *Calle Victoria 3020, at Calle Matamoros* ☎ *867/713–3020* ▭ *AE, MC, V.*

$–$$ ✗ **México Típico.** Mariachis wander in from the street to entertain at this longtime favorite, where the solicitous staff serves up border-town standards like *carne asada* (roasted beef). There's a partially covered patio with a fountain. ✉ *Av. Guerrero 934* ☎ *867/712–1525* ▭ *MC, V.*

$$ ▭ **Fiesta Inn.** Carved wooden statues of San Judas and San Miguel guard the sparkling tiled lobby. The decorative touches—wrought-iron balconies, antique lamps along the walkways—make this reliable chain hotel well worth the 15-minute trip from the city center. The bright, immaculate rooms, overlooking a palm-lined pool area, are as good as it gets in Nuevo Laredo. ✉ *Av. Reforma 5530, 88280* ☎ *867/711–4444* 🖷 *867/717–0402* ⊕ *www.posadas.com* ☞ *111 rooms, 5 suites* ⚷ *Restaurant, room service, cable TV, tennis court, pool, gym, hair salon, basketball, Internet, meeting room* ▭ *AE, MC, V.*

¢ ▭ **La Finca.** A block east of Plaza Hidalgo, this little place is within easy walking distance of all the city's attractions. Simply furnished rooms wrap around a quiet courtyard. ✉ *Calle Reynosa 811, 88000* ☎ *867/712–8883* ☞ *27 rooms* ⚷ *Cable TV* ▭ *No credit cards.*

## Nightlife & the Arts

Most of the popular clubs are on Avenida Guerrero, not far from the International Bridge. It won't be hard to locate them, as insistent doormen practically push you inside. Better choices are only a block or two away. **Cadillac** (✉ Calle Matamoros at Calle Victoria ☎ 867/713–1525) is to the bar scene what its namesake is to the automobile industry: a classic that appeals to a slightly older crowd. Drawing folks across the border since Prohibition, **El Dorado Bar & Grill** (✉ Calle Ocampo at Calle Belden ☎ 867/712–0015) looks a little rough from outside, but it's still a favorite with Texans.

## Shopping

The International Bridge empties into Avenida Guerrero, where you'll find most of Nuevo Laredo's shops. Guerrero is famous for its bargain shoe stores. Most shops stay open until 8 PM. The first stop for many

people is the **Mercado Maclorio Herrero** (✉ Av. Guerrero at Calle Belden). Ceramics and other items are found in dozens of shops on two levels.

## Reynosa

**㉑** *16 km (10 mi) south of McAllen, Texas.*

Because of its manageable size and mellow attitude, Reynosa is a favorite point of entry into Mexico. It's a convenient starting point for a trip south. This industrial town has very limited appeal, but it is still more attractive than most border towns, especially Nuevo Laredo. The heart of the city is tidy **Plaza Hidalgo,** about five blocks beyond the International Bridge. The square has a colonial church and a movie theater.

### Where to Stay & Eat

**$–$$** ✕ **La Fogata.** An imposing pink structure, the facade of La Fogata foreshadows the Herculean portions of food found inside. Slow-roasted cabrito, lamb, and beef are all prepared on a smoky open grill at the back of this popular joint. ✉ *Calle Matamoros Oriente 750, at Calle Chapa* ☎ *899/922–4772* ▭ *AE, MC, V.*

**¢–$** ✕ **Café de Paris.** Cool white-tile floors and strong air-conditioning make this spot an oasis on a hot day. Don't let the name throw you off—you can sample spicy enchiladas as well as a café au lait and a pastry. ✉ *Blvd. Hidalgo Norte 815* ☎ *899/922–5535* ▭ *No credit cards.*

**$$** ☑ **Astromundo.** A short walk to the center and the market, this downtown hotel is perfect for anyone wanting to be close to the action without actually being right smack in the middle of it. The efficient air conditioners in the comfortable, but dim rooms are a blessing. ✉ *Calle Juárez Norte 675, 88500* ☎ *899/922–5625* 📠 *899/922–9888* ↘ *90 rooms, 6 suites* ⚒ *Restaurant, room service, cable TV, gym, bar, Internet, meeting rooms, airport shuttle* ▭ *AE, MC, V* ¶○¶ *CP.*

**$$** ☑ **Hacienda.** About 16 km (10 mi) south of the U.S. border, this elegant hotel is relatively far from the center of town. If you are in search of creature comforts and Mexican charm, this is your best choice. Both the tiled lobby and the light-filled, cheerful rooms are outfitted with carved wooden furniture. ✉ *Blvd. Hidalgo 2013, 88650* ☎ *899/924–6100* 📠 *899/923–5962* ⊕ *www.haciendahotel.com.mx* ↘ *20 rooms, 13 suites* ⚒ *Restaurant, room service, cable TV, bar, meeting room* ▭ *AE, MC, V.*

**$** ☑ **San Carlos.** This five-story hotel overlooking Plaza Hidalgo is a great value. The central location and views of the plaza make up for the simple rooms. The friendly staff is more than happy to help you find your way around or give advice about Reynosa. ✉ *Blvd. Hidalgo Norte 970, 88500* ☎ *899/922–1280* 📠 *899/922–4000* ↘ *69 rooms, 4 suites* ⚒ *Restaurant, room service, cable TV, laundry service* ▭ *MC, V.*

### Nightlife & the Arts

The Zona Dorada, the so-called Golden Zone along Emilio Portés Gel, has the most popular nightspots. Your best bet is **Frida's** (✉ Emilio Portés Gel 1410 ☎ 899/922–2233), popular with a younger crowd.

### Shopping

Colorful **Calle Hidalgo**, a pedestrian mall lined with vendors, leads off from the plaza. You'll find anything from toys to clothes to cowboy boots here. Many Texans save money by having their teeth fixed south of the Río Bravo, hence the many dentists you'll find here.

## Matamoros

**㉒** *1 km (about ½ mi) south of Brownsville, Texas.*

With a much longer history than its neighbors to the west, the 18th-century town of Matamoros is a great place to start your journey to Mexico. It's named for one of the many rebellious priests who were executed by the Spanish during the War of Independence. The first major battle of the Mexican-American War was fought here when Mexican troops began lobbing shells to the other side of the Río Bravo. Shortly afterward, General Zachary Taylor and his men occupied the city and began their march south.

Matamoros prides itself on being the hub of a rich agricultural region and a manufacturing center for multinational corporations. Nowhere is this more evident than in the lively **Plaza Hidalgo** (✉ Calle 6 and Calle Gonzalez). Nearby stands the carefully restored **Teatro de la Reforma** (✉ Calle 6 and Calle Abasolo ☎ 868/812–3788), which first threw open its doors in 1864.

The **Museo Casa Mata** is housed in the remains of Fort Mata, built in 1845 to defend the city against American invasion. It never fulfilled its purpose, though; the fortress wasn't completed when Zachary Taylor's troops marched into town. The museum displays artifacts from the Mexican Revolution. ⊠ *Calle Guatemala and Calle Santos Degollado* ☎ *868/813–5929* ⚏ *Free* ⊗ *Tues.–Fri. 8–4, weekends 9–2.*

### Where to Stay & Eat

**$$–$$$**  ✕ **Garcia's.** Talk about tough decisions—there are over a dozen fine tequilas to choose from here. Hopefully, one of them will help you make up your mind between lobster and steak. An elevator from the garage whisks you up to the restaurant and bar, where there's dancing until the wee hours. ⊠ *Av. Alvaro Obregón 82* ☎ *868/812–3929, 800/769–2470 in the U.S.* ⊟ *AE, D, DC, MC, V.*

**$**  ✕ **Los Norteños.** A *cabrito al pastor* cooking over hot coals is the not-so-subtle advertisement for the best roasted kid in town. Don't let the decor—an odd mix of stately wooden columns and harsh fluorescent lights—make you pass up a tender T-bone weighing in at 12 ounces. ⊠ *Calle Matamoros 109, at Calle 8* ☎ *868/813–0037* ⊟ *No credit cards.*

**$$**  ▦ **Gran Hotel Residencial.** Although it couldn't be called luxurious, this is by far the best lodging in Matamoros. All rooms have private terraces, and the bathrooms have tubs. The lush garden has a children's play area. ⊠ *Av. Alvaro Obregón 249, at Calle Amapola, 87330* ☎ *868/813–9811, 800/718–8230, or 800/528–1234 in the U.S.* ⚏ *868/813–2777* ⊕ *www.geocities.com/hotelresidencial* ☞ *109 rooms, 5 suites* ⚐ *Restaurant, cafeteria, room service, cable TV, pool, bar, baby-sitting, playground, meeting room, car rental, travel services* ⊟ *AE, MC, V.*

**$$**  ▦ **Plaza Matamoros.** The superior service and the location near the center of town make this colonial-style hotel a good choice. Decorated with heavy wooden furniture, the clean, comfortable rooms overlook the central courtyard. ⊠ *Calle 9 1421, at Calle Bravo, 87330* ☎ *868/816–1696* ⚏ *868/816–1687* ⊕ *www.hotelplazamatamoros.com* ☞ *50 rooms* ⚐ *Restaurant, room service, cable TV, bar, shops, laundry service, meeting room* ⊟ *AE, MC, V.*

### Shopping

The most appealing shops line Avenida Alvaro Obregón, which leads into town from the International Bridge. **Aztlan** (⊠ Av. Alvaro Obregón 75 ☎ 868/816–2947) has good-quality jewelry, pewter, and wooden and stone carvings. **Barbara** (⊠ Av. Alvaro Obregón 37 ☎ 868/816–5456) sells attractive handicrafts.

The bustling **Mercado Juárez** (⊠ Calle 9 at Calle Matamoros) is the place to haggle over pretty pottery and other souvenirs.

## Monterrey

*235 km (146 mi) southwest of Nuevo Laredo, 225 km (140 mi) west of Reynosa, 325 km (201 mi) west of Matamoros.*

▶ A brewer of beer and forger of steel, the industrial powerhouse of Monterrey has nothing in the way of a laid-back lifestyle. Some of the country's most powerful captains of industry hold sway here—a fact that earned the city its nickname, the *Sultana del Norte* (Sultan of the North).

With its focus on the future, Monterrey hasn't preserved as much of its past as other cities. Don't expect colonial splendor here; there's just one building, El Obispado, dating from the colonial period, and the Barrio Antiguo, east of the Macroplaza, is the city's only concentration of century-old structures. Still, Monterrey makes up for its lack of tradition with progress and innovation. The city boasts a state-of-the-art planetarium and the prestigious Tecnológico de Monterrey, arguably the best university in all of Latin America.

Although Monterrey is considered an indispensable stop for those headed south, it's also a much overlooked destination in itself. Shop-lined pedestrian malls like Avenida J. M. Morelos are perfect for browsing, while the museums, especially the Museo de Arte Contemporáneo, are among the best in the country. Dining experiences are both innovative and traditional, and the nonstop nightlife might even surpass that of Monterrey's rival to the south, Mexico City. If you're not straying too far from the city center, it's easy to get around town. There's a modern, efficient metro called Metrorrey, which runs along elevated tracks across the city center. Each ride costs less than 50¢. The metro runs from 4:45 AM–midnight daily. Be aware, however, that much of Monterrey is not accessible by Metro. Access to a car helps if you want to explore the best of the metropolitan area.

## The Macroplaza

The city's focal point is the Macroplaza, a swath of concrete connecting two older squares, the rather stark, monumental Plaza 5 de Mayo to the north, and the tranquil, tree-shaded Plaza Zaragoza to the south. It's fringed by the city's best museums; El Faro de Comercio towers above. Designed by Luis Barragán to commemorate the city's 100th anniversary, this postmodern lighthouse's brilliant green beam sweeps the night sky from its ironic location at the edge of the Barrio Antiguo.

A GOOD WALK    Start with a bit of window-shopping at the stores around the Plaza Hidalgo. Facing the shady square is the **Museo Metropolitano de Monterrey** ㉓ ▶, a showcase for Mexican artists. From the museum's east side, you'll see the loveliest section of the Macroplaza. Above the trees you'll spy the spires of the centuries-old **Catedral de Monterrey** ㉔. The rust-color building to the south is the **Museo de Arte Contemporáneo** ㉕.

Next, head north past the gushing Fuente de la Vida to the impressive **Museo de Historia Mexicana** ㉖, filled with exhibits on the country's history. Cool off with a boat ride or sit down for an overpriced drink and a snack at the enticing café on the **Paseo Santa Lucia,** which runs along a tiny river on the museum's southern side. The official-looking edifice to the west of the Museo de Historia is the **Palacio de Gobierno** ㉗.

TIMING    Monterrey can be hot and sticky, especially in the city center, so don't plan on rushing. This walk will take at least a few hours. Note that the museums are closed Mondays.

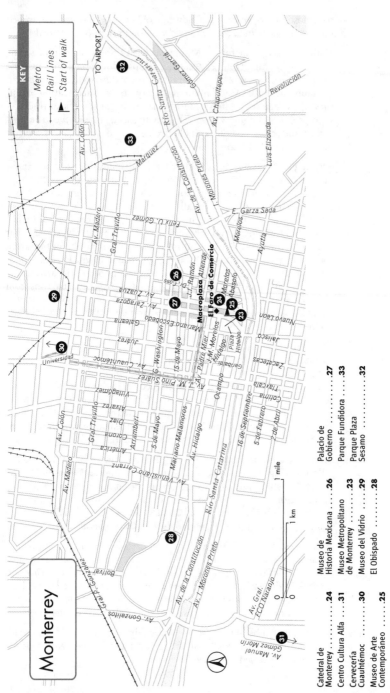

# Monterrey

**KEY**

Metro
Rail Lines
▲ Start of walk

TO AIRPORT

1 km
1 mile

Catedral de
Monterrey . . . . . . . . . **24**

Centro Cultura Alfa . . . **31**

Cervecería
Cuauhtémoc . . . . . . . . **30**

Museo de Arte
Contemporáneo . . . . . **25**

Museo de
Historia Mexicana . . . . **26**

Museo Metropolitano
de Monterrey . . . . . . . **23**

Museo del Vidrio . . . . **29**

El Obispado . . . . . . . . **28**

Palacio de
Gobierno . . . . . . . . . . **27**

Parque Fundidora . . . . **33**

Parque Plaza
Sesamo . . . . . . . . . . . **32**

Macroplaza

El Faro de Comercio

WHAT TO SEE **Catedral de Monterrey.** Construction began in 1600, but the massive cathe-
㉔ dral took 250 years to finish. As a result, a baroque facade is set off by
neoclassical columns and two huge ornate plateresque medallions on
the main door. Murals by local artists frame the main altar. ⌧ *Macroplaza
at Calle Abasolo* ☎ *81/8340–3752.*

㉕ **Museo de Arte Contemporáneo.** Better known as MARCO, this contem-
**Fodor'sChoice** porary art museum was designed by renowned Mexican architect Ri-
★ cardo Legorretta. It has 11 galleries of cutting-edge international art;
recent shows have included works by Frida Kahlo and Diego Rivera.
Juan Soriano's *La Paloma,* a mammoth dove statue, guards the entrance.
Take a break at one of the tables near the marble reflecting pool and
watch the fountain's irregular jets. ⌧ *Macroplaza at Calle Jardón* ☎ *81/
8342–4820* ⊕ *www.marco.org.mx* ☜ *$3.50, free Wed.* ☉ *Tues. and
Thurs.–Sun. 10–6, Wed. 10–8.*

㉖ **Museo de Historia Mexicana.** This Mexican history museum mounts the
country's most complete exhibition on the 1910–20 Revolution. Period
newsreels play in a multimedia show displayed inside a railroad car that
transported the insurgents. Life-size models of the *villistas* (soldiers
under the command of Pancho Villa) sit on the roof of a car "liberated"
from the Mexican army. Other exhibits include the first bottle-capping
machine used by Coca-Cola, a history of Mexican cinema, and pre-
Columbian artifacts. Call ahead for an English-speaking guide. ⌧ *Dr.
Coss 444 Sur* ☎ *81/8345–9898* ⊕ *www.museohistoriamexicana.org.
mx* ☜ *$1.20, 60¢ Sun., free Tues.* ☉ *Tues.–Fri. 10–7, weekends 10–8.*

▶ ㉓ **Museo Metropolitano de Monterrey.** The former Palacio Municipal now
hosts temporary exhibits of prominent Mexican artists. One recent
show by Sergio Rodrígues filled the central courtyard with a giant apple
made of soda bottles. ⌧ *Macroplaza at Av. Zaragoza* ☎ *81/8345–4036*
⊕ *www.museometropolitano.org* ☜ *Free* ☉ *Tues.–Sun. 10–6.*

㉗ **Palacio de Gobierno.** On the northern tip of the Macroplaza sits one of
the city's loveliest buildings. The Government Palace, built in 1908, is
especially striking at night, when its slender neoclassical columns are
beautifully illuminated. From the statue-studded front terrace you have
a splendid view of the entire Macroplaza. ⌧ *Plaza 5 de Mayo.*

## Elsewhere in Monterrey
The rest of Monterrey's sights are spread out. Unless you have a car,
you will have to take a taxi to the others. Although you can take a bus
to El Obispado, it lets you off at the bottom of a steep hill. The Museo
del Vidrio and Cerveceria Cuauhtémoc are near subway stops, but
you'd have to walk through an iffy neighborhood to reach them.

A GOOD TOUR Start out early to see unobstructed views of the city from **El Obispado** ㉘,
on a hill to the west of the city center. To the north is **Museo del Vidrio** ㉙.
**Cerveceria Cuauhtémoc** ㉚ is where they brew up most of the country's
favorite beers.

If you have teenagers with a working knowledge of Spanish, spend the
afternoon at **Centro Cultural Alfa** ㉛. Youngsters will probably prefer **Par-**

que **Plaza Sesamo** ㉜ or to ride bikes around the enormous **Parque Fundidora** ㉝.

TIMING    Factor in plenty of time to get between these sights. It takes 10 to 15 minutes to get to the sights in downtown Monterrey. A ride to the Centro Cultural Alfa or Parque Plaza Sesamo will take 20 to 30 minutes. Note that the Centro Cultural Alfa and the Museo del Vidrio are closed on Monday, and the Cervecería is closed on Sunday.

WHAT TO SEE    **Centro Cultural Alfa.** The country's best science and technology museum, the cylindrical Alfa Cultural Center has an IMAX theater and many fun, hands-on exhibits. There's even a planetarium. Information is in Spanish only. The facility is 7 km (4½ mi) south of Monterrey. ⊠ *Av. Roberto Garza Sada 1000, San Pedro Garza García* ☎ *81/8303–0001* ⊕ *www. planetarioalfa.org.mx* ✑ *$7 for museum and IMAX film, $3.50 for museum only, 2-for-1 admission Wed.* ⊙ *Tues.–Fri. 3–8, weekends 11:30–8.*

㉚ **Cervecería Cuauhtémoc.** The popularity of Mexican beer owes much to this powerful brewery, which opened a century ago. Named after a famous Aztec chief, the brewery is the heart of an industrial empire that produces well-known brands like Carta Blanca and Tecate. The fascinating tour concludes with free beer—obviously the big draw. Call about tours in English. ⊠ *Av. Alfonso Reyes Norte 2202* ☎ *81/ 8328–5355 or 81/8328–5703* ✑ *Free* ⊙ *Weekdays 9–5, Sat. 9–2. Brewery tours by request during business hours.*

㉙ **Museo del Vidrio.** This century-old building is on the property of the glass factory that makes, among other items, the Cuauhtémoc suds bottles. Inside is a museum of the history of glassmaking in Mexico. It also includes a stunning collection of glass by local artists. All information is in Spanish only. ⊠ *Calle Magallanes 517, at Av. Zaragoza* ☎ *81/ 8863–1070* ⊕ *museovidrio.vto.com* ✑ *$1.50* ⊙ *Tues.–Sun. 9–6.*

㉘ **El Obispado.** Built in 1788, the hilltop Bishop's Residence is the city's only remaining colonial landmark. Originally intended as a retirement home for Bishop Fray Rafael José Verger, the domed structure was used as a fort during the Mexican-American War, the French Intervention, and the Revolution. Today the restored structure houses a wonderful museum focusing on the region's history (most info is in Spanish only). From here you'll have a splendid view of Monterrey. ⊠ *Calle Fray Rafael José Verger* ☎ *81/8333–9588* ✑ *$3, Free Sun.* ⊙ *Tues.–Sun. 10–5.*

㉝ **Parque Fundidora.** An enormous green area with numerous playgrounds, shady picnic spots, and soothing fountains is always welcome in a big, industrial city. The well-groomed grounds of Monterrey's historic steel foundry host droves of people who come on weekends to rent bikes and kid-sized electric jeeps or enjoy a leisurely stroll. ⊠ *Avenida Fundidora, Colonia Obrera* ✑ *Free, $2 parking* ⊙ *6 AM–11 PM.*

㉜ **Parque Plaza Sesamo.** The cleverly designed Sesame Plaza theme park, built next to Cintermex on the grounds of Parque Fundidora, has three main areas. One has 17 water toboggans, pint-size pools, and games. A second has a computer center. The last has theaters where the park's Sesame Street characters put on musical shows in Spanish. ⊠ *Calle Agri-*

*cola Oriente 3700–1, Col. Agricola* ☎ *81/8354–5400* ⊕ *www. parqueplazasesamo.com* ✉ *$15* ☯ *Call for hours.*

## Where to Stay & Eat

★ **$$$–$$$$**  ✕ **Luisiana.** In what might be downtown's most elegant and renowned dining room (a favorite of Monterrey's rich and famous), you can taste a Mexican interpretation of New Orleans cuisine. There are no Cajun specialties on the menu, but the popular *huachinango* (red snapper) is divine. ⊠ *Av. Hidalgo Oriente 530* ☎ *81/8340–3753 or 81/8343–1561* ▭ *AE, MC, V.*

★ **$$–$$$**  ✕ **Vitrales.** This dining room in the Sheraton Ambassador has a unique stained-glass ceiling and equally distinctive food. Choose from shrimp, beef, pasta, chicken, sandwiches, or the ubiquitous cabrito. Entrées aren't terribly filling; you might want to start with one of the many appetizers. ⊠ *Av. Hidalgo Oriente 310* ☎ *81/8380–7000* ▭ *AE, MC, V.*

**$**  ✕ **Las Monjitas.** The sight of a white-frocked mother superior in the open-
Fodor'sChoice air kitchen may surprise you as you pass this odd little place. Step down
★ into the colonnaded dining room, where waitresses dressed as nuns rush about serving sinfully delicious comida corrida. You may have to atone for meals like "La Pecadora," thinly sliced grilled chicken topped with mushrooms, fried onions, and melted asadero cheese. There are other branches around the city center, but this one has the best food. ⊠ *Calle Escobedo Sur 903* ☎ *81/8344–6713* ▭ *MC, V.*

¢–$  ✕ **La Casa de Maiz.** On a bustling street in Barrio Antiguo, the House of Corn has a special flair for turning the local cash crop into delicious *sopas* and *sopes* (the former is soup, the latter an appetizer). The funky decor, with brightly colored walls and quirky art, makes this a popular place with young people, who often stop by for a cold beer before hitting the clubs. ⊠ *Calle Abasolo 870, at Montemayor* ☎ *81/8340–4332* ▭ *MC, V.*

¢  ✕ **Gorditas Doña Tota.** This squeaky-clean Mexican fast-food chain originated in Ciudad Victoria, Tamaulipas, in 1952, but it is a favorite now in Monterrey as well. Fill your freshly hand-made flour or corn *gorditas* with Mexican favorites such as *barbacoa* (a slow-roasted, shredded meat dish, often cow tongue), *cochinita pibil* (tender pork in a red sauce), and *chicharrón* (pork rinds), or staples like beans and cheese. ⊠ *Calle Escobedo Sur 831* ☎ *81/8345–6717.*

★ **$$$$**  ⊞ **Quinta Real.** With its aura of a prosperous hacienda, this hotel just outside the city draws the most important officials and executives. The domed lobby welcomes you with huge bowls of flowers, and classic Mexican crafts. Suites have hand-carved furnishings and thoughtful extras like fluffy robes. The excellent restaurant, serving French and Mexican cuisine, has quite a following. ⊠ *Av. Diego Rivera 500, Fracc. Valle Oriente, 66260 San Pedro Garza García* ☎ *81/8368–1000, 800/457–4000 in the U.S.* 🖷 *81/8368–1091* ⊕ *www.quintareal.com* ⇆ *125 suites* ⚘ *Restaurant, room service, minibars, cable TV, gym, sauna, bar, babysitting, laundry service, concierge, business services, free parking, nosmoking rooms* ▭ *AE, MC, V* ❖ *BP.*

**$$**  ⊞ **Fiesta Americana Centro Monterrey.** This massive pink sandstone structure is impossible to overlook. The striking atrium lobby is always abuzz with travelers. The standard rooms are really two generously sized rooms with fold-out sofas, making them an excellent arrangement for families. Rooms facing the plaza have fabulous views of the surrounding mountains and the city. ⊠ *Privada Corregidora Oriente 519, 64000* ☎ *81/8319–0900, 01800/504–5000 toll free in Mexico* 🖷 *81/8319–0980* ⊕ *www.fiestaamericana.com.mx* ⤶ *189 rooms, 18 suites* ♨ *Restaurant, room service, minibars, cable TV, indoor pool, gym, bar, baby-sitting, laundry service, concierge, business services, parking (fee), no-smoking rooms* ≡ *AE, DC, MC, V.*

★ $$ 🏨 **Radisson Plaza Gran Hotel Ancira.** Legend has it that Pancho Villa was so taken with this elegant place, reminiscent of the grand hotels of Europe, that he settled in and stabled his horse in the lobby. A spiral staircase dominates the expansive art deco lobby; elegant hanging bird cages surround the restaurant. The guest rooms have hand-carved furniture and large marble baths. ⊠ *Ocampo 443, 64000* ☎ *81/8150–7000, 800/830–6000 in the U.S.* 🖷 *81/8344–5226* ⊕ *www.hotel-ancira.com* ⤶ *267 rooms, 26 suites* ♨ *Restaurant, minibars, cable TV, pool, gym, hair salon, sauna, bar, shops, baby-sitting, laundry service, concierge floor, car rental, travel services, free parking, no-smoking rooms* ≡ *AE, D, DC, MC, V.*

¢ 🏨 **Hotel Fundador.** Scalloped awnings mark the facade of the only hotel in the Barrio Antiguo—also one of the best values in Monterrey. Rooms could not be described as luxurious, but they are clean, comfortable, and spacious, and those facing the street have pleasant views of the historic neighborhood. There is an old wing and a newer one—rooms in the latter have more in the way of amenities (microwaves, minibars, etc.). ⊠ *Calle Montemayor 802, at Calle Mariano Matamoros, 64000* ☎ *81/8342–0121* 🖷 *81/8342–1694* ⤶ *65 rooms* ♨ *Restaurant, bar* ≡ *MC, V.*

## Nightlife & the Arts

Charming Barrio Antiguo is lined with live music bars and clubs. One interesting dance club is **Fonda San Miguel** (⊠ Av. Morelos Oriente 924 ☎ 81/8040–9557), where you'll find an eclectic mix of people.

These days, **Kokoloco** (⊠ Padre Mier 318 Poniente ☎ 81/8345–1231) is the rage in Monterrey. The basement room houses a young, alternative crowd, while the larger, airier upstairs blares popular dance music. Arrive before 10:30 or wait in a long line to get in.

**Café Iguana** (⊠ Calle Montemayor 927 Sur ☎ 81/8343–0822) is a funky favorite. Live rock bands Wednesday through Saturday attract a young, alternative crowd. The cover charge varies depending on the band. Stop by the charming **La Casa de Pancho Villa** (⊠ Av. Padre Mier, No. 837 Pte. ☎ 81/8401–9549) for an evening of live music and conversation with friends. To taste 15 flavors of the best margaritas in town, head to the trendy **Nueva Luna** (⊠ Padre Mier 808 Ote. ☎ 81/8344–1217 ⊕ www.nuevaluna.com.mx). Live bands playing everything from pop to salsa to typical Norteño music hit the stage every night starting at around 9. There's a $5 cover charge on Saturday.

★ **Café Infinito** (⊠ Calle Raymundo Jardón 904 ☎ 81/989–5252 ⊕ www. cafeinfinito.com) is the perfect place to start the day with a relaxing pancake breakfast, spend a relaxing afternoon with a book and a cup of cappucino, or pass an intellectual evening over a glass of red wine. Browse the tiny selection of used books in the front or cozy up in one of the tiny lofts overlooking the back room. At **Fuenteovejuna** (⊠ Calle Morelos 1011 at Calle Mina. ☎ 81/8344–4002 ⊕ www.fuenteovejuna.com. mx) you can enjoy live theater, poetry readings, and music and dance performances over dinner or a drink. Call for the current calendar of performances. There's usually a $3–$5 cover charge.

## Shopping

In the heart of Monterrey is **Galerías Monterrey** (⊠ Av. Insurgentes 2500), where you'll find the popular department store Liverpool and dozens of smaller shops. In the center of the wealthy suburb of San Pedro Garza García, lies **Centrito Valle**, a pleasant, walkable area packed with elegant furniture stores, boutiques, and generally expensive shops. **Plaza Fiesta San Agustín** (⊠ Av. Real de San Agustín at Calle Lázaro Cárdenas) is an enormous mall where socialites shop for evening gowns,  precious gems, and imported perfumes. The nicest, cleanest, poshest mall in the Monterrey area is **Valle Oriente** (⊠ Lázaro Cárdenas 1000). The movie theaters here are the nicest in the city, and all movies are in English with Spanish subtitles. Go before 3 PM and it's only $3.

In a building that was once one of the city's grand hotels, **Plaza Mexico** (⊠ Av. Morelos 359) is one of the best places to go for souvenirs. The downtown **Mercado Indio** (⊠ Bolívar Norte 1150) is a sprawling two-floor market, but the selection is overpriced and changes little from stall to stall. You can haggle (gently) with the vendors.

Owner Porfirio Sosa handpicks all the items he sells at the upscale **Carápan** (⊠ Av. Hidalgo Oriente 305 ☎ 81/8345–4422). His array of hard-to-find antiques, hand-loomed rugs, and handblown glassware rivals that of stores anywhere in the country.

# Side Trips from Monterrey

Monterrey is so densely packed that it's hard to believe a short drive from the city will bring you relative solitude. Parque Nacional Cumbres has three extremely beautiful sites: Parque Ecológico Chipinque, the Cañon de la Huasteca, and the Cola del Caballo. The Cañon de la Huasteca is nearly deserted during the week; on weekends it's a popular retreat for Monterrey residents. Best of all, it's only a 20-minute drive from the city. The Cascada Cola de Caballo and Grutas de García are slightly more than an hour away, in opposite directions. El Potrero Chico is a longer endeavor, but for rock climbers it's worth the trip.

## Parque Ecológico Chipinque

This beautiful nature reserve lies at the top of a hill. The drive to the park is an attraction in itself, as you can see the whole city below you. You can get maps of the trails at the park's information center or on their Web site. ⊠ *Gómez Morin, 5 km (3 mi) south of Monterrey Center* ☎ *No phone* ⊕ *www.chipinque.org.mx* 🚗 *Cars $2.50, bikes $2.50, pedestrians $1.50* ⊙ *Daily 6 AM–8 PM.*

### Cañon de la Huasteca

The walls of the 1,000-foot-deep gorge of Huasteca Canyon are spectacularly striated. The trails are various and well maintained, and the stunning peaks—with evocative names like Devil's Tower and Cat's Walk—attract climbing enthusiasts. ⊹ *From Monterrey, 20 km (12 mi) west on Hwy. 40 to Santa Catarina, then 3 km (2 mi) south on a nameless but clearly marked road* 🕾 *No phone* ⊠ *$1 per car* ☉ *Daily 9–6.*

### Cascada Cola de Caballo

A highlight of the Parque Nacional Cumbres de Monterrey, tucked into the Sierra Madre, is a view of Horsetail Falls, a dramatic 75-foot-high waterfall that tumbles down from the pine-forested heights. The waterfall is about 1 km (½ mi) from the park's entrance, up a cobblestone road. You can rent a docile horse or burro for about $3 an hour from the local kids who hang out by the ticket booth, or hop on a horse-drawn carriage for $2. Or, for a guided tour, call Tours Gray Line. ⊹ *From Monterrey, take Hwy. 85 southeast 40 km (25 mi) to falls* 🕾 *81/8369–6472 Tours Gray Line* ⊠ *Free* ☉ *Daily 9–7.*

### Grutas de García

The Garcia Caves are an estimated 50–60 million years old and at one time were submerged by an ocean. Petrified sea animals are visible in some of its walls. From the entrance, you can hike the steep 1 km (½ mi) to the caves or hop on a swaying funicular. Guides lead the way through a strenuous mile of underground grottoes and caverns. Osetur's tours cost $5, which includes the funicular. ⊹ *From Monterrey, Hwy. 40 west for 40 km (25 mi), then 9 km (5mi) north to Km 22* 🕾 *81/ 8347–1599 Osetur* ☉ *Daily 9–5.*

### El Potrero Chico

This series of rugged limestone cliffs has become popular with climbing enthusiasts over the past several years. The cliffs stretch on for miles, threaded with more than 300 routes ranging from moderate to difficult. As the area was once under the ocean, the rocks hold plenty of marine fossils. **Posada El Potrero Chico** (⊠ 825 Potrero Chico, Hidalgo Nuevo Leon 🕾 81/8362–6672 ⊕ www.elpotrerochico.com.mx), a campground in Hidalgo Nuevo Leon, sometimes leads expeditions into the rocks. ⊠ *From Monterrey, 35 min on Hwy. 53 towards Monclova* 🕾 *81/8305–8435* ⊠ *Free.*

## Saltillo

**㉞** *85 km (53 mi) southwest of Monterrey.*

While Monterrey shies away from its past, the colonial capital of Saltillo revels in it—it's the only town in the northeastern corner of the country to retain its colonial character. It's hard to imagine a lovelier square than the sedate **Plaza de Armas,** flanked on one side by the Palacio de Gobierno and the other by an ornate cathedral. A few blocks north is noisy **Plaza Manuel Acuña,** the province of men hawking cowboy hats and boys offering to shine your shoes.

A few blocks uphill from the Plaza de Armas is the **Museo de las Aves,** dedicated to the region's amazing bird population. Hundreds of mounted birds are on display in realistic dioramas. ⊠ *Calle Hidalgo and Calle Bolívar* ☎ *844/414–0167* ☜ *$1* ⊙ *Tues.–Sat. 10–6, Sun. 11–6.*

**El Sarape de Saltillo** is a favorite place for buying the intricate woven sarapes typical of the area. ⊠ *Av. Higaldo Sur 305* ☎ *844/412–4889* ⊙ *Closed Sun.*

☺ On a hill in the outskirts of Saltillo, **Parque Las Maravillas** allows a closer
**Fodor'sChoice** look at the city's desert ecosystem. Within the park grounds is the ex-
★ cellent **Museo Del Desierto.** The museum's four interactive pavilions explore the desert and its relationship to man and mammals, as well as the ecosystems of the Chihuauan desert. ⊠ *Prolongación Pérez Treviño 3745* ☎ *844/410–6633* ⊕ *www.museodelsierto.net* ☜ *$2 park, $5 museum* ⊙ *Tues.–Sun. 10–6.*

### Where to Stay & Eat

**$–$$** ✕ **Carlos 'N Charlie's.** The eager-to-please staff make you feel at home in this fun dining room, which recreates a Mexican market—the ceiling is entirely covered with baskets. Each meal opens with a complementary cup of shrimp-flavored broth; turn the tiny traffic light on the table from red to green when you are ready to order. Try the *molcajete de pollo*—chicken, sausage, and queso asadero (cheese browned on the grill). ⊠ *Blvd. Venustiano Carranza 3070* ☎ *844/416–6428* ☐ *MC, V.*

**$–$$** ✕ **El Principal.** Kid roasting over a charcoal grill fills the front window of this rustic restaurant. If you're bold, start off with the kidneys, which locals swear are the best part. There are also plenty of steaks on the menu if you aren't in the mood for cabrito. On Friday, entrées are two for the price of one. ⊠ *Calle Allende 702* ☎ *844/414–3384* ☐ *AE, MC, V.*

**¢** ⬚ **Hotel Urdiñola.** The cheerful yellow facade of this colonial-era charmer beckons travelers. Those who answer the call get convenience (it's just a block away from the main plaza) and value. A gleaming marble staircase stretches up from the lobby. The rooms are spare, but spacious; ask for one in the back, as they're quieter. ⊠ *Calle Victoria 211, 25000* ☎ *844/ 414–0940* ⬚ *844/412–9380* ↩ *55 rooms* ⬚ *Restaurant, room service, fans, bar, laundry service; no a/c* ☐ *MC, V.*

## Tampico

**㉟** *504 km (312 mi) south of Matamoros, 583 km (361 mi) southeast of Monterrey.*

Foreigners seem to be drawn to this port on the Gulf of Mexico. In 1828 the Spanish attempted to reconquer their former colony by landing troops here, but were soundly defeated. After later incursions by the Americans and then the French, the port was ignored until oil was discovered in the region in 1901. The Americans returned, this time with the British, to reap the profits.

Although the city focuses on business and industry, Tampico can also be a pleasure. In the center of town, wrought-iron balconies recall New Orleans. **Plaza de la Libertad,** a stone's throw from the harbor, is surrounded by old colonial-era buildings. A block from laid-back Plaza de la Libertad is the regal **Plaza de Armas,** surrounded by towering palms. On its northern edge stands the cathedral. Begun in 1823, the elegant structure was finally completed with funds from U.S. oil magnate Edward L. Doheny, implicated in the Teapot Dome scandal of the 1920s.

The area near the docks, just south of the Plaza de la Libertad, is also a good place to explore by day. Stroll through the daily market, where you can purchase candles that bring bad luck to your enemies. Steer clear of this area at night, though, as it gets pretty rough.

In the new **Espacio Cultural Metropolitano (Metro)** you'll find a tiny gallery of temporary exhibits, and the thoughtful **Museo de la Cultura Huasteca,** with displays on all aspects of Huastecan culture. Unfortunately, bureaucratic red tape and squabbling between municipalities has as yet prevented the transfer of the oldest and finest artifacts from the old Huastecan culture museum in neighboring Ciudad Madero. Still, the interactive exhibits are worth the trip. ⊠ *López Mateos, on Laguna del Carpintero* ☎ *833/126–0732* 🖾 *$3* ☉ *Tues.–Sun. 10–6.*

## Where to Stay & Eat

**$–$$** ✕ **El Consuelo.** "Full stomach, happy heart" is the motto at this tiny cantina-restaurant, which is stuffed to the brim on weekends with a well-dressed, twenty-something crowd. Glowing metal stars hang from the ceiling, and pictures of famous Mexican actors cover the walls. The *arrachera borrachera* (beef marinated in beer) will put you well on your way to a happy heart. ⊠ *Avenida Hidalgo 1615* ☎ *833/213–1032* ▤ *D, DC, MC, V.*

**$–$$** ✕ **La Troya.** For unbeatable views of Plaza de la Libertad, nab one of the tables on the balcony of this longtime favorite. Many of the exceedingly rich meat and seafood dishes, such as the delicious paella, tip their hat to Spain. The signature dish is the tasty *carne asada tampiqueña* (steak marinated in garlic and spices). ⊠ *Calle Madero Oriente 218, at Av. Juárez, El Centro* ☎ *833/214–1155* ▤ *AE, MC, V.*

**¢** ✕ **Café y Nevería Elite.** This popular gathering spot not far from the Plaza de Armas serves up delicious coffee and ice-cream. For lunch and dinner there is plenty of low-priced local fare. Don't be put off by the noise and the rather worn tables. ⊠ *Av. Díaz Mirón Oriente 211* ☎ *833/212–0364* ▤ *MC, V.*

**$$$** ▦ **Camino Real.** This classy resort about 20 minutes from the city center is the best lodging you'll find in Tampico. Its rooms surround a huge garden overflowing with tropical trees and flowers. Fishing excursions can be booked through the on-site travel agency. ⊠ *Av. Hidalgo 2000, Col. Smith, 89140* ☎ *833/229–3535, 800/570–0000 in U.S.* 🖷 *833/229–3540* ⊕ *www.caminorealtampico.com* 🗗 *100 rooms, 3 suites* 🖒 *Restaurant, room service, minibars, cable TV, tennis court, pool, bar, playground, laundry service, car rental, travel services* ▤ *AE, DC, MC, V.*

**$$** ▦ **Club Maeva.** This big, yellow building right across from Miramar Beach is perfect for those seeking both action and relaxation. During the day, you can take it easy with a drink by the pool. After dark, catch the nightly live show and then head to the popular tropical-theme dance club. The only drawback is the complex's proximity to the Pemex refinery; depending on where you are in the hotel, you may be able to see—or smell—it. ⊠ *Boulevard Costero, s/n Playa Miramar, Ciudad Madero 89540* ☎ *833/230–0202* 🖷 *833/230–0202* ⊕ *www.maevamiramar.com.mx*

↩ *192 rooms* ♦ *Restaurant, room service, tennis courts, pool, wading pool, gym, soccer, volleyball, bar, nightclub, theater, shops, babysitting, meeting rooms, car rental* ⊟ *AE, MC, V* ⍟ *EP.*

¢ ▦ **Posada del Rey.** The posada is in one of the city's oldest buildings, whose art nouveau facade fronts the Plaza de la Libertad. Ask for one of the rooms overlooking the square, as others in the back are a bit shabby. The rooms are dimly lit, but the effect is cozy and quite charming. ✉ *Calle Madero Oriente 218, El Centro 89000* ☎ *833/214–1155* 🖷 *833/212–1077* ↩ *40 rooms* ♦ *Restaurant, bar* ⊟ *AE, MC, V.*

### Sports & the Outdoors

FISHING  Although the Río Pánuco has become too polluted for fishing, those in search of tarpon and snapper can head to **Laguna del Chairel,** in the northern part of the city, where's you'll find boats loaded with all the gear you'll need. Hotels can arrange for excursions.

# THE NORTHEAST A TO Z

### AIR TRAVEL

AIRPORTS  Monterrey has the region's only international airport, Aeropuerto Internacional Mariano Escobedo (MTY), which is 6 km (4 mi) northeast of downtown.

Should you need to fly into Tampico's Aeropuerto General Francisco Javier Mina (TAM), there are very expensive domestic flights available. The airport is about 15 km (9 mi) north of town.

🛈 **Aeropuerto General Francisco Javier Mina** ☎ 833/228-0571. **Aeropuerto Internacional Mariano Escobedo** ☎ 81/8369-0753.

AIRPORT  The only way to get between Monterrey and the airport is by taxi, which
TRANSFERS  will cost about $20.

CARRIERS  From the United States, Continental flies to Monterrey from Chicago, Las Vegas, Los Angeles, Miami, and New York, via Houston. American has six flights a day to Monterrey from Dallas. Aerolitoral has service to Monterrey from McAllen and San Antonio, Texas. Mexicana has flights from Chicago, Denver, Los Angeles, New York, San Antonio, and San Francisco to Monterrey, via Mexico City. Aeroméxico has direct service to Monterrey from Houston and Los Angeles and flights from New York via Mexico City.

From Mexico City, Aeroméxico has service to Matamoros, Tampico, and Reynosa. Mexicana flies to Nuevo Laredo and Tampico, while Aerolitoral has nonstop flights to Tampico.

🛈 **Aerolitoral** ☎ 81/8221-1600 in Monterrey, 833/228-4197, 833/228-0857 in Tampico ⊕ www.aerolitoral.com. **Aeroméxico** ☎ 868/812-2460 in Matamoros, 81/8343-5560 in Monterrey, 833/213-9600 in Tampico, 800/021-4050 elsewhere in Mexico, 800/237-6639 in the U.S. ⊕ www.aeromexico.com. **American** ☎ 81/8363-8380 in Monterrey ⊕ www.aa.com. **Continental** ☎ 81/8369-0838 in Monterrey ⊕ www.continental.com. **Mexicana** ☎ 81/8124-2500 in Monterrey, 833/213-9600 in Tampico, 800/502-2000 in Mexico, 800/531-7921 in the U.S. ⊕ www.mexicana.com.mx.

### BUS TRAVEL TO & FROM THE NORTHEAST

Northeastern Mexico is easy to reach by bus. Greyhound runs several buses a day to the border from San Antonio, Dallas, and Houston. At the border towns of Laredo, McAllen, and Brownsville, buses operated by Transportes del Norte will whisk you down to Monterrey. The trip from the border takes about three hours.

🚌 **Greyhound** ☎ 402/330-8552, 800/229-9424 in the U.S. ⊕ www.greyhound.com. **Transportes del Norte** ☎ 956/686-5479 in McAllen, 956/546-7171 in Brownsville, 81/8318-3738 in Monterrey.

### BUS TRAVEL WITHIN THE NORTHEAST

Monterrey's busy terminal, called the Central de Autobuses, is the hub of bus transportation in the northeast. Transportes del Norte buses cover the region quite thoroughly, with frequent service between Monterrey and all the cities in the region. Omnibus de México sends one bus a day between Monterrey and Tampico and Monterrey and Nuevo Laredo; it also offers frequent daily service to Reynosa.

🚌 Bus Depot **Central de Autobuses** ✉ Av. Colón at Amado Nervo, Monterrey ☎ 81/8374-1648.

🚌 Bus Companies **Omnibus de México** ☎ 81/8375-7121 in Monterrey. **Transportes del Norte** ☎ 81/8318-3738 in Monterrey.

### CAR TRAVEL

Crossing the border in a car is not without its red tape. Many rental companies won't allow you to take their cars across the border, so be sure to inquire in advance. If you plan on taking your own car, remember that your insurance won't cover you south of the border. You must purchase insurance from a Mexican company. Sanborn's Mexican Insurance can help you complete the paperwork before you leave.

If you're making a day trip to a border town, consider leaving your car in the United States. Walking over eliminates the long wait—often a half hour or more—to bring a car back into the country.

When planning your trip, keep in mind that it can take more time than you might expect to drive through this part of Mexico because of the meandering roads through the Sierra Madre Oriente. It generally takes three hours to drive from the border to Monterrey.

Downtown Nuevo Laredo is reached via International Bridge 1, which drops you right into busy Avenida Guerrero. International Bridge 2, just to the east, is favored by those bypassing the city for points south. From Nuevo Laredo, the road splits between the slow Mexico 85 Libre and the speedy Mexico 85 Cuota. Both lead to Monterrey. The latter is better maintained, but costs about $15 in tolls.

From Reynosa, a $15 toll gets you onto Mexico 40, which leads south. The highway, although rather monotonous, is the most convenient route to Monterrey. From Matamoros, Mexico 180 runs down the Gulf coast to Tampico, Veracruz, and beyond. If you're headed to Monterrey, Mexico 2 connects with Reynosa.

Tampico is roughly a seven-hour drive from Matamoros on Mexico 180, or eight hours from Monterrey via Mexico 85. Saltillo is an hour and a half from Monterrey on Mexico 40.

🚩 **Bravo Insurance** ✉ 2212 Santa Ursula St., Laredo, TX 78040 ☎ 956/723-3657 🖷 956/723-0000 ⊕ www.bravoinsurance.biz. **Sanborn's Mexican Insurance** ✉ 2009 S. 10th St., McAllen, TX 78503 ☎ 800/222-0158 in the U.S. 🖷 956/686-0732 ⊕ www.sanbornsinsurance.com.

## EMBASSIES & CONSULATES

🚩 **Canadian Consulate** ✉ Calle Zaragoza 1300 Sur, Edificio Kalos, Monterrey ☎ 81/8344-3200 🖷 81/8344-3048 ⊕ www.canada.org.mx/consular/english/monterrey.asp. **U.S. Consulate** ✉ Calle Primero 2002, Matamoros ☎ 868/812-4402 ✉ Av. Constitución Poniente 411, Monterrey ☎ 81/8343-7124 🖷 81/8343-9399 ⊕ www.usembassymexico.gov/monterrey/monterrey.html ✉ Allende 3330, Nuevo Laredo ☎ 867/714-0512 ✉ Calle Monterrey 390, at Sinaloa, Reynosa ☎ 899/923-9331

## EMERGENCIES

Dial **066** for medical, fire, and other emergencies.

Many pharmacies stay open until 9 or 10 PM. Fenix and Benavides are among the better-known chains. If you must reach a hospital, call the local Cruz Roja, or Red Cross, for ambulance service.

🚩 Ambulances **Monterrey Cruz Roja** ✉ Av. Alfonso Reyes 2503, Monterrey ☎ 81/8375-1212. **Nuevo Laredo Cruz Roja** ✉ Independencia 1619 at San Antonio, Nuevo Laredo ☎ 867/712-0949 or 867/712-0989. **Reynosa Cruz Roja** ☎ 899/922-1314 or 899/922-6250. **Saltillo Cruz Roja** ☎ 844/412-1206. **Tampico Cruz Roja** ☎ 833/212-1333.

🚩 Hospitals **Hospital Murguerza** ✉ Av. Hidalgo 2525 Poniente, Monterrey ☎ 81/8399-3400. **Hospital Nueva Esperanza** ✉ Calle Veracruz 542, Reynosa ☎ 899/922-7710. **Matamoros Cruz Roja Hospital** ✉ García and L. Caballero, Matamoros ☎ 868/812-0044. **Tampico Cruz Roja Hospital** ✉ Tamaulipas and Colegio Militar, El Centro, Tampico ☎ 833/212-1333.

🚩 Police **Matamoros Police** ✉ Pedro Cárdenas, between Longoria and Mexicali, Matamoros ☎ 868/817-2205. **Monterrey Police** ✉ Calle Ocampo 502 Pte., Monterrey ☎ 81/8343-2576. **Nuevo Laredo Police** ✉ Blvd. Camacho and Carretera Anauac, Nuevo Laredo ☎ 867/711-3930. **Reynosa Police** ✉ Morelos between Veracruz and Nayarit ☎ 899/922-0008 or 899/22-0790. **Saltillo Police** ✉ Carretera a Torreón, Km 2.5 ☎ 844/434-0810. **Tampico Police** ✉ Calle Doctor del Alorcón, Tampico ☎ 833/214-3249.

🚩 Pharmacies **Farmacia Benavides** ✉ Av. Morelos 499, at Escobedo, Monterrey ☎ 81/8345-0257. **Farmacia Calderón** ✉ Guerrero 704, Nuevo Laredo ☎ 867/712-5177. **Farmacia Droguería del Pueblo** ✉ Av. Juárez Sur 308, Tampico ☎ 833/212-1542. **Farmacia El Fenix** ✉ Calle Abasolo 806, Matamoros ☎ 868/812-2909.

## MONEY MATTERS

In the border towns, businesses generally accept U.S. dollars; if you're going beyond the border area you'll need to use pesos. Twenty-four-hour ATMs are plentiful all around northeastern Mexico, so getting cash is no problem. Most machines accept bank cards on both the Cirrus and Plus systems. If you need to exchange currency or cash traveler's checks, banks are generally open weekdays 9–2.

In Monterrey, the banks in the downtown area are generally open weekdays 9–3. If you need cash at other times, Eurodivisas is open Monday–Saturday from 10–8 and Sunday from 11–8.

There are plenty of banks in downtown Matamoros, mostly around Plaza Hidalgo. Banorte branches in Nuevo Laredo, Matamoros, and Reynosa are open weekdays 9–3 and can change dollars to pesos and vice versa. Banorte in Saltillo changes money weekdays 9–4 and Saturday 10–2. Banamex on Calle Madero in Tampico is open 9–3.

🚩 **Banamex** ✉ Calle Madero Oriente 403, Tampico ☎ 833/214–0231. **Banorte** ✉ Hidalgo and Morelos, Reynosa ☎ 899/922–4690 ✉ Sexta and Morelos, Matamoros ☎ 868/813–3483 ✉ Arteaga 3720, Nuevo Laredo ☎ 867/712–0477 ✉ Allende 561, Saltillo ☎ 844/414–7829. **Eurodivisas** ✉ Av. Morelos Oriente 359, Monterrey ☎ 81/8340–1683.

## TAXIS

Taxis are pretty scarce and expensive in border towns but plentiful and moderately priced in Monterrey. Hailing a cab is generally considered safe, but for added security you can call a reliable company such as Metro Taxi. In Saltillo, try Radio Taxi for on-call service. Tampico relies on Eco Taxis.

🚩 **Eco Taxis Paraíso** ☎ 844/217–3939. **Metro Taxi** ☎ 81/8342–2069. **Radio Taxi** ☎ 844/412–6760.

## TOURS

Well-regarded agencies include Tours Gray Line and Osetur Tours. Osetur goes to las Grutas de García and Tours Gray Line can show you around the Grutas, the Cola del Caballo, and other destinations around Nuevo León. The staff of these companies speak English.

🚩 **Osetur Tours** ✉ Privada Liendo 703, Colonia Obispado, Monterrey ☎ 81/8347–1599 or 81/8347–1614. **Tours Gray Line** ✉ Cintermex, Avenida Fundidora 501, Office 29, Monterrey ☎ 81/8369–6472 or 81/8369–6473.

## VISITOR INFORMATION

The best sources of information about northeastern Mexico are the Texan border towns' chambers of commerce. You can stop by the offices, open weekdays during business hours.

Not every Mexican town has tourism information handy. Monterrey's tourism office is the best of the bunch; it's open weekdays 8:30–6:30. The staff bends over backwards to help. Or, call the extremely useful and convenient INFORMATEL at 81/8340–0707 or 81/8340–0070.

The lackluster office in Nuevo Laredo, in the Palacio Municipal, is open weekdays 8–8, and Saturday 10–1. The minuscule Tampico office is tucked away in an easy-to-miss module in the Plaza de Armas.

🚩 North of the Border **Brownsville Chamber of Commerce** ✉ 1600 E. Elizabeth St., Brownsville, TX 78520 ☎ 956/542–4341 ⊕ www.brownsvillechamber.com. **Laredo Chamber of Commerce** ✉ 2310 San Bernardo, Laredo, TX 78040 ☎ 956/722–9895 ⊕ www.laredochamber.com. **McAllen Chamber of Commerce** ✉ 1200 Ash St., McAllen, TX 78501 ☎ 956/682–2871 ⊕ www.mcallen.org.

🚩 South of the Border **Monterrey** ✉ Calle Washington 539 Oriente, Amway Building ☎ 81/8041–0106. **Nuevo Laredo** ✉ Galeana, between Mier and González ☎ 867/712–7397 ⊕ www.nuevolaredo.gob.mx. **Tampico** ✉ Plaza de Armas ☎ 833/219–3130.

# THE YUCATÁN PENINSULA

**THERE'S A LONG LIST OF REASONS WHY** the Yucatán Peninsula is a perennial favorite destination: the high-profile sparkle of Cancún; the laid-
back beachcombing of Isla Mujeres; the spectacular seas around Cozumel;
the fascinating Spanish-Maya mix of Mérida; and the evocative Maya
ruins of Tulum, Chichén Itzá, and Uxmal.

Cancún, Mexico's most popular resort area, owes its success to a location on the east coast, which is washed by exquisitely colored Caribbean
waters, lined by unbroken stretches of beach, and blessed with a semitropical climate. The region is also home to the world's second-largest barrier reef, which starts off the coast of the Yucatán Peninsula and runs
all the way to South America.

Cancún incarnates the success formula for sun-and-sand travel: luxury hotels, sandy beaches, hot nightclubs, fine restaurants—not to
mention proximity to compelling Maya ruins. Cozumel's hotels may
not be as showy as those in Cancún, but they're still beloved of scuba
divers. On relaxed Isla Mujeres (*ees*-lah moo-*hair*-ayce; Island of the
Women), you're likely to stay in a rustic bungalow with ceiling fans
and hammocks.

There are also the cities of the Yucatán. Foremost among them is Mérida,
whose well-preserved examples of Moorish-inspired colonial architecture make it seem unaltered by time. In this city, café life is still an art,
and the Maya still follow the customs of their ancestors.

Wildlife is another of the Yucatán's riches. Iguanas, lizards, tapirs, deer,
armadillos, and wild boars thrive on this alternately parched and densely
foliated peninsula. Flamingos and herons, manatees and sea turtles—
they all find idyllic watery habitats in and above the coastline's mangrove swamps, lagoons, and sandbars, acres of which have been made
into national parks.

But perhaps it is the myriad colors that are the peninsula's most remarkable features. From the stark, white, sun-bleached sand, the sea
stretches out like some immense canvas painted in bands of celadon
greens, pale aquas, and deep blues. At dusk the sea and the horizon
meld in the glow of a lavender sunset, the sky just barely tinged with
periwinkle and violet.

Inland, the beige, gray, and amber stones of ruined temples are set off
by riotous greenery. The colors of newer structures are equally intox-
icating: tawny, gray-brown thatched roofs sit atop white oval huts. Colonial mansions favor creamy pastels of bisque, salmon, and
coral—highlighted by elegant white arches, white balustrades, and
white porticos.

Brilliant colors glimmer in carved hardwood doors, variegated tile
floors, brown and green pottery, and rugs affixed to walls. Orchids,
bougainvillea, and poinciana are ubiquitous; dazzling reds and pinks and
oranges and whites rush down the sides of countless buildings and into
countless courtyards. The Yucatán is a treat for all the senses and a place
to both relax and re-energize.

*Numbers in the text correspond to numbers in the margin and on the Cancún, Isla Mujeres, Cozumel, Riviera Maya, State of Yucatán, and Mérida maps.*

**If you have**
# 3 days

Base yourself on the Caribbean coast, at ▦ **Playa del Carmen** ⑱ ►, and relax on the white-sand beach or go diving in nearby reefs. On Day 2, visit the ruins of the Maya city of **Tulum** ⑳ and then climb down to the small beach alongside it for a dip. On Day 3, head for **Akumal** ⑲ for diving, deep-sea fishing, snorkeling, or swimming. Later in the day visit the tiny lagoon of Yalkú.

Alternatively, you could spend two days in ▦ **Mérida** ㉓–㉟ ►, savoring the city's unique character as you make your way among its historic structures. You can easily devote a day to exploring the heart of downtown, including the *zócalo* (main square) and its surroundings. Take a second, more leisurely day to visit the Museo de Antropología y Historia in the Palacio Cantón and, perhaps, the Museo de Arte Contemporáneo. On Day 3, drive or take a tour to one of Yucatán's most famous Maya ruins—**Chichén Itzá** ㊱ or **Uxmal** ㊲. Each is within about two hours of Mérida.

**If you have**
# 7 days

Base yourself at ▦ **Playa del Carmen** ⑱ ►, spending Day 1 on the beach and Day 2 visiting **Tulum** ⑳. On Day 3, tour the Maya ruins of **Cobá** ㉑. Head for **Akumal** ⑲ and its water sports on Day 4. The next day, sign up for a tour of the **Sian Ka'an Biosphere Reserve** ㉒. On Days 6 and 7, head west to the colonial city of ▦ **Mérida** ㉓–㉟. Spend one day in town and the next out at **Chichén Itzá** ㊱ or **Uxmal** ㊲.

On a weeklong trip in and around Mérida, take in the city's sights first and then take two separate overnight excursions. First, head for **Uxmal** ㊲ and overnight at one of the nearby hotels. The next day explore the Ruta Puuc, the series of lost cities south of Uxmal that includes Kabah, Sayil, and Labná, as well as the fascinating Loltún Caves. On the second excursion, to **Chichén Itzá** ㊱, allow as much as a full day so that you can also explore some of the present-day Maya villages along the way.

## Exploring the Yucatán Peninsula

In its entirety, the 113,000-square-km (43,600-square-mi) peninsula encompasses the Mexican states of Yucatán, Campeche, and Quintana Roo, as well as Belize and part of Guatemala. Its north and west sides are lapped by the waters of the Gulf of Mexico; the Caribbean Sea edges it to the east. Within its bounds are tremendous bird-watching, water sports, archaeology, handicrafts, and savory Yucatecan cuisine. Above all, there are the friendly and open Yucatecos themselves.

International airports at Cancún and Cozumel provide nonstop service from several North American cities. The Mérida airport handles primarily domestic flights. Cruise ships call at Cozumel and Calica, south of Playa del Carmen.

## About the Restaurants

In the early days, Yucatecan cuisine was tremendously influenced by French, Cuban, and New Orleans cooking because of continual cultural contact. This multicultural approach resulted in such specialties as *pollo pibíl* (chicken marinated in a sour orange and annatto seed sauce and baked in banana leaves); *poc chuc* (pork marinated in a sour-orange sauce with pickled onions); *tikinchic* (fish marinated in a sour-orange sauce and achiote paste, wrapped in banana leaves, and cooked over an open flame); *panuchos* (fried tortillas filled with black beans and topped with diced turkey, chicken, or pork as well as pickled onions and avocado); *papadzules* (tortillas rolled up with hard-boiled eggs and drenched in a sauce of pumpkin seed and fried tomato); and *codzitos* (rolled tortillas in pumpkin-seed sauce). *Achiote* (annatto seed), cilantro (coriander), and the fiery *chili habañero* are zesty condiments. Along the gulf coast, there's nothing finer than a dish of fresh blue crab, or baby shrimp.

*El desayuno* can be either a breakfast sweet roll and coffee or milk or a full breakfast of an egg dish such as *huevos a la mexicana* (scrambled eggs with chopped tomato, onion, and chilies) or *huevos rancheros* (fried eggs on a tortilla covered with tomato sauce) plus juice and tortillas. Lunch is called *la comida* or *el almuerzo* and is the biggest meal of the day. Traditional businesses close down between 2 PM and 4 PM for this meal. It usually includes soup, a main dish, and dessert. The lighter evening meal is called *la cena*.

## About the Hotels

In Cancún, Cozumel, and Isla Mujeres luxurious international chains have the latest room amenities and lots of restaurants, bars, boutiques, and sports facilities. These beach resort areas also have more-modest accommodations—usually a short walk or a shuttle ride from the water. In the Yucatán's less-populated and -visited areas, accommodations tend to be simpler and more typically Mexican: inexpensive bungalows, campsites, and beachside places to hang a hammock. With the broad range of accommodations comes an equally broad range of travelers: package-tour groups, backpackers, people touring in rental cars.

| WHAT IT COSTS | | | | |
|---|---|---|---|---|
| **$$$$** | **$$$** | **$$** | **$** | **¢** |
| RESTAURANTS over $25 | $15–$25 | $10–$15 | $5–$10 | under $5 |
| HOTELS over $250 | $150–$250 | $75–$150 | $50–$75 | under $50 |

Restaurant prices are for a main course excluding tax and tip. Hotel prices are for two people in a standard double room in high season, based on the European Plan (EP, with no meals) and excluding service and 17% tax.

## Timing

High season in the State of Yucatán consists of Christmastime, Easter week, and July and August. Rainfall is heaviest and humidity most uncomfortable from May to October or November. In Cancún, Cozumel, and Isla Mujeres, the peak tourist times are mid-December through late March and again in August. In less visited towns, levels of service dif-

## Archaeological Sites

The ancient Maya left an incredible mark in the Yucatán. Pick your period and your preference, whether it's for well-excavated sites or overgrown, out-of-the-way ruins barely touched by a scientist's shovel. The major Maya sites are Cobá, Tulum, Chichén Itzá and Uxmal, but smaller sites scattered throughout the peninsula are often equally fascinating.

## Beaches

Along the Caribbean coast, the sands are white, the bays are generally curvaceous, and the coves are often rocky. Playa Chacmool and Playa Tortugas are on the bay side of Cancún, which is calmer if less beautiful than the windward side. Playa Norte on Isla Mujeres is known for its great sunsets. Beaches on Cozumel's east coast—once used by buccaneers—are private but rocky, and the waters off them are treacherous; for wide, sandy beaches, head to the relatively sheltered leeward side. There are also long, crowded stretches of white sand at Puerto Morelos, Akumal, and Playa del Carmen.

## Bird-Watching

Habitats range from wildlife and bird sanctuaries to unmarked lagoons, estuaries, and mangrove swamps. Frigates, tanagers, warblers, and herons inhabit Isla Contoy (off Isla Mujeres) and the Laguna Colombia on Cozumel; there's an even greater variety of species in the Sian Ka'an Biosphere Reserve on the Boca Paila Peninsula south of Tulum. Along the north and west coasts—at Río Lagartos, Laguna Rosada, and Celestún—flamingos, herons, ibis, cormorants, pelicans, and peregrine falcons thrive.

## Fishing

The waters of both the Caribbean and the Gulf of Mexico support hundreds of species of game fish, making them paradise for deep-sea fishing, fly-fishing, and bonefishing. Between April and July in particular, the waters off Cancún, Cozumel, and Isla Mujeres teem with sailfish, marlin, red snapper, tuna, barracuda, wahoo, and other denizens of the deep. Bill fishing is so rich around Cozumel that it's the site of an annual tournament. Farther south, along the Boca Paila peninsula, bonefishing is a hands-down favorite, as is light-tackle saltwater fishing for shad and sea bass. On the north coast, sportfishing for grouper, dogfish, and pompano is quite popular.

## Scuba Diving

Underwater enthusiasts come to Cozumel, Akumal, and other parts of the Caribbean coast for the clear turquoise waters, the colorful and assorted tropical fish, and the exquisite coral formations along the Palancar Reef system. Currents allow for drift diving, and both reefs and offshore wrecks lend themselves to dives, many of which are safe enough for neophytes. The waters off the peninsula also have cenotes, or natural sinkholes, and underwater caverns.

fer drastically between the high and low seasons (when staff and activities may be cut back), so be prepared for the trade-off. The rainy season isn't a bad time to visit if you don't mind the afternoon showers and the sometimes reduced attentions. On the coast, hurricane season is usually September to October, though storms can blow through anytime from July to November.

Thousands of people swarm to Chichén Itzá for the vernal equinox on the first day of spring to see the astronomical phenomenon that makes a shadow resembling a snake—which represented the plumed serpent god Kukulcán—appear on the side of the main pyramid. The phenomenon also occurs on the first day of fall, but autumnal rains tend to discourage visitors.

# CANCÚN

Updated by
Shelagh
McNally

Flying into Cancún, you see nothing but green treetops for miles. It's clear from the air that this resort was literally carved out of the jungle. When development began in the early 1970s, the beaches were deserted except for birds and iguanas. Now luxury hotels, malls, and restaurants line the oceanfront. More vacationers come here than to any other part of Mexico, and many come again and again.

Not much was written about Cancún before its birth as a resort. The Maya people settled the area during the Late Preclassic era, around AD 200, and remained until the 14th or 15th century, but little is known about them. Other explorers seem to have overlooked it—it doesn't appear on early navigators' maps. It was never heavily populated, perhaps because its terrain of mangroves and marshes (and resulting swarms of mosquitoes) discouraged settlement. Some minor Maya ruins were discovered in the mid-19th century, but archaeologists didn't get around to studying them until the 1950s.

In 1967, the Mexican government, under the leadership of Luis Echeverría, commissioned a study to pinpoint the ideal place for an international Caribbean resort. The computer chose Cancún, and the Cinderella transformation began. At the time, the area's only residents were the three caretakers of a coconut plantation. In 1972 work began on the first hotel, and the island and city grew from there.

Today's Cancún has two different sides. On the mainland is the actual Ciudad Cancún (Cancún City). Its commercial center, known as El Centro, offers an authentic glimpse into the sights and sounds of Mexico. The other half, the Zona Hotelera (Hotel Zone), is the tourist heart. It's actually a 22½-km (14-mi) barrier island off the Yucatán Peninsula. A separate northern strip called Punta Sam, north of Puerto Juárez (where some ferries to Isla Mujeres depart), is sometimes referred to as the Zona Hotelera Norte (Northern Hotel Zone).

During the day you can shop, eat, and lounge in the year-round tropical warmth: the sun shines an average of 240 days a year, and temperatures linger at about 27°C (80°F). The reefs off Cancún and nearby Cozumel, Puerto Morelos, and Isla Mujeres are great places to dive, and

Cancún also makes a relaxing base for visiting the ruins of Chichén Itzá, Tulum, and Cobá. At night you can sample Yucatecan food and watch folkloric dance performances, knock back tequila slammers, or listen to great jazz.

Cancún's success hasn't come without a price. Its lagoons and mangrove swamps have been polluted; a number of species, such as conch and lobster, are dwindling; and parts of the coral reef are dead. And although the beaches still appear pristine for the most part, an increased effort will have to be made to preserve the beauty that is the resort's prime appeal.

## Exploring Cancún

The Zona Hotelera is a small island shaped roughly like the numeral 7. The top extends east from the mainland into the Caribbean; the Punta Cancún–Punta Nizuc strip has a slight north–northeast arc. Hotel development began at the north end (close to the mainland), headed east toward Punta Cancún, and then moved south to Punta Nizuc. At the south end of the Zona Hotelera, the road curves west toward the highway and airport. Downtown Cancún—El Centro—is 4 km (2½ mi) west of the Zona Hotelera on the mainland.

Cancún's scenery consists mostly of beautiful beaches and crystal-clear waters, but there are also a few intriguing historical sites tucked away among the modern hotels. In addition to the attractions listed below, two modest vestiges of the ancient Maya civilization are worth a visit, but only for dedicated archaeology buffs. Neither is identified by name. On the 12th hole of Pok-Ta-Pok golf course (Boulevard Kukulcán, Km 6.5)—the name means "ball game" in Maya—stands a ruin consisting of two platforms and the remains of other ancient buildings. And the ruin of a tiny Maya shrine is cleverly incorporated into the architecture of the Hotel Camino Real, on the beach at Punta Cancún.

You don't need a car in Cancún, but if you've rented one to make extended trips, start in the Zona Hotelera at **Ruinas del Rey ❶ ☞**. Drive north to **Yamil Lu'um ❷**, and then stop in at the **Cancún Convention Center ❸**, with its anthropology and history museum, before heading farther north to the **Museo de Arte Popular ❹**, in El Embarcadero marina, and finally turning west to reach **El Centro ❺**.

### What to See

**❸ Cancún Convention Center.** This strikingly modern venue for cultural events is the jumping-off point for a 1-km (½-mi) string of shopping malls that extends west to the Presidente InterContinental Cancún. The **Instituto Nacional de Antropología y Historia** (National Institute of Anthropology and History; ☎ 998/883–0305), a small, ground-floor museum, traces Maya culture with a fascinating collection of 1,000- to 1,500-year-old artifacts from throughout Quintana Roo. Admission to the museum is about $3; it's open Tuesday–Sunday 9–7. Guided tours are available in English, French, German, and Spanish. ✉ *Blvd. Kukulcán, Km 9, Zona Hotelera* ☎ *998/883–0305.*

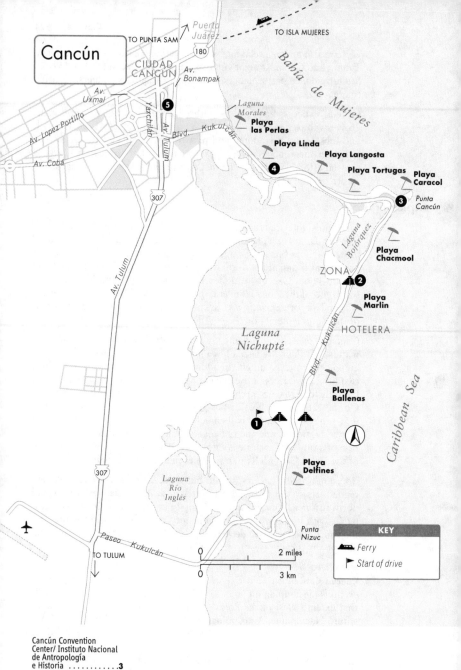

# Cancún

TO PUNTA SAM

Puerto Juárez

TO ISLA MUJERES

180

CIUDAD CANCÚN

Av. Bonampak

*Bahía de Mujeres*

Av. Uxmal

Yaxchilán

Av. Tulum

Av. López Portillo

Blvd. Kukulcán

**5**

Av. Cobá

*Laguna Morales*

**Playa las Perlas**

**Playa Linda**

307

**4**

**Playa Langosta**

**Playa Tortugas**

**Playa Caracol**

**3**

Punta Cancún

*Laguna Bojórquez*

**Playa Chacmool**

ZONA

**2**

**Playa Marlin**

HOTELERA

*Laguna Nichupté*

Blvd. Kukulcán

*Caribbean Sea*

**Playa Ballenas**

Av. Tulum

307

**1**

**Playa Delfines**

*Laguna Río Inglés*

Punta Nizuc

Paseo Kukulcán

TO TULUM

| KEY |
| --- |
| ⛴ Ferry |
| ⚑ Start of drive |

0 ——— 2 miles

0 ——— 3 km

**❺ El Centro.** The downtown area is a combination of markets and malls that offer a glimpse of Mexico's emerging urban lifestyle. Avenida Tulum, the main street, is marked by a huge sculpture of shells and starfish in the middle of a traffic circle. The sculpture, one of Cancún's icons, is particularly dramatic at night when the lights are turned on. It's also home to many restaurants and shops as well as Mercado Veintiocho (Market 28)—an enormous crafts market just off Avenidas Yaxchilán and Sunyaxchén. Bargains can also be found along Avenida Yaxchilán as well as in the smaller shopping centers.

★ **❹ Museo de Arte Popular.** The enormous, entrancing Folk Art Museum is on the second floor of El Embarcadero marina. Original works by the country's finest artisans are arranged in fascinating tableaux; plan to spend a couple of hours here. It's open daily, and admission is $10. Allow time to visit the museum's shop. Other marina complex attractions include two restaurants, a rotating scenic tower, the Teatro Cancún, and ticket booths for Xcaret, a snorkeling park on Isla Mujeres. ⊠ *Blvd. Kukulcán, Km 4, Zona Hotelera* ☎ *998/849–4848* ⊕ *www. elembarcadero.com* 🎫 *$10* ⏲ *Daily 9 AM–9 PM.*

**❶ Ruinas del Rey.** Large signs on the Zona Hotelera's lagoon side, roughly opposite El Pueblito hotel, point out the small Ruins of the King. First entered into Western chronicles in a 16th-century travelogue, then sighted in 1842 by American explorer John Lloyd Stephens and his draftsman, Frederick Catherwood, the ruins were finally explored by archaeologists in 1910, though excavations didn't begin until 1954. In 1975 archaeologists, along with the Mexican government, began restoration work.

Dating from the 3rd to 2nd century BC, del Rey is notable for having two main plazas bounded by two streets—most other Maya cities contain only one plaza. The pyramid here is topped by a platform, and inside its vault are paintings on stucco. Skeletons interred both at the apex and at the base indicate that the site may have been a royal burial ground. Originally named Kin Ich Ahau Bonil, Maya for "king of the solar countenance," the site was linked to astronomical practices in the ancient Maya culture. If you don't have time to visit the major sites, this one will give you an idea of what the ancient cities were like. The ruins are now part of an elaborate dinner show, which you needn't attend to visit the structures. ⊠ *Blvd. Kukulcán, Km 17, Zona Hotelera* ☎ *998/ 883–2080* 🎫 *$4.50* ⏲ *Daily 8–5.*

**❷ Yamil Lu'um.** A small sign at Occidental Caribbean Village directs you to a dirt path leading to this site, which is on Cancún's highest point (the name Yamil Lu'um means "hilly land"). Although it comprises two structures—one probably a temple, the other probably a lighthouse—this is the smallest of Cancún's ruins. Discovered in 1842 by John Lloyd Stephens, the ruins date from the late-13th or early-14th century. ⊠ *Blvd. Kukulcán, Km 12, Zona Hotelera* ☎ *No phone* 🎫 *Free.*

## Beaches

Cancún Island is one long continuous beach. By law the entire coast of Mexico is federal property and open to the public. In reality, security

# CloseUp
# A SHORT HISTORY OF THE MAYA

THE MAYA SETTLED in the lowlands of Guatemala, Mexico, and Belize before they moved north onto the Yucatán Peninsula. That puts the height of the Classic period in the north at a time when the southern centers were being abandoned. The following divisions are commonly used by archaeologists who study the Maya.

**Preclassic Period (2000BC–AD 200):** At this time, farming replaced the nomadic lifestyle as the Maya adopted some of the ways of the Olmec, a more advanced culture. Monumental buildings with corbeled (false) arches and roof combs appeared, as did the first hieroglyphics and a calendar system.

**Classic Period (AD 200–AD 900):** The Maya eventually developed their own art, language, science, and architecture. Trade routes were established helping the economy to grow. With the cult of the ruler, government became centralized; cities began to resemble small kingdoms or city-states. A distinct class system emerged, with the wealthiest living in elaborate ceremonial sites and the peasants in the rural areas. Regents had temples and pyramids constructed to chronicle their feats in war and to honor the gods. Buildings were placed on superstructures atop stepped platforms and were often decorated with bas-reliefs and ornate frescoes. The population's growing dependence on agriculture inspired the creation of the highly accurate Maya calendar, based on planting cycles.

Examples of great Classic architecture are Yaxchilán, Uxmal, and Sayil.

**Postclassic Period (900–1521):** Every flourishing civilization has its decline. Here, increased military activity and the growth of conquest states were the telltale signs. Powers from other Mexican cultures became part of the ruling bodies of the small sovereign states. This led to an increasingly warlike society, more elaborate temples and palaces, and a greater number of human sacrifices—especially after the Aztecs conquered the Yucatán. At the same time, the quality of Maya craftsmanship fell; for example, carved-stone building facades were replaced by carved stucco. Eventually many of the sites were abandoned. Chichén Itzá and Mayapán are representative of Postclassic architecture.

guards discourage locals from using the beaches outside hotels. Some all-inclusives distribute neon wristbands to guests; those without a wristband aren't actually prohibited from being on the beach—just from entering or exiting via the hotel. Everyone is welcome to walk along the beach, as long as you get on or off from one of the public points. Although these points are often miles apart, one way around the situation is to find a hotel open to the public, go into the lobby bar for a drink or snack, and afterward go for a swim along the beach. All of the beaches can also be reached by public transportation; just let the driver know where you are headed.

Most hotel beaches have lifeguards, but, as with all ocean swimming, use common sense—even the calmest-looking waters can have currents and riptides. Overall, the beaches on the windward stretch of the island—those facing the Bahía de Mujeres—are best for swimming; farther out, the undertow can be tricky. *Don't* swim when the red or black danger flags fly; yellow flags indicate that you should proceed with caution, and green or blue flags mean the waters are calm.

Two popular public beaches, Playa Tortugas (Km 7) and Chacmool (Km 10), have restaurants and changing areas, making them especially appealing for vacationers who are staying at the beachless downtown hotels. Be careful of strong waves at Chacmool, where it's tempting to walk far out into the shallow water. South of Chacmool are the usually deserted beaches of Playa Marlin or Playa Ballenas (between Km 15 and Km 16) and Playa Delfines (between Km 20 and Km 21), noted for its expansive views. Swimming can be treacherous in the rough surfs of Ballenas and Delfines, but the beaches are breezy, restful places for solitary sunbathing.

## Where to Eat

Both the Zona Hotelera and El Centro have plenty of great places to eat. There are some pitfalls: restaurants that line Avenida Tulum are often noisy and crowded, gas fumes make it hard to enjoy alfresco meals, and Zona Hotelera chefs often cater to what they assume is a visitor preference for bland food. The key to eating well is to find the local haunts, most of which are in El Centro. The restaurants in the Parque de las Palapas, just off Avenida Tulum, serve expertly prepared Mexican food. Farther into the city center, you can find fresh seafood and traditional fare at dozens of small, reasonably priced restaurants in the Mercado Veintiocho (Market 28).

### Zona Hotelera

**$$$$** ✕ **Club Grill.** The dining room is romantic and quietly elegant—with rich wood, fresh flowers, crisp linens, and courtyard views—and the classic dishes have a distinctly Mexican flavor. The cream of lobster soup infused with coconut is a good starter, and the filet mignon and roast duck with Yucatán honey are excellent entrées. The tasting menu offers a small selection of all the courses paired with wines and followed by wickedly delicious desserts. ✉ *Ritz-Carlton Cancún, Blvd. Kukulcán, Km 14 (Retorno del Rey 36), Zona Hotelera* ☎ *998/881–0808* ▭ *AE, MC, V* ⊙ *No lunch.*

**$$$–$$$$** ✕ **Aioli.** Dining is relaxed and stylish at this restaurant, with its green-and-taupe plaids, white linens, contemporary table settings, and creative Provençal dishes. Try the duck breast in a potato *galette* and lavender sauce or Moroccan-style rack of lamb. Fresh fish is grilled to perfection, and the wine list is extensive. The breakfast buffet is superb. ✉ *Le Meri-*

*dien, Blvd. Kukulcán, Km 14 (Retorno del Rey, Lote 37), Zona Hotel-
era* ☎ *998/881–2260* ▤ *AE, DC, MC, V.*

★ **$$$–$$$$** ✕ **Le Basilic.** The sophisticated dishes served in this elegant oak-and-mar-
ble dining room are the creations of French chef Henri Charvet. The
spinach tart with a hint of curry is the perfect start to a meal; the quail
stew with fresh figs and roast loin of lamb seasoned with bacon are
supremely satisfying. Reservations are recommended. ⊠ *Blvd. Kukul-
cán, Km 9.5, Lote 6, Zona Hotelera* ☎ *998/881–3200 Ext. 4220* ▤ *AE,
MC, V.*

**$$$–$$$$** ✕ **Laguna Grill.** Intricate tile work adorns this restaurant's floors and walls,
Fodor'sChoice and a natural stream divides the open-air dining room, which overlooks
★ the lagoon. The menu here is as imaginative as the setting; culinary wiz-
ard Alex Rudin whips up such innovative appetizers as shrimp and veg-
etable tempura with carrot sherbet and sea scallops with truffle emulsion.
Ingenious entrées include Thai spiced salmon, lamb shank with curry
mash, and rib-eye steak with lobster satay. The wine menu is excellent
as well, and be sure to finish off your meal with a decadent dessert. ⊠ *Blvd.
Kukulcán, Km 15.6, Zona Hotelera* ☎ *998/885–0267* ▤ *AE, MC, V.*

**$$–$$$$** ✕ **Blue Bayou.** Mexico's first Cajun restaurant is still very popular. Five
levels of intimate dining areas are done in wood, rattan, and bamboo—
all set against a backdrop of waterfalls and greenery. Specialties include
Cancún jambalaya, blackened grouper, herb crawfish Louisiana, plantation duckling, and chicken Grand Bayou. There's live jazz nightly and
dancing on weekends. ⊠ *Hyatt Cancún Caribe, Blvd. Kukulcán, Km
10.5, Zona Hotelera* ☎ *998/848–7800* ⚏ *Reservations essential* ▤ *AE,
DC, MC, V* ☯ *No lunch.*

**$$–$$$$** ✕ **La Destileria.** Be prepared to have your perceptions of tequila changed
forever. In what looks like an old-time Mexican hacienda, you can sam-
ple from a list of 100 varieties—in shots or in superb margaritas—while
visiting the tequila museum and store. The traditional Mexican menu
focuses on wonderfully fresh fish and seafood; highlights include the sea
scallops with avocado and habanero chiles, and grilled tuna done Maya
style. ⊠ *Blvd. Kukulcán, Km 12.65 (across from Plaza Kukulcán),
Zona Hotelera* ☎ *998/885–1087* ▤ *AE, MC, V.*

**$$$** ✕ **La Brisa Mesquite Grill.** A winding pathway under a palapa brings you
to this idyllic restaurant alongside Bahía de Mujeres. The view, the sea
breezes, and the large selection of fresh wood-grilled seafood make eating here a feast for the senses. Chilean sea bass, Atlantic turbot, Pacific
mahimahi, and swordfish are just a few of the choices. ⊠ *Blvd. Kukulcán, Km 9, Punta Cancún (next to Camino Real Hotel), Zona Hotelera* ☎ *998/888–7000* ▤ *AE, MC, V.*

**$$–$$$** ✕ **Maria Bonita.** Colorful tile work, ceramics, paintings, and a glass-en-
closed patio with a water view make this the perfect spot to enjoy such
Mexican dishes as chicken almond mole (with chocolate, almonds, and
chiles). The menu explains the different chiles used in many of the regional dishes. The bar is spacious and stocked with fine tequila; be sure
to try the tamarind margaritas. ⊠ *Hotel Camino Real, Punta Cancún,
Blvd. Kukulcán, Km 9, Zona Hotelera* ☎ *998/848–7000* ▤ *AE, D, MC,
V* ☯ *No lunch.*

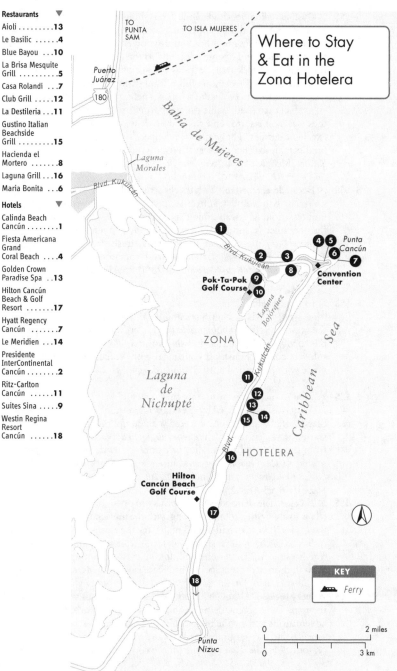

**Restaurants** ▼

Aioli . . . . . . . . . **13**

Le Basilic . . . . . . **4**

Blue Bayou . . . **10**

La Brisa Mesquite
Grill . . . . . . . . . . **5**

Casa Rolandi . . . **7**

Club Grill . . . . . **12**

La Destileria . . . **11**

Gustino Italian
Beachside
Grill . . . . . . . . . **15**

Hacienda el
Mortero . . . . . . . **8**

Laguna Grill . . . **16**

Maria Bonita . . . **6**

**Hotels** ▼

Calinda Beach
Cancún . . . . . . . . **1**

Fiesta Americana
Grand
Coral Beach . . . . **4**

Golden Crown
Paradise Spa . . **13**

Hilton Cancún
Beach & Golf
Resort . . . . . . . **17**

Hyatt Regency
Cancún . . . . . . . **7**

Le Meridien . . . **14**

Presidente
InterContinental
Cancún . . . . . . . . **2**

Ritz-Carlton
Cancún . . . . . . **11**

Suites Sina . . . . . **9**

Westin Regina
Resort
Cancún . . . . . . **18**

TO PUNTA SAM

TO ISLA MUJERES

Where to Stay
& Eat in the
Zona Hotelera

Puerto
Juárez

180

Bahía de Mujeres

Laguna
Morales

Blvd. Kukulcán

Blvd. Kukulcán

Punta
Cancún

Convention
Center

Pok-Ta-Pok
Golf Course

Laguna
Bojórquez

ZONA

Kukulcán

Caribbean

Sea

Laguna
de
Nichupté

HOTELERA

Hilton
Cancún Beach
Golf Course

Blvd.

Punta
Nizuc

KEY

🚢  Ferry

0                    2 miles

0                    3 km

**$–$$$** ✕ **Gustino Italian Beachside Grill.** Everything works in harmony to cre-
**Fodor'sChoice** ate a memorable dining experience at this restaurant. You walk down
★ a dramatic staircase to a brick-and-wood entrance; then continue past
the wine cellar and open-air kitchen to the dining room where leather
furniture and sleek table settings are set off by artistic lighting. Chef
Richard Sylvester's menu is full of tantalizing choices; standout appe-
tizers include*ostriche gustino* (black-shelled oysters with lemon) and
swordfish carpaccio, while the pappardelle pasta with sun-dried toma-
toes, seafood risotto, and roasted lamb wrapped in prosciutto are all
excellent entrées. The waitstaff is impeccable; the violin music adds a
final romantic touch. Reservations are recommended. ⊠ *JW Marriott
Resort, Blvd. Kukulcán, Km 14.5, Zona Hotelera* ☎ *998/848–9600 Ext.
6649* ▤ *AE, MC, V* ☯ *No lunch.*

**$–$$$** ✕ **Hacienda el Mortero.** With its cheerful and welcoming staff, strolling
mariachi band, and traditional menu, this casual restaurant is the
quintessential Mexican dining spot. The tortilla soup is delicious, as is
the beef fillet "chemita" with its four chile peppers. Fish lovers should
definitely try the pescado Veracruzana, fresh grouper prepared Veracruz-style with olives, garlic, and fresh tomatoes. ⊠ *Blvd. Kukulcán,
Km 9, Zona Hotelera* ☎ *998/848–9800* ▤ *AE, MC, V.*

## El Centro

**$–$$$** ✕ **La Habichuela.** Elegant yet cozy, the much-loved Green Bean restau-
rant is full of Maya sculptures and local trees and flowers. Don't miss
the famous *crema de habichuela* (a rich, cream-based seafood soup) or
the *cocobichuela* (lobster and shrimp in a light curry sauce served in-
side a coconut). Finish off your meal with Xtabentun, a Maya liqueur
made with honey and anise. ⊠ *Av. Margaritas 25, Sm 22* ☎ *998/884–
3158* ▤ *AE, MC, V.*

★ **$–$$$** ✕ **Labná.** Yucatecan cuisine reaches new and exotic heights here, with
fabulous dishes prepared by chef Carlos Hannon. The *papadzules*—tor-
tillas stuffed with eggs and covered with pumpkin sauce—are a delicious
starter; for an entrée, try the savory *loganza de Valladolid* (spicy sausage
from the village of Valladolid) or *poc chuc*, tender pork loin in a sour
orange sauce. *Guayaba* (guava) mousse and Xtabentun-infused Maya
coffee make for a happy ending. ⊠ *Av. Margaritas 29, Sm 22* ☎ *998/
892–3056* ▤ *AE, D, MC, V.*

**$–$$$** ✕ **El Cejas.** The seafood is fresh at this fun open-air eatery and the clien-
tele is lively—often joining in song with the musicians who stroll among
the tables. If you've had a wild night, try the *vuelva la vida,* or "return
to life" (conch, oysters, shrimp, octopus, calamari, and fish with a hot
tomato sauce). The ceviche and hot, spicy shrimp soup are both good
as well, though the quality can be inconsistent. ⊠ *Mercado Veintiocho,
Av. Sunyaxchén, Sm 26* ☎ *998/887–1080* ▤ *No credit cards.*

**$–$$** ✕ **Lucky Luciano.** Although it's off the beaten track, this spot is well worth
the trip. The homemade pastas and ravioli are superb. Or you can be
adventurous and try the fillet steak cooked with a pistachio-and-cheese
sauce. Salads are large and fresh. Take a cab here since it's hard to reach
on foot. ⊠ *Calle Tlaquepaque (at the corner of Calle Andres Q. Roo),
Sm 45* ☎ *998/880–5858* ▤ *AE, V.*

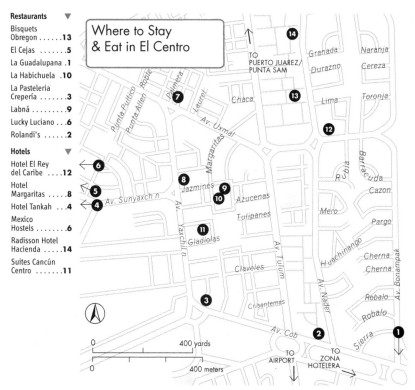

**Restaurants** ▼

Bisquets
Obregon . . . . . .**13**

El Cejas . . . . . . .**5**

La Guadalupana .**1**

La Habichuela .**10**

La Pasteleria
Crepería . . . . . . .**3**

Labná . . . . . . . .**9**

Lucky Luciano . . .**6**

Rolandi's . . . . . .**2**

**Hotels** ▼

Hotel El Rey
del Caribe . . . .**12**

Hotel
Margaritas . . . . .**8**

Hotel Tankah . . .**4**

Mexico
Hostels . . . . . . .**6**

Radisson Hotel
Hacienda . . . . .**14**

Suites Cancún
Centro . . . . . . .**11**

**Where to Stay & Eat in El Centro**

TO
PUERTO JUAREZ/
PUNTA SAM

TO
AIRPORT

TO
ZONA
HOTELERA

0 ——— 400 yards

0 ——— 400 meters

**$–$$** ✕ **La Guadalupana.** Enjoy steak, fajitas, tacos, and other Mexican tra-
ditional dishes at this lively cantina. It's decorated with art and photos
of famous bull fighters—very appropriate since it's alongside a bullring—
and is usually filled with music and an animated crowd. ⊠ *Av. Bonampak (Plaza de Toros), Sm 4* ☎ *998/887–0660* ▭ *MC, V.*

**¢–$** ✕ **Bisquets Obregon.** With its cheery lunch counter and two levels of ta-
bles, this cafeteria-style spot is *the* place to have breakfast downtown.
Begin your day early (food is served starting at 7 AM) with hearty Mexican classics such as huevos rancheros (eggs sunny-side up on tortillas,
covered with tomato salsa). The *cafe con leche* (coffee with hot milk)
is also delicious—and just watching the waiters pour it is impressive.
⊠ *Av. Náder 9, Sm 2* ☎ *998/887–6876* ▭ *MC, V.*

**¢–$** ✕ **La Pasteleria-Crepería.** This small café offers fresh salads and terrific
soups and crepes. The cream of mushroom soup followed by the turkey
breast crepe makes a perfect lunch. There's also a bakery that makes
decadent desserts. ⊠ *Av. Cobá 7 Sm 25* ☎ *998/884–3420* ▭ *AE, V.*

## Where to Stay

You might find it bewildering to choose among the many hotels in Cancún, not least because brochures and Web sites make them sound—and

look—alike. For luxury and amenities, the Zona Hotelera is the place to stay. Boulevard Kukulcán, the district's main thoroughfare, is artfully landscaped with palm trees, sculpted bushes, waterfalls, and tiered pools. The hotels pride themselves on delivering endless opportunities for fun; most have water sports, golf, tennis, kids' clubs, fitness centers, spas, shopping, entertainment, dining, and tours and excursions (along with warm attentive Mexican service). None of this comes cheaply, however; hotels in the Zona Hotelera are expensive.

If proximity to El Centro is a priority, stay in the north end. Many of the malls are within walking distance, and taxis to downtown and to the ferries at Puerto Juárez cost less than from hotels farther south. If you prefer something more secluded, the south end is less developed.

In the modest Centro, local color outweighs facilities. The hotels here are basic and much less expensive than those in the Zona. Many have free shuttle service to the beach, and Ki Huic—Cancún's crafts market—and authentic Mexican restaurants are close by.

## Zona Hotelera

★ $$$$ ⊞ **Fiesta Americana Grand Coral Beach.** This distinctive salmon-color hotel is a perennial favorite. Despite its vastness, it has a cozy lobby with stained-glass skylights, sculptures, plants, and mahogany furniture. Rooms are large and marble-floored, and decorated in tones of soothing slate-blue and beige. Small sitting rooms open onto balconies that overlook the Bahía de Mujeres and gardens. The beach here is small, but there's a 660-foot pool surrounded by a lush exotic flower garden. Exceptional dining is only steps away at the hotel's restaurant, Le Basilic. ⊠ *Blvd. Kukulcán, Km 9.5, Zona Hotelera, 77500* ☎ *998/881–3200 or 800/ 343–7821* 🖷 *998/881–1401* ⊕ *www.fiestaamericana.com* ⤳ *602 rooms, 60 suites ⌂ 5 restaurants, cable TV with video games, pool, health club, hair salon, spa, beach, 5 bars, baby-sitting, children's programs (ages 4–12), Internet, business services, car rental, free parking* ⊟ *AE, D, DC, MC, V.*

$$$$ ⊞ **Hilton Cancún Beach & Golf Resort.** All rooms here have balconies or terraces with views—either of the ocean or of the resort's championship 18-hole, par-72 golf course. Lavish, interconnected pools wind through palm-dotted lawns, ending at the magnificent beach. For total luxury consider staying at the Beach Club, with its 80 oceanfront villas. In the evening enjoy incredible Japanese fare at the romantic seaside restaurant, Mitachi. ⊠ *Blvd. Kukulcán, Km 17 (Retorno Lacandones), Zona Hotelera, 77500* ☎ *998/881–8000 or 800/445–8667* 🖷 *998/881–8080* ⊕ *www.hilton.com* ⤳ *426 rooms, 4 suites ⌂ 2 restaurants, cable TV with video games, 18-hole golf course, 2 tennis courts, 7 pools, fitness classes, gym, hair salon, hot tubs, sauna, beach, 3 bars, lobby lounge, shops, children's programs (ages 4–12), car rental* ⊟ *AE, DC, MC, V* ⦿❘ *CP.*

★ $$$$ ⊞ **Le Meridien.** High on a hill, this refined yet relaxed hotel is an artful blend of art deco and Maya styles; there's lots of wood, glass, and mirrors. Rooms have spectacular ocean views. The many thoughtful extras—such as water of a different temperature in each of the swimming pools—make a stay here special. The Spa del Mar is the area's best, with the latest European treatments and an outdoor hot tub and waterfall. The Aioli restaurant serves fabulous French food. ⊠ *Blvd. Kukulcán, Km 14 (Retorno del Rey, Lote 37), Zona Hotelera, 77500* ☎ *998/881–2200 or 800/543–4300* 🖷 *998/881–2201* ⊕ *www.meridiencancun.com.mx* 🖙 *187 rooms, 26 suites* ♿ *3 restaurants, cable TV with video games, 2 tennis courts, 3 pools, gym, health club, hot tub, spa, beach, 2 bars, shops, children's programs (ages 4–12)* ▭ *AE, MC, V.*

**$$$$** 🏨 **Ritz-Carlton Cancún.** The sumptuous carpets, rich European antiques, and elegant oil paintings may cause you to forget that you're in Mexico. Rooms are done in shades of teal, beige, and rose and have wall-to-wall carpeting, large balconies overlooking the Caribbean, and marble bathrooms with separate tubs and showers. In the evening, the Club Grill serves a wonderful dinner. ⊠ *Blvd. Kukulcán, Km 14 (Retorno del Rey 36), Zona Hotelera, 77500* ☎ *998/881–0808 or 800/241–3333* 🖷 *998/881–0815* ⊕ *www.ritzcarlton.com* 🖙 *365 rooms, 40 suites* ♿ *3 restaurants, 3 tennis courts, pro shop, 2 pools, health club, hot tub, spa, beach, 2 bars, shops* ▭ *AE, D, DC, MC, V.*

**$$$** 🏨 **Hyatt Regency Cancún.** This hotel's 14-story cylindrical tower on Punta Cancún is easy to spot. Inside, the building is striking: a central atrium filled with tropical greenery provides a 360-degree view of the surrounding sea and lagoon; there's also an enormous two-level pool with a waterfall. Cilantro, the hotel's waterfront restaurant, serves a good breakfast buffet. Soothing blue, green, and beige tones prevail in the rooms. The property is close to the convention center and several shopping malls. ⊠ *Blvd. Kukulcán, Km 8.5, Zona Hotelera, 77500* ☎ *998/883–0966 or 800/233–1234* 🖷 *998/883–1349* ⊕ *www.hyatt.com* 🖙 *300 rooms* ♿ *2 restaurants, cable TV with video games, pool, health club, beach, 3 bars, recreation room* ▭ *AE, MC, V.*

**$$$** 🏨 **Presidente InterContinental Cancún.** It's hard to miss the striking yellow entrance of this hotel. Inside, lavish marble and Talavera pottery fill the public areas, and larger-than-average rooms have royal-blue or beige color schemes with wicker furniture and area rugs on stone floors. Most don't have balconies, but those on the first floor have patios and outdoor hot tubs. Suites have contemporary furnishings, in-room VCRs and DVD players, and spacious verandas. The pool has a waterfall in the shape of a Maya pyramid, and the beach is peaceful. ⊠ *Blvd. Kukulcán, Km 7.5, Zona Hotelera, 77500* ☎ *998/848–8700 or 888/567–8725* 🖷 *998/883–2602* ⊕ *www.interconti.com* 🖙 *299 rooms, 6 suites* ♿ *2 restaurants, cable TV with video games, some in-room VCRs, tennis court, 2 pools, gym, hair salon, hot tubs, beach, bar, shops* ▭ *AE, MC, V.*

**$$$** 🏨 **Westin Regina Resort Cancún.** On the southern end of the Zona Hotelera, this low-rise hotel is more secluded than most. The lobby has dramatic sculptures displayed against vivid pink or blue backdrops. Both the stylish lobby bar and the restaurant have stunning ocean views. Rooms are even more elegant, with cozy beds dressed in soft white linens, oak tables and chairs, and pale marble floors extending to ocean-view balconies. This is one of the few hotels with direct access to both the beach and Laguna Nichupté. For added privacy consider staying at the Royal Beach Club, a separate area on the grounds that has 48 rooms. ⊠ *Blvd.*

*Kukulcán, Km 20, Zona Hotelera, 77500* ☎ *998/848–7400 or 888/625–5144* 📠 *998/885–0296* ⊕ *www.starwood.com/westin* 🛏 *278 rooms, 15 suites* ⚐ *4 restaurants, cable TV with video games, 2 tennis courts, 5 pools, gym, health club, 6 hot tubs, beach, 3 bars, children's programs (ages 4–12)* ▭ *AE, MC, V.*

**$$–$$$** 🏨 **Golden Crown Paradise Spa.** Romantic rooms at this all-inclusive, adults-only resort have private Jacuzzis, and are warmly decorated with sunset colors, flower arrangements, and rich wood furniture. Small sitting areas open up onto balconies with ocean or lagoon views. The beach here is small, but there's a comfortable pool area with two tiers of deck chairs and palapas. The spa offers massages and facials and the restaurants are bright and airy. This hotel provides great luxury at a reasonable price. ✉ *Blvd. Kukulcán, Km 14.5 (Retorno Del Rey, Lote 37), Zona Hotelera, 77500* ☎ *998/885–0909 or 800/882–8215* 📠 *998/885–1919* ⊕ *www.crownparadise.com* 🛏 *214 rooms* ⚐ *4 restaurants, cable TV, miniature golf, tennis courts, pools, spa, beach, billiards, 4 bars, Internet, car rental, travel services, free parking; no kids* ▭ *AE, D, DC, MC, V* 🍴 *AI.*

**$$** 🏨 **Calinda Beach Cancún.** At the spot where Laguna Nichupté meets the Caribbean Sea, this otherwise no-frills hotel has one spectacular draw: its beach. It's quiet, with calm waters perfect for swimming, and within walking distance of shops and restaurants. The hotel also has a patio garden surrounding the pool; rooms are on the small side but do have marble floors, comfortable beds, and balconies overlooking the ocean. If you can stand to forego some luxurious extras, this place is a good bargain for the Zona Hotelera. ✉ *Blvd. Kukulcán, Km 8.5, Zona Hotelera, 77500* ☎ *998/849–4510* 📠 *998/883–1857* ⊕ *http://cancún.calinda.beach.hotels-by.com* 🛏 *470 rooms* ⚐ *2 restaurants, cable TV, 2 pools, 3 bars, free parking* ▭ *AE, D, DC, MC, V.*

**$** 🏨 **Suites Sina.** These economical suites are in front of Laguna Nichupté and close to the Pok-Ta-Pok golf course. Each unit has comfortable furniture, a kitchenette, a dining-living room with a sofa bed, a balcony or a terrace, and double beds. Outside is a central pool and garden. ✉ *Club de Golf, Calle Quetzal 33, Zona Hotelera, 77500* ☎ *998/883–1017 or 877/666–9837* 📠 *998/883–2459* 🛏 *33 suites* ⚐ *Kitchenettes, cable TV, pool* ▭ *AE, MC, V.*

## El Centro

**$$** 🏨 **Radisson Hotel Hacienda.** Rooms in this pink, hacienda-style building are on the generic side but do have pleasant Mexican accents like wall prints and flower arrangements. The rooms overlook a large pool surrounded by tropical plants. The gym has state-of-the-art equipment and the business center offers e-mail access. The daily breakfast buffet is popular with locals, and there's a shuttle to the beach. ✉ *Av. Nader 1, Sm 2, 77500* ☎ *998/887–4455 or 888/201–1718* 📠 *998/884–7954* ⊕ *www.radisson.com* 🛏 *248 rooms* ⚐ *2 restaurants, cable TV, tennis court, pool, gym, hair salon, 2 bars, nightclub, laundry facilities, car rental, travel services, business services* ▭ *AE, DC, MC, V.*

**★ $** 🏨 **Hotel El Rey del Caribe.** Thanks to the use of solar energy, a water-recycling system, and composting toilets, this hotel has very little impact on the environment—and its luxuriant garden blocks the heat and noise of downtown. Hammocks hang poolside, and wrought-iron tables and chairs dot the grounds. Rooms are small but pleasant. El Centro's shops and restaurants are within walking distance. ⊠ *Avs. Uxmal and Nader, Sm 2, 77500* ☎ *998/884–2028* 🖷 *998/884–9857* ⊕ *www.reycaribe.com* 🛏 *25 rooms* ♨ *Kitchenettes, cable TV, pool, hot tub* ⊟ *MC, V.*

¢–$ 🏨 **Hotel Margaritas.** This lovely hotel is just steps away from several restaurants and Parque de las Palapas. Its largish rooms are decorated with elegant marble tiles, floral bedspreads, and Mexican folk art. The pool is on the small side but there is a lovely palapa restaurant with a brick oven, which serves great pizza. The buffets are also good and reasonably priced. ⊠ *Av. Yaxchilán 41, Sm 22, 77500* ☎ *998/884–9333* 🖷 *998/884–1324* ⊕ *www.margaritascancún.com* 🛏 *99 rooms, 3 suites* ♨ *Restaurant, cable TV, pool, bar* ⊟ *MC, V.*

¢–$ 🏨 **Suites Cancún Centro.** You can rent suites or rooms by the day, week, or month at this quiet hotel. Even though is abuts the lively Parque de las Palapas, the hotel manages to remain tranquil with a lovely and private courtyard filled with flowers and plants. All the suites open up onto the courtyard. Tiled bathrooms are small but pleasant, and there are king-size as well as single beds. Suites have fully equipped kitchenettes along with sitting and dining areas. Some rooms only have fans, so be sure to ask when you make reservations. ⊠ *Calle Alcatraces 32, Sm 22, 77500* ☎ *998/884–2301* 🖷 *998/884–7270* 🛏 *30 suites* ♨ *Kitchenettes, cable TV, no a/c in some rooms* ⊟ *MC, V.*

¢ 🏨 **Hotel Tankah** Just around the corner from Mercado Veintiocho (Market 28), this basic hotel has clean, simple rooms with comfortable beds, air-conditioning, good showers, and cable TV. Some even have small sitting areas. The lobby is pleasant, with Mexican-style arches and a small garden; the staff is friendly and helpful. ⊠ *Av. Tankah, Lotes 69 and 70, Sm 24, 77500* ☎ *998/884–4446* 🖷 *998/884–3065* 🛏 *40 rooms* ♨ *Cable TV* ⊟ *No credit cards.*

¢ 🏨 **Mexico Hostels.** The cheapest place to stay in Cancún, this clean but cramped hostel is four blocks from the main bus terminal. Some rooms are lined with bunk beds and share baths; others are more private. There are lockers to secure your belongings, and access to a full kitchen, a lounge area, laundry facilities, and the Internet on-site. Those who want to sleep outdoors can share a space with 20 others under a palapa roof. The hostel is open 24 hours. ⊠ *Calle Palmera 30 (off Av. Uxmal), Sm 23, 77500* ☎ *998/887–0191, 212/699–3825 Ext. 7860* 🖷 *425/962–8028* ⊕ *www.mexicohostels.com* 🛏 *64 beds* ♨ *café, lounge, laundry facilities, Internet; no a/c* ⊟ *No credit cards* ❢◯❢ *CP.*

---

## Nightlife & the Arts

### Nightlife

Many restaurants in Cancún double as party centers, and there are also discos with DJs and light shows, and nightclubs where live bands play. There are several familiar chain clubs, including Hard Rock, Margaritaville, and Carlos 'n Charlie's, but there are many other, more unique nightspots that cater to locals as well as tourists.

DISCOS   Cancún wouldn't be Cancún without its glittering discos, which generally start jumping about 10:30. **La Boom** (⊠ Blvd. Kukulcán, Km 3.5, Zona Hotelera ☎ 998/883–1152) is always the last place to close; it has a video bar with a light show and weekly events such as dance contests. The **Bull Dog Night Club** (⊠ Krystal Cancún hotel, Blvd. Kukulcán, Km 9, Lote 9, Zona Hotelera ☎ 998/883–1133) has an all-you-can-drink bar, the latest dance music, and an impressive laser-light show. The wild, wild **Coco Bongo** (⊠ Blvd. Kukulcán, Km 9.5, across the street from Dady'O, Zona Hotelera ☎ 998/883–5061) has no chairs, but there are plenty of tables that everyone dances on. The floor show billed as "Las Vegas meets Hollywood" has some impressive performances.

**Glazz** (⊠ La Isla Shopping Village, Blvd. Kukulcán, Km 12.5, Zona Hotelera ☎ 998/883–1881) is an upscale restaurant and club with a large dance floor, where all kinds of music are played. The menu is ghastly and pretentious, but the dancing and cocktails are terrific. **Hijack** (⊠ Plaza la Fiesta, Blvd. Kukulcán, Km 9, Zona Hotelera ☎ 998/883–5801) plays classic disco so you can indulge your Saturday-night fever, Cancún style. **Dady'O** (⊠ Blvd. Kukulcán, Km 9.5, Zona Hotelera ☎ 998/883–3333) has been around for a while but is still very "in" with the younger set. Next door to Dady'O, **Dady Rock** (⊠ Blvd. Kukulcán, Km 9.5, Zona Hotelera ☎ 998/883–3333) draws a high-energy crowd with live music, a giant TV screen, contests, and food specials. **Fat Tuesday** (⊠ Blvd. Kukulcán, Km 6.5, Zona Hotelera ☎ 998/849–7199), with its large daiquiri bar and live and taped disco music, is another place to dance the night away.

MUSIC   To mingle with locals and hear great music for free, head to the **Parque**
☾   **de las Palapas** (⊠ bordered by Avs. Tulum, Yaxchilán, Uxmal, and Cobá, Sm 22) in El Centro. Every Friday night at 7:30 there's live music that ranges from jazz to salsa to Caribbean. There are often shows on Sunday, too, when families gather at the plaza.

**Azucar** (⊠ Hotel Camino Real, Blvd. Kukulcán, Km 9, Zona Hotelera ☎ 998/883–0100) showcases the very best Latin American bands. Go just to watch the locals dance (the beautiful people tend to turn up here really late). Proper dress is required—no jeans or sneakers. The **Blue Bayou Jazz Club** (⊠ Blvd. Kukulcán, Km 10.5, Zona Hotelera ☎ 998/883–0044), the lobby bar in the Hyatt Cancún Caribe, has nightly jazz. **Mambo Café** (⊠ Av. Tulum, Plaza las Americas, 2nd fl., Sm 4 ☎ 998/887–7894), which opens its doors after 10 PM, plays hot salsa music so you can practice your moves with the locals. El Centro's classy **Roots Bar** (⊠ Av. Tulipanes 26, near Parque de las Palapas, Sm 22 ☎ 998/884–2437) is the place to go for jazz, fusion, flamenco, and blues. The **Royal Bandstand** (⊠ Blvd. Kukulcán, Km 13.5, Royal Sands Hotel, Zona Hotelera ☎ 998/848–8220) is the place for ballroom dancing. Its terrific live band plays golden oldies, romantic favorites, and latest hits. There is a dinner menu offered as well if you get hungry. **Tragar Bar** (⊠ Laguna Grill, Blvd. Kukulcán, Km 15.6, Zona Hotelera ☎ 998/885–0267) in the Laguna Grill has a DJ after 10 PM on weekends; if you show up early, you can sample some terrific cocktails at the plush aquarium bar.

### The Arts

🏛 The **Casa de Cultura** (✉ Prolongación Av. Yaxchilán, Sm 26 ☎ 998/884–8364) hosts local cultural events, including art exhibits, dance performances, plays, and concerts, throughout the year.

🏛 Every weeknight the **Teatro de Cancún** (✉ El Embarcadero, Blvd. Kukulcán, Km 4, Zona Hotelera ☎ 998/849–4848) presents two shows: *Voces y Danzas de Mexico* (*Voices and Dances of Mexico*), a colorful showcase of popular songs and dances from different cities in Mexico, as well as *Tradución del Caribe* (*Caribbean Tradition*), which highlights the rhythms, music, and dance of Cuba, Puerto Rico, and other Caribbean destinations. Tickets for each performance are $29. Dinner packages are also available.

## Sports & the Outdoors

### Boating & Sailing

There are lots of ways to get your adrenaline going on the waters off Cancún. You can arrange to go parasailing (about $35 for eight minutes), waterskiing ($70 per hour), or jet skiing ($70 per hour, or $60 for Wave Runners). Paddleboats, kayaks, catamarans, and banana boats are readily available, too.

🏛 **Aqua Fun** (✉ Blvd. Kukulcán, Km 16.5, Zona Hotelera ☎ 998/885–2930) maintains a large fleet of water toys such as Wave Runners, Jet Skis, speedboats, kayaks, and Windsurfers. **AquaWorld** (✉ Blvd. Kukulcán, Km 15.2, Zona Hotelera ☎ 998/848–8300 ⊕ www.aquaworld.com.mx.) rents boats and water toys and offers parasailing and tours aboard a submarine. **El Embarcadero** (✉ Blvd. Kukulcán, Km 4, Zona Hotelera ☎ 998/849–4848), the marina complex at Playa Linda, is the departure point for ferries to Isla Mujeres and several tour boats.

### Fishing

Some 500 species—including sailfish, wahoo, bluefin, marlin, barracuda, and red snapper—live in the waters off Cancún. You can charter deep-sea fishing boats starting at about $350 for four hours, $450 for six hours, and $550 for eight hours. Rates generally include a captain and first mate, gear, bait, and beverages.

**Marina Barracuda** (✉ Blvd. Kukulcán, Km 14.1, Zona Hotelera ☎ 998/885–343), which has one of Cancún's largest fishing fleets, offers deep-sea and fly-fishing. **Marina Punta del Este** (✉ Blvd. Kukulcán, Km 10.3, Zona Hotelera ☎ 998/883–1210) is right next to the convention center. **Marina del Rey** (✉ Blvd. Kukulcán, Km 15.5, Zona Hotelera ☎ 998/885–0273) offers boat tours and has a small market and a souvenir shop. **Mundo Marino** (✉ Blvd. Kukulcán, Km 5.5, Zona Hotelera ☎ 998/883–0554) is the marina closest to downtown and specializes in deep-sea fishing.

### Golf

Cancún's main golf course is at **Pok-Ta-Pok** (✉ Blvd. Kukulcán between Km 6 and Km 7, Zona Hotelera ☎ 998/883–1230). The club has fine views of both sea and lagoon; its 18 holes were designed by Robert Trent Jones Sr. The club also has a practice green, a swimming pool, tennis courts, and a restaurant. The greens fees start at $80 ($45 after 2 PM); electric cart, $30; and caddies, $20. There is an 18-hole championship golf course at the **Hilton Cancún Beach & Golf Resort** (⊠ Blvd. Kukulcán, Km 17, Zona Hotelera ☎ 998/881–8016); greens fees are $100 ($65 for hotel guests), carts are included, and club rentals run from $20 to $30. The 13-hole executive course (par 53) at the **Gran Meliá Cancún** (⊠ Blvd. Kukulcán, Km 12, Zona Hotelera ☎ 998/885–1160) forms a semicircle around the property and shares its beautiful ocean views. The greens fee is about $20.

### Snorkeling & Scuba Diving

The snorkeling is best at Punta Nizuc, Punta Cancún, and Playa Tortugas, although you should be careful of the strong currents at Tortugas. You can rent gear for about $10 per day from many of the scuba-diving places as well as at many hotels.

Scuba diving is popular in Cancún, though it's not as spectacular as in Cozumel. Look for a scuba company that will give you lots of personal attention: smaller companies are often better at this than larger ones. Regardless, ask to meet the dive master, and check the equipment and certifications thoroughly. A few words of caution about one-hour courses that many resorts offer for free: such courses *do not* prepare you to dive in the ocean, no matter what the high-pressure concession operators tell you. If you've caught the scuba bug, prepare yourself properly by investing in several lessons.

🐚 **Barracuda Marina** (⊠ Blvd. Kukulcán, Km 14, Zona Hotelera ☎ 998/885–3444) has a two-hour Wave Runner jungle tour through the mangroves, which ends with snorkeling at the Punta Nizuc coral reef. The fee (which starts at $35) includes snorkeling equipment, life jackets, and refreshments. **Scuba Cancún** (⊠ Blvd. Kukulcán, Km 5, Zona Hotelera ☎ 998/884–7508) specializes in diving trips and offers NAUI, CMAS, and PADI instruction. It's operated by Luis Hurtado, who has more than 35 years of experience. A two-tank dive starts at $64. **Solo Buceo** (⊠ Blvd. Kukulcán, Km 9.5, Zona Hotelera ☎ 998/883–3979) charges $60 for two-tank dives and has NAUI, SSI, and PADI instruction. The outfit goes to Cozumel, Akumal, and Isla Mujeres. Extended trips are available from $130.

## Shopping

There are many duty-free stores that sell designer goods at reduced prices—sometimes as much as 30% or 40% below retail. Although prices for handicrafts are higher here than in other cities and the selection is limited, you can find handwoven textiles, leather goods, and handcrafted silver jewelry.

A note of caution about tortoiseshell products: the turtles from which they're made are an endangered species, and it's illegal to bring tortoiseshell into the United States and several other countries. Simply refrain from buying anything made from tortoiseshell. Also be aware that there are some restrictions regarding black coral. You must purchase it from a recognized dealer.

Shopping hours are generally weekdays 10–1 and 4–7, although more stores are increasingly staying open throughout the day rather than closing for siesta. Many shops keep Saturday-morning hours, and some are now open on Sunday until 1. Centros comerciales tend to be open weekdays 9 AM or 10 AM to 8 PM or 9 PM.

## Zona Hotelera

There is only one open-air market in the Zona Hotelera. **Coral Negro,** (✉ Blvd. Kukulcán, Km 9, Zona Hotelera) next to the convention center, is a collection of about 50 stalls selling crafts items. It's open daily until late evening. Everything here is overpriced, but bargaining does work.

**Plaza Kukulcán** (✉ Blvd. Kukulcán, Km 13, Zona Hotelera ☎ 998/885–2200) is a seemingly endless mall, with around 80 shops, six restaurants, a liquor store, and a video arcade. The plaza is also notable for the many cultural events and shows that take place in the main public area. The **Huichol Collection** (✉ Forum-by-the-Sea, Blvd. Kukulcán, Km 9.5, Zona Hotelera ☎ 998/883–5856) sells handcrafted beadwork and embroidery made by the Huichol Indians of the West Coast. You can also watch a visiting tribe member doing this amazing work. Leading off Plaza Caracol is the oldest and most varied commercial center in the Zona, **Plaza Mayafair** (✉ Blvd. Kukulcán, Km 8.5, Zona Hotelera ☎ 998/883–2801). Mayafair has a large open-air center filled with shops, bars, and restaurants. An adjacent indoor shopping mall is decorated to resemble a rain forest, complete with replicas of Maya stelae.

The largest and most contemporary of the malls, **Plaza Caracol** (✉ Blvd. Kukulcán, Km 8.5, Zona Hotelera ☎ 998/883–1038) is north of the convention center. It houses about 200 shops and boutiques, including two pharmacies, art galleries, a currency exchange, and folk art and jewelry shops, as well as a café and restaurants. Boutiques include Benetton, Bally, Gucci, and Ralph Lauren, with prices lower than those of their U.S. counterparts. You can rest your feet upstairs at the café, where there are often afternoon concerts, or have a meal at one of the fine restaurants. **Plaza la Fiesta** (✉ Blvd. Kukulcán, Km 9, Zona Hotelera ☎ 998/883–2116) has 20,000 square feet of showroom space, and over 100,000 different products for sale. This is probably the widest selection of Mexican goods in the hotel zone, and includes leather goods, silver and gold jewelry, handicrafts, souvenirs, and swimwear. There are some good bargains here.

## El Centro

There are lots of interesting shops downtown along Avenida Tulum (between Avenidas Cobá and Uxmal). **Fama** (✉ Av. Tulum 105, Sm 21 ☎ 998/884–6586) is a department store that sells clothing, English books and magazines, sports gear, toiletries, liquor, and *latería* (crafts made of tin). The oldest and largest of Cancún's crafts markets is **Ki Huic** (✉ Av. Tulum 17, between Bancomer and Bital banks, Sm 3 ☎ 998/884–3347). It is open daily 9 AM–10 PM and houses about 100 vendors. **Mercado Veintiocho** (Market 28), just off Avenidas Yaxchilán and Sunyaxchén, is a popular souvenir market filled with shops selling many of the same items found in the Zona Hotelera but at half the price. **Ultrafemme**

(✉ Av. Tulum and Calle Claveles, Sm 21 ☎ 998/885–1402) is a popular downtown store that carries duty-free perfume, cosmetics, and jewelry. It also has branches in the Zona Hotelera at Plaza Caracol, Plaza Flamingo, Plaza Kukulcán, and La Isla Shopping Village.

## Cancún A to Z

### ADDRESSES
In Cancún addresses, "Sm" stands for Super Manzana, literally a group of houses. All neighborhoods are classified with an Sm number (Sm 23, Sm 25, and so on). Each Sm has its own park or square, and the area streets are fashioned around the park.

### AIR TRAVEL
AIRPORT The Aeropuerto Internacional Cancún is 16 km (9 mi) southwest of the heart of Cancún and 10 km (6 mi) from the Zona Hotelera's southernmost point.

🖪 **Aeropuerto Internacional Cancún** ✉ Carretera Cancún–Puerto Morelos/Carretera 307, Km 9.5 ☎ 998/886-0028.

AIRPORT TRANSFERS The public-transport options are taxis or *colectivos* (vans); buses aren't allowed into the airport due to an agreement with the taxi union. A counter at the airport exit sells colectivo and taxi tickets; prices range from $15 to $75, depending on the destination and driver. Don't hesitate to barter with the cab drivers. The colectivos have fixed prices and usually wait until they are full before leaving. They start at the far end of the Zona Hotelera, dropping off passengers along the way. It's slow but cheaper than a cab. Getting back to the airport for your departure is less expensive; taxi fares range from about $15 to $22. Hotels post current rates. Be sure to agree on a price before getting into a cab.

CARRIERS Aeroméxico flies nonstop to Cancún from Los Angeles. American has nonstop service from Chicago, New York, Dallas, and Miami. Continental offers daily direct service from Houston. Mexicana's nonstop flights are from Los Angeles and Miami. From Cancún, Mexicana subsidiaries Aerocaribe and Aerocozumel fly to Cozumel, the ruins at Chichén Itzá, Mérida, and other Mexican cities. Aerocosta flies to mainland cities, ruins, and haciendas.

🖪 **Aerocaribe/Aerocozumel** ☎ 998/884-2000 El Centro, 998/886-0083 airport. **Aerocosta** ☎ 998/884-0383. **Aeroméxico** ☎ 998/884-3571 El Centro, 998/886-0161 airport. **American** ☎ 998/883-4460 airport, 800/904-6000. **Continental** ☎ 998/886-0006. **Mexicana** ☎ 998/881-9093 El Centro, 998/886-0068 airport. **United Airlines** ☎ 800/003-0777.

### BOAT & FERRY TRAVEL
From either the Embarcadero dock or the Xcaret dock (both are owned by the same company) in the Zona Hotelera, you can take a shuttle boat to the main dock at Isla Mujeres. Ferries carry vehicles and passengers between Cancún's Punta Sam and Isla's dock, and other ferries carry passengers from Puerto Juárez.

## BUS TRAVEL

Frequent, reliable public buses run between the Zona Hotelera and El Centro from 6 AM to midnight; the cost is 75¢. There are designated stops—look for blue signs with white buses in the middle—but you can also flag down drivers along Boulevard Kukulcán. Take Ruta 8 (Route 8) to reach Puerto Juárez and Punta Sam for the ferries to Isla Mujeres. Take Ruta 1 (Route 1) to and from the Zona Hotelera. Ruta 1 buses will drop you off anywhere along Avenida Tulum, and you can catch a connecting bus into El Centro. Try to have the correct change and be careful of drivers trying to shortchange you. Also, hold on to the tiny piece of paper the driver gives you. It's your receipt, and bus company officers sometimes board buses and ask for all receipts.

First- and second-class buses arrive at the downtown bus terminal from all over Mexico. ADO and Playa Express are the main companies servicing the coast. Buses leave every 20 minutes for Puerto Morelos and Playa del Carmen. Check the schedule for departure times for Tulum, Chetumal, Cobá, Chichén Itzá, and Mérida.

**⚠ ADO** ☎ 998/887-1149. **Bus terminal** ✉ Avs. Tulum and Uxmal, Sm 23 ☎ 998/887-1149. **Playa Express** ☎ 998/884-0994.

## CAR RENTAL

**⚠ Major Agencies Avis** ☎ 998/886-0222.**Budget** ☎ 998/886-0226 airport. **Hertz** ☎ 998/884-1326 airport. **National** ☎ 998/886-0152 airport. **Thrifty** ☎ 998/886-0333 airport.

**⚠ Local Agencies & Contacts Buster Renta Car** ✉ Plaza Nautilus Kukulcán, Km 3.5, Zona Hotelera ☎ 998/849-7221. **Car Rental Association** ✉ La Costa 28, Sm 2 ☎ 998/887-3109. **Econorent** ✉ Av. Bonampak at Av. Cobá, Sm 4 ☎ 998/887-6487. **Executive** ✉ Av. Yaxchilán 160, Sm 20 ☎ 998/884-2699. **Localiza Rent a Car** ✉ Airport, International Terminal ☎ 998/886-0248.**Zipp Rental Cars** ✉ Avalon Grand, Blvd. Kukulcán, Km 11.5, Zona Hotelera ☎ 998/849-4193.

## CAR TRAVEL

Driving in Cancún isn't for the faint of heart. Traffic moves at a breakneck speed; adding to the danger are the many one-way streets, *glorietas* (traffic circles), sporadically working traffic lights, ill-placed *topes* (speed bumps), numerous pedestrians, and large potholes. Be sure to observe speed limits as traffic police are vigilant and eager to give out tickets. As well as being risky, car travel is expensive, since it often necessitates tips for valet parking, gasoline, and costly rental rates.

Although driving in Cancún isn't recommended, exploring the surrounding areas on the peninsula by car is. The roads are excellent within a 100-km (62-mi) radius. Carretera 180 runs from Matamoros at the Texas border through Campeche, Mérida, Valladolid, and into Cancún. The trip from Texas can take up to three days. Carretera 307 runs south from Cancún through Puerto Morelos, Tulum, and Chetumal, then into Belize. Carretera 307 has several Pemex gas stations between Cancún and Playa del Carmen. For the most part, though, the only gas stations are near major cities and towns, so keep your tank full. When approaching any community, watch out for the speed bumps—hitting them at top speed can ruin your transmission and tires.

## CONSULATES

🏛 **Canadian Consulate** ⊠ Plaza Caracol 11, 3rd fl., Zona Hotelera ☎ 998/883-3360, 800/706-2900 emergencies. **U.K. Consulate** ⊠ Royal Sands Hotel, Blvd. Kukulcán, Km 13.5, Zona Hotelera ☎ 998/881-0100.**U.S. Consulate** ⊠ Plaza Caracol, 3rd fl., Zona Hotelera ☎ 998/883-0272.

## EMERGENCIES

🏛Emergency Services **Fire Department** ☎998/884-9480. **General Emergencies** ☎06. **Highway Police** ☎ 998/884-0710. **Immigration Office** ☎ 998/884-1749. **Municipal Police** ☎ 998/884-1913. **Red Cross** ⊠ Avs. Xcaret and Labná, Sm 21 ☎ 998/884-1616. **Traffic Police** ☎ 998/884-0710.

🏛 Hospitals **Ameri Med** ⊠ Plaza las Americas, Sm 4 ☎ 998/881-3400.**Hospital Amat** ⊠ Av. Náder 13, Sm 3 ☎ 998/887-4422. **Hospital Americano** ⊠ Retorno Viento 15, Sm 4 ☎ 998/884-6133.**Total Assist** ⊠ Claveles 5, Sm 22 ☎ 998/884-1092.

🏛 Pharmacies **Farmacia Cancún** ⊠ Av. Tulum 17, Sm 22 ☎ 998/884-1283. **Farmacia Extra** ⊠ Plaza Caracol, Blvd. Kukulcán, Km 8.5, Zona Hotelera ☎ 998/883-2827.**Paris** ⊠ Av. Yaxchilán 32, Sm 3 ☎ 998/884-3005. **Roxanna's** ⊠ Plaza Flamingo, Blvd. Kukulcán, Km 11.5, Zona Hotelera ☎ 998/885-1351.

## MAIL, INTERNET & SHIPPING

The *correos* (post office) is open weekdays 8–5 and Saturday 9–1; there's also a Western Union office in the building and a courier service. Postal service to and from Mexico is extremely slow. Avoid sending or receiving parcels—and never send checks or money through the mail. Invariably they are stolen. Your best bet for packages, money, and important letters is to use a courier service such as DHL or Federal Express.

You can receive mail at the post office if it's marked "Lista de Correos, Cancún, 77500, Quintana Roo, Mexico." If you have an American Express card, you can have mail sent to you at the American Express Cancún office for a small fee. The office is open weekdays 9–6 and Saturday 9–1. To send an e-mail or hop online, try Web@Internet, which is downtown.

Most hotels offer Internet service but at exorbitant rates. Some go as high as $25 per hour. Most of the Internet cafés in the Zona Hotelera charge by the minute and have computers that take at least 10 minutes to boot up. Compu Copy, in the Zona Hotelera, is open daily 9–9. Downtown, the Internet Café is open Monday–Saturday 11–10, and Infonet is open daily 10 AM–11 PM. Rates at all three start at $2 per hour. Head to El Centro if you need to send more than one e-mail.

🏛 Cybercafés **Compu Copy** ⊠ Plaza Kukulcán, Blvd. Kukulcán, Km 13, Zona Hotelera ☎ 998/885-0055. **Infonet** ⊠ Plaza las Americas, Av. Tulum, Sm 4 and Sm 9 ☎ 998/887-9130. **Internet Café** ⊠ Av. Tulum behind Comercial Mexicana, across from the bus station, Sm 2 ☎ 998/887-3167. **Web@Internet** ⊠ Av. Tulum 51, El Centro, Sm 26 ☎ 998/887-2833.

🏛 Mail Services **American Express** ⊠ Av. Tulum 208, at Calle Agua, Sm 4 ☎ 998/884-4554 or 998/884-1999. **Correos** ⊠ Avs. Sunyaxchén and Xel-Há, Sm 26 ☎ 998/884-1418. **DHL** ⊠ Av. Tulum 200, El Centro, Sm 26 ☎ 998/887-1813. **Federal Express** ⊠ Av. Tulum 9, El Centro, Sm 22 ☎ 998/887-3279. **Western Union** ⊠ Avs. Sunyaxchén and Xel-Há, Sm 26 ☎ 998/884-1529.

## MONEY MATTERS

Banks are generally open weekdays 9 to 5; money-exchange desks have hours from 9 to 1:30. Automatic teller machines (ATMs) usually dispense Mexican money; some newer ones also dispense dollars. ATMs at the smaller banks are often out of order, and if your personal identification number has more than four digits, your card may not work. Also, don't delay in taking your card out of the machine. ATMs are quick to eat them up, and it takes a visit to the bank and a number of forms to get them back. If your transactions require a teller, arrive at the bank early to avoid long lines. Banamex and Bital both have El Centro and Zona Hotelera offices and can exchange or wire money.

🏦 Banks **Banamex** Downtown ⊠ Av. Tulum 19, next to City Hall, Sm 1 ☎ 998/884-6403 ⊠ Plaza Terramar, Blvd. Kukulcán, Km 37, Zona Hotelera ☎ 998/883-3100. **Bital** ⊠ Av. Tulum 15, Sm 4 ☎ 998/881-4103 ⊠ Plaza Caracol, Blvd. Kukulcán, Km 8.5, Zona Hotelera ☎ 998/883-4652.

## TAXIS

Taxi rides within the Zona Hotelera cost $5–$9; between the Zona Hotelera and El Centro, they run $8 and up; and to the ferries at Punta Sam or Puerto Juárez, fares are $15–$20 or more. Prices depend on distance, your negotiating skills, and whether you pick up the taxi in front of a hotel or save a few dollars by going onto the avenue to hail one yourself (look for green city cabs). Most hotels list rates at the door; confirm the price with your driver *before* you set out. If you lose something in a taxi or have questions or a complaint, call the Sindicato de Taxistas. Don't be disappointed if your lost item stays lost. Most locals assume that something lost means it doesn't have to be returned. Some drivers ask for such outrageously high fares it's not worth trying to bargain with them. Just let them go and flag down another cab.

🚕 **Sindicato de Taxistas** ☎ 998/888-6985.

## TOURS

BOAT TOURS Day cruises to Isla Mujeres generally include snorkeling, shopping, and lunch. Caribbean Carnaval runs a nightly cruise with music and dinner for $60. Capitán Hook runs a nighttime cruise around the bay with lobster or steak dinner and pirate show; it costs $60 or $70, depending on your dinner choice. Dolphin Discovery sails daily from Playas Langosta and Tortugas to the company's dock on Isla Mujeres; its program includes an instruction video, a 30-minute swim session with the dolphins, and time to explore the island. Tickets start at $75.

🚤 **Capitán Hook** ⊠ Playa Langosta, Blvd. Kukulcán, Km 3, Zona Hotelera ☎ 998/849-4452. **Caribbean Carnaval** ⊠ Fat Tuesday, Blvd. Kukulcán, Km 6.5, Zona Hotelera ☎ 998/884-3760. **Dolphin Discovery** ⊠ Playa Langosta, Local 16, Blvd. Kukulcán, Km 3, Zona Hotelera ☎ 998/849-4748 or 998/883-0780.

ECOTOURS The 500,000-acre Reserva Ecológica El Edén, 48 km (30 mi) northwest of Cancún, is in the area known as Yalahau. The reserve was established by one of Mexico's leading naturalists, Arturo Gómez-Pompa, and his nephew, Marco Lazcano-Barrero, and is dedicated to research and conservation. It offers excursions for people interested in exploring wetlands, mangrove swamps, sand dunes, savannas, and tropical forests. Activities include bird-watching, animal-tracking, stargazing, and archaeology. Rates are based on activities and the number of nights you stay at the station. For more information on tours contact **Reserva Ecológica El Edén** (⬦ Box 770, 77500 Cancún, Quintana Roo 🖀🖀 998/880–5032 ⊕ http://maya.ucr.edu/pril/el_eden/home.html).

Eco Colors runs adventure tours to the wildlife reserves at Isla Holbox and Sian Ka'an, El Eden and to remote ruins on the peninsula. It also offers bird-watching, kayaking, camping, and biking excursions around the peninsula.
🚹 **Eco Colors** ⊠ Calle Camarón 32, Sm 27 🖀🖀 998/884–9580 ⊕ www.ecotravelmexico. com.

**TRAVEL AGENCIES**
🚹 **Local Agent Referrals Travel Agency Association** ⊠ Plaza México, Av. Tulum 200, Suite 301, Sm 5 🖀 998/887–1670 🖷 998/884–3738.
🚹 **Local Agents Intermar Caribe** ⊠ Avs. Tulum and Cobá, Sm 4 🖀 998/884–4266. **Mayaland Tours** ⊠ Av. Robalo 30, Sm 3 🖀 998/987–2450. **Olympus Tours** ⊠ Av. Bonampak 107, Sm 3 🖀 998/881–9030.

**VISITOR INFORMATION**
🚹 **Cancún Visitors and Convention Bureau Visitor** ⊠ Avs. Nader and Cobá, Sm 5 🖀 998/884–6531 ⊕ www.ovccancún.org. **Quintana Roo State Tourism Office** ⊠ Calle Pecari 23, Sm 20 🖀 998/881–9000.

# ISLA MUJERES

Updated by
Shelagh
McNally

No one knows who named Isla Mujeres (Island of Women). Many believe it was the ancient Maya, who were said to use the island as a religious center for worshipping Ixchel (ee-*shell*), the Maya goddess of rainbows, the moon, and the sea, and the guardian of fertility and childbirth. Another popular legend has it that the Spanish conquistador Hernández de Córdoba named the island when he landed here in 1517 and found hundreds of female-shape clay idols dedicated to Ixchel and her daughters. Others say the name dates from the 17th century, when pirates stashed their women on Isla before heading out to rob the high seas.

After its popularity waned with buccaneers and smugglers, Isla settled into life as a quiet fishing village. In the 1950s it became a favorite vacation spot for Mexicans. Americans discovered it soon afterward, and in the 1960s Isla became well known among hippies and backpackers. As Cancún grew so did Isla. During the late 1970s, the number of day-trippers coming over from the mainland increased, turning the island into a small-scale tourist haven.

Although Isla continues to undergo development, it still primarily attracts visitors who prefer such seaside pleasures as scuba diving, snorkeling, and relaxing on the beach to spending time in fast-paced Cancún. And its inhabitants, *isleños* (islanders; pronounced ees-*lay*-nyos), cherish Isla's history and culture. Most wish to continue the legacy of Ramon Bravo, the late shark expert, ecologist, and filmmaker who fought to keep Isla a peaceful, authentically Mexican getaway.

## Exploring Isla Mujeres

To get your bearings, think of Isla Mujeres as an elongated fish, the head being the southeastern tip, the northwest prong the tail. The minute you step off the boat, you get a sense of how small Isla is. Directly in front of the ferry piers is the only town, known simply as El Pueblo. It extends the full width of the northern "tail" and is sandwiched between sand and sea to the south, west, and northeast, with no high-rises to block the views.

**a good tour**

The best way to explore the entire island is to take a taxi or rent a moped or golf cart. You can walk to Isla's historic **Cementerio** ⑥ by going northwest from the ferry piers on Avenida López Mateos. Then head southeast (by car or other vehicle) along Avenida Rueda Medina past the piers to reach the Mexican naval base, where you can see flag ceremonies at sunrise and sunset. Just don't take any pictures—it's illegal to photograph military sites in Mexico. Continue southeast; 2½ km (1½ mi) out of town is **Laguna Makax** ⑦, on the right.

At the lagoon's southeast end, a dirt road on the left leads to the remains of the **Hacienda Mundaca** ⑧. About a block west, where Avenida Rueda Medina splits, is a statue of Ramon Bravo, the first diver to explore the Cave of the Sleeping Sharks. Bravo, who passed away in 1998, was Isla's first environmentalist; he started campaigning to protect the island's natural treasures as early as 1950. He remains a hero to many islanders. If you turn right (northwest) and follow the road for about ½ km (¼ mi), you'll reach Playa Tiburon. If you turn left (southwest), you'll see Playa Lancheros almost immediately. Both are good swimming beaches.

Continue southeast past Playa Lancheros to **El Garrafón National Park** ⑨. Slightly more than ½ km (¼ mi) farther along the same road, on the windward side of the tip of Isla Mujeres, is the site of a small Maya ruin, once a temple dedicated to Ixchel, the Santuario Maya a la Diosa Ixchel. Although little remains here, the ocean and bay views are still worth the stop—although you must pay to see them. Follow the paved eastern perimeter road northwest back into town. Known as either the Corredor Panorámico (Panoramic Highway) or Carretera Perimetral al Garrafón (Garrafón Perimeter Highway), this is a scenic drive with a few pull-off areas along the way. This side of the island is quite windy, with strong currents and a rocky shore, so swimming is not recommended. The road curves back into Avenida Rueda Medina near the naval base.

### What to See

⑥ **El Cementerio** Isla's unnamed cemetery, with its century-old gravestones, is on Avenida López Mateos, the road that runs parallel to Playa Norte. Many of the tombstones are covered with carved angels and flowers; the most elaborate and beautiful mark the graves of children. Hidden among them is the tomb of the notorious Fermín Mundaca. This 19th-century slave trader—who's often billed more glamorously as a pirate—carved his own skull-and-crossbones gravestone with the ominous epitaph: AS YOU ARE, I ONCE WAS; AS I AM, SO SHALL YOU BE. Mundaca's grave is empty, however; his remains lie in Mérida, where he died. The monument is tough to find—ask a local to point out the unidentified marker.

(☉ ❾ **El Garrafón National Park.** Much of the coral reef at this national marine park has died—a result of too many snorkelers—and so the fish have to be bribed with food. There's no longer much for snorkelers here, but the park does have kayaks and ocean playground equipment, as well as a three-floor facility with restaurants, bathrooms, and gift shops. Be prepared to spend big money here. The basic entry fee doesn't include snorkel gear, lockers, or food; the deluxe package is overpriced. Bring a book if you intend to spend a whole day here. (The Garrafón Beach Club next door is a much cheaper alternative; the snorkeling is at least equal to that available in the park.)

The park also has the **Santuario Maya a la Diosa Ixchel,** the sad vestiges of a Maya temple once dedicated to the goddess Ixchel. Unsuccessful attempts to restore it were made after Hurricane Gilbert greatly damaged the site in 1988. A lovely walkway around the area remains, but the natural arch beneath the ruin has been blasted open and "repaired" with concrete badly disguised as rocks. The views here are spectacular, though: you can look to the open ocean on one side and the Bahía de Mujeres (Bay of Women) on the other. On the way to the temple there is a cutesy re-creation of a Caribbean village selling overpriced jewelry and souvenirs. Just before you reach the ruins you will pass the sculpture park with its abstract blobs of iron painted in garish colors. Inside the village is an old lighthouse, which you can enter for free. Climb to the top for an incredible view to the south; the vista in the other direction is marred by a tower from a defunct amusement ride. Ixchel would not be pleased. The ruin, which is open daily 9 to 5:30, is at the point where the road turns northeast into the Corredor Panorámico. Admission is $3 to the ruins and sculpture park. Admission to the village is free. ✢ *Carretera El Garrafón, 2½ km (1½ mi) southeast of Playa Lancheros* ☎ *998/884–9420 in Cancún, 998/877–1100 to the park* ⊕ *www.garrafon.com* ⊡ *$29* ☉ *Daily 9–5:30.*

(☉ ❽ **Hacienda Mundaca.** A dirt drive and stone archway mark the entrance to what's left of a mansion constructed by 19th-century slave trader–turned–pirate Fermín Mundaca de Marechaja. When the British navy began cracking down on slavers, Mundaca settled on the island. He fell in love with a local beauty nicknamed La Trigueña (The Brunette). To woo her, Mundaca built a sprawling estate with verdant gardens. Apparently unimpressed, La Trigueña instead married a young islander— and legend has it that Mundaca went slowly mad waiting for her to change her mind. He ended up dying in a brothel in Mérida.

The actual hacienda has vanished. All that remains are a rusted cannon and a ruined stone archway with a triangular pediment carved with the following inscription: HUERTA DE LA HACIENDA DE VISTA ALEGRE MDCC-CLXXVI (Orchard of the Happy View Hacienda 1876). The gardens are also suffering from neglect, and the animals in a small on-site zoo seem as tired as the rest of the property. Mundaca would, however, approve of the cover charge; it's piracy. ⊠ *East of Av. Rueda Medina (take main*

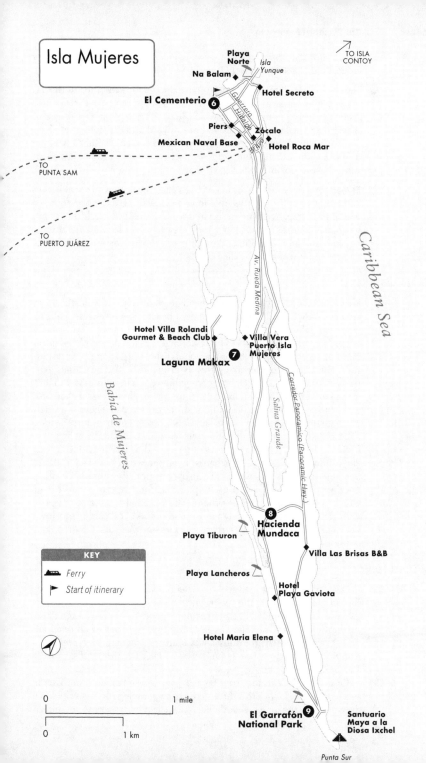

# Isla Mujeres

Playa Norte

*Isla Yunque*

TO ISLA CONTOY

Na Balam

Hotel Secreto

**El Cementerio** ⑥

Piers

Zócalo

Mexican Naval Base

Hotel Roca Mar

TO PUNTA SAM

*Caribbean Sea*

TO PUERTO JUÁREZ

*Av. Rueda Medina*

Hotel Villa Rolandi Gourmet & Beach Club

Villa Vera Puerto Isla Mujeres

⑦ **Laguna Makax**

*Bahía de Mujeres*

*Corredor Panorámico (Panoramic Hwy.)*

*Salina Grande*

⑧ **Hacienda Mundaca**

Playa Tiburon

Villa Las Brisas B&B

Playa Lancheros

Hotel Playa Gaviota

**KEY**

Ferry

Start of itinerary

Hotel Maria Elena

0                    1 mile

0                    1 km

**El Garrafón National Park** ⑨

Santuario Maya a la Diosa Ixchel

*Punta Sur*

*road southeast from town to S-curve at end of Laguna Makax and turn left onto dirt road)* ☎ *No phone* ✉ *$2.50* ◎ *Daily 9 AM–dusk.*

**❼ Laguna Makax.** Pirates are said to have anchored their ships in this lagoon while waiting to ambush hapless vessels crossing the Spanish Main (the geographical area in which Spanish treasure ships trafficked). These days the lagoon houses a local shipyard and provides a safe harbor for boats during hurricane season. It's off Avenida Rueda Medina about 2½ km (1½ mi) south of town, across the street from a Mexican naval base and some *salinas* (salt marshes).

**❻ El Malecón.** To enjoy the drama of Isla's eastern shore while soaking up some rays, stroll along this mile-long boardwalk. It's the beginning of a long-term improvement project and will eventually encircle the island. Currently, it runs from Half Moon Bay to El Colonia, with several benches and look-out points. You can visit El Monumento de Tortugas (Turtle Monument) along the way.

## Beaches

**Playa Norte** is easy to find: simply head north on any of the north–south streets in town until you hit this superb beach. The turquoise sea is as calm as a lake here, and you can wade out for 40 yards in waist-deep water. There are two beaches between Laguna Makax and El Garrafón National Park. **Playa Lancheros** is a popular spot with an open-air restaurant where locals gather to eat freshly grilled fish. The beach has grittier sand than Playa Norte, but more palm trees. The calm water makes it the perfect spot for children to swim—although it's best if they stay close to shore, since the ocean floor drops off steeply. There is a small pen with domesticated and quite harmless *tiburones gatos*—nurse sharks. (These sharks are tamer than the *tintoreras,* or blue sharks, which live in the open seas, have seven rows of teeth, and weigh up to 1,100 lbs.) **Playa Tiburon,** like Playa Lancheros, is on the west coast facing Bahía de Mujeres, and so its waters are also exceptionally calm. It's a more developed beach with a large, popular seafood restaurant (through which you actually enter the beach). This beach also has two sea pens with the sleepy and relatively tame nurse sharks. You can have a low-key and very safe swim with these sharks—and get your picture taken doing so—for $2.

## Where to Eat

★ **$$–$$$$** ✕ **Casa Rolandi.** Of the many delicious items on the northern Italian menu, the carpaccio *di tonno alla Giorgio* (thin slices of tuna with extra-virgin olive oil and lime juice) is particularly good, as are the lasagna and shrimp-filled black ravioli. The restaurant extends out to an open-air deck over the beach; the sunset views are spectacular. ✉ *Hotel Villa Rolandi Gourmet & Beach Club, Fracc. Laguna Mar Makax, Sm 7* ☎ *998/877–0100* ▭ *AE, D, MC, V.*

**$–$$$** ✕ **Casa O's.** The entrance to this casual yet stylish restaurant crosses a
**Fodor'sChoice** small stream and down to a three-tiered circular dining room overlooking
★ the bay. Enjoy the sunset while dining on excellent fresh snapper or grouper

or on fresh lobster chosen from the on-site pond. The Black Angus steaks will satisfy your beef cravings; the roasted lamb is equally delicious. Be sure to try the incredible key lime pie. The restaurant is named for its waiters—all their names end in the letter "o." ⊠ *Carretera El Garrafón s/n* ☎ *998/888–0170* ▭ *MC, V.*

**$–$$$** ✕ **Rolandi's Pizzeria.** It serves consistently good pizzas, calzones, and pastas. The grilled fresh fish and shrimp are also recommended, and so is the garlic bread—a puffed pita oozing butter and garlic. It's a friendly, casual spot in the heart of downtown, the perfect stop for a drink and some people-watching. ⊠ *Av. Hidalgo 110, between Avs. Francisco Madero and Abasolo* ☎ *998/877–0430* ▭ *AE, D, MC, V.*

**$–$$$** ✕ **Velazquez.** This family-owned restaurant on the beach is open until dusk and serves the island's freshest seafood. You haven't eaten Yucatecan until you've tried the regional specialty *tikinchic* (fish marinated in a sour-orange sauce and chile paste then cooked in a banana leaf over an open flame). Feasting on fish while you sit outside and watch the boats go by is the true Isla experience. ⊠ *Av. Rueda Medina, 2 blocks northwest of ferry docks* ☎ *No phone* ▭ *No credit cards.*

**$–$$$** ✕ **Zazil Ha.** This consistently good restaurant serves both vegetarian and traditional Mexican dishes. You can dine downstairs under the trees or upstairs under a palapa roof. Enjoy fresh couscous with vegetables, stuffed red peppers with polenta, or grapefruit and avocado salad. The breakfast menu includes Mexican egg dishes, beans, tortillas, and other choices. ⊠ *Na Balam hotel, Calle Zazil-Ha 118* ☎ *998/877–0279* ▭ *AE, MC, V.*

**¢–$** ✕ **Taquería.** For delicious Yucatecan specialties—*sabutes* (fried corn tortillas smothered in chicken and salsa), *tortas* (sandwiches), panuchos, or tamales—check out this hole-in-the-wall eatery. The two sisters who do the cooking don't speak English but can communicate using sign language. ⊠ *Av. Juárez, 1 block south of cemetery* ☎ *No phone* ▭ *No credit cards.*

## Where to Stay

In general, modest budget hotels can be found in town, while the more expensive resorts are around Punta Norte or the peninsula near the lagoon. Local travel agents can provide information about luxury condos and residential homes for rent—an excellent option if you're planning a long stay.

**$$$$** ▭ **Hotel Villa Rolandi Gourmet & Beach Club.** A private yacht delivers you from Cancún's Embarcadero Marina to this property. Each of its elegant, brightly colored suites has an ocean view, a king-size bed, and a sitting area that leads to a balcony with a heated whirlpool bath. Showers have *six* adjustable heads and can be converted into saunas. Both the Casa Rolandi restaurant and the garden pool overlook the Bahía de Mujeres; a path leads down to an intimate beach. ⊠ *Fracc. Laguna Mar Makax, 77400* ☎ *998/877–0700 or 998/877–0500* 🖷 *998/877–0100* ⊕ *www.rolandi.com* ⤴ *20 suites* ⚖ *Restaurant, in-room hot tubs, cable TV, pool, gym, spa, beach, dock, boating; no kids under 13, no smoking* ▭ *AE, MC, V* ¶⊙¶ *MAP.*

**$$$$** ⊞ **Villa Vera Puerto Isla Mujeres.** Yachties love this hideaway. Rooms are awash in rose and blue and have cozy seating areas. The large pool, which has a fountain and swim-up bar, is surrounded by a garden and lawn. Paths lead to the dock and the lagoon, where a shuttle boat ferries you to a beach club that faces Cancún. Families are warmly welcomed. ⊠ *Puerto de Abrigo, Laguna Makax, 77400* ☎ *998/287–3340 or 800/ 508–7923* ⊕ *www.puertoislamujeres.com* ⥲ *17 suites, 4 villas* ⚿ *Restaurant, in-room hot tubs, some kitchenettes, cable TV, in-room VCRs, 3 pools, beach, marina* ⊟ *AE, MC, V* |O| *CP.*

**$$$–$$$$** ⊞ **Na Balam.** Each room in the main building has a thatched palapa roof,
**Fodor's**Choice Mexican folk art, a large bathroom, an eating area, and a spacious bal-
★ cony or patio facing the ocean. The beach here is private, with its own bar serving snacks and drinks. Across the street are eight more spacious rooms surrounding a pool, a garden, and a meditation room where yoga classes are held. ⊠ *Calle Zacil-Ha 118, 77400* ☎ *998/877–0279* 🖷 *998/ 877–0446* ⊕ *www.nabalam.com* ⥲ *31 rooms* ⚿ *Restaurant, pool, beach, bar; no room phones, no room TVs* ⊟ *AE, MC, V.*

★ **$$$** ⊞ **Hotel Secreto.** It's airy, modern, and intimate. It's also not such a se-
cret anymore, so reserve far in advance. All rooms have floor-to-ceiling windows, veiled king-size four-poster beds, and balconies overlooking Half Moon Bay. Mexican artwork really pops out from predominantly white backdrops. The cozy dining room is alongside a small ocean-side pool. ⊠ *Sección Rocas, Lote 11, Half Moon Bay, 77400* ☎ *998/ 877–1039* 🖷 *998/877–1048* ⊕ *www.hotelsecreto.com* ⥲ *9 rooms* ⚿ *Restaurant, pool, bar; no a/c, no room phones, no room TVs* ⊟ *AE, MC, V* |O| *CP.*

**$$** ⊞ **Villa Las Brisas B&B.** The ocean views are dramatic from this roman-
tic eastern-coast hideaway. Rooms have king-size beds, hammocks, conch-head showers, ceiling fans, and refrigerators. A restaurant and a small pool are on-site. It's a bit of a jaunt to downtown, but the hotel can arrange for a taxi or a golf-cart rental for you. ⊠ *Carretera Perime-tral al Garrafón, 77400* ☎ *998/888–0342* ⊕ *www.villalasbrisas.com* ⥲ *6 rooms* ⚿ *Fans, refrigerators; no a/c, no room phones, no room TVs* ⊟ *MC, V* |O| *CP.*

**$–$$** ⊞ **Hotel Roca Mar.** You can smell, hear, and see the ocean from the simply furnished guest rooms of this quintessential beach hotel. The court-yard—filled with plants, birds, and benches—overlooks the ocean, too. ⊠ *Calle Nicolas Bravo, Zona Maritima, 77400* ☎ *998/877–0101* ⊕ *http://mjmnet.net/hotelrocamar/home.htm* ⥲ *31 rooms* ⚿ *Restau-rant, fans, pool, beach, snorkeling; no a/c in some rooms, no room phones, no room TVs* ⊟ *AE, MC, V.*

**$** ⊞ **Playa Gaviota.** The real plus at this hilltop hotel is the beach, with its
barbecue area, palapas, and gorgeous sunset views. Each blue-and-white suite has a kitchenette, two queen-size beds, a small dining area, and a large terrace facing the ocean. There are also smaller and older (but still comfortable) cabins on the beach. The owners, a quiet Mexi-can family, live on-site. ⊠ *Carretera El Garrafón, Km 4.5, 77400* ☎ *998/877–0216* ⊕ *www.lostoasis.net/gaviota.htm* ⥲ *10 suites, 3 cabins* ⚿ *Fans, kitchenettes, beach, cable TV; no room phones* ⊟ *No credit cards* |O| *CP.*

¢ ⊞ **Hotel Maria Elena.** Rooms are bright and cheery in this south-end hotel. All have king-size beds and balconies overlooking the bay. There's also a small garden and a deck. ⊠ *Carretera El Garrafón, Km 5.5, 77400* ☎☎ *998/888–0471* ⤵ *28 rooms* ⚲ *Fans; no room phones* ☰ *No credit cards.*

## Nightlife

Isla has developed a healthy nightlife with a variety of clubs from which to choose. **La Adelita** (⊠ Av. Hidalgo Norte 12A, ☎ no phone) is a popular gathering spot for enjoying local music while trying out a variety of tequila and cigars. **Jax Bar & Grill** (⊠ Av. Adolfo Mateos 42, near the lighthouse ☎ 998/887—1218) has live music, cold beer, good bar food, and satellite TV with ESPN. Dance the night away with the locals at **Nitrox** (⊠ Av. Matamoros 87, ☎ no phone). Wednesday night is salsa night and the weekend is a blend of disco, techno, and house.

## Sports & the Outdoors

### Boating

**Puerto Isla Mujeres** (⊠ Puerto de Abrigo, Laguna Makax ☎ 998/877–0330 ⊕ www.puerto-isla.co) is a full-service marina for vessels up to 170 feet&. Services include mooring, a fuel station, a 150-ton lift, customs assistance, hookups, 24-hour security, laundry and cleaning services, and boatyard services. If you prefer to sleep on land, the Villa Vera Puerto Isla Mujeres resort is steps away from the docks. The shallow waters of Playa Norte make it a pleasant place to kayak. You can rent kayaks—as well as sailboats and paddleboats starting at $20 for the day—from **Tarzan Water Sports** located in the middle of Playa Norte.

### Fishing

**Captain Anthony Mendillo Jr** (⊠ Av. Arq. Carlos Lazo 1 ☎ 998/877–0213) provides specialized fishing trips aboard his 29-foot vessel, the *Keen M.* **Sea Hawk Divers** (⊠ Av. Arq. Carlos Lazo ☎ 998/877–0296) runs fishing trips—for barracuda, snapper, and smaller fish—that start at $200 for a half day. The **Sociedad Cooperativa Turistica** (☎ 998/877–0239) provides four hours of fishing close to shore for $100; eight hours farther out is $240.

### Snorkeling & Scuba Diving

DIVE SITES  Most area dive spots are also described in detail in *Dive Mexico* magazine, which is available in many local shops. The coral reefs at El Garrafón National Park have suffered tremendously because of human negligence, boats dropping their anchors (now an outlawed practice), and the effects of Hurricane Gilbert in 1988. Some good snorkeling can be had near Playa Norte on the north end.

Isla is a good place for learning to dive, since the snorkeling is close to shore. Offshore, there's excellent diving and snorkeling at Xlaches (pronounced *ees*-lah-chayss) reef, due north on the way to Isla Contoy. One of Contoy's most alluring dives is the Cave of the Sleeping Sharks, east of the northern tip. The cave was discovered by an island fisherman known as Vulvula and extensively explored by Ramon Bravo, a local diver, cin-

# CloseUp
# SHHH . . . DON'T WAKE THE SHARKS

THE UNDERWATER CAVERNS *off Isla Mujeres attract a dangerous species of shark—though nobody knows exactly why. Stranger still, once the sharks swim into the caves they enter a state of relaxed nonaggression seen nowhere else. Naturalists have two explanations, both involving the composition of the water inside the caves—it contains more oxygen, more carbon dioxide, and less salt. According to the first theory, the decreased salinity causes the parasites that plague sharks to loosen their grip, which allows the remora fish (the sharks' personal vacuum cleaner) to eat the parasites more easily. Perhaps the sharks relax in order to facilitate the cleaning, or maybe their deep state of relaxation is a side effect of having been scrubbed clean.*

*Another theory is that the caves' combination of fresh- and saltwater may produce a euphoric feeling in the sharks,* *similar to the effect scuba divers experience on extremely deep dives (most divers call the feeling "getting narc'd"). Whatever the sharks experience while "sleeping" in the caves, they pay a heavy price for it: A swimming shark breathes automatically and without effort (water is forced through the gills as the shark swims), but a stationary shark must laboriously pump water to continue breathing. If you dive in the caves of the sleeping sharks, be cautious: Many of the creatures are reef sharks, the species responsible for the largest number of attacks on humans. Dive with a reliable guide and be on your best diving behavior.*

ematographer, and Mexico's foremost expert on sharks. The cave is a fascinating 150-foot dive for experienced divers only.

At 30 feet to 40 feet deep and 3,300 feet off the southwestern coast, the coral reef known as Los Manchones is a good dive site. During the summer of 1994, an ecology group hoping to divert divers and snorkelers from El Garrafón commissioned the creation of a 1-ton, 9¾-foot bronze cross, which was sunk here. Named the Cruz de la Bahía (Cross of the Bay), it's a tribute to everyone who has died at sea. Another option is the Barco L-55 and C-58 dive, which takes in sunken World War II boats just 20 minutes off the coast of Isla.

DIVE SHOPS The PADI-affiliated **Coral Scuba Dive Center** (✉ Av. Matamoros 13A ☎ 998/877–0763) sells two-tank dives ($60), shipwreck dives, and snorkel trips. **Mundaca Divers** (✉ Av. Francisco Madero 10 ☎ 998/877–0607) has a good reputation with professional divers and employs a PADI instructor. A two-tank dive costs $60. **Sea Hawk Divers** (✉ Av. Arq. Carlos Lazo ☎ 998/877–0296) runs dive ($55 for two tanks) and snorkel trips, has a PADI instructor, and will also set up accommodations for divers in pleasant rooms starting at $45 per day during low season, $65 during high. **Seafriends** (✉ Playa Norte ☎ no phone) is a small cooperative dive operation that runs dives ($55 for two tanks); the PADI introduction course is available for $65.

## Shopping

Aside from seashell art and jewelry, Isla produces few local crafts. The streets are filled with souvenir shops selling T-shirts, garish ceramics, and seashells glued onto a variety of objects. But amidst all the junk, you may find good Mexican folk art, hammocks, textiles, and silver jewelry. Most stores are small family operations that don't take credit cards, but everyone gladly accepts American dollars. Stores that do take credit cards sometimes tack on a fee to offset the commission they must pay. Hours are generally Monday–Saturday 10–1 and 4–7, although many stores stay open during siesta hours (1–4).

### Crafts

**Artesanías El Nopal** (⊠ Avs. Guerrero and Matamoros ☎ 998/877–0555) has fine Mexican handicrafts hand-picked by the owner. Many local artists display their works at the public **Artesanías Market** (⊠ Avs. Matamoros and Arq. Carlos Lazo ☎ no phone) where you can find plenty of bargains.

## Isla Mujeres A to Z

### BIKE, MOPED & GOLF CART TRAVEL

You can rent bicycles on Isla, but keep in mind that it's hot here and the roads have plenty of speed bumps. Don't ride at night; many roads don't have streetlights, so drivers have a hard time seeing you. Most moped rental places carry bicycles starting at about $5.50 an hour.

Mopeds are the most popular mode of transportation. Most rental places charge $22–$27 a day, or $5.50–$11 per hour, depending on the moped's make and age. Most tourist prefer golf carts—a fun way to get around the island, especially when traveling with children. Ciro's Motorent and P'pe's Rentadora have rates as low as $40 for 24 hours. Although motorists are generally accommodating, be prepared to move to the side of the road to let vehicles pass. Whether walking or driving, exercise caution when traveling through the streets—the locals like to drive their mopeds at breakneck speeds.

🚩 **Ciro's Motorent** ⊠ Av. Guerrero Norte 11, at Av. Matamoros ☎ 998/877–0578. **Cardenas Rent-a-car** ⊠ Av. Guerrero 105 ☎ 998/877–0079.**El Sol** ⊠ Av. Francisco Madero 5 ☎ 998/877–0068. **P'pe's Rentadora** ⊠ Av. Hidalgo 19 ☎ 998/877–0019.

### BOAT & FERRY TRAVEL

The Isla ferries are actually speedboats that run between the main dock on the island and Puerto Juárez on the mainland. *Miss Valentina* and *Caribbean Lady* are small air-conditioned cruisers able to make the crossing in just under 20 minutes, depending on weather. A one-way ticket costs $3.50 and the boats leave daily, every 30 minutes from 6:30 AM to 8:30 PM with a late ferry at 11:30 PM for those returning from partying in Cancún. Don't buy your ticket from anyone on the dock; all official tickets are sold on board by young girls easily identified by their uniforms and money belts. They accept American dollars but your change will be given in Mexican pesos.

Always check the times posted at the dock. Schedules are subject to change, depending on the season and weather. Boats also wait until there are enough passengers to make the crossing worthwhile, but this delay never lasts long. Both docks have porters who will carry your luggage and load it on the boat for a tip. (They're easy to spot; they're the ones wearing T-shirts with the slogan "Will carry bags for tips.") One dollar per person for between 1–3 bags is the usual gratuity. To avoid long lines with Cancún day-trippers, catch the early-morning ferry or the ferry after 5 PM. The docks get busy from 11 AM until 3 PM.

Fast, expensive shuttles to Isla's main dock leave from El Embarcadero marina complex in Cancún's Zona Hotelera and from the Xcaret office complex. The cost is between $10 and $15 round-trip, and the voyage takes about 30 minutes.

Municipal ferries carry vehicles (although you don't really need a car on the island) and passengers between Isla's dock and Punta Sam, north of Cancún. The ride takes about 45 minutes, and the fare is $1.50 per person and about $15–$20 per vehicle, depending on the size of your car. The ferry runs four times a day and docks just a few steps from the main dock.

🚢 **Isla Ferry office** ☎ 998/877-0065. **Isla Shuttle service** ☎ 998/883-3448.

### BUS TRAVEL
Municipal buses run at 20- to 30-minute intervals daily between 6 AM and 10 PM, generally following the ferry schedule. The route goes from the Hotel Posada del Mar on Avenida Rueda Medina out to Colonia Salinas (an area of salt marshes near the naval base) on the windward side. The service does not continue farther south to any of the beaches or hotels past El Colonia village. Service is slow because the buses make frequent stops to let passengers on and off. Fares are about 25¢.

🚌 **Municipal buses** ☎ 998/877-0307 on Isla, 998/884-5542 in Cancún.

### CAR TRAVEL
There aren't any car-rental agencies on the island, and there's little reason to bring a car here. Taxis are inexpensive, and the island is small, making bikes, mopeds, and golf carts good ways to get around.

### EMERGENCIES
🏥 **Centro de Salud** (Health Center) ✉ Av. Guerrero 5, on the plaza ☎ 998/877-0001. **Police** ☎ 998/877-0082. **Port Captain** ☎ 998/877-0095. **Red Cross Clinic** ✉ Colonia La Gloria, south side of island ☎ 998/877-0280. **Tourist/Immigration Department** ✉ Av. Rueda Medina ☎ 998/877-0307.

💊 **Late-Night Pharmacies Farmacia Isla Mujeres** ✉ Av. Juárez 8 ☎ 998/877-0178. **Farmacia Lily** ✉ Av. Francisco Madero 17 ☎ 998/877-0116.

## MAIL, INTERNET & SHIPPING

The *correos* (post office) is open weekdays 8–7 and Saturday 9–1. You can have mail sent to "Lista de Correos, Isla Mujeres, Quintana Roo, Mexico"; the post office will hold it for 10 days, but note that it can take up to 12 weeks to arrive. There aren't any courier services on the island; for Federal Express or DHL, you have to go to Cancún.

Internet service is available in downtown stores, hotels, and offices. The average price is 15 pesos per hour. Cafe Internet and Cosmic Cosas have the fastest computers.

🔢 Cybercafés **Cafe Internet** ✉ Av. Hidalgo 15 ☎ 998/877–0461. **Cosmic Cosas** ✉ Av. Matamoros 82 ☎ 998/877–0349.

🔢 Services **Correos** ✉ Avs. Guerrero and López Mateos, ½ block from market ☎ 998/877–0085.

## MONEY MATTERS

Bital, the island's only bank, is open weekdays 8:30–6 and Saturday 9–2. Its ATM often runs out of cash or has a long line, especially on Sunday, so plan accordingly. Bital exchanges currency Monday–Saturday 10–noon. You can also exchange money at Cunex Money Exchange, which is open weekdays 8:30–7 and Saturday 9–2.

🔢 Bank **Bital** ✉ Av. Rueda Medina 3 ☎ 998/877–0005.

🔢 Exchange Service **Cunex Money Exchange** ✉ Av. Francisco Madero 12A, at Av. Hidalgo ☎ 998/877–0474.

## TAXIS

Taxis line up by the ferry dock around the clock. Fares run $2 to $3 from the ferry to hotels along Playa Norte. A taxi to the south end of the island should be about $5.50. You can also hire a taxi for an island tour for about $16.50 an hour. Some taxis have begun overcharging in an effort to recoup revenue lost to golf-cart rentals. Always establish the price before getting into the cab. If it seems too high, decline the ride; you'll always be able to find another. If you think you've been overcharged or mistreated, contact the taxi office.

🔢 **Sitio de Taxis** (Taxi Syndicates) ✉ Av. Rueda Medina ☎ 998/877–0066.

## TOURS

Cooperativa Lanchera runs four-hour trips to the lighthouse, the turtles at Playa Lancheros, the coral reefs at Los Manchones, and El Garrafón for about $28 per person, including lunch. Cooperativa Isla Mujeres rents boats for a maximum of four hours and six people ($120). An island tour with lunch (minimum six people) costs $20 per person. Sundreamers has full- and half-day tours around the island on its 52-foot catamaran. Prices start at $30 per person and include food and drinks.

Sociedad Cooperativa Isla Mujeres and La Isleña launch boats to Isla Contoy daily at 8:30 AM and return at 4 PM. Groups are a minimum of 6 and a maximum of 12 people. Captain Jaime Avila Canto, a local Isla Contoy expert, provides an excellent tour for large groups aboard his boat the *Anett*.

The trip to Isla Contoy takes about 45 minutes, depending on the weather and the boat; the cost is $38–$50. Sociedad Cooperativa Isla

Mujeres tour operators provide a fruit breakfast on the boat and stop at Xlaches reef on the way to Isla Contoy for snorkeling (gear is included). As you sail, your crew trolls for the lunch it cooks on the beach—you may be in for anything from barracuda to snapper (beer and soda are also included). While the catch is being barbecued, you have time to explore the island, snorkel, check out the small museum and biological station, or just laze under a palapa.

🎣 Operators **Captain Jaime Avila Canto** ✉ Av. Lic Jesús Martínez Ross 38 ☎ 998/877-0478. **Cooperativa Isla Mujeres** ✉ Av. Rueda Medina ☎ 998/877-0274. **Cooperativa Lanchera** ✉ Waterfront near dock ☎ no phone. **La Isleña** ✉ Avs. Morelos and Juárez, ½ block from pier ☎ 998/877-0578. **Sociedad Cooperativa Isla Mujeres** ✉ Pier ☎ 998/877-0500. **Sonadoras del Sol** (Sundreamers) ✉ Av. Juárez 9 ☎ 998/877-0736 ⊕ www.sundreamers.com.

### VISITOR INFORMATION

The Isla Mujeres tourist office is open weekdays 8–8 and weekends 8–noon and has general information about the island.

🎣 **Isla Mujeres Tourist Office** ✉ Av. Rueda Medina 130 ☎📠 998/877-0307 ⊕ www.isla-mujeres.net.

# COZUMEL

Updated by
Maribeth
Mellin

The name of this island, 9 km (12 mi) east of the Yucatán peninsula, comes from the Maya word *Ah-Cuzamil-Peten,* which means "land of the swallows." For the Maya, Cozumel was a sacred site of the fertility goddess Ixchel and a trade and navigational center. For the 16th-century Spanish, it made a great naval base. Pirates appreciated its harbors and the catacombs and tunnels left by the Maya. The island went through several periods of settlement and abandonment. It saw an economic boom based on the island's abundant supply of zapote trees, which produce chicle, a chewing-gum industry staple. But when Jacques Cousteau discovered its incredible reefs in 1961, Cozumel's trajectory was set.

Cozumel strikes a balance between the sophistication of Cancún and the relaxed lifestyle of Isla Mujeres. The island has white-sand beaches, excellent snorkeling and scuba diving, luxury resorts and modest hotels, fine restaurants and family eateries, great shops, and a few Maya ruins. It's particularly popular among underwater enthusiasts, who come to explore some of the world's best coral reefs.

## Exploring Cozumel

Taxis have become so costly that it's worth renting a vehicle for a day or two to explore this 53-km-long (33-mi-long) and 15-km-wide (9-mi-wide) island. It's mostly flat, with an interior covered by parched scrub, dense jungle, and marshy lagoons. Several minor Maya ruins dot the eastern coast. One of them, El Caracol, served as an ancient lighthouse. There are also a couple of minuscule ruins—El Mirador (The Balcony) and El Trono (The Throne)—identified by roadside markers. White, sandy beaches with calm waters and spectacular reefs line the leeward (western) side. The windward (eastern) side, facing the Caribbean Sea, has powerful surf and rocky strands.

Hotels in the town of San Miguel tend to be inexpensive. The Zona Hotelera Norte, north of town, has the best swimming beaches as well as coral reefs and coves that are good for snorkeling. The hotels in this area tend to be large and popular with families. The Zona Hotelera Sur attracts divers, as it's south of town and closer to the best reefs. This area is home to a cluster of large all-inclusives.

**a good tour**

Head south from **San Miguel** ➤ ⑩ to **Parque Chankanaab** ⑪. Continue past the park to reach the beaches: Playa Corona, Playa San Clemente, Playa San Francisco, and Playa Sol. Stay on the road to reach the village of **El Cedral** ⑫. A red arch on the left marks the turnoff.

Back on the coast road, continue south until you reach the turnoff for Playa del Palancar, where the famous reef lies offshore. Continue to the island's southernmost tip to reach **Parque Punta Sur** ⑬. The park encompasses Laguna Colombia and Laguna Chunchacaab as well as an ancient Maya lighthouse, El Caracol, and the modern lighthouse, Faro de Celarain. Leave your car at the gate and use the public buses or bicycles to enter the park.

At Punta Sur the road swings north. Not far from the Parque Punta Sur entrance are the minuscule ruins of **El Mirador** (The Balcony) and **El Trono.** (The Throne). The road also passes several beaches: Playa Paraíso, Punta Chiqueros, Playa de San Martín, and Punta Morena. At Punta Este, the coast road intersects with Avenida Juárez, which crosses the island to the opposite coast. Follow this road back to San Miguel.

North of Punta Morena, an inaccessible dirt road runs along the rest of the windward coast to **Punta Molas.** Don't try to drive here; instead, arrange for an off-road-vehicle tour. The area includes several marvelously deserted beaches, including Ixpal Barco, Los Cocos, Hanan Reef, and Ixlapak. Beyond them is **Castillo Real** ⑭, a small Maya site. Farther north are a few other minor ruins, including a lighthouse, **Punta Molas Faro** ⑮, at the island's northern tip.

Take Avenida Juárez from Punta Este past the Army airfield to the turnoff for the ruins of **San Gervasio** ⑯. Turn right and follow this well-maintained road for 7 km (4½ mi) to reach the ruins. To return to San Miguel, go back to Avenida Juárez and keep driving west.

## What to See

 ⑭ **Castillo Real.** A Maya site on the coast near the island's northern end, the "royal castle" includes a lookout tower, the base of a pyramid, and a temple with two chambers capped by a false arch. The waters here harbor several shipwrecks, and it's a fine spot for snorkeling because there are few visitors to disturb the fish. Note, however, that you can't get here by car; plan to explore the area on a guided tour.

 ⑫ **El Cedral.** Spanish explorers discovered this site, once the hub of Maya life on Cozumel, in 1518. Later, it became the island's first official city, founded in 1847. Today it's a farming community with small houses

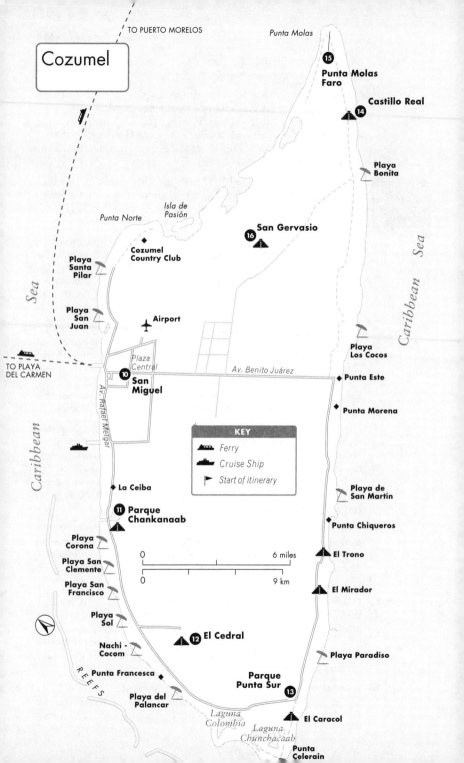

and gardens that show little evidence of its past glory. Conquistadores tore down much of the temple and, during World War II, the U.S. Army Corps of Engineers destroyed the rest to make way for the island's first airport. All that remains of the Maya ruins is one small structure with an arch; look inside to see faint traces of paint and stucco. Nearby is a green-and-white cinder-block church, decorated inside with crosses shrouded in embroidered lace; legend has it that Mexico's first Mass was held here. Each May there's a fair here with dancing, bullfights, and a cattle show. More small ruins are hidden in the surrounding jungle, but you need a guide to find them. Check with nearby locals who offer excellent tours on horseback. ⊠ *Turn at Km 17.5 off Carretera Sur or Av. Rafael E. Melgar, then drive 3 km (2 mi) inland to the site* 🕾 *No phone* 🖾 *Free* ⊙ *Daily dawn–dusk.*

⛰ ★ ☾ ⓫ **Parque Chankanaab.** A short drive from San Miguel, Chankanaab (which means "small sea") is a national park with a saltwater lagoon, an archaeological park, and a botanical garden. Established in 1980, it's among Mexico's oldest marine parks.

Scattered throughout the archaeological park are reproductions of a Maya village, and of Olmec, Toltec, Aztec, and Maya stone carvings. The botanical garden has more than 350 plant species. Enjoy a cool walk through pathways leading to the lagoon, home to 60-odd species of marine life, including fish, coral, turtles, and various crustaceans.

Swimming is no longer allowed in the lagoon; the area's ecosystem has become quite fragile since the collapse of the underwater tunnels that linked the lagoon to the sea. But you can swim, scuba dive, or snorkel at the beach. Sea Trek and Snuba programs allow nondivers to spend time underwater while linked up to an above-water oxygen system (there's an extra charge for this activity). There's plenty to see under the sea: a sunken ship, crusty old cannons and anchors, a statue of Maya Chacmool (the revered rain god), and a sculpture of the Virgin del Mar (Virgin of the Sea). Hordes of brilliantly colored fish swim around the coral reef. To preserve the ecosystem, park rules forbid touching the reef or feeding the fish.

Close to the beach are four dive shops, two restaurants, three gift shops, a snack stand, and dressing rooms with lockers and showers. There's also a sea-lion enclosure and an aviary. A small but worthwhile museum nearby offers exhibits on coral, shells, and the park's history as well as some sculptures. Arrive early—the park fills up fast, particularly when the cruise ships dock. ⊠ *Carretera Sur, Km 9* 🕾 *987/872–2940* ⊕ *www.cozumelparks.com.mx* 🖾 *$10* ⊙ *Daily 7–5.*

☾ ⓭ **Parque Punta Sur.** The 247-acre national preserve, at Cozumel's southernmost tip, has numerous birds and animals, including crocodiles, flamingos, egrets, and herons. Cars aren't allowed, so use park transportation: bicycles or public buses. From observation towers you can spot crocodiles and birds in **Laguna Colombia** or **Laguna Chunchacaab.** Or visit the ancient Maya lighthouse, **El Caracol,** constructed to whistle when the wind blows in a certain direction. At the park's (and the island's) southernmost point is the **Faro de Celarain,** a lighthouse that is now a museum of navigation. Climb the 134 steps to the top; it's a steamy effort, but the views are incredible. Beaches here are wide and deserted, and there's great snorkeling offshore. Snorkeling equipment is available for rent, as are kayaks. The park also has an excellent restaurant, an information center, a small souvenir shop, and restrooms. In summer, when the turtles are nesting, the park runs a special evening program; it costs $55 per person to see a film on sea turtles and then watch them nesting. Without a rental car, expect to pay about $40 for a round-trip taxi ride from San Miguel. Food and drinks are not allowed. ⊠ *Southernmost point in Punta Sur Park and the coastal road* ☎ *987/ 872–2940 or 987/872–0914* ⊕ *www.cozumelparks.com.mx* 🎫 *$10* ⏱ *Daily 9–5.*

**⑮ Punta Molas Faro** (Molas Point Lighthouse). The lighthouse, at Cozumel's northernmost point, is an excellent spot for sunbathing and bird-watching. The jagged shoreline and open sea offer magnificent views, making it well worth the cost of a guided tour. Don't try to get here on your own; the narrow, rutted road is impassable in a car.

🏛 **⑯ San Gervasio.** Surrounded by a forest, these remarkable ruins comprise Cozumel's largest remaining Maya and Toltec site. San Gervasio was once the island's capital and ceremonial center, dedicated to the fertility goddess Ixchel. The Classic- and Postclassic-style buildings were continuously occupied from AD 300 to AD 1500. Typical architectural features include limestone plazas and arches atop stepped platforms, as well as stelae and bas-reliefs. Be sure to see the "hands" temple with red handprints all over its altar. Plaques clearly describe each ruin in Maya, Spanish, and English. At the entrance there's a snack bar and craft shops. ⊠ *From San Miguel, take the cross-island road (follow signs to the airport) east to San Gervasio access road; turn left and follow road for 7 km (4½ mi)* 🎫 *$5.50* ⏱ *Daily 8–5.*

★ **⑩ San Miguel.** Although highly commercialized and packed with tourists, Cozumel's only town has retained some of the flavor of a Mexican village. Stroll along the malecón and take in the ocean breeze. The main square is where townspeople and visitors hang out, particularly on Sunday night, when musical groups join the assortment of food and souvenir vendors.

# Beaches

Cozumel's beaches vary from long, treeless, sandy stretches to isolated coves and rocky shores. Most stretches have concessions that charge a fee for use of facilities such as showers, beach chairs, and umbrellas. The fee may be waived if you have a meal there. Much of the development is on the leeward (western) side, where the coast is relatively sheltered by the proximity of the mainland 19 km (12 mi) to the west.

Several good sand beaches lie along 5 km (3 mi) of the southern half of Cozumel's leeward side. Playa Corona has good snorkeling. At Playa San Clemente you'll find wide, sandy beaches and shallow waters. Playa San Francisco is considered one of Cozumel's longest and finest beaches. Playa del Palancar is near the reef of the same name and is fronted by all-inclusive hotels. Punta Celarain is now part of Parque Sur; you must pay admission to the park to access it.

Reaching beaches on the windward (eastern) side is more difficult and requires transportation, but you'll be rewarded with solitude. Near El Mirador is Playa Paradiso (also known as Playa Bosh), the southernmost of the windward beaches. North of Playa Paradiso, Punta Chiqueros is a moon-shape cove sheltered from the sea by an offshore reef. Where the paved road toward Punta Molas Faro ends lies a long stretch of deserted beaches, including Playa Bonita, which extends to Punta Molas at the island's northern tip. It's unspoiled and quite beautiful—perfect for sunbathing and communing with nature.

## Where to Eat

★ **$$$–$$$$**  ✕ **Arrecife.** Some locals celebrate every special occasion with dinner at this subtly elegant restaurant, where a guitarist plays familiar ballads—listen for the Beatles and Eric Clapton in the mix. The unusual and delicious warm lobster salad served over mashed potatoes is a full meal for light eaters; any beef dish will satisfy a hearty yet discerning appetite. Save room for one of the special flambéed coffees, prepared table-side. Reservations are recommended. ⊠ *Carretera Chankanaab, Km 6.5* ☎ *987/872–0322* ⊟ *AE, D, DC, MC, V* ☉ *No lunch.*

**$$–$$$**  ✕ **La Veranda.** Romantic and intimate, this wooden Caribbean house has comfortable rattan furniture, soft lighting, and good music. Sit inside or enjoy the evening out on the terrace. Start with poblano chiles stuffed with goat cheese or Roquefort quesadillas, then move on to shrimp curry or jerk chicken. The menu changes as the chef experiments with new dishes, which are sometimes overambitious. ⊠ *Calle 4 Norte 140, between Avs. 5 and 10 Norte* ☎ *987/872–4132* ⊟ *MC, V.*

**$–$$$**  ✕ **La Cocay.** The name is Maya for "firefly," and like its namesake, this place is a bit magical. The chef creates a new menu every four to five weeks; dishes might include seared tuna or rack of lamb with a red-onion sauce. The sophisticated restaurant has wood tables, wrought-iron chairs, soft lighting, and an open kitchen. Desserts are fantastic, and the wine list has a good selection. ⊠ *Calle 19 No.1100, at Av. 25* ☎ *987/872–5533* ⊟ *No credit cards* ☉ *Closed Sun. and Mon. and Oct. No lunch.*

**$–$$**  ✕ **Plaza Leza.** Let the hours slip away as you savor great Mexican food and watch the action in the square. For more privacy, go indoors to the somewhat secluded, cozy inner patio for everything from *poc chuc,*(tender pork loin in a sour orange sauce), enchiladas, and lime soup to chicken sandwiches and coconut ice cream. Breakfast is available here as well. ⊠ *Calle 1 Sur, south side of Plaza Central* ☎ *987/872–1041* ⊟ *MC, V.*

**$–$$**  ✕ **Las Tortugas.** The motto at this simple eatery is "delicious seafood at accessible prices," and Las Tortugas lives up to it. The menu consists primarily of fish, lobster, and conch caught by local fishermen, and it changes according to what's available. Fajitas and other traditional Mexican dishes are also options. ⊠ *Av. 30 and Calle 19 Sur* ☎ *987/872–1242* ⊟ *MC, V* ☉ *Closed Mon.*

**$**  ✕ **La Perlita** The ceviche and whole fried fish are as fresh as can be at this neighborhood seafood market and restaurant. Lunch is the main meal and the crowd is largely made up of families and local workers on break. Take a taxi—it's far from downtown and hard to find. ⊠ *Av. 65 Norte 49, between Calles 8 and 10* ☎ *987/872–3452* 🖃 *MC, V* ⊗ *No dinner.*

**¢–$$$** ✕ **La Choza.** Purely Mexican in design and cuisine, this family-owned restaurant is a favorite for mole *rojo* (with cinnamon and chiles) and *cochinita pibíl* (marinated pork baked in banana leaves). Leave room for the chilled chocolate pie or the equally intriguing avocado pie. ⊠ *Calle Adolfo Rosado Salas 198, at Av. 10* ☎ *987/872–0958* 🖃 *AE, MC, V.*

★ **¢–$** ✕ **Jeanie's Waffles & Raul's Tacos** This is a wonderful place to start the day. Tables in the dining room and on the terrace face the sea; sidewalk tables have a view of traffic and travelers walking to and from town. The waffles are fresh, light, and yummy, and available in more variations than you can imagine. Jeanie's husband Raul takes over in the evening with a menu of ceviche, tacos, and other reasonably priced Mexican dishes. ⊠ *Av. Rafael E. Melgar and Calle 11* ☎ *044–987–871–2133 cell phone* 🖃 *No credit cards.*

★ ☾ **¢–$** ✕ **Playa Bonita.** Locals gather on Sunday afternoons at this casual beach café. The water is usually calm here, and families alternate between swimming and lingering over long lunches of ceviche and fried fish. Weekdays are quieter, and this is a good place to spend the day if you want access to food, drinks, and showers, but aren't into the rowdy beach-club scene. ⊠ *East-coast road* ☎ *No phone* 🖃 *No credit cards* ⊗ *No dinner.*

**¢–$** ✕ **Rock 'n Java Caribbean Café.** The extensive breakfast menu includes such delights as whole-wheat French toast and cheese blintzes. For lunch or dinner consider the vegetarian tacos or linguine with clam sauce, or choose from more than a dozen salads. There are also scrumptious pies, cakes, and pastries baked here daily. Enjoy your healthful meal or sinful snack while sitting on the wrought-iron studio chairs. ⊠ *Av. Rafael E. Melgar 602-6* ☎ *987/872–4405* 🖃 *No credit cards* ⊗ *Closed Sun.*

**¢–$** ✕ **El Turix.** Off the beaten track, about 10 minutes by cab from downtown, this simple place is worth the trip for a chance to experience true Yucatecan cuisine served by the amiable owners, Rafael and Maruca. Don't miss the pollo pibíl or the poc chuc. There are also daily specials, and paella is available on request (call 24 hours ahead). ⊠ *Av. 20 Sur between Calles 17 and 19* ☎ *987/872–5234* 🖃 *No credit cards* ⊗ *Closed Oct. No lunch.*

## Where to Stay

All of Cozumel's hotels are on the leeward (west) and south sides of the island, though construction has begun on some small properties on the windward (east) side. The larger resorts are north and south of San Miguel; the less expensive places are in town. Divers and snorkelers tend to congregate at the southern properties, while swimmers and families prefer the hotels to the north, where smooth white-sand beaches face calm, shallow water.

### Zona Hotelera Norte

**$$$** 🏨 **Meliá Cozumel All-Inclusive Golf & Beach Resort.** A long white-sand beach with clear, shallow water fronts this full-scale resort. Spacious rooms are cool and comfortable, with ocean-view balconies. Families congregate around the kids' club and pool; grown-ups go for the quieter pool by the beach. The golf course is across the street. The fresh french fries are in big demand at the grill, and the food at the buffets is better than in the specialty restaurant. ⊠ *Carretera Costera Norte, Km 5.8, 77600* ☎ *987/872–9870 or 800/336–3542* 🖷 *987/872–1599* ⊕ *www.solmelia. com* 📑 *147 rooms* ♦ *2 restaurants, snack bar, in-room safes, refrigerators, cable TV, 2 tennis courts, 2 pools, gym, fitness classes, steam bath, beach, dive shop, snorkeling, windsurfing, boating, bicycles, horseback riding, 5 bars, theater, children's programs (ages 2–12), laundry service, meeting rooms, car rental* ▭ *AE, MC, V* ¶⧠ *AI.*

★ **$$$** ▦ **Playa Azul Golf and Beach Resort.** The bright airy rooms of this boutique hotel face the ocean or gardens and have mirrored niches, wicker furnishings, and sun-filled terraces. Master suites have hot tubs. Small palapas shade lounge chairs on the beach, and you can arrange snorkeling and diving trips at the hotel's own dock. The Palma Azul restaurant serves Continental meals, and all rooms have coffeemakers. Golf packages are available. ⊠ *Carretera Costera Norte, Km 4, 77600* ☎ *987/ 872–0043* 🖷 *987/872–0110* ⊕ *www.playa-azul.com* 📑 *34 rooms, 16 suites* ♦ *Restaurant, room service, in-room safes, some in-room hot tubs, minibars, pool, beach, dive shop, dock, snorkeling, billiards, 2 bars, laundry service, car rental* ▭ *AE, MC, V.*

## Zona Hotelera Sur

**$$$** ▦ **Iberostar.** Jungle greenery surrounds this all-inclusive resort at Cozumel's southernmost point. Rooms are small but pleasant, with wrought-iron details, one king-size or two queen-size beds, and a terrace or patio with hammocks. There isn't much privacy, though, as paths through the resort wind around the rooms. But this is the most enjoyable all-inclusive on the south coast. Guests don sandals and cover-ups to dine, but otherwise are utterly casual and relaxed. ⊠ *Carretera Chankanaab, Km 17, past El Cedral turnoff, 77600* ☎ *987/872–9900 or 888/923–2722* 🖷 *987/872–9909* ⊕ *www.iberostar.com* 📑 *300 rooms* ♦ *3 restaurants, in-room safes, 2 tennis courts, 2 pools, health club, hot tub, spa, beach, dive shop, dock, windsurfing, boating, bicycles, 3 bars, theater, children's programs (ages 4–12), car rental* ▭ *AE, D, MC, V* ¶⧠ *AI.*

**$$$** ▦ **Presidente InterContinental Cozumel.** The long driveway edged by FodorsChoice palms and vines lets you know that this comfortable luxury resort pro-
★ tects its guests' privacy and serenity. Rooms are stylish and contemporary, with white cedar furnishings and private terraces or balconies; most overlook the ocean. Splurge on an oceanfront suite; terraces lead right to quiet sands. Couples and families often opt for at least one private candlelit dinner on the beach. The pool is modest, but the snorkeling and dive shop are superb, and the restaurants are highly recommended. ⊠ *Carretera Chankanaab, Km 6.5, 77600* ☎ *987/872–9500 or 800/ 327–0200* 🖷 *987/872–2928* ⊕ *www.interconti.com* 📑 *253 rooms, 7 suites* ♦ *2 restaurants, snack bar, room service, in-room safes, minibars, 2 tennis courts, pool, gym, hot tub, beach, dive shop, dock, snorkeling, 3 bars, shops, children's programs (ages 4–12), laundry service, concierge, Internet, business services, meeting rooms, car rental, no-smoking rooms* ▭ *AE, DC, MC, V.*

**$$** ⊞ **Fiesta Americana Cozumel Dive Resort.** A walkway over the road links this hotel to the dive shop, dock, beach, pool, and restaurant. Standard rooms are large, with light-wood furnishings; all have oceanfront balconies, some with hammocks. Casitas along jungle paths have balconies with hammocks and outdoor lockers for dive gear. ⊠ *Carretera Chankanaab, Km 7.5, 77600* ☎ *987/872–2622 or 800/343–7821* 📠 *987/ 872–2666* ⊕ *www.fiestaamericana.com* ↙ *172 rooms, 54 casitas* ♿ *3 restaurants, room service, in-room safes, minibars, 2 tennis courts, 2 pools, gym, hot tub, beach, dive shop, dock, snorkeling, 3 bars, laundry service, meeting room, car rental, travel services* ☰ *AE, MC, V.*

**$$** ⊞ **Villablanca Garden Beach Hotel.** The architecture is striking here—from the hotel's white facade to the guest rooms with sleeping and living areas separated by archways. All rooms have sunken bathtubs; some include refrigerators and private terraces. The hotel's beach club, which is across the street from the main building, has three dive shops. An innovative meal plan includes vouchers for dinner at several popular restaurants. ⊠ *Carretera Chankanaab, Km 3, 77600* ☎ *987/872–0730 or 888/ 599–3483* 📠 *987/872–0865* ⊕ *www.villablanca.net* ↙ *25 superior rooms, 15 standard rooms, 1 penthouse, 5 villas* ♿ *Restaurant, fans, some kitchens, some refrigerators, tennis court, pool, beach, dock, bicycles, laundry service* ☰ *AE, D, MC, V* ⊙ *MAP.*

## San Miguel

**$** ⊞ **Charrita's.** This bed-and-breakfast is in a residential neighborhood 11 blocks from the beach. Each of the three comfortable rooms is individually decorated and has a private bath. Upstairs there's a terrace for sunbathing or taking in sunsets. Guests rave about the huge Mexican breakfast included in the room rate. The on-site restaurant, open to the public, serves burritos, chile con carne, and other Tex-Mex food, and it stocks 50 brands of tequila. ⊠ *Calle 11 and Av. 55 Bis, 77600* ☎ *987/872–4760* ⊕ *www.cozumelbandb.com* ↙ *3 rooms* ♿ *Restaurant* ☰ *No credit cards* ⊙ *BP.*

**$** ⊞ **Hacienda San Miguel.** Continental breakfast is delivered to your room at this small gem of a hotel, where two-story buildings surround a lush courtyard. Extra in-room touches include bathrobes, coffeemakers, purified water, wrought-iron balconies, and hand-carved furnishings. The management arranges car rentals at lower-than-usual rates, and guests get discounts at the affiliated Mr. Sancho's Beach Club. You can use the office phone, but you won't be able to hook up your laptop. ⊠ *Calle 10 Norte 500, at Av. 5, 77600* ☎ *987/872–1986* 📠 *987/872–7043* ⊕ *www. haciendasanmiguel.com* ↙ *7 studios, 3 junior suites, 1 master suite* ♿ *In-room safes, kitchenettes, car rental; no room phones* ☰ *MC, V.*

**¢–$** ⊞ **Tamarindo Bed & Breakfast.** The owners have blended elements of Mexico and France. Many rooms have hammocks; all rooms are pleasantly furnished. Bungalows and apartments are for rent closer to the waterfront. The staff arranges diving expeditions, and there's a rinse tank as well as gear-storage facilities. Breakfast includes French-pressed coffee, and guests can use the communal outdoor kitchenette with barbecue. ⊠ *Calle 4 Norte 421, between Avs. 20 and 25, 77600* ☎☎ *987/872– 3614* ⊕ *www.cozumel.net/bb/tamarind/* ↙ *5 rooms* ♿ *Fans, massage, bicycles, laundry service; no a/c in some rooms* ☰ *MC, V* ⊙ *CP.*

# Nightlife

### Bars

Sports fans come to bet on their favorite teams, watch the games, and catch the ESPN news at **All Sports** (⊠ Av. 5 Norte and Calle 2 ☎ 987/869–2246).**Cactus** (⊠ Av. Rafael E. Melgar 145 ☎ 987/872–5799) has a disco, live music, and a bar that stays open until 5 AM. **Señor Frog's and Carlos 'n Charlie's** (⊠Av. Rafael E. Melgar and Punta Langosta ☎987/872–0191) attract lively crowds who want loud rock and a liberated, anything-goes dancing scene.

### Discos

Cozumel's oldest disco, **Neptune Dance Club** (⊠ Av. Rafael E. Melgar and Av. 11 ☎ 987/872–1537) is the island's classiest night spot, with a dazzling light-and-laser show. **Viva Mexico** (⊠ Av. Rafael E. Melgar ☎ 987/872–0799) has a DJ who spins Latin and American dance music until the wee hours. There's also an extensive snack menu.

### Live Music

Sunday evenings 8–10, locals head for the zócalo to hear mariachis and island musicians playing tropical tunes. Salsa bands perform on some nights, adding a Latin beat to the night scene at **Cafe Salsa** (⊠ Av. 10 between Av. Juárez and Calle 2 ☎ no phone). For sophisticated jazz, ★ smart cocktails, and great cigars, check out the **Havana Club** (⊠ Av. Rafael E. Melgar between Calles 6 and 8, 2nd fl. ☎ 987/872–1268). Beware of ordering imported liquors such as vodka and scotch; drink prices are very high.

The food isn't the draw at **Joe's Lobster House** (⊠ Av. Rafael E. Melgar, across from the ferry pier ☎ 987/872–3275), but the reggae and salsa bring in the crowds nightly, from 10:30 until dawn.

# Sports & the Outdoors

Most people come to Cozumel for the water sports—scuba diving, snorkeling, and fishing are particularly popular. Services and equipment rentals are available throughout the island, especially through major hotels and water-sports centers such as **Scuba Du** (⊠ at the Presidente InterContinental and El Cozumeleño hotels ☎ 987/872–0050).

Because dive shops tend to be competitive, it's well worth your while to shop around. Many hotels have their own on-site operations, and there are dozens of dive shops in town. **ANOAAT** (Aquatic Sports Operators Association; ☎ 987/872–5955) has listings of affiliated dive operations. Before signing on, ask experienced divers about the place, check credentials, and look over the boats and equipment.

### Fishing

Deep-sea fishing for tuna, barracuda, wahoo, and dorado is good year-round. You can go bottom-fishing for grouper, yellowtail, and snapper on the shallow sand flats at the island's north end; you can fly-fish for bonefish, tarpon, snook, grouper, and small sharks in the same area. Regulations forbid commercial fishing, sportfishing, spear fishing, and collecting marine life in certain areas around Cozumel. It's illegal to kill certain species within marine reserves, including billfish, so be prepared to return some prize catches to the sea.

CHARTERS You can charter high-speed fishing boats for $400 for a half day or $550 for a full day (with a maximum of six people). Your hotel can help arrange daily charters—some offer special deals, with boats leaving from their own docks. **Albatros Deep Sea Fishing** (☎ 987/872–7904 or 888/ 333–4643) is a local outfit specializing in fishing trips. Full-day rates include the boat and crew, tackle and bait, and lunch with beer and soda. **Marathon Fishing & Leisure Charters** (☎ 987/872–1986) is popular with fishermen. Full-day rates include the boat and crew, tackle and bait, and lunch with beer and soda.

## Golf

The **Cozumel Country Club** (✉ Carretera Costera Norte, Km 5.8 ☎ 987/ 872–9570 ⊕ www.cozumelcountryclub.com.mx) has an 18-hole championship golf course. The gorgeous fairways amid mangroves and a lagoon are the work of the Nicklaus Design Group. The greens fee is $149, which includes a golf cart. Many hotels offer golf packages.

## Scuba Diving

The options for divers on Cozumel include deep dives, drift dives, shore dives, wall dives, and night dives, as well as theme dives focusing on ecology, archaeology, sunken ships, and photography. More than 100 shops serve divers, so look for high safety standards and documented credentials. The best places offer small groups and individual attention. Next to your equipment, your dive master is the most important consideration for your adventure, particularly if you're new to the sport. Make sure he or she has PADI or NAUI certification (or FMAS, the Mexican equivalent). Be sure to bring your own certification card; all reputable shops require customers to show them before diving. If you forget, you may be able to call the agency that certified you and have the card number faxed to the shop. If you feel ill during or after your dive, tell the instructor, who may refer you to a medical center specializing in such problems.

There's a reputable recompression chamber at the **Buceo Médico Mexicano** (✉ Calle 5 Sur 21B ☎ 987/872–1430 24-hr hotline). The **Cozumel Recompression Chamber** (✉ San Miguel Clinic, Calle 6 between Avs. 5 and 10 ☎987/872–3070) is a fully equipped recompression center. These chambers, which aim for a 35-minute response time from reef to chamber, treat decompression sickness, commonly known as "the bends," which occurs when you surface too quickly and nitrogen bubbles form in the bloodstream. Recompression chambers are also used to treat nitrogen narcosis, collapsed lungs, and overexposure to the cold. Consider getting DAN (Divers Alert Network) insurance, which covers accidents.

Much of the reef area off Cozumel is included in a National Marine Park. Boats aren't allowed to anchor around the reefs, and visitors can't touch the coral or take anything from the reefs. When diving, stay at least 3 feet above the reef—not just because coral can sting or cut you, but also because it's easily damaged and grows very slowly; it has taken 2,000 years to reach its present size. Some dive operators do not allow customers to wear gloves or carry dive knives as an extra measure to protect reefs and marine life.

### Dive Shops & Operators

Most dive shops can provide everything you need for an underwater adventure. Equipment rental is relatively inexpensive, ranging from $6 for tanks or a lamp to about $8–$10 for a regulator and BC. Underwater-camera rentals can cost as much as $35, video-camera rentals run about $75, and professionally shot and edited videos of your own dive are about $160. You can choose from two-tank boat trips and specialty dives ranging from $45 to $60. Most companies also offer one-tank afternoon and night dives for $30–$35. The dive shops handle more than 1,000 divers per day; many run "cattle boats" packed with lots of divers and gear. It's worth the extra money to go out with a smaller group on a fast boat, especially if you're experienced.

**Aqua Safari** (✉ Av. Rafael E. Melgar 429, between Calles 5 and 7 Sur ☎ 987/872–0101) is among the island's oldest and most professional shops. It provides PADI certification, classes on night diving, deep diving and other interests, and individualized dives. **Blue Bubble** (✉ Av. 5 Sur and Calle 3 Sur ☎ 987/872–1865) offers several departure times in the morning—a blessing for those who hate early wake-up calls. **Del Mar Aquatics** (✉ Carretera Costera Sur, Km 4 ☎ 987/872–5949) offers dive instructions and boat and shore dives. It operates at El Cid La Ceiba hotel, among the best places for shore and night dives. **Dive Cozumel** (✉ Calle Adolfo Rosado Salas 72, at Av. 5 Sur ☎ 987/872–4567) specializes in cave diving for highly experienced divers, along with regular open-water dives for the less proficient.

### Snorkeling

Snorkeling equipment is available at nearly all hotels and beach clubs as well as at Parque Chankanaab, Playa San Francisco, and Parque Punta Sur. Gear rents for less than $10 a day. Snorkeling tours run about $60 and take in the shallow reefs off Palancar, Chankanaab, Colombia, and Yucab.

**Cozumel Sailing** (✉ Carretera Norteat the marina ☎ 987/869–2312) offers sailing tours with open bar, lunch, snorkeling and beach time for $60. Sunset cruises aboard *El Tucan* are also available; they include unlimited drinks and live entertainment and cost about $25. **Fury Catamarans** (✉ Carretera Surbeside Casa del Mar hotel ☎ 987/872–5145) runs snorkeling tours from its 45-foot catamarans. Rates begin at about $58 per day and include equipment, a guide, soft drinks, beer, and margaritas and a beach party with lunch.

## Shopping

Cozumel's main shopping area is downtown on the waterfront along Avenida Rafael E. Melgar and on some side streets around the plaza; there are more than 150 shops in this area alone. There are also small clusters of shops at Plaza del Sol (east side of the main plaza), Villa Mar (north side of the main plaza), and Plaza Confetti (south side of the main plaza).

★ ☾  There's a **crafts market** (⊠ Calle 1 Sur behind the plaza) in town, which sells a respectable assortment of Mexican wares. The market across the street from **Puerto Maya,** where some cruise ships dock, has some crafts at good prices. Bargains are best after the ships have departed.

### Specialty Stores

CLOTHING  Several trendy sportswear stores line Avenida Rafael E. Melgar between Calles 2 and 6. **Exotica** (⊠ Av. Juárez at the plaza ☎ 987/872–5880) has high-quality sportswear and shirts with nature-theme designs. **Poco Loco** (⊠ Av. Rafael E. Melgar 18, at Juárez 2A ☎ 987/872–5499) sells casual wear and beach bags.

CRAFTS  **Bugambilias** (⊠ Av. 10 Sur between Calles Adolfo Rosado Salas and 1
★ ☾  Sur ☎ 987/872–6282) sells handmade Mexican linens. **Los Cinco Soles** (⊠ Av. Rafael E. Melgar and Calle 8 Norte ☎ 987/872–0132) is the best one-stop shop for crafts from around Mexico. Several display rooms, covering almost an entire block, are filled with clothing, furnishings, home decor items, and jewelry. The **Hammock House** (⊠ Av. 5 and Calle 4 ☎ no phone) has long been a local curiosity thanks to its bright-blue exterior and the inventory that hangs out front. Manuel Azueta Vivas has been selling hammocks here for more than four decades. **Talavera** (⊠ Av. 5 Sur 349 ☎ 987/872–0171) carries tiles from the Yucatán, masks from Guerrero, brightly painted wooden animals from Oaxaca, and carved chests from Guadalajara.

JEWELRY  **Diamond Creations** (⊠ Av. Rafael E. Melgar Sur 131 ☎ 987/872–5330) lets you custom-design a piece of jewelry from a collection of loose diamonds, emeralds, rubies, sapphires, or tanzanite. The shop and its affiliates, Tanzanite International, Diamond Creations, and Silver International, have multiple locations along the waterfront and in the shopping malls—in fact, you can't avoid them. Look for silver, gold, and coral jewelry—especially bracelets and earrings—at **Joyería Palancar** (⊠ Av. Rafael E. Melgar Norte 15 ☎ 987/872–1468). Quality gemstones and striking designs are the strong points at **Rachat & Romero** (⊠ Av. Rafael E. Melgar 101 ☎ 987/872–0571).

## Cozumel A to Z

### AIR TRAVEL

AIRPORT  The **Aeropuerto Internacional de Cozumel** is 3 km (2 mi) north of San Miguel.
🛈 **Aeropuerto Internacional de Cozumel** ☎ 987/872-0928.

AIRPORT  At the airport, the *colectivo,* a van that seats up to eight, takes arriving
TRANSFERS  passengers to their hotels; the fare is about $7–$20. If you want to avoid waiting for the van to fill or for other passengers to be dropped off, you can hire an *especial*—an individual van. A trip in one of these to hotel

zones costs about \$20–\$25; to the city it's about \$10; and to the all-inclusives at the far south it's about to \$30. Taxis to the airport cost between \$10 and \$30 from the hotel zones and approximately \$5 from downtown.

CARRIERS    Continental has two nonstop flights from Houston on Saturday and one daily nonstop flight from Houston the rest of the week. US Airways flies nonstop daily from Charlotte, North Carolina, to Cozumel and nonstop from Philadelphia on Saturday. American Airlines has seasonal nonstop flights daily from Dallas. Aerocaribe flies between Cozumel, Cancún, and Mexico City twice daily. Charter flights to Chichén Itzá, Tulum, Palenque, and Belize can be arranged through Aerolamsa.

🛈 **Aerocaribe** ☎ 987/872-0503. **Aerolamsa** ☎ 987/872-1781. **American** ☎ 800/882-8880. **Continental** ☎ 987/872-0847. **US Airways** ☎ 800/622-1015.

## BOAT & FERRY TRAVEL

Passenger-only ferries to Playa del Carmen leave Cozumel's main pier approximately every hour on the hour from 5 AM to 10 PM (no ferries at 11 AM, 1, 7, and 9 PM). They leave Playa del Carmen's dock also about every hour on the hour, from 6 AM to 11 PM (no service at 7 AM, noon, 2 PM, and 8 PM). The trip takes 45 minutes. Call to verify the times. Bad weather sometimes prompts cancellations.

There are car ferries from Puerto Morelos and Punta Venado. The trip takes three to five hours. Service is more frequent from Punta Venado. The fare starts at about \$60 for small cars (more for larger vehicles) and \$6 per passenger.

🛈 **Car Ferry** ☎ 987/872-0950. **Cozumel's main pier** ☎ 987/872-1508 or 987/872-1588. **Playa del Carmen dock** ☎ 987/873-0067.

## BUS TRAVEL

Public buses do not operate in the hotel zones along the leeward coast; local bus service runs mainly within the town of San Miguel, although there is a route from town to the airport. Service is irregular but inexpensive.

## CAR RENTAL

🛈 **Major Agencies Avis** ☎ 987/872-0219. **Hertz** ☎ 987/872-3888.

🛈 **Local Agencies Aguila Rentals** ✉ Av. Rafael E. Melgar 685 ☎ 987/872-0729. **Fiesta** ✉ Calle 11 No. 598 ☎ 987/872-0433.

## CAR TRAVEL

There are several excellent paved roads, but dirt roads—such as the one to Punta Molas—aren't well maintained; proceed with great caution, especially after rain. Most car-rental companies have a policy that voids your insurance when you leave the paved roads and journey to off-road points. If you rent a four-wheel-drive vehicle, make sure it works properly.

## EMERGENCIES

🛈 **General Emergency Numbers Air Ambulance** ☎ 987/872-4070. **Police** ✉ Anexo del Palacio Municipal ☎ 987/872-0409.

🛈 **Hospitals & Clinics Centro Medico de Cozumel** (Cozumel Medical Center) ✉ Calle 1 Sur 101, corner of Av. 50 ☎ 987/872-3545 or 987/872-5370. **Centro de Salud** ✉ Av. 20 Sur and Calle 11 ☎ 987/872-0140. **Medical Specialties Center** ✉ Av. 20 Norte 425

☎ 987/872-1419 or 987/872-2919. **Red Cross** ⊠ Calle Adolfo Rosada Salas and Av. 20 Sur ☎ 987/872-1058.

🚩 Late-Night Pharmacies **Farmacia Canto** ☎ 987/872-5377. **Farmacia Dori** ⊠ Calle Adolfo Rosado Salas between Avs. 15 and 20 Sur ☎ 987/872-0559. **Farmacia Joaquin** ⊠ North side of plaza ☎ 987/872-2520.

🚩 Recompression Chambers **Buceo Médico Mexicano** ⊠ Calle 5 Sur 21B ☎ 987/872-1430 24-hr hotline. **Cozumel Recompression Chamber** ⊠ San Miguel Clinic, Calle 6 between Avs. 5 and 10 ☎ 987/872-3070.

### MAIL, INTERNET & SHIPPING

The local correos (post office), six blocks south of the plaza, is open weekdays 8–8, Saturday 9–5, and Sunday 9–1. For packages and important letters, you're better off using DHL. You can hop online at Coffee Net.

🚩 Cybercafés **Calling Station** ⊠ Av. Rafael E. Melgar 27, at Calle 3 Sur ☎ 987/872-1417. **Coffee Net** ⊠ Av. Rafael E. Melgar s/n ☎ 987/872-6394.

🚩 Mail Services **Correos** ⊠ Calle 7 Sur and Av. Rafael E. Melgar ☎ 987/872-0106. **DHL** ⊠ Av. Rafael E. Melgar and Av. 5 Sur ☎ 987/872-3110.

### MONEY MATTERS

Most of the banks are in the main square and are open weekdays 9 to 4 or 5. Many change currency all day. Most have ATMs. The American Express exchange office is open weekdays 9–5. After hours, you can change money at Promotora Cambiaria del Centro, which is open Monday–Saturday 8 AM–9 PM.

🚩 Banks **Banamex** ⊠ Av. 5 Norte at the plaza ☎ 987/872-3411. **Bancomer** ⊠ Av. 5 Norte at the plaza ☎ 987/872-0550. **Banco Serfín** ⊠ Calle 1 Sur between Avs. 5 and 10 Sur ☎ 987/872-0930. **Bancrecer** ⊠ Calle 1 Sur, between Avs. 5 and 10 ☎ 987/872-4750. **Bital** ⊠ Av. Rafael E. Melgar 11 ☎ 987/872-0142.

🚩 Exchange Services **American Express** ⊠ Punta Langosta, Av. Rafael E. Melgar 599 ☎ 987/869-1389. **Promotora Cambiaria del Centro** ⊠ Av. 5 Sur between Calles 1 Sur and Adolfo Rosado Salas ☎ no phone.

### TAXIS

Cabs wait at all the major hotels, and you can hail them on the street. The fixed rates run about $2 within town; $8–$20 between town and either hotel zone; $10–$30 from most hotels to the airport; and about $20–$40 from the northern hotels or town to Parque Chankanaab or Playa San Francisco. The cost from the cruise-ship terminal by La Ceiba to San Miguel is about $10.

Drivers quote prices in pesos or dollars—the peso rate may be cheaper. Tipping isn't necessary. Despite the established taxi fares, many of the younger and quite aggressive cab drivers have begun charging double or even triple these rates. Be firm on a price before getting into the car. Drivers carry a rather complicated rate sheet with them that lists destinations by zone. Ask to see the sheet if the price seems unreasonably high.

### TOURS

BOAT & SUBMARINE TOURS Atlantis Submarine runs 1½-hour submarine rides that explore the Chankanaab Reef and surrounding area; tickets for the tours are $72.

🚩 **Atlantis Submarines** ⊠ Carretera Sur, Km 4, across from Hotel Casa del Mar ☎ 987/872-5671 ⊕ www.goatlantis.com.

HORSEBACK   Aventuras Naturales runs two-hour guided horseback tours. Prices start
TOURS   at $50 and visit Maya ruins and the jungle. Rancho Buenavista provides
four-hour rides through the jungle starting at $65 per person.
🏇 **Aventuras Naturales** ✉ Av. 35 No. 1081 ☎ 987/872-1628. **Rancho Buenavista** ✉ Av.
Rafael E. Melgar and Calle 11 Sur ☎ 987/872-1537.

ORIENTATION   Tours of the island's sights, including the San Gervasio ruins, El Cedral,
Parque Chankanaab, and the Museo de la Isla de Cozumel, cost about
$50 a person and can be arranged through travel agencies. Fiesta Hol-
idays, which has representatives in most major hotels, sells several tours.
Another option is to take a private tour of the island via taxi, which
costs about $70 for the day.
🏇 **Fiesta Holidays** ✉ Calle 11 Sur 598, between Avs. 25 and 30 ☎ 987/872-0923.

**TRAVEL AGENCIES**
🏇 **Local Agents Fiesta Holidays** ✉ Calle 11 Sur 598, between Avs. 25 and 30 ☎ 987/
872-0923. **IMC** ✉ Calle 2 Norte 101-8 ☎ 987/872-1535. **Turismo Aviomar** ✉ Av. 5 Norte
8, between Calles 2 and 4 ☎ 987/872-5445.

**VISITOR INFORMATION**
The state tourism office, Fidecomiso, is open weekdays 9–2:30. The
Cozumel Island Hotel Association provides information on affiliated ho-
tels and tour operators.
🏇 **Cozumel Island Hotel Association** ✉ Calle 2 Norte and Av. 15 ☎ 987/872-3132.
**Fidecomiso** ✉ Upstairs at Plaza del Sol, at east end of main square ☎🖥 987/872-
0972 ⊕ www.islacozumel.com.mx.

# THE RIVIERA MAYA

Updated by
Patricia Alisau

South of Cancún, the coast of the Yucatán Peninsula has many tropical possibilities. The beaches are beloved by scuba divers, snorkelers,
birders, and beachcombers, and there are accommodations to suit every
budget. Puerto Morelos retains the relaxed atmosphere of a Mexican
fishing village, while the once laid-back town of Playa del Carmen has
resorts as glitzy as those in Cancún. Secluded Boca Paila in the Sian Ka'an
Biosphere Reserve has excellent bonefishing and superb diving on virgin reefs. At the same time this coast is one of the most threatened by
development; environmentalists are supporting programs that get visitors involved in saving the threatened sea-turtle population.

Against this backdrop is the Maya culture. The modern Maya live in
the cities and villages along the coast; the legacies of the ancients inhabit
the ruins. The dramatic remains of Tulum are on a bluff overlooking
the Caribbean. A short distance inland, at Cobá, towering jungle-
shrouded pyramids are testament to the site's importance as a leading
center of commerce in the ancient Maya world.

The coast is divided into two areas: from just south of Puerto Morelos
to Punta Allen it's called the Riviera Maya; farther south it's referred
to as the Costa Maya. Most of the hotels and ancient sites are between
Puerto Morelos and Tulum; south of here civilization thins out considerably. This chapter covers the shores as far as the Sian Ka'an Biosphere

Reserve, just below Tulum. If you venture farther along, you'll be rewarded by remote beaches, coves, inlets, lagoons, and tropical landscapes.

## Puerto Morelos

⑰ *8 km (5 mi) south of Punta Tanchacté.*

For years, Puerto Morelos was known as the small, relaxed coastal town where the car ferry left for Cozumel. This lack of regard actually helped it avoid overdevelopment, though now the construction of all-inclusive resorts nearby may spoil the fishing-village aura. And more people are discovering that Morelos, exactly halfway between Cancún and Playa del Carmen, makes a great base for exploring the region.

In ancient times this was one of the points of departure for pregnant Maya women making pilgrimages by canoe to Cozumel, the sacred isle of the fertility goddess, Ixchel. Remnants of Maya ruins exist along the coast here, but nothing has been restored. The town itself is small but colorful, with a central plaza surrounded by shops and restaurants; its trademark is a leaning lighthouse. Puerto Morelos's greatest appeal lies out at sea: a superb coral reef only 1,800 feet offshore is an excellent place to snorkel and scuba dive. Its proximity to shore means that the waters here are calm and safe, though the beach isn't as attractive as others as it isn't regularly cleared of seaweed and turtle grass. Still, you can walk for miles here and see only a few people. In addition, the mangroves in back of town are home to 36 species of birds, making it a great place for bird-watchers.

### Where to Stay & Eat

★ **$–$$$** ✕ **Casa del Mar.** The food at this family-run restaurant is some of the town's best. Choices include delicious empanadas, chicken fajitas, fresh salads, pastas, and incredible steaks that rival anything at the larger steak houses in Cancún (and for half the price). There's a palapa bar on a terrace that leads down to the beach. ⊠ *Calle Heriberto Frias 6* ☎ *998/871–0522* ☱ *D, MC, V.*

**$$$$** ▦ **Ceiba del Mar Hotel & Spa.** For peace and quiet, this resort on a secluded beach is just the ticket. Rooms are in eight thatched-roof buildings, and all have ocean-view terraces. Painted tiles, wrought ironwork, and bamboo details complement hardwood furnishings from Guadalajara. The whole effect is very Maya, though. A first-class spa offers massage and beauty treatments. There's also butler service, and your Continental breakfast is discreetly delivered to your room through a hidden closet chamber. ⊠ *Av. Niños Heroes s/n* ☎ *998/872–8060 or 877/545–6221* ☷ *998/872–8061* ⊕ *www.ceibadelmar.com* ⤲ *120 rooms, 6 suites* ♧ *2 restaurants, in-room safes, cable TV with movies, tennis court, pool, hot tub, spa, beach, dive shop, bar, shop, laundry service, concierge, meeting room, car rental, travel services* ☱ *AE, MC, V* ⦿⧫ *CP.*

FodorśChoice
★

**$$$$** ▦ **Presidente InterContinental Paraiso de la Bonita Resort and Thalasso.** Eclectic is the byword at this luxury all-suites hotel. A pair of stone dragons guards the entrance, and the spacious two-room guest quarters—all with sweeping sea and jungle views—are outfitted with furnishings from

FodorśChoice
★

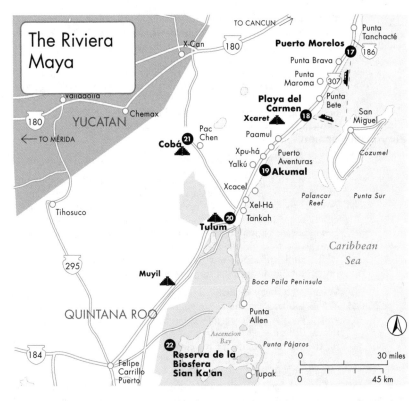

The Riviera
Maya

TO CANCUN

Punta
Tanchacté

X-Can  180

**Puerto Morelos** ⑰  186

Punta Brava

Punta
Maroma  307

**Playa del
Carmen** ⑱

Punta
Bete

San
Miguel

Xcaret

vauaaoua

Chemax

YUCATAN

180

← TO MÉRIDA

Pac
Chen

Paamul

**Cobá** ㉑

Xpu-há
Yalkú

Puerto
Aventuras

**Akumal** ⑲

Cozumel

Xcacel

Xel-Há

Tankah

Palancar
Reef

Punta Sur

Tihosuco

**Tulum** ⑳

*Caribbean
Sea*

295

**Muyil**

*Boca Paila Peninsula*

QUINTANA ROO

Punta
Allen

*Ascencion
Bay*

*Punta Pájaros*

184

Felipe
Carrillo
Puerto

㉒ **Reserva de la
Biosfera
Sian Ka'an**

Tupak

0                30 miles

0                45 km

Asia, Africa, the Mediterranean, or the Caribbean. The restaurants, which are among the best in the Riviera Maya, adroitly blend Asian and Mexican flavors. The knockout spa has thalassotherapy treatments, some of which take place in specially built saltwater pools. ⊠ *Carretera 307, Km 328* ☎ *998/872–8300 or 800/327–7777* 🖷 *998/872–8301* ⊕ *www. paraisodelabonitaresort.com* ➷ *90 suites △ 2 restaurants, in-room data ports, in-room safes, cable TV, golf privileges, tennis court, pool, health club, hot tub, massage, sauna, spa, steam room, beach, snorkeling, fishing, bar, laundry service, Internet, meeting room, airport shuttle, car rental, travel services, free parking; no kids under 13* ⊟ *AE, DC, MC, V.*

$  🏨 **Casa Caribe.** This small hotel is a few blocks from the town center and five minutes from the beach. Breezy rooms have king-size beds, coffeemakers, and large tile baths. Terraces have hammocks and views of the ocean or the mangroves. You can use the large kitchen, huge terrace, and the lounge area. The grounds include a walled courtyard and a fragrant tropical garden. ⊠ *Avs. Javier Rojo Gómez and Ejercito Mexicano, 3 blocks north of town* ☎ *998/871–0049, 763/441–7630 in U.S.* ⊕ *www.us-webmasters.com/casa-caribe* ➷ *6 rooms △ Fans, refrigerators, bar; no a/c, no room phones, no room TVs* ⊟ *No credit cards.*

### Sports & the Outdoors

Enrique at the PADI-affiliated **Almost Heaven Adventures** (☎998/871–0230), in the main square by the currency exchange office, can set up snorkeling and diving trips. Instruction ranges from an $85 beginner course to a $275, four-day, open-water course; dives cost $45 for one tank, $65 for two tanks. **Brecko's** (✉ Casita del Mar, Calle Heriberto Frias 6 ☎998/ 871–0301) offers snorkeling and deep-sea fishing in a 25-foot boat. Snorkeling trips start at $15–$20 and fishing trips at $200.

## Playa del Carmen

**⑱**  *10 km (6 mi) south of Punta Bete, 68 km (42 mi) south of Cancún.*

Once upon a time, Playa del Carmen was a fishing village with a ravishing deserted beach. The villagers fished and raised coconut palms to produce copra, and the only foreigners who ventured here were beach bums. These days, however, it's one of Latin America's fastest-growing communities, with a population of more than 135,000 and a pace almost as hectic as Cancún's. The beach is still delightful—alabaster-white sand, turquoise-blue waters—it's just not deserted. Hotels, restaurants, and shops multiply faster than you can say "Kukulcán."

### Where to Stay & Eat

★ $$–$$$  ✕ **Blue Lobster.** You can chose your dinner live from a tank and if it's grilled, you pay by the weight—the average is $10–$50 a platter. At night, the candlelit dining room draws a good crowd. People come not only for the lobster but also for the ceviche, mussels, jumbo shrimp, or imported T-bone steak. Ask for a table on the terrace overlooking the street. ✉ *Calle 12 and Av. 5* ☎ *984/873–1360* ☐ *AE, MC, V* ☺ *No lunch.*

$–$$$  ✕ **Casa del Agua.** Gunther Spath, the patriarch of the Swiss family that
**Fodor'sChoice**  founded this restaurant, learned his trade as manager of Las Palapas hotel
★  north of Playa del Carmen. His praiseworthy German, Italian, and Swiss dishes include sliced chicken Zurich with spaetzle and mushroom gravy and the ever-popular steak Roquefort. Finish up with Mama Spath's Hot Love, an ice-cream-and-hot-blueberry dessert. ✉ *Av. 5 and Calle 2* ☎ *984/803–0232* ☐ *MC, V.*

$–$$$  ✕ **Sur.** This two-story enclave of food from the Pampas region of Argentina is a trendy spot. Sky-blue tablecloths and plants complement hardwood floors in the intimate upstairs dining room. Entrées come with four sauces, dominant among them *chimichurri,* made with oil, vinegar, and finely chopped herbs. Start off with meat or spinach empanadas or Argentine sausage, followed by a sizzling half-pound *churrasco* (top sirloin steak). Finish the meal with warm caramel crepes. ✉ *Calle Corozonbetween Calles 12 and 14* ☎ *984/803–2995* ☐ *D, MC, V* ☺ *No lunch Sun.*

★ $–$$$  ✕ **Yaxche.** One of Playa's best restaurants has copies of hand-carved stelae from famous ruins and murals of Maya gods and kings. Maya dishes such as *halach winic* (chicken in a spicy four-pepper sauce) are superb. Finish your meal with a Maya Kiss (Kahlúa and Xtabentun, the local liqueur flavored with anise and honey). ✉ *Calle 8 and Av. 5* ☎ *984/ 873–2502* ☐ *AE, MC, V.*

★ $$$$  ▦ **Royal Hideaway.** On a breathtaking stretch of beach, this 13-acre resort has exceptional amenities and superior service. Art and artifacts from around the world fill the lobby, and streams, waterfalls, and fountains dot the grounds. Rooms are in two- and three-story colonial-style villas, each with its own concierge, who will make reservations for you at the five on-site restaurants. Gorgeous rooms have two queen-size beds, sitting areas, and ocean-view terraces. The resort is wheelchair accessible. ⊠ *Fracc. Playacar, Lote 6, Playacar* ☎ *984/873–4500 or 800/858–2258* 🖷 *984/873–4506* ⊕ *www.allegroresorts.com* ⌁ *192 rooms, 8 suites* ⌂ *5 restaurants, in-room data ports, cable TV, 2 tennis courts, 2 pools, exercise equipment, hot tub, spa, beach, snorkeling, windsurfing, bicycles, 3 bars, library, recreation room, theater, shops, laundry service, concierge, meeting rooms, Internet, travel services, free parking; no kids* ⊟ *AE, MC, V* ⎟◎⎟ *AI.*

★ **$$$** 🏨 **Lunata.** An elegant entrance, Spanish-tile floors, and hand-tooled furniture from Guadalajara greet you at this classy inn. Guest rooms have sitting areas, dark hardwood furnishings, high-quality crafts, orthopedic mattresses, and terraces—some with hammocks. Service is personal and gracious. Breakfast is laid out in the garden each day. ⊠ *Av. 5 between Calles 6 and 8* ☎ *984/873–0884* 🖷 *984/873–1240* ⊕ *www. lunata.com* ⌁ *10 rooms* ⌂ *Refrigerators, cable TV, laundry service, car rental* ⊟ *AE, MC, V* ⎟◎⎟ *CP.*

**$$** 🏨 **Mosquito Blue.** It's simultaneously casual, exotic, and elegant. The lobby and guest quarters have Indonesian details, mahogany furniture, and soft lighting. King-size beds and great views round out the rooms. The open-air bar is a soothing spot—it's sheltered by a thatched roof and surrounded by pastel walls in a cloistered courtyard near one of the swimming pools. The restaurant serves Mexican and Italian cuisine. ⊠ *Calle 12 between Avs. 5 and 10* ☎☎ *984/873–1335* ⊕ *www. mosquitoblue.com* ⌁ *46 rooms, 1 suite* ⌂ *Restaurant, cable TV, 2 pools, massage, dive shop, bar, laundry service, car rental, travel services; no kids under 16* ⊟ *AE, MC, V.*

**$–$$** 🏨 **Baal Nah Kah.** True to its Maya name, which means "home hidden among the gum trees," this small hotel is quite homey. You can use the large kitchen, the sitting room, and the barbecue pit. The five bedrooms and one studio are on different levels, affording complete privacy. Two rooms have spacious balconies with ocean views; all have tile baths, double or king-size beds, and Mexican details. There's a small café next door, and the beach is a block away. ⊠ *Calle 12 near Av. 5* ☎ *984/873–2343* 🖷 *984/873–0050* ⊕ *www.playabedandbreakfast. com* ⌁ *5 rooms, 1 studio* ⌂ *Fans; no a/c in some rooms, no TV in some rooms* ⊟ *No credit cards.*

**$$** 🏨 **Hacienda del Caribe.** This hotel evokes an old Yucatecan hacienda—albeit a colorful one—with wrought-iron balconies, stained-glass windows, and Talavera tile work. Guest rooms have such unique details as headboards with calla lily motifs and painted tile sinks. The pool is right off the lobby and surrounded by a small restaurant. The beach is a half block away. ⊠ *Calle 2 between Avs. 5 and 10* ☎ *984/873–3132* 🖷 *984/ 873–1149* ⊕ *www.haciendadelcaribe.com* ⌁ *27 rooms, 5 suites* ⌂ *Restaurant, fans, in-room safes, cable TV, pool, car rental, free parking* ⊟ *D, MC, V.*

**$** 🏨 **Posada Mariposa.** Not only is this Italian-style property in the quiet north end of town impeccable and comfortable, but it's also well priced.

Rooms center on a garden with a small fountain. All have ocean views, queen-size beds, wall murals, luxurious bathrooms, and shared patios. Suites have full kitchens. Sunset from the rooftop is spectacular, and the beach is five minutes away. ⊠ *Av. 5 No. 314, between Calles 24 and 26* 🏠 *984/873–3886* ⊕ *www.posada-mariposa.com* ➷ *18 rooms, 6 suites* ⌂ *Cable TV; no room phones* ⊟ *No credit cards.*

**$$** 🏨 **Tierra Maya.** The Spanish owners have transformed this small inn just three blocks from the beach into a little work of art, with burned-orange and ocher color schemes, stucco Maya masks, batik wall hangings, and rustic wood-frame beds. All guest rooms have balconies overlooking the garden and pool area, which also has a thatched-roof restaurant, a reading pavilion, and a *temazcal* (sweat lodge). The temazcal ceremony led by a shaman costs $70 and includes purification rituals, massage, and fruit juices. The apartment and the suite have kitchenettes. ⊠ *Calle 24 between Avs. 5 and 10* 🏠 *984/873–3960* ⊕ *www.hoteltierra maya.com* ➷ *21 rooms, 1 suite, 1 apartment* ⌂ *Restaurant, fans, in-room safes, some kitchenettes, cable TV, pool, massage, bar, concierge, Internet, free parking* ⊟ *MC, V.*

**¢** 🏨 **Posada Marina.** Popular with Italian budget travelers, this friendly, three-story, family–style hotel in the tranquil north part of Avenida 5 has small rooms done in shades of yellow as well as a patio garden with benches. Each floor has a sitting area looking out to sea. The cozy restaurant serves Italian cuisine. ⊠ *Av. 5 Norte between Calles 22 and 24* ☎ *984/873–3240* ⊕ *www.alphauniversal.com/posadamarina* ➷ *20 rooms* ⌂ *Restaurant; no a/c, no room phones, no room TVs* ⊟ *No credit cards.*

## Nightlife

**Alux** (⊠ Av. Juárez and Calle 55 Sur ☎ 984/803–0713) has a bar, disco, and restaurant and is built into a cavern. **Apasionado** (⊠ Av. 5 ☎ 984/803–1101) has live jazz Wednesday through Sunday nights. **Capitán Tutix** (⊠ Calle 4 Norte near Av. 5 ☎ 984/803–1595) is a beach bar designed to resemble a ship. Good drink prices and live music keep things humming until dawn. To party off the beach check out **Coco Bongo** (⊠ Calle 6 between Avs. 5 and 10 ☎ 984/973–3189), a dance club that plays the latest Cuban sounds.

## Sports & the Outdoors

SCUBA DIVING   The PADI-affiliated **Abyss** (⊠ Calle 12 ☎ 984/873–2164) offers training ($80 for an introductory course) in addition to dive trips ($38 for one tank, $56 for two tanks) and packages. The oldest shop in town, **Tank-Ha Dive Shop** (⊠ Av. 5 between Calles 8 and 10 🏠 984/873–5037) has PADI-certified teachers and runs diving and snorkeling trips to the reefs and caverns. A one-tank dive costs $35; for a two-tank trip it's $55; and for a cenote two-tank trip it's $90. Dive packages are also available. **Yucatek Divers** (⊠ Av. 15 Norte between Calles 2 and 4 ☎ 984/873–1363), which is affiliated with PADI, specializes in cenote dives and diving packages and works with divers who have disabilities. Introductory courses start at $75 for a one-tank dive and go as high as $350 for a four-day beginner course in open water.

## Shopping

Avenida 5 between Calles 4 and 10 is the best place to shop along the coast. Boutiques sell folk art and textiles from around Mexico, and clothing stores carry lots of sarongs and beachwear made from Indonesian batiks. A shopping area called Calle Corozon, between Calles 12 and 14, has a pedestrian street, art galleries, restaurants, and boutiques.

**Amber Mexicano** (⊠ Av. 5 between Calles 4 and 6 ☎☎ 984/873–2357) has amber jewelry crafted by a local designer who imports the amber from Chiapas. **Telart** (⊠ Av. Juárez 10 ☎ 984/873–0066) carries textiles from all over Mexico.

# Akumal

**19** *37 km (23 mi) south of Playa del Carmen.*

In Maya, Akumal (pronounced ah-koo-maal) means "place of the turtle," and for hundreds of years this beach has been a nesting ground for turtles (the season is June–August and the best place to see them is on Half Moon Bay). The place first attracted international attention in 1926, when explorers discovered the *Mantanceros,* a Spanish galleon that sank in 1741. In 1958, Pablo Bush Romero, a wealthy businessman who loved diving these pristine waters, created the first resort, which became the headquarters for the club he formed—the Mexican Underwater Expeditions Club (CEDAM). Akumal soon attracted wealthy underwater adventurers who flew in on private planes and searched for sunken treasures.

These days Akumal is probably the most Americanized community on the coast. It consists of three areas: Half Moon Bay, with its pretty beaches, terrific snorkeling, and large number of rentals; Akumal Proper, a large resort with a market, grocery stores, laundry facilities, a pharmacy; and Akumal Aventuras, to the south, with more condos and homes. The original Maya community has been moved to a planned town across the highway.

Devoted snorkelers may want to walk the unmarked dirt road to **Yalkú,** a couple of miles north of Akumal in Half Moon Bay. A series of small lagoons that gradually reach the ocean, Yalkú is an eco-park that's home to schools of parrot fish in superbly clear water with visibility to 160 feet. It has restrooms and an entrance fee of about $8.

## Where to Stay & Eat

**$–$$** ✕ **Que Onda.** A Swiss-Italian couple created this northern Italian restaurant at the end of Half Moon Bay. Dishes are served under a palapa and include great homemade pastas, shrimp flambéed in cognac with a touch of saffron, and vegetarian lasagna. Que Onda also has a neighboring six-room hotel that's creatively furnished with Mexican and Guatemalan handicrafts. ⊠ *Caleta Yalkú, Lotes 97–99; enter through Club Akumal Caribe, turn left, and go north to very end of road at Half Moon Bay* ☎ 984/875–9101 ☐ MC, V ☉ Closed Tues.

**$$–$$$$** ☷ **Villas Akumal.** These white-stucco, thatched-roof condos in a beach-side residential development offer all the comforts of home and are perfect for extended stays (there are special rates if you book for a week). Units vary in size and configuration but most have cool tile floors, fabrics in tropical colors and prints, wicker furniture, and well-equipped kitchens. Many also have terraces with dynamite sea views—especially beautiful on evenings when the moon is full. On summer nights you can watch nesting sea turtles. ⊠ *Carretera Cancún–Tulum, Km 104, Fracc. Akumal C, Playa Jade* ☎ *55/5202–3600 Ext. 224 in Mexico City* 🖷 *55/ 5202–8200 in Mexico City* ⊕ *www.lasvilasakumal.com* 🛏 *8 3-bedroom suites, 10 2-bedroom suites, 8 studios* ♨ *Kitchen, cable TV, pool, beach, snorkeling, boating, concierge, airport shuttle, car rental, travel services, free parking* ⊟ *AE, MC, V.*

$$ 🏨 **Club Akumal Caribe & Villas Maya.** Pablo Bush Romero established this resort in the 1960s to house his diving buddies, and it still has pleasant accommodations and a congenial staff—not to mention some of the best rates along the Riviera Maya. Rooms have rattan furniture, large beds, tile work, and ocean views. The bungalows are surrounded by gardens and have lots of beautiful Mexican tile. The secluded one-, two-, and three-bedroom units, called Villas Flamingo, are on Half Moon Bay and have kitchenettes as well as a separate beach and pools. Dive and meal-plan packages available. ⊠ *Carretera 307, Km 104* ☎ *984/875– 9012, 800/351–1622 in U.S. and Canada, 800/343–1440 in Canada* 🖷 *915/581–6709* ⊕ *www.hotelakumalcaribe.com* 🛏 *21 rooms, 40 bungalows, 4 villas, 1 condo* ♨ *Restaurant, ice cream parlor, pizzeria, snack bar, fans, some kitchenettes, refrigerators, pool, beach, 2 dive shops, bar, baby-sitting, children's programs (ages 2–12); no room phones, no TV in some rooms* ⊟ *AE, MC, V.*

### Sports & the Outdoors
The **Akumal Dive Center** (⊠ About 10 mins north of Club Akumal Caribe ☎ 984/875–9025) is the area's oldest and most experienced dive operation, offering reef or cenote diving, fishing, and snorkeling. Dives cost from $33 (one tank) to $110 (four tanks); a two-hour fishing trip for as many as four people runs $99.

## Tulum

🔥 ⑳ *2 km (1 mi) south of Tankah, 130 km (81 mi) south of Cancún.*

Fodor'sChoice
★

Tulum (pronounced tool-lum) is the Yucatán Peninsula's most-visited Maya ruin, attracting more than 2 million people annually. This means you have to share the site with roughly half of the tourist population of Quintana Roo on any given day, even if you arrive early. Though most of the architecture is of unremarkable Postclassic (AD 1000–AD 1521) style, the amount of attention that Tulum receives is not entirely undeserved. Its location by the blue-green Caribbean is breathtaking.

At the entrance you can hire a guide, but keep in mind that some of their information is more entertaining than historically accurate. (Disregard that stuff about virgin sacrifices atop the altars.) Because you aren't allowed to climb or enter the fragile structures—only three really merit close inspection anyway—you can see the ruins in two hours. You might, however, want to allow extra time for a swim or a stroll on the beach.

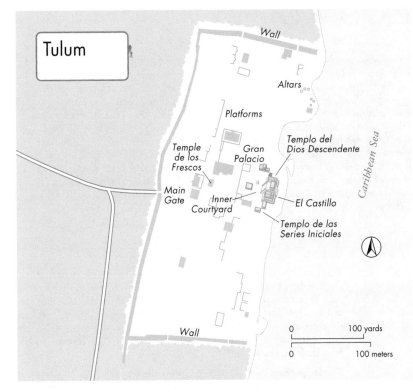

Tulum is one of the few Maya cities known to have been inhabited when the conquistadores arrived in 1518. In the 16th century, it functioned as a safe harbor for trade goods from rival Maya factions; it was considered neutral territory where merchandise could be stored and traded in peace. The city reached its height when traders, made wealthy through the exchange of goods, for the first time outranked Maya priests in authority and power. When the Spaniards arrived, they forbade the Maya traders to sail the seas, and commerce among the Maya died.

Tulum has long held special significance for the Maya. A key city in the League of Mayapán (AD 987–AD 1194), it was never conquered by the Spaniards, although it was abandoned about 75 years after the conquest. For 300 years thereafter, it symbolized the defiance of an otherwise subjugated people; it was one of the last outposts of the Maya during their insurrection against Mexican rule in the War of the Castes, which began in 1846. Uprisings continued intermittently until 1935, when the Maya ceded Tulum to the government.

The first significant structure is the two-story **Templo de los Frescos,** to the left of the entryway. The temple's vault roof and corbel arch are examples of classic Maya architecture. Faint traces of blue-green frescoes outlined in black on the inner and outer walls refer to ancient

# CASTE WARS

When Mexico achieved independence from Spain in 1821, the Maya didn't celebrate. The new government didn't return their lost land, and it didn't treat them with respect. In 1846, a Maya rebellion began in Valladolid. A year later, they had killed hundreds and the battle raged on. (The Indians were rising up against centuries of being relegated to the status of "lower caste" people. Hence the conflict was called the Guerra de las Castas or Caste Wars.

Help for the embattled Mexicans arrived with a vengeance from Mexico City, Cuba, and the United States. By 1850, the Maya had been mercilessly slaughtered, their population plummeting from 500,000 to 300,000. Survivors fled to the jungles and held out against the government until its troops withdrew in 1915. The Maya controlled Quintana Roo from Tulum, their headquarters, and finally accepted Mexican rule in 1935.

Maya beliefs (the clearest frescoes are hidden from sight now that you can't walk into the temple). Reminiscent of the Mixtec style, the frescoes depict the three worlds of the Maya and their major deities and are decorated with stellar and serpentine patterns, rosettes, and ears of maize and other offerings to the gods. One scene portrays the rain god seated on a four-legged animal—probably a reference to the Spaniards on their horses.

The largest and most famous building, the **Castillo** (Castle), looms at the edge of a 40-foot limestone cliff just past the Temple of the Frescoes. Atop it, at the end of a broad stairway, is a temple with stucco ornamentation on the outside and traces of fine frescoes inside the two chambers. (The stairway has been roped off, so the top temple is inaccessible.) The front wall of the Castillo has faint carvings of the Descending God and columns depicting the plumed serpent god, Kukulcán, who was introduced to the Maya by the Toltecs. To the left of the Castillo is the **Templo del Dios Descendente**—so called for the carving of a winged god plummeting to earth over the doorway.

The tiny cove to the left of the Castillo and Temple of the Descending God is a good spot for a cooling swim, but there are no changing rooms. A few small altars sit atop a hill at the north side of the cove and have a good view of the Castillo and the sea. On the highway about 4 km (2½ mi) south of the ruins is the present-day village of Tulum. As Tulum's importance as a commercial center increases, markets, restaurants, shops, services, and auto-repair shops continue to spring up along the road. Growth hasn't been kind to the pueblo, however: it's rather unsightly, with a wide four-lane highway running down the middle. Despite this blight, it has a few good restaurants. 🖼 *$9; use of video camera extra* ☉ *Daily 8–5.*

### Where to Stay & Eat

★ **$$–$$$$** ✕ **Restaurante Oscar y Lalo.** A couple of miles outside Tulum, at Bahías de Punta Soliman, is this wonderful restaurant run by two friends, Oscar and Lalo. The seafood is excellent—this is supposedly the only place for miles that serves king crab—and the pizza is divine. If you're inspired to sleep on the beach, there are campsites. RVs are also welcome, though there aren't any hookups. ⊠ *Carretera 307 north of Tankah (look for faded white sign)* ☎ *984/871–2209* ▭ *No credit cards.*

★ **$$$** ✕▥ **Las Ranitas.** Stylish and ecologically correct Las Ranitas (The Little Frogs) creates its own power through wind-generated electricity, solar energy, and recycled water. Each chic room has gorgeous tile and fabric from Oaxaca. Terraces overlook gardens and the ocean, and jungle walkways lead to the breathtaking beach. The pièce de résistance is the French chef, who creates incredible French and Mexican cuisine ($$–$$$). ⊠ *Carretera Tulum–Boca Paila, Km 9 (last hotel before the Reserva de la Biosfera Sian Ka'an)* ☎🖷 *984/877–8554* ⊕ *www.lasranitas. com* ➦ *13 rooms, 2 suites* ⬧ *Restaurant, pool, beach, snorkeling, paddle tennis; no a/c, no room phones* ▭ *No credit cards* ❍ *CP* ☉ *Closed mid-Sept.–mid-Nov.*

**$$** ✕▥ **Zamas.** On the wild, isolated Punta de Piedra (Rock Point), with ocean views as far as the eye can see, this kick-back-and-groove hotel draws Americans. The romantically rustic cabanas—with bare-bulb lighting, mosquito nets over spartan beds, big tile bathrooms, and bright Mexican colors—are nicely distanced from one another. The restaurant ($–$$$) has an eclectic Italian-Mexican-Yucatecan menu and fresh fish. ⊠ *Carretera Tulum–Boca Paila, Km 5* ☎ *984/871–2067, 415/387–9806 in U.S.* ⊕ *www.zamas.com* ➦ *15 cabanas* ⬧ *Restaurant, beach, bar, snorkeling, car rental; no a/c, no room phones* ▭ *No credit cards.*

**¢–$$** ▥ **Cabañas Copal.** At this sensational eco-hotel on a rugged cliff, you
FodorsChoice   can sleep in dirt- or cement-floored palapas sheltered from the jungle
★   elements by mosquito nets and thatched roofs. Some baths are shared, and there's no electricity in some. Rooms are bigger and more elegant than palapas, with hardwood floors, hand-carved furniture, and a kind of primitive whirlpool bath. At night thousands of candles light the walkways and grounds. Wellness programs, exercise classes, and spa treatments include yoga, dream classes, and Maya massages; there's also a flotation chamber and a temazcal (sweat lodge). ⊠ *Carretera Tulum Ruinas, Km 5 (turn right at fork in highway; hotel is less than 1 km (½ mi) on right),* ☎ *984/806–4406 or 984/806–8247* ⊕ *www.cabanascopal. com* ➦ *45 palapas, 15 rooms* ⬧ *Restaurant, fitness classes, massage, beach, snorkeling, fishing, bar, Internet; no a/c, no room phones, no room TVs* ▭ *No credit cards.*

# Cobá

🏛 ❷¹   *49 km (30 mi) northwest of Tulum.*

FodorsChoice
★   Cobá (pronounced ko-*bah*), Maya for "water stirred by the wind," flourished from AD 800 to AD 1100, with a population of as many as 55,000. Now it stands in solitude, with the jungle having taken many of its build-

ings. Cobá is often overlooked by visitors who opt, instead, to visit better-known Tulum. But this site is much grander and less crowded, giving you a chance to really immerse yourself in ancient culture. Cobá exudes stillness, the silence broken by the occasional shriek of a spider monkey or the call of a bird. Processions of huge army ants cross the footpaths as the sun slips through openings between the tall hardwood trees, ferns, and giant palms.

Near five lakes and between coastal watchtowers and inland cities, Cobá exercised economic control over the region through a network of at least 16 *sacbéob* (white stone roads), one of which measures 100 km (62 mi) and is the longest in the Maya world. The city once covered 70 square km (27 square mi), making it a noteworthy sister state to Tikal in northern Guatemala, with which it had close cultural and commercial ties. It's noted for its massive temple-pyramids, one of which is 138 feet tall, the largest and highest in northern Yucatán. The main groupings of ruins are separated by several miles of dense vegetation, so the best way to get a sense of the immensity of the city is to scale one of the pyramids. It's easy to get lost here, so stay on the main road; *don't* be tempted by the narrow paths that lead into the jungle unless you have a qualified guide with you.

The first major cluster of structures, to your right as you enter the ruins, is the **Cobá Group,** whose pyramids are around a sunken patio. At the near end of the group, facing a large plaza, is the 79-foot-high temple, which was dedicated to the rain god, Chaac; some Maya people still place offerings and light candles here in hopes of improving their harvests. Around the rear to the left is a restored ball court, where a sacred game was once played to petition the gods for rain, fertility, and other boons.

Farther along the main path to your left is the **Chumuc Mul Group,** little of which has been excavated. The principal pyramid here is covered with the remains of vibrantly painted stucco motifs (*chumuc mul* means "stucco pyramid"). A kilometer (½ mi) past this site is the **Nohoch Mul Group** (Large Hill Group), the highlight of which is the pyramid of the same name, the tallest at Cobá. It has 120 steps—equivalent to 12 stories—and shares a plaza with Temple 10. The Descending God (also seen at Tulum) is depicted on a facade of the temple atop Nohoch Mul, from which the view is excellent.

Beyond the Nohoch Mul Group is the **Castillo,** with nine chambers that are reached by a stairway. To the south are the remains of a ball court, including the stone ring through which the ball was hurled. From the main route follow the sign to **Las Pinturas Group,** named for the still-discernible polychrome friezes on the inner and outer walls of its large, patioed pyramid. Take the minor path for 1 km (½ mi) to the Macanxoc Group, not far from the lake of the same name. The main pyramid at Macanxoc is accessible by a stairway.

Cobá is a 35-minute drive northwest of Tulum along a pothole-filled road that leads straight through the jungle. You can comfortably make your way around Cobá in a half day, but spending the night in town is highly advised, as doing so will allow you to visit the ruins in solitude when they open at 8 AM. Even on a day trip, consider taking time out for lunch to escape the intense heat and mosquito-heavy humidity of the ruins. Buses depart to and from Cobá for Playa del Carmen and Tulum at least twice daily. Taxis to Tulum are still reasonable (about $16). ⊠ *$4; use of video camera $6; $2 fee for parking* ⊙ *Daily 8–5.*

### Where to Stay & Eat

¢–$   ✗ **El Bocadito.** The restaurant closest to the ruins is owned and run by a gracious Maya family, which serves simple, traditional cuisine. A three-course fixed-price lunch costs $4. Look for such classic dishes as *pollo pibíl* (chicken baked in banana leaves) and *cochinita pibíl* (pork baked in banana leaves). ⊠ *On road to ruins* ☎ *987/874–2087* ▭ *No credit cards* ⊙ *No dinner.*

$   ▦ **Uolis Nah.** This small thatched-roof complex has extra-large, quiet rooms with high ceilings, two beds, hammocks, and tile floors. You're less than 2 km (1 mi) from the Tulum highway but away from the noise, and there's lots of privacy. An extra person in a double room costs $11 more. ⊠ *On road to ruins* ☎ *984/879–5685* ⊕ *www.uolisnah.com* ⇩ *7 rooms* ⚵ *Fans, kitchenettes, car rental; no a/c, no room phones, no room TVs* ▭ *No credit cards.*

## Reserva de la Biosfera Sian Ka'an

★ ㉒   *15 km (9 mi) south of Tulum to the Punta Allen turnoff and within Sian Ka'an.*

The Sian Ka'an ("where the sky is born," pronounced see-an caan) region was first settled by the Maya in the 5th century AD. In 1986 the Mexican government established the 1.3-million-acre Reserva de la Biosfera Sian Ka'an as an internationally protected area. The next year, it was named a World Heritage Site by the United Nations Educational, Scientific, and Cultural Organization (UNESCO); later, it was extended by 200,000 acres. The Riviera Maya and Costa Maya split the biosphere reserve; Punta Allen and north belong to the Riviera Maya, and everything south of Punta Allen is part of the Costa Maya.

The Sian Ka'an reserve constitutes 10% of the land in Quintana Roo and covers 100 km (62 mi) of coast. Hundreds of species of local and migratory birds, fish, other animals and plants, and fewer than 1,000 residents (primarily Maya) share this area of freshwater and coastal lagoons, mangrove swamps, cays, savannas, tropical forests, and a barrier reef. There are approximately 27 ruins (none excavated) linked by a unique canal system—one of the few of its kind in the Maya world in Mexico. This is one of the last undeveloped stretches of North American coast. To see its sites you must take a guided tour. Several kinds of tours, including bird-watching and kayaking trips, are offered on site through the reserve's visitor center; other privtaely-run tours are also available.

Many species of the once-flourishing wildlife have fallen into the endangered category, but the waters here still teem with rooster fish, bonefish, mojarra, snapper, shad, permit, sea bass, and crocodiles. Fishing the flats for wily bonefish is popular, and the peninsula's few lodges also run deep-sea fishing trips.

## Where to Stay

**$$$$**   🏨 **Boca Paila Fishing Lodge.** Home of the "grand slam" (fishing lingo for catching three different kinds of fish in one trip), this charming lodge has nine cottages, each with two double beds, couches, bathrooms, and screened-in sitting areas. Boats and guides for fly-fishing and bonefishing are provided; you can rent tackle at the lodge. Meals consist of fresh fish dishes and Maya specialties, among other things. From January through June and October through December a 50% deposit is required, and the minimum stay is one week (there's no required deposit and only a three-night minimum stay the rest of the year). ⊠ *Boca Paila Peninsula* ☍ *reservations: Frontiers, Box 959, Wexford, PA 15090* ☎ *724/935–1577 or 800/245–1950* ⊕ *www.frontierstravel.com* ⊲ *9 cottages* ⚲ *Restaurant, beach, snorkeling, fishing, bar, laundry service, airport shuttle; no a/c in some rooms, no room phones, no room TVs* ⊟ *No credit cards unless arranged with Frontiers* ¶⊙¶ *AI.*

★ **$$$$**   🏨 **Casa Blanca Lodge.** This American-managed lodge is on a rocky outcrop on remote Punta Pájaros Island—reputed to be one of the best places in the world for light-tackle saltwater fishing. Modern guest rooms have tile-and-mahogany bathrooms. An open-air thatched-roof bar welcomes anglers with drinks, fresh fish dishes, fruit, and vegetables at the start and end of the day. Only weeklong packages can be booked March through July. Rates include a charter flight from Cancún, all meals, a boat, and a guide; nonfishing packages are cheaper. A 50% prepayment fee is required. ⊠ *Punta Pájaros* ☍ *reservations: Frontiers, Box 959, Wexford, PA 15090* ☎ *724/935–1577, 800/245–1950 to Frontiers* ⊕ *www.frontierstravel.com* ⊲ *9 rooms* ⚲ *Restaurant, beach, snorkeling, fishing, bar, laundry service; no room phones, no room TVs* ⊟ *MC, V* ¶⊙¶ *AI.*

# The Riviera Maya A to Z

### BOAT & FERRY TRAVEL

Passenger-only ferries and two enormous speedboats depart from the dock at Playa del Carmen for the 45-minute trip to the main pier in Cozumel. They leave daily, approximately every hour on the hour 5 AM–11 PM, with no ferries at noon, 2, 8, or 10. Return service to Playa runs every hour on the hour 4 AM–10 PM, with no ferries at 5, 11 AM, 1, 7, or 9 PM. Call ahead, as the schedule changes often.

🛈 **Playa del Carmen passenger ferry** ☎ 984/872-1508, 984/872-1588, or 984/872-0477.

### BUS TRAVEL

Buses traveling all points except Cancún stop at the terminal Avenida 20 and Calle 12. Buses headed to and from Cancún use the main bus terminal downtown (Avenida Juárez and Avenida 5). ADO runs express, first-class, and second-class buses to major destinations.

🔢 Bus Information **ADO** 📞 984/873-0109. **Caribe Express** 📞 984/832-7889.

## CAR RENTAL

🔢 Major Agencies **Budget** ✉ Continental Plaza, Playa del Carmen 📞 984/873-0100. **Hertz** ✉ Plaza Marina, Playa del Carmen 📞 984/873-0702. **Thrifty** ✉ Calle 8 between Avs. 5 and 10, Playa del Carmen 📞 984/873-0119.

## CAR TRAVEL

The entire 382-km (237-mi) coast from Punta Sam near Cancún to the main border crossing to Belize at Chetumal is traversable on Carretera 307—a straight, paved highway. Puerto Morelos, Playa del Carmen, Tulum, Puerto Felipe Carrillo, Bacalar, and Chetumal have gas stations.

Good roads that run into Carretera 307 from the west are Carretera 180 (from Mérida and Valladolid), Carretera 295 (from Valladolid), Carretera 184 (from central Yucatán), and Carretera 186 (from Villahermosa and, via Carretera 261, from Mérida and Campeche). There's an entrance to the *autopista* toll highway between Cancún and Mérida off Carretera 307 just south of Cancún. Approximate driving times are as follows: Cancún to Felipe Carrillo Puerto, 4 hours; Cancún to Mérida, 4½ hours (3½ hours on the autopista toll road, $27); Puerto Felipe Carrillo to Chetumal, 2 hours; Puerto Felipe Carrilloto Mérida, about 4½ hours; Chetumal to Campeche, 6½ hours.

## EMERGENCIES

In Puerto Morelos, there are two drugstores in town on either side of the gas station on Carretera 307. In Playa del Carmen, there's a pharmacy at the Plaza Marina shopping mall; several others are on Avenida 5 between Calles 4 and 12. There are two pharmacies on Avenida Juárez between Avenidas 20 and 25.

🔢 **Centro de Salud** ✉ Av. Juárez and Av. 15, Playa del Carmen 📞 984/873-1230 Ext. 147. **Police** ✉ Av. Juárez between Avs. 15 and 20, Playa del Carmen 📞 984/873-0291. **Red Cross** ✉ Av. Juárez and Av. 25, Playa del Carmen 📞 984/873-1233.

## INTERNET, MAIL & SHIPPING

Many of the more remote places on the Caribbean coast rely on e-mail and the Internet as their major forms of communication. In Playa del Carmen, Internet service is cheap and readily available. The best places charge $3 per half hour and include Cyberia Internet Café and Atomic Internet Café. In Tulum, try the Internet Club.

The Playa del Carmen correos (post office) is open weekdays 8–7. If you need to ship packages or important letters, go through the shipping company Estafeta.

🔢 Cybercafés **Atomic Internet Café** ✉ Av. 5 and Calle 8, Playa del Carmen. **Cyberia Internet Café** ✉ Calle 4 and Av. 15, Playa del Carmen. **Internet Club** ✉ Av. Oriente 89, Tulum.

🔢 Services **Correos** ✉ Av. Juárez, next to the police station, Playa del Carmen 📞 983/873-0300. **Estafeta** ✉ Calle 20, Playa del Carmen 📞 984/873-1008.

### MONEY MATTERS

🗐 Banks **Banamex** ✉ Av. Juárez between Avs. 20 and 25, Playa del Carmen ☎ 984/873-0825. **Bancomer** ✉ Av. Juárez between Calles 25 and 30, Playa del Carmen ☎ 984/873-0356 ✉ Av. Alvaro Obregón 222, at Av. Juárez, Chetumal ☎ 984/832-5300. **Bancrecer** ✉ Av. 5 by the bus station, Playa del Carmen ☎ 984/873-1561. **Bital** ✉ Av. Juárez between Avs. 10 and 15, Playa del Carmen ☎ 984/873-0272 ✉ Av. 30 between Avs. 4 and 6, Playa del Carmen ☎ 984/873-0238. **Scotiabank Inverlat** ✉ Av. 5 between Avs. Juárez and 2, Playa del Carmen ☎ 984/873-1488.

### TAXIS

You can hire taxis in Cancún to go as far as Playa del Carmen, Tulum, or Akumal, but the price is steep unless you have many passengers. Fares run about $65 or more to Playa alone; between Playa and Tulum or Akumal, expect to pay at least another $25–$35. It's much cheaper from Playa to Cancún, with taxi fare running about $30; negotiate before you hop into the cab. Getting a taxi along Carretera 307 can take a while. Ask your hotel to call one for you. You can walk to just about everything in Playa. If you need to travel along the highway or farther north than Calle 20, a reliable taxi service is Sitios Taxis.

🗐 Taxis **Sitios Taxis** ✉ Playa del Carmen ☎ 984/873-0032.

### TOURS

Although some guided tours are available in this area, the roads are quite good for the most part, so renting a car is an efficient and enjoyable alternative. Most of the sights along this stretch are natural, and you can hire a guide at the ruins. If you'd like someone else to do the planning and driving for you, contact Maya Sites Travel Services, which offers inexpensive personalized tours.

You can visit the ruins of Cobá and the Maya villages of Pac-Chen and Chi Much—deep in the jungle—with Alltournative Expeditions. The group offers other ecotours as well. ATV Explorer offers two-hour rides through the jungle on all-terrain vehicles; explore caves, see ruins, and snorkel in a cenote. Tours start at $38.50. Based in Playa del Carmen, Tierra Maya Tours runs trips to the ruins of Chichén Itzá, Uxmal, Palenque, and Tikal. It can also help you with transfers, tickets, and hotel reservations.

Tres Palmas runs a day tour to the Reserva de la Biosfera Sian Ka'an that includes a visit to a typical Maya family living in the biosphere, a tamale breakfast, a visit to the Maya ruins at Muyil, a jungle trek to a lookout point for bird-watching, a boat trip through the lagoon and mangrove-laden channels (where you can jump into one of the channels and float downstream), lunch on the beach beside the Maya ruins at Tulum, and a visit to nearby cenotes for a swim and snorkeling. The staff picks you up at your hotel; the fee of $129 per person includes a bilingual guide.

🗐 **Alltournative Expeditions** ✉ Av. 10 No. 1, Plaza Antigua, Playa del Carmen ☎ 984/873-2036 ⊕ www.alltournative.com. **ATV Explorer** ✉ Carretera 307, 1 km [½ mi] north of Xcaret ☎ 984/873-1626. **Maya Sites Travel Services** ☎ 719/256-5186 or 877/620-8715 ⊕ www.mayasites.com. **Tierra Maya Tours** ✉ Av. 5 and Calle 6, Playa del Carmen ☎ 984/873-1385. **Tres Palmas** ✉ Main plaza beside church, Puerto Morelos ☎ 998/871-0709, 044-998-845-4083 cell ⊕ www.trespalmasweb.com.

## TRAVEL AGENCIES

There are more major travel agencies and tour operators along the coast than ever, and first-class hotels in Playa del Carmen, Puerto Aventuras, and Akumal usually have their own in-house travel services.

🚩 Local Agent Referrals **Alltournative Expeditions** ✉ Av. 10 No. 1, Plaza Antigua, Playa del Carmen ☎ 984/873-2036. **IMC** ✉ Plaza Antigua, Playa del Carmen ☎ 984/873-1439 🖶 984/873-1439 ⊕ www.imcplay.com. **Turistica Maya de Quintana Roo** ✉ Holiday Inn Puerta Maya, Chetumal ☎ 984/832-0555 or 984/832-2058 🖶 984/832-9711.

## VISITOR INFORMATION

The tourist information booths in Chetumal are open weekdays 8:30–2:30 and 6–9. In Playa del Carmen the booth is open Monday–Saturday 8 AM–9 PM.

🚩 Tourist Information **Chetumal** ✉ Calles Cinco de Mayo and Carmen Ochoa ☎ 983/832-2031 ✉ Calle 22 de Enero and Av. Reforma ☎ 983/832-6647. **Playa del Carmen** ✉ Av. Juárez by the police station, between Calles 15 and 20, Playa del Carmen ☎ 983/873-2804 in Playa del Carmen, 888/955-7155 in U.S., 604/990-6506 in Canada, 800/731-6148 in U.K.

# MÉRIDA & ENVIRONS

Updated by
Jane Onstott

Mérida, and the surrounding State of Yucatán, represent the juxtaposition of two powerful civilizations—that of the Maya and that of transplanted Europeans. Culturally, it is one of the richest parts of Mexico. Vestiges of the past are evident in this land of oval, thatched-roof adobe huts and sober Franciscan mission churches. Once-great cities, many abandoned at the height of their power, rise above the low tropical forests that have engulfed them over more than a millennium. Mysterious caves harbor subterranean swimming holes; fishing villages hug beaches untouched by the tourist industry.

The celebrated Maya ruins—including Chichén Itzá, Uxmal, and a spate of smaller sites—bring most people to the State of Yucatán. Indeed, the Puuc hills south of Mérida have one of the highest concentrations of archaeological sites in the hemisphere.

Travelers to Mérida are a loyal bunch, content to return again and again to favorite restaurants, neighborhoods, and museums. The hubbub of the city can be frustrating, particularly after a peaceful stay on the coast or at one of the archaeological sites, but Mérida's merits far outweigh its flaws. Mérida is the cultural and intellectual center of the peninsula and its museums, shops, and attractions can provide great insight into the history and character of the Yucatán.

**a good walk**

Start at the **zócalo** ㉓: see the **Casa de Montejo** ㉔ (now a Banamex bank), on the south side; the **Centro Cultural de Mérida Olimpo** ㉕ and the **Palacio Municipal** ㉖, on the west side; the **Palacio del Gobierno** ㉗, on the northeast corner, and, catercorner, the **Catedral de San Ildefonso** ㉘; and the **Museo de Arte Contemporáneo** ㉙ on the east side. Step out on Calle 60 from the cathedral and walk north to **Parque Hidalgo** ㉚ and the **Iglesia de la Tercera Orden de Jesús** ㉛, which is across Calle 59. Continue north along Calle 60 for a short block to the **Teatro Peón Contreras** ㉜, which lies on the east side of the street; the entrance to the **Universidad Autónoma de Yucatán** ㉝ is on the west side of Calle 60 at Calle 57. A block farther north on the west side of Calle 60 is the Parque Santa Lucía. From the park, walk north four blocks and turn right on Calle 47 for two blocks to **Paseo Montejo** ㉞. Once on this street, continue north for two long blocks to the **Palacio Cantón** ㉟. From here look either for a *calesa* (horse-drawn carriage) or cabs parked outside the museum to take you back past the zócalo to the Mercado Municipal—or walk if you're up to it.

## What to See

㉔ **Casa de Montejo.** This stately palace sits on the south side of the plaza, on Calle 63. Francisco de Montejo—father and son—conquered the peninsula and founded Mérida in 1542; they built their "casa" 10 years later. The property remained with the family until the late 1970s, when it was restored by banker Agustín Legorreta and converted to a bank. Built in the French style, it represents the city's finest—and oldest—example of colonial plateresque architecture, which typically has elaborate ornamentation. A bas-relief on the doorway—the facade is all that remains of the original house—depicts Francisco de Montejo the younger, his wife, and daughter as well as Spanish soldiers standing on the heads of the vanquished Maya. Even if you have no banking to do, step into the building weekdays between 9 and 5 to glimpse the leafy inner patio.

㉘ **Catedral de San Ildefonso.** Begun in 1561, St. Ildefonso is the oldest cathedral in Mexico and the second oldest on the North American mainland. It took several hundred Maya laborers, working with stones from the pyramids of the ravaged Maya city, 36 years to complete it. Designed in the somber Renaissance style by an architect who had worked on the Escorial in Madrid, its facade is stark and unadorned, with gunnery slits instead of windows, and faintly Moorish spires. Inside, the black Cristo de las Ampollas (Christ of the Blisters) occupies a side altar to the left of the main one. The statue is a replica of the original, which was destroyed during the Revolution. According to one of many legends, the Christ figure burned all night yet appeared the next morning unscathed—except that it was covered with the blisters for which it is named. ☒ *Calles 60 and 61, Centro* 🕾 *No phone* ⊙ *Daily 7–11:30 and 4:30–8.*

㉕ **Centro Cultural de Mérida Olimpo.** Referred to as simply Olimpo, this is the best venue in town for free cultural events. The beautiful porticoed cultural center was built adjacent to City Hall in late 1999, occupying what used to be a parking lot. The marble interior is a showcase for top international art exhibits, classical-music concerts, conferences, and theater and dance performances. Next door, a movie house renovated to its 1950s look, shows art films most nights. The complex also includes a bookstore and a wonderful cybercafé-restaurant; 90-minute shows explaining the solar system are presented at the planetarium for $3 (Tuesday–Saturday at 10, noon, 5, and 7; Sunday at 10 and noon). ☒ *Calle 62 between Calles 61 and 63, Centro* 🕾 *999/928–0000* ☒ *Free* ⊙ *Tues.–Sun. 10–10.*

㉛ **Iglesia de la Tercera Orden de Jesús.** Just north of Parque Hidalgo is one of Mérida's oldest buildings and the first Jesuit church in the Yucatán.

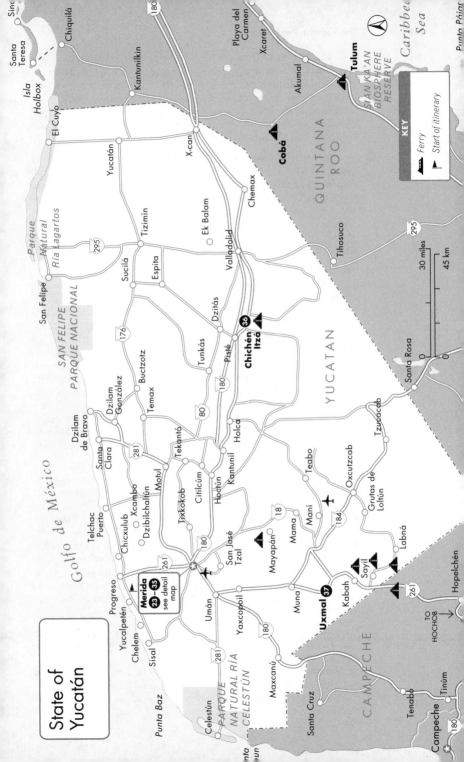

# State of Yucatán

**KEY**

Ferry

Start of itinerary

Caribbean Sea

QUINTANA ROO

YUCATAN

CAMPECHE

Golfo de México

**Merida** 23 – 35 see detail map

**Chichén Itzá** 36

**Uxmal** 37

Cobá

Tulum

SIAN KA'AN BIOSPHERE RESERVE

Punta Páiam

Santa Teresa

Sinc

Chiquilá

Isla Holbox

Kantunilkin

Playa del Carmen

Xcaret

Akumal

El Cuyo

Yucatán

X-can

Chemax

Parque Natural Ría Lagartos

San Felipe

Tizimín

Ek Balam

Valladolid

SAN FELIPE PARQUE NACIONAL

Sucilá

Espita

Dzitás

Pisté

Tihosuco

Santa Rosa

Dzilam de Bravo

Dzilam González

Buctzotz

Temax

Tunkás

Holca

Tzucacab

Santa Clara

Tekantó

Citilcúm

Hoctún

Kantunil

Teabo

Oxcutzcab

Grutas de Loltún

Chicxulub

Xcambo

Dzibilchaltún

Motul

Tixkokob

Mayapán

Mamá

Maní

Labná

Telchac Puerto

San José Tzal

Muna

Kabah

Sayil

Progreso

Yucalpetén

Chelem

Sisal

Umán

Yaxcopoil

Punta Baz

Maxcanú

PARQUE NATURAL RÍA CELESTÚN

Celestún

Santa Cruz

Tenabó

Tínúm

Campeche

Hopelchén

TO HOCHOB

295

180

176

281

80

18

184

261

180

30 miles

45 km

It was built in 1618 from the limestone blocks of a dismantled Maya temple, and faint outlines of ancient carvings are still visible on the west wall. Although a favorite place for society weddings because of its antiquity, the church interior is not very ornate. The former convent rooms in the rear of the building now host the small Pinoteca Juan Gamboa Guzmán, a collection of artwork. ⊠ *Calle 59 between Calles 58 and 60, Centro* ☎ *No phone* ☎ *$3* ☉ *Tues.–Sat. 8–8, Sun. 8–2.*

**㉙ Museo de Arte Contemporáneo.** Originally designed as an art school but used until 1915 as a seminary, this enormous two-story building is full of light, just perfect for an art museum. It showcases the works of contemporary Yucatecan artists such as Gabriel Ramírez Aznar and Fernando García Ponce on the ground-floor and second-floor galleries. There's also a café (closed Sunday and Tuesday). ⊠ *Pasaje de la Revolución 1907, between Calles 58 and 60 on the main square, Centro* ☎ *999/928–3236 or 999/928–3258* ☎ *$2* ☉ *Wed.–Mon. 10–5:30.*

**㉟ Palacio Cantón.** The most compelling of the mansions on **Paseo Montejo**, the pale-peach palacio houses the air-conditioned **Museo de Antropología y Historia.** Designed by Enrique Deserti, who also did the blueprints for the Teatro Peón Contreras, the building has a grandiose air that seems more characteristic of a mausoleum than a home, but in fact it was built for a general between 1909 and 1911. There is marble everywhere, as well as Doric and Ionic columns and other Italianate Beaux Arts flourishes. From 1958 to 1967 the mansion served as the residence of the state governor; in 1977 it became a museum dedicated to the archaeology and history of the Maya. Although not as impressive as its counterparts in other Mexican cities, it's nonetheless an introduction to ancient Maya culture. Exhibits show conch shells, stones, and quetzal feathers used for trading and explain the Maya practice of dental mutilation and incrustation. ⊠ *Calle 43 and Paseo Montejo, Paseo Montejo* ☎ *999/923–0557* ☎ *$3.50* ☉ *Tues.–Sat. 8–8, Sun. 8–2.*

**㉗ Palacio del Gobierno.** Occupying the northeast corner of the main square, the seat of state government was built in 1885 on the site of the Casa Real (Royal House). The upper floor of the State House contains Fernando Castro Pacheco's vivid murals of the bloody history of the conquest of the Yucatán, painted in 1978. On the main balcony (visible from outside on the plaza) stands a reproduction of the Bell of Dolores Hidalgo, on which Mexican independence rang out on the night of September 15, 1810, in the town of Dolores Hidalgo in Guanajuato. On the anniversary of the event, the governor rings the bell to commemorate the occasion. ⊠ *Calle 61 between Calles 60 and 62, Centro* ☎ *999/930–3101* ☎ *Free* ☉ *Daily 9–9.*

**㉖ Palacio Municipal.** The west side of the main square is occupied by City Hall, a 17th-century building painted pale yellow and trimmed with white arcades, balustrades, and the national coat of arms. Originally erected on the ruins of the last surviving Maya structure, it was rebuilt in 1735 and then completely reconstructed along colonial lines in 1928. It remains the headquarters of the local government, and houses the municipal tourist office. ⊠ *Calle 62 between Calles 61 and 63, Centro* ☎ *999/928–2020* ☉ *Daily 9–8.*

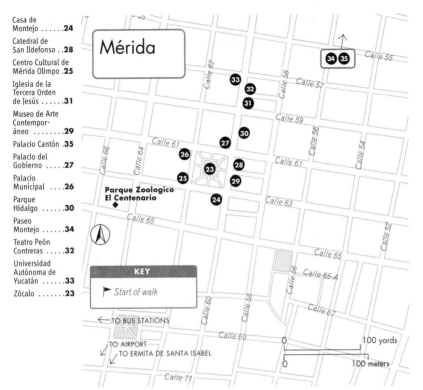

**❸❹ Paseo Montejo.** North of downtown, this 10-block-long street was *the* place to reside in the late 19th century, when wealthy plantation owners sought to outdo each other with the opulence of their elegant mansions. Inside, the owners typically displayed imported Carrara marble and antiques, opting for the decorative styles popular in New Orleans, Cuba, and Paris rather than the style in Mexico City. The broad boulevard, lined with tamarinds and laurels, has lost much of its former panache; many of the once-stunning mansions have fallen into disrepair. Others, however, are being restored as part of a citywide, privately funded beautification program.

**❸❷ Teatro Peón Contreras.** This 1908 Italianate theater was built along the same lines as grand turn-of-the-20th-century European theaters and opera houses. In the early 1980s the marble staircase, dome, and frescoes were restored. Today, in addition to performing arts, the theater also houses the Centro de Información Turística, providing maps, brochures, and details about attractions in the city and state. A café serving cappuccino and other coffees, plus snacks and light meals, spills out to a patio from inside the theater next to the information center. ⊠ *Calle 60 between Calles 57 and 59, Centro* ☎ *999/923–7354, 999/924–9290 tourist-information center* ☉ *Theater daily 7 AM–1 AM; tourist-information center daily 8 AM–9 PM.*

㉝ **Universidad Autónoma de Yucatán.** The arabesque university plays a major role in the city's cultural and intellectual life. The folkloric ballet performs on the patio of the main building most Fridays at 9 PM ($3), and less often during the low season of September and October. A Jesuit college built in 1618 previously occupied the site; the present building, which dates from 1711, has crenellated Moorish ramparts and archways. ⊠ *Calle 60 between Calles 57 and 59, Centro* ☎ *999/924–8000.*

㉓ **Zócalo.** Meridanos traditionally refer to this main square as the Plaza de la Independencia, or the Plaza Principal. Whichever name you prefer, it's a good spot from which to begin a tour of the city. The plaza was laid out in 1542 on the ruins of T'hó, the Maya city demolished to make way for Mérida, and is still the focal point around which the most important public buildings cluster. *Confidenciales* (S-shape benches designed for tête-à-têtes), stationed under ancient, geometrically pruned laurel trees, invite lingering. Lampposts keep the park beautifully illuminated at night. ⊠ *Bordered by Calles 60, 62, 61, and 63, Centro.*

## Where to Stay and Eat

★ **$$–$$$** ✕ **Alberto's Continental Patio.** The striking architecture of this dining spot dates from 1727, and was constructed on the site of a Maya temple. It's adorned with the original temple stones and mosaic floors from Cuba; the two air-conditioned dining rooms have handsome antiques, stone sculptures, and candles glowing in glass lanterns. A courtyard surrounded by rubber trees decked in white lights is ideal for starlit dining. There's lots of delicious Lebanese food: shish kebab, fried *kibi* (meatballs of ground beef, wheat germ, and spices), cabbage rolls, hummus, eggplant dip, and tabbouleh; and don't forget the almond pie and Turkish coffee. ⊠ *Calle 64 No. 482, at Calle 57, Centro* ☎ *999/928– 5367* ☰ *AE, MC, V.*

★ **$$–$$$** ✕ **La Habichuela.** Custom-made hardwood furniture, marble floors, and lots of leaded-glass accents make this a favorite power-lunch spot for local businessmen; at night, it's filled with families and couples. The menu is inventive, and includes such appetizers as seafood crepes and salmon pâté; the chicken breast stuffed with cheese and served with a rose-petal sauce is a standout entrée. The chocolate-mousse cake is the undisputed star of the dessert menu. Sax music lends a mellow air on weekend evenings. ⊠ *Calle 21 No. 416, at Calle 8 (about 20 mins by car from main square), Col. México Oriente* ☎ *999/926–3626* ☰ *AE, D, MC, V.*

★ **$–$$$** ✕ **Hacienda Teya.** This beautiful hacienda just outside the city has some of the best regional food in the area. Most patrons are well-to-do Meridanos enjoying a leisurely lunch, so you'll want to dress up a bit. A guitarist serenades from 2 to 5 on weekends. After a fabulous lunch of *cochinita pibíl,* you can stroll in the orchard, or wander through the surrounding botanical gardens. If you find yourself wanting to stay longer, the hacienda also has six handsome lodging suites available. ⊠ *13 km (8 mi) east of Mérida on Carretera 180, Kanasín* ☎ *999/924–3800, 999/924– 3880 in Mérida* ⚱ *Reservations essential* ☰ *AE, MC, V* ☾ *No dinner.*

**$–$$** ✕ **El Pórtico del Peregrino.** At the Pilgrim's Porch, a Mérida institution
**Fodor'sChoice** for 30 years, you can choose among three dining areas. Smokers get the
★ street view, while nonsmokers share the dining room stuffed with an-

tiques (both these rooms have air-conditioning); groups gather on the small, fern-draped interior patio. Start your meal with a warming, traditional lime soup before zeroing in on the *zarzuela de mariscos*—a yummy dish containing lobster tails or crab claws (depending on the season), squid, octopus, fish, and shrimp baked with white wine and garlic. Or try the baked eggplant layered with Italian sauce, chicken, and grated cheese. The homemade flan or coconut ice cream bathed in coffee liqueur makes for a fine finish. ⊠ *Calle 57 No. 501, between Calles 60 and 62 Centro* ☎ *999/928–6163* ⊟ *AE, MC, V.*

$$$–$$$$ ⊡ **Hacienda Xcanatun.** The furnishings at this beautifully restored henequen hacienda include African and Indonesian antiques, locally made lamps, and oversize comfortable couches and chairs from Puebla. The rooms come with cozy sleigh beds, fine sheets, and fluffy comforters, and are decorated with art from Mexico, Cuzco, Peru, and other places the owners have traveled. Bathrooms are luxuriously large. An in-house restaurant serves a small menu of eclectic dishes. ⊠ *Carretera 261, Km 12, 8 mi north of Mérida, 97300* ☎ *999/941–0213 or 888/883–3633* 🖷 *999/941–0319* ⊕ *www.xcanatun.com* 🗺 *18 suites* ☼ *Restaurant, room service, fans, some in-room hot tubs, minibars, 2 pools, spa, steam room, 2 bars, laundry service, meeting room, airport shuttle, free parking; no room TVs* ⊟ *AE, MC, V.*

$$–$$$ ⊡ **Fiesta Americana Mérida.** The facade of this posh hotel echoes the grandeur of the mansions on Paseo Montejo. The spacious lobby is filled with colonial accents and gleaming marble; there's also a 300-foot-high stained-glass atrium. Floral prints and larger-than-life proportions lend period elegance to the guest rooms, which are inspired by late-19th-century design, and which have such extras as balconies, bathtubs, hair dryers, and coffeemakers. Specially equipped rooms for people with disabilities are available, and guests on the business floor have access to the Fiesta Club for morning breakfast or afternoon appetizers. ⊠ *Av. Colón 451, Paseo Montejo, 97127* ☎ *999/942–1111 or 800/343–7821* 🖷 *999/942–1122* ⊕ *www.fiestaamericana.com* 🗺 *323 rooms, 27 suites* ☼ *Restaurant, coffee shop, room service, in-room data ports, minibars, cable TV with movies, golf privileges, tennis court, pool, gym, massage, bar, lounge, shops, baby-sitting, dry cleaning, laundry service, concierge, concierge floor, business services, car rental, travel services, free parking, no-smoking rooms* ⊟ *AE, D, DC, MC, V.*

$$ ⊡ **Casa del Balam.** This pleasant hotel two blocks from the zócalo is owned by the Barbachano family, pioneers of Yucatán tourism since the 1960s. The rooms here include colonial touches, like carved cedar doors and rocking chairs on the wide verandas; but they also have such modern-day conveniences as double-pane windows to keep out the noise. The rich decor and thoughtful details, like the hand-painted plates, make this place seem more like a home than a hotel. Guests have access to a golf and tennis club about 15 minutes away by car. ⊠ *Calle 60 No. 488, Centro 97000* ☎ *999/924–8844 or 800/624–8451* 🖷 *999/924–5011* ⊕ *www.yucatanadventure.com.mx* 🗺 *44 rooms, 3 suites* ☼ *Restaurant, room service, minibars, refrigerators, cable TV, golf privileges, pool, bars, car rental, travel services, free parking, no-smoking rooms* ⊟ *AE, D, DC, MC, V.*

¢–$ 🏠 **Casa Mexilio.** Four blocks from the main square is this eclectic B&B. Middle Eastern wall hangings, French tapestries, and colorful tile floors crowd the public spaces; individually decorated rooms have tile sinks and folk-art furniture. Some find the intimacy of this inn private and romantic, although others may find it a bit too small for their liking. A two-night minimum stay is required. ⊠ *Calle 68 No. 495, between Calles 57 and 59, Centro, 97000* ☎ *800/538–6802 in U.S. and Canada* 📠 *999/928–2505* ⊕ *www.mexicoholiday.com* ⤴ *8 rooms, 1 penthouse* ⚄ *Dining room, pool; no a/c in some rooms, no room phones, no room TVs* ⊟ *MC, V* ⑩ *CP.*

★ ¢ 🏠 **Casa San Juan.** This homey B&B in a restored colonial mansion, just a few blocks from the zócalo, is popular with travelers who appreciate an informal friendly environment. Original design elements include 10-foot-high wooden doors and tiled floors. Affable host Pablo da Costa, a hotelier from Cuba, can give you tips on visiting the city—in five languages. A two-night minimum stay is required. Guests are given front-door keys; if you're arriving in the afternoon, call ahead to make sure someone can let you in. ⊠ *Calle 62 No. 545A, between Calles 69 and 71, Centro 97000* ☎ *999/986–2937* 📠 *999/986–2937* ⊕ *www.casasanjuan.com* ⤴ *8 rooms* ⚄ *Fans, travel services; no a/c in some rooms; no room phones, no room TVs* ⊟ *AE, MC, V (when booked from the U.S, Canada or Europe)* ⑩ *CP.*

★ ¢ 🏠 **Dolores Alba.** The newer wing of this comfortable cheerful hotel has spiffy rooms with quiet yet strong air-conditioning, comfortable beds, and many amenities; rooms in this section have large TVs, balconies, and telephones. Although even the older and cheaper rooms have air-conditioning, they also have fans, which some people prefer to use. The big rectangular pool is surrounded by lounge chairs and shaded by giant trees, and there's a comfortable restaurant and bar at the front of the property. Different meal plans packages are available, so be sure to ask when you make reservations. ⊠ *Calle 63 No. 464, between Calles 52 and 54, Centro 97000* 📠 *999/928–5650* ⊕ *www.doloresalba.com* ⤴ *95 rooms* ⚄ *Restaurant, some fans, pool, bar, free parking* ⊟ *No credit cards* ⑩ *MAP, FP.*

## Nightlife & the Arts

Mérida has an active and diverse cultural life, which features free government-sponsored music and dance performances many evenings, as well as sidewalk art shows in local parks. On Saturday evenings, the Fiesta Mexicana (corner of Paseo Montejo and Calle 47), hosts different musical and and cultural events. On Sunday, six blocks around the zócalo are closed off to traffic, and you can see performances—often mariachi and marimba bands or folkloric dancers—at Plaza Santa Lucía, Parque Hidalgo, and the main plaza.

DANCING ★ Part bar, restaurant, and stage show **Eladios** (⊠ Calle 24 No. 100, Col. Itzimná ☎ 999/927–2126), with its peaked palm-thatch room and ample dance floor, is a lively place often crammed with local families and couples even midweek. **Pancho's** (⊠Calle 59 No. 509, between Calles 60 and 62, Centro ☎ 999/923–0942), open daily 6 PM–2:30 AM, has a lively bar and a restaurant. It also has a small dance floor that attracts locals and foreigners for a mix of live salsa and western music.

FOLKLORIC
SHOWS
★
Paseo Montejo hotels such as the Fiesta Americana, Hyatt Regency, and Holiday Inn stage dinner shows with folkloric dances; check with concierges for schedules. The **Ballet Folklórico de Yucatán** (⊠ Calles 57 and 60, Centro ☎ 999/924–7260) presents a combination of music, dance, and theater every Friday at 9 PM at the university; tickets are $3. (Performances are every other Friday in the off-season, and there are no shows from August 1 to September 22 and the last two weeks of December.)

## Sports & the Outdoors

The 18-hole championship golf course at **Club de Golf La Ceiba** (⊠ Carretera Mérida–Progreso, Km 14.5 ☎ 999/922–0053) is open to the public. It is about 16 km (10 mi) north of Mérida on the road to Progreso; greens fees are about $60, carts are an additional $25, and clubs can be rented. The pro shop is closed Monday.

## Shopping

MARKETS
The **Mercado Municipal** (⊠ Calles 56 and 67, Centro) has crafts, food, flowers, and live birds, among many other items. If you're interested in handicrafts, **Bazar García Rejón** (⊠ Calles 65 and 62, Centro) has rows of indoor stalls that sell items like leather goods, palm hats, and handmade guitars. Visit the government-run **Casa de las Artesanías** (⊠ Calle 63 No. 503A, between Calles 64 and 66, Centro ☎ 999/928–6676) for folk art from throughout Yucatán. There's a showcase of hard-to-find traditional filigree jewelry in silver, gold, and gold-dipped versions.

SPECIALTY
STORES
Pick up a Panama hat at **El Becaleño** (⊠ Calle 65 No. 483, between Calles 56 and 58, Centro ☎ 999/985–0581), and be sure to try your bargaining skills. You might not wear a guayabera to a business meeting as some men in Mexico do, but the shirts are cool, comfortable, and attractive; for a good selection, try **Camisería Canul** (⊠ Calle 62 No. 484, between Calles 57 and 59, Centro ☎ 999/923–0158). **Mexicanísimo** (⊠ Calle 60 No. 496, at Parque Hidalgo, Centro ☎ 999/923–8132) sells expensive designer cotton and linen clothing inspired by regional dress.

# Chichén Itzá

🏛 ㊱   *120 km (74 mi) east of Mérida, 1 km (½ mi) east of Pisté.*

Fodor's Choice
★
One of the four most magnificent Maya ruins—along with Palenque in Chiapas in Mexico, Tikal in Guatemala, and Copán in Honduras—Chichén Itzá was the most important city in Yucatán from the 10th through the 12th century. Its architectural mélange shows the influence of several different Maya groups. As epigraphers have been able to translate many of the Chichén inscriptions, the site's history has become clearer to archaeologists.

At one time it was believed that Chichén Itzá was dominated by the Toltecs of central Mexico; now historians believe that the city was indeed influenced by trade with the north, although not by conquest. Chichén *was* altered by successive waves of inhabitants, and archaeologists are able to date the arrival of these waves by the changes in the architecture and information contained in inscriptions. However, the long gaps of time when the buildings seem to have been uninhabited remain a mystery.

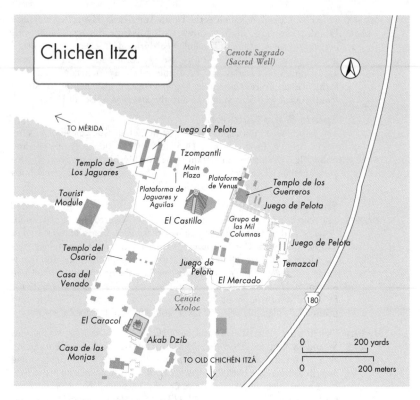

The site is believed to have been first settled in AD 432, abandoned for an unknown period of time, then rediscovered in 868 by the Maya-speaking Itzás, who migrated north from the region of the Petén rain forest around Tikal, in what is now northern Guatemala. The latest data point to the city's having been refounded by not only the Itzás but also by two other groups—one from the Valley of Mexico (near present-day Mexico City) and another from Ek Balam. The trio formed a ruling triumvirate. The Itzás may have also abandoned the site, but they were the dominant group until 1224, when the city appears to have been abandoned for all time.

Chichén Itzá means "the mouth of the well of the Itzás." The enormousness, grace, and functionality of this site are unforgettable. It encompasses approximately 6 square km (2½ square mi), though fewer than a quarter of the site's several hundred structures and buildings have been fully explored. It's divided into two parts, called Chichén Viejo (old) and Chichén Nuevo (new), although architectural motifs from the Classic period are found in both sections. A more convenient distinction is topographical, since there are two major complexes of buildings separated by a dirt path.

The martial, imperial architecture of the Itzás and the more cerebral architecture and astronomical expertise of the earlier Maya are married in the 98-foot-tall pyramid called **El Castillo**—The Castle—which dominates the site and rises above all the other buildings. Atop this structure is a temple dedicated to Kukulcán (also known as Quetzalcóatl), the legendary Toltec priest-king from Tula in the Valley of Mexico who was held to be an incarnation of the mystical plumed serpent. Open-jawed serpent statues adorn the balustrades of each stairway, and serpents reappear at the top of the temple as sculptured columns. At the spring and fall equinoxes, the afternoon light strikes one of these balustrades in such a way as to form a shadow representation of Kukulcán undulating out of his temple and down the pyramid to bless the fertile earth. (Thousands of people travel to Chichén Itzá to see this phenomenon, so if you're planning to witness it, you'll need to make hotel reservations many months in advance.) At the base of the temple on the northwest side, you can enter a passageway and climb a humid claustrophobic staircase to see two particularly ancient statues within—one of a jaguar and the other of a minor god, Chacmool. Each evening there's a sound-and-light show that highlights the architectural details in El Castillo and other buildings, though its accompanying narration is more dramatic than fact filled.

West of the temple is Chichén Itzá's largest **juego de pelota,** one of seven ball courts on the site. Its two parallel walls are each 272 feet long, with two stone rings on each side, and 99 feet apart. The game played here was something like soccer (no hands were used), but it had a religious and socio-political significance. Bas-relief carvings at the court depict a player being decapitated, the blood spurting from his neck fertilizing the earth. Other bas-reliefs show two teams of opposing players pitted against each other during the ball game.

Between the ball court and El Castillo stands the **Anexo del Templo de los Jaguares,** where bas-relief carvings represent several deities. On the bottom left column, Tlaloc's tears represent rain. In the central opening of the structure is a statue of Chacmool. West of the Jaguars' Temple is a **tzompantli,** a stone platform carved with rows of human skulls. These carvings are thought to depict the heads of enemies impaled on stakes.

One kilometer (½ mi) north of El Castillo at the end of a *sacbé* (white road), the **Cenote Sagrado** was used for human sacrifices. Some 37 skeletons have been recovered from the muddy bottom of the 65-yard-wide pool. Many archaeologists think the ritual sacrifices were carried out by local chiefs hundreds of years after Chichén Itzá was abandoned. Thousands of artifacts made of gold, jade, and other precious materials, most of them not of local provenance, have also been recovered from the sinkhole's brackish depths.

East of El Castillo is the **Grupo de las Mil Columnas,** or Group of the Thousand Columns. Part of this group, the **Templo de los Guerreros**—a masterful example of the Itzá influence at Chichén Itzá—was used as a meeting place for the high lords of the council that ruled the city.

The temple-top sculpture of the reclining Chacmool—its head turned to the side, the offertory dish carved into its middle—is probably the most photographed symbol of the Maya. Murals of everyday village life and scenes of war are here, although climbing up to see them is no longer permitted.

To get to the less-visited cluster of structures at Chichén Nuevo, take the main path south from the Jaguars' Temple past El Castillo and turn right onto a small path opposite the ball court. Archaeologists have been restoring several buildings in this area, including the **Templo del Osario,** where several tombs with skeletons and offerings were found, and the northern part of the site, which was used for military training and barracks. The most impressive structure within this area is the astronomical observatory called **El Caracol.** The name, meaning the Snail, refers to the spiral staircase at the building's core. Built in several stages, El Caracol is one of the few round buildings constructed by the Maya. Judging by the eight tiny windows oriented toward the compass points, and the structure's alignment with the planet Venus, it was used for observing the heavens. Since astronomy was the province of priests and used to determine rituals and predict the future, the building undoubtedly served a religious function.

After leaving El Caracol, continue south several hundred yards to the **Grupo de las Monjas** (The Nunnery). Traditional to the Puuc style prevalent in southern Yucatán, the facades of this structure and of the adjacent annex are plain below their friezes, but richly decorated with masks above.

At Chichén Viejo, the architecture shows less outside influence. A combination of Puuc and Chenes Maya styles dominates, with playful latticework, masks, and gargoylelike serpents on the cornices. One highlight here is the Grupo de las Fechas, or Date Group, so named because of its complete series of hieroglyphic dates. If you ask, guides will lead you down the path by an old narrow-gauge railroad track to even more ruins, which are barely unearthed. A small museum includes information on the migration patterns of the ancient Maya and some small sculptures recovered from the site. The site draws some 3,000 visitors a day; most of the tour groups arrive in the morning. ☒ *$9 (includes museum and sound-and-light show, $4 on Sun.); parking $2; use of video camera $3* ⊙ *Daily 8–5; sound-and-light show Apr.–Oct., daily just after dusk.*

## Where to Stay

**$$–$$$**   🏨 **Hacienda Chichén.** A converted 16th-century hacienda with its own
**Fodor's Choice**   entrance to the ruins, this hotel once served as the headquarters for the
★   Carnegie expedition to Chichén Itzá. Rustic-chic cottages are simply but beautifully furnished in colonial Yucatecan style, with handwoven bedspreads and dehumidifiers; all of the ground-floor rooms have verandas, but only master suites have hammocks. There's a satellite TV in the library. An enormous old pool and a chapel now used for weddings grace the gardens. Meals are served on the patio overlooking the grounds, or in the air-conditioned restaurant. ☒ *Carretera 180, Km 120* ☎ *985/ 851–0045, 999/924–2150 reservations, 800/624–8451* 📠 *999/924–*

*5011* ⊕ *www.haciendachichen.com.mx* ⟿ *24 rooms, 4 suites* ♿ *Restaurant, some minibars, pool, bar, laundry service, free parking; no room phones, no room TVs* 🖃 *AE, DC, MC, V.*

★ **$$–$$$** 🏨 **Mayaland.** This charming property is in a large garden, and close enough to the ruins to have its own entrance; you can actually see part of Chichén Viejo from here. Colonial-style guest rooms have decorative tiles; ask for one with a balcony, which doesn't cost extra. Bungalows have thatched roofs as well as wide verandas with hammocks. The simple Maya-inspired "huts" near the front of the property, built in the 1930s, are the cheapest option, but are for groups only. Snacks served poolside are an alternative to the rather expensive meals in the restaurants. ✉ *Carretera 180, Km 120* ☎ *999/924–2099 or 800/235–4079* 🖷 *999/924–6290* 🖷🖷 *985/851–0129* ⊕ *www.mayaland.com* ⟿ *60 bungalows, 30 rooms, 10 suites* ♿ *4 restaurants, room service, fans, minibars, cable TV, tennis court, 3 pools, volleyball, 2 bars, shop, laundry service, free parking* 🖃 *AE, D, DC, MC, V.*

## Uxmal

🏞 **㊲** *78 km (48 mi) south of Mérida on Carretera 261.*

**Fodor's**Choice
★

If Chichén Itzá is the most expansive Maya ruin in Yucatán, Uxmal is arguably the most elegant. The architecture here reflects the Late Classical renaissance of the 7th to the 9th century and is contemporary with that of Palenque and Tikal, among other great Maya cities of the southern highlands.

The site is considered the finest and most extensively excavated example of Puuc architecture, which embraces such details as ornate stone mosaics and friezes on the upper walls, intricate cornices, rows of columns, and soaring vaulted arches. Although most of Uxmal hasn't been restored, three buildings in particular merit attention:

At 125 feet high, the **Pirámide del Adivino** is the tallest and most prominent structure at the site. Unlike most other Maya pyramids, which are stepped and angular, the Temple of the Magician has a softer and more refined round-corner design. This structure was rebuilt five times over hundreds of years, each time on the same foundation, so artifacts found here represent several different kingdoms. The pyramid has a stairway on its western side that leads through a giant open-mouthed mask to two temples at the summit. During restoration work in 2002, the grave of a high-ranking Maya official, a ceramic mask, and a jade necklace were discovered within the pyramid. Continuing excavations have revealed exciting new finds that are still being studied.

West of the pyramid lies the **Cuadrángulo de las Monjas,** considered by some to be the finest part of Uxmal. The name was given to it by the conquistadores because it reminded them of a convent building in Old Spain. According to research, what's called the Nunnery was actually the palace and living quarters of a high lord of Uxmal named Chaan Chak, which means "abundance of rain." You may enter the four buildings; each comprises a series of low, gracefully repetitive chambers that look onto a central patio. Elaborate and symbolic decorations—masks, geometric patterns, coiling snakes, and some phallic figures—blanket the upper facades.

Heading south from the Nunnery, you'll pass a small ball court before reaching the **Palacio del Gobernador,** which archaeologist Victor von Hagen considered the most magnificent building ever erected in the Americas. Interestingly, the palace faces east, while the rest of Uxmal faces west. Archaeologists believe this is because the palace was built to allow observation of the planet Venus. Covering 5 acres and rising over an immense acropolis, it lies at the heart of what may have been Uxmal's administrative center.

Today, you can watch a sound-and-light show at the site that recounts Maya legends. The colored light brings out details of carvings and mosaics that are easy to miss when the sun is shining. The show is performed nightly in Spanish; earphones ($2.50) provide an English translation. ⌧ *Site, museum, and sound-and-light show $8.50 ($3.50 for foreigners on Sun.); parking $2; use of video camera $3* ☉ *Daily 8–5; sound-and-light show just after dusk.*

## Where to Stay & Eat

**$$$–$$$$** ⌧ **Lodge at Uxmal.** The outwardly rustic, thatched-roof buildings here have glossy red-tile floors, carved and polished hardwood doors and rocking chairs, and local weavings. The effect is comfortable yet luxuriant. All rooms have bathtubs and screened windows; suites have king-size beds and jet baths. Tennis and volleyball are available at the hotel's sister property, Hacienda Uxmal. ⌧ *Carretera Uxmal, Km 78* ☎ *800/235–4079* 🖷 *998/884–4510 in Cancún* ⊕ *www.mayaland.com* ⇨ *40 suites* ⚒ *2 restaurants, fans, some in-room hot tubs, some minibars, cable TV, 2 pools, hot tub, bar, free parking* ⊟ *AE, MC, V.*

**$$** ⌧ **Hacienda Uxmal.** The first hotel built in Uxmal, this pleasant colonial-style building has lovely floor tiles, ceramics, and iron grillwork. The rooms are fronted with wide, furnished verandas; the courtyard has two pools surrounded by gardens. Each room has an ample bathroom with tub, comfortable beds, and coffeemaker. Ask about packages that include free or low-cost car rentals, or comfortable minivans traveling to Mérida, Chichén, or Cancún. ⌧ *Carretera 261, Km 78* ☎ *997/976–2012 or 800/235–4079* 🖷 *997/976–2011, 998/884–4510 in Cancún* ⊕ *www.mayaland.com* ⇨ *80 rooms, 7 suites* ⚒ *2 restaurants, room service, some in-room hot tubs, cable TV, 2 pools, billiards, bar, shop, laundry service, free parking* ⊟ *AE, MC, V.*

**$** ✕⌧ **Villas Arqueológicas Uxmal.** Rooms in this pretty two-story Club Med

Fodor'sChoice  property are small but functional, with wooden furniture and cozy twin
★  beds that fit nicely into alcoves. Half of the bright, hobbit-hole rooms have garden views. Since rooms are small, guests tend to hang out in the comfy library with giant-screen TV and lots of reading material, or at thatch-shaded tables next to the pool. The indoor restaurant ($$–$$$)—classy or old-Europe fussy, depending on your tastes—serves both regional fare and international dishes, like stuffed squid, chicken in tarragon, or roast chicken with french fries and steamed veggies. ⌧ *Carretera 261, Km 76* ☎ *997/974–6020 or 800/258–2633* 🖷 *997/976–2040*

⊕ *www.clubmedvillas.com* ⊃ *40 rooms, 3 suites* ⌂ *Restaurant, in-room safes, tennis court, pool, billiards, bar, library, shop, laundry service, free parking; no room TVs* ▭ *AE, MC, V.*

## Mérida & Environs A to Z

*To research prices, get advice from other travelers, and book travel arrangements, visit www.fodors.com.*

### AIR TRAVEL

AIRPORT  The Mérida airport, Aeropuerto Manuel Crescencio Rejón, is 7 km (4½ mi) west of the city on Avenida Itzaes, a 20- to 30-minute cab ride.
🔢 **Aeropuerto Manuel Crescencio Rejón** ☎ 999/946-1300 or 999/946-1340.

AIRPORT  A private taxi from the airport costs about $8. Bus 79 (40¢) goes from
TRANSFERS  the airport to downtown and vice versa, departing from Calle 67 between Calles 60 and 62 about every 25 minutes; the ride takes about 45 minutes. It's very inexpensive, but a hassle if you've got more than a day pack or small suitcase.

CARRIERS  Aerocaribe, a subsidiary of Mexicana, has flights from Cancún, Cozumel, Mexico City, Oaxaca City, Tuxtla Gutiérrez, and Villahermosa, with additional service to Central America. Aeroméxico flies direct to Mérida from Miami with a stop (but no plane change) in Cancún. Aeroméxico's affiliate, AeroMaya, connects Chichén Itzá, Cozumel, Mérida, and Chetumal with Cancún. Aviacsa flies from Mérida to Mexico City, Villahermosa, and Monterrey with connects to Los Angeles, Las Vegas, Chicago, Miami, Ciudad Juárez, Houston, and Tijuana, among other destinations. Mexicana has direct flights to Cancún from Los Angeles and Miami, and a number of other connecting flights from Chicago and a number of other U.S. cities via Mexico City.
🔢 **Aerocaribe** ☎ 999/928-6790 ⊕ www.aerocaribe.com.**AeroMaya** ☎ 999/946-9450. **Aeroméxico** ☎ 999/920-1293 or 01800/021-4000 toll-free in Mexico ⊕ www.aeromexico.com. **Aviacsa** ☎ 999/925-6890, 01800/006-2200 toll-free in Mexico ⊕ www.aviacsa.com.mx. **Mexicana** ☎ 999/946-1332 ⊕ www.mexicana.com.mx.

### BUS TRAVEL

Mérida's municipal buses run daily 5 AM–midnight. In the downtown area buses go east on Calle 59 and west on Calle 61, north on Calle 60 and south on Calle 62. You can catch a bus heading north to Progreso on Calle 56. There's no direct bus service from the hotels around the plaza to the long-distance bus station; however, taxis are reasonable.

There are several first-class bus lines offering deluxe buses with air-conditioning and comfortable seats. ADO and UNO have direct buses to Cancún, Chichén Itzá, Playa del Carmen, Tulum, Uxmal, Valladolid, and other Mexican cities, with intermediate service to Izamal. They depart from the first-class CAME bus station. ADO and UNO also have direct buses to Cancún, Chetumal, and Playa del Carmen from their terminal at the Fiesta Americana hotel, on Paseo Montejo. Regional bus lines to intermediate or more out-of-the-way destinations leave from the second-class terminal. The most frequent destination of tourists using Autotransportes del Sureste (ATS), which departs from the second-class station, is Uxmal. Buses to Celestún depart from the Autobuses del Occidente station; those to Progreso are found at the Terminal de Autobuses a Progreso. Clase Elite/Nuevos Horizontes have first-class buses to destinations in Quintana Roo but depart from the second-class bus station.

⚑ : **ADO/UNO at Fiesta Americana** ✉ Av. Colón 451, Paseo Montejo, Mérida ☎ 999/920-4444.**Autobuses de Occidente** ✉ Calles 50 and 67, Centro Mérida ☎ 999/924-8391 or 999/924-9741.**CAME** ✉ Calle 70 No. 555, at Calle 71, Centro Mérida ☎ 999/924-8391 or 999/924-9130. **Terminal de Autobuses a Progreso** ✉ Calle 62 No. 524, between Calles 65 and 67, San Juan Mérida ☎ 999/924-8941 or 999/928-3965. **Terminal de Autobuses de 2da clase** ✉ Calle 69 No. 544, between Calles 68 and 70, Centro Mérida ☎ 999/923-2287.

## CAR RENTAL

⚑ **Major Agencies Budget** ✉ Holiday Inn, Av. Colón No. 498, at Calle 60 Centro, Mérida ☎ 999/925-6877 Ext. 516 ✈ airport ☎ 999/946-1323. **Hertz** ✉ Fiesta Americana, Av. Colón 451, Paseo Montejo, Mérida ☎ 999/925-7595 ✈ airport ☎ 999/946-1355. **Mundo Maya** ✉ Calle 60 No. 486A, Centro, Mérida ☎ 999/926-3351. **Thrifty** ✉ Calle 55 No. 508, at Calle 60, Centro, Mérida ☎ 999/923-2040 or 999/928-0966.

## CAR TRAVEL

Driving in Mérida can be frustrating because of the narrow one-way streets and dense traffic. But having your own wheels is the best way to take excursions from the city. For more relaxed sightseeing, consider hiring a cab for short excursions. Most charge approximately $12 per hour. Carretera 180, the main road along the Gulf coast from the Texas border, passes through Mérida en route to Cancún. Mexico City is 1,550 km (961 mi) west, Cancún 320 km (198 mi) due east.

The autopista is a four-lane toll highway between Mérida and Cancún. Beginning at the town of Kantuníl, 55 km (34 mi) southeast of Mérida, it runs somewhat parallel to Carretera 180. The toll road cuts driving time between Mérida and Cancún—around 4½ hours on Carretera 180—by about an hour and bypasses about four dozen villages. Access to the toll highway is off old Carretera 180 and is clearly marked. The highway has exits for Valladolid and Pisté (Chichén Itzá), as well as rest stops and gas stations. Tolls between Mérida and Cancún total about $25.

## CONSULATE

⚑ **United States** ✉ Paseo Montejo 453, at Av. Colón, Centro Mérida ☎ 999/925-5011.

## EMERGENCIES

⚑ **Doctors & Hospitals:** English-speaking doctors can be found at **Centro de Especialidades Médicas** ✉ Calle 60 No. 329, at Av. Colón, Centro Mérida ☎ 999/920-4040.**Centro Médico de las Américas** ✉ Calle 54 No. 365, between Calle 33A and Av. Pérez Ponce, Centro Mérida ☎ 999/927-3199.

⚑ Emergency Services **Fire, police, Red Cross, and general emergency** ☎ 060.

⚑ **Pharmacies Farmacia de Ahorros** ✉ Calles 60 and 63, Centro Mérida ☎ 999/928-5027. **Farmacia Yza** ☎ 999/926-6666 information and delivery.

## MAIL, INTERNET & SHIPPING

Mérida's post office is open weekdays 8–3 and Saturday 9–1. You can, however, buy postage stamps at some handicrafts shops and newspaper and magazine kiosks. Cybercafés are ubiquitous, though particularly prevalent along Mérida's main square and Calles 61 and 63. Most charge $1–$3 per hour.

**Cybercafés Express Internet** ⊠ Café Express, Calle 60 No. 502, at Calle 59, Centro Mérida ☎ 999/928-1691. **Vía Olimpo Café** ⊠ Calles 62 and 61, Centro Mérida ☎ 999/923-5843.

**Mail Service Correo** ⊠ Calles 65 and 56, Centro Mérida ☎ 999/928-5404 or 999/924-3590.

## MONEY MATTERS

Most banks throughout Mérida are open weekdays 9–4. Banamex has its main offices, open weekdays 9–4 and Saturday 9–1:30, in the handsome Casa de Montejo, on the south side of the main square, with branches at the airport and the Fiesta Americana hotel. All have ATMs. Several other banks, including Bital, can be found on Calle 65 between Calles 62 and 60, and on Paseo Montejo.

**Banks Banamex** ⊠ Calle 59 No. 485, Mérida ☎ 01800/226-2639 toll-free in Mexico. **Bital** ⊠ Paseo Montejo 467A, Centro Mérida ☎ 999/942-2378 ⊠ Calle 58 No. 524, between Calles 63 and 65 Centro Mérida ☎ 999/923-4572. **Serfin** ⊠ Paseo Montejo 467A Centro Mérida ☎ 999/942-2378.

## TAXIS

Taxis charge beach-resort prices, which makes them a little expensive for this region of Mexico. They cruise the streets for passengers and are available at 13 taxi stands (*sitios*) around the city, or in front of major hotels like the Hyatt Regency, Holiday Inn, and Fiesta Americana. The minimum fare is $3, which should get you from one downtown location to another, or from downtown to Paseo Montejo or the first- or second-class bus stations.

**Taxi Company Sitio 14** ☎ 999/924-5918.

## TOURS

Mérida has more than 50 tour operators, who generally go to the same places. Beware the *piratas* (street vendors) who stand outside the offices of reputable tour operators and offer to sell you a cheaper trip. They have been known to take your money and not show up; most also do not carry liability insurance.

A two- to three-hour group tour of the city, including museums, parks, public buildings, and monuments, costs $20 to $35 per person. Or you can pick up an open-air sightseeing bus at Parque Santa Lucía for $8 (departures are Monday–Saturday at 10, 1, 4, and 7 and Sunday at 10 and 1). Free guided tours are offered daily by the Municipal Tourist Office. These depart from City Hall, on the main plaza at 9:30 AM. Call 999/928-2020 Ext. 833 for information. A day trip to Chichén Itzá, including guide service, entrance to the ruins, and lunch goes for $60–$70 and departs from Cancún or Mérida. For about the same price you can see the ruins of Uxmal and Kabah in the Puuc region. Early afternoon departures to Uxmal allow you to take in the sound-and-light show at the ruins and return by 11 PM for about $63 (including dinner). Another option is a tour of Chichén Itzá followed by a drop-off in Cancún, for about $80. Most tour operators take credit cards.

If you don't have your own wheels, a great option for seeing the ruins of the Ruta Puuc is the unguided ATS tour that leaves Mérida at 8 AM from the second-class bus station. The tour stops for half an hour each at the ruins of Labná, Xlapak, Sayil, and Kabah, giving you just enough time to scan the plaques, climb a few crumbling steps, and poke your nose into a crevice or two. You get almost two hours at Uxmal before heading back to Mérida at 2:30 PM. The trip costs $9 per person, is unguided, and does not include entrance to the ruins.Ecoturismo Yucatán leads kayaking tours out of Mérida that begin in Celestún and enable you to explore the mangroves and estuaries of the western coast. It also offers bird-watching and biking adventures, and custom trips to suit the needs and abilities of its clients.

🖪 Tour Operators **Amigo Travel** ⊠ Av. Colón 508C, Col. García Ginerés Mérida ☎ 999/920-0101 or 999/920-0107. **Ecoturismo Yucatán** ⊠ Calle 3 No. 235, between Calles 32A and 34, Col. Pensiones, Mérida ☎ 999/920-2772 ⊕ www.ecoyuc.com. **Mayaland Tours** ⊠ Calle Robalo 30, Sm 3, Cancún ☎ 998/887-2495 in Cancún, 01800/719-5465 toll-free from elsewhere in Mexico, 800/235-4079. **Ricardía Tours** ☎ 999/923-6431.Yucatán Trails ⊠ Calle 62 No. 502, between Calles 57 and 59 ☎ 999/928-2582.

## VISITOR INFORMATION

The Mérida city, municipal, and state tourism departments are open daily 8–8. Those outside Mérida are generally open weekdays 9–7 and Saturday 9–1.

🖪 **City Tourist Information Center** ⊠ Calle 62 between Calles 61 and 63 on the ground floor of the Palacio Municipal, Centro Mérida ☎ 999/928-2020 Ext. 133.

# UNDERSTANDING MEXICO

MEXICO ENTERED THE 21ST CEN-TURY with a new regime, finally booting out the party that had lorded over Mexican politics for 71 years. The PRI, or Institutional Revolutionary Party, grew out of the Mexican Revolution, and kept its hold on power through a combination of political maneuvering, co-optation, and outright electoral fraud. In July 2000, however, Mexican voters—armed with new electoral laws and fed up with official corruption and economic hardship—dethroned the PRI. With 43% of the vote (compared with the PRI's 36%), the swashbuckling businessman Vicente Fox, from the center-right National Action Party (PAN), became the first opposition president of modern Mexico. The Guanajuato-born president stands tall (six-foot-five) and in striking contrast to those who came before him: he talks colloquially instead of using the stiff speech of traditional *políticos;* he dons cowboy boots and a giant silver belt buckle that reads F-O-X; he entered office a divorced man, then made his presidential campaign adviser the First Lady. He pledged to run the country much like he used to run Coca-Cola de México. The changes President Fox promised during his campaign, however, have been excruciatingly slow in coming, and many Mexicans today question whether or not they're truly any better off than before. Nonetheless, he has taken some important steps toward modernizing the country's economy, battling corruption, and strengthening relations with the United States.

For all its ancient history, Mexico is a young country. About a third of the population is between 15 and 29 years old. Many of these young people were raised in economic and political turmoil. Mexicans today are tired of seeing themselves as downtrodden. Many prefer to look for inspiration to actress Salma Hayek—a Veracruz native—or to the successful young Harvard Business School entrepreneur Miguel Angel Davila, who started the Cinemex movie chain. Signs of modern Mexico are everywhere: cash machines even in some small towns, *People en Español,* and the proliferation of cell phones. But, as ever, modernity does not come all at once. In much of Mexico, a brand-new SUV may share the road with a burro. The nation's struggle with progress is like a Latin dance: two steps forward, one step back.

As the country opened economically over the past two decades, a slow push for political opening followed. Those growing up are often dubbed the NAFTA generation, after the free-trade agreement: they're more outward-looking, more free-enterprise savvy, and more cynical about traditional (often corrupt) politics. The old one-party system failed them when the bottom fell out of the economy just after the 1994 presidential election, and the memory of what Mexicans simply call *la crisis* is very much alive. Many people are still shy of bank accounts, credit cards, and home loans, which were practically nonexistent for years after the peso crashed. Wages remain below what they were before the crisis, full-time jobs are always in short supply, and the new government has tightened the belt even further, raising sales taxes and cutting government assistance. Much of Mexico, however, appears to be booming. Exports—driven by the free-trade agreement with the United States—are thriving in some sectors. Investors have returned, betting on the perennial comeback. The economy is still vulnerable to global recession, as shown by the layoffs following the recent U.S. economic recession, but it's much more stable than it was before la crisis.

Emphasizing his experience as a former CEO of Coca-Cola in Mexico, Fox promised to improve Mexico's economy by running the country more like a business. He even announced he'd improve efficiency by placing the government on a "matrix-style management plan." As his term draws to an end, however, most of Fox's efforts to create jobs and jump-start the economy have been frustrated by the economic recession on this side of the border and by an oppositional Congress.

During the first three years of his presidency, Fox met an unprecedented number of times with his newly elected U.S. counterpart, lobbying both George W. Bush and the U.S. Congress for a major liberalization of immigration laws between the two countries. Mexico's 3,141-km (1,952-mi) border with the United States, which serves as a pressure valve during hard times, has always made for tricky politics between the two nations. Although the U.S. Congress at first seemed receptive to the fiery new president's proposals, the September 11, 2001, terrorist attacks delayed talk of loosening immigration laws.

Although change may seem painstakingly slow, it's clear the 2000 political upset has opened a whole new can of worms, politically speaking. In state and local politics, the PRI has lost considerable ground in recent years. Fox's conservative PAN has won the governorships in 8 of Mexico's 31 states, whereas the liberal Revolution Democratic Party (PRD) controls four states and Mexico City. In the states of Chiapas and Nayarit, the diametrically opposed PAN and PRD formed an alliance to unseat the PRI governors in 1999 and 2000. Opposition parties have also achieved real power in congress for the first time in modern Mexican history. Congressmen used to be called *levantadedos* (finger lifters) because all they did was vote as the president wished. Today, there's competition—even the occasional fistfight—on the House floor.

Democratic reform has also brought an end to the extreme formality of Mexican politics. No one used to look the Mexican president in the eye, such was his power. Today, some political commentators use the informal *tú* (you) when addressing President Fox, a tradition that began with Fox's PRI predecessor, former President Ernesto Zedillo. Fox is pilloried regularly in political cartoons. The press have angered him by poking fun at everything from his cowboy boots, his occasional mispronunciation of words, and the lavish charity benefits thrown by First Lady Martha Sahagun. During the first half of Fox's presidency, his unruly advisers were dubbed the "Montessori Cabinet."

Much of the credit for Mexico's new democracy is owed to former President Zedillo (1994–2000), who paved the way for his own party's fall from power. Zedillo was often called the "accidental candidate" because he stepped into the presidential race at the last minute after front-runner Luis Donaldo Colosio was assassinated in 1994, a tragedy from which Mexico has never fully recovered. But during his *sexenio* (six-year term), Zedillo proved himself more of an accidental reformer. By not playing the role of ironclad president, he opened the door to the opposition. He expanded political funding for all parties, returned some power and money to the country's 31 states, and relinquished his traditional right to name his successor. This PRI tradition of handpicking the next president, called the *dedazo* (literally "the finger-pointing"), existed from the time the PRI took power in 1929 until 1999, when the party held its first-ever primaries to choose its presidential candidate.

But the PRI's continued power and influence in the new political landscape should not be underestimated. During its seven decades of power, the party showed an uncanny ability to learn from its mistakes and to remake itself to fit the national mood.

Many older Mexicans yearn for the security the party once provided. In some states, the PRI seems to be gaining popularity by moving away from its technocrats—the term refers to the cocky young reformers epitomized by former president Carlos Salinas de Gortari (1988–94). The "Harvard-trained economist," as he was invariably described, brought Mexico free trade, privatization, and all the promises of neoliberalism.

Salinas also brought discredit on his party and his country. Not only did his dream of First World membership die with the peso crisis, but his administration is now considered one of the most corrupt in Mexican history. Salinas lives in self-imposed exile in Dublin, Ireland, but he is still called Mexico's favorite villain. Street vendors sell masks of his face with his inimitable big ears. Bankers who cashed in under Salinas's privatizations have gone on the lam. And Salinas's older brother, Raúl, has been sentenced to 27 years in prison for masterminding the murder of a former PRI leader. Meanwhile, Swiss investigators seized $114 million from Raúl's Swiss bank accounts in 1998, arguing that the money came from drug trafficking. In the ongoing legal proceedings, Mexican prosecutors claim that the fortune was built on corrupt political practices.

There has been a kind of don't-ask-don't-tell attitude about drug trafficking in Mexico for years. Since the country became the main transportation route for Colombian cocaine growers in the 1980s, drug cartels have insinuated themselves into Mexican life, and Mexican cartels are now as powerful as their Colombian counterparts. Although two top drug lords were arrested in 2002 and 2003, the cartels remain formidable. Drug use is up, and drug culture, touching everything from clothing to music, is spreading. People wink and nudge each other about the gaudy hotels and new shopping complexes, especially along the U.S. border, that they assume

were built with drug money. But they shrug it off. Drug violence hasn't hurt the average citizen enough (except in border cities such as Juárez and Tijuana) for Mexicans to get really angry about it. But increased crime has. Most Mexicans' biggest concern, they'll tell you, is public safety. Although crime is still no worse than in many big U.S. cities, poor policing and weak courts make it seem that way.

As in much of Latin America, hard-liners are making a comeback. Some Mexicans are beginning to clamor for the death penalty, something almost unheard of in Catholic countries. The army has been called in to help fight street crime, drugs, and guerrillas. And the human-rights situation, especially in states considered guerrilla-friendly, is bleak. In December 1997, paramilitary forces massacred 45 peasants thought sympathetic to the Zapatista rebels in Acteal in the southern state of Chiapas. Digna Ochoa, a leading human-rights attorney who had defended Zapatista sympathizers and environmentalists, was murdered in 2001 in her Mexico City office; her murderers left a note warning her colleagues to stop their work. Peace talks with the Zapatistas, who sprang up in 1995, are stalled even though the cease-fire holds.

The Zapatistas, or Ejército Zapatista de Liberación Nacional (EZLN), are only the most publicity-savvy of a few small guerrilla groups. They—with their charismatic spokesman Subcomandante Marcos—are still a leftist cause célèbre. At first, Mexicans had a brief romance with the pipe-smoking Marcos because he seemed to speak for the downtrodden. Now, they say they are mostly weary of the violence. President Fox boasted during his campaign that he could solve the Zapatista conflict in 15 minutes. Sadly, this is another goal he has not been able to achieve. Indeed, because of congressional resistance, consensus has become nearly impossible. Fox has been unable to make good on promises of tax reform, revamped labor laws, and a partially privatized electricity industry.

One thing is certain, however. The change in climate represented by the 2000 presidential elections, along with the growth of nonprofit and civic organizations, has had a tremendous impact on Mexican politics, economics, and culture. There's greater debate from the ballot box to the boardrooms to the kitchen tables every day. From the scathing editorials in the increasingly free press to the customer-service hot lines at once-indifferent monopolies, the county is going through a dramatic transition. In the 2006 presidential elections, Mexicans are sure to weigh recent revelations of previously suspected voter fraud and other improprieties by the once-powerful PRI against the inability of Fox's PAN to deliver much-needed quality-of-life improvements to the majority of Mexicans. The transition continues.

— Martha Brandt and Paige Bierma
updated by Jane Onstott

# CHRONOLOGY

## Pre-Columbian Mexico

ca. 40,000 BC    Asian nomads cross land bridge over the Bering Strait to North America, gradually migrate south.

ca. 7000 BC– 2000 BC    Archaic period, which marked the beginnings of agriculture and village life.

ca. 2000 BC– AD 100    Formative or Preclassic period: development of pottery, incipient political structures. (The late Preclassic period runs from 400 BC to AD 100.)

500 BC–900 BC    The powerful and sophisticated Olmec civilization develops primarily along the Gulf of Mexico in the present-day states of Veracruz and Tabasco. Olmec culture, the "mother culture" of Mexico, flourishes along Gulf coast.

AD 100– AD 1000    Classic period: height of Mesoamerican culture. Totonac-speaking people build the city of Teotihuacán (near Mexico City); the powerful and cultured Zapotecs rule in Oaxaca, and the Maya advance math and astronomy in the Yucatán. Ruling dynasties produce impressive art and architecture; powerful priests perform elaborate ceremonies based on their interpretation of signs and celestial events. (The late Classic period runs from 800 to 1000.)

650–900    Fall of Teotihuacán ca. 650 leads to competition among other city-states, exacerbated by migrations of tribes from the harsh northern deserts.

ca. 900–1150    Toltecs, a northern tribe, establish a flourishing culture at their capital of Tula under the legendary monarch Topiltzin-Quetzalcóatl.

1000–1521    Postclassic period: with the decline of the monarchy, rule passes to tribal councils. Cultural achievements wane; many once-flourishing cities have by now been abandoned.

1111    The unlettered Aztecs migrate to mainland from island home off the Nayarit coast. They are not welcomed by the peoples of central Mexico.

ca. 1200    Rise of Mixtec culture at Zapotec sites of Monte Albán and Mitla; notable for production of picture codices, which include historical narratives.

1150–1350    Following the fall of Tula, the Chichimecs and then the Tepanecs assert hegemony over central Mexico. The Tepanec tyrant Tezozómoc (1320–1426), like his contemporaries in Renaissance Italy, establishes his power with murder and treachery.

1320    The Aztec city of Tenochtitlán is built in the middle of Lake Texcoco.

1420–1519    Aztecs extend their rule to much of central and southern Mexico. A warrior society, they build a great city at Tenochtitlán.

1502    Moctezuma II (1502–1520) assumes throne at the height of Aztec culture and political power.

1517 Spanish expedition under Francisco Hernandez de Córdoba (1475–1526) lands on Yucatán coast.

1519 Hernán Cortés (1485–1547) lands in Cozumel, founds Veracruz, and determines to conquer. Steel weapons, horses, and smallpox, combined with a belief that Cortés was the resurrected god Quetzalcóatl, minimize Aztec resistance. Cortés and his men stay for months as somewhat captive guests at Tenochtitlán before taking Moctezuma hostage.

## The Colonial Period

1521 Tenochtitlán falls to Cortés after Moctezuma is killed in 1520. The last Aztec emperor, Cuauhtémoc, is tortured to reveal hidden gold; he doesn't, and is later executed.

1528 Juan de Zumarraga (1468–1548) arrives as bishop of Mexico City, gains title "Protector of the Indians"; conversions to Catholicism increase.

1535 First Spanish viceroy arrives in Mexico.

1537 Pope Paul III issues a papal bull declaring that Mesoamerica's indigenous people are indeed human and not beasts. First printing press arrives in Mexico City.

1546–48 Silver deposits discovered at Zacatecas.

1547 Spanish conquest of Aztec Empire—now known as "New Spain"—completed, at enormous cost to native peoples.

1553 Royal and Pontifical University of Mexico, first university in the New World, opens.

1571 The Spanish Inquisition established in New Spain; it is not abolished until 1820.

1609 Northern capital of New Spain established at Santa Fe (New Mexico).

1651 Birth of Sor (Sister) Juana Inés de la Cruz, greatest poet of colonial Mexico (d. 1695).

1718 Franciscan missionaries settle in Texas, which becomes part of New Spain.

1765 Charles III of Spain (1716–88) sends José de Galvez to tour New Spain and propose reforms.

1769 Franciscan Junípero Serra establishes missions in California, extending Spanish hegemony.

1788 Death of Charles III; his reforms improved administration, but also raised social and political expectations among the colonial population, which were not fulfilled.

1808 Napoléon invades Spain, leaving a power vacuum in New Spain.

## The War of Independence

1810   September 16: Father Miguel Hidalgo y Costilla (1753–1811) and co-conspirators launch the War of Independence against the Spanish crown.

1811   Hidalgo is captured and executed; leadership of the movement passes to Father José María Morelos y Pavón (1765–1815).

1813   Morelos calls a congress at Chilpancingo, which drafts a Declaration of Independence.

1815   Morelos is captured and executed.

## The Early National Period

1821   Vicente Guerrero, a rebel leader, and Agustín de Iturbide (1783–1824), a Spanish colonel, sign a peace accord, rejuvenating the Independence movement. Spain soon recognizes Mexican independence with the Treaty of Córdoba.

1822   Iturbide is named Emperor of Mexico, which stretches from California to Central America.

1823   After 10 months in office, Agustín de Iturbide is turned out.

1824   A new constitution creates a federal republic, the Estados Unidos Mexicanos; modeled on the U.S. Constitution, the Mexican version retains the privileges of the Catholic Church and gives the president extraordinary "emergency" powers.

1829   President Vicente Guerrero abolishes slavery. A Spanish attempt at reconquest is halted by General Antonio López de Santa Anna (1794–1876), already a hero for his role in the overthrow of de Iturbide.

1833   Santa Anna is elected president by a huge majority; by 1855, he has held the office for 11 of its 36 changes of hands.

1836   Although voted in as a liberal, Santa Anna abolishes the 1824 constitution. Already dismayed at the abolition of slavery, Texas—whose population is largely American—declares its independence. Santa Anna successfully besieges the Texans at the Alamo. But a month later he is captured by Sam Houston following the Battle of San Jacinto. Texas gains its independence as the Lone Star Republic.

1846   The U.S. decision to annex Texas leads to war.

1848   The treaty of Guadalupe Hidalgo reduces Mexico's territory by half, ceding present-day Texas, New Mexico, Arizona, California, Nevada, Utah, and part of Colorado to the United States.

1853   Santa Anna agrees to the Gadsden Purchase, ceding a further 48,000 square km (30,000 square mi) to the United States.

## The Reform & French Intervention

1855  The Revolution of Ayutla topples Santa Anna and leads to the period of The Reform.

1857  The liberal Constitution of 1857 disestablishes the Catholic Church, among other measures.

1858–61  The Civil War of the Reform ends in liberal victory. Benito Juárez (1806–72) is elected president. France, Spain, and Britain agree jointly to occupy the customhouse at Veracruz to force payment of Mexico's huge foreign debt.

1862  Spain and Britain withdraw their forces; the French, seeking empire, march inland. On May 5, General Porfirio Díaz repulses the French at Puebla.

1863  Strengthened with reinforcements, the French occupy Mexico City. Napoléon III of France appoints Archduke Ferdinand Maximilian of Austria (1832–67) as Emperor of Mexico.

1864  Maximilian and his empress Charlotte, known as Carlotta, land at Veracruz.

1867  With U.S. assistance, Juárez overthrows Mexico's second empire. Maximilian is executed; Carlotta, pleading his case in France, goes mad.

1872  Juárez dies in office. The Mexico City–Veracruz railway is completed, symbol of the new progressivist mood.

## The Porfiriato

1876  Porfirio Díaz (1830–1915) comes to power in the revolution of Tuxtepec; he holds office nearly continuously until 1911. With his advisers, the *científicos,* he forces modernization and balances the budget for the first time in Mexican history. But the social cost is high.

1886  Birth of Diego Rivera (d. 1957).

1890  José Schneider, who is of German ancestry, founds the Cerveceria Cuauhtémoc, brewer of Carta Blanca beer.

1900  Jesús, Enrique, and Ricardo Flores Magón publish the anti-Díaz newspaper *La Regeneración*. Suppressed, the brothers move their campaign to the United States, first to San Antonio, then to St. Louis.

1906  The Flores Magón group publish their Liberal Plan, a proposal for reform. Industrial unrest spreads.

## The Second Revolution

1907  Birth of the renowned painter Frida Kahlo (d. 1954).

1910  On the centennial of the Revolution, Díaz wins yet another rigged election. Revolt breaks out.

1911   Rebels under Pascual Orozco and Francisco (Pancho) Villa (1878–1923) capture Ciudad Juárez; Díaz resigns. Francisco Madero is elected president; calling for land reform, Emiliano Zapata (1879–1919) rejects the new regime. Violence continues.

1913   Military coup: Madero is deposed and murdered. In one day Mexico has three presidents, the last being General Victoriano Huerta (1854–1916). Civil war rages.

1914   American intervention leads to dictator Huerta's overthrow. Villa and Zapata briefly join forces at the Convention of Aguascalientes, but the revolution goes on. Birth of poet-critic Octavio Paz.

1916   Villa's border raids lead to an American punitive expedition under Pershing. Villa eludes capture.

1917   Under a new constitution, Venustiano Carranza, head of the Constitutionalist Army, is elected president. Zapata continues his rebellion, which is brutally suppressed.

1918   CROM, the national labor union, is founded.

1919   On order of Carranza, Zapata is assassinated.

1920   Carranza is assassinated; Alvaro Obregón (1880–1928), who helped overthrow dictator Huerta in 1914, is elected president, beginning a period of reform and reconstruction. Schools are built and land is redistributed. In the next two decades, revolutionary culture finds expression in the art of Diego Rivera and José Clemente Orozco (1883–1949), the novels of Martin Luis Guzmán and Gregorio López y Fuentes, and the music of Carlos Chávez (1899–1978).

1923   Pancho Villa is assassinated. The United States finally recognizes the Obregón regime.

1926–28   Catholics react to government anticlericalism in the Cristero Rebellion.

1934–40   The presidency of Lázaro Cárdenas (1895–1970) leads to the fullest implementation of revolutionary reforms.

1938   Cárdenas nationalizes the oil companies, removing them from foreign control.

1940   On August 20, exiled former Soviet leader Leon Trotsky is murdered in his Mexico City home.

## Post-Revolutionary Mexico

1951   Mexico's segment of the Pan-American Highway is completed, confirming the industrial growth and prosperity of postwar Mexico. Culture is increasingly Americanized; writers such as Octavio Paz and Carlos Fuentes express disillusionment with the post-revolution world.

1968   The Summer Olympics in Mexico City showcase Mexican prosperity, but hundreds of student activists are murdered or jailed during a massive demonstration. The government denies and suppresses this information.

1981–82  Recession and a drop in oil prices severely damage Mexico's economy. The peso is devalued.

1985  Thousands die in the Mexico City earthquake.

1988  American-educated economist Carlos Salinas de Gortari is elected president; for the first time since 1940, support for the PRI, the national political party, seems to be slipping.

1993  North American Free Trade Agreement (NAFTA) is signed with United States and Canada.

1994  Uprising by the indigenous peoples of Chiapas, led by the Zapatistas and their charismatic ski-masked leader, Subcomandante Marcos; election reforms promised as a result.

Popular PRI presidential candidate Luis Donaldo Colosio assassinated while campaigning in Tijuana. Ernesto Zedillo, generally thought to be more of a technocrat and "old boy" PRI politician, replaces him and wins the election.

Zedillo, blaming the economic policies of his predecessor, devalues the peso in December.

1995  Recession sets in as a result of the peso devaluation. Ex-President Carlos Salinas de Gortari is linked to scandels surrounding the assassinations of Colosio and another high-ranking government official; Salinas moves to the United States.

1996  Mexico's economy, bolstered by a $28 billion bailout program led by the United States, turns upward, but the recovery is fragile. The opposition National Action Party (PAN), which is committed to conservative economic policies, gains strength. New details of scandals of the former administration continue to emerge.

1997  Mexico's top antidrug official is arrested on bribery charges. Nonetheless, the United States recertifies Mexico as a partner in the war on drugs. The Zedillo administration faces midterm party elections.

1998  Death of Octavio Paz.

1999  Raúl Salinas, brother of the former president Carlos Salinas de Gortari, sentenced to prison for the murder of a PRI leader.

2000  Spurning the long-ruling PRI, Mexicans elect opposition candidate Vicente Fox president.

2001  U.S.-Mexico relations take on increased importance as Fox meets repeatedly with George W. Bush to discuss immigration reform and economic programs.

President Fox frees imprisoned Zapatista rebel sympathizers and signs into law a controversial Indian rights bill in hopes of bringing peace to southern Chiapas state; however, peace talks remain stalled.

Human-rights attorney Digna Ochoa is assassinated, opening the country to accusations of failing to investigate human-rights abuses by the military and police. The case is unsolved.

2002   Under President Fox's orders, the federal Human Rights Commission investigates and confirms that hundreds of people, most suspected leftist rebels, disappeared at the hands of the state after being arrested in the 1960s, '70s, and '80s. Fox also signs into law a freedom of information act and releases nearly 80 million secret intelligence files collected by the government.

To help fight crime in Mexico City, the local government hires former New York City Mayor Rudolph Giuliani as a consultant. City officials also create a special force of English-speaking mounted police officers to patrol the downtown tourist area.

2003   High hopes for NAFTA corrode as hundreds of factories relocate from Mexico to the Far East, where labor is even cheaper.

2004   In his autobiography *Change of Course,* former president Miguel de la Madrid admits that the government rigged the 1988 presidential election in favor of PRI candidate Carlos Salinas de Gortari. According to De la Madrid, opposition candidate Cuauhtémoc Cárdenas, son of agrarian reformist Lázaro Cárdenas, was likely to win according to an early count of electronic ballots.

# MEXICO AT A GLANCE

## Fast Facts

**Name in local language:** México
**Capital:** Mexico City (a.k.a. Distrito Federal or Federal District)
**National anthem:** *Mexicanos, al grito de guerra!* (*Mexicans, to the cry of war!*), by Francisco González Bocanegra and music by Jaime Nunó
**Type of government:** Federal republic
**Administrative divisions:** 31 states and 1 federal district
**Independence:** September 16, 1810 (from Spain)
**Constitution:** February 5, 1917
**Legal system:** Mixture of U.S. constitutional theory and civil law system, with judicial review of legislative acts
**Suffrage:** 18 years of age; universal and compulsory
**Legislature:** Bicameral National Congress of a Senate (128 seats; 96 are elected by popular vote to serve six-year terms, and 32 are allocated on the basis of each party's popular vote) and Federal Chamber of Deputies (500 seats; 300 members are directly elected by popular vote to serve three-year terms; remaining 200 members are allocated on the basis of each party's popular vote, also for three-year terms)
**Population:** 104.9 million
**Population density:** 141 people per square mi
**Median age:** Male 22.9, female: 24.6
**Life expectancy:** Male 69.3, female 75.5
**Infant mortality rate:** 23.7 deaths per 1,000 live births

**Literacy:** 92.2%
**Language:** Spanish (official). Regional indigenous languages include Mayan and Nahuatl
**Ethnic groups:** Mestizo 60%; Amerindian or predominantly Amerindian 30%; white 9%; other 1%
**Religion:** Roman Catholic 89%, Protestant 6%, other 5%
**Discoveries & Inventions:** Zero (665), 365-day calendar (800), color television (1940)

*The phenomenon of corruption is like the garbage. It has to be removed daily.*
—Ignacio Pichardo Pagaza, Comptroller General of Mexico 1983–87

*In its male, in its public, its city aspect, Mexico is an arch-transvestite, a tragic buffoon. Dogs bark and babies cry when Mother Mexico walks abroad in the light of day. The policeman, the Marxist mayor— Mother Mexico doesn't even bother to shave her mustachios. Swords and rifles and spurs and bags of money chink and clatter beneath her skirts. A chain of martyred priests dangles from her waist, for she is an austere, pious lady. Ay, how much—clutching her jangling bosoms; spilling cigars— how much she has suffered.*
—Richard Rodriguez

## Geography & Environment

**Land area:** 1.9 million square km (.7 million square mi), almost three times the size of Texas
**Coastline:** 9,330 km (3,602 mi) along Pacific and Atlantic Oceans, the Gulf of Mexico, and the Gulf of California

**Terrain:** High, rugged mountains; low coastal plains; high plateaus; desert (highest point is Volcan Pico de Orizaba, 18,410 feet)
**Islands:** Isla Angel de la Guarda, Isla Cedros, Isla Tiburon, Isla San Jose, Isla

del Carmen, Cozumel, Isla Mujeres, Islas Marias, Isla Margarita, Isla Magdalena, Isla Cerralvo, Isla Espiritu Sancto, Isla Guadalupe, Islas Revillagigedos
**Natural resources:** Copper, gold, lead, natural gas, petroleum, silver, timber, zinc
**Natural hazards:** Tsunamis along the Pacific coast; volcanoes and earthquakes in the center and south; and hurricanes on the Pacific, Gulf of Mexico, and Caribbean coasts
**Environmental issues:** Scarcity of hazardous waste disposal facilities; natural fresh water resources scarce and polluted in north, inaccessible and poor quality in center and extreme southeast; raw sewage and industrial effluents polluting rivers in urban areas; deteriorating agricultural lands, especially groundwater depletion in the Valley of Mexico; serious air and water pollution, especially in the national capital where pollutants in the city's air exceed World Health Organization guidelines by more than a factor of two, and in urban centers along the U.S.–Mexico border.

## Economy

**Currency:** Peso
**Exchange rate:** 11 pesos = $1
**GDP:** 6.8 trillion pesos ($601.51 billion)
**Per capita income:** 66,013 pesos ($5,920)
**Inflation:** 10.7%
**Unemployment:** 3.92%
**Work force:** 41.4 million
**Debt:** 1.7 trillion pesos ($153.9 billion)
**Economic aid:** 13.2 billion pesos ($1.2 billion)
**Major industries:** Food and beverages, iron and steel, mining, motor vehicles, petroleum, textiles
**Agricultural products:** Beans, beef, corn, fruit, rice, wheat
**Exports:** 174.2 trillion pesos ($158.4 billion)

**Major export products:** Coffee, cotton, fruits, manufactured goods, oil and oil products, silver, vegetables
**Export partners:** U.S. 82.7%; Canada 5.4%; Japan 1.1%
**Imports:** 185.2 trillion pesos ($168.4 billion)
**Major import products:** Agricultural machinery, electrical equipment, car parts for assembly, metalworking machines, repair parts for motor vehicles, aircraft, and aircraft parts, steel mill products
**Import partners:** U.S. 70.6%; Germany 3.5%; Japan 2.7%

## Political Cimate

Mexico's relationship with the United States dominates national politics. The U.S. is Mexico's largest trading partner by far, as well as its largest cultural influence. Both sides are working to improve upon inroads made since the North American Free Trade Agreement (NAFTA) was signed in 1994 and their effects on income and government. In elections in 1997 and 2000, opposition parties defeated the Institutional Revolutionary Party (PRI) for the first time since the 1910 Mexican Revolution. Change has been slow since the upheaval, and it's unclear whether the electorate is happy with the change. Immigration and the treatment of Mexican nationals in the U.S. is a perennial issue. Indigenous groups continue to pressure the government for greater rights. An indigenous rights law passed in 2001 fell short of giving Mexico's Indians political autonomy.

*In Mexico an air-conditioner is called a politician because it makes a lot of noise but doesn't work very well.*
—Len Deighton

## Did You Know?

• Mexico's 30 major newspapers give it an air of vigorous news gathering, but most are heavily subsidized by the government. A 2001 study estimated that 9 out of 10 would fold without the aid.

• Mexico has the greatest number of universities, colleges, and other institutions of higher education in the world, with 10,341.

• As you might expect, Mexico holds the record for the world's largest taco. During the 100th anniversary celebrations of the city of Mexicali in 2003 a 35-foot, 1,654-pound taco was made by residents. Using 1,183 pounds of beef, 186 pounds of dough, 179 pounds of onion, and 106 pounds of cilantro, it took 80 people six hours to finish.

• With nearly 105 million people, Mexico is the world's largest Spanish-speaking country by far. Colombia, Spain, and Argentina are next, with about 40 million inhabitants each.

• Remittances from Mexicans living in the U.S. recently passed tourism and foreign investment to become Mexico's second most important source of income. Only oil brings in more money.

• International law limits the production of tequila to a specific region of Mexico, but most of the tequila distilled there is shipped in bulk to the U.S., where it's bottled.

• A Cardon cactus (Pachycereus pringlei) holds the world record for being the tallest cactus, at 63 feet tall, in the Sonoran Desert of Baja California, Mexico.

# BOOKS & MOVIES

## Books

Some of the titles described below may be out of print and available only in libraries.

### Pre-Columbian & Colonial Works & Histories

If the pre-Columbian way of thinking has any appeal to you, Dennis Tedlock's superb translation of the Maya creation myth, *Popol Vuh*, is essential reading. Good general reference works can deepen your understanding of Mexico's indigenous peoples and enrich your trips to the many marvelous archaeological sites in Mexico. These include *The Conquest of the Yucatán* by celebrated ethnographer and champion of indigenous cultural survival Frans Blom; *The Maya* and *Mexico*, by Michael D. Coe; *The Toltec Heritage*, by Nigel Davies; *The Last Lords of Palenque: The Lacandon Mayas of the Mexican Rain Forest*, by Victor Perera and Robert D. Bruce; *The Blood of Kings: Dynasty & Ritual in Maya Art*, by Linda Schele and Mary Ellen Miller; *Secrets of the Maya* from the editors of *Archaeology* magazine; and the colorful *Ancient Mexico*, by Maria Longhena.

Mary Miller has also collaborated with Karl Taube to produce a useful glossary-style handbook called *The Gods and Symbols of Ancient Mexico and the Maya*. R. C. Padden's *The Hummingbird and the Hawk* paints a fascinating picture of the Aztec's transformation from a group of illiterate nomads to powerful and learned kingdom, and explains how this mighty empire could be defeated by Cortés's tiny expedition. Written by one of Cortés's own soldiers, Bernal de Diaz, *History of the Conquest of New Spain*, provides a detailed first-hand account of events. For a more zingy historical fiction depicting life among the Aztecs, read Gary Jennings's historical novel *Aztec*.

A number of fascinating first-hand accounts of the colonial period by some of its most important figures have been translated and published. Of these, the most compelling may be *Letters from Mexico*, by conquistador Hernán Cortés, and *In Defense of the Indians*, an unsparing account of Spanish brutality toward the native population by the outspoken Catholic priest Bartolomé de las Casas. Although no 19th-century history of the conquest of Mexico could be reconciled with our contemporary view of the conquistadors' barbarism, Prescott's *The Conquest of Mexico* is no less intriguing for its dated conceits.

For decades, the standard texts written by scholars for popular audiences have been *A History of Mexico*, by Henry B. Parkes; *Many Mexicos*, by Lesley Byrd Simpson; and *A Compact History of Mexico*, an anthology published by the Colegio de México. Michael C. Meyer and William L. Sherman's *The Course of Mexican History* and Eric Wolf's *Sons of the Shaking Earth* are also good survey works. Alan Knight has contributed works on the Mexican Revolution and a three-volume history text spanning the Spanish Conquest through the 20th century.

### Contemporary Histories

Enrique Krauze's ambitious *Mexico: Biography of Power* begins its romantic sweep with the Insurgent priests of the early 1800s. Jorge Castañeda's 1995 *The Mexican Shock* is an important study of the financial and political crisis in Mexico and its ramifications for United States–Mexico relations. His previous works, *Utopia Unarmed* and, with American political scientist Robert A. Pastor, *Limits to Friendship: The United States and Mexico*, are also excellent resources. *Opening Mexico* (2004), by reporters Julia Preston and Samuel Dillon, is a highly acclaimed book about the end of the PRI's stranglehold on Mexican politics.

A number of journalists have made important contributions to the literature on historical and contemporary Mexico. Pulitzer Prize–winning *Miami Herald* Latin

American correspondent Andres Oppenheimer's *Bordering on Chaos: Mexico's Roller-Coaster Journey to Prosperity* (1996) chronicles two of the most tumultuous years in recent Mexican history. The book investigates the country's descent into turmoil following the 1994 Zapatista uprising, two shocking 1994 political assassinations, the presidential elections, and the 1995 peso crisis. William Langewiesche's *Cutting for Sign* examines life along the Mexican–U.S. border, and *Los Angeles Times* correspondent Sam Quiñones's *True Tales from Another Mexico: The Lynch Mob, the Popsicle Kings, Chalino, and the Bronx* (2001) recounts engaging stories about everyday Mexican people that manage to reveal the complexities and peculiarities of Mexico's social, economic, and political situations.

Alan Riding's *Distant Neighbors: A Portrait of the Mexicans* is a classic description of Mexican politics, society, and finance from the *New York Times* correspondent who lived there during the 1980s. Another former *New York Times* journalist, Jonathan Kandell, penned *La Capital: The Biography of Mexico City* in 1988, a fascinating and detailed history of the city from pre-Hispanic times to modern day. Elena Poniatowska, better known in the English-speaking world for her fiction, is one of Mexico's most highly respected journalists. *Massacre in Mexico*, her account of government repression of a demonstration in Mexico City in 1968, is an enlightening and disturbing work. Bill Weinberg writes of oppression and rebellion in one of Mexico's poorest states in *Homage to Chiapas*. Setting Chiapas's indigenous movement of resistance in a broad historical context, it's also an education in Mexican politics, economics, and traditional culture. More academic works on Mexico's modern history include Hector Aguila Camín's *In the Shadow of the Mexican Revolution*, Roderic A. Camp's *Politics in Mexico*, and Merilee Grindle's *Bureaucrats, Politicians and Peasants in Mexico*.

## Ethnography

Excellent ethnographies include Oscar Lewis's classic works on the culture of poverty *The Children of Sanchez* and *Five Families*; *Juan the Chamula*, by Ricardo Pozas, about a small village in Chiapas; *Mexico South: The Isthmus of Tehuantepec*, by Miguel Covarrubias, which discusses Indian life in the early 20th century; Gertrude Blom's *Bearing Witness*, on the Lacandones of Chiapas; and *Maria Sabina: Her Life and Chants*, an autobiography of a shaman in the state of Oaxaca. Beginning in the early 1970s, Carlos Castaneda wrote a series of philosophical, controversial books beginning with *The Teachings of Don Juan: A Yaqui Way of Knowledge*. Each book recounted the author's purported apprenticeship with the wise old shaman from northern Mexico, Don Juan.

## Food

Perhaps one of the most unusual and delightful books published on Mexican cookery in recent years is *Recipe of Memory: Five Generations of Mexican Cuisine* (1995). Written by Pulitzer Prize–winning food journalist Victor Valle and his wife, Mary Lau Valle, this book reproduces recipes the couple found in an antique chest passed down through the Valle family and in the process weaves an intriguing family and social history. Patricia Quintana's lushly photographed cookbooks, which capture the culinary history and culture of Mexico, include *The Taste of Mexico* (1993). Diana Kennedy's culinary works are also wildly popular, including her classic *The Art of Mexican Cooking* (1989) and *The Essential Cuisines of Mexico* (2000).

Chef Rick Bayless is another staunch champion of Mexican regional cuisine; his books include *Mexico: One Plate at a Time* (2000) and *Mexican Kitchen* (1996). Marita Adair's *The Hungry Traveler Mexico* (1997), with descriptions of Mexican foods and their origins, goes beyond the typical food list. *Frida's Fiestas: Recipes and Recollections of Life with Frida Kahlo*

(1994) is a cookbook memoir by the artist's stepdaughter, Guadalupe Rivera Marín. It assembles photos, a personal account of important events in Kahlo's life, and recipes for over 100 dishes Kahlo used to serve to family and friends.

## Travelogues

Two of the more straightforward accounts from the early 19th century are the letters of Frances Calderón de la Barca (*Life in Mexico*) and John Lloyd Stephens's *Incidents of Travel in Central America, Chiapas and Yucatán*. Foreign journalists have described life in Mexico during and after the revolution: John Reed (*Insurgent Mexico*); John Kenneth Turner (*Barbarous Mexico*); Aldous Huxley (*Beyond the Mexique Bay*); and Graham Greene (*The Lawless Roads,*) a superbly written narrative about Tabasco and Chiapas, which served as the basis for *The Power and the Glory*). In much the same vein, but more contemporary, are works by Patrick Marnham (*So Far from God*), about Central America and Mexico, and Hugh Fleetwood, whose *A Dangerous Place* is informative despite its cantankerousness.

Alice Adams's *Mexico: Some Travels and Some Travelers There*, which includes an introduction by Jan Morris, is available in paperback; James A. Michener's novel, *Mexico,* captures the history of the land and the personality of the people. Probably the finest travelogue-cum-guidebook is Kate Simon's *Mexico: Places and Pleasures. Into a Desert Place,* chronicling Graham Mackintosh's trek along the Baja coast. So entranced by San Miguel de Allende that he decided to stay, Tony Cohan recounts a gringo's daily life there in *On Mexican Time.* James O'Reilly and Larry Habegger have edited a diverse collection of articles and essays by contemporary writers in *Travelers' Tales Mexico.* Ron Butler's *Dancing Alone in Mexico: From the Border to Baja and Beyond* recounts the author's capricious travels across the country. *Cartwheels in the Sand,* by Ann Hazard, tells of the author's adventures with friends up and down the Baja peninsula.

## Contemporary Literature

The late poet-philosopher Octavio Paz was the dean of Mexican intellectuals. His best works are *Labyrinth of Solitude*, a thoughtful, far-reaching dissection of Mexican culture, and *Sor Juana*, the biography of Sor Juana Inés de la Cruz, a 17th-century nun and poet. For more on Sor Juana, including her own writings, see Alan Trueblood's *A Sor Juana Anthology*. Other top authors include Carlos Fuentes (*The Death of Artemio Cruz* and *The Old Gringo* are among his most popular novels), Juan Rulfo (his classic is *Pedro Páramo*), Jorge Ibarguengoitia (*Two Crimes, The Dead Girls*), Elena Poniatowska (*Dear Diego, Here's to You Jesusa,* and *Tinisima* among others), Rosario Castellanos (*The Nine Guardians* and *City of Kings*), Elena Garros (*Recollections of Things to Come*), Gregorio López y Fuentes (*El Indio*), Angeles Mastretta (*Mexican Bolero*), and José Emilio Pacheco (*Battles in the Desert and Other Stories*).

Recent biographies of the artist couple Frida Kahlo and Diego Rivera (by Hayden Herrera and Bertram D. Wolfe, respectively) provide glimpses into the Mexican intellectual and political life of the 1920s and '30s. Laura Esquivel's recipe-enhanced novel *Like Water for Chocolate* captures the passions and palates of Mexico during the revolution. Edited by Juana Ponce de León, *Our Word Is Our Weapon* contains writings by the Subcomandante Insurgente Marcos. They range from communiqués made on behalf of the Zapatista movement to Marcos's own stories and poetry. The Subcomandante has even written a celebrated children's book, *The Story of Colors: A Bilingual Folktale from the Jungles of Chiapas.*

D. H. Lawrence's *The Plumed Serpent* is probably the best-known foreign novel about Mexico, although its noble savage theme is quite offensive. Lawrence recorded his travels in Oaxaca in *Mornings in Mexico,* also in a rather condescending tone. A far greater piece of literature is Malcolm Lowry's *Under the Volcano.* The mysterious recluse B. Traven, whose fame rests largely on his *Treasure of the Sierra Madre,* wrote brilliantly and passionately about Mexico in *Rebellion of the Hanged* and *The Bridge in the Jungle.* Also noteworthy is John Steinbeck's *The Log from the Sea of Cortez. The Reader's Companion to Mexico,* edited by Alan Ryan, includes material by Langston Hughes, D. H. Lawrence, and Paul Theroux. The characters of Cormac McCarthy's *Border Trilogy* weave back and forth across the Texas–Mexico border in the 1940s. The prize-winning *Sky Over El Nido,* by C. M. Mayo, is a collection of contemporary short stories. Harriet Doerr's novels *Stones for Ibarra* and *Consider This, Señora* tell of newcomers' experiences in rural Mexico.

## Movies

Mexican cinema cut its teeth during the Mexican Revolution, when both Mexican and U.S. cameramen braved the battlefields to catch the generals in action. Legend has it that American cameramen helped Pancho Villa "choreograph" the Battle of Celaya for on-screen (and military) success. For an early Hollywood portrayal of the Revolution shot partially in Mexico, check out director Elia Kazan's *Viva Zapata!* (1952), written by John Steinbeck and starring Marlon Brando as Emiliano Zapata.

It wasn't long after Kazan's epic that directors of Hollywood westerns hit on Durango state as a cheap, accessible alternative to the usual "Old West" locales north of the border. The quintessential cinema cowboy, John Wayne, made eight movies in the area, including *True Grit* (1969), for which he won an Oscar.

John Huston directed one of the earliest American movies shot in Mexico, the un-forgettable prospecting adventure *The Treasure of the Sierra Madre* (1948), filmed in Michoacán state. In 1964, Huston set an adaptation of Tennessee Williams's play *The Night of the Iguana* in Puerto Vallarta. And in 1984, Huston made the beautiful, intense *Under the Volcano,* adapted from Malcolm Lowry's novel. The movie was shot in Morelos, near Cuernavaca, and shows the local Día de los Muertos celebrations.

Hollywood's presence in Mexico continued throughout the 1990s and the early 2000s. After *Titanic* (1997) and parts of *Pearl Harbor* (2001) were filmed in Rosarito, some began referring to the area as "Baja Hollywood." Other recent blockbusters that were shot south of the border include: *Frida* (2002), with Salma Hayek as the Mexican artist, and gorgeous settings in Mexico City's Coyoacán neighborhood; Steven Soderbergh's *Traffic* (2001), which trolls some of the tougher areas of Tijuana and other border towns; and Ted Demme's *Blow* (2001), with Johnny Depp and Penélope Cruz, filmed in glitzy Acapulco. *The Mask of Zorro* (1998), starring Antonio Banderas and Anthony Hopkins, gallops across several locations in central Mexico. Robert Rodriguez made his name with his tales of a mariachi musician dragged into a world of crime. The films *El Mariachi* (1992) and *Desperado* (1995) were capped by *Once Upon a Time in Mexico,* starring Antonio Banderas, Johnny Depp, and Salma Hayek, in 2003.

The predominance of Hollywood films in Mexico has not been without controversy. In 1998, Mexico passed a law requiring movie theaters to reserve 10% of their screen time for domestic films. The government also directed funds to support homegrown Mexican cinema and the effort is already paying off, as recent films gain international attention. Director Carlos Carrera's *El Crimen del Padre Amaro (The Crime of Father Amaro,* 2002) courted scandal with its story of a priest's love affair, becoming Mexico's highest-grossing domestic film in the process. *Y Tu Mamá También (And Your Mother Too,* 2001) swept film festivals across Europe and Latin America. The funny, very sexual coming-of-age tale of two teenage boys was shot in Mexico City and the Oaxaca coast. *Amores Perros (Love's a Bitch,* 2000) is a Mexico City thriller about a car accident and the intertwining stories of loss and regret among the principal characters. For a delicious romance set in early-20th-century Mexico, see *Como Agua Para Chocolate (Like Water for Chocolate,* 1992), based on the novel by Laura Esquivel.

Guillermo del Toro's *Cronos* won the equivalent of the Mexican Academy Awards and allowed the director to create Hollywood successes like *Blade II* and 2004's comic book adaptation *Hellboy.* Less mainstream films that have won critical acclaim in recent years include the 2002 films *Amarte Duele (Love Hurts),* a modern love story with a rock 'n roll soundtrack, and *Asesino en Serio (A Serious Killer),* a sexy murder mystery laced with references to Aztec ritual. Jaime Humberto Hermosillo, Mexico's first openly gay director, made the campy black comedy *El Misterio de los Almendros (Mystery of the Almonds,* 2003).

# VOCABULARY

| | English | Spanish | Pronunciation |
|---|---|---|---|
| **Basics** | | | |
| | Yes/no | Sí/no | see/no |
| | Please | Por favor | pore fah-*vore* |
| | May I? | ¿Me permite? | may pair-*mee*-tay |
| | Thank you (very much) | (Muchas) gracias | (*moo*-chas) *grah*-see-as |
| | You're welcome | De nada | day *nah*-dah |
| | Excuse me | Con permiso | con pair-*mee*-so |
| | Pardon me/what did you say? | ¿Como?/Mánde? | ko-mo/mahn-dey |
| | Could you tell me? | ¿Podría decirme? | po-*dree*-ah deh-*seer*-meh |
| | I'm sorry | Lo siento | lo see-*en*-toe |
| | Hello | Hola | *oh*-lah |
| | Good morning! | ¡Buenos días! | *bway*-nohs *dee*-ahs |
| | Good afternoon! | ¡Buenas tardes! | *bway*-nahs *tar*-dess |
| | Good evening! | ¡Buenas noches! | *bway*-nahs *no*-chess |
| | Goodbye! | ¡Adiós!/¡Hasta luego! | ah-dee-*ohss*/ ah-stah-*lwe*-go |
| | Mr./Mrs. | Señor/Señora | sen-*yor*/sen-*yore*-ah |
| | Miss | Señorita | sen-yo-*ree*-tah |
| | Pleased to meet you | Mucho gusto | *moo*-cho *goose*-to |
| | How are you? | ¿Cómo está usted? | *ko*-mo es-*tah* oo-*sted* |
| | Very well, thank you. | Muy bien, gracias. | *moo*-ee bee-en, grah-see-as |
| | And you? | ¿Y usted? | ee oos-*ted* |
| | Hello (on the telephone) | Bueno | *bwen*-oh |
| **Numbers** | | | |
| | 1 | un, uno | oon, *oo*-no |
| | 2 | dos | dos |
| | 3 | tres | trace |
| | 4 | cuatro | *kwah*-tro |
| | 5 | cinco | *sink*-oh |
| | 6 | seis | sace |
| | 7 | siete | see-*et*-ey |
| | 8 | ocho | *o*-cho |

| 9 | nueve | new-*ev*-ay |
|---|---|---|
| 10 | diez | dee-*es* |
| 11 | once | *own*-sey |
| 12 | doce | *doe*-sey |
| 13 | trece | *tray*-sey |
| 14 | catorce | kah-*tor*-sey |
| 15 | quince | *keen*-sey |
| 16 | dieciséis | dee-es-ee-*sace* |
| 17 | diecisiete | dee-*es*-ee-see-*et*-ay |
| 18 | dieciocho | dee-*es*-ee-o-cho |
| 19 | diecinueve | *dee-es*-ee-new-*ev*-ay |
| 20 | veinte | *bain*-tay |
| 21 | veinte y uno/ veintiuno | *bain*-te-oo-no |
| 30 | treinta | *train*-tah |
| 32 | treinta y dos | train-tay-*dose* |
| 40 | cuarenta | kwah-*ren*-tah |
| 43 | cuarenta y tres | kwah-*ren*-tay-*trace* |
| 50 | cincuenta | seen-*kwen*-tah |
| 54 | cincuenta y cuatro | seen-*kwen*-tay *kwah*-tro |
| 60 | sesenta | sess-*en*-tah |
| 65 | sesenta y cinco | sess-*en*-tay *seen*-ko |
| 70 | setenta | set-*en*-tah |
| 76 | setenta y seis | set-*en*-tay *sace* |
| 80 | ochenta | oh-*chen*-tah |
| 87 | ochenta y siete | oh-*chen*-tay see-*yet*-ay |
| 90 | noventa | no-*ven*-tah |
| 98 | noventa y ocho | no-*ven*-tah o-cho |
| 100 | cien | see-*en* |
| 101 | ciento uno | see-en-toe *oo*-no |
| 200 | doscientos | doe-see-*en*-tohss |
| 500 | quinientos | keen-*yen*-tohss |
| 700 | setecientos | set-eh-see-*en*-tohss |
| 900 | novecientos | no-veh-see-*en*-tohss |
| 1,000 | mil | meel |
| 2,000 | dos mil | dose meel |
| 1,000,000 | un millón | oon meel-*yohn* |

## Colors

| | | |
|---|---|---|
| black | negro | *neh*-grow |
| blue | azul | ah-*sool* |
| brown | café | kah-*feh* |
| green | verde | *vair*-day |
| pink | rosa | *ro*-sah |
| purple | morado | mo-*rah*-doe |
| orange | naranja | na-*rahn*-hah |
| red | rojo | *roe*-hoe |
| white | blanco | *blahn*-koh |
| yellow | amarillo | ah-mah-*ree*-yoh |

## Days of the Week

| | | |
|---|---|---|
| Sunday | domingo | doe-*meen*-goh |
| Monday | lunes | *loo*-ness |
| Tuesday | martes | *mahr*-tess |
| Wednesday | miércoles | me-*air*-koh-less |
| Thursday | jueves | who-*ev*-ess |
| Friday | viernes | vee-*air*-ness |
| Saturday | sábado | *sah*-bah-doe |

## Months

| | | |
|---|---|---|
| January | enero | eh-*neh*-ro |
| February | febrero | feh-*brair*-oh |
| March | marzo | *mahr*-so |
| April | abril | ah-*breel* |
| May | mayo | *my*-oh |
| June | junio | *hoo*-nee-oh |
| July | julio | *who*-lee-yoh |
| August | agosto | ah-*ghost*-toe |
| September | septiembre | sep-tee-*em*-breh |
| October | octubre | oak-*too*-breh |
| November | noviembre | no-vee-*em*-breh |
| December | diciembre | dee-see-*em*-breh |

## Useful Phrases

| | | |
|---|---|---|
| Do you speak English? | ¿Habla usted inglés? | *ah*-blah oos-*ted* in-*glehs* |
| I don't speak Spanish | No hablo español | no *ah*-blow es-pahn-*yol* |

| I don't understand (you) | No entiendo | no en-tee-*en*-doe |
|---|---|---|
| I understand (you) | Entiendo | en-tee-*en*-doe |
| I don't know | No sé | no *say* |
| I am from the United States/ British | Soy de los Estados Unidos/ inglés(a) | soy deh lohs ehs-*tah*-dohs oo-*nee*-dohs/ in-*glace*(ah) |
| What's your name? | ¿Cómo se llama usted? | *koh*-mo say *yah*-mah oos-*ted* |
| My name is . . . | Me llamo . . . | may *yah*-moh |
| What time is it? | ¿Qué hora es? | keh o-rah es |
| It is one, two, three . . . o'clock. | Es la una; son las dos, tres | es la oo-nah/sone lahs dose, trace |
| How? | ¿Cómo? | *koh*-mo |
| When? | ¿Cuándo? | *kwahn*-doe |
| This/Next week | Esta semana/ la semana que entra | es-tah seh-*mah*-nah/ lah say-*mah*-nah keh *en*-trah |
| This/Next month | Este mes/el próximo mes | es-tay mehs/el *proke*-see-mo mehs |
| This/Next year | Este año/el año que viene | es-tay *ahn*-yo/el *ahn*-yo keh vee-*yen*-ay |
| Yesterday/today/ tomorrow | Ayer/hoy/mañana | ah-*yair*/oy/mahn-*yah*-nah |
| This morning/ afternoon | Esta mañana/tarde | es-tah mahn-*yah*-nah/*tar*-day |
| Tonight | Esta noche | es-tah *no*-cheh |
| What? | ¿Qué? | keh |
| What is this? | ¿Qué es esto? | keh es *es*-toe |
| Why? | ¿Por qué? | pore *keh* |
| Who? | ¿Quién? | kee-*yen* |
| Where is . . . ? | ¿Dónde está . . . ? | *dohn*-day es-*tah* |
| the train station? | la estación del tren? | la es-tah-see-*on* del *train* |
| the subway station? | la estación del Metro? | la es-ta-see-*on* del *meh*-tro |
| the bus stop? | la parada del autobús? | la pah-*rah*-dah del oh-toe-*boos* |
| the bank? | el banco? | el *bahn*-koh |
| the ATM? | el cajero automática? | el *kah*-hehr-oh oh-toe-*mah*-tee-kah |
| the . . . hotel? | el hotel . . . ? | el oh-*tel* |
| the store? | la tienda . . . ? | la tee-*en*-dah |
| the cashier? | la caja? | la *kah*-hah |

| the . . . museum? | el museo . . . ? | el moo-*seh*-oh |
| the hospital? | el hospital? | el ohss-pea-*tal* |
| the elevator? | el ascensor? | el ah-*sen*-sore |
| the bathroom? | el baño? | el *bahn*-yoh |
| Here/there | Aquí/allá | ah-*key*/ah-*yah* |
| Open/closed | Abierto/cerrado | ah-be-*er*-toe/<br>ser-*ah*-doe |
| Left/right | Izquierda/derecha | iss-key-*er*-dah/<br>dare-*eh*-chah |
| Straight ahead | Derecho | der-*eh*-choh |
| Is it near/far? | ¿Está cerca/lejos? | es-*tah sair*-kah/<br>*leh*-hoss |
| I'd like . . . | Quisiera . . . | kee-see-air-ah |
| a room | un cuarto/una<br>habitación | oon *kwahr*-toe/<br>oo-nah ah-bee-<br>tah-see-*on* |
| the key | la llave | lah *yah*-vay |
| a newspaper | un periódico | oon pear-ee-oh-<br>dee-koh |
| I'd like to buy . . . | Quisiera<br>comprar . . . | kee-see-*air*-ah<br>kohm-*prahr* |
| cigarettes | cigarrillo | ce-gar-*reel*-oh |
| matches | cerillos | ser-*ee*-ohs |
| a dictionary | un diccionario | oon deek-see-oh-<br>*nah*-ree-oh |
| soap | jabón | hah-*bone* |
| a map | un mapa | oon *mah*-pah |
| a magazine | una revista | *oon*-ah reh-*veess*-tah |
| paper | papel | pah-*pel* |
| envelopes | sobres | *so*-brace |
| a postcard | una tarjeta postal | *oon*-ah tar-*het*-ah<br>post-*ahl* |
| How much is it? | ¿Cuánto cuesta? | *kwahn*-toe *kwes*-tah |
| Do you accept<br>credit cards? | ¿Aceptan tarjetas<br>de crédito? | ah-*sehp*-than<br>tahr-*heh*-tahs deh<br>*creh*-dee-toh? |
| A little/a lot | Un poquito/<br>mucho . . . | oon poh-*kee*-toe/<br>*moo*-choh |
| More/less | Más/menos | mahss/*men*-ohss |
| Enough/too<br>much/too little | Suficiente/de-<br>masiado/muy poco | soo-fee-see-*en*-tay/<br>day-mah-see-*ah*-<br>doe/*moo*-ee *poh*-koh |
| Telephone | Teléfono | tel-*ef*-oh-no |
| Telegram | Telegrama | teh-leh-*grah*-mah |
| I am ill/sick | Estoy enfermo(a) | es-*toy*<br>en-*fair*-moh(ah) |

| | | |
|---|---|---|
| Please call a doctor | Por favor llame un médico | pore fa-*vor ya*-may oon *med*-ee-koh |
| Help! | ¡Auxilio! ¡Ayuda! | owk-*see*-lee-oh/ ah-*yoo*-dah |
| Fire! | ¡Encendio! | en-*sen*-dee-oo |
| Caution!/Look out! | ¡Cuidado! | kwee-*dah*-doh |

## On the Road

| | | |
|---|---|---|
| Highway | Carretera | car-ray-*ter*-ah |
| Causeway, paved highway | Calzada | cal-*za*-dah |
| Speed bump | Tope | *toh*-pay |
| Toll highway | Carretera de cuota | car-ray-*ter*-ha day dwoh-tah |
| Toll booth | Caseta | kah-*set*-ah |
| Route | Ruta | *roo*-tah |
| Road | Camino | cah-*mee*-no |
| Street | Calle | *cah*-yeh |
| Avenue | Avenida | ah-ven-*ee*-dah |
| Broad, tree-lined boulevard | Paseo | pah-*seh*-oh |
| Waterfront promenade | Malecón | mal-lay-*cone* |
| Wharf | Embarcadero | em-bar-cah-*day*-ro |

## In Town

| | | |
|---|---|---|
| Church | Templo/Iglesia | *tem*-plo/e-*gles*-se-*ah* |
| Cathedral | Catedral | cah-tay-*dral* |
| Neighborhood | Barrio | *bar*-re-o |
| Foreign exchange shop | Casa de cambio | *cas*-sah day *cam*-be-o |
| City hall | Ayuntamiento | ah-yoon-tah-mee-*en*-toe |
| Main square | Zócalo | *zo*-cal-o |
| Traffic circle | Glorieta | glor-e-*ay*-tah |
| Market | Mercado (Spanish)/ Tianguis (Indian) | mer-*cah*-doe/ tee-*an*-geese |
| Inn | Posada | pos-*sah*-dah |
| Group taxi | Colectivo | co-lec-*tee*-vo |
| Mini-bus along fixed route | Pesero | pi-*seh*-ro |

## Dining Out

| | | |
|---|---|---|
| I'd like to reserve a table | Quisiera reservar una mesa. | kee-*syeh*-rah rreh-sehr-*vahr* oo-nah *meh*-sah |
| A bottle of . . . | Una botella de . . . | oo-nah bo-*tay*-yah deh |
| A cup of . . . | Una taza de . . . | oo-nah *tah*-sah deh |
| A glass of . . . | Un vaso de . . . | oon *vah*-so deh |
| Ashtray | Un cenicero | oon sen-ee-*seh*-roh |
| Bill/check | La cuenta | lah *kwen*-tah |
| Bread | El pan | el pahn |
| Breakfast | El desayuno | el day-sigh-*oon*-oh |
| Butter | La mantequilla | lah mahn-tay-*key*-yah |
| Cheers! | ¡Salud! | sah-*lood* |
| Cocktail | Un aperitivo | oon ah-pair-ee-*tee*-voh |
| Mineral water | Agua mineral | *ah*-gwah mee-neh-*rahl* |
| Beer | Cerveza | sehr-*veh*-sah |
| Dinner | La cena | lah *seh*-nah |
| Dish | Un plato | oon *plah*-toe |
| Dish of the day | El platillo de hoy | el plah-*tee*-yo day oy |
| Enjoy! | ¡Buen provecho! | bwen pro-*veh*-cho |
| Fixed-price menu | La comida corrida | lah koh-*me*-dah co-*ree*-dah |
| Is the tip included? | ¿Está incluida la propina? | es-*tah* in-clue-*ee*-dah lah pro-*pea*-nah |
| Fork | El tenedor | el ten-eh-*door* |
| Knife | El cuchillo | el koo-*chee*-yo |
| Spoon | Una cuchara | oo-nah koo-*chah*-rah |
| Lunch | La comida | lah koh-*me*-dah |
| Menu | La carta | lah *cart*-ah |
| Napkin | La servilleta | lah sair-vee-*yet*-uh |
| Please give me | Por favor déme | pore fah-*vor* *day*-may |
| Pepper | La pimienta | lah pea-me-*en*-tah |
| Salt | La sal | lah sahl |
| Sugar | El azúcar | el ah-*sue*-car |
| Waiter!/Waitress! | ¡Por favor Señor/Señorita! | pore fah-*vor* sen-*yor*/sen-yor-*ee*-tah |

# INDEX